Fundamental Problems in Organic Chemistry for NEET

Shubh Karan Choudhary
Formerly, Vice President, Sarvottam Career Institute, Kota;
Formerly, Senior Chemistry Faculty, ALLEN Career Institute, Kota

Rohit Agrawal
Formerly, Joint Director, Nucleus, Kota;
Formerly, Faculty, ALLEN Career Institute, Kota

Universities Press

FUNDAMENTAL PROBLEMS IN ORGANIC CHEMISTRY FOR NEET

UNIVERSITIES PRESS (INDIA) PRIVATE LIMITED

Registered Office
3-6-747/1/A & 3-6-754/1, Himayatnagar, Hyderabad 500 029, Telangana, India
info@universitiespress.com; www.universitiespress.com

Distributed by
Orient Blackswan Private Limited

Registered Office
3-6-752 Himayatnagar, Hyderabad 500 029 Telangana, India

Other Offices
Bengaluru / Chennai / Guwahati / Hyderabad / Kolkata
Mumbai / New Delhi / Noida / Patna

First published 2025

ISBN 978-93-93330-77-2

502173

Typeset in Minion Pro 9.5 points *by*
Cameo Corporate Services Limited, Coimbatore

Printed in India by
B.B. Press, Tronica City, Ghaziabad, UP 201 103

Published by
Universities Press (India) Private Limited
3-6-747/1/A & 3-6-754/1, Himayatnagar, Hyderabad 500 029, Telangana, India

Preface and Acknowledgements

This book is a comprehensive compendium of exercises and problems in Organic Chemistry with an emphasis on the new NEET syllabus. The questions featured in this book have been carefully selected from NCERT, NCERT Exemplar and previous NEET exams. We have differentiated them as Level-1 and Level-2, based on their degree of difficulty. We have also provided detailed solutions, with step-by-step explanations as well as relevant diagrams and reactions, or hints to most of the questions. Our aim in doing so is to enable students to assess and improve their problem-solving ability.

We owe a debt of gratitude to the many people who have helped us in our endeavours to bring this book into existence.

Our special thanks to 'guru' Akshay Choudhary, for shaping this book.

Shubh Karan Choudhary sincerely acknowledges the support of his family: mother, Chandrapathi Choudhary; father, Baljeet Singh; sister, Saroj; brother, Vishwanath; wife, Anandhi; and charming son, Kanish.

Rohit Agrawal gratefully acknowledges the encouragement and immense support of his mother, Sunita Agrawal; father, Bhupendra Agrawal; sister, Richa; and Yati. His family has been a source of inspiration to him throughout the process of preparing this book.

We would also like to acknowledge our colleagues, Ashish Bansal, Ajay Kumar Mishra, Prateek Jain, Narendra Kumar Yadav, Ramesh Sharda, Mohit Dadheech and Gaurav, for their invaluable feedback. We also wish to thank Mangilal Choudhary for providing the solutions and for checking the entire book.

We welcome all suggestions and constructive criticism for enhancing this book.

Shubh Karan Choudhary
Rohit Agrawal

Contents

CHAPTER 1

Nomenclature of Organic Compounds

Level-1

1. The number of σ and π bonds in the following molecule are:

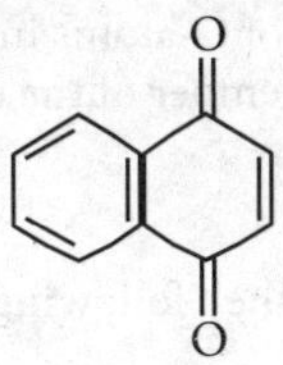

(a) 19, 7 (b) 20, 7
(c) 19, 6 (d) 18, 6

2. The total number of secondary C-atoms in the structure given below is:

$$CH_3-\underset{\displaystyle CH_3}{\underset{|}{CH}}-CH_2-CH_2-CH_3$$

(a) 1 (b) 4
(c) 3 (d) 2

3. A compound has the molecular formula $C_nH_{2n}O_2$. It cannot have:
(a) One carboxylic acid
(b) Two aldehydes
(c) One hydroxy ketone
(d) One ester

4. Which of the following has only 2° H-atoms?

(a) 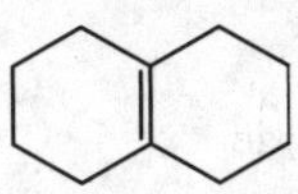

(b) 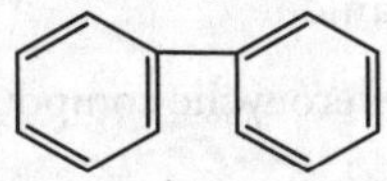

(c) 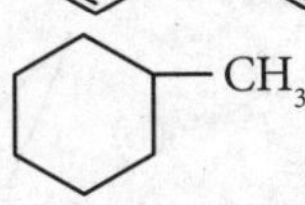

(d) 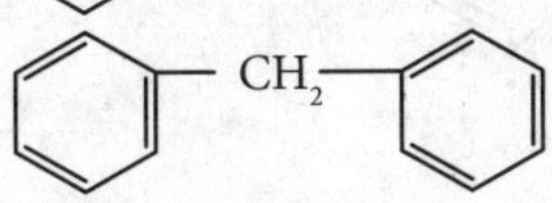

The correct code is:
(a) Only (a) and (b)
(b) (a), (b) and (d)
(c) (a), (c) and (d)
(d) All of them

5. Isobutyl chloride is:
(a) $CH_3CH_2CH_2CH_2Cl$
(b) $(CH_3)_2CHCH_2Cl$
(c) $CH_3CH_2CHClCH_3$
(d) $(CH_3)_3C-Cl$

6. The Cl–C–Cl bond angle in 1,1,2,2-tetrachloroethene and tetrachloromethane will, respectively, be:
(a) 120° and 109.28° (b) 90° and 109.28°
(c) 109.28° and 90° (d) 109.28° and 120°

7. Which of the following is allyl alcohol?

(a) 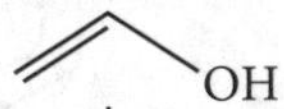

(b) 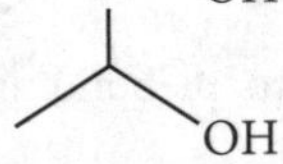

(c) 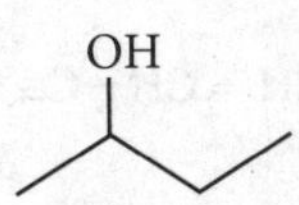

(d) 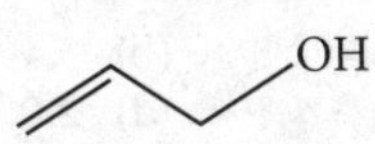

8. The minimum number of carbon atoms in an alkane having only 1°-, 2°- and 3°-degree carbon is:
(a) 4 (b) 8
(c) 5 (d) 6

9. Which of the following is not the bond line structure of

$$CH_3-CH=CH-\underset{\displaystyle CH_3}{\underset{|}{CH}}-CH=CH_2?$$

(a) 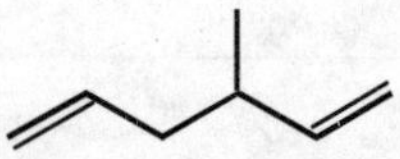

(b) 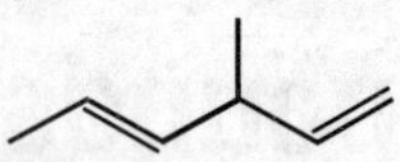

(c) 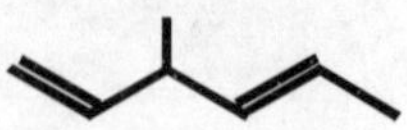

(d) 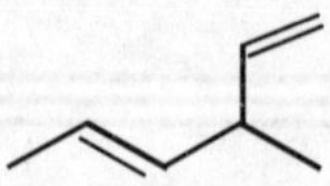

10. The ratio of σ bond to π bond in benzene is:

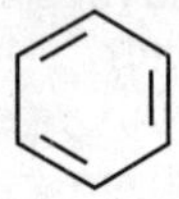

(a) 2 (b) 3
(c) 5 (d) 4

11. The homologue of phenol is:

(a) 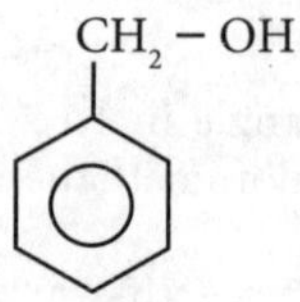
(b) 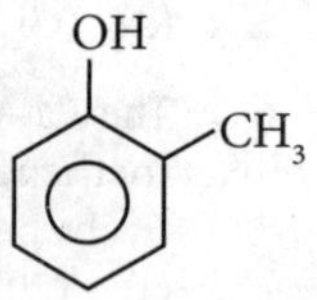
(c) 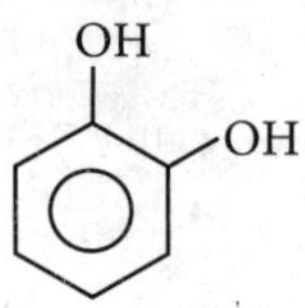
(d) 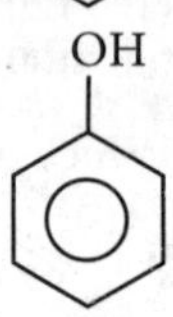

12. The ratio of sigma to pi bond in the given compound is:

$$CH_2=CH-\underset{\underset{O}{\|}}{C}-CH=CH-C\equiv N$$

(a) 2.4 (b) 3.4
(c) 2.2 (d) 2.0

13. Which of the following represents the given mode of hybridization sp^2-sp^2-sp-sp from left to right?

(a) $H_2C=CH-C\equiv CH$

(b) $HC\equiv C-C\equiv CH$

(c) $H_2C=CH-CH=CH_2$

(d) $H_2C=C=C=CH_2$

14. How many carbon atoms are present in the second homologue of methyl ether?

(a) 3 (b) 5
(c) 2 (d) 6

15. What is the hybridization of each carbon atom in the following compound?

$$HC\equiv C-CH_2-CH_2-CH_3$$

(a) sp, sp^2, sp^2, sp^2, sp^3
(b) sp, sp, sp^2, sp^2, sp^3
(c) sp, sp, sp^3, sp^3, sp^3
(d) sp^3, sp^3, sp^3, sp, sp

16. The number of C-atoms in the next homologue of the first member of the ester family is:

(a) 5 (b) 4
(c) 3 (d) 2

17. Which of the following is a heterocyclic compound?

(a) 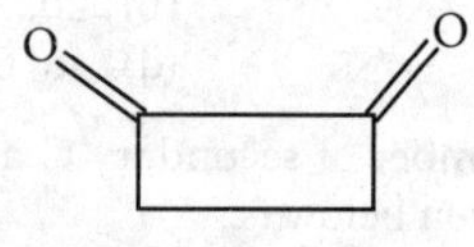
(b) 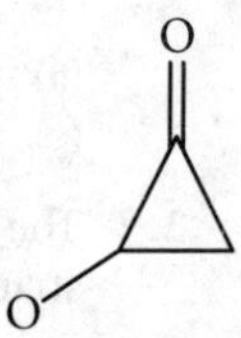
(c) 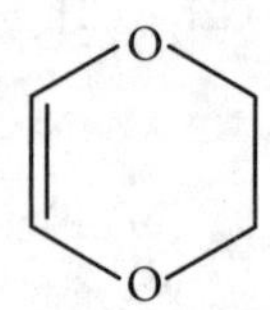
(d) 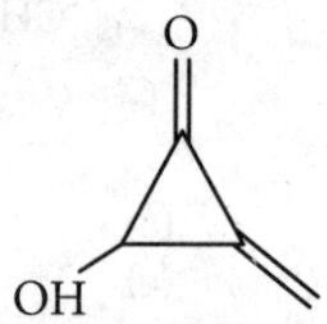

18. The functional groups present in (I) and (II) are, respectively:

$$\underset{\text{(I)}}{CH_3-\overset{\overset{O}{\|}}{C}-NH_2} \xrightarrow{PCl_5} \underset{\text{(II)}}{CH_3-C\equiv N}$$

(a) Cyanide, Amide
(b) Acid, Cyanide
(c) Amide, Isocyanide
(d) Amide, Cyanide

19. The saturated heterocyclic compound is:

(a) 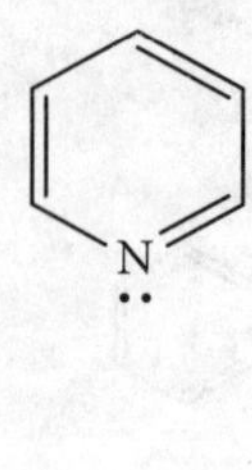
(b) 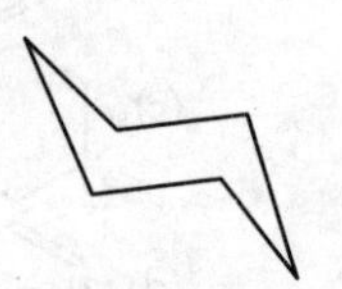

(c) 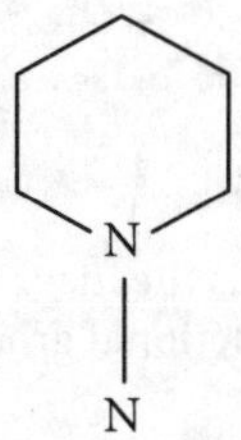

(d) 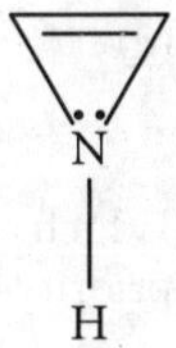

20. Which of the following homologous series has an incorrect general formula?
(a) Alkyne C_nH_{2n-2}
(b) Alkanol $C_nH_{2n+2}O$
(c) Alkanal $C_nH_{2n+1}O$
(d) Carboxylic acid $C_nH_{2n}O_2$

21. According to IUPAC, which of the following priority orders is correct?
(a) –CHO > –CN > –OH > $–NH_2$
(b) –CN > –CHO > –OH > $–NH_2$
(c) –CHO > –CN > $–NH_2$ > –OH
(d) –CN > –CHO > $–NH_2$ > –OH

22. The third member of the homologous series of aliphatic aldehydes has the structure:
(a) CH_3CH_2CHO
(b) $CH_3(CH_2)_2CHO$
(c) $H_3COCH_2CH_3$
(d) CH_3COCH_3

23. Which of the following names is incorrect?

$$\underset{\displaystyle Cl}{CH_2} - \underset{\displaystyle Cl}{CH_2}$$

(a) Ethylidene chloride
(b) 1,2-Dichloroethane
(c) Vicinal dihalide
(d) Ethylene dichloride

24. Which is the incorrect IUPAC name?

(a) 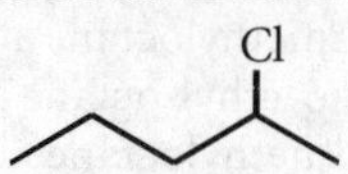
2-Chloropentane

(b) 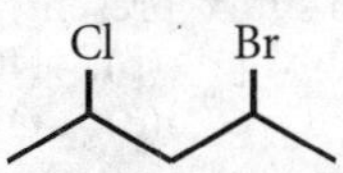
2-Chloro-4-bromopentane

(c) 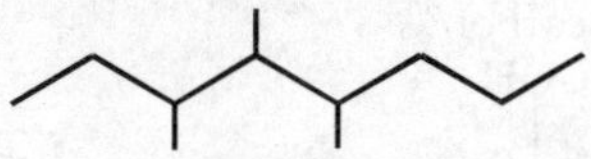
3,4,5-Trimethyloctane

(d) 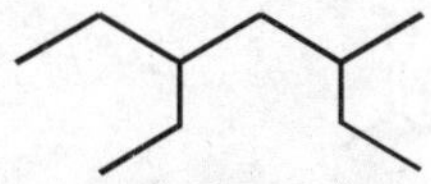
3-Ethyl-5-methylheptane

25. Which of the following functional groups is incorrectly matched with their prefix?
(a) –CHO ⇒ Formyl
(b) $–CONH_2$ ⇒ Carbamoyl
(c) –CN ⇒ Nitrile
(d) –COOH ⇒ Carboxy

26. Which of the following sets belongs to the same homologous series?
(a) C_3H_7Cl, $C_7H_{13}Cl$, $C_8H_{17}Cl$
(b) H–OH, CH_3–OH, CH_3CH_2–OH
(c) $CH_3–NH_2$, $CH_3–NH–CH_3$, $(CH_3)_3N$
(d) HCHO, CH_3–CHO, CH_3CH_2CHO

27. Which of the functional groups is not present in the following compound?

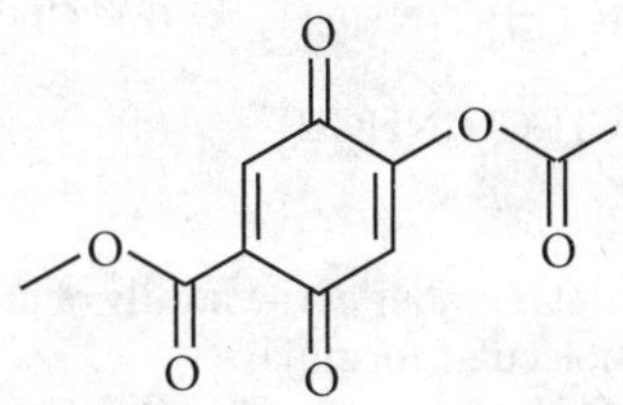

(a) Ketone (b) Ester
(c) Alkene (d) Ether

28. Which of the following functional groups has an odd number of degree of unsaturation?
(a) Acid anhydride (b) Cyanide
(c) Carboxylic acid (d) Sulphonic acid

29. The first member of the homologous series of aliphatic ketones has the structure:
(a) CH_3CH_2CHO
(b) $CH_3(CH_2)_2CHO$
(c) $CH_3COCH_2CH_3$
(d) CH_3COCH_3

30. Which of the following compounds contains alcohol as a functional group?

(a) 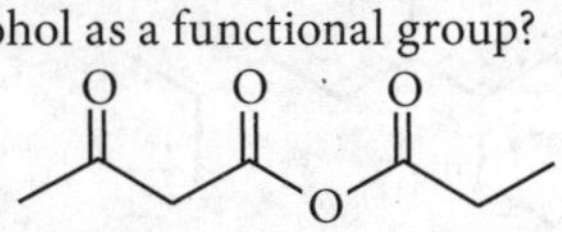

(b) 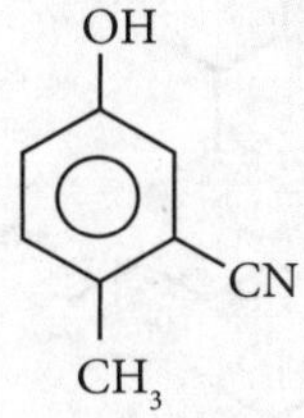

(c) 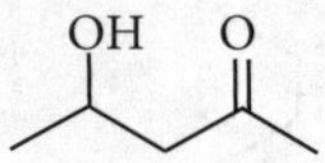

(d) 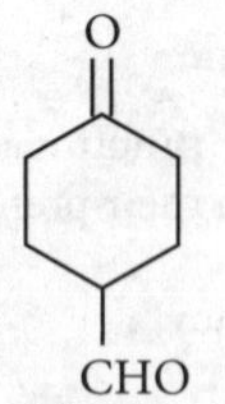

31. Which of the following is a vinyl radical?
(a) $CH_2=CH-$
(b) $(CH_3)_3C-$
(c) C_6H_5-
(d) $CH_3-(CH_2)_2-CH_2-$

32. Which of the following compounds contains 2° amine and 1° carbon only?
(a) $(CH_3)_3C-NHCH_3$ (b) CH_3NH_2
(c) $CH_3CH_2NHCH_3$ (d) 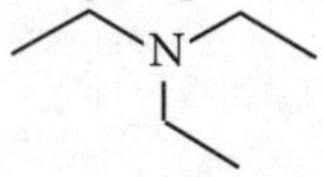

33. The first member of the family of alkenynes has the molecular formula:
(a) C_6H_6 (b) C_4H_4
(c) C_4H_6 (d) C_3H_2

34. In the IUPAC nomenclature of compounds, the correct priority order of groups is:
(i) $-CONH_2$ (ii) $-COOH$
(iii) $-COCl$ (iv) $-CHO$
(v) $-C\equiv N$
(a) ii > i > iii > iv > v
(b) ii > iii > i > v > iv
(c) ii > iii > v > i > iv
(d) ii > iii > i > iv > v

35. The correct structure of 6-ethyl-2,3,5-trimethylnonane is:
(a) 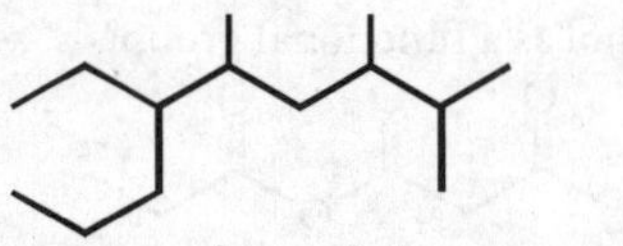

(b) 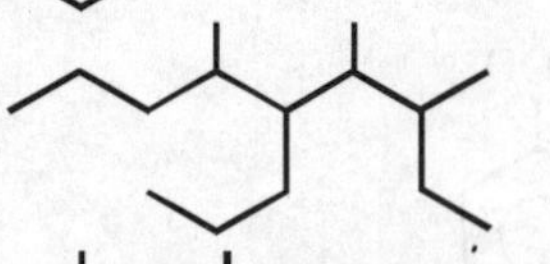

(c) 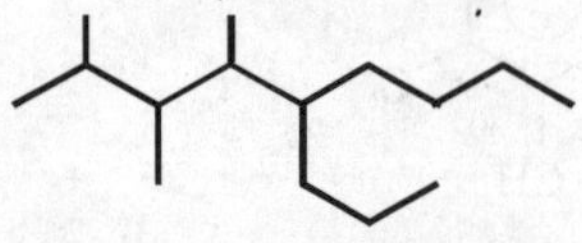

(d) 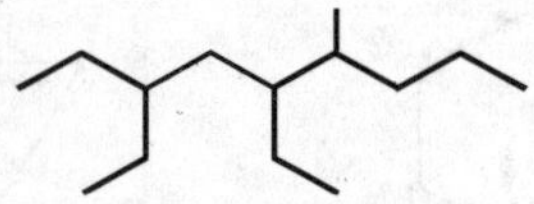

36. Which of the following is the incorrect order of priority of principal functional groups?
(a) $-\overset{\overset{O}{\|}}{C}-OH > -\overset{\overset{O}{\|}}{C}-H > -OH$
(b) $-CN > -\overset{\overset{O}{\|}}{C}-H > -NH_2$
(c) $-\overset{\overset{O}{\|}}{C}-H > -\overset{\overset{O}{\|}}{C}-NH_2 > -SH$
(d) $-\overset{\overset{O}{\|}}{C}-OR > -\overset{\overset{O}{\|}}{C}-Cl > -\overset{\overset{O}{\|}}{C}-H$

37. The σ/π ratio in the following compound is:

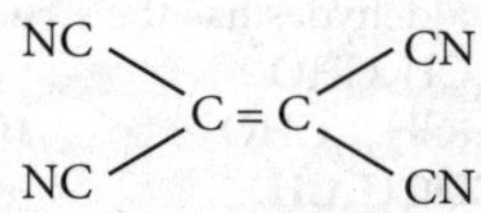

(a) 2 (b) 1
(c) 3 (d) 4

38. The correct IUPAC name of the following compound is:

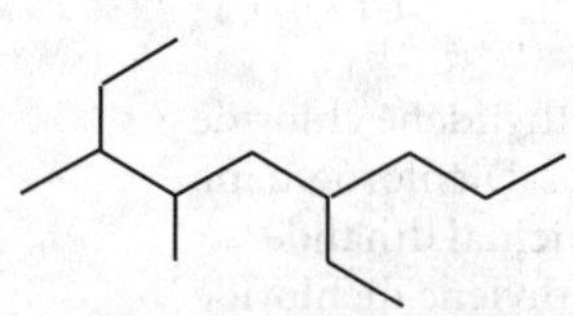

(a) 2,5-Diethyl-3-methylheptane
(b) 3-Ethyl-5,6-dimethyloctane
(c) 3,4-Dimethyl-6-ethyl-octane
(d) 6-Ethyl-3,4-dimethyloctane

39. Which of the following functional groups has only prefix, and no suffix, present?
(a) –COOCO– (b) $-NO_2$
(c) –SH (d) –OH

40. Which of the following is a homocyclic hydrocarbon?
(a) 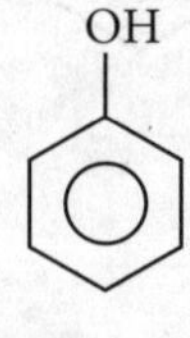
(b) 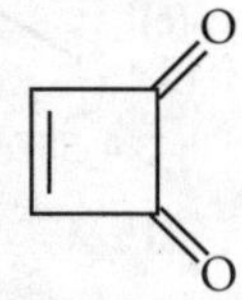

(c) 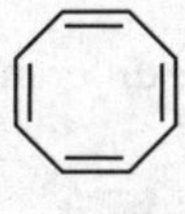 (d) Furan

41. Choose the correct IUPAC name of the following compound:

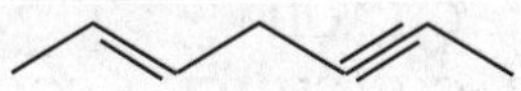

(a) Hept-2-yn-6-ene
(b) Hept-5-yn-2-ene
(c) Hept-5-en-2-yne
(d) Hept-2-en-5-yne

42. In the following compound, the hybridization of C_1–C_2 and C_3–C_4 is:

(a) sp^2-sp^2, sp^3-sp^3 (b) sp-sp, sp^2-sp^2
(c) sp^2-sp^2, sp-sp (d) sp^2-sp, sp-sp^2

43. A student named a certain compound as 2,3-diethylbutane. Its correct IUPAC name is:
(a) 2,3-Dimethylhexane
(b) 3,4-Dimethylhexane
(c) 2-Ethyl-3-methylpentane
(d) 2-Ethylbutane

44. Which is the incorrect structure of 2,3,4-trimethylhexane?

(a) 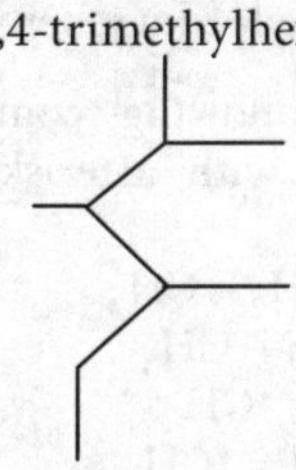

(b) 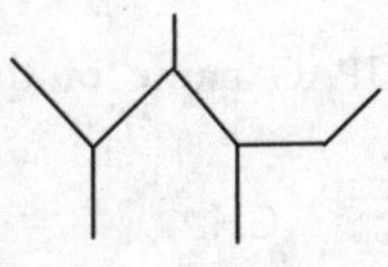

(c) 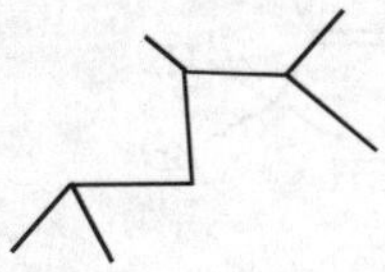

(d) 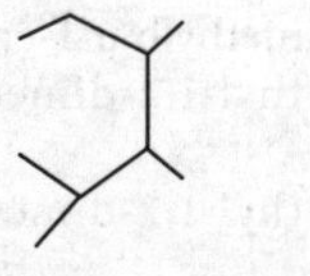

45. Which of the following is the correct IUPAC name?
(a) 3-Ethyl-4,4-dimethylheptane
(b) 4,4-Dimethyl-3-ethylheptane
(c) 5-Ethyl-4,4-dimethylheptane
(d) 4,4-Bis(methyl)-3-ethylheptane

46. The IUPAC name for the given compound is:

$$CH_3-\overset{O}{\overset{\|}{C}}-CH_2-CH_2-\overset{O}{\overset{\|}{C}}-OH$$

(a) 1-Hydroxypentane-1,4-dione
(b) 1,4-Dioxopentanol
(c) 1-Carboxybutan-3-one
(d) 4-Oxopentanoic acid

47. The IUPAC name for the given compound is:

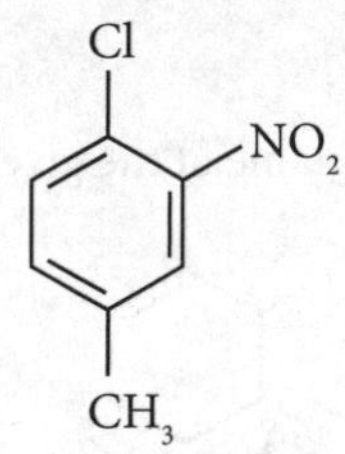

(a) 1-Chloro-2-nitro-4-methylbenzene
(b) 1-Chloro-4-methyl-2-nitrobenzene
(c) 2-Chloro-1-nitro-5-methylbenzene
(d) m-Nitro-p-chlorotoluene

48. The IUPAC name for the given compound is:

$$H_3C-\underset{C_2H_5}{\underset{|}{CH}}-\underset{C_2H_5}{\underset{|}{CH}}-CH_3$$

(a) 2-Ethyl-3-methylpentane
(b) 3,4-Dimethylhexane
(c) 2-Sec-butylbutane
(d) 2,3-Dimethylbutane

49. What is the correct structure of 3-bromo-2-chloro-6-methylcyclohexene-carboxylic acid:

(a) 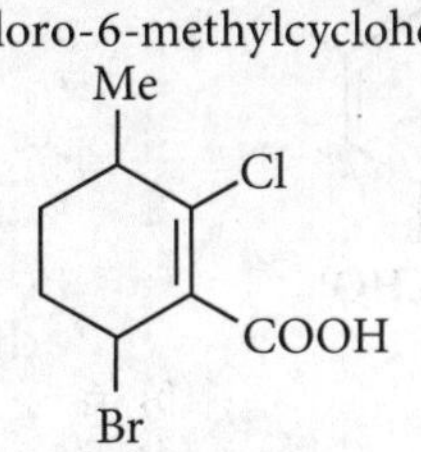

(b) 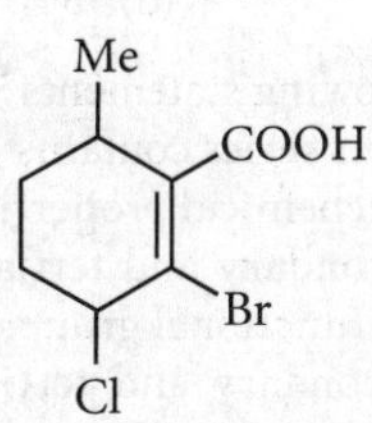

(c) 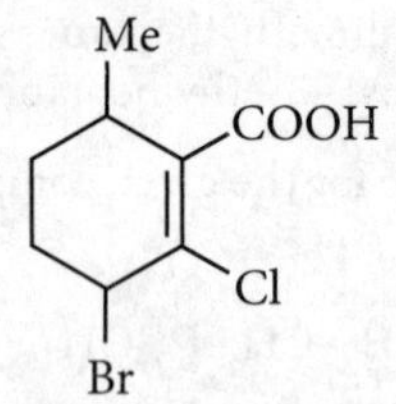

(d) 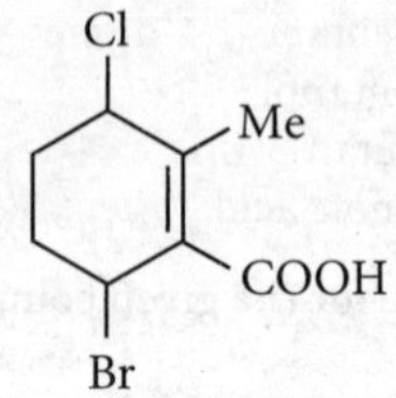

50. The IUPAC name of the given compound is:

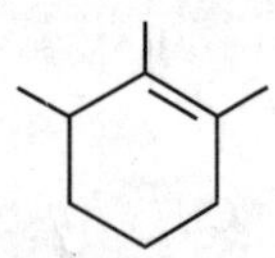

(a) 1,2,6-Trimethylcyclohexene
(b) 1,2,3-Trimethylcyclohexene
(c) 1,2,3-Trimethylcyclohex-2-ene
(d) 1,5,6-Trimethylcyclohex-1-ene

51. In which of the following is functional group isomerism not possible?
(a) Alcohols
(b) Aldehydes
(c) Alkyl halides
(d) Cyanides

52. The double-bond equivalent of the given compound is:

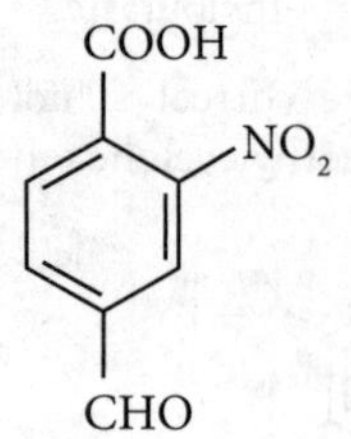

(a) 7 (b) 6
(c) 4 (d) 5

53. Which of the following statements is incorrect?
(a) A homologous series contains compounds with similar chemical properties.
(b) Primary, secondary and tertiary alcohols are different functional groups.
(c) Primary, secondary and tertiary amines are different functional groups.
(d) Phenol and alcohol are different functional groups.

54. The IUPAC name of the following compound is:

$$H_3C-\underset{\displaystyle CH_3}{CH}-\underset{\displaystyle OH}{CH}-CH_2-COOH$$

(a) 4-Methyl-1-3-hydroxypentanoic acid
(b) 2-methyl-1-3-hydroxypentan-5-oic acid
(c) 4,4-Dimethyl-1-3-hydroxybutanoic acid
(d) 3-Hydroxy-4-methylpentanoic acid

55. The correct IUPAC name of the following compound is:

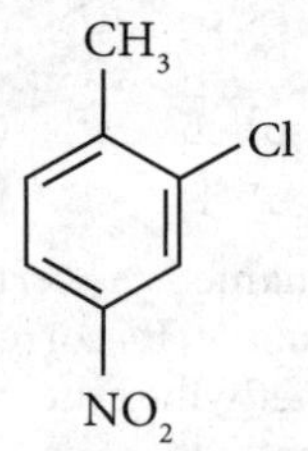

(a) 2-Methyl-5-nitro-1-chlorobenzene
(b) 3-Chloro-4-methyl-1-nitrobenzene
(c) 5-Chloro-4-methyl-1-nitrobenzene
(d) 2-Chloro-1-methyl-4-nitrobenzene

56. In which of the following compounds is the carbon marked with asterisk the most electronegative?
(a) $CH_3-CH_2-{}^*CH_2-CH_3$
(b) $CH_3-{}^*CH=CH-CH_3$
(c) $CH_3-CH_2-C\equiv{}^*CH$
(d) $CH_3-CH_2-CH={}^*CH_2$

57. What is the IUPAC name of the following compound?

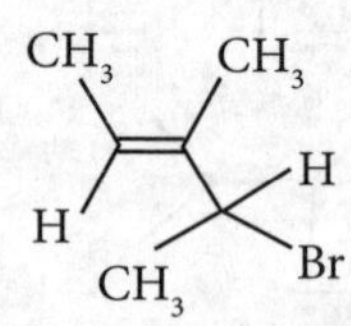

(a) 3-Bromo-1,2-dimethylbut-1-ene
(b) 3-Bromo-3-methyl-1,2-dimethylprop-1-ene
(c) 3-Bromo-3-methyl-1,2-dimethylprop-1-ene
(d) 4-Bromo-3-methylpent-2-ene

58. In which of the following compounds is the IUPAC numbering correct?

(a) 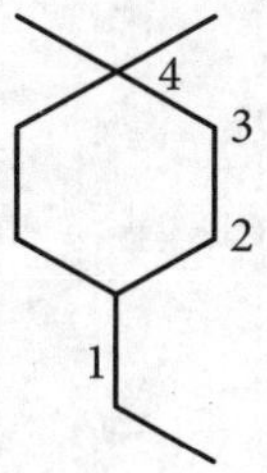

(b) 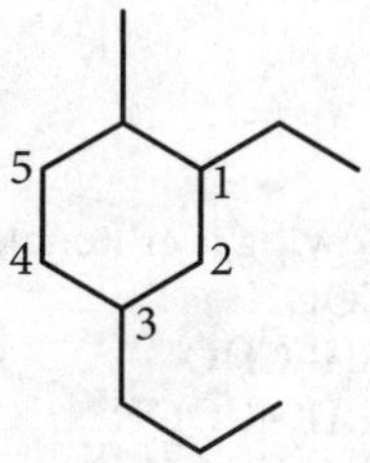

(c) 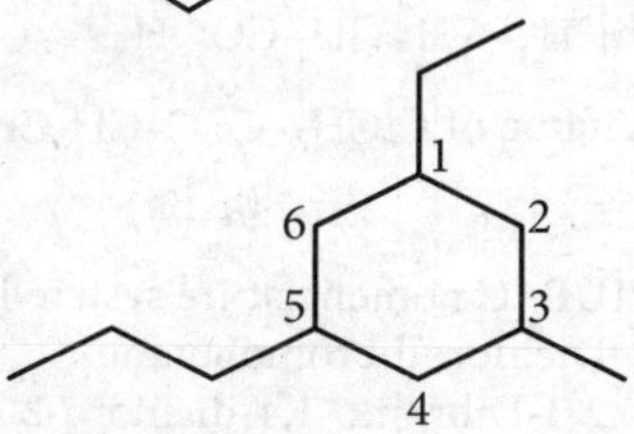

(d) 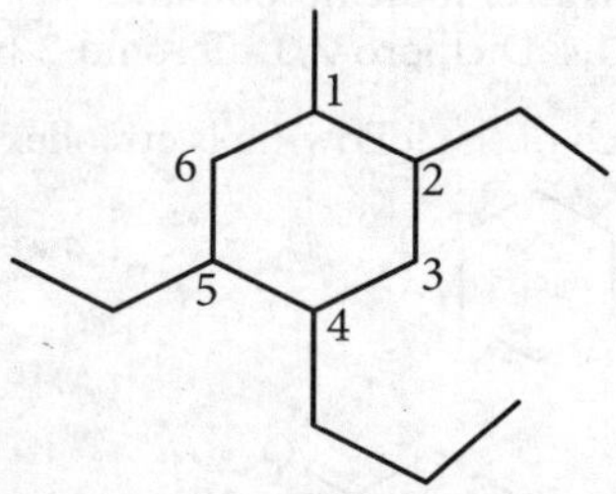

59. The degree of unsaturation in a compound with molecular formula Ph_2C_2 is:

(a) 6 (b) 7
(c) 8 (d) 10

60. Which of the following compounds has only sp^2-hybridized carbon atom?

(a) CH_3COOH
(b) CH_3COCH_3
(c) CH_3CH_2CN
(d) $CH_2{=}CH{-}CH{=}CH_2$

61. Which of the following cannot be used as the IUPAC name as well as the common name?

(a) Phenol (b) Benzoic acid
(c) Toluene (d) Acetic acid

62. In the following compound, the correct lowest set of locants is:

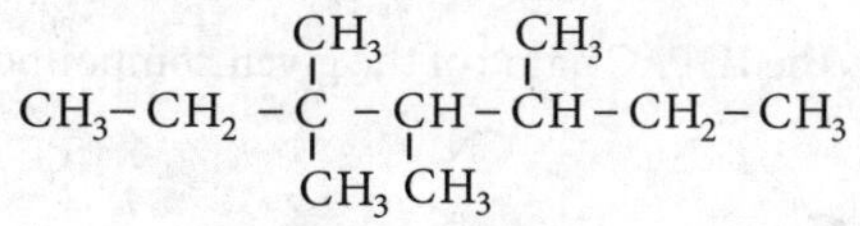

(a) 3,3,4,5 (b) 3,4,5,5
(c) 4,5,3,3 (d) 5,5,4,3

63. The correct IUPAC name of the given compound is:

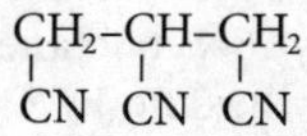

(a) 1,2,3-Tricyano propane
(b) 3-Cyanopentane dinitrile
(c) 1,2,3-Tricarbonitrile propane
(d) Propane-1,2,3-tricarbonitrile

64. The IUPAC name of the given compound is:

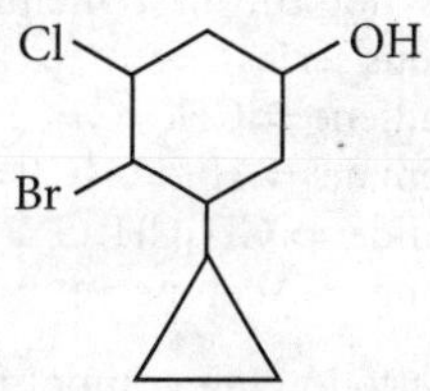

(a) 1-Hydroxy-3-chloro-4-bromo-5-cyclopropyl cyclohexane
(b) 4-Bromo-3-chloro-5-cyclopropyl cyclohexanol
(c) 4-Bromo-3-chloro-5-cyclopropyl cyclohexanal
(d) 1-Hydroxy-4-bromo-3-chloro-5-cyclopropyl cyclohexane

65. For the following compound, choose the correct IUPAC name:

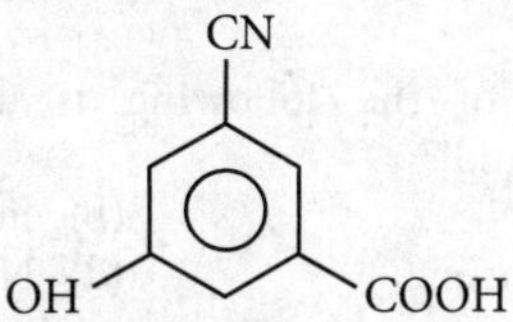

(a) 3-Carboxy-5-cyanophenol
(b) 3-Carboxy-5-hydroxybenzene carbonitrile
(c) 3-Cyano-5-hydroxybenzene carboxylic acid
(d) 3-Hydroxy-5-cyanobenzene carboxylic acid

66. The IUPAC name of the given compound is:

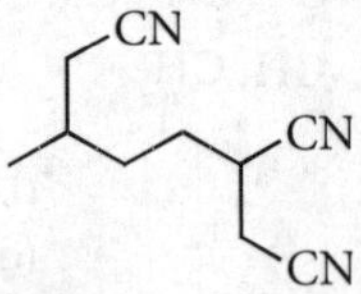

(a) 2-Methylhexane-1,5,6-tricarbonitrile
(b) 6-Methyl-3-cynoctane-1,8-dinitrile
(c) 3-Methyl-6-cynoctane-1,8-dinitrile
(d) 5-Methylhexane-1,2,6-tricarbonitrile

67. The IUPAC name for tertiary butyl chloride is:
(a) 2-Methyl-2-chlorobutane
(b) 2-Chloro-2-methylpropane
(c) 1-Chloro-2-methylpropane
(d) 2-Methyl-3-chloropropane

68. Which is not the first member of the given homologous series?
(a) Alkadiene ⇒ $CH_2=C=CH_2$
(b) Alkenyne ⇒ $HC\equiv C-CH=CH_2$
(c) Cyanide ⇒ CH_3CH_2CN
(d) Ketone ⇒ Acetone

69. Select the following compounds in which the prefix 'cyclo' is used in IUPAC nomenclature:

(a) 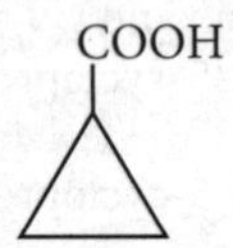
(b) 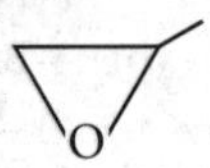
(c) 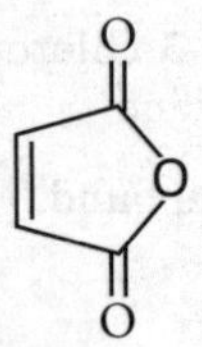
(d) All of these

70. Which of the following is a heterocyclic compound?
(a) Phenol
(b) Furan
(c) Benzene
(d) Naphthalene

71. Which of the following sets does not belong to the same homologous series?
(a) $CH_3Br, C_2H_5Br, C_3H_7Br$
(b) $CH_3-O-CH_3, CH_3-OC_2H_5, CH_3CH_2-OC_2H_5$
(c) $PhNH_2, PhNHCH_3, PhN(CH_3)_2$
(d) $HCHO, CH_3CHO, CH_3CH_2CHO$

72. Which of the following compounds is benzyl chloride?

(a) 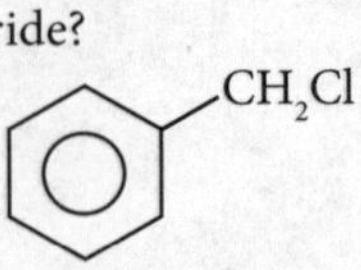
(b) 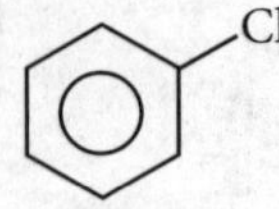
(c) 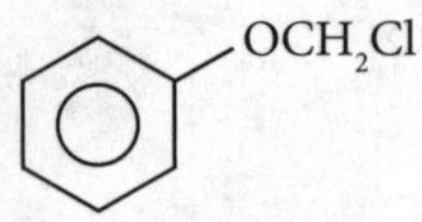
(d) 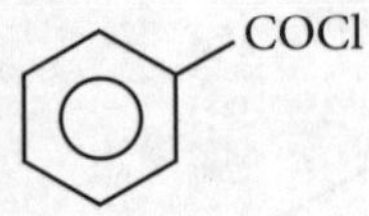

73. Which of the following is crotonaldehyde?
(a) $CH_2=CH-COOH$
(b) $CH_3-CH=CH-CHO$
(c) $CH_3-CH_2-CH_2-COOH$
(d) $CH_3-CH=CH-COOH$

74. The name of $ClCH_2-\underset{Br}{C}=\underset{Br}{C}-CH_2Cl$ according to the IUPAC nomenclature system is:
(a) Dichlorodibromobutane
(b) 2,3-Dibromo-1,4-dichloro-2-butene
(c) Dibromodichlorobutane
(d) 1,4-Dichloro-2,3-dibromo-2-butane

75. Which of the following is cyclohexanedione?

(a) 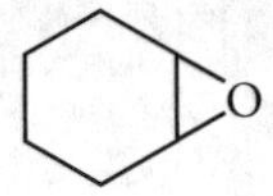
(b) 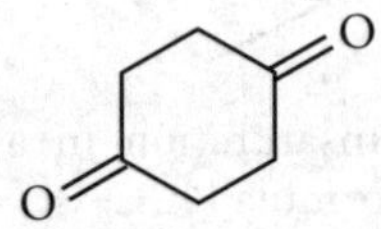
(c) 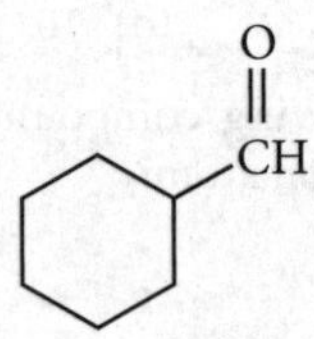
(d) 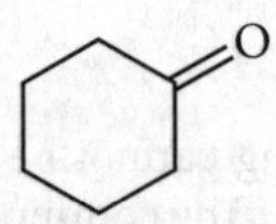

76. Which of the following compounds is a homocyclic hydrocarbon?

(a) 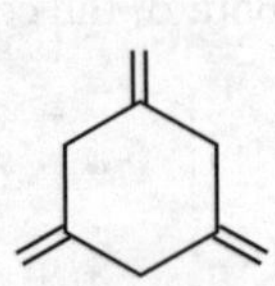
(b) 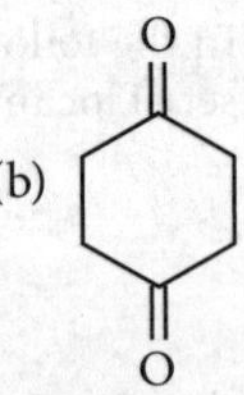

(c) 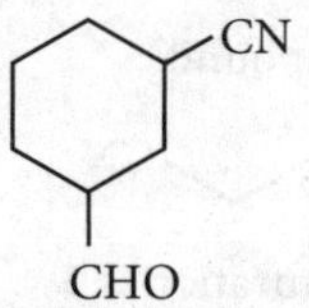
(d) 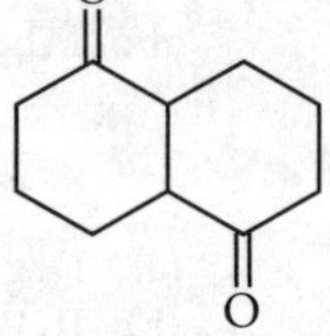

77. Choose the incorrect IUPAC name:
(a) 4,5-Dimethylhexane
(b) 2,2,4-Trimethylpentane
(c) 1-Cyclobutyl-1-cyclopropylpentane
(d) 2-Methyl-3-ethylpentane

78. The correct IUPAC name of the following compound is:

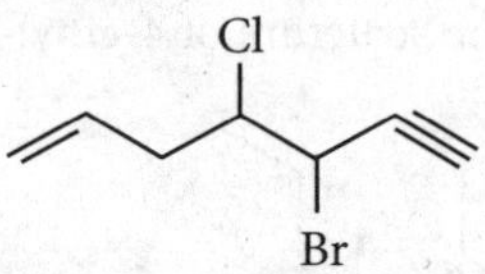

(a) 3-Bromo-4-chlorohept-1-en-6-yne
(b) 5-Bromo-4-chlorohept-1-en-6-yne
(c) 3-Bromo-4-chlorohept-6-en-1-yne
(d) 5-Bromo-4-chlorohept-6-en-1-yne

79. The IUPAC name of $(CH_3CO)_2O$ is:
(a) Acetic anhydride
(b) Methanoic anhydride
(c) Ethanoic methanoic anhydride
(d) Ethanoic anhydride

80. Which of the following esters uses the alkoxy carbonyl prefix?

(a) 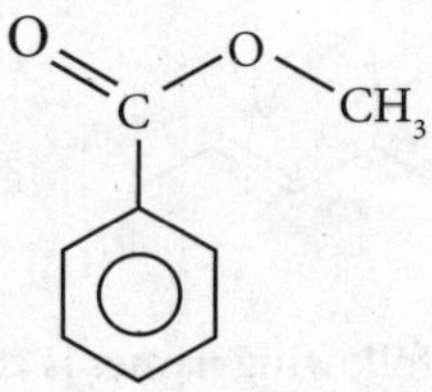

(b) 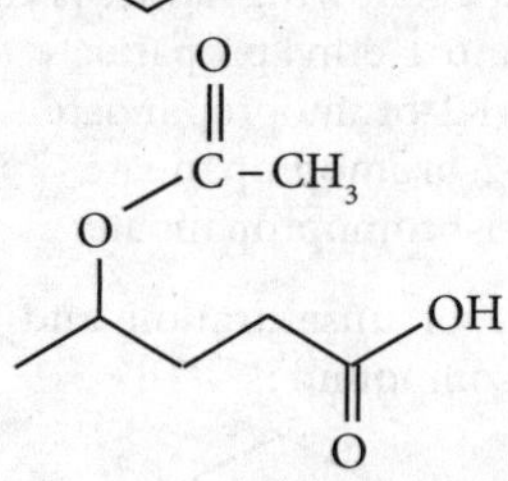

(c) 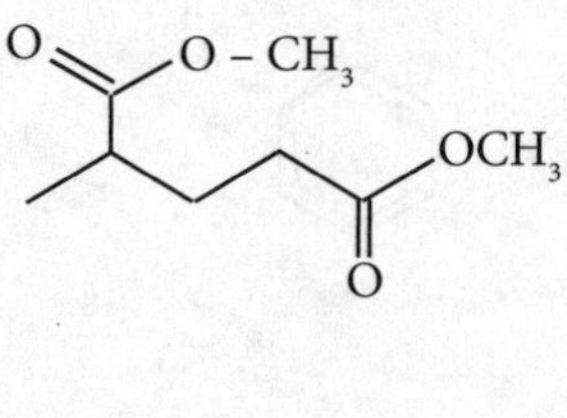

(d) 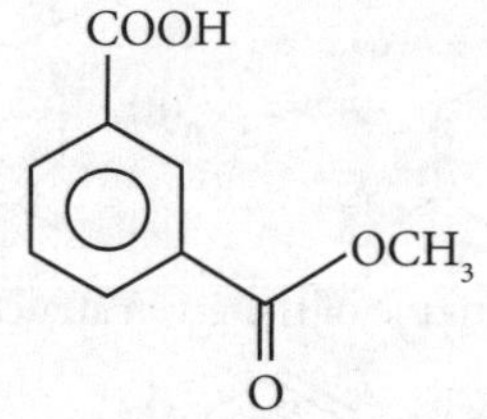

81. Among the following, find out the incorrect statement:
(a) CH_3–$CHCl_2$ is an example of gem-dihalide
(b) Penta-1,4-diene contain sp^2 and sp^3 carbon
(c) Isopentane has 4 carbons
(d) Toluene is a homocyclic compound

82. Select the structure with the correct numbering in the chain:
(a) $\overset{5}{C}H_2=\overset{4}{C}H-\overset{3}{C}H_2-\overset{2}{C}\equiv\overset{1}{C}H$
(b) $\overset{1}{C}H_3-\overset{2}{C}H=\overset{3}{C}H-\overset{4}{C}\equiv\overset{5}{C}H$
(c) $\overset{7}{C}H_2=\overset{6}{C}H-\overset{5}{C}H=\overset{4}{C}H-\overset{3}{C}H_2-\overset{2}{C}H=\overset{1}{C}H_2$
(d) $\overset{1}{C}H_2=\overset{2}{C}H-\overset{3}{C}H=\overset{4}{C}H-\overset{5}{C}H_2-\overset{6}{C}\equiv\overset{7}{C}H$

83. Which of the following compounds is homocyclic?
(a) 
(b) 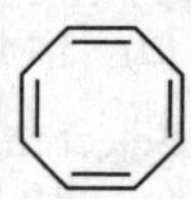
(c) 
(d) All of these

84. Which of the following compounds does not have a secondary suffix?
(a) $PhOCH_3$
(b) CH_3NH_2
(c) CH_3CH_2OH
(d) C_6H_5CHO

85. Choose the correct IUPAC name of following compound:

CH_3–CH–CH_2–CH–CH_2–CH–CH_3
with CH_3 on C-2, CH_2–CH_3 on C-4 and CH_2–CH_3 on C-6

(a) 2,4-Diethyl-6-methylheptane
(b) 3,7-Dimethyl-5-ethyloctane
(c) 5-Ethyl-3,7-dimethyloctane
(d) 4-Ethyl-2,6-dimethyloctane

86. Which of the following compounds has an unequal number of 1°, 2° and 3° carbons?

(a) 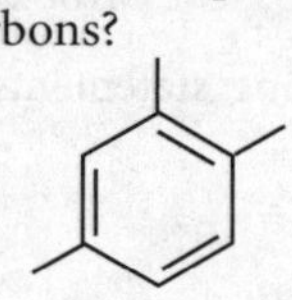
(b) 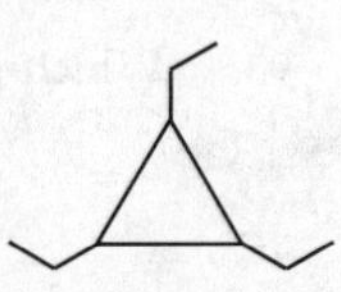

(c) 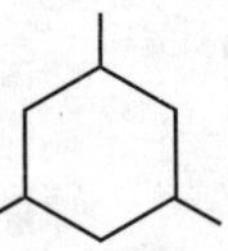 (d) 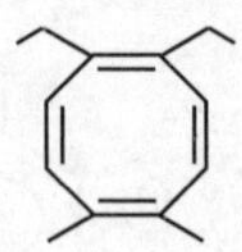

87. The IUPAC name of the given structure is:

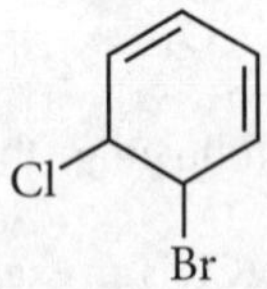

(a) 6-Bromo-5-chloro-1,3-cyclohexadiene
(b) 1-Bromo-2-chloro-3,5-cyclohexadiene
(c) 5-Bromo-6-chloro-1,3-cyclohexadiene
(d) 2-Bromo-1-chloro-3,5-cyclohexadiene

88. 1°, 2°, 3° and 4° carbon atoms are not present in:
(a) 2,2,3-Trimethylpentane
(b) 2,3,4-Trimethylpentane
(c) 3-Ethyl-2,3-trimethylpentane
(d) 1,1,2-Trimethylcyclohexane

89. Which of the following IUPAC names is correct?
(a) 2-Ethylpentane
(b) 4-Methylbutan-1-ol
(c) 5-Ethyl-3-methylheptane
(d) 3-Methylhexane

90. Select the incorrect IUPAC name:
(a) Pentan-1-amine
(b) Pentan-2-ol
(c) Pent-2-ene
(d) 1-Methylbutanamine

91. A primary amine has an amino group ($-NH_2$) attached to:
(a) Primary carbon
(b) Secondary carbon
(c) Tertiary carbon
(d) All of these

92. Which of the following is the correct IUPAC name of the given compound:

$$CH_3-\underset{\displaystyle CH_3}{\underset{|}{CH}}-CH_2-\underset{\displaystyle CH_3}{\underset{|}{C}}=CH-COOH$$

(a) 3,5-Dimethylhexanoic acid
(b) 3,5-Dimethylhex-2-enoic acid
(c) 2,4-Dimethylhex-2-enoic acid
(d) 3,5-Dimethylhex-2-ene carboxylic acid

93. Which of the following statements is correct about the given compound?

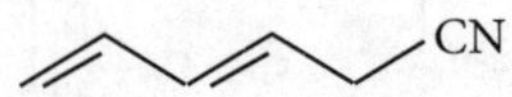

(a) Degree of unsaturation is 3
(b) IUPAC name is Hexa-3,5-dien-1-nitrile
(c) It is an saturated compound
(d) Hybridization of all carbons is sp^2

94. The correct IUPAC name of succinic acid is:
(a) Propane-1,3-dioic acid
(b) Ethane-1,2-dioic acid
(c) Butane-1,4-dioic acid
(d) 2-Hydroxybutane-1,4-dioic acid

95. Select the structure of 4-ethyl-2,3-dimethyl-2-heptene:

(a) 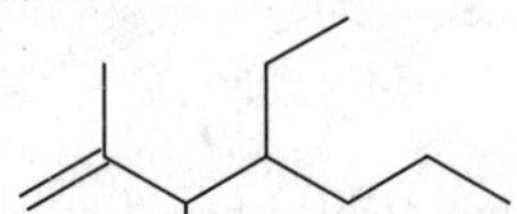

(b) 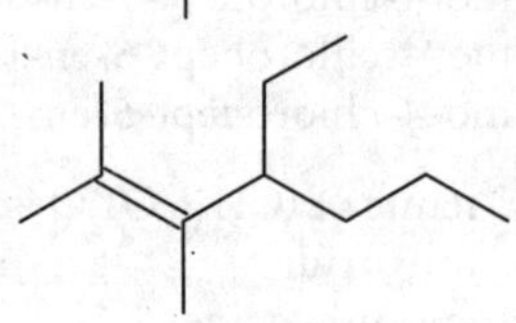

(c) 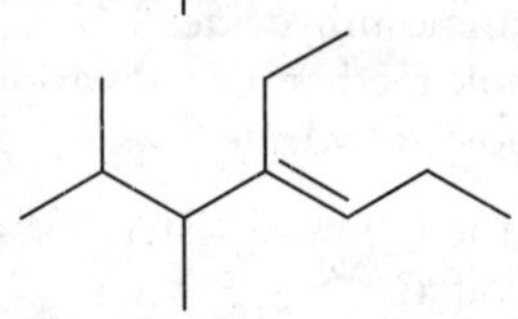

(d) 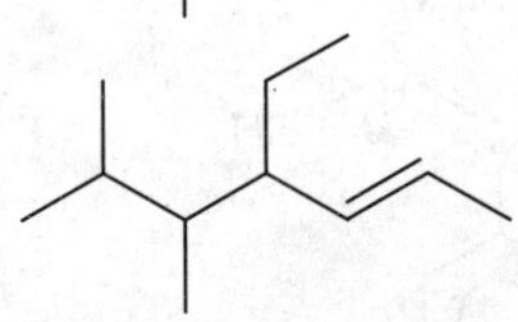

96. Which of the following names is correct?
(a) 2-Bromo-1-ethyl propanoate
(b) 1-Ethyl-2-bromopropanoate
(c) Ethyl-2-bromopropanoate
(d) Ethyl-1-bromopropanoate

97. The degree of unsaturation and type of the following compound is:

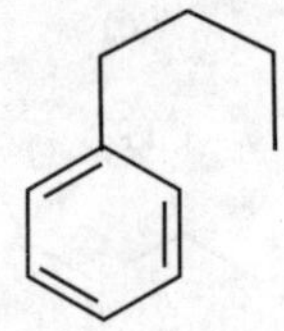

(a) 4, Homocyclic (b) 5, Homocyclic
(c) 5, Heterocyclic (d) 4, Heterocyclic

98. The incorrect statement about homologous series is:
(a) The homologues shows difference in physical properties due to change in molecular mass.
(b) The homologues shows difference in chemical properties due to change in functional group.
(c) All the members of a homologous series have the same general formula.
(d) The two adjacent members differ by a $-(CH_2)-$ group or (14) atomic mass unit.

99. The homocyclic compound is:

(a) 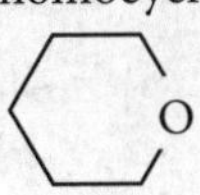

(b) 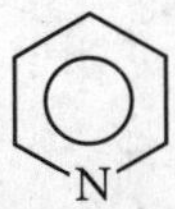

(c) 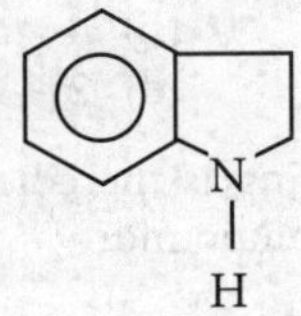

(d) 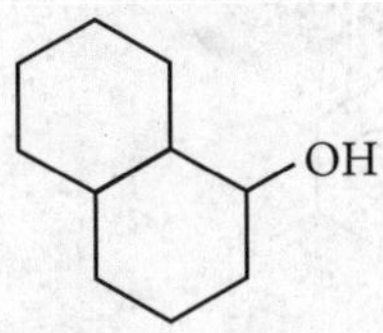

100. The correct IUPAC name of 2-ethyl-3-pentyne is:
(a) 3-Methyl hexyne-4
(b) 4-Ethyl pentyne-2
(c) 4-Methyl hexyne-2
(d) None of these

Level-2

1. The IUPAC name of $CH_3-CH=C=CH-C\equiv CH$ is:
(a) 2-Hexen-4-yne
(b) Hexa-2,3-dien-1-yne
(c) Hexa-3,4-dien-1-yne
(d) None of these

2. The IUPAC name of the compound shown below is:

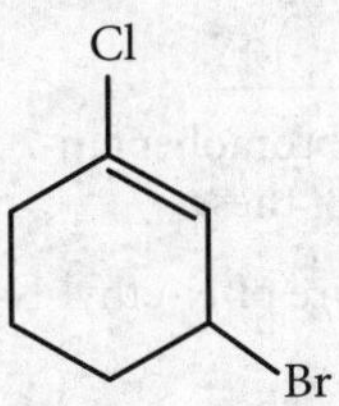

(a) 2-Bromo-6-chlorocyclohex-1-ene
(b) 6-Bromo-2-chlorocyclohexene
(c) 3-Bromo-1-chlorocyclohexene
(d) 1-Bromo-3-chlorocyclohexene

3. The correct IUPAC name of the following is:

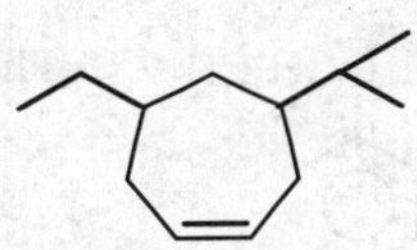

(a) 4-Ethyl-6-(1-methylethyl)cycloheptene
(b) 4-(1-Methylethyl)-6-ethylcycloheptene
(c) 4-Ethyl-6-isopropylcycloheptene
(d) None of these

4. How many compounds among the following contain tertiary carbon atoms?

(i) 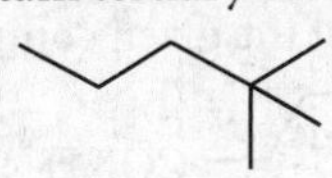

(ii) 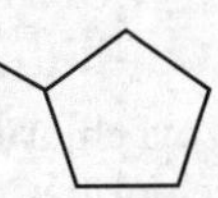

(iii) 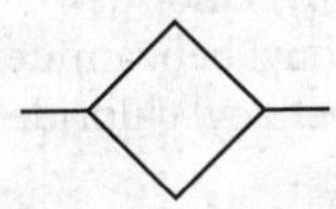

(iv) 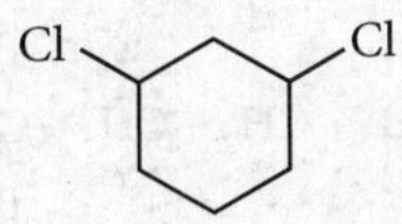

(a) 1 (b) 4
(c) 3 (d) 2

5. Which of the following is the correct IUPAC name for the given compound?

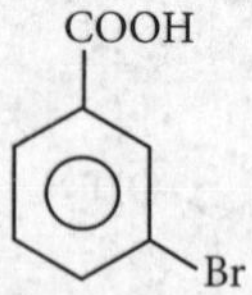

(a) 3-Bromobenzene carboxylic acid
(b) m-Bromobenzoic acid
(c) 3-Bromobenzoic acid
(d) Both (a) and (c)

6. Which of the following sets is incorrectly matched?

	Compound	Common name	IUPAC name
(a)	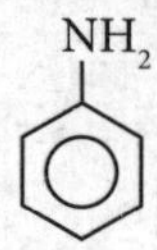	Aniline	Aniline
(b)	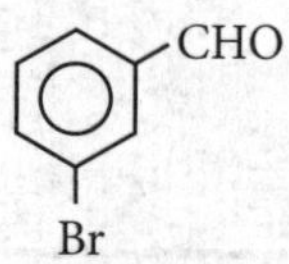	m-Bromobenzaldehyde	3-Bromobenzaldehyde
(c)	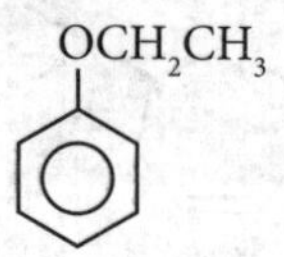	Phenetole	Ethyl phenyl ether
(d)	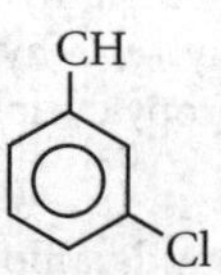	m-Chlorotoluene	3-Chlorotoluene

7. The IUPAC name of the given compound is:

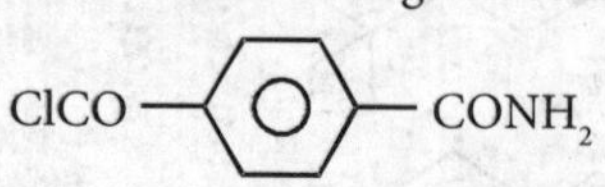

(a) 4-Carbamoyl benzoyl chloride
(b) 4-Amino benzoyl chloride
(c) 4-Chloro carbonyl benzamide
(d) 4-Acetamide benzoyl chloride

8. The IUPAC name of

$$CH_3-\underset{\displaystyle OH}{\underset{|}{CH}}-CH_2-CH_2-CH_2-\overset{\displaystyle Br}{\overset{|}{\underset{\displaystyle Br}{\underset{|}{C}}}}-CH_3 \text{ is:}$$

(a) 6,6-Dibromoheptan-2-ol
(b) 2,2-Dibromoheptan-6-ol
(c) 6,6-Dibromoheptan-2-al
(d) None of these

9. The structure of N-ethyl-N-phenylbutanamide is:

(a) $CH_3CH_2CH_2-\overset{\displaystyle O}{\overset{||}{C}}-N\begin{matrix} C_6H_5 \\ CH_3 \end{matrix}$

(b) $CH_3CH_2CH_2-\overset{\displaystyle O}{\overset{||}{C}}-N\begin{matrix} C_6H_5 \\ CH_2-CH_3 \end{matrix}$

(c) $C_6H_5-CH_2CH_2CH_2-\overset{\displaystyle O}{\overset{||}{C}}-\underset{\displaystyle H}{\underset{|}{N}}-CH_2-CH_3$

(d) $CH_3CH_2-\overset{O}{\overset{\|}{C}}-CH_2-N\begin{matrix} C_6H_5 \\ CH_2-CH_3 \end{matrix}$

10. The correct structure of 6-amino-4-hydroxycylohex-2-ene-1-sulphonic acid is:

(a)

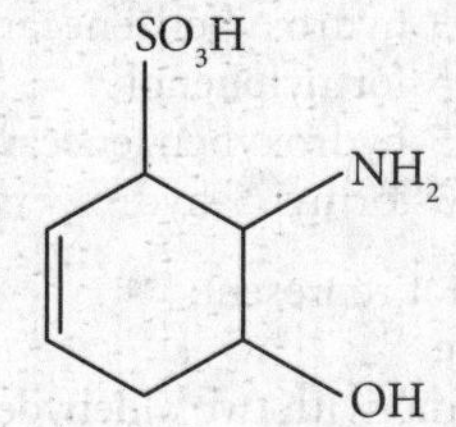

(b)

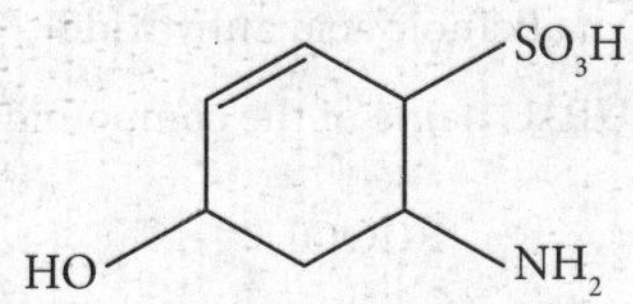

(c)

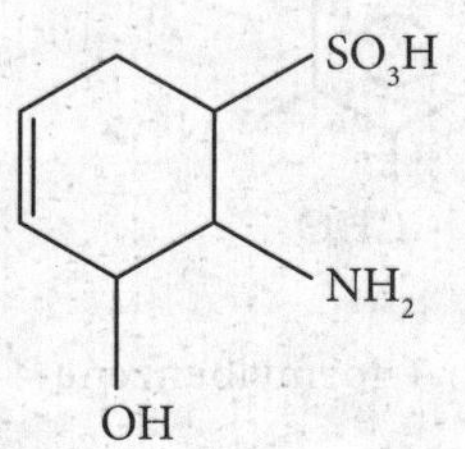

(d)

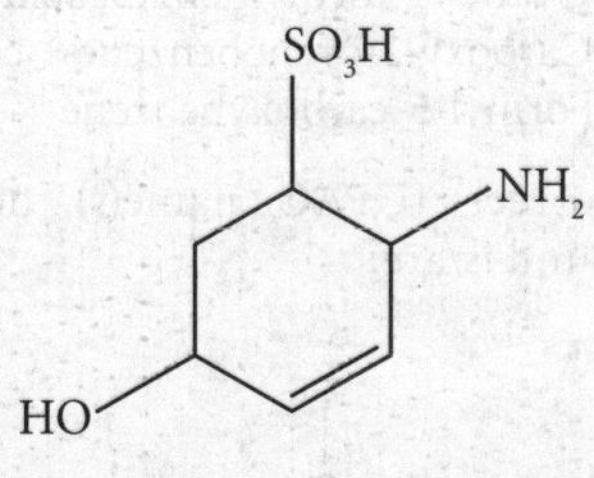

11. Identify the correct order of priority of functional groups:

(a) $-CHO > \;\rangle C{=}O > -COX > -CN$

(b) $-COX > -CHO > \;\rangle C{=}O > -CN$

(c) $-CHO > -CN > -COX > \;\rangle C{=}O$

(d) $-COX > -CN > -CHO > \;\rangle C{=}O$

12. Which of the following is not a dicarboxylic acid?

(a) Lactic acid (b) Oxalic acid
(c) Malonic acid (d) Adipic acid

13. Which of the following statements is correct for the given compound?

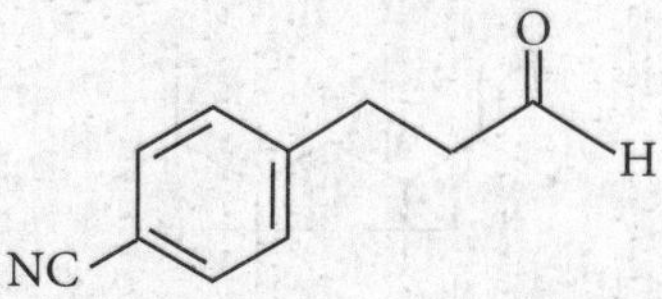

(a) The degree of unsaturation for the given compound is eight
(b) The compound has two primary carbon atoms and six secondary carbon atoms
(c) The number of π bonds in the given compound is seven
(d) The compound has an aldehyde group according to priority

14. The IUPAC name of the compound

$CH_3-NH-\underset{CH_3}{\underset{|}{CH}}-CH_2-\underset{CH_3}{\underset{|}{CH}}-CH_3$ is:

(a) 2-(N-methylamino)-4-methyl pentane
(b) N-methyl-4-methylpentan-2-amine
(c) 2-(N-methylamino)-3-isopropylpropane
(d) 2-(N-methylamino)-1,4,4-trimethylbutane

15. The correct IUPAC name of following compound is:

$CH_3-\underset{C_2H_5}{\underset{|}{CH}}-\overset{O}{\overset{\|}{C}}-O-CH_3$

(a) Methyl-2-ethylpropanoate
(b) Methylbutane-2-carboxylate
(c) Methyl-2-methylbutanoate
(d) Methoxypentanone

16. For the molecular formula C_6H_{14}, how many compounds are possible which contain three different types of carbon (1°, 2°, 3° only)?

(a) 4 (b) 3
(c) 6 (d) 2

17. The IUPAC name of the given compound is:

(a) 4-Carbamoylbenzoic acid
(b) 4-Aminobenzoic acid
(c) 4-Carboxy benzamide
(d) 4-Acetamidebenzoic acid

18. The total number of carbon atoms present in the principal carbon chain according to IUPAC is:

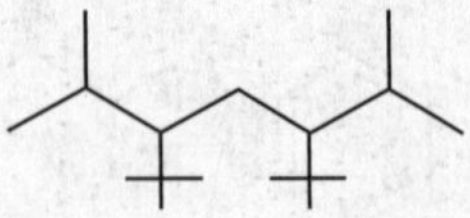

(a) 6 (b) 7
(c) 8 (d) 5

19. Choose the correct IUPAC name of the compound:

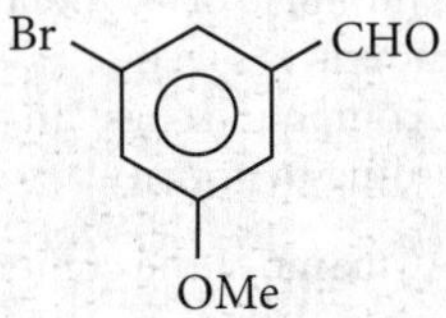

(a) 3-Methyl-5-bromobenzene carbaldehyde
(b) 3-Formyl-5-bromophenyl methyl ether
(c) 3-Bromo-5-methoxy benzeldehyde
(d) 3-Formyl-5-bromo-1-methoxy benzene

20. Which of the following represents the correct IUPAC name?
(a) 2-Ethylbutane
(b) But-3-en-1-ol
(c) 2-Chloro-3-fluoro-1,4-epoxy-but-3-ene
(d) Cyclopentanoic acid

21. The IUPAC name of the given compound is:

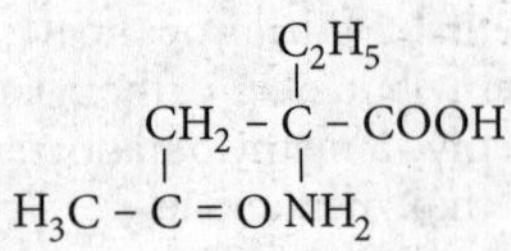

(a) 2-Oxo-4-amino-4-ethyl pentanoic acid
(b) 2-Amino-4-oxo-2-ethyl pentanoic acid
(c) 3-Amino-3-carboxy-5-hexanone
(d) 2-Amino-2-ethyl-4-oxopentanoic acid

22. The IUPAC name of the following compound is:

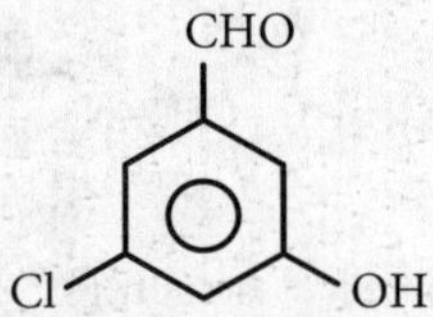

(a) 5-Chloro-3-hydroxybenzenecarbaldehyde
(b) 3-Chloro-5-formylphenol
(c) 3-Chloro-5-hydroxybenzenecarbaldehyde
(d) 1-Chloro-3-formyl-5-hydroxy benzene

23. $C_4H_6O_2$ does not represent:
(a) A diketone
(b) A compound with two aldehydes
(c) An alkenoic acid
(d) An alkanoic acid anhydride

24. The IUPAC name of the compound is:

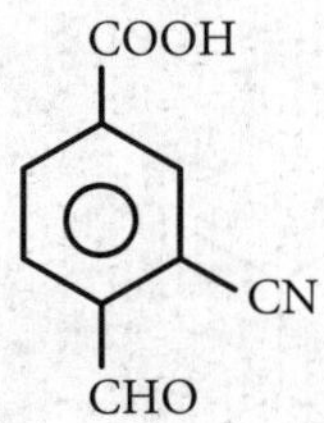

(a) 2-Cyano-1-formylbenzene-4-carboxylic acid
(b) 3-Cyano-4-formylbenzoicacid
(c) 4-Carboxy-2-cyanobenzene-1-carbaldehyde
(d) 2-Formyl-5-carboxybenzene-1-carbonitrile

25. The correct IUPAC name(s) of following compound is/are:

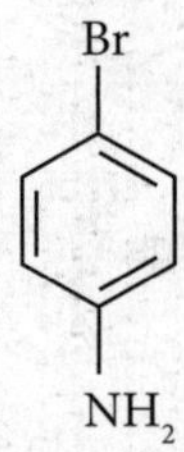

(a) p-Bromoaniline
(b) 4-Bromoaniline
(c) 4-Bromobenzenamine
(d) Both (b) and (c)

26. Which of the following IUPAC names is correct?
(a) 2-Ethyl-3-methylheptane
(b) 2-Bromo-1-chlorocyclohexane
(c) Pent-2-en-4-ol
(d) 1-Chloro-4-methyl benzene

27. Which of the following compounds is not a dicarboxylic acid?
(a) Maleic acid
(b) Succinic acid
(c) Phthalic acid
(d) Picric acid

28. How many carbons are present in the parent carbon chain of the following compound?

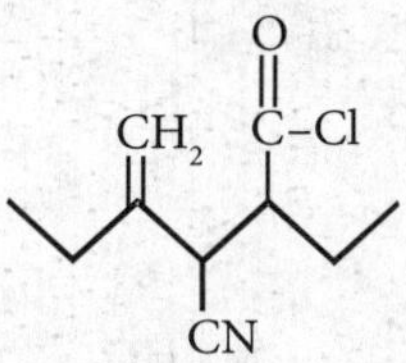

(a) 4 (b) 6
(c) 5 (d) 8

29. The sum of the positions of –OH and –Br in the given compound is:

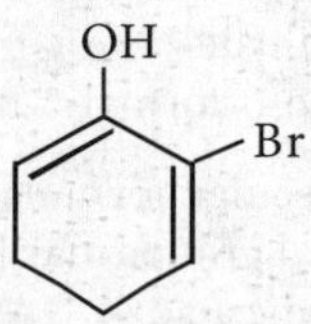

(a) 3 (b) 5
(c) 6 (d) 7

30. The correct IUPAC name of the compound is:

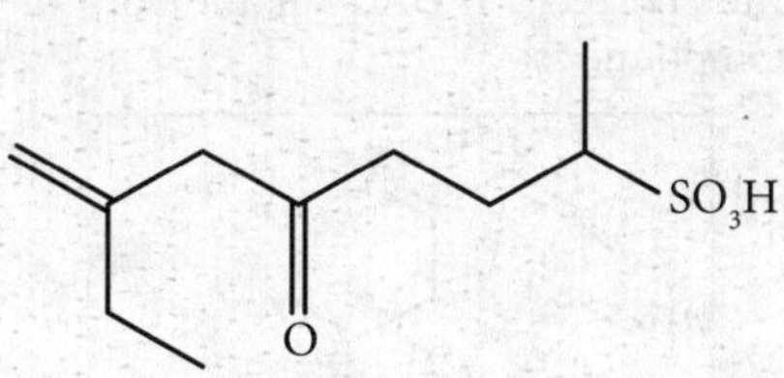

(a) 6-Ethyl-1-methyl-4-oxohept-6-ene-1-sulphonic acid
(b) 7-Ethyl-5-oxooct-7-ene-2-sulphonic acid
(c) 2-Ethyl-7-sulphooct-1-ene-4-one
(d) 7-Methylene-5-oxononane-2-sulphonic acid

31. The IUPAC name of

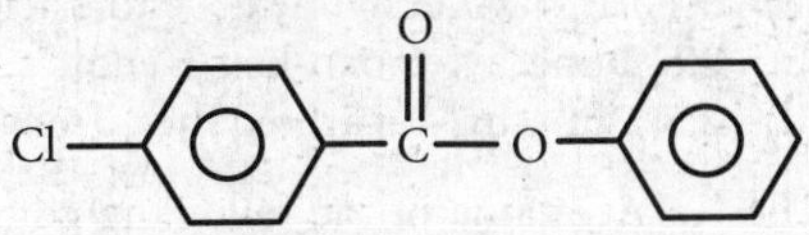

is:

(a) 4-Chlorophenyl benzoate
(b) Phenyl-4-chlorobenzoate
(c) Benzyl-4-chlorobenzenecarboxylate
(d) 4-Chlorodiphenyl carboxylate

32. The IUPAC name of

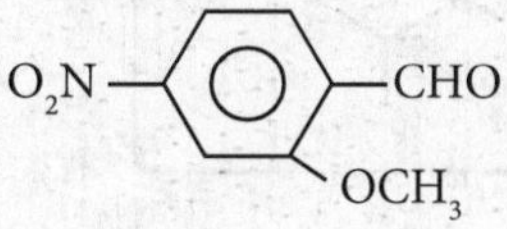

is:

(a) 2-Methoxy-4-nitrobenzaldehyde
(b) 4-Nitroanisaldehyde
(c) 3-Methoxy-4-formyl nitro benzene
(d) 2-Formyl-4-nitro anisole

33. The molecular formula $C_nC_{2n-4}O_2$ can have:
(a) Three aldehydes
(b) One acid anhydride
(c) Hydroxy alkanal
(d) One aldehyde and one ketone

34. Among the following, choose the incorrect option:
(a) Phenyl group has 4 double bond equivalent.
(b) Primary, secondary and tertiary amides are different functional groups.
(c) Urea was first formed by Friedrich Wohler in the laboratory.
(d) Phenol is a homocyclic compound as well as a hydrocarbon.

35. For a homologous series, which functional group is incorrectly matched with their general formula?
(a) Ether ⇒ $C_nH_{2n+2}O$
(b) Carboxylic acid ⇒ $C_nH_{2n}O_2$
(c) Cyanide⇒ $C_nH_{2n+1}N$
(d) Halogen ⇒ $C_nH_{2n+1}X$

36. The IUPAC name for the following compound is:

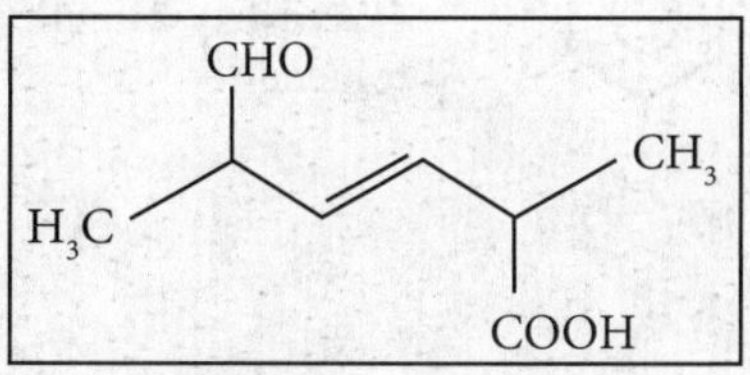

(a) 2,5-Dimethyl-5-carboxy-hex-3-enal
(b) 6-Formyl-2-methyl-hex-3-enoic acid
(c) 2,5-Dimethyl-6-oxo-hex-3-enoic acid
(d) 2,5-Dimethyl-6-carboxy-hex-3-enal

37. The IUPAC name of the following compound is:

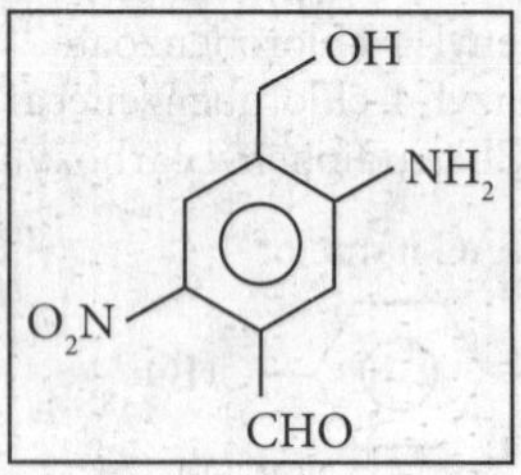

(a) 3-Amino-4-hydroxymethyl-5-nitrobenzaldehyde
(b) 2-Nitro-4-hydroxymethyl-5-aminobenzaldehyde
(c) 4-Amino-2-formyl-5-hydroxymethylnitrobenzene
(d) 5-Amino-4-hydroxymethyl-2-nitrobenzaldehyde

38. The IUPAC name of the compound 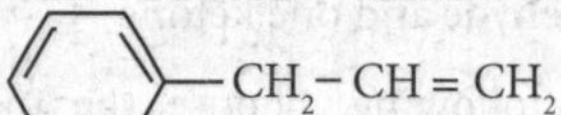 is:

(a) 1-Phenylprop-2-ene
(b) 3-Phenylprop-1-ene
(c) 1-(Prop-1-enyl) benzene
(d) 1-(Prop-2-enyl) benzene

39. Which of the following is the correct IUPAC name?

(a) 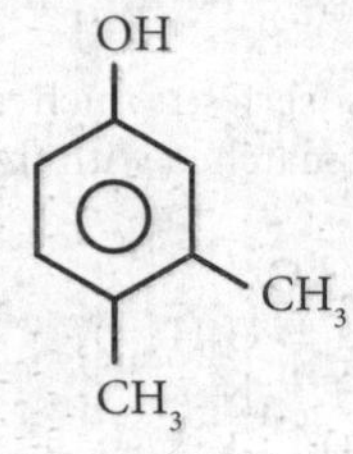 3, 4-Dimethylphenol

(b) 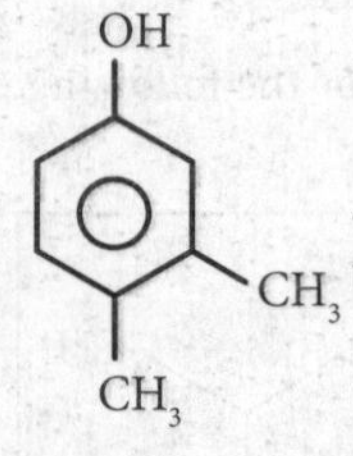 4-Hydroxy-2-methyl toluene

(c) 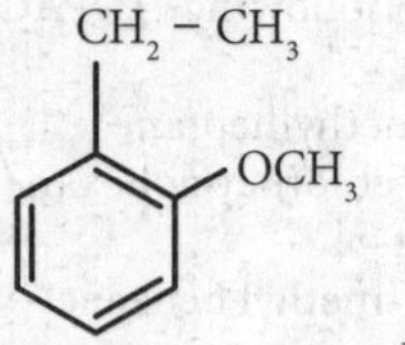 1-Ethyl-2-anisole

(d) 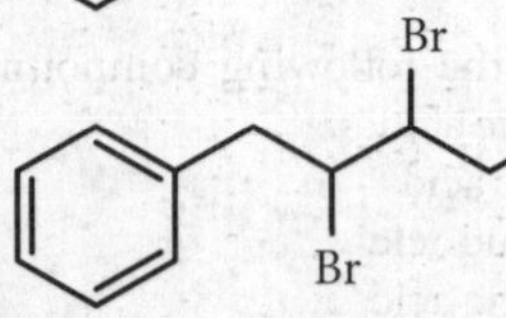

1-(2,3-Dibromopentyl) benzene

40. The correct IUPAC name of the following compound is:

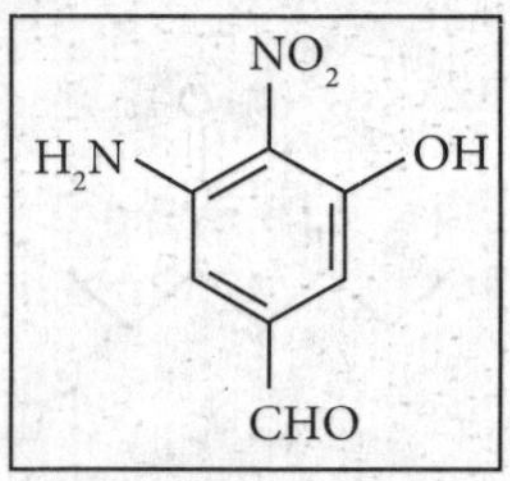

(a) 5-Amino-3-hydroxy-4-nitrobenzene carbaldehyde
(b) 3-Amino-5-formyl-2-nitrobenzene carbaldehyde
(c) 3-Amino-5-hydroxy-4-nitrobenzene carbaldehyde
(d) 3-Amino-5-formyl-2-nitrophenol

41. For the molecular formula $C_nH_{2n}O$, which of the functional groups may be possible?
(a) Carboxylic acid
(b) Anhydride
(c) Aldehyde
(d) Ester

42. The correct IPUAC name of the given compound is:

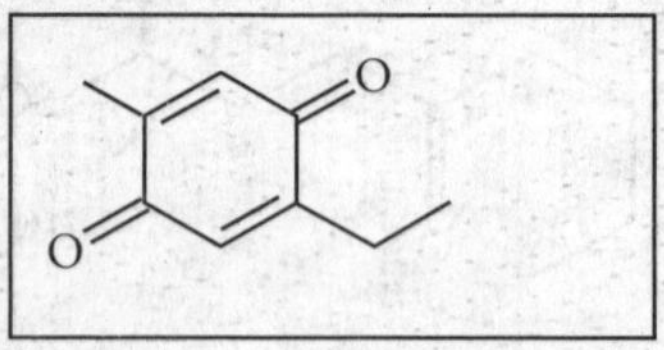

(a) 5-Ethyl-2-methylcyclohexa-2,5-diene-1,4-dione
(b) 2-Ethyl-5-methylcyclohexa-2,5-diene-1,4-dione

(c) 2-Ethyl-5-methyl cyclohex-2,5-diene-1,4-dione
(d) 2-Ethyl-5-ethyl cyclohex-2,5-diene-1,4-dione

43. The correct IUPAC name of the following compound is:

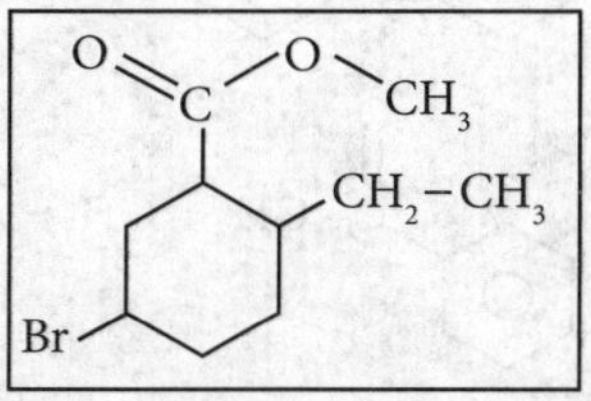

(a) Methyl-5-bromo-2-ethyl cyclohexane carboxylate
(b) 5-Bromo-2-ethylmethyl cyclohexane carboxylate
(c) Methyl-3-bromo-5-ethyl cyclohexane carboxylate
(d) Methyl-2-bromo-5-ethyl cyclohexane carboxylate

44. The (2-propenyl) group is:
(a) $CH_2=CH-CH_2-$
(b) $CH_3-CH=CH-$
(c) Both (a) and (b)
(d) None of these

45. The compound 2-carbamoyl-pent-3-enedioic acid contains how many carbons having sp^2-hybridization?
(a) 2 (b) 3
(c) 4 (d) 5

46. What would be the sum of the positions of the chlorine and bromine atoms according to IUPAC?

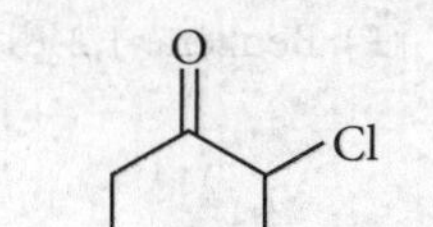

(a) 6 (b) 5
(c) 9 (d) 11

47. Which of the following names is not correct for the given compound?

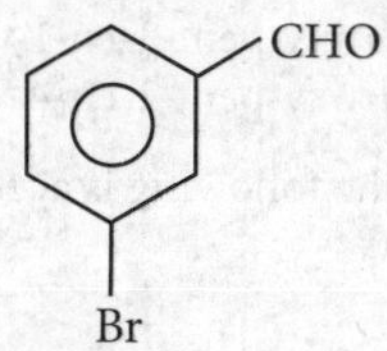

(a) 3-Bromobenzaldehyde
(b) 3-Bromobenzenecarbaldehyde
(c) 3-Formylbromobenzene
(d) m-Bromobenzaldehyde

48. The IUPAC name of the following compound is:

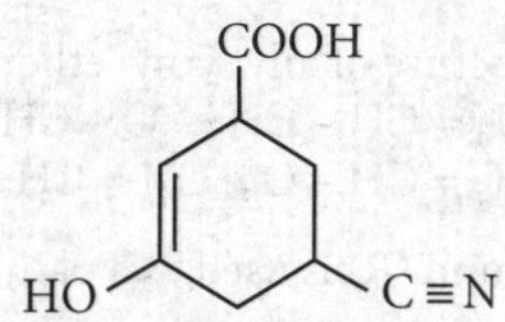

(a) 5-Cyano-3-hydroxycyclohex-2-enecarboxylicacid
(b) 3-Hydroxy-5-cyanocyclohex-5-enoicacid
(c) 3-Hydroxy-5-cyanocyclohex-2-enoicacid
(d) 3-Carboxy-5-hydroxycyclohex-5-enecarbonitrile

49. The structure of the (2,2-dimethyl-3-ethylpentyl) group is:

(a) $CH_3-C(CH_3)(CH_3)-CH(C_2H_5)-CH_2-CH_2-$

(b) $CH_3-CH(C_2H_5)-C(CH_3)(CH_3)-CH_2-CH_2-$

(c) $CH_3-CH_2-CH(C_2H_5)-C(CH_3)(CH_3)-CH_2-$

(d) None of these

50. The IUPAC name of the following compound is:

$HC\equiv C-C(OH)=CH-CH_3$

(a) 3-Hydroxy-pent-3-en-1-yne
(b) Pent-3-en-1-yn-3-ol
(c) 3-Hydroxy-pent-2-en-4-yne
(d) Pent-2-en-4-yn-3-ol

51. Which of the following is acetophenone?

(a) $CH_3-\underset{\underset{O}{\|}}{C}-CH_3$

(b) 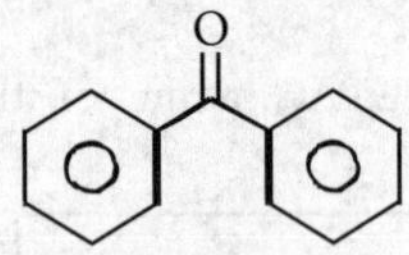

(c) 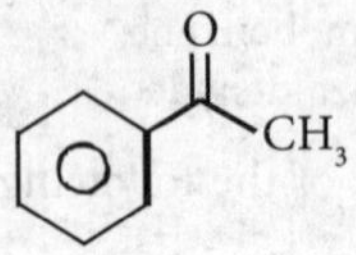

(d) 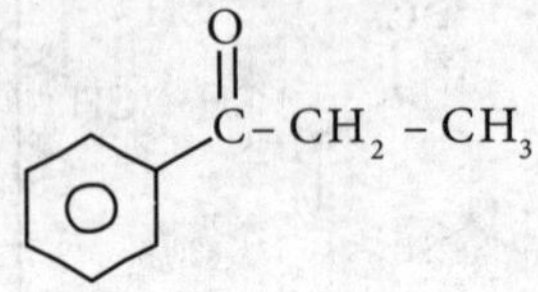

52. The structure of allyl vinyl ether is:

(a) $CH_2=CH-CH_2-O-CH_2-CH=CH_2$
(b) $CH_2=CH-O-CH_2-CH=CH_2$
(c) $CH_2=CH-O-CH=CH_2$
(d) $CH_3-CH=CH-O-CH=CH_2$

53. Compound (R) is used as a painkiller known as aspirin.

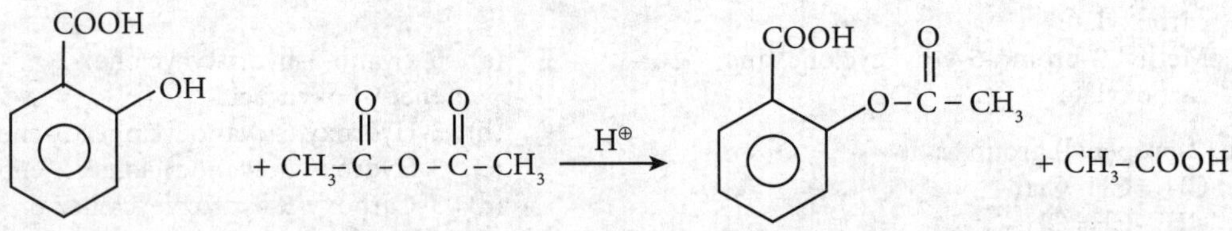

(P) (Q) (R) (S)

Which of the following is correctly matched with their IUPAC name?

(a) P ⇒ 2-Carboxy phenol
(b) Q ⇒ Ethanoic anhydride
(c) S ⇒ Acetic acid
(d) All of these

54.

Column-1 (Aromatic compound)	Column-2 (Common name)	Column-3 (IUPAC name)
(I) 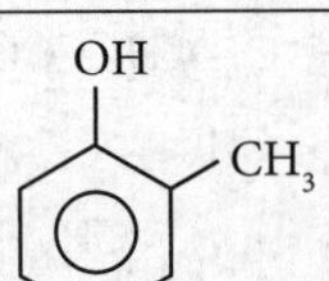	(i) p-Xylene	(P) Benzene-1,2-dicarboxylic acid
(II) 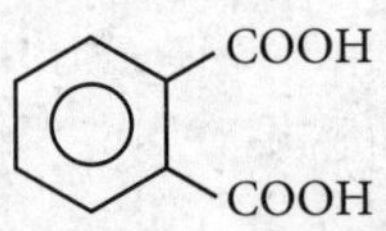	(ii) o-Cresol	(Q) 2-Methylphenol
(III) 	(iii) m-Chlorotoluene	(R) 1-Chloro-3-methylbenzene

(IV) 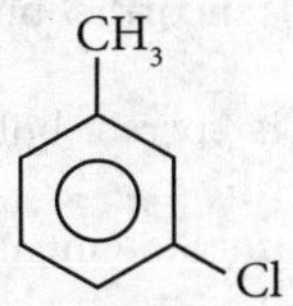

(iv) Pthalic acid

(S) 1,4-Dimethylbenzene

Which of the following options is the only correct combination?

(a) III, ii and S (b) IV, ii and R
(c) I, ii and Q (d) III, ii and Q

55. Which of the following is the structure of picric acid?

(a) 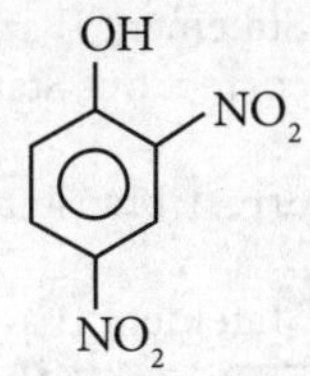

(b) 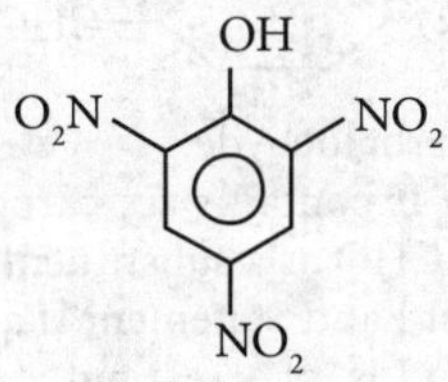

(c) 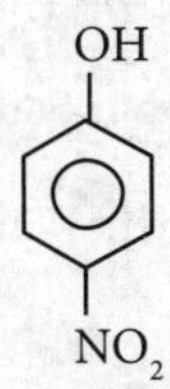

(d) 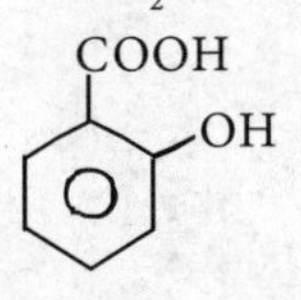

56. Which of the following is the structure of aspirin?

(a) 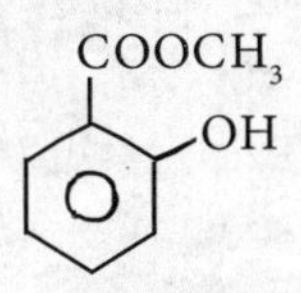

(b) 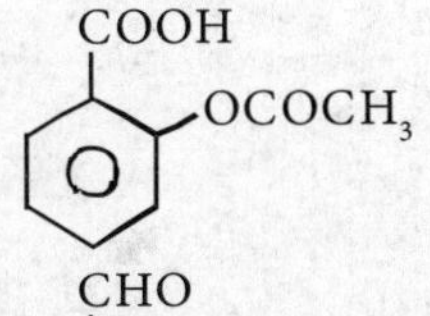

(c) 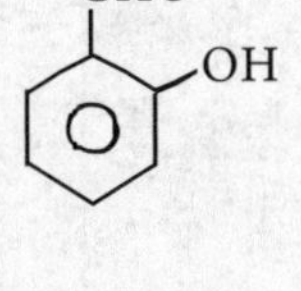

(d) 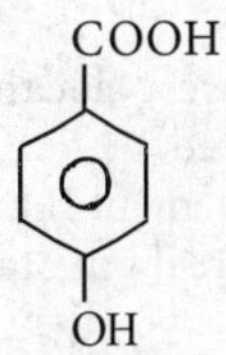

57. The IUPAC name of the neopentyl group is:
(a) 2,2-Dimethylbutyl
(b) 2,2-Dimethylpropyl
(c) 1,1-Dimethylbutyl
(d) 1,2-Dimethylpropyl

58. The IUPAC name of the given compound is:

$$HO-C(=O)-CH_2-C(OH)(COOH)-CH_2-C(=O)-OH$$

(a) 3-Carboxy-3-hydroxybutanedioic acid
(b) 2-Hydroxypropane-1,2,3-tricarboxylic acid
(c) 3-Hydroxybutanedioic acid
(d) 2-Bis(carboxymethyl)-2-hydroxyethanoic acid

59. Examine the following structures:

(A) $CH_3-C(CH_3)_2-OH$ (B) $CH_3-C(CH_3)_2-NH_2$

Which of the following statements is correct?
(a) A is tertiary alcohol while B is tertiary amine
(b) A is primary alcohol while B is primary amine
(c) A is tertiary alcohol while B is primary amine
(d) A is primary alcohol while B is tertiary amine

60. Which is not the first member of the given homologous series?

(a) Alkadiene $CH_2=C=CH_2$
(b) Alkenyne $HC\equiv C-CH=CH_2$
(c) Ethyl ester $CH_3-CH_2-O-\underset{\underset{O}{||}}{C}-CH_3$

(d) Ketone $CH_3-\overset{\overset{O}{||}}{C}-CH_3$

61. **Statement I:** The IUPAC name of $CH_3-CH=CH-C\equiv C-H$ is pent-3-en-1-yne but not pent-2-en-4-yne.
Statement II: The lowest locant rule for multiple bonds is preferred.
(a) Statement I and Statement II are correct
(b) Statement I is incorrect but Statement II is correct
(c) Statement I is correct but Statement II is incorrect
(d) Statement I and Statement II are incorrect

62. **Statement I:** The IUPAC name for

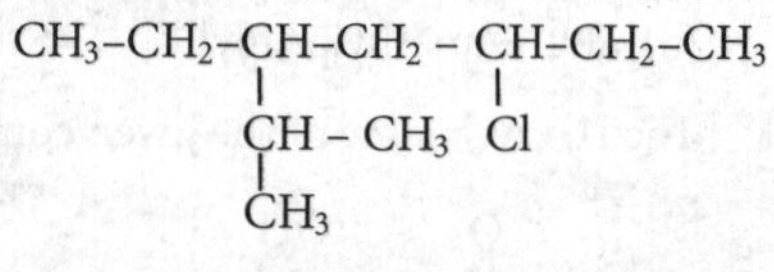

is 5-chloro-3-ethyl-2-methylheptane but not 3-chloro-5-isopropylheptane.
Statement II: The parent carbon chain should contain more alkyl substituents.
(a) Statement I and Statement II are correct
(b) Statement I is incorrect but Statement II is correct
(c) Statement I is correct but Statement II is incorrect
(d) Statement I and Statement II are incorrect

63. **Statement I:** The IUPAC name of

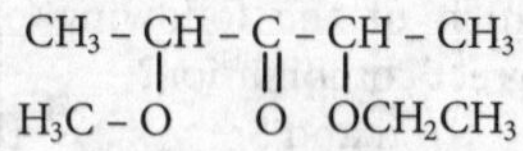

is 2-ethoxy-4-methoxypentan-3-one.
Statement II: Larger substituents are assigned lower locants.
(a) Statement I and Statement II are correct
(b) Statement I is incorrect but Statement II is correct
(c) Statement I is correct but Statement II is incorrect
(d) Statement I and Statement II are incorrect

64. **Statement I:** CHO is called cyclohexanecarbaldehyde.
Statement II: It contains six carbon atoms in the ring with CHO as a substituent.
(a) Statement I and Statement II are correct
(b) Statement I is incorrect but Statement II is correct
(c) Statement I is correct but Statement II is incorrect
(d) Statement I and Statement II are incorrect

Answer Key

Level-1

1. (c)	**2.** (d)	**3.** (b)	**4.** (b)	**5.** (b)	**6.** (a)	**7.** (d)	**8.** (c)
9. (a)	**10.** (d)	**11.** (b)	**12.** (a)	**13.** (a)	**14.** (a)	**15.** (c)	**16.** (c)
17. (c)	**18.** (d)	**19.** (c)	**20.** (c)	**21.** (b)	**22.** (a)	**23.** (a)	**24.** (b)
25. (c)	**26.** (d)	**27.** (d)	**28.** (c)	**29.** (d)	**30.** (c)	**31.** (a)	**32.** (c)
33. (b)	**34.** (b)	**35.** (a)	**36.** (c)	**37.** (b)	**38.** (d)	**39.** (b)	**40.** (c)
41. (d)	**42.** (c)	**43.** (b)	**44.** (c)	**45.** (a)	**46.** (d)	**47.** (b)	**48.** (b)
49. (c)	**50.** (b)	**51.** (c)	**52.** (a)	**53.** (b)	**54.** (d)	**55.** (d)	**56.** (c)
57. (d)	**58.** (c)	**59.** (d)	**60.** (d)	**61.** (d)	**62.** (a)	**63.** (d)	**64.** (b)
65. (c)	**66.** (d)	**67.** (b)	**68.** (c)	**69.** (a)	**70.** (b)	**71.** (c)	**72.** (a)
73. (b)	**74.** (b)	**75.** (b)	**76.** (a)	**77.** (a)	**78.** (c)	**79.** (d)	**80.** (d)
81. (c)	**82.** (d)	**83.** (d)	**84.** (a)	**85.** (d)	**86.** (d)	**87.** (c)	**88.** (b)
89. (d)	**90.** (d)	**91.** (d)	**92.** (b)	**93.** (b)	**94.** (c)	**95.** (b)	**96.** (c)
97. (a)	**98.** (b)	**99.** (d)	**100.** (c)				

Level-2

1. (c)	**2.** (c)	**3.** (a)	**4.** (d)	**5.** (d)	**6.** (c)	**7.** (a)	**8.** (a)
9. (b)	**10.** (b)	**11.** (d)	**12.** (a)	**13.** (b)	**14.** (b)	**15.** (c)	**16.** (d)
17. (a)	**18.** (b)	**19.** (c)	**20.** (b)	**21.** (d)	**22.** (c)	**23.** (d)	**24.** (b)
25. (d)	**26.** (d)	**27.** (d)	**28.** (c)	**29.** (d)	**30.** (b)	**31.** (b)	**32.** (a)
33. (c)	**34.** (d)	**35.** (c)	**36.** (c)	**37.** (d)	**38.** (b)	**39.** (a)	**40.** (c)
41. (c)	**42.** (b)	**43.** (a)	**44.** (a)	**45.** (d)	**46.** (c)	**47.** (c)	**48.** (a)
49. (c)	**50.** (b)	**51.** (c)	**52.** (b)	**53.** (b)	**54.** (c)	**55.** (b)	**56.** (b)
57. (b)	**58.** (b)	**59.** (c)	**60.** (c)	**61.** (a)	**62.** (a)	**63.** (c)	**64.** (c)

Solutions

Level-1

1. 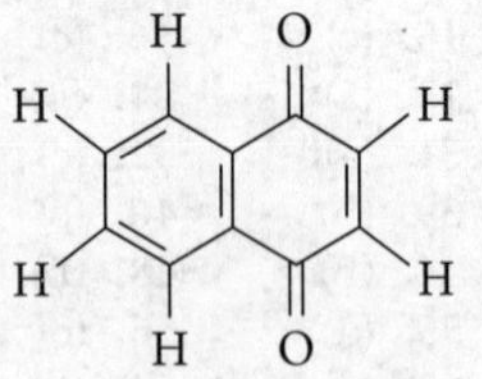

σ bonds present between every two atoms

2. $CH_3-CH(CH_3)-CH_2-CH_2-CH_3$ (the two CH_2 carbons marked 2°, 2°)

3. $C_nH_{2n}O_2$
This formula has DU = 1 and two oxygen atoms. So, it is not possible in two aldehydes.

$H-\overset{\displaystyle O}{\overset{\|}{C}}-CH_2-\overset{\displaystyle O}{\overset{\|}{C}}-H$

4. 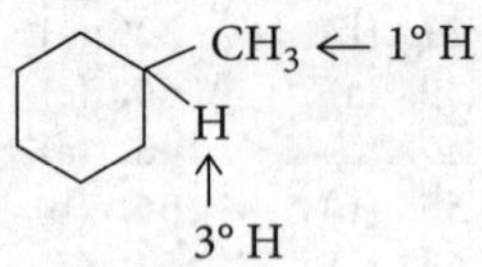

5. $CH_3-CH(CH_3)-CH_2-$
Isobutyl

6. 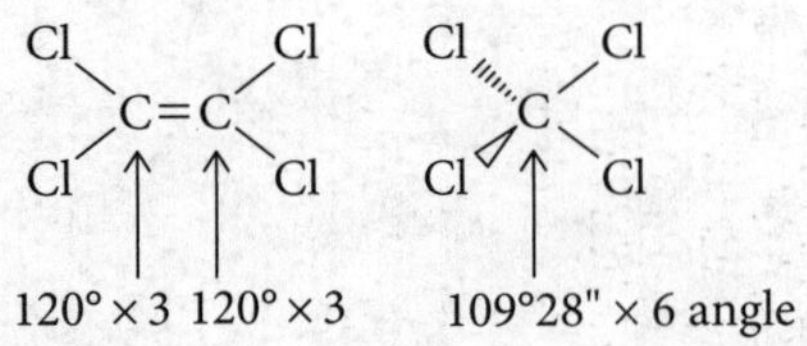

7. $CH_2=CH-CH_2-$
Allyl

8. 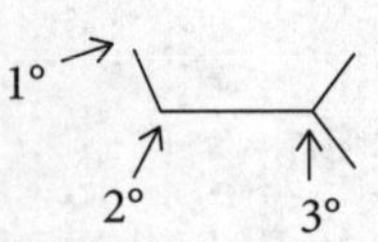

9. $CH_2=CH-CH_2-CH(CH_3)-CH=CH_2$

10. $\pi = 3, \sigma = 12$

$\frac{\sigma}{\pi} = \frac{12}{3} = 4$

11. 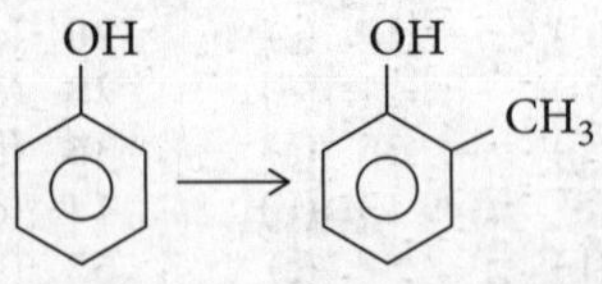

Phenol It is phenol (functional group) and CH_2 difference. So it is homologous.

12. $\sigma = 12, \pi = 5$ Ratio $= \frac{12}{5} = 2.4$

13. $CH_2=CH-C\equiv CH$
sp^2 sp^2 sp sp

14. CH_3-O-CH_3 (methyl ether)
$CH_3-CH_2-O-CH_3$ (IInd homologous)

15. Single bond carbons are sp^3 and one-double bond carbons are sp^2.

16. $H-C(=O)-O-CH_3$
It is the 1st member of esters. The next homologue is $CH_3-C(=O)-O-CH_3$

17. Other than carbon atom in the ring

19. Single bond (C–C) and hetero atom in the ring

20. Alkanal → $CH_3-C(=O)-H \rightarrow C_nH_{2n}O$

22. $H-C(=O)-H$, $CH_3-C(=O)-H$, $CH_3-CH_2-C(=O)-H$
Ist IInd IIIrd

23. $CH_3-CH<$
Ethylidene

24. 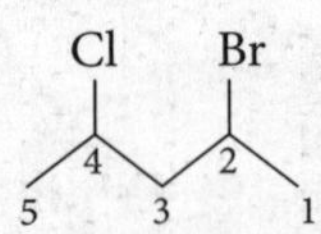

Alphabetical order

25. $-CN \Rightarrow$ Cyano

26. For homologous, the functional group and DU must be the same and there should be a difference of CH_2 or n × CH_2.

27.

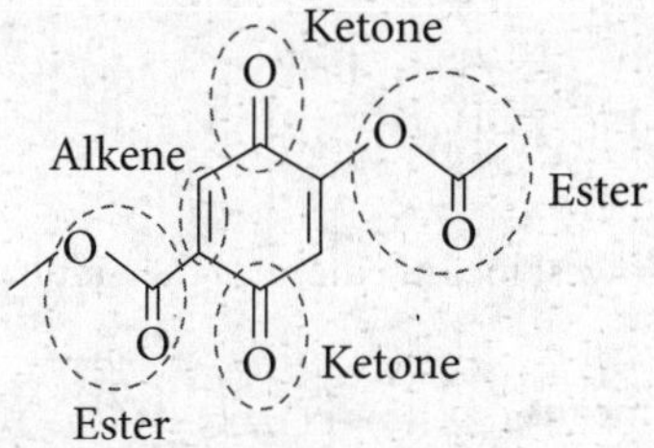

28. $CH_3-\underset{\underset{O}{\|}}{C}-OH$

Carboxylic acid has only one DU.

29. $CH_3-\underset{\underset{O}{\|}}{C}-CH_3$

First member of ketone

30.

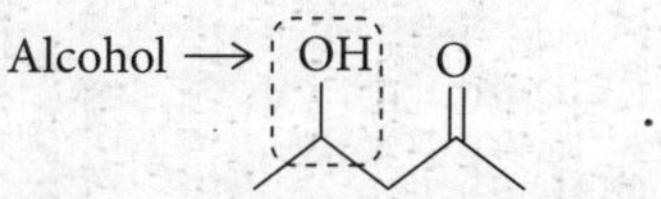

OH directly attached to benzene is phenol, not alcohol.

31. $CH_2 = CH$ – Vinyl

32. $CH_3 - CH_2 - NH - CH_3$

1°C 1°C 2° amine 1°C

33. Enyne means $CH_2 = CH - C \equiv CH$

35.

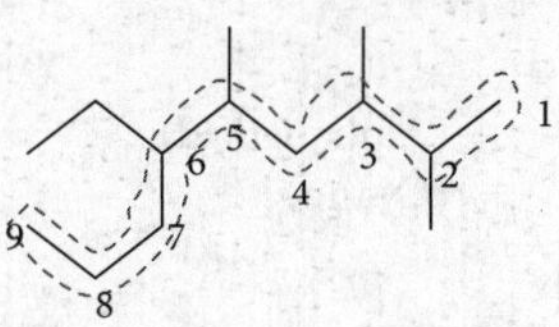

36. Amide has higher priority than aldehyde

37. $\sigma = 9$

$\pi = 9$

38.

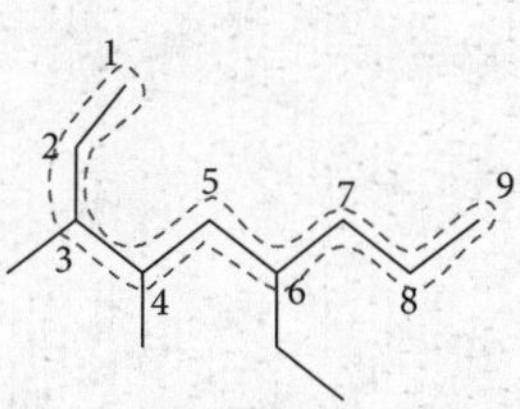

39. Nitro group (NO_2) has only prefix = nitro.

40. Homocyclic hydrocarbon means not other atoms; only hydrogen and carbons.

41.

42. One-double-bond containing carbons are sp^2 and one-triple-bond containing carbons are sp, and the numbering is from ene and not from yne.

43. 2,3-Diethyl butane means PCC will be

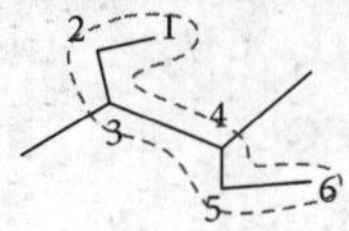

44.

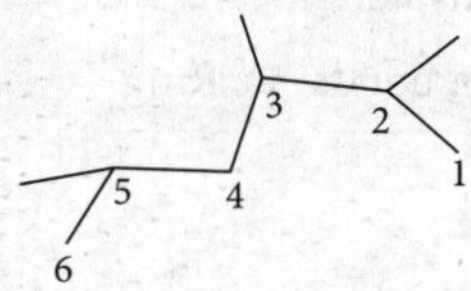

2, 3, 5-Trimethylhexane

45.

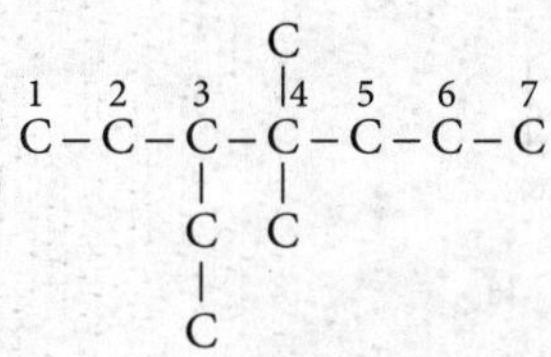

46.

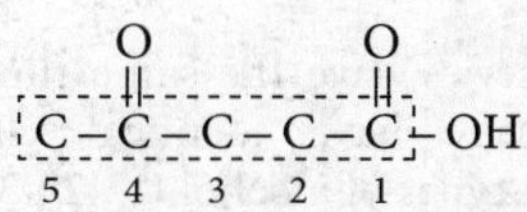

47.

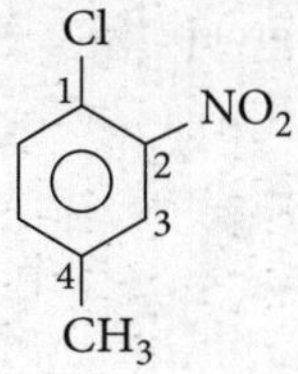

48.

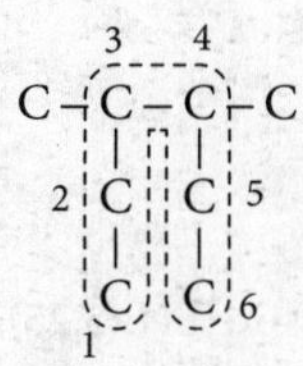

49. Lowest number to –COOH and closed multiple bonds in sequence of numbering.

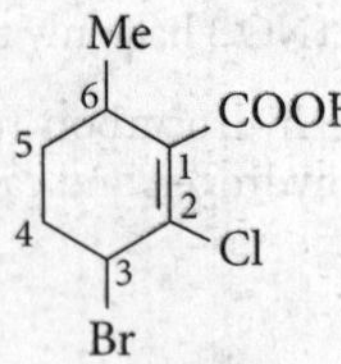

50. 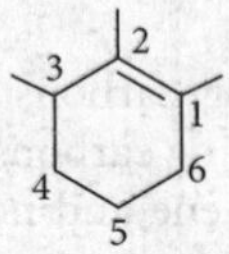

51. CH_3–CH_2–Cl → Alkyl halide is never a constituent of another functional group.
But CH_3CH_2OH and CH_3OCH_3

CH_3CH_2CHO and CH_3COCH_3

CH_3CN and CH_3NC

52. Double-bond equivalent means DU.

DU = No. of π bonds + Ring
(No. of π bonds = 6; Ring = 1)

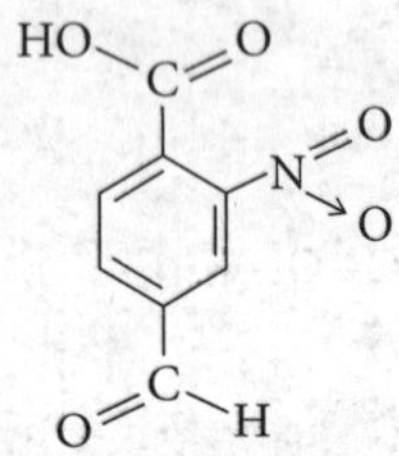

53. Homologous series have the same functional group. So, they have identical chemical properties. All types of alcohol (1°, 2°, 3°) have identical chemical properties because they have the same functional group.

54. 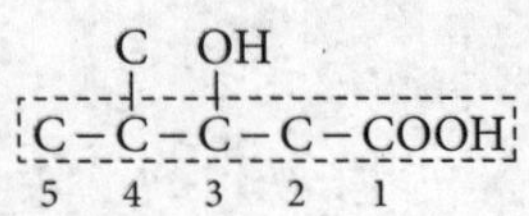

55. 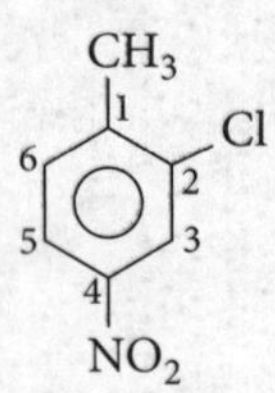

56. $CH_3 - CH_2 - C \equiv CH$ ← More EN (3.25)

57.

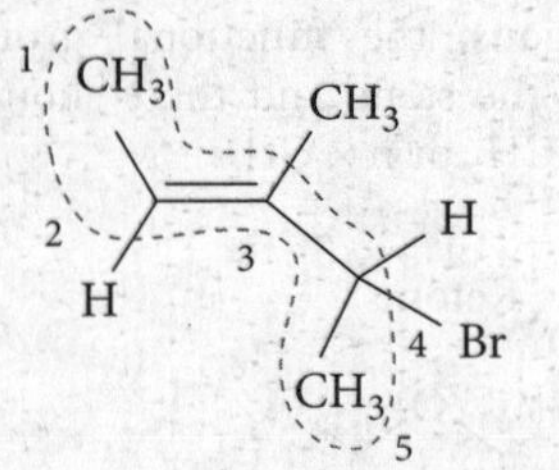

58. Apply lowest locant rule, and then alphabetical.

59. Ph_2C_2 means 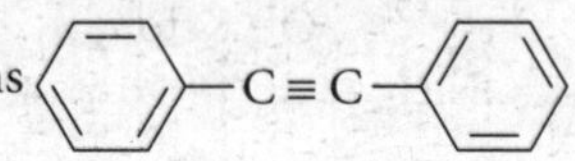

DU = π + ring
(π = 8; ring = 2)

60. One-double-bond containing carbons.

61. Acetic acid → $CH_3 - COOH$ → IUPAC name is ethanoic acid.

62. 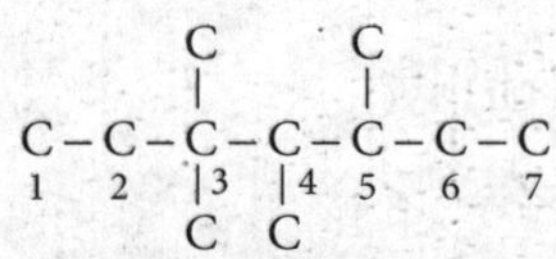

(3, 3, 4, 5) lowest locant

63. 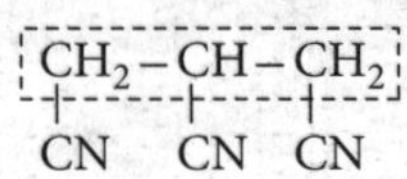 PCC selection

64.

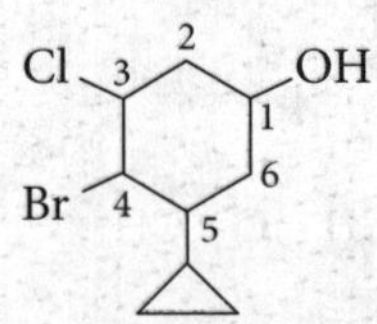

Used alphabetical
Chloro > Cyclopropyl

65.

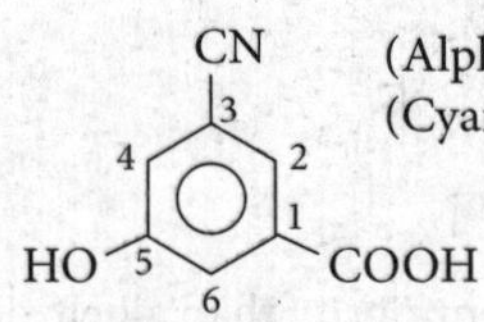

(Alphabetical)
(Cyano)

66.

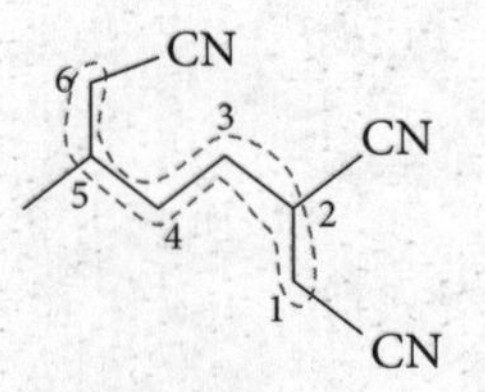

67.

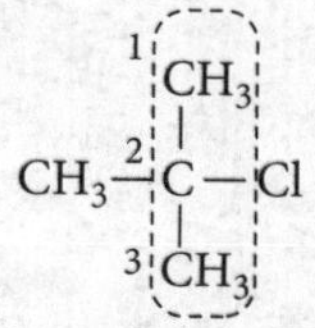

68. Cyanide, first member is H – CN

69.

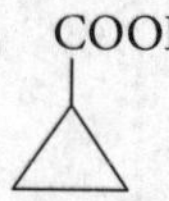

→ Cyclopropane carboxylic acid

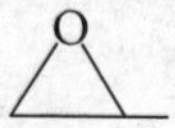

→ 1, 2-Epoxypropane

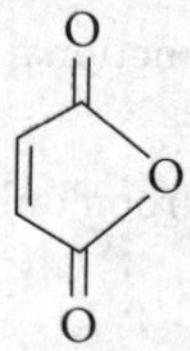

→ Butene-1, 4-dioic anhydride

70.

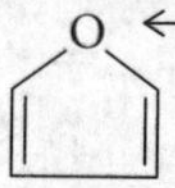

← Other atom oxygen in the ring

71. Primary, secondary and tertiary amines are considered as different functional groups.

72.

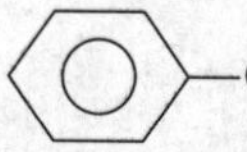

$-CH_2-$ (Benzyl)

(Phenyl)

73. $CH_3 - CH = CH - (C)$

PCC = Croton

74.

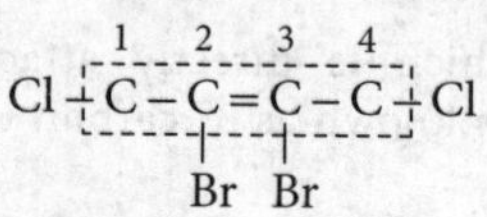

75. Diketone

76. All carbons in the ring means homocyclic series. No other atoms means only hydrogens and carbons are present in the molecule.

77.

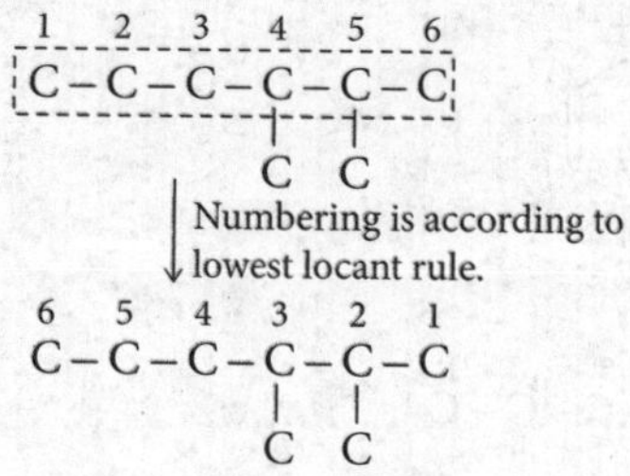

78.

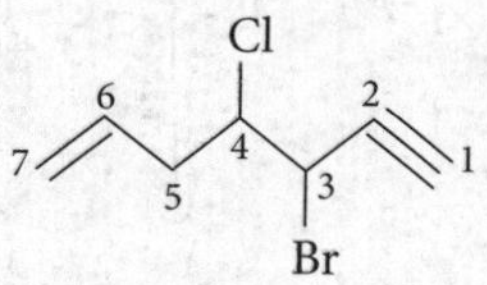

Multiple bonds locant is the same but lowest locant of substituent

79. $CH_3-\overset{\overset{O}{||}}{C}-O-\overset{\overset{O}{||}}{C}-CH_3$

PCC of the same number of carbons on both sides; so ethanoic anhydride.

80.

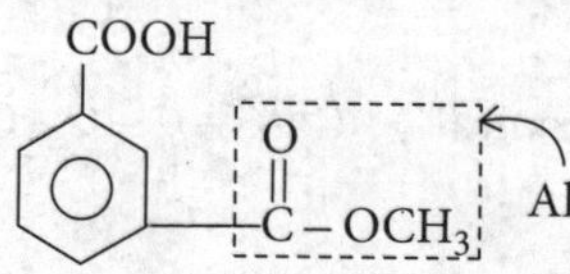

Alkoxy carbonyl

81. $CH_3-\underset{\underset{CH_3}{|}}{CH}-CH_2-CH_3$ has 5 carbon atoms

82. Lowest locant rule for multiple bonds is 1, 3, 6.

84. Amine, aldehyde and alcohol are the top '13' function groups which have a suffix, but ether is always considered as substituent.

85.

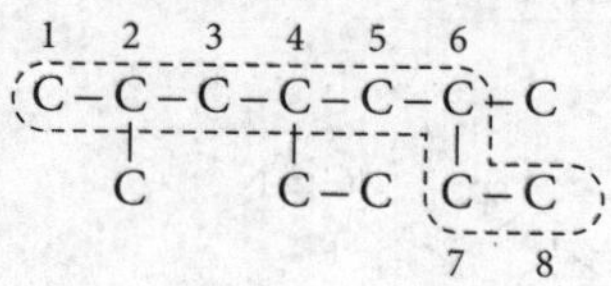

86. 1° C = 4
2° C = 6
3° C = 4

87. 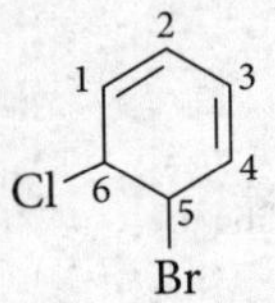

88. 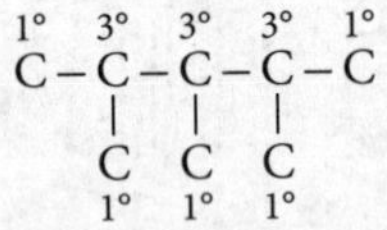

1°, 2°, 3°, 4°
✓ × ✓ ×

89. 2-Ethylpentane (×) 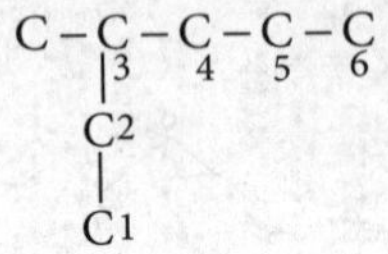

4-Methyl butan-l-ol (×) 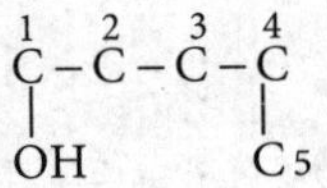

5-Ethyl-3-methyl heptane (×)

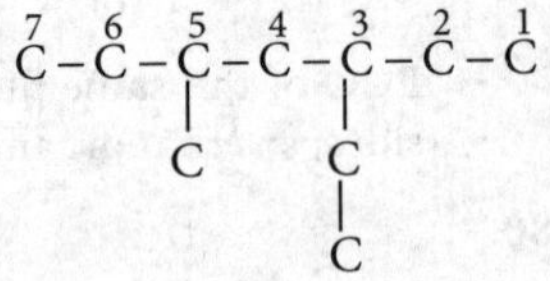

3-Methyl hexane (✓) 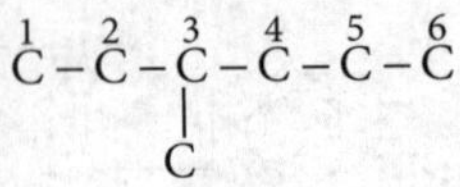

90. 1-Methyl butanamine

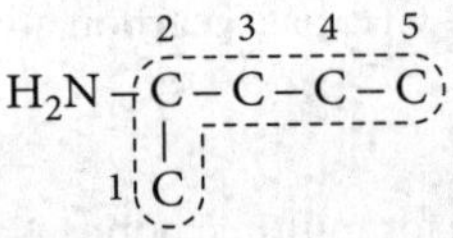 → Pentan-2-amine

91. The number of carbons directly attached to nitrogen determines the degree of amines.

92. 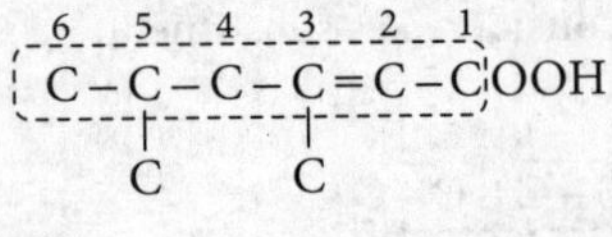

93. 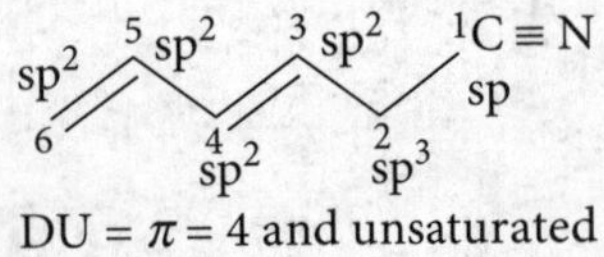

DU = π = 4 and unsaturated compound

94.

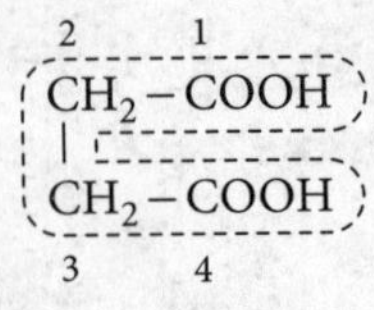 Succinic acid

95. 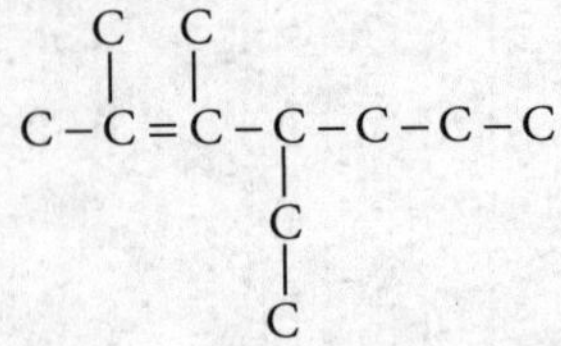

96. 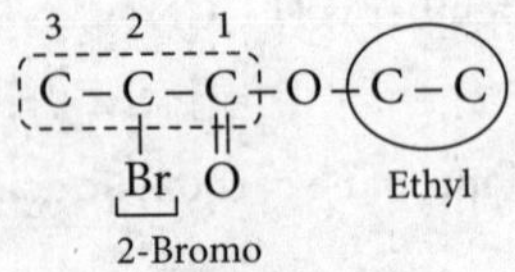

97. DU = π + ring
↓ ↓
3 1

98. Homologues have the same functional group, so the same chemical properties.

99. In the ring, all the atoms are carbon only.

100. 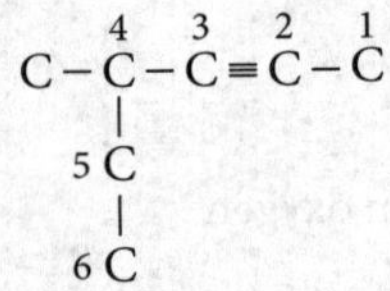

LEVEL-2

1. $CH_3–CH=C=CH–C\equiv CH$
6 5 4 3 2 1

2. 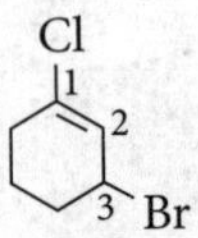

3. Ethyl 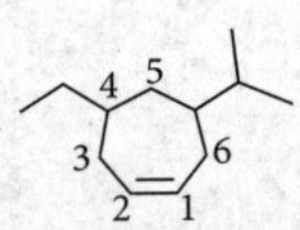 [1-Methylethyl]

4. The carbon which is directly attached to three carbons is known as 3° carbon (tertiary carbon).

5. 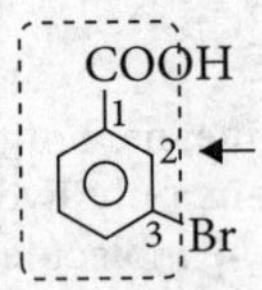 ← Considered benzoic acid

6. 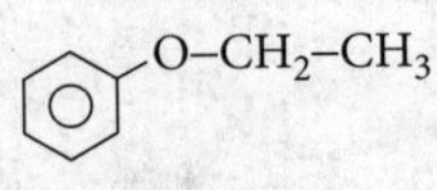

IUPAC name is ethoxy benzene.

7. 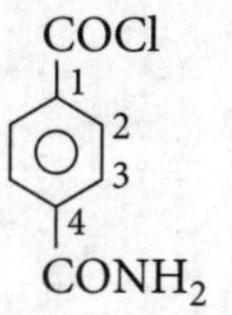

Acid chloride is principal functional group and amide is substituent.

8. 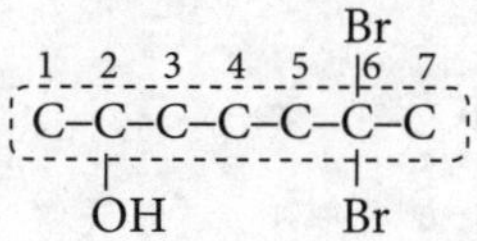

9. 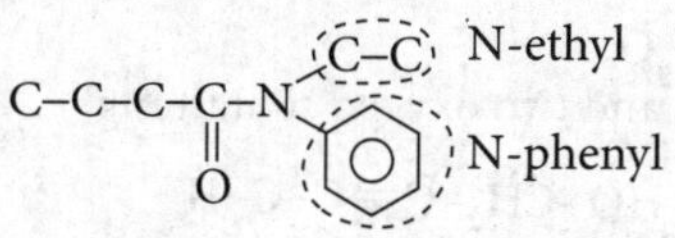

10. 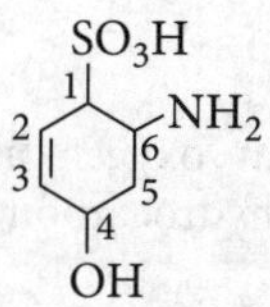

12. 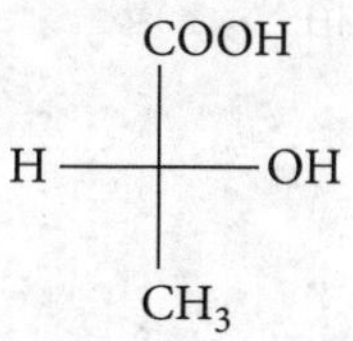 Lactic acid

13.

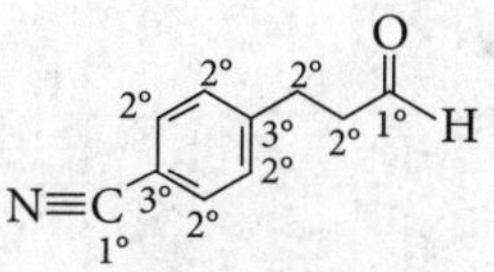

DU = π + ring = 6 + 1 = 7

14. 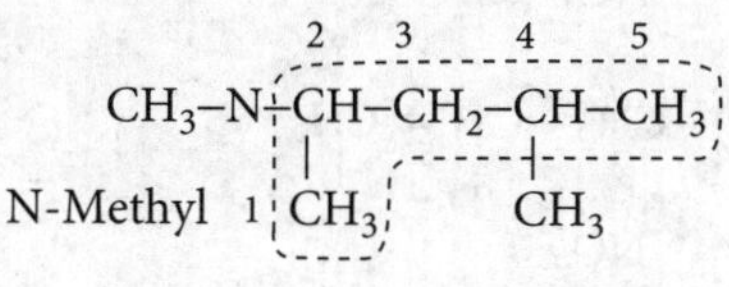

15. 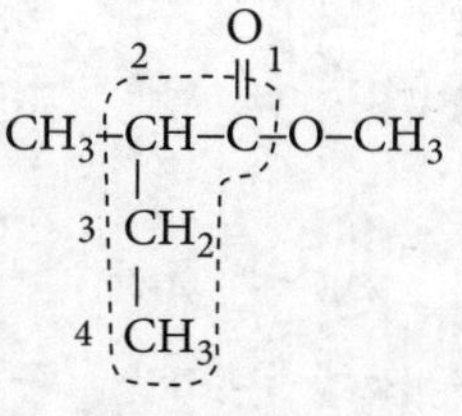

16. 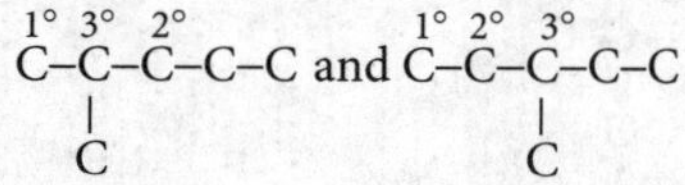

17. 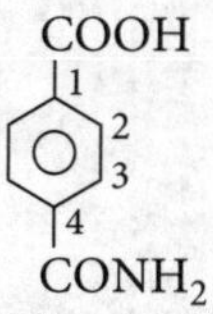

18. 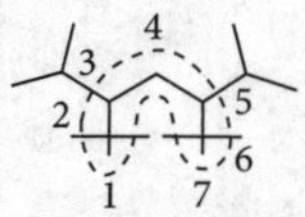

19. Alphabetical 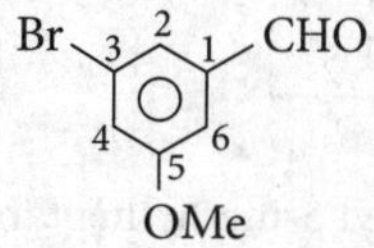

20. 2-Ethylbutane (✗) 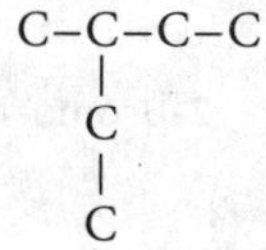

But-3-en-1-ol (✓) 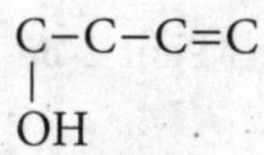

2-Chloro-3-fluoro-1, 4-epoxy-but-3-ene (✗) 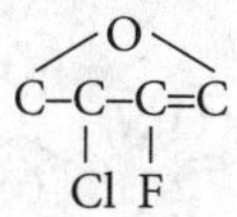

Cyclopentanoic acid (✗)

21. 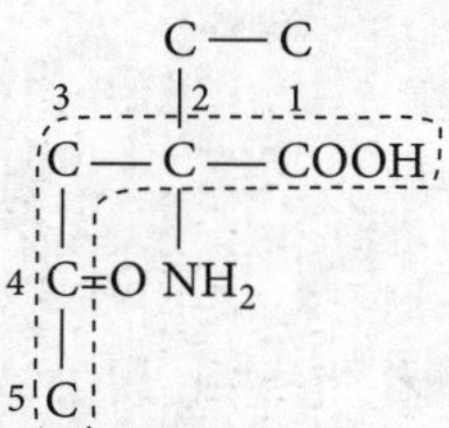

22. 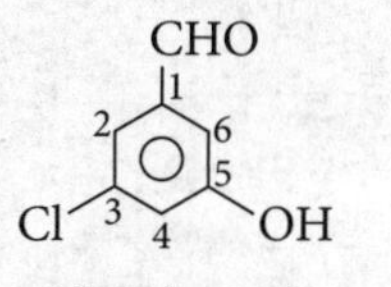

Alphabetical

23. $C_4H_6O_2$

→ DU=2 and two oxygen containing compounds

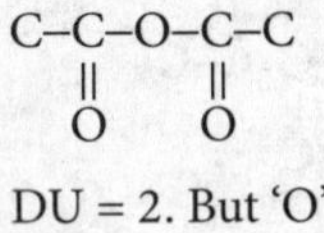

DU = 2. But 'O' is 3.

24. 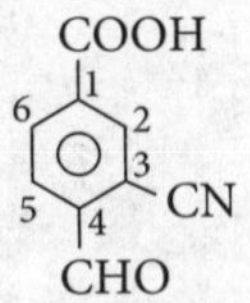

25. 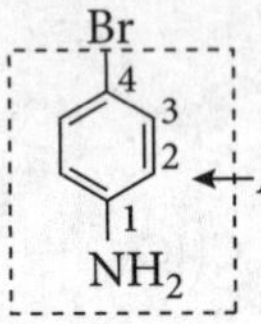 ←Aniline or Benzenamine

26. 2-Ethyl-3-methylheptane (✗) 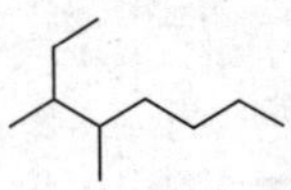

2-Bromo-1-chlorocyclohexane (✗) 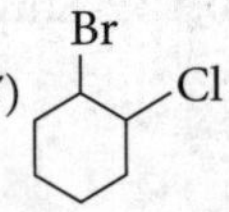

Pent-2-en-4-ol (✗) 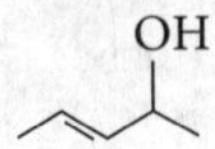

27. 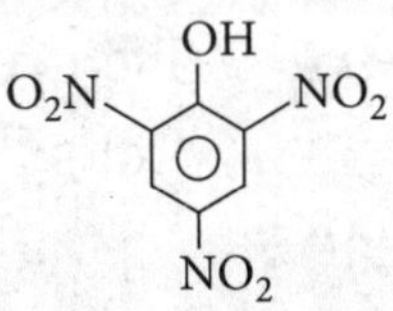

28. 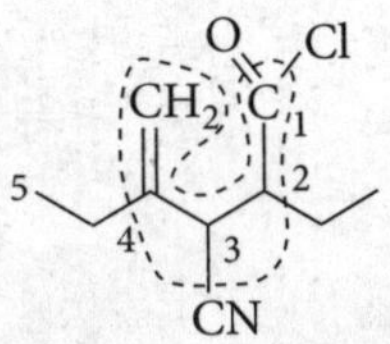

29. 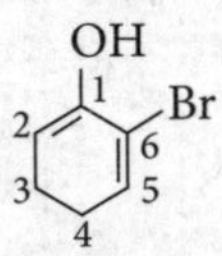

1 + 6 = 7

30. 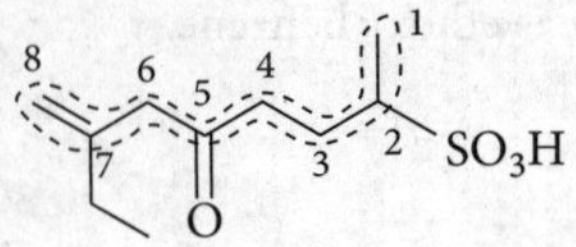

31. 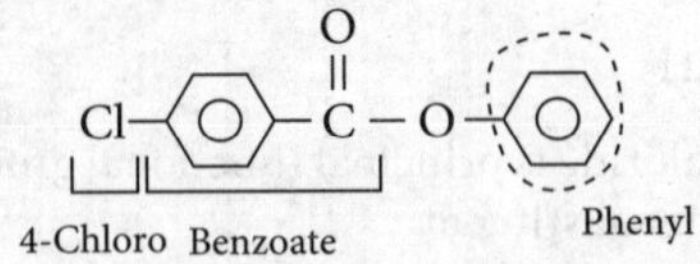

32. 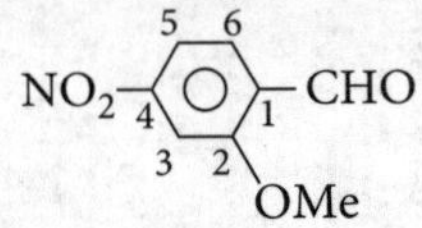

33. $C_nH_{2n-4}O_2$
DU = 3 and two oxygen containing

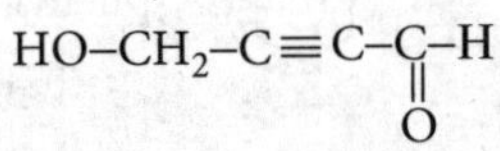

34. Phenol is homocyclic, but oxygen atom is present. So phenol is not a hydrocarbon.

35. Alkyl cyanide
$C_nH_{2n+2-4+1}N = C_nH_{2n-1}N$

36. 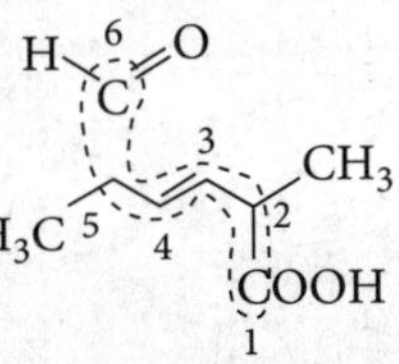

37. 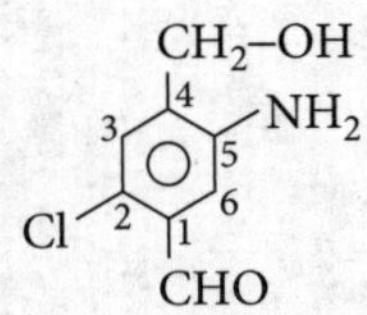

38. 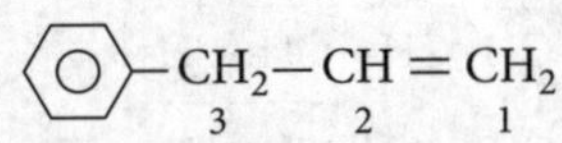

40. 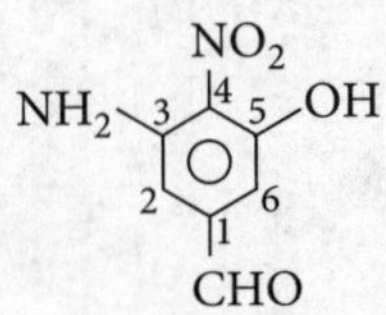

41. $C_nH_{2n}O_1$
DU = 1 and one oxygen containing

42. 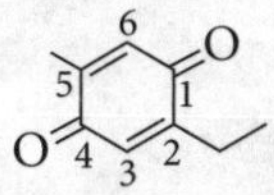 Substituent at 2 and 5

43. 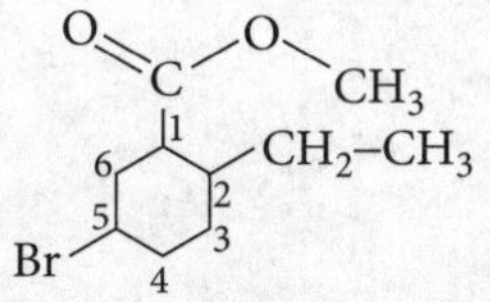

44. $\underset{3}{CH_2}=\underset{2}{C}-\underset{1}{CH_2}-$ Prop-2-enyl

45. 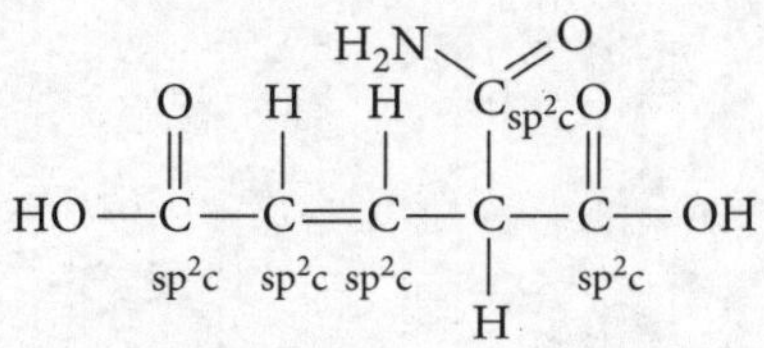

46. 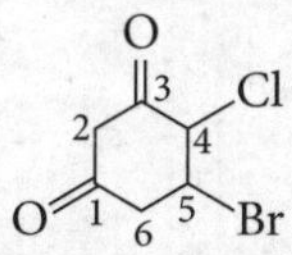

47. 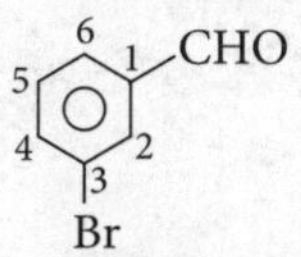

Aldehyde is the principal functional group in the given compound, and will not be a substituent.

48. 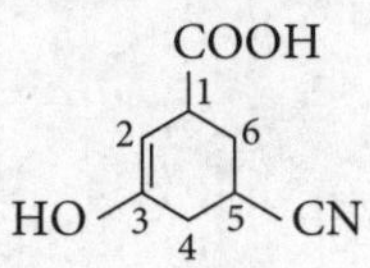

49. 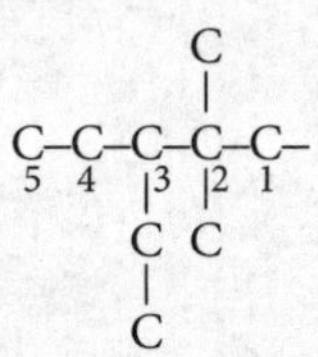

50. $\overset{1}{HC}\equiv\overset{2}{C}-\overset{3}{C}(OH)=\overset{4}{CH}-\overset{5}{CH_3}$

52. 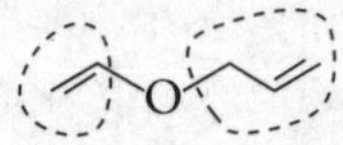

Vinyl Allyl

57. 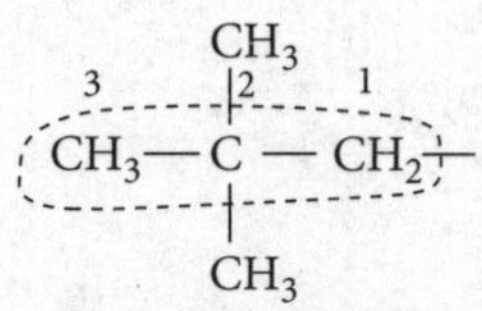

2,2-Dimethylpropyl is neopentyl.

58. 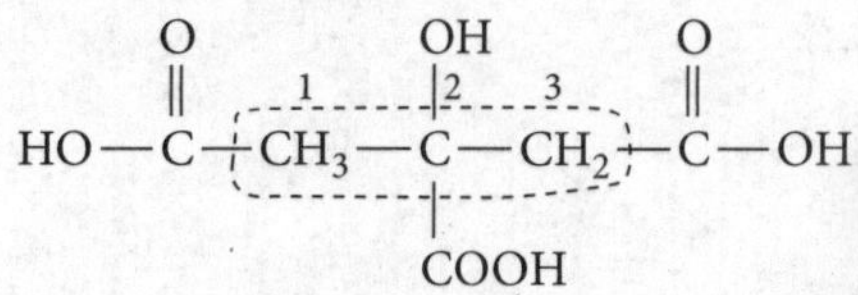

59. Number of carbons directly connected to the 'N' atom determines the degree of amine and these are different functional groups.

60. First member of ethyl ester is

$$H-\underset{\underset{O}{\|}}{C}-O-CH_2-CH_3$$

61. $\underset{5}{CH_3}-\underset{4}{CH}=\underset{3}{CH}-\underset{2}{C}\equiv\underset{1}{CH}$

(Lower locant for multiple bonds)

62. 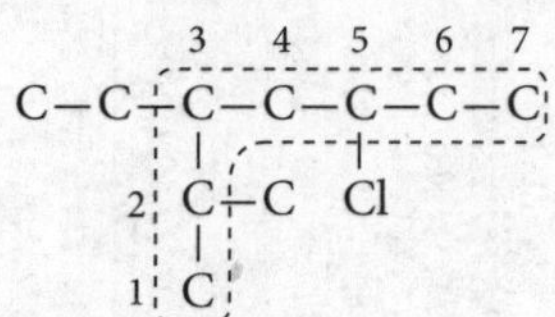

Numbering in PCC is by the lowest locant rule (2, 3, 5).

63. 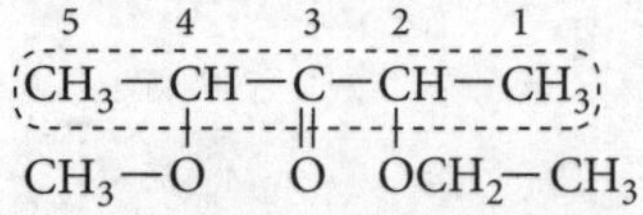

Numbering will be from the right because alphabetically Ethoxy > Methoxy. Numbering is not by size of substituent.

64. '6' carbons is PCC and CHO (aldehyde) is principal functional group and not substituent.

CHAPTER **2**

General Organic Chemistry

Level-1

1. At normal temperature, X and Y are:

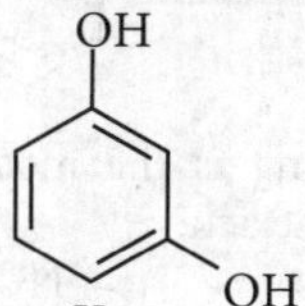

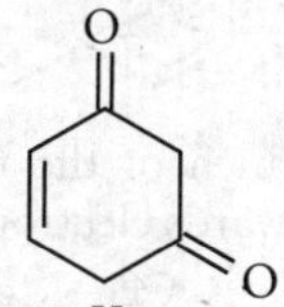

X Y

(a) Resonance structures
(b) Tautomers
(c) Functional isomers
(d) Positional isomers

2. The number of π and σ bonds present in the given compound is:

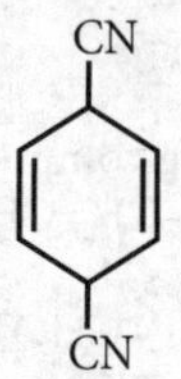

(a) $\pi = 6, \sigma = 16$ (b) $\pi = 4, \sigma = 16$
(c) $\pi = 6, \sigma = 14$ (d) $\pi = 4, \sigma = 14$

3. Positive charge is localized in which of the following groups?

(a) 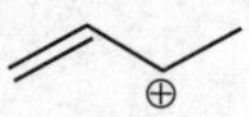 (b) 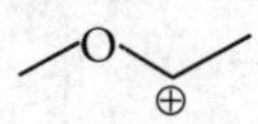

(c) 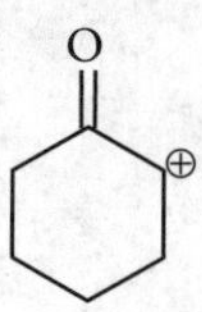 (d) 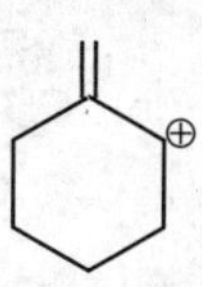

4. Inductive effect is not observed in:
(a) $CH_3 - CH_2 - OH$ (b) $CH_3 - C \equiv N$
(c) $CH_3–CH_2–CH=CH_2$ (d) $CH_3–CH_2–CH_3$

5. The factor which is not favourable for homolysis is:
(a) Presence of heat and light
(b) Presence of peroxide
(c) If the attacking reagent is a free radical
(d) Polar medium

6. The correct relationship between the given compounds is:

(I) 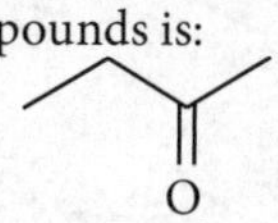 (II) 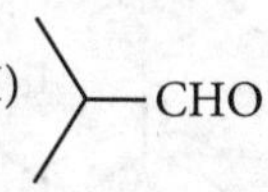

(III) 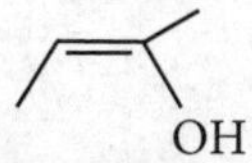 (IV) 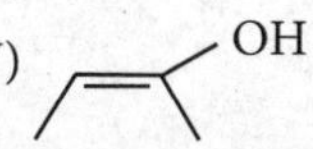

(a) (I) and (II) are tautomers of each other
(b) (III) and (IV) are alkenols of compound (II)
(c) (II) and (III, IV) are functional isomers
(d) (I) and (II) will give the same alkenol form

7. The correct order of inductive effect is:
(a) $-\overset{\oplus}{N}H_3 > -\overset{\oplus}{N}R_3 > -\overset{\oplus}{N}F_3$ (–I effect)
(b) $-CH_3 > -CD_3 > -CT_3$ (+I effect)
(c) $-F > -OH > -NR_2$ (–I effect)
(d) $-\overset{\ominus}{O} > -NH_2 > -CH_3$(+I effect)

8. Which of the following statements is correct?
(a) Free radicals are diamagnetic in nature.
(b) Hybridizations of $\overset{\oplus}{C}H_3$ and $\overset{\ominus}{C}H_3$ are the same.
(c) For homolytic fission, electronegativity difference must be zero.
(d) Structures of $\overset{\oplus}{C}H_3$ and $\dot{C}H_3$ are trigonal planar.

9. The incorrect statement for inductive effect is:
(a) It is a permanent effect.
(b) It arises due to difference in electronegativity.
(c) It decreases with increase in distance.
(d) It causes temporary polarisation in the molecule.

10. Which of the following can show +R/+M effect?
(a) $-NH_3^+$ (b) $-CONHCH_3$
(c) $-NO_2$ (d) $-NHCOCH_3$

11. The most unlikely representation of the resonance structure of the given compound is:

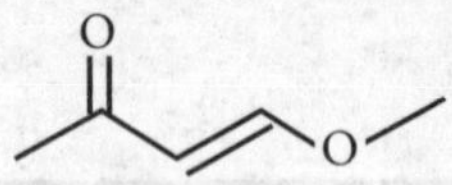

(a) 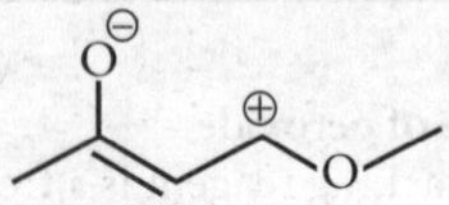

(b) 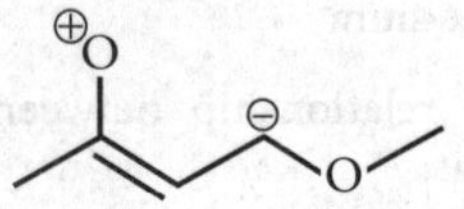

(c) 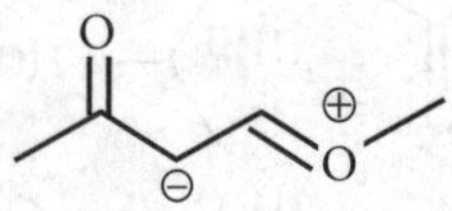

(d) 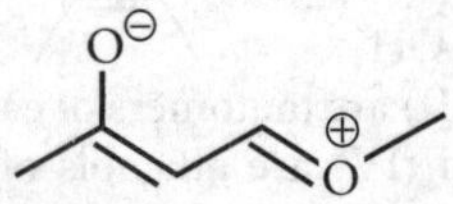

12. Which of the following resonating structures of the given compound is not correct?

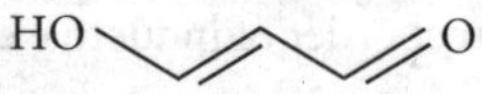

(a) 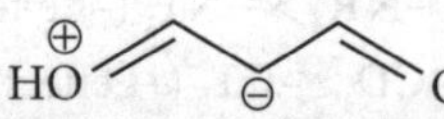

(b) 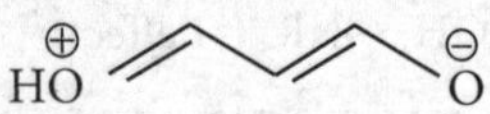

(c) 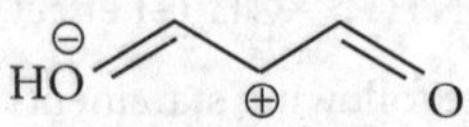

(d) 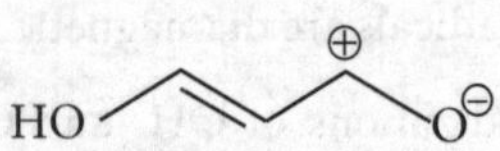

13. Which among the following carbanions is not resonance stabilized?

(a) 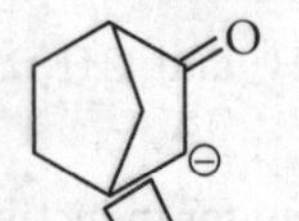 (b) 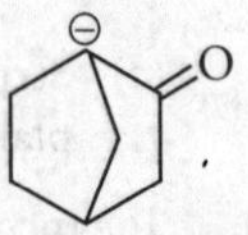

(c) 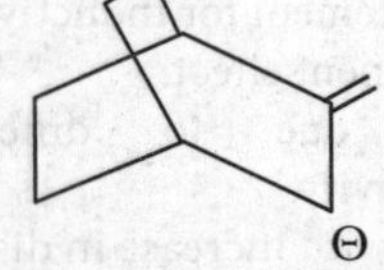 (d) 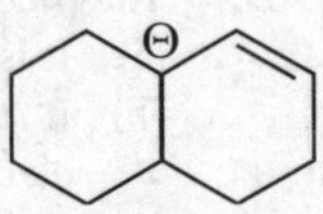

14. Which of the following orders is incorrect?
(a) $-NO_2 > -CN > -F$ (–I)
(b) $-NH_2 > -OH > -NHCOCH_3$ (+R/+M)
(c) $-CT_3 > -CD_3 > -CH_3$(+H)
(d) $-\overset{\ominus}{N}H > -O^{\ominus} > -COO^{\ominus}$(+I)

15. Among the following resonating structures, in which pair is (II) more stable?

(a) $\overset{\oplus}{C}H_2-OCH_3 \longleftrightarrow CH_2=\overset{\oplus}{O}-CH_3$

(b) 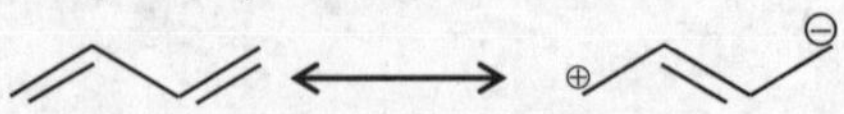

(c) 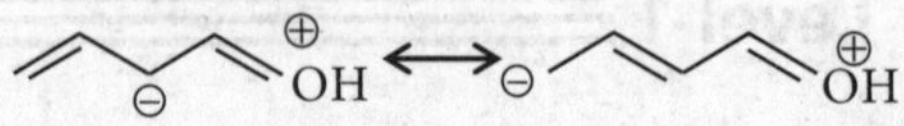

(d) 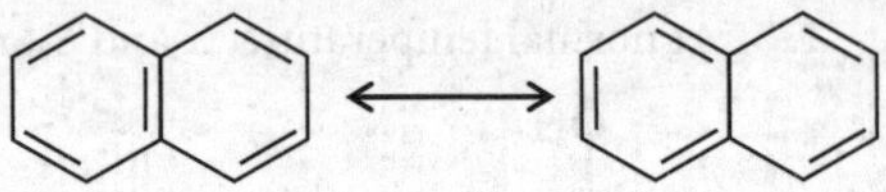

16. Which of the following is the most reactive towards electrophilic attack?

(a) 

(b) 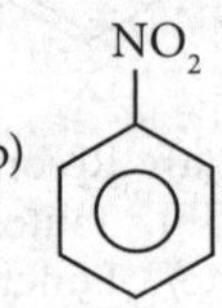

(c) 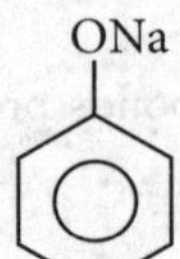

(d) 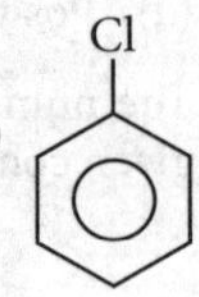

17. In the following compound, flow of $\pi e^{\ominus}$ is:
$H_2N-CH=CH-CH=CH-CHO$
(a) Towards $-NH_2$
(b) Away from –CHO
(c) Towards –CHO
(d) All of these

18. Mesomeric effect is observed in:

(a) 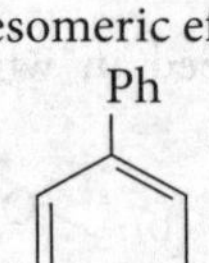

(b) $CH_2=CH-CH=CH_2$

(c) 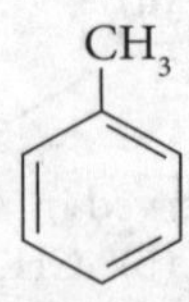

(d) 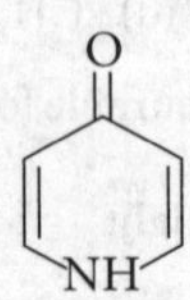

19. Which of the following is aromatic in nature?

(a) 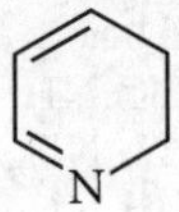 (b) 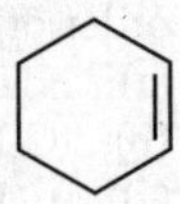

(c) 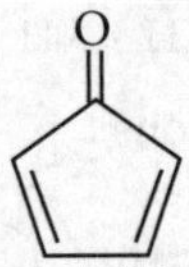 (d) 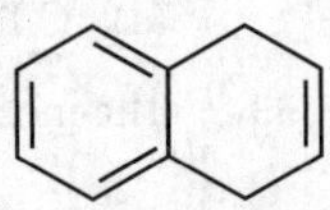

20. Which of the following orders of stability is correct?

(a) 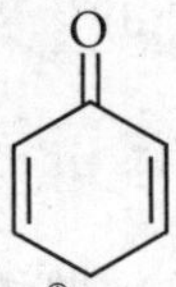 > 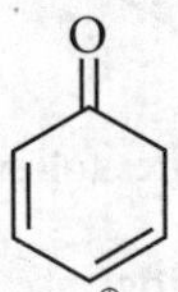

(b) $\overset{\oplus}{C}H_2-F > CH_2=\overset{\oplus}{F}$

(c) 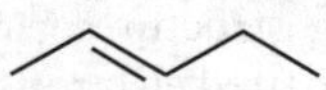 > 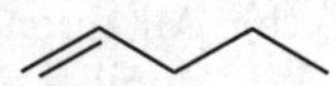

(d) 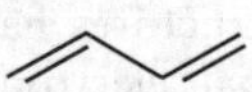 < 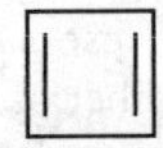

21. The stability order of the given resonating structures is:

$CH_3\overset{\oplus}{O}=CH-CH=C(NH_2)-\overset{\ominus}{O}$ (I)

$CH_3O-CH=CH-C(=\overset{\oplus}{N}H_2)-\overset{\ominus}{O}$ (II)

$CH_3O-\overset{\ominus}{C}H-\overset{\oplus}{C}H-C(NH_2)=O$ (III)

$CH_3O-\overset{\oplus}{C}H-\overset{\ominus}{C}H-C(NH_2)=O$ (IV)

(a) I > II > III > IV (b) II > I > IV > III
(c) IV > III > II > I (d) II > I > III > IV

22. Which of the following is incorrect for imidazole?

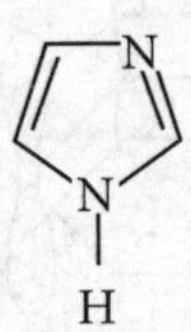

(a) It contains five p_π orbitals in resonance
(b) It is aromatic in nature
(c) Two lone pairs are localized
(d) It contains six π electrons in conjugation

23. The conjugated base of which compound will be the most stable?
(a) $CH_3CH_2-NO_2$
(b) $CH_3-CH(NO_2)-CH_3$
(c) $O_2N-CH_2-NO_2$
(d) $NC-CH_2-CN$

24. Which of the following can show resonance phenomenon?
(a) $H_2C=C=CH_2$
(b) Hex-2-en-1-ol
(c) CH_3COOH
(d) 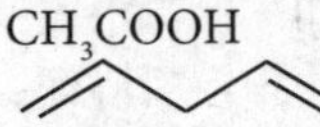

25. Which of the following compounds does not exhibit tautomerism?

(a) 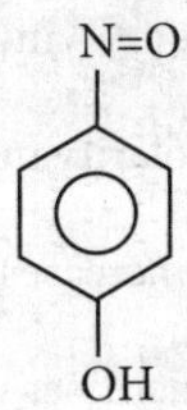 (b) 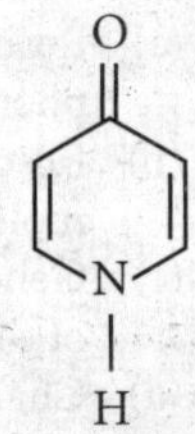

(c) 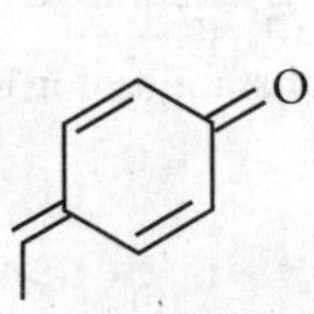 (d) 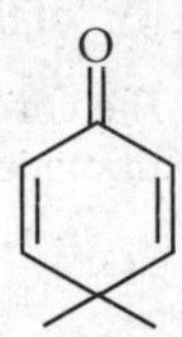

26. Which of the following compounds does not have sp^2 nitrogen?

(a) 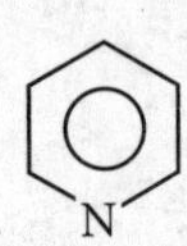 (b) 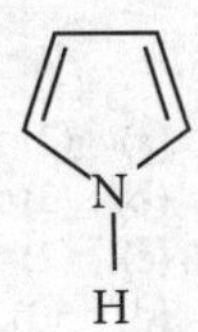

(c) 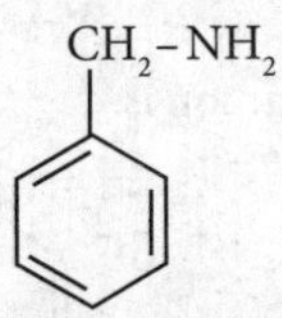 (d) 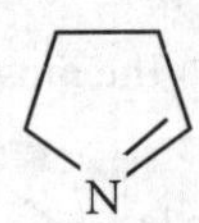

27. In which of the following compounds is the C–H bond dissociation energy the lowest?

(a) 

(b) 

(c) 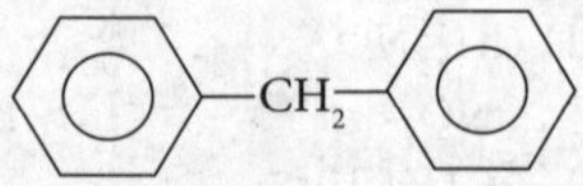

(d) $CH_3-CH=CH_2$

28. The stability order of the following resonating structures is:

$$\underset{\text{I}}{CH_2=CH-\underset{\underset{O}{\|}}{C}-OH} \qquad \underset{\text{II}}{\overset{\oplus}{C}H_2-CH=\underset{\underset{O^{\ominus}}{|}}{C}-OH} \qquad \underset{\text{III}}{CH_2=CH-\underset{\underset{O^{\ominus}}{|}}{C}=\overset{\oplus}{O}H}$$

(a) II > III > I (b) I > II > III
(c) III > I > II (d) I > III > II

29. Select the correct statement:
(a) Resonance is an intermolecular phenomenon.
(b) Resonance induces polarity in a non-polar molecule.
(c) Generally resonance increases the stability of the molecule.
(d) Charge separation increases the stability of the resonating structures.

30. The correct order of stability for the following alkoxides is:

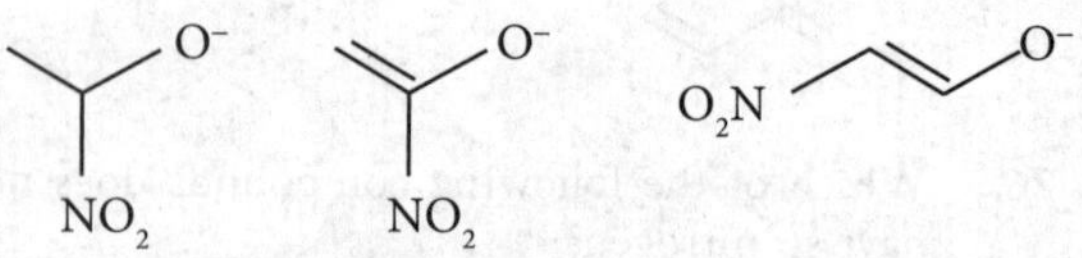

(1) (2) (3)

(a) (2) > (1) > (3)
(b) (3) > (2) > (1)
(c) (2) > (3) > (1)
(d) (3) > (1) > (2)

31. The most stable carbanion is:

(a) 
(b) 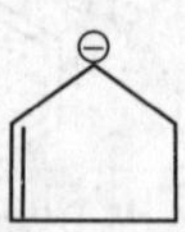
(c) 
(d) 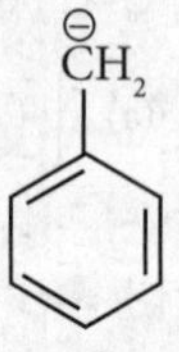

32. In the following compounds, the decreasing order of basic strength will be:
(a) $NH_3 > C_2H_5NH_2 > (C_2H_5)_2NH$
(b) $(C_2H_5)_2NH > C_2H_5NH_2 > NH_3$
(c) $(C_2H_5)_2NH > NH_3 > C_2H_5NH_2$
(d) $C_2H_5NH_2 > NH_3 > (C_2H_5)_2NH$

33. The most stable carbocation is:

(a) 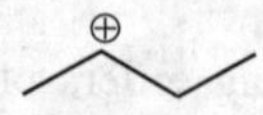
(b) 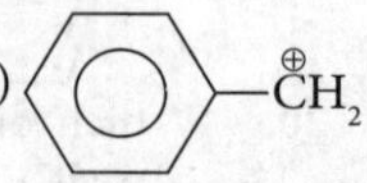
(c) 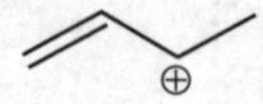
(d) 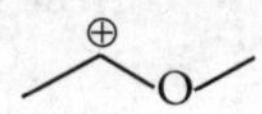

34. Which of the following is incorrect about resonance?
(a) Resonating structures have the same energy and the same contribution.
(b) All resonating structures have the same number of unpaired electrons.
(c) All resonating structures have the same number of bond pair electrons.
(d) All resonating structures have the same amount of net charge.

35. Which of the following compounds has localized lone pair electrons?

(a) 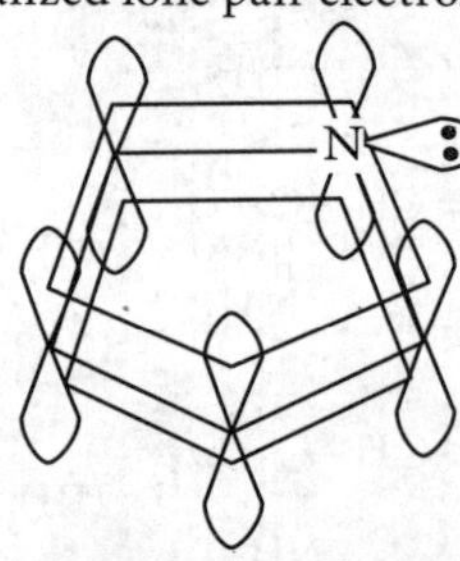

(b) 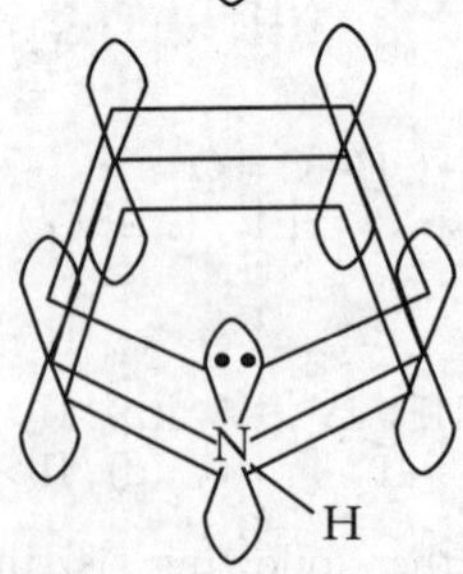

(c) 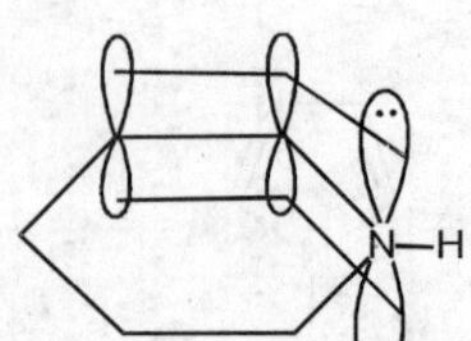

(d) 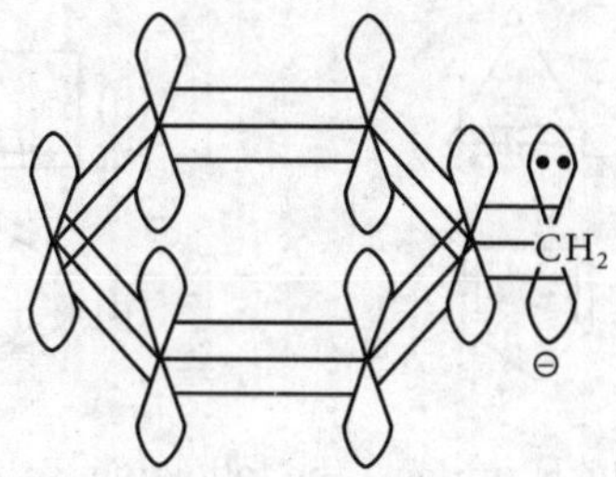

36. Among the following compounds, the correct increasing order of the Ka value is:

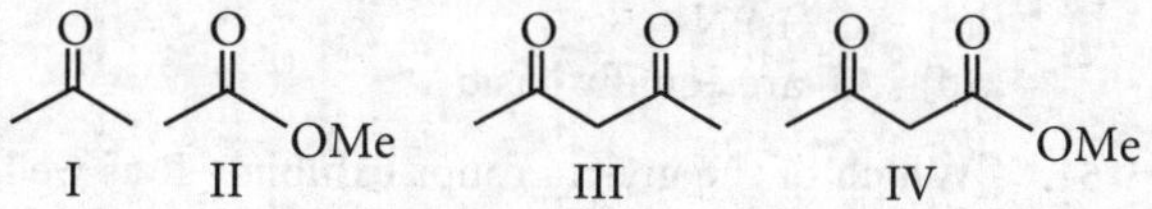

I II III IV

(a) I < II < IV < III (b) II < I < IV < III
(c) III < I < IV < II (d) IV < I < III < II

37. In the given compounds, the correct increasing order of heat of hydrogenation is:

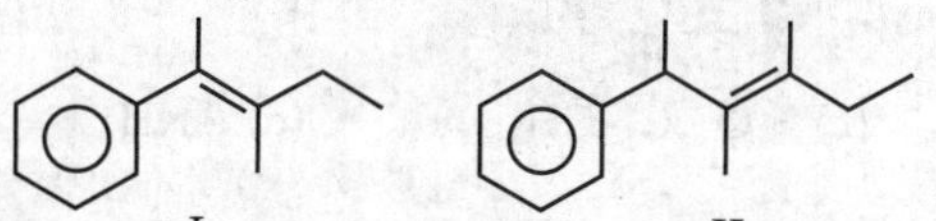

I II

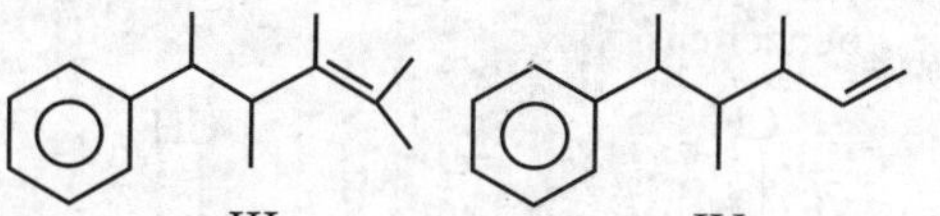

III IV

(a) I < II < III < IV (b) I < III < II < IV
(c) IV < III < I < II (d) I < II < IV < III

38. Compare the resonance energy of the following species:

(I) (II) (III)

(a) III > II > I (b) II > III > I
(c) III > I > II (d) II > I > III

39. Which of the following methyl-substituted anilines is the least basic?
(a) Ortho (b) Meta
(c) Para (d) N-substituted

40. Which of the following stability orders is correct?

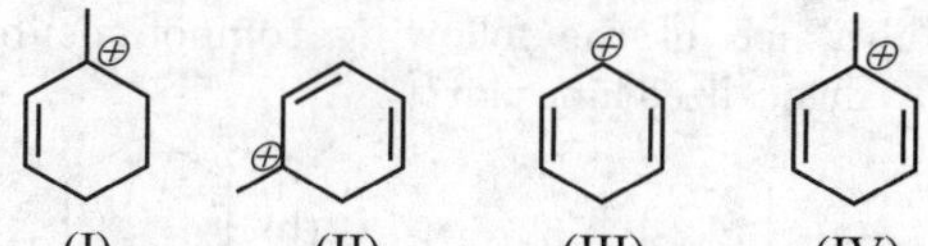

(I) (II) (III) (IV)

(a) I > II > III > IV (b) II > IV > III > I
(c) IV > II > III > I (d) IV > III > II > I

41. Among the following, which compound has the lowest heat of combustion?

(a) 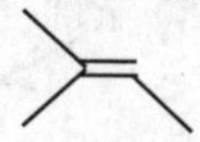 (b) 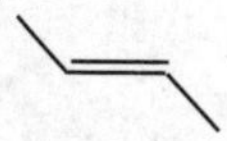

(c)  (d) 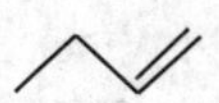

42. Which of the following pairs are resonance structures of each other?

(a) 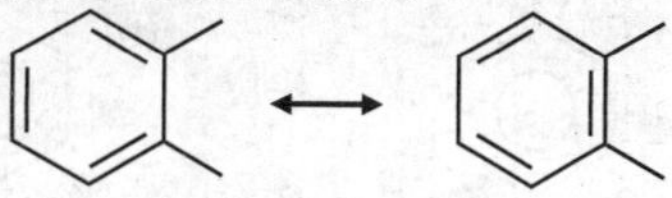

(b) 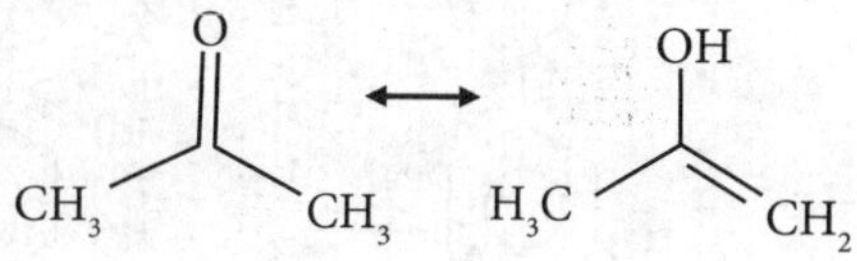

(c) 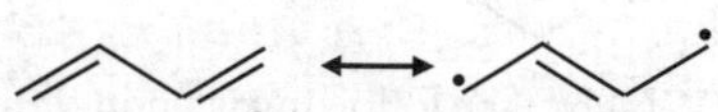

(d) All of these

43. Choose the correct order of stability of the following carbanions:

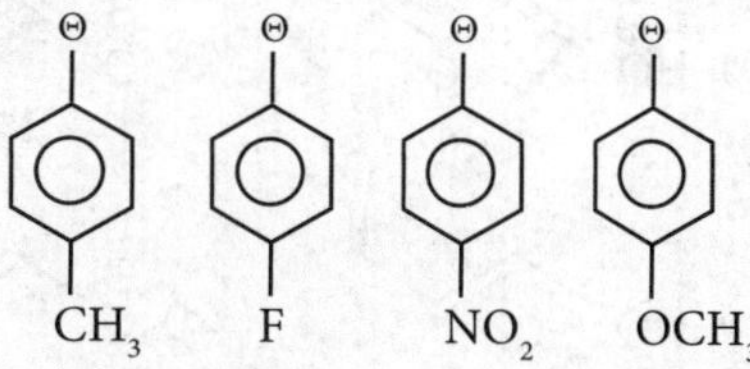

(P) (Q) (R) (S)

(a) R > P > Q > S
(b) P > R > Q > S
(c) R > Q > P > S
(d) P > Q > R > S

44. Which compound among the following has the lowest heat of hydrogenation per π bond?

(a) 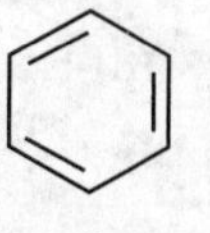 (b) 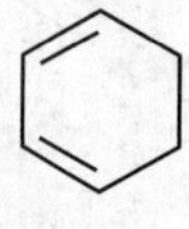

(c) 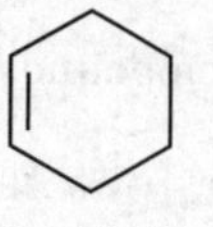 (d) 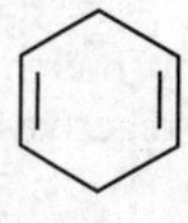

45. Which of the following compounds has a delocalized lone pair?

(a) 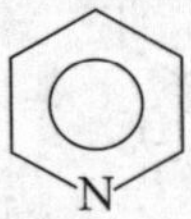 (b) 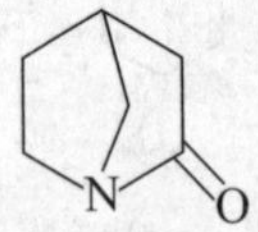

(c) 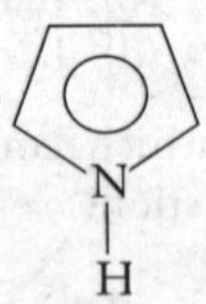 (d) 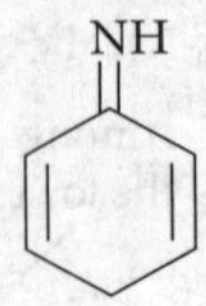

46. Which of the following is less reactive for electrophilic attack than benzene?

(a) 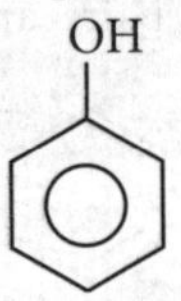 (b) 

(c) 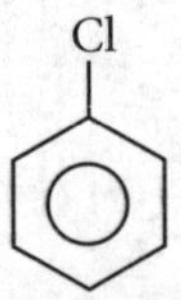 (d) 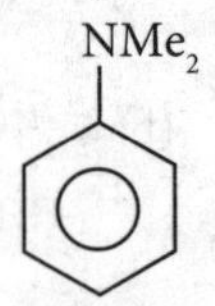

47. Which of the following is a non-valid resonating structure of "3-hydroxyprop-2-enal"?

(a) 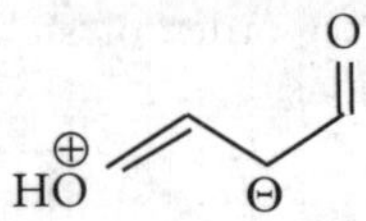 (b) 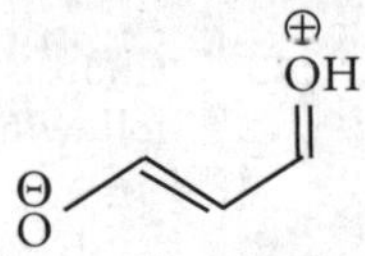

(c) 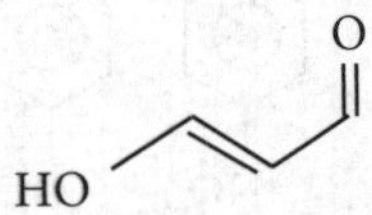 (d) 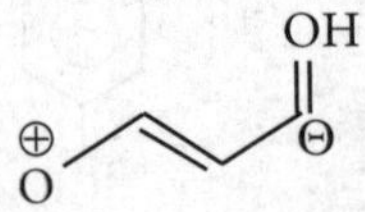

48. Which of the following intermediates is the most stable?

(a) 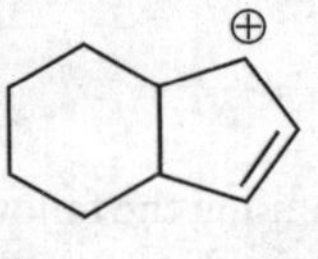 (b) 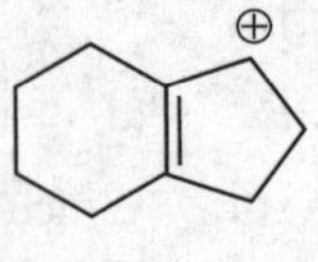

(c) 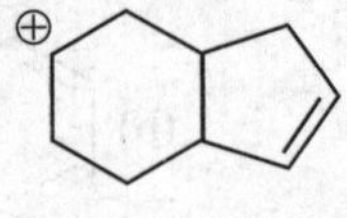 (d) 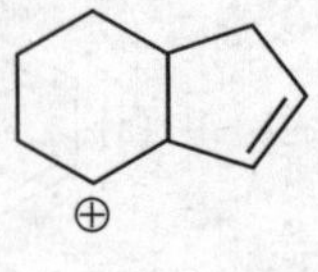

49. Which of the following compounds is the most reactive to a strong base?

(a)  (b) 

(c)  (d) 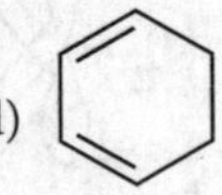

50. Which amongst the following is the least basic in nature in H_2O?
(a) $C_2H_5NH_2$
(b) $(C_2H_5)_2NH$
(c) $(C_2H_5)_3N$
(d) All are equally basic

51. Which of the given groups exhibits +R as well as –R effect when attached with a suitable group?

(a) $-\overset{\overset{\displaystyle O}{\|}}{S}-CH_3$ (b) $-\overset{\overset{\displaystyle O}{\|}}{C}-OH$

(c) $-O-\overset{\overset{\displaystyle O}{\|}}{C}-CH_3$ (d) $-NH_2$

52. Among the following, the most electron-rich benzene is:

(a) 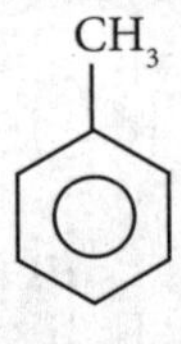 (b) 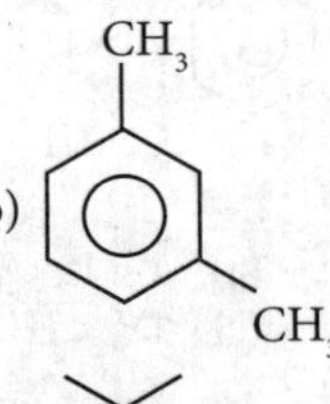

(c) 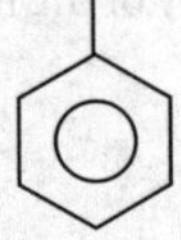 (d) 

53. The non-aromatic compound among the following is:

(a)  (b) 

(c) 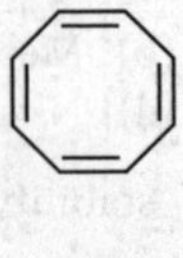 (d) 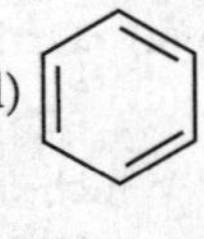

54. Which of the following has the highest stability?

(a) 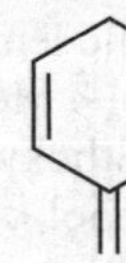 (b) 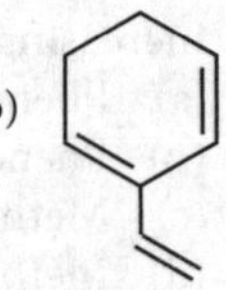

(c) 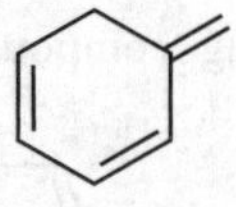 (d) 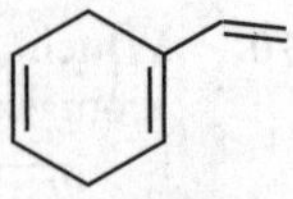

55. The given theoretical potential energy profile diagram shows the position of the resonating structures of ethanoic acid. The structure of C is:

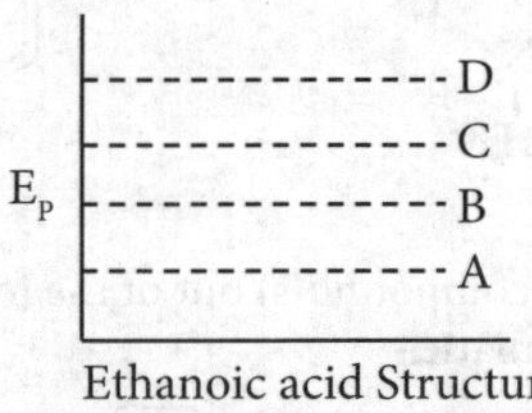

(a) $CH_3–C(=O)–OH$ (A)

(b) $CH_3–C(–\overset{\ominus}{O})=\overset{\oplus}{O}–H$ (B)

(c) $CH_3–\overset{\oplus}{C}(–\overset{\ominus}{O})–OH$ (C)

(d) $CH_3–\overset{\ominus}{C}(–\overset{\oplus}{O})–OH$ (D)

56. Which of the following can show resonance phenomenon?
(a) Cyclohex-2-enol
(b) Cyclopent-3-en-1-one
(c) 6-Hydroxyhex-3-enal
(d) Pentanoic acid

57. The group having both +R and –R effect is:
(a) –C≡N (b) –F
(c) –N=O (d) –OMe

58. Which of the following rings is more reactive for electrophile attack than benzene?

 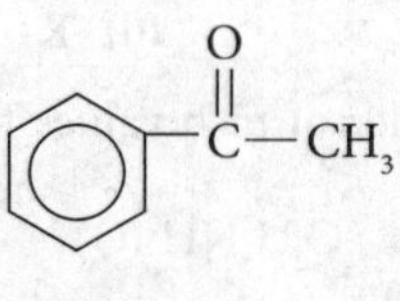 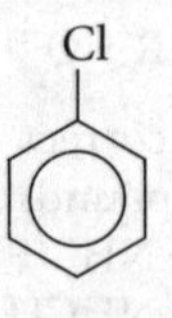 

P Q R S

(a) P, R (b) Q, S
(c) Q, R (d) P, S

59. Which of the following compounds has 6 hyper-conjugating structures involving C–H bonds?
(a) 1-Butene
(b) 2-Methylpropene
(c) 2-Pentene
(d) 1-Methylcyclohexene

60. Which of the following encircled groups participates in resonance?

(a) 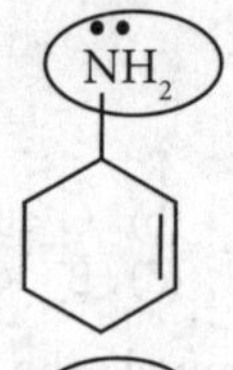 (b) 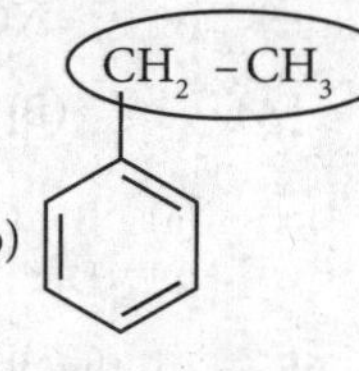

(c) 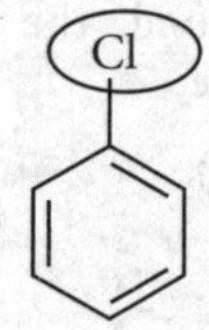 (d) 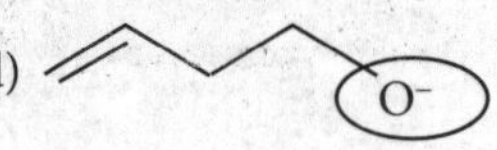

61. The correct statement about compounds (I) and (II) is:

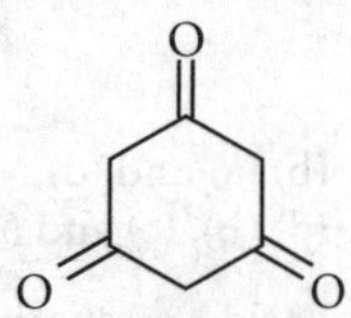 > 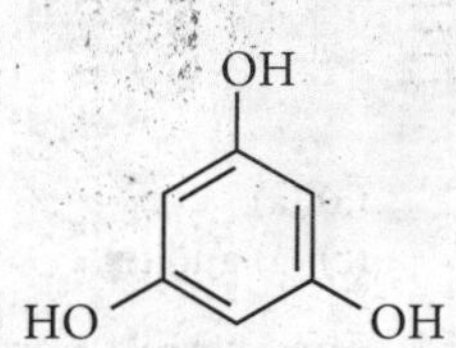

(I) (II)

(a) I shows geometrical isomerism (GI)
(b) II shows geometrical isomerism
(c) I and II are positional isomers
(d) I and II are tautomers

62. Which amongst the following is the strongest acid?
(a) CHI_3 (b) $CHCl_3$
(c) $CHBr_3$ (d) $CH(CN)_3$

63. The increasing basicity order of the following compounds in aqueous medium is:
(a) $CH_3CH_2NH_2$
(b) $(CH_3CH_2)_2NH$
(c) $(CH_3)_3N$
(d) $PhNHCH_3$
(a) (d) < (c) < (b) < (a)

(b) (a) < (b) < (d) < (c)
(c) (a) < (b) < (c) < (d)
(d) (d) < (c) < (a) < (b)

64. The increasing order of pKa values of the following compounds is:

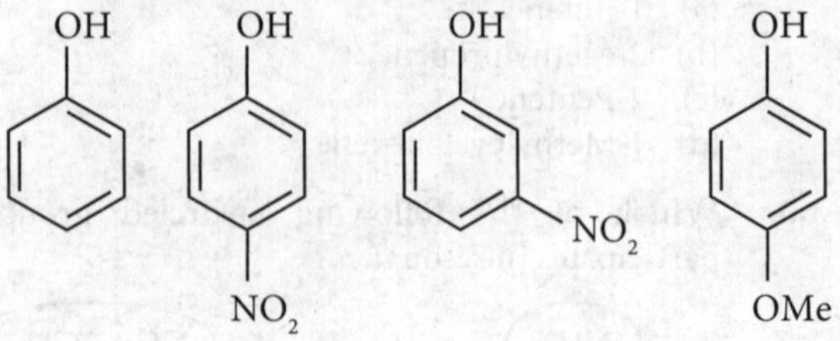

(A) (B) (C) (D)

(a) B < C < D < A
(b) C < B < A < D
(c) D < A < C < B
(d) B < C < A < D

65. In the following compound, the favourable site/s for protonation is/are:

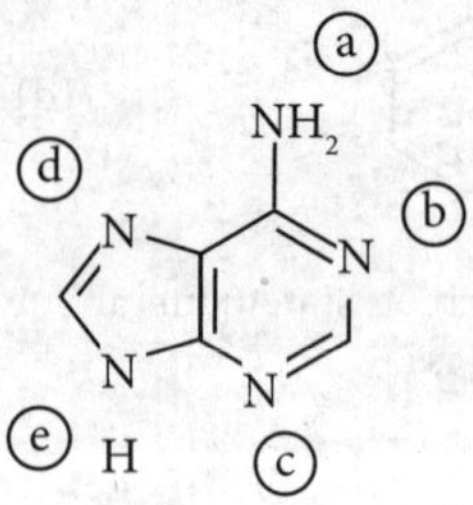

(a) (a)
(b) (a) and (d)
(c) (a) and (e)
(d) (b), (c) and (d)

66. The correct order for acid strength of compounds is:

CH≡CH, CH_3–C≡CH and CH_2=CH_2

(a) CH ≡ CH > CH_2 = CH_2 > CH_3–C ≡ CH
(b) HC ≡ CH > CH_3–C≡ CH > CH_2 = CH_2
(c) CH_3–C ≡ CH > CH_2 = CH_2 > HC ≡ CH
(d) CH_3–C ≡ CH > CH ≡ CH > CH_2 = CH_2

67. The number of sp^2-hybrid orbitals in a molecule of benzene is:
(a) 6
(b) 24
(c) 18
(d) 12

68. Which of the following has the shortest C–Cl bond?
(a) Cl–CH ≡ CH
(b) C1–CH = CH–CH_3
(c) C1–CH = CH_2
(d) Cl–CH = CH–NO_2

69. Arrange the following compounds in increasing order of C–OH bond length:
(a) Phenol < p-Ethoxyphenol < Methanol
(b) Phenol < Methanol < p-Ethoxyphenol
(c) Methanol < p-Ethoxyphenol < Phenol
(d) Methanol < Phenol < p-Ethoxyphenol

70. Which of the following compounds is not aromatic?

(a) 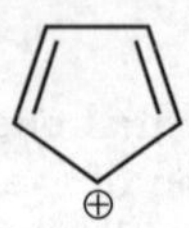
(b) 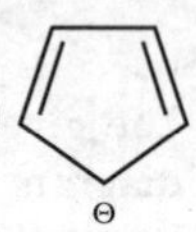
(c) 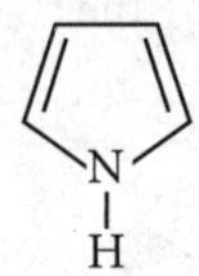
(d) 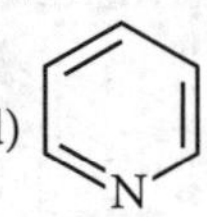

71. Which compound(s) out of the following is/are not aromatic?

 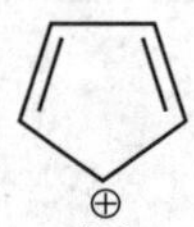 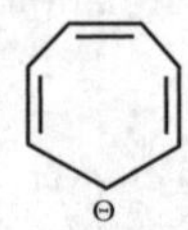 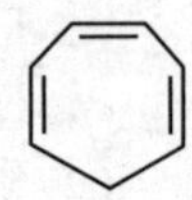

(A) (B) (C) (D)

(a) (A) and (B)
(b) (B), (C) and (D)
(c) (C) and (D)
(d) (B)

72. Among the following, select the incorrect statement:
(a) If only Kekule structures are considered, then the bond order of benzene is 1.5
(b) Resonance effect is a distance-independent permanent effect
(c) Resonance effect arises due to difference in electronegativity only
(d) Resonating structures are hypothetical and resonance hybrid is real

73. The correct order of the C–N bond length is:
P : CH_3CN Q : HNCO R : CH_3CONH_2
(a) P > Q > R
(b) P = Q = R
(c) R > Q > P
(d) R > P > Q

74. The correct order of pKb values for the given compounds is:
$C_6H_5NH_2$ (P) $C_2H_5NH_2$(Q)
$C_6H_5NHCH_3$(R)

(a) R > Q > P (b) P > R > Q
(c) Q > R > P (d) R > P > Q

75. Which of the following has the lowest value of heat of combustion?
(a) 1-Heptene
(b) 2,4-Dimethyl-1-pentene
(c) 2,4-Dimethyl-2-pentene
(d) 4,4-Dimethyl-2-pentene

76. The compound that contains the most acidic hydrogen is:
(a) $H_2C=CH_2$ (b) HC≡CH
(c) $H_2C=C=CH_2$ (d) $H_3C–CH_3$

77. Which of the following is non-aromatic?
(a) Pyrrole (b) Thiophene
(c) Furan (d) Pyran

78. The correct order of the acidic strength of the following acids is:
(I) $ClCH_2COOH$
(II) O_2NCH_2COOH
(III) $CHCl_2COOH$
(IV) CCl_3COOH
(a) I > II > III > IV (b) II > IV> III > I
(c) IV > III > II > I (d) II > IV > I > III

79. Among the following, the correct statement is:
(a) Most stable resonating structures contribute less to resonance hybrid
(b) Inductive effect involves migration of electrons from one orbital to another
(c) Resonance involves permanent displacement of π electron density due to σ bond
(d) Acetate ion contains identical resonating structures

80. Which of the following options is incorrect?
(a) H_2O is the conjugate base of H_3O^+ (hydronium ion)
(b) Ethene does not undergo resonance but 1,3-butadiene undergoes resonance
(c) Generally alkyl group shows +I effect
(d) $–O^{\ominus}$ (oxide ion group) and –OH (hydroxyl group) both show –I effect

81. Among the following, which is the most basic?
(a) NaOMe (b) NaOEt
(c) $NaOCHMe_2$ (d) $NaOCMe_3$

82. Which of the following can show +I effect?
(a) –CN (b) $–CH_3$
(c) –COOH (d) $–NH_2$

83. Which of the following compounds has maximum rotational energy barrier about the indicated bond?
(a) $CH_3 – CH \overset{\downarrow}{=} CH_2$
(b) $(CH_3)_2C \overset{\downarrow}{=} CH_2$
(c) $CH_2=CH–CH \overset{\downarrow}{=} CH_2$
(d) $CH_3–CH_2 \overset{\downarrow}{–} CH_3$

84. Which of the following options is correct?
(a) Cyclopentadienyl anion is very stable because of aromatic character
(b) Cycloheptatrienyl cation is very stable because of aromatic character
(c) Cyclic de-localisation of (4n+2) π electron is more stable than acyclic de-localisation of (4n+2)
(d) All of these

85. Among the following, which is the incorrect option for *?

$CH_2 = CH–\overset{*}{O}H$ (A) $CH_2 = CH – \overset{*}{N}H^{\ominus}$ (C)

$CH_3–CH_2–\overset{*}{O}H$ (B) $CH_3–CH_2–\overset{*}{N}H^{\ominus}$ (D)

(a) Group in A shows +M, –I effect
(b) Group in B shows +I, +M effect
(c) Group in C shows –I effect
(d) Group in D shows –I effect

86. The increasing order of basicity for the following intermediates is (from weak to strong):

$(CH_3)_3C^{\ominus}$ (i) $CH_2 = CH – \overset{\ominus}{C}H_2$ (ii) $CH \equiv C^{\ominus}$ (iii) $CN^{\ominus}$ (iv) $CH_3^{\ominus}$ (v)

(a) (v) < (i) < (iv) < (ii) < (iii)
(b) (iii) < (iv) < (ii) < (i) < (v)
(c) (iii) < (i) < (ii) < (iv) < (v)
(d) (iv) < (iii) < (ii) < (v) < (i)

87. Which of the following canonical structures is the most stable?

(a) 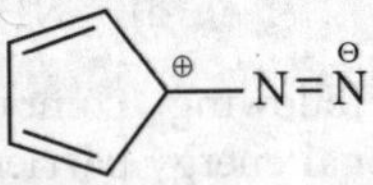

(b) 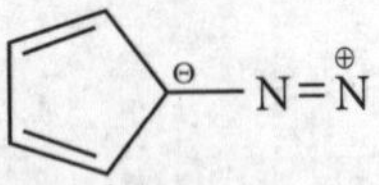

(c) 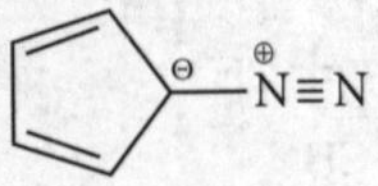

(d) All are equally stable

88. Which of the following is the correct order of stability?

(a) 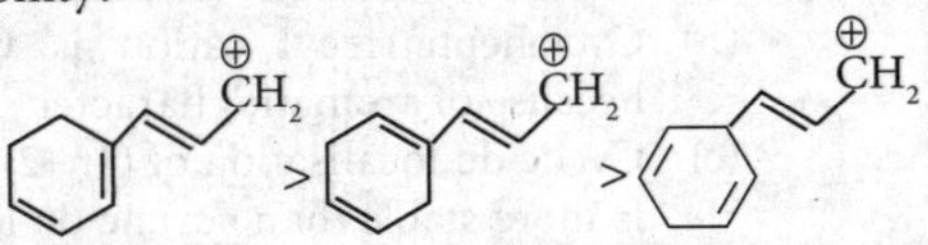 (Carbocation)

(b) 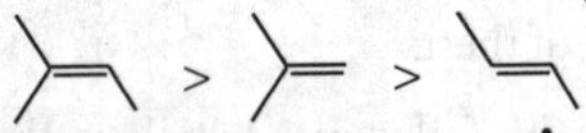 (Alkene)

(c) 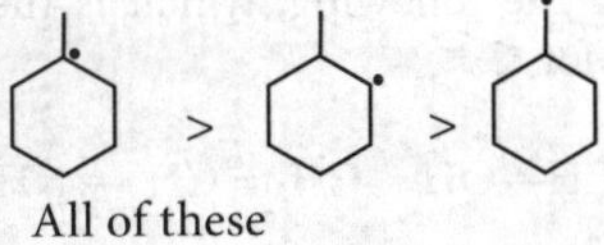 (Free radical)

(d) All of these

89. The correct order of heat of hydrogenation is:

(a) 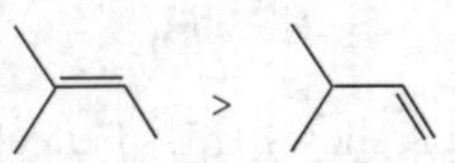

(b) 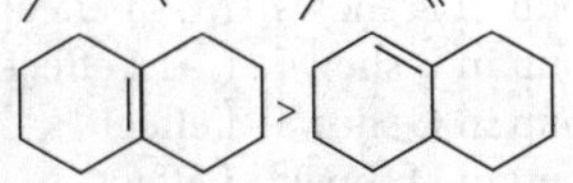

(c) 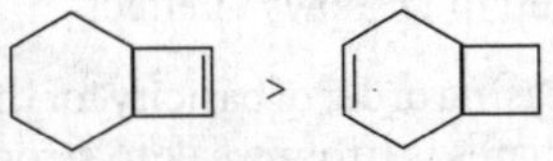

(d) 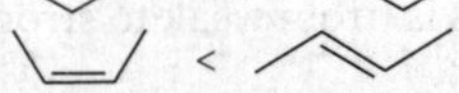

90. The correct stability order of the following resonating structures is:

(a) 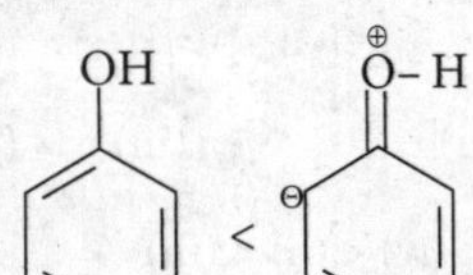

(b) 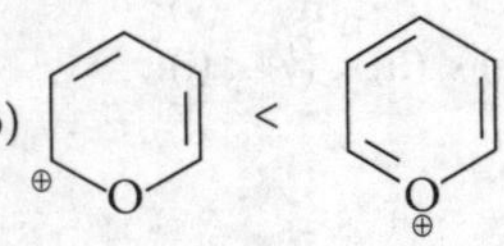

(c) 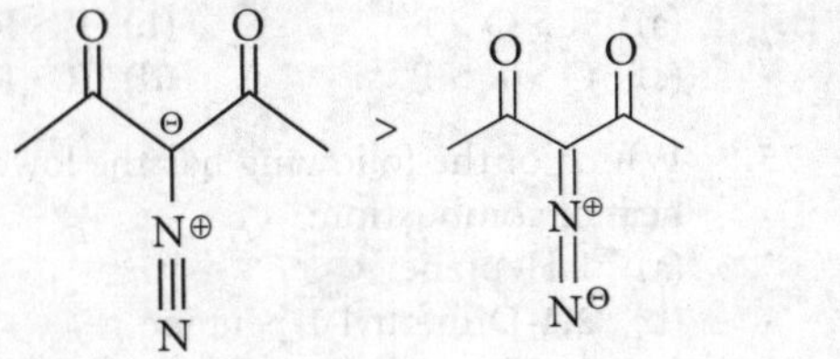

(d) 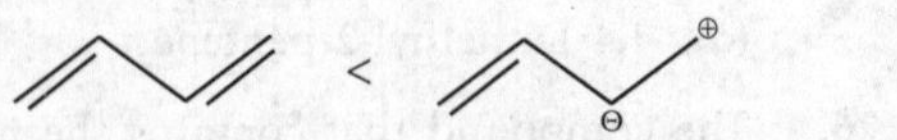

91. Which of the following compounds has the maximum heat of combustion?

(a) 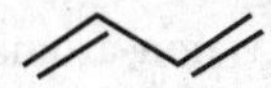
(b) 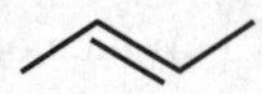
(c) 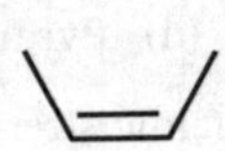
(d) 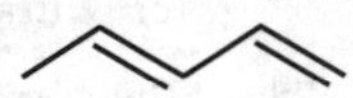

92. Compare the carbocation stability:

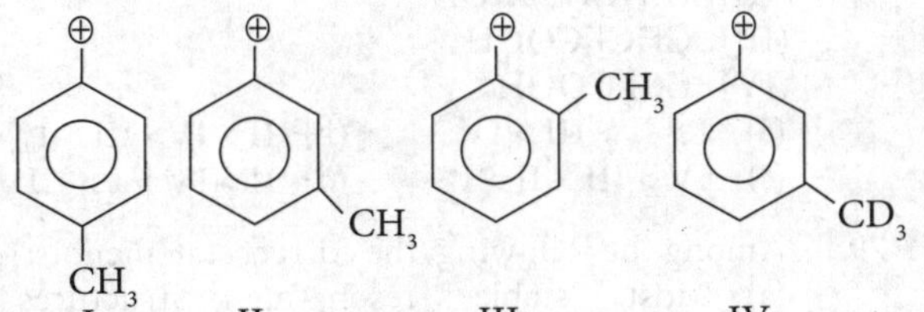

I II III IV

(a) IV > I > III > II
(b) III > I > IV > II
(c) I > IV > III > II
(d) I > IV > II > III

93. The most basic anion is:

(a) HCOONa
(b) HC≡CNa
(c) $NaNH_2$
(d) CH_3CH_2Na

94. The acidic strength of p-substituted phenol is maximum when the group at para is:

(a) $-NO_2$
(b) $-CH_3$
(c) –Cl
(d) $-CO_2H$

95. Which of the following shows the acidic character of n-butyl alcohol?

(a) Na
(b) NaOH
(c) $NaHCO_3$
(d) NaOPh

96. SIR effect is observed in:

(a) 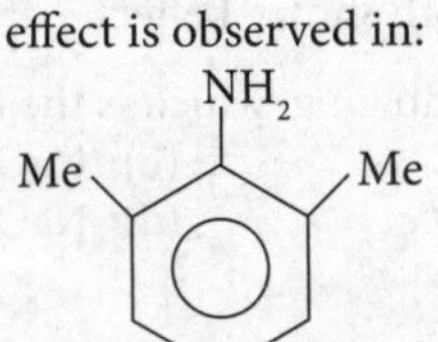

(b) 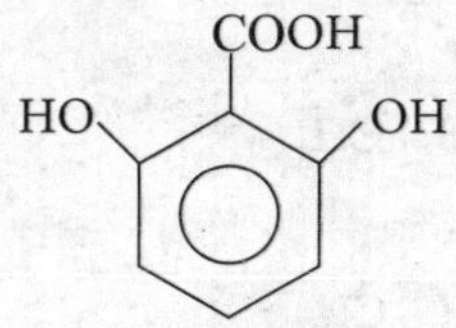

(c) 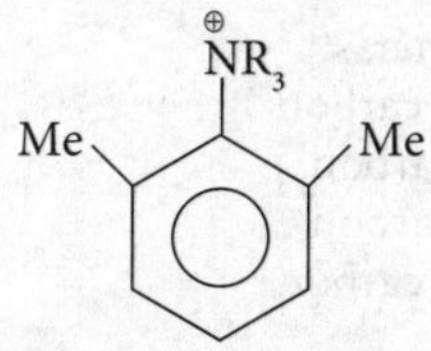

(d) 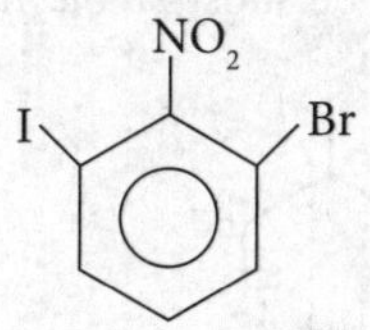

97. The most stable carbocation is:

(a) 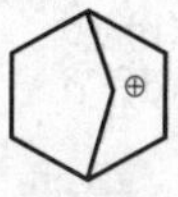 (b) 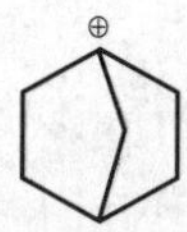

(c) 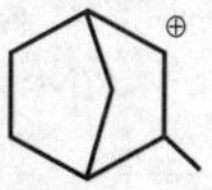 (d) 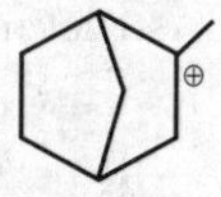

98. The compound with the least pKb is:

(a) CH_3NHCH_3 (b) CH_3NH_2

(c) 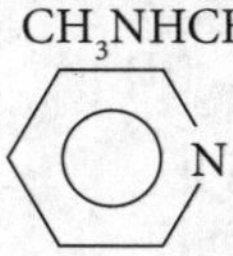 (d) 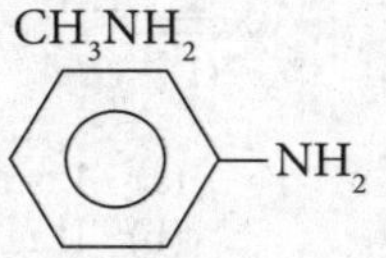

99. The most stable carbocation is:

(a) 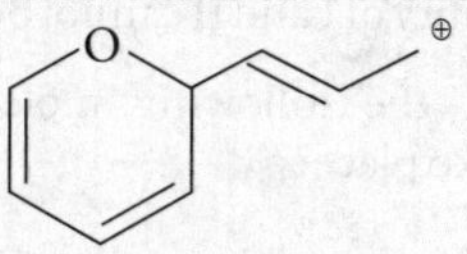

(b) 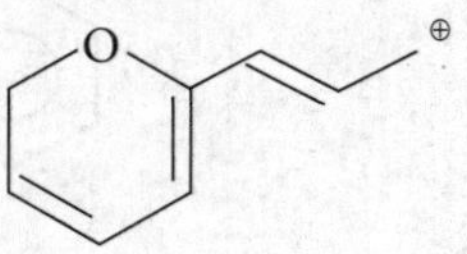

(c) 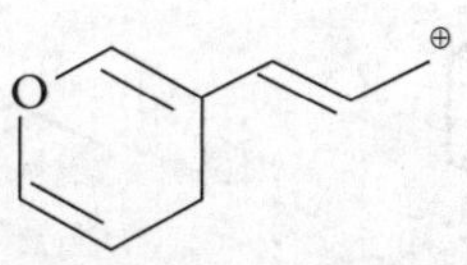

(d) 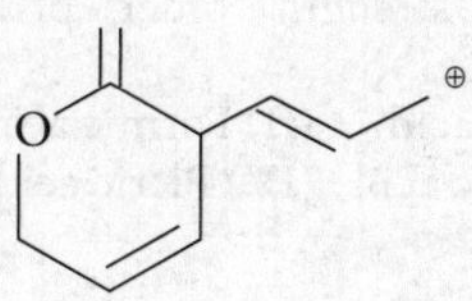

100. Which nitrogen is protonated readily in the given molecule?

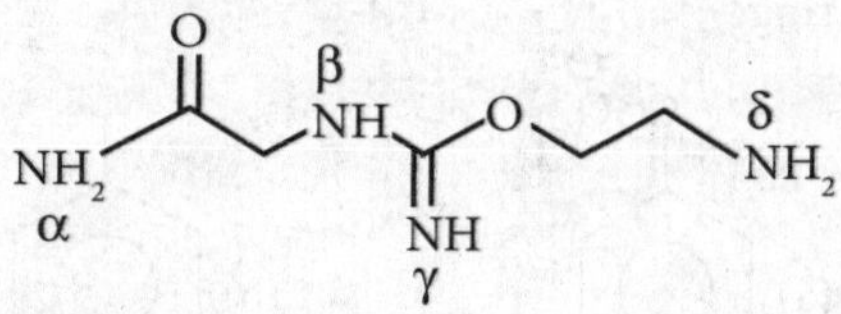

(a) α (b) β
(c) γ (d) δ

101. Compare the carbocation stability orders:

(a) 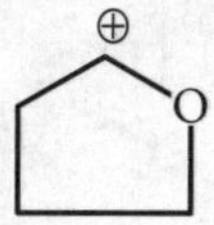 (b) 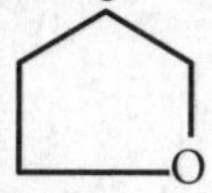 (c) 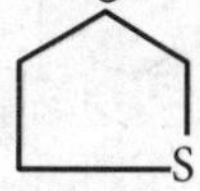 (d) 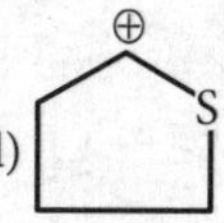

(a) (d) > (a) > (b) > (c)
(b) (a) > (d) > (c) > (b)
(c) (d) >(a) > (c) > (b)
(d) (a)> (d) > (b) > (c)

102. Which of the following is the most stable ?

(a) 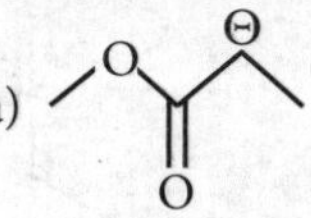 (b) 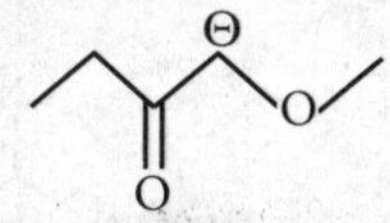

(c) 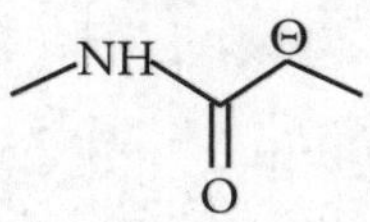 (d) 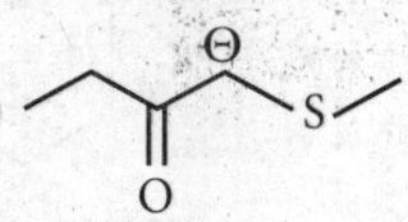

103. The most stable anion is:

(a) 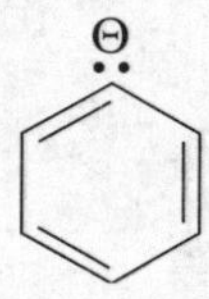 (b) $CH_2=\ddot{C}H^{\ominus}$

(c) $CH_3-\ddot{C}H_2^{\ominus}$ (d) $CH_3-\ddot{O}^{\ominus}$

104. Which of the following is not a valid pair of resonating structures?

(a) $CH_3-\overset{O}{\overset{\|}{C}}-\ddot{N}H^{\ominus} \longleftrightarrow CH_3-\overset{\ominus\ddot{O}}{\overset{|}{C}}=\overset{\oplus}{N}H$

(b) 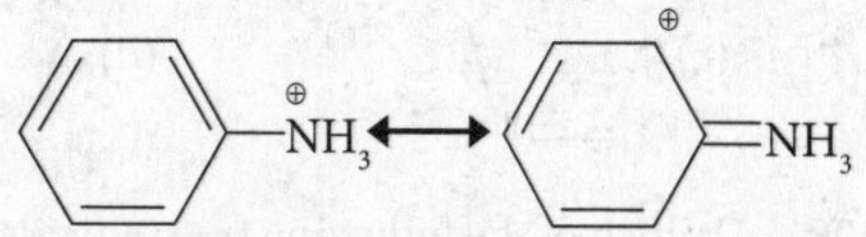

(c) $H_2\overset{\oplus}{C}-CH=O \longleftrightarrow H_2C=CH-\overset{\oplus}{O}$

(d) All of these

105. In which of the following is the molecule electron density maximum in the benzene ring?

(a) 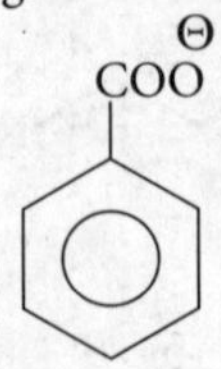 (b) 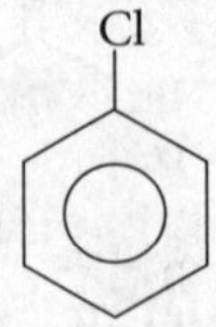

(c) 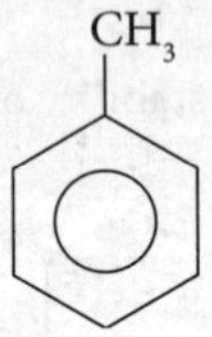 (d) 

106. Ortho effect is observed in:

(a) 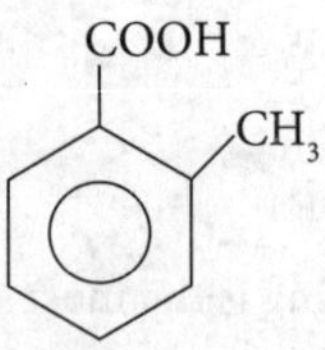 (b) 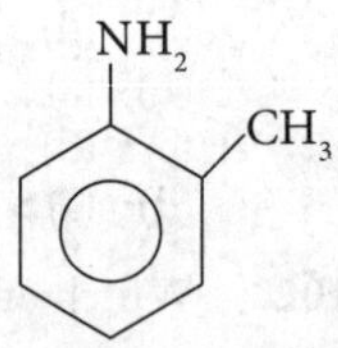

(c) 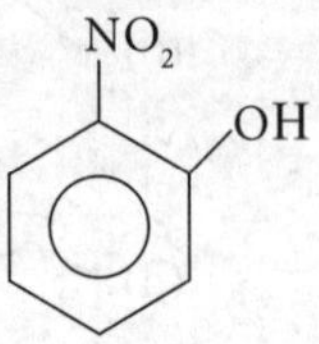 (d) 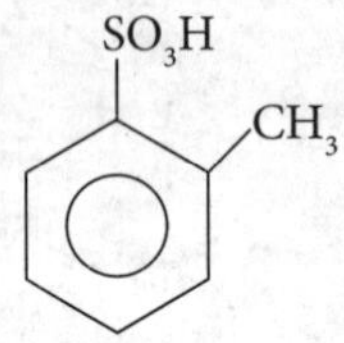

107. Which of the following is true?

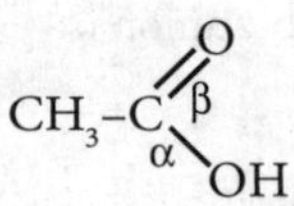

(a) $\alpha = \beta$
(b) $\alpha > \beta$
(c) $\alpha < \beta$
(d) Cannot be compared

108. The most stable carbocation is:

(a) 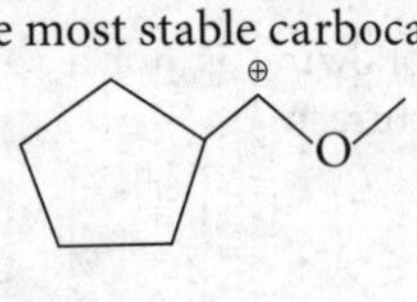 (b) 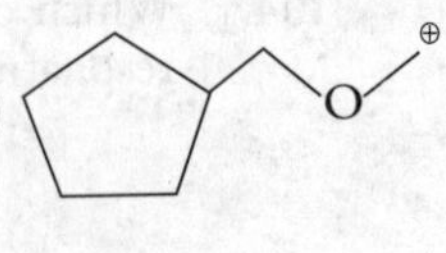

(c) 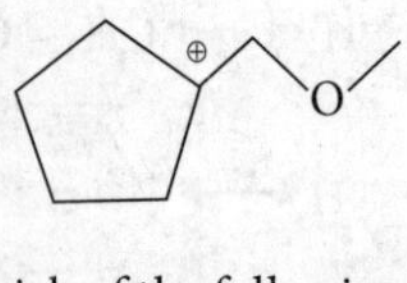 (d) 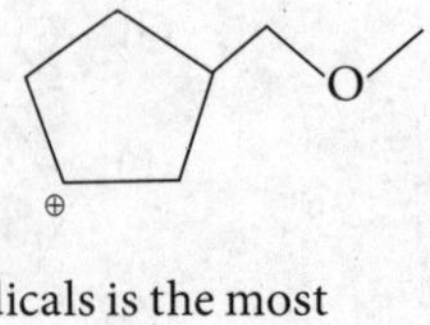

109. Which of the following free radicals is the most stable?

(a) $Ph-\dot{C}H_2$
(b) $CH_2=CH-\dot{C}H_2$
(c) $(CH_3)_3\dot{C}$
(d) $CH_3-\dot{C}H-CH_3$

110. Allyl carbanion has:
(a) $sp^2$and sp^3 carbon
(b) Only sp^3 carbon
(c) Only sp^2 carbon
(d) sp and sp^2 carbon

111. Carbocation will be most stable in the given molecule if it is on:

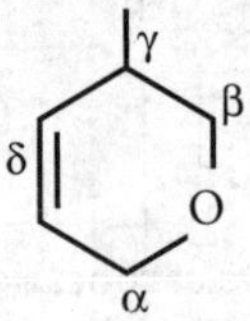

(a) α (b) β
(c) γ (d) δ

112. Which is true for the given resonating structures?

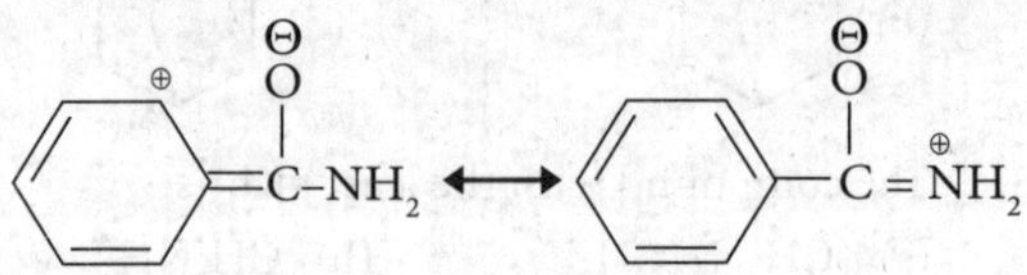

(I) (II)

(a) I is more stable than II
(b) II is more stable than I
(c) I and II are equally stable
(d) The stability of I and II cannot be compared

113. In which of the following molecules does resonance take place?

(a) 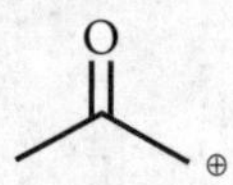 (b) 

(c) 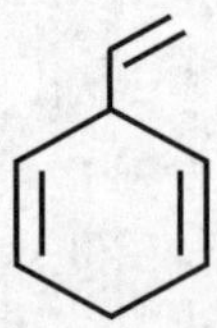 (d) 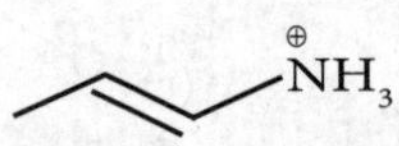

114. The acidic strength order of the given compounds is:
(I) Acetic acid (II) Formic acid
(III) Benzoic acid (IV) Picric acid

(a) IV > II >III > I
(b) IV > II > I > III
(c) II > III > I> IV
(d) II > IV > III > I

115. Compare the stability of the following carbanions:

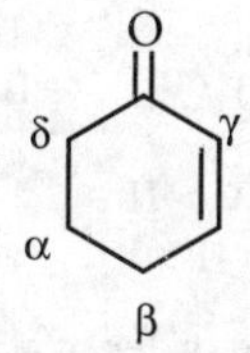

(a) $\beta > \delta > \gamma > \alpha$
(b) $\gamma > \delta > \beta > \alpha$
(c) $\gamma > \beta > \delta > \alpha$
(d) $\beta > \gamma > \delta > \alpha$

116. The order of basicity of amines in benzene solvent is:
(a) 3° > 2° > NH_3> 1°
(b) 2° > 1° > 3° > NH_3
(c) 3° > 2° > 1° > NH_3
(d) 2° > 3° > 1° > NH_3

117. Hyper-conjugation effect is not observed in:
(a) $CH_3-\overset{\oplus}{C}H_2$ (b) $CH_3-\dot{C}H_2$
(c) CH_3–CH=CH_2 (d) $CH_3-\overset{\ominus}{\ddot{C}}H_2$

118. Which of the following carbanions is resonance stabilized?

(a) 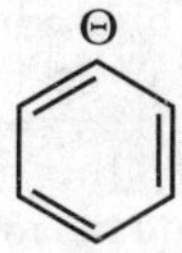 (b) 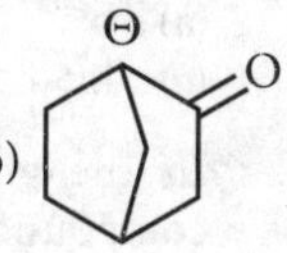

(c) 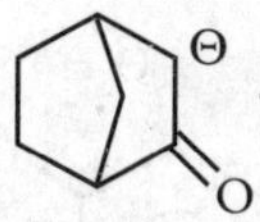 (d) 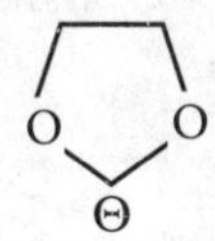

119. Which order among the following is incorrect about alkenol content?

(a) 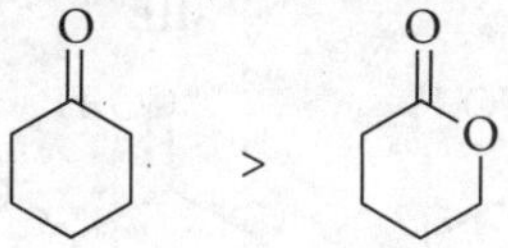

(b) 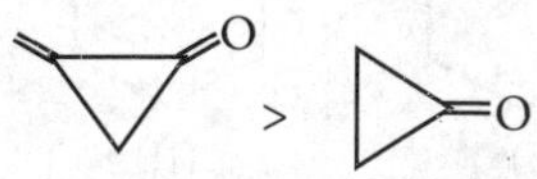

(c) 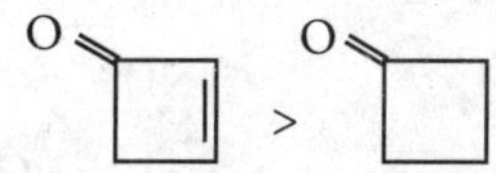

(d) 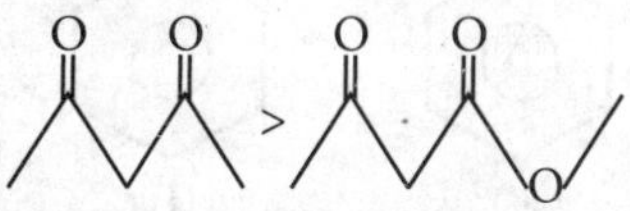

120. Which of the following compounds can show geometrical isomerism and tautomerism?
(a) But-3-en-2-one
(b) 2,2,6,6-Tetramethylcyclohexanone
(c) 4,4-Dimethyl-pent-2-enal
(d) Cyclooct-2-enone

Level-2

1. Which statement is incorrect?
(a) The C–Cl bond in vinyl chloride is stronger than in chloroethane
(b) The carbon–carbon bond length in ethene is shorter than in CH_2 = CH – OCH_3
(c) CH_3OH is a stronger acid than CH_3SH
(d) $CH_3CH_2NH_2$ is a stronger base than CH_2 = CH NH_2

2. Arrange the following compounds in decreasing order of their basic strength:

a 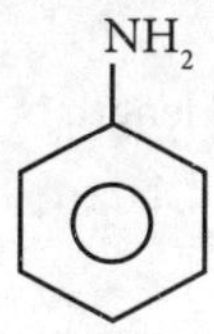 b 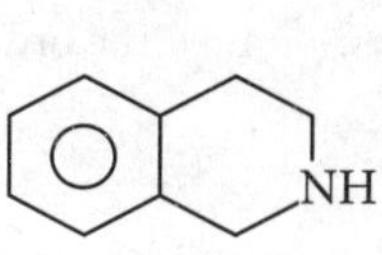

c 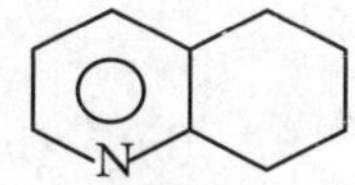 d 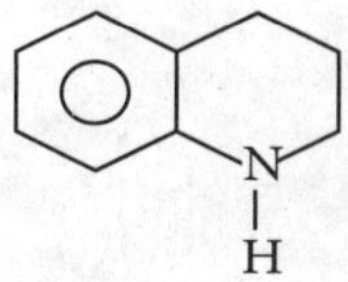

(a) b > c > d > a (b) c > b > d > a
(c) b > c > a > d (d) c > b > a > d

3. In the given pair, identify the most acidic compound in (A) and (B) and the most basic in (C) and (D):

(A) 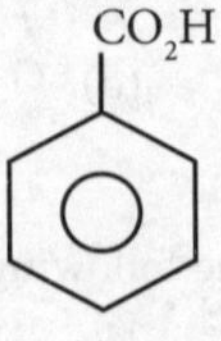 (I) 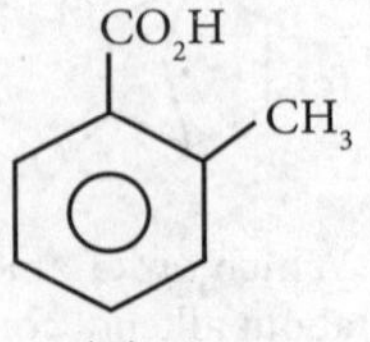 (II)

(B) 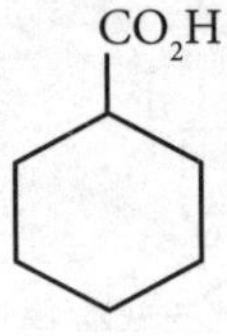 (I) 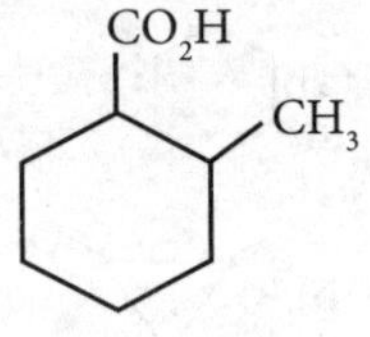 (II)

(C) 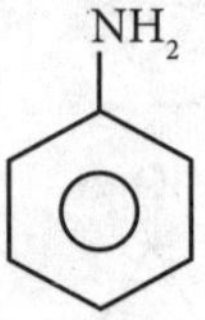 (I) 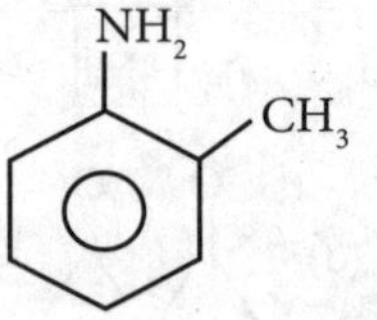 (II)

(D) 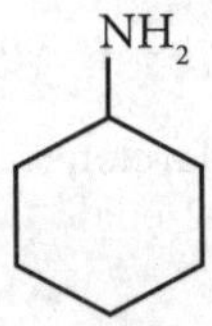 (I) 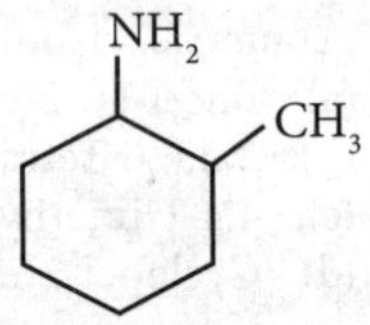 (II)

(a) A-I, B-II, C-I, D-II
(b) A-II, B-I, C-I, D-II
(c) A-II, B-II, C-II, D-II
(d) A-I, B-II, C-I, D-I

4. The order of marked bond length is:

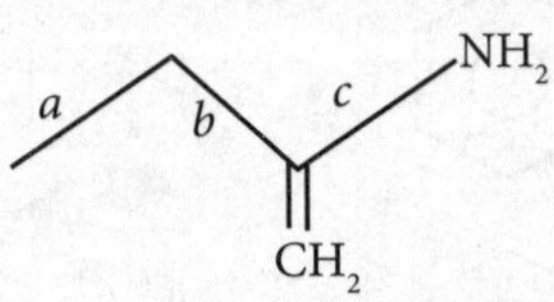

(a) c > a > b (b) a > b > c
(c) a > c > b (d) c > b > a

5. Which is the correct order of basic strength of the following compounds?

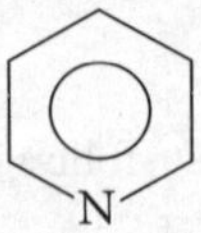 (I) 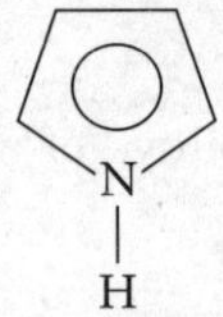 (II) 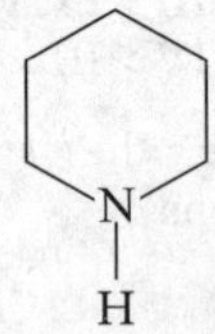 (III) 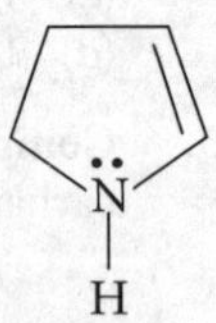 (IV)

(a) III > I > IV > II (b) IV > III > I > II
(c) III > IV > II > I (d) I > III > IV > II

6. The decreasing order of acidity of the following hydrogen atoms is:

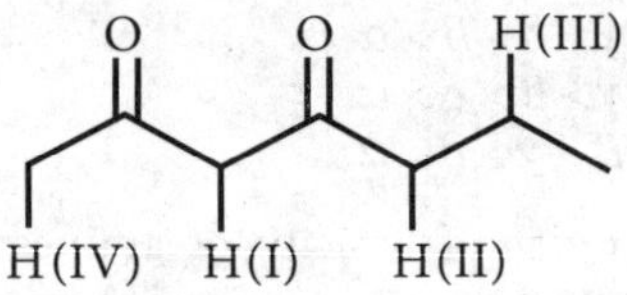

(a) IV > I > III > II (b) I > IV > II > III
(c) I > IV > III > II (d) IV > I > II > III

7. Compare the C–N bond length in the following species:

(i) 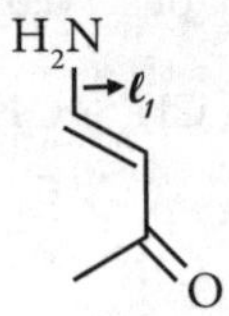 (ii) 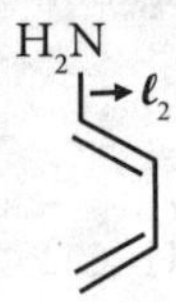 (iii) 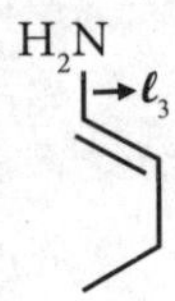

(a) $l_1 > l_2 > l_3$ (b) $l_3 > l_2 > l_1$
(c) $l_3 > l_1 > l_2$ (d) $l_2 > l_1 > l_3$

8. Which of the functional groups does not give hydrogen gas with sodium metal?
(a) $CH_3 - CH_2 - OH$
(b) $CH_3 - C \equiv CH$
(c) $(CH_3)_3N$
(d) $CH_3 - COOH$

9. The correct order of heat of hydrogenation for the given compounds is:

a  b 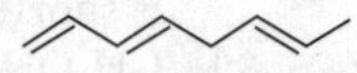

c 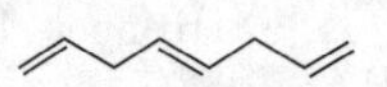 d 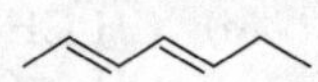

(a) c > b > a > d (b) a > b > c > d
(c) c > d > b > a (d) c > b > d > a

10. Among the following, the correct order is:

(a) 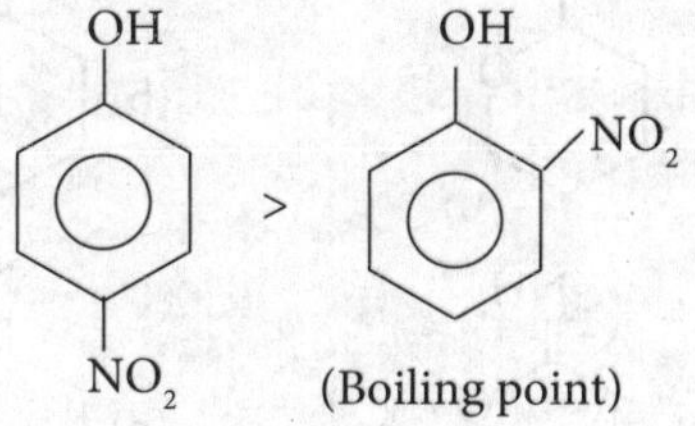

(Boiling point)

(b) 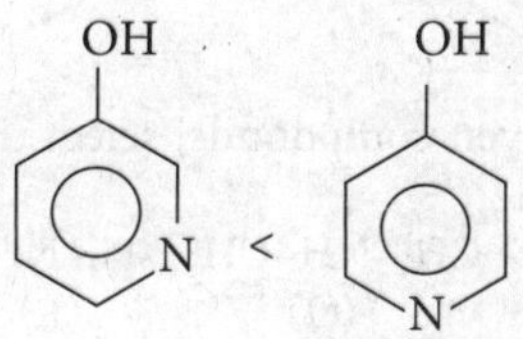

(Acidic strength)

(c) 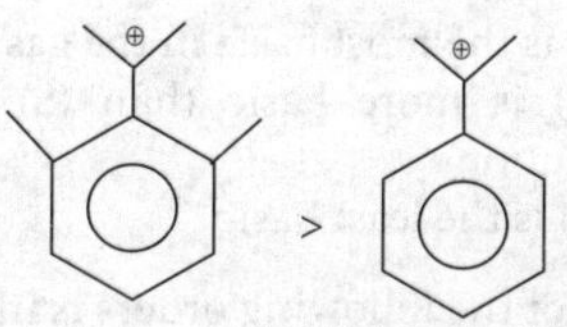

(Cation stability)

(d) $\overset{\ominus}{C}H(CN)_2 > \overset{\ominus}{C}H(NO_2)_2$

(Carbanion stability)

11. The correct statement for the given compound is:

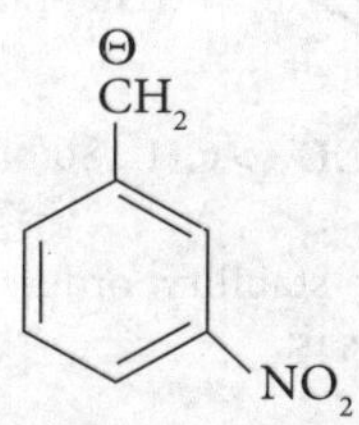

(a) –M effect of $-NO_2$ operates on the benzene ring but not on the carbanion
(b) –M effect of $-NO_2$ operates on the carbanion but not on the benzene ring
(c) –M effect of $-NO_2$ operates on the carbanion as well as on the benzene ring
(d) Only the –I effect of $-NO_2$ operates on the carbanion as well as the benzene ring

12. The carbanion is most stable on which site?

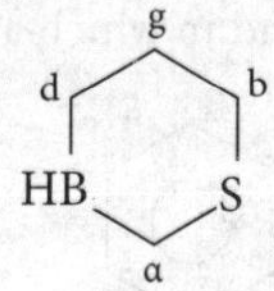

(a) α (b) β
(c) γ (d) δ

13. The compound with the least pKa is:

(a) 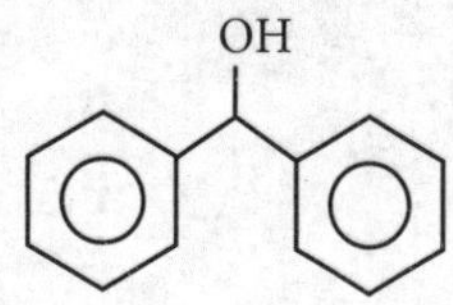

(b) 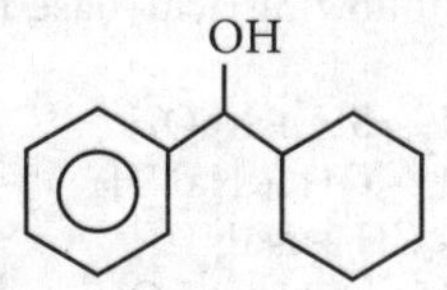

(c) 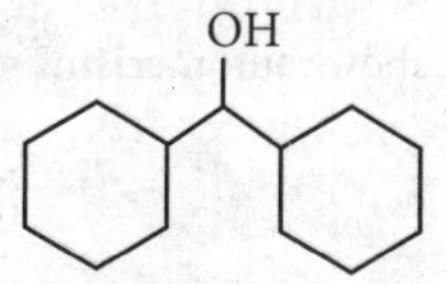

(d) 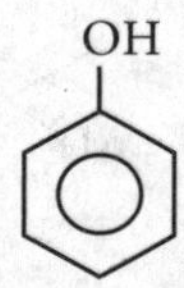

14. The reaction in which aromatic product is obtained is:

(a) 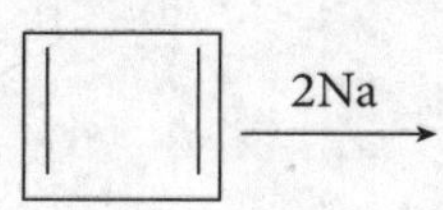

(b) 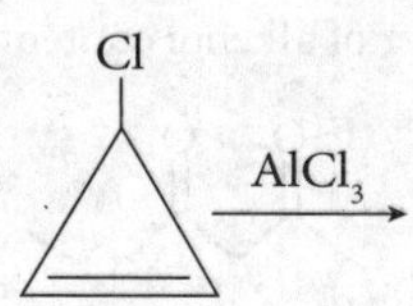

(c) 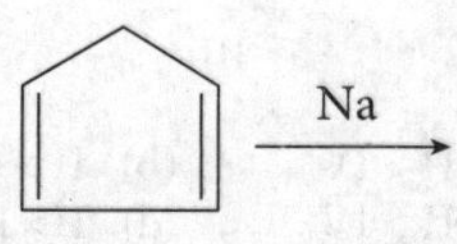

(d) All of these

15. The compound in which all C–C bond lengths are the same is:

(a) 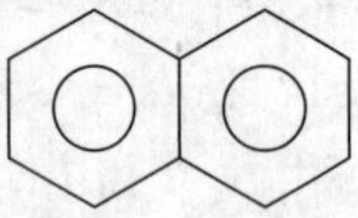

(b) $CH_2=CH-CH=CH_2$

(c) $CH_2=CH-\overset{\ominus}{C}H_2$

(d) 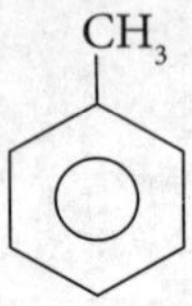

16. Which of the following acid–base reactions is not feasible?

(a) $CH_3-CH_2-SH + NaOH$

(b) $CH_3-CH_2-OH + NaNH_2$

(c) $CH_3-C\equiv CH + NaNH_2$

(d) $C_6H_5-CH_2-OH + NaOH$

17. Which cannot show tautomerism?

(a) 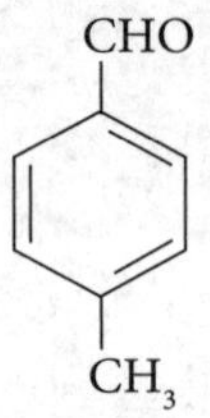

(b) 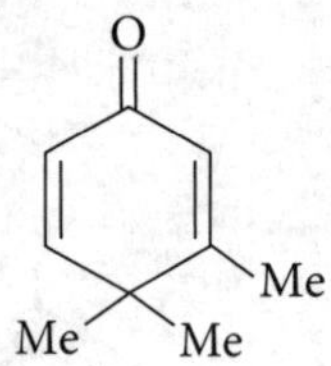

(c) 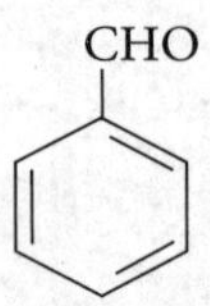

(d) 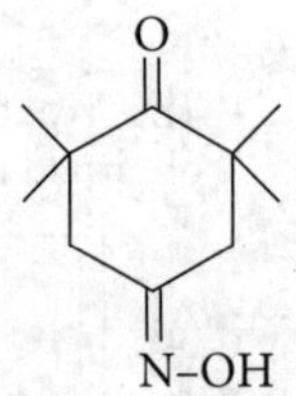

18. The correct order of alkenol content is:

I

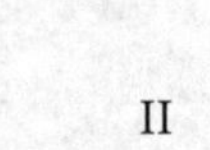

II

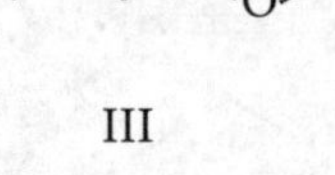

III

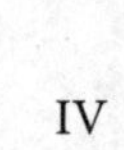

IV

(a) I > II > III > IV (b) II > I > III > IV

(c) I > III > II > IV (d) II> III > I > IV

19. Which of the following is the most basic?

(a) 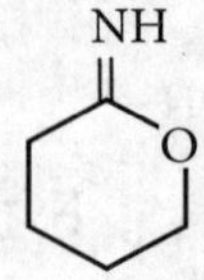

(b) 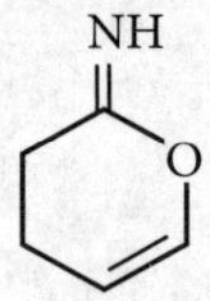

(c) 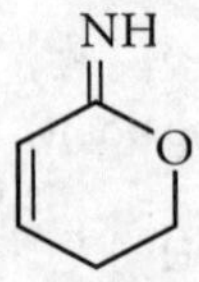

(d) 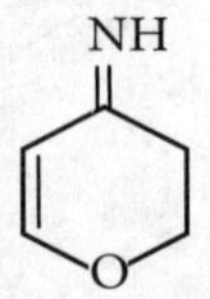

20. For the given compounds, select the incorrect statement:

CH_3-NH_2 (P) $CH_3-NH-CH_3$ (Q) $Ph-NH_2$ (R) $(CH_3)_3N$ (S)

(a) (S) is more basic than (P) in aqueous solution

(b) (S) is the most basic in the gas phase

(c) (Q) is more basic than (S) in aqueous solution

(d) (R) is the least basic

21. Which of the following orders is incorrect?

(a) $\overset{\ominus}{C}H_3 > \overset{\ominus}{N}H_2 > \overset{\ominus}{O}H > \overset{\ominus}{F}$ (Basic strength)

(b) HI > HBr > HCl > HF (Acidic strength)

(c) 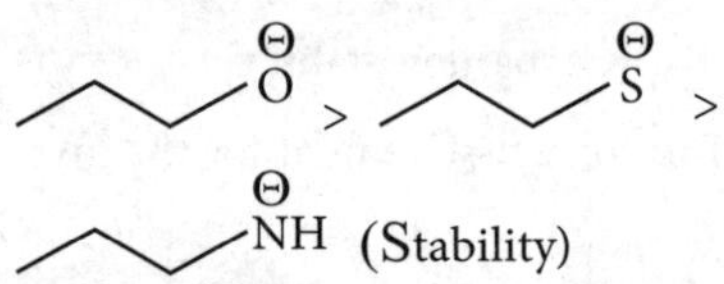

(d) $\overset{\oplus}{C}T_3 > \overset{\oplus}{C}D_3 > \overset{\oplus}{C}H_3$ (Stability of cation)

22. The correct stability order of the following carbocations is:

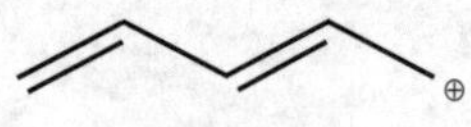

I

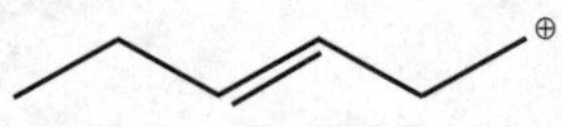

II

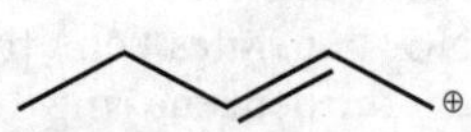

III

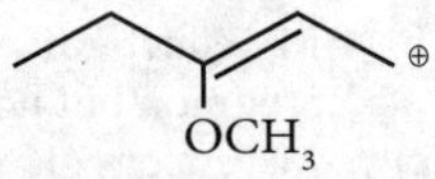

IV

(a) IV > I > III > II (b) I > VI > III > II

(c) I > VI > II > III (d) VI > I > II > III

23. Which one is the correct order of acidity of the following compounds?

H_2O	HBr	HC≡CH	HCl
(I)	(II)	(III)	(IV)

(a) I > IV>II >III (b) II > IV >I >III
(c) I >II > IV >III (d) II >I > IV >III

24. If 1 mole of H_2 is reacted with 1 mole of compound, which double bond will be hydrogenated?

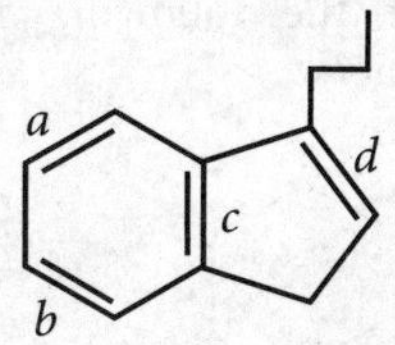

(a) c (b) b
(c) a (d) d

25. The correct order of bond length is:

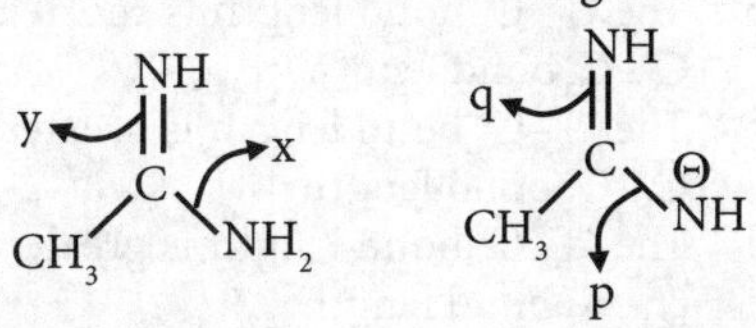

(a) x > p > q > y (b) x > p = q > y
(c) y > p = q > x (d) q > y > x > p

26. The most stable carbanion is:

(a) 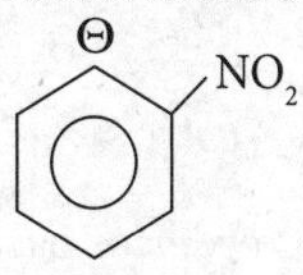

(b) 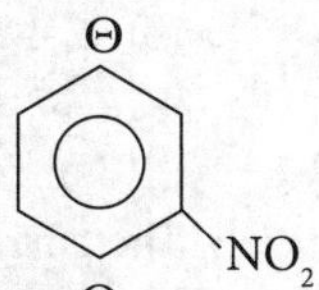

(c) 

(d) 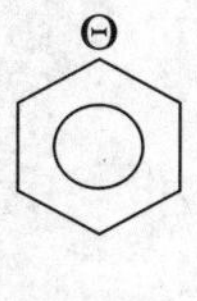

27. Which of the following compounds is the most basic?

(a) 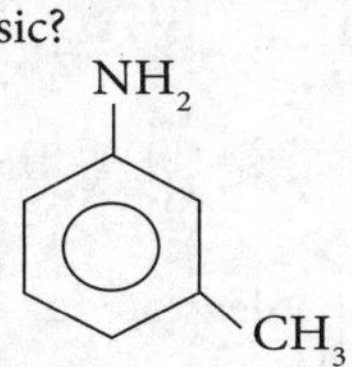

(b) 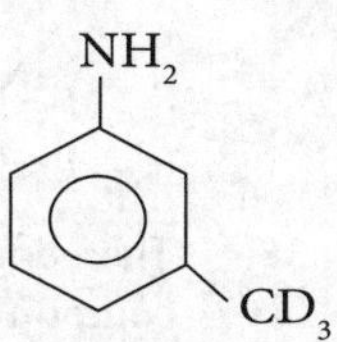

(c) 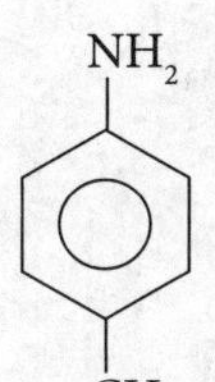

(d) 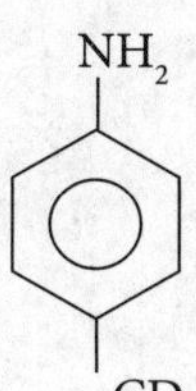

28. Compare the indicated bond lengths:

(i) CH_3–O–CH = CH–C(=O)–CH_3 (indicated bond: CH = CH)

(ii) CH_2 = CH–C(=O)–CH_3 (indicated bond: CH_2 = CH)

(iii) CH_2 = CH –C(=O)–O–CH_3 (indicated bond: CH_2 = CH)

(iv) CH_2 = CH_2 (indicated bond: CH_2 = CH_2)

(a) II > III > I > IV (b) I > II > III > IV
(c) I > III > II > IV (d) II > I > III > IV

29. Which of the following compounds has the highest dipole moment?

(a) 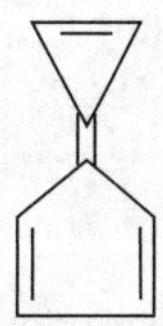

(b) 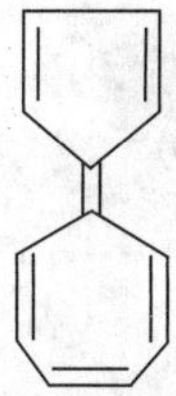

(c) 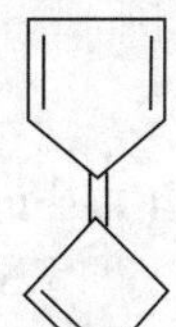

(d) 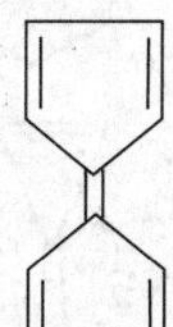

30. Compare the heat of hydrogenation of the following compounds:

(i) 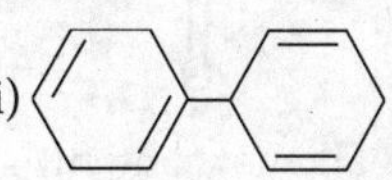

(ii) 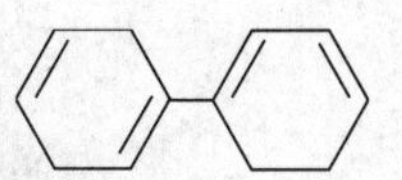

(iii) 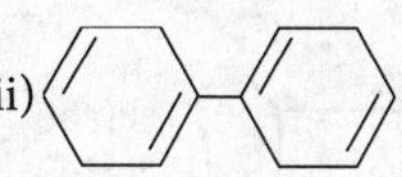

(iv) 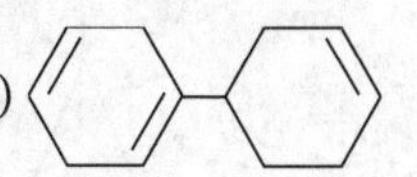

(a) i > iii > ii > iv (b) iv > i > iii > ii
(c) i > ii > iii > iv (d) iv > ii > iii > i

31. In which of the following statements is hydrogen bonding not a dominating phenomenon?

(a) p-Hydroxybenzoic acid is less acidic than o-hydroxybenzoic acid
(b) Secondary alkyl amine is more basic than tertiary amine in aqueous solution
(c) m-Nitrophenol is less acidic than o-nitrophenol

(d) Maleic acid is a stronger acid than fumaric acid

32. The correct order of the C–N bond length in the given compounds is:

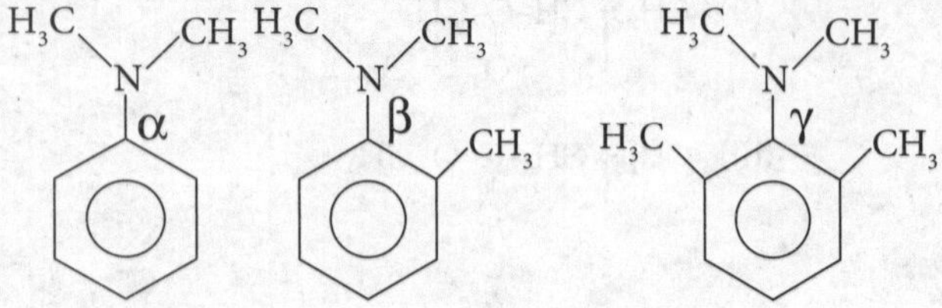

(a) $\gamma > \beta > \alpha$ (b) $\alpha > \beta > \gamma$
(c) $\beta > \gamma > \alpha$ (d) $\gamma > \alpha > \beta$

33. Select the incorrect option:

(a) 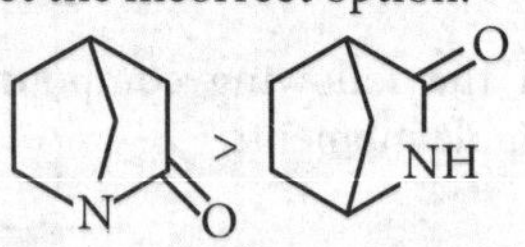

(Basic strength)

(b) $CH_3CO\overset{\oplus}{C}H_2 < CH_3O\overset{\oplus}{C}H_2$ (Stability)

(c) 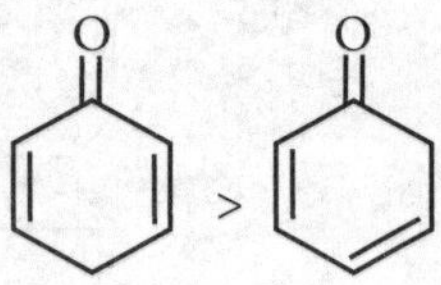

(C–O bond length)

(d) 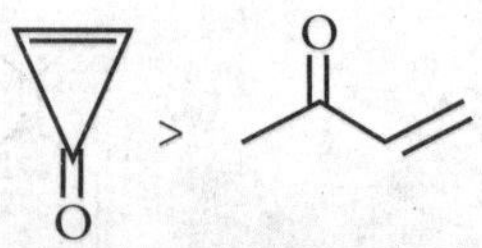

(Resonance energy)

34. Select the incorrect order:

(a) 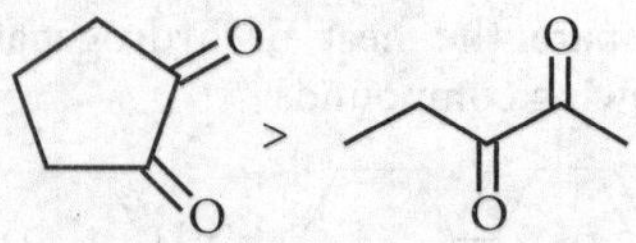

(Percentage of alkenol content)

(b) 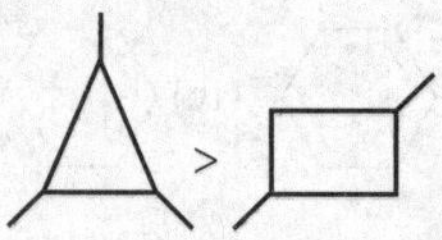 (Heat of combustion)

(c) 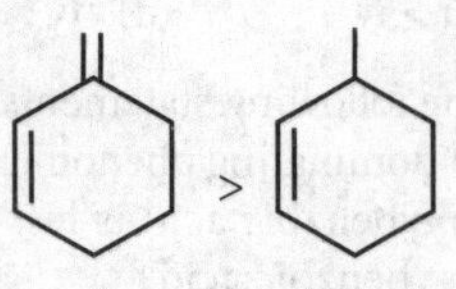 (Heat of hydrogenation)

(d) 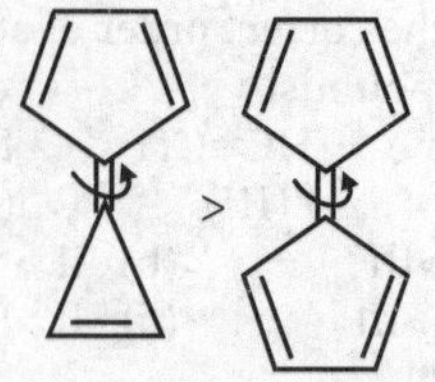

(Rotational energy barrier)

35. Which of the following is correct about naphthalene?

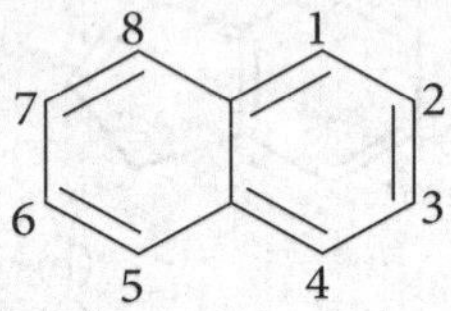

(a) All the C–C bond lengths are the same
(b) The C_1–C_2 bond length is shorter than the C_2–C_3 bond length
(c) The C_1–C_2 bond length is greater than the C_2–C_3 bond length
(d) The C_1–C_2 bond length is greater than the C_7–C_8 bond length

36. Which of the following has the most acidic hydrogen?
(a) 3-Hexanone
(b) 2,4-Hexanedione
(c) 2,5-Hexanedione
(d) 2,3-Hexanedione

37. The correct increasing order of basic strength of the structure labelled N is:

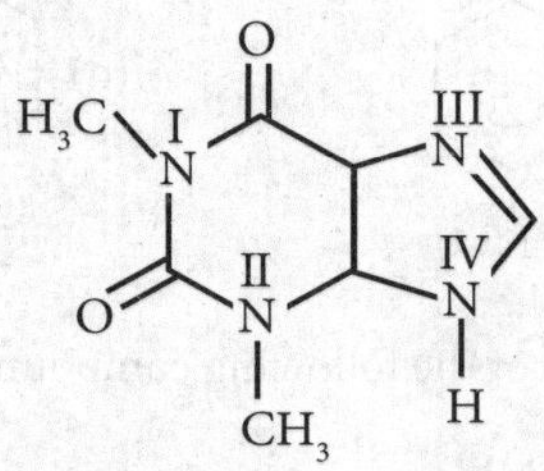

(a) I < II < III < IV (b) I <II < IV < III
(c) I < III < IV < II (d) IV < III < II < I

38. The bond length order of the following compound is:

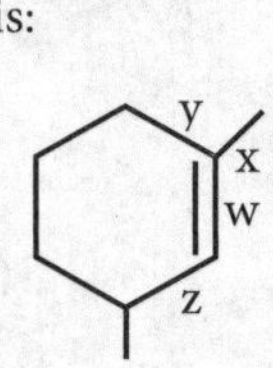

(a) x > y > z > w (b) z > y > x > w
(c) y > z > x > w (d) z > x > y > w

39. The stability order of the following carbocations is:

(I) 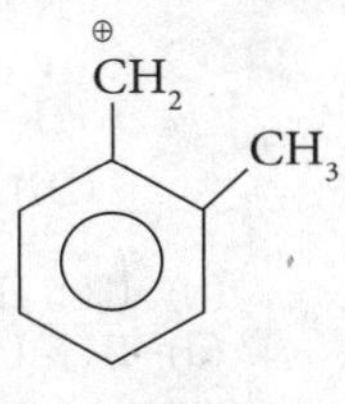 (II) 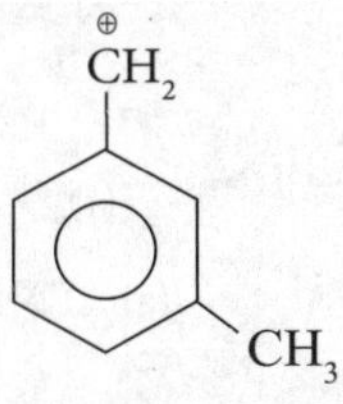

(III) 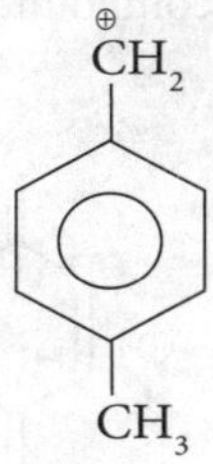 (IV) 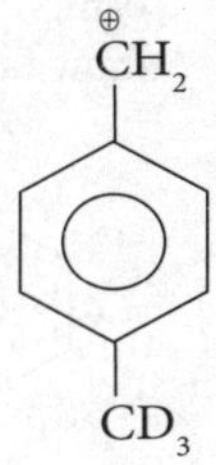

(a) I > II > III > IV (b) IV > I > III > II
(c) I > III > IV > II (d) IV > III > I > II

40. The increasing order of the acidity of the α-hydrogen of the following compounds is:

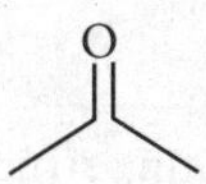
(A)

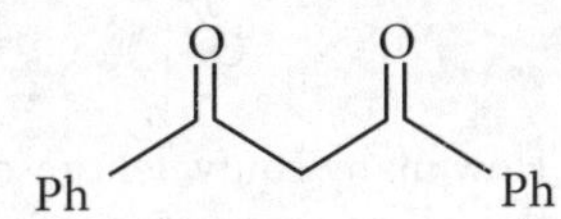
(B)

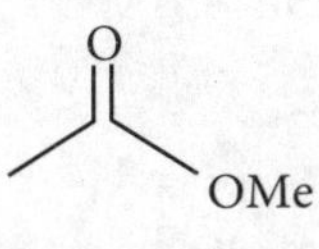
(C)

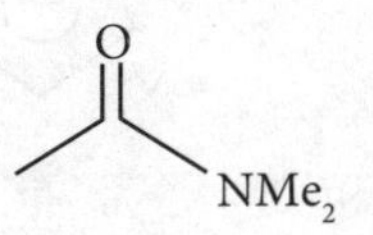
(D)

(a) (D) < (C) < (A) < (B)
(b) (A) < (C) < (D) < (B)
(c) (C) < (A) < (B) < (D)
(d) (B) < (C) < (A) < (D)

41. The increasing order of basicity of the following compounds is:

(a) 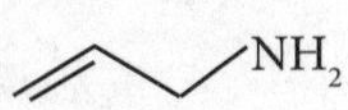 (b) 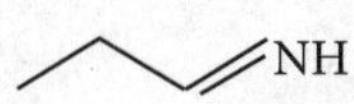

(c) 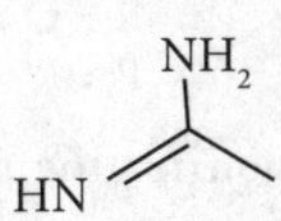 (d) 

(a) (d) < (b) < (a) < (c)
(b) (a) < (b) < (c) < (d)
(c) (b) < (a) < (c) < (d)
(d) (b) < (a) < (d) < (c)

42. Arrange the following labelled hydrogens in decreasing order of acidity:

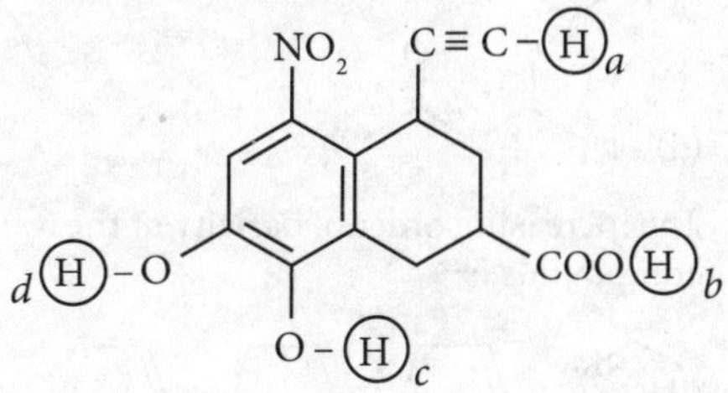

(a) b > a > c > d (b) c > b > d > a
(c) c > b > a > d (d) b > c > d > a

43. The increasing order of pKb values of the following compounds is:

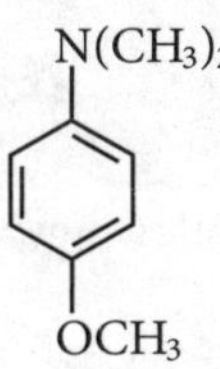
I

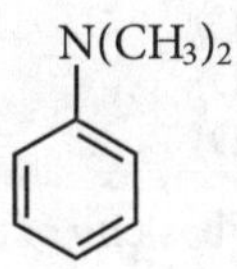
II

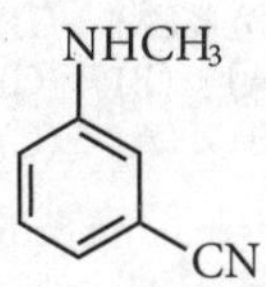
III

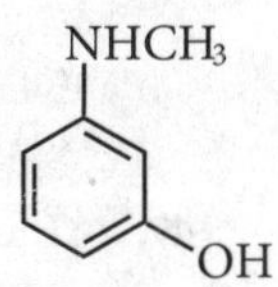
IV

(a) II < I < III < IV (b) II < IV < III < I
(c) I < II < IV < III (d) I < II < III < IV

44. The increasing order of pKb for the following compounds will be:

$NH_2–CH=NH$ (A)

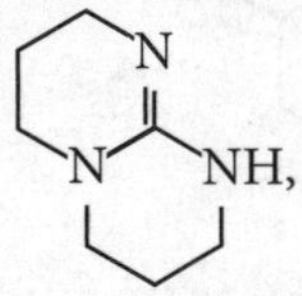
(B)

CH_3NHCH_3 (C)

(a) (B) < (A) < (C)
(b) (C) < (A) < (B)
(c) (B) < (C) < (A)
(d) (A) < (B) < (C)

45. Which of the following possesses less alkenol form than the corresponding keto form?

(a) 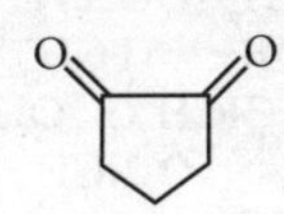

(b) 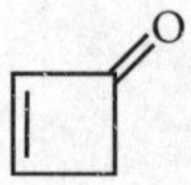

(c) 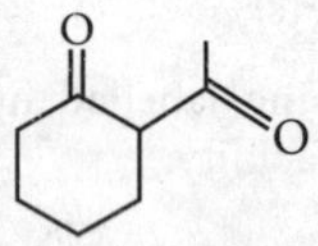

(d) 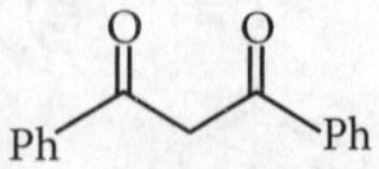

46. The increasing order of basicity of the following compounds is:

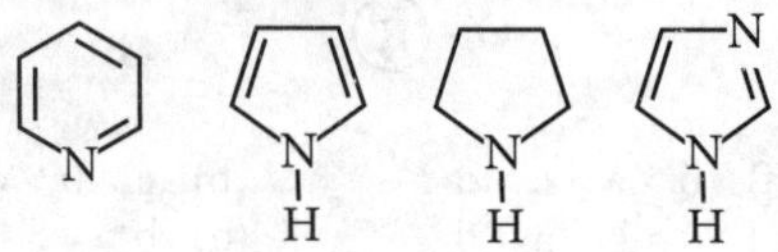

(A) (B) (C) (D)

(a) (D) < (A) < (B) < (C)
(b) (B) < (A) < (D) < (C)
(c) (A) < (B) < (C) < (D)
(d) (B) < (A) < (C) < (D)

47. The decreasing order of basicity of the following amines is:

(I) 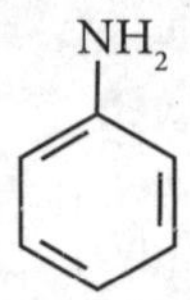

(II) 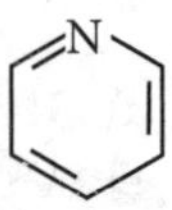

(III) 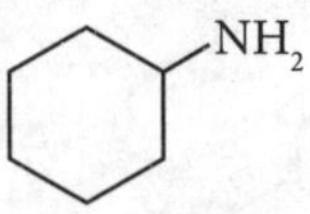

(IV) 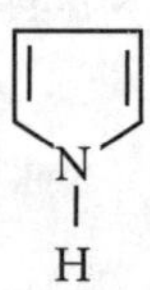

(a) (III) > (I) > (II) > (IV)
(b) (III) > (II) > (I) > (IV)
(c) (II) > (III) > (IV) > (I)
(d) (I) > (III) > (IV) > (II)

48. The correct decreasing order for acid strength is:
(a) $NO_2CH_2COOH > NCCH_2COOH > FCH_2COOH > ClCH_2COOH$
(b) $FCH_2COOH > NCCH_2COOH > NO_2CHCOOH > ClCH_2COOH$
(c) $NO_2CH_2COOH > FCH_2COOH > CNCH_2COOH > ClCH_2COOH$
(d) $CNCH_2COOH > O_2NCH_2COOH > FCH_2COOH > ClCH_2COOH$

49. Arrange the following amines in decreasing order of basicity:

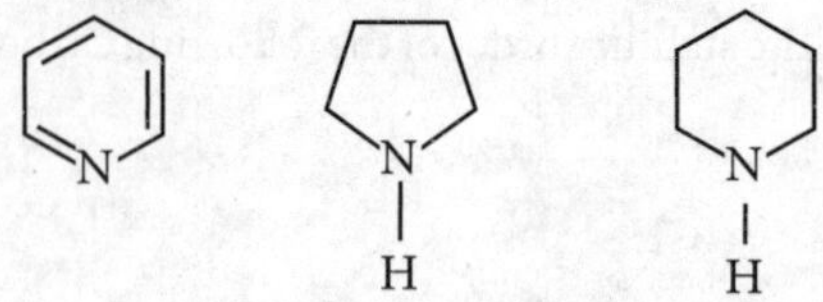

(I) (II) (III)

(a) I > II > III (b) III > II > I
(c) I > III > II (d) III > I > II

50. Which of the following compounds does not show tautomerism?

(a) 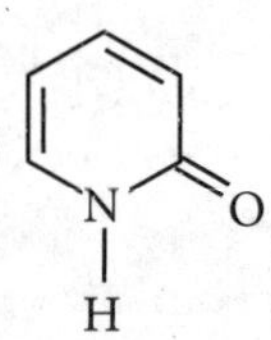

(b) 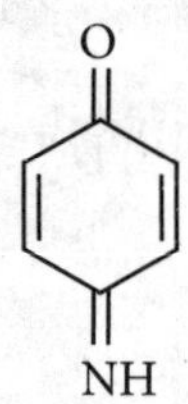

(c) 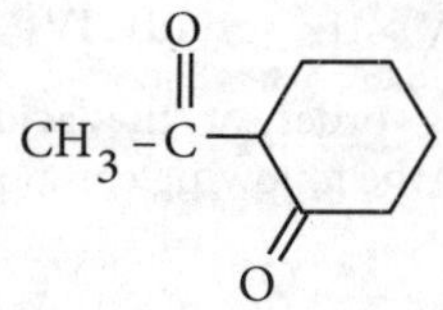

(d) 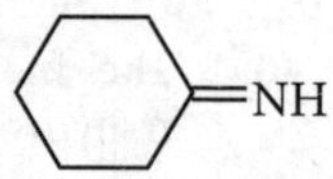

51. How many equivalent resonating structures of the following compound are possible?

(a) 3 (b) 4
(c) 5 (d) 6

52. For the following compounds, select the correct order of resonance energy:

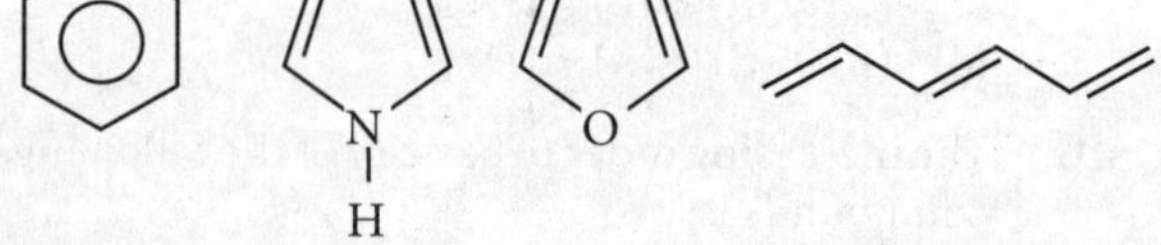

(P) (Q) (R) (S)

(a) Q > R > P > S (b) R > Q > P > S
(c) P > Q > R > S (d) P > R > Q > S

53. Select the incorrect option for the following compound:

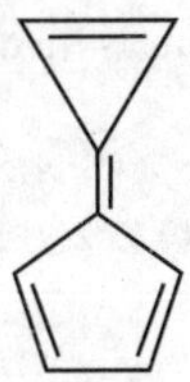

(a) It is an aromatic compound
(b) Dipole moment is from larger to smaller ring
(c) It is soluble in water
(d) C=C between two rings is larger than in ethene

54. Select the incorrect option for the following compound:

(a) It reacts with sodium and produces aromatic compound
(b) It has more resonance energy than

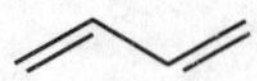

(c) It contains 4pπ and 4π electrons in resonance
(d) It exists in dimer form like

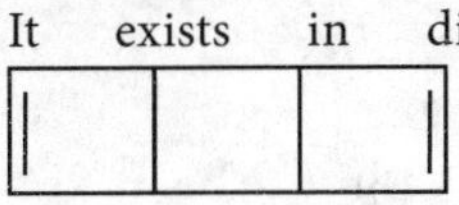

at room temperature

55. Which of the following orders is correct?

(a) 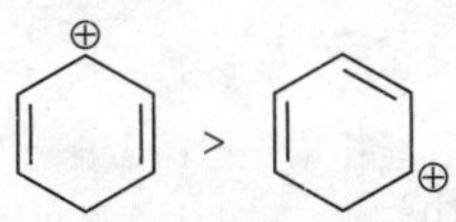 (Resonance energy)

(b) $-NH_2 > -OH$ (+R/+M effect)

(c) 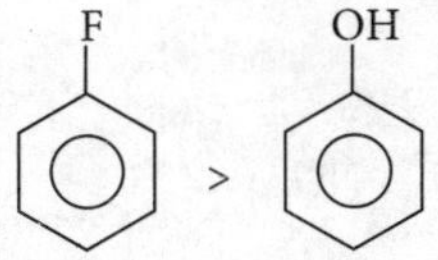 (Electrophilic attack)

(d) 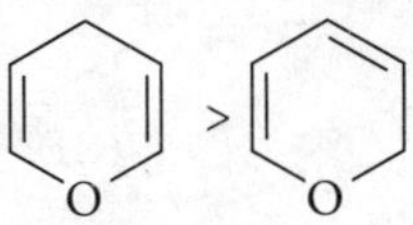 (Stability)

56. Compare the acidic strength of the following:

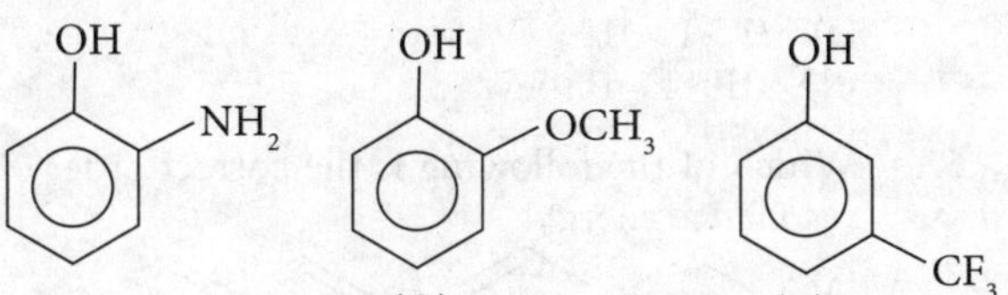

(P) (Q) (R)

(a) R > Q > P (b) P > Q > R
(c) Q > P > R (d) P > R > Q

57. Among the following, the incorrect statement is:
(a) The pKa value of benzoic acid is more than formic acid
(b) Heat of hydrogenation of cyclohexa-1,3-diene is more than cyclohexa-1,4-diene
(c) Resonance energy of acetate ion is more than phenoxide
(d) Tropylium cation is aromatic in nature

58. Which of the following orders is incorrect?

(a) 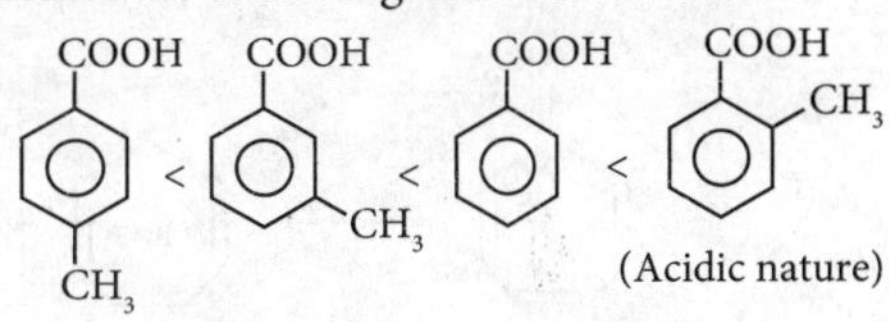 (Acidic nature)

(b) HCl > 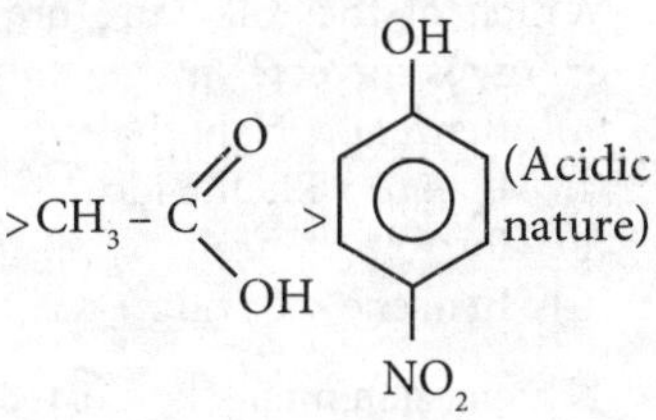 (Acidic nature)

(c) 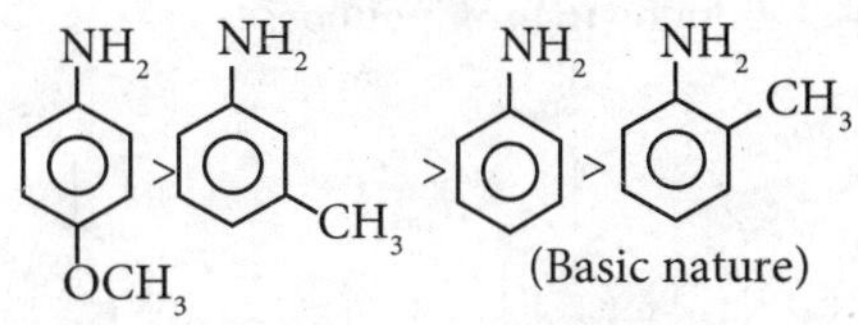 (Basic nature)

(d) $CH_3OH < HCO_2^{\ominus} < CO_3^{--} < HCHO$
(C–O bond length)

59. Which of the following orders is correct?

(a) 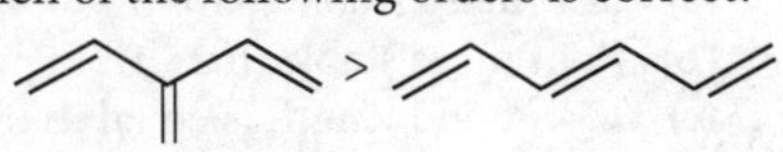
(Resonance energy)

(b) 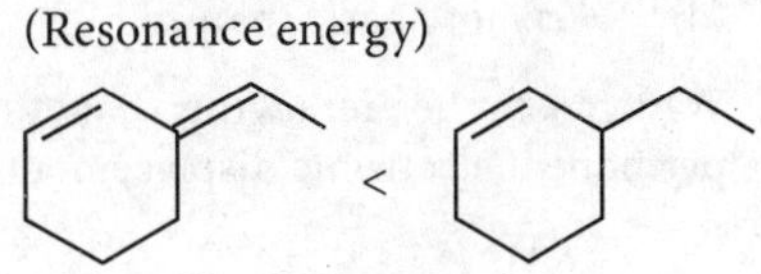
(Heat of hydrogenation)

(c) 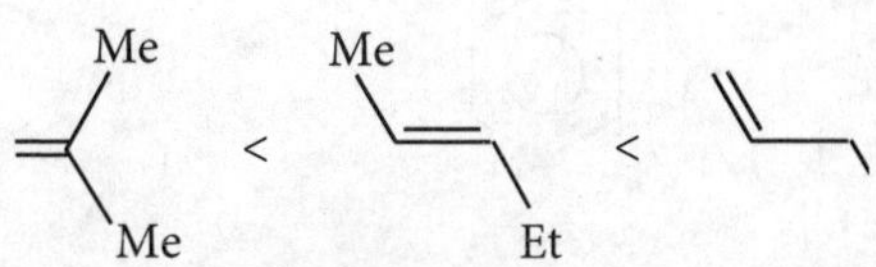
(Heat of combustion)

(d) $Ph_3C{-}CPh_3 < CH_3{-}CH_3$
(Bond energy of C–C bond)

60. In which of the following pairs does the first have less stability than the second?

(a) 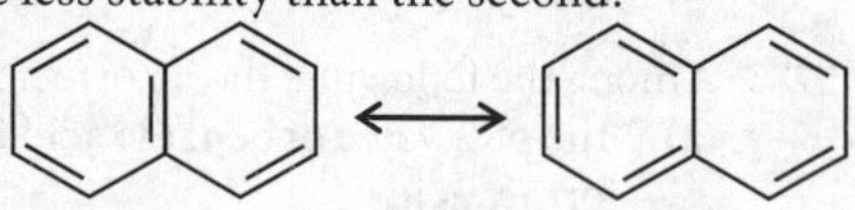

(b) 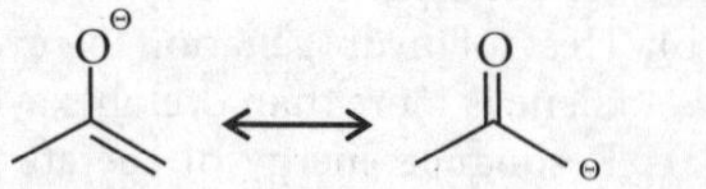

(c) 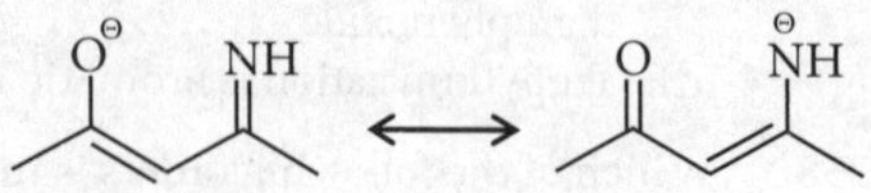

(d) 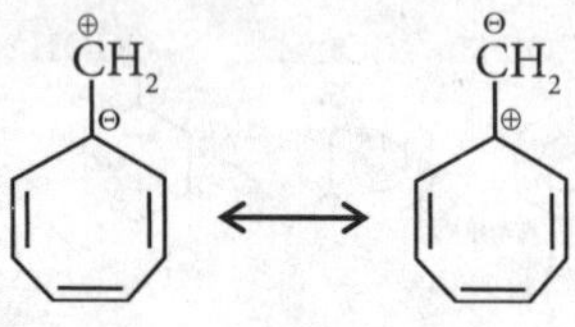

61. Which of the following orders of resonance energy is correct?
(a) Benzene > Naphthalene
(b) Phenol > Phenoxide
(c) Pyrrole > Furan
(d) Benzene < Pyridine

62. Which statement is correct regarding the following compounds?

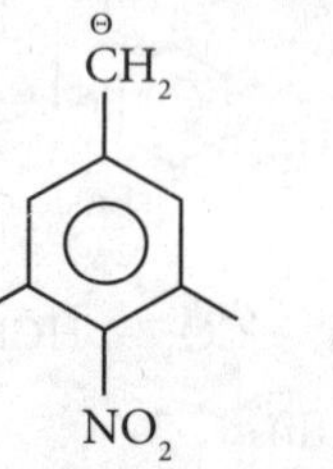
(a)

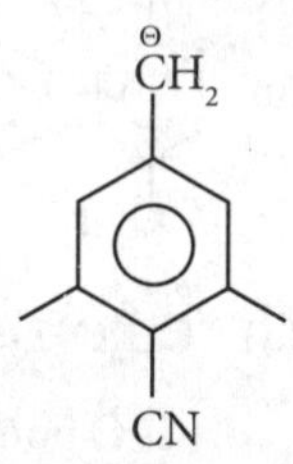
(b)

(a) 'a' is more stable than 'b'
(b) 'b' is more stable than 'a'
(c) C–N bond length is equal in both
(d) 'b' is more basic than 'a'

63. Which of the following has all types of permanent electronic displacement effect?

(a) 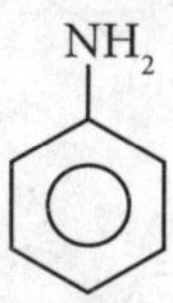

(b) 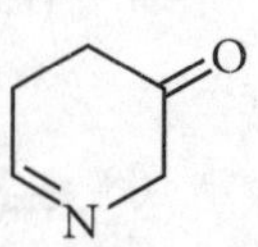

(c) 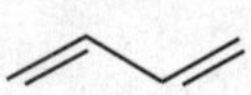

(d) 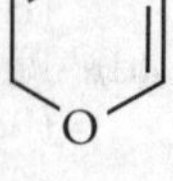

64. Which statement is incorrect?

(a) 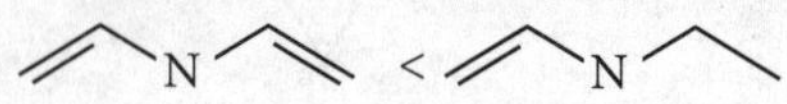
(Basic strength)

(b) 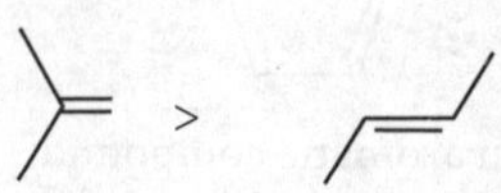
(Stability of alkene)

(c) 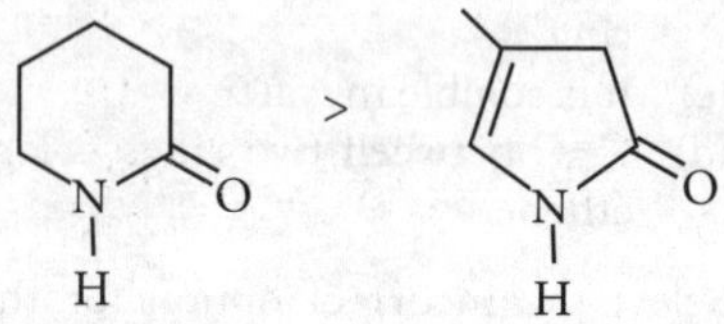
(Percentage of alkenolic form)

(d) 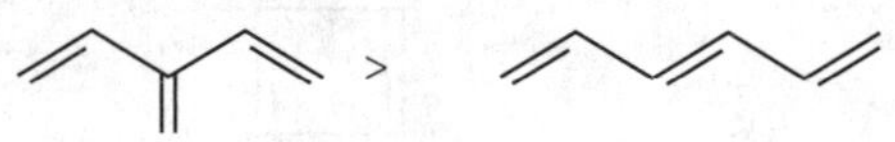
(Heat of combustion)

65. The correct order of heat of combustion for the following alkadienes is:

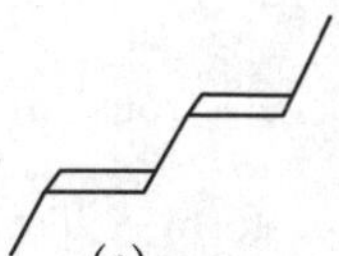
(a)

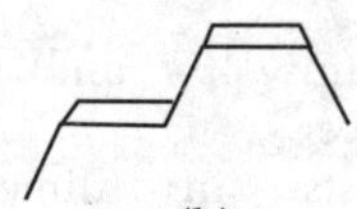
(b)

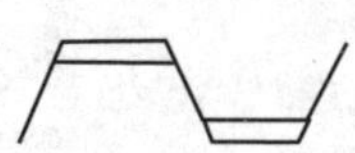
(c)

(a) (a) < (c) < (b)
(b) (b) < (c) < (a)
(c) (a) < (b) < (c)
(d) (c) < (b) < (a)

66. Which of the following orders is correct for acidic strength?

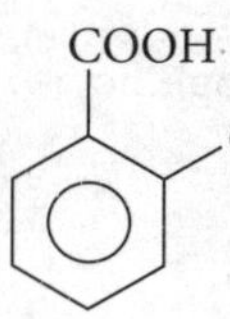
(I)

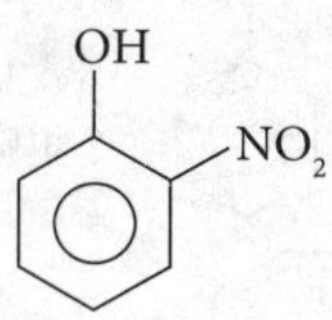
(II)

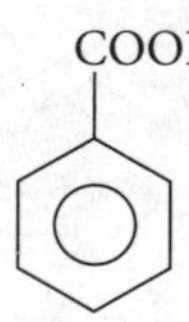
(III)

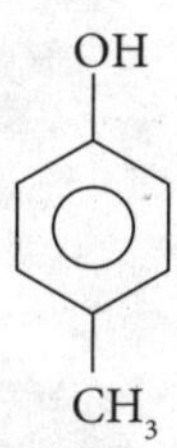
(IV)

(a) I > III > IV > II
(b) I > III > II > IV
(c) II > I > III > IV
(d) III > I > II > IV

67. Which of the following is the correct order of resonance energy?

(a) 

(b) 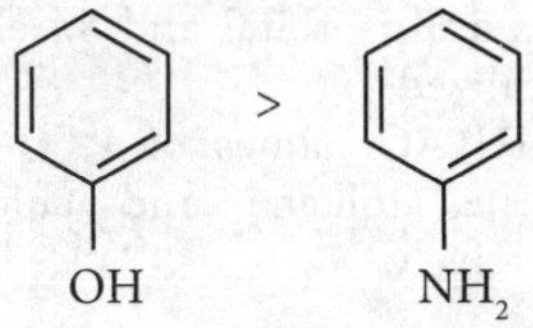

(c) 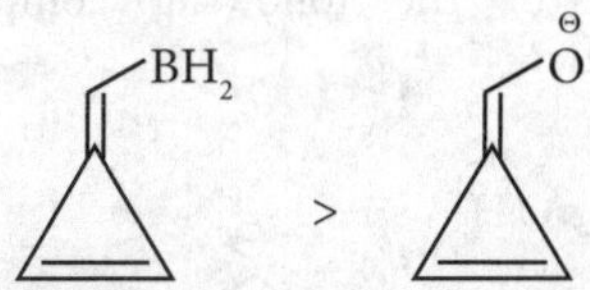

(d) 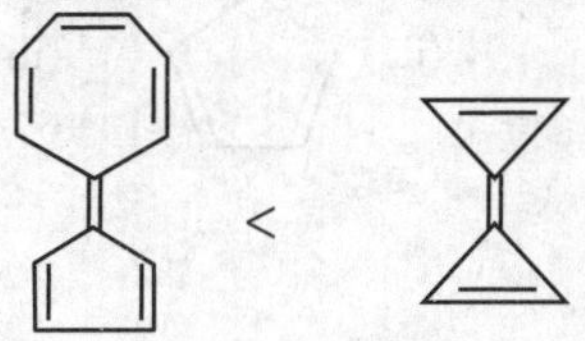

68. Which of the following compounds is not aromatic?

(a) 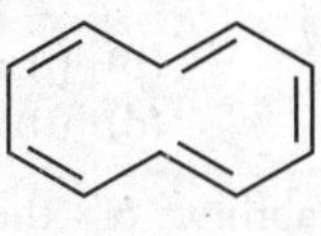 (b) 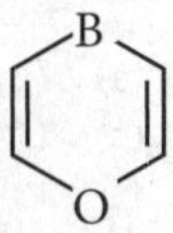

(c) 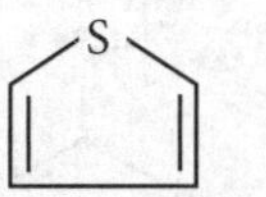 (d) 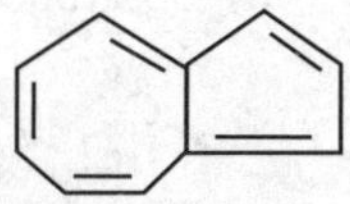

69. Out of following, the most basic isomers of the formula C_4H_7N are:

(a) $HC{\equiv}C{-}CH_2{-}CH_2{-}NH_2$

(b) $H_3C{-}C{\equiv}C{-}CH_2{-}NH_2$

(c) $CH_3{-}CH_2{-}CH{=}CH{-}NH_2$

(d) 

70. For the following reaction, find the resonance energy of buta-1,3-diene:

(I) 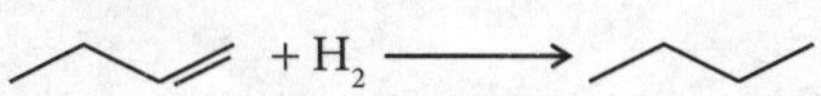

$\Delta H = -28$ kcal / mol

(II) 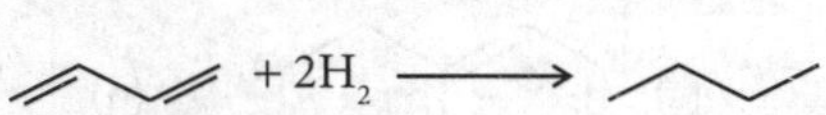

$\Delta H = -54$ kcal / mol

(a) –26 kcal/mol
(b) +3 kcal/mol
(c) –2 kcal/mol
(d) +2 kcal/mol

71. Which of the following compounds can show tautomerism?

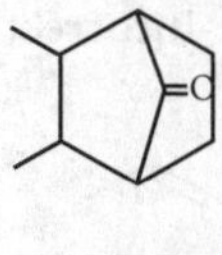

(I)

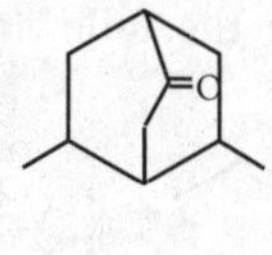

(II)

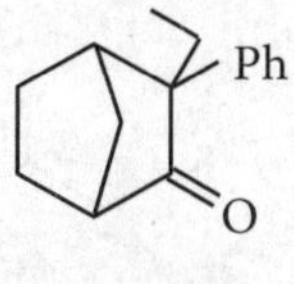

(III)

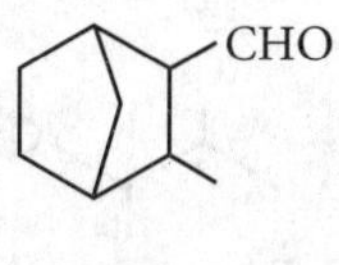

(IV)

(a) (I) and (II) (b) (II) and (III)
(c) (II) and (IV) (d) (III) and (IV)

72. The correct order of basic strength is:

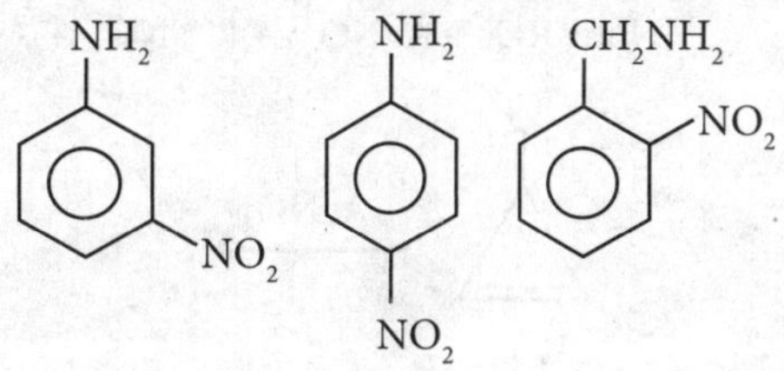

(P) (Q) (R)

(a) P > Q > R (b) Q > P > R
(c) R > P > Q (d) P > R > Q

73. The decreasing order of basicity of the three isomers of nitro aniline is:

(a) p-Nitroaniline > o-Nitroaniline > m-Nitroaniline
(b) p-Nitroaniline > m-Nitroaniline > o-Nitroaniline
(c) m-Nitroaniline > p-Nitroaniline > o-Nitroaniline
(d) m-Nitroaniline > o-Nitroaniline > p-Nitroaniline

74. Which of the following would not produce effervescence of CO_2 (g) with sodium bicarbonate?

(a) 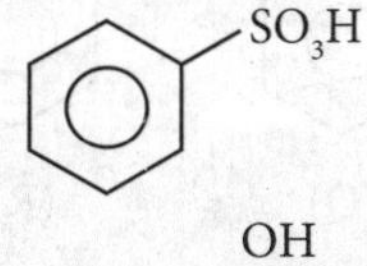 (b) $CH_3{-}COOH$

(c) 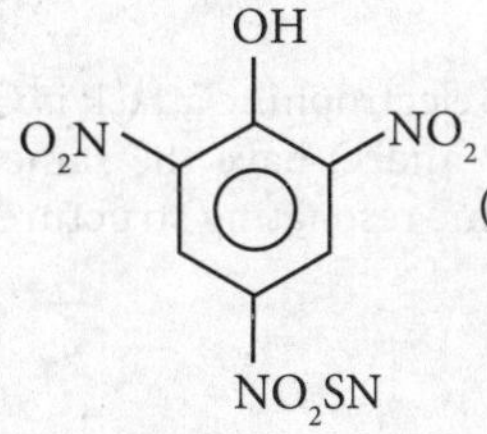 (d) 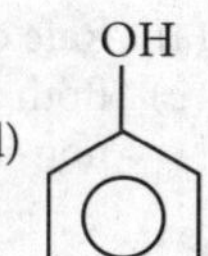

75. Among the following, the incorrect stability order is:

(a) 

(b) 

(c) 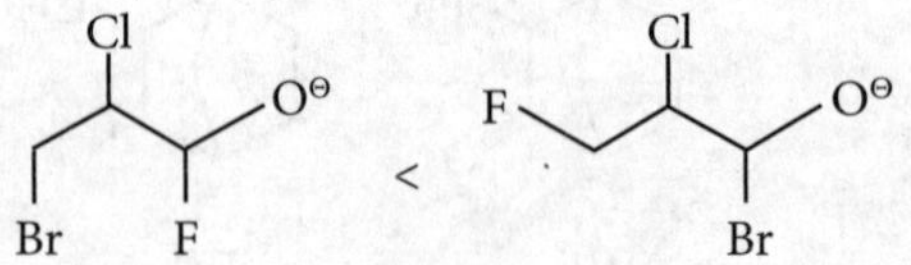

(d) 

76. The reaction which gives aromatic product is:
[Note: R–X + $AgNO_3 \rightarrow R^{\oplus}) NO_3^{\ominus} + AgX$]

(a) 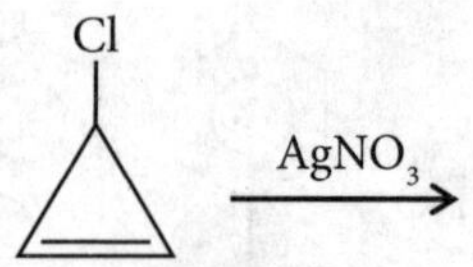

(b) 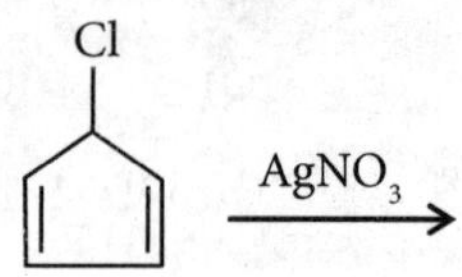

(c) 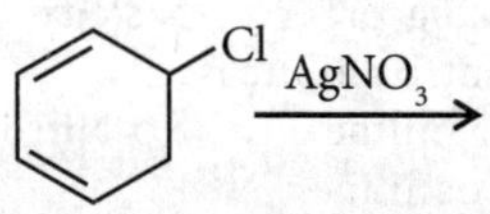

(d) 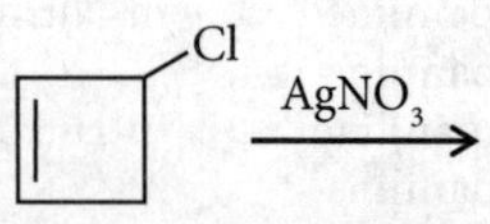

77. Which of the following is incorrect for the given compounds?

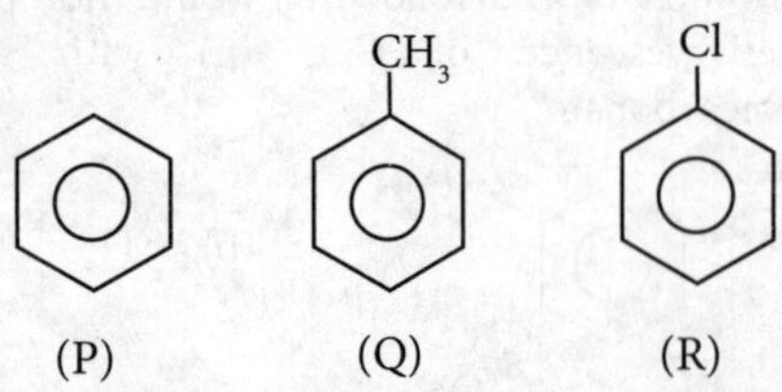

(P) (Q) (R)

(a) Rate of electrophilic attack is Q > P > R
(b) Both P and Q have the same number of non-ionic resonating structures
(c) R has a 6-p orbital and 8π electrons are delocalized
(d) The IUPAC names of P, Q and R are benzene, toluene and chlorobenzene, respectively

78. Which of the following compounds are aromatic?

(i) 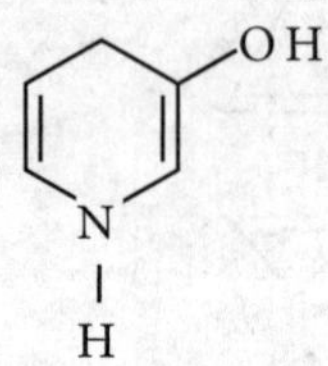 (ii)  (iii) 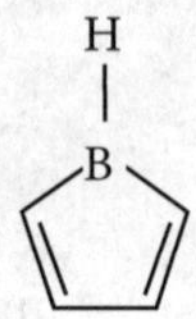

(iv) 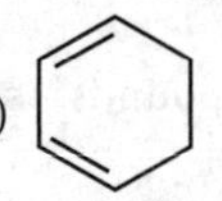 (v) 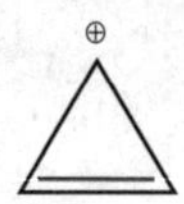 (vi) 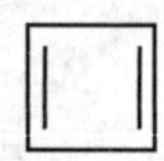

(a) (iii) and (iv) (b) (i) and (v)
(c) (iv) and (v) (d) (ii) and (v)

79. The order of stability of the following carbocations is:

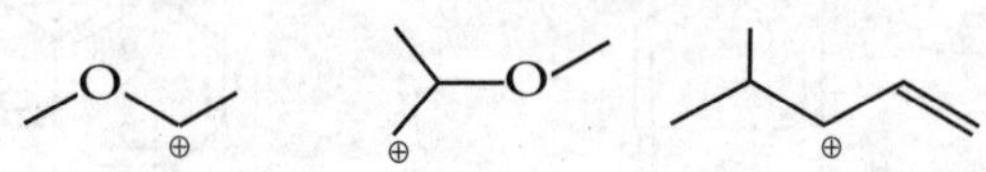

(I) (II) (III)

(a) I > II > III (b) III > II > I
(c) III > I > II (d) I > III > II

80. Which of the following does not have five resonating structures?

(a) 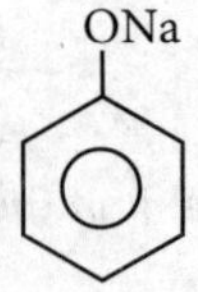 (b) 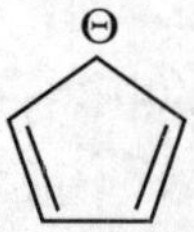

(c) 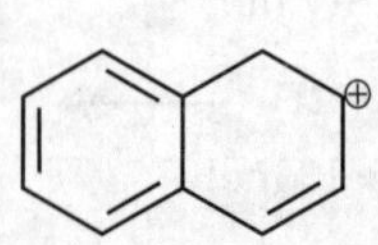 (d) 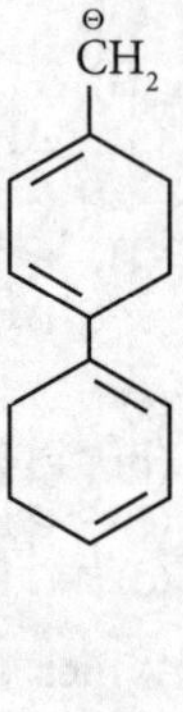

81. The compound with the localized lone pair is:

(a) 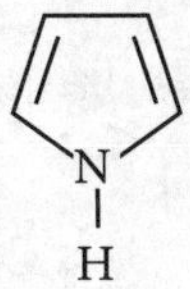 (b) 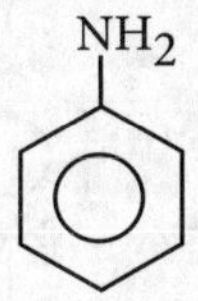

(c) 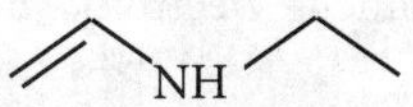 (d) 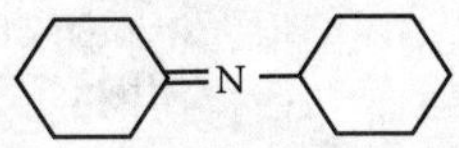

82. In which of the following pairs is (I) more stable than (II)?

(a) $CH_3-\overset{\oplus}{C}=O \longleftrightarrow CH_3-C\equiv\overset{\oplus}{O}$

(b) $\overset{\ominus}{C}H_2-CHO \longleftrightarrow CH_2{=}CH-\overset{\ominus}{O}$

(c)  and 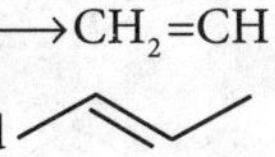

(d) 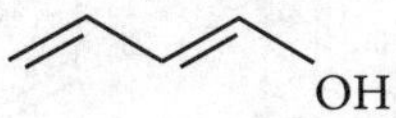 and 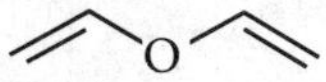

83. For the given compounds, select the correct order(s):

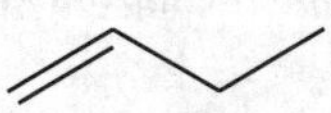 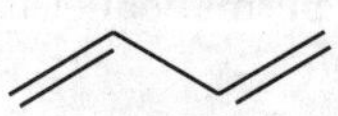 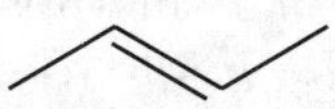

(P) (Q) (R)

(a) R > P > Q (Stability)
(b) Q > P > R (Heat of combustion)
(c) P > R > Q (Heat of hydrogenation per mole of H_2)
(d) P > Q > R (Rotational bond energy barrier about C_2–C_3)

84. Which of the following statements is false about azulene?

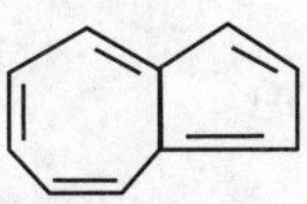

(a) Five-membered ring is electron-rich
(b) Seven-membered ring is electron-deficient
(c) It is aromatic in nature
(d) It has zero dipole moment

85. Which of the following is incorrectly matched with the total number of non-polar resonating structures?
(a) Benzene → 2
(b) Naphthalene → 3
(c) Anthracene → 4
(d) Phenanthrene → 4

86. When acetaldehyde reacts with NaOD/D_2O for a long time, the total number of D present in the alkenol form of acetaldehyde is:
(a) 4 (b) 5
(c) 3 (d) 0

87. Which of the following reactions is non-spontaneous?
(a) $HC\equiv CH + KOH \longrightarrow$
(b) 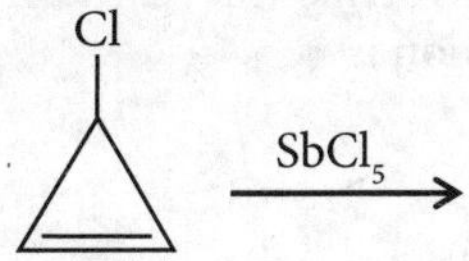
(c) 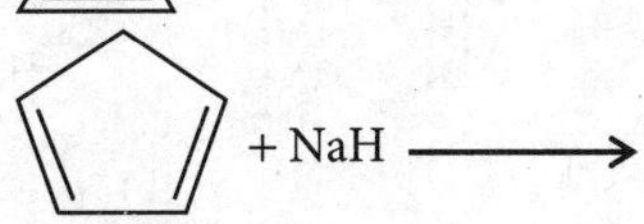
(d) 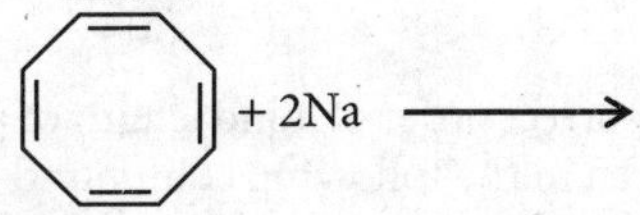

88. Which of the following compounds is aromatic in nature?

(a) 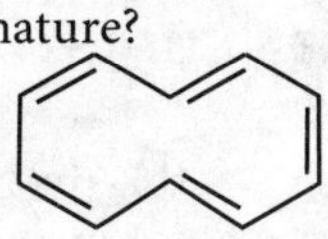 (b) 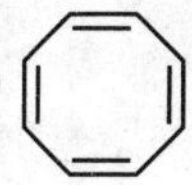

(c) 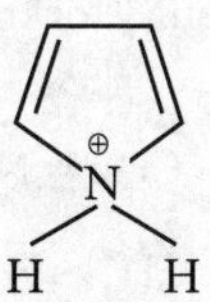 (d) 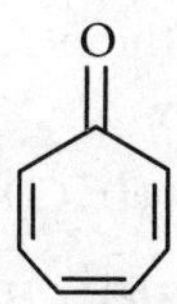

89. In which of the following pairs is the second compound/species more stable than the first?

(a) 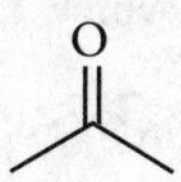 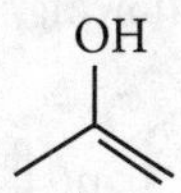

(b) 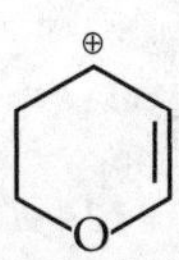 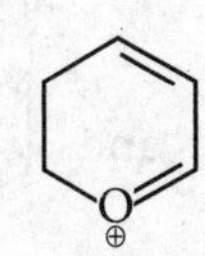

(c) 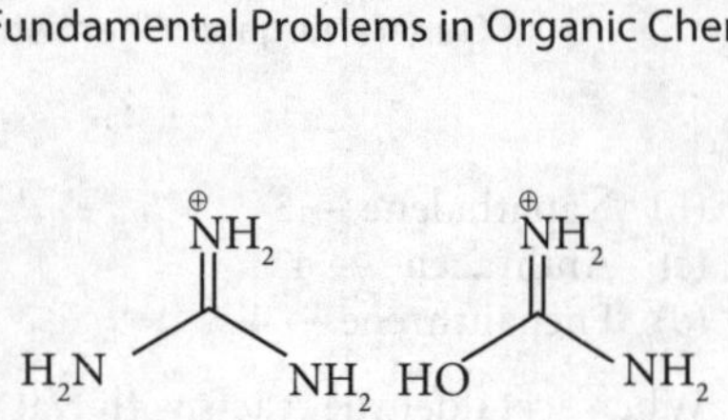

(d) 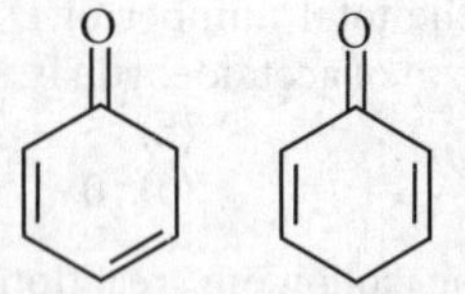

90. The total number of hyper-conjugating structures involving the C–H bond for the following cation is:

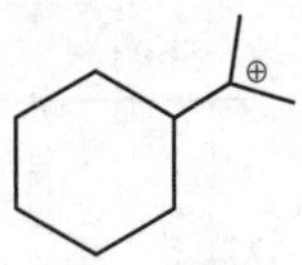

(a) 5 (b) 8
(c) 6 (d) 7

91. The correct order of bond length of p, q, r, x and y given in the following compound is:

$CH_3-\overset{O}{\overset{\|}{C}}\overset{x}{-}\overset{\ominus}{O}$ $CH_3-\overset{O}{\overset{\|q}{C}}\underset{p}{-}OH$ $CH_2=C\overset{r}{=}O$ $CH_3\overset{y}{-}OH$

(a) $y > x > p > q > r$ (b) $p > x > y > q > r$
(c) $y > p > x > q > r$ (d) $p > y > x > q > r$

92. The incorrect order of stability for the following is:

(I) $\overset{\ominus}{C}H_2-\overset{\oplus}{N}\equiv N$ (II) $CH_2=\overset{\oplus}{N}=\overset{\ominus}{N}$

(III) $\overset{\ominus}{C}H_2-N=\overset{\oplus}{N}$ (IV) $\overset{\oplus}{C}H_2-N=\overset{\ominus}{N}$

(a) I > II (b) IV > III
(c) II > III (d) I > IV

93. Among the following, in which is (II) more stable than (I)?

(a) 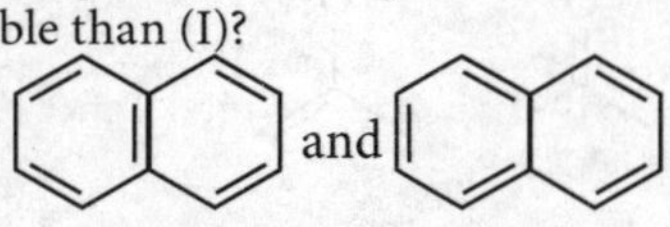

(b) 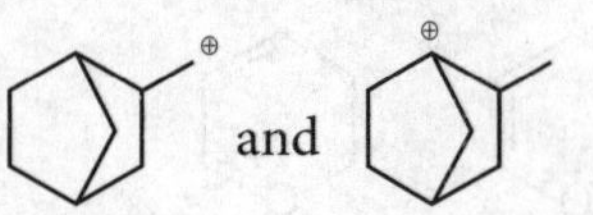

(c) 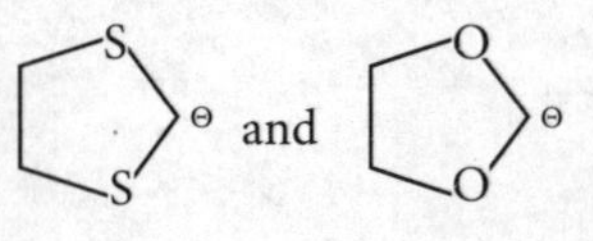

(d) 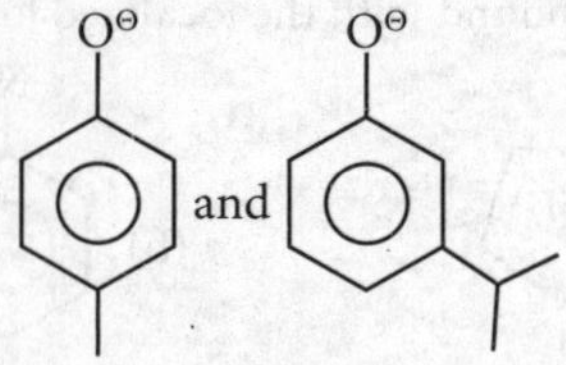

94. Which of the following compounds has all types of permanent electronic displacement effects?

(a) 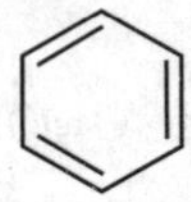 (b) 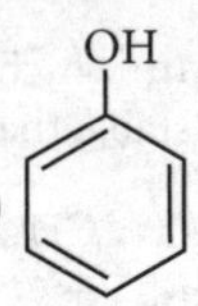

(c) 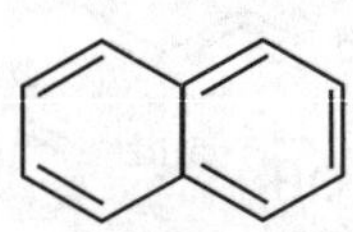 (d) 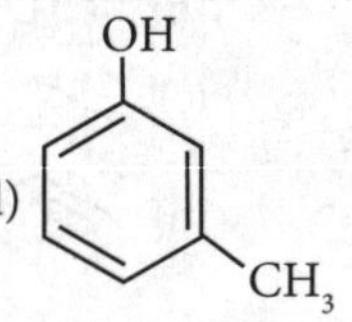

95. Which of following compounds does not have all types of permanent electronic displacement effects?

(a) 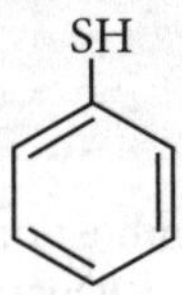 (b) 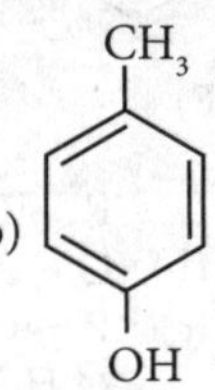

(c) 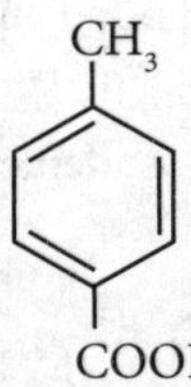 (d) 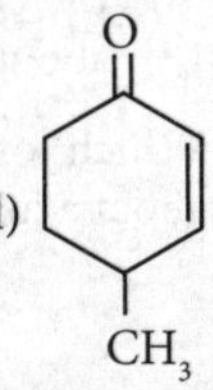

96. The tautomer of which compound will not form an aromatic compound?

(a) 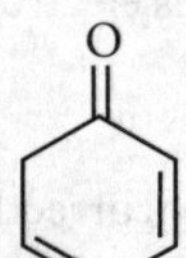 (b) 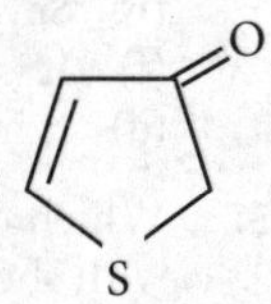

(c) 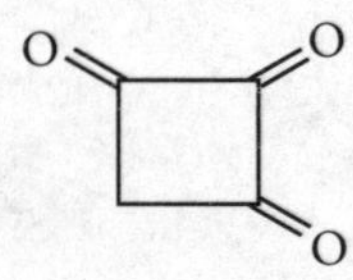 (d) 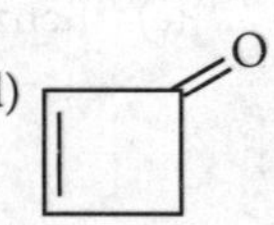

97. Which of the following statements is incorrect for the following compounds?

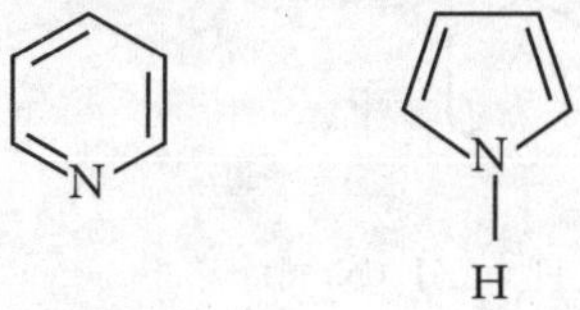

(P) (Q)

(a) Both P and Q are aromatic in nature.
(b) Pyrrole is more basic than pyridine.
(c) Resonance energy of P is more than of Q.
(d) P is known as pyridine while Q is known as pyrrole.

98. Phenanthrene is a polycyclic aromatic hydrocarbon composed of benzene rings. In its pure form, it is found in cigarette smoke and is a known irritant, photosensitizing skin to light. Its structure is given below.

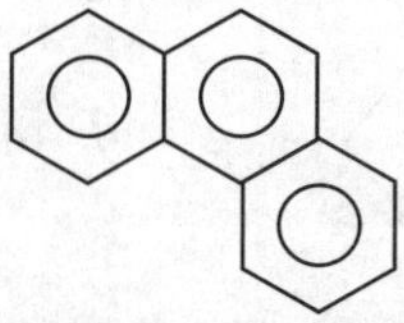

The most stable resonating structure of phenanthrene is:

(a) 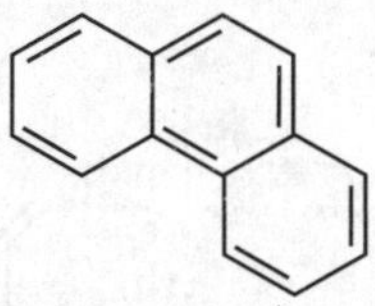 (b) 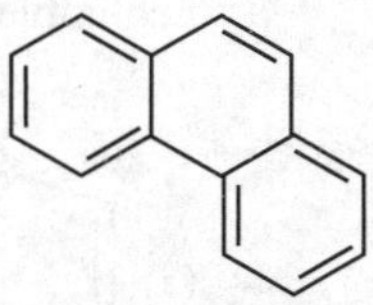

(c) 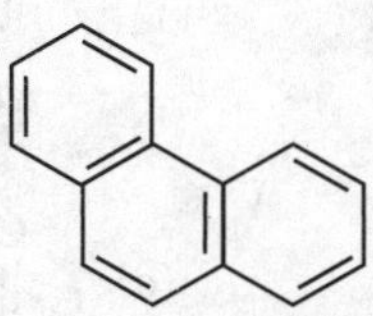 (d) 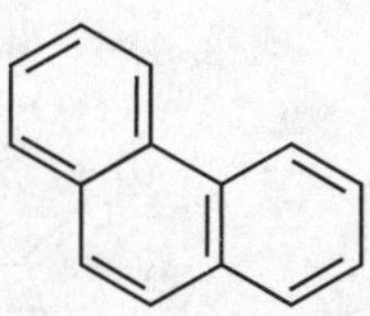

99. Hydroxychloroquine, sold under the brand name Plaquenil, among others, is a medication used to prevent and treat malaria in areas where malaria remains sensitive to chloroquine. Hydroxychloroquine is being studied to prevent and treat COVID-19. Which of the following orders is correct about basic strength?

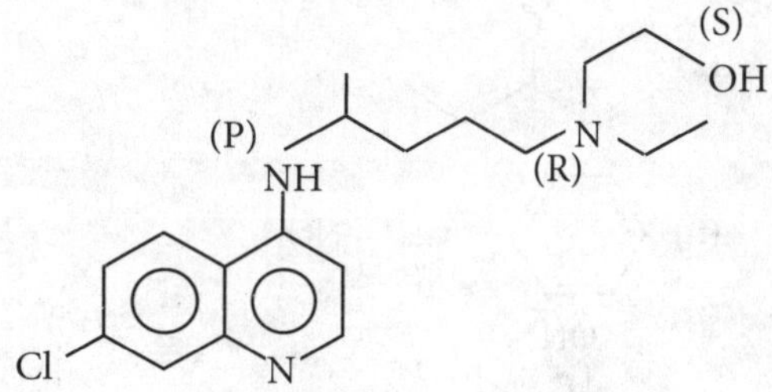

(Q)

(a) P > Q (b) P > R
(c) S > R (d) Q > S

100. Purine is a heterocyclic compound with four nitrogen atoms, as shown below. The number of localized lone pairs in purine is:

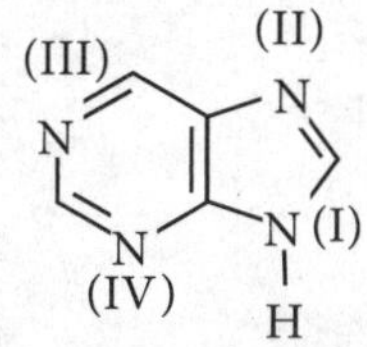

(a) 4 (b) 3
(c) 2 (d) 1

101. Alkenol in the given reaction should be:

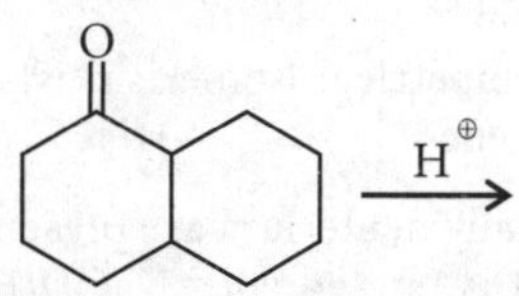

(a) 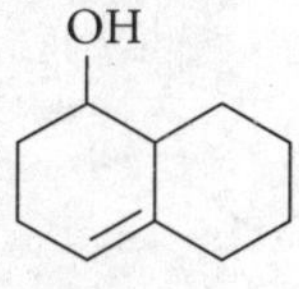 (b) 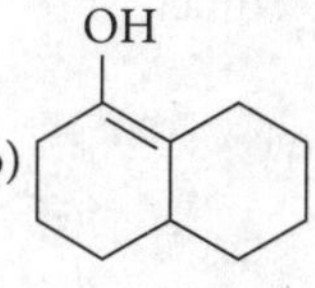

(c) 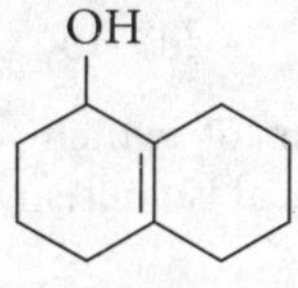 (d) 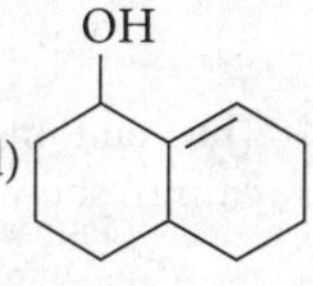

102. Which of the following cannot show tautomerism?

(a) 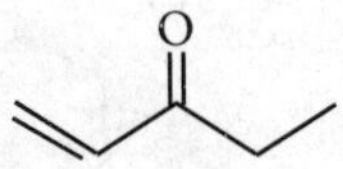

(b) 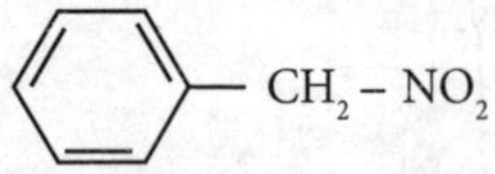

(c) 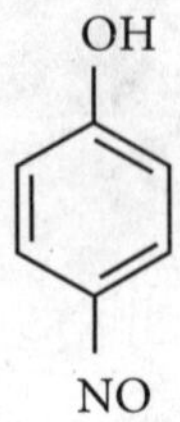

(d) 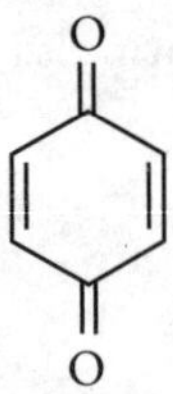

103. Which of the following statements is correct?
(a) Metamerism belongs to the category of structural isomerism
(b) Tautomeric structures are the resonating structures of a molecule
(c) Keto form is always more stable than enol form
(d) Geometrical isomerism is shown only by alkenes

104. How many deuterium are present in enol form when it is treated with NaOD/D_2O for a long time?

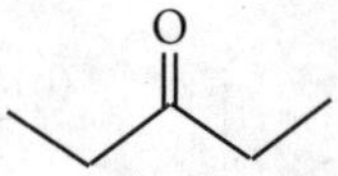

(a) 2 (b) 4
(c) 5 (d) 10

105. The tautomeric form of which compound cannot show geometrical isomerism?
(a) 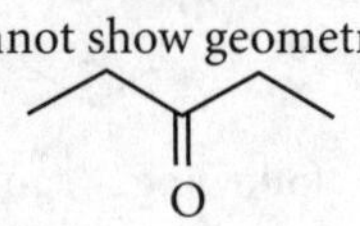

(b) 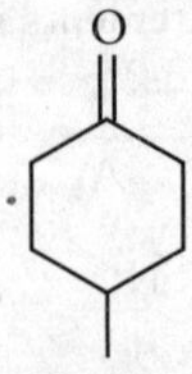

(c) $CH_3-CH_2-N=O$
(d) CH_3-CH_2-CHO

106. Which of the following compounds can show tautomerism as well as geometrical isomerism?

(a) 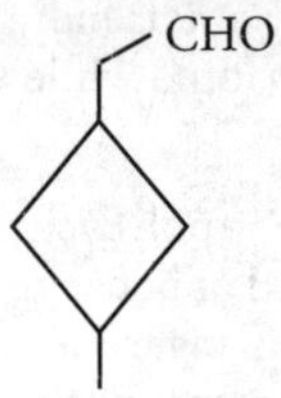

(b) 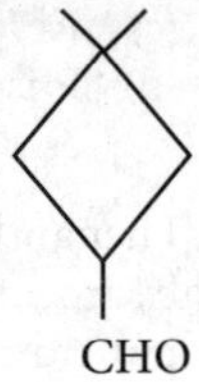

(c) 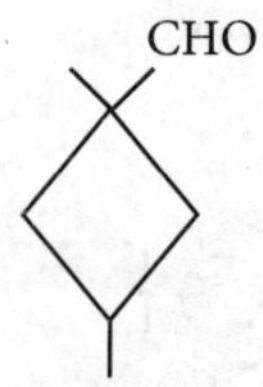

(d) 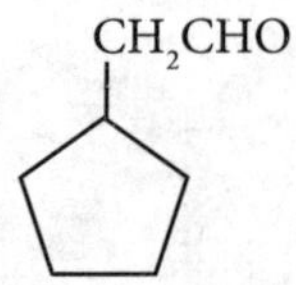

107. Which of the following compounds has negligible enol?

(a) 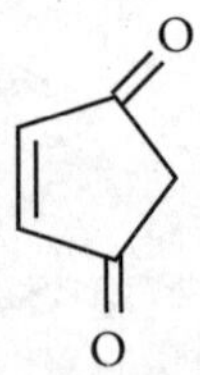

(b) 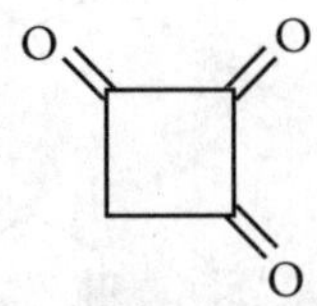

(c) 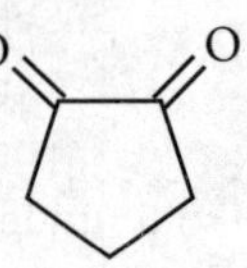

(d) 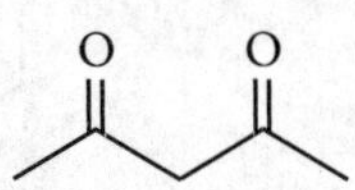

108. Which of the following has more enol content than keto in liquid form?
(a) Acetaldehyde
(b) Cyclohexanone
(c) Acetylacetone
(d) $CH_3COCH_2CO_2CH_3$

Answer Key

Level-1

1. (b)	2. (a)	3. (c)	4. (d)	5. (d)	6. (c)	7. (c)	8. (d)
9. (d)	10. (d)	11. (b)	12. (c)	13. (b)	14. (c)	15. (a)	16. (c)
17. (c)	18. (d)	19. (d)	20. (c)	21. (b)	22. (c)	23. (c)	24. (c)
25. (d)	26. (c)	27. (c)	28. (d)	29. (c)	30. (b)	31. (c)	32. (b)
33. (d)	34. (c)	35. (a)	36. (b)	37. (b)	38. (c)	39. (a)	40. (b)
41. (b)	42. (a)	43. (c)	44. (a)	45. (c)	46. (c)	47. (d)	48. (b)
49. (c)	50. (a)	51. (a)	52. (b)	53. (c)	54. (c)	55. (c)	56. (d)
57. (c)	58. (d)	59. (b)	60. (c)	61. (d)	62. (d)	63. (d)	64. (d)
65. (d)	66. (b)	67. (c)	68. (d)	69. (a)	70. (a)	71. (b)	72. (c)
73. (c)	74. (b)	75. (c)	76. (b)	77. (d)	78. (c)	79. (d)	80. (d)
81. (d)	82. (b)	83. (a)	84. (d)	85. (d)	86. (d)	87. (c)	88. (d)
89. (c)	90. (b)	91. (d)	92. (b)	93. (d)	94. (a)	95. (a)	96. (d)
97. (d)	98. (a)	99. (c)	100. (c)	101. (b)	102. (d)	103. (d)	104. (d)
105. (d)	106. (a)	107. (b)	108. (a)	109. (a)	110. (c)	111. (a)	112. (b)
113. (b)	114. (a)	115. (a)	116. (c)	117. (d)	118. (c)	119. (c)	120. (d)

Level-2

1. (c)	2. (a)	3. (b)	4. (b)	5. (a)	6. (b)	7. (b)	8. (c)
9. (a)	10. (a)	11. (a)	12. (a)	13. (d)	14. (d)	15. (c)	16. (d)
17. (c)	18. (a)	19. (d)	20. (a)	21. (c)	22. (a)	23. (b)	24. (d)
25. (b)	26. (a)	27. (c)	28. (b)	29. (b)	30. (a)	31. (c)	32. (a)
33. (c)	34. (d)	35. (b)	36. (b)	37. (b)	38. (b)	39. (c)	40. (a)
41. (d)	42. (d)	43. (c)	44. (a)	45. (b)	46. (d)	47. (b)	48. (a)
49. (b)	50. (b)	51. (c)	52. (c)	53. (b)	54. (b)	55. (b)	56. (a)
57. (b)	58. (d)	59. (d)	60. (d)	61. (c)	62. (b)	63. (d)	64. (c)
65. (c)	66. (b)	67. (c)	68. (a)	69. (a)	70. (c)	71. (c)	72. (c)
73. (c)	74. (d)	75. (c)	76. (a)	77. (c)	78. (d)	79. (d)	80. (c)
81. (d)	82. (d)	83. (c)	84. (d)	85. (d)	86. (c)	87. (a)	88. (d)
89. (b)	90. (d)	91. (c)	92. (a)	93. (d)	94. (d)	95. (a)	96. (d)
97. (b)	98. (c)	99. (d)	100. (b)	101. (b)	102. (d)	103. (a)	104. (b)
105. (b)	106. (a)	107. (a)	108. (c)				

Solutions

LEVEL-1

1. Enol molecule converts to keto molecule, so it shows tautomerism.

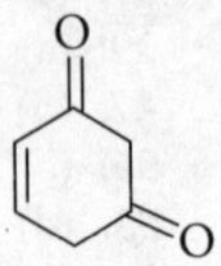

2.

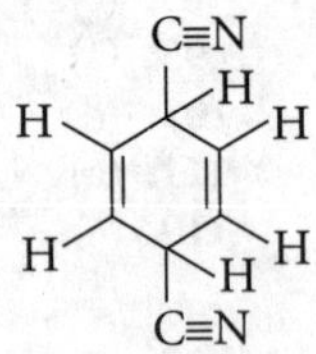

3.

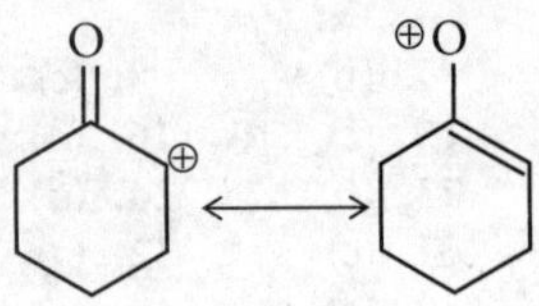

Positive on oxygen is not favourable.

4. $CH_3–CH_2CH_3 \Rightarrow$ All carbon atoms have equal EN.

5. Polar medium (solvent)-induced ionization in bonds.

6. All are isomers.
→ I and II have different functional groups (ketone and aldehyde); so functional isomers.
→ III and IV are tautomers [enol] of I isomers but III and IV are geometrical isomers to each other.

7. According to EN difference

8. $\overset{\oplus}{C}H_3$ and $\overset{\ominus}{C}H_3$ have the same sp^2 hybridization, so they have the same structures.

9. I-effect causes permanent polarization in molecules.

10. $\overset{\ominus}{N}H–\underset{\underset{O}{\|}}{C}–CH_3$ (lone pair containing)

11.

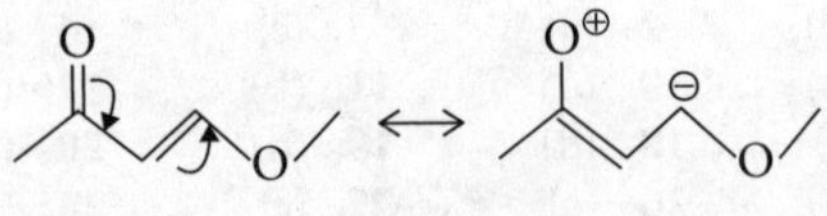

Polar π bond never delocalizes from more EN atom.

12. Oxygen does not have vacant orbital to accept electron of π bond.

13. Bridgehead carbon atom will never be sp^2 hybridized according to Bredt's Rule.

14. C–T bond is strong, so hyper-conjugation is weak.

15. Carbon has incomplete octet.

16. In phenoxide, $(–\overset{\ominus}{O})$ is a strong activating group because of better resonance.

17. –CHO has polar π bond and electron withdrawing group.

18. Resonance is due to lone pair; it gives +M effect to non-polar π bond.

19. 4n + 2π electrons in cyclic resonance

20. Due to hyper-conjugation

21. II > I > IV > III

II: +ve on N; I: +ve on O — Octet of all atoms complete

IV: –ve in resonance; III — Octet of C incomplete

22.

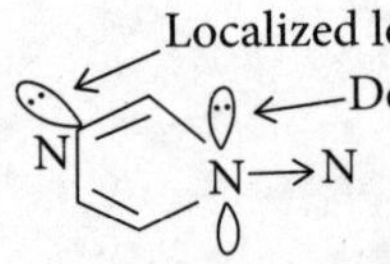

23. $\underset{-M}{O_2N}–\overset{\ominus}{C}H–\underset{-M}{NO_2}$

24. 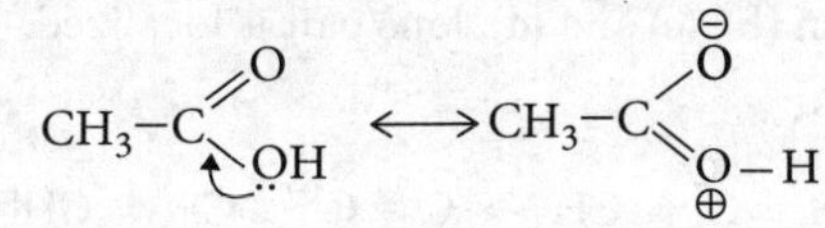

25. 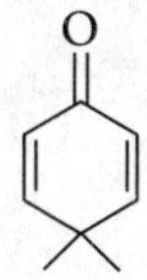 Absence of α-hydrogen

26. 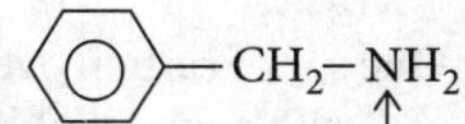

sp^3 nitrogen because localized lone pair

27. 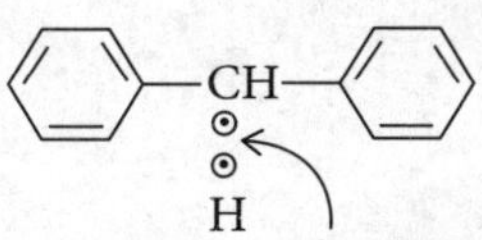

hν (least energy required)
Because resonance stable
Carbon free radical is formed

28. I > III > II

(I: Octet complete and neutral; II: Incomplet octet)

30. c b > a

(c: +ve in extended resonance; b: +ve in resonance; a: –ve not in resonance)

31. Negative in aromaticity.

32. Electron density on 'N' increases basicity.

33. Back bonding

34. In resonating structure, new bond formation may occur, like $\overset{\oplus}{C}H_2 - OH \longleftrightarrow CH_2 = \overset{\oplus}{O}H$

35. Lone pair of nitrogen is perpendicular to p-orbital of the ring.

36. $K_a \propto$ Stability of carbanion of acid

37. Heat of hydrogenation $\propto \dfrac{1}{\text{Stability of alkene}}$

Stability of alkenes identified by resonance and hyper-conjugation.

38. III > I > II

(Aromatic > Non-aromatic > Anti-aromatic)

39. At the para position, the methyl group increases electron density on 'N' by hyper-conjugation and does not give SIP effect.

40. Resonance and hyper-conjugation are involved in stability.

41. Heat of combustion $\propto \dfrac{\text{No. of 'c' atoms}}{\text{Stability of compound}}$

43. $-OCH_3$ destablized by +M and $-CH_3$ destabilized by +H, but $-NO_2$ mostly stabilized by –M and –F is stabilized by –I. So the stability order is

R > Q > P > S

44.  Every π bond is stabilized by aromaticity resonance; so for the π bond, heat of hydrogenation is the least.

45. 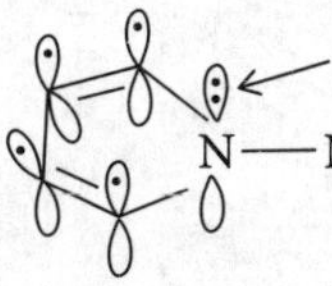 Lone pair of electrons delocalized

46. Chlorine in chlorobenzene acts as a deactivating group due to –I.

47. It is not a resonating structure.

48. Resonance and hyper-conjugation

49. 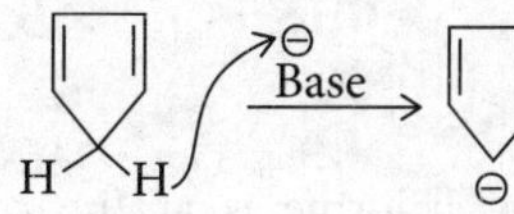

50. I-effect and solvation effect are both considered.

51. 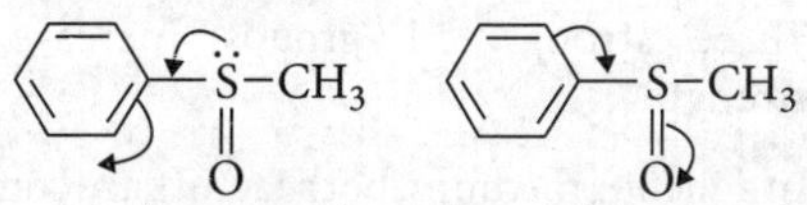

+M by lone pair; –M by polar π bond

52.

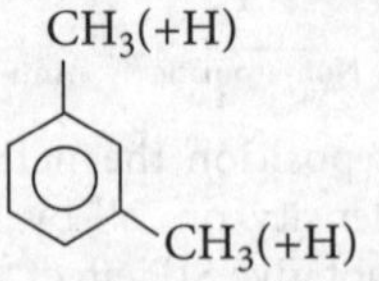

6 α-H by hyper-conjugation, increases electron density in the ring.

53.  Non-aromatic because in tub shape, cyclic resonance is restricted.

54. Extended and more resonance

55. Stability of R.S. $\propto \dfrac{1}{\text{Potential energy}}$

56.

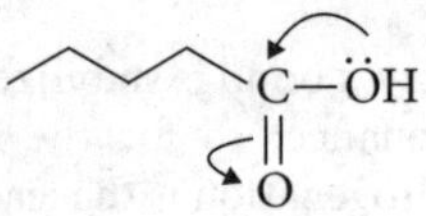

57.

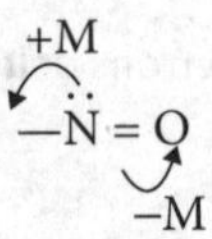

Lone pair and polar π bond

58. $-CH_3$ and –OH are activating groups by +H and +M, respectively.

59.

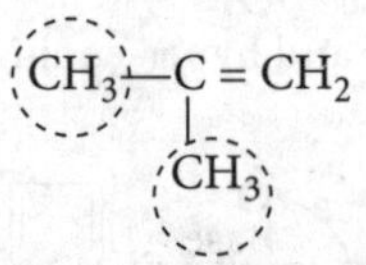

60. Lone pair of chlorine is at the conjugated position of the π bond of the ring.

61. Keto $\rightleftharpoons$ enol forms

62. Three strong –M groups increase acidic strength.

63. In aqueous medium, both factors are considered (+I effect and solvation effect)

64. $-NO_2$ at the para position increases the acidity of phenol by –M and at the meta position by –I. But $-OCH_3$ at the para position decreases the acidic strength of phenol.

65. In (b), (c) and (d), lone pair is localized.

66.

$$\underset{sp}{CH \equiv C^{\ominus}} > \underset{+I}{CH_3} \rightarrow \underset{sp}{C \equiv C^{\ominus}} > \underset{sp^2}{CH_2 = CH^{\ominus}}$$

67.

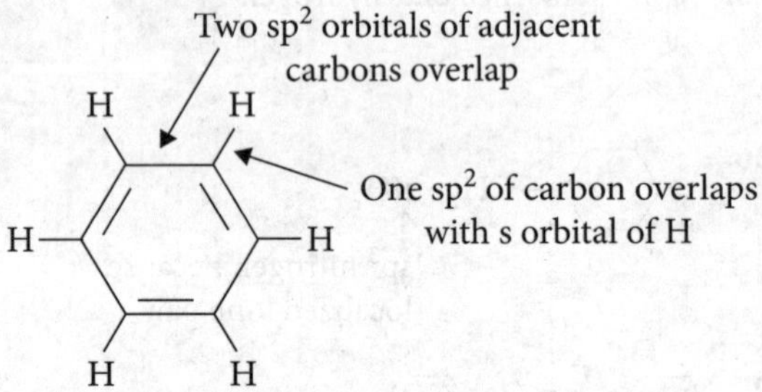

$6 \times 2 = 12$
$6 \times 1 = 6$
$12 + 6 = 18$

68.

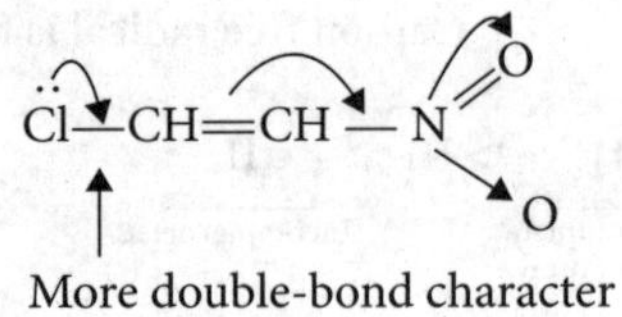

69.

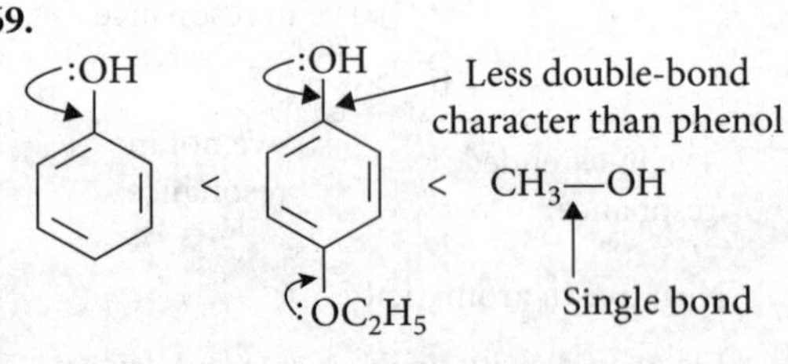

70. (4n + 2) π electrons are not in cyclic resonance; so it is an anti-aromatic.

71. B is anti-aromatic but C and D are non-aromatic.

72. Resonance arises due to delocalization of the p-orbital.

73.

$$CH_3—C \equiv N < H — N = C = O < CH_3—\underset{\underset{O}{\|}}{C}—NH_2$$

triple double single

74.

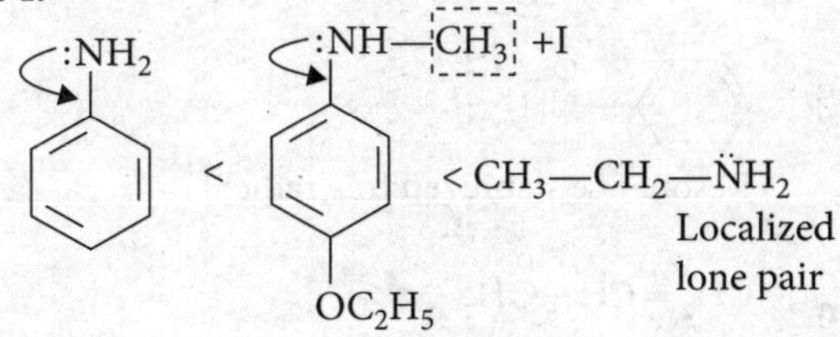

75. Heat of combustion $\propto \dfrac{\text{No. of carbons}}{\text{Stability of compound}}$

Stability of alkene ∝ Hyper-conjugation

76. $CH \equiv C \leftarrow H \rightleftharpoons CH \equiv C^{\ominus} + H^{\oplus}$
Most stable anion

77.

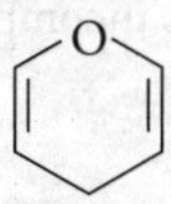

In pyran, cyclic resonance is absent.

78. Distance, number, power rules apply for (–I) group.

79.

$$CH_3-\overset{\overset{\displaystyle O}{\|}}{C}-O^- \longleftrightarrow CH_3-\overset{\overset{\displaystyle O^-}{|}}{C}=O$$

80. $-O^{\ominus}$ is +I due to –ve charge.
–OH is –I due to electronegative oxygen atom.

81.

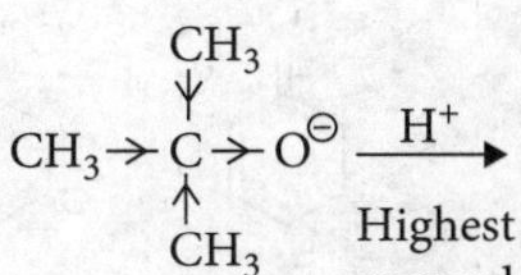

Highest electron density, so good base

82. Saturated alkyl group shows +I.

83. $CH_3-CH=CH_2$
Least single-bond character, so highest rotational energy barrier.

85.

$$CH_3—CH_2 \leftarrow \overset{\ominus}{N}H$$

Anion shows +I

86. ⇒ Considering electronegativity of atoms and inductive effect.

87. Octet complete for all atoms.

88. (a) by extended resonance
(b) by hyper-conjugation
(c) by hyper-conjugation

89. Use concept of hyper-conjugation

$HOH \propto \dfrac{1}{\text{Stability of alkenes}}$

90. Complete octet of all atoms

91. Heat of combustion ∝ Number of 'c' atoms.

92.

III	>	I	>	IV	>	II
3α-H and +I more		3α-H and +I less		+I more		+I less

93. $CH_3-\overset{\ominus}{C}H_2$
Less EN atom is more likely to donate lone pair.

94. $-NO_2$ is the most withdrawing group (–M) at the para position; increases acidic strength.

95.

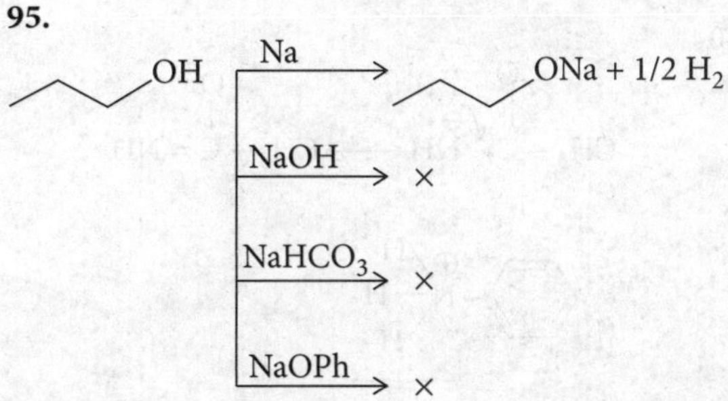

96.

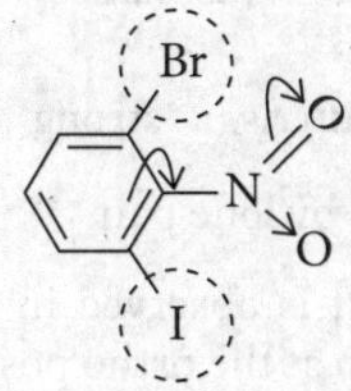

Ortho-substituted group inhibits resonance.

97. 5-α-hydrogen

98. $CH_3-\ddot{N}H-CH_3$

2° amines have localized lone pair and sp^3 'N'

99.

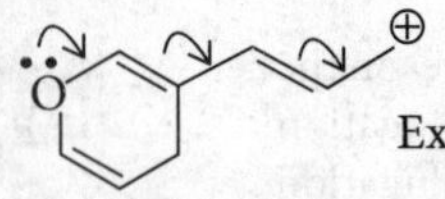

Extended resonance

100. γ-Nitrogen has localized lone pair and conjugated acid stabilized by equivalent resonance.

101.

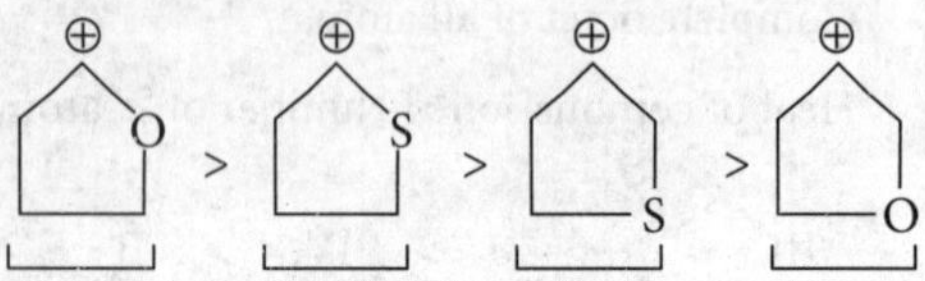

Back-bonding | Weak back-bonding | Weak –I | Strong –I

102.

Resonance

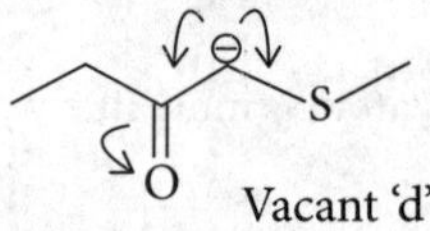

Vacant 'd' orbital

103. Negative on more EN atom is more stable.

104.

$$CH_3-\overset{O}{\overset{\|}{C}}-\overset{\ominus}{N}H \longleftrightarrow CH_3-\overset{O^{\ominus}}{\overset{|}{C}}=NH$$

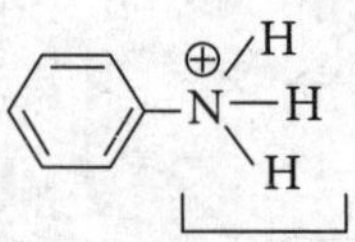

Not vacant orbital, so $-\overset{\oplus}{N}H_3$
Not involved in resonance

105. $-\ddot{N}H_2$ group is a strong electron releasing group (+M) by lone pair.

106. Ortho effect is observed in benzoic acid with bulky group at the ortho position.

107.

$$CH_3-\overset{O}{\overset{\|}{C}}-\ddot{O}-H \longleftrightarrow CH_3-\overset{O^{\ominus}}{\overset{|}{C}}=\overset{\oplus}{O}-H$$

108. Back-bonding + Hyper-conjugation

109.

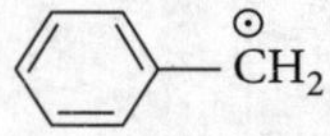

Resonance stabilized free radical

110. $CH_2=CH-\overset{\ominus}{C}H_2$

Delocalized negative, so sp^2

111.

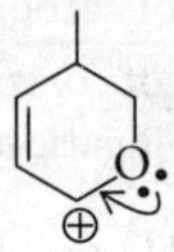

Back-bonding + Resonance

112. 'II' has complete octet of all atoms. But in 'I', carbocation has incomplete octet.

113.

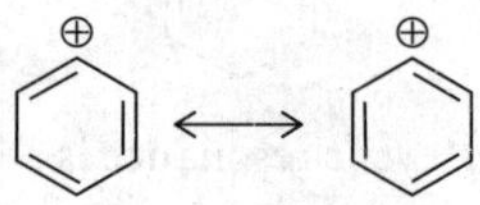

114.

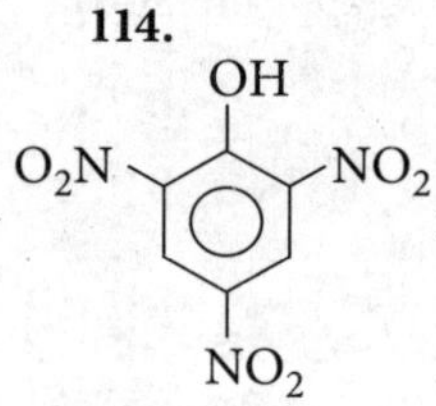

> H – COOH >

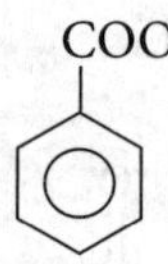

> CH_3–COOH

Picric acid has 3 (–M) groups.

115.

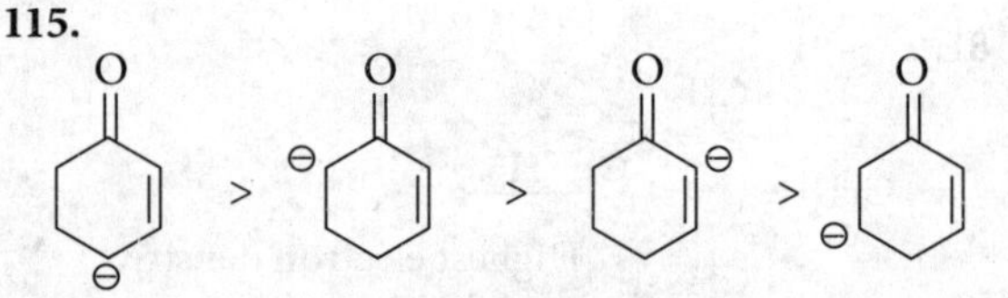

Extended resonance | Resonance | Negative on more EN atom | Negative on less EN atom

116. Benzene is a non-polar solvent, so basicity order depends on +I effect only.
3° > 2° > 1° > NH_3

117.

$$\overset{\ominus}{C}H_2-C(H)(H)(H)$$

Not vacant orbital nor electron withdrawing tendency.

118.

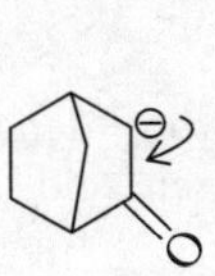

Resonance

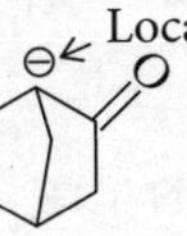

Localized (–ve)

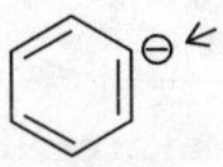

Out of p-orbital, so localized

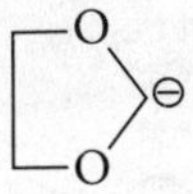

Localized (–ve)

119.

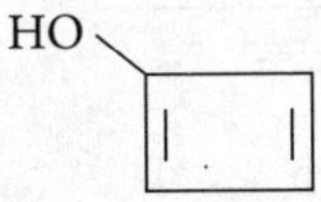

Anti-aromatic enol form not formed.

120.

(a) $CH_3-\underset{\underset{O}{\|}}{C}-CH=CH_2$ GI × Tautomer ✓

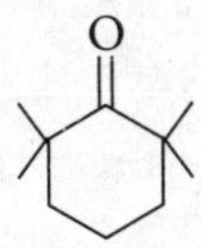

GI × Tautomer ×

$C-\underset{\underset{C}{|}}{\overset{\overset{C}{|}}{C}}-C=C-\underset{\underset{O}{\|}}{C}-H$ GI ✓ Tautomer ×

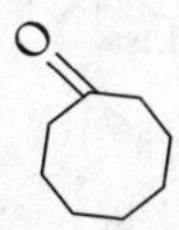

GI ✓ Tautomer ✓

Level-2

1. Conjugate base R–S$^\ominus$ is weak base, so R–SH is a stronger acid than R–OH. This is because of its size.

2.

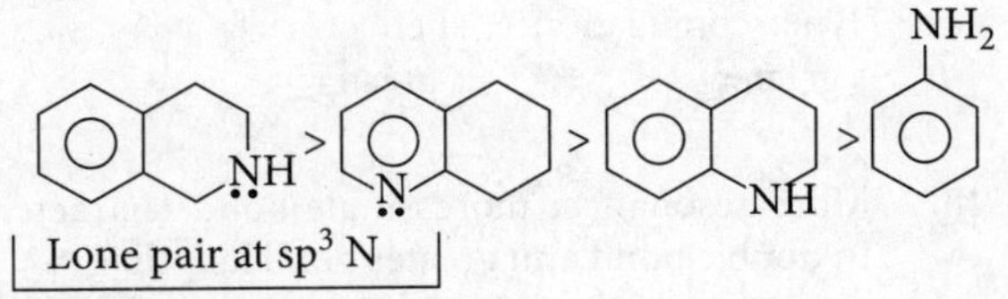

Localized lone pair.

3. In A → II > I (Ortho effect)
In B → I > II (+I effect)
In C → I > II (SIP)
In D → II > I (+I effect)

4.

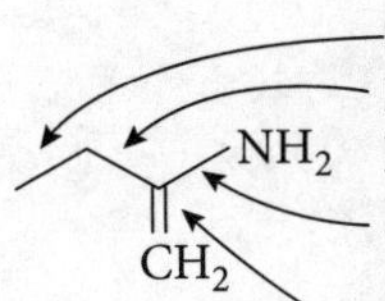

Single bond.
Double-bond character in single bond by hyper-conjugation (2α-H).
Double-bond character in single bond by resonance.
Single-bond character in double bond by both resonance and hyper-conjugation.

5. Localized lone pair containing (I and III) more basic (less EN nitrogen has more tendency to donate lone pair).
In II (pyrrole), lone pair is delocalized in aromaticity. So it is a poor base.

6. Anion stability after less of the hydrogen atom determines the acidic character of 'H'.

7.

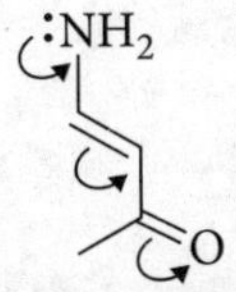

In l_1, more double-bond character due to polar π bond resonance. So it is the smallest bond length.

8. Active hydrogen (more acidic) gives hydrogen gas with metal.

9. Heat of hydrogenation ∝ number of π bonds. When π bond is the same, it is inversely proportional to the stability of alkene.

10. Boiling point ∝ Intermolecular H-bonding.
Phenoxide stability ∝ Acidic strength of phenol.
SIR decreases delocalization of +ve charge.
NO_2 more stabilized to carbanion.

11.

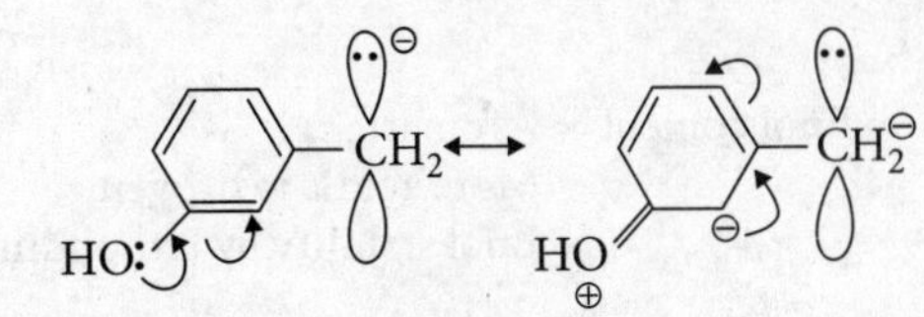

Resonance by meta group does not operate at carbanion, whereas its resonance operates the conjugate carbon of the phenyl ring.

12.

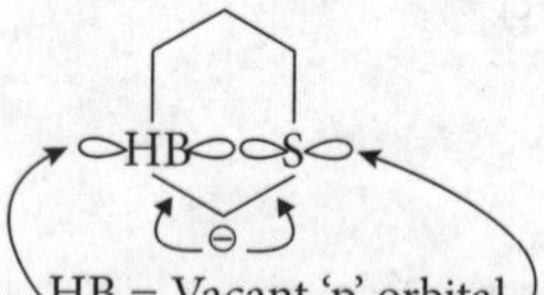

HB = Vacant ‘p’ orbital.
S = Vacant ‘d’ orbital.

13.

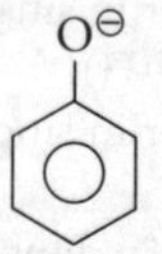

Stable anion has highest Ka and least pKa.

14.

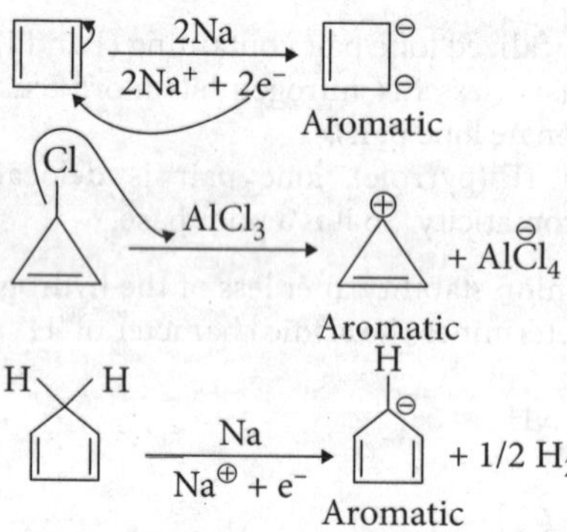

15. $CH_2 = CH - \overset{\ominus}{C}H_2 \longleftrightarrow \overset{\ominus}{C}H_2 - CH = CH_2$

Equal stable RS.

16.

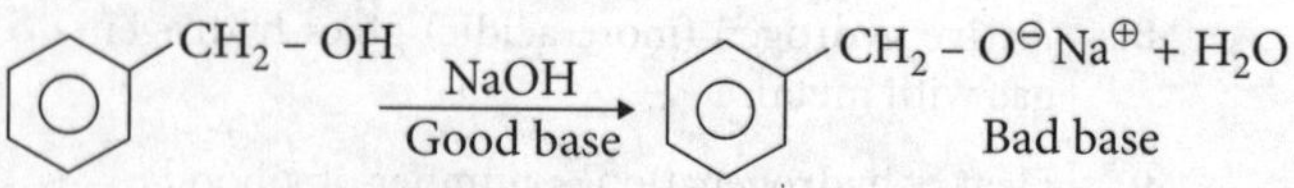

Good base to bad base reaction does not follow.

17. α-hydrogen (hydrogen attached to single-bond atom and conjugated with polar π bond required for tautomerism)

$\underset{\underset{H}{|}}{CH_2} - CH = CH - \underset{\underset{O}{\|}}{C} - H$

18. Enol content ∝ Aromaticity
∝ More acidic hydrogen
∝ Enol stability by H-bonding

19.

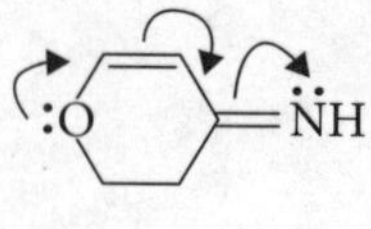

High electron density or stable conjugate acid

20.

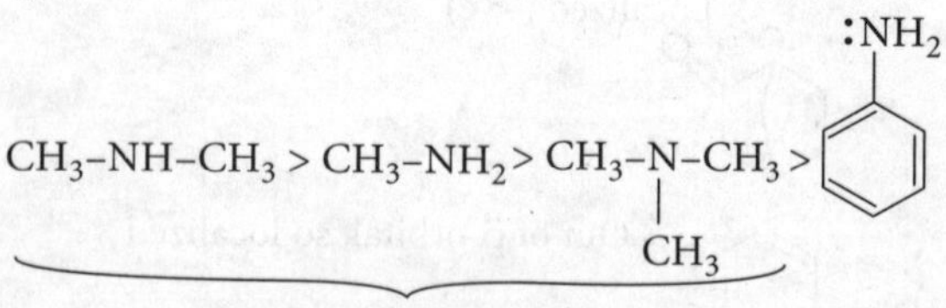

Localized lone pair, so better than aniline; also consider the solution and I effects.

21.

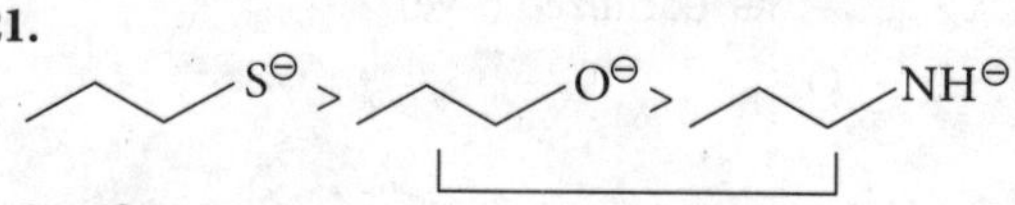

Size factor more dominant than EN factor.

EN factor

22.

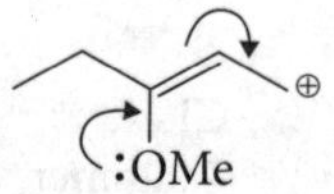

Extended back-bonding and resonance considered.

23. $\underbrace{HBr > HCl}_{\text{Size factor}} > \underbrace{H_2O > CH \equiv CH}_{\text{EN factor}}$

24. Unstable π bond is more reactive.

25. X > q = p > Y
X: Double-bond character is less.
q = p: Equal stable RS, so bond length is equal.
Y: Single-bond character is less.

26. Anion is not in resonance, so the –I effect of NO_2 depends on distance.

27.

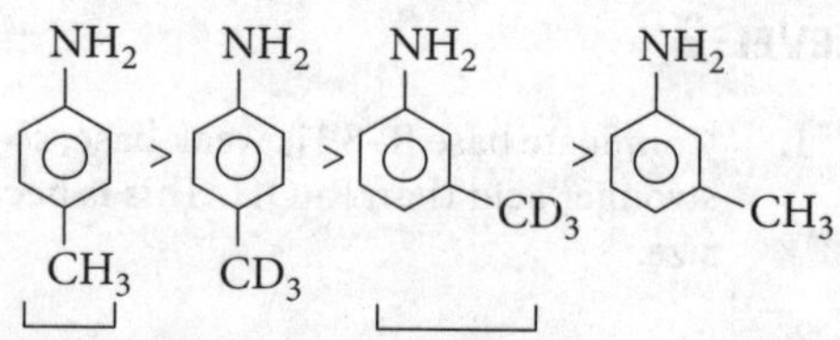

(+H) Hyper-conjugation is greater

+I effect is greater

28. More resonance, more single-bond character in double bond and greater bond length.

29. 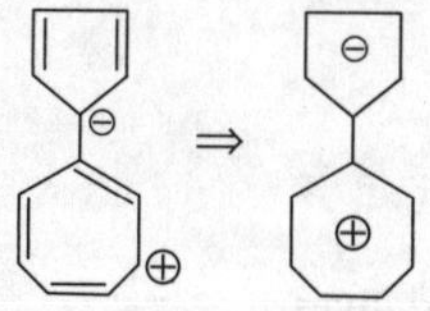

In polar condition, the molecule gets aromaticity; so it is more polar.

30. HOH $\propto$ No. of π bonds $\propto \dfrac{1}{\text{Stability of alkene}}$.

31. –M effect and –I effect considered for acidic strength, not H-bonding.

32. SIR (steric inhibition of resonance) decreases resonance of the lone pair of 'N' with the ring, so double-bond formation decreases and bond length increases.

33. (a) 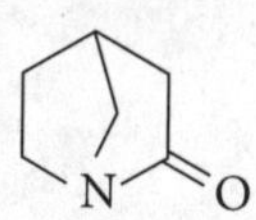

Lone pair of 'N' not delocalized because of Bredt's Rule, so more basic

(b) Back-bonding carbocation more stable.

(c) 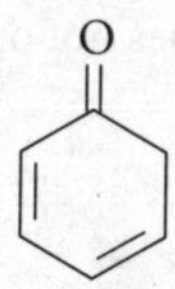

Extended resonance increases C–O bond length by single-bond character.

(d) Aromatic compound has more resonance energy.

34. (a) 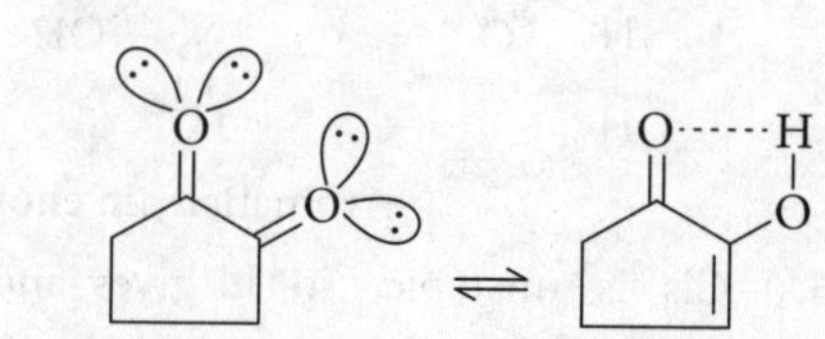

Lone pairs repulsion makes it unstable — H bonding makes it stable

(b) HOC $\propto$ No. of carbons × Instability (due to strain)

(c) HOH $\propto$ No. of π bonds

(d) 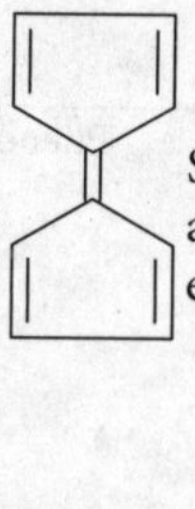 Stable because of avoiding anti-aromaticity; so more rotational energy barrier.

35. 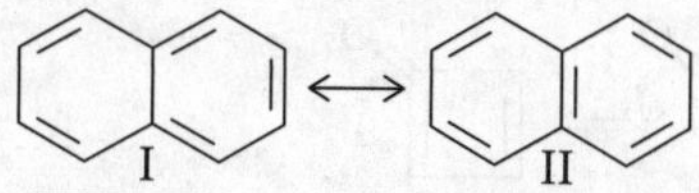

I: NA + A = A — II: A + A = A

II is the more stable aromatic, so all the properties are considered by this.

36. 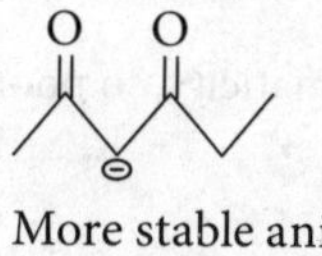

More stable anion form or bad conjugate base

37. Basicity $\propto \dfrac{\text{Localized lone pair}}{\text{Delocalized in quality resonace}}$

38. Hyper-conjugation considered

39. +H of CH_3 is greater than CD_3 and hyper-conjugation is dominant over inductive effect.

40. Anionic stability × Acidity

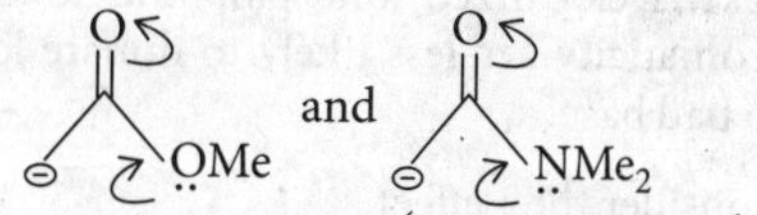

(more resonance)

Lone pair resonance decreases anion stability.

41. 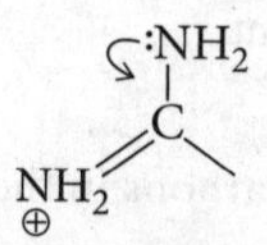

Conjugate acid is stabilized by the lone pair of 'N'.

42. 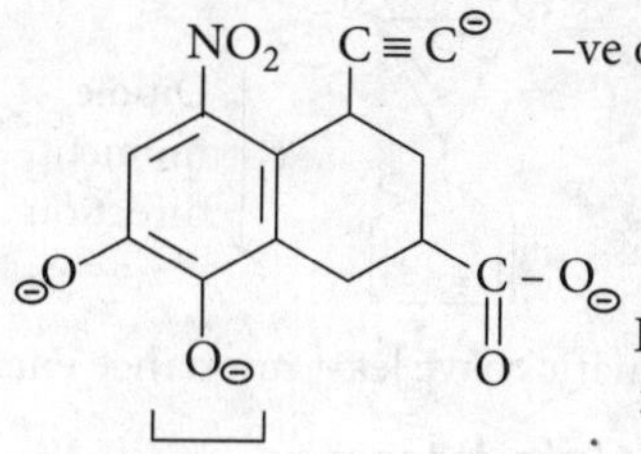

–ve on less EN

Equivalent resonance

Resonance and –M of NO_2 operate

43. Consider the –I effect and +M of $-OCH_3$

44. Equivalent resonance in conjugated acid (b > a)

45. 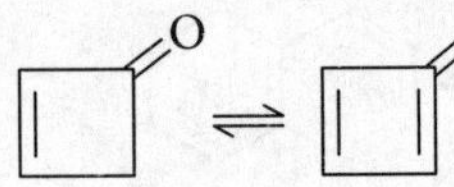

Anti-aromatic enol is not formed.

46. 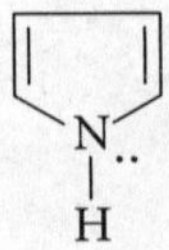 Lone pair in aromaticity, so poor base.

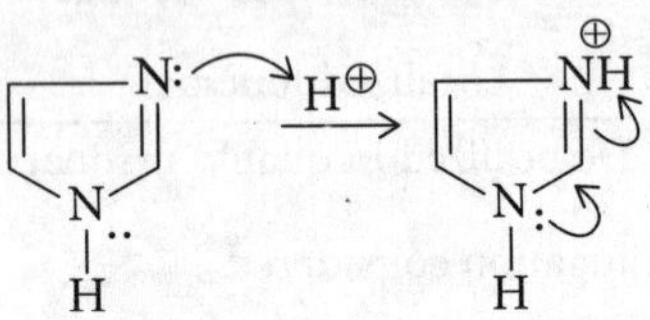

Stable conjugate acid

47. Localized lone pair and less EN atom is more likely to donate lone pair, so good base. Delocalized lone pair and lone pair in aromaticity are less likely to donate lone pair; so bad base.

48. Consider the I effect.

49. Less EN has more tendency to donate lone pairs; consider the I effect.

50. α-Hydrogen must be present.

51. 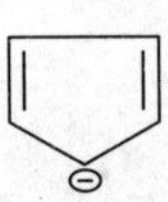 R.S. = Number of carbons in the ring

52. Aromaticity ∝ Resonance energy.

53. 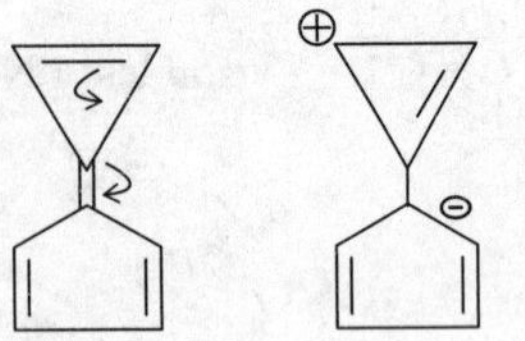 Dipole moment direction

54. Anti-aromatics have least resonance energy.

55. (a) Extended resonance
(b) Less EN atom has more tendency to donate lone pairs
(c) Halogens deactivate ring by –I
(d) Extended resonance

56. Consider +M of $-NH_2$ and –OH and –I of CF_3.

57. 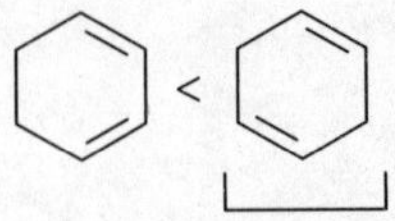

Unstable π bond gives more HOH.

58. Bond length ∝ Less double-bond character, means single-bond character.

59. Less stable carbon free radical ($\dot{C}H_3$) formed, so more bond energy.

60. Aromatic more stable.

61. Pyrrole has more aromaticity than Furan because the lone pair has less EN nitrogen.

62. 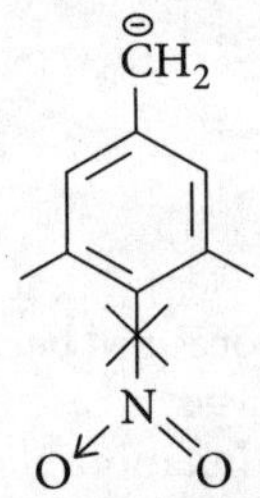

Due to SIR, –M of $-NO_2$ does not operate.

63. 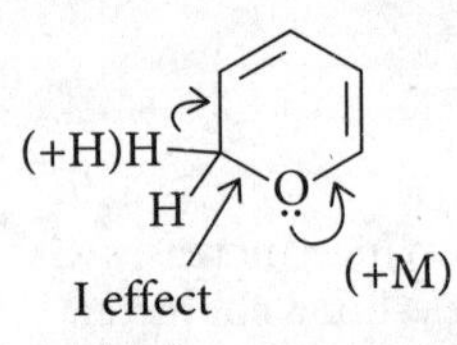

64. 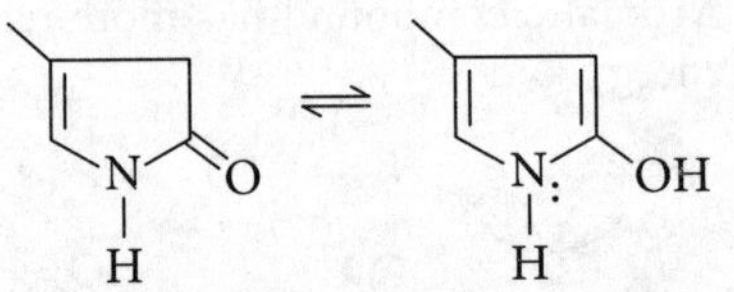

Aromaticity in enol

65. Cis is unstable, so it gives more heat of combustion.

66. 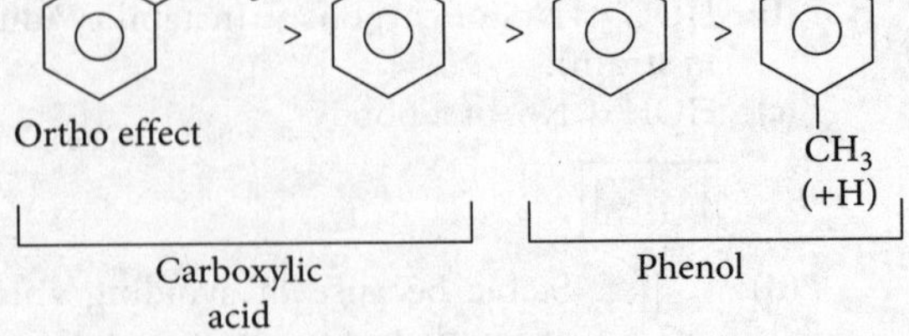

67.

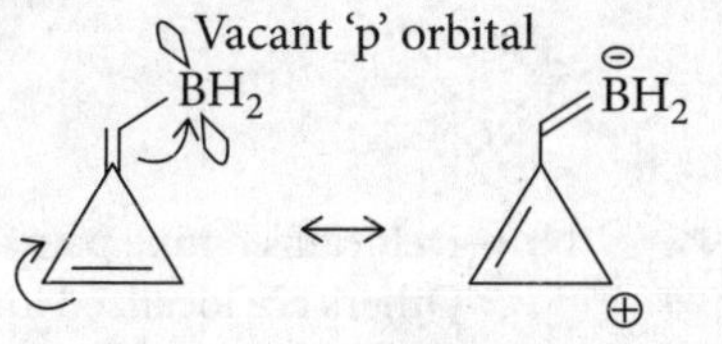

Gets aromaticity

68.

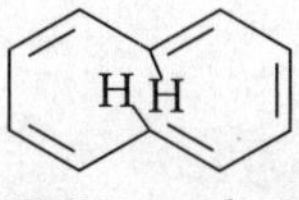

H–H repulsion in the molecule, so it goes out of the plane.

69. (–I) of $CH \equiv C$ is less

70. $1\pi \rightarrow -28$ Kcal

$2\pi \rightarrow -56$ Kcal (theoretical value)

Resonance energy = Theoretical value – Practical Value

$= -56 - (-54)$

$= -2$ Kcal

71. Hydrogen of bridgehead carbon does not show tautomerism.

72. R = Localized lone pair

P = Basicity decreases by –I of NO_2 (at meta position)

Q = Basicity decreases by –M of NO_2 (at para position)

73.

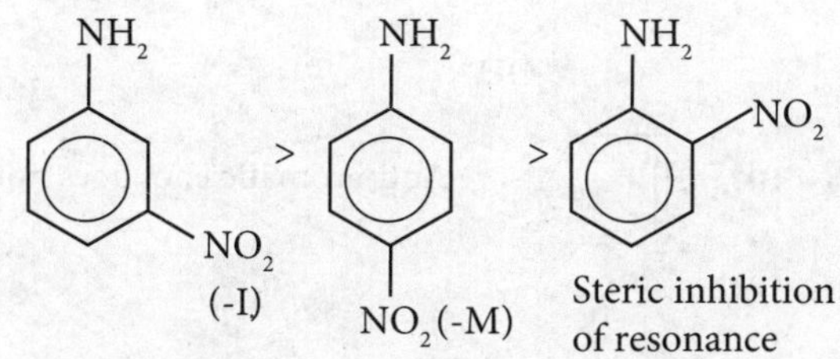

74. Phenol does not gives proton to $NaHCO_3$ because phenol is less acidic than H_2CO_3.

75. –I of fluorine is higher than in others.

76.

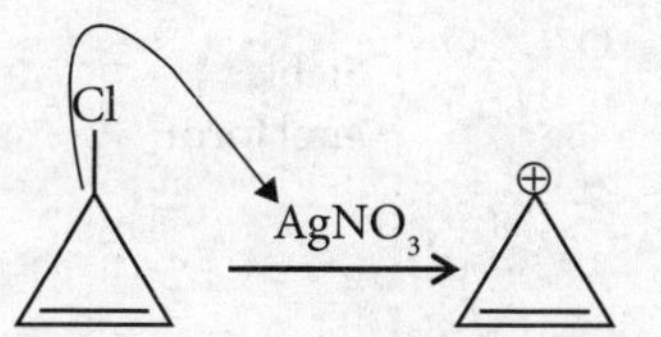

Aromatic

77.

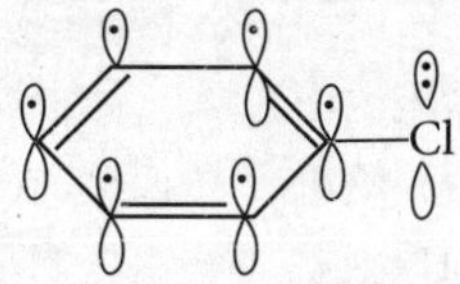

7 p-orbital
8 π electrons

78.

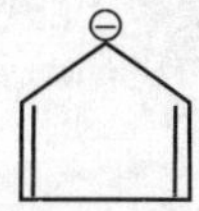 → 6π electrons in cyclic resonance

 → 2π electrons in cyclic resonance

4n + 2π electrons in cyclic resonance; this obeys Huckel's Rule and is aromatic.

79. Back-bonding and resonance stabilized carbocation

81. In (d), lone pairs are not conjugated with the π bond or vacant orbital.

82. Extended resonance > Cross resistance.

83. $\pi \text{ bond stability} \propto \dfrac{1}{\text{Heat of hydrogenation per mole of } H_2}$

84.

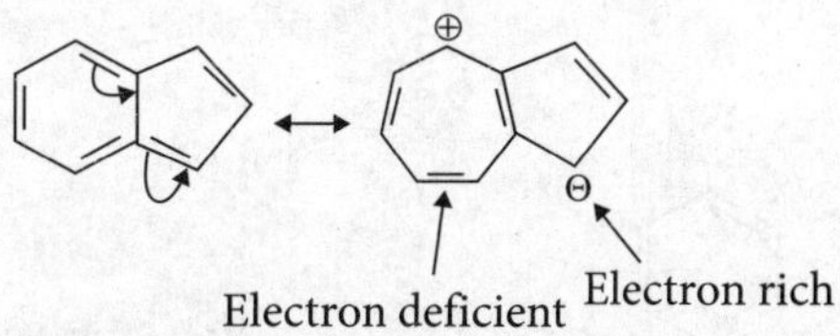

Polar, so dipole moment is non-zero.

85. Phenanthrene has 5 R.S. in neutral form.

86.

$$CH_3-\underset{\underset{O}{\parallel}}{C}-H \xrightleftharpoons{\overset{\ominus}{O}D/D_2O} CD_3-\underset{\underset{O}{\parallel}}{C}-H \rightleftharpoons CD_2=\underset{\underset{OD}{|}}{C}-H$$

Keto ⇌ Enol

87. $HC{\equiv}CH + KOH \rightarrow HC{\equiv}\overset{\ominus}{C}\overset{\oplus}{K} + H_2O$

Less stable anion, so non-feasible.

88.

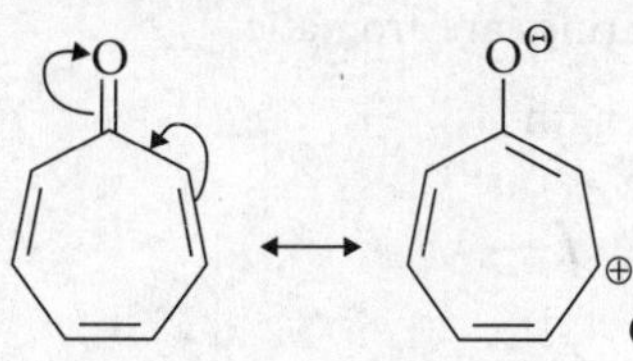

Quasi-aromatic

89. First carbocation has incomplete octet.

90. 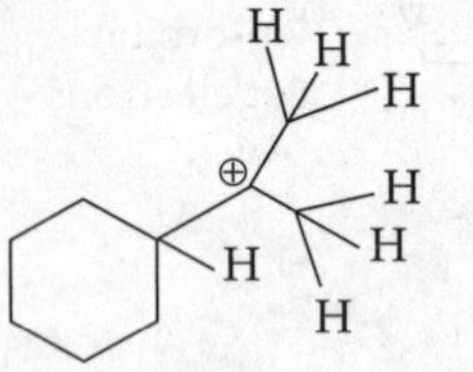

91. $CH_2=C=\ddot{O} \leftrightarrow \overset{\ominus}{C}H_2-C\equiv\overset{\oplus}{O}$

'r' is triple-bond character.

92. II is more stable than I because in II negative charge on more EN atom.

93. 

CH_3(+H) unstabilized to anion

94. 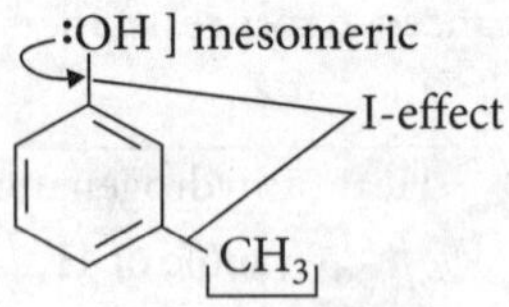

Hyper-conjugation

95. 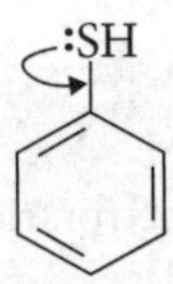

Mesomeric and inductive is present but hyper-conjugation is absent.

96. Anti-aromatic enol highly unstable, so does not form.

97. 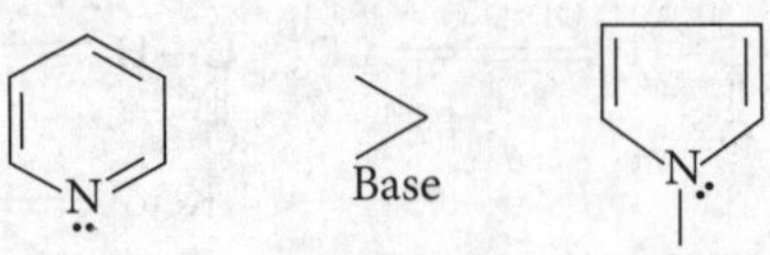

Lone pair localized in pyridine

Lone pair is in aromaticity

98. In (c), all rings are aromatic.

99. Basic strength
$R > Q > P > S$

100. 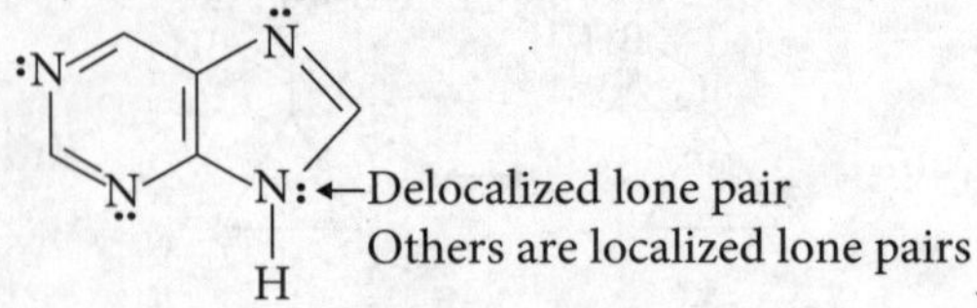

101. 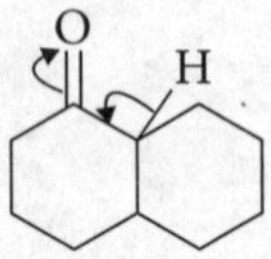

102. α-hydrogen is absent.

104. 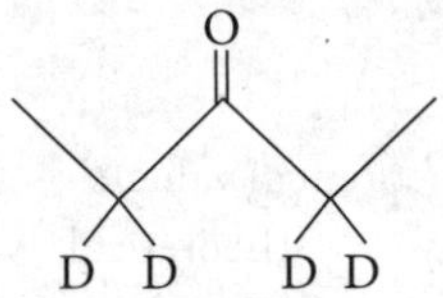

105. π bond of the ring shows geometric isomerism only when the ring is of 8 or more members.

106. 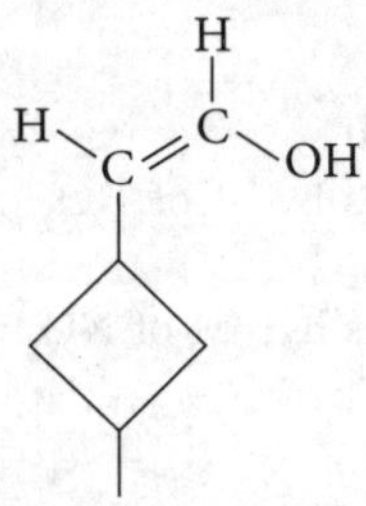

107. 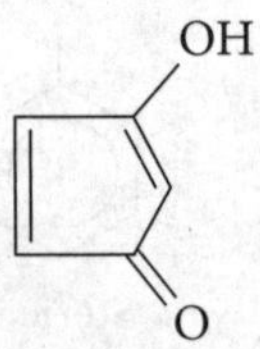 Anti-aromatic enol does not exist

108. $CH_3-\underset{\underset{O}{\|}}{C}-CH_2-\underset{\underset{O}{\|}}{C}-CH_3$

$\Downarrow$

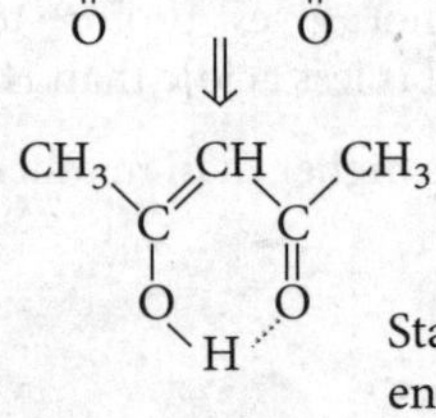

Stable enol form

CHAPTER **3**

Isomerism

Level-1

STRUCTURAL ISOMERISM

1. 2-Methylbutane and 2,2-dimethylpropane are:
(a) Chain isomers
(b) Position isomers
(c) Metamers
(d) Functional isomers

2. Cycloalkanes are isomeric with:
(a) Alkadienes (b) Alkynes
(c) Aromatics (d) Olefins

3. Among the following, the correct match is:

LIST – I	LIST – II
(A) Dimethyl ether, Ethyl alcohol	1. Ring chain isomers
(B) Acetaldehyde, Acetone	2. Metamers
(C) 2-Pentanone, 3-Pentanone	3. Functional isomers
(D) Propene, Cyclopropane	4. Chain isomers
	5. Non-isomers

	A	B	C	D
(a)	5	3	2	1
(b)	3	5	2	1
(c)	2	3	1	4
(d)	3	2	1	5

4. Which one of the following pairs are position isomers?
(a) CH_2 (OH) CH_2COOH and CH_3–CH(OH) COOH
(b) C_2H_5OH and CH_3OH
(c) CH_3 – NH – CH_3 and CH_3CH_2 – NH_2
(d) 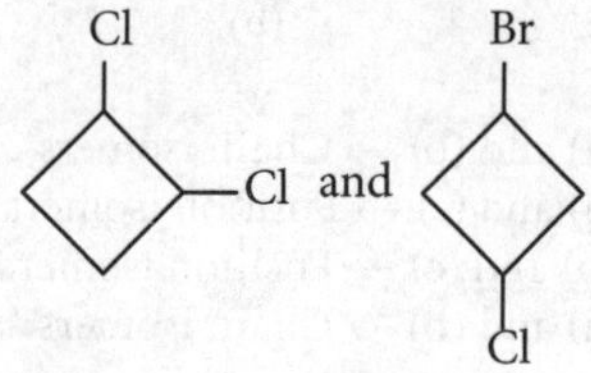

5. Which of the following is not a chain isomer of n-hexane?
(a) 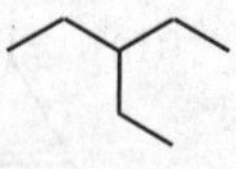 (b) 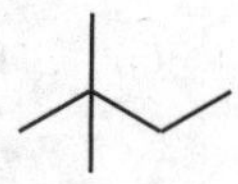
(c) 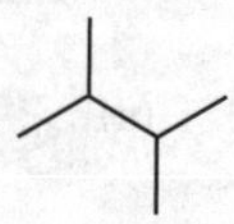 (d) 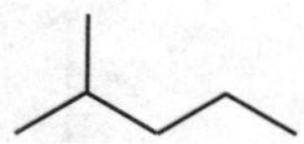

6. Which of the following are related as position isomers?
(a) CH_3CO_2Et and $CH_3CH_2CO_2CH_3$
(b) Pentanal and 2-Pentanone
(c) 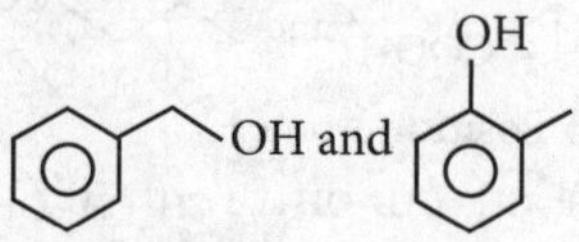
(d) $CH_3CH_2CH_2NH_2$ and $CH_3CH(NH_2)CH_3$

7. Which of the following can show tautomerism?
(a) 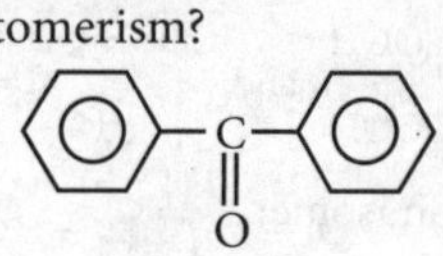 (b) 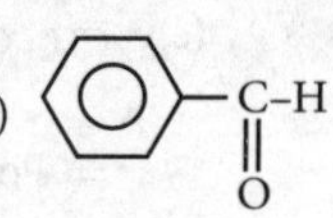
(c) 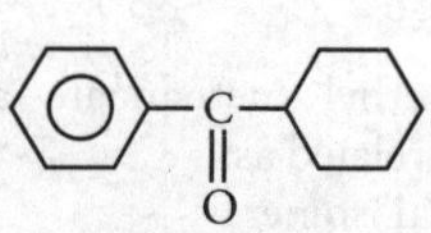 (d) None of these

8. The isomerism exhibited due to the difference in the chain of alkyl groups attached to the bivalent functional group is:
(a) Tautomerism
(b) Stereoisomerism
(c) Metamerism
(d) Optical isomerism

9. The following compounds are related as:

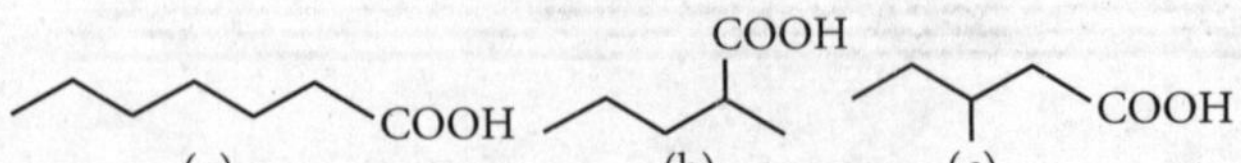

(a) (b) (c)

(a) (a) and (b) → Chain isomers
(b) (a) and (c) → Position isomers
(c) (b) and (c) → Position isomers
(d) (a) and (b) → Chain isomers

10. Which of the following is not an isomer of the others?

(a) $CH_3-C\equiv C-CH_3$

(b) 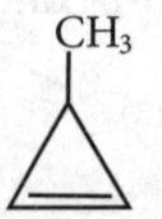

(c) 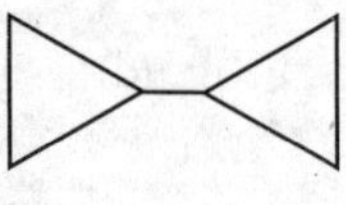

(d) 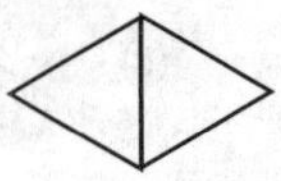

11. Which of the following are incorrectly matched?

(a) 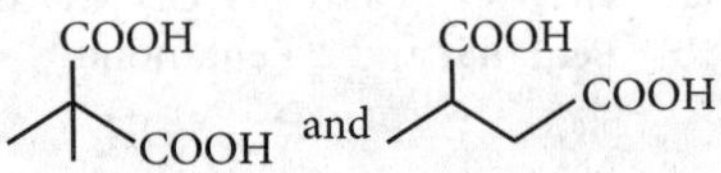

⇒ Position isomer

(b) $CH_3-CH_2-CH_2-OH$ and $CH_3CH(CH_3)-OH$

⇒ Metamers

(c) $CH_2=C(COOH)_2$ and $COOH-CH=CH-COOH$

⇒ Position isomer

(d) All of these

12. Compounds ethyl methanoate and methyl ethanoate are related as:
(a) Functional isomers
(b) Positional isomers
(c) Metamers
(d) Chain isomers

13. The following compounds are related as:

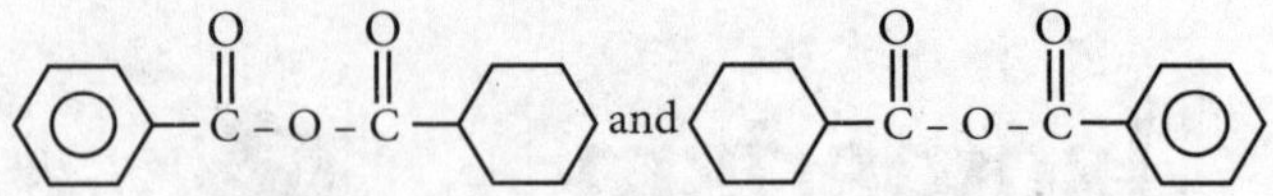

(a) Functional isomers (b) Chain isomers
(c) Identical isomers (d) Metamers

14. The number of possible position isomers for dichlorobenzene is:
(a) 2 (b) 3
(c) 4 (d) 5

15. Diethyl ether and n-propyl methyl ether are:
(a) Metamers
(b) Tautomers
(c) Functional isomers
(d) Optical isomers

16. How many optically active stereoisomers are possible for butane-2,3-diol?
(a) 1 (b) 2
(c) 3 (d) 4

17. Which of the following compounds exhibits stereoisomerism?
(a) 2-Methylbutene-1
(b) 3-Methylbutyne-1
(c) 3-Methylbutanoic acid
(d) 2-Methylbutanoic acid

18. Which of the following molecules is achiral?
(a) 2-Chlorobutane
(b) 2,3-Dihydroxypropanal
(c) Bromo-chloro-iodo methane
(d) 2-Bromoethanoic acid

19. Which of the following has a plane of symmetry and centre of symmetry?

(a) 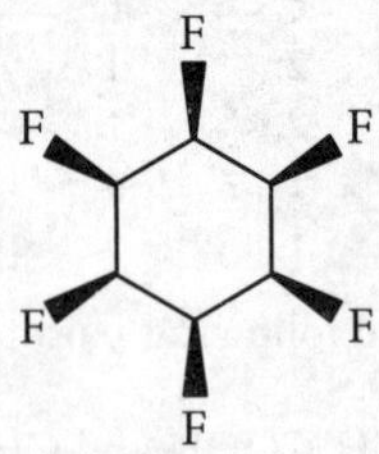

(b) 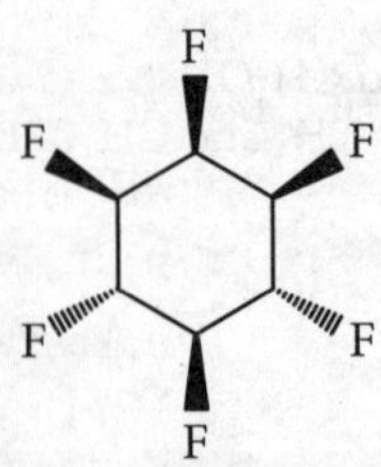

(c) 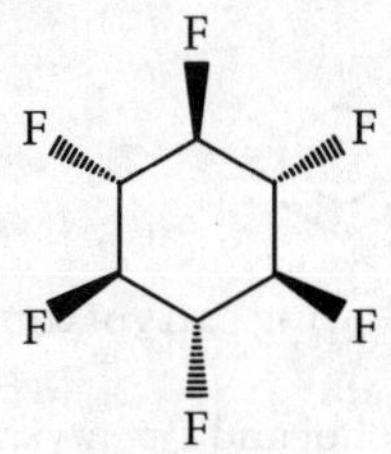

(d) 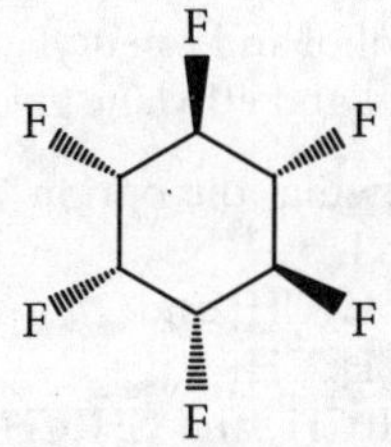

20. Which of the following can show chain isomerism as well as position isomerism?
(a) n-Butane
(b) n-Pentane
(c) n-Hexane
(d) Dichloropropane

21. Which of the following classes of organic compounds shows metamerism?
(a) Ethers
(b) Secondary amines
(c) Ketones
(d) Any of the three

22. Which compound is not the isomer of 3-ethyl-2-methylpentane?
(a) 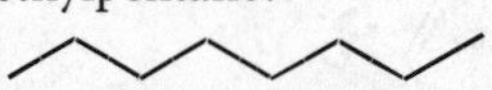
(b) 
(c) 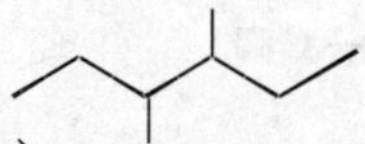
(d) 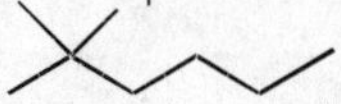

23. Find out the incorrect relation in the following pairs of compounds:
(a) 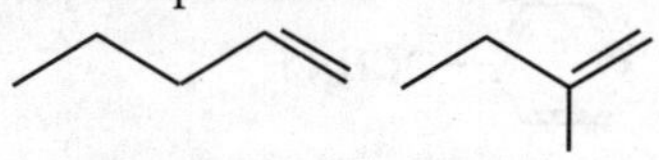 (Chain)
(b) 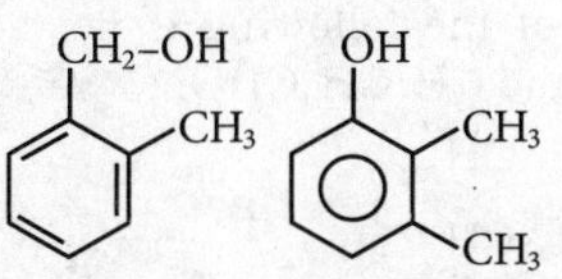

(Functional)
(c) 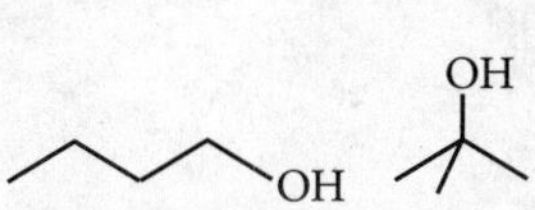

(Positional)

(d) None of these

24. What are the groups X and Y in the given Newman projection of 2,2-dimethylbutane?

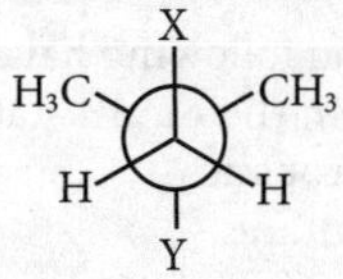

(a) $X = -H; Y = -C_2H_5$
(b) $X = -C_2H_5; Y = -H$
(c) $X = -CH_3; Y = -C_2H_5$
(d) $X = -C_2H_5; Y = -CH_3$

25. How many conformations are less stable than the anti form of butane?
(a) 2 (b) 3
(c) 4 (d) Infinite

26. Which of the given set of molecules has similar molecular formula?
(a) Nonane and 2-methylheptane
(b) 3-Isopropylcyclopent-1-ene and 3-methylhexane
(c) 3-Methylcyclopent-1-ene and penta-1,3-diene
(d) Ethylcyclohexane and oct-2-ene

27. The molecular formula which is correctly matched with the total number of structural isomers is:
(a) $C_3H_5Cl_3$ – 5 isomers
(b) $C_3H_6Br_2$ – 4 isomers
(c) C_3H_7Br – 4 isomers
(d) All of these

28. Of the following, the alkene that exhibits optical isomerism is:
(a) 2-Methyl-2-hexene
(b) 3-Methyl-2-hexene
(c) 5-Methyl-1-hexene
(d) 3-Methyl-1-hexene

29. Consider the following compounds and select the correct statement:

(I) 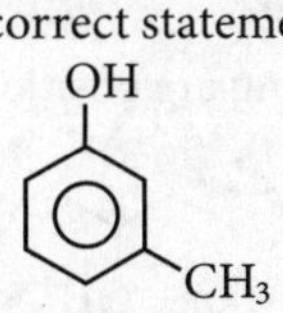

(II) 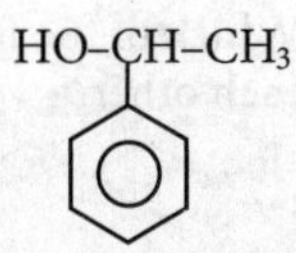

(III) 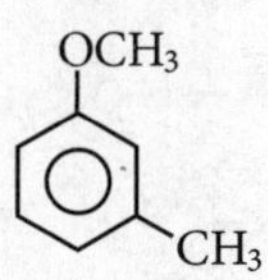

(IV) 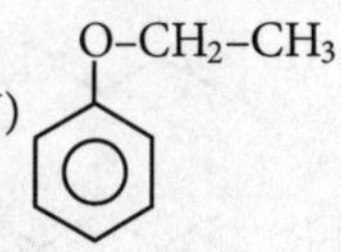

(a) I and II are position isomers
(b) III and IV are chain isomers
(c) III and IV are metamers
(d) I, II, III and IV are isomers

30. Which of the following have all carbons in the same plane in their most stable conformation?
(a) Cyclopropane
(b) Cyclobutane
(c) Cyclopentane
(d) Cyclohexane

31. Among the following, the incorrect relationship is:

(a) 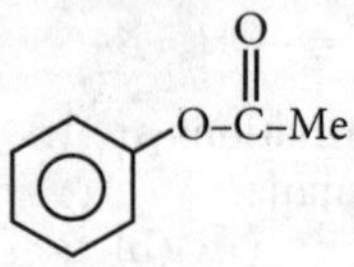 and 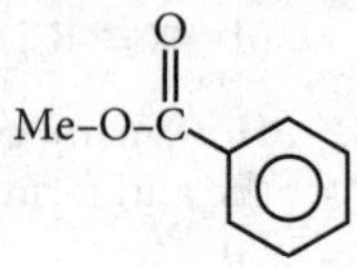
Metamers

(b) 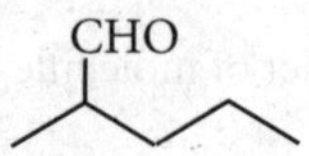 and 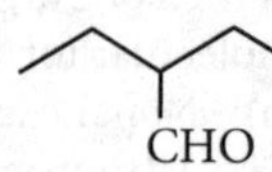
Positional isomers

(c) 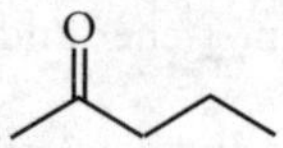 and 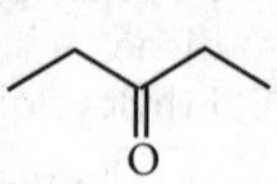
Positional isomers

(d)  and 
Chain isomers

32. Which of the following is not an isomer of CH_3-CH_2-CHO?
(a) 
(b) 
(c) $CH_2=CH-CH_2-OH$
(d) $CH_3-CH_2-O-CH_3$

33. Which of the following are position isomers to each other?
(a) 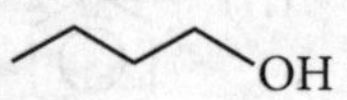 , 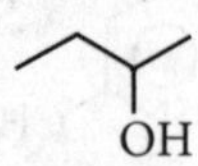
(b) 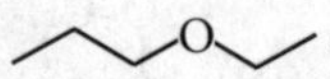 , 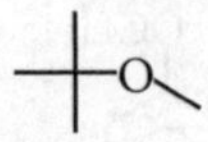
(c) 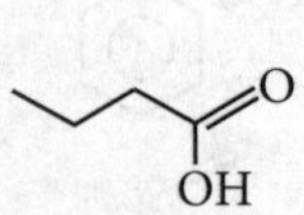 , 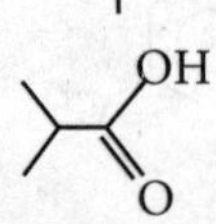
(d) 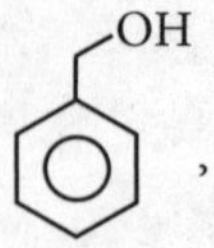 , 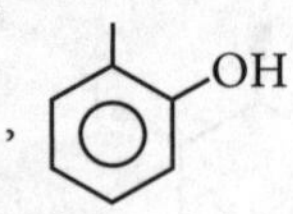

34. Which of the following pairs of compounds are chain isomers?
(a) Isobutyl alcohol and s-pentyl alcohol
(b) Isobutyl alcohol and t-butyl alcohol
(c) s-Pentyl alcohol and t-pentyl alcohol
(d) Ethyl alcohol and ethylene glycol

35. Among the following, the option that is not a pair of metamers is:
(a) $CH_3OCH_2CH_2CH_3$ and $CH_3CH_2OCH_2CH_3$
(b) $CH_3CH_2CH_2CH_3$ and $CH_3CH(CH_3)_2$
(c) $CH_3NHCH_2CH_2CH_3$ and $CH_3CH_2NHCH_2CH_3$
(d) $CH_3CO(CH_2)_2CH_3$ and $CH_3CH_2COCH_2CH_3$

36. The minimum number of C-atoms required by a hydrocarbon alkane, alkene and alkyne, respectively, to show chain isomerism are:
(a) 4, 4, 4 (b) 4, 4, 3
(c) 4, 4, 5 (d) 4, 3, 3

37. The metamer of compound B is:

B: 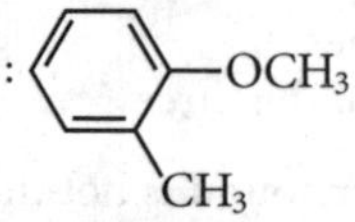

(a) 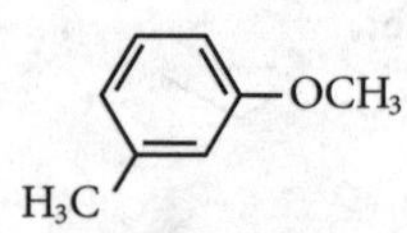
(b) 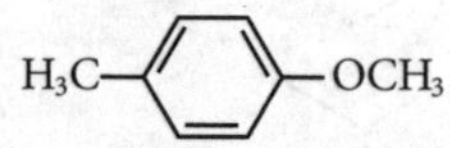
(c) 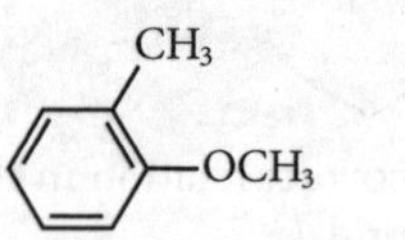
(d) 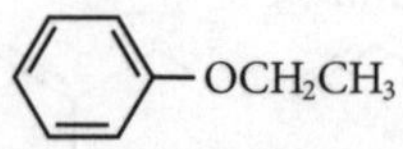

38. Which of the following is not an isomer of compound CH_3CH_2CHO?
(a) $CH_3-\underset{}{CH}(OH)-CH_3$
(b) 

(c) 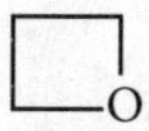

(d) CH_2=CH–CH_2–OH

39. But-2-ene can exist in two forms, P and Q. P has zero dipole moment. Then the configuration of Q is:
(a) Cis and Z (b) Trans and E
(c) Cis and E (d) Trans and Z

40. Which of the following on reaction with NH_2OH will form two isomeric oximes?
(a) Acetone (b) Cyclobutanone
(c) Butanone (d) 3-Pentanone

41. Saturated acyclic ethers are isomeric with:
(a) Aldehydes
(b) Ketones
(c) Both aldehydes and ketones
(d) Alcohols

42. Which of the following pairs is correctly related?

(a) 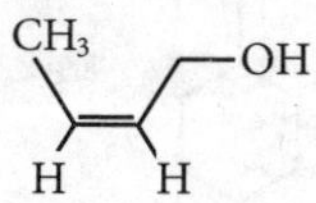 and 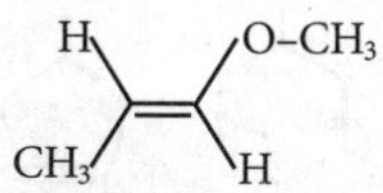
(Geometrical isomers)

(b) 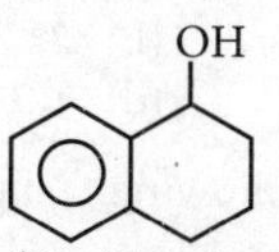 and 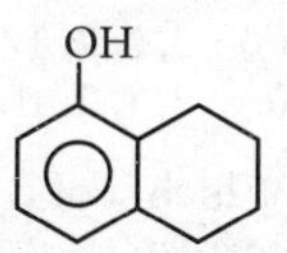
(Position isomers)

(c) 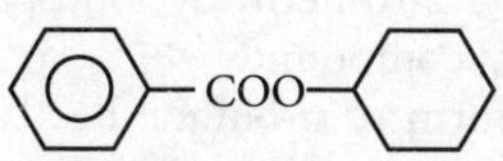 and 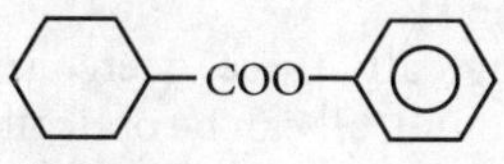
(Metamers)

(d) CH_3CO_2Et and $CH_3CH_2CO_2CH_3$
(Position isomers)

Stereoisomerism

43. In eclipsed conformation of ethane, by rotating the front carbon by 180° and the rear carbon by 60° clockwise, the conformation obtained is:
(a) Eclipsed
(b) Staggered
(c) Both (a) and (b)
(d) None of these

44. The correct order of priority according to the CIP rule is:
(a) –H > –D > –T
(b) –CH_2Cl > –CH_2CH_2Cl > –CH_2F
(c) –Ph > –CH=CH_2 > –OH
(d) –Cyclobutyl > –Cyclopropyl

45. Which of the following can show geometrical isomerism?
(a) 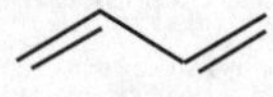
(b) 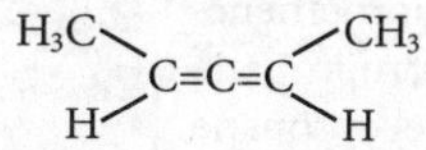
(c) 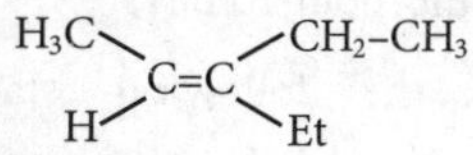
(d) 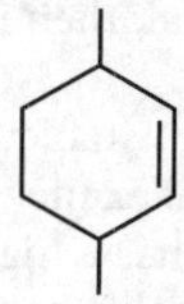

46. The incorrect statement about the given compound is:

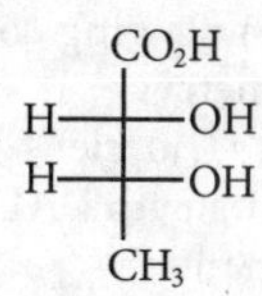

(a) It is an erythro optical isomer
(b) It has 2R, 3R configuration
(c) It is a meso form
(d) All of these

47. The least stable conformation of cyclohexane is:
(a) Boat (b) Chair
(c) Twist boat (d) Half chair

48. The correct configuration of the following compound is:

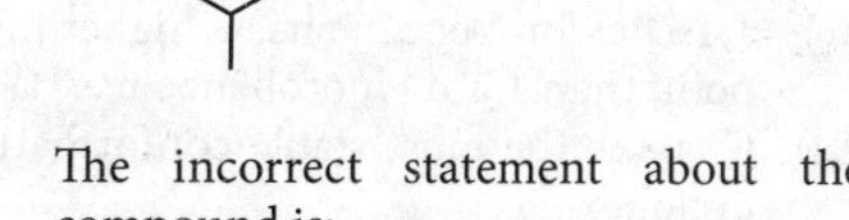

(a) 3Z, 5E, 7Z (b) 3Z, 5Z, 7E
(c) 3Z, 5E, 7E (d) 3E, 5E, 7Z

49. Geometrical isomers result from the:
(a) Free rotation about C–C
(b) Restricted rotation about C=C
(c) Restricted rotation about C–C

(d) Free rotation about C=C

50. Two geometrical isomers are given by the following compound:
(a) Ethylidene bromide
(b) Acetylene tetrachloride
(c) Acetylene tetrabromide
(d) Acetylene dibromide

51. Which of the following can show geometrical isomerism?
(a) 1,1-Dicholoroethene
(b) 3,3-Dichloropropene
(c) 2,3-Dichloropropene
(d) 1,2-Dichlorobut-1-ene

52. Which of the following statements is incorrect?
(a) If a compound is chiral, then it must have a chiral carbon.
(b) Twist boat is more stable than boat conformation of cyclohexane.
(c) 1,4-Dichlorobenzene has a higher melting point than 1,2-dichlorobenzene.
(d) Chair is the most stable conformation of cyclohexane.

53. Which of the following compounds contains a plane of symmetry?
(a) Children's tricycle
(b) Coffee mug with DAD opposite the handle
(c) Human hand
(d) Coffee mug with MOM opposite the handle

54. Among the following, the incorrect statement is:
(a) Functional group isomers differ in physical and chemical properties.
(b) Geometrical isomers differ in physical properties.
(c) Enantiomers have the same physical properties but differ towards plane-polarized light.
(d) Molecules having asymmetric carbons are compulsorily optically active.

55. Ordinary light is converted into plane-polarized light by passing it through a:
(a) Nickel prism (b) Glass prism
(c) Nicol prism (d) Glass slab

56. The correct stereochemical formula of trans-3-chloro-1-phenyl but-1-ene is:

(a) 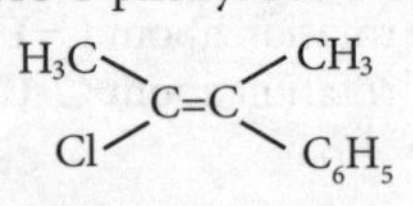

(b) 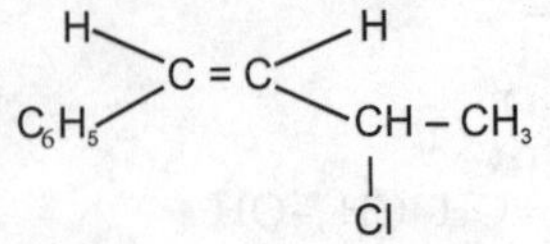

(c) 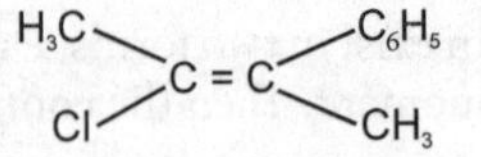

(d) 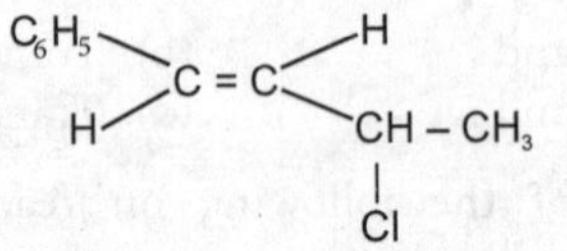

57. Which of the following can show geometrical isomerism?
(a) 1,3-Dibromo-1-chlorocyclopentane
(b) 2,3,4,5-Heptatetraene
(c) 1,4-Dimethylcyclohexene
(d) 2-Hydroxycyclobutanone

58. The number of chiral carbon atoms in the compounds W, X, Y and Z would be:

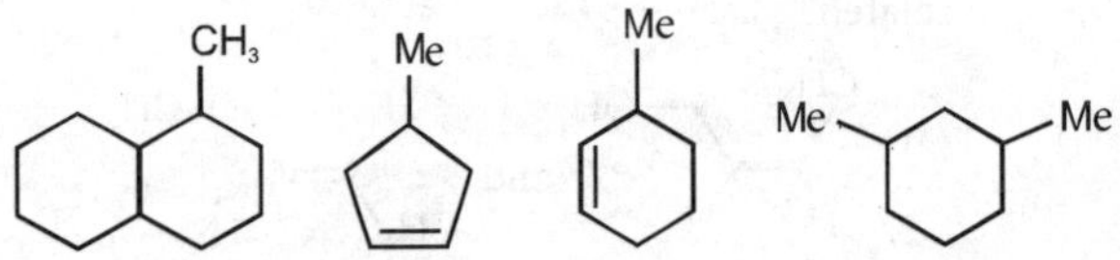

W X Z Y

(a) 3, 0, 2, 1 (b) 2, 1, 0, 1
(c) 3, 1, 2, 1 (d) 1, 1, 2, 0

59. Which of the following statements is correct?
(a) Trans-1,2-dimethylcyclopropane is an achiral compound.
(b) Anti form of n-butane has two planes of symmetry.
(c) Among all three stereoisomers of a compound, all can be optically active.
(d) Mesotartaric acid shows optical isomerism.

60. Which of the following is polar?
(a) Naphthalene
(b) Trans-2-butene
(c) 1,4-Dichlorobenzene
(d) Quinol

61. Which of the following compounds has a chiral carbon?
(a) 1,3-Dimethylcyclopentane
(b) 2-Methylbutane
(c) Butan-1-ol
(d) 1,3-Dichlorocyclobutane

62. The best method to distinguish between a pair of enantiomers is to determine their:
(a) Melting point
(b) Angle of rotation
(c) Refractive index
(d) Boiling point

63. Which of the following compounds cannot show geometrical isomerism?

(a) 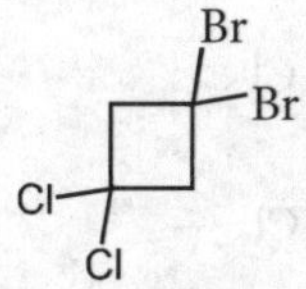 (b) 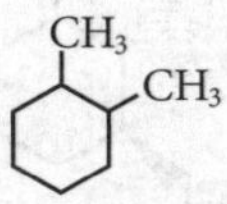

(c) 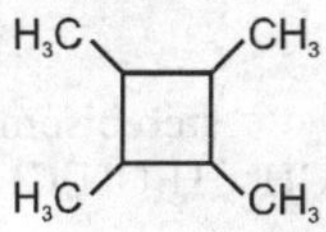 (d) 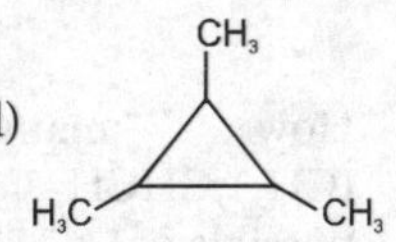

64. Among the following, a pair of resolvable configurational enantiomers is given by:
(a) cis-1,2-Dimethylcyclohexane
(b) cis-1,3-Dimethylcyclohexane
(c) trans-1,4-Dimethylcyclohexane
(d) trans-1,3-Dimethylcyclohexane

65. Among the given compounds, identify the pair of geometrical isomers:

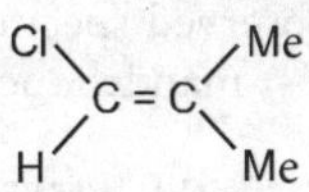
I

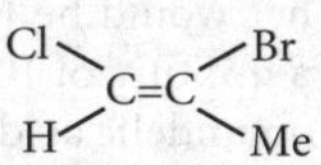
II

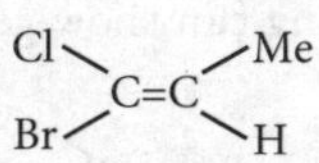
III

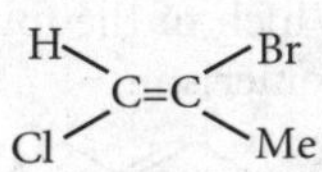
IV

(a) I and II (b) I and III
(c) II and IV (d) III and IV

66. The compound not having two chiral centres is:

(a) 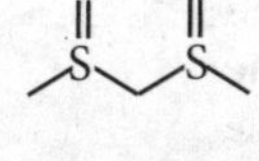 (b) 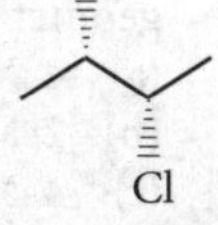

(c) 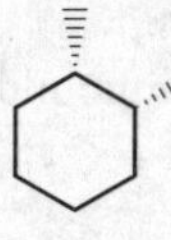 (d) 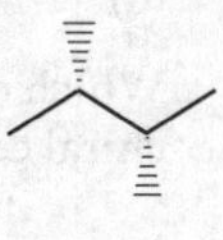

67. Which of the following compound(s) contains a plane of symmetry but not a centre of symmetry?

(a) 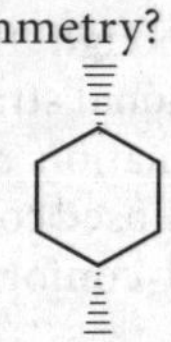

(b) 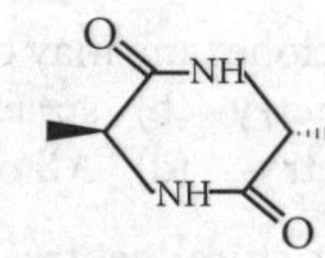

(c) 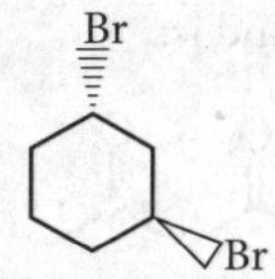

(d) 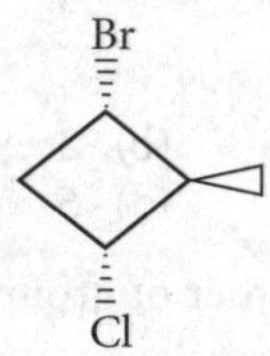

68. Which of the following is the correct statement?
(a) Geometrical isomers are mirror image isomers mostly.
(b) A compound having double bond always shows geometrical isomerism.
(c) Cyclic compounds having single bond can show geometrical isomerism.
(d) Cyclodecene cannot show cis and trans isomerism.

69. The compound for which meso stereoisomer is possible is:
(a) 2,3-Dimethylbutane
(b) 1,3-Dichloropentane
(c) 2,4-Pentane-diol
(d) 2,3-Dichloroheptane

70. The correct statement regarding the comparison of staggered and eclipsed conformations of ethane is:
(a) The staggered conformation of ethane is less stable than the eclipsed conformation, because the staggered conformation has torsional strain.
(b) The eclipsed conformation of ethane is more stable than the staggered conformation, because the eclipsed conformation has no torsional strain.

(c) The eclipsed conformation of ethane is more stable than the staggered conformation even though the eclipsed conformation has torsional strain.

(d) The staggered conformation of ethane is more stable than the eclipsed conformation because the staggered conformation has no torsional strain.

71. Cis-1,3-dimethyl cyclohexane may contain:
(a) Centre of symmetry (b) sp^2 atom
(c) Plane of symmetry (d) All of these

72. The total number of chiral centres present in the following compound is:

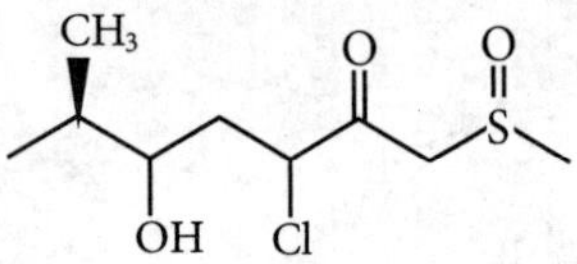

(a) 2 (b) 3
(c) 4 (d) 5

73. The correct priority order of groups according to the CIP rule is:
(a) $-F > -CH_2Cl > -CH_2CH_2-Br$
(b) $-CH{=}O > -CN > -CH_2-NH_2$
(c) $-CH_2CD_3 > -CH_3 > -T > -H$
(d) All of these

74. Which of the following compounds does not have a plane of symmetry?

(a) 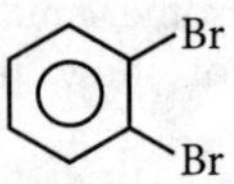

(b) 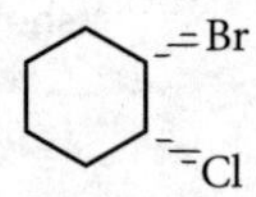

(c) 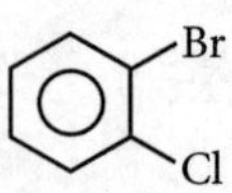

(d) 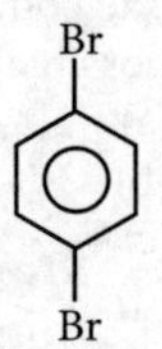

75. Which compound has a centre of symmetry?

(a) 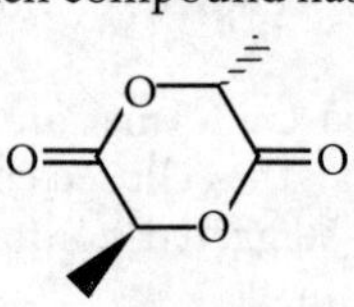

(b) 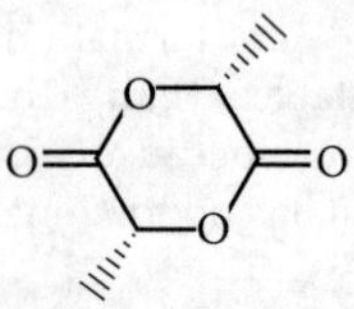

(c) 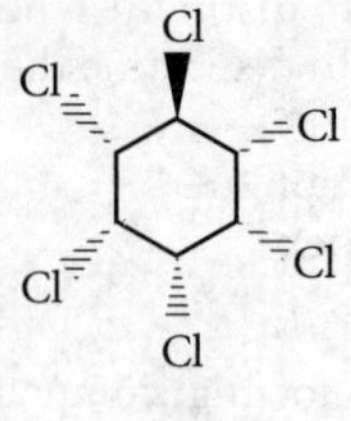

(d) 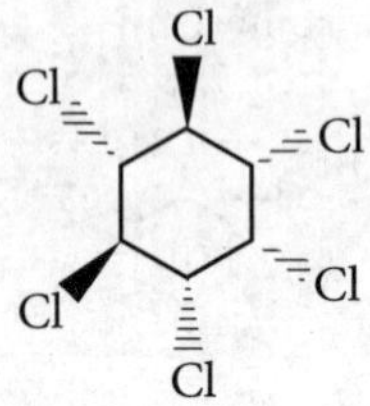

76. How many stereoisomers of $(CH_3)_2CHCH{=}CHCH_2CH(OH)CH_2Br$ are possible ?
(a) 2 (b) 3
(c) 4 (d) 5

77. Which of the following sets are chiral?
(a) 3-Heptanol and 4-heptanol
(b) 2-Heptanol and 3-heptanol
(c) 2-Heptanol, 3-heptanol and 4-heptanol
(d) All are chiral

78. (+)-Mandelic acid has a specific rotation of 158°. What would be the observed specific rotation of a mixture of 100% (–)-mandelic acid and 0% (+)-mandelic acid?
(a) +158° (b) –158°
(c) –79° (d) 0°

79. Which of the following can show geometrical isomerism?

(a) 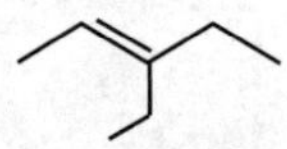

(b) 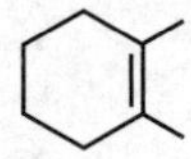

(c) 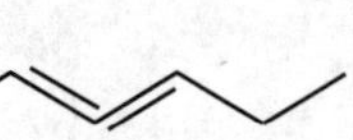

(d) 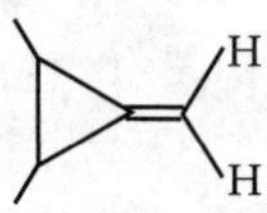

80. Which of the following compounds shows geometrical isomerism?
(a) 4-Methylpent-1-ene
(b) 2-Methylpent-2-ene
(c) 4-Methylpent-2-ene
(d) 2-Methylpent-1-ene

81. Which of the following compounds possesses a chiral centre?

(a) 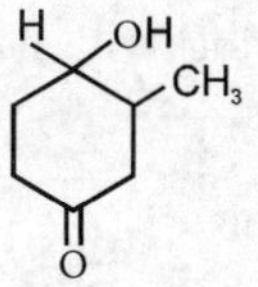 (b) 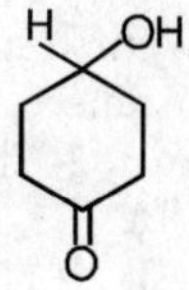

(c) 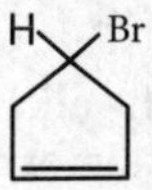 (d) 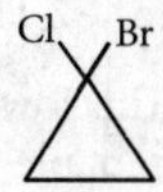

82. Which of the following statements is incorrect?
(a) The process of conversion of enantiomer into a racemic mixture is known as racemization.
(b) If all the substituents attached to a carbon are different, then such a carbon is a chiral centre.
(c) The sign of optical rotation is necessarily related to the absolute configuration of the molecule.
(d) The (+) sign indicates a dextrorotatory and the (–) sign indicates a laevorotatory compound.

83. Which of the following statements must be true for two pure chiral isomers?
(a) They must be enantiomers
(b) They must be diastereomers
(c) They must be stereoisomers
(d) They must be optically active

84. The total number of isomers possible by replacing one hydrogen atom of propane with chlorine is:
(a) 2 (b) 3
(c) 4 (d) 5

85. Which of the following compounds has non-zero dipole moment?

(a) 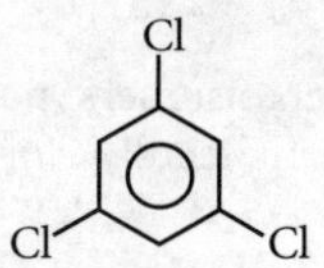 (b) 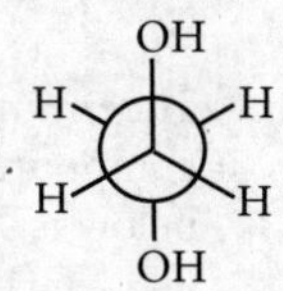

(c) 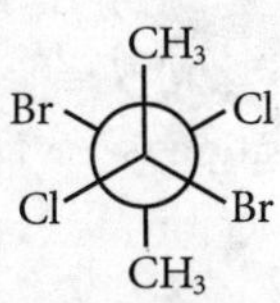 (d) 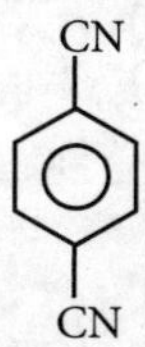

86. What is the relation between the following compounds?

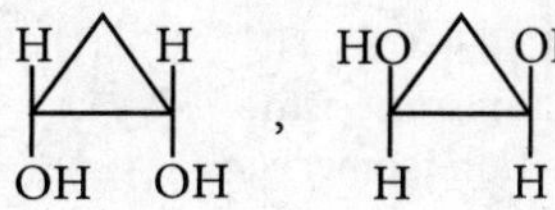

(a) Enantiomers
(b) Identical
(c) Diastereomers
(d) Constitutional isomers

87. The optically inactive form in the following is:
(a) 2-Chloropropanal
(b) 2-Chlorobutane
(c) 2-Chloro-2-methylbutane
(d) 2-Chloropentane

88. The absolute configuration is:

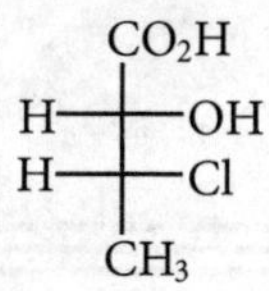

(a) (2R, 3R) (b) (2R, 3S)
(c) (2S, 3R) (d) (2S, 3S)

89. Which of the following can show geometrical but not optical isomerim?

(a) 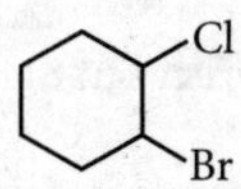

(b) 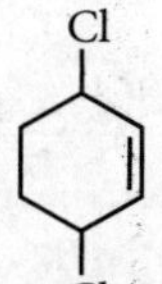

(c) 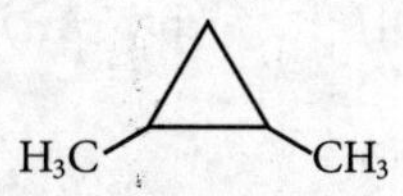

(d) None of the above

90. If the specific rotation of (+)-2-butanol is +12°, then the specific rotation of mesotartaric acid is:
(a) + 12°
(b) –12°
(c) 0°
(d) Cannot be predicted

91. The following types of compounds I and II are studied in terms of isomerism in:

(I) $CH_3CH=CHCH_3$ (II) Butan-2-ol

(a) Chain isomerism
(b) Position isomerism
(c) Conformers
(d) Stereoisomerism

92. Identify which compound has a plane of symmetry:

(a) 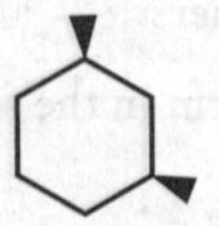

(b) 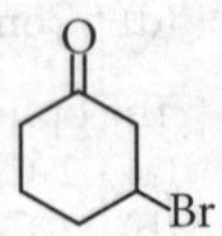

(c) 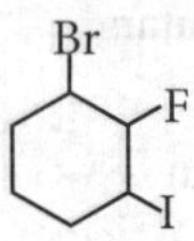

(d) All of the above

93. Which of the following will have a meso isomer?

(a) 2-Chlorobutane
(b) 2,3-Dichlorobutane
(c) 2,3-Dichloropentene
(d) 2-Hydroxypropanoic acid

94. The lowest molecular weight alkane which is capable of showing enantiomorphism must have:

(a) Four carbons (b) Five carbons
(c) Six carbons (d) Seven carbons

95. The lowest molecular weight alkyne capable of showing optical activity is:

(a) 2-Heptyne
(b) 3-Methyl-1-pentyne
(c) 3-Methyl-1-butyne
(d) 3-Hexyne

Level-2

1. **Statement I:** Ethanol cannot show position isomerism.
Statement II: Ethanol cannot show isomerism.

(a) Both Statement I and Statement II are incorrect
(b) Statement I is correct but Statement II is incorrect
(c) Statement I is incorrect but Statement II is correct
(d) Both Statement I and Statement II are correct

2. Among the following pairs, which has the first compound achiral?

(a) 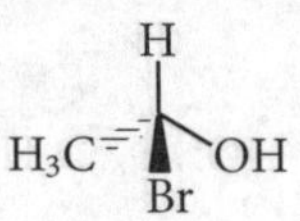 , 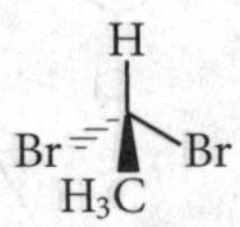

(b)  , 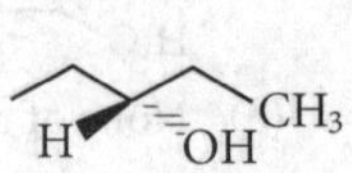

(c) $CH_3-CH(Br)CH_2CH_3$ and $CH_3CH_2CH_2CH_2Br$

(d) 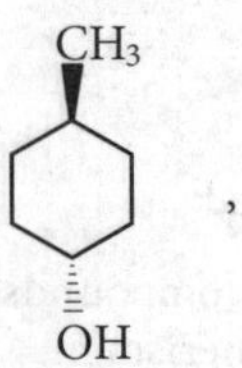 , 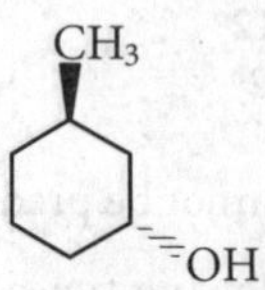

3. For the following, select the incorrect statement:

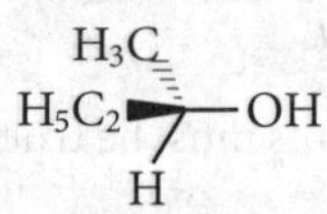
(P)

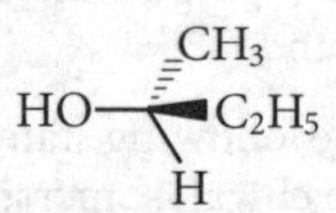
(Q)

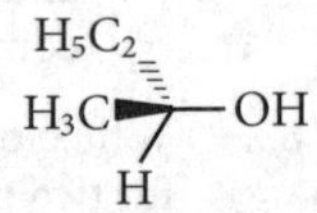
(R)

(a) (R) is obtained by rotating (Q) by 180°.
(b) (R) is non-superimposable on its mirror image (P).
(c) Refractive index of (Q) is the same as that of (P).
(d) Equimolar mixture of (Q) and (R) is known as racemic mixture.

4. The number of optically active isomers for 2,3,4-trichloropentane is:

(a) 2 (b) 3
(c) 4 (d) 6

5. The number of stereoisomers possible for a compound of the molecular formula given below is:

$CH_3-CH=CH-CH(OH)-Me$

(a) 4 (b) 6
(c) 3 (d) 2

6. The absolute configuration is:

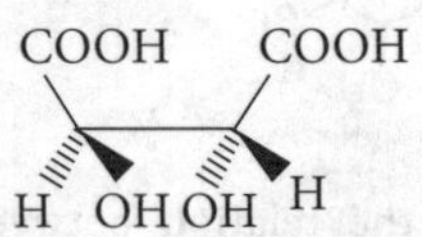

(a) S, S (b) R, R
(c) R, S (d) S, R

7. **Statement I:** Molecules that are non-superimposable on their mirror images are chiral.
Statement II: All chiral molecules have a chiral carbon.
(a) Both Statement I and Statement II are incorrect
(b) Statement I is correct but Statement II is incorrect
(c) Statement I is incorrect but Statement II is correct
(d) Both Statement I and Statement II are correct

8. The correct configuration of the following compound is:

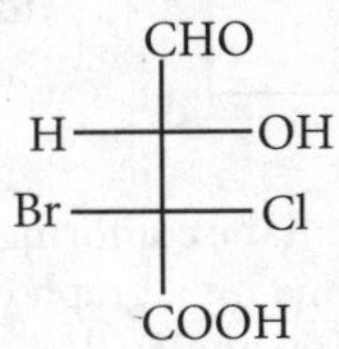

(a) 2R, 3S (b) 2S, 3S
(c) 2R, 3R (d) 2S, 3R

9. If the given conformation is D-glucose, then the correct representation of L-glucose is:

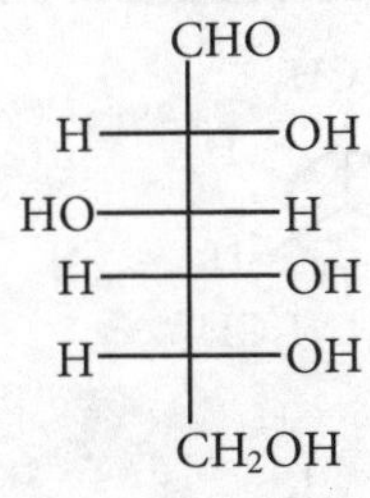

(a) 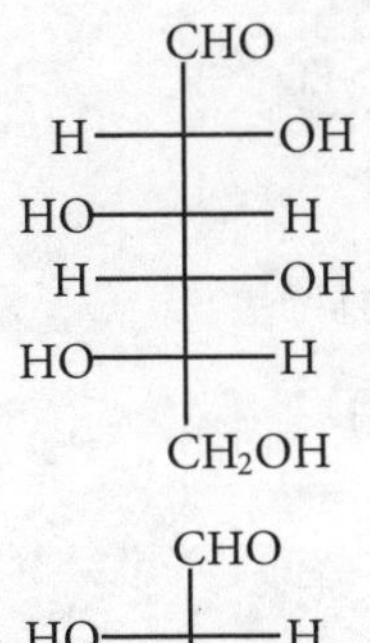 (b) 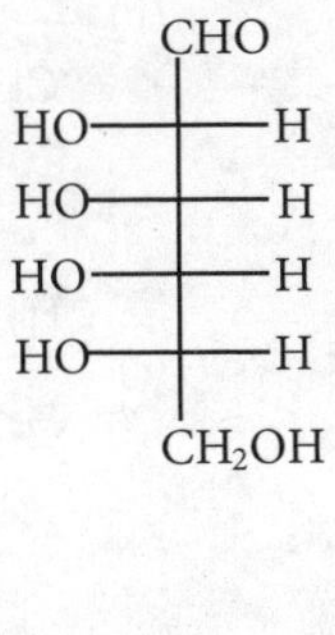

(c) 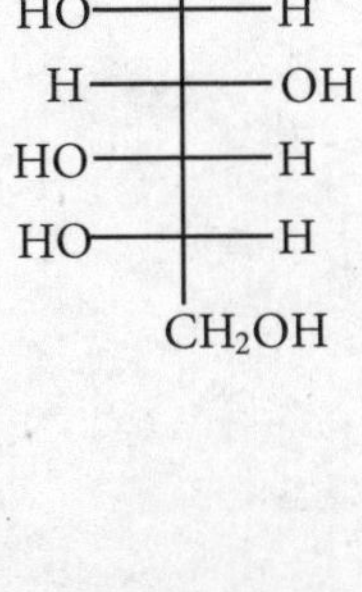 (d) All of these

10. **Statement I:** All geometrical isomer are diasteromers.
Statement II: Diasteromers are non-mirror image stereoisomers.
(a) Statement I is True, Statement II is True; Statement II is a correct explanation for Statement I
(b) Statement I is True, Statement II is True; Statement II is NOT a correct explanation
(c) Statement I is True, Statement II is False.
(d) Statement I is False, Statement II is True.

11. The incorrect statement concerning the structures E, F and G is:

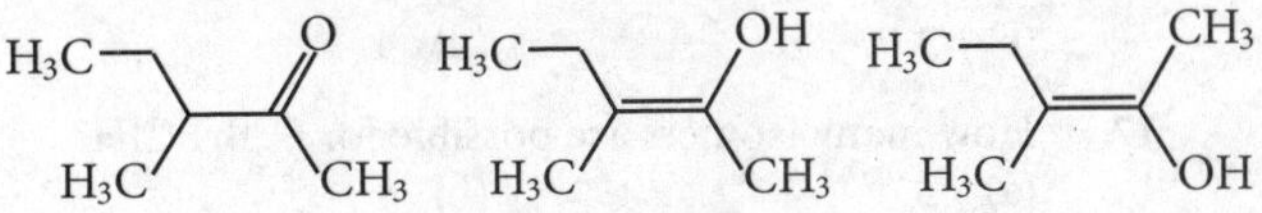

(E) (F) (G)

(a) E, F and G are resonance structures
(b) E, F and E, G are tautomers
(c) F and G are geometrical isomers
(d) F and G are diastereomers

12. Which of the following is an isomer of molecular formula C_5H_{10} and can show geometrical isomerism?

(a) 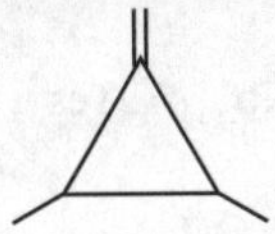 (b) 

(c) 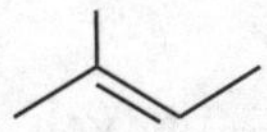 (d) 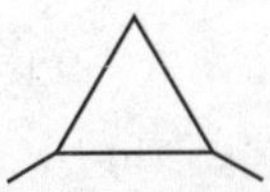

13. How many structural isomers are possible when one hydrogen is replaced by a chlorine atom in the following?

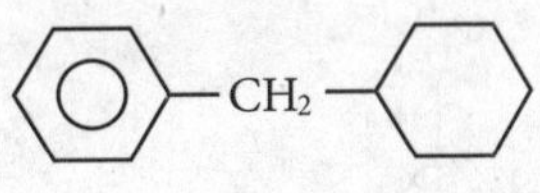

(a) 4 (b) 6
(c) 7 (d) 8

14. Which of following has S configuration on at least one chiral centre?

(a) 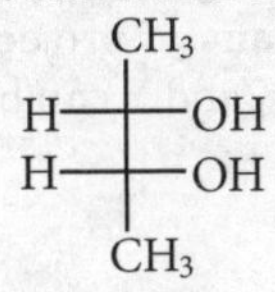 (b) 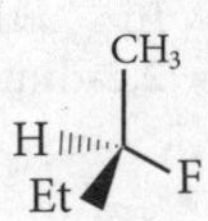

(c) 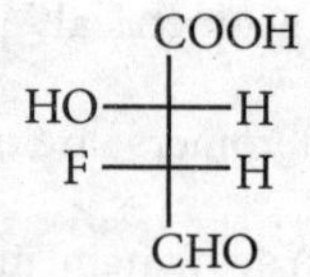

(d) 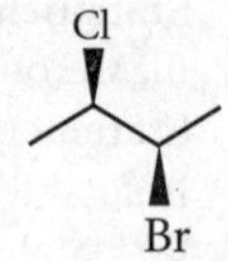

15. Compound CH_2Cl_2 contains:
(a) Plane of symmetry
(b) Centre of symmetry
(c) Axis of symmetry
(d) Both (a) and (c)

16. How many isomeric dibromobenzenes are possible?
(a) 1 (b) 2
(c) 3 (d) 4

17. How many isomers are possible for $C_2BrFClH$?
(a) 3 (b) 4
(c) 6 (d) 5

18. The total number of stereoisomers possible for 2,3-dichlorobutane is:
(a) 2 (b) 3
(c) 4 (d) 5

19. Among the following, which is a correct match?

	Compound	POS	COS	Active
(a)	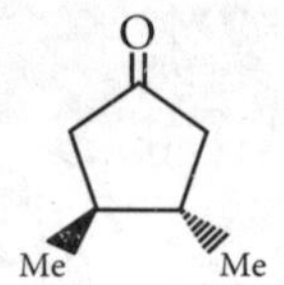	No	Yes	Yes
(b)	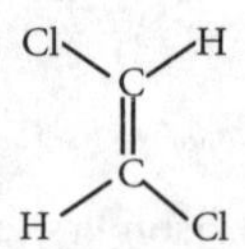	Yes	Yes	No
(c)	CH_4	Yes	Yes	No
(d)	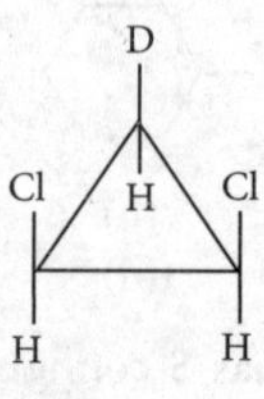	Yes	No	Yes

20. In the Newman projection for 2,2-dimethylbutane, X and Y can be:

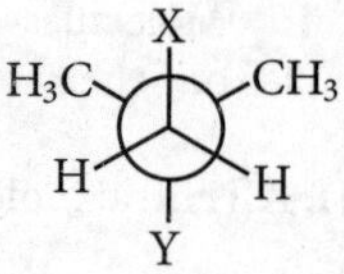

(a) H and H (b) H and C_2H_5
(c) C_2H_5 and H (d) CH_3 and C_2H_5

21. Which of the following is a chiral compound?

(a) 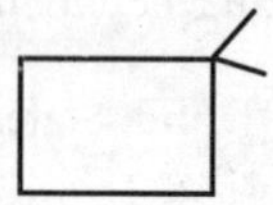 (b) 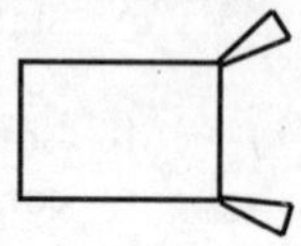

(c) 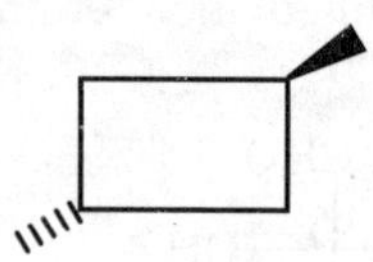 (d) 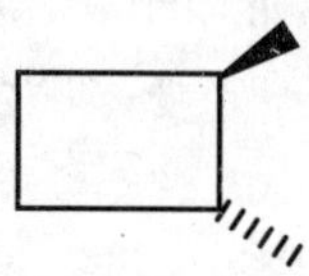

22. Among the butane conformers, which occurs at energy minima on a graph of potential energy versus dihedral angle?
(a) Gauche
(b) Fully eclipsed
(c) Anti
(d) Partially eclipsed

23. Identify the conformer of 2-methylpentane:

(a) 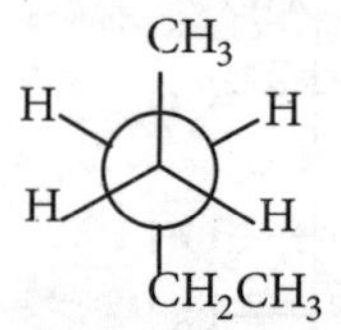

(b) 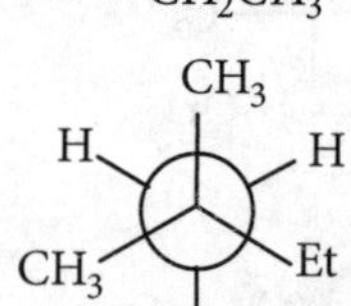

(c) 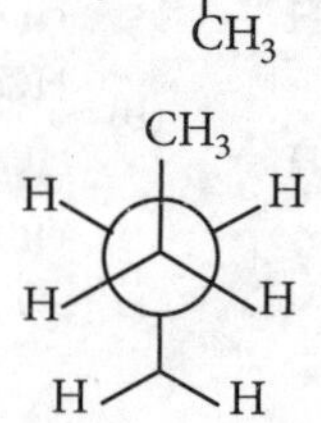

(d) 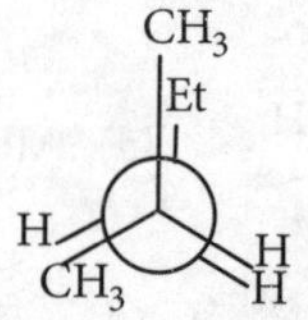

24. 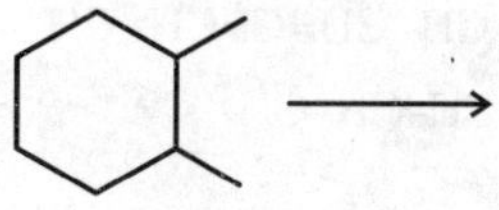 a (stereoisomers)

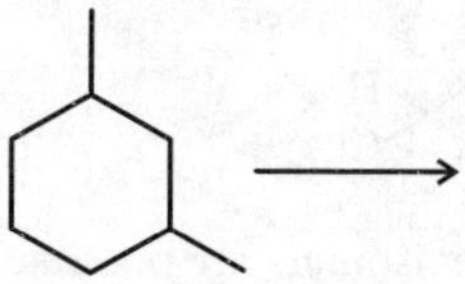 b (stereoisomers)

a and b are stereoisomers; sum of ($a + b$ = ?):

(a) 4 (b) 6
(c) 8 (d) 12

25. Which of the following can show geometrical and optical isomerism?

(a) 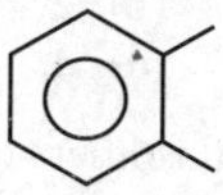 (b) 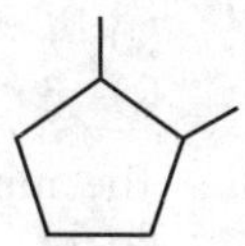

(c) 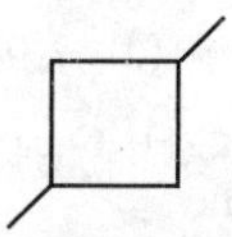 (d) 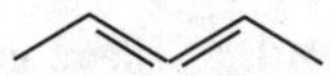

26. How many stereoisomers of the following molecule are possible?
HOOC.CH=C=CH.COOH

(a) Two optical isomers
(b) Two geometrical isomers
(c) Two optical and two geometrical isomers
(d) None of the above

27. The number of optically active compounds in the isomers of C_4H_9Br is:

(a) 1 (b) 2
(c) 3 (d) 4

28. The configuration of the given compound is:

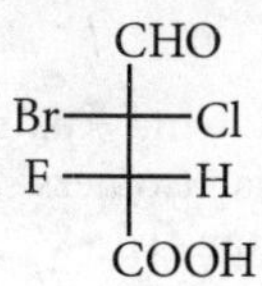

(a) 2S, 3S (b) 2R, 3S
(c) 2R, 3R (d) 2S, 3R

29. Which can show geometrical isomerism?

(a) $CH_2 = CH–CH_2–CH_3$
(b) $CH_3 - \underset{\underset{\displaystyle Cl}{|}}{C} = CH - CH_3$
(c) $CH_3 - \underset{\underset{\displaystyle CH_3}{|}}{C} = CH - CH_3$
(d) $CH_3 - \underset{\underset{\displaystyle CH_3}{|}}{C} = \underset{\underset{\displaystyle C_2H_5}{|}}{C} - C_2H_5$

30. 'R' and 'S' configurations of chiral centres in the following compound are:

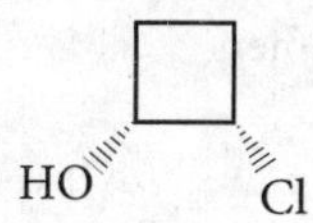

(a) (1R), (2S) (b) (1R), (2R)
(c) (1S), (2R) (d) (1S), (2S)

31. Which of the following can show optical activity?

(a) $CH_3 - CH_2 - CH_2 - CH_2 - OH$
(b) $CH_3 - CH_2 - \underset{\underset{\displaystyle OH}{|}}{CH} - CH_3$
(c) $CH_3 - \overset{\overset{\displaystyle CH_3}{|}}{CH} - CH_2 - OH$
(d) $(CH_3)_3\,C - OH$

32. Which of the following compounds could be optically active?

(a) Isobutyl alcohol
(b) t-Butyl alcohol
(c) s-Butyl alcohol
(d) n-Butyl alcohol

33. Which of the following is optically inactive?

(a) 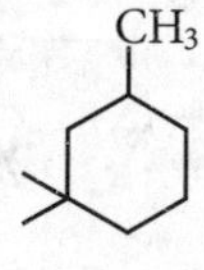

(b) 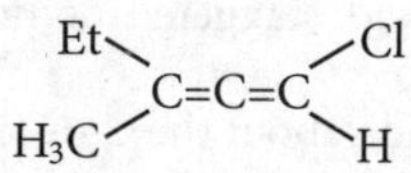

(c) 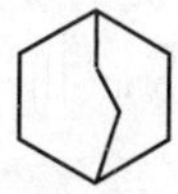

(d) 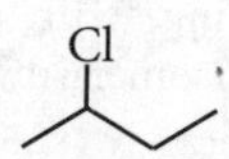

34. The pair of compounds with correct relation is:

(a) 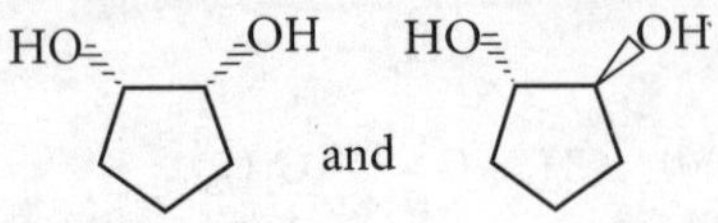

Diastereomers

(b) 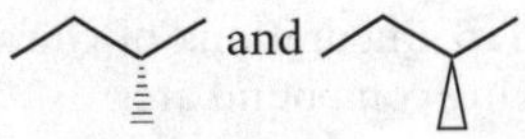

Enantiomers

(c) 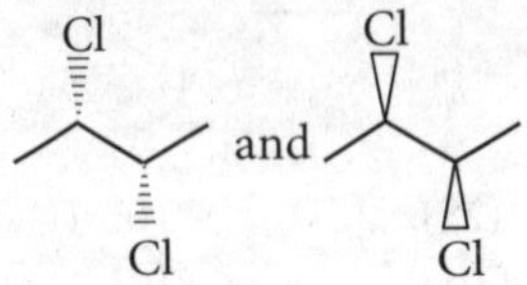

Diastereomers

(d) 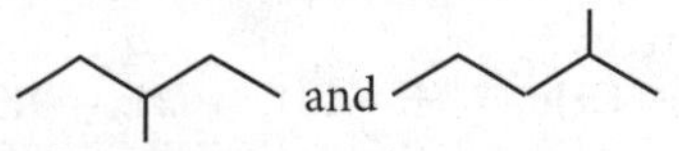

Chain isomers

35. Optical and geometrical isomerism can be shown by:

(a) 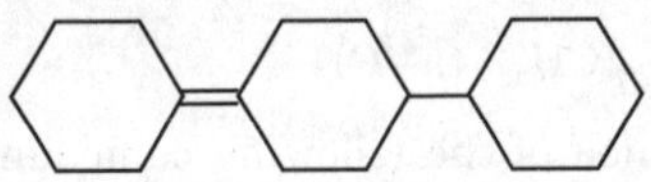

(b) 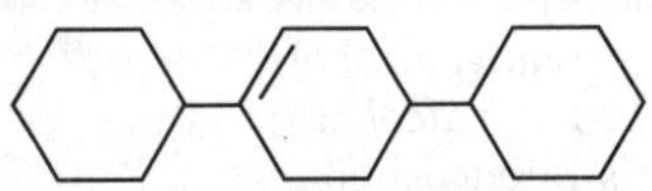

(c) 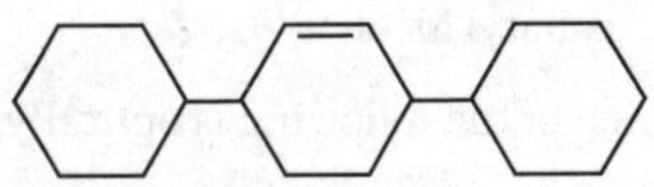

(d) 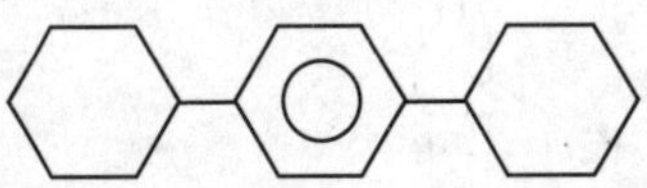

36. The eclipsed and staggered conformation of ethane is due to:
(a) Free rotation about the C–C single bond
(b) Restricted rotation about the C–C single bond
(c) Absence of rotation about the C–C bond
(d) None of the above

37. Which of the following will show both geometrical and optical isomerism?

(a) $CH_2=CH-CH(Cl)(Br)$

(b) $CH_3-CH=CH-CH=C=CH-CH_3$

(c) $CH_3-CH=CH-CH(Me)-CH_3$

(d) 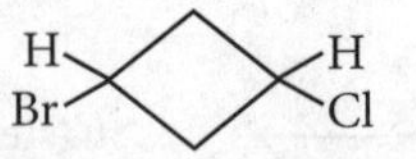

38. How many stereoisomers are possible with the following structure?

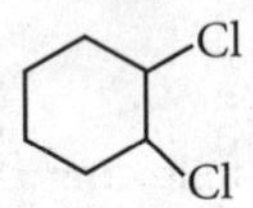

(a) 1 (b) 2
(c) 3 (d) 4

39. The number of structural isomers for C_3H_9N is:
(a) 3 (b) 4
(c) 5 (d) 2

40. The molecular formula $C_5H_{10}O$ can have:
(a) 6-aldehyde, 4-ketone
(b) 5-aldehyde, 3-ketone
(c) 4-aldehyde, 3-ketone
(d) 5-aldehyde, 2-ketone

41. **Statement I:** Neopentyl bromide and 2-bromo-2-methylbutane are enantiomers.
Statement II: Both have the same molecular formula as well as structural formula.
(a) Both Statement I and Statement II are incorrect
(b) Statement I is correct but Statement II is incorrect
(c) Statement I is incorrect but Statement II is correct
(d) Both Statement I and Statement II are correct

42. In the following pairs of compounds/conformational isomers, in which one is (II) more stable than (I)?

(a) 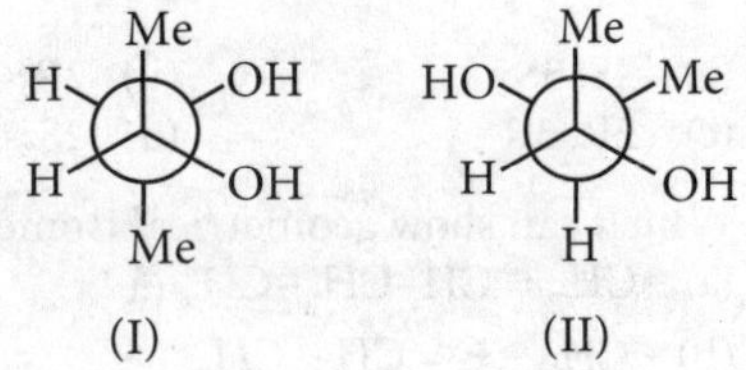

(I) (II)

(b) 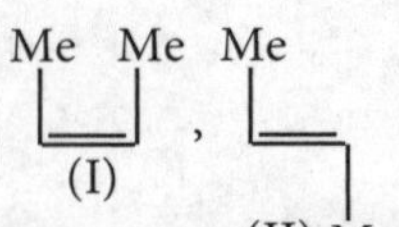

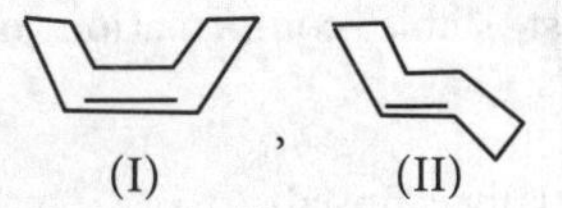

(c) (I) , (II)

(d) All of these

43. **Statement I:** Diastereomers are not mirror images of each other.
Statement II: Diastereomers may be optically active.
(a) Both Statement I and Statement II are incorrect
(b) Statement I is correct but Statement II is incorrect
(c) Statement I is incorrect but Statement II is correct
(d) Both Statement I and Statement II are correct

44. **Statement I:** Racemic mixture is optically inactive.
Statement II: Racemic mixture is a mixture of meso structures.
(a) Both Statement I and Statement II are incorrect
(b) Statement I is correct but Statement II is incorrect
(c) Statement I is incorrect but Statement II is correct
(d) Both Statement I and Statement II are correct

45. The compound which possess a centre of symmetry is:

(a) 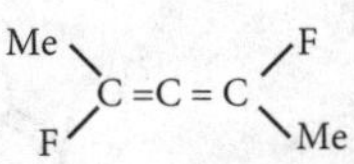 (b) 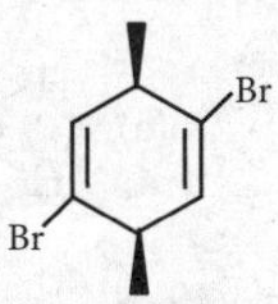

(c) 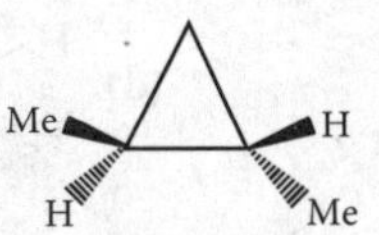 (d) 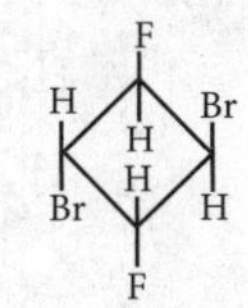

46. **Statement I:** An organic compound is optically active only when its mirror image is non-superimposable irrespective of whether it contains a chiral carbon atom or not.
Statement II: Organic compounds which do not contain chiral carbon atoms cannot be optically active.
(a) Both Statement I and Statement II are incorrect
(b) Statement I is correct but Statement II is incorrect
(c) Statement I is incorrect but Statement II is correct
(d) Both Statement I and Statement II are correct

47. The following compounds are related as:

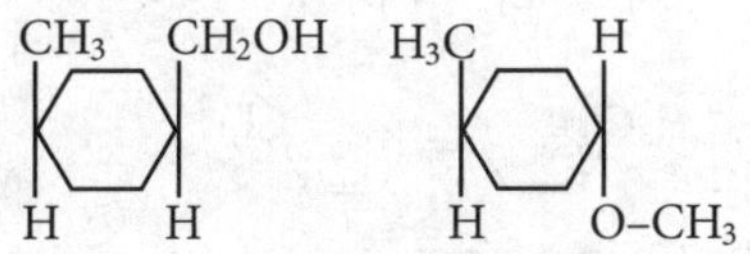

(a) Geometrical isomers
(b) Metamers
(c) Position isomers
(d) Functional isomers

48. Which of the following compounds has non-zero dipole moment?

(a) 

(b) $H_3C-C\equiv C-CH_3$

(c) 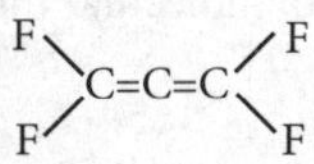

(d) 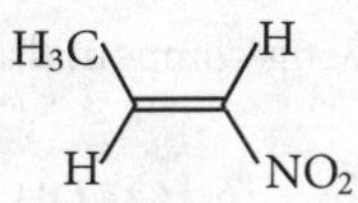

49. Among the following, the chiral compound is:

(A) 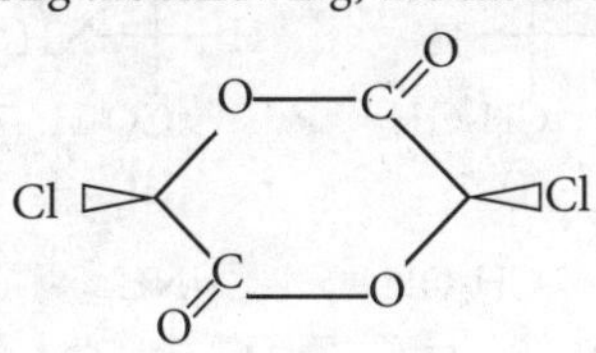

(B) 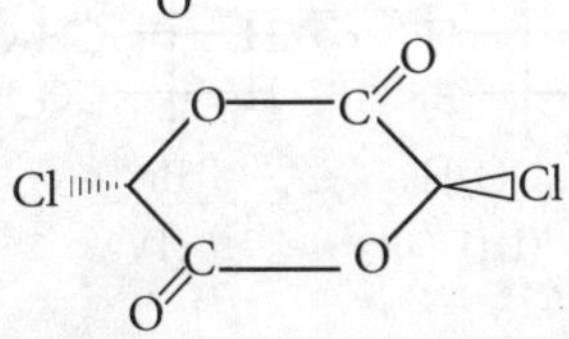

(a) Only A (b) Only B
(c) Both A and B (d) None A and B

50. Which of the given molecules/species is chiral?

(a) 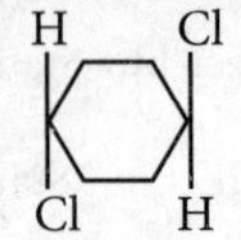

(b) 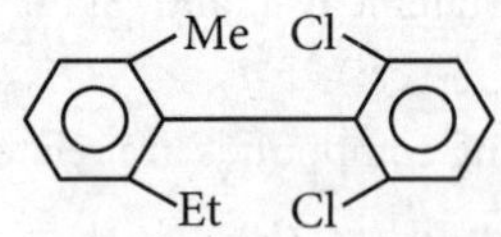

(c) 

(d) Ceiling fan

51. Which of the following statements can be true for the compound filled in a polarimeter tube?

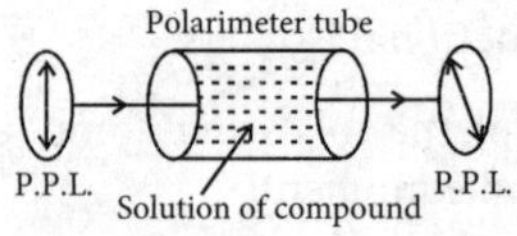

(a) Compound does not show optical isomerism.
(b) Compound is optically inactive.
(c) Solution is an equimolar mixture of d and l isomers.
(d) Compound is optically active.

52. How many isomers of molecular formula C_5H_{10} are optically active?

(a) 4 (b) 5
(c) 3 (d) 2

53. Among the following compounds, the pair of diastereomers is:

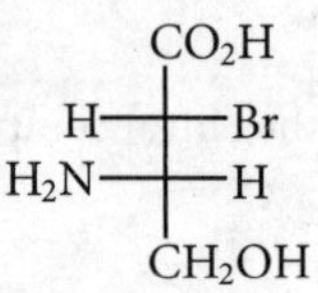
(I)

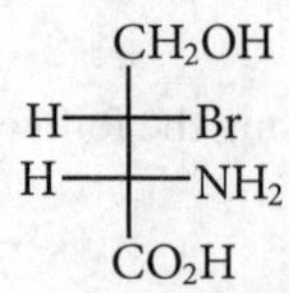
(II)

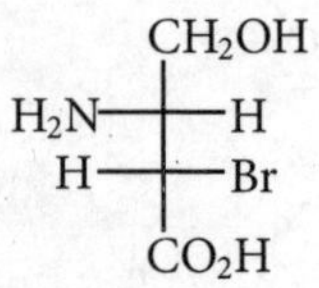
(III)

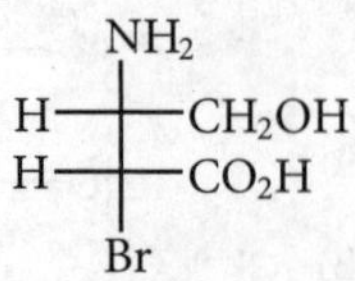
(IV)

(a) I and IV (b) I and III
(c) II and III (d) II and IV

54. The most stable conformation of 2-fluoro-ethanol is:
(a) Gauche
(b) Partially eclipsed
(c) Fully eclipsed
(d) Anti

55. Which of the following is a pair of enantiomers?

(a) 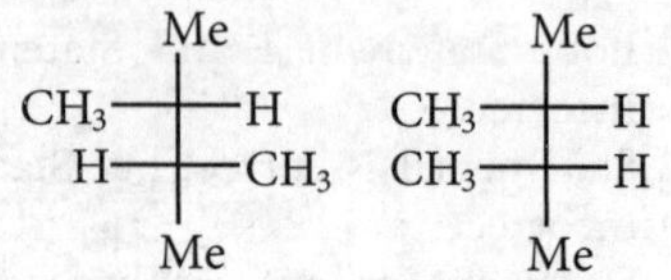

(b) 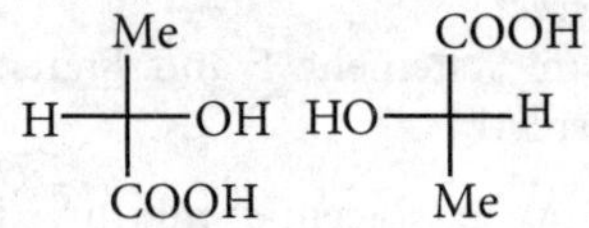

(c) 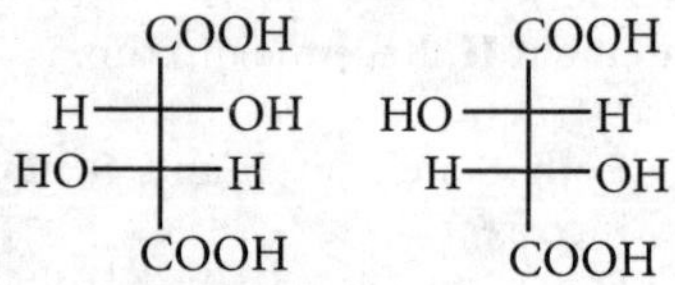

(d) 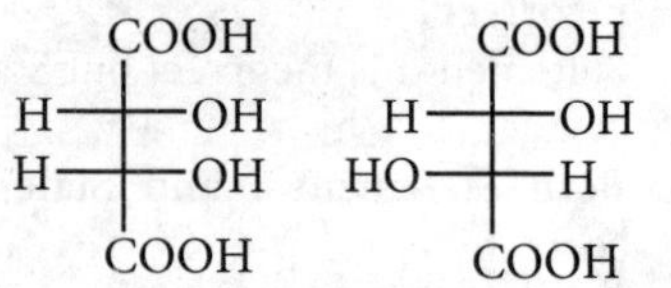

56. Gauche conformation of pentane is:

(a) 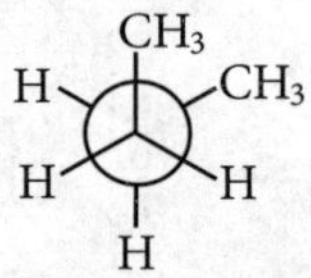

(b) 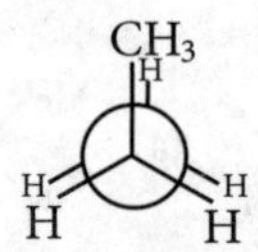

(c) 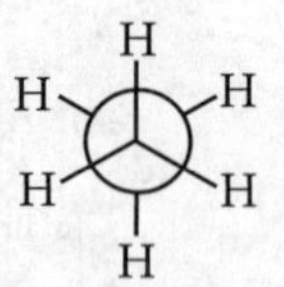

(d) 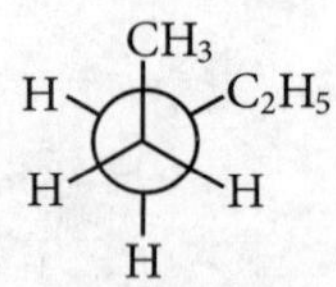

57. Which of the following compounds can show geometrical and optical isomerism?
(a) 3-Methyl-1-pentene
(b) 4-Methyl-2-hexene
(c) 3-Methyl-2-pentene
(d) 2-Methyl-1-pentene

58. **Statement I:** 1,2-Propadiene exhibits optical isomerism.

Statement II: It has one chiral carbon.
(a) Both Statement I and Statement II are incorrect
(b) Statement I is correct but Statement II is incorrect
(c) Statement I is incorrect but Statement II is correct
(d) Both Statement I and Statement II are correct

59. In the complete rotation of butane from 0° to 360°, gauche conformation appears:
(a) Once (b) Twice
(c) Thrice (d) Four times

60. In the following structures, which two forms are staggered conformations of ethane?

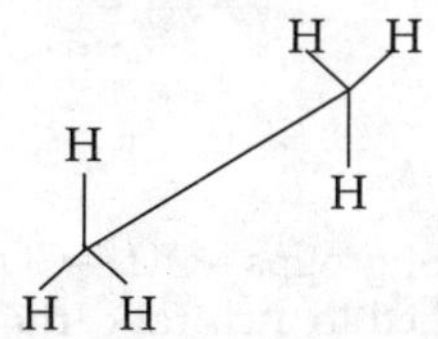
(1)

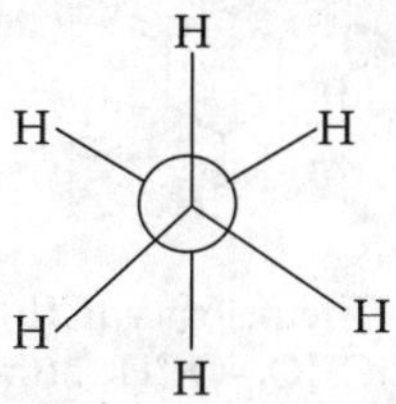
(2)

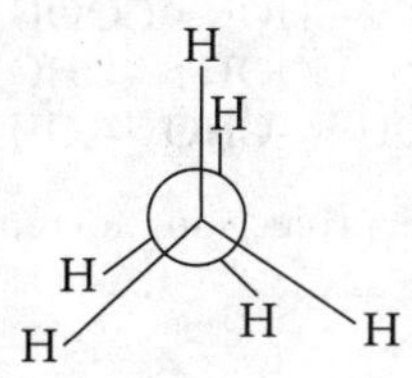
(3)

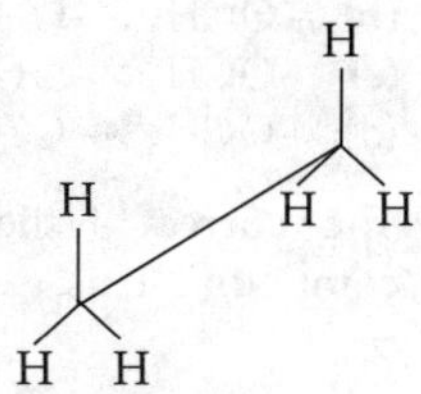
(4)

(a) 1 and 4 (b) 2 and 3
(c) 1 and 2 (d) 1 and 3

61. The most stable conformer of 2-fluoro ethanol is:

(a) 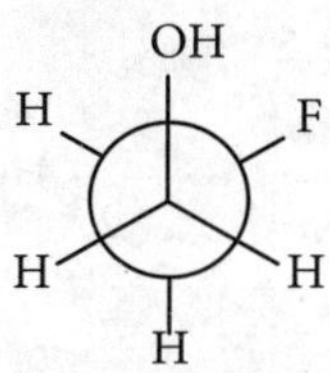

(b) 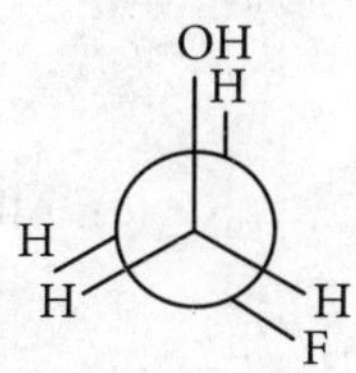

(c) 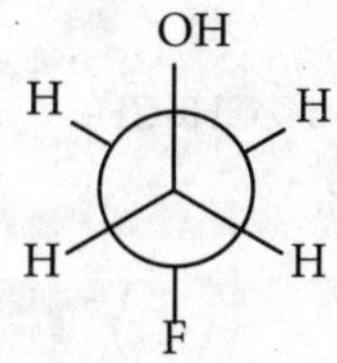

(d) 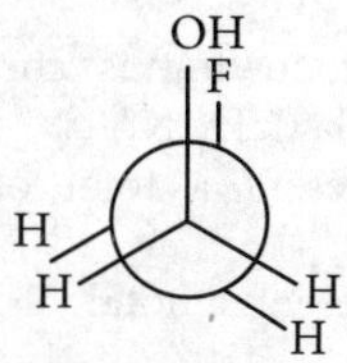

62. For the Newman projection of n-butane, which pair of (X, Y) is not possible?

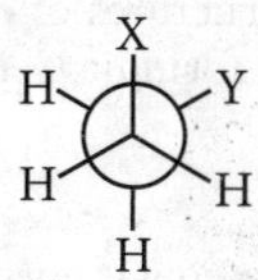

(a) (Et, H) (b) (CH_3, CH_3)
(c) (H, Et) (d) (CH_3, H)

63. The absolute configuration of the following compound is:

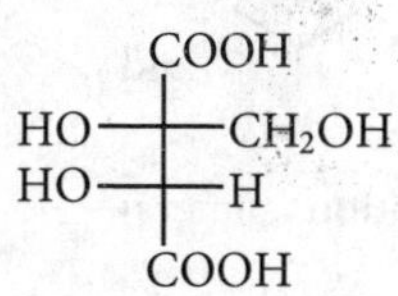

(a) 2R, 3S (b) 2S, 3R
(c) 2R, 3R (d) 2S, 3S

64. In the given compounds, which can show optical but not geometrical isomerism?

(a) 
(b) 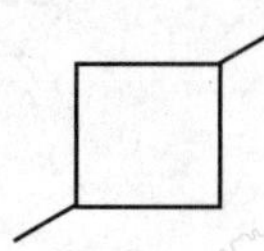
(c) 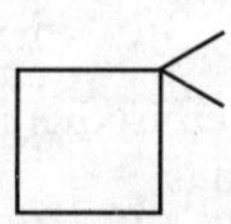
(d) 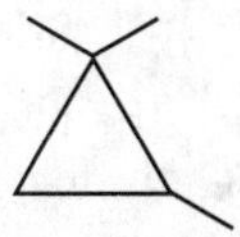

65. The total number of stereoisomers in the following compound is:

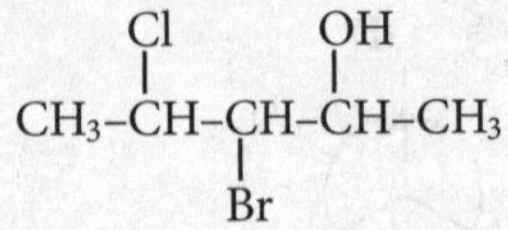

(a) 6 (b) 4
(c) 8 (d) 16

66. Which of the following is correct for the molecular formula $C_4H_{11}N$?
(a) It can represent a total of 4 primary amines.
(b) It can represent a total of 2 secondary amines.
(c) It represents a total of 1 tertiary amine.
(d) It represents a total of 8 isomeric amines.

67. How many structures of ether are possible for the molecular formula $C_4H_{10}O$?
(a) 4 (b) 5
(c) 3 (d) 2

68. Which of following is correctly matched?

(a) 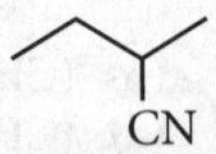 and 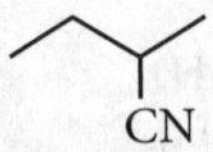
(Chain isomers)

(b) 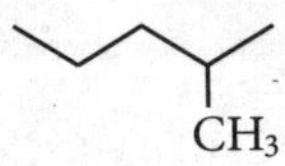 and 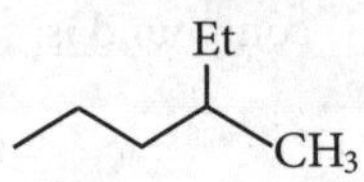
(Position isomers)

(c) 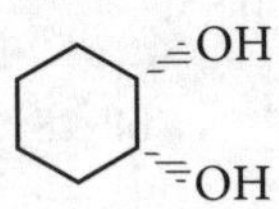 and 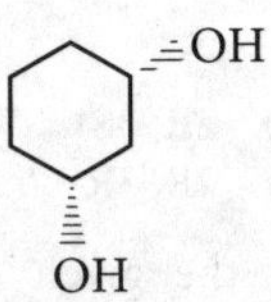
(Geometrical isomers)

(d) 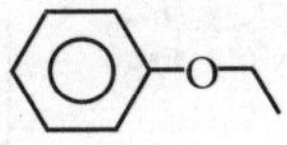 and 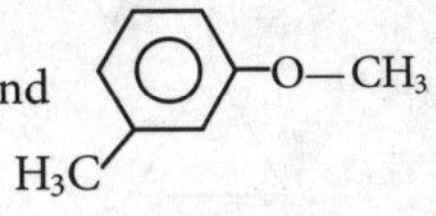
(Metamers)

69. The total number of steroisomers possible in the following compound is:

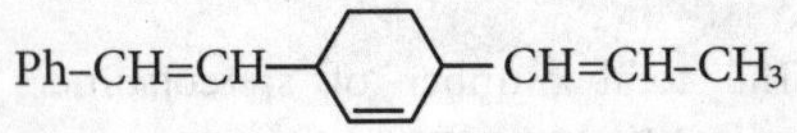

(a) 2 (b) 16
(c) 6 (d) 8

70. Which of the following compounds shows geometrical isomerism?

(a) 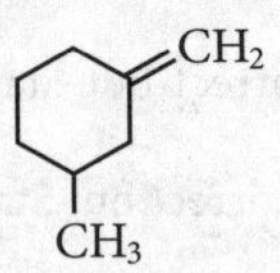

(b) 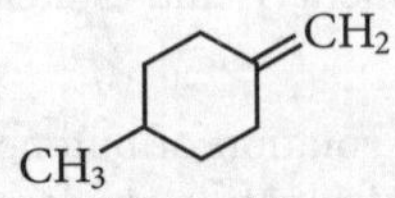

(c) 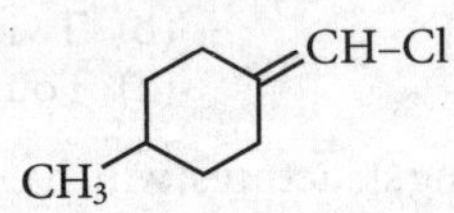

(d) 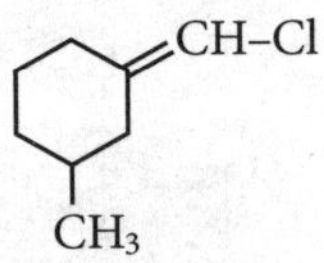

71. The priority (CIP) of groups –OH, –COOH, –CHO,–OCH_3 attached to a chiral carbon is in the order:
(a) –OH > –COOH > –CHO > –OCH_3
(b) –OCH_3 > –OH > –CHO > –COOH
(c) –OCH_3 > –OH > –COOH > –CHO
(d) –OCH_3 > –COOH > –CHO > –OH

72. The correct Fisher projection formula for compound 'P' is:

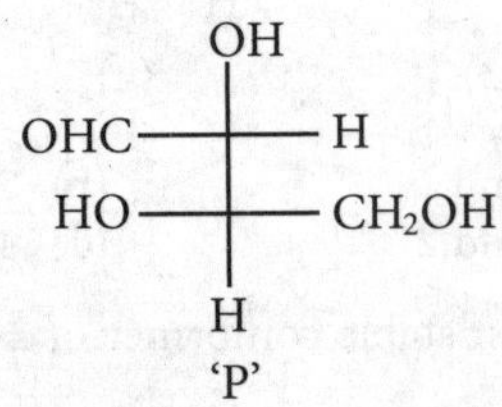
'P'

(a) 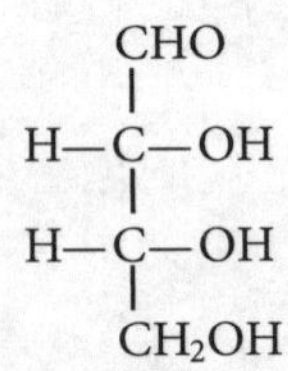

(b) 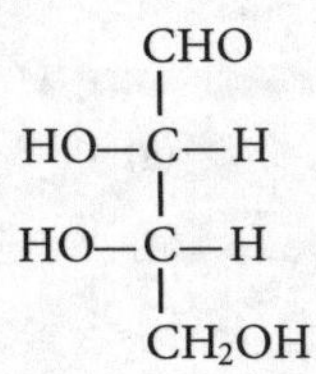

(c) 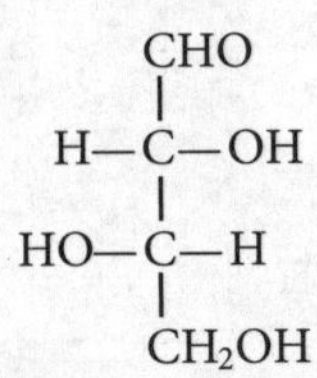

(d) All of these

73. Which of the following is optically active?

(a) 

(b) 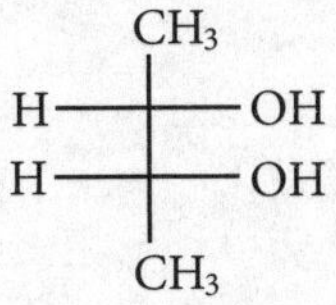

(c) 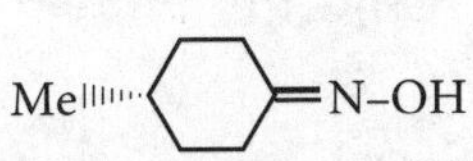

(d) 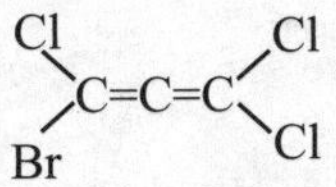

74. Which of the following is a chiral molecule?

(a) 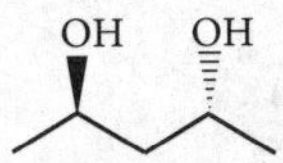

(b) 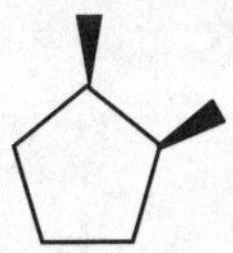

(c) 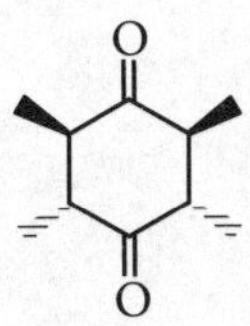

(d) 

75. The compound which shows both optical and geometrical isomerism is:

(a) 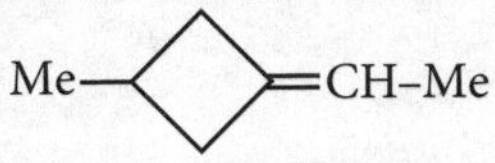

(b) 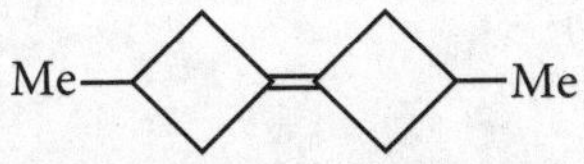

(c) CHO–CHOH–CHOH–CH_2OH

(d) 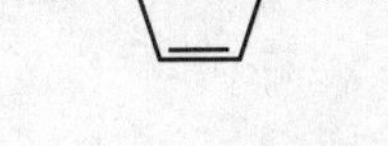

76. Which of the following compounds is optically active?

(a) 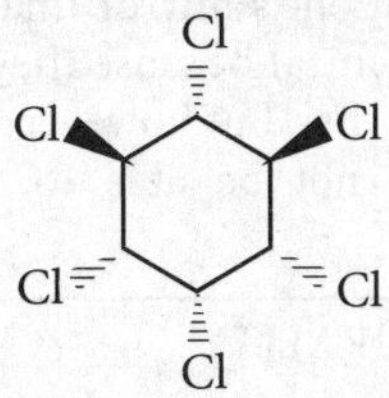

(b) 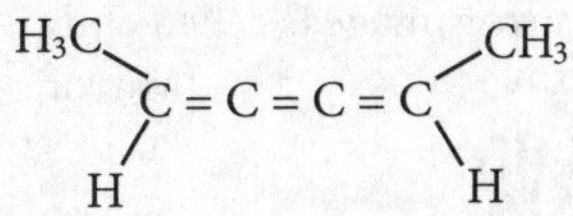

(c) 

(d) CH_2Cl_2

77. Which of the following molecules is expected to rotate plane-polarized light?

(a) 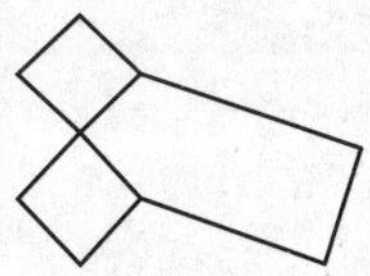

(b) 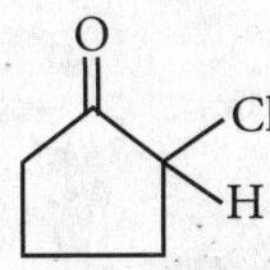

(c) 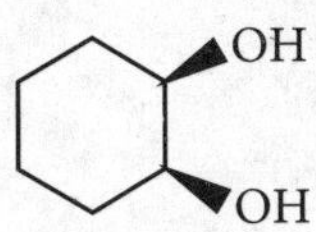

(d) 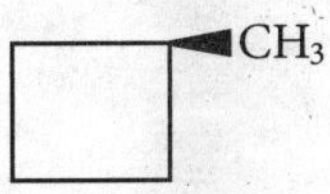

78. Which of the following has 'E' configuration?

(a) 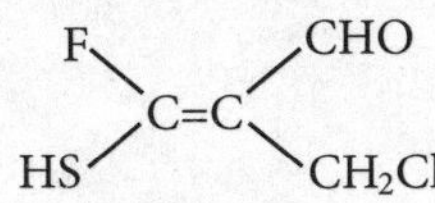

(b) 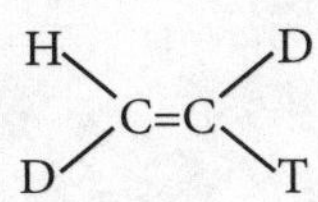

(c) 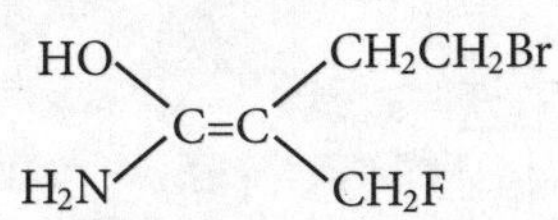

(d) 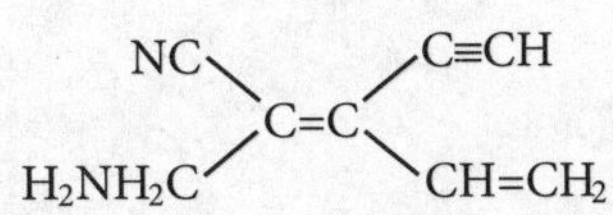

79. In chemistry, the term 'chiral' (from the Greek word for *hand*) describes the property of not overlapping with one's mirror image. Left and right hands are chiral because they are mirror images of each other, but however you reorient them, you will not be able to make them overlap.

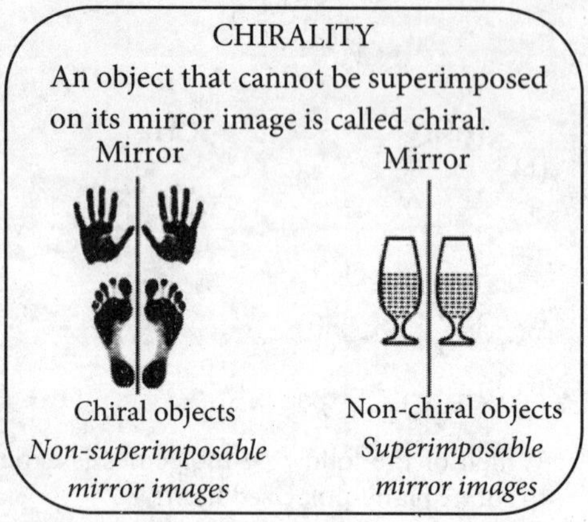

Which of the following is an achiral compound?

(a) 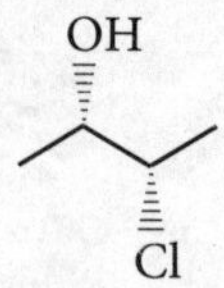

(b) 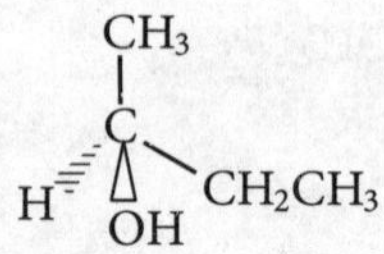

(c) 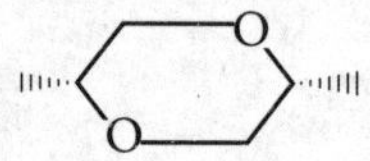

(d) 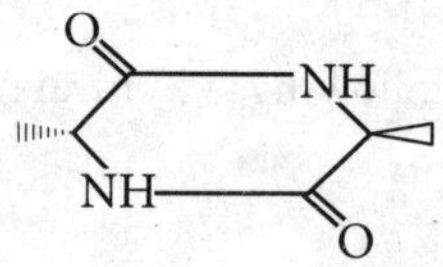

Answer Key

Level-1

1. (a)	**2.** (d)	**3.** (b)	**4.** (a)	**5.** (a)	**6.** (d)	**7.** (c)	**8.** (c)
9. (c)	**10.** (c)	**11.** (d)	**12.** (c)	**13.** (c)	**14.** (b)	**15.** (a)	**16.** (b)
17. (d)	**18.** (d)	**19.** (c)	**20.** (c)	**21.** (d)	**22.** (b)	**23.** (c)	**24.** (a)
25. (d)	**26.** (d)	**27.** (d)	**28.** (d)	**29.** (c)	**30.** (a)	**31.** (b)	**32.** (d)
33. (a)	**34.** (c)	**35.** (b)	**36.** (c)	**37.** (d)	**38.** (a)	**39.** (a)	**40.** (c)
41. (d)	**42.** (c)	**43.** (a)	**44.** (d)	**45.** (d)	**46.** (c)	**47.** (d)	**48.** (b)
49. (b)	**50.** (d)	**51.** (d)	**52.** (a)	**53.** (d)	**54.** (d)	**55.** (c)	**56.** (d)
57. (a)	**58.** (a)	**59.** (d)	**60.** (d)	**61.** (a)	**62.** (b)	**63.** (a)	**64.** (d)
65. (c)	**66.** (d)	**67.** (a)	**68.** (c)	**69.** (c)	**70.** (d)	**71.** (c)	**72.** (b)
73. (d)	**74.** (b)	**75.** (a)	**76.** (c)	**77.** (b)	**78.** (b)	**79.** (d)	**80.** (c)
81. (a)	**82.** (c)	**83.** (d)	**84.** (a)	**85.** (b)	**86.** (b)	**87.** (c)	**88.** (c)
89. (d)	**90.** (c)	**91.** (d)	**92.** (a)	**93.** (b)	**94.** (d)	**95.** (b)	

Level-2

1. (b)	**2.** (d)	**3.** (d)	**4.** (a)	**5.** (a)	**6.** (b)	**7.** (b)	**8.** (a)
9. (c)	**10.** (a)	**11.** (a)	**12.** (d)	**13.** (d)	**14.** (a)	**15.** (d)	**16.** (c)
17. (c)	**18.** (b)	**19.** (b)	**20.** (b)	**21.** (d)	**22.** (c)	**23.** (d)	**24.** (b)
25. (b)	**26.** (a)	**27.** (b)	**28.** (d)	**29.** (b)	**30.** (a)	**31.** (b)	**32.** (c)
33. (c)	**34.** (a)	**35.** (c)	**36.** (a)	**37.** (b)	**38.** (c)	**39.** (b)	**40.** (c)
41. (a)	**42.** (b)	**43.** (d)	**44.** (b)	**45.** (d)	**46.** (b)	**47.** (d)	**48.** (d)
49. (a)	**50.** (d)	**51.** (d)	**52.** (d)	**53.** (a)	**54.** (a)	**55.** (c)	**56.** (d)
57. (b)	**58.** (a)	**59.** (b)	**60.** (c)	**61.** (a)	**62.** (d)	**63.** (b)	**64.** (d)
65. (c)	**66.** (d)	**67.** (c)	**68.** (d)	**69.** (b)	**70.** (d)	**71.** (c)	**72.** (a)
73. (c)	**74.** (a)	**75.** (d)	**76.** (c)	**77.** (b)	**78.** (c)	**79.** (d)	

Solutions

Level-1

1. Parent carbon chains are different; so chain isomers.

2. 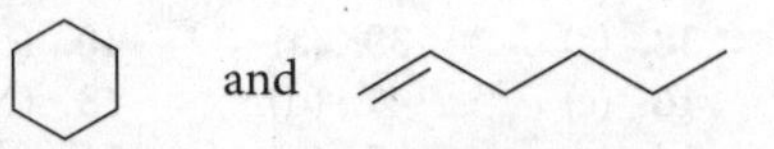

Cycloalkane DU = 1 and Olefins (alkene) DU = 1

Isomers having the same molecular formula

4. For position isomers, the functional groups are the same.

5. First count the number of carbon atoms.

6. Functional groups with parent chain and side chain must be the same. Only the position of the functional group, multiple bond or substituent is different.

7. At least one α-hydrogen must be on sp3 carbon and must conjugate with the polar π bond.

8. $\underbrace{CH_3}_{1\,C} - O - \underbrace{CH_2 - CH_2 - CH_3}_{3\,C}$ and

$\underbrace{CH_3 - CH_2}_{2\,C} - O - \underbrace{CH_2 - CH_3}_{2\,C}$

9. The positions of methyl on the parent chain are different.

10. For isomers, the molecular formula will be the same. The 'C' number is different.

12. 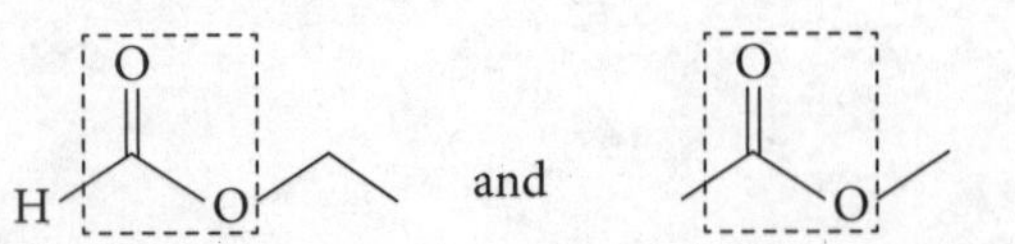

zero 'C' 2 'C' and 'C' 1 'C'

Change in carbon numbers in bivalent group

14. 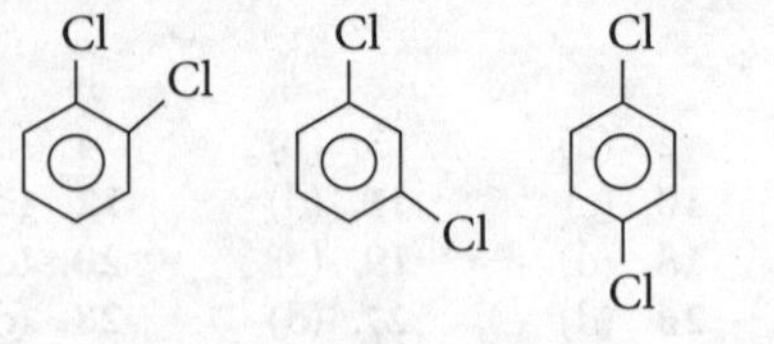

15. Change in carbon number in bivalent position

16. 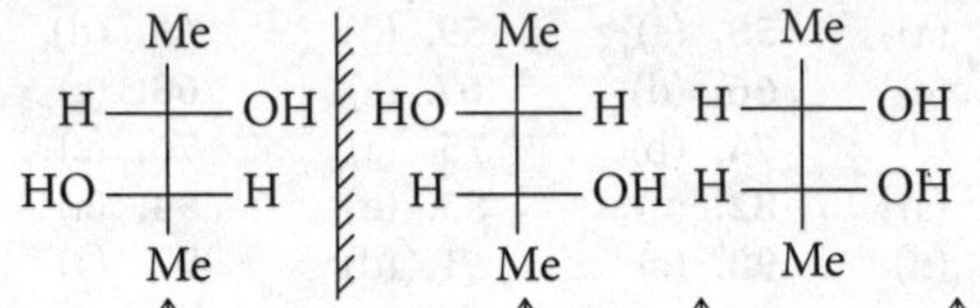

Active d and l = 2 Meso (inactive)

17. $CH_3 - CH_2 - \overset{H}{\underset{CH_3}{C^*}} - COOH$ Chiral carbon

18. Achiral means inactive compound

$\underset{Br}{CH_2} - COOH$ (Not chiral carbon)

20. C–C–C–C–C–C and

$C-C-\underset{C}{C}-C-C$ [C.I.]

$C-\underset{C}{C}-C-C-C$ and $C-C-\underset{C}{C}-C-C$ [P.I.]

21.

—O—	Ether	All three are bivalent F. group
—NH—	Secondary Amine	
$-\overset{O}{\overset{\|\|}{C}}-$	Ketone	

22. 3-Ethyl-2-methylpentane has 8 carbons but option (b) has 6 carbons. So, that is not an isomer.

23. The parent carbon chains are different in both alcohols. So they are chain isomers, not position isomers.

24.

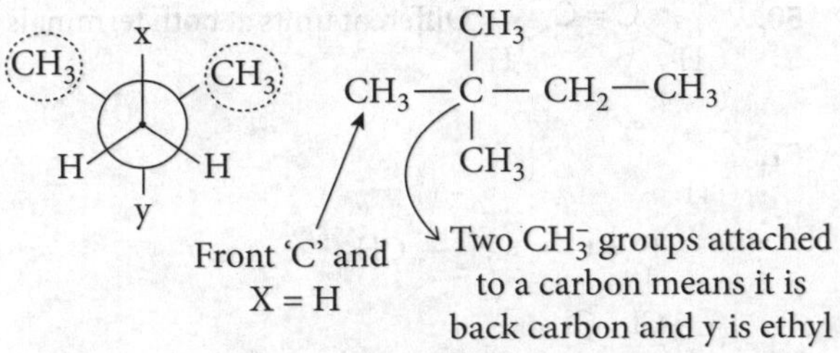

25. Conformers have free rotation about a single bond. So they can form infinite conformers.

27.

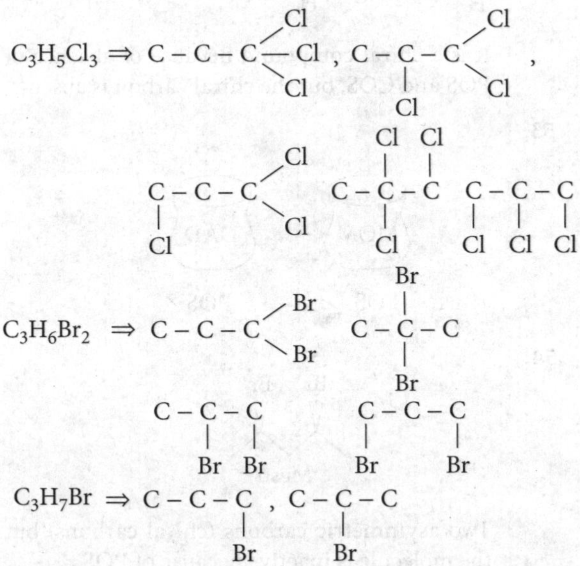

28. Chiral carbon containing

29. Number of carbons must be the same for isomers. Change in carbon number at bivalent position is called metamer.

30.

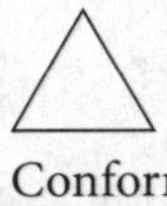

Conformers are not possible, so all the atoms are in a plane.

31. The parent carbon chains are different. So, CI, not PI.

32. DU is different, so the molecular formula is different.

33. Parent carbon chains are the same, but the position of –OH is different.

34.

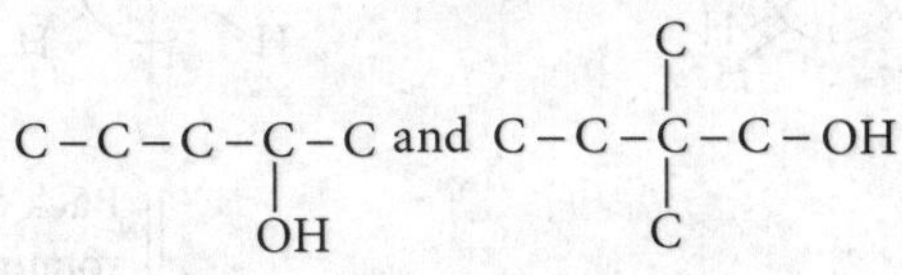

Different PCC (parent carbon chains)

35. Polyvalent functional groups (like –O–,

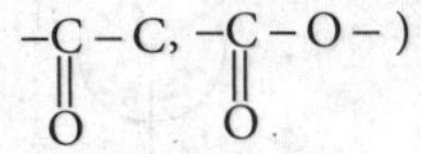

) show metamerism.

36.

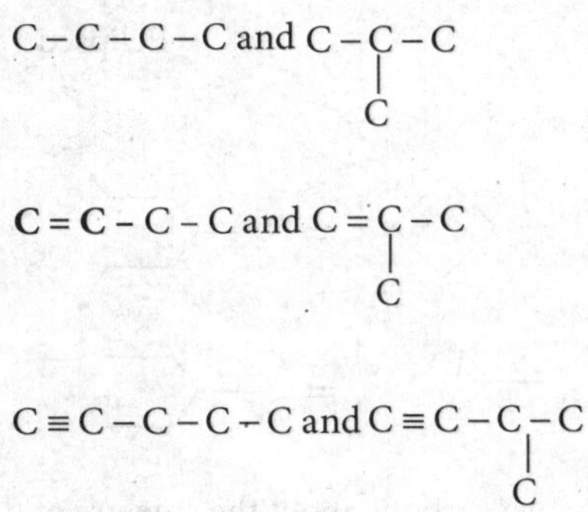

37.

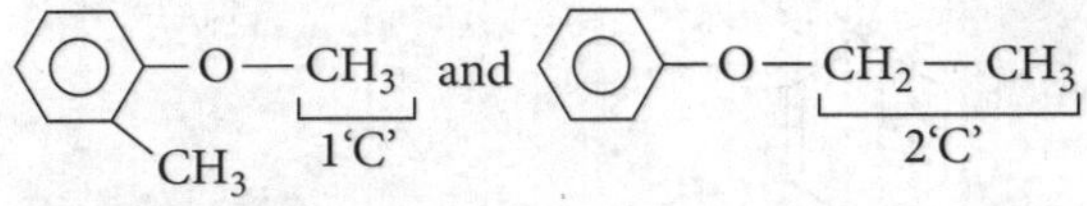

38. Degree of unsaturation is the same for isomers.

39.

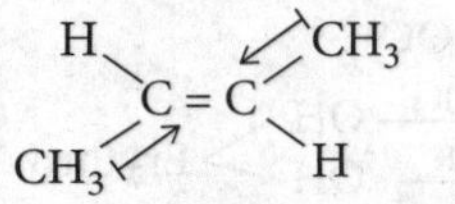

, $\mu = 0$

'P' has trans and E configuration and 'Q' will be the opposite of 'P'.

40. Unsymmetrical carbonyl compound gives two different geometrical isomers, syn and anti.

41. C – C – O – C and C – C – C – OH
DU = 0 and one oxygen; DU = 0 and one oxygen

42. Change on bivalent terminals

43.

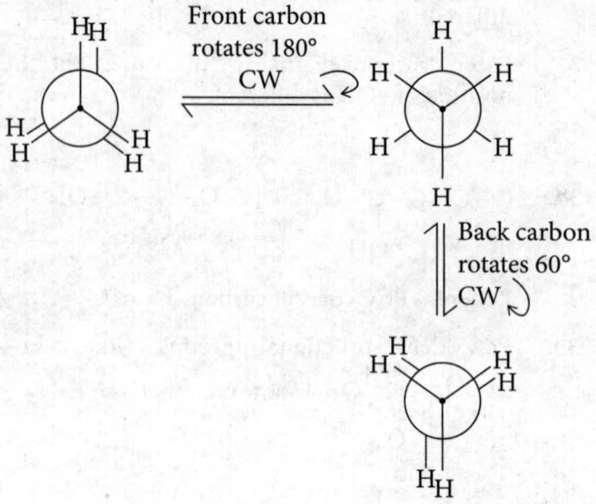

Eclipsed

44.

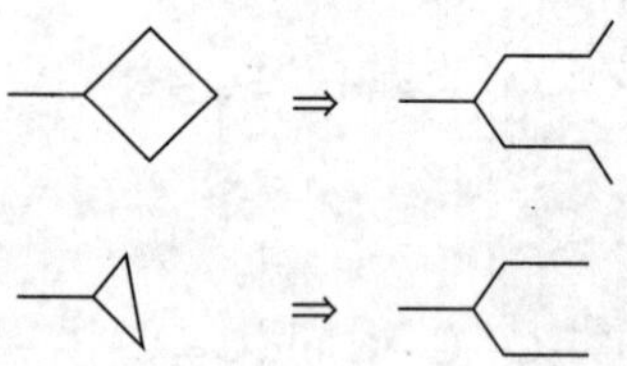

45. The two carbons about the ring are of different units.

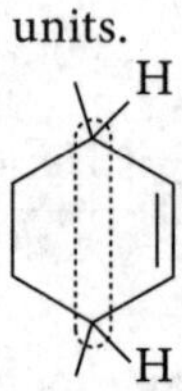

46.

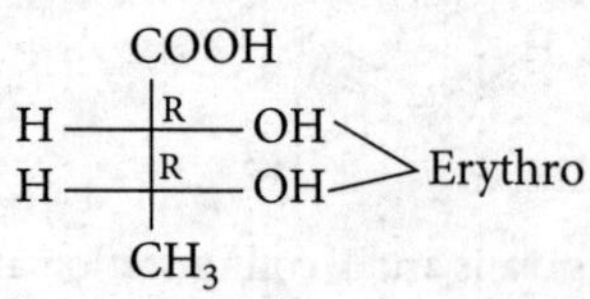

But not meso because POS and COS are absent.

48.

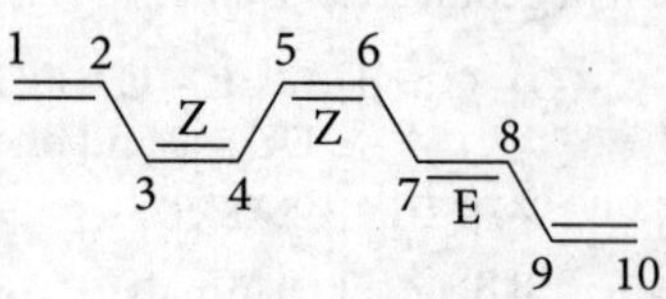

49.  Double bond is restricted.

50. 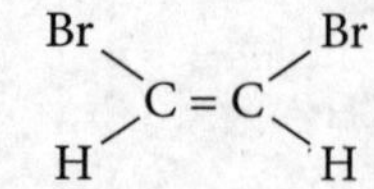 Different units at both terminals

51.

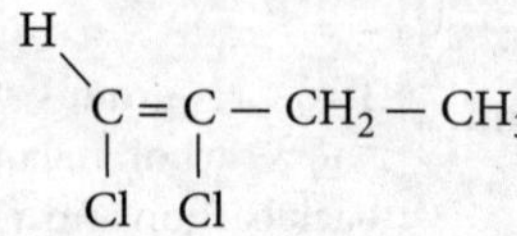

→ Different units at both terminals.

52. 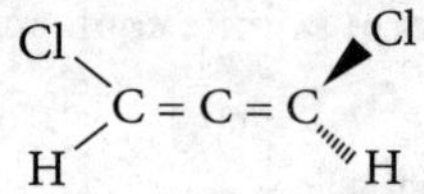

It is a chiral compound because of absence of POS and COS, but the chiral carbon is absent.

53.

POS ✓ POS ×

54.

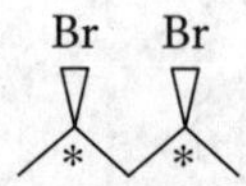

Meso

Two asymmetric carbons (chiral carbons) but the molecule is inactive because of POS.

57.

Two carbons (sp^3 C) of the ring have different units.

58.

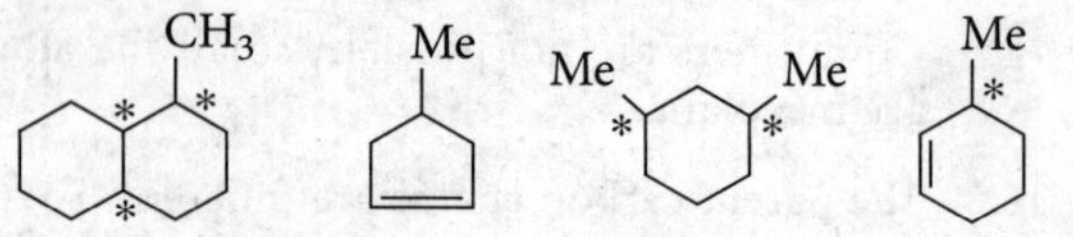

3 0 2 1

59.

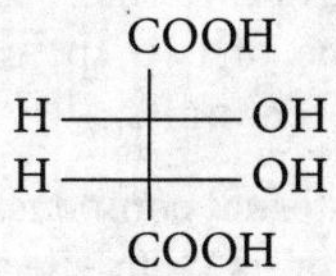

Due to the presence of two chiral carbons, meso-tartaric acid shows optical isomerism but is an inactive optical isomer.

60.

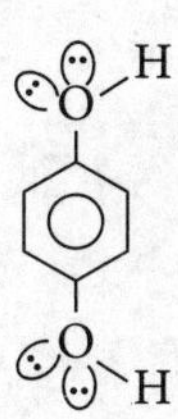

$\mu \neq 0$

61.

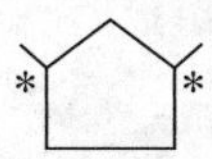

62. All the physical properties of enantiomers are the same.

63. At least two sp^3 carbons of different units or groups is required to show GI in the ring.

64.

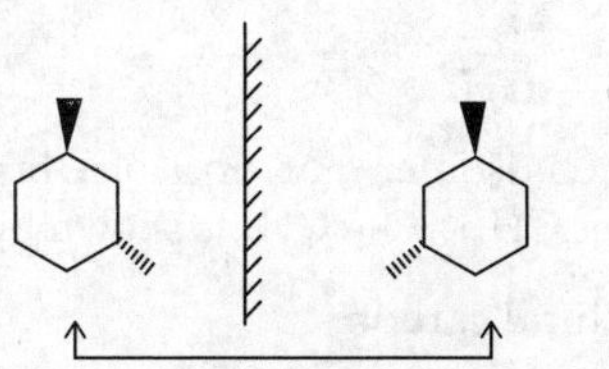

Enantiomers = Resolvable

65. II and IV are geometrical isomers of each other [Z and E]

66. Same methyl group

67.

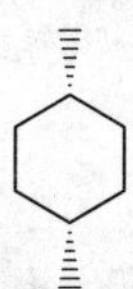

← POS ✓
COS ×

68.

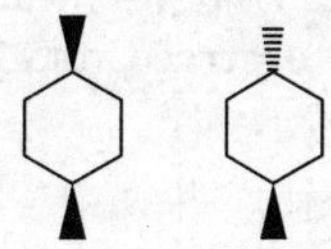

Cis Trans

69. Chiral carbon containing symmetrical molecules can show meso form.

$CH_3 - \overset{*}{C}H(OH) - CH_2 - \overset{*}{C}H(OH) - CH_3 \rightarrow$

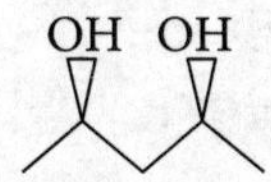

71.

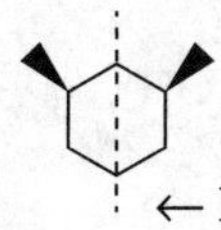

← POS ✓

72.

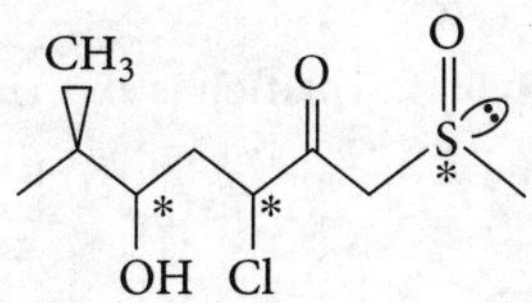

74.

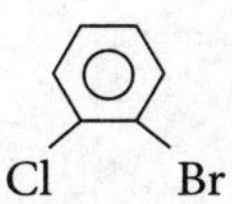

Whole molecule is planar, so it has POS.

76.

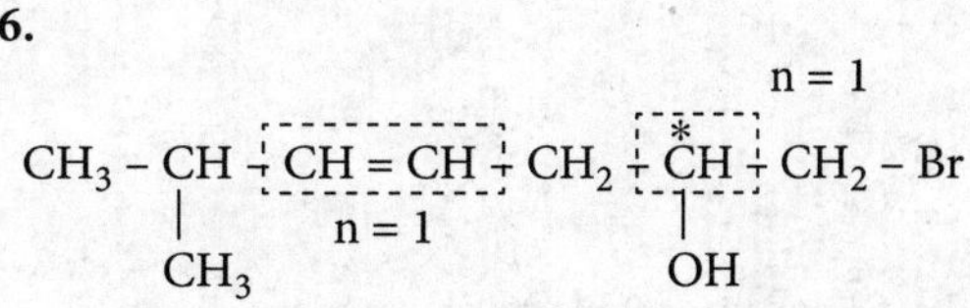

n = 2 Unsymmetrical molecule. So
$2^n = 2^2 = 4$

77.

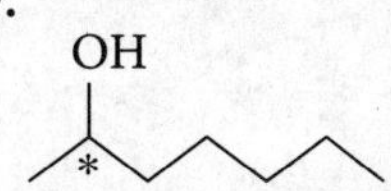

and

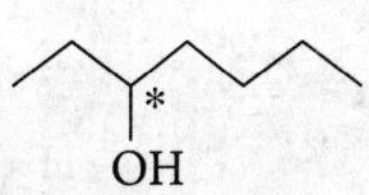

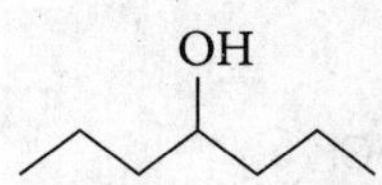

← Not chiral carbon

78. Mixture is 100% of (–) means mixture is laevo only. So the observed rotation of the mixture will be –158°.

79. Due to ring 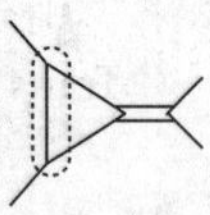

80.

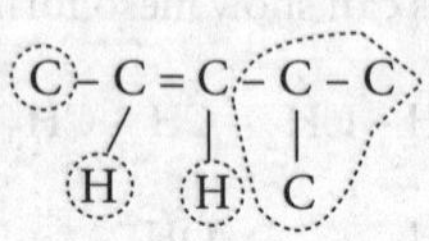

Different units at both terminals

81.

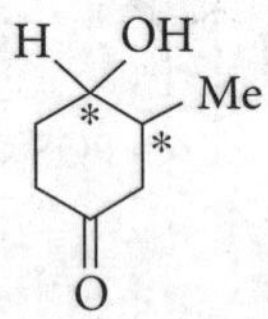

82. The sign of the rotation is experimental.

83. Optically active means 100% chiral molecule.

84. 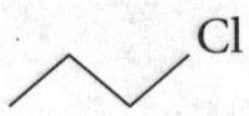 and 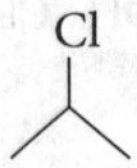

85.

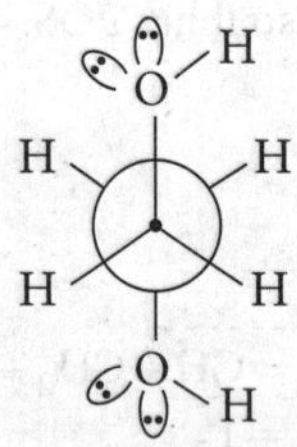

86. Super-imposable mirror image

87. 2-Chloro-2-methylbutane does not have chiral carbon, but the rest have chiral carbon.

88.

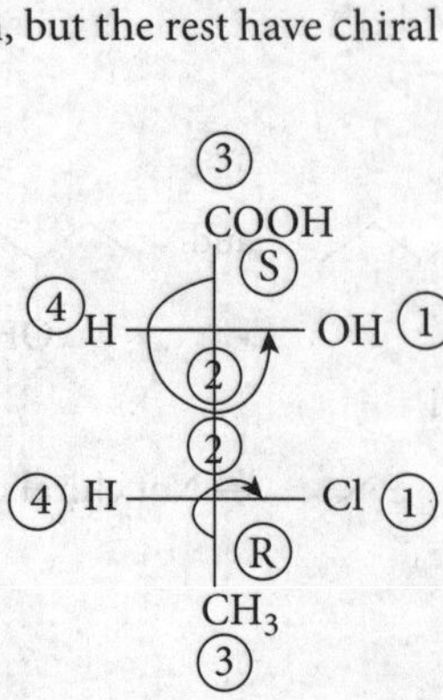

89. All have chiral carbons to show optical isomers and presence of two sp^3 carbons of the ring having different units.

90. Meso has internal compensation, so inactive or due to POS or COS. Its specific rotation is zero.

91. I shows GI due to restricted π bond. II shows OI due to chiral carbon.

92. 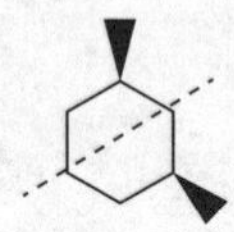 POS ✓

93. 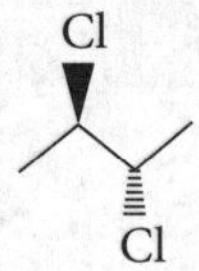 COS ✓

94. 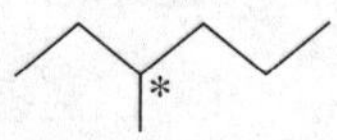

95. Chiral carbon 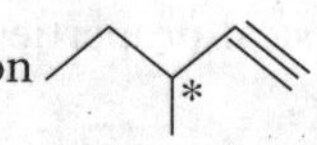

LEVEL-2

1. CH_3-CH_2-OH

Position isomer not possible, but functional isomer CH_3-O-CH_3 is shown by it.

2. Not chiral carbon

3.

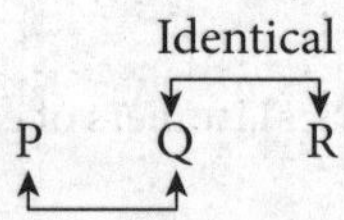

4.

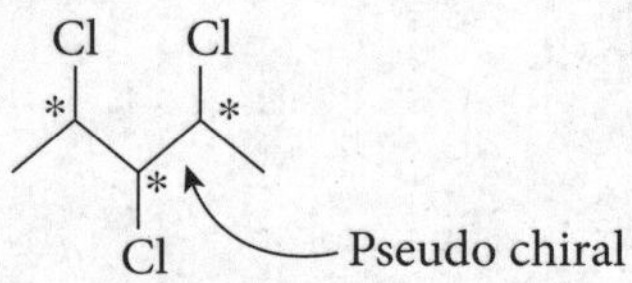

For symmetrical molecules (n = 3, odd)

$$\underbrace{2^{n-1}}_{\text{Total isomers}} - \underbrace{2^{\frac{n-1}{2}}}_{\text{Meso}} = \text{Active isomers}$$

4 – 2 = 2 (Active)

5.

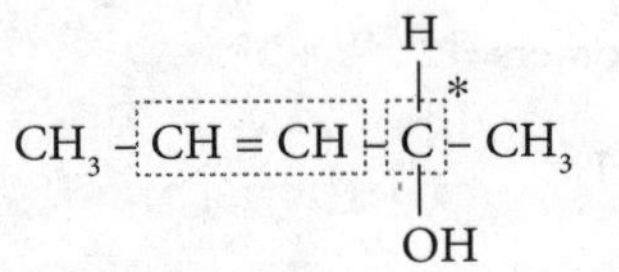

$n = 2$
Unsymmetrical molecule 4
$2^n = 2^2 = 4$

6. Find out using CIP rule

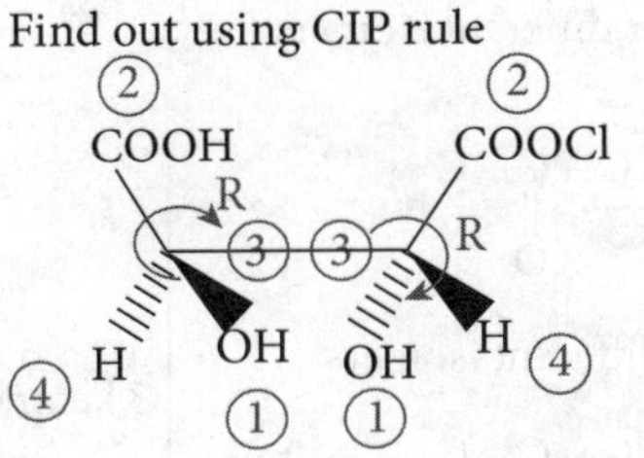

7.

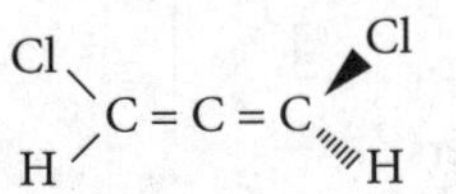

Chiral molecule but not a chiral carbon.

8. Find out using CIP rule.

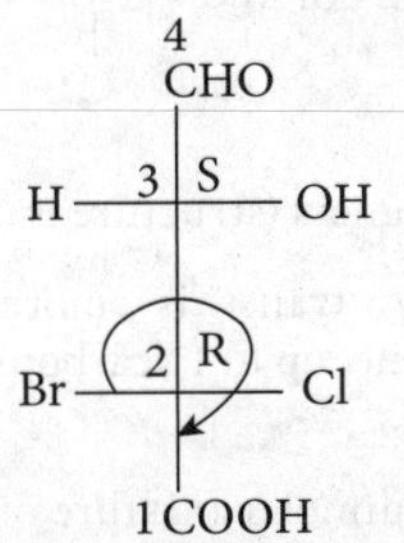

9. L-glucose will be complete mirror of D-glucose

10. Cis and trans not mirror image.

11. F and G are enol tautomer forms of E (keto form) and are geometrical isomers of each other.

12. (a) has two DU. So it is not an isomer of the rest. In (d), two carbons are of different groups; so it gives GI.

13.

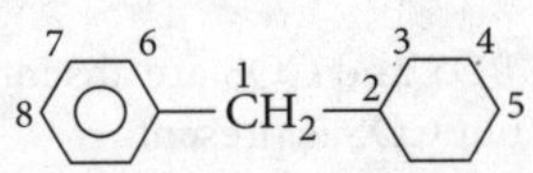

14. Using CIP rule, meso compound has one chiral 'R' and the other 'S'.

15.

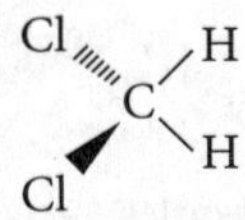

POS ✓
COS ×
AOS ✓

16.

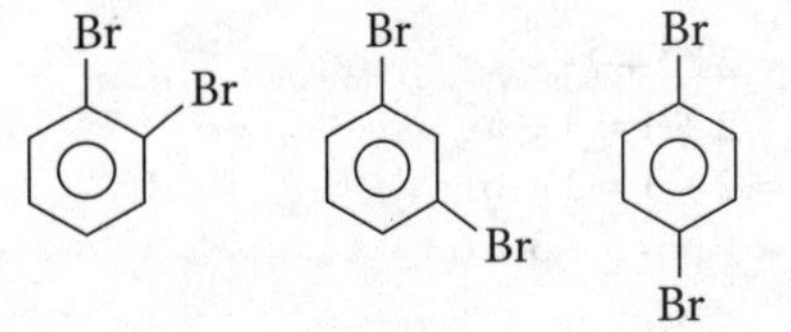

17.

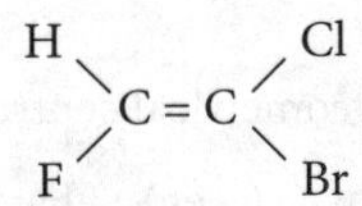

and GI

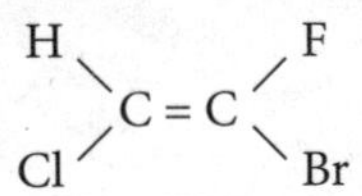

and GI

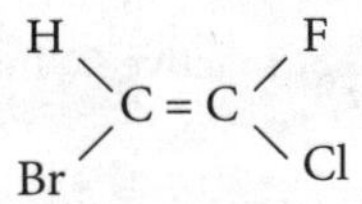

and GI

18. $n = 2$ (two chiral carbon)
Molecule is symmetrical

$= 2^{n-1} + 2^{\frac{n}{2}-1}$ = Total optical isomers

20.

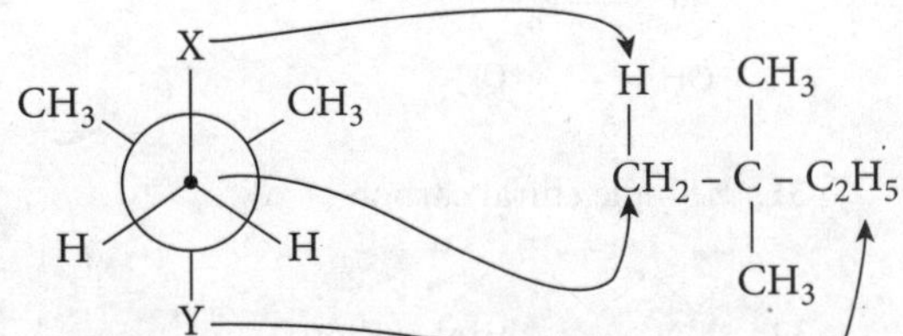

21. If POS and COS are absent, it is a chiral molecule.

22.

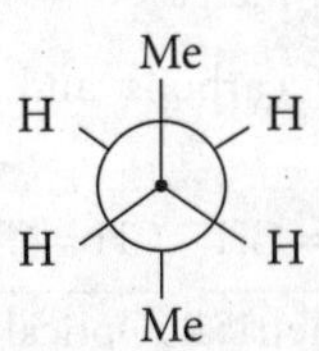

Anti form has the least steric strain and the least torsional strain.

23. $CH_3-\underset{\displaystyle CH_3}{\underset{|}{CH}} \leftarrow CH_2-Et$

24. For symmetrical molecules

n = 2 (even) for both structures, n = 2

$= 2^{n-1} + 2^{\frac{n}{2}-1}$

$= 2 + 1 = 3 \leftarrow a$

$= 2 + 1 = 3 \leftarrow b$

$a + b = 3 + 3 = 6$

25. 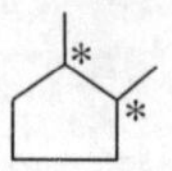

Chiral carbon and geometrical centre present.

26. Cumulated system (even) has optical isomerism.

27.

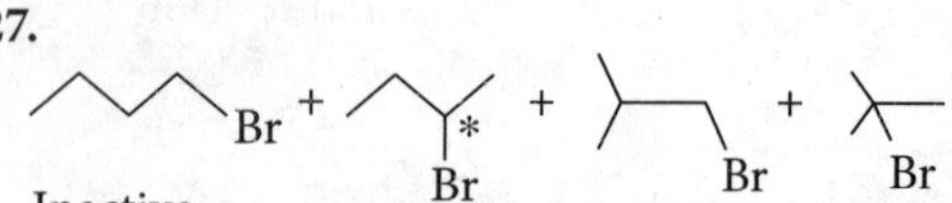

Inactive + d + *l* Active = 2 + Inactive + Inactive

28. Using CIP rule, like in Q8.

30. Using CIP rule

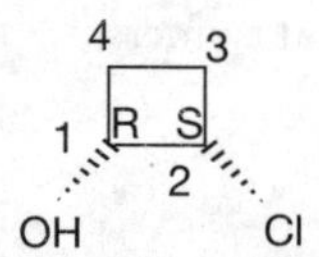

31. Single chiral carbon

32. 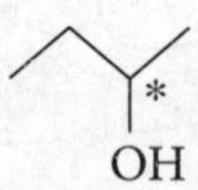 chiral carbon

33. Symmetric molecule without chiral carbon.

34. Non-mirror image

35. Two chiral carbons and geometrical centre present.

37. $CH_3 - CH = CH - CH = C = CH - CH_3$

$CH = CH$: Geometrical centre; $CH = C = CH$: Optical centre

38. Two chiral carbons (n = 2)

Optical isomers $= 2^{(n+1)} + 2^{\frac{n}{2}-1}$

39. 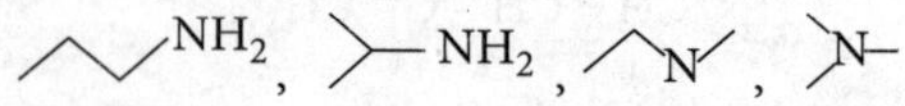

40.

$\underbrace{C-C-C-C}_{4\,C}-\underset{\displaystyle O}{\underset{\|}{C}}-H$ = 4 aldehyde

so four different isomers

$\underbrace{C-C-C}_{3\,C}-\underset{\displaystyle O}{\underset{\|}{C}}-C$] 2

so two different isomers

$\underbrace{C-C}_{2\,C}-\underset{\displaystyle O}{\underset{\|}{C}}-C-C$] 1

so single isomers

(2 + 1 = 3 ketone)

41. $C-\underset{\displaystyle C}{\underset{|}{\overset{\displaystyle C}{\overset{|}{C}}}}-C-Br$ and $C-\underset{\displaystyle C}{\underset{|}{\overset{\displaystyle Br}{\overset{|}{C}}}}-C-C$

Chain isomers (structure is different)

42. Normally trans is more stable, but in cycloalkene, up to 11 carbons, cis is more stable than trans.

44. RM is equimolar mixture of dextro and laevo. So net rotation of PPL is zero.

45. Diagonally, the same group is present at the same distance.

46. Compound can be optically active even in the absence of chiral carbon.

47. Function group is different

48. 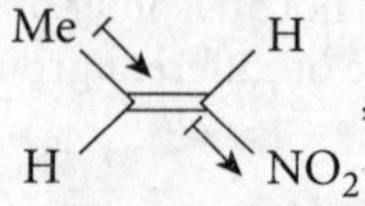

, $\mu \neq 0$

49. In [A], POS and COS are absent. In [B], POS is absent but COS is present.

50. Ceiling fan does not have POS and COS.

51. PPL rotates, then the molecule is active.

52. 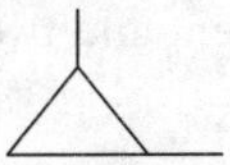

It shows two active enantiomers and one inactive meso.

53. Non-mirror image stereoisomers

54. Hydrogen bonding at gauche position.

55. Mirror image, but does not super-impose.

56. (d) has five carbons in parent carbon chain.

57.

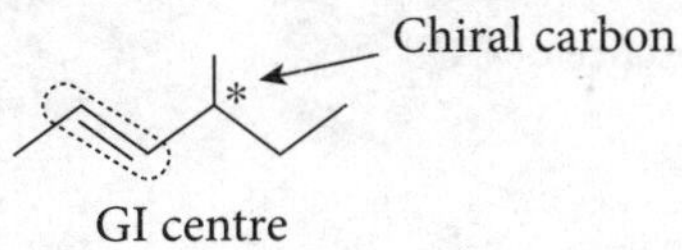

58. 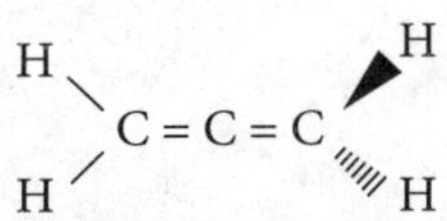

Presence of POS, so not an optical isomer.

60. Least repulsion of hydrogen atom gives staggered form.

61. Hydrogen bonding at the gauche position between hydrogen of [OH] and lone of 'F'

62.

$CH_3 - CH_2 - CH_2 - CH_3$

front carbon can be any of them

63.

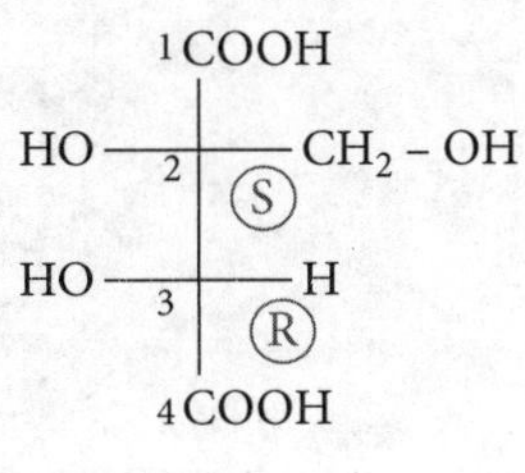

64. 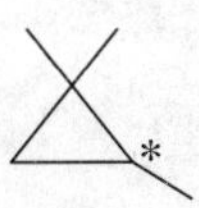

Chiral carbon but not geometrical centre in the ring because two carbons by different units are not present.

65. Three chiral carbons and the molecule is unsymmetrical. So $2 = 2^3 = 8$

66.

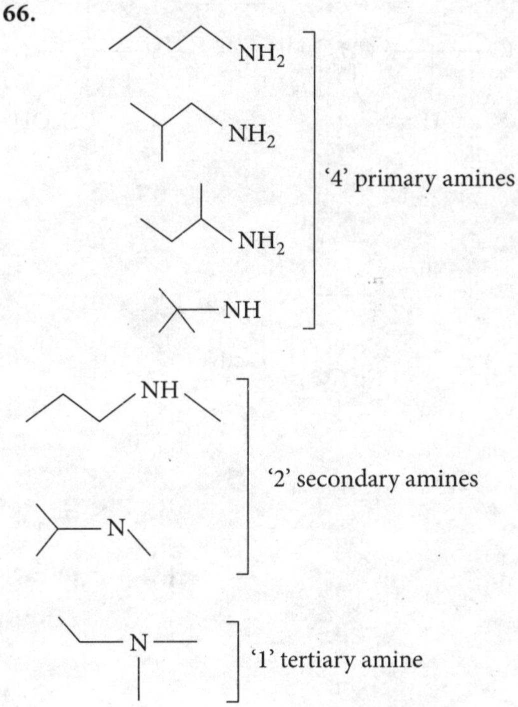

67.

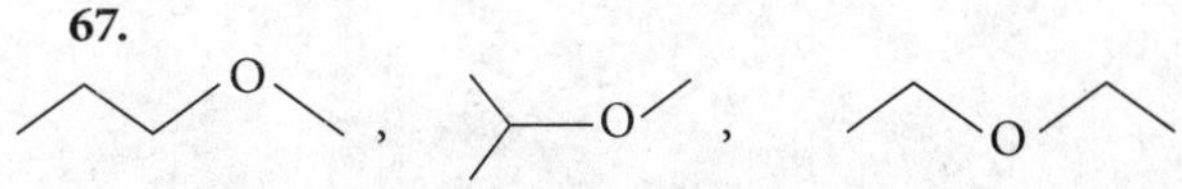

68. Different groups on valency of oxygen

69. 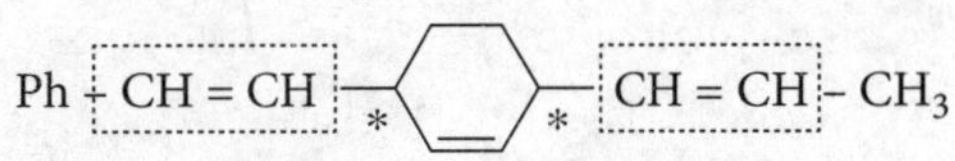

$n = 4, 2^n = 2^4 = 16$

70.

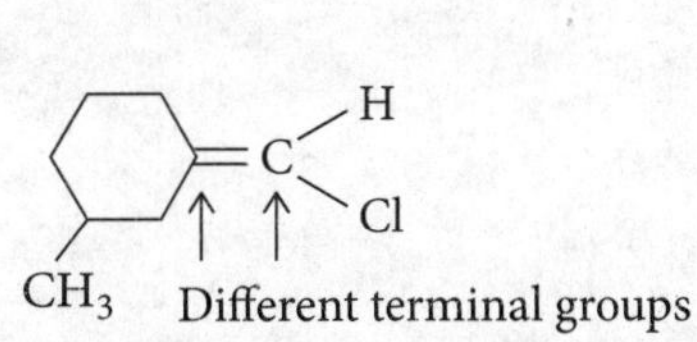

71. CIP rule, first higher atomic number, then next atom of higher atomic number.

72.

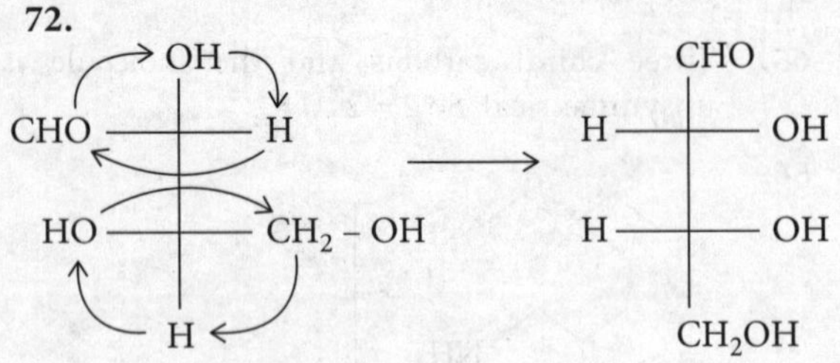

73.

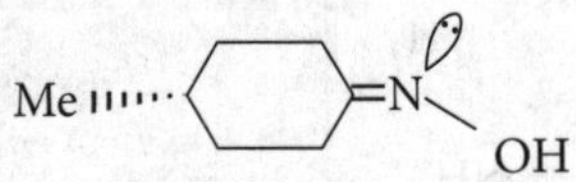

No POS
No COS — So active

74. Both POS and COS are absent and two chiral carbons.

75. Two chiral carbons and geometrical centre about the ring.

76. Tetrahedral system at the spiro ring. So POS and COS absent.

77. Single chiral carbon always gives net rotation of PPL and shows optical activity.

78. Higher priority groups (according to the CIP rule) are at opposite sides.

79. Presence of COS

CHAPTER 4

Hydrocarbons

Level-1

ALKANE

1. Which of the following methods is used to synthesize alkanes having even number of carbon atoms from carboxylic salts?
(a) The Wurtz reaction
(b) The Kolbe electrolysis method
(c) Dehydration
(d) None of the above

2. Based on branching, isomers of hexane are shown as below:

(a) 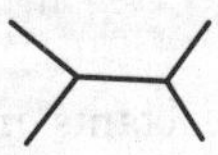 (b) 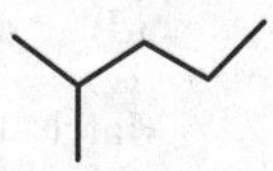

(c) 

The correct order of their boiling point is:
(a) a > b > c (b) c > b > a
(c) b > c > a (d) c > a > b

3. Which of the following are appropriate conditions for halogenation?
(a) High temperature (573–773 K)
(b) Presence of diffused light
(c) Presence of ultraviolet radiation
(d) All of the above

4. Which of the following is a termination step in halogenation?
(a) $Cl-Cl \xrightarrow{h\nu} \dot{C}l + \dot{C}l$
(b) $CH_4 + Cl \xrightarrow{h\nu} \dot{C}H_3 + HCl$
(c) $CH_3Cl + \dot{C}l \longrightarrow \dot{C}H_2Cl + HCl$
(d) $H_3\dot{C} + \dot{C}l \longrightarrow CH_3Cl$

5. The rate of replacement of a hydrogen of an alkane in the bromination process is:
(a) $1^o > 2^o > 3^o$ (b) $1^o > 3^o > 2^o$
(c) $2^o > 1^o > 3^o$ (d) $3^o > 2^o > 1^o$

6. Iodination of alkanes is always carried out in the presence of some oxidizing agents like HIO_3. This is because:
(a) It is a very fast process.
(b) It is a reversible reaction.
(c) The I–I bond is very weak.
(d) All of the above.

7. The reactants involved in the general combustion equation for any alkane is represented as:
(a) $C_nH_{2n+2} + \left(\frac{3n+2}{2}\right)O_2$
(b) $C_nH_{2n} + \left(\frac{3n-1}{2}\right)O_2$
(c) $C_nH_{2n} + \left(\frac{3n+2}{2}\right)O_2$
(d) $C_nH_{2n+2} + \left(\frac{3n+1}{2}\right)O_2$

8. Which of the following is formed during incomplete combustion of alkanes with insufficient amount of air of dioxygen?
(a) Carbon dioxide
(b) Carbon black
(c) Water
(d) None of the above

9. Considering the following reaction, reagent X can be:
$CH_4 + O_2 \xrightarrow[\Delta]{'X'} HCHO + H_2O$
(a) Mo_2O_3 (b) Cu/523 K
(c) Both (a) and (b) (d) $Mn(OAc)_2$

10. In the presence of X, ordinary alkanes resist oxidation but alkanes having a tertiary H-atom can be easily oxidized to alcohols. Identify 'X':
(a) Cu/523 K (b) Mo_2O_3
(c) $KMnO_4$ (d) $(CH_3COO)_2Mn$

11. Name the process in which n-hexane on heating to 773 K at 10–20 atm pressure in the presence of oxides of vanadium, molybdenum or chromium supported by alumina produces benzene:
(a) Reforming (b) Reduction
(c) Aromatization (d) Both (a) and (c)

12. Select the incorrect statement:
(a) Lower alkanes do not undergo nitration and sulphonation.
(b) Combustion of alkane is highly exothermic.
(c) Methane reacts with steam at 1273 K to produce syngas.
(d) Isomerization of alkanes requires Cr_2O_3 as catalyst.

13. Which of the following statements is correct?
(a) Alkanes are polar molecules.
(b) Alkanes are ionic in nature.
(c) Alkanes are inert towards acids and bases.
(d) Alkanes are very reactive.

14. Which of the following statements are correct regarding Kolbe's electrolysis process?
(a) Alkanes containing even number of C-atoms are prepared.
(b) Sodium or potassium salts of carboxylic acids are taken as substrate.
(c) Methane can be prepared by this method.
(d) H_2 gas is liberated at the anode.
Choose the correct statement:
(a) Both (a) and (b) (b) Both (b) and (c)
(c) Both (a) and (c) (d) All of the above

15. Arrange in the correct sequence for the mechanism of chlorination of methane:
(a) $CH_4 + Cl^{\bullet} \longrightarrow \dot{C}H_3 + H-Cl$
(b) $Cl-Cl \xrightarrow{h\nu} 2\dot{C}l$
(c) $\dot{C}H_3 + Cl_2 \longrightarrow CH_3 - Cl + Cl^{\bullet}$
(d) $\dot{C}l + \dot{C}l \longrightarrow Cl-Cl$
$\dot{C}H_3 + \dot{C}H_3 \longrightarrow CH_3 - CH_3$
Choose the correct option:
(a) (b), (a), (c) and (d)
(b) (a), (b), (c) and (d)
(c) (d), (c), (b) and (a)
(d) (b), (c), (a) and (d)

16. Which of the following is the correct match regarding controlled oxidation of alkane and the catalysts used in the reactions?

Column I	Column II
A. $CH_4 + O_2 \longrightarrow CH_3OH$	a. Cu/523 K/100 atm
B. $CH_4 + O_2 \longrightarrow HCHO$	b. Mo_2O_3, Δ
C. $2CH_3CH_3 + 3O_2 \longrightarrow 2CH_3COOH + 2H_2O$	c. $(CH_3COO)_2Mn$ /Δ
D. $(CH_3)_3CH \longrightarrow (CH_3)_3COH$	d. $KMnO_4$

Codes

	A	B	C	D
(a)	b	c	d	a
(b)	a	b	c	d
(c)	b	a	c	d
(d)	d	c	b	a

17. Match the following reactants in Column I with the corresponding reaction products in Column II and select the correct answer using the codes given below:

Column I	Column II
A. $Alkane + X_2 \xrightarrow{h\nu}$	a. Water + Carbon dioxide
B. $Alkane + O_2 \xrightarrow{\Delta}$	b. Alkanal
C. $Alkane + O_2 \xrightarrow[\Delta]{Mo_2O_3}$	c. Haloalkane
D. n-hexane $\xrightarrow[10-20\ atm]{Cr_2O_3/Al_2O_3, \Delta, 773\ K}$	d. Benzene

Codes

	A	B	C	D
(a)	a	b	c	d
(b)	a	b	d	c
(c)	c	a	b	d
(d)	c	a	d	b

18. $RCOONa \xrightarrow[2.H^+]{1.NaOH+CaO/\Delta} R-H + CO_2$

This decarboxylation reaction occurs through the generation of:
(a) $R^{\ominus}$
(b) $R^{\oplus}$
(c) $R^{\bullet}$
(d) None of the above

19. $\underset{}{CH_4} + \underset{\text{(Halogen)}}{X_2} \xrightarrow{\Delta} CH_3X + HX$

In this reaction, X_2 exhibits which of the following reactivity orders?
(a) $F_2 > Cl_2 > Br_2 > I_2$
(b) $I_2 > Br_2 > Cl_2 > F_2$
(c) $Br_2 > Cl_2 > F_2 > I_2$
(d) $Cl_2 > F_2 > Br_2 > I_2$

20.

$CH_3—\underline{H}$ (I) $CH_3—CH_2—\underline{H}$ (II)

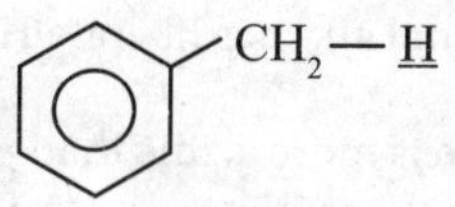

III

Which of the following orders is correct for the reactivity of the indicated H-atoms among these compounds in monochlorinations?
(a) I > II > III (b) III > II > I
(c) II > III > I (d) II > I > III

Alkene and Alkyne

21. Which of the following acts as a Lindlar catalyst?
(a) Palladium
(b) $Zn-H_2SO_4$
(c) Partially deactivated palladised charcoal
(d) Zn amalgam

22. Consider the given reactions:

(i) $CH_3C \equiv CC_2H_5 + H_2 \xrightarrow[\text{Sulphur}]{\text{Pd/C}} A$

(ii) $CH_3C \equiv CC_2H_5 + H_2 \xrightarrow{\text{Na/liq. NH}_3} B$

A and B are, respectively:
(a) Cis- and trans-alkene
(b) Trans- and cis-alkene
(c) Alkane and alkene
(d) Alkene and alkane

23. 2-Methylpropan-2-ol is obtained by the reaction of X with water in the presence of concentrated H_2SO_4. The compound X is:
(a) 2-Methylbut-2-ene
(b) 2,2-Dimethylhexane
(c) 2-Methylprop-1-ene
(d) 2-Methylbutane

24. The major product formed when 3,3-dimethylbutan-2-ol is heated with concentrated sulphuric acid is:
(a) 2,3-Dimethylbut-1-ene
(b) 2,3-Dimethylbut-2-ene
(c) 3,3-Dimethylbut-1-ene
(d) 2,3-Dimethylbutane

25. Which of the following is the correct reason for the addition reactions on alkenes?
(a) Loosely held π-electrons
(b) Tightly held π-electrons
(c) Loosely held σ-electrons
(d) Tightly held σ-electrons

26. The addition of cold concentrated H_2SO_4 to alkenes is an example of:
(a) Electrophilic substitution reaction
(b) Nucleophilic substitution reaction
(c) Electrophilic addition reaction
(d) Nucleophilic addition reaction

27. Consider the following reaction:
$CH_3CH = CH_2 + HOSO_2OH \longrightarrow$
The product obtained and the colour is:
(a) $CH_3-\underset{\underset{OSO_2H}{|}}{CH}-CH_3$ (yellow)
(b) $CH_3-CH_2-\underset{\underset{OSO_2H}{|}}{CH_2}$ (yellow)
(c) $CH_3-\underset{\underset{OSO_3H}{|}}{CH}-CH_3$ (yellow)
(d) $CH_3-CH_2-\underset{\underset{OSO_3H}{|}}{CH_2}$ (yellow)

28. Choose the correct option regarding A and B:
$CH_2 = CH_2 \xrightarrow[\text{273 K}]{\text{Dil. KMnO}_4} A$

$CH_3 - CH = CH_2 \xrightarrow[\text{273 K}]{\text{Dil. KMnO}_4} B$

	A	B
(a)	$CH_2(OH)-CH_3$	$CH_3CH_2CH_2OH$
(b)	CH_3CH_2OH	$CH_3CHOHCH_3$
(c)	$CH_3CH(OH)CH_3$	$CH_3CH(OH)CH_2OH$
(d)	$CH_2(OH)CH_2(OH)$	$CH_3CH(OH)CH_2OH$

29. Which of the following is an example of polythene?
(a) $n(CH\equiv CH)$
(b) $-\!(CH_2-CH_2)\!-_n$
(c) $-\!(C\equiv C)\!-_n$
(d) $-\!(CH_2=CH_2)\!-_n$

30. The major and minor product in electrophilic addition is determined by applying:
(a) Zaitsev's rule (b) Hofmann's rule
(c) Markovnikov's rule (d) Bredt's rule

31.

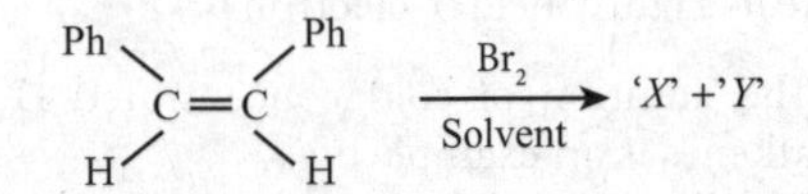

The isomeric relation between X and Y is:
(a) Enantiomers (b) Diastereomers
(c) Identical (d) Geometrical

32.

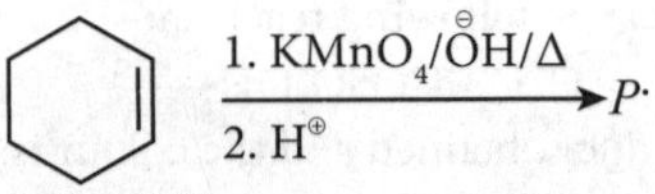

P should be:

(a) 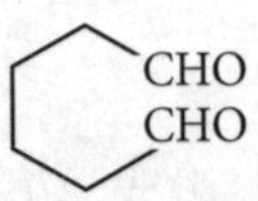

(b) 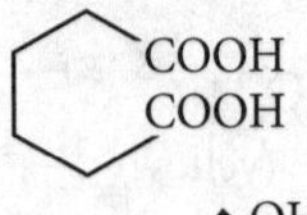

(c) 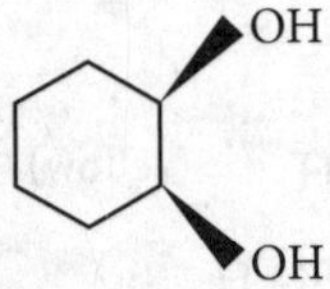

(d) None of the above

33. A, B and C in the following reaction would be:
$Mg_2C_3 + H_2O \longrightarrow A$
$Al_4C_3 + H_2O \longrightarrow B$
$CaC_2 + H_2O \longrightarrow C$

(a) $A = C_3H_6$ $B = C_3H_6$ $C = CH_4$
(b) $A = CH_4$ $B = C_3H_4$ $C = C_2H_2$
(c) $A = C_3H_4$ $B = CH_4$ $C = C_2H_2$
(d) $A = CH_4$ $B = C_3H_4$ $C = C_2H_4$

34. Which of the following reactions depicts an incorrect product?
(a) $CH_3-C\equiv CH + NaNH_2 \longrightarrow CH_3-C\equiv CNa + NH_3$
(b) $CH_3-C\equiv CH \xrightarrow[Pt/Pd/Ni]{H_2(Excess)} CH_3-CH_2-CH_3$
(c) $CH_3-C\equiv CH \xrightarrow[333\ K]{Hg^{2+}/H^+} CH_3-CH_2-CHO$
(d) $CH\equiv CH \xrightarrow{HBr(2\ moles)} CH_3-CHBr_2$

35. Which of the following statements is correct?
(a) Terminal alkynes liberate H_2 with sodium metal.
(b) Ethene is more acidic than ethyne.
(c) Mercuric catalyzed hydration of ethyne produces ethanol.
(d) Alkynes are more reactive than alkenes with respect to electrophilic addition.

36. When $CH_3-C\equiv CH$ reacts with one mole of HBr, the product obtained is:
(a) Bromoethane
(b) Dibromopropane
(c) 2-Bromopropene
(d) 1-Bromopropane

37. Which of the following reactions will yield 2,2-dibromopropane?
(a) $CH_3-CH=CH_2 + HBr \longrightarrow$
(b) $CH_3-C\equiv CH + 2HBr \longrightarrow$
(c) $CH_3-CH=CHBr + HBr \longrightarrow$
(d) $CH\equiv CH + 2HBr \longrightarrow$

38. Predict the correct intermediate and product in the following reaction:
$H_3C-C\equiv CH \xrightarrow[HgSO_4]{H_2O/H_2SO_4}$ Intermediate $(A) \rightarrow$ Product (B)
(a) $A = H_3C-\underset{SO_4H}{\underset{|}{C}}=CH_2$ $B = H_3C-\underset{O}{\underset{\|}{C}}-CH_3$
(b) $A = H_3C-\underset{OH}{\underset{|}{C}}=CH_2$
$B = H_3C-CH_2-CHO$

(c) $A = H_3C-\underset{\underset{O}{\|}}{C}-CH_3 \quad B = CH_3-CH=CH_2$

(d) $A = H_3C-\underset{\underset{OH}{|}}{C}=CH_2, \; B = H_3C-\underset{\underset{O}{\|}}{C}-CH_3$

39. Consider the following reaction,

$$H_3C-C\equiv CH \xrightarrow[873\text{ K}]{\text{Red hot iron tube}} A$$

The number of sigma (σ) bonds present in the product A is:

(a) 21 (b) 9

(c) 24 (d) 18

40. Which of the following orders is correct regarding the acidic character of the hydrocarbons given below?

(a) $CH\equiv CH > CH_2=CH_2 > CH_3-CH_3$

(b) $HC\equiv CH > CH_3C\equiv CH > CH_3C\equiv CCH_3$

(a) Only (a)

(b) Only (b)

(c) Both (a) and (b)

(d) None of the above

41. Match Column I with Column II and choose the correct option from the codes given below:

Column I	Column II
(A) $RC\equiv CR \xrightarrow[\text{(ii)}H_2O_2/OH^-]{\text{(i)}BH_3,THF}$	(a) $CH_3-C\equiv CNa$
(B) $RC\equiv CR \xrightarrow[H_2]{Pd/Ni}$	(b) $R-CH_2-\underset{\underset{O}{\|}}{C}-R$
(C) $\underset{\underset{Br}{|}}{C}H_2CH_2Br \xrightarrow[NaNH_2]{Alc.KOH}$	(c) $CH\equiv CH$
(D) $CH_3C\equiv CH \xrightarrow{NaNH_2}$	(d) $R-CH_2-CH_2-R$

Codes

	A	B	C	D
(a)	b	d	c	a
(b)	b	d	a	c
(c)	b	c	d	a
(d)	d	b	c	a

42.

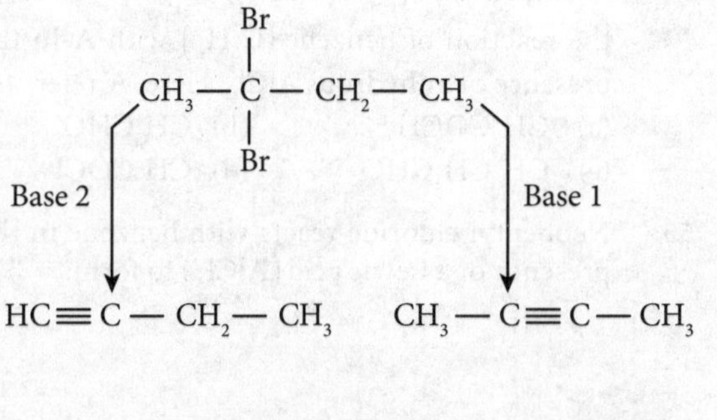

Base 1 and Base 2 should, respectively, be:

(a) KOH and $NaNH_2$

(b) $NaNH_2$ and KOH

(c) Either KOH or $NaNH_2$ can be used for both reactions

(d) None of the above

43. $Ph-C\equiv C-CH_3 \xrightarrow{HgSO_4/H_2SO_4,H_2O} P$

P should be:

(a) $Ph-\overset{\overset{O}{\|}}{C}-CH_2-CH_3$

(b) $Ph-CH_2-\overset{\overset{O}{\|}}{C}-CH_3$

(c) Both in equal proportion

(d) $Ph-\underset{\underset{OH}{|}}{C}=CH-CH_3$

44. **Assertion:** CH_4 does not react with Cl_2 in the dark.

Reason: Chlorination of CH_4 takes place in sunlight.

(a) Assertion is correct, reason is correct; reason is a correct explanation for assertion.

(b) Assertion is correct, reason is correct; reason is not a correct explanation for assertion

(c) Assertion is correct, reason is incorrect

(d) Assertion is incorrect, reason is correct.

45. **Assertion:** Iodination of alkanes is reversible.

Reason: The byproduct HI is a strong reducing agent, and reduces alkyl iodide.

(a) Assertion is correct, reason is correct; reason is a correct explanation for assertion.

(b) Assertion is correct, reason is correct; reason is not a correct explanation for assertion

(c) Assertion is correct, reason is incorrect

(d) Assertion is incorrect, reason is correct.

46. Match List-I with List-II and select the correct answer:

List-I (Reaction)	List-II (Reagent)
(A) $CH_3-CH=CH_2 \rightarrow CH_3-CHBr-CH_3$	(P) HBr
(B) $CH_3-CH=CH_2 \rightarrow CH_3-CH_2-CH_2Br$	(Q) Br_2/CCl_4
(C) $CH_3-CH=CH_2 \rightarrow BrCH_2-CH=CH_2$	(R) HBr/Peroxide

(D) $CH_3-CH=CH_2 \rightarrow$ $CH_3-CHBr-CH_2Br$	(S) NBS

(a) A-P, B-R, C-S, D-Q
(b) A-R, B-P, C-Q, D-S
(c) A-P, B-S, C-R, D-Q
(d) A-Q, B-P, C-S, D-R

AROMATICS

47. Which reaction confirms the presence of three double bonds in benzene?
(a) Oxidation reaction
(b) Hydrolysis reaction
(c) Triozonolysis reaction
(d) Addition reaction

48. Read the statements below:
(a) Aromatic hydrocarbons are immiscible with water but readily miscible with organic solvents.
(b) Benzene reacts with excess Cl_2 in the presence of anhydrous $AlCl_3$ to produces C_6Cl_6.
(c) Acylium ion is a resonance stabilized electrophile.
Choose the option containing correct statements:
(a) (a), (b) (b) (b), (c)
(c) (a), (c) (d) (a), (b) and (c)

49. For an electrophilic substitution reaction, the presence of a halogen atom in the benzene ring:
(a) Deactivates the ring by inductive effect.
(b) Deactivates the ring by resonance.
(c) Decreases the electron density at the ortho and para positions by resonance.
(d) Directs the incoming electrophile to the meta position by increasing the charge density relative to the ortho and para positions.

50. Consider the reaction given below:

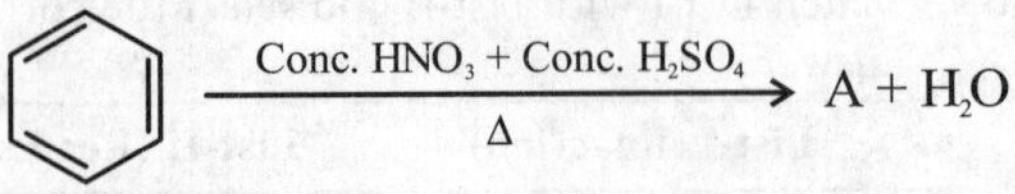

Here, A refers to:

(a)
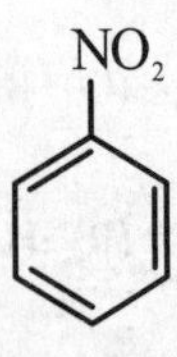

(b)
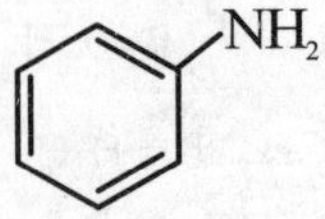

(c)
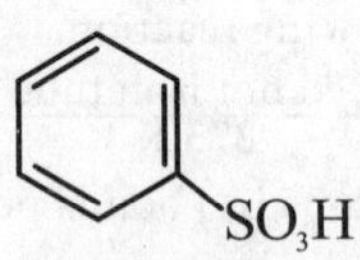

(d) All of the above

51. In an electrophilic substitution reaction of nitrobenzene, the presence of the nitro group:
(a) Activates the ring by resonance effect.
(b) Activates the ring by inductive effect.
(c) Decreases the charge density at the ortho and para positions of the ring relative to the meta position by resonance.
(d) Increases the charge density at the meta position relative to the ortho and para positions of the ring by resonance.

52. Consider the reaction given below:

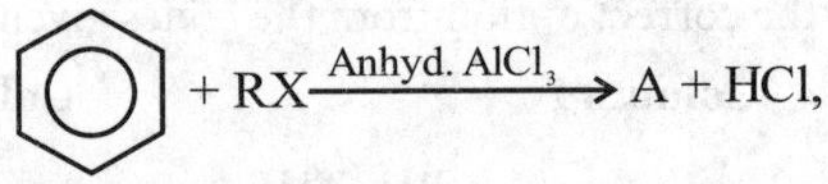

Here, A is:
(a) Methylbenzene
(b) Toluene
(c) Alkylbenzene
(d) Ethylbenzene

53. In the reaction,

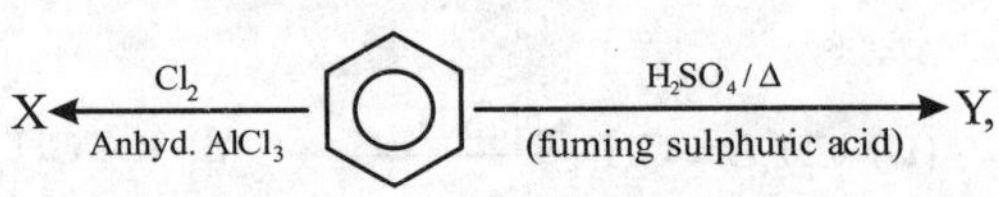

X and Y are, respectively:
(a) C_6H_5Cl and $C_6H_5SO_3H$
(b) C_6H_5Cl and C_6H_5OH
(c) $C_6H_4Cl_2$ and $C_6H_5SO_2$
(d) C_6H_5Cl and C_6H_5CHO

54. Acetophenone $(C_6H_5COCH_3)$ is prepared from the reaction of benzene (C_6H_6) with A in the presence of anhydrous $AlCl_3$. Here, A refers to:
(a) CH_3COCH_3 (b) CH_3CHO
(c) CH_3CH_2CHO (d) CH_3COCl

55. Neopentyl chloride reacts with benzene in the presence of a Lewis acid $(AlCl_3)$ to form:

(a) 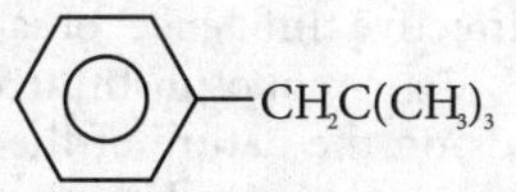

(b) 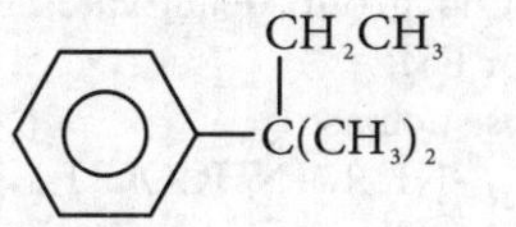

(c) 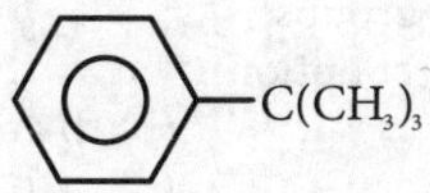

(d) 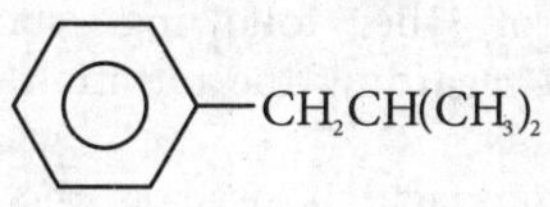

56. During nitration of benzene, the attacking electrophile is:
(a) NO_3^- (b) NO_2^-
(c) NO_2^+ (d) HNO_3

57. Consider the reaction given below:

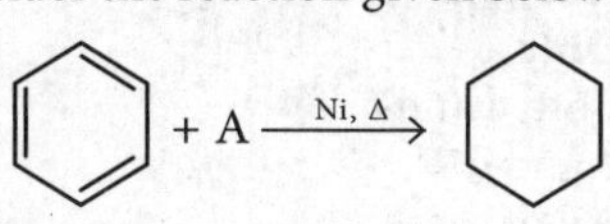

Here, A is:
(a) H_2 (b) $2H_2$
(c) $3H_2$ (d) $4H_2$

58. Benzene hexachloride is obtained by the addition of X moles of Cl_2 with C_6H_6 in the presence of UV / 500 K. The value of X is:
(a) 2 (b) 6
(c) 3 (d) 8

59. When benzene is heated in air, it burns with a sooty flame, producing X and Y, as shown in the reaction: $C_6H_6 + \frac{15}{2}O_2 \longrightarrow X + Y$
Here, X and Y refer to:
(a) C_6H_5-OH, CO (b) CO_2, H_2O
(c) C_6H_{14}, CO_2 (d) C_6H_5OH, H_2

60. Which of the following sets of functional groups is meta-directing?
(a) $-NO_2, -NH_2, -COOH, -COOR$
(b) $-NO_2, -CHO, -SO_3H, -COR$
(c) $-CN, -CHO, -NHCOCH_3, -COOR$
(d) $-CN, -NH_2, -NHR, -OCH_3$

61. In nitrobenzene, X attacks the comparatively electron-rich meta position, resulting in Y substitution. Here, X and Y refer to:
(a) Electrophile, meta
(b) Nucleophile, meta
(c) Deactivating group, para
(d) Activating group, meta

62. The correct order of the electrophilic substitution reaction is:

(a) 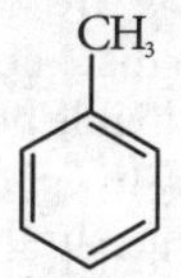

(b) 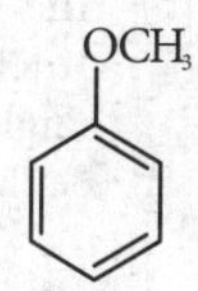

(c) 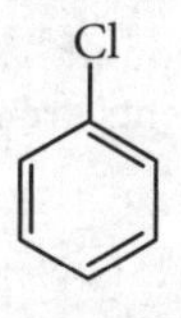

(d) 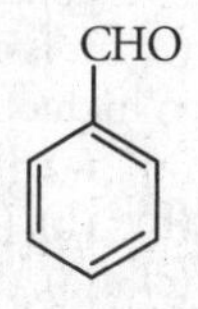

(a) a > b > c > d
(b) d > b > a > c
(c) b > a > c > d
(d) b > a > d > c

63. Polynuclear hydrocarbons are formed by an incomplete process of organic materials. This process is termed:
(a) Addition (b) Cracking
(c) Elimination (d) Substitution

64. Which one of these is incorrect for benzene?
(a) It forms only one type of monosubstituted product.
(b) There are three C–C single bonds and three C–C double bonds.
(c) The heat of hydrogenation of benzene is less than the theoretical value.
(d) The bond angle between the C–C bond is 120°.

65. Which of the following statements are correct regarding the structure of benzene?
(a) All the six carbons in benzene are sp^2 hybridized.
(b) The sp^2-hybridized orbital of carbon overlaps with another sp^2-hybridized orbital of carbon to give a C–C sigma bond.

(c) The C–H σ-bond is formed by the lateral overlapping of the sp^2-hybridized orbital of C and the ls orbital of the H-atom.

Choose the correct statements:
(a) (a), (b) and (c) are correct
(b) (a) and (b) are correct
(c) (a) and (c) are correct
(d) (b) and (c) are correct

66. An X-ray diffraction study of benzene reveals that:
(a) It is a planar molecule.
(b) The C–C bond lengths are of the same order, which is intermediate between C–C single bond and C–C double bond.
(c) Benzene is reluctant to participate in the addition reaction under normal conditions.
(d) It is an aromatic compound.

Which of the above statements are true?
(a) (a), (b) and (c)
(b) (b), (c) and (d)
(c) (a), (b) and (d)
(d) All of the above

67. Which of the following is carcinogenic?

(a) 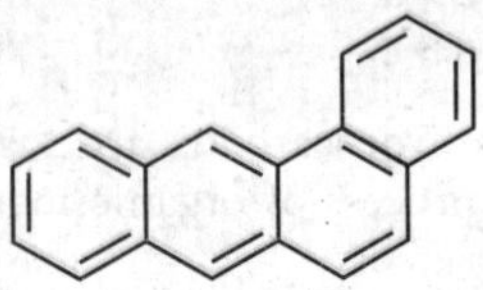

1,2-Benzanthracene

(b) 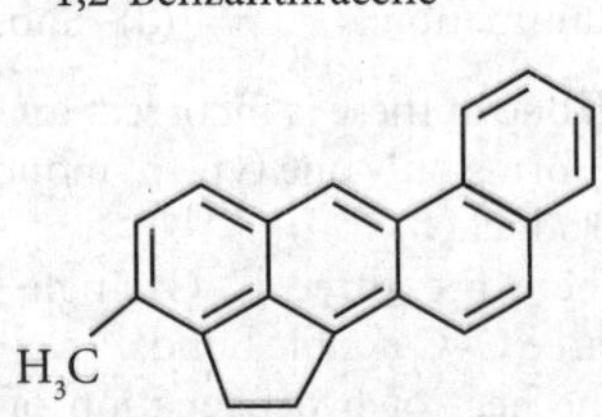

3-Methylcholanthrene

(c) 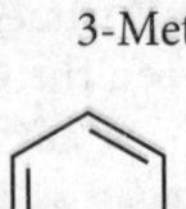

Benzene

Choose the correct option:
(a) a and b (b) b and c
(c) a and c (d) a, b, c

68. Consider the following statements:
(a) The-OH group present in phenol is ortho- and para-directing.
(b) The directive influence of a functional group in monosubstituted benzene depends on the nature of the substituent already present in the benzene ring.
(c) The –OH group deactivates the benzene ring for ESR.
(d) Groups such as $-NH_2, -NHR, -NHCOCH_3, -OCH_3, -CH_3, -C_2H_5$ are examples of activating groups.

Select the correct option:
(a) a and b (b) b and c
(c) b, c and d (d) a, b, d

69. Which of the following statements is incorrect regarding the nitration of aromatic compounds?
(a) Nitrous acid is used as the reagent for nitration of benzene.
(b) The rate of nitration of toluene is greater than that of benzene.
(c) The rate of nitration of chlorobenzene is greater than that of benzene.
(d) Nitration is an electrophilic substitution reaction.
(a) Only a
(b) Both a and c
(c) b and d
(d) All of these

70. **Assertion (A):** The compound cyclooctatetraene has the following structural formula:

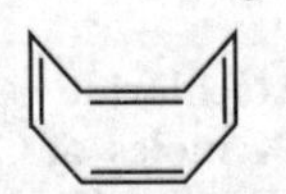

It is a cyclic and non-aromatic compound.
Reason (R): $(4n+2)\pi$-electron rule does not hold good and the ring is non-planar.
(a) Both A and R are correct, R is the correct explanation of A.
(b) Both A and R are correct, R is not the correct explanation of A.
(c) A is correct, R is incorrect.
(d) A is incorrect, R is correct.

71. **Assertion (A):** Nitration of benzene with nitric acid requires the use of concentrated sulphuric acid.
Reason (R): The mixture of concentrated sulphuric acid and concentrated nitric acid produces the electrophile, NO_2^+.
(a) Both A and R are correct, R is the correct explanation of A.

(b) Both A and R are correct, R is not the correct explanation of A.
(c) A is correct, R is incorrect.
(d) A is incorrect, R is correct.

72. **Assertion (A):** In the electrophilic substitution of aryl halides, the incoming electrophile gets attached to the meta position.
Reason (R): Aryl halides are moderately deactivating.
(a) Both A and R are correct, R is the correct explanation of A.
(b) Both A and R are correct, R is not the correct explanation of A.
(c) A is correct, R is incorrect.
(d) A is incorrect, R is correct.

73. Identify the conditions under which hydrogenation of benzene produces cyclohexane:
(a) High temperature, High pressure, Nickel catalyst.
(b) Low temperature, Low pressure, Ziegler–Natta catalyst.
(c) High temperature, Low pressure, Anhydrous $AlCl_3$.
(d) Low temperature, Low pressure, Anhydrous $AlCl_3$.

74. Match the reactants in Column I with the corresponding reaction products in Column II and choose the correct option from the codes given below:

A. $C_6H_6 + Cl_2 \xrightarrow{AlCl_3}$ — a. Benzenesulphonic acid
B. $C_6H_6 + CH_3Cl \xrightarrow{AlCl_3}$ — b. Methyl phenyl ketone
C. $C_6H_6 + CH_3COCl \xrightarrow{AlCl_3}$ — c. Toluene
D. $C_6H_6 \xrightarrow{H_2SO_4}$ — d. Chlorobenzene

Codes

	A	B	C	D
(a)	d	c	b	a
(b)	d	c	a	b
(c)	c	d	a	b
(d)	c	d	b	a

75. The product in the reaction below is:

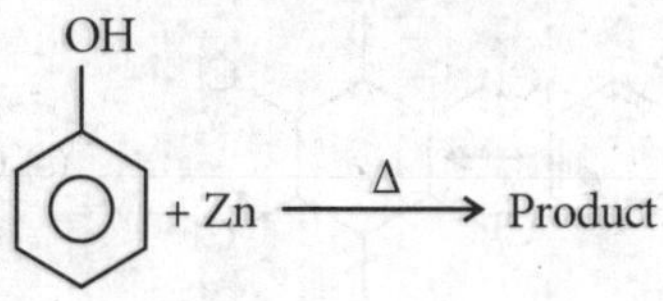

(a) 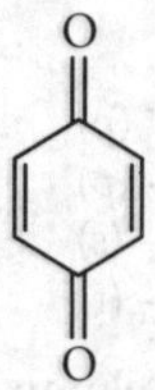

(b) 
(c) 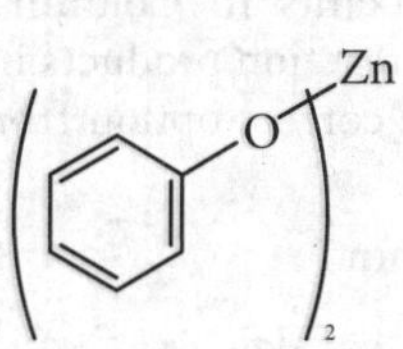

(d) 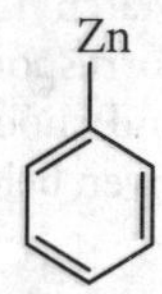

76. During the nitration of benzene, in the process of generation of nitronium ion, sulphuric acid behaves as a/an ______ and nitric acid behaves as a/an _________.
(a) Base, acid
(b) Acid, base
(c) Strong acid, weak acid
(d) Weak acid, strong acid

77. Match the columns:

Column I	Column II
(A) 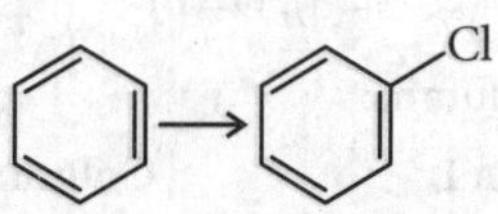	(p) Cl_2, UV/500 K
(B) 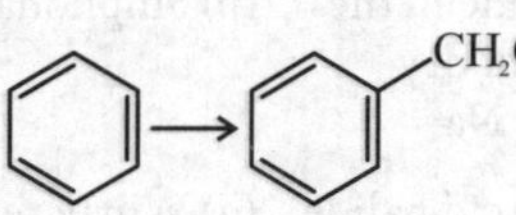	(q) Cl_2/ Anhydrous $AlCl_3$
(C) 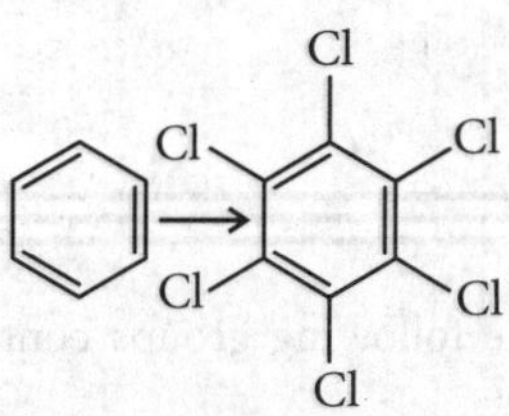	(r) CH_2Cl_2, anhydrous $AlCl_3$

(D) 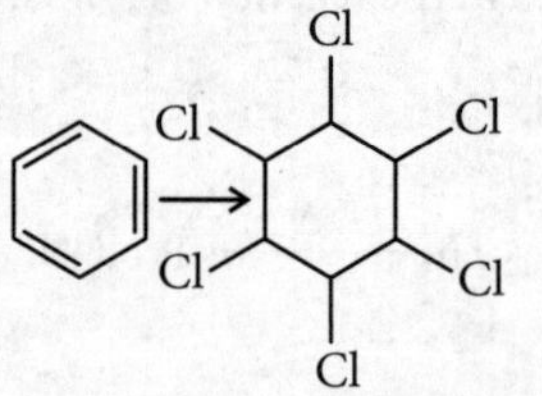 (s) Cl_2, anhydrous $AlCl_3$ (Dark, Cold)

(a) A–(s), B–(r), C–(q), D – (p)
(b) A–(q), B–(r), C–(s), D – (p)
(c) A–(r), B–(p), C–(q), D – (s)
(d) A–(q), B–(p), C–(s), D – (r)

78. Match the reactants in Column I with the corresponding reaction products in Column II and choose the correct option from the codes given below:

Column I	Column II
(A) Benzene + $Cl_2 \xrightarrow{AlCl_3}$	(p) Benzoic acid
(B) Benzene + $CH_3Cl \xrightarrow{AlCl_3}$	(q) Methyl phenyl ketone
(C) Benzene + $CH_3COCl \xrightarrow{AlCl_3}$	(r) Toluene
(D) Toluene $\xrightarrow{KMnO_4/NaOH}$	(s) Chlorobenzene

(a) A–(s), B–(r), C–(q), D–(p)
(b) A–(s), B–(r), C–(p), D–(q)
(c) A–(r), B–(s), C–(p), D–(q)
(d) A–(r), B–(s), C–(q), D–(p)

79. Match the columns:

Column I	Column II
(A) Alkyl halide in the presence of dry ether and Na	(p) Sulphonation
(B) Arene + Acid halide in the presence of $AlCl_3$	(q) Wurtz reaction
(C) Arene + Fuming sulphuric acid	(r) Catalytic hydrogenation
(D) Arene + Hydrogen in the presence of Ni	(s) Friedel–Crafts reaction

(a) A-(p), B-(r), C-(q), D-(s)
(b) A-(s), B-(q), C-(r), D-(p)
(c) A-(r), B-(p), C-(s), D-(q)
(d) A-(q), B-(s), C-(p), D-(r)

80. Match the columns:

Column I (Reactants)	Column II (No. of chlorinated products)
(A) Benzene $\xrightarrow{Cl_2,\ UV/500\ K}$	p. Three compounds
(B) Toluene $\xrightarrow{Cl_2,\ light}$	q. Four compounds
(C) Methane $\xrightarrow{Cl_2,\ light}$	r. Single monochloro derivative
(D) Benzene $\xrightarrow{Cl_2,\ AlCl_3}$	s. Hexachloro derivative

(a) A-(r), B-(p, r), C-(q, r), D-(s)
(b) A-(s), B-(p, r), C-(q, r), D-(r)
(c) A-(p, r), B-(s), C-(q, r), D-(r)
(d) A-(s), B-(p, r), C-(r), D-(q, r)

81. (i) Chlorobenzene and (ii) Benzene hexachloride are obtained from benzene by the reaction of chlorine, in the presence of:
(a) (i) UV or 500 K and (ii) Anhydrous $AlCl_3$ (Dark and Cold)
(b) (i) Sodium hydroxide and (ii) Sulphuric acid
(c) (i) UV or 500 K and (ii) Anhydrous $FeCl_3$
(d) (i) Anhydrous $AlCl_3$ and (ii) UV or 500 K

Level-2

1. Which of the following groups contains only electrophiles?
(a) BF_3, NH_3, H_2O
(b) $AlCl_3$, SO_3, $\overset{\oplus}{NO_2}$
(c) $\overset{\oplus}{NO_2}$, $\overset{\oplus}{CH_3}$, $\overset{\oplus}{Na}$
(d) $\overset{\ominus}{C_2H_5}$, $\overset{\odot}{C_2H_5}$, $\overset{\oplus}{C_2H_5}$

2. Which of the following is an electron-seeking species?
(a) CH≡ CH (b) Ammonia
(c) Acetaldehyde (d) C_2H_5OH

3. Which of the following orders is correct for the electrophilic addition reaction of these substrates:

$CH_2=CH_2$ (A) $\quad CH\equiv CH$ (B) $\quad CH_3-C\equiv CH$ (C)

(a) A > B > C (b) C > A > B
(c) A > C > B (d) C > B > A

4. Which of the following carbocations does not undergo rearrangement?

(a) 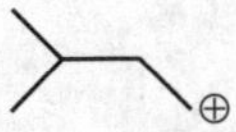 (b) 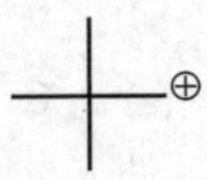

(c) 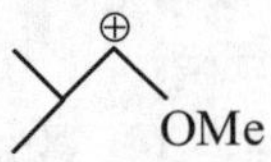 (d) $Ph-CH_2-\overset{\oplus}{C}H_2$

5. The intermediate during the addition of HBr to propene in the absence of peroxide is:

(a) $CH_3\dot{C}H\,CH_2Cl$ (b) $CH_3\overset{\oplus}{C}H-CH_3$
(c) $CH_3-CH_2-\overset{\oplus}{C}H_2$ (d) $CH_3\dot{C}H\,CH_2$

6. The electrophilic addition reaction is not observed according Markovnikov's rule in:
(a) $CH_3-CH=CH_2$
(b) $Ph-CH=CH_2$
(c) $Cl_3C-CH=CH_2$
(d) $CH_3O-CH=CH_2$

7. Arrange the alkenes in decreasing order of the rate of electrophile addition reaction with HCl:

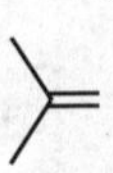 (P), 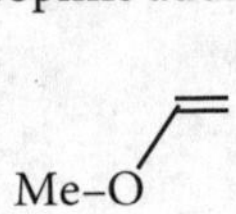 (Q), 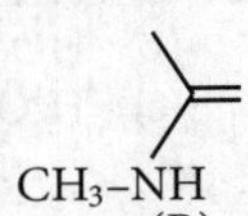 (R)

(a) P > Q > R (b) Q > R > P
(c) R > Q > P (d) P = Q = R

8. Which of the following carbocations are most likely to rearrange:

(i) 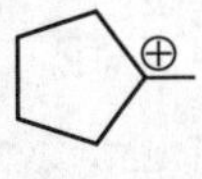 (ii) 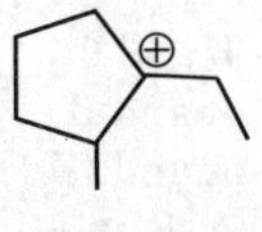

(iii)  (iv) 

(a) III, IV (b) II, III, IV
(c) II, IV (d) I, III

9. In which of the following reactions does the first compound act as an electrophile?

(a) 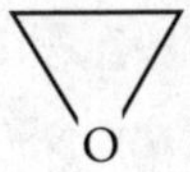 $+ PCl_5 \longrightarrow$

(b) $CH_2=CH_2 + Br_2 \longrightarrow$

(c) $NaSH + CH_3-I \longrightarrow$

(d) 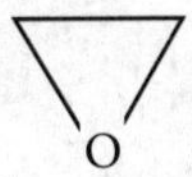 $+ NaOH \longrightarrow$

10. The increasing order of nucleophilicity of the following nucleophiles is:
(a) $CH_3CO_2^{\ominus}$
(b) H_2O
(c) $CH_3SO_3^{\ominus}$
(d) $\overset{\ominus}{O}H$
(a) (b) < (c) < (d) < (a)
(b) (b) < (c) < (a) < (d)
(c) (a) < (d) < (c) < (b)
(d) (d) < (a) < (c) < (b)

11. Which one of the following carbocations would you expect to rearrange:

(a) 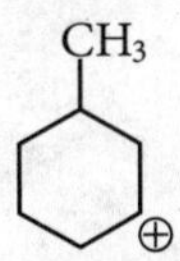 (b) 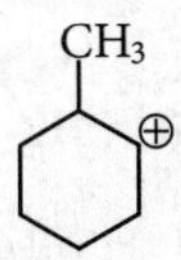

(c) 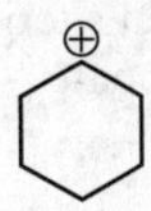 (d) 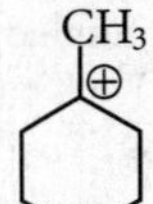

12. The electrophilic addition reaction proceeds in two steps. The first step involves the addition of an electrophile. Name the type of intermediate formed in the first step of the addition reaction:

$$H_3C-HC=CH_2 + H^+ \rightarrow$$

(a) 2° Carbanion
(b) 1° Carbocation
(c) 2° Carbocation
(d) 1° Carbanion

13. How many 1,2-shifts are involved in the course of the following reaction?

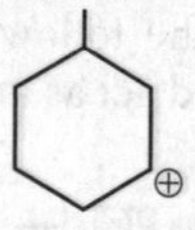

(a) 1 (b) 2
(c) 3 (d) 0

14. A covalent bond can undergo fission in two different ways. The correct representation involving a heterolytic fission of CH_3—Br is:

(a) 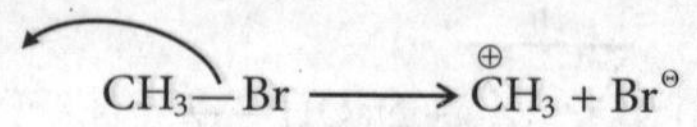

(b) 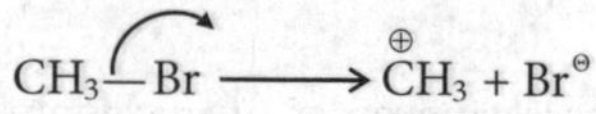

(c) 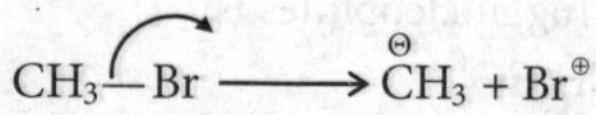

(d) 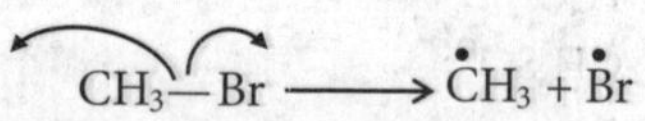

15. The addition of HCl to an alkene proceeds in two steps. The first step is the attack of H^+ ions to the alkene portion, which can be shown as:

(a) 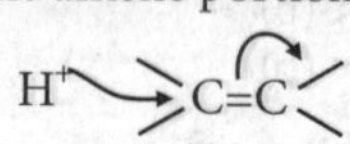

(b) 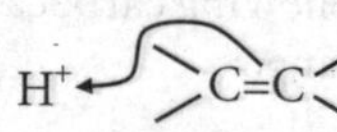

(c) 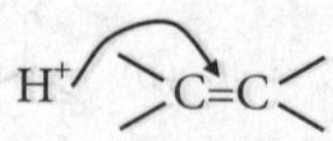

(d) All of these are possible

16. A nucleophile is a species that should have:
(a) A pair of electrons to donate
(b) Positive charge
(c) Vacant orbital
(d) Electron-deficient species

17. The following order is incorrect for:

$$I^{\ominus} > Br^{\ominus} > Cl^{\ominus} > F^{\ominus}$$

(a) Leaving group tendency
(b) Basic strength
(c) Stability
(d) Nucleophilicity in water

18. Which statement is incorrect?
(a) On the increasing nucleophilicity of alkene, the reactivity of the reaction with Br_2 increases.
(b) Ethene is more reactive than ethyne towards electrophilic addition reaction.
(c) Buta-1,3-diene on reaction with 1 equivalent of HBr gives 1-bromo-but-2-ene as a major product.
(d) When acetylene reacts with methylmagnesium bromide, hydrogen is evolved.

19. The compound with the highest leaving group tendency is:

(a) 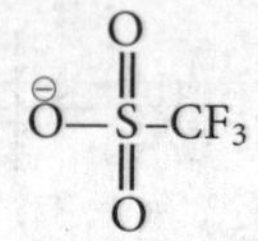 (b) 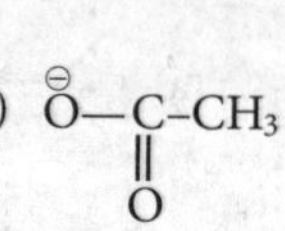

(c) 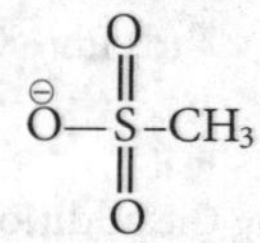 (d) 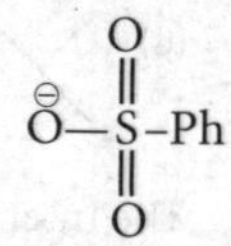

20. Select the correct option for the given solvent:

	Polar protic solvent	Polar aprotic solvent	Non-polar solvent
(a)	CH_3COCH_3	CH_3COOH	n-Hexane
(b)	CH_3COOH	CH_3COCH_3	n-Hexane
(c)	n-Hexane	CH_3COCH_3	CH_3COOH
(d)	CH_3COOH	n-Hexane	CH_3COCH_3

21. Which of the following is the correct order of nucleophilicity?
(a) $NH_3 > H_2N^-$
(b) $HO^- > H_2N^-$
(c) $H_2O > HO^-$
(d)

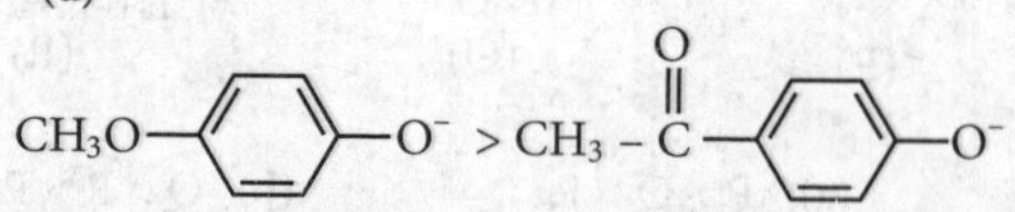

22. Which of the following compounds gives a white precipitate with ammoniacal $AgNO_3$?

$CH_2 = CH_2$ (A) $CH \equiv CH$ (B) $CH_3 - C \equiv CH$ (C)

(a) B and C
(b) A and B
(c) A and C
(d) A, B and C

23. Which of the following compounds will produce 2 moles of CO_2 with oxidative ozonolysis?
(a) 1,4-Pentadiene

(b) 1,3,4-Pentatriene
(c) 1,2,3-Pentatriene
(d) Pent-1-en-3-yne

24. Which of the following alkenes is the most reactive for hydration?
(a) Ethene (b) 2-Butene
(c) Isobutane (d) 1-Pentene

25. Which of the following is the best reagent to convert 3-methyl-1-butene into 3-methyl-2-butanol?
(a) Dil.H_2SO_4
(b) B_2H_6, H_2O_2/NaOH
(c) $Hg(OAc)_2/H_2O$,$NaBH_4$
(d) All of the above

26. Arrange the alkenes in decreasing order of the rate of electrophile addition reaction with HCl:

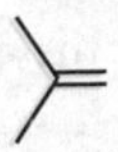 , 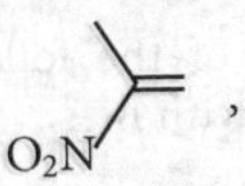 , 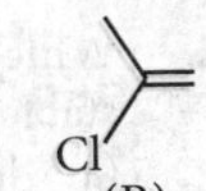
(P) (Q) (R)

(a) P > Q > R (b) Q > R > P
(c) R > Q > P (d) P > R > Q

27. The major product of the following reaction is:

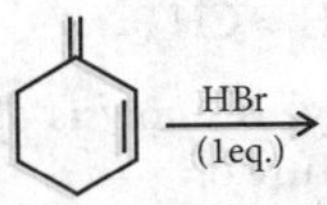

(a) 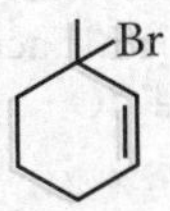 (b) 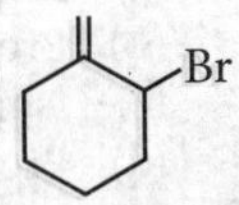
(c) 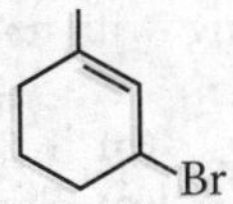 (d) 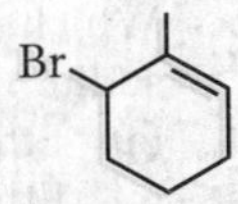

28. The major product of the following sequence is:

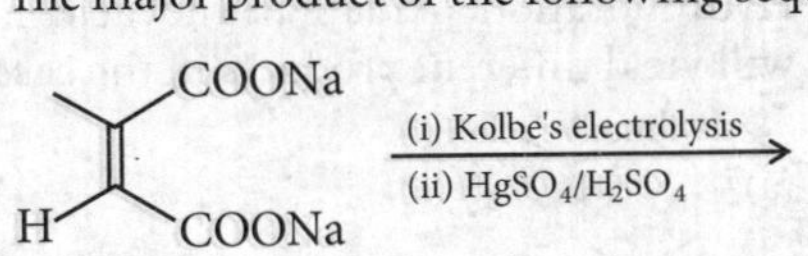

(a) 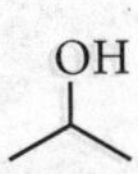 (b) 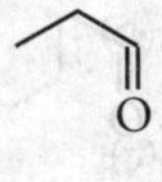
(c) 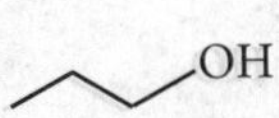 (d) 

29. Which of the following compounds will not give 3° alcohol as a major product with dilute H_2SO_4?

(a) 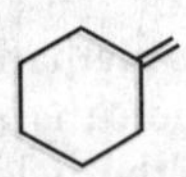 (b) 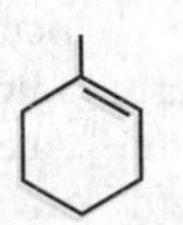
(c) 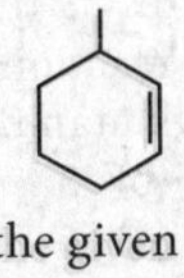 (d) 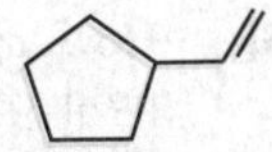

30. In the given reaction, [X] will be:

$$CH_3-CH=CH_2 \xrightarrow{Hg(OAc)_2/HOH} [X]$$

(a) $CH_3-CH_2-CH_2-OH$
(b) $CH_3-\underset{\displaystyle OH}{\underset{|}{CH}}-CH_3$
(c) $CH_3-\underset{\displaystyle OH}{\underset{|}{CH_2}}-CH_2-HgOAc$
(d) $CH_3-CH_2-CH_2-HgOAc$

31. Which of the following statements is incorrect?
(a) Neohexene is less reactive than n-pentene for HI.
(b) Neohydrocarbons contain a quaternary carbon atom in chain.
(c) Benzene cannot show addition reaction with dilute sulphuric acid.
(d) Alkenes can give nucleophilic addition reaction with hydrochloric acid.

32. Which of the following reactions involves Markovnikov's rule?
(a) $CH_2=CH_2 \xrightarrow[CCl_4]{HBr}$
(b) 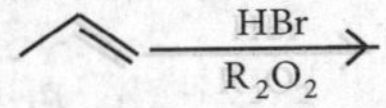
(c) 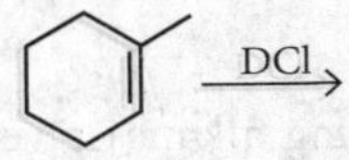
(d) 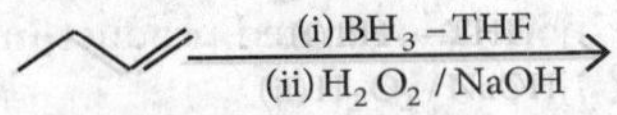

33. Which of the following will not give a colourless compound with bromine?

(a) 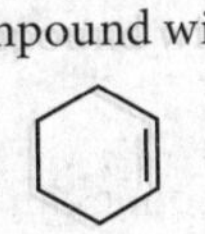 (b) 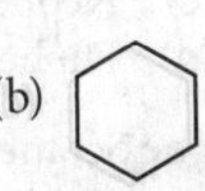
(c) $CH_3-C\equiv CH$ (d) 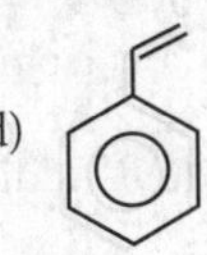

34. Which of the following statements is incorrect?
(a) An unsaturated compound has a higher octane number.
(b) LPG mainly contains methane.
(c) Acetylene is more acidic than ethylene.
(d) Reforming decreases the yield of gasoline.

35. How many alkenes on reaction with HBr produce 2-bromo-2-methylbutane?
(a) 4 (b) 3
(c) 5 (d) 6

36. Which of the following compounds will produce a precipitate with $AgNO_3$?

(a) 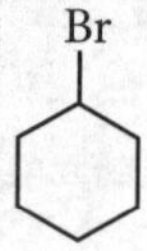

(b) 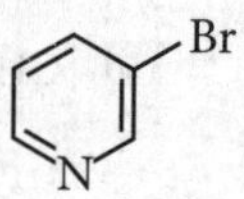

(c) 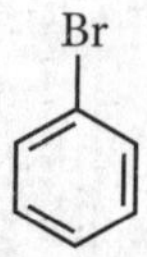

(d) 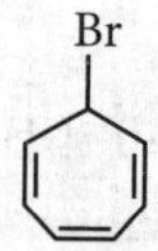

37. Which of the following is an incorrect statement about oxymercuration-demercuration?
(a) In the first step, oxymercuration occurs, that is, water and $Hg(OAc)_2$ add to the double bond.
(b) In the second step, demercuration occurs, that is, $NaBH_4$ reduces the –HgOAc group to hydrogen.
(c) The net reaction is addition of water according to anti-Markovnikov's rule.
(d) Rearrangement does not take place.

38. Which of the following cannot decolourise 1% alkaline $KMnO_4$?
(a) 1-Butyne (b) Propene
(c) 3-Hexene (d) Cyclohexane

39. Which of following alkanes gives more than one monohalogenated product in the presence of $X_2/h\nu$?
(a) Ethane
(b) Propane
(c) Neopentane
(d) Diphenylmethane

40. The octane number of gasoline can be increased by:
(a) Isomerization (heating with Al_2O_3)
(b) Aromatization
(c) Adding anti-knocking agent
(d) All of the above

41. The major product of the following addition reaction is:
$H_3C-CH=CH_2 \xrightarrow{Cl_2/H_2O}$
(a) $CH_3-CH(Cl)-CH_2(OH)$
(b) $H_3C-CH(OH)-CH_2(Cl)$
(c) 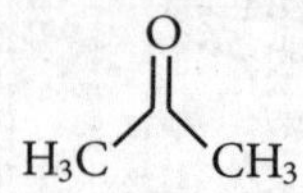
(d) 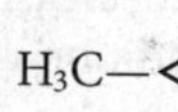

42. Which one of the following gives the most stable NCC with Br_2?
(a) Isobutene (b) Propene
(c) Ethene (d) Pentane

43. Which of the alkenes when treated with HCl yields majorly an anti-Markovnikov product?
(a) $F_3C-CH=CH_2$
(b) $H_2N-CH=CH_2$
(c) $CH_3O-CH=CH_2$
(d) $Cl-CH=CH_2$

44. The oxidative ozonolysis of 3-methyl-1-butene gives a mixture of:
(a) Isopropanoic acid and formic acid
(b) Propanoic acid and formic acid
(c) Isopropanoic acid and CO_2
(d) Propanoic acid and CO_2

45. Which of the following will not react with sodium metal?
(a) Ethyne (b) 1-Butyne
(c) Ethanol (d) Ethane

46. Hydroboration oxidation and acid hydration will yield different products in the case of:
(a) 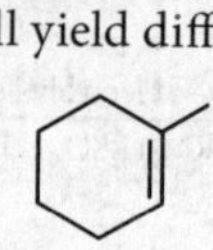
(b) 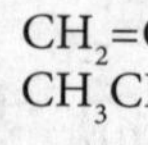
(c) $CH_2=CH_2$
(d) $CH_3CH=CHCH_3$

47. Which of the following reactions does not give a major product?

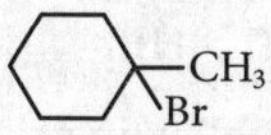

(a) 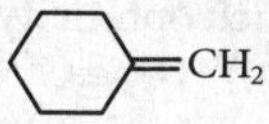 with HBr / H_2O_2

(b) 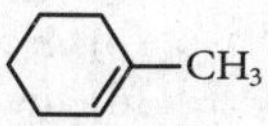 with HBr

(c) 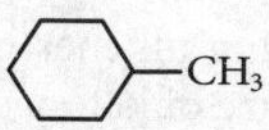 with $Br_2/h\nu$

(d) 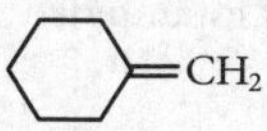 with HBr

48. Which of the following compounds will produce different major products with HBr?

(a) 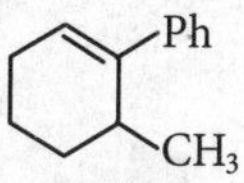 (b) 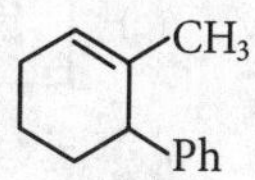

(c) 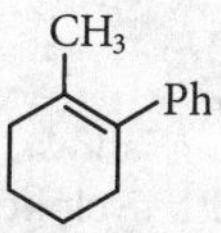 (d) 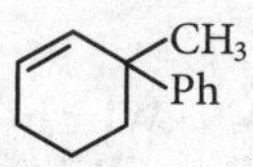

49. Which of the following cannot be used for the preparation of propane?

(a) $CH_3CH{=}CH_2 \xrightarrow[2.CH_3COOH]{1.B_2H_6}$

(b) $CH_3CH_2CH_2Cl \xrightarrow[2.H_2O]{1.\ Mg/ether}$

(c) $CH_3CH_2CH_2COONa \xrightarrow[\Delta]{NaOH/CaO}$

(d) $CH_3CH_2CH_2Cl \xrightarrow{Na/ether}$

50. Which of the following compounds contains a lower leaving tendency than acetate?

(a) 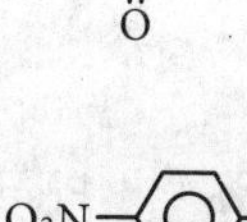 (b) 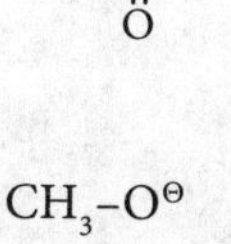

(c) 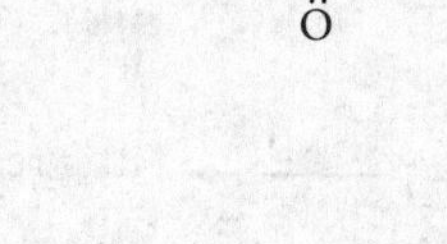 (d) $CH_3-O^{\ominus}$

51. Which of the following reactions produces secondary halides as a major product?

(a) 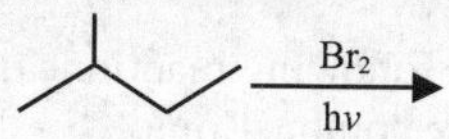

(b) 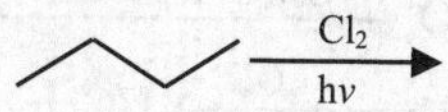

(c) 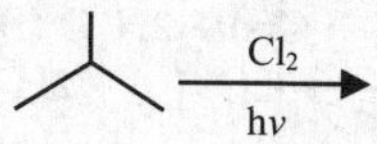

(d) 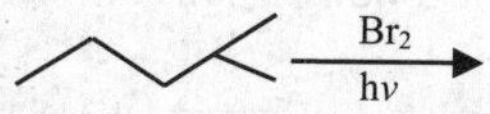

52. Arrange the following in decreasing order of their boiling points:

(i) n-Butane (ii) 2-Methylbutane
(iii) n-Pentane (iv) 2,2-Dimethylpropane

(a) i > ii > iii > iv (b) ii > iii > iv > i
(c) iv > iii > ii > i (d) iii > ii > iv > i

53. The intermediate carbocation formed in the reactions of HI, HBr and HCl with propene is the same and the order of reactivity of these halogen acids is HI >HBr>HCl. The bond energy of HCl, HBr and HI in kJ mol^{-1} is:

(a) 430.5, 363.7 and 296.8
(b) 363.7, 296.8 and 430.5
(c) 296.8, 363.7 and 430.5
(d) 430.5, 296.8 and 363.7

54. Arrange the halogens F_2, Cl_2, Br_2, I_2 in the order of their increasing reactivity with alkanes:

(a) $I_2 < Br_2 < Cl_2 < F_2$
(b) $Br_2 < Cl_2 < F_2 < I_2$
(c) $F_2 < Cl_2 < Br_2 < I_2$
(d) $Br_2 < I_2 < Cl_2 < F_2$

55. The increasing order of reduction of alkyl halides with zinc and dilute HCl is:

(a) R–Cl< R–I < R–Br
(b) R–Cl< R–Br < R–I
(c) R–I < R–Br < R–Cl
(d) R–Br < R–I < R–Cl

56. The double bond which is most reactive towards electrophile is:

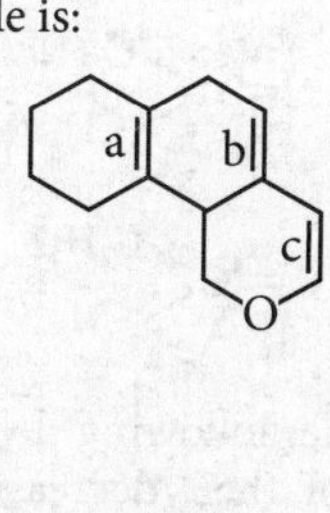

(a) a (b) c
(c) b (d) All are equal

57. Which of the following reactions of methane is an incomplete combustion?
(a) $2CH_4 + O_2 \xrightarrow{Cu/523\ K/100\ atm} 2CH_3OH$
(b) $CH_4 + O_2 \xrightarrow{Mo_2O_3} HCHO + H_2O$
(c) $CH_4 + O_2 \longrightarrow C(s) + 2H_2O\ (l)$
(d) $CH_4 + 2O_2 \longrightarrow CO_2\ (g) + 2H_2O\ (l)$

58. Which of the following is a controlled oxidation reaction?
(a) $CH_4(g) + 2O_2(g) \longrightarrow CO_2(g) + 2H_2O(l)$
(b) $CH_4(g) + O_2(g) \longrightarrow C(s) + 2H_2O(l)$
(c) $CH_4(g) + O_2(g) \xrightarrow{Mo_2O_3} HCOOH + H_2O$
(d) $2CH_4(g) + O_2(g) \xrightarrow{Cu/523\ K/100\ atm} 2CH_3OH$

59. The addition of HBr to 1-butene gives a mixture of products A, B and C. The mixture consists of:

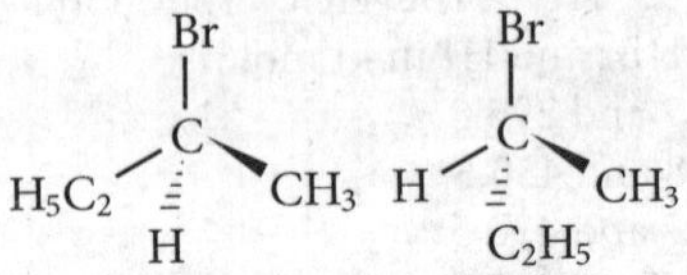

$CH_3–CH_2–CH_2–CH_2–Br$

(A) (B) (C)

(a) A and B as major and C as minor products
(b) B as major, A and C as minor products
(c) B as minor, A and C as major products
(d) A and B as minor and C as major products

60. Which of the following is the most reactive towards bromine water?

(a) 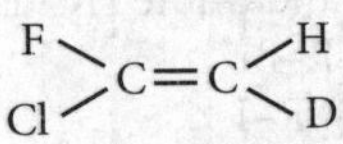

(b) 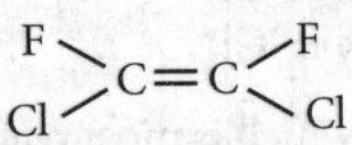

(c) 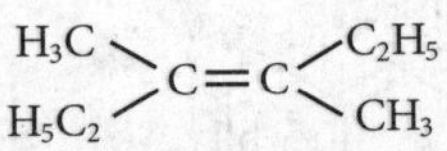

(d) 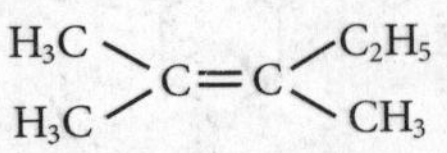

61. Arrange the following hydrogen halides in the order of their decreasing reactivity with propene:
(a) HCl > HBr > HI
(b) HBr > HI > HCl
(c) HI > HBr > HCl
(d) HCl > HI > HBr

62. Arrange the following carbanions in the order of their decreasing nucleophilicity:
(i) $H_3C–C{\equiv}C^-$ (ii) $H–C{\equiv}C^-$
(iii) $H_3C–CH_2^-$
(a) i > ii > iii (b) ii > i > iii
(c) iii > ii > i (d) iii > i > ii

63. Which of the following alkenes on ozonolysis does not give a mixture of ketones only?
(a) 1,2-Dimethyl cyclopentene
(b) $CH_3–C(CH_3)–CH=CH_2$
(c) 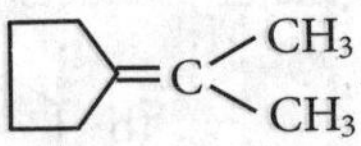
(d) $(CH_3)_2C=C(CH_3)_2$

64. Which of the following shows free radical substitution reaction with cyclohexene?
(a) HBr/H_2O_2
(b) Br_2/CCl_4
(c) NBS
(d) HBr/CCl_4

65. An alkane C_8H_{18} is obtained as the only product on subjecting a primary alkyl halide to Wurtz reaction. On monobromination, this alkane yields a single isomer of a tertiary bromide. The structure of the alkane is:
(a) 2-Bromo-2-methylpropane
(b) 1-Bromobutane
(c) 2-Bromobutane
(d) 1-Bromo-2-methylpropane

66. Which of the following reactions is incorrectly matched?

(a) 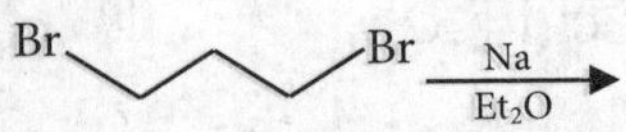
Wurtz reaction

(b) 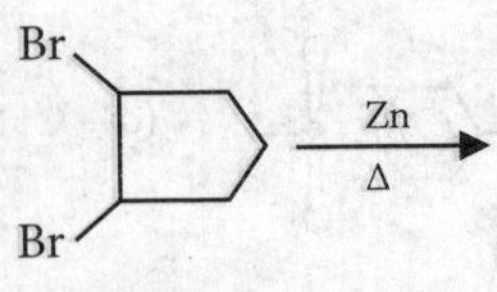
Frankland reaction

(c) 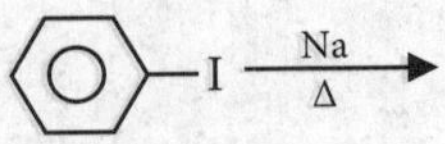
Fittig reaction

(d) 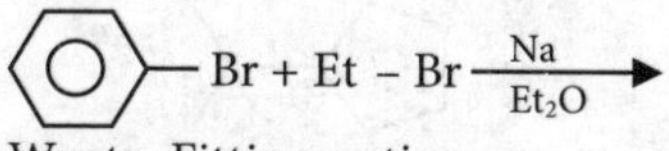

Wurtz–Fittig reaction

67. The major product obtained from the following reaction is:

$$\text{Propyne} \xrightarrow[\text{(ii) } H_2O_2/\overset{\ominus}{O}H]{\text{(i) } BD_3 \cdot THF}$$

(a) $H_3C{-}CO{-}CD_3$
(b) $H_3C{-}CH_2{-}COD$
(c) $H_3C{-}CD_2{-}COD$
(d) $CH_3{-}CH(D){-}CHO$

68. Which of the following reactions is correctly matched with the major product?

(a) $CH_3{-}C{\equiv}CH \xrightarrow[\text{dil.} H_2SO_4]{1\% \, HgSO_4} CH_3{-}\overset{O}{\overset{\|}{C}}{-}CH_3$

(b) 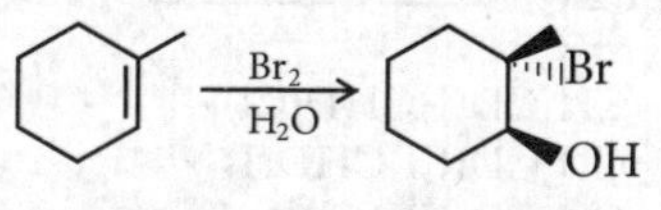

(c) 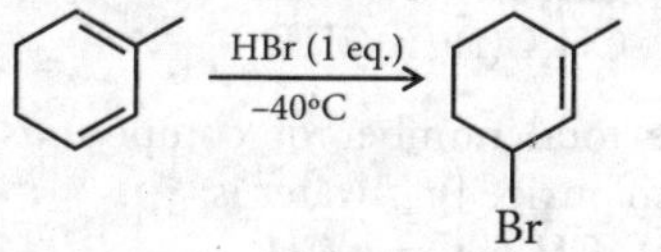

(d) 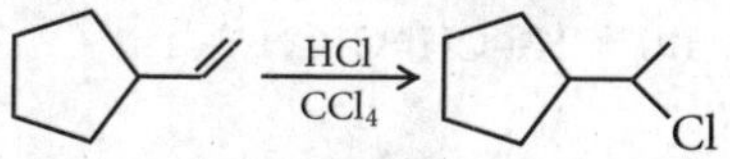

69. Product (B) is not the same when (A) is:

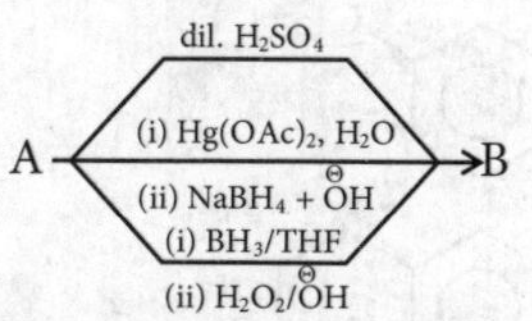

(a) Me–CH=CH–Me (b) Me–CH=CH_2

(c)  (d) 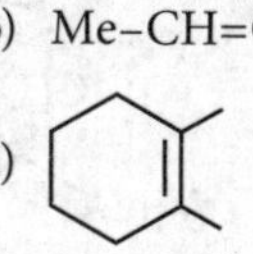

70. The reaction in which ethane is not obtained is:

(a) $CH_3{-}Cl \xrightarrow[\text{in ether}]{Na}$

(b) $CH_3{-}Br \xrightarrow[\text{(ii) } H{-}CHO]{\text{(i) } Mg}$

(c) $CH_3{-}COONa + H_2O \xrightarrow{\text{electrolysis}}$

(d) $CH_3{-}CH_2{-}Cl \xrightarrow[\text{(ii) } H_2O]{\text{(i) } Mg}$

71. In the following sequence of hydration reaction, X and Y are:

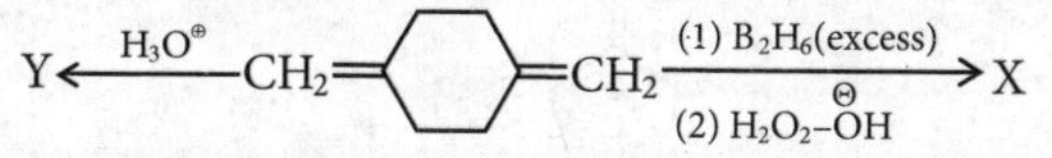

(a) 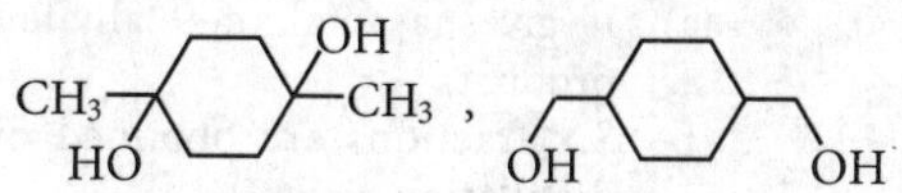

(b) 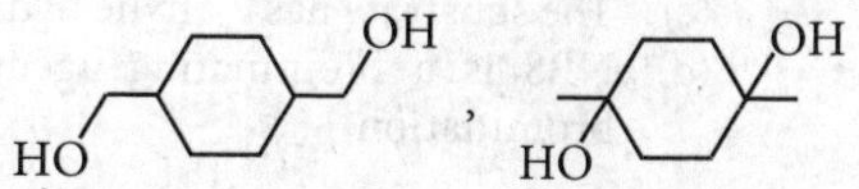

(c) 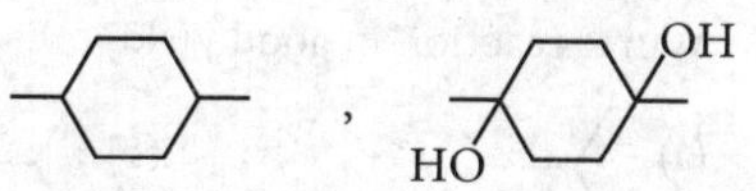

(d) 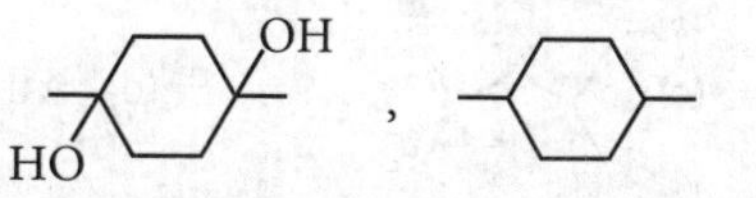

72. For the following reactions, identify the value of X + Y:

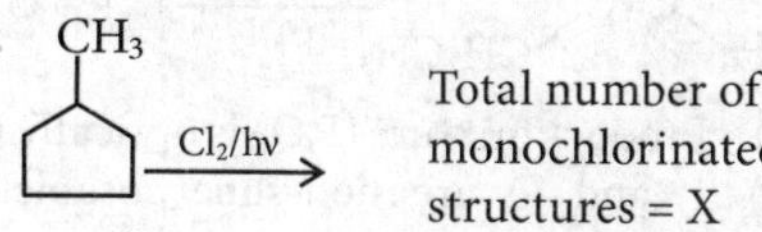

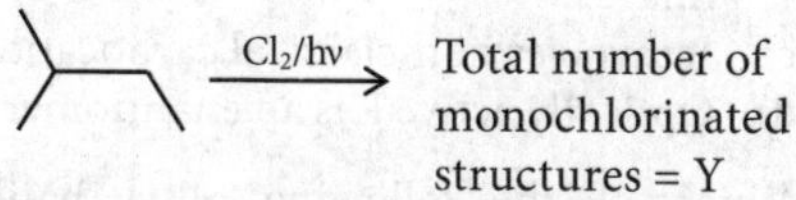

(a) 8 (b) 9
(c) 11 (d) 10

73. Which of the following can be obtain by the Wurtz reaction in good yield by a single reactant?

(a) 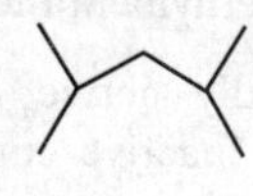

(b) 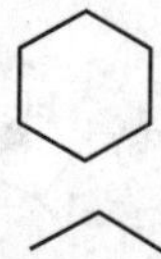

(c) 

(d) 

74. In the given reaction, find out the correct statement:

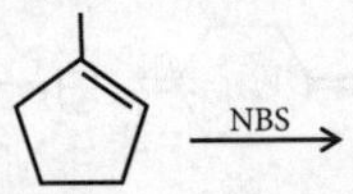

(a) It gives a total of 9 allylic brominated products
(b) Six fractions are obtained on fractional distillation
(c) The substrate has 7 allylic hydrogens
(d) NBS is a brominating agent for allylic bromination

75. Which of the following can be produced by the Wurtz reaction in good yield?

(a) 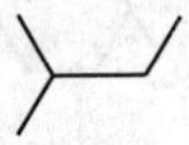

(b) 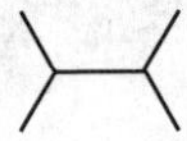

(c) 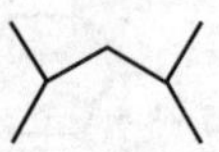

(d) All of these

76. Which of the following statements is incorrect?

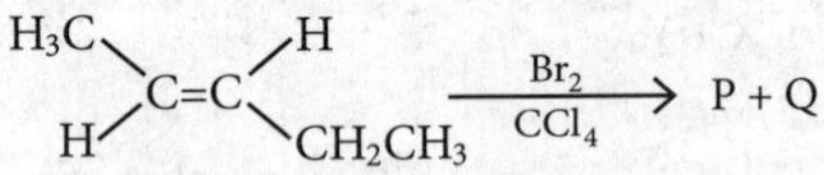

(a) Product mixture (P,Q) is optically inactive
(b) P and Q are non-superposable mirror images
(c) It involves non-classical carbocation
(d) Optically active P is an enantiomer with Q

77. Which of the following alkyl halides on reaction with sodium metal in dry ether give alkene:
(a) 1-Chloro-3-methyl butane
(b) 1-Chloro-2-methylbutane
(c) 2-Chloro-2,3-dimethyl pentane
(d) 1-Chloro-2,3-dimethylpentane

78. Which of the optically active compounds produces an optically inactive compound on hydrogenation?

(a) 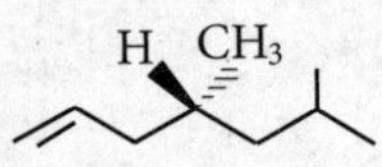

(b) 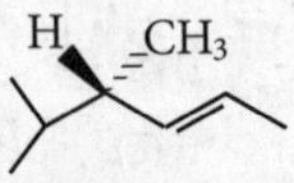

(c) 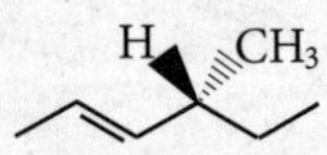

(d) 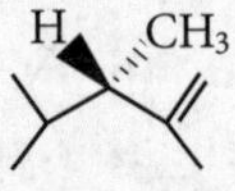

79. For maximum stability, how many 1,2-shifts will occur in the following carbocations?

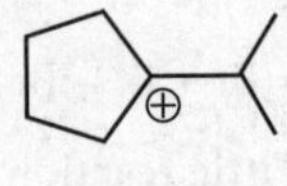

(a) 2 (b) 1
(c) 0 (d) 3

80. The incorrect statement for the monochlorinated products of the following reaction is:

$$CH_2{=}CH{-}CH_2{-}CH_3 \xrightarrow{Cl_2/500^\circ C}$$

(a) Five different products are formed
(b) Two optically active products are formed.
(c) The same can be made by the reaction of HCl.
(d) The reaction path is free radical substitution.

81. The major product of the following reaction is:

$$CH_3C\equiv CH \xrightarrow[\text{(ii) DI}]{\text{(i) DCl(1 eq.)}}$$

(a) $CH_3CD(I)CHD(Cl)$
(b) $CH_3CD(Cl)CHD(I)$
(c) $CH_3CD_2CH(Cl)(I)$
(d) $CH_3C(I)(Cl)CHD_2$

82. The total number of compounds which can decolourize Br_2 / water is:
(i) $CH_3-CH=CH_2$
(ii) $CH_3-CH=\underset{\underset{CH_3}{|}}{C}-CH_3$
(iii) $CH_2=CH_2$
(iv) 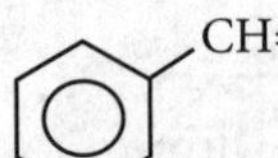
(v) 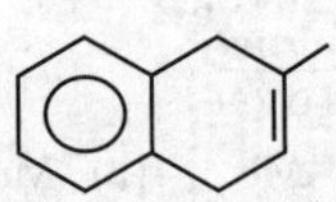
(vi) $CH_3-C\equiv C-H$
(vii) 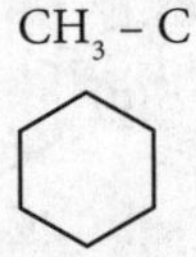
(viii) 
(ix) 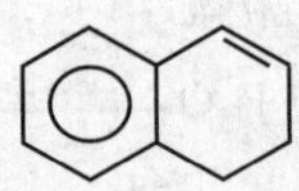

(a) 7 (b) 6
(c) 8 (d) 5

83. Acid catalysed hydration of alkenes, except ethene, leads to the formation of:
(a) Secondary or tertiary alcohol
(b) Primary alcohol
(c) Mixture of secondary and tertiary alcohols
(d) Mixture of primary and secondary alcohols

84. Phenylmagnesium bromide reacts with methanol to give:
(a) A mixture of anisole and Mg(OH)Br
(b) A mixture of benzene and Mg(OMe)Br
(c) A mixture of toluene and Mg(OH)Br
(d) A mixture of phenol and Mg(Me)Br

85. Anti-Markovnikov's addition of HBr is not observed in:
(a) Cyclohexene (b) Isobutene
(c) Propene (d) Hex-2-ene

86. Which of the following compounds is not obtained by ozonolysis of o-xylene?
(a) CHO–CHO
(b) CH_3–CO–CH_3
(c) CH_3–CO–CO–CH_3
(d) CH_3–CO–CHO

87. The major products when methylcyclopentene reacts with ozone followed by zinc are:

(a) 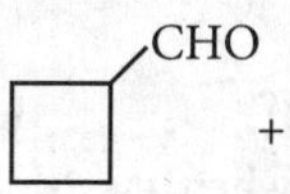 + HCHO

(b) 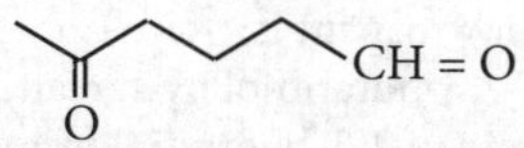

(c) 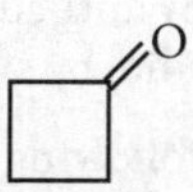 + CH_3CHO

(d) 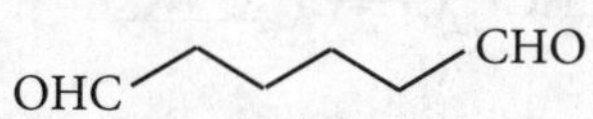

88. The synthesis of 3-octyne is achieved by adding a bromoalkane into a mixture of sodium amide and an alkyne. The bromoalkane and alkyne are, respectively:
(a) $BrCH_2CH_2CH_2CH_2CH_3$ and $CH_3CH_2C{\equiv}CH$
(b) $BrCH_2CH_2CH_3$ and $CH_3CH_2CH_2C{\equiv}CH$
(c) $BrCH_2CH_2CH_2CH_2CH_3$ and $CH_3C{\equiv}CH$
(d) $BrCH_2CH_2CH_2CH_3$ and $CH_3CH_2C{\equiv}CH$

89. Compound (A) on oxidation with hot $KMnO_4$/NaOH gives two compounds.

$$CH_3-\underset{\displaystyle CH_3}{\underset{|}{CH}}-COOH \quad \text{and} \quad CH_3-\overset{\displaystyle O}{\overset{\|}{C}}-CH_2CH_2CH_3$$

Then A is:

(a) $CH_3CH_2-\underset{\displaystyle CH_3}{\underset{|}{C}}=\underset{\displaystyle CH_3}{\underset{|}{C}}-CH_2CH_3$

(b) $CH_3-\underset{\displaystyle CH_3}{\underset{|}{CH}}-CH=\underset{\displaystyle CH_3}{\underset{|}{C}}-CH_2CH_2CH_3$

(c) $CH_3\underset{\displaystyle CH_3}{\underset{|}{CH}}-C\equiv C-CH_3$

(d) $CH_3-\underset{\displaystyle CH_3}{\underset{|}{CH}}-C\equiv C-\underset{\displaystyle CH_3}{\underset{|}{CH}}-CH_3$

90. Isomers of hexane, based on their branching, can be divided into three distinct classes, as shown in the figure. The correct order of their boiling points is:

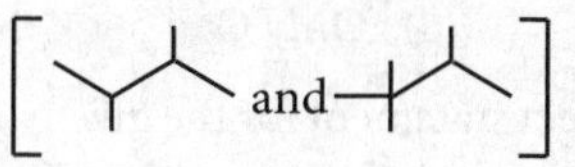
(I)

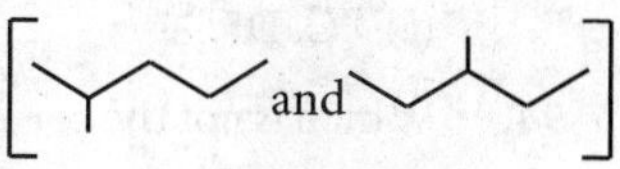
(II)

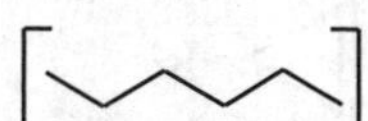
(III)

(a) I > II > III (b) III > II > I
(c) II > III > I (d) III > I > II

91. A compound that on hydrogenation produces an optically active compound is:

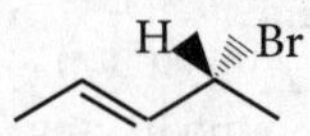
(A)

(B)

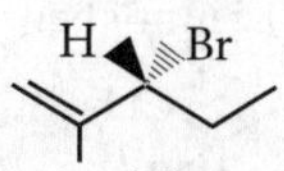
(C)

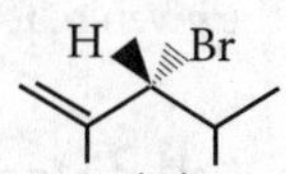
(D)

(a) All (b) Only A, C
(c) A, B, C (d) B, C, D

92. R_1 and R_2 in the following reaction can be, respectively:

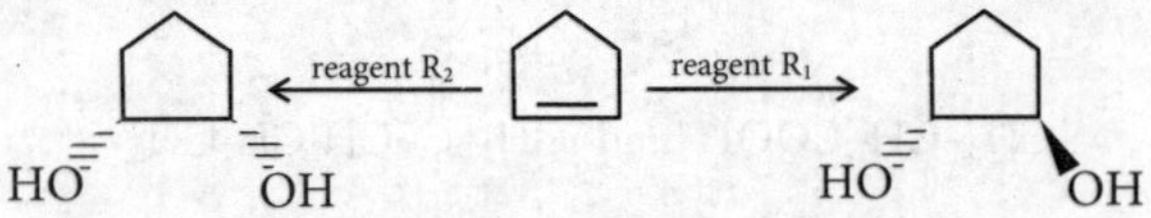

(a) Cold alkaline $KMnO_4$, $OsO_4/NaHSO_3$
(b) (i) $C_6H_5CO_3H$ (ii) $H_3\overset{\oplus}{O}$, cold $KMnO_4$
(c) $OsO_4/NaHSO_3$, $(CH_3)_2O_2$
(d) $C_6H_5CO_3H$, HCO_3H

93. Which of the following reactions produces propane as a major product?

(A) 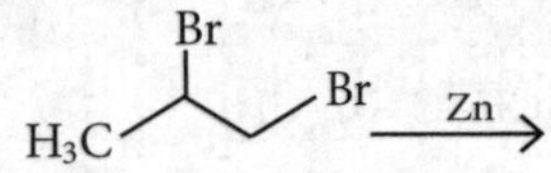

(B) 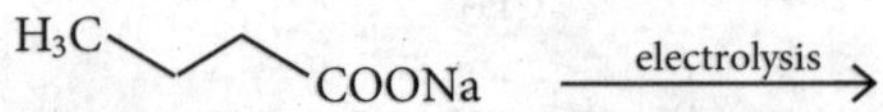

(C) 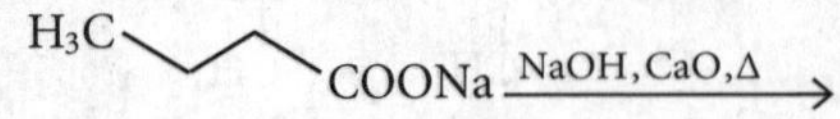

(D) 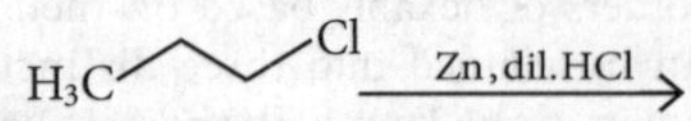

(a) A, C, D (b) B, C, D
(c) C, D (d) Only C

94. Which is not the correct statement for the given compound?

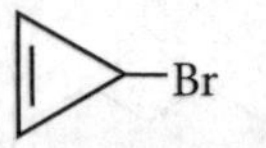

(I)

(a) I is more soluble than bromocyclopropane.
(b) I gives a pale yellow precipitate on addition of $AgNO_3$.
(c) I has lower dipole moment than bromocyclopropane.
(d) On reaction with $AlBr_3$, I will produce an aromatic compound having three resonating structures.

95. In the given reaction, (X) cannot be:

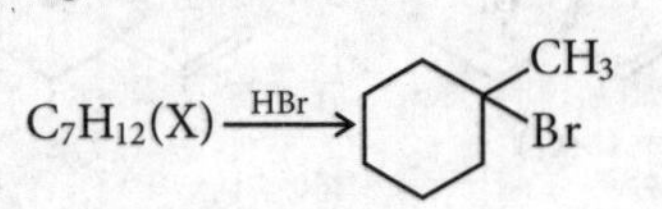

(a) 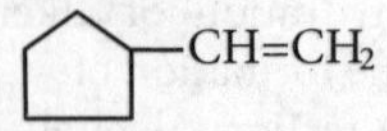

(b) 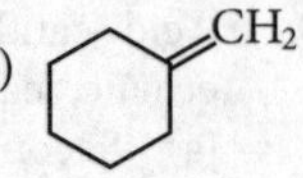

(c) 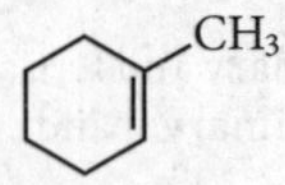

(d) 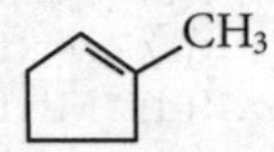

96. Which of the following is the correct set of nucleophiles?
(a) Br_2, H_2O, NH_3
(b) ROH, RNH_2, CO_2
(c) 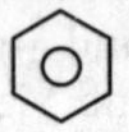 , $CH_2{=}CH_2$, NaOH
(d) $CH_3{-}NH_2$, $CH_3{-}OH$, $CH_3{-}\overset{O}{\overset{\|}{C}}{-}Cl$

97. For the following steps, Ea_1 and Ea_2 are activation energies. Then choose the correct alternative:

(i) $CH_3{-}CH_2{-}CH_3 + \dot{B}r \xrightarrow{Ea_1} CH_3{-}CH_2{-}\dot{C}H_2 + HBr$

(ii) $CH_3{-}CH_2{-}CH_3 + \dot{B}r \xrightarrow{Ea_2} CH_3{-}\dot{C}H{-}CH_3 + HBr$

(a) $Ea_1 = Ea_2$
(b) $Ea_1 > Ea_2$
(c) $Ea_1 < Ea_2$
(d) None of the above

98. The major product when cis-2-butene reacts with Baeyer's reagent is:
(a) Meso-2,3-butandiol by syn addition
(b) Racemic of 2,3-butandiol by anti-addition
(c) Meso-2,3-butandiol by anti-addition
(d) Racemic of 2,3-butandiol by syn addition

99. The major product of the following reaction is:
$CH_2{=}CHCH_2CH{=}CH_2 \xrightarrow{NBS}$

(a) $CH_2{=}CH\underset{Br}{\underset{|}{C}}HCH{=}CH_2$
(b) $CH_2{=}CHCH{=}CH{-}CH_2Br$
(c) $CH_2{=}CHCH_2CH{=}CHBr$
(d) $CH_2{=}CH\underset{Br}{\underset{|}{C}}HCH{=}CH_2$

100. The major product in the following reaction is:

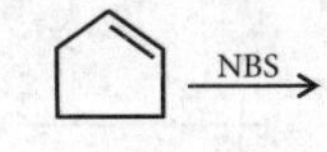

(a) 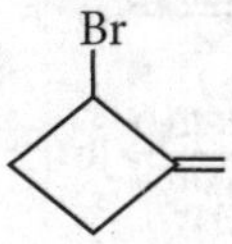

(b) 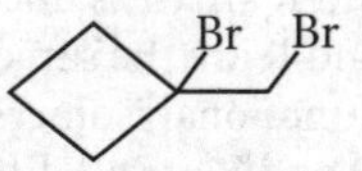

(c) 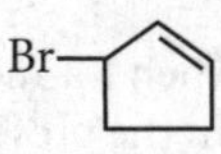

(d) 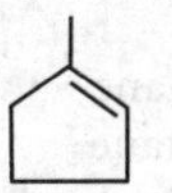

101. Among the isomeric alkanes of molecular formula C_5H_{12}, which of the following yields four structures of monochlorides on photochemical chlorination?

(a)  (b) 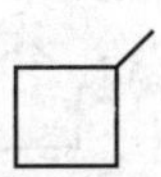

(c)  (d) 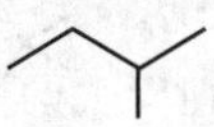

102. The reaction of cyclooctyne with $HgSO_4$ in the presence of aqueous H_2SO_4 gives:

(a) 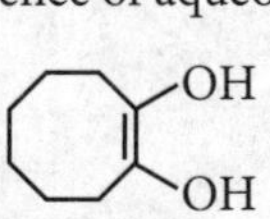 (b) 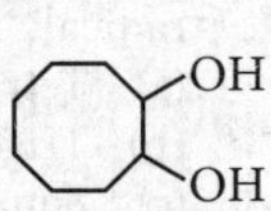

(c) 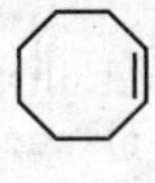 (d) 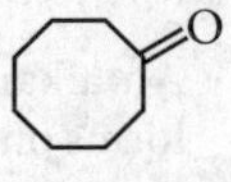

103. The major product of the following reaction is:

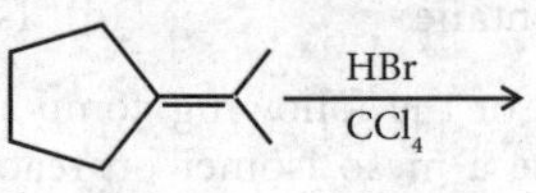

(a) 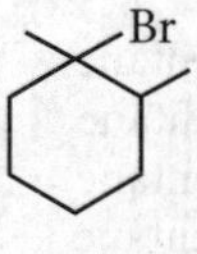

(b) 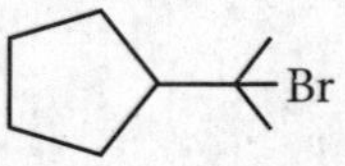

(c) 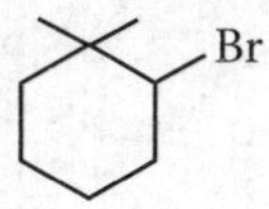

(d) 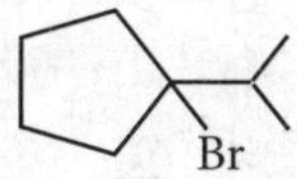

104. Among the following, select the incorrect statement:

(a) I_2 does not react with ethane at room temperature.
(b) Free radical addition and electrophilic addition reaction on propene are identical.
(c) The rate of bromination of methane is less than that of isobutane.
(d) Allylic chloride reacts faster than vinylic chloride for electrophilic addition.

105. Which reagent is the most useful for distinguishing compound I from the rest of the compounds?

$CH_3CH_2C{\equiv}CH$ (I) $CH_3C{\equiv}CCH_3$ (II)

$CH_3CH_2CH_2CH_3$ (III) $CH_3CH{=}CH_2$ (IV)

(a) Alk. $KMnO_4$ (b) Br_2/CCl_4
(c) Br_2/CH_3COOH (d) Cu_2Cl_2/NH_4OH

106. B and C are identical when A is:

$$C \xleftarrow[H_2O_2/OH^-]{BH_3/THF} A \xrightarrow[H_2SO_4]{HgSO_4} B$$

(a) Ethyne (b) Propyne
(c) 2-Pentyne (d) 1-Butyne

107. The major product of the following reaction is:

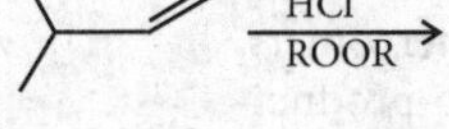

(a)  (b) 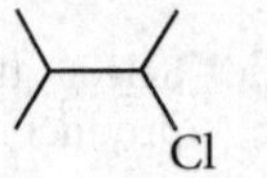

(c) 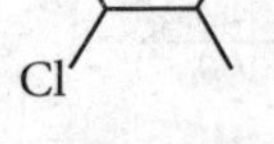 (d) 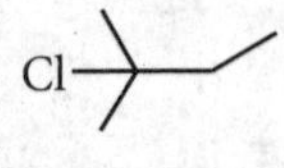

108. The major product of the following reaction is:

$Ph{-}CH = CH_2 + BrCCl_3 \rightarrow$

(a) 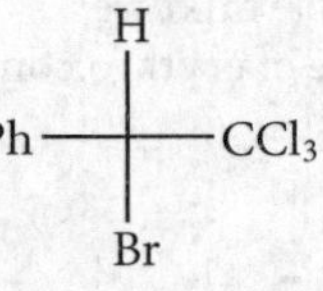

(b) 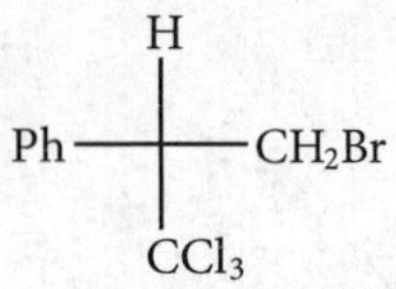

(c) 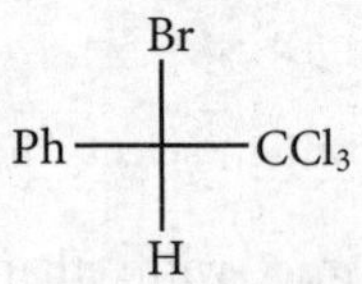

(d) 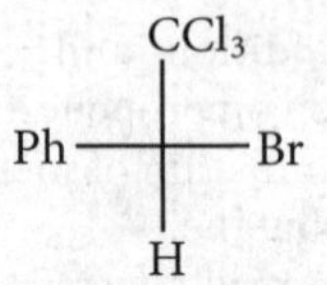

109. Arrange the following compounds in decreasing order of electrophilic addition:

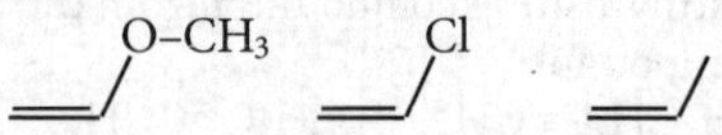

'P' 'Q' 'R'

(a) P > Q > R (b) P > R > Q
(c) R > P > Q (d) R > Q > P

110. The major product mixture of the following reaction is :

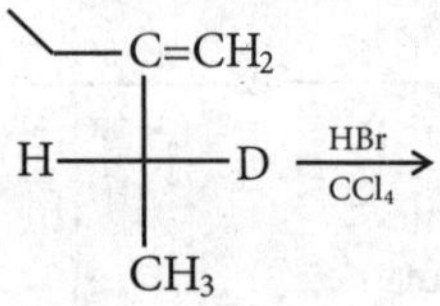

(a) Racemic mixture
(b) Optically inactive
(c) Diastereomers
(d) Meso-product

111. Select the incorrect statement about the product mixture in the following reaction:

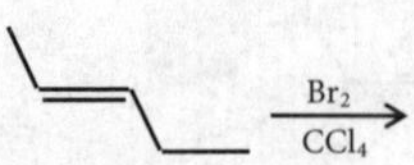

(a) It is optically active
(b) It is a racemic mixture
(c) It is a resolvable mixture
(d) It is a mixture of erythro compounds

112. The correct statement regarding products P, Q and R is:

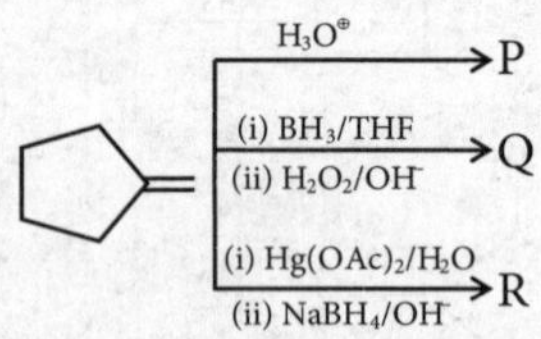

(a) Products P and R are the same
(b) Products Q and R are the same
(c) P and Q are functional isomers
(d) Products P, Q and R are all different

113. The major product when 2-methylbutane undergoes bromination in the presence of light is:
(a) 1-Bromo-2-methylbutane
(b) 2-Bromo-2-methylbutane
(c) 2-Bromo-3-methylbutane
(d) 1-Bromo-3-methylbutane

114. The alkane which cannot give only one monochloro derivative on reaction with chlorine in sunlight is:

(a)  (b) 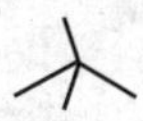

(c) 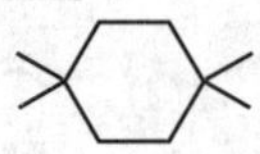 (d) 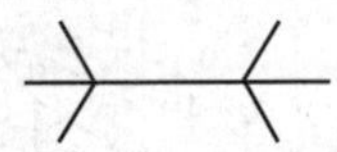

115. 2-Chloropentane gives 2,3-dichloropentane with Cl_2. What will be the structure of the free radical?
(a) Tetrahedral
(b) Trigonal planar
(c) Square planar
(d) Pyramidal

116. An alkane with chlorine and ultraviolet light forms only one monochloro alkane. The alkane is:
(a) Neopentane (b) Propane
(c) Pentane (d) Isopentane

117. Which of the following compounds does not produce a meso isomer on reaction with Na/Et_2O?
(a) 2-Bromo-2-methylpentane
(b) 1-Bromo-2-methylpentane
(c) 1-Bromo-3-methylpentane
(d) 2-Bromo-3-methylpentane

118. The correct order of the rate of photochlorination for the following compounds is:

(I) CH_3-CH_3 (II) CD_3-CD_3
(III) Neopentane

(a) III < II < I (b) I < II < III
(c) III < I < II (d) II < III < I

119. The number of reactions which produces hydrocarbon as a major product is:

(i) $CH_3-CH_2-Cl \xrightarrow[Et_2O]{Na}$

(ii) $CH_3-\overset{O}{\overset{\|}{C}}-OK \xrightarrow{Electrolysis}$

(iii) $\underset{Cl}{\underset{|}{CH_2}}-\underset{Cl}{\underset{|}{CH_2}} \xrightarrow[dust]{Zn}$

(iv) 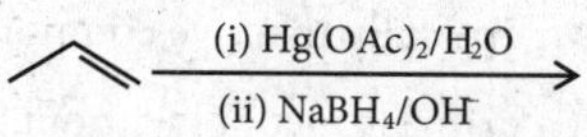

(v) 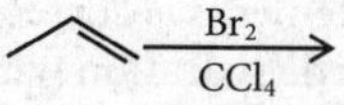

(vi) $CH_3CH_2-CH=CH_2 \xrightarrow[(ii)\ CH_3COOH/H_2O]{(i)\ B_2H_6-THF}$

(a) 2 (b) 4
(c) 5 (d) 6

120. Find out the correct order of the rate of reaction towards free radical allylic substitution:

(I) $CH_3-CH=CH_2$
(II) $CH_3-CH_2-CH=CH_2$
(III) $CH_3-\underset{}{\overset{CH_3}{\overset{|}{CH}}}-CH=CH_3$

(a) I > II > III (b) II > I > III
(c) III > II > I (d) III > I > II

121. The correct order of the rate of the Wurtz reaction is:

(I) 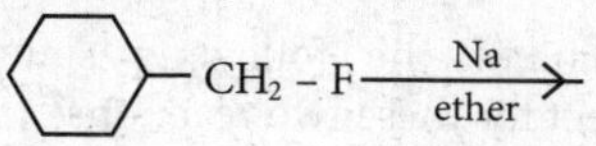

(II) 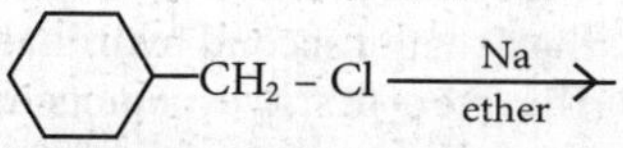

(III) 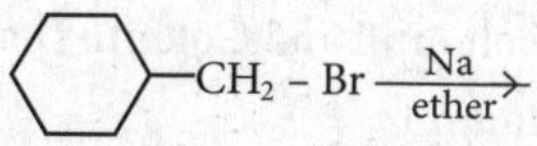

(IV) 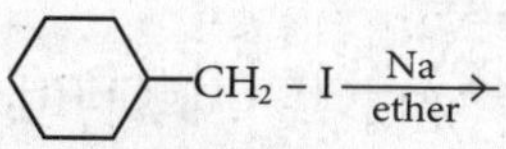

(a) I > II > III > IV
(b) II > I > III > IV
(c) IV > III > II > I
(d) In all, the rate is the same

122. Consider the reaction given below:

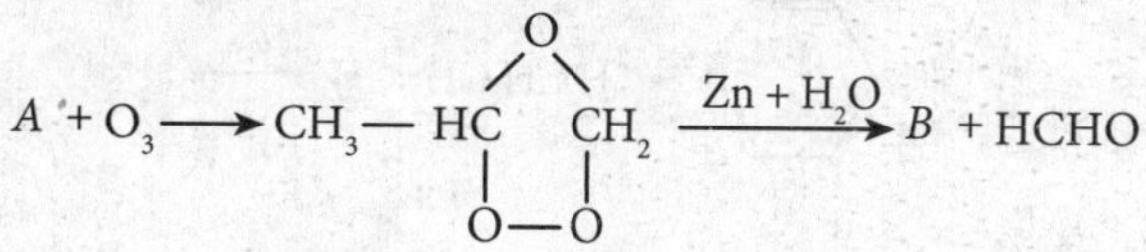

Here, *A* and *B* are, respectively:

(a) Propene and methanol
(b) Propane and ethanal
(c) Propene and ethanol
(d) Propene and ethanal

123. **Assertion (A):** 1-Butene on reaction with HBr in the presence of a peroxide produces 1-bromobutane.
Reason (R): It involves the formation of a primary radical.

(a) Both A and R are correct, R is the correct explanation of A.
(b) Both A and R are correct, R is not the correct explanation of A.
(c) A is correct, R is incorrect.
(d) R is correct, A is incorrect.

124. **Assertion (A):** Propene reacts with HI in the presence of peroxide to give 1-iodopropane.
Reason (R): 1° free radical is less stable than 2° free radical.

(a) Both A and R are correct, R is the correct explanation of A.
(b) Both A and R are correct, R is not the correct explanation of A.
(c) A is correct, R is incorrect.
(d) A is incorrect, R is correct.

125. Match Column I and Column II and choose the correct option from the codes given below:

Column I	Column II
(A) 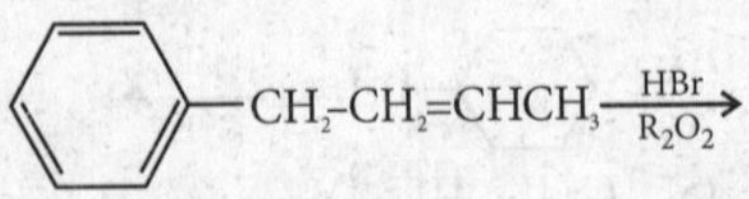	(a) 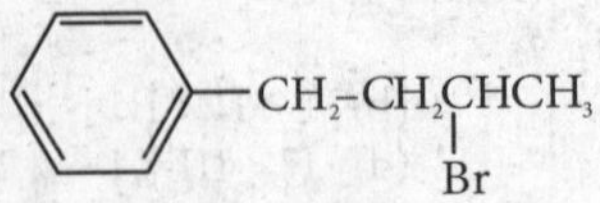
(B) 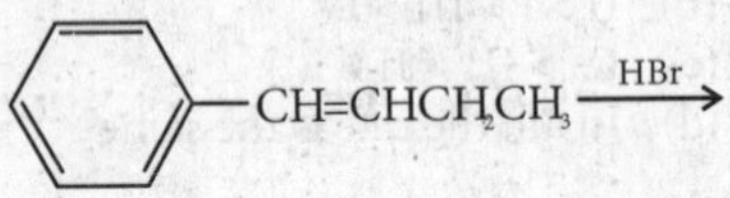	(b) 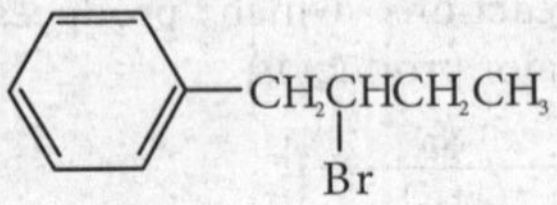
(C) 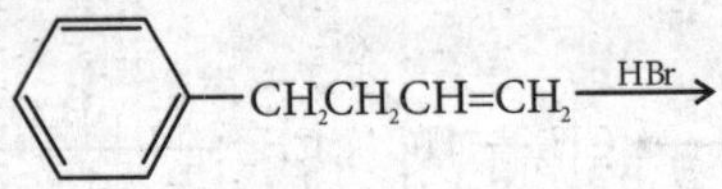	(c) 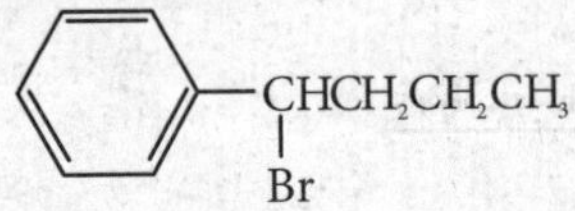

Codes

	A	B	C
(a)	b	c	a
(b)	a	b	c
(c)	a	c	b
(d)	c	b	a

126. Which of the following statements is true about the catalytic hydrogenation of alkenes and alkynes?
(a) Reaction is exothermic, but catalyst is required to reduce the activation energy.
(b) Reaction is exothermic, but catalyst is required to increase the activation energy.
(c) Reaction is endothermic, but catalyst is required to reduce the activation energy.
(d) Reaction is endothermic, but catalyst is required to increase the activation energy.

127.

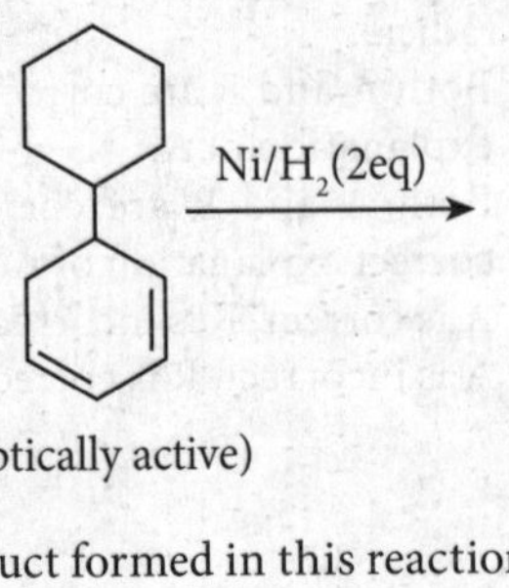

(Optically active)

The product formed in this reaction will be:
(a) An optically active compound
(b) A racemic mixture
(c) A mixture of diastereomers
(d) An optically inactive compound

128. About a primary alcohol without β-H, which of the following statements is correct?
(a) It undergoes dehydration with rearrangement.
(b) It fails to undergo dehydration.
(c) It undergoes dehydration in basic condition, not in acidic condition.
(d) None of the above.

129. $R-C\equiv CH \xrightarrow{HX} R-C(X)=CH_2$ (Vinyl halide) $\xrightarrow{HX} R-CX_2-CH_3$

Which of the following statements is/are correct for these two reactions?
(a) The rate of first hydrohalogenation is faster than that of second hydrohalogenation.
(b) The rate of first hydrohalogenation is slower than that of second hydrohalogenation.
(c) Alkynes are more reactive than vinyl halide toward an electrophile.
(d) Both (a) and (c)

Answer Key

Level-1

Alkane

1. (b)	2. (b)	3. (d)	4. (d)	5. (d)	6. (b)	7. (d)	8. (b)
9. (a)	10. (c)	11. (d)	12. (d)	13. (c)	14. (a)	15. (a)	16. (b)
17. (c)	18. (a)	19. (a)	20. (b)				

Alkene and Alkyne

21. (c)	22. (a)	23. (c)	24. (b)	25. (a)	26. (c)	27. (c)	28. (d)
29. (b)	30. (c)	31. (a)	32. (b)	33. (c)	34. (c)	35. (a)	36. (c)
37. (b)	38. (d)	39. (a)	40. (c)	41. (a)	42. (a)	43. (a)	44. (b)
45. (a)	46. (a)						

Aromatics

47. (c)	48. (d)	49. (a)	50. (a)	51. (c)	52. (c)	53. (a)	54. (d)
55. (b)	56. (c)	57. (c)	58. (c)	59. (b)	60. (b)	61. (a)	62. (c)
63. (b)	64. (b)	65. (b)	66. (d)	67. (d)	68. (d)	69. (b)	70. (a)
71. (a)	72. (d)	73. (a)	74. (a)	75. (b)	76. (b)	77. (b)	78. (a)
79. (d)	80. (b)	81. (d)					

Level-2

1. (b)	2. (c)	3. (c)	4. (c)	5. (b)	6. (c)	7. (c)	8. (c)
9. (d)	10. (b)	11. (b)	12. (c)	13. (d)	14. (b)	15. (b)	16. (a)
17. (b)	18. (d)	19. (a)	20. (b)	21. (d)	22. (a)	23. (a)	24. (b)
25. (c)	26. (d)	27. (c)	28. (d)	29. (c)	30. (c)	31. (d)	32. (c)
33. (b)	34. (d)	35. (b)	36. (d)	37. (c)	38. (d)	39. (b)	40. (d)
41. (b)	42. (a)	43. (a)	44. (c)	45. (d)	46. (a)	47. (a)	48. (d)
49. (d)	50. (d)	51. (b)	52. (d)	53. (a)	54. (a)	55. (b)	56. (c)
57. (c)	58. (d)	59. (a)	60. (d)	61. (c)	62. (d)	63. (b)	64. (c)
65. (d)	66. (b)	67. (d)	68. (a)	69. (b)	70. (b)	71. (b)	72. (a)
73. (b)	74. (b)	75. (b)	76. (a)	77. (c)	78. (d)	79. (d)	80. (c)
81. (d)	82. (a)	83. (a)	84. (b)	85. (a)	86. (b)	87. (b)	88. (d)
89. (b)	90. (b)	91. (b)	92. (b)	93. (c)	94. (c)	95. (d)	96. (c)
97. (b)	98. (a)	99. (b)	100. (c)	101. (d)	102. (d)	103. (a)	104. (b)
105. (d)	106. (a)	107. (d)	108. (b)	109. (b)	110. (c)	111. (a)	112. (a)
113. (b)	114. (c)	115. (b)	116. (a)	117. (a)	118. (a)	119. (b)	120. (c)
121. (c)	122. (d)	123. (c)	124. (d)	125. (a)	126. (a)	127. (d)	128. (a)
129. (d)							

Solutions

Level-1

1.

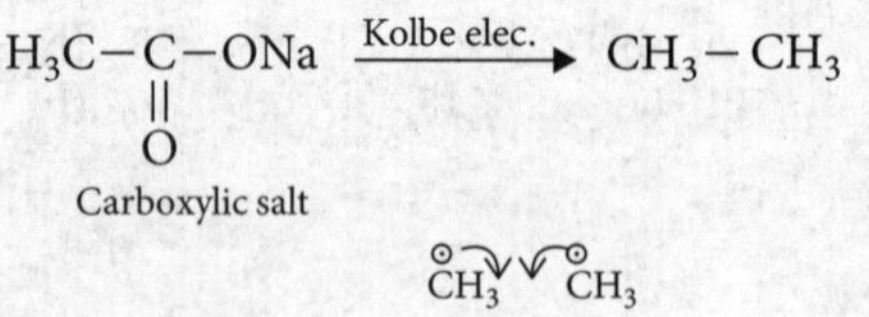

2. Boiling point $\propto \frac{\text{Surface area}}{\text{Branching}}$

3.

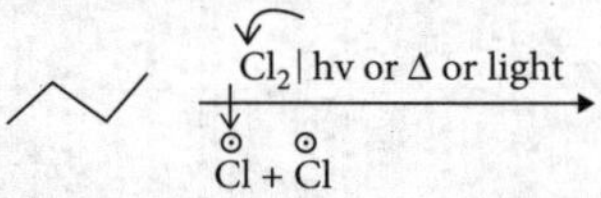

4. Free radical intermediate combines in chain termination step.

5.

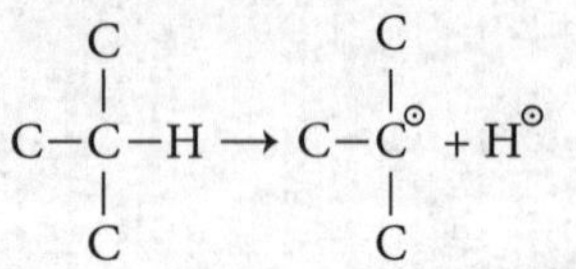

More stable carbon-free radical formed

6. HI is formed in iodination. It is a reducing agent and it is reduced to R-I which is reversible. So to remove HI, HIO_3 oxidising agent is added.

8.

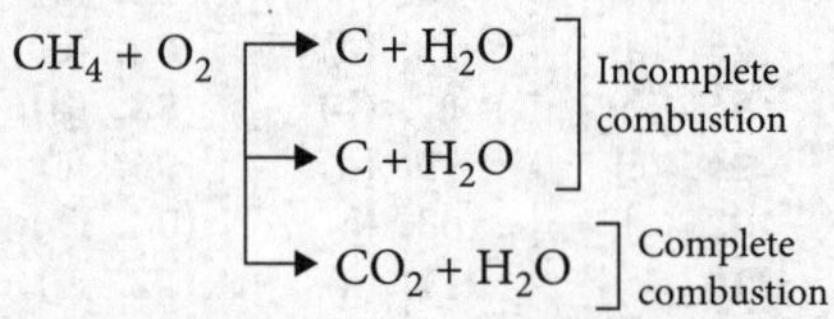

9. Mo_2O_3 is a catalytic controlled oxidizing agent used to form H-CHO from methane in the presence of heat.

10. Alkane is less reactive and does not oxidize, but strong oxidizing agent $KMnO_4$ oxidises only the alkane having 3° hydrogens.

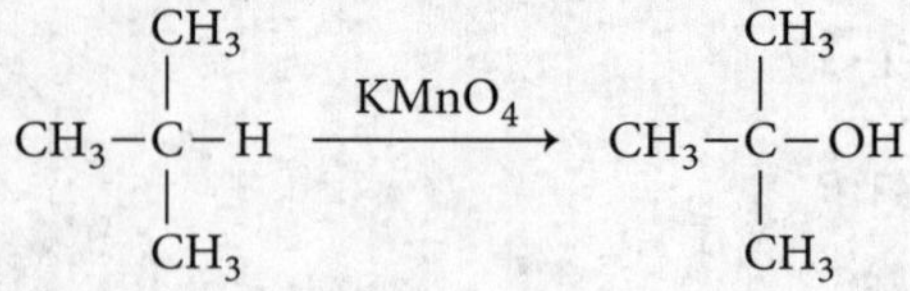

12.

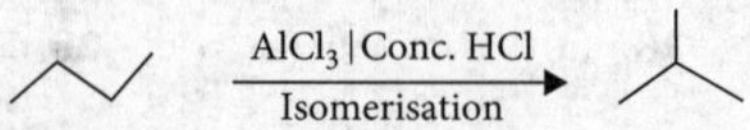

13. Alkanes are less reactive; so also known as paraffins.

14.

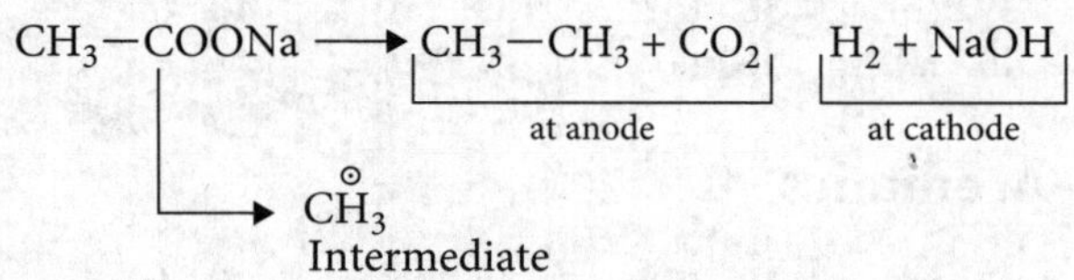

17. (A)

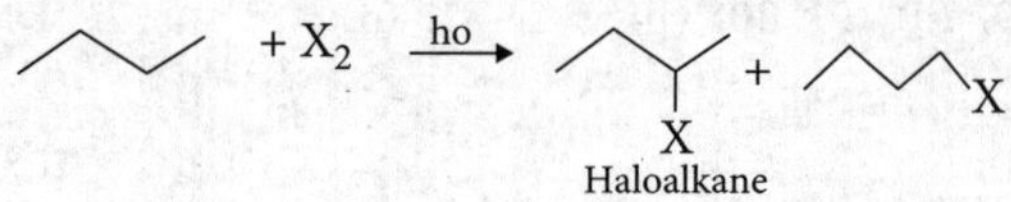

(B)

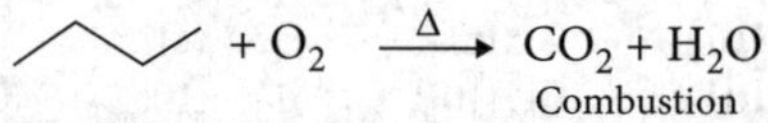

(C)

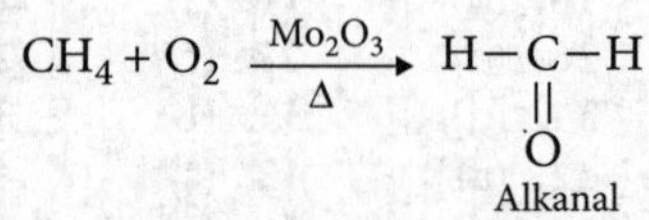

(D)

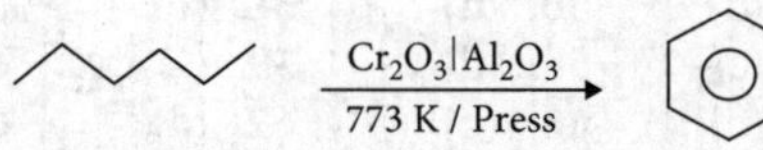

18.

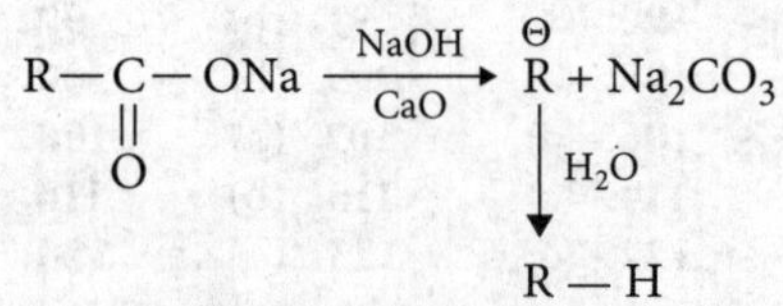

19. HF > HCl > HBr > HI
Strong bond formation of side product.

20. Stability of intermediate free radical.

21. Partial reducing agent = Lindlar catalyst

22.

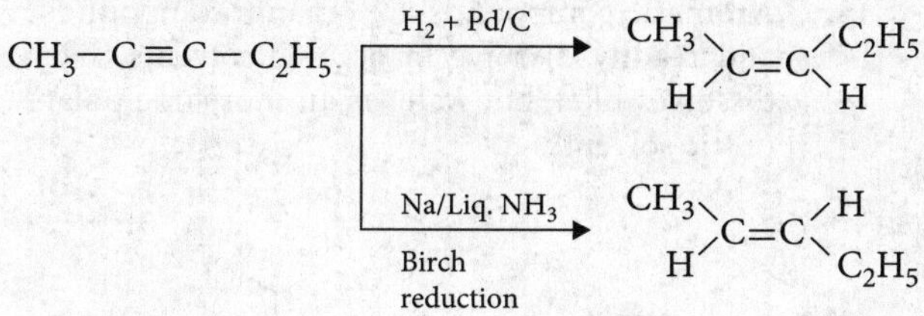

23.

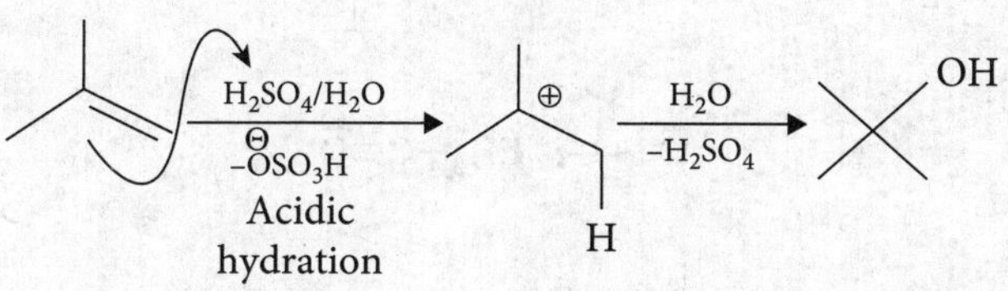

24.

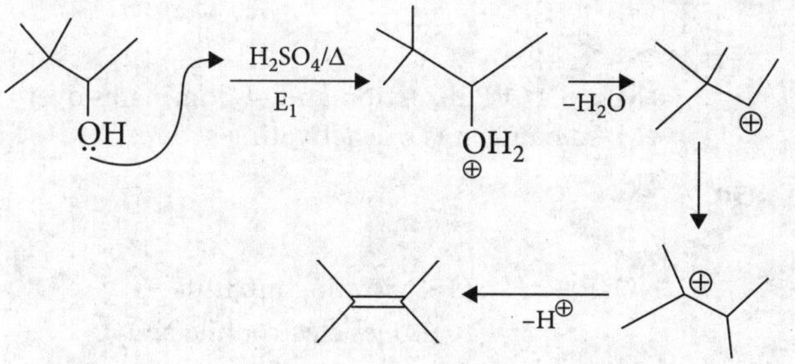

25.

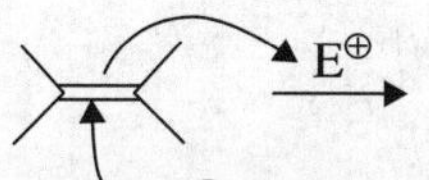

Octet complete and loosely bonded π bond

26. EAR is characteristic reaction of alkene.

27.

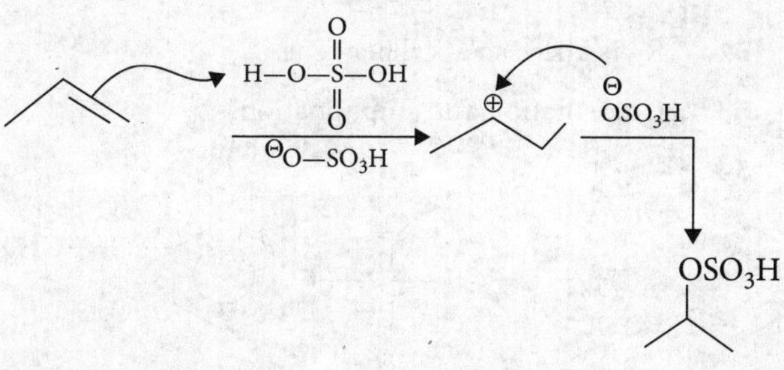

28. Cold (273 K), dilute $KMnO_4$ with Baeyer's reagent oxidizes alkene and alkyne and forms a syn addition of diol.

29.

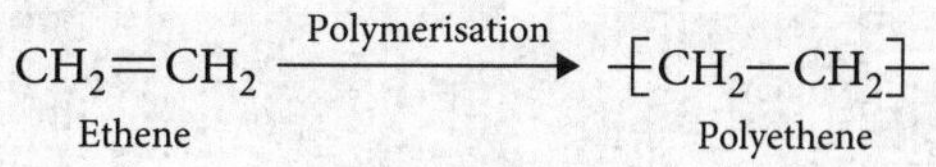

31.

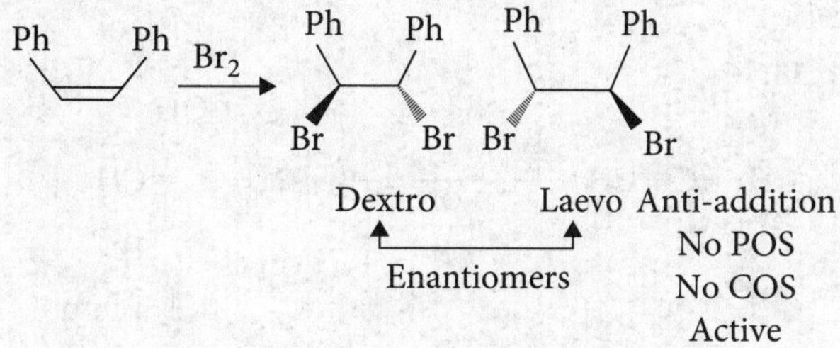

32. Oxidation ozonolysis gives acids.

33. Metal carbide hydrolysis gives hydrocarbon. Like $Mg_2C_3 + H_2O \rightarrow CH_3\text{-}C{\equiv}CH$

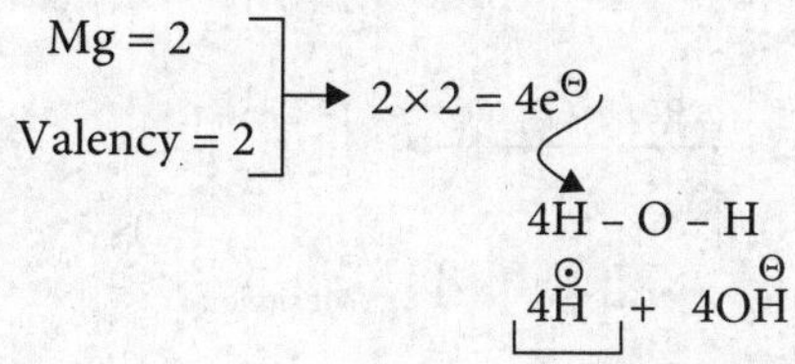

4 hydrogen atoms combine with 3 carbon atoms $H_3C{-}C{\equiv}CH$

34.

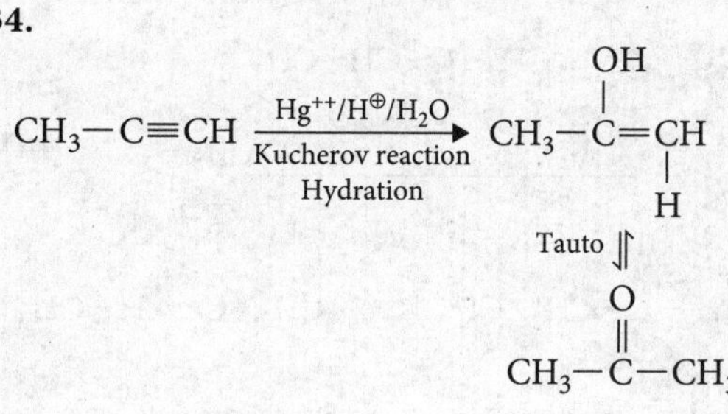

35.

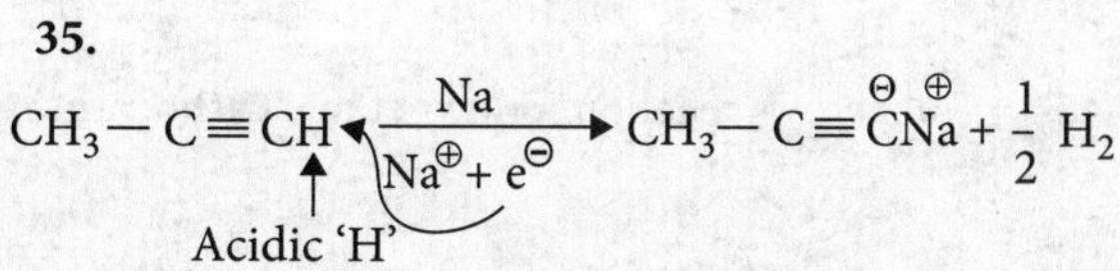

36. 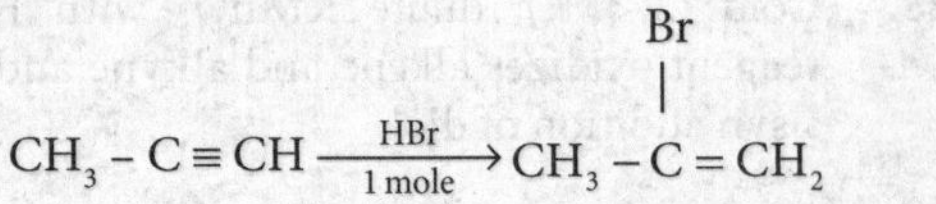

37. 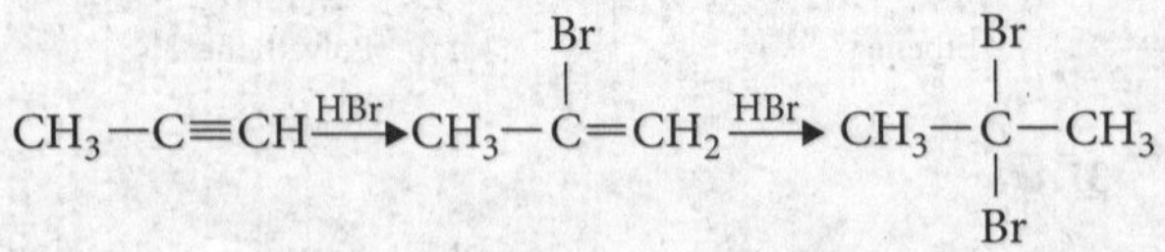

38. 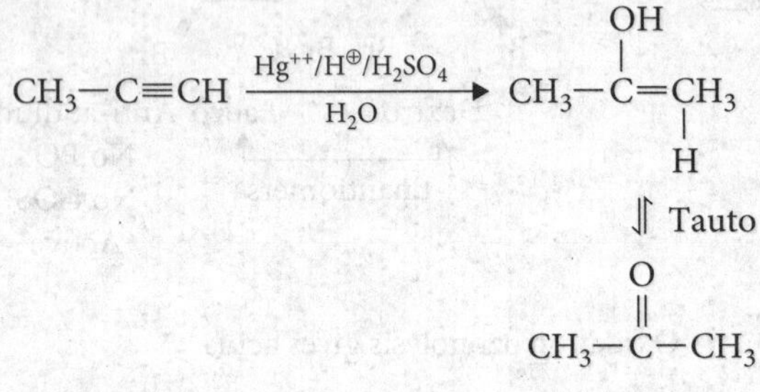

39. 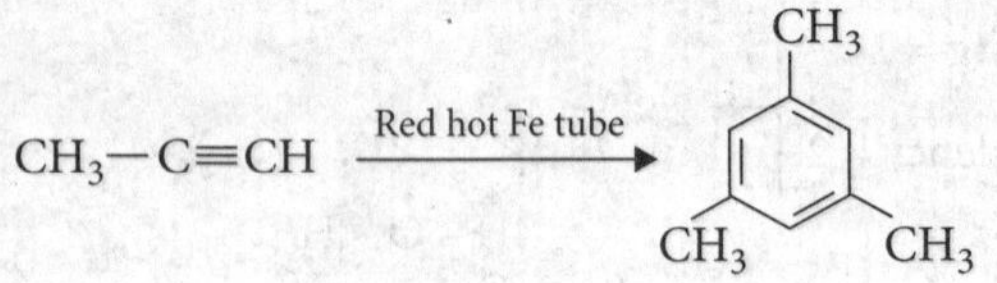

Mesitylene

40. Anion stability ∝ Acidic strength

42. 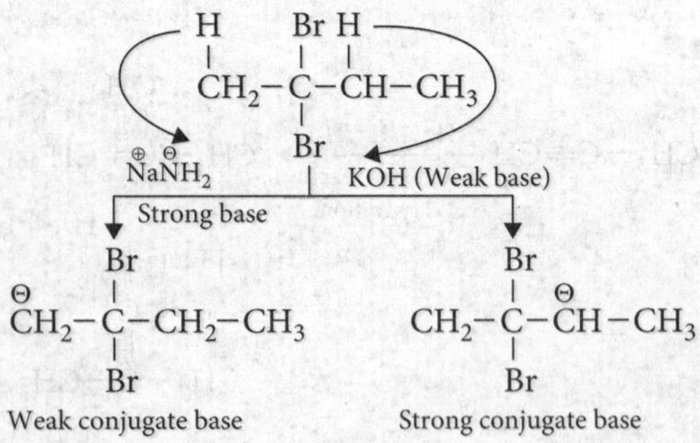

43. Kucherov's reaction follows stable carbocation.

44. $CH_4 + Cl_2 \xrightarrow[\text{is required for this reaction}]{\text{hv (proton)}} CH_3Cl + HCl$

Without photon, free radical does not form.

47. Ozonolysis is used to detect the presence of π bond and resonance in molecules.

48. Aromatic compounds are organic compounds and readily dissolve in organic solvents (like dissolves like), but water is an inorganic polar protic solvent.

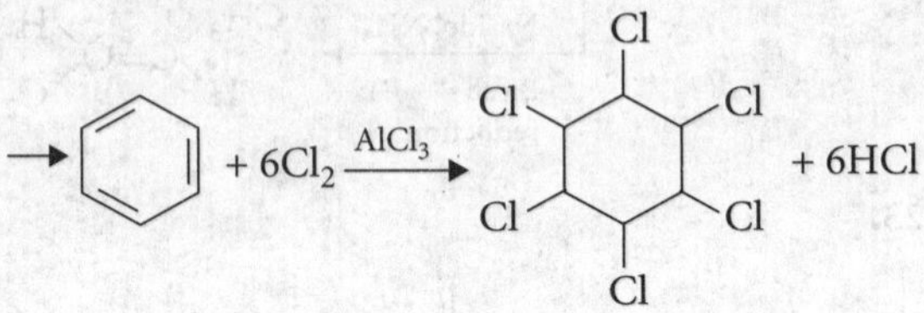

49. 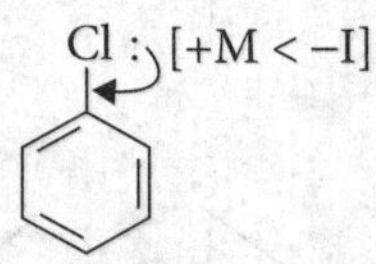

+M gives O/P direction and –I dominates over +M; so halogen is a deactivating group.

50. 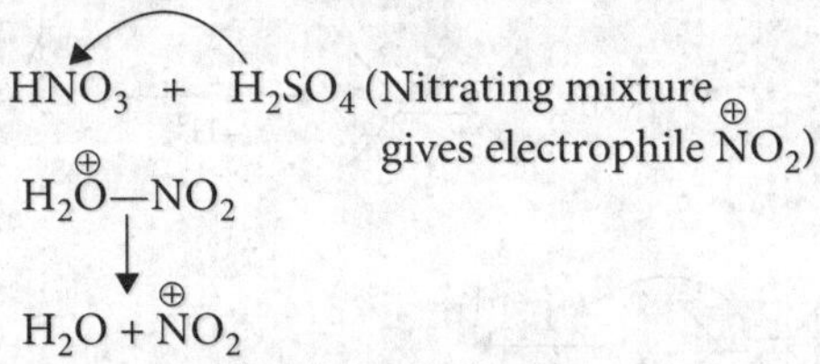

51. 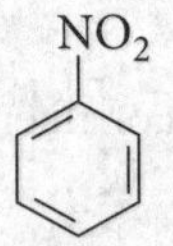

–M group deactivates to ring for electrophilic substitution reaction and meta directive

52. R– is alkyl; so alkyl benzene.

53. Chlorination and sulphonation.

54. 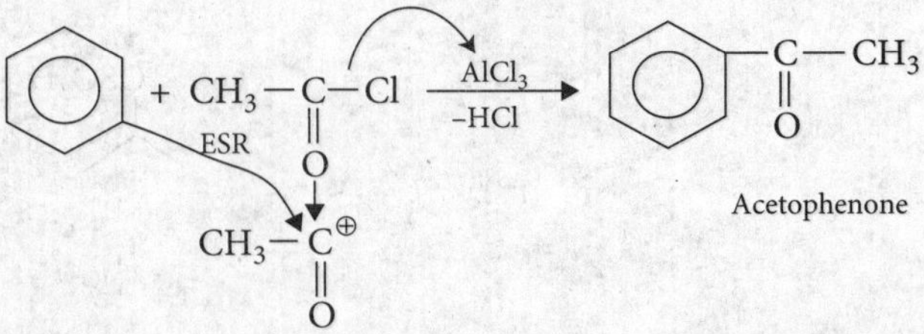

Acetophenone

55.

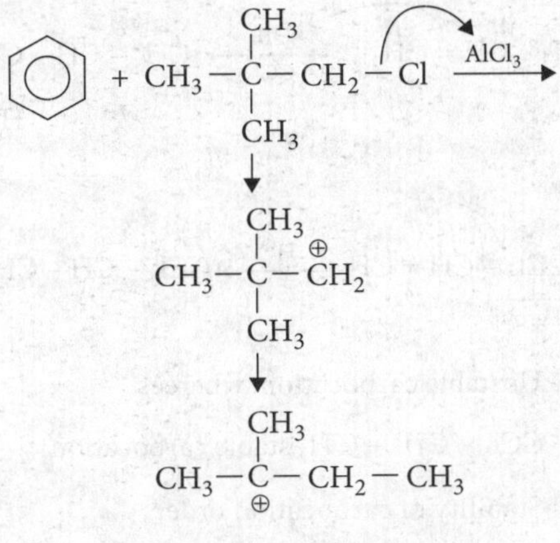

56. $HNO_3 \xrightarrow[\text{or } H_2SO_4]{HNO_3} H_2O + \overset{\oplus}{N}O_2$ (Electrophile)

57. 3π bonds reduced by $3H_2$ molecules.

58.

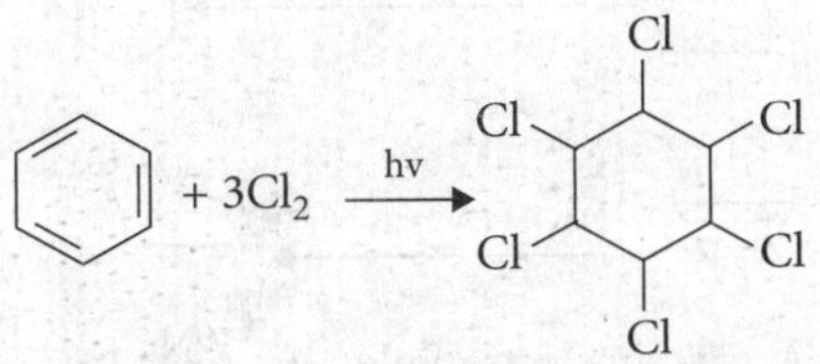

59. By complete combustion, $CO_2 + H_2O$ is formed.

60. All deactivating groups ($-NO_2$, $-CHO$, $-SO_3H$, $-COR$) are meta-directing groups.

61. In electrophilic substitution reaction, electrophile attacks and $-NO_2$ is the metadirecting group b/c by –M; it decreases electron density at the O/P position.

62. ESR $\propto$ Electron density tendency (+M, +H, +I, –I, –H, –M in order)

63. By pyrolysis (cracking), higher organic hydrocarbon is converted into lower hydrocarbon.

64. Due to resonance, all C–C bonds are partial double bond character.

65. C–H bond formed by axial–axial overlapping of sp^2 of 'C' and 1s of 'H'.

66. To retain aromaticity, benzene shows electrophilic substitution reaction.

67. Aromatic compounds are cancer causing agents.

68. –OH is lone pair containing; activating group by +M.

70. 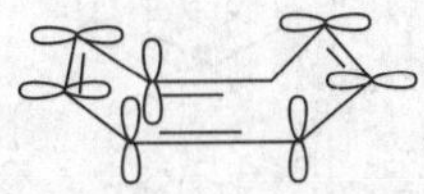

The P-orbital goes out of the plane, so cycle resonance is absent; therefore, non-aromatic.

71.

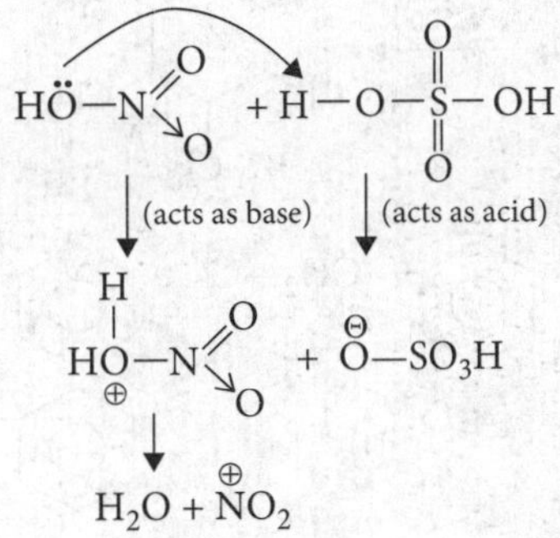

72.

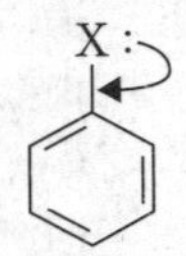

Aryl halide is lone pair containing, so it is ortho, para directing by +M; due to weak +M and more dominant –I, it is a weak deactivating group.

74.

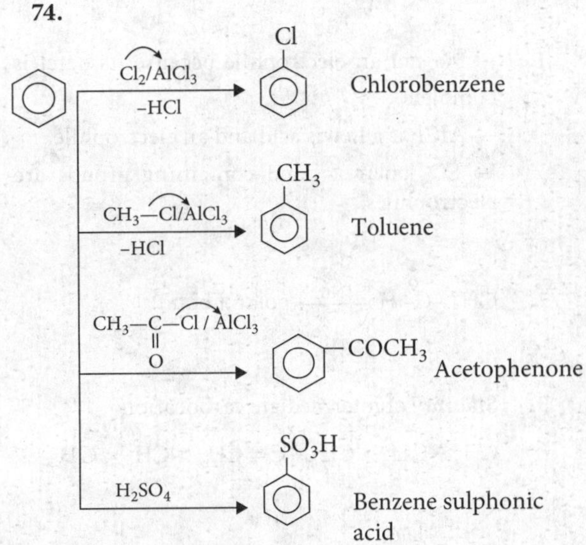

75. $Zn \rightarrow ZnO$.

76. See Q71.

78.

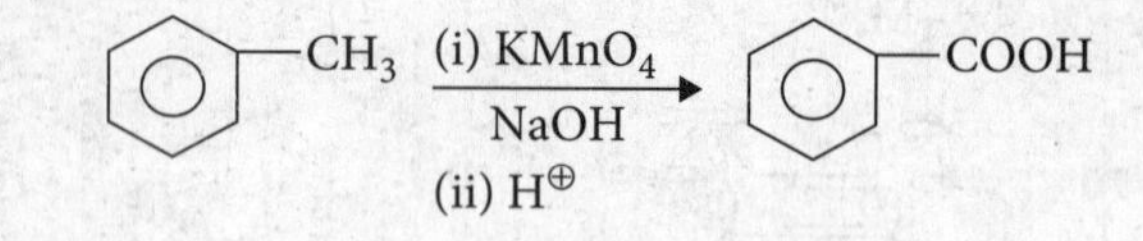

80.

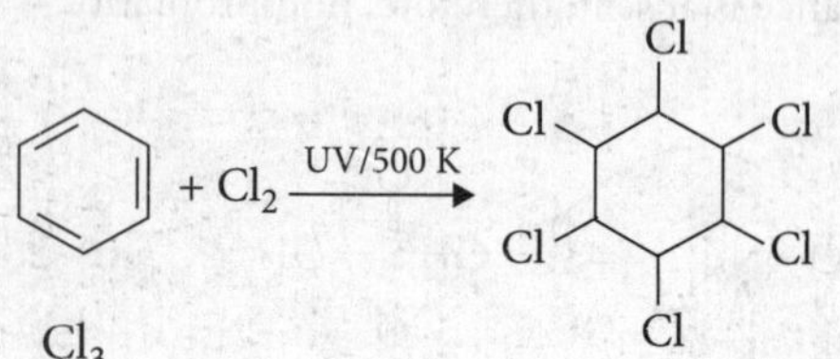

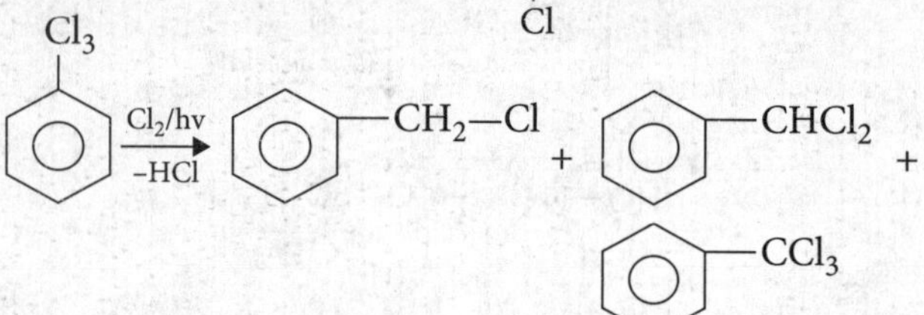

$$CH_4 \xrightarrow[-HCl]{Cl_2/hv} CH_3Cl + CH_2Cl_2 + CHCl_3 + CCl_4$$

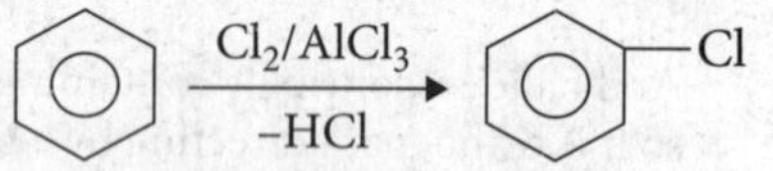

Level-2

1. → $\overset{+}{Na}$ not an electrophile because its octet is complete.
   → $AlCl_3$ is a Lewis acid and an electrophile.
   → SO_3 polar π bond containing groups are electrophiles.

2. $CH_3-\overset{+\delta}{\underset{\|}{C}}-H \xrightarrow{\overset{\ominus}{Nu}}$ polar π bond. (C=O)

3. Stability of intermediate carbocation
   $CH_3-\overset{\oplus}{C}H_2 > CH_3-\overset{\oplus}{C}=CH_2 > CH_2=\overset{\oplus}{C}H$

4. 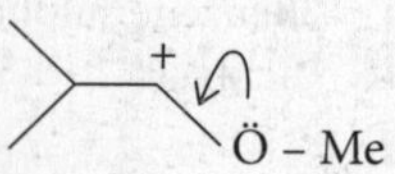

   (Back-bonding, most stable carbocation)

5. $CH_3-CH=CH_2 \xrightarrow[CCl_4]{HBr} CH_3-\overset{\oplus}{C}H-\underset{|}{C}H_2$ (H on CH_2)

6. $\underbrace{CCl_3}_{-H\ group}-CH=CH_2 \xrightarrow{H^\oplus} CCl_3-\overset{\oplus}{C}H-CH_3$

   Unstable carbocation, whereas
   $CCl_3-CH_2-\overset{\oplus}{C}H_2$ stable carbocation.

7. Stability of carbocation order.

8. 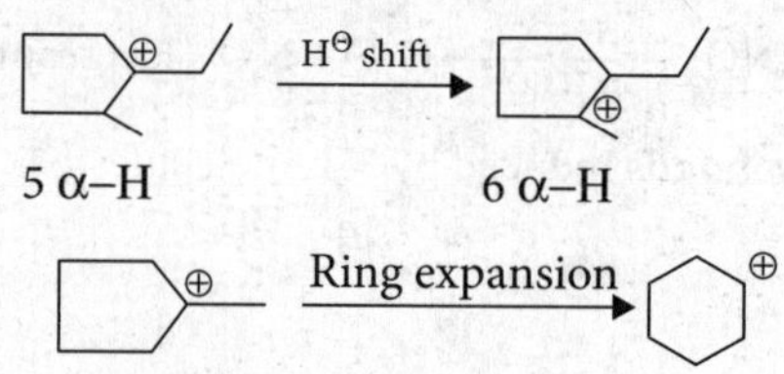

9. 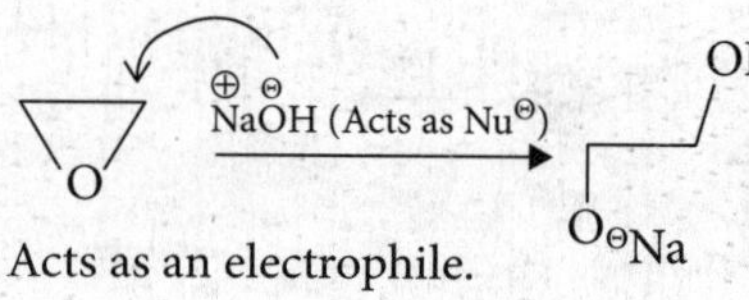

   Acts as an electrophile.

10. $\underbrace{H_2O}_{\text{Neutral, so bad nucleophile}} < \underbrace{CH_3-\overset{O}{\underset{O}{\overset{\|}{\underset{\|}{S}}}}-\overset{\ominus}{O} < CH_3-\underset{O}{\underset{\|}{C}}-\overset{\ominus}{O} < \overset{\ominus}{O}H}_{\text{Anion is good nucleophile and unstable anion is better nucleophile}}$

11. 2° carbocation → 3° carbocation more stable

12. $CH_3-CH=CH_2 \xrightarrow{H^\oplus} CH_3-\overset{\oplus}{C}H-CH_3$
    2° carbocation.

13. 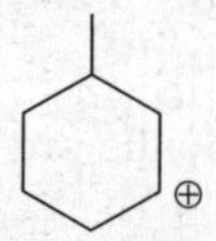

    2° carbocation and 4α – H not rearranged for 2° carbocation and 3α – H.

14. $CH_3-Br \rightarrow \overset{\oplus}{C}H_3 + Br^-$
    More EN

16. Arrow always from electron-rich (nucleophile alkene) to electron-deficient (electrophile $H^{\oplus}$)

17. Basicity $\propto$ Electron density.

18.

$$CH_3MgBr \xrightarrow{CH \equiv CH} \underset{\text{Methane gas}}{CH_4} + CH \equiv C\,MgBr$$

19. Stable anion is a good leaving group.

20. $CH_3-COOH \leftarrow$ polar ($\mu \neq 0$) and $H^{\oplus}$ donor
$CH_3-\underset{\underset{O}{\parallel}}{C}-CH_3 \leftarrow$ polar ($\mu \neq 0$) but does not have $H^{\oplus}$ donor

 $\leftarrow \mu = 0$

21. $\overset{\ominus}{O}H > H_2O$

Anion is a good nucleophile.

22. $CH{\equiv}CH \xrightarrow[\text{Acidic hydrogen}]{AgNO_3+NH_4OH} \underset{\text{White ppt}}{CH \equiv \overset{\ominus}{C}Ag^{+}}$

23.

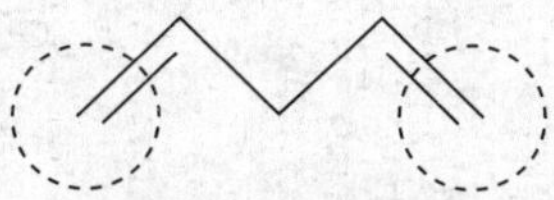

Terminal unsaturated carbon releases CO_2 by oxidative ozonolysis.

24. Stable intermediate $(CH_3-\overset{\oplus}{C}H-CH_2-CH_3)$ and higher nucleophilicity.

25.

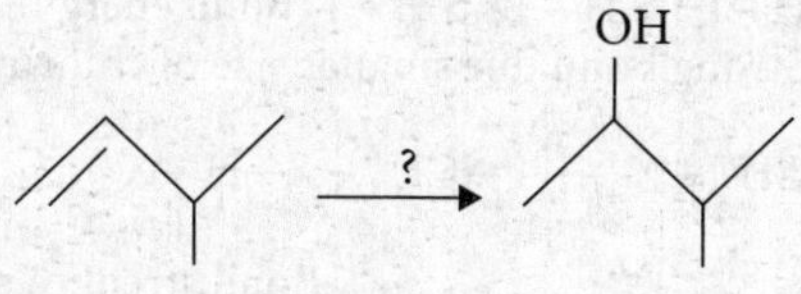

In oxymercuration-demercuration reaction, rearrangement does not occur and it follows the MR rule.

26.

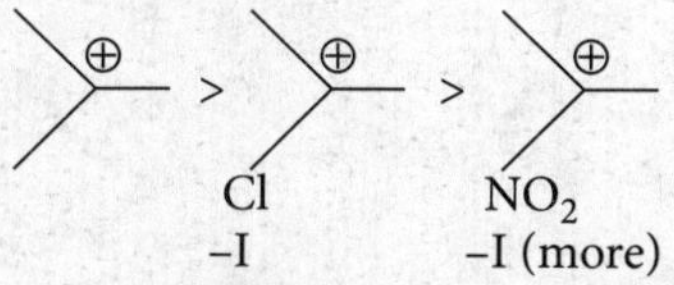

$\rightarrow$ Rate depends on intermediate carbocation.

27.

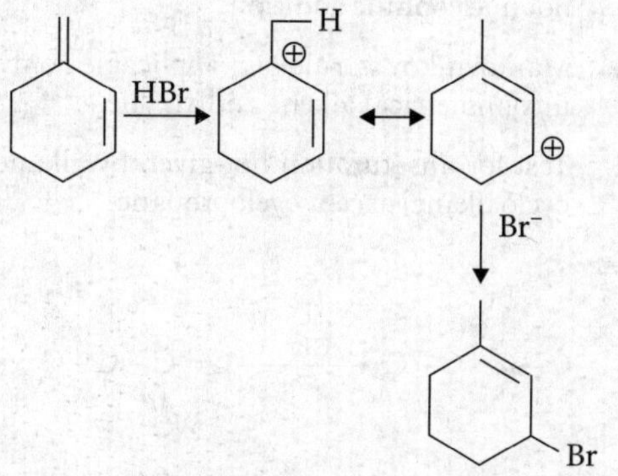

28.

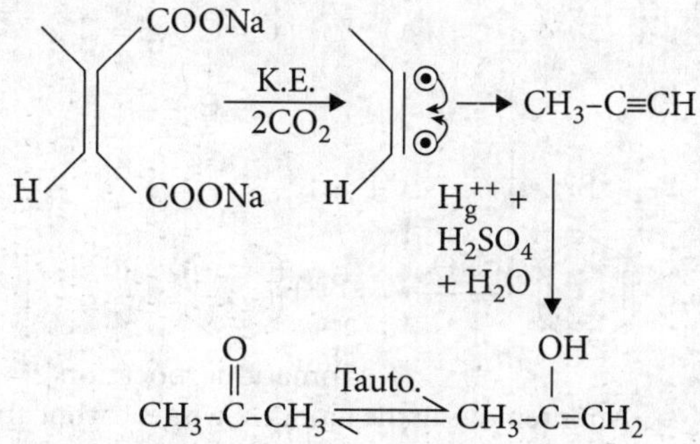

29.

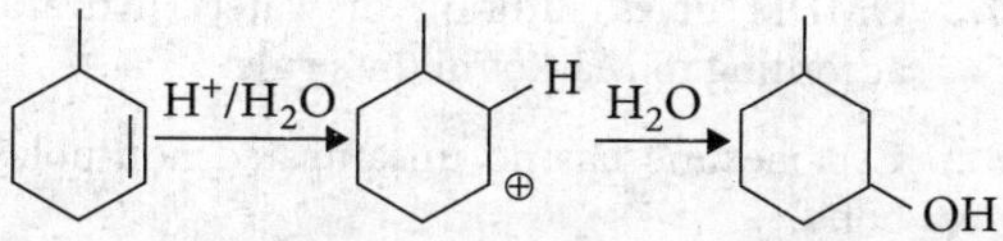

More stable carbocation is formed and there is no rearrangement.

30.

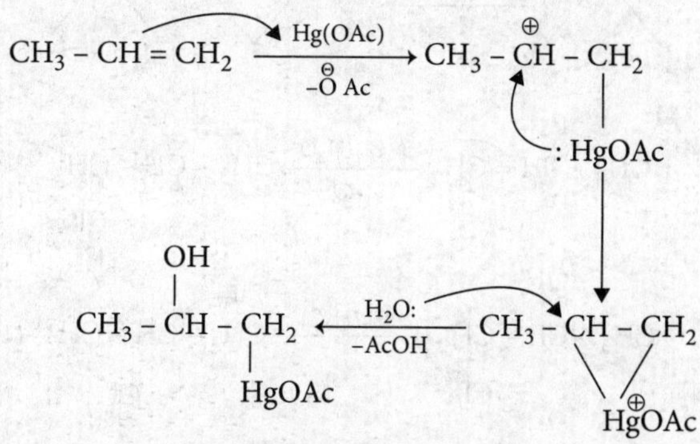

31. Alkene gives electrophilic addition reaction, not nucleophilic addition.

32. Markovnikov's rule is applicable only for unsymmetrical alkene and alkyne.

33. Test for unsaturation not given by alkane and cycloalkane, except cyclopropane.

35.

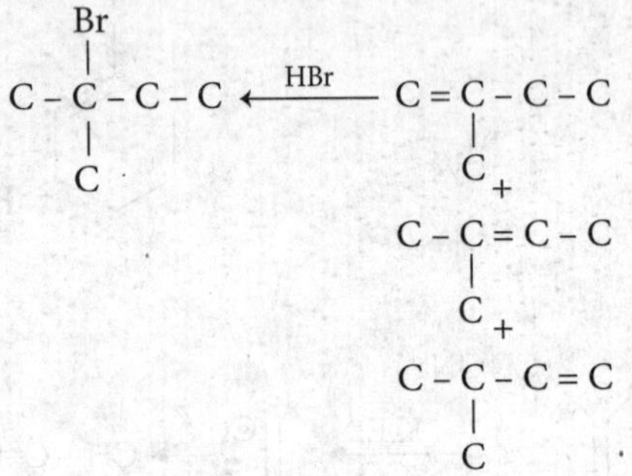

36.

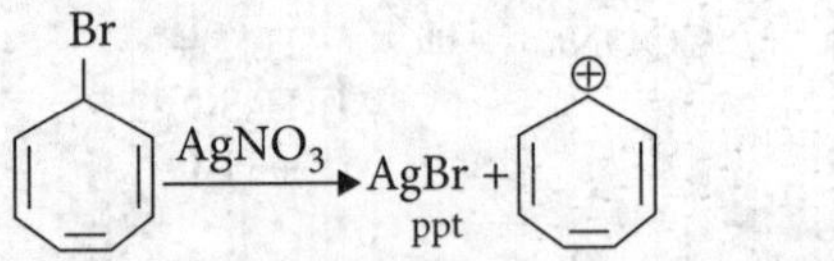

Aromatic carbocation

After removing the halogen, we get carbocation 3° or resonance stable or more stable carbocation; then AgBr (ppt) is formed.

37. OMDM gives addition of water (hydration) according to Markovnikov's rule.

38. Cyclohexane has no unsaturated non-polar π bond.

39.

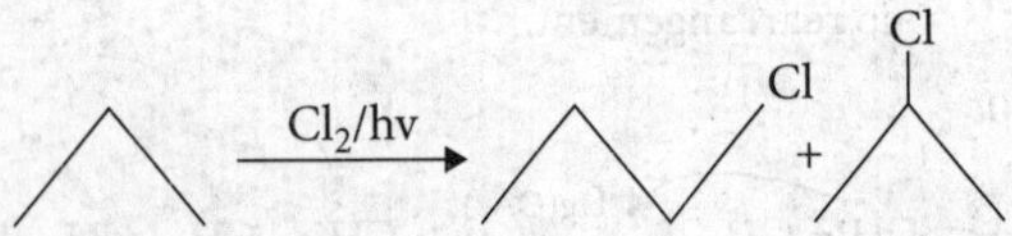

41.

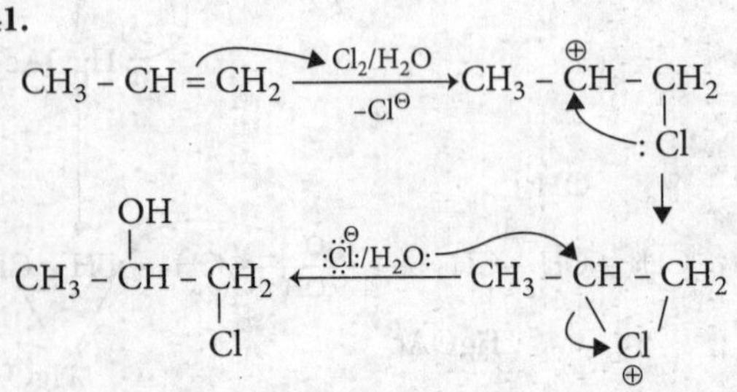

42. Stable intermediate carbocation.

43.

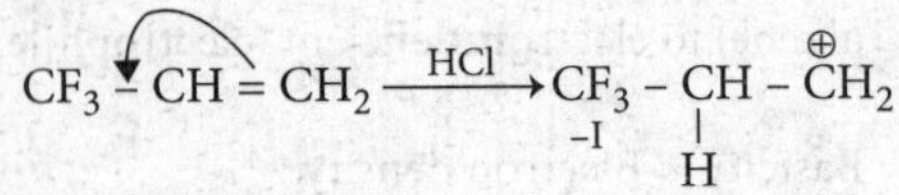

Stable carbocation.

44.

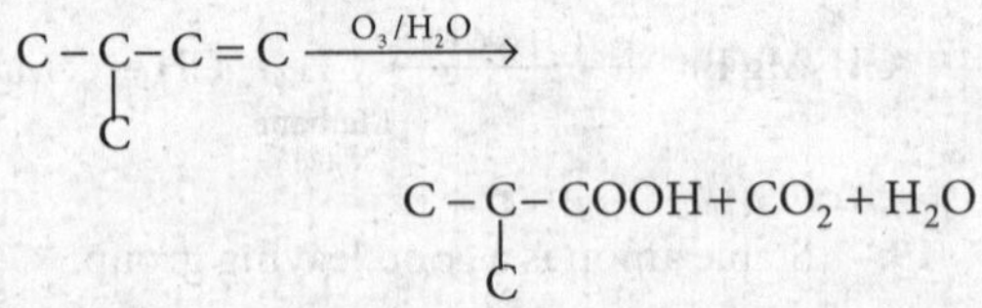

45. For metal test, acidic 'H' is required.

46. HBO gives anti-MR product and acidic hydration gives MR product. It is observed only in unsymmetrical alkene.

47. HBr with peroxide gives anti-Markovnikov's product.

48. The molecules in which rearrangement is possible give different products.

49. Wurtz reaction gives radical combination products of double carbon number.

50. $CH_3-\overset{\ominus}{O}$ not more stable than $CH_3-\underset{\underset{O}{\|}}{C}-\overset{\ominus}{O}$.

51.

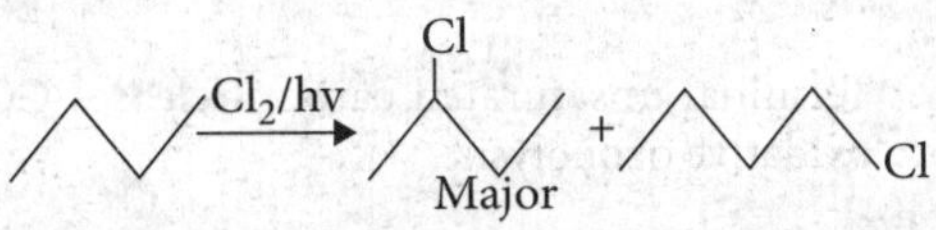

52. Boiling point $\propto \frac{1}{\text{Branching}}$.

53. H – Cl > H – Br > H – I (Bond energy)
Strong bond due smaller size of chlorine

54. $CH_4 + X_2 \xrightarrow{hv} CH_3 - X + H - X$
↑ Bond strength decides reactivity

55. Leaving tendency of halogen ∝ Reactivity.

56.

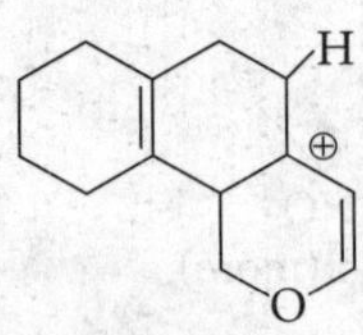

Most stable carbocation.

57. a, b are oxidation reactions

$CH_4 + O_2 \rightarrow C + H_2O$ Incomplete combustion

$CH_4 + O_2 \rightarrow CO_2 + H_2O$ Complete combustion

59. Stable intermediate gives major product and it can give two stereoproducts because of planar carbocation.

60. Stable intermediate.

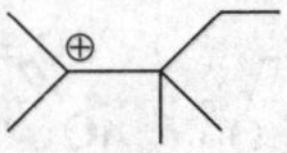

61. $C-C=C \xrightarrow{H-X} C-\overset{\oplus}{C}-\overset{H}{C}-C + X^{\ominus}$

Leaving group stability

$I^{\ominus} > Br^{\ominus} > Cl^{\ominus}$

62. Unstable anion is good nucleophile.

63. $C-\underset{C}{C}-C=C \xrightarrow[\text{ii) } H_2O/Zn]{\text{i) } O_3}$

$C-\underset{C}{C}-C=O + O=CH_2$

64. NBS gives free radical substitution reaction with allylic and benzylic hydrogen only.

65.

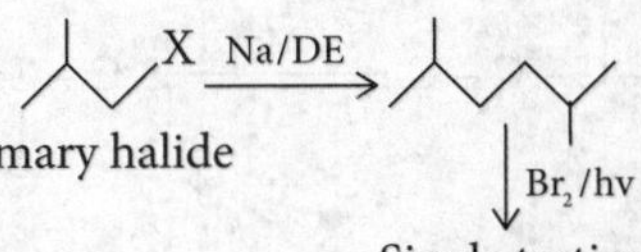

Primary halide

Single tertiary bromide possible

66.

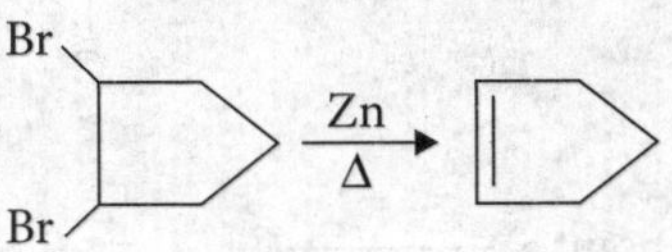

This is dehalogenation reaction [E_2]

67.

$CH_3-C\equiv CH \xrightarrow[\text{ii) } H_2O_2/\overset{\ominus}{O}H]{\text{i) } BD_3, THF} CH_3-\underset{D}{C}=\underset{OH}{CH} \xrightarrow{\text{Tauto.}}$

$CH_3-\underset{D}{CH}-\underset{O}{\overset{\|}{C}}-H$

68. (b)

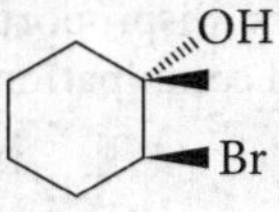

MR rule and anti-addition

(c)

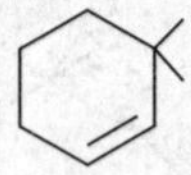

Kinetically controlled product

(d)

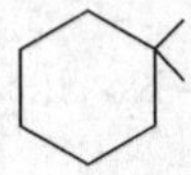

Rearrangement possible

69. Unsymmetrical alkene gives different products.

70. $CH_3-Br \xrightarrow{\text{i) Mg/DE}} CH_3MgBr$

$\xrightarrow[\text{NAR}]{\text{(ii) } H-\overset{O}{\overset{\|}{C}}-H} CH_3-\underset{OH}{CH_2}$

71. $H_3O^{\oplus}$ gives MR rule hydration reaction but (i) B_2H_6 followed H_2O_2 / OH^- (oxidation) gives anti-MR rule hydration reaction.

72.

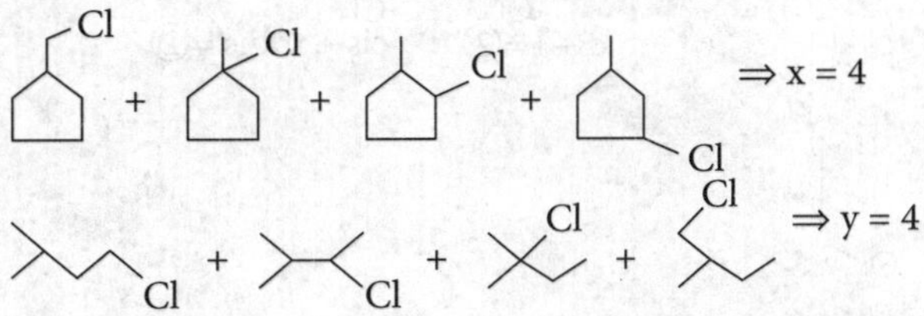

73. Wurtz reaction gives radical combination of even number of carbons and symmetrical alkanes.

74.

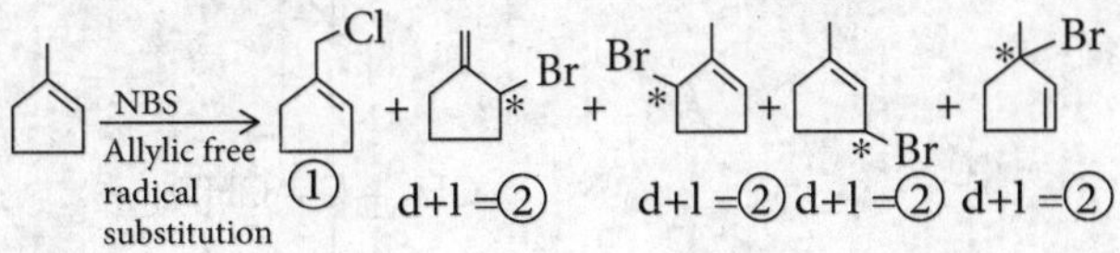

75. Symmetrical alkane

76.

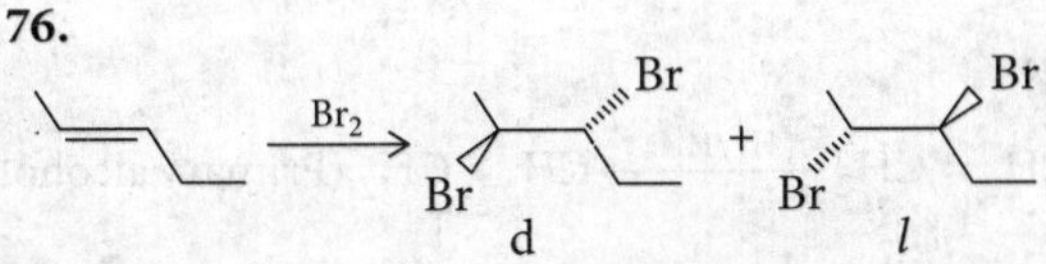

Enantiomers = R.M.

77. 3° alkyl halide gives disproportional major products than radical combination products.

78.

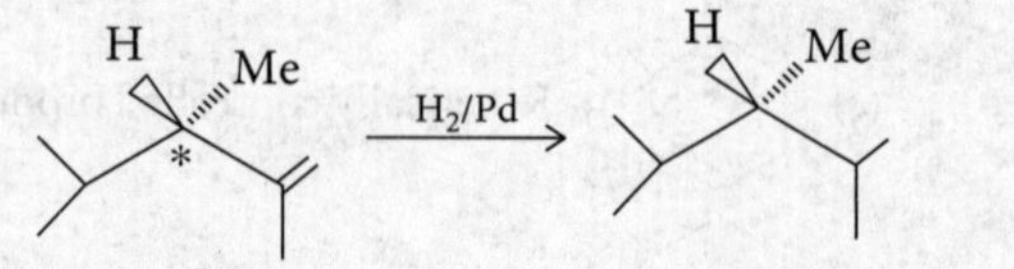

Chiral carbon   No chiral carbon

79.

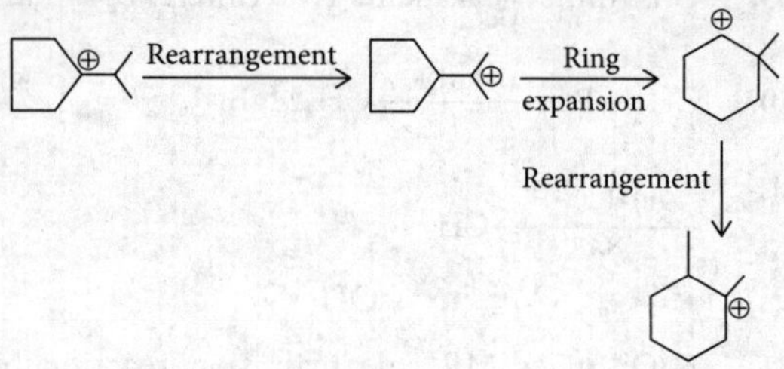

80.

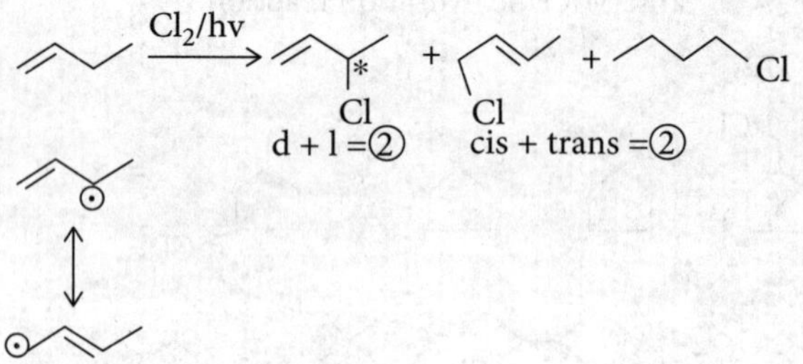

81.

$$CH_3-C\equiv CH \xrightarrow{DCl} CH_3-\underset{Cl}{\underset{|}{C}}=\underset{D}{\underset{|}{CH}} \xrightarrow{DI} CH_3-\overset{I}{\overset{|}{\underset{Cl}{\underset{|}{C}}}}-CHD_2$$

82. (i), (ii), (iii), (iv), (v), (vi) and (ix) = 7

83.

$$CH_2=CH_2 \xrightarrow{H^{\oplus}/H_2O} CH_3-\underset{OH}{\underset{|}{CH_2}} \text{ (Primary alcohol)}$$

But all others give secondary or tertiary alcohol.

84.

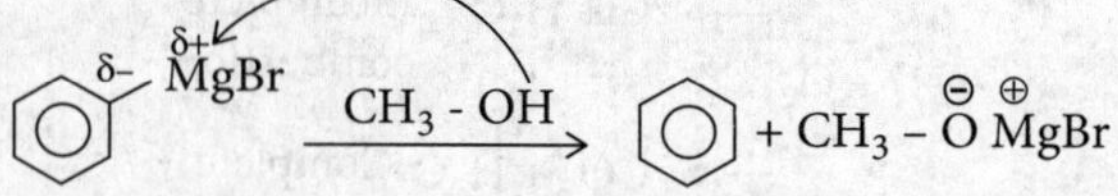

85. In symmetrical alkene, MR rule is not observed.

86.

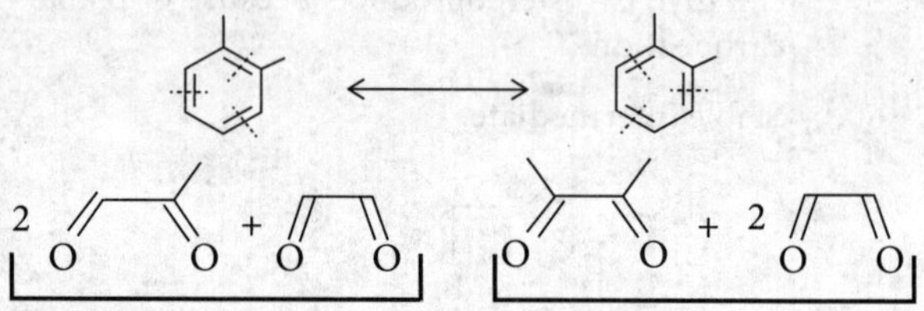

87.

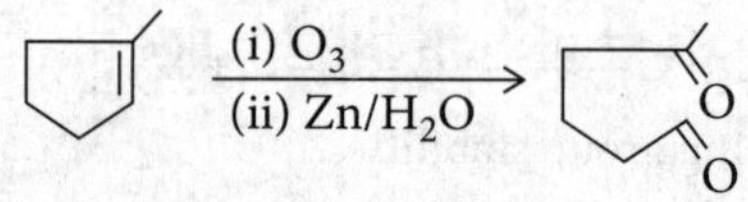

88.

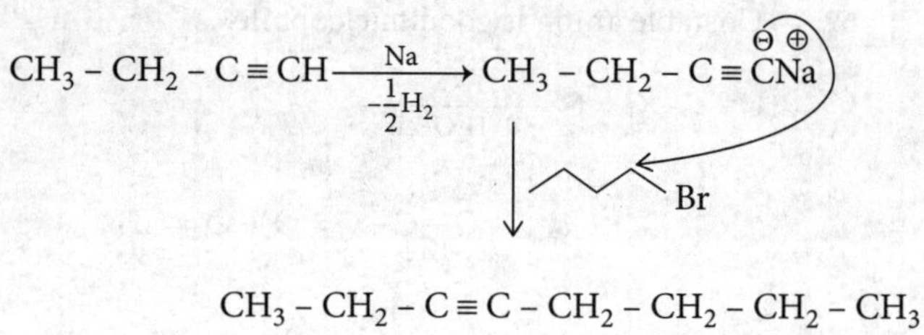

89.

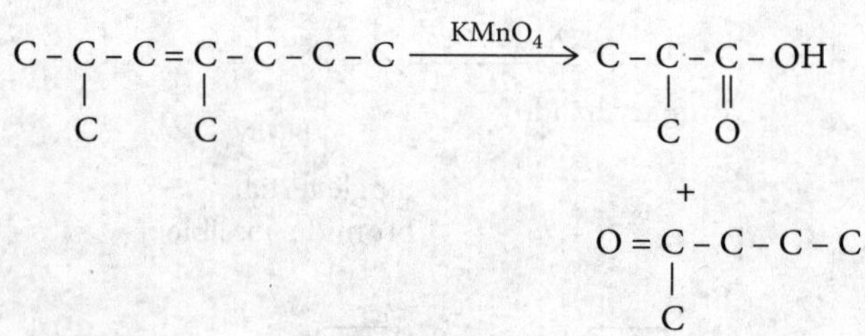

90. $\text{Boiling point} \propto \dfrac{1}{\text{Branching}}$

91. After hydrogenation

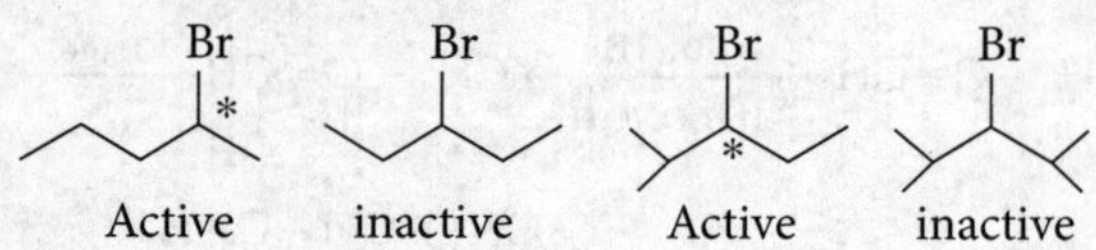

92. Cold $KMnO_4$ gives syn diol but per acid (mCPBA) followed by acidic hydrolysis, it gives anti-diol product.

93. (A) gives propene by dehalogenation
(B) gives n-hexane by radical combination
(C) gives propane by decarboxylation
(D) gives propane by reduction

94.

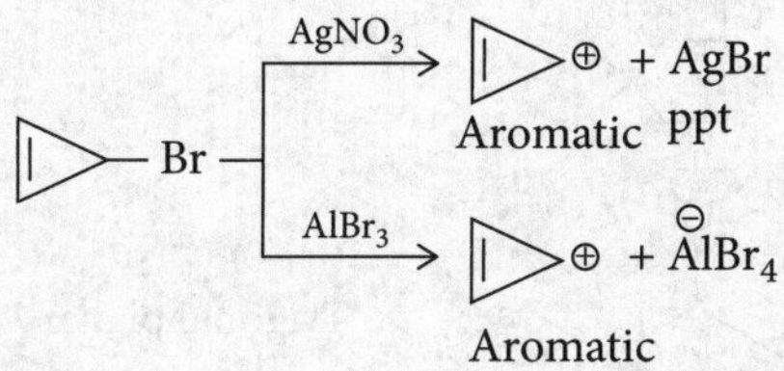

95. In EAR, rearrangement is possible.

96. Br_2 acts as electrophile and CO_2 and $CH_3-\overset{O}{\overset{\|}{C}}-Cl$ polar π bonds are also electrophiles, but 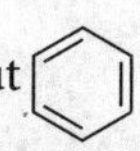, $CH_2=CH_2$ non-polar π bonds act as nucleophiles.

97. Unstable intermediate having higher activation energy.

98.

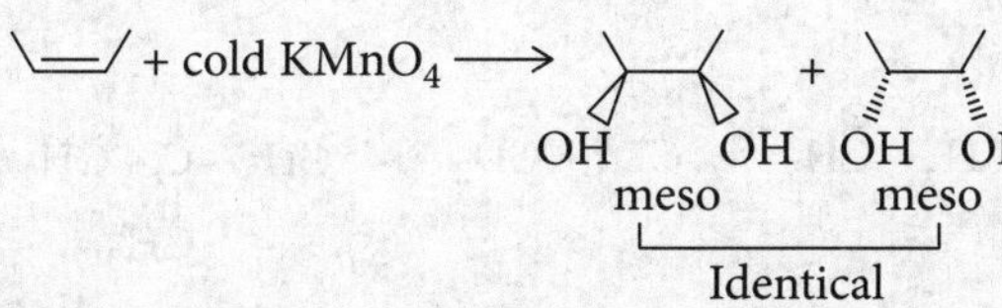

99.

$$CH_2{=}CH{-}CH_2{-}CH{=}CH_2 \xrightarrow{NBS} CH_2 = CH - \overset{\odot}{C}H - CH = CH_2$$

$$\updownarrow$$

$$CH_2 = CH - CH = CH - \underset{\odot}{C}H_2$$

$$\downarrow NBS$$

$$CH_2 = CH - CH = CH - \underset{Br}{C}H_2$$

Resonance stable alkene
Major

100.

101. 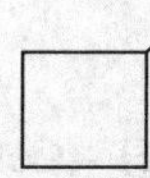 is not an isomer of the other three; so its product is not considered.

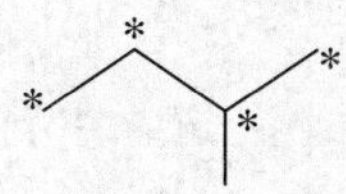

102.

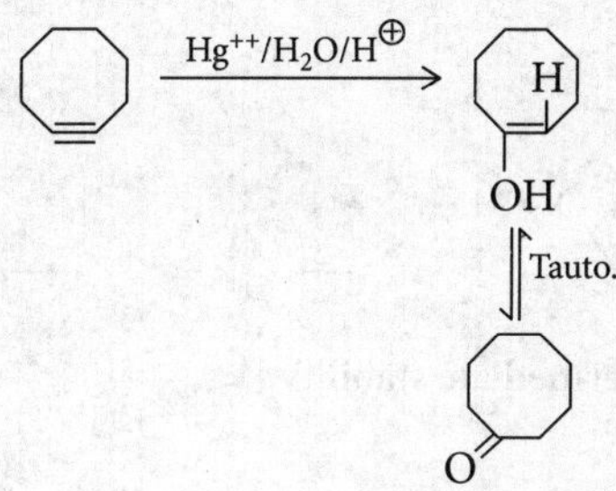

103.

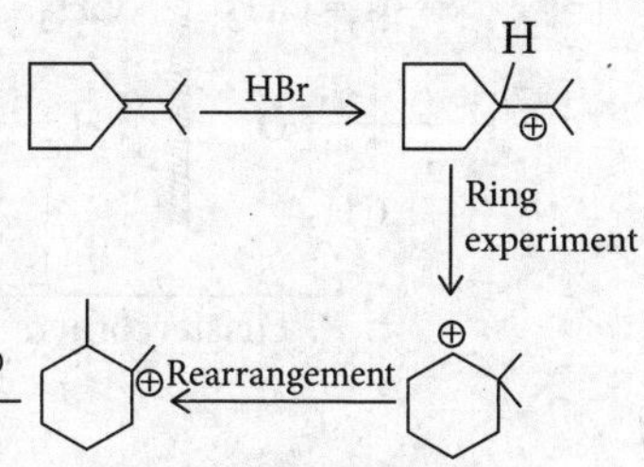

104. In free radical addition by Kharasch effect, $\overset{\odot}{Br}$ radical added 1st to propene with anti-Markovnikov's rule.

105. Like Tollens' reagent, Cu_2Cl_2/NH_4OH reacts with terminal alkyne ($CH_3-CH_2-C{\equiv}CH$) to give red precipitate of $CH_3CH_2-C\equiv\overset{\ominus}{C}\overset{\oplus}{Cu}$

106. In ethyne, internal carbon is absent. So the same product of acetaldehyde (CH_3CHO) is formed.

107.

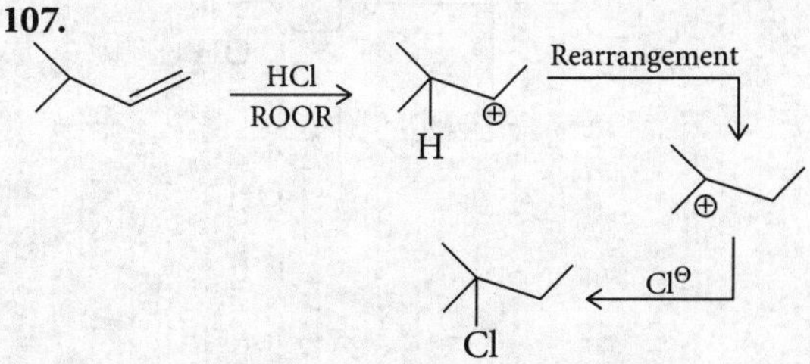

Peroxide effect not observed in HCl

108.

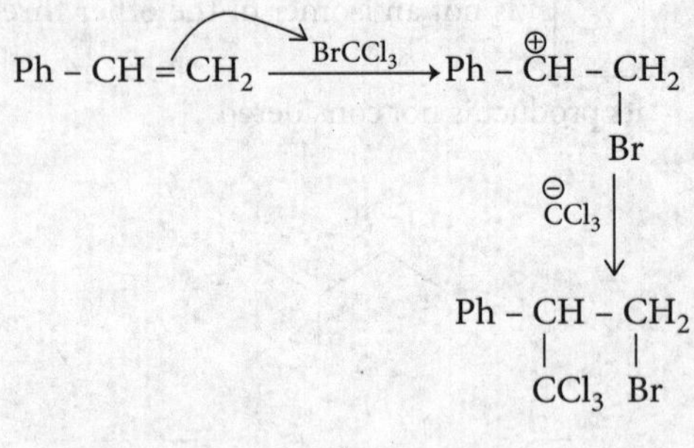

109.

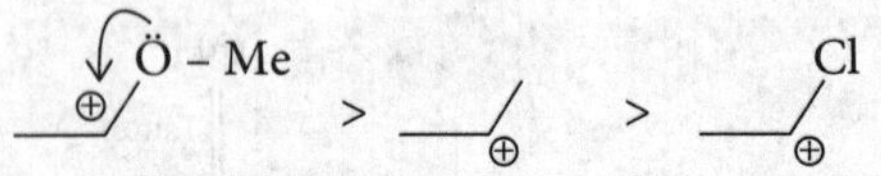

Intermediate stability

110.

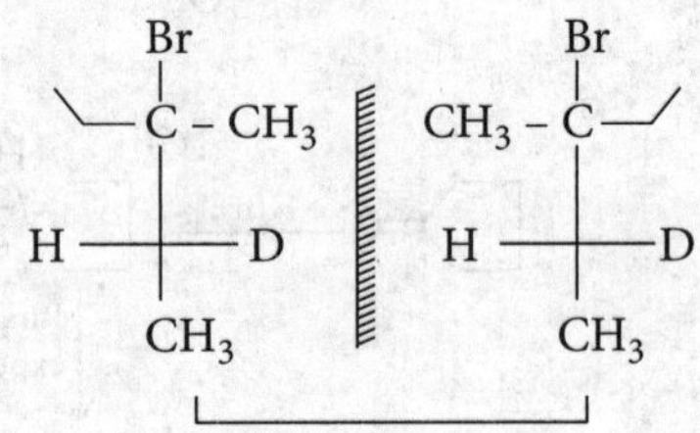

Diastereomers

111.

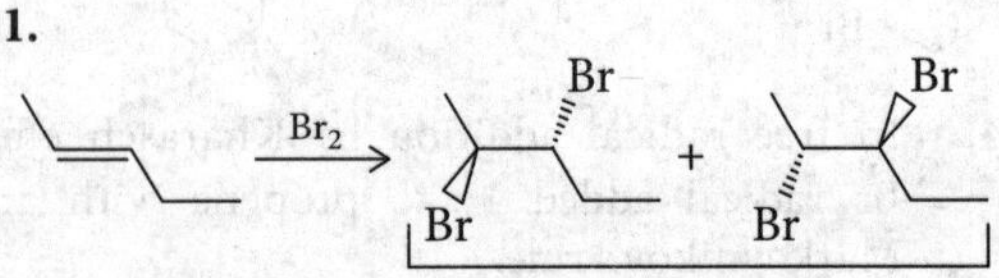

R.M. is inactive

112.

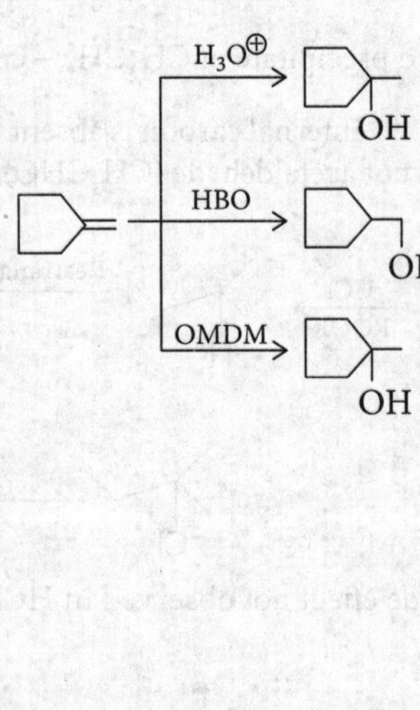

113.

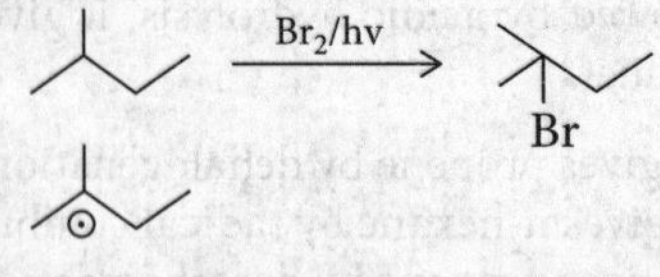

Stable free radical gives major product

114. 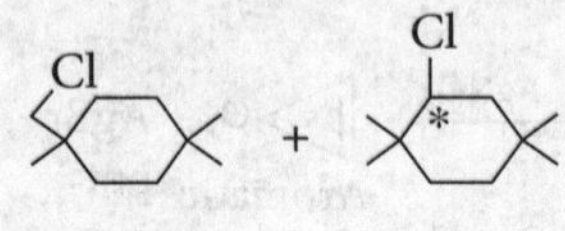

115. 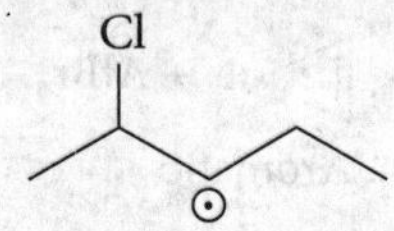 Trigonal planar

116. 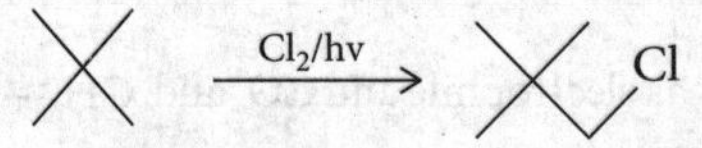

117. 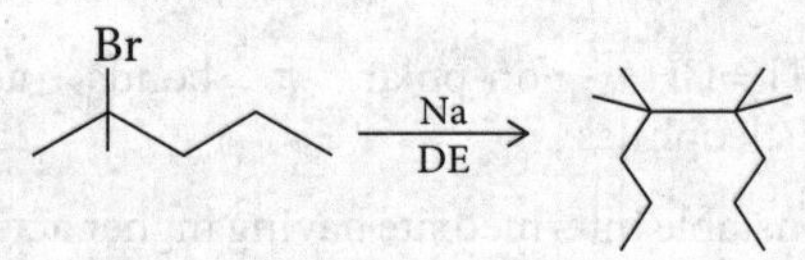

Not chiral carbon

118.

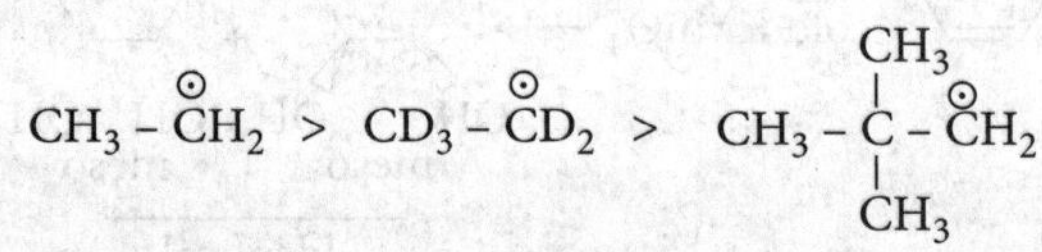

119. (i)  by Wurtz reaction

(ii) $CH_3 - CH_3$ by Kolbe's electrolysis

(iii) $CH_2 = CH_2$ by dehalogenation

(iv) 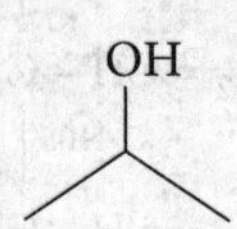 by OMDM

(v) 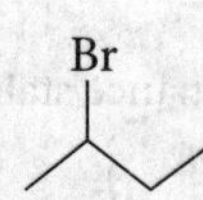 by halogenation

(vi) 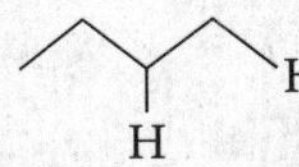 by hydroboration reduction

120. Stable free radical

121. Leaving group tendency

122. Reductive ozonolysis

123.

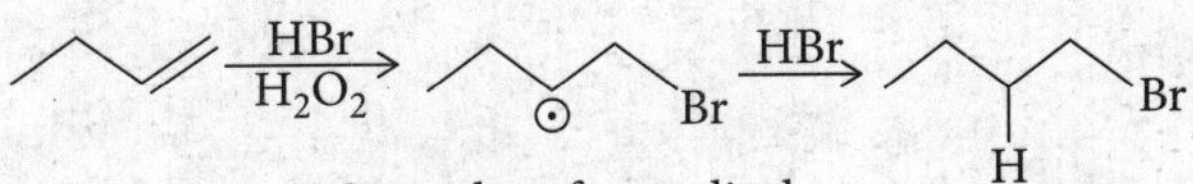

Secondary free radical

124.

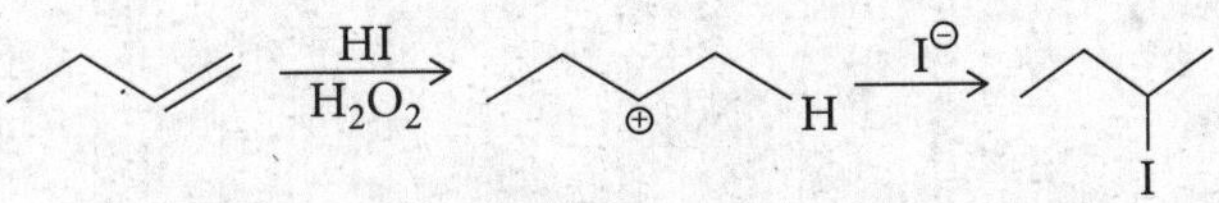

HI does not give peroxide effect.

126. In hydrogenation, two σ bonds are formed and one π bond breaks. So net energy is released, hence exothermic.

127.

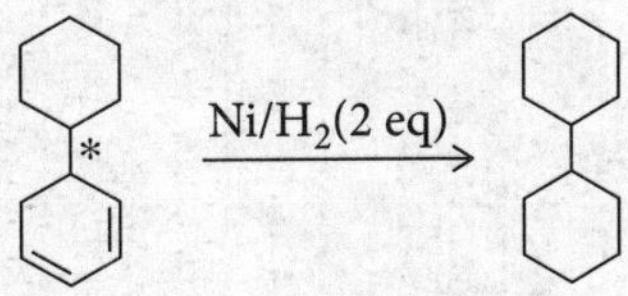

Active Inactive

128.

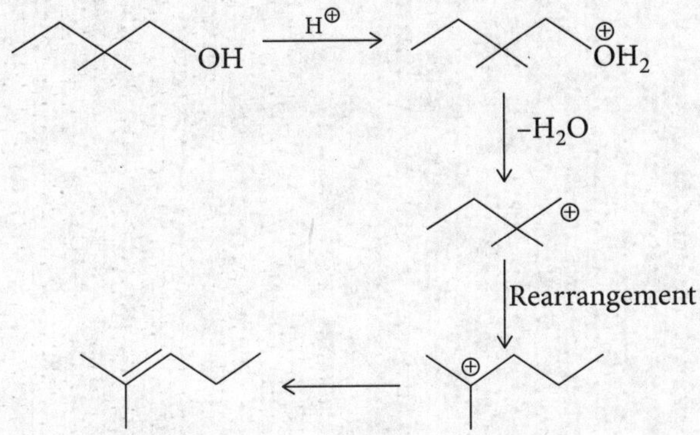

CHAPTER 5

Purification Methods, Qualitative and Quantitative Analysis

1. Naphthalene can be easily purified by:
(a) Sublimation (b) Crystallization
(c) Distillation (d) Vaporization

2. Which of the following can be used to remove an impurity that imparts colour to the solution?
(a) Activated palladium
(b) Activated charcoal
(c) Activated nickel
(d) All of the above

3. Aniline and chloroform are easily separated by the technique of:
(a) Sublimation
(b) Crystallization
(c) Distillation
(d) Solvent extraction

4. A mixture of acetone and methanol can be separated by:
(a) Vacuum distillation
(b) Steam distillation
(c) Fractional distillation
(d) Simple distillation

5. Which of the following processes is used to separate a volatile liquid from non-volatile impurities?
(a) Distillation
(b) Sublimation
(c) Differential extraction
(d) Crystallization

6. Which of the following distillations is used if the difference in the boiling points of two liquids is not much?
(a) Steam distillation
(b) Simple distillation
(c) Fractional distillation
(d) Distillation under reduced pressure

7. Which of the following is fitted over the mouth of a round-bottomed flask in a simple distillation apparatus to convert it to a fractional distillation apparatus?
(a) Capillary tube
(b) Octadecyl column
(c) C-18 column
(d) Fractionation column

8. **Assertion (A):** If one of the substances in a mixture is water and the other a water-insoluble substance, the mixture will boil close to but lower than 373 K.
Reason (R): In the presence of an insoluble substance, the boiling point of water decreases.
(a) Both A and R are correct; R is the correct explanation of A.
(b) Both A and R are correct; R is not correct explanation of A.
(c) A is correct; R is incorrect.
(d) Both A and R are incorrect.

9. A substance which decomposes below its boiling point can be best purified by:
(a) Simple distillation
(b) Steam distillation
(c) Fractional distillation
(d) Distillation under reduced pressure.

10. What are the technological applications of fractional distillation?
(a) To separate different fractions of crude oil in the petroleum industry
(b) To separate different fractions of volatile and non-volatile solvents
(c) To separate a mixture of amino acids
(d) No technological application of fractional distillation

11. Which of the following processes is suitable for the purification of aniline?
(a) Simple distillation
(b) Fractional distillation
(c) Fractional crystallization
(d) Steam distillation

12. A mixture of o-nitrophenol and p-nitrophenol can be separated by

(a) Fractional distillation
(b) Sublimation
(c) Chemical separation
(d) Steam distillation

13. **Assertion (A):** A liquid boils at a temperature at which its vapour pressure is lower than the external pressure.
Reason (R): Glycerol can be separated from spent-lye in the soap industry by using the technique of distillation under reduced pressure.
(a) Both A and R are correct; R is the correct explanation of A.
(b) Both A and R are correct; R is not correct explanation of A.
(c) A is correct; R is incorrect.
(d) R is correct; A is incorrect.

14. The technique in which extraction of a compound takes place on the basis of greater solubility of one compound in another solvent is:
(a) Differential extraction
(b) Chromatography
(c) Sublimation
(d) Crystallization

15. What do A and B refer to in the figure of differential extraction?

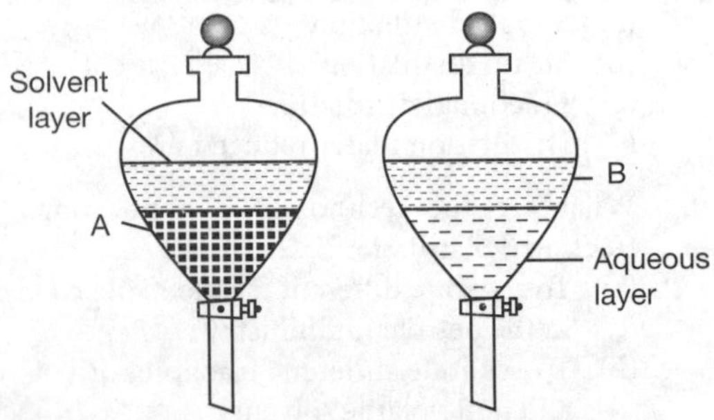

Choose the correct option:
(a) A → Organic compound in aqueous layer
B → Organic compound in solvent layer
(b) A → Organic compound in solvent layer
B → Organic compound in aqueous layer
(c) A → Inorganic compound in aqueous layer
B → Inorganic compound in aqueous layer
(d) A → Inorganic compound in aqueous layer
B → Inorganic compound in aqueous layer

16. **Assertion (A):** In steam distillation, the liquid boils when the sum of vapour pressures due to the organic liquid (p_1) and water (p_2) becomes equal to the atmospheric pressure (p), that is, $p = p_1 + p_2$.
Reason (R): If p_1 is lower than p, the organic liquid vaporizes at a lower temperature than its boiling point.
(a) Both A and R are correct; R is the correct explanation of A.
(b) Both A and R are correct; R is not correct explanation of A.
(c) A is correct; R is incorrect.
(d) R is correct; A is incorrect.

17. In which technique is the same solvent repeatedly used for extraction of the compound?
(a) Continuous extraction
(b) Non-continuous extraction
(c) Diffraction extraction
(d) Non-differential extraction

18. Which type of chromatography is based on the fact that different compounds are adsorbed on an adsorbent to different degrees?
(a) Partition chromatography
(b) Adsorption chromatography
(c) Absorption chromatography
(d) Paper chromatography

19. Match the items in Column I with the items in Column II and choose the correct option from the codes given below:

Column I	Column II
A. Adsorbent	1. Silica gel or alumina
B. R_f value	2. Brown spots
C. Spots of colourless compounds, which are invisible to the eye	3. Ninhydrin solution
D. Crystals of iodine	4. Fluorescent in ultraviolet light

Column I	Column II
E. Spraying reagent	5. Acts as stationary phase
F. Chromatography paper contains water trapped in it	6. $\frac{\text{Distance moved by the substance from base line (x)}}{\text{Distance moved by the solvent from base line (y)}}$

Codes

	A	B	C	D	E	F
(a)	5	6	4	2	3	1
(b)	6	4	5	1	3	2
(c)	2	3	4	5	6	1
(d)	1	6	4	2	3	5

20. Which of the following absorbents is used in thin layer chromatography?
(a) Silica gel
(b) Alumina
(c) Sodium benzoate
(d) Both (a) and (b)

21. The compound that acts as an adsorbent in column chromatography is:
(a) Na_2O (b) Na_2SO_4
(c) Al_2O_3 (d) NaCl

22. The correct match between Item I and Item II is:

Item I (Mixture)	Item II (Separation method)
A. H_2O : Sugar	P. Sublimation
B. H_2O : Aniline	Q. Recrystallization
C. H_2O : Toluene	R. Steam distillation
	S. Differential extraction

(a) (A) → (Q); (B) → (R); (C) → (S)
(b) (A) → (Q); (B) → (R); (C) → (P)
(c) (A) → (S); (B) → (R); (C) → (P)
(d) (A) → (R); (B) → (P); (C) → (S)

23. Look at the figure of column chromatography. The labels A and B are:

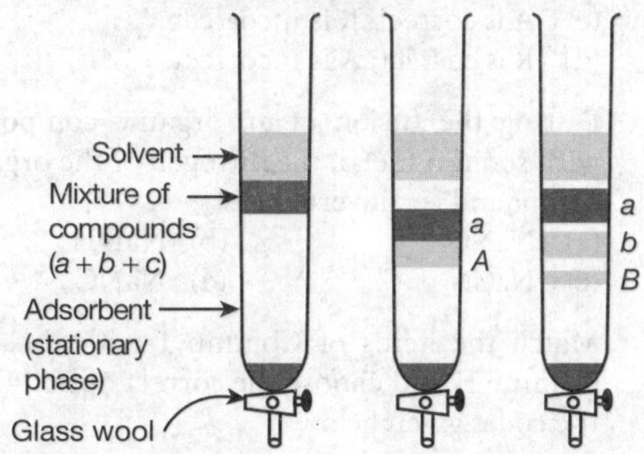

(a) A = b + c, B = c
(b) A = K (constant), B = b + c
(c) A = a, B = b
(d) A = no component, B = a

24. The paper used in paper chromatography selectively retains different components according to their differing partitions in the two phases. The paper strip so developed is known as:
(a) Chroma paper
(b) Chromatogram
(c) Chromatography
(d) Chroma

25. In chromatography, which of the following statements is incorrect for R_f?
(a) R_f value depends on the type of chromatography
(b) Higher R_f value means higher adsorption
(c) R_f value is dependent on the mobile phase
(d) The value of R_f cannot be more than 1

26. Which of the following should be added to the compound for the detection of carbon and hydrogen?
(a) Cu(I) oxide
(b) Cu(II) oxide
(c) Zn dust
(d) Activated charcoal

27. **Assertion (A):** Carbon and hydrogen are detected by heating the compound with copper(II) oxide.
Reason (R): Carbon and hydrogen present in the compound are oxidised to carbon dioxide and water, respectively.
(a) Both A and R are correct; R is the correct explanation of A.

(b) Both A and R are correct; R is not correct explanation of A.
(c) A is correct; R is incorrect.
(d) R is correct; A is incorrect.

28. During the fusion of an organic compound with sodium metal, the nitrogen of the organic compound is converted to:
(a) $NaNO_2$ (b) $NaNH_2$
(c) NaCN (d) NaNC

29. Match the items of Column I with those of Column II and choose the correct option from the codes given below:

Column I (Test for element)	Column I (Products involved in the chemical reaction)
A. Test for nitrogen	1. $(NH_4)_3PO_4 \cdot 12MoO_3$ Ammonium phosphomolybdate
B. Test for sulphur	2. $Fe_4[Fe(CN)_6]_3 \cdot xH_2O$ Prussian blue
C. Test for both nitrogen and sulphur	3. AgX
D. Test for halogens	4. $[Fe(SCN)]^{2+}$ Blood red
E. Test for phosphorus	5. PbS Black

Codes

	A	B	C	D	E
(a)	1	2	3	4	5
(b)	2	5	4	3	1
(c)	5	3	4	2	1
(d)	4	2	3	1	5

30. In Lassaigne's test, a blue colour is obtained if the organic compound contains nitrogen. The blue colour is due to the formation of:
(a) $K_4[Fe(CN)_6]$ (b) $Fe_4[Fe(CN)_6]_3$
(c) $Na_3[Fe(CN)_6]$ (d) $Cu_2[Fe(CN)_6]$

31. **Assertion (A):** Phosphorus present in the organic compound is oxidised to phosphoric acid. It is precipitated as ammonium phosphomolybdate by adding ammonium hydroxide.
Reason (R): Phosphoric acid may be precipitated as $MgNH_4PO_4$ by adding magnesia mixture which on ignition yields $Mg_2P_2O_7$.
(a) Both A and R are correct; R is the correct explanation of A.
(b) Both A and R are correct; R is not correct explanation of A.
(c) A is correct; R is incorrect.
(d) R is correct; A is incorrect.

32. Acidified sodium fusion extract on addition of ferric chloride solution gives blood red colouration. This confirms the presence of which of the following element(s)?
(a) Both S and Cl (b) Both N and S
(c) Only N (d) Only S

33. In phosphorus detection of an organic compound, the oxidized phosphorus compound solution is boiled with nitric acid and treated with ammonium molybdate. Yellow colour is due to the formation of:
(a) $(NH_4)_3PO_3 \cdot MoO_3$
(b) $(NH_4)_3PO_4 \cdot 12MoO_3$
(c) $NH_4[Mo(NH_4)_3 \cdot PO_3]$
(d) None of these

34. Lassaigne's test is not used for the detection of which element?
(a) Carbon (b) Halogens
(c) Nitrogen (d) Sulphur

35. Which of the following statements is true for calculation of the volume of nitrogen at STP in the Dumas method?

I. Volume of nitrogen at STP = $\dfrac{p_1V_1 \times 273}{760 \times T_1}$
II. p_1 and V_1 are the pressure and volume of nitrogen.
III. p_1 is different from atmospheric pressure at which nitrogen gas is collected
p_1 = Atmospheric pressure – Aqueous tension

Choose the correct option:
(a) I and II (b) II and III
(c) I and III (d) I, II and III

36. On complete combustion, 0.246 g of an organic compound gave 0.198 g of carbon dioxide and 0.1014 g of water. The percentage compositions of carbon and hydrogen in the compound are:

	%C	%H
(a)	21.95	4.58
(b)	21.95	5.58
(c)	11.95	5.58
(d)	11.95	4.58

37. Observe the figure given below carefully for the Dumas method. Here, A and B refer to:

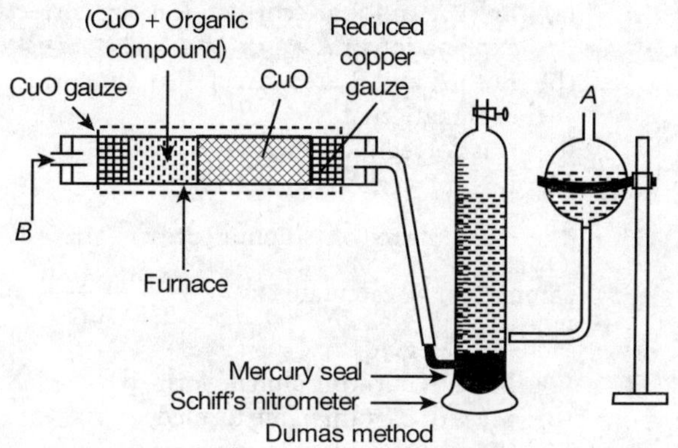

	A	B
(a)	CO_2	Nitrogen
(b)	Nitrogen	CO_2
(c)	Neon	KOH
(d)	Nitrogen	Oxygen

38. How many grams is equal to 22400 mL N_2 at STP?
(a) 26 g (b) 27 g
(c) 28 g (d) 29 g

39. An organic compound was estimated through the Dumas method and was found to have evolved 6 moles of CO_2, 4 moles of H_2O and 1 mole of nitrogen gas. The formula of the compound is:
(a) C_6H_8N (b) $C_{12}H_8N$
(c) $C_{12}H_8N_2$ (d) $C_6H_8N_2$

40. The quantitative measurement of nitrogen in an organic compound is done by:
(a) The Berthelot method
(b) The Beilstein method
(c) The Lassaigne method
(d) The Kjeldahl method

41. **Assertion (A):** The percentage of carbon can be estimated by using the formula $\frac{12 \times m_2 \times 100}{44 \times m}$
Reason (R): The molar mass of carbon dioxide is 12.
(a) Both A and R are correct; R is the correct explanation of A.
(b) Both A and R are correct; R is not correct explanation of A.
(c) A is correct; R is incorrect.
(d) R is correct; A is incorrect.

42. The Kjeldahl method cannot be used to estimate nitrogen for which of the following compounds?
(a) $C_6H_5NO_2$
(b) $NH_2-\overset{\overset{\displaystyle O}{\|}}{C}-NH_2$
(c) $CH_3CH_2-C\equiv N$
(d) $C_6H_5NH_2$

43. Which of the following compounds will be suitable for the Kjeldahl method for nitrogen estimation?

(a) 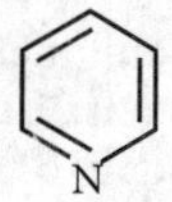

(b) 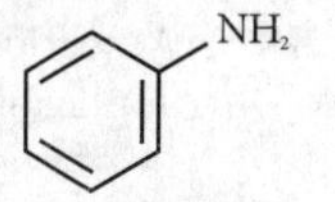

(c) 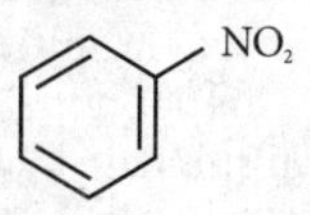

(d) 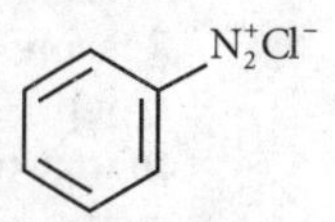

44. **Assertion (A):** In the Dumas method, the nitrogen-containing organic compound, when heated with copper oxide in an atmosphere of carbon dioxide, yields free nitrogen in addition to carbon dioxide and water.
Reason (R): The correct equation representing this method is

$$C_xH_yN_z + (2x + y/2)\, CuO \longrightarrow xCO_2 + y/2\, H_2O + z/2N_2 + (2x + y/2)Cu$$

(a) Both A and R are correct; R is the correct explanation of A.
(b) Both A and R are correct; R is not correct explanation of A.
(c) A is correct; R is incorrect.
(d) R is correct; A is incorrect.

45. The percentage of N in the Kjeldahl method

$$= \frac{1.4 \times M \times \left(V - \frac{V_1}{2}\right)}{m}$$

What does V_1 represent in the above formula?
(a) Volume of NaOH of molarity, M, used for titration of excess of sulphuric acid
(b) Volume of NaOH of normality, N, used for titration of excess of sulphuric acid
(c) Volume of H_2SO_4 of molarity, M
(d) Volume of H_2SO_4 of molarity, N

46. In the Kjeldahl method for estimation of nitrogen present in a soil sample, the ammonia evolved from a 0.75-g sample neutralised 10 mL of 1 M H_2SO_4. The percentage of nitrogen in the soil is:

(a) 37.33 (b) 45.33
(c) 35.33 (d) 45.33

47. In the Carius method of estimation of halogens, 250 mg of an organic compound gave 141 mg of AgBr. The percentage of bromine in the compound is (atomic mass Ag = 108 and Br = 80):

(a) 24 (b) 36
(c) 48 (d) 60

48. **Assertion (A):** The Kjeldahl method is not applicable to compounds containing nitrogen in the form of nitro and azo groups and nitrogen present in the ring (such as pyridine).
Reason (R): Nitrogen of the nitro- and azo-group-containing compounds does not change to ammonium sulphate by the Kjeldahl method.

(a) Both A and R are correct; R is the correct explanation of A.
(b) Both A and R are correct; R is not correct explanation of A.
(c) A is correct; R is incorrect.
(d) R is correct; A is incorrect.

49. Which method is used to find halogens in an organic compound?

(a) The Dumas method
(b) Liebig's method
(c) The Kjeldahl method
(d) The Carius method

50. What is the name of the tube in which a known mass of an organic compound is heated for the quantitative analysis of sulphur?

(a) Borosil tube (b) Carius tube
(c) Kjeldahl tube (d) None of these

51. In the estimation of sulphur, which reagent is heated along with the organic compound in a Carius tube?

(a) Sodium peroxide
(b) Dilute nitric acid
(c) Silver nitrate
(d) Sodium hydroxide

52. **Assertion (A):** The percentage of phosphorus in an organic compound can be estimated by the formula

$$\frac{31 \times m_1 \times 100}{1887 \times m}$$

Reason (R): Molar mass of $(NH_4)_3PO_4 \cdot 12MoO_3 = 1877$ g

(a) Both A and R are correct; R is the correct explanation of A.
(b) Both A and R are correct; R is not correct explanation of A.
(c) A is correct; R is incorrect.
(d) R is correct; A is incorrect.

53. The percentage of sulphur present in any sample can be calculated as $= \frac{32 \times m_1 \times 100}{233 \times m}$.
Here, m_1 refers to:

(a) Mass of barium sulphate formed
(b) Mass of barium oxide formed
(c) Mass of barium chloride formed
(d) None of the above

54. In sulphur estimation, 0.157 g of an organic compound gave 0.4813 g of barium sulphate. The percentage of sulphur in the compound is:

(a) 42.10 (b) 52.10
(c) 21.05 (d) 40.01

55. Match the items of Column I with the items of Column II and choose the correct option from the codes given below:

Column I	Column II
A. Carius method	1. $\frac{1.4 \times M \times 2(V - V_1/2)}{m}$
B. Percentage of sulphur	2. $\frac{62 \times m_1 \times 100}{222 \times m}\%$
C. Percentage of phosphorus	3. $\frac{\text{Atomic mass X} \times m_1 \times 100}{\text{Molecular mass of AgX} \times m}$
D. Percentage of halogen	4. $\frac{32 \times m_1 \times 100}{233 \times m}$
E. Percentage of nitrogen	5. Organic compound is heated with fuming nitric acid in the presence of silver nitrate

Codes

	A	B	C	D	E
(a)	5	4	2	3	1
(b)	2	4	3	1	5
(c)	4	5	2	1	3
(d)	3	1	5	2	4

56. In the crystallization process, impurities which impart colour to the solution are removed by which of the following?
(a) Repeated crystallization
(b) Activated charcoal
(c) Bleaching agent
(d) Sand

57. The best method for the separation of naphthalene and benzoic acid from their mixture is:
(a) Distillation (b) Sublimation
(c) Chromatography (d) Crystallization

58. A liquid decomposes at its boiling point. It can be purified by:
(a) Steam distillation
(b) Fractional distillation
(c) Vacuum distillation
(d) Sublimation

59. Glycerol can be separated from spent-lye in the soap industry by which of the following methods?
(a) Steam distillation
(b) Fractional distillation
(c) Distillation under reduced pressure
(d) Differential extraction

60. In paper chromatography:
(a) Moving phase is liquid and stationary phase is solid
(b) Moving phase is liquid and stationary phase is liquid
(c) Moving phase is solid and stationary phase is solid
(d) Moving phase is solid and stationary phase is liquid

61. Which of the following statements are correct for fractional distillation?
(i) Fractional distillation is used if the two liquids have sufficiently large difference in their boiling points.
(ii) A fractionating column provides many surfaces for heat exchange between the ascending vapours and the descending condensed liquid.
(iii) Each successive condensation and vaporization unit in the fractionating column is called a theoretical plate.
(iv) Fractional distillation is used to separate different fractions of crude oil in the petroleum industry.
(a) (i), (ii) and (iv)
(b) (ii), (iii) and (iv)
(c) (i), (ii) and (iii)
(d) (i), (ii), (iii) and (iv)

62. Which of the following sequences of T and F are correct for the given statements. Here 'T' stands for True and 'F' stands for False:
(i) The relative adsorption of each component of a mixture is expressed in terms of its retardation factor (R_F).
(ii) Retardation factor is given as:

$$R_F = \frac{\text{Distance moved by the solvent from the base line}}{\text{Distance moved by the substance from the base line}}$$

(iii) In TLC, the spots of colourless compounds can be detected by ultraviolet light.
(iv) Spots of amino acids may be detected by iodine.
(a) TTTF (b) TFFF
(c) TTTT (d) TFTF

63. **Assertion (A):** Simple distillation can help in separating a mixture of propan-1-ol (boiling point 97°C) and propanone (boiling point 56°C).
Reason (R): Liquids with a difference of more than 20°C in their boiling points can be separated by simple distillation.
(a) Both A and R are correct; R is the correct explanation of A.
(b) Both A and R are correct; R is not correct explanation of A.
(c) A is correct; R is incorrect.
(d) R is correct; A is incorrect.

64. Match the columns:

Column I	Column II
A. Separation of sublimable compounds from non-sublimable compounds	(p) Steam distillation
B. Method based on the difference in the solubilities of the compound and the impurities in a suitable solvent	(q) Sublimation

Column I	Column II
C. Separation of liquids having sufficient difference in their boiling points	(r) Distillation
D. Separation of substances which are steam-volatile and are immiscible with water	(s) Crystallization

(a) A – (q), B – (s), C – (r), D – (p)
(b) A – (q), B – (r), C – (p), D – (s)
(c) A – (s), B – (q), C – (r), D – (p)
(d) A – (q), B – (s), C – (p), D – (r)

65. During the hearing of a court case, the judge suspected that some changes had been carried out in the documents. He asked the forensics department to check the ink used at two different places. According to you, which technique can give the best results?
(a) Column chromatography
(b) Solvent extraction
(c) Distillation
(d) Thin layer chromatography

66. Which of the following is used for the detection of carbon and hydrogen?
(a) $Ca(OH)_2$ (b) CuO
(c) $CaCl_2$ (d) KOH

67. In a sodium fusion test of organic compounds, the nitrogen of the organic compound is converted to:
(a) Sodamide
(b) Sodium cyanide
(c) Sodium nitrite
(d) Sodium nitrate

68. Which of the following compounds does not show Lassaigne's test for nitrogen?
(a) Urea (b) Hydrazine
(c) Phenylhydrazine (d) Azobenzene

69. The compound formed in the positive test for nitrogen with the Lassaigne solution of an organic compound is:
(a) $Fe_4[Fe(CN)_6]_3$
(b) $Na_3[Fe(CN)_6]$
(c) $Fe(CN)_3$
(d) $Na_4[Fe(CN)_5NOS]$

70. In the quantitative analysis of carbon and hydrogen, the mass of water produced is determined by passing the mixture through a weighed U-tube containing X and carbon dioxide is absorbed in a concentrated solution of Y:
(a) $X = CaCl_2$, $Y = NaOH$
(b) $X = Ca(OH)_2$, $Y = CuSO_4$
(c) $X = CuSO_4$, $Y = Ca(OH)_2$
(d) $X = CaCl_2$, $Y = KOH$

71. Match the columns:

Column I (Element)	Column II (Colour of precipitate formed in Lassaigne's test)
A. Nitrogen	(p) Yellow
B. Sulphur	(q) Prussian blue
C. Chlorine	(r) Violet
D. Phosphorus	(s) White

(a) A – (q), B – (r), C – (p), D – (s)
(b) A – (r), B – (q), C – (p), D – (s)
(c) A – (q), B – (r), C – (s), D – (p)
(d) A – (r), B – (q), C – (s), D – (p)

72. In Lassaigne's test, the organic compound is fused with a piece of sodium metal in order to:
(a) Increase the ionization of the compound
(b) Decrease the melting point of the compound
(c) Increase the reactivity of the compound
(d) Convert the covalent compound into a mixture of ionic compounds

73. Lassaigne's extract is boiled with dilute HNO_3 before testing for halogens because:
(a) Silver halides are soluble in HNO_3
(b) Na_2S and NaCN are decomposed by HNO_3
(c) Ag_2S is soluble in HNO_3
(d) AgCN is soluble in HNO_3

74. Lassaigne's test cannot be used for the detection of:
(a) Nitrogen (b) Halogen
(c) Carbon (d) Phosphorous

75. The chemical formula of Prussian blue is:
(a) $Fe_3 [Fe(CN)_6] . xH_2O$
(b) $Fe_4 [Fe(CN)_4] . xH_2O$
(c) $Fe_3 [Fe(CN)_4] . xH_2O$
(d) $Fe_4 [Fe(CN)_6] . xH_2O$

76. The Kjeldahl method is not applicable to which of the following?
(a) Nitro compounds
(b) Azo compounds
(c) Pyridine
(d) All of the above

77. In the Kjeldahl method of estimation of nitrogen, K_2SO_4 acts as:
(a) Oxidizing agent
(b) Catalytic agent
(c) Hydrolyzing agent
(d) Boiling point elevator

78. The percentage of sulphur in an organic compound whose 0.32 g produces 0.233 g of $BaSO_4$ [Atomic weight Ba = 137, S = 32] is:
(a) 1.0 (b) 10.0
(c) 23.5 (d) 32.1

79. An organic compound contains C = 40%, H = 13.33% and N = 46.67%. Its empirical formula would be:
(a) CHN (b) C_2H_2N
(c) CH_4N (d) C_3H_7N

80. 2.79 g of an organic compound, when heated in a Carius tube with concentrated HNO_3 and H_3PO_4, formed $MgNH_4 \cdot PO_4$ precipitate. The precipitate on heating gave 1.332 g of $Mg_2P_2O_7$. The percentage of P in the compound is:
(a) 23.33% (b) 13.33%
(c) 33.33% (d) 26.66%

81. A compound contains 38.8% C, 16% H and 45.2% N. The formula of the compound would be:
(a) CH_3NH_2 (b) CH_3CN
(c) C_2H_5CN (d) $CH_2(NH_2)_2$

82. In the estimation of percentage of oxygen, a mixture of gaseous products containing oxygen is passed over red hot coke. All the oxygen is converted to A. This mixture is passed through B when A is converted to C.
What are A, B and C in the above statement?
(a) A = CO_2, B = KOH, C = pure O_2
(b) A = CO, B = I_2O_5, C = CO_2
(c) A = CO, B = I_2, C = CO_2
(d) A = CO_2, B = $Ca(OH)_2$, C = $CaCO_3$

83. In the Kjeldahl method for the estimation of N_2, potassium sulphate and copper sulphate are used. On the basis of their functions, which of the following statement(s) is/are correct?
(i) Potassium sulphate raises the boiling point and ensures complete reaction.
(ii) Copper sulphate acts as catalyst.
(iii) Potassium sulphate acts as catalyst and copper sulphate raises the boiling point.
(a) Only (iii) is correct.
(b) (i) and (ii) are correct.
(c) Only (ii) is correct.
(d) None are correct.

84. In the estimation of carbon and hydrogen by the combustion method, which of the following is/are correct?
(i) A spiral of copper is introduced at the right extreme of the combustion tube if the organic compound contains nitrogen.
(ii) A spiral of silver is introduced if the organic compound contains halogens.
(iii) The copper oxide in the combustion tube is replaced by lead chromate if the organic compound contains sulphur.
(a) (i) and (ii) are correct.
(b) (i) and (iii) are correct.
(c) (ii) and (iii) are correct.
(d) All are correct.

85. Match the columns:

Column I	Column II
A. The Dumas method	(p) $\frac{80 \times m_1 \times 100}{188 \times m}$
B. The Kjeldahl method	(q) $\frac{31 \times m_1 \times 100}{1877 \times m}\%$
C. The Carius method for bromine	(r) $\frac{1.4 \times M \times 2\left(v - \frac{V_1}{2}\right)}{m}\%$
D. Percentage of phosphorus	(s) $\frac{28 \times V \times 100}{22400 \times m}\%$

(a) A – (s), B – (r), C – (p), D – (q)
(b) A – (r), B – (s), C – (q), D – (p)
(c) A – (s), B – (p), C – (q), D – (r)
(d) A – (p), B – (r), C – (q), D – (s)

Answer Key

1. (a)	**2.** (b)	**3.** (c)	**4.** (c)	**5.** (a)	**6.** (c)	**7.** (d)	**8.** (d)
9. (d)	**10.** (a)	**11.** (d)	**12.** (d)	**13.** (d)	**14.** (a)	**15.** (a)	**16.** (b)
17. (a)	**18.** (b)	**19.** (d)	**20.** (d)	**21.** (c)	**22.** (a)	**23.** (a)	**24.** (b)
25. (b)	**26.** (b)	**27.** (a)	**28.** (c)	**29.** (b)	**30.** (b)	**31.** (d)	**32.** (b)
33. (b)	**34.** (a)	**35.** (d)	**36.** (a)	**37.** (b)	**38.** (c)	**39.** (d)	**40.** (d)
41. (c)	**42.** (a)	**43.** (b)	**44.** (a)	**45.** (a)	**46.** (a)	**47.** (a)	**48.** (a)
49. (d)	**50.** (b)	**51.** (a)	**52.** (a)	**53.** (a)	**54.** (a)	**55.** (a)	**56.** (b)
57. (b)	**58.** (c)	**59.** (c)	**60.** (b)	**61.** (b)	**62.** (d)	**63.** (a)	**64.** (a)
65. (d)	**66.** (b)	**67.** (b)	**68.** (b)	**69.** (a)	**70.** (c)	**71.** (c)	**72.** (d)
73. (b)	**74.** (c)	**75.** (d)	**76.** (d)	**77.** (d)	**78.** (b)	**79.** (c)	**80.** (b)
81. (a)	**82.** (d)	**83.** (b)	**84.** (d)	**85.** (a)			

Solutions

1. Naphthalene is a sublimable compound which goes into vapour without passing through a liquid phase.

2. Activated charcoal is a good adsorbent.

3. Both liquids have sufficient difference between boiling points; so simple distillation is used.

4. Acetone and methanol have very close boiling points; so for separation, fractional distillation is used.

5. Simple distillation may used.

8. In the presence of an insoluble substance, the boiling point of the solvent is unchanged.

9. Under reduced pressure, the boiling point of the liquid decreases; the liquid boils at a lower temperature.

11. Aniline is immiscible in water, so steam distillation is used.

12. O-nitrophenol is steam volatile but P-nitrophenol is not steam volatile because of intramolecular H-bonding and intermolecular H-bonding, respectively.

13. A liquid boils at a temperature at which its vapour pressure is equal to external pressure (atmospheric pressure).

14. Organic compounds have greater solubility in organic solvents than water.

16. If the vapour pressure of the liquid (P_1) is lower than atmospheric pressure (P), the liquid is not vaporized.

20. Silica gel and alumina are good adsorbents and act as solid stationary phase.

21. Al_2O_3 (Alumina).

22. Sugar dissolves in water and after saturated solution, on cooling, sugar crystallises.
Aniline and water are immiscible and aniline vapour pressure is not sufficient for volatility. So steam distillation is used.
Toluene (organic compound) in water is less soluble, but toluene in organic solvent is more soluble.

23. In the sample compound, A is effectively adsorbed on silica gel (adsorbent). So A = b + c.

26. $\underset{(C+H)}{\text{Sample}} \xrightarrow[\text{Cupric oxide } (Cu^{+2})]{CuO/\Delta} CO_2 + H_2O$

28. N + C (in sample) $\xrightarrow{Na}$ NaCN (Ionic compound) (Lassaigne's extract)

30. $Fe_4[Fe(CN)_6]_3$ (Prussian blue)

31.

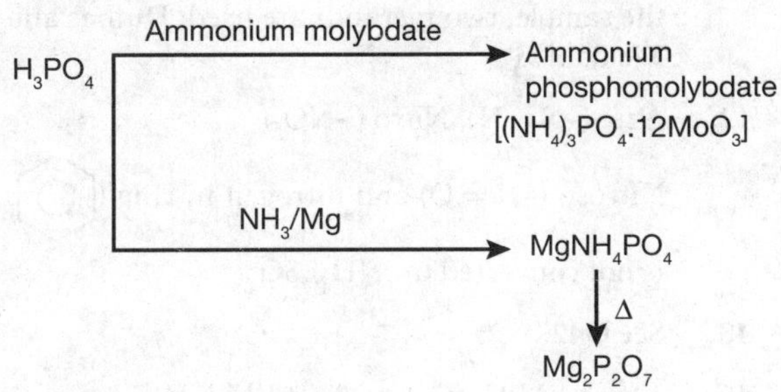

32. N + S (in sample) $\xrightarrow{Na}$ NaSCN $\xrightarrow{FeCl_3}$ $Fe(SCN)_3$
(Blood red colour)

33. Sample P $\xrightarrow{Na_2O_2}$ $Na_3PO_4 \xrightarrow{HNO_3} H_3PO_4$
$H_3PO_4 \xrightarrow{(NH_4)_2MoO_4} (NH_4)_3PO.12MoO_3$
(yellow ppt)

35. $$\frac{P_1V_1}{T_1} = \frac{P_2V_2}{T_2}$$

P_1 = Pressure of nitrogen after removal of aqueous tension.
V_1 = Volume of N_2 gas collected.
T_1 = The temperature at which these are obtained and P_2V_2 and T_2 are at STP value.

36. $$\%c = \frac{12}{44} \times \frac{W_{CO_2}}{W_{Sample}} \times 100$$

$$\%H = \frac{2 \times W_{H_2O}}{18 \times W_{sample}} \times 100$$

37. B = Excess CO_2
A = Collected N_2 gas

38. 22400 ml N_2 = 1 mole N_2 = 28 g N_2

39. Sample: $C + H + N \xrightarrow{CuO} \underset{6}{CO_2} + \underset{4}{H_2O} + \underset{1}{N_2}$

$$C = \frac{6}{1} = 6$$

$$H = \frac{4}{1} \times 2 = 8$$

$$N = \frac{1}{1} \times 2 = 2$$

40. For quantitative measurement of nitrogen in the sample, two methods are used: Dumas and Kjeldahl's.

42. Azo, (–N = N), Nitro ($-NO_2$)

Nitroso (–N = O) and nitrogen in ring (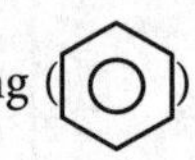)

is not converted in $(NH_4)_2SO_4$.

43. See Q42.

46. 10 ml, 1 M $H_2SO_4 \rightarrow$ 20 ml 1 M NH_3.
1000 ml 1 M $NH_3 \rightarrow$ 1 mole NH_3 = 14 g N

$$= \frac{14 \times 20}{1000 \times 0.75} \times 100 = 37.33$$

47. 188 g $\rightarrow$ 80 g

$$= \frac{80 \times 141}{188 \times 250} \times 100 = 24$$

49. Carius method is also used for estimation of sulphur, phosphorus and halogens.

51. Sample of S + $Na_2O_2 \rightarrow H_2SO_4$

53. $BaSO_4 = m_1$

54. $\frac{32 \times 0.4813}{233 \times 0.157} \times 100 = \%$ of sulphur

56. Activated charcoal is a good adsorbent.

57. Sublimable compound (naphthalene) is separated from non-sublimable compound.

58. In vacuum distillation, the boiling point of the liquid decreases. So the liquid boils at a lower boiling point.

59. Glycerol has high boiling point. It decomposes before its boiling point.

60. Water trapped in cellulose paper acts as stationary phase; solvent (mobile phase) is also liquid.

65. In thin layer chromatography, their adsorption determines the type of ink used.

66. (C + H in sample) $\xrightarrow{CuO} CO_2 + H_2O$.

67. NaCN

68.

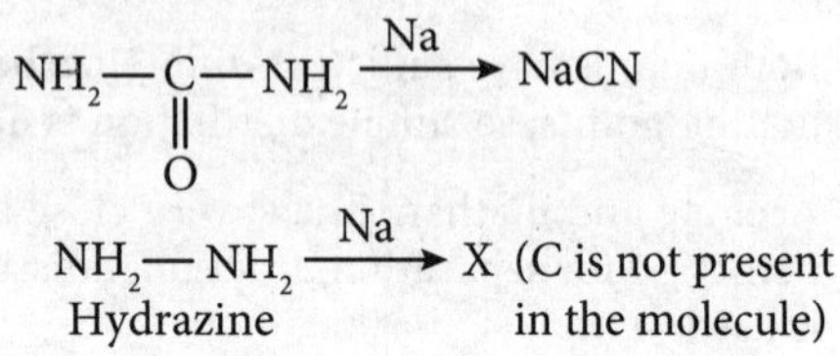

69. Prussian blue = $Fe_4[Fe(CN)_6]_3$

70.

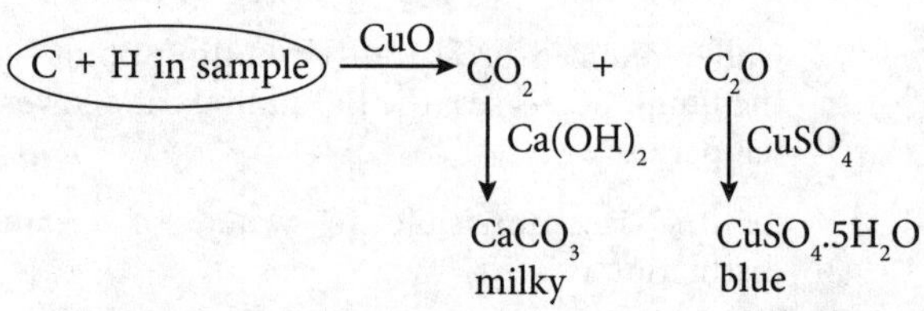

71. N $\rightarrow$ Prussian blue $[Fe_4Fe(CN)_6]_3$
S $\rightarrow$ Violet $[Fe_4[Fe(CN)_5NOS]^{+2}$
Cl $\rightarrow$ White ppt [AgCl]
P $\rightarrow$ Yellow $[(NH_4)_3PO_4.12MoO_3]$

73.

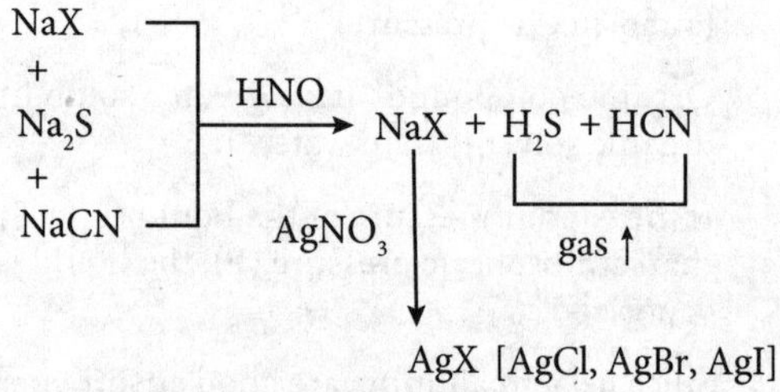

76.

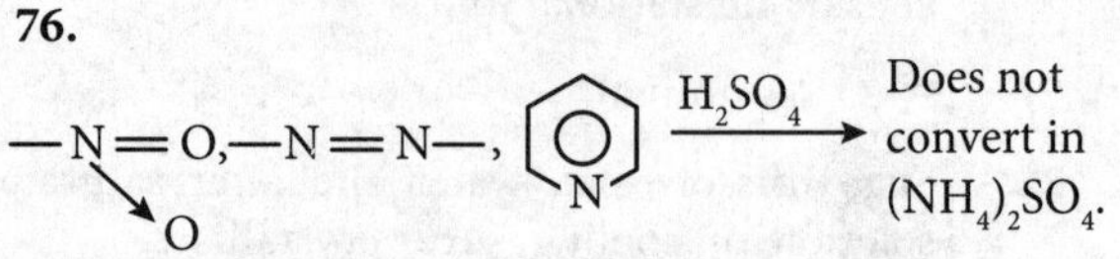

77. K_2SO_4 increases the boiling point of H_2SO_4; so K_2SO_4 acts as boiling point elevator.

78. $S\% = \frac{32 \times m_1}{233 \times m} \times 100$

m_1 = Weight of $BaSO_4$.
m = Weight of sample.

79. $C = \frac{40}{12} = \frac{3.33}{3.33} = 1$

$H = \frac{13.33}{1} = \frac{13.33}{3.33} = 4$

$N = \frac{416.67}{14} = \frac{3.33}{3.33} = 4$

80. $P\% = \frac{62 \times m_1}{222.55 \times m} \times 100$

m_1 = Mass of $Mg_2P_2O_7$.
m = Mass of sample.

81. $C = \frac{38.8}{12} = \frac{3.33}{3.33} = 1$

$H = \frac{16}{1} = \frac{16}{3.33} = 5$

$N = \frac{45.2}{14} = \frac{3.33}{3.33} = 1$

$CH_5N \Rightarrow CH_3 - NH_2$

CHAPTER **6**

Haloalkanes and Haloarenes

Level-1

HALOALKANES

1. The reaction conditions leading to the best yields of C_2H_5Cl are:
(a) $C_2H_6 \text{ (excess)} + Cl_2 \xrightarrow{\text{UV light}}$
(b) $C_2H_6 + Cl_2 \xrightarrow[\text{Room temperature}]{\text{Dark}}$
(c) $C_2H_6 + Cl_2 \text{ (excess)} \xrightarrow{\text{UV light}}$
(d) $C_2H_6 + Cl_2 \xrightarrow{\text{UV light}}$

2. The addition of bromine in CCl_4 to an alkene results in:
(a) Gem-dibromide
(b) Cyclic dibromide
(c) Alkane
(d) Vic-dibromide

3. Read the following statements:
(a) The –OH of an alcohol is replaced by –X (halogen) on reaction with concentrated HX, PX_3 or $SOCl_2$.
(b) The Lucas test is used to distinguish among 1°, 2° and 3° alkyl halides.
(c) Good yields of RI may be obtained by heating alcohols with NaI or KI in 95% orthophosphoric acid.
In light of the above statements, which set of statements is correct?
(a) (a), (b) (b) (b), (c)
(c) (a), (c) (d) (a), (b) and (c)

4. Which of the following is incorrect with respect to the physical properties of alkyl halides?
(a) Alkyl halides are colourless but alkyl bromide and iodides develop colour when exposed to light.
(b) Though alkyl halides are polar, they are still very slightly soluble in water.
(c) The nature of intermolecular forces in alkyl halides are dipole-dipole and Van der Waals forces.
(d) The boiling point of isomeric haloalkanes increases with increase in branching.

5. Which of the following will have the maximum dipole moment?
(a) CH_3F (b) CH_3Cl
(c) CH_3Br (d) CH_3I

6. Read the following statements and choose the correct option:
(i) Many volatile halogen compounds have a sweet smell.
(ii) With increase in the size and mass of a halogen atom, the magnitude of Van der Waals forces increases.
(a) Both statements (i) and (ii) are correct
(b) Statement (i) is correct and (ii) is incorrect
(c) Statement (ii) is correct and (i) is incorrect
(d) Both statements (i) and (ii) are incorrect

7. Which of the following statements is correct?
(a) S_N2 reactions of optically active halides are accompanied by inversion of configuration.
(b) S_N1 reactions of optically active halides are accompanied by racemisation.
(c) Carbocation formed in S_N1 reaction is sp^2 hybridized.
(d) All of the above.

8. Read the following statements and choose the correct option:
(i) S_N1 reactions are carried out through formation of carbocation as an intermediate.
(ii) S_N1 reactions are two-step reactions in which step 1 is fast and irreversible.
(iii) Step 1 involves breaking of the C–X bond which obtains energy through solvation of halide.
(iv) S_N1 reactions are two-step reactions in which step 2 is slow and reversible.
(v) Allylic and benzylic halides show high reactivity towards S_N1 reactions.
(a) (i), (iii) and (v) are correct
(b) (ii), (iii) and (v) are correct

(c) (i), (iii) and (iv) are correct
(d) (i), (ii) and (iv) are correct

9. Read the following statements and choose the correct code:

(i) S_N2 reactions proceed with complete stereochemical inversion.
(ii) S_N1 reactions proceed with racemisation.
(iii) A dextrorotatory compound rotates the plane-polarized light to the left.
(iv) A laevorotatory compound rotates the plane-polarized light to the right

(a) TFTT (b) TTFF
(c) FFTT (d) TFTF

10.

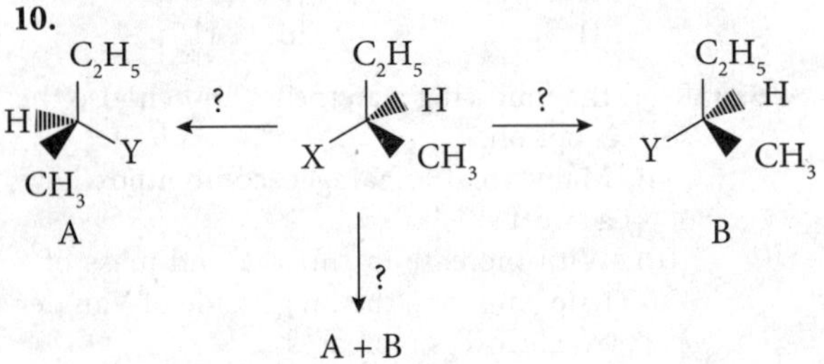

For the reaction scheme given above, some statements are given. Read the statements and choose the correct option:

(i) If (A) is the only compound obtained, the process is called inversion of configuration.
(ii) If (B) is the only compound obtained, the process is called retention of configuration.
(iii) If a 50 : 50 mixture of the above two is obtained, the process is called racemisation.
(iv) The product (A + B) is optically active.

(a) TTTF (b) TFTF
(c) TTFF (d) TFFT

11. The reactivity order of halides for dehydrohalogenation is:

(a) R-F > R-Cl > R-Br > R-I
(b) R-I > R-Br > R-Cl > R-F
(c) R-I > R-Cl > R-Br > R-F
(d) R-F > R-I > R-Br > R-Cl

12. Which is the main product of the following reaction?

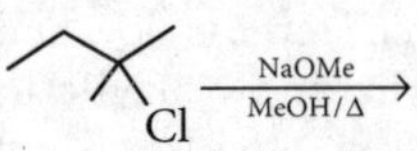

(a)  (b) 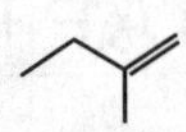

(c) 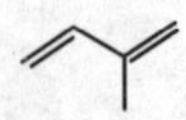 (d) 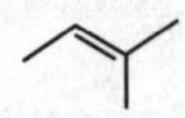

13. Elimination reactions of compounds 1 and 2 with sodium ethoxide give two alkenes, A and B, but with different selectivity. Which of the following statements best indicates the most probable outcome?

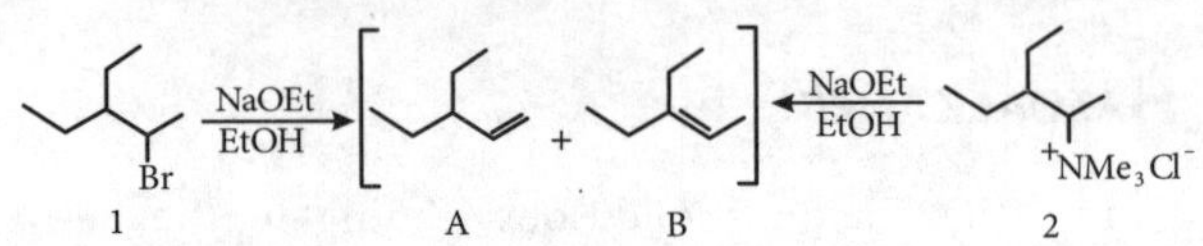

(a) A both from 1 and 2
(b) B both from 1 and 2
(c) A from 1 and B from 2
(d) B from 1 and A from 2

14. **Assertion (A):** In the preparation of alkyl halides from alcohols, thionyl chloride is preferred over other reagents.
Reason (R): The other two products produced during the reaction, apart from alkyl halides, are escapable gases.

(a) Both A and R are correct; R is the correct explanation of A
(b) Both A and R are correct; R is not the correct explanation of A
(c) A is correct; R is incorrect
(d) R is correct; A is incorrect

15. **Assertion (A):** H_3PO_4 is used during the reaction of alcohol with KI.
Reason (R): H_3PO_4 is a non-oxidising agent.

(a) Both A and R are correct; R is the correct explanation of A
(b) Both A and R are correct; R is not the correct explanation of A
(c) A is correct; R is incorrect
(d) R is correct; A is incorrect

16. Select the byproduct formed in the reaction:

$ROH + PCl_5 \longrightarrow RCl + \text{Byproducts}$

(a) $POCl_3 + HCl$ (b) H_3PO_3
(c) $H_3PO_3 + HCl$ (d) $POCl_3$

17. Alkyl halides are not prepared from alcohols by treating with:

(a) $HCl + ZnCl_2$ (b) Red P + Br_2
(c) $H_2SO_4 + KI$ (d) PCl_5

18. How many monochloro derivatives are obtained when isobutane is chlorinated?
(a) 1 (b) 2
(c) 3 (d) 4

19. **Assertion (A):** The yield of an alkyl halide which is formed by free radical halogenation is low.
Reason (R): Free radical halogenation leads to the formation of a mixture of isomeric mono- and poly-haloalkanes.
(a) Both A and R are correct; R is the correct explanation of A
(b) Both A and R are correct; R is not the correct explanation of A
(c) A is correct; R is incorrect
(d) R is correct; A is incorrect

20. Identify the structure of the hydrocarbon if its molecular mass is 72 g mol^{-1}, which on chlorination gives a single dichloro derivative:
(a) CH_3-CH_3
(b) $CH_3-CH_2-CH_2-CH_2-CH_3$
(c) 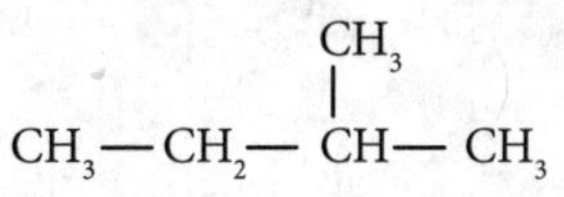
(d) 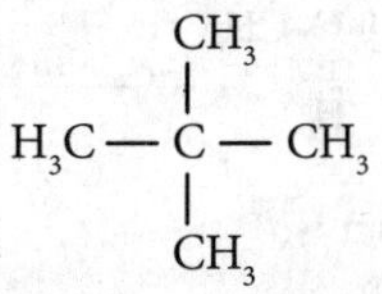

21. Which of the following statements is/are true?

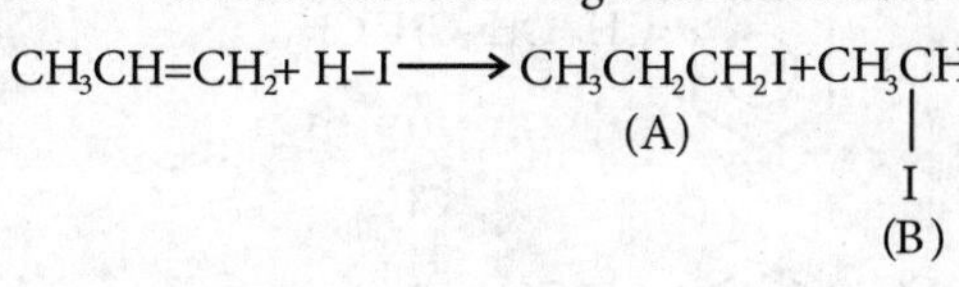

(a) A product is due to Markovnikov's rule
(b) B product is due to Markovnikov's rule
(c) A product is due to anti-Markovnikov's rule
(d) Both (b) and (c)

22. Identify A, B and C in the given sequence of reactions:

$$\underset{(B)}{H_2C=CH_2 + Br_2} \xrightarrow{(A)} \underset{(C)}{BrCH_2CH_2Br}$$

(a) CCl_4, Colourless, Reddish brown
(b) CCl_4, Reddish brown, Colourless
(c) H_2O, Colourless, Reddish brown
(d) Colourless, H_2O, Reddish brown

23. Select the correct options regarding the reaction, $R\text{-}X + NaI \rightleftharpoons R\text{-}I + NaX$
(a) The solvent used in the reaction is dry acetone.
(b) Precipitation of NaCl or NaBr might occur.
(c) The forward reaction is facilitated by Le Chatelier's principle.
(d) All of the above.

24. Arrange the following compounds in increasing order of their density:
(i) CH_2Cl_2 (ii) $CHCl_3$ (iii) CCl_4
(a) (iii) < (ii) < (i) (b) (iii) < (i) < (ii)
(c) (iii) < (i) < (ii) (d) (i) < (ii) < (iii)

25. Which of the following statements is/are best suited for the following figure?

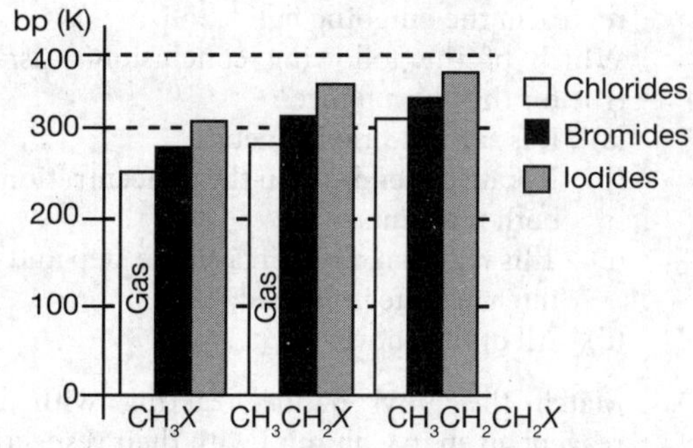

(a) The attraction is stronger as molecules get bigger in size.
(b) The boiling point of alkyl halide is in the order of RI > RBr > RCl > RF.
(c) The magnitude of Van der Waals forces increases as the mass of the halogen atom increases.
(d) All of the above.

26. **Assertion (A):** The boiling points of chlorides, bromides and iodides are considered to be higher than for hydrocarbons.
Reason (R): Due to greater polarity and higher molecular mass, the intermolecular forces of attraction are weaker in halogen derivatives as compared to hydrocarbons.
(a) Both A and R are correct; R is the correct explanation of A
(b) Both A and R are correct; R is not the correct explanation of A
(c) A is correct; R is incorrect
(d) R is correct; A is incorrect

27. **Assertion (A):** Haloalkanes are very slightly soluble in water.
Reason (R): New intermolecular attraction between haloalkanes and solvent molecules have much more strength than intermolecular attraction between haloalkanes molecules.
(a) Both A and R are correct; R is the correct explanation of A
(b) Both A and R are correct; R is not the correct explanation of A
(c) A is correct; R is incorrect
(d) R is correct; A is incorrect

28.

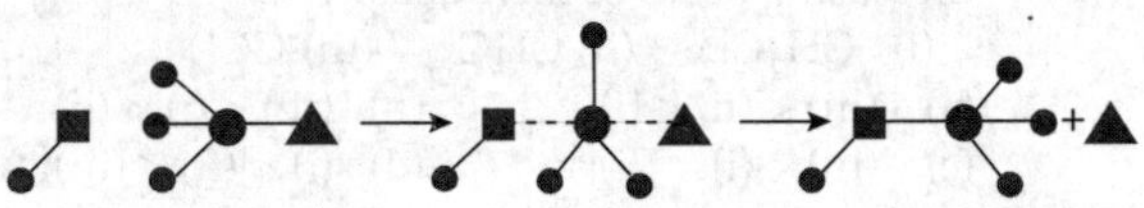

The square dots represent the incoming hydroxide ion, while the triangular dots represent the outgoing halide ion.
Which of the following conclusion(s) is/are true for the given figure?
(a) It is second-order kinetics.
(b) Its rate depends upon the concentration of both reactants.
(c) This reaction occur in a single step and no intermediate is formed.
(d) All of the above.

29. Match the alkyl halide reacting with the reagent given in Column I with their respective substituted product given in Column II and choose the correct option from the codes given below:

Column I	Column II
A. KCN	p. RH
B. AgCN	q. RCN
C. KNO_2	r. RNC
D. $LiAlH_4$	s. R–O–N=O
E. $AgNO_2$	t. $R–NO_2$

Codes

	A	B	C	D	E
(a)	q	r	t	p	S
(b)	r	q	t	p	S
(c)	q	r	s	p	t
(d)	r	q	s	p	t

30. Match Column I representing alkyl halide with the statement given in Column II and choose the correct option from the codes given below:

Column I	Column II
A. Primary alkyl halide	p. S_N2 or elimination depending upon the strength of the base/nucleophile
B. Secondary alkyl halide	q. Prefers S_N2 reaction
C. Tertiary alkyl halide	r. S_N1 or elimination depending upon the stability of carbocation or more substituted alkene

Codes:

	A	B	C
(a)	q	p	r
(b)	p	q	r
(c)	q	r	p
(d)	p	r	q

31.

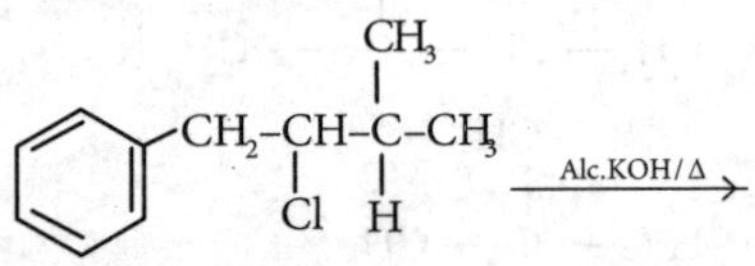

The major product is:

(a)
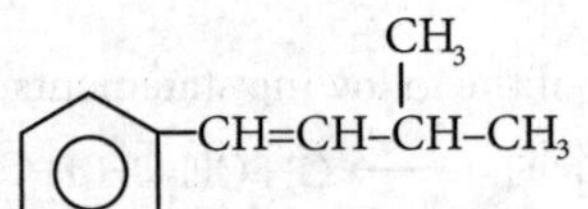

(b)
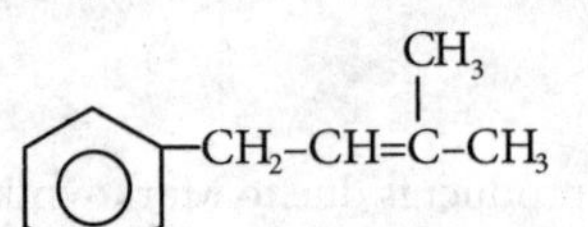

(c)
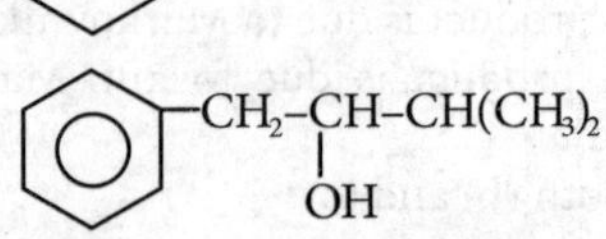

(d)
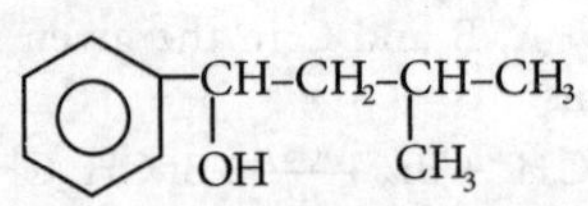

32. Which of the following is incorrect regarding the Grignard reagent?

(a) Dry ether is used as a solvent in the formation of the Grignard reagent.
(b) The carbon–magnesium bond is partially covalent in nature.
(c) The Grignard reagent reacts with water to give the corresponding hydrocarbon.
(d) The alkyl part of the Grignard reagent acts as an electrophile.

33. Identify D and E in the following reactions:

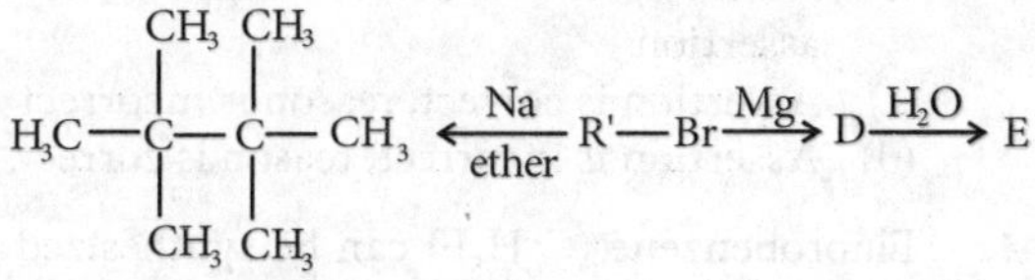

(a) $CH_3-\overset{CH_3}{\overset{|}{C}H}-MgBr$ $\quad$ $CH_3-\overset{CH_3}{\overset{|}{C}H}-H$

(b) $CH_3-\overset{CH_3}{\overset{|}{C}H}-MgBr$ $\quad$ $CH_3-\overset{CH_3}{\overset{|}{C}H}-OH$

(c) $CH_3-C(CH_3)_2-MgBr$ $\quad$ $CH_3-C(CH_3)_2-H$

(d) $CH_3-C(CH_3)_2-MgBr$ $\quad$ $CH_3-C(CH_3)_2-OH$

34. **Assertion (A):** It is necessary to avoid traces of moisture in the Grignard reagent.
Reason (R): The Grignard reagent reacts with water and forms hydrocarbons.
(a) Both A and R are correct; R is the correct explanation of A
(b) Both A and R are correct; R is not the correct explanation of A
(c) A is correct; R is incorrect
(d) R is correct; A is incorrect

35. 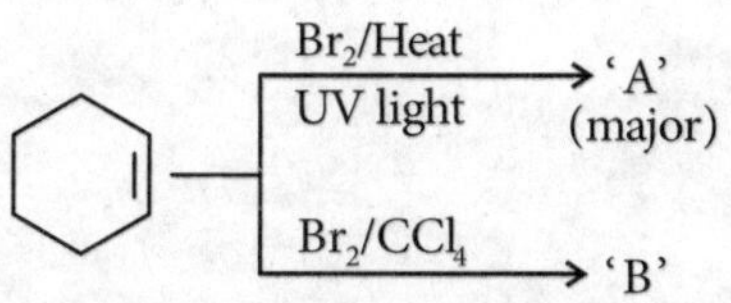

About products 'A' and 'B', which sets of statement is/are correct?
I. 'A' is an inactive racemic mixture.
II. 'B' is an inactive racemic mixture.
III. 'A' comprises substitution products whereas 'B' comprises addition products.
(a) I, II (b) II, III
(c) I, III (d) I, II, III

36. Which would be the major product from the following reaction?

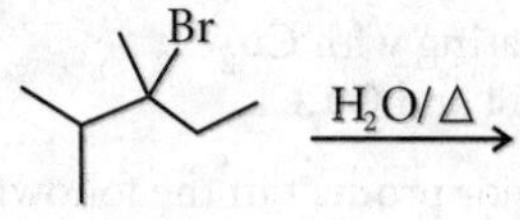

(a) 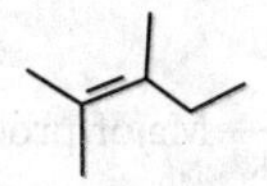 (b) 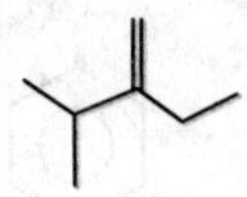

(c) 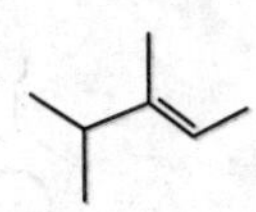 (d) 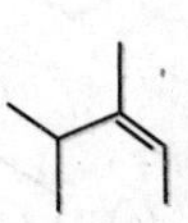

37. Match Column I (statement) with Column II (corresponding halide) and choose the correct option from the codes given below:

Column I	Column II
A. The halogen atom is bonded to an sp^3-hybridized carbon atom next to an aromatic ring.	p. Aryl halide
B. The halogen atom is bonded to an sp^2-hybridized carbon atom of a carbon–carbon double bond.	q. Vinylic halide
C. The halogen atom is bonded to an sp^2-hybridized carbon atom of an aromatic ring.	r. Benzylic halide

Codes

	A	B	C
(a)	p	q	r
(b)	r	p	q
(c)	r	q	p
(d)	q	p	r

Haloarenes

38. In the preparation of chlorobenzene from aniline, the most suitable reagent is:
(a) Chlorine in the presence of ultraviolet light
(b) Chlorine in the presence of $AlCl_3$
(c) Nitrous acid ($HCl + NaNO_2$) followed by heating with Cu_2Cl_2
(d) HCl and Cu_2Cl_2

39. The major product in the following reaction is:

 $+Cl_2 \xrightarrow[\text{Dark}]{\text{Fe}}$ Major product

(a) 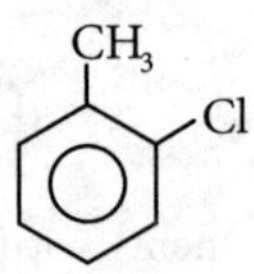 (b) 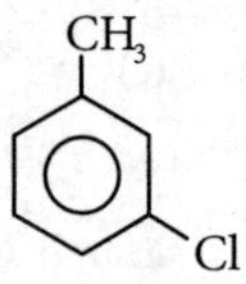

(c) 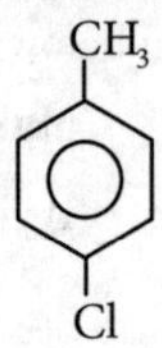 (d) 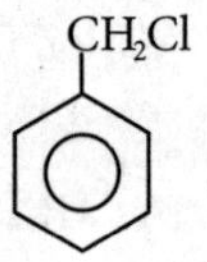

40. **Assertion (A):** Aryl halides are difficult to prepare by replacement of an –OH group in phenol with an –X group.
Reason (R): The carbon–oxygen bond in phenol has a partial double-bond character.
(a) Assertion is correct, reason is correct; reason is a correct explanation for assertion.
(b) Assertion is correct, reason is correct; reason is not a correct explanation for assertion
(c) Assertion is correct, reason is incorrect
(d) Assertion is incorrect, reason is correct.

41. Fluorobenzene (C_6H_5F) can be synthesized in the laboratory in good yield:
(a) By direct fluorination of benzene with F_2 gas.
(b) By reacting bromobenzene with NaF solution.
(c) By heating phenol with HF and KF.
(d) From an aniline by diazotisation followed by heating the diazonium salt with HBF_4.

42. Match the columns:

Column I	Column II
A. 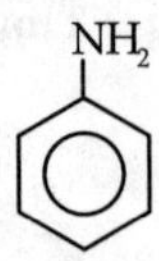 $\xrightarrow[\text{(ii) Cu/HBr}]{\text{(i) NaNO}_2\text{/HCl/0°–5°C}}$	p. The Balz–Schiemann reaction
B. $C_6H_5NH_2 \xrightarrow[\text{273–278 K}]{\text{NaNO}_2\text{+HCl/Cu}_2\text{Cl}_2} C_6H_5Cl$	q. The Gattermann reaction
C. Aniline $\xrightarrow[\text{(ii)NaBF}_4\text{/}\Delta]{\text{(i)Nitrous acid/0°–5°C}}$	r. Electrophilic aromatic substitution
D.  $\xrightarrow{\text{Br}_2\text{/Fe}}$	s. The Sandmeyer reaction

(a) A – (q), B – (s), C – (p), D – (r)
(b) A – (q), B – (r), C – (p), D – (s)
(c) A – (r), B – (p), C – (s), D – (q)
(d) A – (s), B – (r), C – (p), D – (q)

43. Which of the following statements is correct regarding the preparation of aryl halides from arenes by electrophilic substitution reaction?
(a) Aryl chlorides and bromides can be easily prepared by electrophilic substitution of arenes.
(b) Preparation of aryl iodide requires the presence of an oxidising agent.
(c) Aryl fluorides cannot be prepared by this method due to high reactivity of fluorine.
(d) All of these.

44. Which of the following statements is incorrect regarding the Sandmeyer reaction?
(a) It involves preparation of haloarenes from benzenediazonium halide.
(b) Replacement of the diazonium group by iodine requires the presence of cuprous iodide.
(c) Reaction of benzenediazonium chloride with cuprous bromide gives bromobenzene.
(d) The reaction takes place very easily because of the very high leaving tendency of nitrogen.

45. Which of the following possesses the highest melting point?
(a) Chlorobenzene
(b) m-Dichlorobenzene
(c) o-Dichlorobenzene
(d) p-Dichlorobenzene

46. Read the following statements and choose the correct answer:
(i) Alkyl iodide gives yellow precipitate with aqueous $AgNO_3$ while aryl iodide does not.
(ii) Among isomeric dihalobenzenes, the para-isomer has a higher melting point than the ortho- and meta-isomers.
(iii) The isomeric dihalobenzenes have a large difference in their boiling and melting points.
(iv) The isomeric dihalobenzenes have nearly the same boiling point.
(a) (i), (ii) and (iii) are correct
(b) (i) and (iii) are correct
(c) (ii) and (iv) are correct
(d) (i), (ii) and (iv) are correct

47. Aryl halides are much less reactive towards nucleophilic substitution than alkyl halides. Which of the following accounts for this?
(i) Due to resonance in aryl halides.
(ii) In alkyl halides, the carbon atom in the C–X bond is sp^2 hybridized whereas in aryl halides, the carbon atom in the C–X bond is sp^3 hybridized.
(iii) Due to the greater stability of the phenyl cation.
(iv) Due to possible repulsion, there is less chance for the nucleophile to approach the electron-rich arenes.
(a) (i), (ii) and (iv) (b) (i), (ii) and (iii)
(c) (i) and (iv) (d) (ii), (iii) and (iv)

48. Select the correct statement about the nucleophilic substitution reaction of haloarenes:
(a) Haloarenes are more reactive than alkyl halides.
(b) Nucleophilic substitution is more favourable than electrophilic substitution.
(c) The presence of an electron withdrawing group such as $-NO_2$ decreases the reactivity.
(d) Haloarenes are much less reactive towards nucleophilic substitution reactions.

49. The replacement of chlorine in chlorobenzene to give phenol requires drastic conditions, but the chlorine of 2,4-dinitrochlorobenzene is readily replaced since:
(a) Nitro groups make the aromatic ring electron rich at the ortho/para positions.
(b) Nitro groups withdraw electrons from the meta position of the aromatic ring.
(c) Nitro groups donate electrons at the meta position.
(d) Nitro groups withdraw electrons from the ortho/para positions of the aromatic ring.

50. Chlorobenzene reacts with Mg in dry ether to give a compound (A) which further reacts with ethanol to yield:
(a) Phenol (b) Benzene
(c) Ethylbenzene (d) Anisole

51. On sulphonation of C_6H_5Cl:
(a) Benzene sulphonic acid is formed.
(b) Meta-chlorobenzenesulphonic acid is formed.
(c) Ortho-chlorobenzenesulphonic acid is formed.
(d) Ortho- and para-chlorobenzenesulphonic acids are formed.

52. Haloarenes are ortho- and para-directing due to:
(a) Resonance effect of the halogen atom
(b) – I effect of the halogen atom
(c) + I effect of the halogen atom
(d) Both (a) and (b)

53. **Statement-I:** Aryl halides are less reactive than benzene towards ESR.
Statement-II: Aryl halides are more reactive than alkyl halides towards nucleophilic substitution.
(a) Both Statement-I and Statement-II are correct
(b) Statement-I is correct but Statement-II is incorrect
(c) Statement-I is incorrect but statement-II is correct
(d) Both Statement-I and Statement-II are incorrect

54. Which of the following is incorrectly matched with the name of the reaction?

(a) 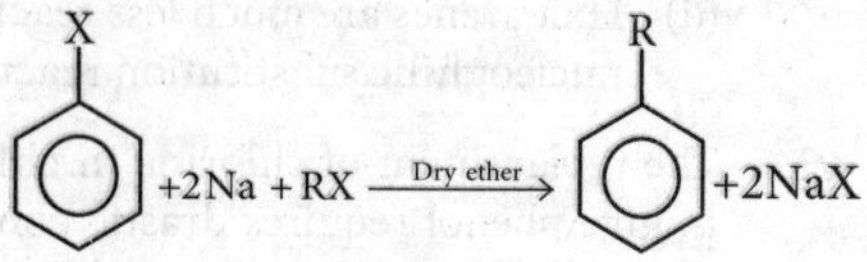

⇒ Wurtz–Fittig reaction

(b) 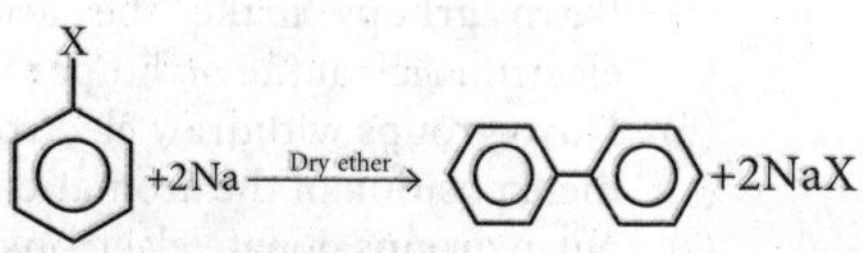

⇒ Fittig reaction

(c) 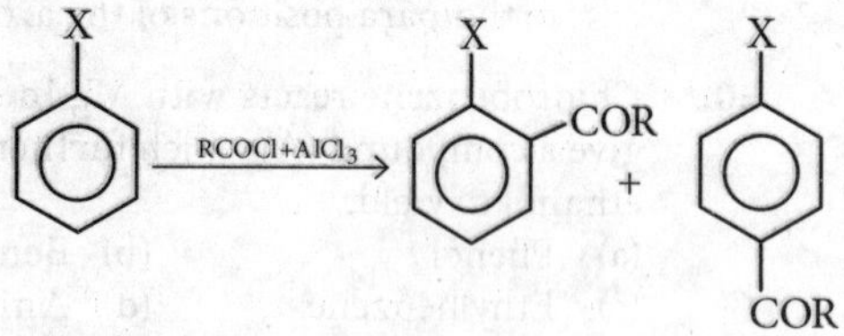

⇒ Friedel–Crafts alkylation

(d) 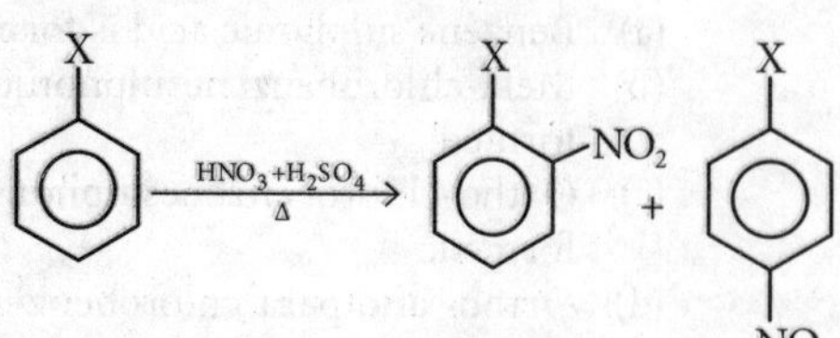

⇒ Nitration

55. Read the statements given below:
(a) Haloarenes require drastic conditions for nucleophilic substitution reaction (NSR).
(b) The presence of the electron withdrawing group increases the reactivity of haloarenes towards NSR.
(c) Electrophilic substitution of haloarenes is slower than in benzene.
Choose the option containing the correct set of statements:
(a) (a), (b) (b) (b), (c)
(c) (a), (c) (d) (a), (b), (c)

56. Consider the following haloarenes:

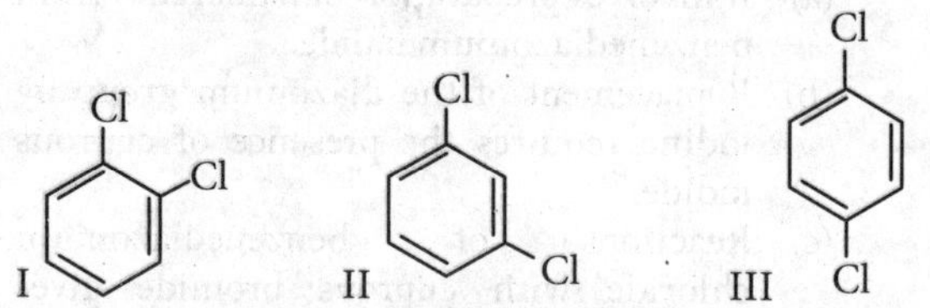

(I) B.P. of II is more than that of I.
(II) B.P. of II is the least among the given.
(III) M.P. of III is the highest among the given.
(IV) M.P. of I is greater than that of II.
Choose the correct option:
(a) Only I (b) II, III and IV
(c) Only IV (d) Both I and IV

57. Name the reagent used in this reaction:

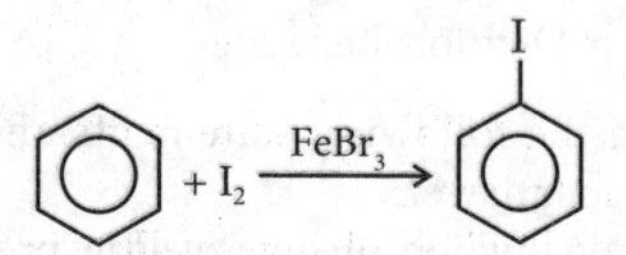

(a) HNO_3 (b) HF
(c) H_2O (d) SO_2

58.

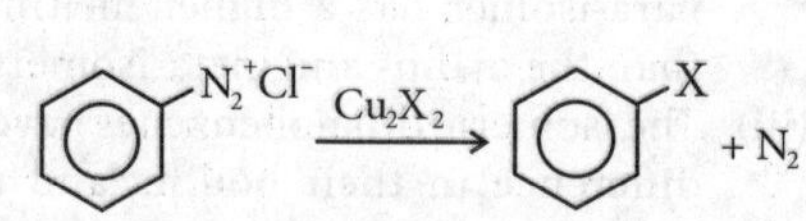

Which of the following do/does not match the equation?
(a) X=Cl
(b) X=Br
(c) X=I
(d) Both (a) and (b)

59. When a primary aromatic amine dissolved in cold aqueous mineral acid (HCl) is treated with sodium nitrite, the product formed is:
(a) Aryl halide

(b) Diazonium salt
(c) 2° aromatic amine
(d) Benzyl chloride

60. Aryl halides are much less reactive towards nucleophilic substitution reaction due to:
(a) Resonance effect
(b) Instability of the phenyl cation
(c) Repulsion between the π-cloud of the benzene ring and the incoming nucleophile
(d) All of the above

61.

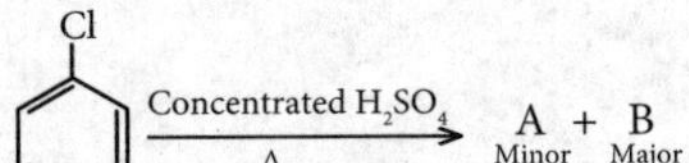

A and B are, respectively:

(a) 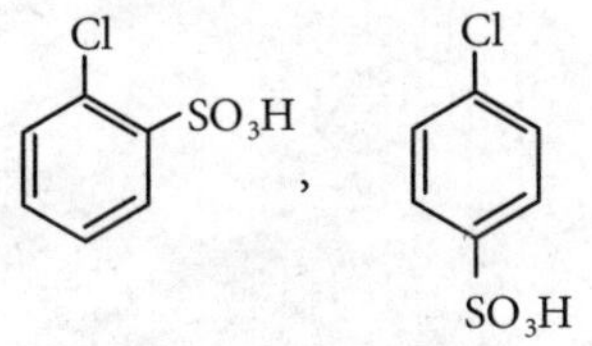

(b) 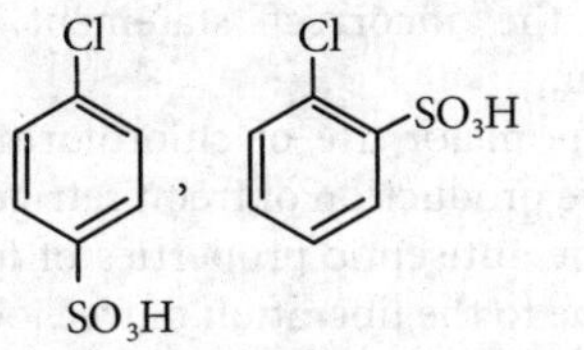

(c) 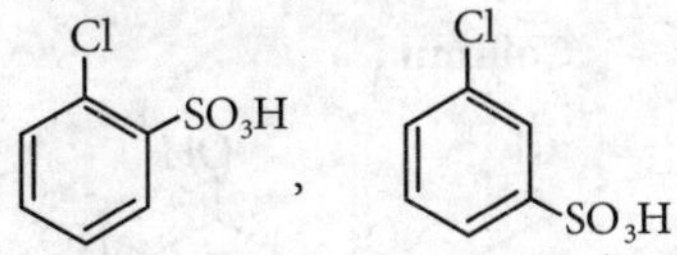

(d) 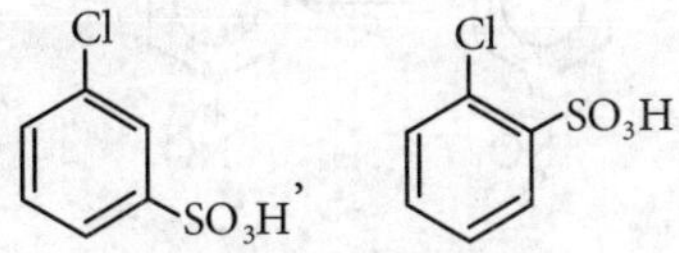

62. **Assertion (A):** The presence of the nitro group at the ortho or para position increases the reactivity of haloarenes towards nucleophilic substitution.
Reason (R): The $-NO_2$ group stabilises intermediate carbanion by resonance in nucleophilic substitution of haloarenes.
(a) Both A and R are correct; R is the correct explanation of A
(b) Both A and R are correct; R is not the correct explanation of A
(c) A is correct; R is incorrect
(d) R is correct; A is incorrect

63. **Assertion (A):** Electrophilic substitution reactions in haloarenes occur slowly and under drastic conditions.
Reason (R): Haloarenes are more activated as compared to benzene.
(a) Both A and R are correct; R is the correct explanation of A
(b) Both A and R are correct; R is not the correct explanation of A
(c) A is correct; R is incorrect
(d) R is correct; A is incorrect

64. Match the conditions given in Column I with Column II and choose the correct option from the codes given below:

Column I	Column II
A. 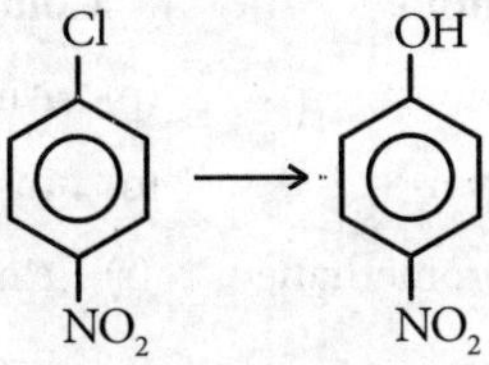	p. NaOH, 443 K, H^+

Column I	Column II
B. 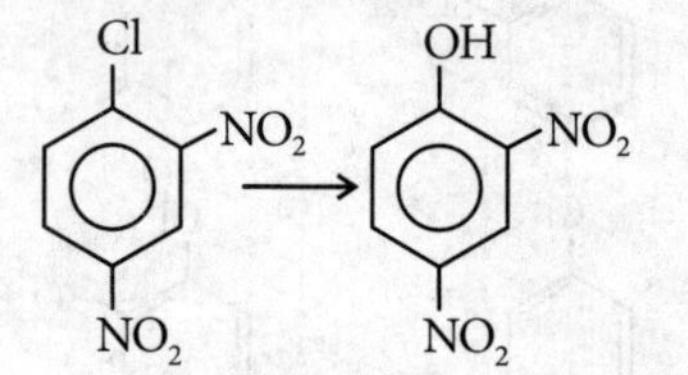	q. NaOH, 368 K, H^+
C. 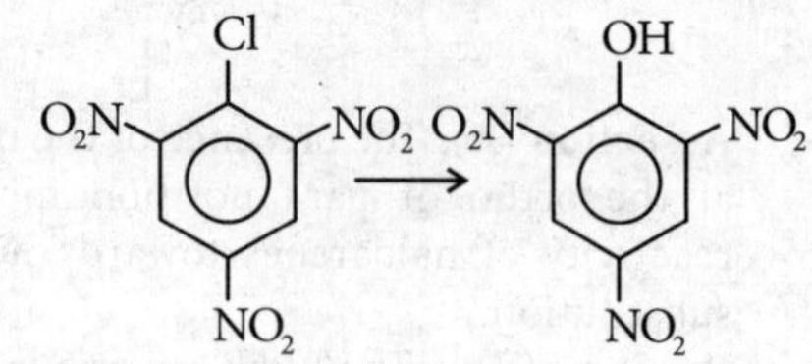	r. Warm H_2O

Codes

	A	B	C
(a)	r	p	q
(b)	p	r	q
(c)	p	q	r
(d)	r	q	p

Polyhalogen Compounds

65. The use of chlorofluorocarbons is not encouraged because:
(a) They are harmful to the eyes of people who use it.
(b) They damage refrigerators and air conditioners.
(c) They affect the food chain in the oceans.
(d) They upset the ozone balance in the stratosphere.

66. Which of the following is used in fire extinguishers?
(a) CH_4 (b) $CHCl_3$
(c) CH_2Cl_2 (d) CCl_4

67. The uses of dichloromethane include:
(a) Paint remover
(b) Solvent in drugs manufacturing
(c) Metal cleansing and finishing solvent
(d) All of the above

68. When chloroform is exposed to light and air, it forms:
(a) Chlorine gas
(b) Methyl chloride
(c) Phosgene gas
(d) Carbon tetrachloride

69. Select the incorrect statement among the following:
(a) The major use of chloroform today is in the production of freon refrigerant R-22.
(b) The antiseptic properties of iodoform are due to the liberation of free iodine.
(c) Freon-12 is CCl_3F.
(d) Due to prolonged ingestion, DDT builds up within animals (biological magnification).

70. The full form of DDT is:
(a) p, p'-Dichlorodiphenyltrichloroethane
(b) p, p'-Dichlorodifluorotrichloroethane
(c) p, p'-Diphenyldichlorotribromoethane
(d) None of the above

71. Match the columns:

Column I	Column II
(a) Chloroform	(p) Antiseptic
(b) Iodoform	(q) Insecticide
(c) Dichloromethane	(r) Anaesthetic
(d) DDT	(s) Propellant

(a) a – (s), b – (p), c – (r), d – (q)
(b) a – (r), b – (p), c – (s), d – (q)
(c) a – (q), b – (s), c – (p), d – (q)
(d) a – (r), b – (s), c – (p), d – (q)

72. Match the columns:

Column I (Haloalkane/ Haloarene)	Column II (Application)
(a) Iodoform	(p) CCl_2F_2
(b) BHC	(q) Antiseptic
(c) Freon-12	(r) Poisonous gas
(d) DDT	(s) Biological magnification
(e) Phosgene	(t) Termite pesticide

(a) a – (q), b – (s), c – (t), d – (r), e – (p)
(b) a – (q), b – (t), c – (p), d – (s), e – (r)
(c) a – (r), b – (s), c – (q), d – (p), e – (t)
(d) a – (p), b – (r), c – (t), d – (q), e – (s)

73. Match the columns:

Column I	Column II
(a) Chloramphenicol	(p) Goitre
(b) Thyroxine	(q) Surgery
(c) Chloroquine	(r) Typhoid
(d) Halothane	(s) Malaria

(a) a – (q), b – (p), c – (s), d – (r)
(b) a – (r), b – (p), c – (s), d – (q)
(c) a – (s), b – (r), c – (q), d – (p)
(d) a – (p), b– (s), c – (q), d – (r)

74. Choose the incorrect alternative among the following:
(a) In polyhalogen compounds, more than one halogen atom is present.
(b) Dichloromethane is used as a paint remover.
(c) Chloroform is used as anaesthetic in surgery.
(d) Chloroform is used as a paint remover.

75. Why is chloroform stored in closed dark-coloured bottles completely filled with it?
(a) It is slowly reduced by air in the presence of light to carbonyl chloride.
(b) It is slowly oxidised by air in the absence of light to carbonyl chloride.
(c) It is slowly reduced by air to carbonyl chloride.
(d) It is slowly oxidised by air in the presence of light to carbonyl chloride.

76. The solvent which is used in the synthesis of chlorofluorocarbons is:
(a) Iodoform
(b) Chloroform
(c) Carbon tetrachloride
(d) Methylene chloride

77. When freon is manufactured by tetrachloromethane, the reaction involved in this process is called:
(a) Sandmeyer reaction
(b) Swarts' reaction
(c) Finkelstein reaction
(d) All of the above

78. Freons, hydrofluorocarbons and fluorocarbons are stable in the stratosphere; they are used in:
(a) Aerosol propellants
(b) Air-conditioning equipment
(c) Refrigeration
(d) All of the above

Level-2

1. Which compound undergoes hydrolysis by the S_N1 mechanism at the fastest rate?

(a)
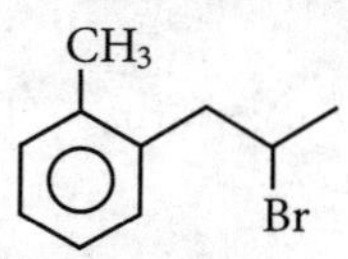

(b)
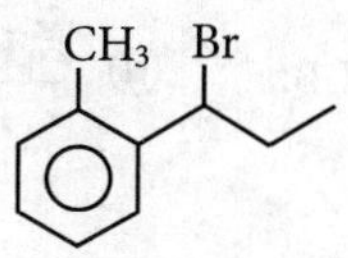

(c)
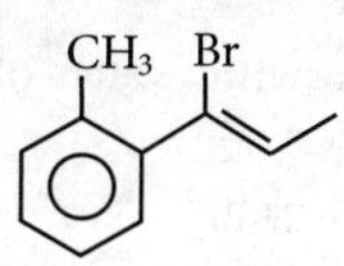

(d)
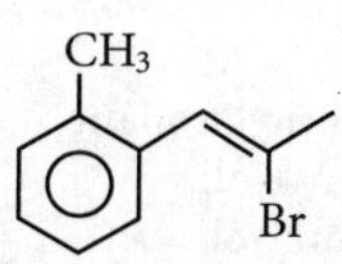

2. The decreasing order of reactivity of the following organic molecules towards the S_N1 reaction is:

(i) 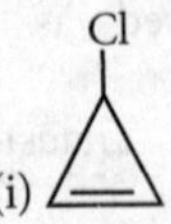 (ii) CH_3CHCH_3 with Cl on the central carbon

(a) (i) > (ii) (b) (i) = (ii)
(c) (ii) > (i) (d) Cannot say

3. Which reagent will you use for the following reaction?
$CH_3CH_2CH_2CH_3 \rightarrow CH_3CH_2CH_2CH_2Cl + CH_3CH_2CHClCH_3$
(a) Cl_2/UV light (b) NaCl + H_2SO_4
(c) Cl_2 gas in the dark (d) NaCl

4. Arrange the following compounds in the increasing order of their densities:

(a)  (b) 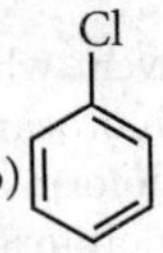

(c) 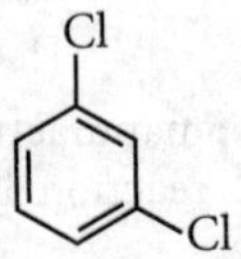 (d) 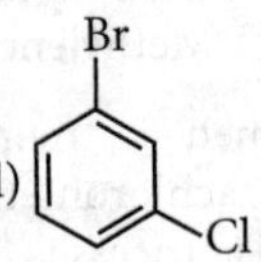

(a) (a) < (b) < (c) < (d)
(b) (a) < (c) < (d) < (b)
(c) (d) < (c) < (b) < (a)
(d) (b) < (d) < (c) < (a)

5. Which of the following compounds is most rapidly hydrolysed by the S_N1 mechanism?
(a) C_6H_5Cl
(b) $Cl-CH_2-CH=CH_2$
(c) $(C_6H_5)_3CCl$
(d) $C_6H_5CH_2Cl$

6. The rate of the S_N2 mechanism depends on:
(a) [Nucleophile] (b) [R-X]
(c) Leaving group (d) All of these

7. The S_N1 reaction with water of the given compound produces:

CH_3CHCH_2Br with C_2H_5 on the central carbon

(a) 1-Hydroxy-2-ethylpropane
(b) 2-Methylbutan-1-ol
(c) 2-Methylbutan-2-ol
(d) 2-Ethylpropan-1-ol

8. Among the bromides I–III given below, the order of reactivity in the S_N1 reaction is:

(I) 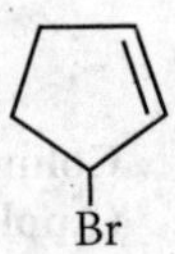 (II) 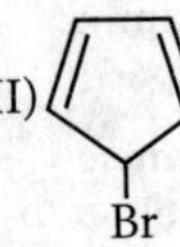 (III) 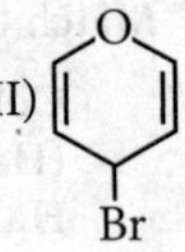

(a) III > I > II
(b) III > II > I
(c) II > III > I
(d) II > I > III

9. In which pair is the first compound more reactive than the second towards the S_N1 reaction?

(a) 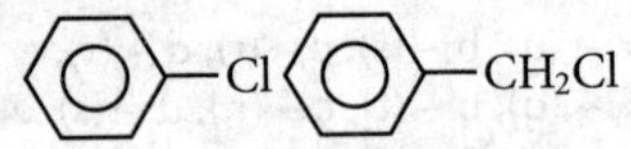

(b) 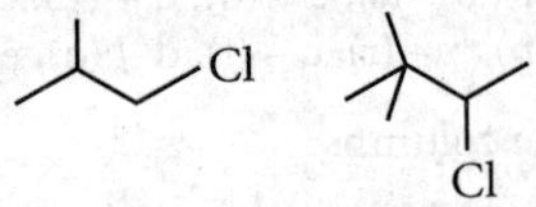

(c) 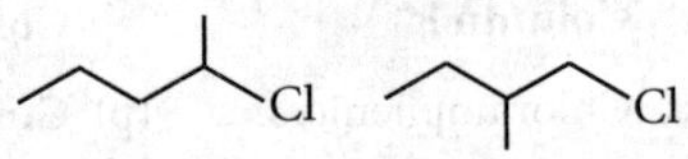

(d) 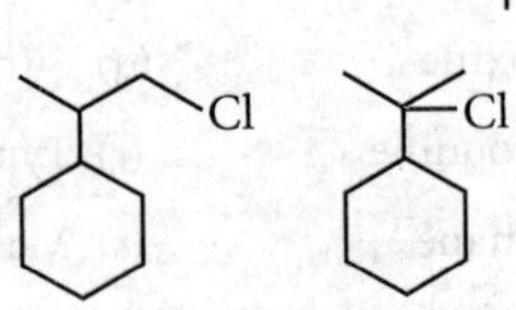

10. Which of the following compounds can be classified as aryl halides?
(a) p-$ClC_6H_4CH_2CH(CH_3)_2$
(b) p-$CH_3CHCl(C_6H_4)CH_2CH_3$
(c) o-$BrH_2C-C_6H_4CH(CH_3)CH_2CH_3$
(d) $C_6H_5-CH_2Cl$

11. Alkyl fluorides cannot be synthesised by heating an alkyl chloride/bromide in the presence of:
(a) CaF_2 (b) CoF_2
(c) Hg_2F_2 (d) AgF

12. Which of the following compounds will show retention on nucleophilic substitution by the OH^- ion?
(a) $CH_3-CH(CH_3)-Br$ (b) $CH_3-CH(C_6H_5)-Br$
(c) $CH_3-CH(C_2H_5)-CH_2Br$ (d) $CH_3-C(Br)(C_6H_{13})-H$

13. Which of the following is the most reactive towards S_N2?

(a) 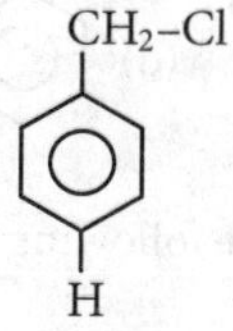

(b) 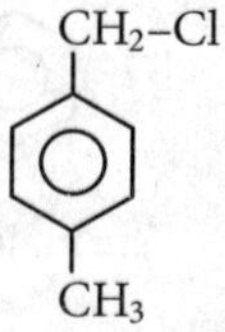

(c) 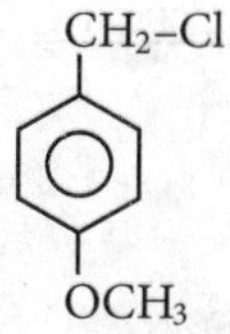

(d) 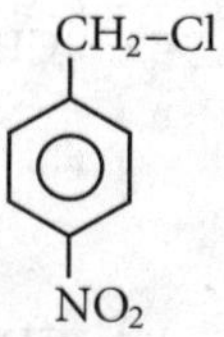

14. How many monochloro isomers will be formed on free radical chlorination of 2-methylbutane?
(a) 4
(b) 6
(c) 8
(d) 5

15. For the given reaction, the rate of reaction is given by the expression:
$CH_3Br + OH^- \rightarrow CH_3OH + Br^-$
(a) Rate = k $[CH_3Br]$
(b) Rate = k $[OH^-]$
(c) Rate = k $[CH_3Br][OH^-]$
(d) Rate = k $[CH_3Br]^\circ [OH^-]^\circ$

16. Which of the following has the fastest rate of hydrolysis?
(a) 3-Bromopentane
(b) 2-Bromopentane
(c) 1-Bromo-3-methylbutane
(d) 1-Bromopentane

17. Which of the following statements is incorrect?
(a) Aryl halides cannot be prepared by the reaction of phenol with HCl in the presence of $ZnCl_2$.
(b) Allyl chloride is hydrolysed more readily than n-propyl chloride.
(c) It is necessary to avoid even traces of moisture during the use of the Grignard reagent.
(d) KCN reacts with methyl chloride to give methyl isocyanide.

18. The major product in the following reaction is:

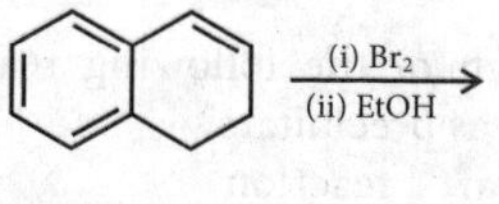

(a) 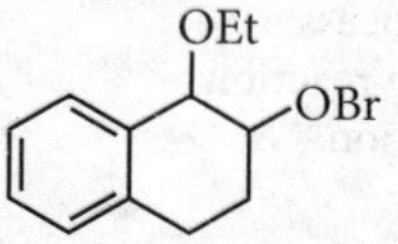

(b) 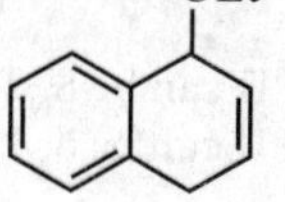

(c) 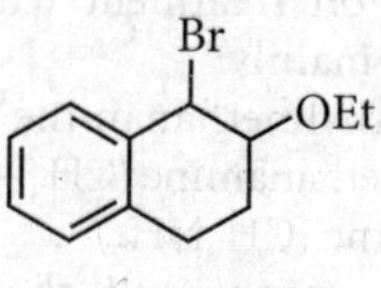

(d) 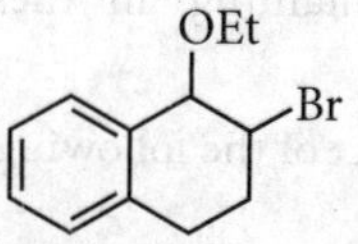

19. The correct order of the S_N1 solvolysis of the following halides in aqueous formic acid is:

(I) 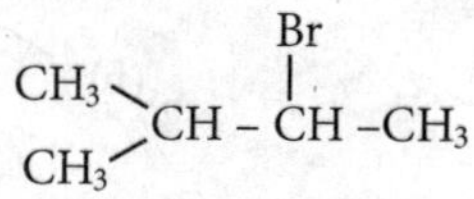
(II) 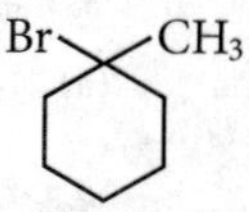

(III) 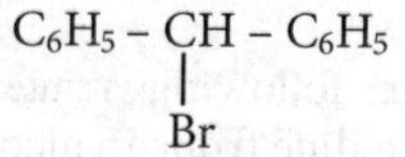
(IV) 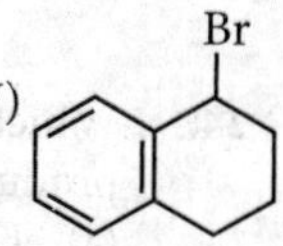

(a) III > IV > II > I
(b) II > IV > I > III
(c) I > II > III > IV
(d) III > I > II > IV

20. The reaction of toluene with NBS in the presence of light yields:

(a) 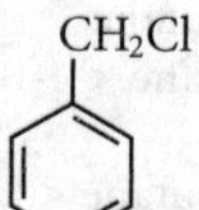

(b) 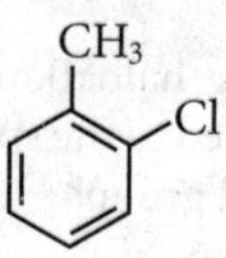

(c) 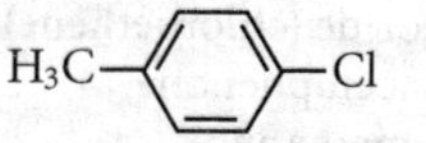

(d) Mixture of (b) and (c)

21. For the given reaction, the correct option regarding the mechanism involved is:

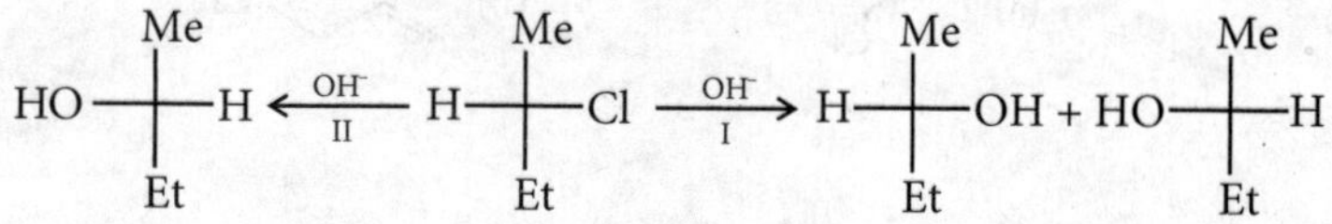

(a) I cannot be S_N1
(b) II cannot be S_N2
(c) I can be S_N1 and II can be S_N2
(d) I can be S_N2 and II can be S_N1

22. Chloromethane on treatment with excess of ammonia yields mainly:
(a) N, N-Dimethylmethanamine
(b) N-Methylmethanamine (CH_3—NH—CH_3)
(c) Methanamine (CH_3NH_2)
(d) Mixture containing all these in equal proportion

23. The major product of the following reaction is:

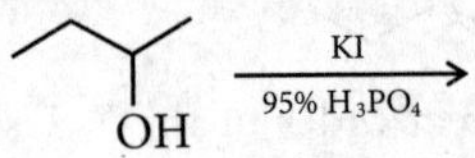

(a)  (b) 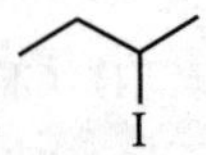

(c) 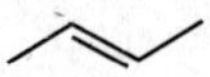 (d) 

24. Which of the following reagents will not produce alkyl halide from an alcohol?
(a) Concentrated HBr (b) $SOCl_2$
(c) RedP/Br_2 (d) NaI/H_2SO_4

25. Which is the correct increasing order of boiling points of the following compounds?
(a) Butane < 1-Chlorobutane < 1-Bromobutane < 1-Iodobutane
(b) 1-Iodobutane < 1-Bromobutane < 1-Chlorobutane < Butane
(c) Butane < 1-Iodobutane < 1-Bromobutane < 1-Chlorobutane
(d) Butane < 1-Chlorobutane < 1-Iodobutane < 1-Bromobutane

26. Which of the following haloalkanes contains the halogen atom attached to the sp^2-hybridized carbon atom of an alkyl group?
(a) 2-Bromopentane
(b) Vinyl chloride (chloroethene)
(c) 2-Chloroacetophenone
(d) Trichloromethane

27. In which of the following is replacement of Cl^- the most difficult?

(a) 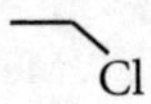

(b) 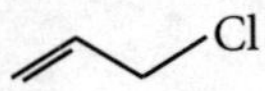

(c) 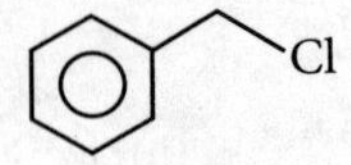

(d) 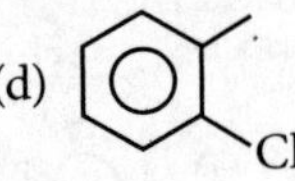

28. The major product of the following reaction is:

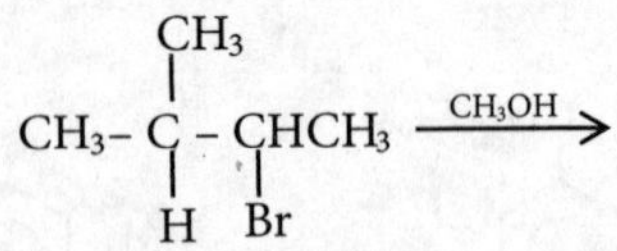

(a) 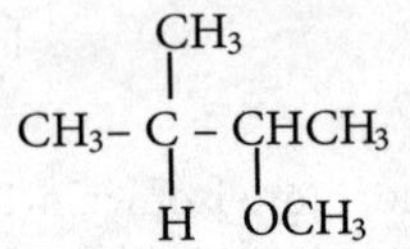

(b) 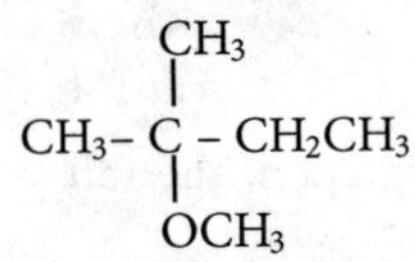

(c) 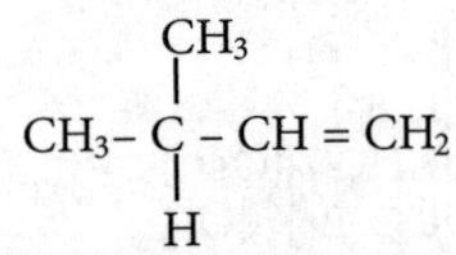

(d) 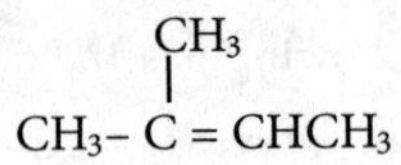

29. Arrange these compounds in the order of increasing S_N2 reaction rate:

(I) 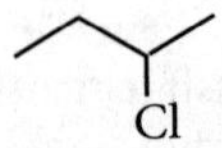

(II) 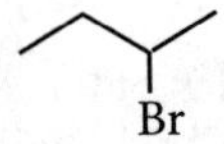

(III) 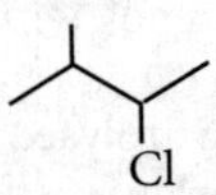

(IV) 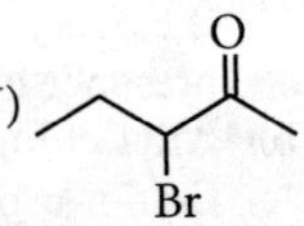

(a) III < I < II < IV (b) III < II < I < IV
(c) IV < III < I < II (d) III < IV < I < II

30. How many dihalogen derivatives of propane are possible?
(a) 4 (b) 5
(c) 6 (d) 8

31. In which of the following reactions is NaCl formed as precipitate?
(a) Swarts' reaction
(b) Darzen process
(c) Finkelstein reaction
(d) HVZ reaction

32. Which reaction proceeds faster with NaI in DMSO?

(a) 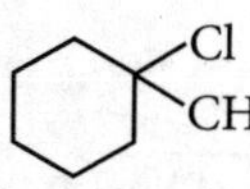
(b) 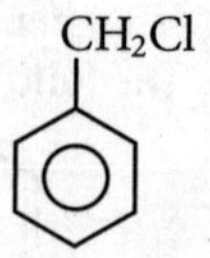
(c) 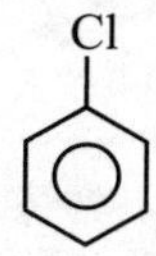
(d) 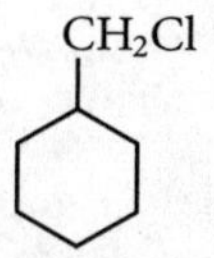

33. The correct order for the density of the given compound is:

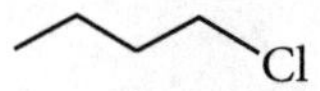 CH_2Cl_2 CCl_4 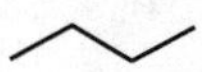

(P) (Q) (R) (S)

(a) R > Q > P > S
(b) P > S > Q > R
(c) P > Q > R > S
(d) R > Q > S > P

34. Increasing rate of S_N1 reaction in the following compounds is:

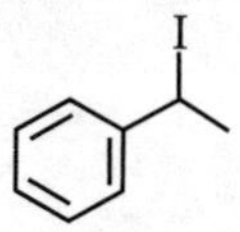
(A)

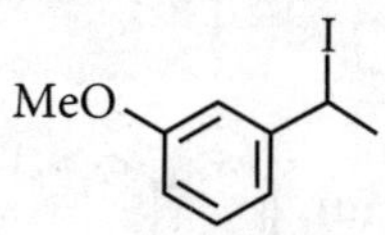
(B)

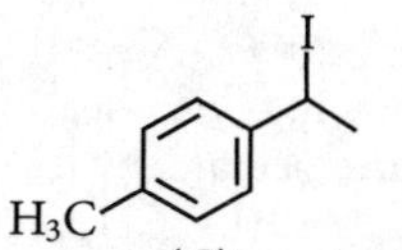
(C)

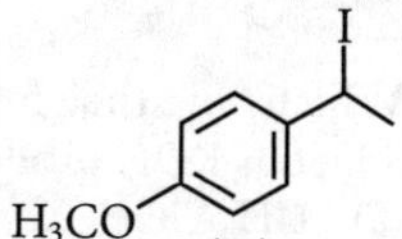
(D)

(a) (B) < (A) < (C) < (D)
(b) (A) < (B) < (C) < (D)
(c) (B) < (A) < (D) < (C)
(d) (A) < (B) < (D) < (C)

35. The compound CH_3–O–CH_2–Cl gives a slower rate of nucleophilic substitution reaction than:
(a) CH_3Cl
(b) CH_3CH_2Cl
(c) $PhCH_2Cl$
(d) CH_3OCH_2Br

36. The correct order of boiling point in the given compounds is:
1-Chloropropane (P)
Isopropyl chloride (Q)
1-Chlorobutane (R)
(a) P > Q > R
(b) R > P > Q
(c) P > R > Q
(d) R > Q > P

37. **Assertion (A)**: Vinyl halides do not undergo nucleophilic substitution easily.
Reason (R): Even though the intermediate carbocation is stabilized by loosely held π-electrons, the cleavage is difficult because of strong bonding.
(a) (A) is a correct statement but (R) is an incorrect statement.
(b) Both (A) and (R) are correct statements but (R) is not the correct explanation of (A).
(c) Both (A) and (R) are incorrect statements
(d) Both (A) and (r) are correct statements and (R) is the correct explanation of (A).

38. For the given reaction, which substrate will give maximum racemisation?

$$R-C(R_1)(R_2)-X \xrightarrow{HOH} R-C(R_1)(R_2)-OH$$

(a) $C_6H_5-C(CH_3)(C_2H_5)-Br$

(b) $CH_2=CH-C(CH_3)(C_2H_5)-Br$

(c) 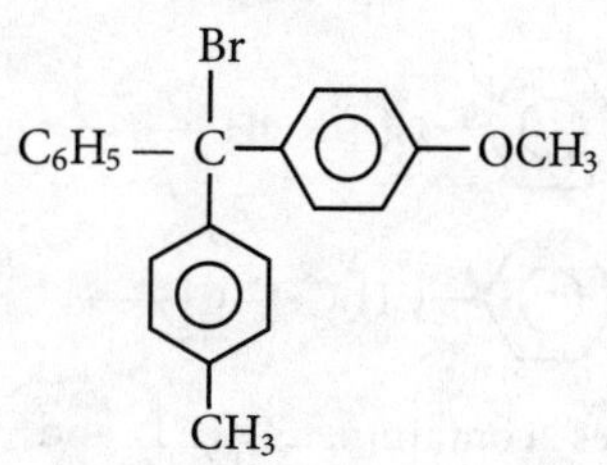

(d) 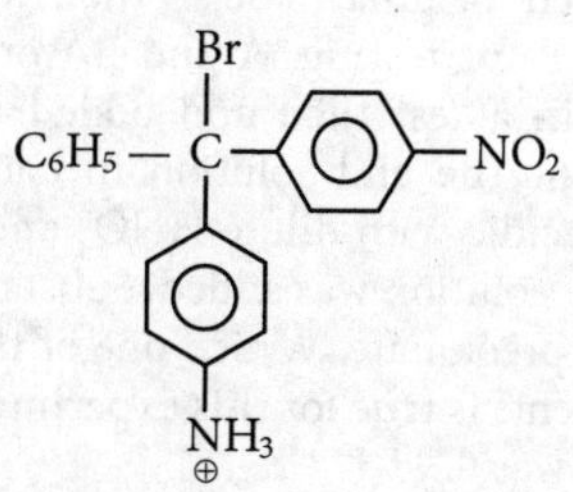

39. The increasing order of reactivity of the following compounds for S_N1 substitution is:

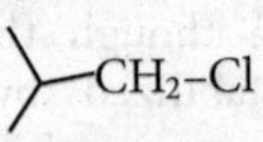
(A)

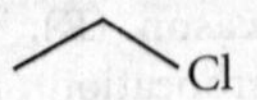
(B)

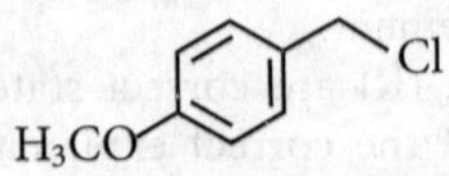
(C)

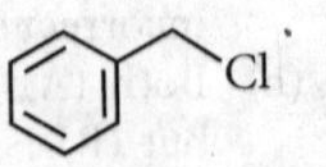
(D)

(a) B < A < D < C (b) B < C < A < D
(c) B < C < D < A (d) A < B < D < C

40. Heating an alkyl chloride/bromide in the presence of metallic fluoride is known as:
(a) Swarts' reaction
(b) Darzen process
(c) Finkelstein reaction
(d) HVZ reaction

41. The following reaction is an example of:
$(CH_3)_3C\text{–}Br + H_2O \rightarrow (CH_3)_3C\text{–}OH + HBr$
(a) Elimination reaction
(b) Free radical substitution
(c) Nucleophilic substitution
(d) Electrophilic substitution

42. The S_N1 reaction is feasible in:

(a) 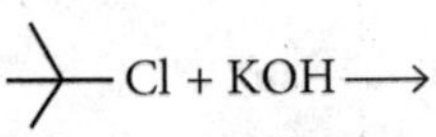

(b) 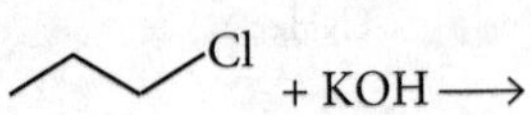

(c) 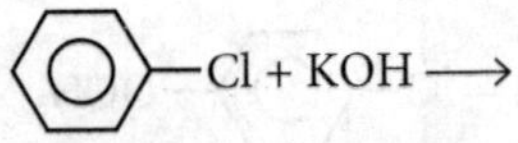

(d) 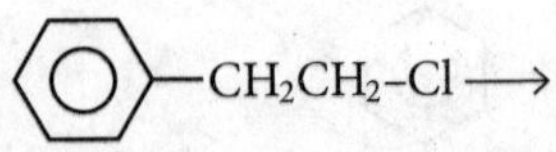

43. Bottles containing C_6H_5I and $C_6H_5\text{–}CH_2I$ lost their original labels. They were labelled A and B for testing. A and B were separately taken in a test tube and boiled with NaOH solution. The end solution in each tube was made acidic with dilute HNO_3 and then some $AgNO_3$ solution was added. Substance B gave a yellow precipitate. Which one of the following statements is true for this experiment?
(a) A was C_6H_5I
(b) A was $C_6H_5CH_2I$
(c) B was C_6H_5I
(d) B produces yellow precipitate of AgBr

44. The structure of the major product formed in the following reaction is:

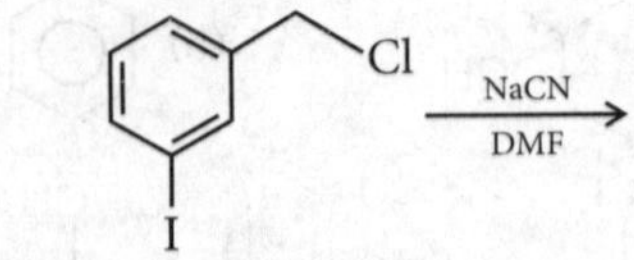

(a) 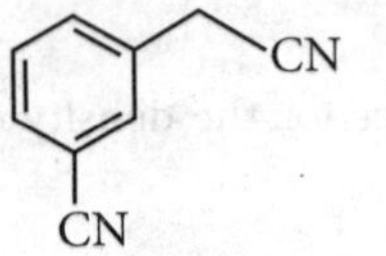

(b) 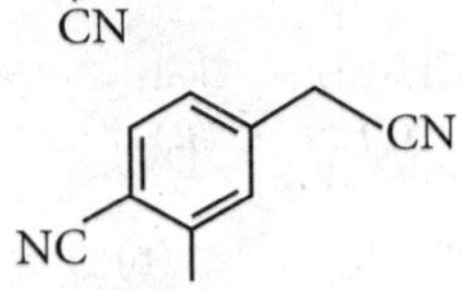

(c) 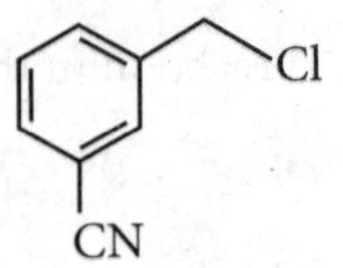

(d) 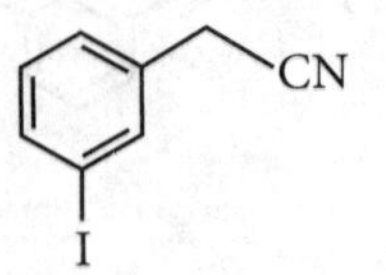

45. Which of the following on heating with aqueous KOH produces acetaldehyde?
(a) CH_2ClCH_2Cl (b) CH_3CHCl_2
(c) CH_3COCl (d) CH_3CH_2Cl

46. Consider the following bromides. The correct order of S_N1 reactivity is:

(A)

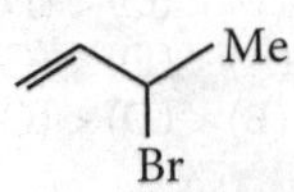
(B)

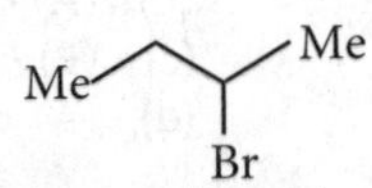
(C)

(a) A > B > C (b) B > C > A
(c) B > A > C (d) C > B > A

47. Which of the following is the most reactive towards the S_N1 reaction?

(a) 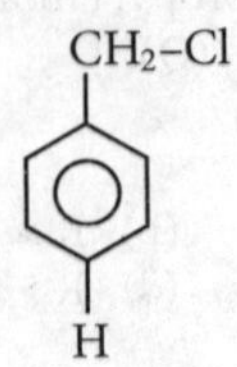

(b) 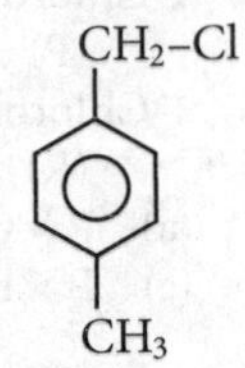

(c) 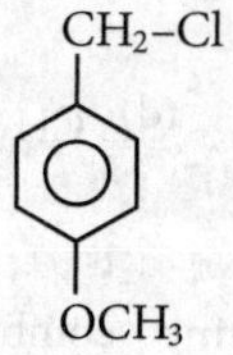 (d) 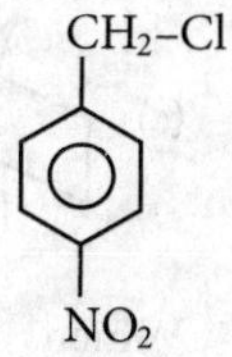

48. The increasing order of the reactivity of the following halides for the S_N1 reaction is:

$CH_3CH(Cl)CH_2CH_3$ (I) $CH_3CH_2CH_2Cl$ (II) p-H_3CO–C_6H_4–CH_2Cl (III)

(a) (III) < (II) < (I)
(b) (II) < (I) < (III)
(c) (I) < (III) < (II)
(d) (II) < (III) < (I)

49. Arrange the following compounds in decreasing order of their reactivity for the hydrolysis reaction:

(I) C_6H_5–CH_2–Br

(II) C_6H_5–CH(Cl)–C_2H_5

(III) 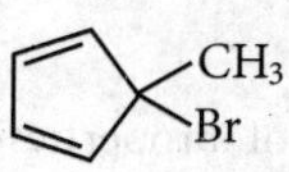

(IV) 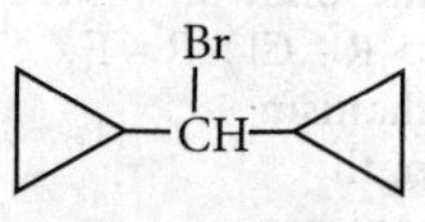

(a) I > II > III > IV
(b) IV > II > I > III
(c) III > IV > II > I
(d) IV > III > II > I

50. The major product of the following reaction is:

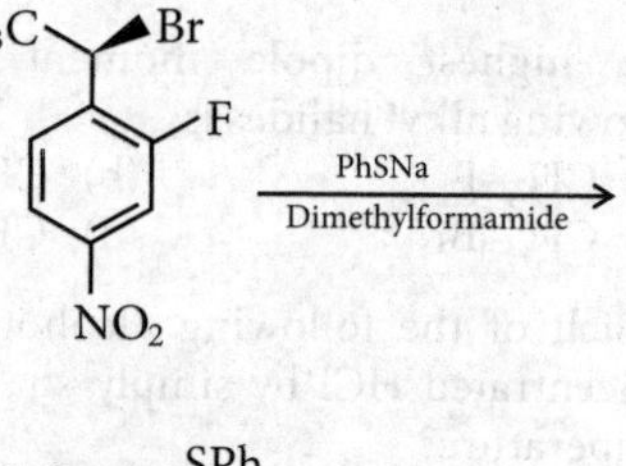

(a) 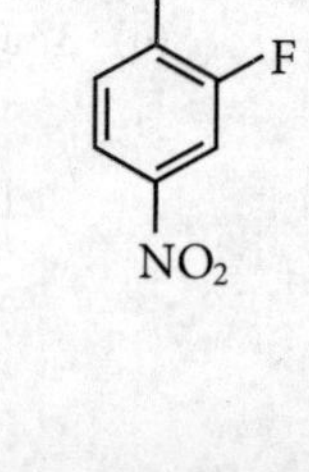

(b) 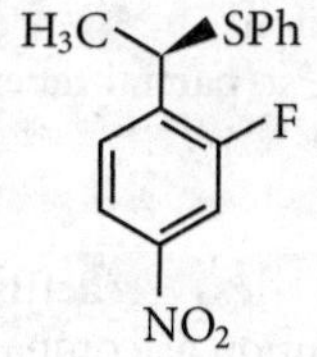

(c) 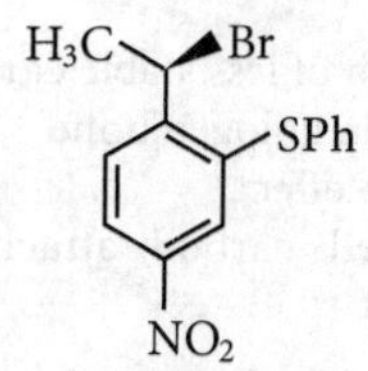

(d) 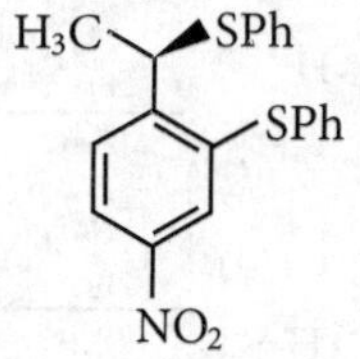

51. The order of reactivity of the following alkyl halides for an S_N2 or S_N1 reaction is:
(a) R–F > R–C > R–Br > R–I
(b) R–F > R–Br > R–Cl> R–I
(c) R–Cl> R–Br > RF > RI
(d) R–I >RBr> R–Cl> R–F

52. $(CH_3)_3CMgCl$ reaction with D_2O produces:
(a) $(CH_3)_3CD$ (b) $(CH_3)_3OD$
(c) $(CD_3)_3CD$ (d) $(CH_3)_3OD$

53. Among the following alcohols, which would react fastest with concentrated HCl and anhydrous $ZnCl_2$?
(a) 1-Butanol
(b) 2-Butanol
(c) 2-Methylpropan-2-ol
(d) 2-Methylpropanol

54. When the concentration of alkyl halide is doubled and H_2O is reduced to half, the rate of S_N1 increases by:
(a) 3 times (b) 2 times
(c) 1.5 times (d) 6 times

55. If we doubled the concentration of aklyl halide and the nucleophile, the rate of the S_N2 reaction would increase by:
(a) 2 times
(b) 4 times
(c) 8 times
(d) No change

56. In an S_N1 reaction on chiral centres, there is:

(a) 100% racemization
(b) Inversion, more so partial racemization
(c) 100% retention
(d) 100% inversion

57. Aryl halides are less reactive towards nucleophilic substitution as compared to alkyl halides due to:
(a) The formation of less stable carbanion
(b) Longer carbon halogen bond
(c) The inductive effect
(d) sp^2-hybridized carbon attached to the halogen

58. Which of the following relations is incorrect?

(I) 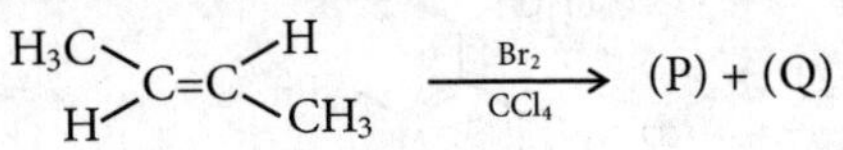

(II) 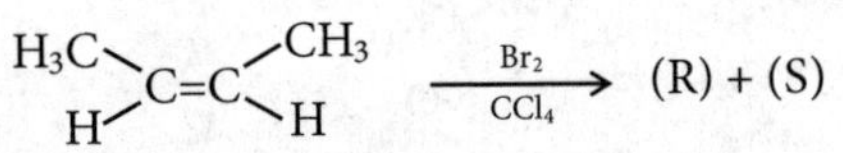

(a) P and Q ⇒ Enantiomer
(b) R and S ⇒ Enantiomer
(c) P and R ⇒ Diastereomer
(d) Q and S ⇒ Diastereomer

59. Which of the following is used in the synthesis of alkyl fluoride to produce the best yield?
(a) Swarts' reaction
(b) Finkelstein reaction
(c) Darzen process
(d) Dehydration of alcohol

60. The correct order of the leaving ability of the given groups in decreasing order for the S_N2 reaction is:

$R-O-SO_2-CH_3$ (I)	$R-O-SO_2-CF_3$ (II)
$R-O-H$ (III)	$R-O-CO-CH_3$ (IV)

(a) I > II > III > IV
(b) I > II > IV > III
(c) II > I > IV > III
(d) IV > III > II > I

61. Which one of the following tertiary halides will not give an S_N1 reaction?

(a) $CH_3-C(C_6H_5)(CH_3)-X$

(b) $CH_3-C(C_6H_5)(C_6H_5)-Br$

(c) 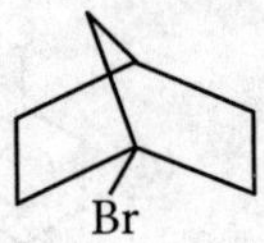

(d) $CH_3-C(CH_3)(CH_3)-Cl$

62. Which of the following combinations is correctly matched?

(a) $CH_3-C(H)(D)-Cl$, S_N1, Walden inversion

(b) $CH_3-C(H)(D)-Cl$, S_N2, Walden inversion

(c) $C_6H_5-C(C_2H_5)(CH_3)-Cl$, S_N1, only retention

(d) $C_6H_5-C(C_2H_5)(CH_3)-Cl$, S_N1, only inversion

63. The total number of properties/mechanisms which shows the following order is:
$R-I > R-Br > R-Cl > R-F$
(i) S_N1 mechanism
(ii) Bond length
(iii) E_2 mechanism
(iv) S_N2 mechanism
(v) Dipole moment
(vi) Boiling point
(vii) E_1 mechanism
(viii) Bond strength
(a) 6 (b) 5
(c) 7 (d) 8

64. The highest dipole moment among the following alkyl halides is:
(a) CH_3-F (b) CH_3-Cl
(c) CH_3-Br (d) CH_3-I

65. Which of the following alcohols reacts with concentrated HCl by simply shaking at room temperature?
(a) 1° alcohol (b) 2° alcohol
(c) Vinyl alcohol (d) 3° alcohol

66. How many alkenes will be obtained when 2-chloro-3-methylpentane reacts with alcoholic potash?
(a) 4 (b) 5
(c) 3 (d) 2

67. Which of the following reactions confirms the presence of vicinal product?
(a) Alkene + HX $\rightarrow$
(b) Alkene + HX $\xrightarrow{\text{Peroxide}}$
(c) Alkene + Br_2 $\xrightarrow{CCl_n}$
(d) Alkane + $\underset{\text{(excess)}}{Cl_2}$ $\xrightarrow{h\nu}$

68. Para-isomer has a higher melting point than ortho- and meta-isomers due to:
(a) Large surface area
(b) Better fit in lattice
(c) Lower dipole moment
(d) Better resonance

69. Among the following, select the incorrect statement:
(a) Electron donating group increases the rate of S_N1 reaction
(b) Cyclohexene and hexane can be distinguished by Br_2/H_2O
(c) Rate of Cl_2 is faster than Br_2 for electrophilic addition
(d) Electron withdrawing group decreases the rate of S_N2 reaction

70. The major products P and Q formed in the given reaction are:

(A) 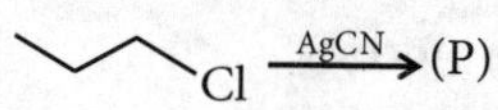

(B) 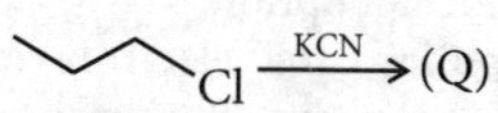

(a) Identical
(b) Chain isomers
(c) Position isomers
(d) Functional isomers

71. The major product formed in the given reaction is:

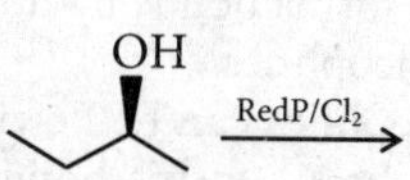

(a) 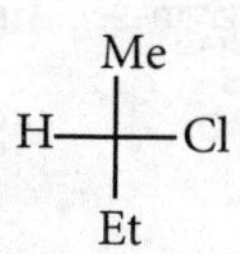 (b) 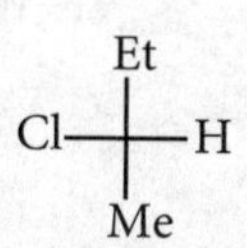

(c) 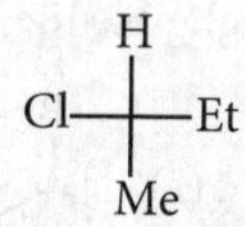 (d) None of these

72. Which of these reactions will give different products in the presence of peroxide and in the absence of peroxide?
(a) 2-Butene, HCl
(b) 1-Butene, HBr
(c) 2-Butene, HBr
(d) Cyclohexene, HCl

73. The total number of α-H in the major product obtained in following reaction is:

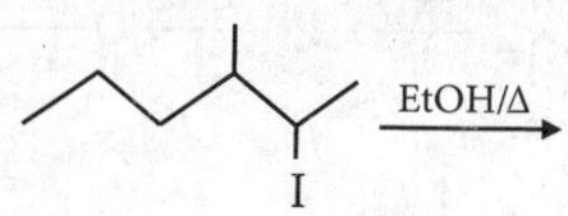

(a) 8 (b) 7
(c) 4 (d) 6

74. The product 'P' obtained in the following reaction is:
$CH_3 - CH_2 - CH_2 - OH \xrightarrow[H_2SO_4]{NaI}$ 'P'
(a) $CH_3 - CH_2 - I$
(b) $CH_3CH(I)CH_3$
(c) $CH_2 = CH - CH_3$
(d) None of these

75. Which of the following statements is correct?
(a) Chlorofluorocarbon compounds of methane and ethane are known as freons.
(b) The boiling point of alcohols is less than ether due to H–bonding.
(c) The Finkelstein reaction is an S_N1 reaction.
(d) Williamson synthesis is an example of S_N1.

76. The compound which can never show the S_N1 as well as the S_N2 mechanism is:

(a) 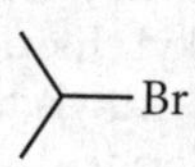

(b) 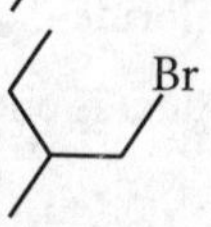

(c) 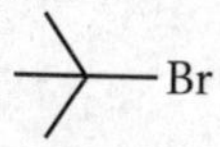

(d) 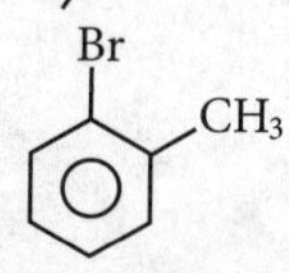

77. The rate of S_N2 will be negligible in:

(a) 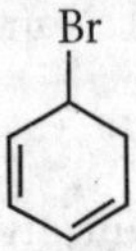
(b) 
(c) 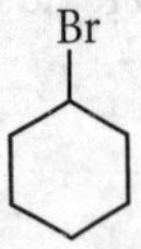
(d) 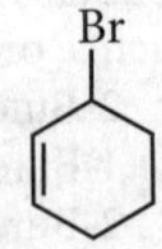

78. For the given sequence, choose the correct option:

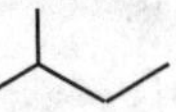 $\xrightarrow[h\nu]{Br_2}$ P $\xrightarrow{EtONa}$ Q $\xrightarrow[H_2O_2]{HBr}$ R

(a) R is 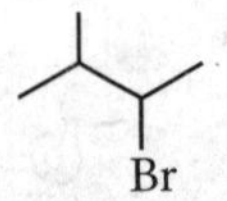
(b) P is 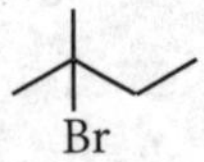
(c) Q is 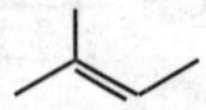
(d) All of these

79. The major product of the following reaction is:

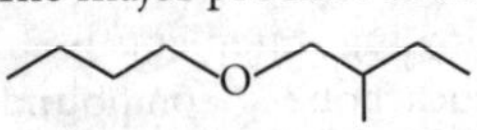 $\xrightarrow{\text{Concentrated HI}}$

(a) 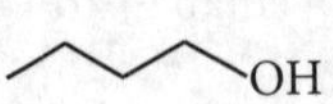
(b) 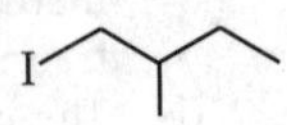
(c) 
(d) 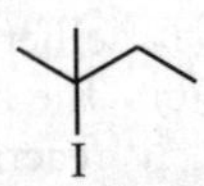

80. Which of the following reactions is incorrectly matched with the major product of the reaction?
(a) Swarts' reaction ⇒ Alkyl fluoride
(b) Darzen process ⇒ Alkyl chloride
(c) Finkelstein reaction ⇒ Alkyl chloride
(d) Lucas test ⇒ Alkyl chloride

81. Alkylarene as a major product is obtained in:
(a) Wurtz reaction
(b) Fittig reaction
(c) Reeds reaction
(d) Wurtz–Fittig reaction

82. The major product of which reaction cannot show stereoisomerism?

(a) $(CH_3)_2CH\text{-}CH\text{=}CH_2 \xrightarrow[\text{(ii)}NaBH_4/NaOH]{\text{(i)}Hg(OAc)_2/H_2O}$

(b) 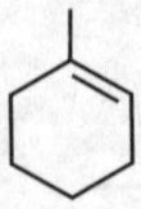 $\xrightarrow[\text{(ii)}H_2O_2/NaOH]{\text{(i)}B_2H_6\text{-THF}}$

(c) 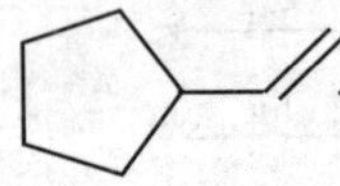 $\xrightarrow[CCl_4]{HBr}$

(d) $CH_3\text{-}CH_2\text{-}CH\text{=}CH_2 \xrightarrow[CCl_4]{Br_2}$

83. Which of the following reactions is incorrectly matched with the major product and name of the reaction?

(a) 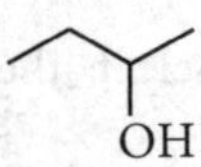 $\xrightarrow{SOCl_2}$ 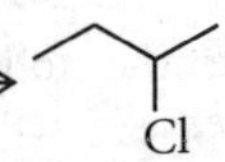
(Darzen process)

(b) $CH_3\text{-}CH_2\text{-}Br \xrightarrow[\text{acetone}]{NaI} CH_3\text{-}CH_2\text{-}I$
(Finkelstein reaction)

(c) 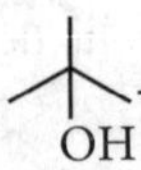 $\xrightarrow[ZnCl_2]{HCl}$ 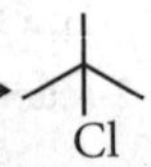 (Lucas test)

(d) $CH_3\text{-}CH_2\text{-}Cl \xrightarrow{AgF} CH_3\text{-}CH_2\text{-}F$
(Grove's process)

84. Choose the correct option:
(a) Electrophiles are electron-rich species which can form bonds by accepting electrons from nucleophiles.
(b) Nucleophiles are electron-seeking species which can form bonds by donating electrons to neutral or positively charged species.
(c) Electrophiles can be Lewis acid in nature which forms bonds by donating electrons to nucleophiles.
(d) Nucleophiles can be Lewis base in nature which can form bonds by donating electrons to any electron-seeking species.

85. Which of the following is incorrectly matched with their major product?

(a) 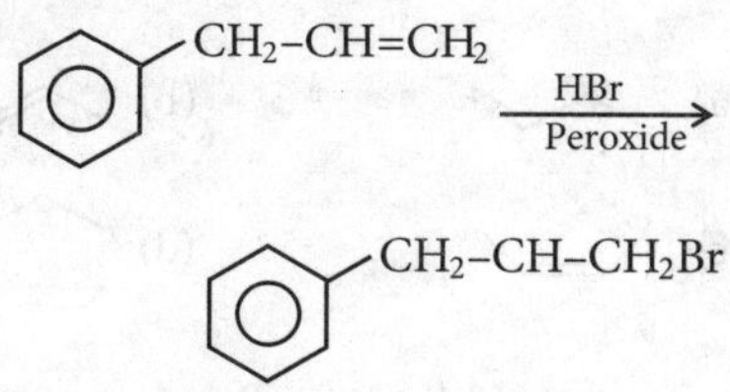

(b) 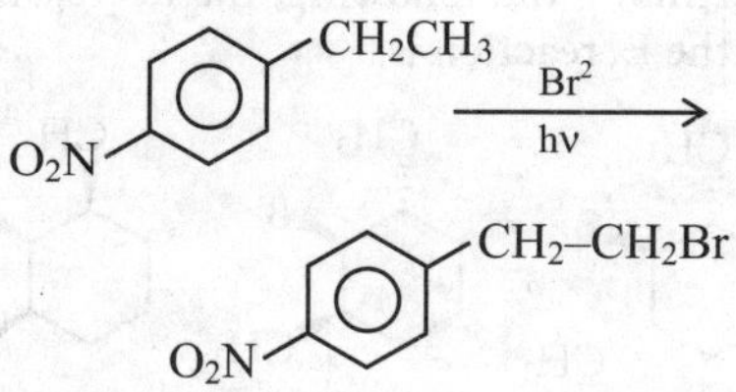

(c) 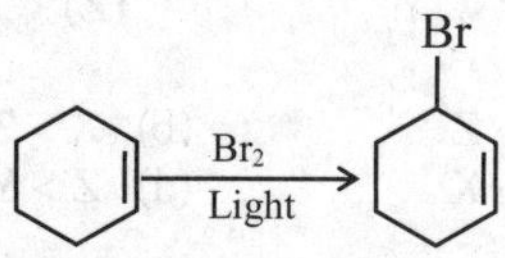

(d) 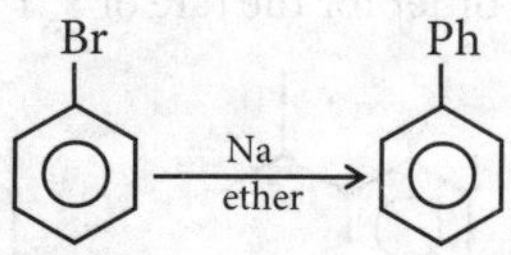

86. The incorrect order for compounds P, Q and R is:

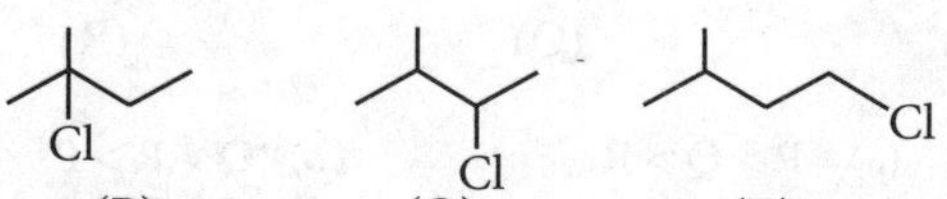

(P) (Q) (R)

(a) Reactivity towards S_N1 reaction P > Q > R
(b) Reactivity towards S_N2 reaction P > Q > R
(c) Reactivity towards E_1 reaction P > Q > R
(d) Reactivity towards E_2 reaction P > Q > R

87. In the given pairs, which pair represents the correct order of rate of dehydrohalogenation reaction?

(a) 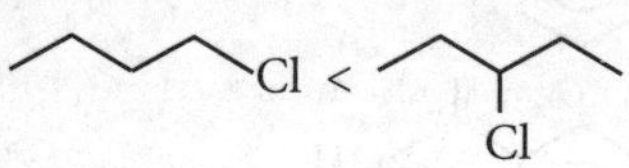

(b) 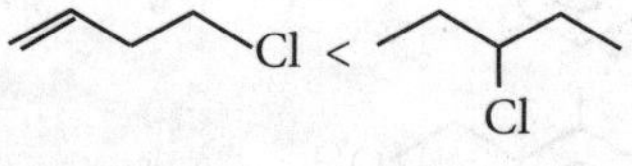

(c) 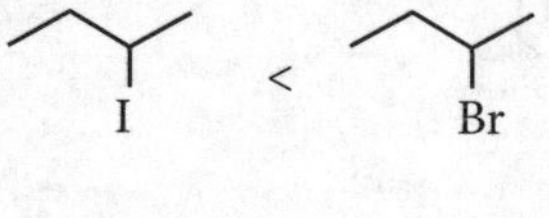

(d) $CH_3-CH_2-Cl < CD_3-CD_2-Cl$

88. The decreasing order of reactivity towards dehydrohalogenation (E_1) reaction is:

(A) 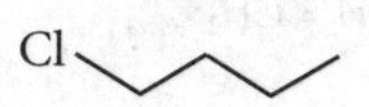

(B) 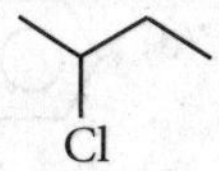

(C) 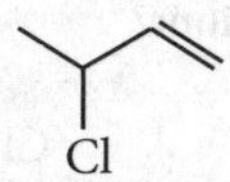

(a) B > C > A (b) B > A > C
(c) C > B > A (d) C > A > B

89. Which of the following cannot give an E_1 reaction easily?

(a) 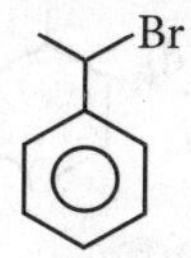

(b) 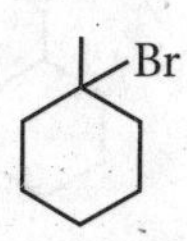

(c) 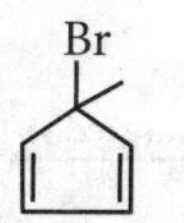

(d) 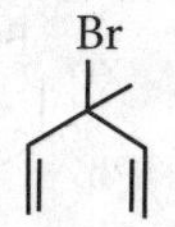

90. Consider the following reactions. Which of these reaction(s) will not produce Saytzeff's product?

(A) $(CH_3)_3CCH(OH)CH_3 \xrightarrow{\text{conc. } H_2SO_4}$

(B) $(CH_3)_2CHCH(Br)CH_3 \xrightarrow{\text{alc. KOH}}$

(C) $(CH_3)_2CHCH(Br)CH_3 \xrightarrow{(CH_3)_3O^{\ominus}K^{\oplus}}$

(D) $(CH_3)_2\underset{\substack{|\\OH}}{C}-CH_2-CHO \xrightarrow{\Delta}$

(a) (B) and (D) (b) (C) only
(c) (D) only (d) (A), (C) and

91. The major product of the following reaction is:

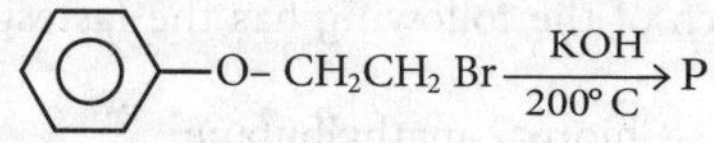

(a) 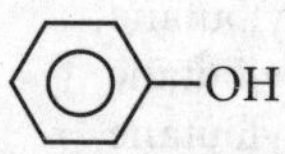

(b) 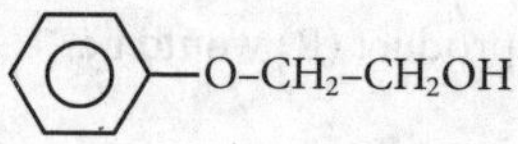

(c) 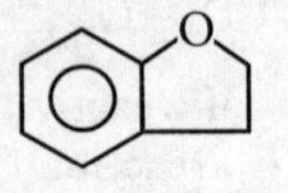

(d) 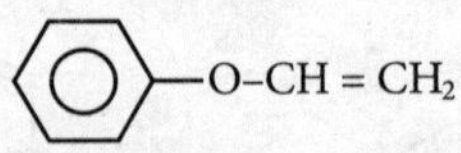

92. Which one of the following compounds will be most reactive for E_1 reactions?

(a) 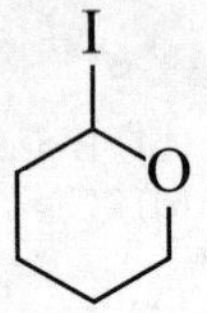

(b) 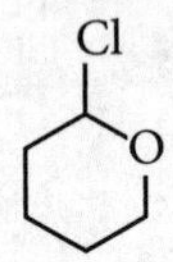

(c) 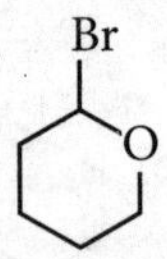

(d) 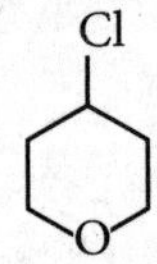

93. The major product of the following reaction is:

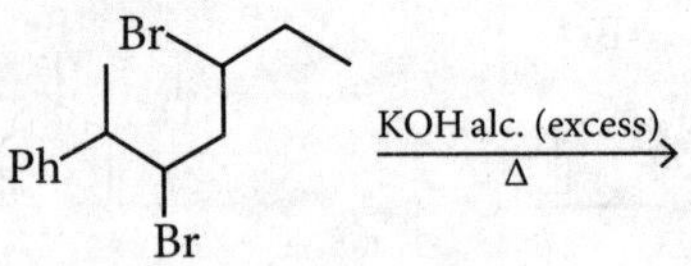

(a) 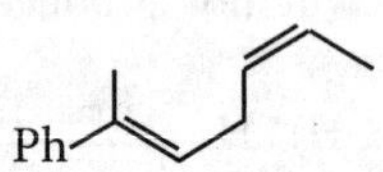

(b) 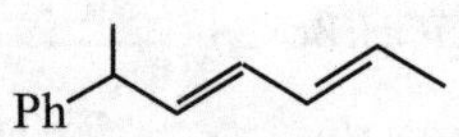

(c) 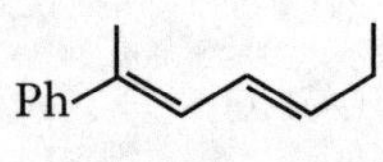

(d) 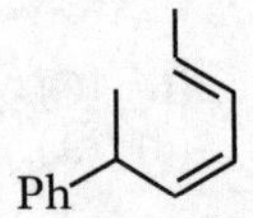

94. Which of the following has the fastest rate of E_1?

(a) 1-Chloro-2-methylbutane
(b) 1-Chloro-3-methylbutane
(c) 2-Chloro-3-methylbutane
(d) 2-Chloro-2-methylbutane

95. The major product (R) would be:

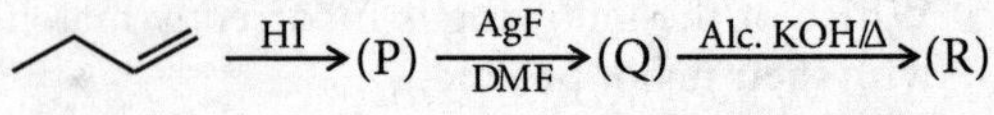

(a) 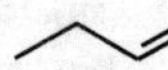

(b) 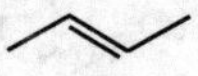

(c) 

(d) 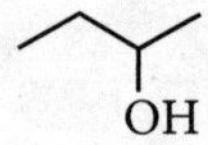

96. Among the following, the decreasing order of the E_2 reaction is:

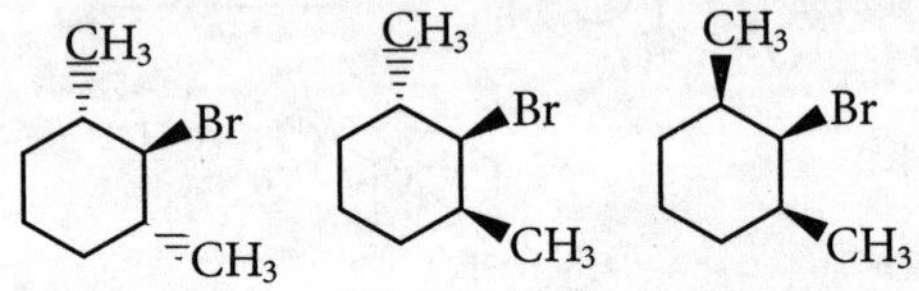

(X) (Y) (Z)

(a) X > Y > Z
(b) X > Z > Y
(c) Y > Z > X
(d) Z > Y > X

97. The correct order for the rate of S_N1 reaction is:

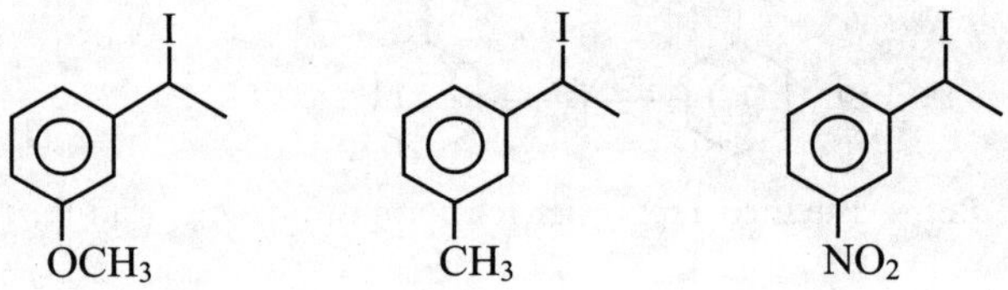

(P) (Q) (R)

(a) P > Q > R
(b) Q > R > P
(c) P > R > Q
(d) Q > P > R

98. The major product of the following reaction is:

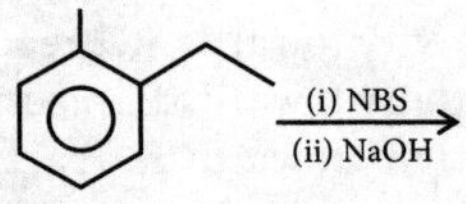

(a) 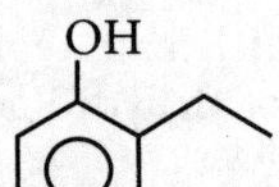

(b) 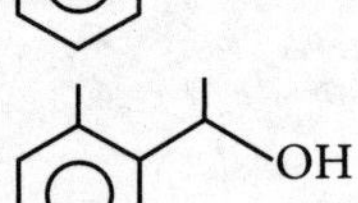

(c) 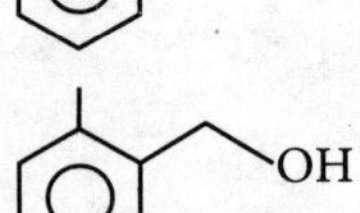

(d) 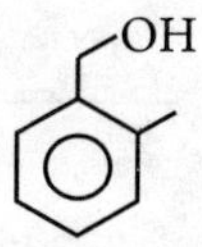

99. The major product of the following reaction is:

$$\underset{\text{Br}}{\text{CH}_3\text{CH}_2\text{CH}}-\underset{\text{Br}}{\text{CH}_2} \xrightarrow[\text{(ii) NaNH}_2 \text{ in liq. NH}_3]{\text{(i) KOH alc.}}$$

(a) $CH_3CH=CHCH_2NH_2$
(b) $CH_3CH=C=CH_2$
(c) $\underset{\text{NH}_2}{\text{CH}_3\text{CH}_2\text{CH}}-\underset{\text{NH}_2}{\text{CH}_2}$
(d) $CH_3CH_2C\equiv CH$

100. The major product obtained if 2,2,3-trimethyl-3-bromopentane reacts with sodium ethoxide is:

(a) 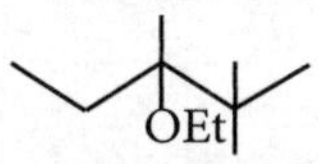
(b) 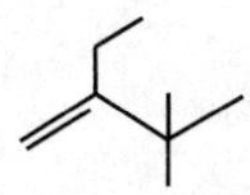
(c) 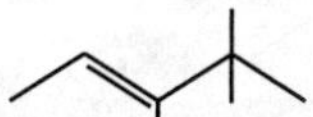
(d) 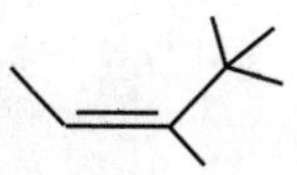

101. When ethanol is treated with sulphuric acid at 413 K, the major product formed and mechanism followed is:
(a) Ethene, E_2
(b) Ethoxy Ethane, S_N1
(c) Ethene, S_N2
(d) Ethoxy Ethane, S_N2

102. Which of the following reactions is incorrectly matched?
(a) $R-OH + HCl/ZnCl_2 \rightarrow R-Cl$ (Lucas test)
(b) $(CH_3)(H)C=C(CH_3)(H) + HI \rightarrow CH_3CH(H)-CH(I)CH_3$
(Electrophilic addition reaction)
(c) $R-OH + NaI/H_2SO_4 \rightarrow RI$
(Nucleophilic substitution reaction)
(d) 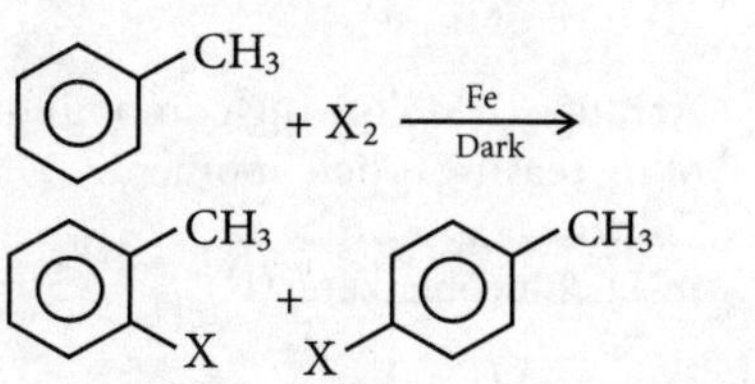
(Electrophilic substitution reaction)

103. The major product when chlorobenzene reacts with methyl chloride in the presence of sodium metal is:

(a) 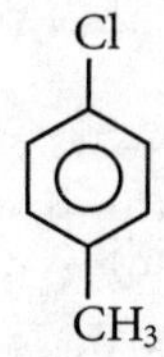
(b) 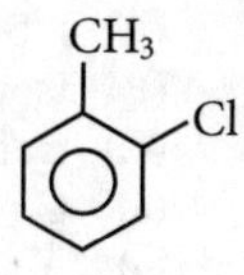
(c) 
(d) 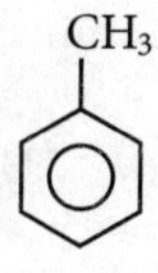

104. The mechanism of the S_N1 reaction is given as:

$$R-X \longrightarrow \underset{\text{Ion pair}}{R^{\oplus}X^{\ominus}} \longrightarrow \underset{\text{Solvent Separated ion pair}}{R^{\oplus}\,||\,X^{\ominus}} \xrightarrow{Y^{\ominus}} R-Y + X^{\ominus}$$

A student writes the general characteristics based on the given mechanism, so the correct statement is:
(A) The reaction is favoured by weak nucleophiles.
(B) $R^{\oplus}$ would be easily formed if the substituents are bulky.
(C) The reaction is accompanied by racemization.
(D) The reaction is favoured by non-polar solvents.
(a) (A) and (C)
(b) (A), (B) and (C)
(c) (B) and (C)
(d) (A) and (B)

105. Among the following, the incorrect statement is:

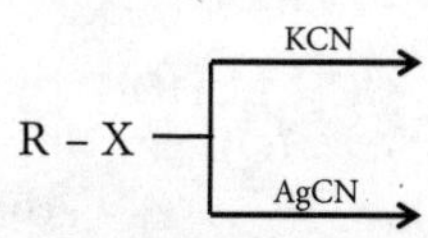

(a) KCN is predominantly ionic in nature
(b) AgCN is mainly covalent in nature
(c) In KCN, carbon is the donor atom
(d) In AgCN, carbon is the donor atom

106. The increasing order of the boiling points of the major products A, B and C of following reactions will be:

(A) 1-Butene + HBr $\xrightarrow{(CH_3COO)_2}$ A
(B) Isobutene + HBr $\rightarrow$ B
(C) trans-2-Butene + HBr $\rightarrow$ C

(a) C < A < B (b) B < C < A
(c) A < B < C (d) A < C < B

107. The major product obtained from E_2 elimination of 3-bromo-2-fluoropentane is:

(a) $CH_3-CH_2-\overset{Br}{\overset{|}{C}}=CH-CH_3$

(b) $CH_3CH_2CH=\underset{CH_3}{\underset{|}{C}}-F$

(c) $CH_3-CH=CH-\overset{F}{\overset{|}{CH}}-CH_3$

(d) $CH_3CH_2-\overset{Br}{\overset{|}{CH}}-CH=CH_2$

108. Consider the reaction sequence given below. Which of the following statements is true?

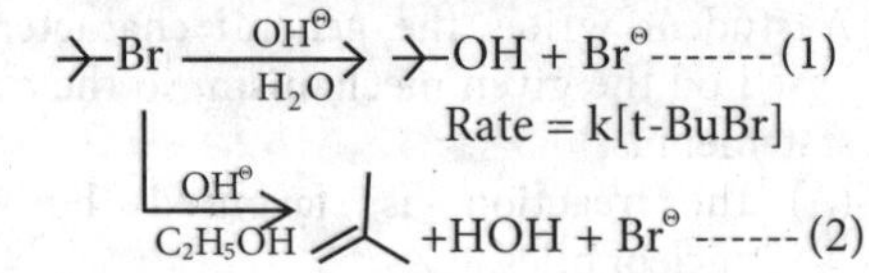

Rate = k[t-BuBr][OH$^{\ominus}$]

(a) Changing the concentration of the base will have no effect on reaction (1).
(b) Doubling the concentration of the base will double the rate of both the reactions.
(c) Changing the base from OH$^{\ominus}$ to $^{\ominus}$OR will have no effect on reaction (2).
(d) Changing the concentration of the base will have no effect on reaction (2).

109. The correct order of the rate of reaction for the following compounds with concentrated HBr is:

CH_3OH (P) $(CH_3)_2CHOH$ (Q) $(CH_3)_3COH$ (R)

(a) P > R > Q (b) P > Q > R
(c) R > P > Q (d) R > Q > P

110. The major product 'Y' in the following reaction is:

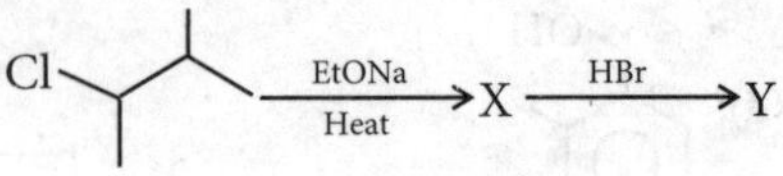

(a) 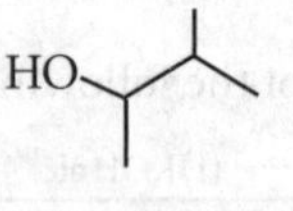

(b) 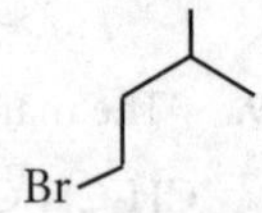

(c) 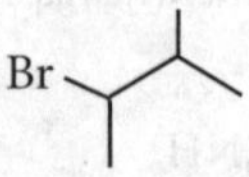

(d) 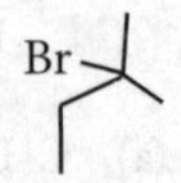

111. Heating of 2-chloro-1-phenylbutane with EtOK/EtOH gives X as the major product. Reaction of X with $Hg(OAc)_2/H_2O$ followed by $NaBH_4$ gives Y as the major product. Y is:

(a) 

(b) 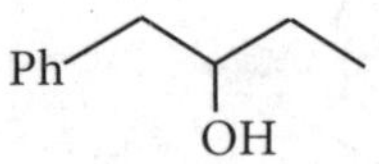

(c) 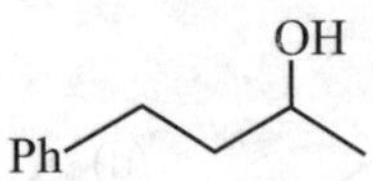

(d) 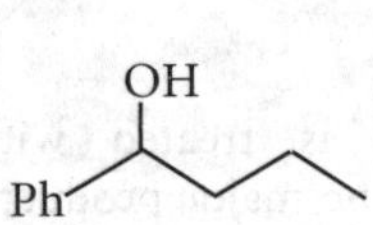

112. For the following compounds, the correct statement with respect to nucleophilic substitution reactions is:

(I) 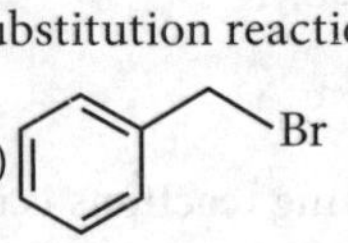

(II) 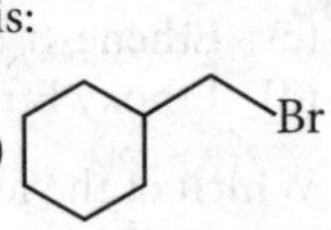

(III) $CH_3-\underset{CH_3}{\overset{CH_3}{C}}-Br$ (IV) 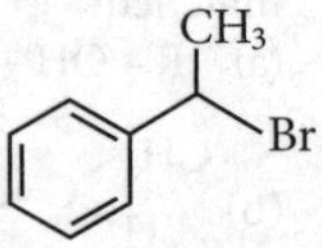

(a) Compound IV shows inversion
(b) I and II can follow S_N2 mechanism
(c) I and III can follow S_N1 mechanism
(d) All of these

113. Arrange the following compounds in the order of increasing dipole moment:
Toluene (I)
m-Dichlorobenzene (II)

o-Dichlorobenzene(III)
p-Dichlorobenzene(IV)

(a) I < IV < II < III (b) IV < I < II < III
(c) IV < I < III < II (d) IV < II < I < III

114. Which of the following compounds is incorrectly matched with the number of alkenes formed by dehydrohalogenation with sodium ethoxide in ethanol and the major alkene obtained?

(a) 1-Bromo-1-methylcyclohexane ⇒2, 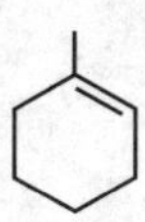

(b) 2-Chloro-2-methylbutane⇒

2, 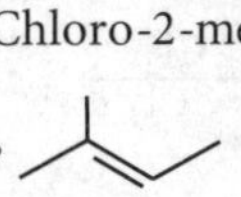

(c) 3-Bromo-2,2,3-trimethylpentane

⇒ 4, 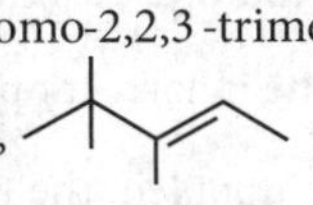

(d) 2-Chloro-3-methylpentane⇒ 4, 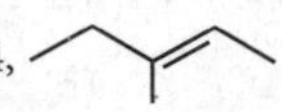

115. Which of the following reactions is correctly matched with its major product?

(a) $R-X \xrightarrow{KCN} RNC$

(b) $R-X \xrightarrow{AgCN} R-CN$

(c) $R-X \xrightarrow{KNO_2} R-O-N=O$

(d) $R-X \xrightarrow{AgNO_2} R-O-N=O$

116. RCl is treated with Li in ether to form R–Li. R–Li reacts with water to form isopentane. R–Cl also reacts with sodium to form 2,7–dimethyloctane. The structure of R–Cl is:

(a) 1-Chloro-2-methylbutane
(b) 2-Chloro-2-methylbutane
(c) 2-Chloro-3-methylbutane
(d) 1-Chloro-3-methylbutane

117. Which of the following reactions will not give but-1-ene as the major product?

(a) $CH_3CH(F)CH_2CH_3 + KOH \xrightarrow{EtOH}$

(b) $CH_3\underset{\underset{+NMe_3}{|}}{C}HCH_2CH_3 + NaOEt \xrightarrow[\Delta]{EtOH}$

(c) $CH_3CH_2CH(Cl)CH_3 + Me_3CO^-K^+ \xrightarrow{\Delta}$

(d) $CH_3CH_2CH(OH)CH_3 \xrightarrow[\Delta]{\text{Concentrated } H_2SO_4}$

118. Which of the following reactions is correctly matched with the major product?

(a) Benzyl ethyl ether + HI → $PhCH_2OH + CH_3CH_2I$
(b) 3-Methylbutane-2-ol + HBr → 2-Bromo-3-methylbutane
(c) Ethanol + H_2SO_4 at 413 K → Ethoxy ethane
(d) Tertiary butyl bromide + Methoxide → t-Butyl methyl ether

119. Which of the following statements is true?

(a) $CH_3-CH_2-CH_2-I$ will react more readily than $(CH_3)_2CHI$ for S_N1 reactions.
(b) $CH_3-CH_2-CH_2-Cl$ will react more readily than $CH_3-CH_2-CH_2-Br$ for S_N2 reactions.
(c) $CH_3-CH_2-CH_2-CH_2-Br$ will react more readily than $(CH_3)_3C-CH_2-Br$ for S_N2 reactions.
(d) $CH_3-O-C_6H_4-CH_2Br$ will react more readily than $NO_2-C_6H_5-CH_2Br$ for S_N2 reactions.

120. S_N1 and S_N2 are not favourable in:

(a) $MeO-CH_2-Cl$
(b) $Ph-CH_2-Cl$
(c) $Ph-Cl$
(d) $H_2C=CH-CH_2-Cl$

121. Which of the following is incorrectly matched:

(a) 

(S_N2 reaction)

(b) 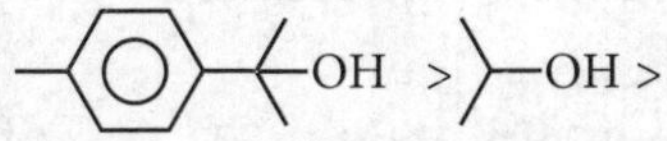 > CH_3OH

(Lucas reagent)

(c) 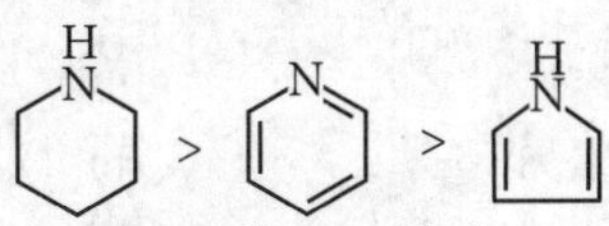

(Nucleophilicity order)

(d) $F_2 > Cl_2 > Br_2 > I_2$ (Free radical substitution)

122. Which of the following reactions is not feasible?

(a) 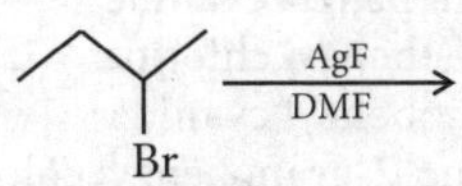

(b) 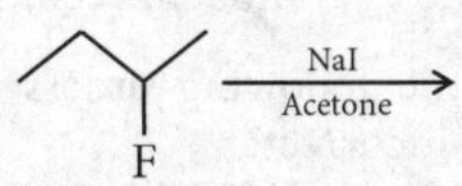

(c) 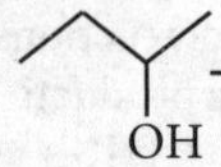 $\xrightarrow[H_2SO_4]{NaCl}$

(d) 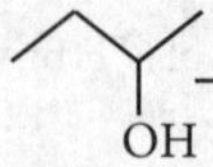 $\xrightarrow[H_3PO_4]{NaI}$

123. Which of the following is a correct statement?
(a) As polarity increases, the rate of S_N1 decreases
(b) In S_N1 reaction, 100% racemisation occurs
(c) In S_N2 reaction, 'R' must be inverted to 'S'
(d) R–CHO with PCl_5 gives gem-dichloride

124. Among the following, select the incorrect statement:
(a) S_N1 reaction involves intimate ion pair
(b) Benzene does not give Br_2/H_2O test
(c) CHI_3 is an anaesthetic and $CHCl_3$ is an antiseptic
(d) Chloroform is used to produce freon R-22

125. The correct order of reactivity of the following compounds towards the S_N1 reaction is:

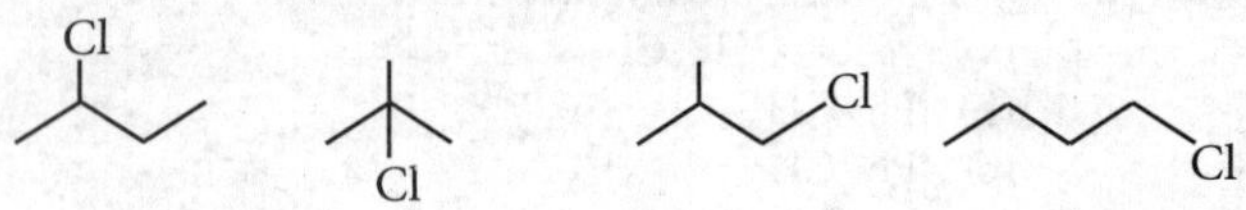

(P) (Q) (R) (S)

(a) P > Q > R > S (b) Q > P > R > S
(c) Q > P > S > R (d) Q > R > P > S

126. Among the following, which can show fastest S_N1 and S_N2, respectively?

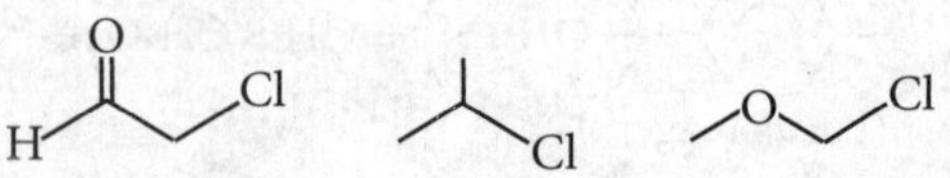 $CH_3–Cl$

(P) (Q) (R) (S)

(a) R, S (b) Q, S
(c) R, P (d) S, P

127. The reaction of 4-bromobenzyl chloride with NaCN in ethanol leads to:
(a) 4-Bromobenzyl cyanide
(b) 4-Cyanobenzyl chloride
(c) 4-Cyanobenzyl cyanide
(d) 4-Bromo-2-cyanobenzyl chloride

128. Which of the following orders of the given reactions is incorrect?
(a) HI > HBr > HCl > HF (Reaction with Ethene)
(b) $OHC–CH_2–Cl > CH_3–Cl > CH_2–CH_2–Cl$ (Reaction with NaOH)
(c) $CH_2 = CH_2 > CH_2 = CH–Cl > CH_2=CH–NO_2$ (Reaction with HBr)
(d) $Ph–CH_2OH > Ph–OH > (CH_3)_2CH–OH$ (Reaction with H_2SO_4, Δ)

129. The major product of which reactions can show stereoisomerism?
(a) $CH_3–CH_2Br \xrightarrow[\Delta]{Zn}$
(b) $CH_3–CH=CH_2 \xrightarrow[H_2SO_4]{dilute}$
(c) $CH_2=CH_2 \xrightarrow[CCl_4]{HBr}$
(d) 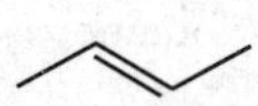 $\xrightarrow[CCl_4]{Cl_2}$

130. The rate for the S_N2 reaction is $r = K[R–Cl][\overset{\ominus}{O}H]$. Select the incorrect option:
(a) If $[\overset{\ominus}{O}H]$ is doubled, the rate will double
(b) If both [R–Cl] and $[\overset{\ominus}{O}H]$ are doubled, the rate will double
(c) If [R–X] is halved, the rate will halve
(d) If [R–X] is doubled and $[\overset{\ominus}{O}H]$ is halved, the rate will be the same

131. Select the correct statement regarding the major product of the following reaction:

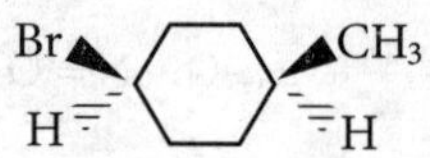

$\xrightarrow[Ethanol]{KOH}$

(a) Only a single alkene is formed
(b) A pair of geometrical isomers is formed
(c) A pair of enantiomers is formed
(d) A pair of diastereomers is formed

132. In which pair is (II) more reactive than (I) for the S_N2 mechanism?
(a) $CH_3CH_2CH_2CH_2Br$ and $CH_3CH_2CH(Br)CH_3$
(b) $CH_3CH_2CH(CH_3)CH_2Br$ and $CH_3CH(CH_3)CH_2CH_2Br$
(c) 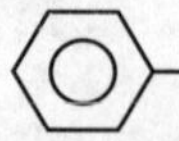 $–CH_2Cl$ and 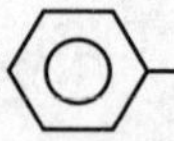 $–Cl$
(d) $C_6H_5CH_2Br$ and $C_6H_5CH(CH_3)Br$

133. Choose the correct option regarding the given reaction:

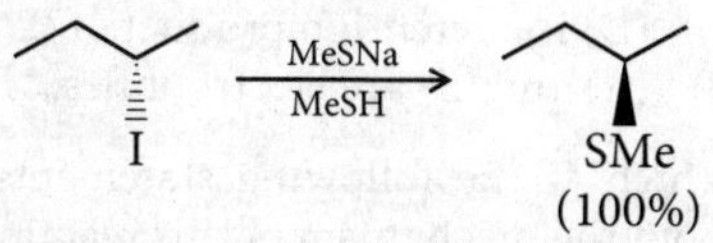

(a) Carbocation is formed as intermediate
(b) Reaction follows first order kinetics
(c) Reaction is S_N2
(d) Same mechanism with $(CH_3)_3CONa$

134. Which of the following factors cannot increase the percentage of racemisation in the S_N1 reaction:
(a) By increasing the polarity of the solvent
(b) By increasing the leaving group tendency
(c) By decreasing the stability of carbocation
(d) By decreasing the nucleophilicity of nucleophiles

135. Which of the following sets of reagents can be used for the given transformation as a major product?
$CH_3-CH_2-CH=CH_2 \rightarrow$ trans-2-Butene
(a) (i) Dilute H_2SO_4 (ii) $SOCl_2$ (iii) $(Me)_3CONa$
(b) (i) HBr, H_2O_2 (ii) Aqueous NaOH (iii) H_2SO_4 Δ
(c) (i) NaCl ,H_2SO_4 (ii) AgF (iii) Alcohol KOH, Δ
(d) (i) AcOH / H^+ (ii) Δ

136. Which of the following figures correctly represents the structure of the transition state?

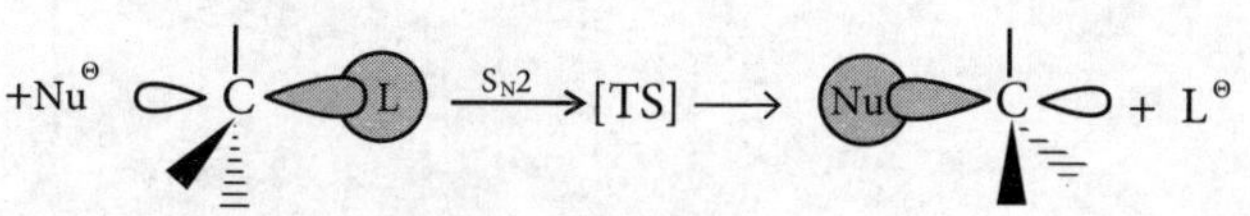

(a) 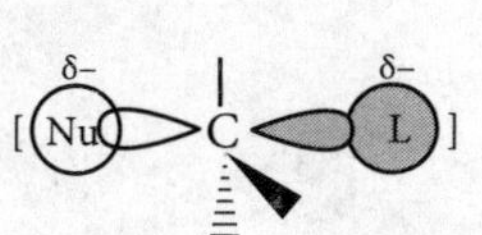

(b) 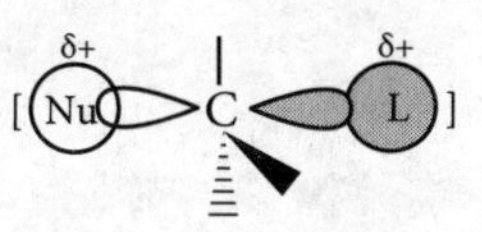

(c) 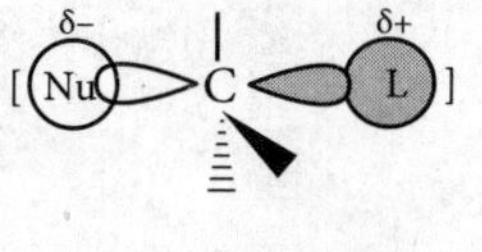

(d) 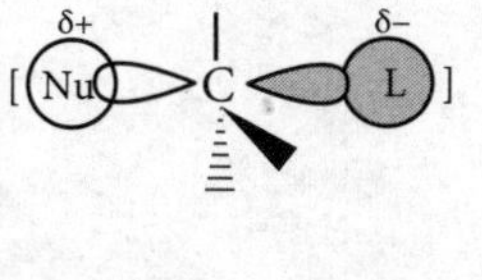

137. The correct increasing order of reactivity towards the S_N1 mechanism is:
(i) $C_6H_5C(CH_3)(C_6H_5)Br$
(ii) $C_6H_5CH(C_6H_5)Br$
(iii) $C_6H_5CH(CH_3)Br$
(iv) $C_6H_5CH_2Br$
(a) (iv) > (iii) > (ii) > (i)
(b) (i) > (ii) > (iii) > (iv)
(c) (i) > (ii) > (iv) > (iii)
(d) (ii) > (i) > (iii) > (iv)

138. Which alkene is not obtained during dehydrohalogenation of (+)3-chloro-3-methylhexane?
(a) 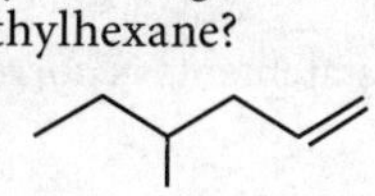
(b) 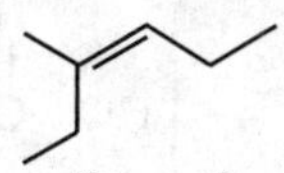
(c) 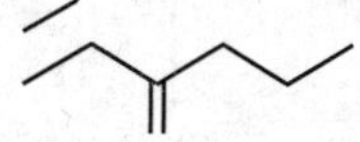
(d) 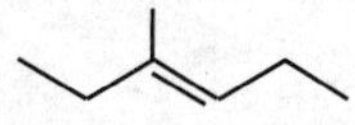

139. Arrange the following compounds in the order of decreasing rate of hydrolysis for the S_N1 reaction:

(I) 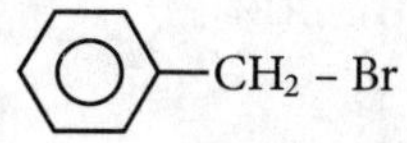

(II) 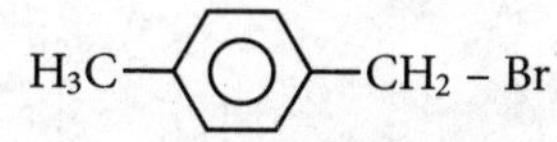

(III) 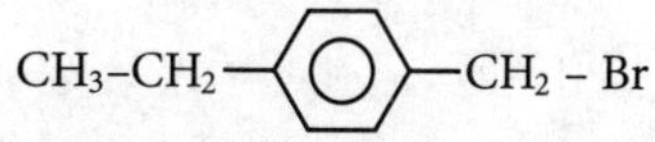

(IV) 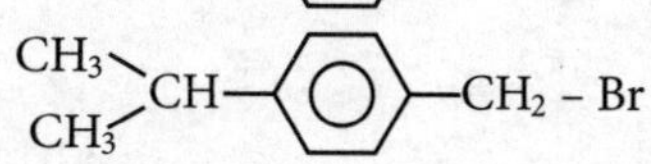

(a) II > III > IV > I
(b) IV > III > II > I
(c) III > IV > II > I
(d) I > II > III > I

140. The correctly matched relative rate of bimolecular nucleophilic substitution for the given substrate is:

Compound	Rate
(A) $(CH_3)_3C-X$	(P) 1
(B) CH_3-CH_2X	(Q) 30
(C) $(CH_3)_2CH-X$	(R) 0
(D) CH_3-X	(S) 0.02

(a) A → Q (b) B → P
(c) C → R (d) D → S

141. For the following conversion, the correct sequence of reagent is:

$CH_3CH_2OH \rightarrow CH_3{-}CH_2{-}C{\equiv}CH$

(1) Br_2/CCl_4
(2) CH_3CH_2I
(3) $H^{\oplus}$
(4) H_2SO_4, Δ
(5) $NaNH_2$ (4 equivalent)

(a) 3, 1, 4, 5, 2 (b) 4, 2, 5, 1, 3
(c) 4, 1, 5, 2, 3 (d) 4, 5, 2, 3

142. Which of these statements is correct about the reactions?

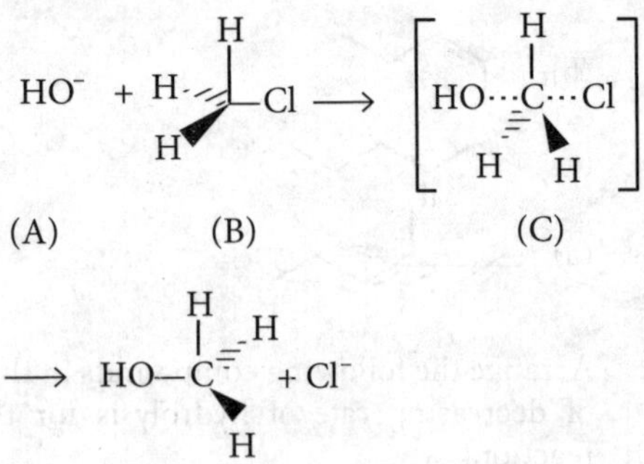

(A) (B) (C) (D) (E)

(a) (A) and (E) are nucleophiles.
(b) In (C), a carbon atom is sp^3 hybridized.
(c) (D) is a retention product of B.
(d) (A) and (E) are electrophiles.

143. Which of the following statements is correct about the mechanism of this reaction:

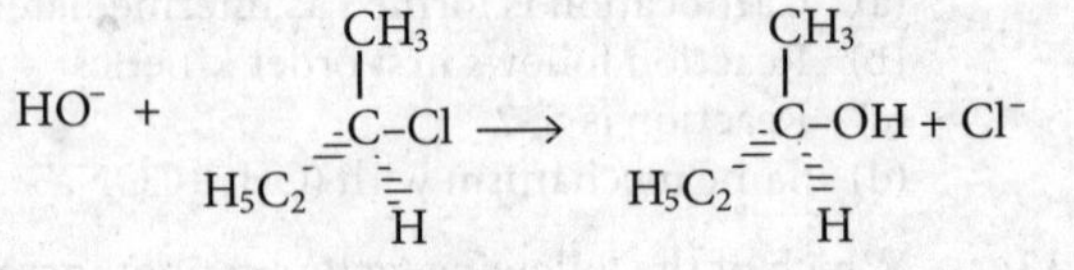

(a) (b) (c) (d)

(a) A carbocation will be formed as an intermediate in the reaction.
(b) OH^- will attach the substrate (b) from one side and Cl^- will leave it simultaneously from the other side.
(c) An unstable intermediate will be formed in which OH^- and Cl^- will be attached by weak bonds.
(d) The reaction proceeds through the S_N2 mechanism.

Answer Key

Level-1

Haloalkanes

1. (a) 2. (d) 3. (c) 4. (d) 5. (b) 6. (a) 7. (d) 8. (a)
9. (b) 10. (a) 11. (b) 12. (d) 13. (d) 14. (a) 15. (a) 16. (a)
17. (c) 18. (b) 19. (a) 20. (d) 21. (d) 22. (b) 23. (d) 24. (d)
25. (d) 26. (c) 27. (c) 28. (d) 29. (c) 30. (a) 31. (a) 32. (d)
33. (c) 34. (a) 35. (d) 36. (a) 37. (c)

Haloarenes

38. (c) 39. (c) 40. (a) 41. (d) 42. (a) 43. (d) 44. (b) 45. (d)
46. (d) 47. (c) 48. (d) 49. (d) 50. (b) 51. (d) 52. (a) 53. (b)
54. (c) 55. (d) 56. (b) 57. (a) 58. (c) 59. (b) 60. (d) 61. (a)
62. (a) 63. (c) 64. (c)

Polyhalogen Compounds

65. (d) 66. (d) 67. (d) 68. (c) 69. (c) 70. (a) 71. (b) 72. (b)
73. (b) 74. (d) 75. (d) 76. (c) 77. (b) 78. (d)

Level-2

1. (b) 2. (a) 3. (a) 4. (c) 5. (c) 6. (d) 7. (c) 8. (a)
9. (c) 10. (a) 11. (a) 12. (c) 13. (d) 14. (b) 15. (c) 16. (b)
17. (d) 18. (d) 19. (a) 20. (a) 21. (c) 22. (c) 23. (b) 24. (d)
25. (a) 26. (b) 27. (d) 28. (b) 29. (a) 30. (b) 31. (c) 32. (b)
33. (a) 34. (a) 35. (d) 36. (b) 37. (a) 38. (c) 39. (a) 40. (a)
41. (c) 42. (a) 43. (a) 44. (d) 45. (b) 46. (b) 47. (c) 48. (b)
49. (b) 50. (a) 51. (d) 52. (a) 53. (c) 54. (b) 55. (b) 56. (b)
57. (d) 58. (a) 59. (a) 60. (c) 61. (c) 62. (b) 63. (a) 64. (b)
65. (d) 66. (c) 67. (c) 68. (b) 69. (d) 70. (d) 71. (c) 72. (b)
73. (a) 74. (d) 75. (a) 76. (d) 77. (b) 78. (d) 79. (c) 80. (c)
81. (d) 82. (c) 83. (d) 84. (d) 85. (b) 86. (b) 87. (a) 88. (c)
89. (c) 90. (b) 91. (d) 92. (a) 93. (c) 94. (d) 95. (a) 96. (d)
97. (d) 98. (b) 99. (d) 100. (c) 101. (d) 102. (c) 103. (d) 104. (b)
105. (d) 106. (b) 107. (b) 108. (a) 109. (d) 110. (d) 111. (d) 112. (d)
113. (b) 114. (c) 115. (c) 116. (d) 117. (d) 118. (c) 119. (c) 120. (c)
121. (a) 122. (b) 123. (d) 124. (c) 125. (b) 126. (c) 127. (a) 128. (d)
129. (d) 130. (b) 131. (c) 132. (b) 133. (c) 134. (c) 135. (b) 136. (a)
137. (b) 138. (a) 139. (a) 140. (b) 141. (c) 142. (a) 143. (a)

Solutions

Level-1

1. Excess of CH_3–CH_3 does not give the polysubstitution and UV rays required for the reaction.

2.

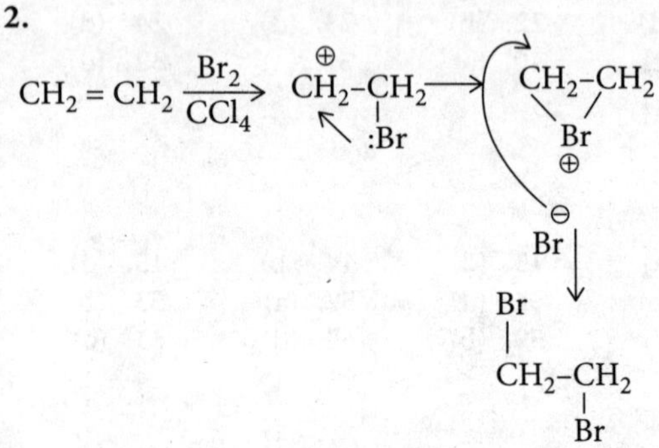

3. Lucas test (conc. HCl + $ZnCl_2$) is used for distinguishing 1°, 2° and 3° alcohols.

4. Boiling point $\propto \dfrac{1}{\text{Branching}}$

5. Dipole moment $\propto$ q. d.
(q ↑ Charge, d ↑ Distance)

For CH_3–Cl, the charge is reduced, but the distance is increased.

8. The first step is slow (RDS) and reversible, and intermediate carbocation is formed; allylic and benzylic carbocations are resonance stabilized.

11. In dehydrohalogenation, leaving tendency is directly proportional to the rate of reaction.

12.

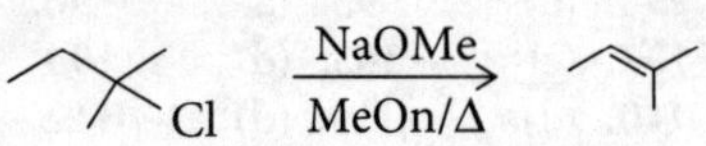

Alkoxide in solvent alcohol with heat gives elimination reaction [E_2], with Saytzeff product.

13. Hofmann product is the major product in the pyrolysis of tetra alkyl ammonium salt.

14. In Darzen's process, byproducts SO_2 and HCl are gaseous. So they escape out and pure alkyl halide is obtained.

15. KI is a reducing agent. So for protonation. H_2SO_4 (oxidising agent) is replaced by H_3PO_4 (non-oxiding agent)

17. $CH_3-CH_2-OH \xrightarrow{H_2SO_4+KI} \times$

$H_2SO_4 \rightarrow$ Oxidising agent
KI $\rightarrow$ Reducing agent

18.

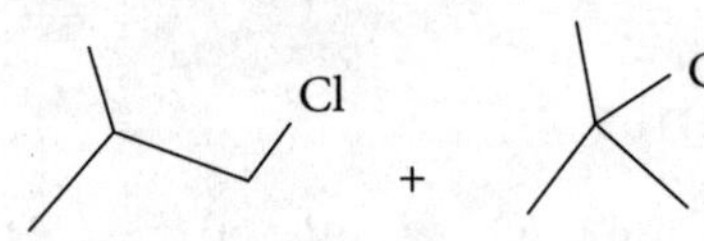

20. Molecular weight 72 amu; so 5 carbons may be

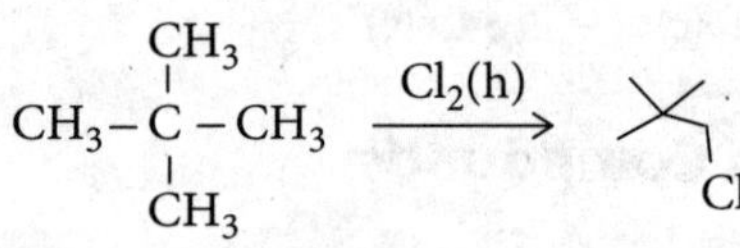

Single product

22. Br_2 is reddish brown in colour and it loses this colour and a colourless solution is obtained in solvent CCl_4 after reaction with alkene.

23. Finkelstein reaction

24. Density $\propto$ Molecular weight

26. Greater polarity and greater molecular mass accompanied by higher boiling point.

28. It is the S_N2 reaction.

29.

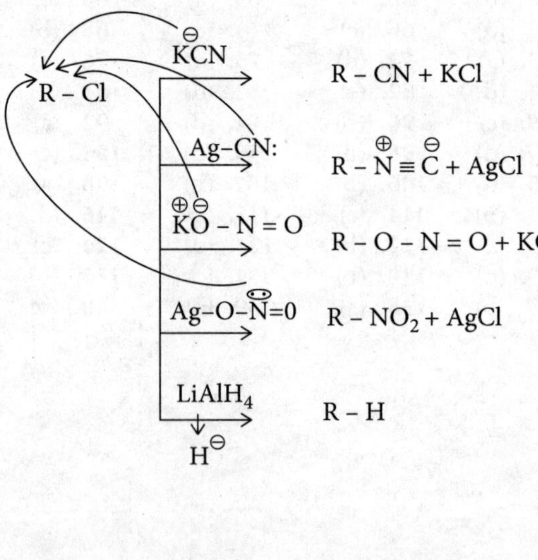

30.

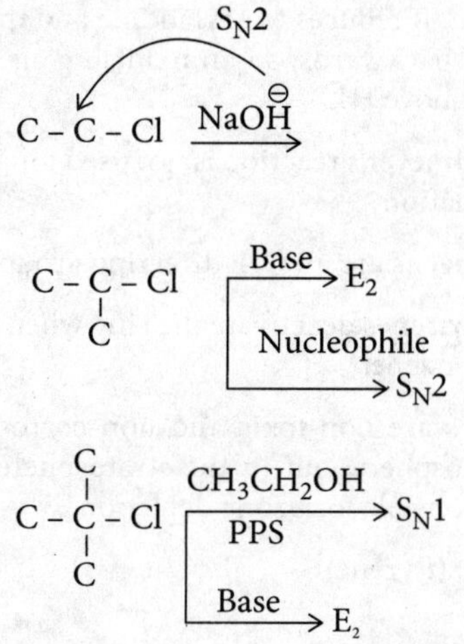

31. Alcoholic KOH means alkoxide in alkanol prefers E_2.

32.

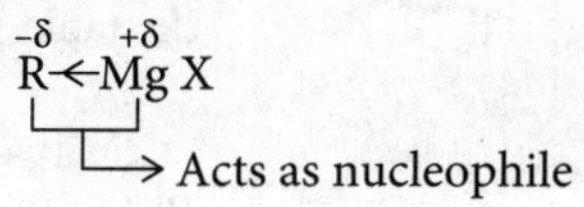

33.

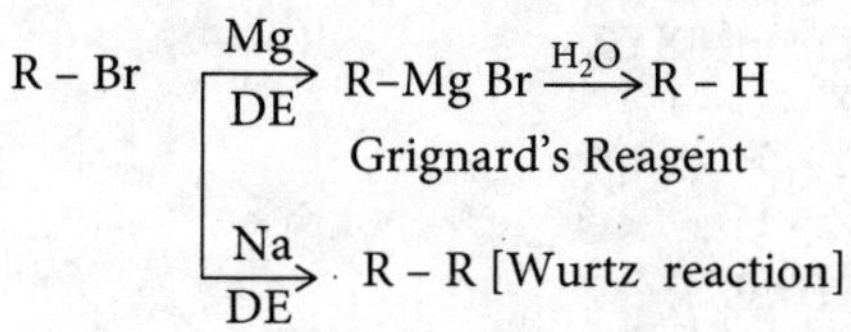

35.

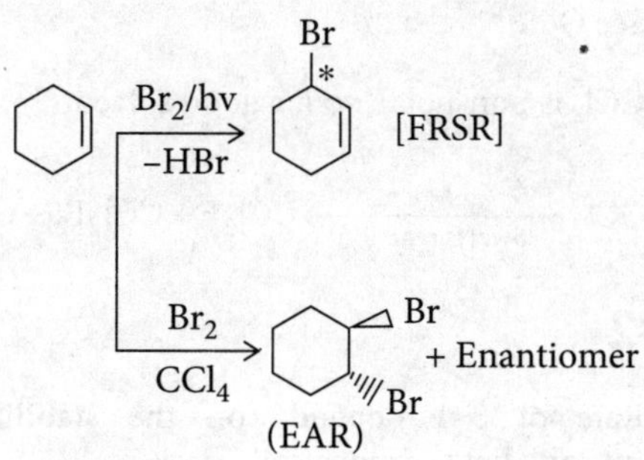

36. Bad base and PPS [H_2O] forms intermediate carbocation and the most stable alkene will be formed after removal of proton; it is the E_1 reaction.

37.

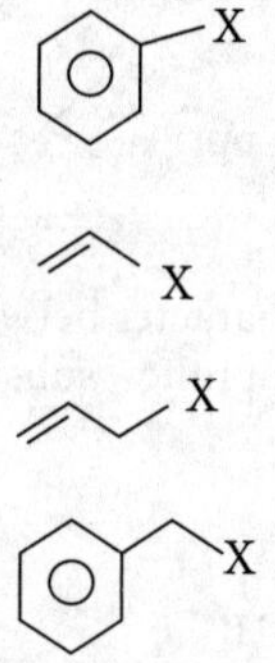

Aryl halide

Vinyl halide

Allyl halide

Benzyl halide

38.

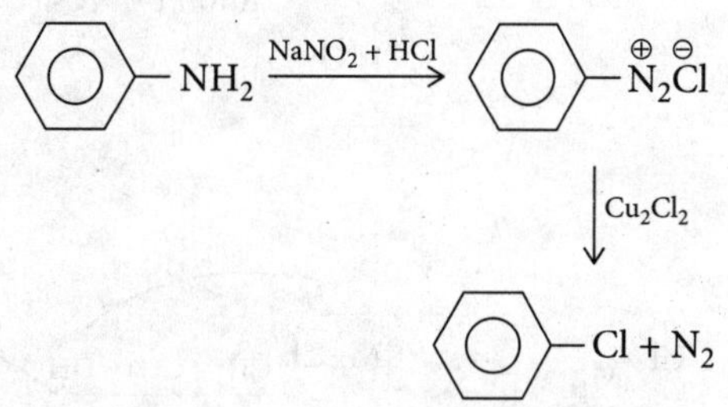

39. Alkyl group is O/P directing and para is major, due to steric hindrance at ortho.

41. Aryl substitution is difficult but after diazotization, N_2 becomes a good leaving group.

44.

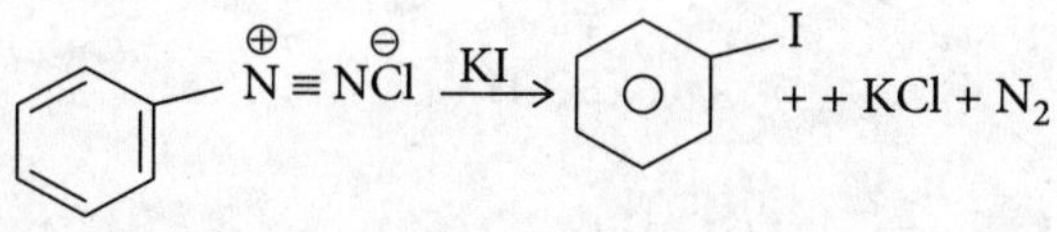

45.

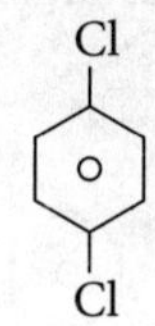

Symmetrical compound having greater packing capacity. So, greater melting point.

46.

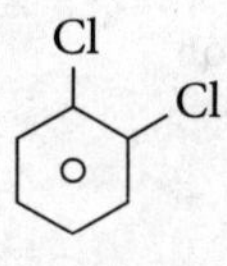

Greater dipole moment, having greater pole–pole attraction. This results in higher boiling point.

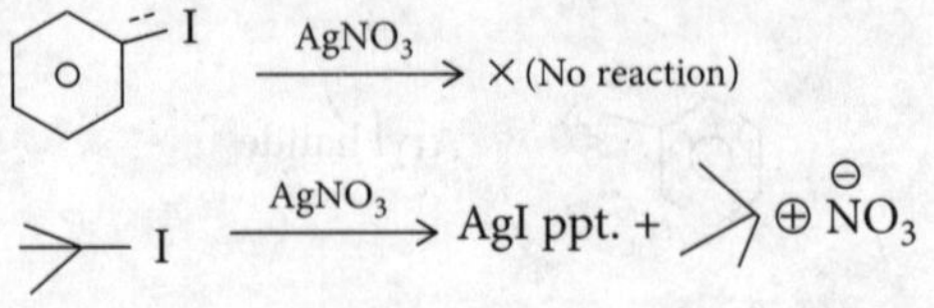

48. Due to double-bond character between carbon and halogen, nucleophilic substitution is difficult.

49.

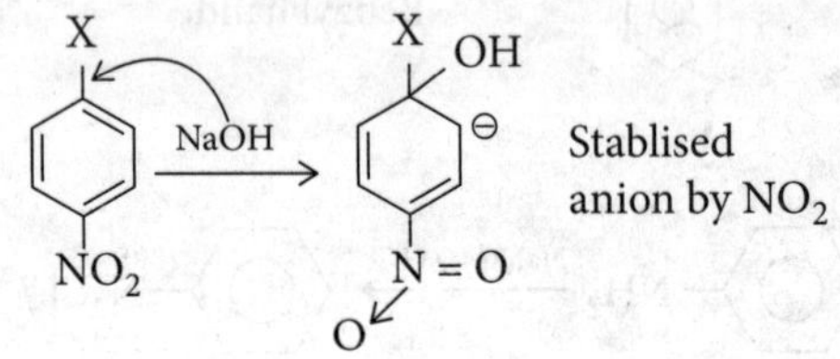

50.

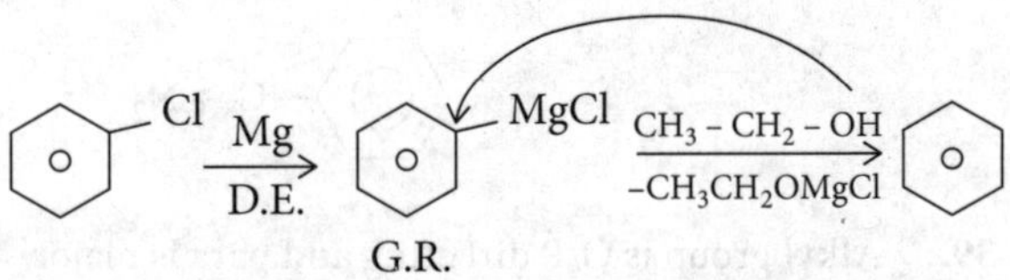

51.

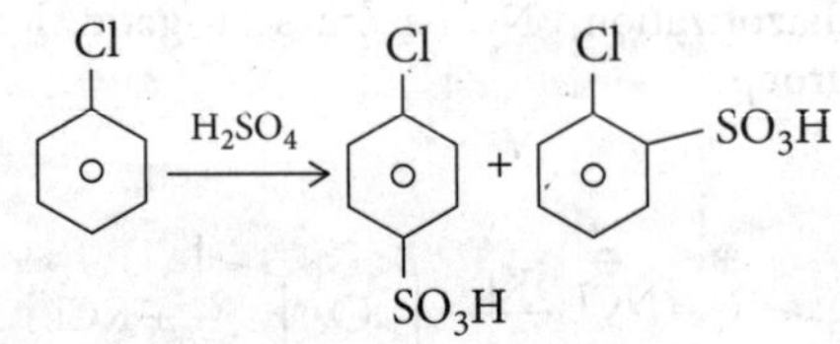

53. In aryl halide, halogen deactivates the ring due to -I being dominant over +M. Aryl halides are less reactive than alkyl halides due to partial double bond.

54.

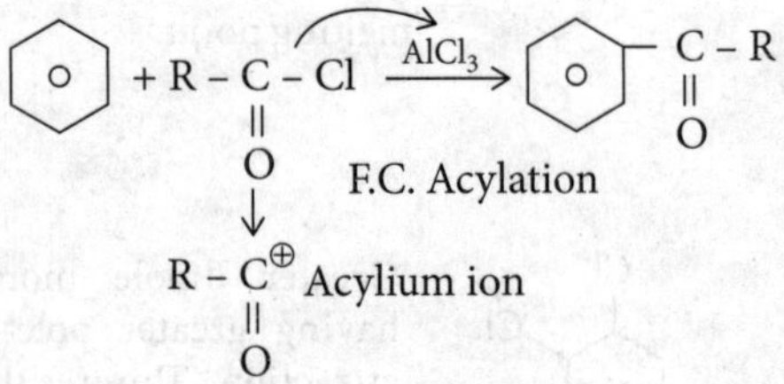

57. In iodination, byproduct HI is a reducing agent. It reduces to aryl iodide and the reaction goes backwards, so an oxidising agent is used to remove HI.

58. Sandmeyer's reaction is not used for aryl iodide formation.

61. Halogens are an O/P directing group.

63. Haloarenes deactivate the ring when compared to benzene.

65. CFCs are non-toxic and non-corrosive in the troposphere, but in the stratosphere, they are responsible for ozone depletion.

66. CCl_4 (Pyrene)

68.

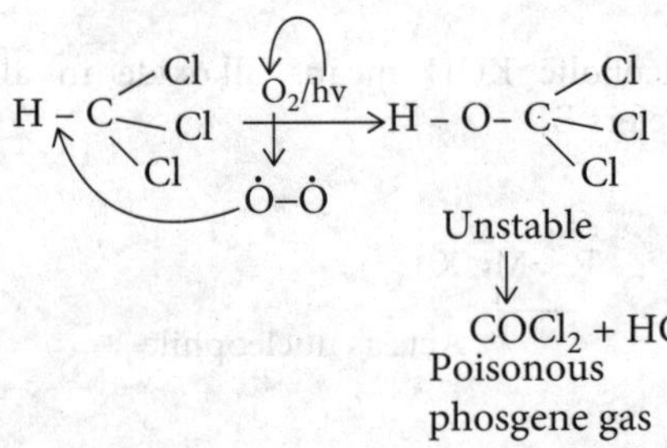

69. Freon – XYZ
X = C – 1
Y = H + 1
Z = F
Freon–012
= CF_2Cl_2

74. CH_2Cl_2 is used as a paint remover.

75. See Q68

76. CCl_4 is non-polar, so it a good solvent.

77. $CCl_4 \xrightarrow[\text{Swarts reaction}]{AgF} CCl_3F + CCl_2F_2 + CClF_3$

Level-2

1. Rate of S_N1 depends on the stability of intermediate carbocation

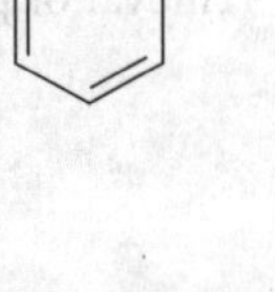

2.

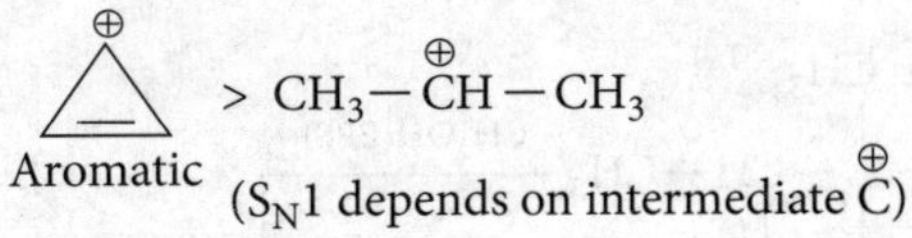

3.

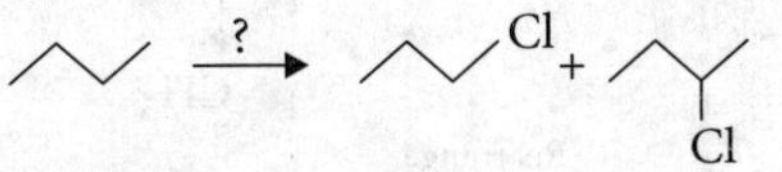

Free radical substitution reaction occurs in the presence of light or hv and Cl_2 gas.

4. Net withdrawing power (+M and –I compare) of bromine is higher than that of chlorine.

5.

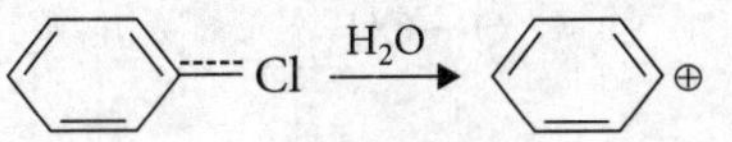

Unstable carbocation
(It does not give S_N1)

6.

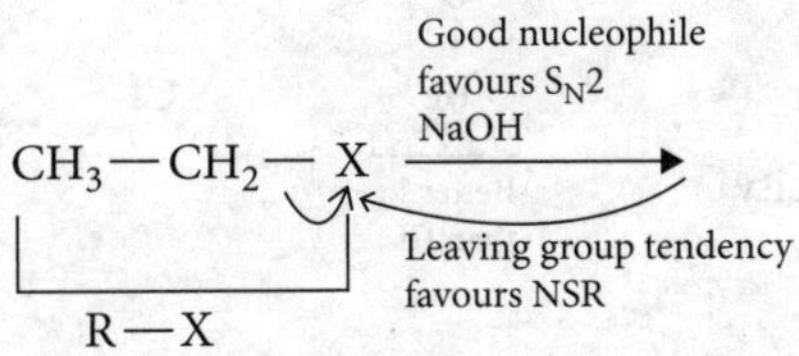

7.

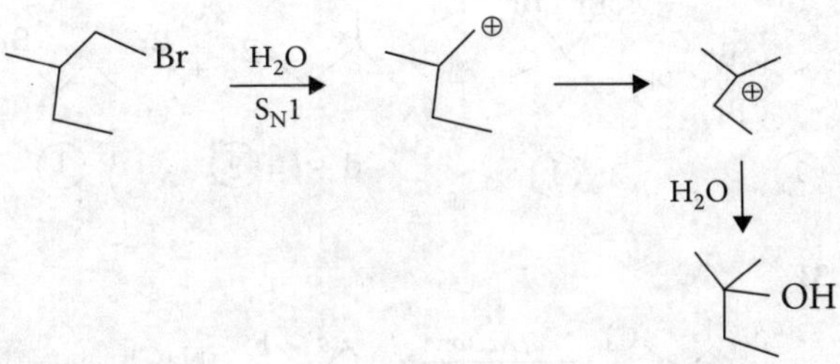

8.

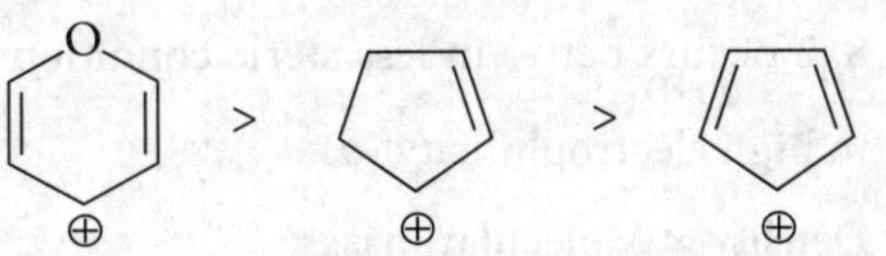

Aromatic carbocation | Resonance | Anti-aromatic carbocation

9.

$5\alpha - H$ $\quad$ $1\alpha - H$

10. Halogen is directly attached to the aromatic (benzene) ring.

11. Due to high EN of $\overset{\ominus}{F}$, a solid crystal of CaF_2 does not dissolve in water.

12.

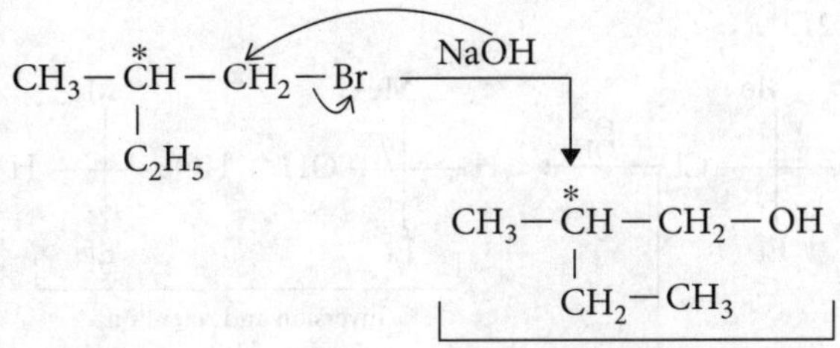

Stereo chemistry of chiral carbon does not change.

13.

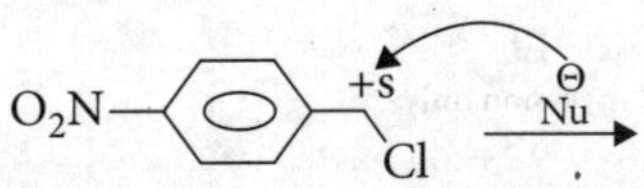

S_N2 also depends on electrophicity.

14.

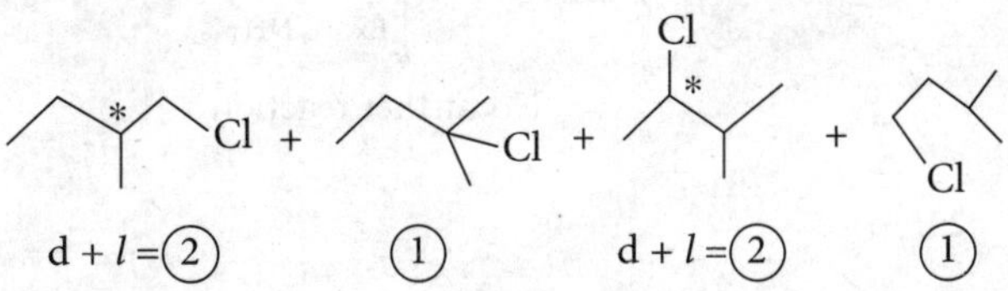

15. S_N2

16. Stable intermediate carbocation

17.

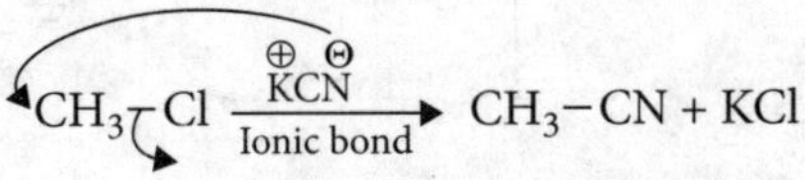

18.

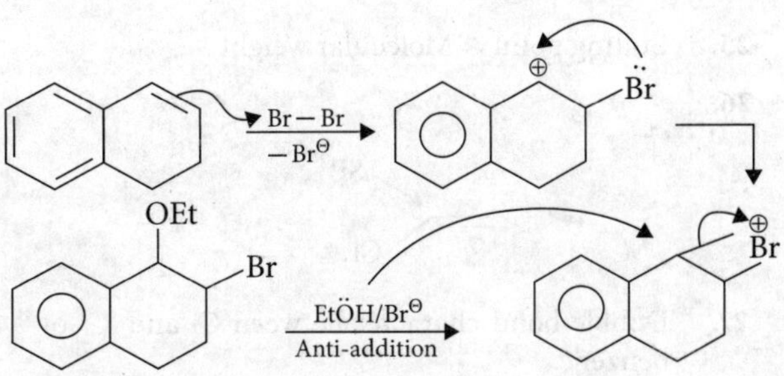

19. Stability of carbocation ∝ S_N1 (solvolysis).

20.

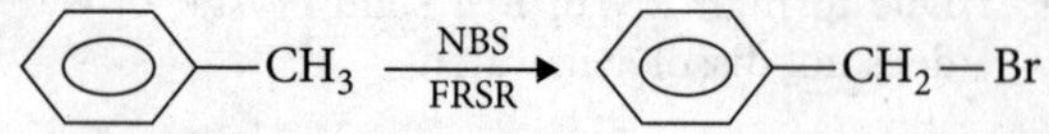

21.

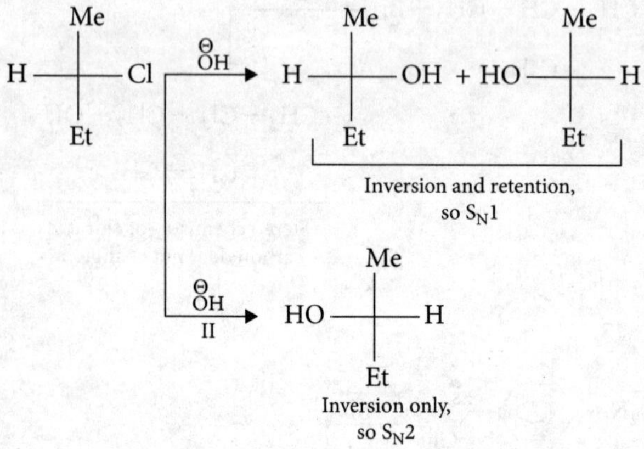

22.

$$CH_3-Cl \xrightarrow[Excess]{NH_3} CH_3-NH_2 + HCl$$

↓ Excess NH_3

No further reaction

23.

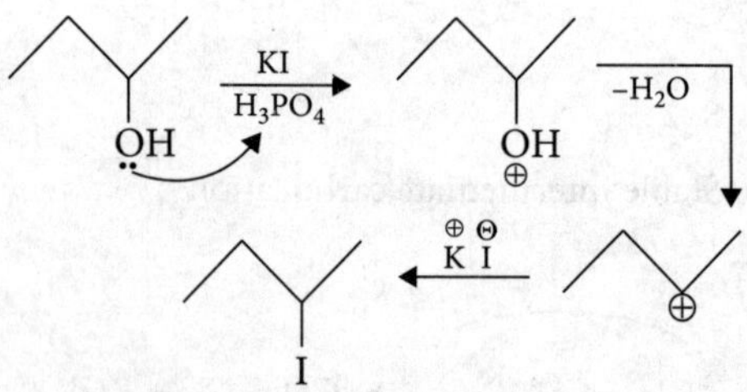

24. NaI is a reducing agent and H_2SO_4 is an oxidizing agent.

25. Boiling point ∝ Molecular weight

26.

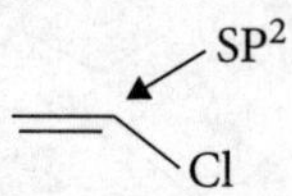

27. Double-bond character between Cl and 'C' of benzene.

28.

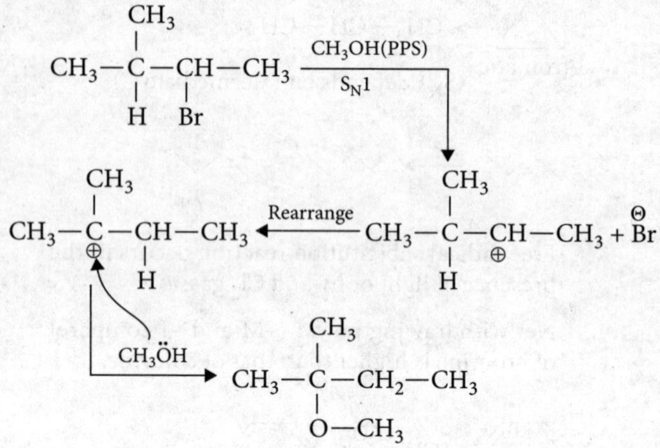

29.

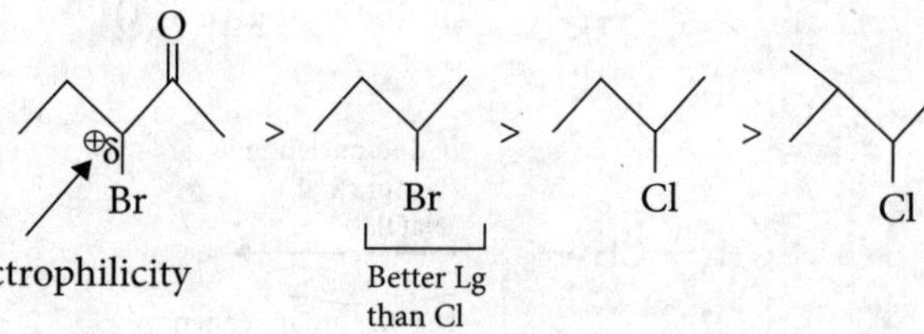

30.

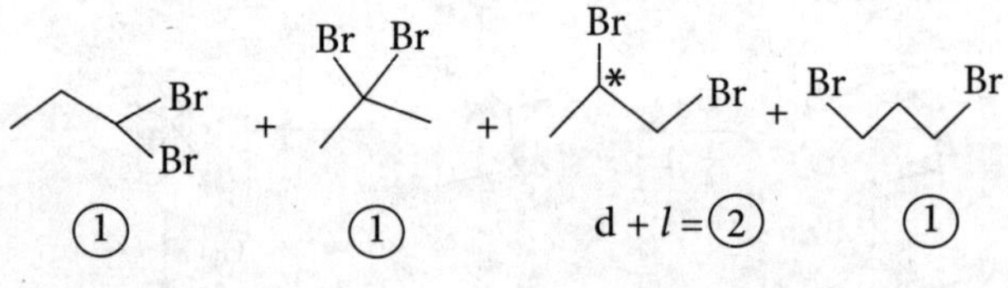

31.

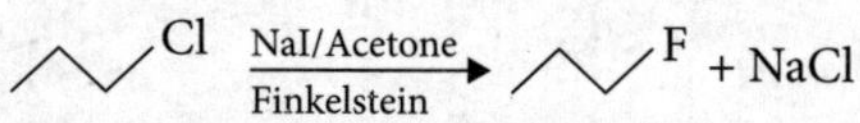

32. S_N2 occurs better in less steric conditions and in high electrophilicity ($\overset{\oplus}{\delta}$).

33. Density ∝ Molecular mass

34. Intermediate carbocation stability

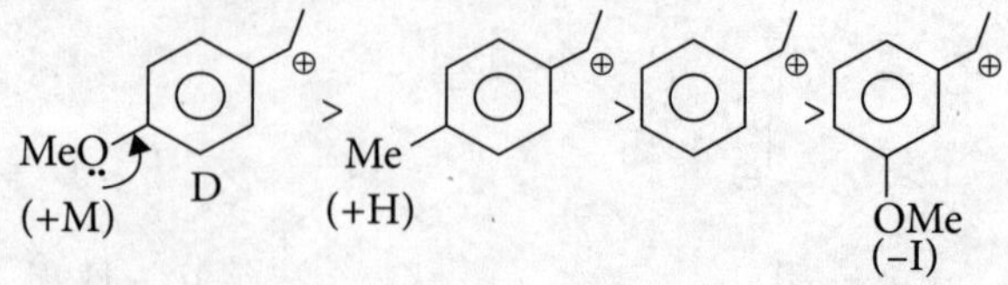

35. $CH_3-\ddot{O}-\overset{\oplus}{C}H_2 + \overset{\ominus}{Br}$ (Better Lg)

36. Boiling point ∝ Molecular mass ∝ $\dfrac{1}{\text{Branching}}$.

37.

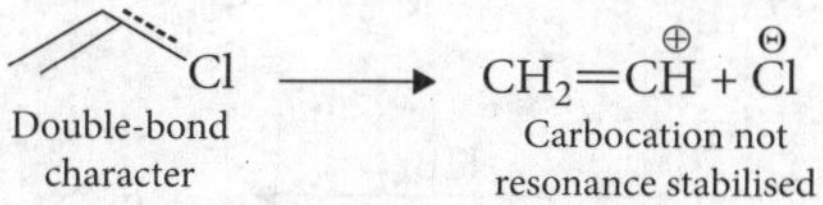

38. Most stable carbocation ∝ R.M

39. S_N1 ∝ Intermediate carbocation

41. $Br^{\ominus}$ [$Nu^{\ominus}$] substituted (replaced) by $\overset{\ominus}{O}H$ [$Nu^{\ominus}$]; so NSR.

42. 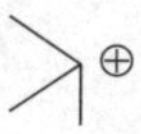 ⊕ Most stable carbocation.

43.

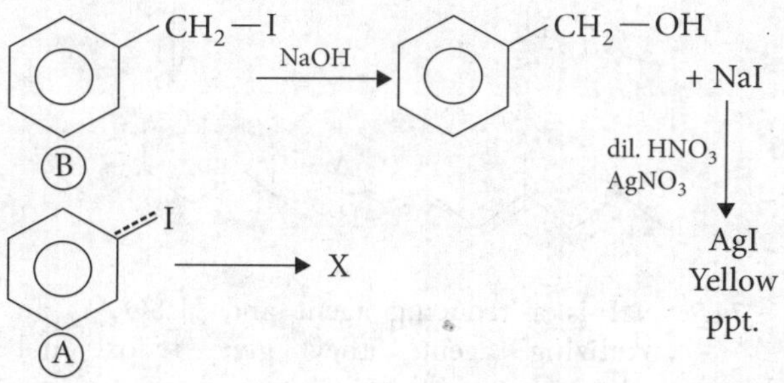

44.

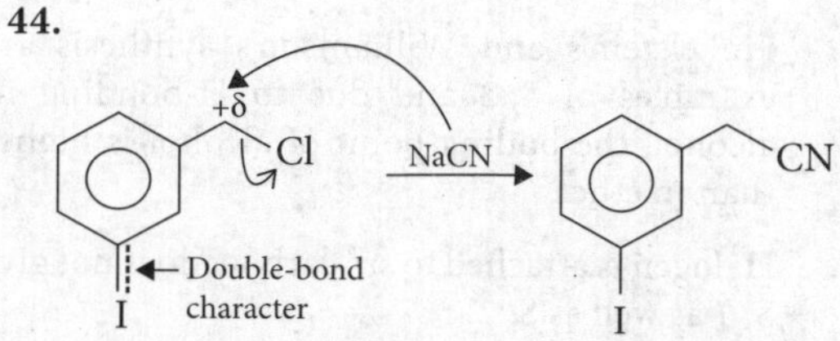

45.

$$CH_3-CH(Cl)-Cl \xrightarrow[\text{Hydrolysis}\ -2KCl]{2\ KOH} CH_3-CH(OH)_2 \longrightarrow CH_3-\underset{\underset{O}{\|}}{C}-H + H_2O$$

46. Intermediate carbocation stability ∝ S_N1

47. Carbocation stability ∝ S_N1

48. Carbocation stability ∝ S_N1

49.

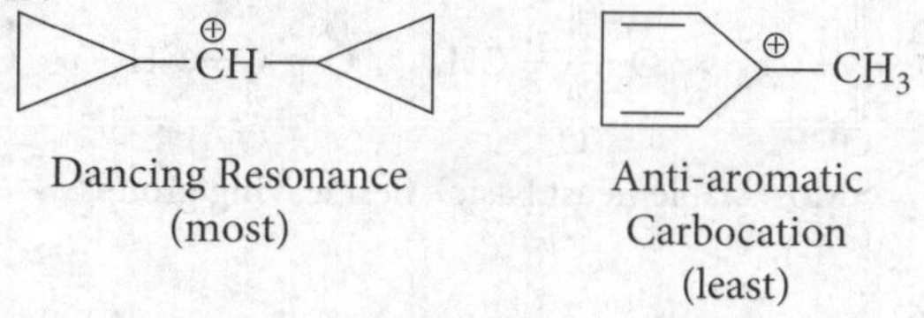

50. S_N2 gives inversion; this means $Ph\overset{\ominus}{S}$ ($\overset{\ominus}{N}u$) will be on the dash opposite the wedge ($Br^{\ominus}$) and C–F will have double-bond character. They are poor leaving groups and so are not affected.

51. After leaving, the leaving groups' anion stability is directly proportional to the rate of reactivity for both S_N1 and S_N2.

52.

$$CH_3-\overset{\overset{CH_3}{|}}{\underset{\underset{CH_3}{|}}{\overset{\ominus\delta}{C}}}-\overset{+\delta}{Mg}Br \xrightarrow{D_2O} CH_3-\overset{\overset{CH_3}{|}}{\underset{\underset{CH_3}{|}}{C}}-D + Mg(OD)Br$$

53. Rate of reaction with Lucas's reagent ∝ Stability of carbocation.

54. For S_N1, Rate ∝ $[R{-}X]^1[H_2O]^0$
So, the rate is directly proportional to only alkyl halide; not on water concentration.

55. For S_N2, Rate ∝ $[R{-}X]^1[\text{Nucleophile}]^1$

$$\frac{r_1}{r_2} = \frac{[C_1]}{[2C_1]}\frac{[C_2]}{[2C_2]} = \frac{1}{4}$$

$r_2 = 4r_1$

56. Partial racemization, because before formation of carbocation, some molecules give inverted products because of planarity.

58.

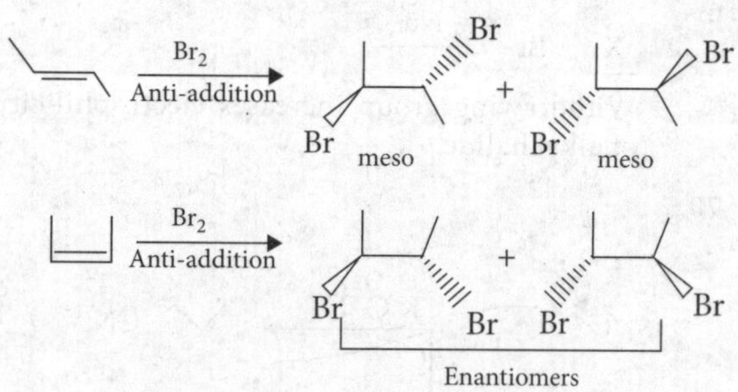

60.

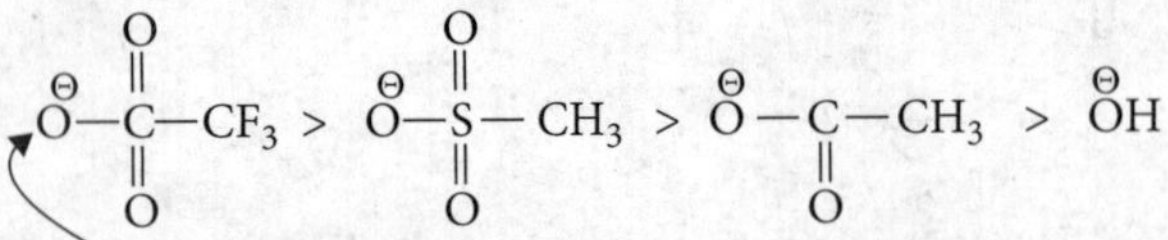

Most stable (least basic), best leaving group

61.

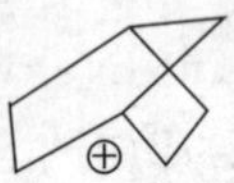

Bridgehead carbon can never be sp^2, as per Bredt's Rule.

62. S_N2 gives Walden inversion.

63. (i) S_N1 mechanism, (ii) Bond length, (iii) E_2 mechanism, (iv) S_N2 mechanism, (vi) Boiling point, (vii) E_1 mechanism - correct for R–I > R–Br > R–Cl > R–F.

64. $\mu \propto$ Charge distance (For CH_3–Cl)

decrease But more increase

65. 3° alcohol gives the most stable carbocation.

66.

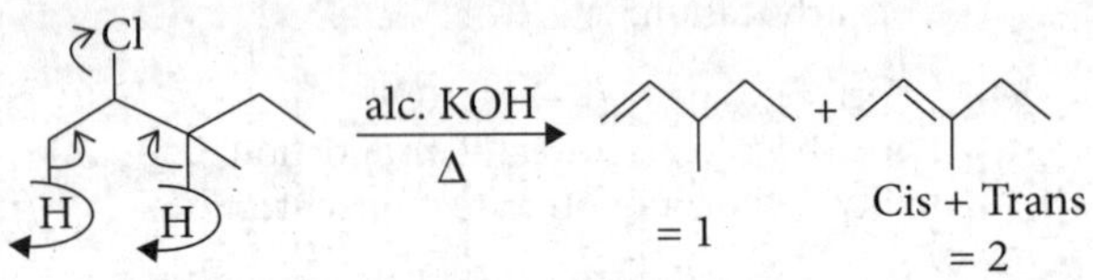

67.

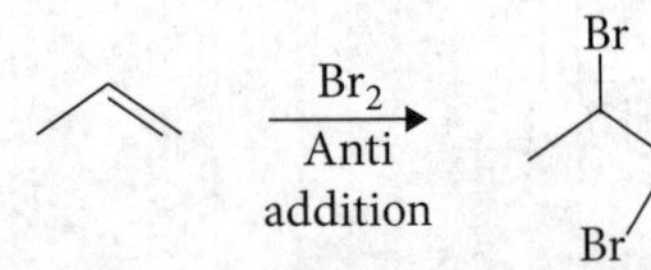

68. Symmetrical compound having better fit in the lattice.

69.

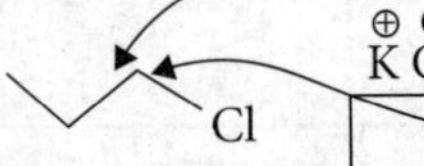

Withdrawing group increases electrophilicity of alkyl halide.

70.

71.

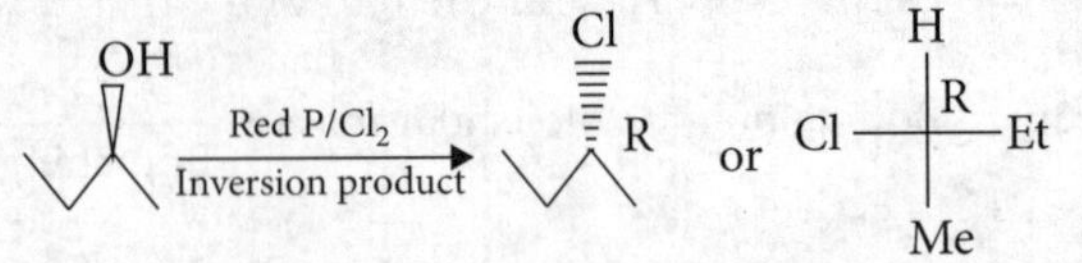

72.

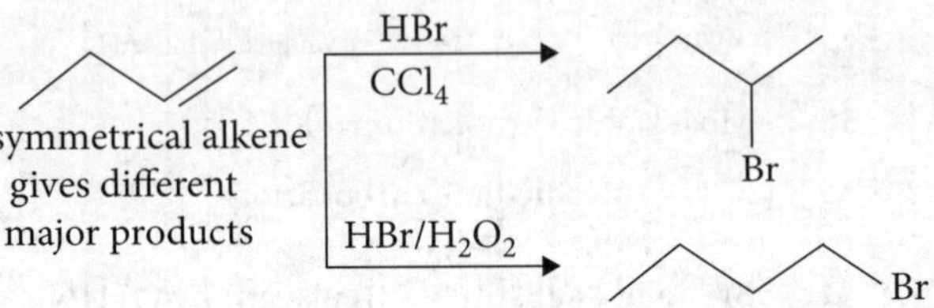

73.

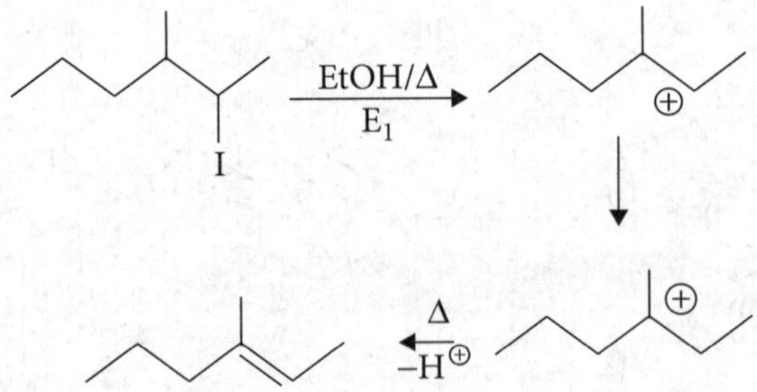

74. NaI is a reducing agent and H_2SO_4 is an oxidizing agent. They give redox, not substitution of alcohol.

75. Finkelstein's and Williamson's synthesis are examples of S_N2 and due to H-bonding in alcohol, the boiling point of alcohol is higher than in ether.

76. Halogen is attached to sp^2 carbon, does not give S_N1 as well as S_N2.

77. 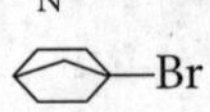 Inversion not possible.

78.

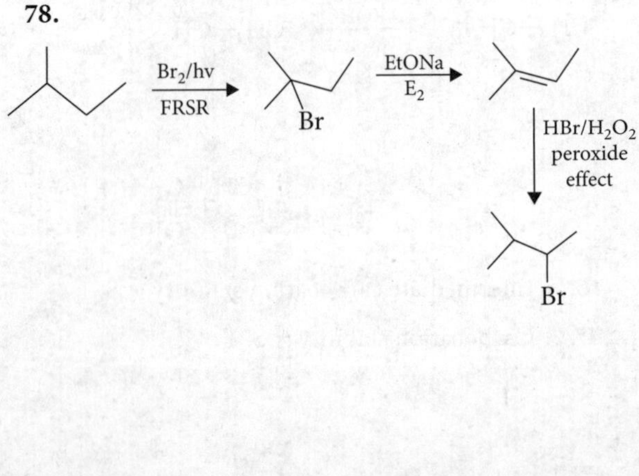

79.

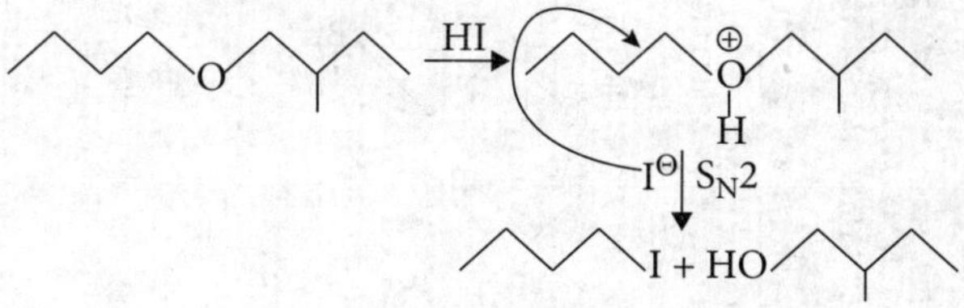

80. Finkelstein reaction for R–I (mostly).

81.

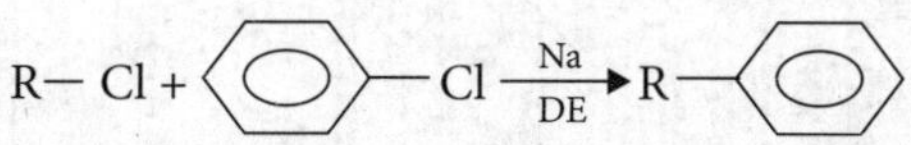

82.

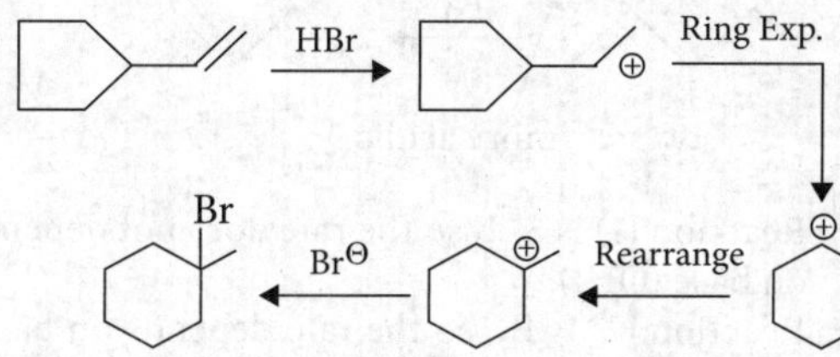

83. $CH_3–CH_2–Cl \xrightarrow[\text{Swarts reaction}]{AgF} CH_3–CH_2–F +$ AgCl

85.

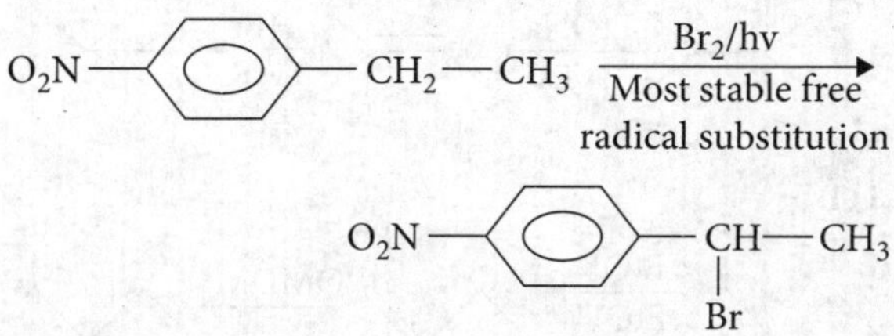

86.

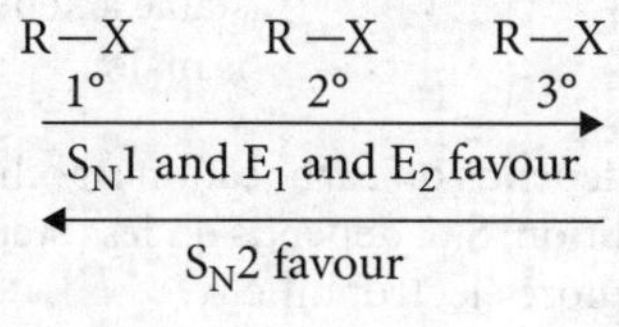

87. E_2 rate ∝ 3° R – X > 2° R – X > 1° R – X

88. E_1 ∝ Stability of carbocation and stability of product alkene.

89.  Anti-aromatic carbocation will not be formed.

90.

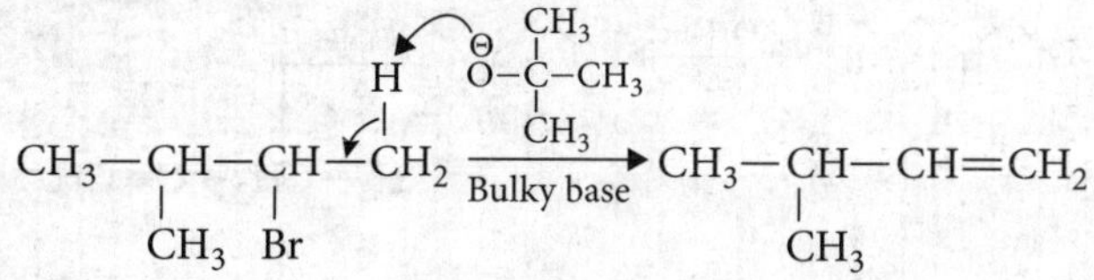

91. Gives dehydrohalogenation [E_2].

92. Better leaving group and most stable carbocation by back-bonding.

93.

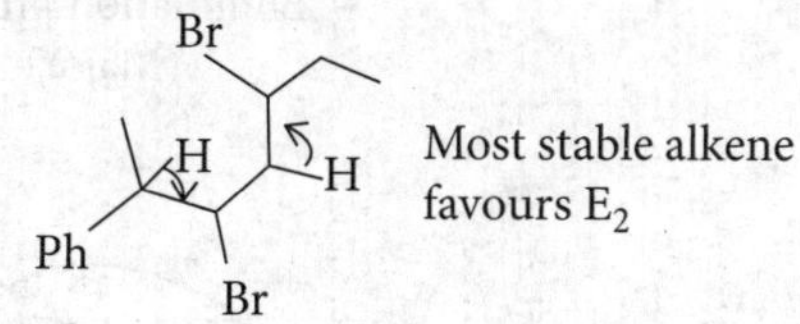

94. 3° alkyl chloride gives fastest E_1.

95.

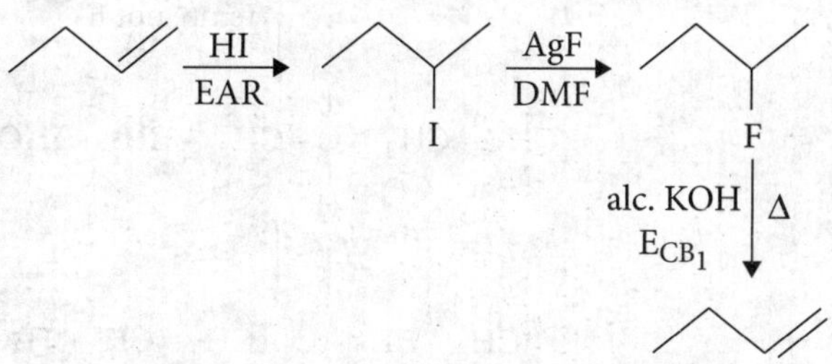

Poor leaving group gives Hoffmann's product by E1cB.

96. For E_2, anti-elimination occurs.
So rate of E2 ∝ Presence of anti-hydrogen (proton) with respect to halogen.

97. Intermediate carbocation stability

98.

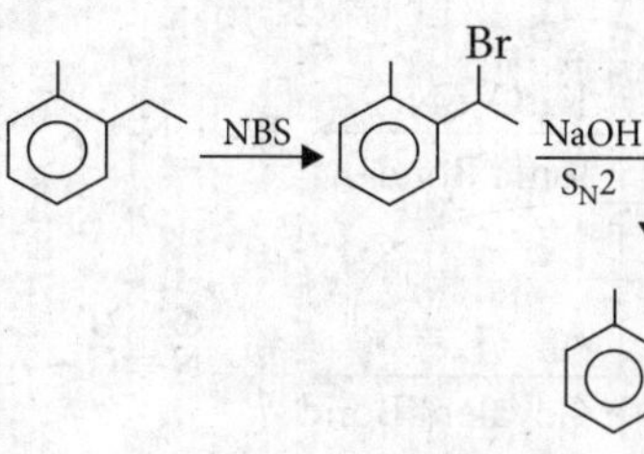

99.

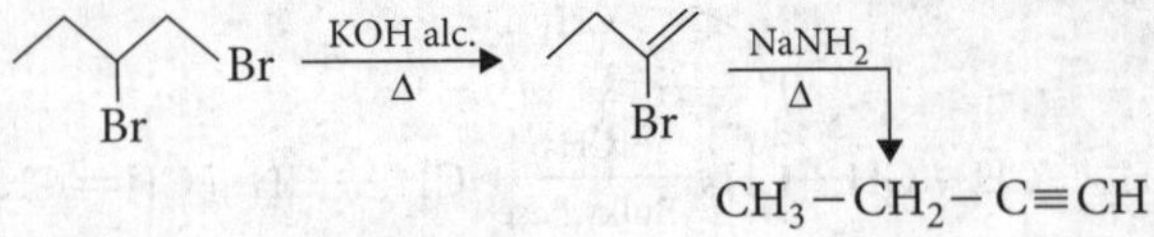

100.

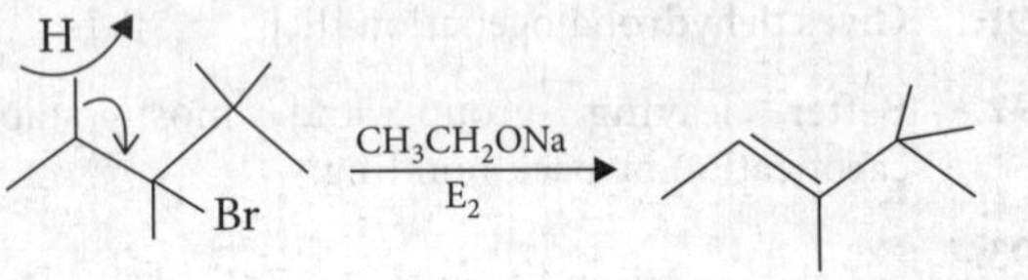

Elimination product (Major)

101.

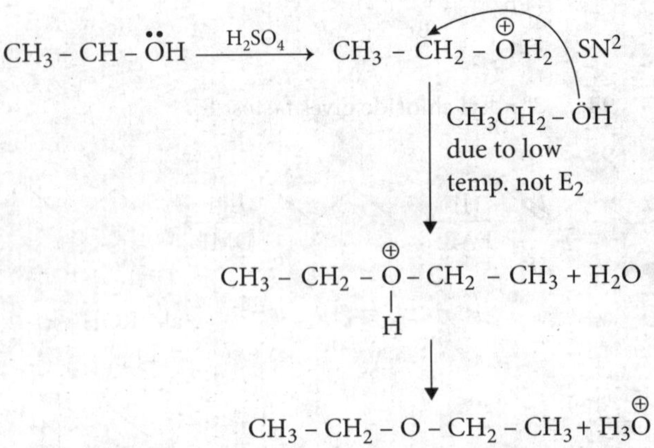

102. NaI is a reducing agent and H_2SO_4 is an oxidizing agent.. They give redox and not NSR.

103. Wurtz–Fittig reaction

104. Polar protic solvent (like H_2O, CH_3CH_2-OH) favours S_N1.

105.

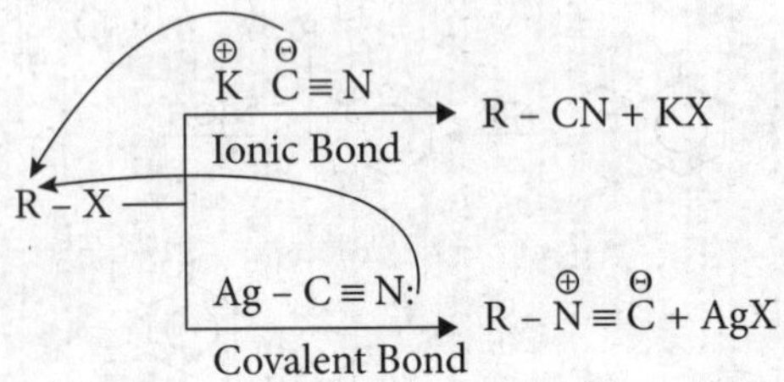

106.

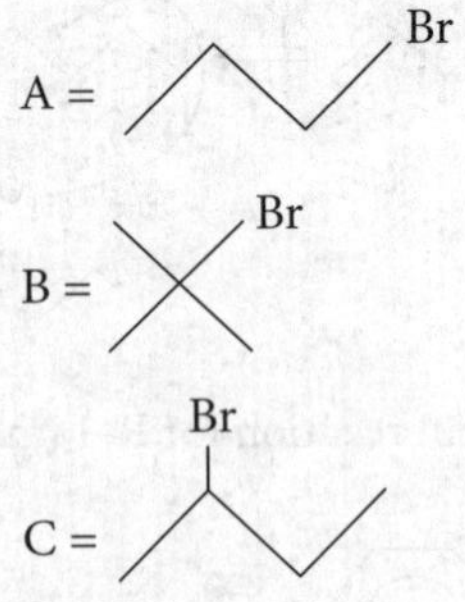

107.

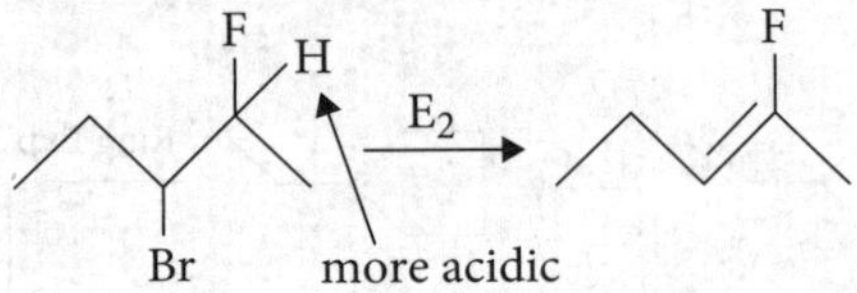

108. Reaction (1) is S_N1, so the rate does not depend on base (OH^-).
Reaction (2) is E_2, so the rate depends on base (OH^-).

109. NSR of alcohol with HX depends on intermediate carbocation.

110.

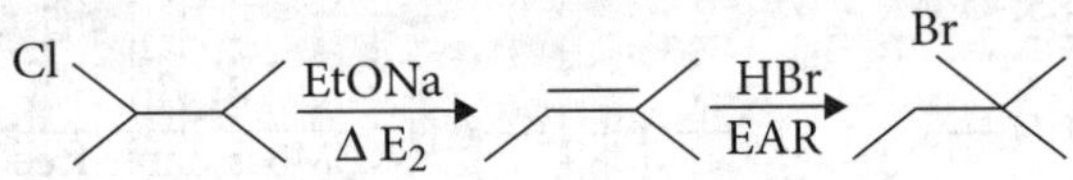

111.

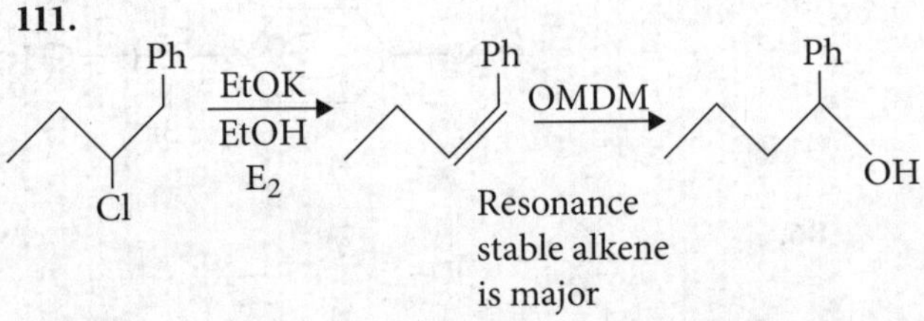

112. S_N1 depends on carbocation stability and steric condition; S_N2 depends on less steric condition and more electrophilicity.

113.

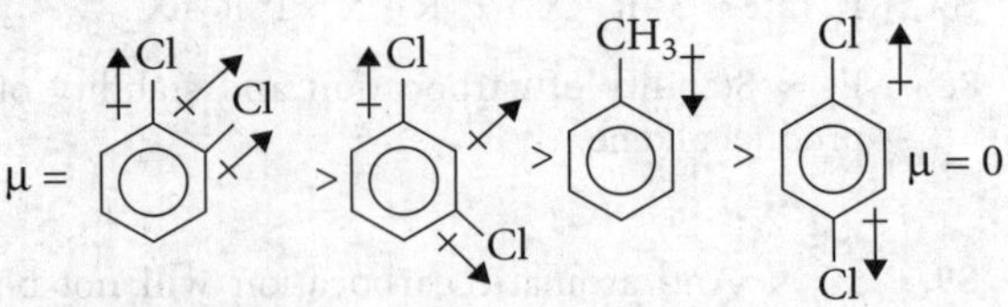

114. (a) 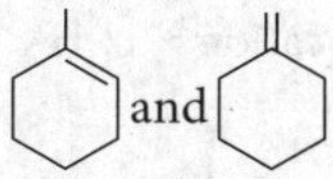

(b) 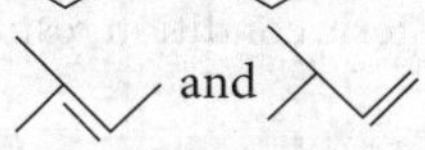

(c) 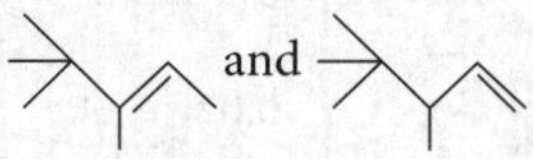

$\frac{\text{cis + trans}}{2} + (1)$

(d) 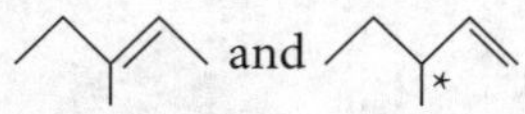

cis + trans = 2 d + *l* = 2

115. 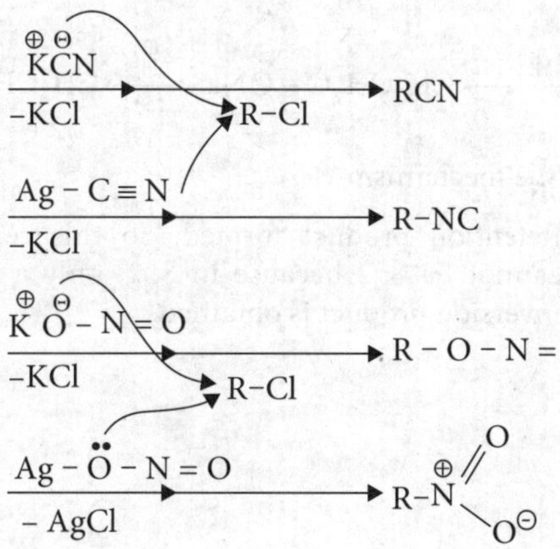

116. 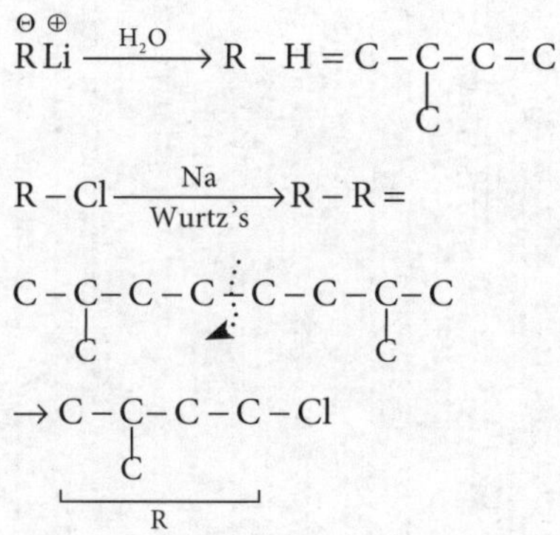

117. E_1 gives Saytzeff's major product; means stable alkene.

118. (a) Follow S_N1
(b) Follow S_N1 and rearrangement
(c) Due to low temperature of 413 K, it does not give E_2; it gives Williamson's continuous ether synthesis (S_N2)
(d) 3° alkyl bromide gives E_2 and forms alkene.

119. S_N2 favours less steric condition; so true.

120. Double-bond character or chlorine attached to sp^2 carbon.

121. 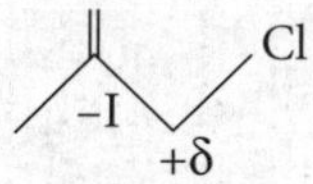

Due to distance –I, greater increase in electrophilicity (+δ) favours nucleophilic attachment.

122. Fluorine is a poor leaving group. So it does not give S_N2 for Finkelstein reaction.

123. As polarity increases, formation of intermediate carbocation will increase.

$$CH_3-\underset{\underset{O}{\|}}{C}-H \xrightarrow[-HCl]{PCl_5 \; - POCl_3} CH_3-C(H)(Cl)Cl$$

124. CHI_3 (Iodoform) shows antiseptic property in the form of I_2; chloroform ($CHCl_3$) is an anesthetic.

125. Stable intermediate carbocation favours S_N1.

126. 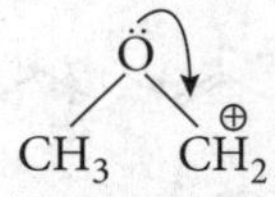 Stable carbocation by back-bonding.

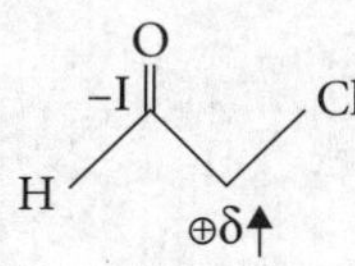

for S_N2

127. 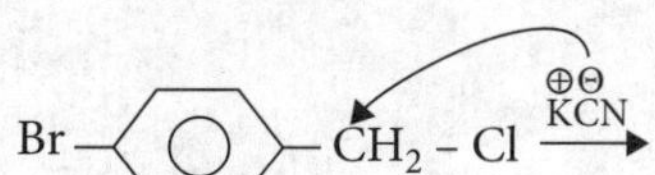

128. 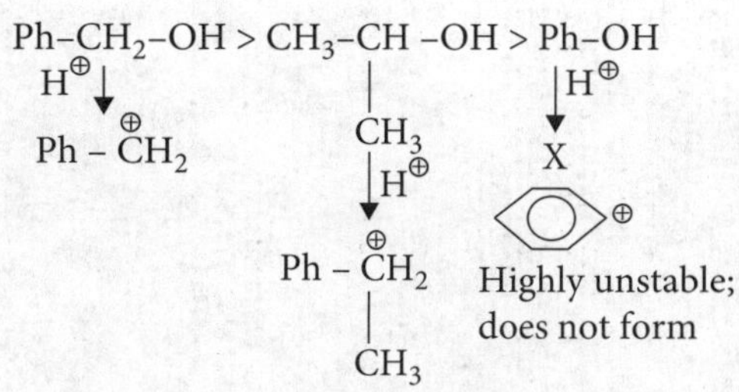

129.

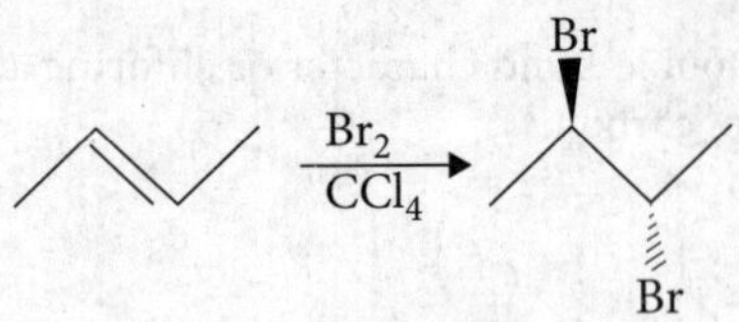

131.

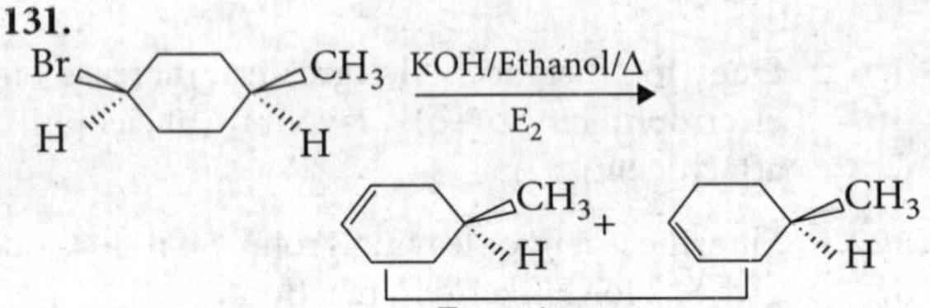

Enantiomers

132. Less steric condition favours S_N2

134. More stable carbocation increases the chances of racemization.

135. H_2SO_4 or H^+ is a catalyst for isomerisation of the unstable alkene to a more stable alkene, and the given reagent is also used.

137. Stable carbocation $\propto S_N1$

138.

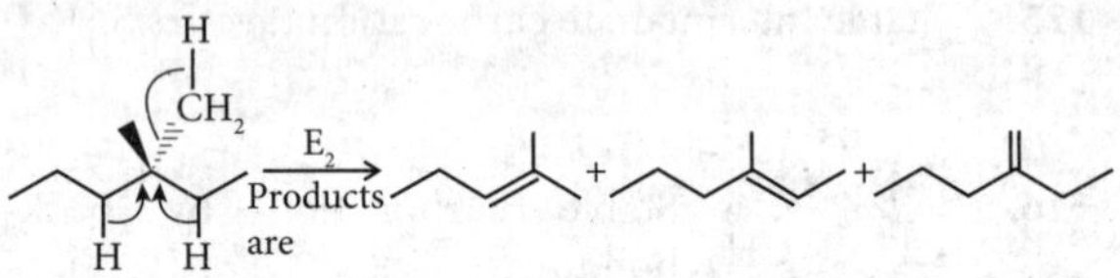

139. Intermediate carbocation $\propto$ α-H of hyperconjugation.

140. For S_N2, more steric condition results in a lower rate (o)

A → 0

B → 1

C → 0.02

D → 30

141. $CH_3-CH_2-OH \xrightarrow[(4)]{H_2SO_4/\Delta} CH_2=CH_2 \xrightarrow[(1)]{Br_2} \underset{Br}{CH_2}-\overset{Br}{CH_2} \xrightarrow[(5)]{4NaNH_2} NaC\equiv CNa$

$\xrightarrow[(2)]{CH_3-CH_2-I} CH_3CH_2C\equiv \overset{\ominus\ \oplus}{C\,Na} \xrightarrow[(3)]{\overset{\oplus}{H}} CH_3CH_2C\equiv CH$

142. S_N2 mechanism

143. Retention product formed. So this reaction cannot be S_N2 because in S_N2, only a single inversion product is obtained.

CHAPTER 7

Alcohol, Phenol and Ether

Level-1

Alcohol

1. Commercially, carboxylic acids are reduced to alcohols by converting them to:
(a) Esters (b) Aldehydes
(c) Ketones (d) Amines

2. $ClCH_2CH_2OH$ is a stronger acid than CH_3CH_2OH because the:
(a) –I effect of Cl increases the negative charge on the O-atom of alcohol.
(b) –I effect of Cl disperses the negative charge on the O-atom to produce a more stable cation.
(c) –I effect of Cl disperses the negative charge on the O-atom to produce a more stable anion.
(d) None of these

3. **Statement I:** Esterification of alcohol involves cleavage of the O–H bond in alcohol.
Statement II: Alcohols liberate hydrogen gas on reaction with metallic sodium.
In the light of the above statements, choose the most appropriate answer from the options given below:
(a) Both statement I and statement II are correct.
(b) Statement I is correct but statement II is incorrect.
(c) Statement I is incorrect but statement II is correct.
(d) Both statement I and statement II are incorrect.

4. Which of the following statements are correct regarding esterification of alcohols?
I. Alcohols react with carboxylic acids, acid chlorides and acid anhydrides to form esters.
II. The reaction with carboxylic acid and acid anhydride is carried out in the presence of a small amount of concentrated H_2SO_4.
III. The reaction with acid chloride is carried out in the presence of a base (pyridine) so as to neutralize the side-product HCl.
IV. The reaction with carboxylic acid and acid anhydride is reversible while that with acid chloride is irreversible.
(a) I, II and III (b) II and III
(c) I, II and IV (d) I, II, III and IV

5. Three moles of ethanol react with one mole of phosphorus tribromide to form three moles of bromoethane and one mole of X. Which of the following is X?
(a) H_3PO_4 (b) H_3PO_2
(c) HPO_3 (d) H_3PO_3

6. Read the following statements and choose the correct option:
(a) Ethanol on dehydration at 443 K gives ethene.
(b) Ethanol on dehydration at 413 K gives diethyl ether.
(c) The dehydration of 2° and 3° alcohols to give their corresponding ethers is unsuccessful as elimination competes over substitution.
(d) 1° alcohol > 2° alcohol > 3° alcohol (Ease of dehydration)
(a) TTFF (b) TFTF
(c) TTTF (d) FTTF

7. Which of the following statements are correct regarding dehydration of alcohols?
I. Concentrated H_2SO_4 or concentrated H_3PO_4 or anhydrous $ZnCl_2$ or Al_2O_3 can be used as dehydrating alcohol.
II. The mechanism involves Protonation → Formation of carbocation → Deprotonation
III. Primary alcohols are the easiest to dehydrate.
IV. Formation of carbocation is the rate determining step.
(a) I, II, III

(b) II and IV
(c) I, II, IV
(d) I, II, III and IV

8. Select the option containing the incorrect statement:
(a) Mild oxidizing agents such as PCC or anhydrous CrO_3 oxidize alcohols to their corresponding carbonyl compounds.
(b) With heated copper, primary and secondary alcohols are oxidized while tertiary alcohols are dehydrated.
(c) At elevated temperatures, tertiary alcohols react with $KMnO_4$ to produce a mixture of carboxylic acids.
(d) PCC is a complex of chromium(III) chloride with pyridine.

9. Which of the following statements are correct?
(a) In phenols, the —OH group is attached to the sp^2-hybridized carbon of an aromatic ring.
(b) The carbon–oxygen bond length (136 pm) in phenol is slightly more than that in methanol.
(c) Partial double bond character in the C–O bond of phenol is due to conjugation of an unshared electron pair of oxygen with the aromatic ring.
(d) The –OH group in phenol shows +M-effect.
(a) (a), (b) and (v) (b) (a), (b) and (c)
(c) (a), (c) and (d) (d) (a) and (d)

10. An industrial method of preparation of methanol is:
(a) Catalytic reduction of carbon monoxide in the presence of $ZnO–Cr_2O_3$.
(b) By reacting methane with steam at 900°C with a nickel catalyst.
(c) By reducing formaldehyde with lithium aluminium hydride.
(d) By reacting formaldehyde with aqueous sodium hydroxide solution.

11. Widespread deaths because of liquor poisoning occur due to:
(a) Presence of carbonic acid in liquor.
(b) Presence of ethyl alcohol in liquor.
(c) Presence of methyl alcohol in liquor.
(d) Presence of lead compounds in liquor.

12. Select the incorrect statement about fermentation in the preparation of wine:
(a) When grapes are crushed, sugar and enzymes come in contact and fermentation starts.
(b) Fermentation takes place in anaerobic conditions.
(c) Carbon monoxide is released during fermentation.
(d) If air gets into the fermentation mixture, the oxygen in air oxidises ethanol to ethanoic acid, which in turn spoils the taste of alcoholic drinks.

13. In order to make alcohol undrinkable, pyridine and methanol are added to it. The resulting alcohol is called:
(a) Power alcohol
(b) Proof spirit
(c) Denatured spirit
(d) Poison alcohol

14. Denaturation of alcohol is the:
(a) Mixing of $CuSO_4$ (a foul smelling solid) and pyridine (to give colour) to make commercial alcohol unfit for drinking.
(b) Mixing of $CuSO_4$ (to give colour) and pyridine (a foul smelling solid) to make commercial alcohol unfit for drinking.
(c) Mixing of $Cu(OAc)_2$ and ammonia to make commercial alcohol unfit for drinking.
(d) Mixing of $Cu(OAc)_2$ and pyridine to make commercial alcohol unfit for drinking.

15. **Assertion (A):** Methanol is also known as wood spirit.
Reason (R): Once, it was produced by the destructive distillation of wood.
(a) Both the assertion and reason are true and the reason is the correct explanation of the assertion.
(b) Both the assertion and reason are true and the reason is not the correct explanation of the assertion.
(c) The assertion is true but the reason is false.
(d) Both the assertion and reason are false.

16. Read the following statements regarding methanol:
I. Today, most methanol is produced by catalytic hydrogenation of CO at high temperature and pressure in the presence of the $ZnO–Cr_2O_3$ catalyst.
II. Ingestion of small quantities of methanol causes blindness and large quantities causes death.
III. Methanol is used as a solvent in paints, varnishes and is chiefly used in making formaldehyde.

Choose the option containing correct statements:
(a) I, II (b) I, III
(c) II, III (d) I, II and III

17. Read the following statements regarding ethanol:
I. Ethanol is obtained commercially by fermentation.
II. Fermentation takes plaçe in aerobic conditions.
III. Commercial alcohol is denatured with copper sulphate and pyridine.
Choose the option containing the correct statements:
(a) I, II (b) I, III
(c) II, III (d) I, II and III

18. Which of the following reactions depicts the correct product?
(a) $CO + H_2 \xrightarrow[\substack{200-300\text{ atm} \\ 573\text{ K}-673\text{ K}}]{ZnO-Cr_2O_3} CH_3OH$
(b) $C_{12}H_{22}O_{11} + H_2O \xrightarrow{\text{Invertase}} \underset{\text{Glucose}}{C_6H_{12}O_6} + \underset{\text{Fructose}}{C_6H_{12}O_6}$
(c) $C_6H_{12}O_6 \xrightarrow{\text{Zymase}} 2C_2H_5OH + 2CO_2$
(d) All of these

19. Select the incorrect statement:
(a) Both methanol and ethanol are colourless liquids.
(b) Methanol boils at a lower temperature than ethanol.
(c) In wine-making, grapes are the source of sugars and yeast.
(d) Alcoholic drinks contain methanol as a major ingredient.

20. Which of the following statement(s) is(are) correct about hydroboration oxidation?
(a) Diborane reacts with alkenes to give trialkyl boranes as addition product, which is oxidised to alcohol by H_2O_2 in the presence of aqueous NaOH.
(b) The alcohol so formed can also be obtained by the addition of water to the alkene by Markovnikov's rule.
(c) Alcohol is obtained in poor yield.
(d) All of the above.

21. On reduction of aldehydes and ketones, the compounds formed are, respectively:
(a) 1° alcohol; 2° alcohols
(b) 2° alcohols; 1° alcohol
(c) 1° alcohol; 3° alcohols
(d) 3° alcohols; 1° alcohol

22. The acid-catalysed hydration of alkenes involves the following three steps:
I. Nucleophilic attack of water on carbocation.
II. Protonation of alkene to form carbocation by the electrophilic attack of H_3O^+.
III. Deprotonation to form an alcohol.
Identify the sequence for the mechanism of reaction in the acid-catalysed hydration of alkenes:
(a) I, II and III (b) II, I and III
(c) III, I and II (d) III, II and I

23. **Assertion (A):** Commercially, acids are reduced to alcohols by converting them to esters, followed by their reduction using catalytic hydrogenation.
Reason (R): $LiAlH_4$ can also reduce carboxylic acids to primary alcohols, but $LiAlH_4$ is an expensive reagent and is used for preparing special chemicals only.
(a) Both A and R are correct; R is the correct explanation of A.
(b) Both A and R are correct; R is not the correct explanation of A.
(c) A is correct; R is incorrect.
(d) R is correct; A is incorrect.

24. **Assertion (A):** Alcohols and phenols are soluble in water.
Reason (R): The solubility of alcohol and phenol in water is due to their ability to form hydrogen bonds with water molecules.
(a) Both A and R are correct; R is the correct explanation of A.
(b) Both A and R are correct; R is not the correct explanation of A.
(c) A is correct; R is incorrect.
(d) R is correct; A is incorrect.

25. The reaction of the Grignard reagent with a carbonyl compound is a nucleophilic addition reaction. This reaction on hydrolysis produces:
(a) Ester (b) Alcohol
(c) Carboxylic acid (d) Ether

26. Select the incorrect option from the following regarding the physical properties of alcohol and phenol:
(a) The boiling points of alcohols and phenols are higher in comparison to hydrocarbons,

ethers, haloalkanes and haloarenes of comparable molecular mass.
(b) Ethanol and propane have similar boiling points but differ only in the molecular mass.
(c) The OH group in alcohols and phenols is involved in intermolecular hydrogen bonding.
(d) The trend of boiling point is Ethanol > Methoxymethane > Propane.

27. Which of the following is not correctly matched with the properties mentioned?
(a) CH_3CH_2OH > $CH_3CH_2CH_2OH$ > $CH_3CH_2CH_2CH_2OH$
(Solubility)
(b) CH_3CH_2OH < $CH_3CH_2CH_2OH$ < $CH_3CH_2CH_2CH_2OH$
(Boiling point)
(c) $CH_3CH_2CH_2CH_2OH > (CH_3)_2CH-CH_2OH$
$> CH_3-\overset{\overset{\large CH_3}{|}}{\underset{\underset{\large CH_3}{|}}{C}}-OH$
(Boiling point)
(d) $CH_3-O-CH_3 > CH_3-CH_2-OH$
(Extent of hydrogen bonding)

28. The correct statement about alcohol and ether (CH_3CH_2OH and CH_3OCH_3) is:
(a) The boiling point of alcohol is greater than that of ether whereas the solubility of ether is greater than that of alcohol.
(b) The solubility of alcohol is greater than that of ether whereas the boiling point of ether is greater than that of alcohol.
(c) Both boiling point and solubility of alcohol are greater than that of ether.
(d) Both boiling point and solubility of ether are greater than that of alcohol.

29. **Assertion (A):** In alcohols, the boiling point decreases with increase in the branching of the carbon chain.
Reason (R): There is an increase in Van der Waals forces between the molecules with branching.
(a) Both A and R are correct; R is the correct explanation of A.
(b) Both A and R are correct; R is not the correct explanation of A.
(c) A is correct; R is incorrect.
(d) R is correct; A is incorrect.

30. Which of the following reactions is correct?

(a) $\underset{\text{Acid}}{B} + \underset{\text{Base}}{H\ddot{\underset{..}{O}}R} \longrightarrow \underset{\text{Conjugate base}}{BH^+} + \underset{\text{Conjugate acid}}{\bar{O}R}$

(b) $\underset{\text{Base}}{B} + \underset{\text{Acid}}{H\ddot{\underset{..}{O}}R} \longrightarrow \underset{\text{Conjugate acid}}{BH^+} + \underset{\text{Conjugate base}}{\bar{O}R}$

(c) $\underset{\text{Acid}}{B} + \underset{\text{Base}}{H\ddot{\underset{..}{O}}R} \longrightarrow \underset{\text{Conjugate acid}}{BH^+} + \underset{\text{Conjugate base}}{\bar{O}R}$

(d) $\underset{\text{Base}}{B} + \underset{\text{Acid}}{H\ddot{\underset{..}{O}}R} \longrightarrow \underset{\text{Conjugate base}}{BH^+} + \underset{\text{Conjugate acid}}{\bar{O}R}$

31. Alcohols and phenols react with active metals to yield:
(a) Alkoxides/Phenoxides
(b) Hydrogen gas
(c) Nitrogen gas
(d) Both (a) and (b)

32. Consider the following statements:
I. Solubility decreases with increase in the size of the alkyl/aryl groups.
II. Alcohols and phenols react with metals like Na and K to produce the corresponding alkoxides or phenoxides.
III. Alcohols act as a Bronsted acid in the presence of a strong acid.
IV. Alcohols react as nucleophiles and electrophiles.
Choose the correct option:
(a) Only II (b) II and III
(c) I, II and IV (d) All of these

33. **Assertion (A):** Increasing order of acid strength of alcohol is 1° alcohol > 2° alcohol > 3° alcohol.
Reason (R): An electron releasing group increases the electron density on oxygen which tends to decrease the polarity of the O–H bond.
(a) Both A and R are correct; R is the correct explanation of A.
(b) Both A and R are correct; R is not the correct explanation of A.
(c) A is correct; R is incorrect.
(d) R is correct; A is incorrect.

34. Which of the following substrates reacts with alcohols and phenols to form esters?
(a) Carboxylic acids
(b) Acid chlorides

(c) Acid anhydrides
(d) All of the above

35. The reaction of alcohol/phenol with acid chloride is carried out in the presence of pyridine in order to:
(a) Neutralise HCl which is formed during the reaction
(b) Shift the equilibrium to the right
(c) Both (a) and (b)
(d) None of the above

36. An unknown alcohol is treated with the Lucas reagent to determine whether the alcohol is primary, secondary or tertiary. Which alcohol reacts fastest and by what mechanism?
(a) Secondary alcohol by S_N1
(b) Tertiary alcohol by S_N2
(c) Secondary alcohol by S_N2
(d) Tertiary alcohol by S_N1

37. Consider the following reactions:

I. $CH_3-CH(CH_3)-CH(OH)CH_3 \xrightarrow{H^+/Heat}$ A (Major product) + B (Minor product)

II. A $\xrightarrow[\text{In the absence of peroxide}]{\text{HBr, Dark}}$ C (Major product) + D (Minor product)

The major products (A) and (C) are, respectively:
(a) $CH_2=C(CH_3)-CH_2CH_3$ and $CH_3-C(CH_3)(Br)-CH_2CH_3$
(b) $CH_2=C(CH_3)-CH_2CH_3$ and $CH_2(Br)-CH(CH_3)-CH_2CH_3$
(c) $CH_3-C(CH_3)=CH-CH_3$ and $CH_3-C(CH_3)(Br)-CH_2CH_3$
(d) $CH_3-C(CH_3)=CHCH_3$ and $CH_3-CH(CH_3)-CH(Br)-CH_3$

38. $RCH_2CH_2OH \xrightarrow{?} RCH_2CH_2CH_2NH_2$
Identify the sequence of the reagents in order to carry out the above conversion:
(a) (i) PBr_3 (ii) KCN (iii) $LiAlH_4$
(b) (i) PBr_3 (ii) KCN (iii) $NaBH_4$
(c) (i) HCN (ii) PBr_3 (iii) $LiAlH_4$
(d) (i) HCN (ii) $LiAlH_4$

39. Consider the following steps:
Step I: Formation of ethene by elimination of a proton.
Step II: Formation of protonated ethanol.
Step III: Formation of carbocation.
Arrange the following steps in the sequence in which they are involved in the mechanism of dehydration of ethanol:
(a) I → II → III (b) II → I → III
(c) II → III → I (d) I → III → II

40. **Assertion (A):** Alcohols do not react with NaBr, but when H_2SO_4 is added, they form alkyl bromides.
Reason (R): Protonation of the –OH group by H_2SO_4 converts it into the $-\overset{\oplus}{O}H_2$ group which has better leaving tendency.
(a) Both A and R are correct; R is the correct explanation of A.
(b) Both A and R are correct; R is not the correct explanation of A.
(c) A is correct; R is incorrect.
(d) R is correct; A is incorrect.

41. Consider the following reactions:

I. $C_2H_5OH \xrightarrow{(A)} CH_2=CH_2 + H_2O$

II. $H_3C-CH(OH)-CH_3 \xrightarrow{(B)} H_3C-CH=CH_2 + H_2O$

III. $H_3C-C(CH_3)_2-OH \xrightarrow{(C)} H_3C-C(CH_3)=CH_2 + H_2O$

Identify A, B and C in the given reactions:

	A	B	C
(a)	20% H_3PO_4, 358 K	85% H_3PO_4, 440 K	H_2SO_4, 443 K
(b)	85% H_3PO_4, 440 K	H_2SO_4, 443 K	20% H_3PO_4, 358 K
(c)	H_2SO_4, 443 K	85% H_3PO_4, 440 K	20% H_3PO_4, 358 K
(d)	H_2SO_4, 443 K	20% H_3PO_4, 358 K	85% H_3PO_4, 440 K

42. Which of the following option is/are true?
(a) $CH_3-CH=CH-CH_2OH \xrightarrow{PCC} CH_3CH_2CH_2CHO$

(b) 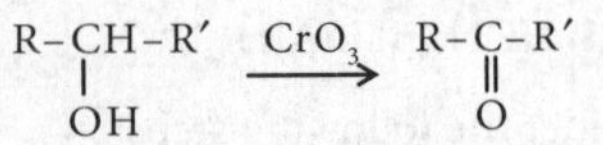

(c) 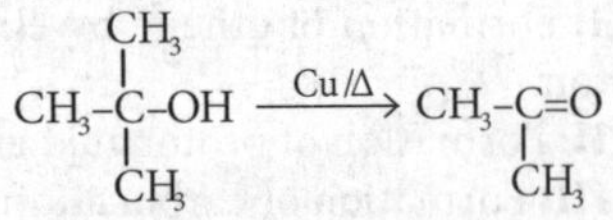

(d) All of the above

43. PCC is the:

(a) Complex of chromium trioxide with pyridine and HCl
(b) Complex of chromium trioxide with ammonia and HCl
(c) Complex of chromium dioxide with pyridine and HCl
(d) Complex of chromium dioxide with ammonia and HCl

44. Identify an appropriate reagent for the conversion of alcohol to carboxylic acid:

(a) PCC
(b) Anhydrous CrO_3
(c) Cu / 573 K
(d) $KMnO_4 / H^{\oplus}$

45. Regarding the given sequence of reactions:

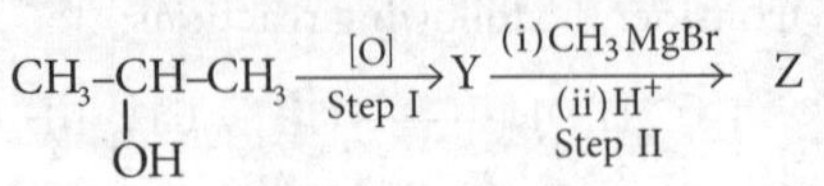

Choose the correct option from the following:

(a) Product Z is 2-methylpropan-2-ol
(b) Product Y is acetone
(c) Step II is nucleophilic addition followed by hydrolysis
(d) Step I is oxidation of alcohol into the corresponding carboxylic acid

(a) a, b (b) a, b, c
(c) a, b, c, d (d) b, c, d

46. Match the alcohols given in Column I with the product formed during their reaction with Cu/573 K in Column II and choose the correct option from the codes given below:

Column I (Alcohol)	Column II (Product)
A. 1° alcohol	a. Ketone
B. 2° alcohol	b. Alkene
C. 3° alcohol	c. Aldehyde

Codes

	A	B	C
(a)	c	a	b
(b)	b	a	c
(c)	b	c	a
(d)	c	b	a

47. $R-OH \xrightarrow{HX} R-X+H_2O$

In this reaction, the reactivity of hydrogen halide (HX) is in the order:

(a) HF > HCl > HBr > HI
(b) HI > HBr > HCl > HF
(c) HI > HCl > HBr > HF
(d) HBr > HCl > HI > HF

48. $R-OH+HCl \xrightarrow[K_1]{} R-Cl+H_2O$

$R-OH+HCl \xrightarrow[K_2]{ZnCl_2} R-Cl+H_2O$

K_1 and K_2 are the rates of these reactions. Now, the magnitudes of K_1 and K_2 follow the order:

(a) $K_1 = K_2$ (b) $K_1 > K_2$
(c) $K_2 > K_1$ (d) $K_2 = 2K_1$

49. Which of the following statements is correct for the Lucas reagent?

(a) Taking advantage of the relative reactivity of alcohols (3°>2°>1°) in reactions with HCl, the Lucas reagent can be used to identify 3°, 2° and 1° alcohols at room temperature.
(b) Alcohols with fewer than six carbon atoms are soluble in the Lucas reagent. But the R-Cl formed is insoluble in the Lucas reagent. Therefore, the mixture becomes cloudy.
(c) Since 3° alcohols are the most reactive, the solution turns cloudy quickly. In the case of 2° alcohols, cloudiness takes about five minutes to appear. On the other hand, since 1° alcohol is the least reactive, the solution remains clear at room temperature for a long time.
(d) All of these

50.

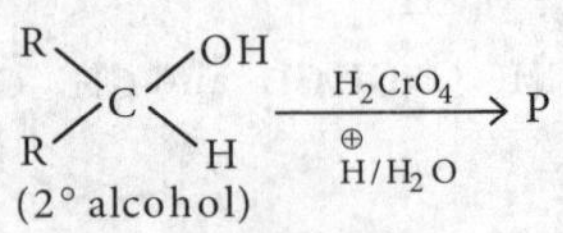

Which of the following statements is correct about this oxidation reaction?

(a) It stops at the ketonic stage. This is because further oxidation of ketone is difficult since it requires cleavage of the C–C bond.
(b) This oxidation goes all the way to RCOOH because oxidation of ketone is easy since it requires cleavage of the C–C bond.
(c) Both ketone and acid (RCOOH) will be formed in equal proportions.
(d) None of these.

51. **Assertion (A):** The dipole moment of phenol is smaller than that of methanol.
Reason (R): In phenol, the C–O bond is less polar whereas in methanol, the C–O bond is more polar.
(a) Both A and R are correct; R is the correct explanation of A.
(b) Both A and R are correct; R is not the correct explanation of A.
(c) A is correct; R is incorrect.
(d) R is correct; A is incorrect.

52. Which of the following is also known as wood spirit?
(a) Ethanol (b) Propanol
(c) Methanol (d) Butanol

53. $X + H_2 \xrightarrow[\substack{200-300\ \text{atm} \\ 573-673\ \text{K}}]{Y} CH_3OH$

What is X and Y in the given reaction?

	X	Y
(a)	CO_2	$ZnO-CrO_3$
(b)	CO	$ZnO-Cr_2O_3$
(c)	CO_2	$ZnO-Cr_2O_3$
(d)	CO	$ZnO-CrO_3$

54. Ethanol is commercially obtained by:
(a) Destructive distillation
(b) Fermentation
(c) Vacuum distillation
(d) All of these

55. $\underset{\text{(found in molasses)}}{\text{Sugar}} + H_2O \xrightarrow{X} \text{Glucose + Fructose}$

$\text{Glucose/Fructose} \xrightarrow[\text{(found in yeast)}]{Y} \text{Ethanol} + CO_2$

Select the enzyme used in the above reactions:
(a) X→ invertase, Y→ zymase
(b) X→ zymase, Y→ invertase
(c) X and Y→ invertase
(d) X and Y→ zymase

56. The action of zymase is inhibited during fermentation if the percentage of alcohol formed exceeds:
(a) 5% (b) 7%
(c) 10% (d) 14%

57. **Assertion (A):** A methanol poisoned patient is treated by giving intravenous infusion of diluted ethanol.
Reason (R): Ethanol reduces the action of the enzyme which converts methanol into toxic products, by competitive inhibition, thus allowing time for the kidneys to excrete methanol.
(a) Both A and R are correct; R is the correct explanation of A.
(b) Both A and R are correct; R is not the correct explanation of A.
(c) A is correct; R is incorrect.
(d) R is correct; A is incorrect.

58. I. Methanol is a colourless liquid and highly poisonous in nature.
II. Ingestion of small quantities of methanol can cause blindness and of large quantities can cause death.
III. Methanol is used as a solvent in paints and varnishes and is chiefly used in making formaldehyde.

Which of the following statement(s) is/are correct?
(a) Only I (b) Only II
(c) Only III (d) All of these

59. **Assertion (A):** Methanol poisoned patients are prone to blindness and death.
Reason (R): In the body, methanol is oxidised first to methanoic acid and then to methanol, which may cause blindness and death.
(a) Both A and R are correct; R is the correct explanation of A.
(b) Both A and R are correct; R is not the correct explanation of A.
(c) A is correct; R is incorrect.
(d) R is correct; A is incorrect.

PHENOL

60. Match the columns:

	Column I	Column II
A.	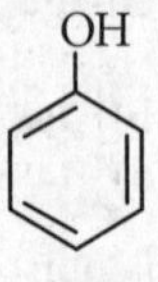	p. Quinol
B.	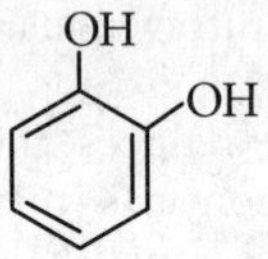	q. Phenol
C.	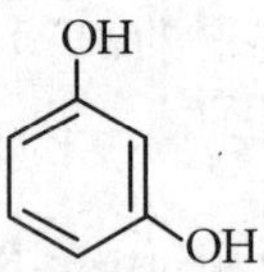	r. Catechol
D.	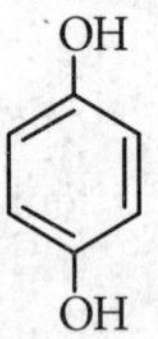	s. Resorcinol

(a) A – q, B – p, C – s, D – r
(b) A – r, B – p, C – s, D – q
(c) A – s, B – q, C – p, D – r
(d) A – q, B – r, C – s, D – p

61. Which of the following reagents can be used for the preparation of cumene?
(a) C_6H_6, $(CH_3)_3CH$, $AlCl_3$
(b) C_6H_6, $CH_3CH_2CH_2Cl$, $AlCl_3$
(c) C_6H_6, $CH_3CHClCH_3$, $AlCl_3$
(d) C_6H_6, CH_3CH_2Cl, $AlCl_3$
(a) (a) and (b) (b) (b) and (c)
(c) (a), (b) and (c) (d) (b) and (d)

62. Which of the following reactions will yield phenol?

(a) 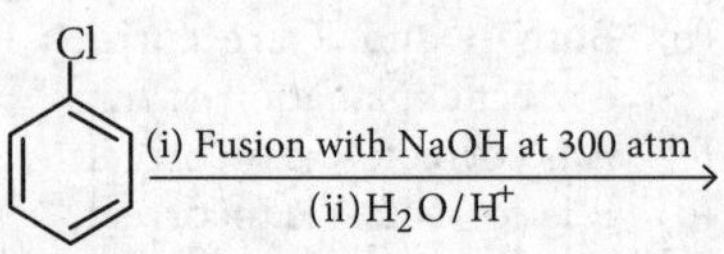

(b) 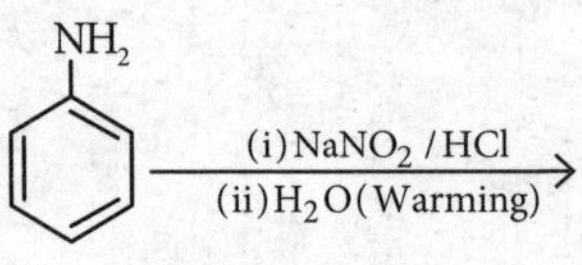

(c) 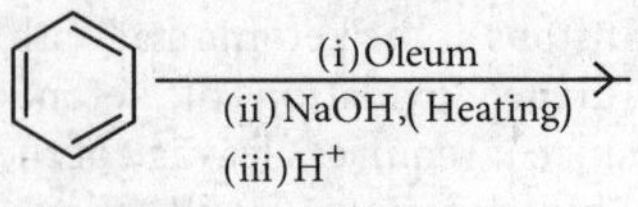

(d) 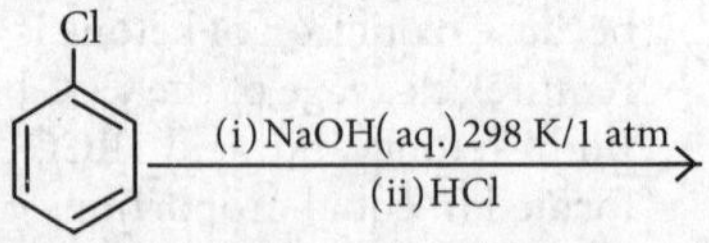

(a) (a), (b) and (c) (b) (a) and (c)
(c) (a), (c) and (d) (d) (b), (c) and (d)

63. Select the incorrect statement:
(a) o-Nitrophenol is steam volatile.
(b) o-Nitrophenol and p-nitrophenol can be separated by steam distillation.
(c) o-Nitrophenol has a higher boiling point than p-nitrophenol.
(d) o-Nitrophenol has higher vapour pressure than p-nitrophenol.

64. Which of the following would not produce phenol as the final product?
(a) Acidification of sodium benzene sulphonate.
(b) Hydrolysis of benzenediazonium chloride.
(c) Oxidation of toluene by hot alkaline $KMnO_4$.
(d) Dow process.

65. Choose the incorrect statement among the following:
(a) The properties of phenol are chiefly due to the hydroxyl group.
(b) The –OH group in phenol is involved in intra-molecular hydrogen bonding.
(c) Phenol is soluble in water.
(d) The boiling point of phenol is higher than that of haloarenes of comparable molecular mass.

66. When phenol is heated with $CHCl_3$ and alcoholic KOH, salicylaldehyde is produced. This reaction is known as:
(a) Rosenmund reaction
(b) Reimer–Tiemann reaction
(c) Friedel–Crafts reaction
(d) Sommelet reaction

67. In the given reaction:

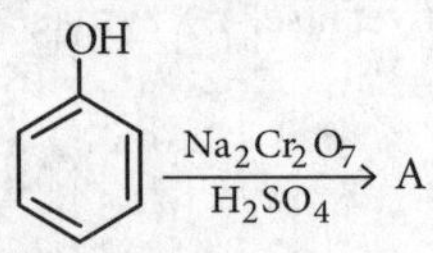

A is:

(a) 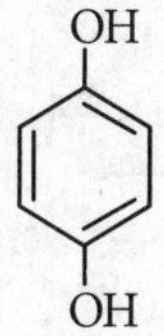 (b) 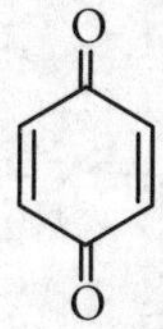

(c) 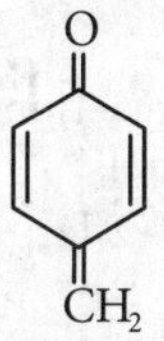 (d) 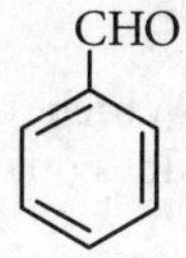

68. Identify which is/are the correct method(s) to synthesize phenol?

(a) 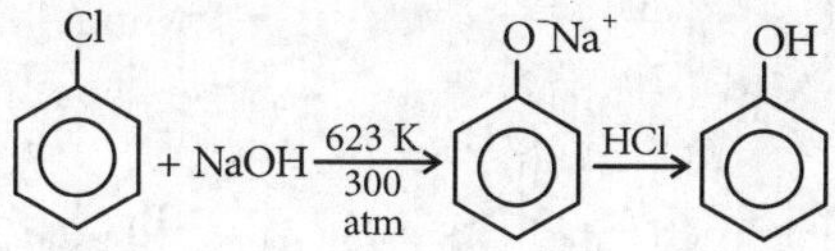

(b) 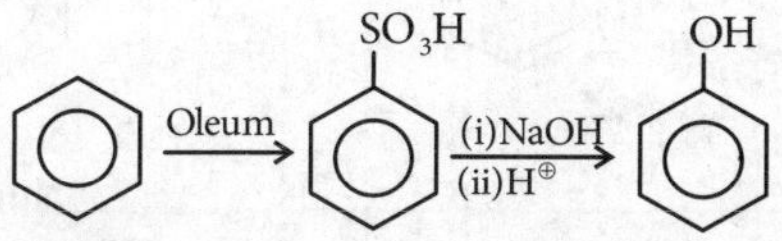

(c) 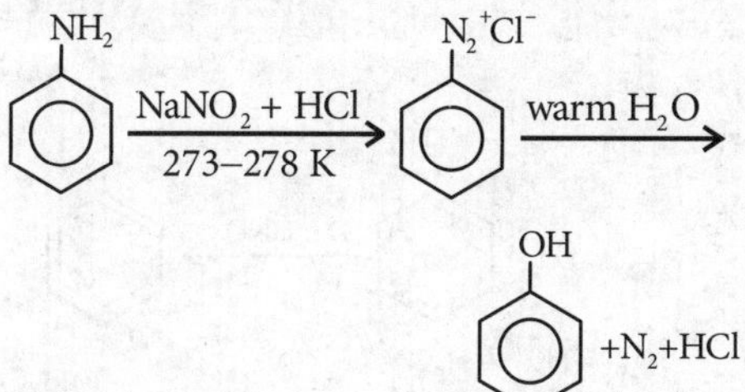

(d) All of the above

69. In the given reaction:

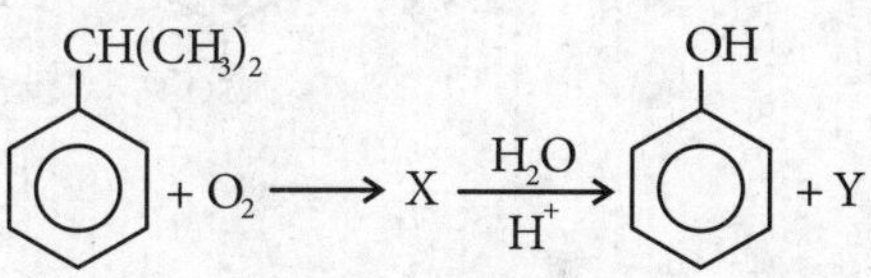

Choose 'X' and 'Y' for the reaction:

(a) 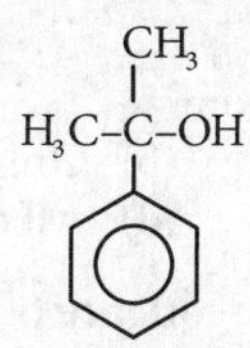 ; $CH_3CH_2CH_3$

(b) 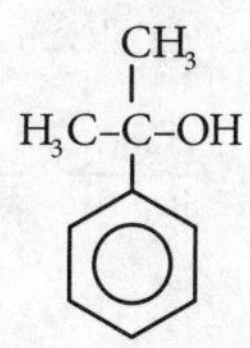 ; CH_3COCH_3

(c) 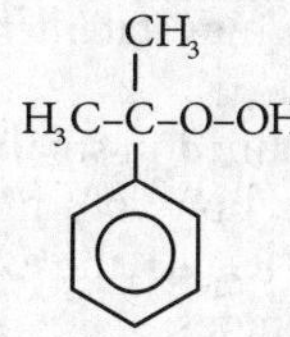 ; $CH_3CH_2CH_3$

(d) 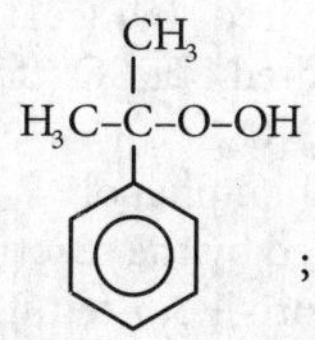 ; CH_3COCH_3

70. Cresols are less acidic than phenols because:

(a) Electron releasing groups favour the formation of phenoxide ion, resulting in decrease in acidic strength

(b) Electron withdrawing groups favour the formation of phenoxide ion, resulting in decrease in acidic strength

(c) Electron releasing groups do not favour the formation of phenoxide ion, resulting in decrease in acidic strength

(d) Electron withdrawing groups do not favour the formation of phenoxide ion, resulting in decrease in acidic strength

71. Electrophilic substitution reaction is given by the –OH group attached to the ring. It directs the incoming group at which positions of the ring?

(a) Ortho and meta

(b) Ortho and para

(c) Ortho, meta and para

(d) Meta and para

72.

Select the product(s) formed in the given reaction:

(a) 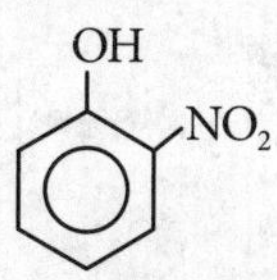 (b) 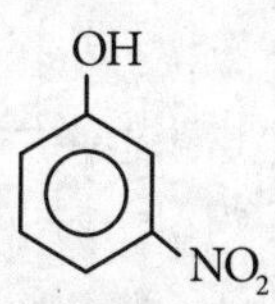

(c)  (d) Both (a) and (c)

73. Which of the following statements is false about picric acid?

(a) Picric acid is obtained in smaller quantity during the reaction of phenol with concentrated HNO_3 as the oxidised by-product predominates.

(b) It is also prepared by treating phenol with concentrated H_2SO_4 followed by concentrated HNO_3.

(c) It is less acidic than phenol.

(d) It can be obtained by the reaction of warm H_2O with 2-chloro-1,3,5-trinitrobenzene.

74. What is(are) the major product(s) formed by the mononitration of 3-methylphenol?

(a) 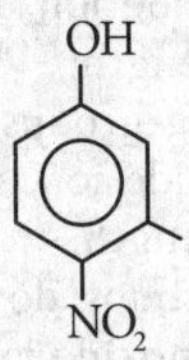

(b) 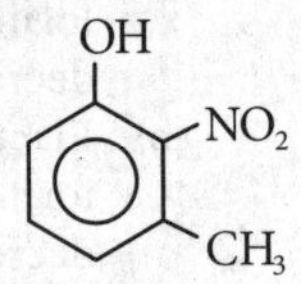

(c) 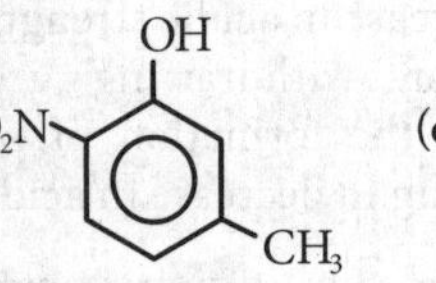

(d) Both (a) and (c)

75.

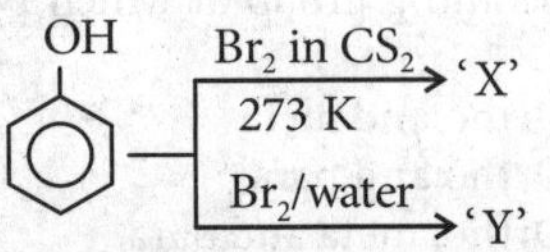

What are X and Y in the above reaction?

(a) X ⟶ 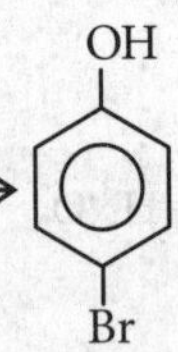 Y ⟶ 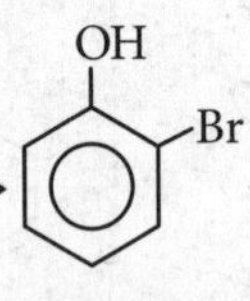

(b) X ⟶ 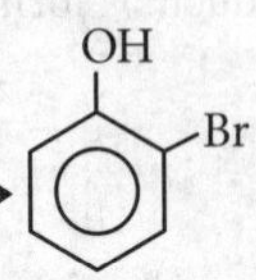 Y ⟶ 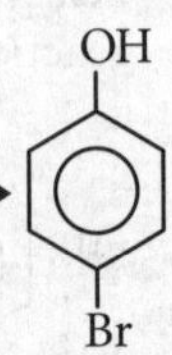

(c) X ⟶ 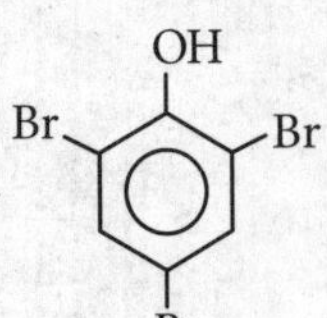 Y ⟶ 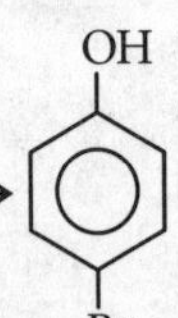

(d) X ⟶ 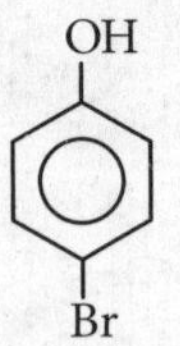 Y ⟶ 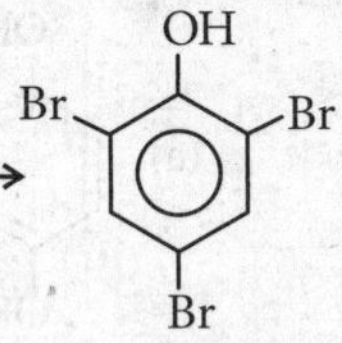

76. Which of the following reaction conditions does not hold good for phenols?

I. 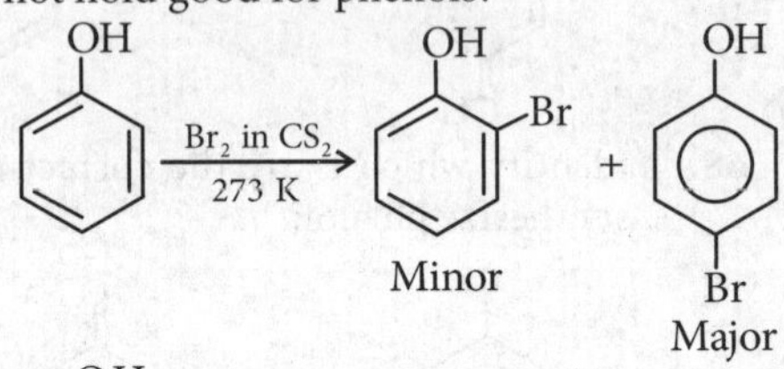

II. 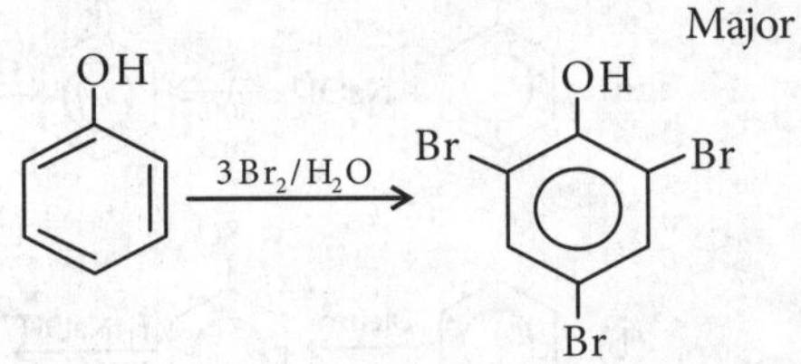

2,4,6-Tribromophenol (White precipitate)

$+ 3HBr$

III. 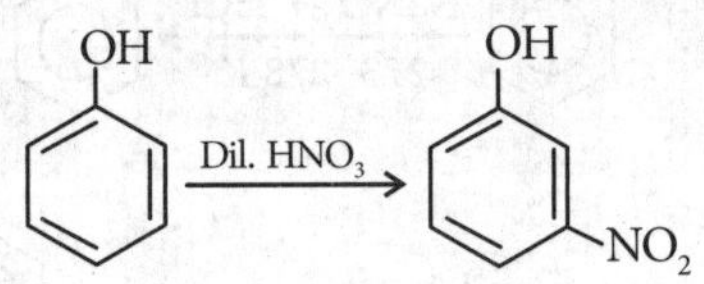

IV. 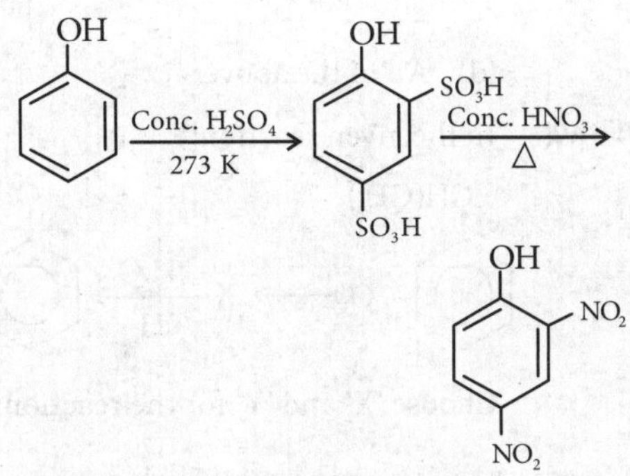

Choose the correct option:

(a) Only II
(b) Only III and IV
(c) I and II
(d) All of the above

77. Consider the following sequence of reactions:

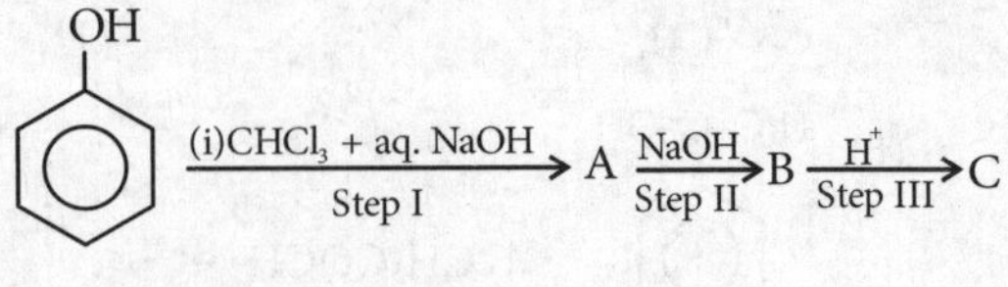

Choose the correct option:

(a) In Step I, the electrophile generated is dichlorocarbene.

(b) In Step II, the –CHO group is introduced at the ortho position of the benzene ring.

(c) Product C is salicylaldehyde.

(d) This reaction is known as Friedel–Crafts alkylation.

(a) a, b, c (b) a, b, c, d

(c) a, b (d) b, c

78. Select the incorrect statement about Kolbe's reaction:

(a) Phenoxide ion is less reactive than phenol towards electrophilic aromatic substitution

(b) A weak electrophile CO_2 is used in this reaction

(c) Ortho-hydroxybenzoic acid is formed as the main product

(d) Acetylation of the major product results in the formation of aspirin

79.

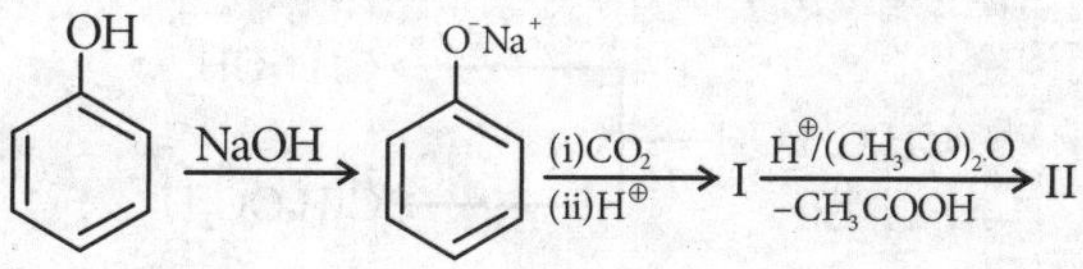

Identify I and II in the above reaction:

(a) (I) 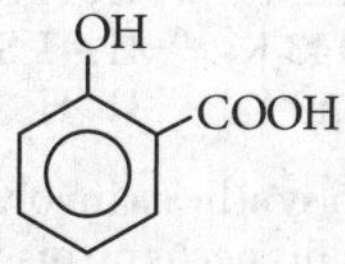 (II) 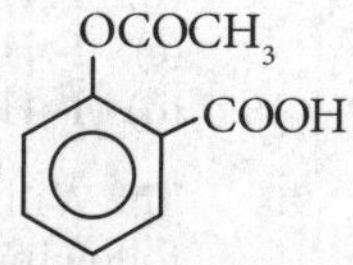

(b) (I) 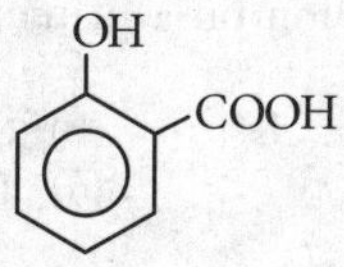 (II) 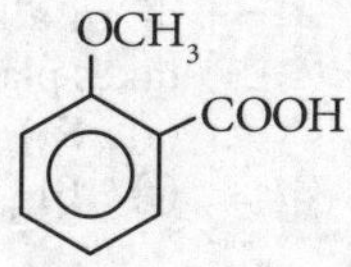

(c) (I) 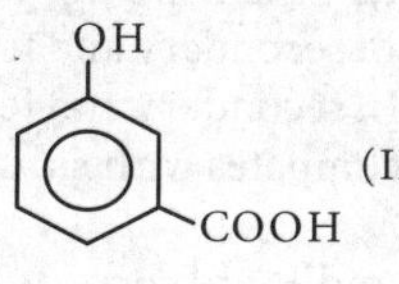 (II) 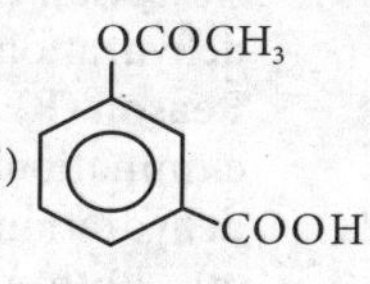

(d) (I) 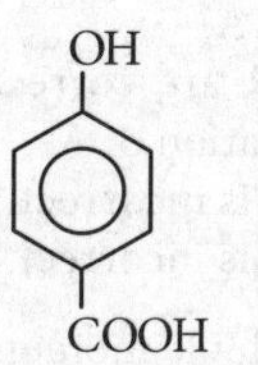 (II) 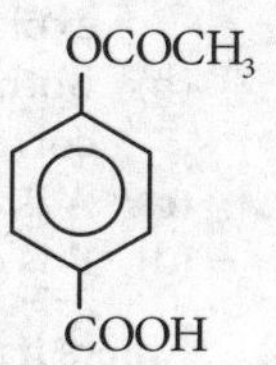

80. Choose the correct pair of reactions and their name:

(a) $CH_3CH{=}CH_2 + H_2O \overset{H^+}{\rightleftharpoons} CH_3\text{–}\underset{\displaystyle OH}{\underset{|}{CH}}\text{–}CH_3$;

(Anti-Markovnikov's electrophilic addition)

(b) 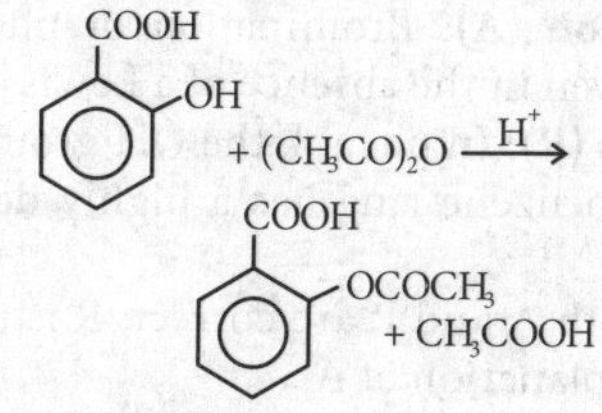

(Acetylation)

(c) 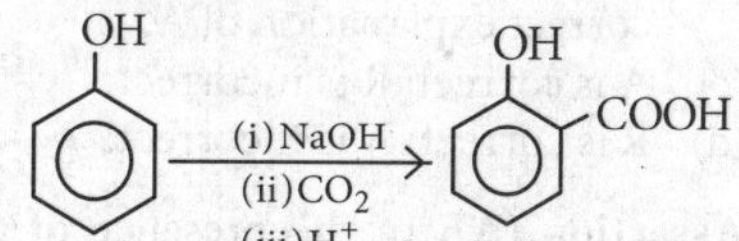

(Kolbe's reaction)

(d) 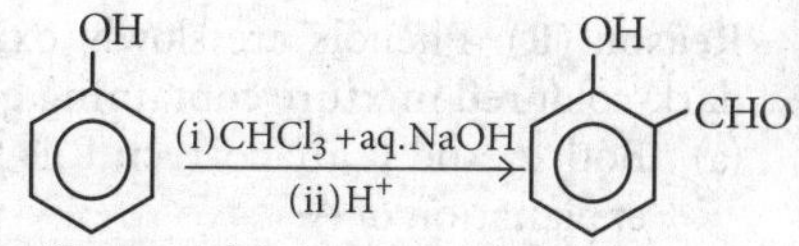

(Reimer–Tiemann reaction)

(a) a, b (b) a, b, c

(c) b, c, d (d) a, b, c, d

81. Phenols show the cleavage of the C–O bond with:

(a) Na (b) K

(c) Zn (d) Ca

82. Match the reactants and reagents given in Column I with the products given in Column II and choose the correct option from the codes given below:

Column I	Column II
A. 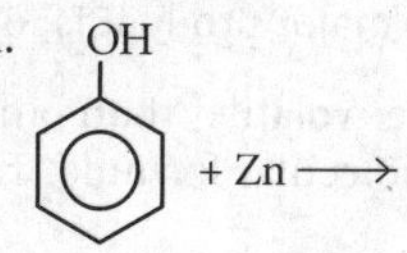	a. Benzene
B. 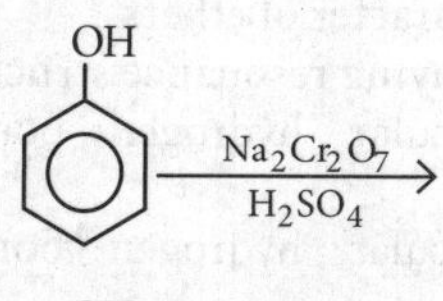	b. Salicylaldehyde
C. 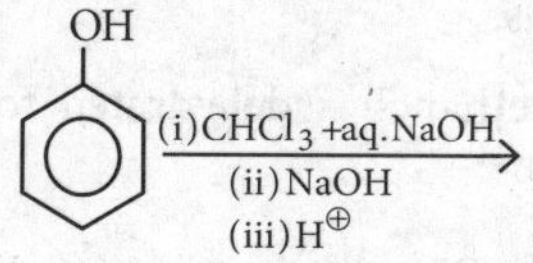	c. Benzoquinone

Codes

	A	B	C
(a)	c	a	b
(b)	a	c	b
(c)	a	b	c
(d)	c	b	a

83. **Assertion (A):** Bromination of phenol takes place even in the absence of a Lewis acid.
Reason (R): In phenol, the OH group attached to the benzene ring has a highly deactivating effect.
(a) Both A and R are correct; R is the correct explanation of A.
(b) Both A and R are correct; R is not the correct explanation of A.
(c) A is correct; R is incorrect.
(d) R is correct; A is incorrect.

84. **Assertion (A):** In the presence of air, phenol mixture becomes dark in colour.
Reason (R): Phenols are slowly oxidised to a dark-coloured mixture containing quinones.
(a) Both A and R are correct; R is the correct explanation of A.
(b) Both A and R are correct; R is not the correct explanation of A.
(c) A is correct; R is incorrect.
(d) R is correct; A is incorrect.

ETHER

85. In the Williamson synthesis, if tertiary alkyl halide is used, then:
(a) Ether is obtained in good yield.
(b) Alcohol is obtained in good yield.
(c) Alkene is the only major product.
(d) A mixture of alkene as a minor product and ether as a major product is formed.

86. An ether is more volatile than an alcohol having the same molecular formula. This is due to:
(a) Dipolar character of ethers.
(b) Alcohols having resonance structures.
(c) Inter-molecular hydrogen bonding in ethers.
(d) Inter-molecular hydrogen bonding in alcohols.

87. At 413 K, ethanol is dehydrated to produce ethoxyethane:

$$CH_3-CH_2-OH \xrightarrow[413\ K]{H_2SO_4} C_2H_5OC_2H_5$$

Read the statements given below, and choose the option containing the correct statements:
I. Such reaction is suitable for preparation of ethers having primary alkyl groups only.
II. The mechanism involves the following sequence: Protonation of alcohol → Attack of another alcohol molecule on the protonated alcohol → Deprotonation
III. At 443 K, the same reaction would produce ethene as the major product.
(a) I, II (b) II, III
(c) I, III (d) I, II, and III

88. Which of the following methods is used for the preparation of symmetrical and unsymmetrical ether?
(a) Williamson synthesis
(b) Reimer–Tiemann reaction
(c) Kolbe's reaction
(d) None of these

89. Identify the reaction condition for this reaction to occur:

$$CH_3CH_2OH \xrightarrow{I} CH_2{=}CH_2$$
$$CH_3CH_2OH \xrightarrow{II} C_2H_5OC_2H_5$$

(a) I→H_2SO_4, 443 K; II→H_2SO_4, 443 K
(b) I→H_2SO_4, 413 K; II→H_2SO_4, 413 K
(c) I→H_2SO_4, 443 K; II→H_2SO_4, 413 K
(d) I→H_2SO_4, 413 K; II→H_2SO_4, 443 K

90. The Williamson synthesis involves which of the following types of mechanisms when an attack of an alkoxide ion on a primary alkyl halide takes place?
(a) S_N1 (b) S_N2
(c) E1 (d) E2

91. **Assertion (A):** Ethers are not obtained during dehydration of secondary and tertiary alcohols.
Reason (R): In secondary and tertiary alcohols, elimination competes with substitution during dehydration.
(a) Both A and R are correct; R is the correct explanation of A.
(b) Both A and R are correct; R is not the correct explanation of A.
(c) A is correct; R is incorrect.
(d) R is correct; A is incorrect.

92. Ethers have a net dipole moment because:
(a) C–O bonds in ethers are non-polar

(b) C–O bonds in ethers are polar
(c) C–C bonds in ethers are polar
(d) C–C bonds in ethers are non-polar

93. Select the correct increasing order of boiling point:
(a) n-Pentane, ethoxyethane, butan-1-ol
(b) Ethoxyethane, n-pentane, butan-1-ol
(c) Butan-1-ol, n-pentane, ethoxyethane
(d) Ethoxyethane, butan-1-ol, n-pentane

94. The large difference in the boiling points of alcohols and ethers is due to the presence of:
(a) Van der Waals forces in alcohols
(b) Dipole–dipole interactions in alcohols
(c) Hydrogen bonding in alcohols
(d) Ion–ion interactions in alcohols

95. **Assertion (A):** An alcohol is more volatile than an ether having the same molecular formula.
Reason (R): There is intermolecular hydrogen bonding in alcohols.
(a) Both A and R are correct; R is the correct explanation of A.
(b) Both A and R are correct; R is not the correct explanation of A.
(c) A is correct; R is incorrect.
(d) R is correct; A is incorrect.

96. **Assertion (A):** 7.5 g of ethoxyethane and 9 g of butan-1-ol is miscible to almost the same extent while pentane is essentially immiscible with water.
Reason (R): Alcohols and ethers can form hydrogen bonds with the water molecule.
(a) Both A and R are correct; R is the correct explanation of A.
(b) Both A and R are correct; R is not the correct explanation of A.
(c) A is correct; R is incorrect.
(d) R is correct; A is incorrect.

97. **Assertion (A):** Cleavage of the C–O bond in ethers takes place under drastic conditions with excess of hydrogen halides.
Reason (R): Ethers are the most reactive among all the functional groups.
(a) Both A and R are correct; R is the correct explanation of A.
(b) Both A and R are correct; R is not the correct explanation of A.
(c) A is correct; R is incorrect.
(d) R is correct; A is incorrect.

98. The mechanism for the reaction of ether with concentrated HI is as follows:

Step-I

$$CH_3-\ddot{O}-CH_2CH_3 + H-I \rightleftharpoons CH_3-\overset{H}{\overset{|}{O^+}}-CH_2CH_3 + I^-$$

Step-II

$$I^- + CH_3-\overset{H}{\overset{|}{O^+}}-CH_2CH_3 \longrightarrow \left[I^{-}\text{---}CH_3\text{---}\overset{H}{\overset{|}{O^+}}-CH_2CH_3\right] \longrightarrow CH_3\text{–}I + CH_3CH_2\text{–}OH$$

Step-III

$$CH_3CH_2-\ddot{O}-H + H-I \rightleftharpoons CH_3CH_2-\overset{H}{\overset{|}{O^+}}-H + I^-$$

$$I^- + \overset{CH_3}{\overset{|}{CH_2}}-\overset{+}{O}H_2 \longrightarrow CH_3CH_2I + H_2O$$

Which of the following statement(s) is(are) true about the above mechanism?
I. The reaction takes place with HBr or HI because these reagents are sufficiently acidic.
II. Iodide is a good nucleophile. It attacks the least substituted carbon of the oxonium ion formed in Step I and displaces an alcohol molecule by the S_N2 mechanism.
III. When primary and secondary alkyl groups are present, it is the lower alkyl group that forms alkyl iodide (S_N2 reaction).

The correct choice is:
(a) I and II
(b) II and III
(c) I and III
(d) I, II and III

99. In the given reaction:

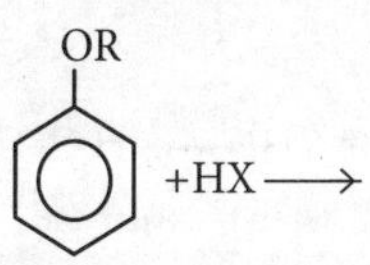

The product(s) is(are):

(a) 

+ RX

(b) 

+ RX

(c) 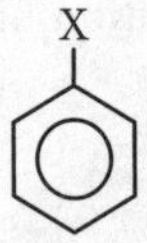 + ROH (d) 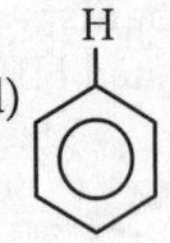 + ROX

100. The order of reactivity of hydrogen halides with ether is as follows:
(a) HBr > HI > HCl
(b) HCl > HBr > HI
(c) HI > HBr > HCl
(d) HCl > HI > HBr

101. The reaction of anisole with HI gives phenol rather than iodobenzene because:
(a) The bond between O–CH_3 is weaker than between O–C_6H_5
(b) The carbon of the phenyl group is sp^2-hybridized and has a partial double bond character
(c) Both (a) and (b)
(d) None of the above

102. **Assertion (A):**

$$H_3C-C(CH_3)_2-Br + \overset{\oplus}{Na}\overset{\ominus}{O}CH_3 \longrightarrow$$

$$H_3C-C(CH_3){=}CH_2 + NaBr + CH_3OH$$

Reason (R): Alkoxides are not only nucleophiles but also a strong base, so they can react with alkyl halide to form the elimination product.
(a) Both A and R are correct; R is the correct explanation of A.
(b) Both A and R are correct; R is not the correct explanation of A.
(c) A is correct; R is incorrect.
(d) R is correct; A is incorrect.

103. **Assertion (A):** Consider the reaction,

$$H_3C-C(CH_3)_2-O-CH_3 + HI \longrightarrow H_3C-OH + H_3C-C(CH_3)_2-I$$

Reason (R): The departure of the leaving group creates a more stable carbocation and the reaction follows the S_N1 mechanism.
(a) Both A and R are correct; R is the correct explanation of A.
(b) Both A and R are correct; R is not the correct explanation of A.
(c) A is correct; R is incorrect.
(d) R is correct; A is incorrect.

104. Anisole with hot HI gives:
(a) 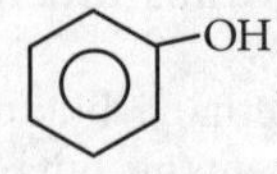 , CH_3–OH
(b) 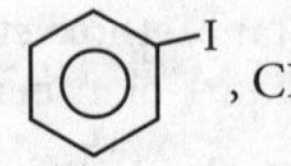 , CH_3–I
(c) 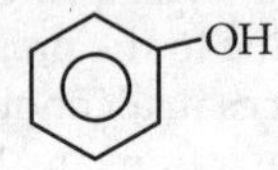 , CH_3–I
(d) 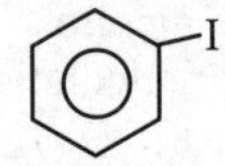 , CH_3–OH

105.

$$CH_3-CH_2-C(CH_3)_2-O-CH_3 \xrightarrow{H^{\oplus}/H_2O}$$

The product(a) is(are):
(a) $CH_3CH_2C(CH_3)_2OH$ only
(b) CH_3OH only
(c) Both $CH_3CH_2C(CH_3)_2OH$ and CH_3OH
(d) $CH_3-CH_2-O-C(CH_3)_2-CH_3$

106. Identify the minor products formed in the given reaction and choose the correct option from the codes given below:

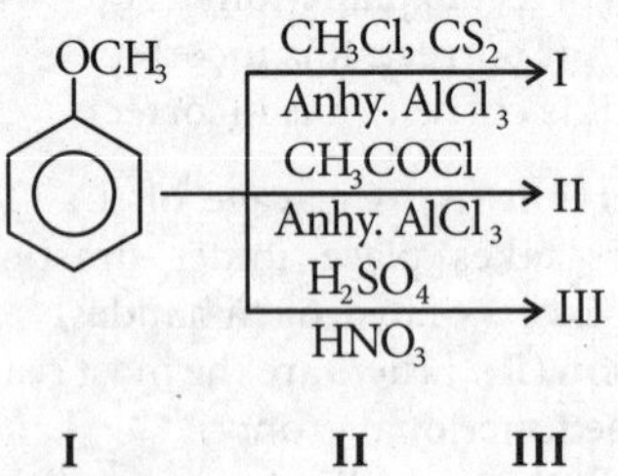

	I	II	III
(a)	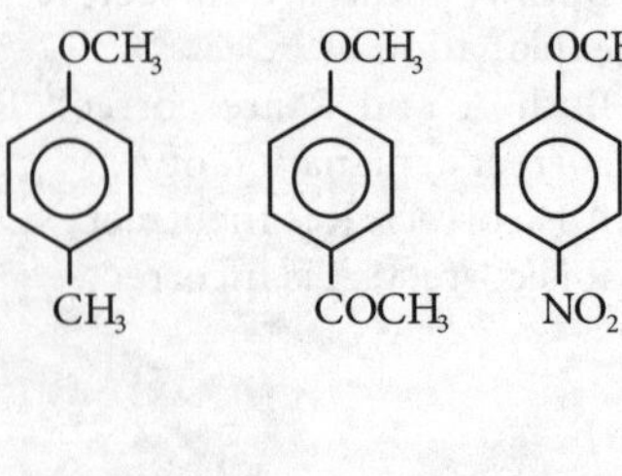		

(b) C–O bonds in ethers are polar
(c) C–C bonds in ethers are polar
(d) C–C bonds in ethers are non-polar

93. Select the correct increasing order of boiling point:
(a) n-Pentane, ethoxyethane, butan-1-ol
(b) Ethoxyethane, n-pentane, butan-1-ol
(c) Butan-1-ol, n-pentane, ethoxyethane
(d) Ethoxyethane, butan-1-ol, n-pentane

94. The large difference in the boiling points of alcohols and ethers is due to the presence of:
(a) Van der Waals forces in alcohols
(b) Dipole–dipole interactions in alcohols
(c) Hydrogen bonding in alcohols
(d) Ion–ion interactions in alcohols

95. **Assertion (A):** An alcohol is more volatile than an ether having the same molecular formula.
Reason (R): There is intermolecular hydrogen bonding in alcohols.
(a) Both A and R are correct; R is the correct explanation of A.
(b) Both A and R are correct; R is not the correct explanation of A.
(c) A is correct; R is incorrect.
(d) R is correct; A is incorrect.

96. **Assertion (A):** 7.5 g of ethoxyethane and 9 g of butan-1-ol is miscible to almost the same extent while pentane is essentially immiscible with water.
Reason (R): Alcohols and ethers can form hydrogen bonds with the water molecule.
(a) Both A and R are correct; R is the correct explanation of A.
(b) Both A and R are correct; R is not the correct explanation of A.
(c) A is correct; R is incorrect.
(d) R is correct; A is incorrect.

97. **Assertion (A):** Cleavage of the C–O bond in ethers takes place under drastic conditions with excess of hydrogen halides.
Reason (R): Ethers are the most reactive among all the functional groups.
(a) Both A and R are correct; R is the correct explanation of A.
(b) Both A and R are correct; R is not the correct explanation of A.
(c) A is correct; R is incorrect.
(d) R is correct; A is incorrect.

98. The mechanism for the reaction of ether with concentrated HI is as follows:

Step-I

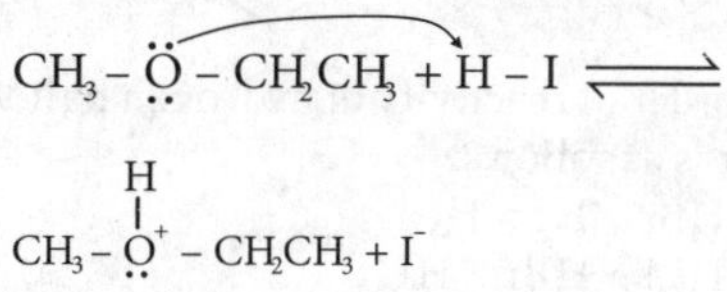

Step-II

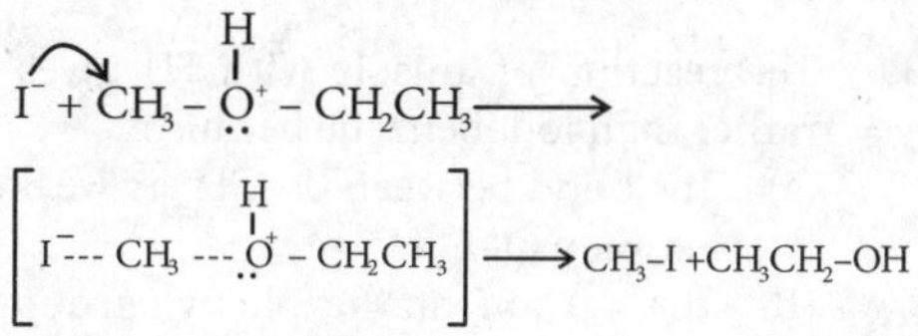

Step-III

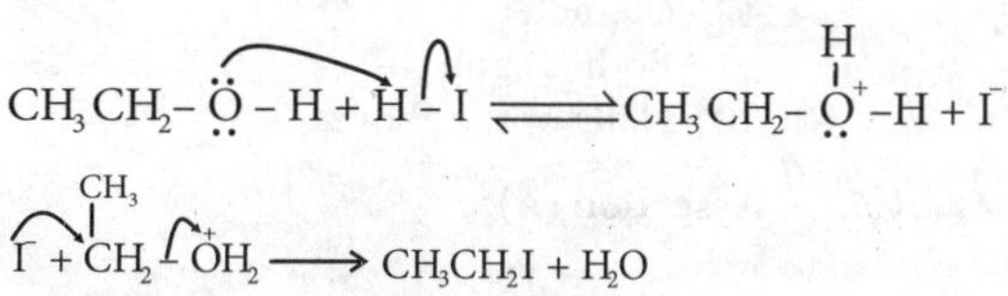

Which of the following statement(s) is(are) true about the above mechanism?
I. The reaction takes place with HBr or HI because these reagents are sufficiently acidic.
II. Iodide is a good nucleophile. It attacks the least substituted carbon of the oxonium ion formed in Step I and displaces an alcohol molecule by the S_N2 mechanism.
III. When primary and secondary alkyl groups are present, it is the lower alkyl group that forms alkyl iodide (S_N2 reaction).

The correct choice is:
(a) I and II
(b) II and III
(c) I and III
(d) I, II and III

99. In the given reaction:

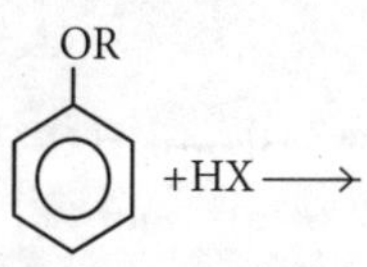

The product(s) is(are):

(a) 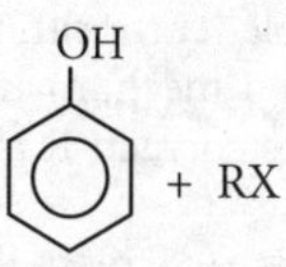

(b) 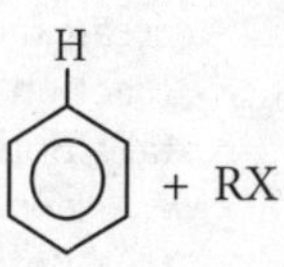

(c)  + ROH (d)  + ROX

100. The order of reactivity of hydrogen halides with ether is as follows:
(a) HBr > HI > HCl
(b) HCl > HBr > HI
(c) HI > HBr > HCl
(d) HCl > HI > HBr

101. The reaction of anisole with HI gives phenol rather than iodobenzene because:
(a) The bond between O–CH_3 is weaker than between O–C_6H_5
(b) The carbon of the phenyl group is sp^2-hybridized and has a partial double bond character
(c) Both (a) and (b)
(d) None of the above

102. **Assertion (A):**

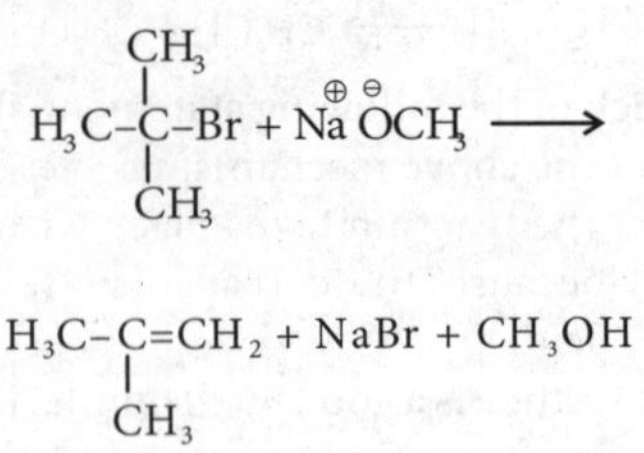

Reason (R): Alkoxides are not only nucleophiles but also a strong base, so they can react with alkyl halide to form the elimination product.
(a) Both A and R are correct; R is the correct explanation of A.
(b) Both A and R are correct; R is not the correct explanation of A.
(c) A is correct; R is incorrect.
(d) R is correct; A is incorrect.

103. **Assertion (A):** Consider the reaction,

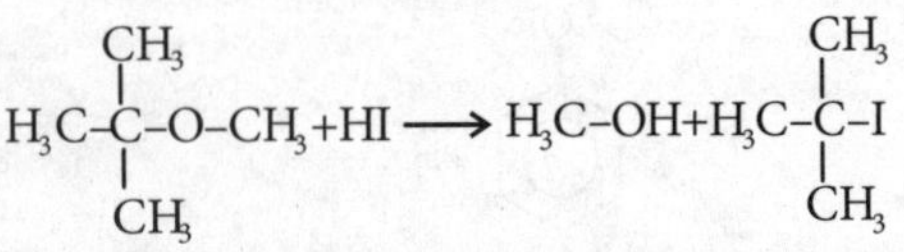

Reason (R): The departure of the leaving group creates a more stable carbocation and the reaction follows the S_N1 mechanism.
(a) Both A and R are correct; R is the correct explanation of A.
(b) Both A and R are correct; R is not the correct explanation of A.
(c) A is correct; R is incorrect.
(d) R is correct; A is incorrect.

104. Anisole with hot HI gives:
(a) 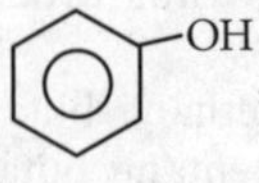 , CH_3–OH
(b) 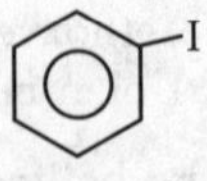 , CH_3–I
(c) 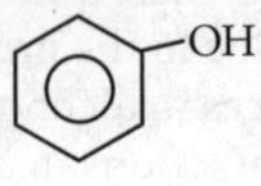 , CH_3–I
(d) 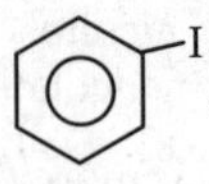 , CH_3–OH

105.

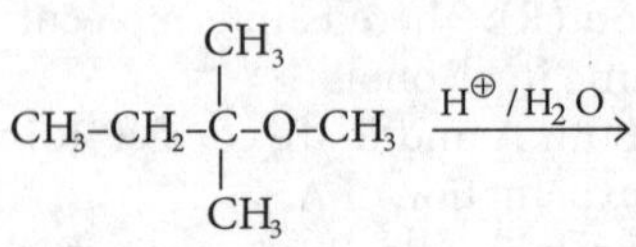

The product(a) is(are):
(a) $CH_3CH_2C(CH_3)_2OH$ only
(b) CH_3OH only
(c) Both $CH_3CH_2C(CH_3)_2OH$ and CH_3OH
(d) 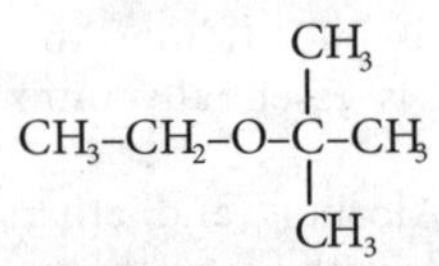

106. Identify the minor products formed in the given reaction and choose the correct option from the codes given below:

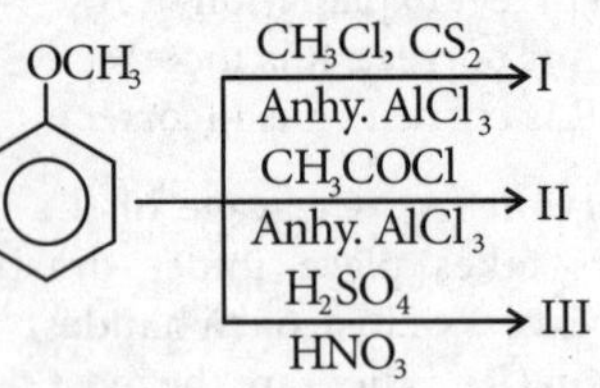

I II III

(a) 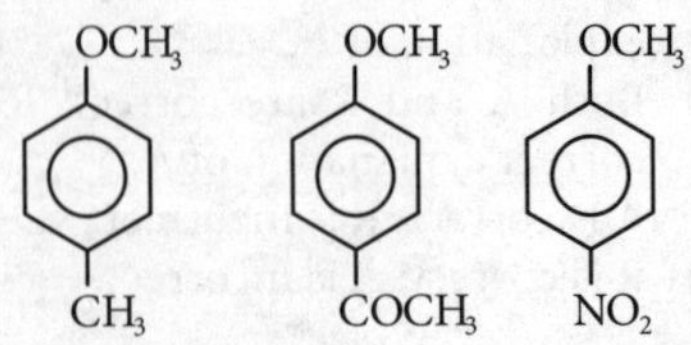

(b) 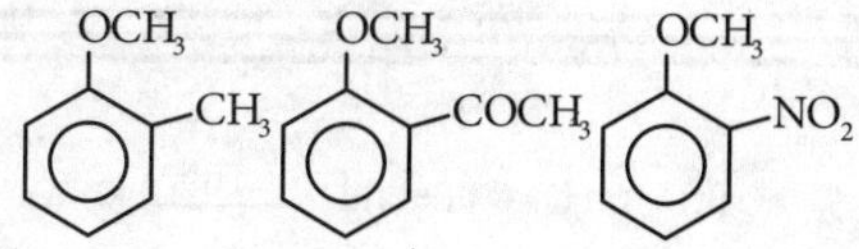

(c) 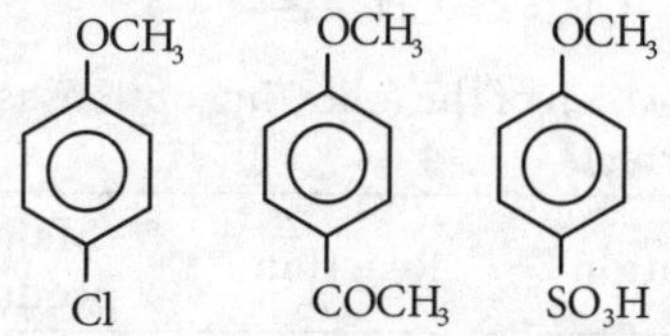

(d) 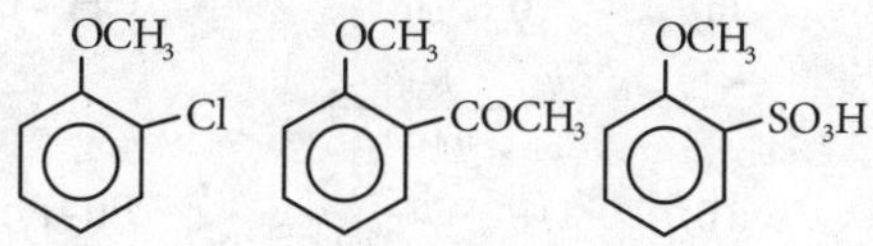

107. In the given reaction:

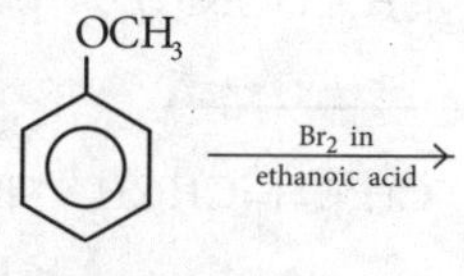

The product formed is:

(a) 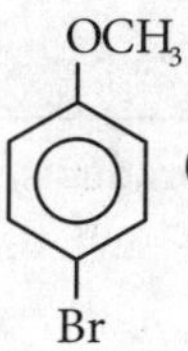 (90% yield)

(b) 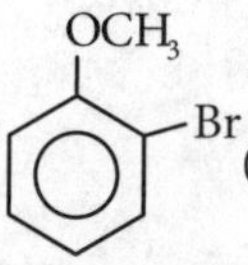 (90% yield)

(c) 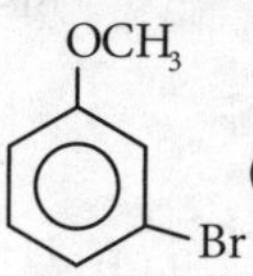 (90% yield)

(d) 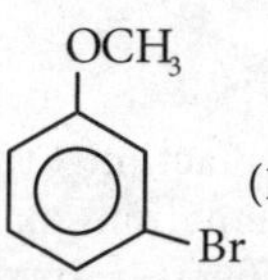 (10% yield)

108. Predict the major product of the following reaction:

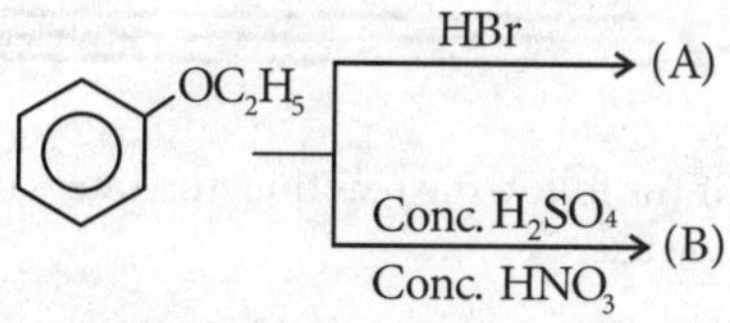

Choose the option with appropriate products from the codes given below:

(A) (B)

(a) 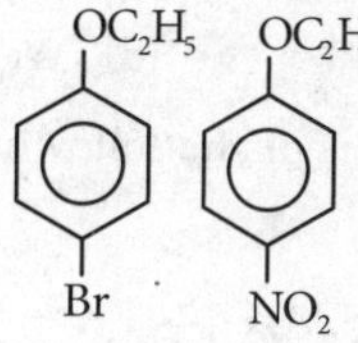

(b) 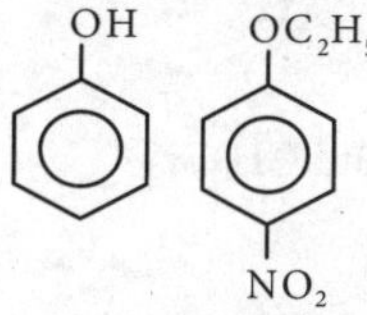

(c) 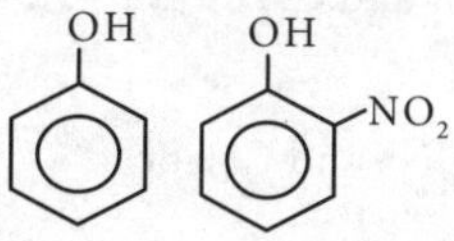

(d) 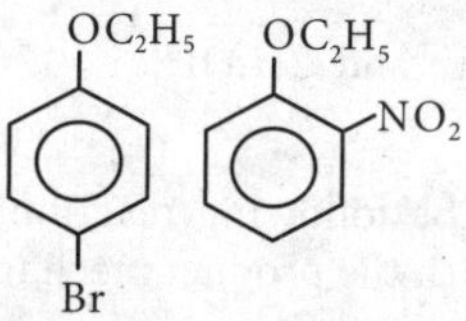

109. Consider the following statements:

I. Alcohols undergo dehydration in the presence of protic acids such as H_2SO_4, H_3PO_4.

II. Dehydration of alcohols is the best method for the preparation of unsymmetrical ethers.

III. Phenols can be easily converted into ethers by the Williamson synthesis.

IV. Ethers are used as industrial solvents for oils, resins, gum, etc.

Choose the correct option:

(a) Only I (b) III and IV

(c) I, III and IV (d) All of these

Level-2

1. For the following reaction, the rate will increase if we use:

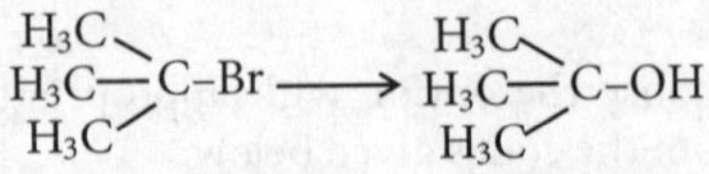

(a) Acetone (b) DMF
(c) DMSO (d) Water

2. For the formation of the following ether, the best set would be:

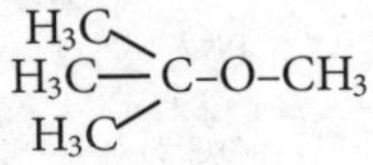

(a) 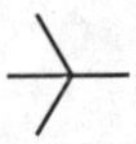 OH and CH_3Br

(b) 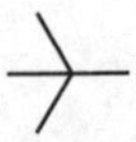 Br and $CH_3O^{\ominus}Na^{\oplus}$

(c)  ONa and CH_3Br

(d) 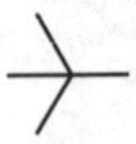 Br and CH_3OH

3. Which of the following reactions is correctly matched with the product mechanism?

(a)  Br + CH_3OH → 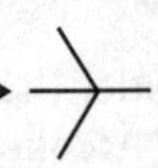 OH (S_N1)

(b) CH_3–I + aq. NaOH → CH_3–OH (S_N2)

(c) CH_3–OH + PCl_5 → CH_3–Cl (S_N1)

(d) CH_3CH_2–Br + NaI $\xrightarrow{\text{Acetone}}$ CH_3CH_2–I (S_N2)

4. Which of the following compounds will not produce methane on reaction with CH_3MgBr?

(a) $CH_3C{\equiv}CH$ (b) H_2O

(c) $CH_3-\overset{O}{\overset{\|}{C}}-CH_2-\overset{O}{\overset{\|}{C}}-H$ (d) 

5. Which of the following will produce 1-bromopropane as the major product?

(a) CH_3–C≡CH $\xrightarrow{\text{HBr}}$

(b)  $\xrightarrow{\text{HBr}}$

(c) CH_3–CH=CH_2 $\xrightarrow{\text{HBr}}$

(d) CH_2=C=CH_2 $\xrightarrow{\text{HBr}}$

6. In which of the following options is each match correct?

Option	Reaction	Major product	Name
(a)	CH_3–Br $\xrightarrow[Et_2O]{Mg}$	CH_3–CH_3	Wurtz reaction
(b)	Ph–Br $\xrightarrow[\Delta]{Cu}$	Ph–Ph	Fittig reaction
(c)	CH_3COONa $\xrightarrow{\text{Electrolysis}}$	CH_4	Kolbe's reaction
(d)	$CH_3CH{=}CHCH_3$ $\xrightarrow[Zn+H_2O]{O_3}$	CH_3CHO	Ozonolysis

7. Which of the following products will never be obtained in the given reaction?

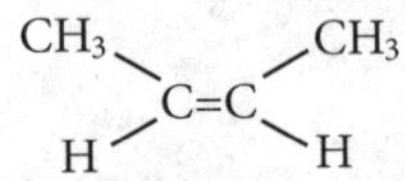 $\xrightarrow[\text{In NaCl}]{Br_2.H_2O}$

(a) 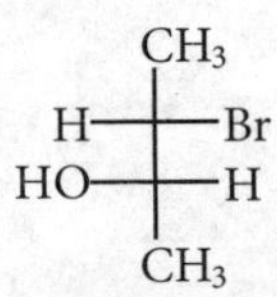 (b) 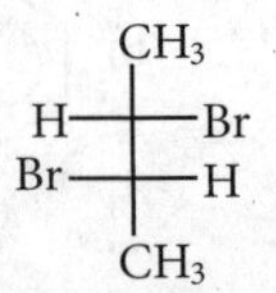

(c) 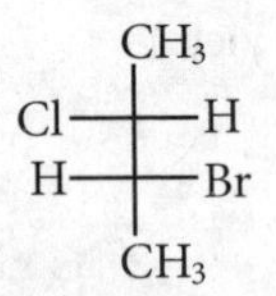 (d) 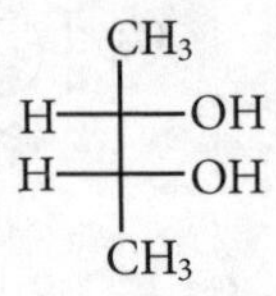

8. For the following reaction, the reactivity of reaction and orientation of product are controlled by which effects, respectively?

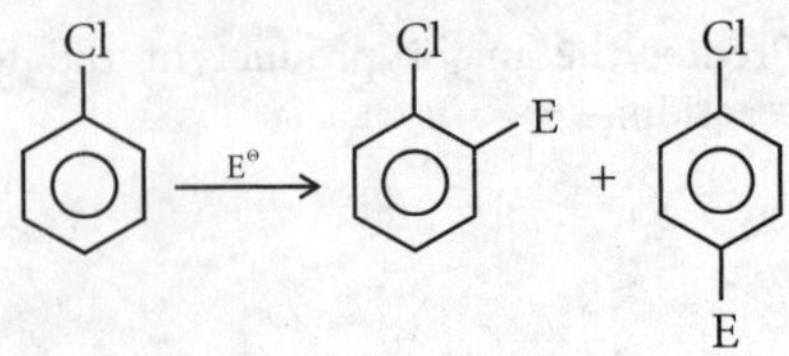

(a) Inductive, Inductive

(b) Resonance, Inductive
(c) Inductive, Resonance
(d) Resonance, Resonance

9. Which of the following is the most correct electron displacement for a nucleophilic reaction to takes place?

(a) 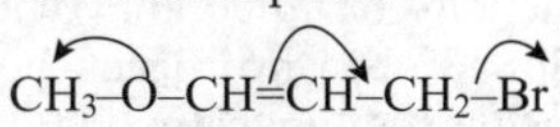

(b) 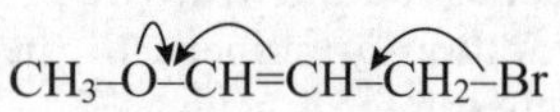

(c) 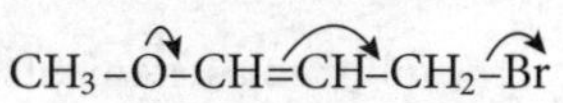

(d) 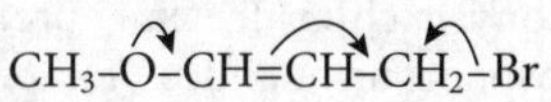

10. Which of the following sets is most appropriate to prepare 1-methoxy-4-nitrobenzene?

(a) 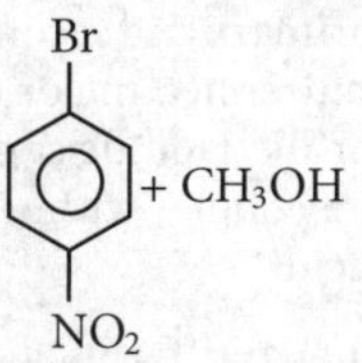
(b) 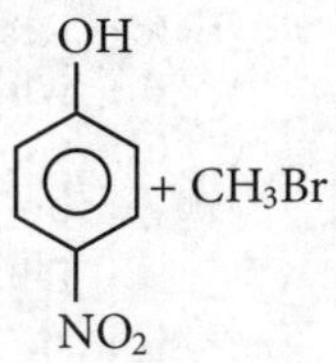

(c) 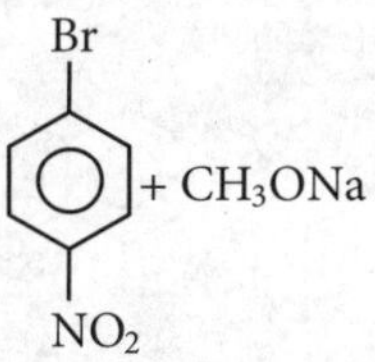
(d) 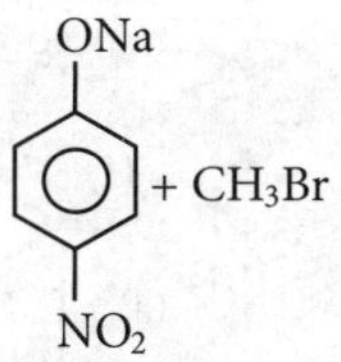

11. When t-butanol and n-butanol are separately treated with a few drops of dilute $KMnO_4$, the purple colour disappears and a brown precipitate is formed. Which of the two alcohols gives the above reaction?
(a) t-Butanol
(b) n-Butanol
(c) (a) and (b)
(d) None of the above

12. Which of the following is the correct method for synthesising methyl-t-butyl ether?
(i) $(CH_3)_3CBr + NaOMe \rightarrow$
(ii) CH_3Br + tert-BuONa $\rightarrow$
(a) (i)
(b) (ii)
(c) (a) and (b)
(d) None of the above

13. Which of the following will produce the same major product with HI and HI(excess)?
(a) CH_3–O–CH_3 (b) Ph–O–Ph
(c) CH_3–O–$C(CH_3)_3$ (d) CH_3–O–Ph

14. Which of the following acid derivatives will not produce acetyl chloride with PCl_5?
(a) Acetamide
(b) Acetic anhydride
(c) Methyl acetate
(d) Acetic acid

15. Monochlorination of toluene in sunlight followed by hydrolysis with aqueous NaOH yields:
(a) o-Cresol
(b) m-Cresol
(c) 2,4-Dihydroxytoluene
(d) Benzyl alcohol

16. How many compounds can be prepared by the Williamson ether synthesis in good yield?

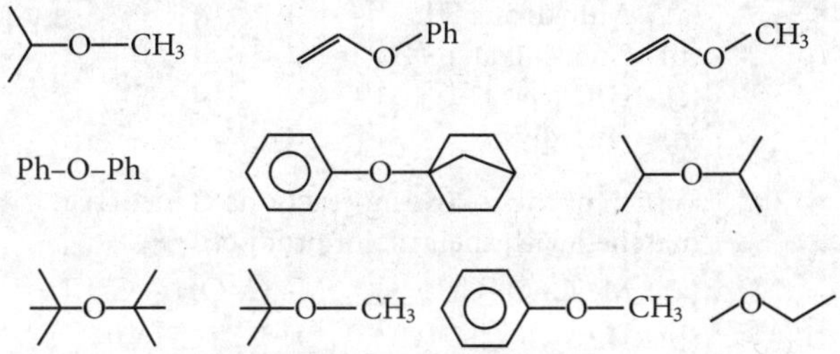

(a) 4 (b) 3
(c) 6 (d) 5

17. Among the given compounds, the correct dehydration order is:

(I) 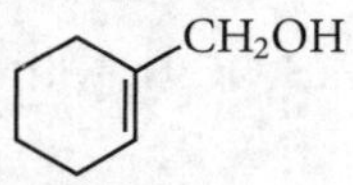

(II) 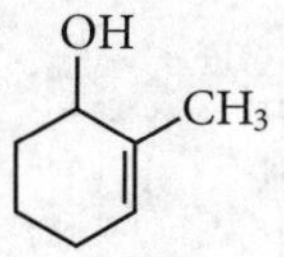

(III) 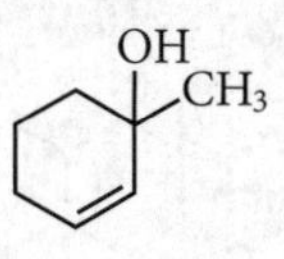

(IV) 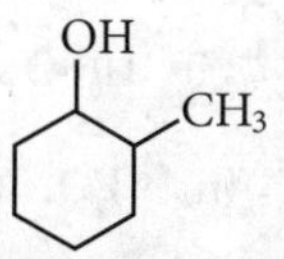

(a) I < II < III < IV (b) II < III < IV < I
(c) I < III < IV < II (d) IV < I < II < III

18. Among the following, which statement is correct?

(a) Sulphuric acid is used during the reaction of alcohol with KI to form R-I.
(b) The dipole moment of cyclohexyl chloride is less than that of chlorobenzene.
(c) Alcohols are insoluble in the Lucas reagent while their halides are soluble.
(d) Preparation of ether by acid dehydration of secondary alcohol is not suitable.

19. Which of the following reagents is correct for the given path and product?

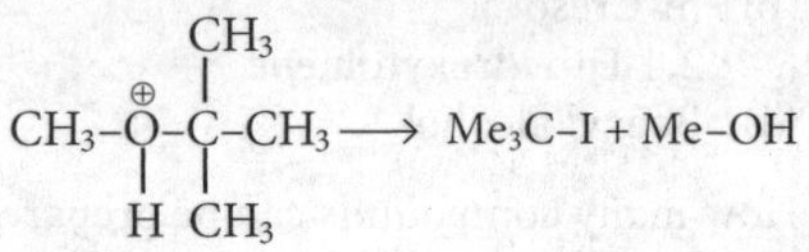

(a) Anhydrous HI
(b) Concentrated HI
(c) HI(excess)
(d) Hydrolysis

20. Which of the following reactions is incorrectly matched with their major product?
(a) $Me_3C-O-CH_3 \xrightarrow{HI} Me_3C-OH + CH_3I$
(b) $H_3C-O-CH_2-CH_3 \xrightarrow{HI} CH_3OH + ICH_2CH_3$
(c) 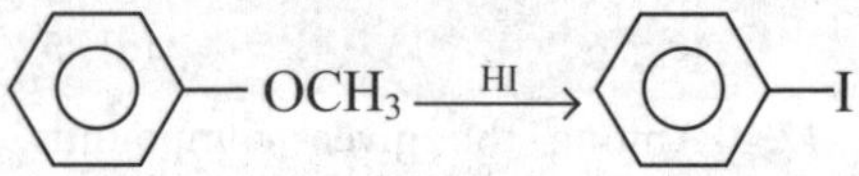
(d) All of these

21. The reaction of $CH_3OC_2H_5$ with concentrated HI mainly gives:
(a) $CH_3I + C_2H_5I$
(b) $CH_3OH + C_2H_5OH$
(c) $CH_3I + C_2H_5OH$
(d) $C_2H_5I + CH_3OH$

22. Which combinations of reagents cannot bring about the following conversion?

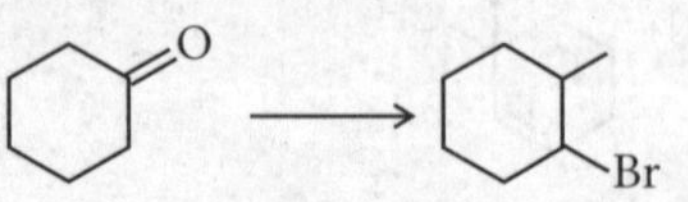

(a) (i) $MeMgBr/H^{\oplus}$ (ii) H_2SO_4/Δ (iii) HBr/H_2O_2
(b) (i) $MeMgBr/H^{\oplus}$ (ii) Al_2O_3 (iii) HBO (iv) $SOBr_2$
(c) (i) $MeMgBr/H^{\oplus}$ (ii) H_2SO_4/Δ (iii) HBr/CCl_4
(d) (i) $MeMgBr/H^{\oplus}$ (ii) $POCl_3$ (iii) B_2H_6 (iv) Br_2

23. Which of the following will produce a homologue of 2-butanol?
(a) Reaction of 1-butene with hydrogen bromide and hydrogen peroxide followed by sodium hydroxide.
(b) Reaction of propanone with methylmagnesium bromide followed by hydrolysis.
(c) Reaction of diborane with 1-butene followed by hydrogen peroxide and aqueous sodium hydroxide.
(d) Hydration of propene in the presence of dilute sulphuric acid.

24. Which of the following statements is incorrect?
(a) Thionyl chloride is preferred over phosphorous halides to prepare alkyl chloride from alcohol.
(b) Sulphuric acid can be used during the reaction of alcohol with KI.
(c) Reaction of primary and secondary alcohol with HCl requires heating or catalyst.
(d) Good yield of alkyl iodide can be obtained by heating alcohols with NaI in 95% phosphoric acid

25. Which of the following forms a di-iodide on reaction with HI(excess)?

(I) 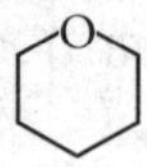 (II) 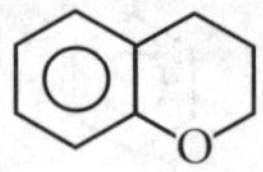

(a) I and II
(b) II only
(c) I only
(d) None of the above

26. The major product of the following reaction is:

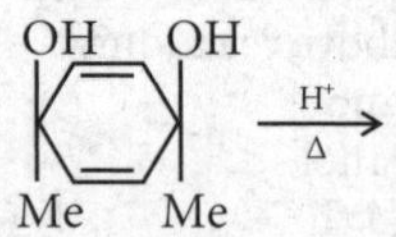

(a) 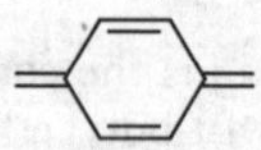
(b) 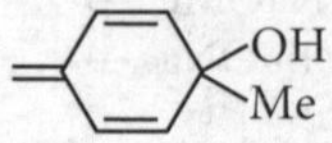
(c) 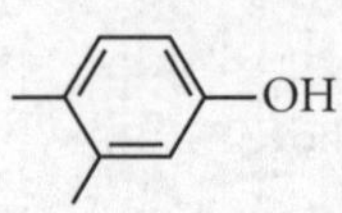
(d) 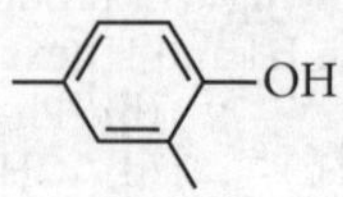

27. For the given diol, choose the correct option:

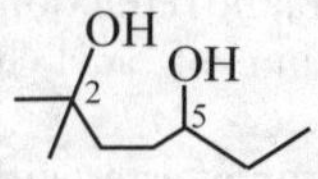

(a) OH at C_2 is more basic than C_5
(b) Compound can be cleaved by HIO_4
(c) Forms 6-member ring with H^+(1equivalent)
(d) OH at C_2 is more acidic than C_5

28. For the following reaction, the total number of α-H present in the major product is:

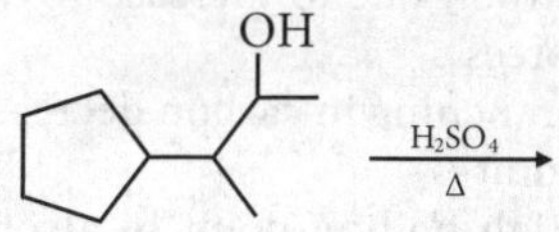

(a) 9 (b) 10
(c) 5 (d) 3

29. Which of the following reactions is not involved in the following sequence?

$$CH_3-CH_2-OH \xrightarrow{SOCl_2} P \xrightarrow[Acetone]{NaI} Q \xrightarrow{AgF} R \xrightarrow[\Delta]{EtO^-} S$$

(a) Swarts' reaction
(b) Williamson ether synthesis
(c) Finkelstein reaction
(d) Darzen process

30. Which of the following reactions will give the best yield of t-butyl methyl ether?

(a) $(CH_3)_3C-OH \xrightarrow[140°C]{H_2SO_4}$
(b) $(CH_3)_3C-Br + CH_3OH \rightarrow$
(c) $(CH_3)_3C-Br + CH_3\overset{\ominus}{O}\overset{\oplus}{Na} \rightarrow$
(d) $(CH_3)_3C-\overset{\ominus}{O}\overset{\oplus}{K} + CH_3Br \rightarrow$

31. Select the correct schemes A, B, C :
I. Acid-catalysed hydration
II. HBO
III. Oxymercuration–demercuration

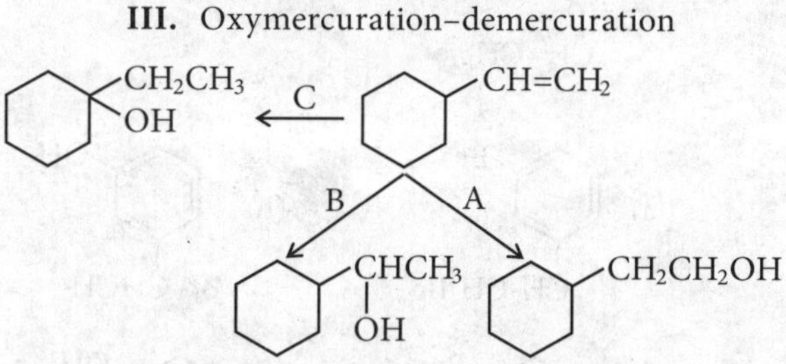

(a) I in all cases (b) I, II, III
(c) II, III, I (d) III, I, II

32. The major product in the following conversion is:

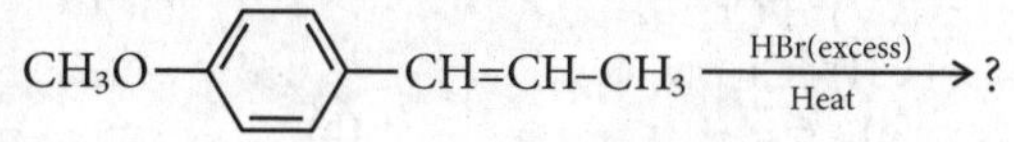

(a) 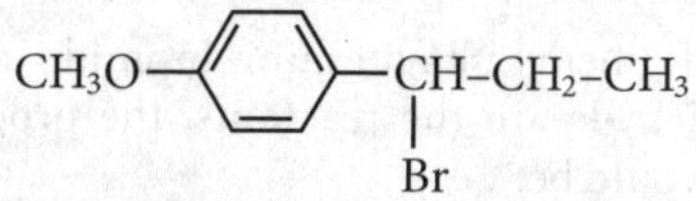

(b) 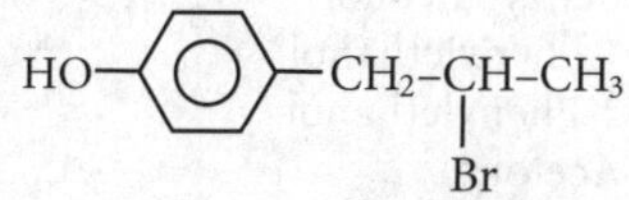

(c) 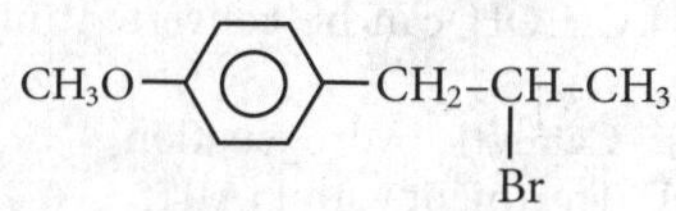

(d) 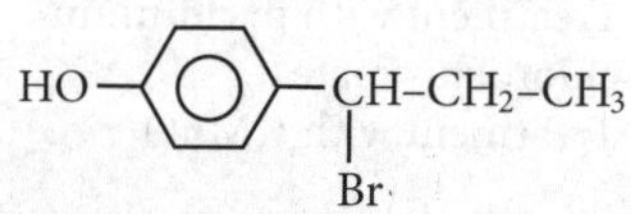

33. Allyl phenyl ether can be prepared by heating:
(a) $CH_2{=}CH-CH_2-Br + C_6H_5ONa$
(b) $C_6H_5-CH{=}CH-Br + CH_3-ONa$
(c) $C_6H_5Br + CH_2{=}CH-CH_2-ONa$
(d) $CH_2{=}CH-Br + C_6H_5-CH_2-ONa$

34. What is the correct order of reactivity of alcohols in the following reaction?

$$R-OH + HCl \xrightarrow{ZnCl_2} R-Cl + H_2O$$

(a) 1° > 2° > 3° (b) 1° < 2° > 3°
(c) 3° > 2° > 1° (d) 3° > 1° > 2°

35. 2-Methyl-2-hexanol can be prepared by:
(a) CH_3MgI and 3-hexanone
(b) C_2H_5MgI and 2-pentanone
(c) C_3H_7MgI and 2-butanone
(d) C_4H_9MgI and propanone

36. Which of the following is a benzylic alcohol?
(a) $C_6H_5-CH_2-CH_2OH$
(b) C_6H_5-OH
(c) $C_6H_5-\underset{CH_3}{\underset{|}{CH}}-OH$
(d) $C_6H_5-CH_2-\underset{CH_3}{\underset{|}{CH}}-OH$

37. The number of reagents that can be used for the following conversion is:

$$R-CH_2-OH \xrightarrow{?} R-CH_2-X \text{ (X is Halogen)}$$

(I) $HCl + ZnCl_2$ (II) HBr
(III) HI (IV) PCl_3
(V) PCl_5 (VI) $SOCl_2$
(VII) Cl_2
(a) 6 (b) 5
(c) 7 (d) 4

38. If phenyl magnesium bromide and formaldehyde are the reactants, the product formed would be:
(a) Benzyl alcohol
(b) 1-Phenylethanol
(c) 2-Phenylethanol
(d) Acetone

39. CH_3CH_2OH can be converted into CH_3CHO by:
(a) Catalytic hydrogenation
(b) Treatment with $LiAlH_4$
(c) Treatment with pyridinium chlorochromate
(d) Treatment with $KMnO_4$

40. Which will dehydrate at the fastest rate by H_3PO_4?
(a) 2-Methyl pentan-2-ol
(b) 3-Methyl pentan-2-ol
(c) Pentan-1-ol
(d) 2-Methyl pentan-1-ol

41. The functional group present in major product B is:

$$RMgX \xrightarrow[\text{(ii) HCl·H}_2\text{O}]{\text{(i) CH}_3\text{CN}} (A) \xrightarrow[\text{(ii)NH}_4\text{Cl}]{\text{RMgX}} (B)$$

(a) 1° Amine (b) 3° Alcohol
(c) 3° Amine (d) Alkene

42. The process of converting alkyl halides into alcohols involves:
(a) Addition reaction
(b) Substitution reaction
(c) Dehydrohalogenation reaction
(d) Rearrangement reaction

43. Compare the rate of reaction towards pinacol to pinacolone rearrangement:

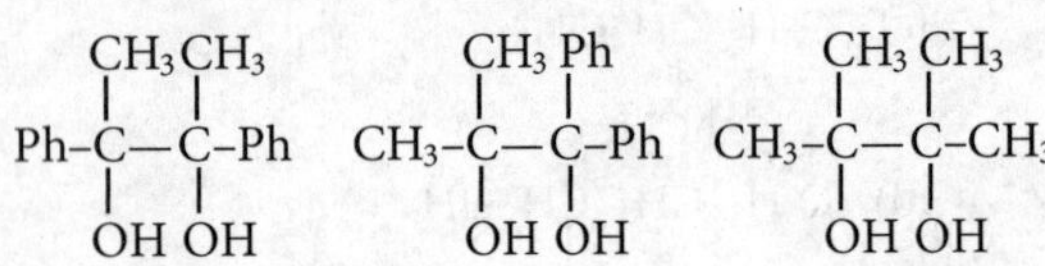

(I) (II) (III)

(a) II > III > I (b) III > II > I
(c) II > I > III (d) I > II > III

44. Which of the following reactions is called the Bouveault–Blanc reduction?
(a) Reduction of acyl halide with H_2,Pd/$BaSO_4$
(b) Reduction of ester with Na/C_2H_5OH
(c) Reduction of anhydride with $LiAlH_4$
(d) Reduction of carbonyl compounds with Na/Hg, HCl

45. Among the following, choose the incorrect statement:
(a) Boiling point increases with increase in carbon due to increase in Van der Waals forces
(b) Branching in carbon decreases the boiling point
(c) High boiling point of alcohols is mainly due to the pressure of intermolecular H-bonding
(d) Methoxymethane has a higher boiling point than ethanol and propane

46. The increasing order of boiling points for the following compounds is:

$\underset{\text{(I)}}{C_2H_5OH}$ $\underset{\text{(II)}}{C_2H_5Cl}$ $\underset{\text{(III)}}{C_2H_5CH_3}$ $\underset{\text{(IV)}}{C_2H_5OCH_3}$

(a) (III) < (IV) < (II) < (I)
(b) (IV) < (III) < (I) < (II)
(c) (II) < (III) < (IV) < (I)
(d) (III) < (II) < (I) < (IV)

47. Williamson synthesis of ether is an example of:
(a) Nucleophilic addition
(b) Electrophilic substitution
(c) Nucleophilic substitution
(d) Electrophilic addition

48. The major product of the following reaction is:

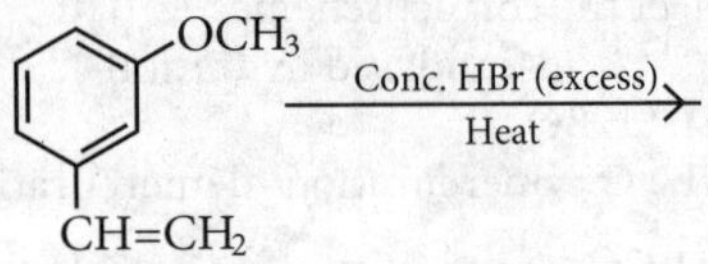

(a) 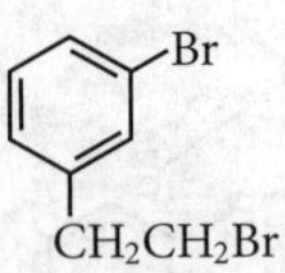
(b) 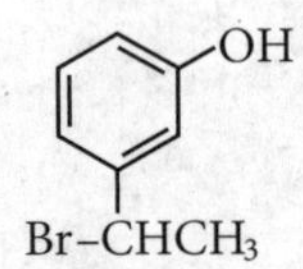
(c) 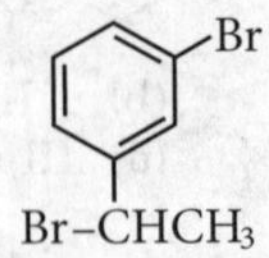
(d) 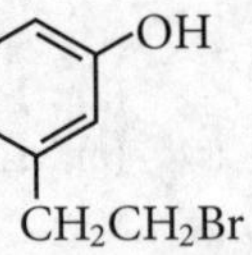

49. The major product of the following reaction is:

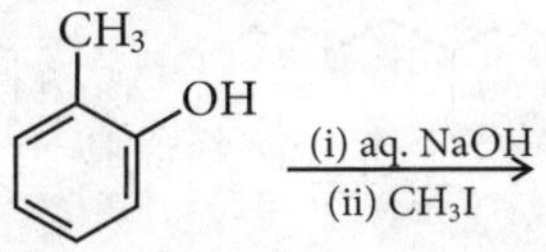

(a) 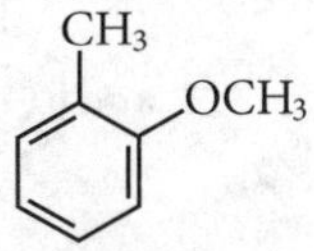 (b) 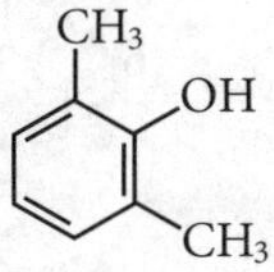

(c) 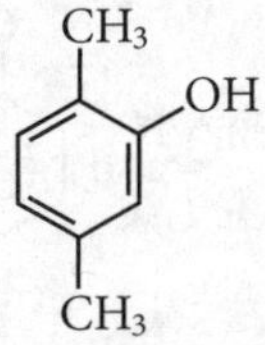 (d) 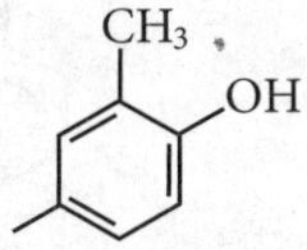

50. Which of the following orders is incorrect:
(a) $CH_3-CH_2-OH > CH_3-CH_2-CH_2-OH > CH_3-CH_2-CH_2-CH_2-OH$ (Solubility in H_2O)
(b) $CH_3-CH_2-OH > CH_3-O-CH_3 > CH_3-CH_2-CH_3$ (Boiling point)
(c) Pentan-1-ol > Pentanal > Ethoxyethane (Boiling point)
(d) $CH_3-OH > CH_3-CH_2-OH > CH_3-CH_2-CH_2-OH$ (Boiling point)

51. Ethoxyethane and butan-1-ol are miscible to almost the same extent (7.5 and 9 g per 100 ml water) because:
(a) Same molecular mass
(b) They are isomers
(c) Both can form hydrogen bonds with water
(d) Water is a universal solvent

52. Which of the following will not give immediate turbidity with the Lucas reagent?
(a) $Ph-CH_2-OH$ (b) $(CH_3)_3C-OH$
(c) 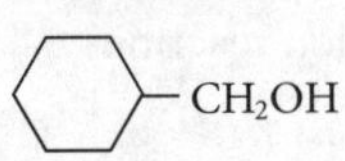 (d) 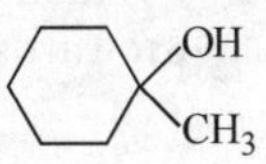

53. In the given reaction (X) and (Y) are, respectively:

$$CH_3-\underset{CH_3}{\overset{CH_3}{\underset{|}{\overset{|}{C}}}}-O-CH_2-CH_3 \xrightarrow[\text{(1 eq.)}]{HI} X + Y$$

(a) $CH_3-\underset{CH_3}{\overset{CH_3}{\underset{|}{\overset{|}{C}}}}-OH$ and CH_3-CH_2-OH

(b) $CH_3-\underset{CH_3}{\overset{CH_3}{\underset{|}{\overset{|}{C}}}}-OH$ and CH_3-CH_2-I

(c) $CH_3-\underset{CH_3}{\overset{CH_3}{\underset{|}{\overset{|}{C}}}}-I$ and CH_3-CH_2-OH

(d) $CH_3-\underset{CH_3}{\overset{CH_3}{\underset{|}{\overset{|}{C}}}}-I$ and CH_3-CH_2-I

54. The Lucas test is used to make a distinction between 1°, 2° and 3° alcohols. Choose the incorrect option:

$$ROH + \underset{\text{conc.}}{HCl} \xrightarrow{\text{Anhydrous } ZnCl_2} \underset{\text{White turbidity}}{RCl\downarrow} + H_2O$$

(a) Tertiary alcohols produce turbidity immediately and follow the S_N1 mechanism
(b) The greater the value of pKa (alcohol), the lower the reactivity with concentrated HCl
(c) RCl is immiscible in the Lucas reagent and produces white turbidity in solution
(d) Primary alcohols do not produce turbidity at room temperature and they follow the S_N2 mechanism

55. Consider the following groups. The order of leaving group nature is:
(I) –OAc (II) –OMe
(III) $-OSO_2Me$ (IV) $-OSO_2CF_3$
(a) I > II > III > IV
(b) IV > III > I > II
(c) III > II > I > IV
(d) II > III > IV > I

56. For the reaction sequence, choose the incorrect option:

$$CaC_2 \xrightarrow{H_2O} P \xrightarrow[Hg^{+2}]{\text{dil. } H_2SO_4} Q \xrightarrow[Ni]{H_2} R$$

(a) P and R can be differentiated by bromine water test and Tollens' test

(b) R on reaction with sulphuric acid at 453 K produces ethene
(c) Both P and R produce hydrogen gas with sodium metal
(d) Q is more reactive than P for catalytic hydrogenation reaction

57. Which of the following cannot be used to convert RCHO into RCH_2OH?
(a) H_2/Pd (b) $LiAlH_4$
(c) $NaBH_4$ (d) RMgX

58. Which of the following reactions gives primary alcohol?
(a) $CH_3-CH=O \xrightarrow[(2)\ H_3O^{\oplus}]{(1)\ CH_3MgBr}$
(b) $CH_3-CH=CH_2 \xrightarrow[(2)\ NaBH_4]{(1)\ (CH_3COO)_2Hg,\ H_2O}$
(c) $CH_3-CH=CH-CH_3 \xrightarrow[(2)\ H_2O_2/\overset{\ominus}{O}H(aq.)]{(1)\ BH_3,THF}$
(d) 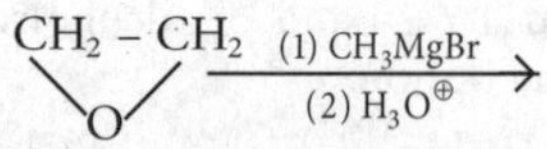

59. When ethyl bromide is treated with moist Ag_2O, the main product is:
(a) Ethyl ether (b) Ethanol
(c) Ethoxyethane (d) All of these

60. The reactants required to prepare 2-methoxy-2-methyl propane using the Williamson ether synthesis are:
(a) 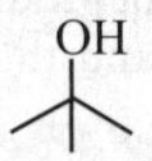 + CH_3–OH
(b)  + CH_3ONa
(c) 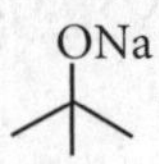 + CH_3–I
(d) 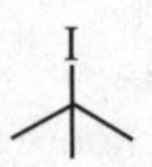 + CH_3OH

61. In the following reaction sequence, the structures of A and B will be:

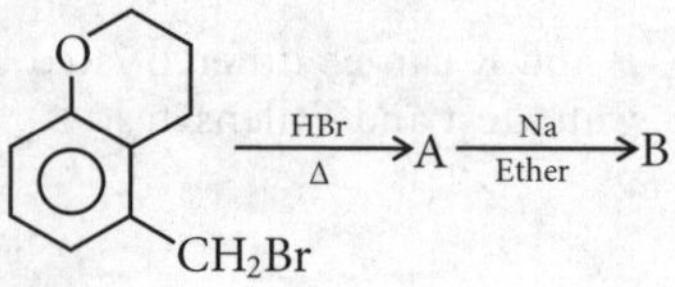

(a) 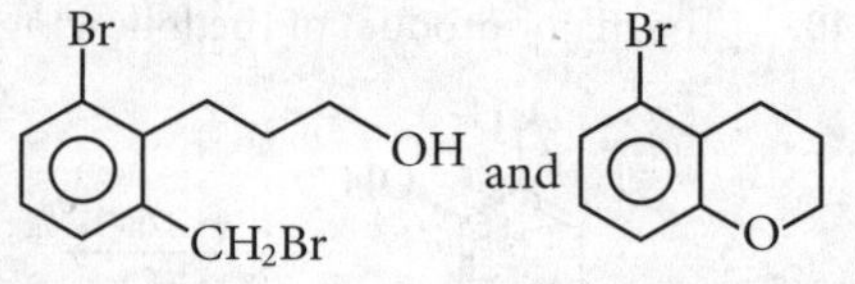
(b) 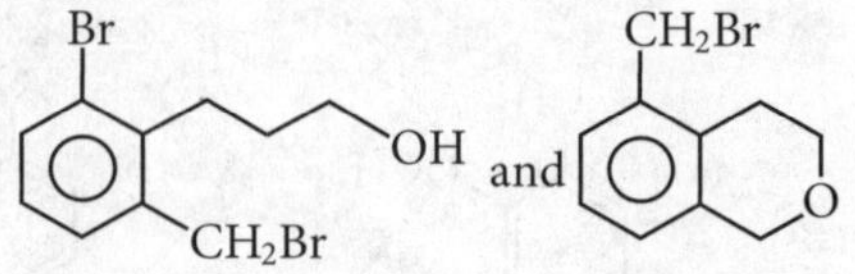
(c) 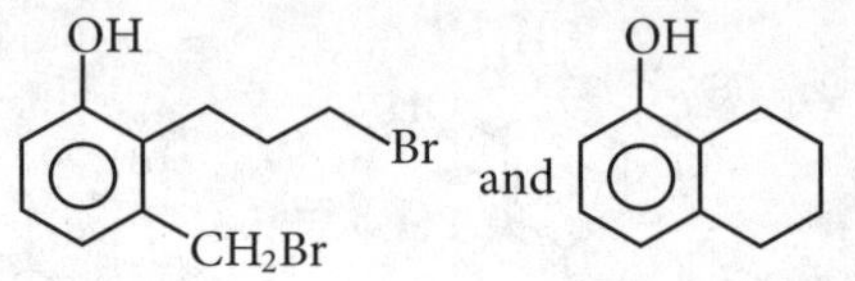
(d) 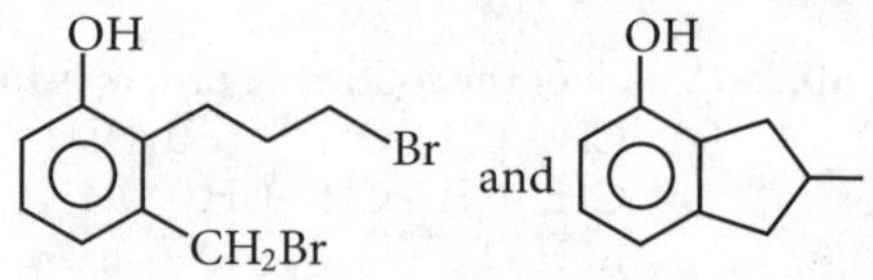

62. Among the following, choose the incorrect option:
(a) Tertiary alcohol will give immediate turbidity of the halide in the Lucas reagent.
(b) Reaction of R–OH with $SOCl_2$ in the presence of pyridine follows the S_N1 mechanism.
(c) Tertiary radical can show disproportion reaction and produce alkane and alkene.
(d) Iodine radical is more stable than chlorine radical.

63. When ethyl bromide is treated with dry Ag_2O, the main product is:
(a) Ethyl ether (b) Ethanol
(c) Ethoxyethane (d) All of these

64. Which one of the following is more reactive towards dehydration reaction?
(a) 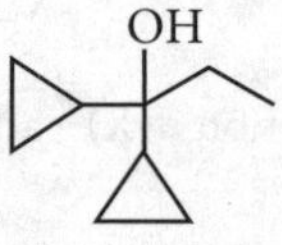 (b) 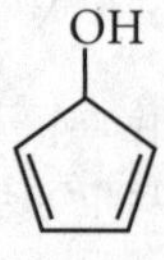
(c) 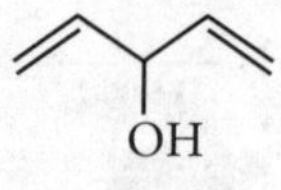 (d) 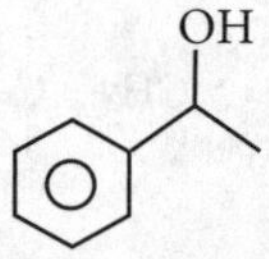

65. Which of the following reagents cannot be used to oxidise primary alcohols to aldehydes?

(a) CrO_3 in anhydrous medium
(b) $KMnO_4$ in acidic medium
(c) Pyridinium chlorochromate
(d) Heat in the presence of Cu at 573 K

66. Phenol cannot be distinguished from ethanol by reactions with:
(a) Br_2/water
(b) Na
(c) Neutral $FeCl_3$
(d) Victor Meyer test

67. An unknown alcohol is treated with the Lucas reagent to determine whether the alcohol is primary, secondary or tertiary. Which alcohol gives turbidity in 5 minutes and by what mechanism?
(a) Secondary alcohol by S_N1
(b) Tertiary alcohol by S_N1
(c) Secondary alcohol by S_N2
(d) Tertiary alcohol by S_N2

68. Which of the following compounds will react with sodium hydroxide solution in water?
(a) C_6H_5OH (b) $C_6H_5CH_2OH$
(c) $(CH_3)_3COH$ (d) C_2H_5OH

69. The major product formed in the following reaction is:

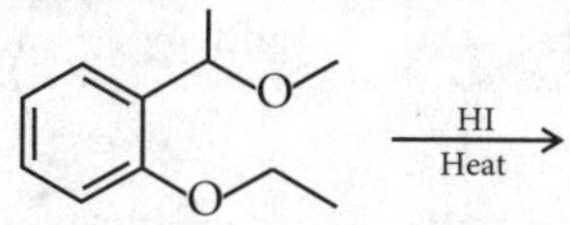

(a) 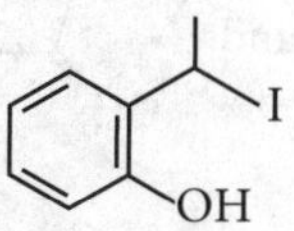

(b) 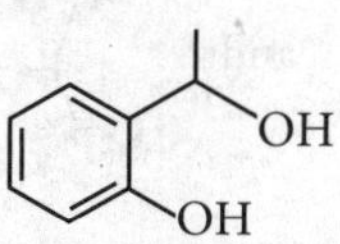

(c) 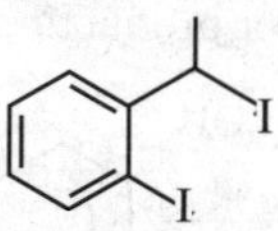

(d) 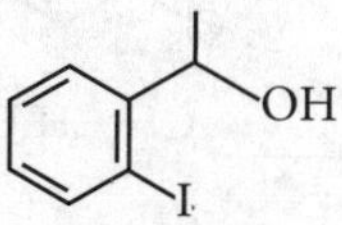

70. The acidic hydrolysis of ether (X) shown below is fastest when:

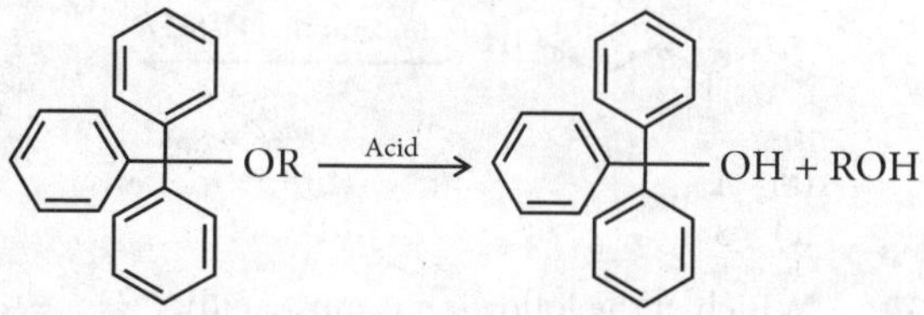

(a) One phenyl group is replaced by a para-methylphenyl group
(b) One phenyl group is replaced by a para-methoxyphenyl group
(c) One phenyl groups are replaced by para-nitrophenyl group
(d) No structural change is made to X

71. The major product of the following reaction is:

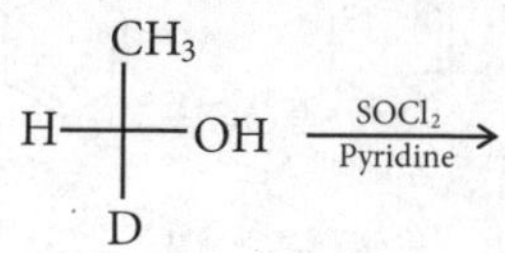

(a) 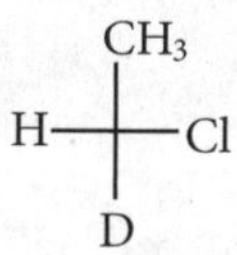

(b) 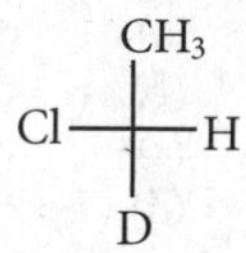

(c) $H_2C = CH_2$

(d) 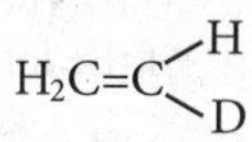

72. The major products Q and R of the following sequence are:

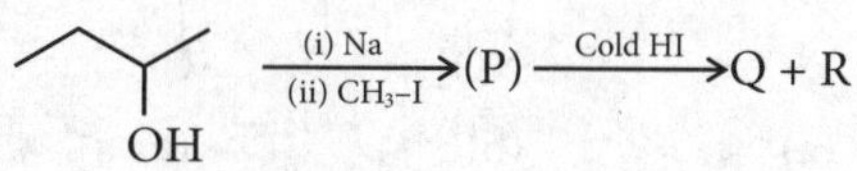

(a) 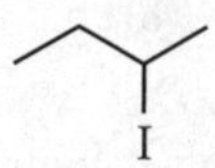 + CH_3–OH

(b) 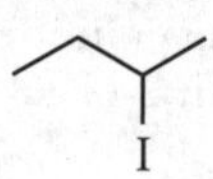 + CH_3–I

(c) 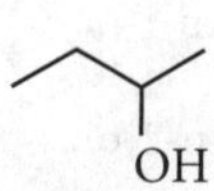 + CH_3–I

(d) 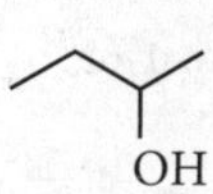 + CH_3–OH

73. The total number of hyper-conjugating structures possible for the major product is:

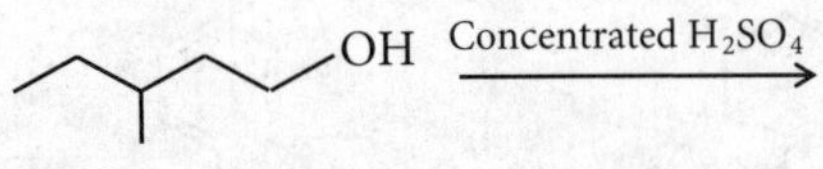

(a) 4 (b) 5
(c) 8 (d) 7

74. Which of the following is most acidic?
(a) Benzyl alcohol
(b) Cyclohexanol
(c) Phenol
(d) m-Chlorophenol

75. Mark the correct order of decreasing acid strength of the following compounds:

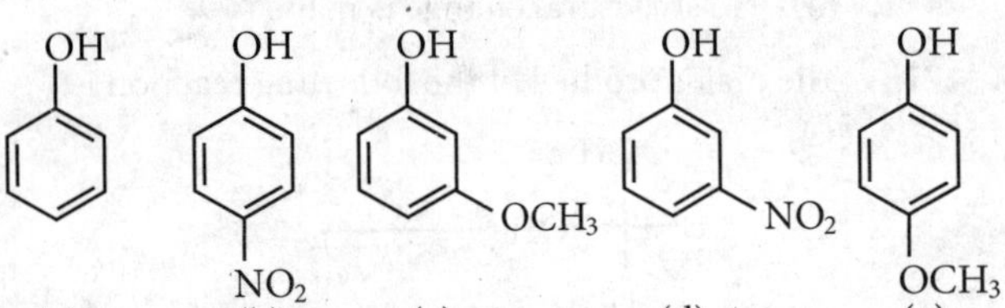

(a) (b) (c) (d) (e)

(a) e > d > b > a > c
(b) b > d > c > a > e
(c) b > d > a > c > e
(d) e > d > c > b > a

76. Mark the correct increasing order of reactivity of the following compounds with HBr/HCl:

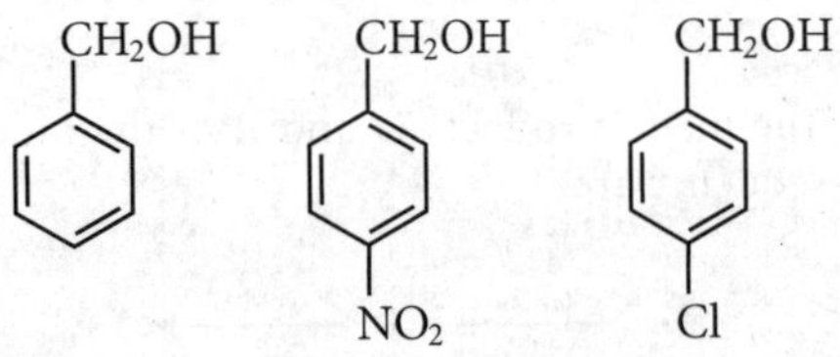

(a) (b) (c)

(a) a< b < c (b) b < a < c
(c) b < c < a (d) c < b < a

77. Arrange the following compounds in increasing order of boiling point:
(a) Propan-1-ol, butan-2-ol, butan-1-ol, pentan-1-ol
(b) Propan-1-ol, butan-1-ol, butan-2-ol, pentan-1-ol
(c) Pentan-1-ol, butan-2-ol, butan-1-ol, propan-1-ol
(d) Pentan-1-ol, butan-1-ol, butan-2-ol, propan-1-ol

78. Which of the following orders is incorrect?

(a) 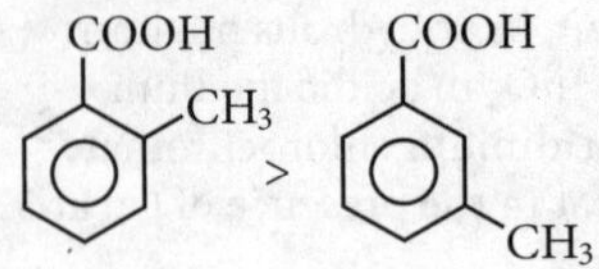 (Acid)

(b) HI > HBr > HCl (Electrophilic addition)

(c) 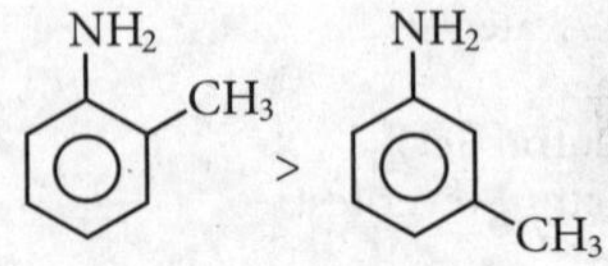 (Base)

(d) 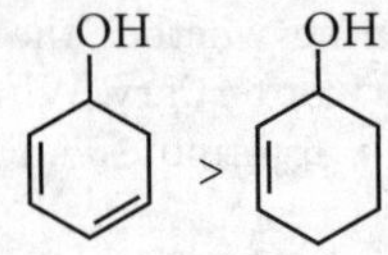 (Rate of dehydration)

79. When neopentyl alcohol is heated with an acid, it is slowly converted into an 85:15 mixture of alkenes A and B, respectively. What are these alkenes?

(a) 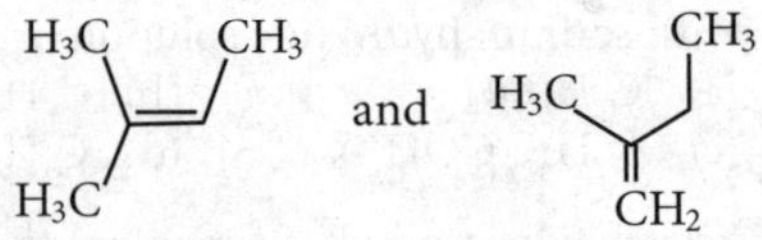

(b) 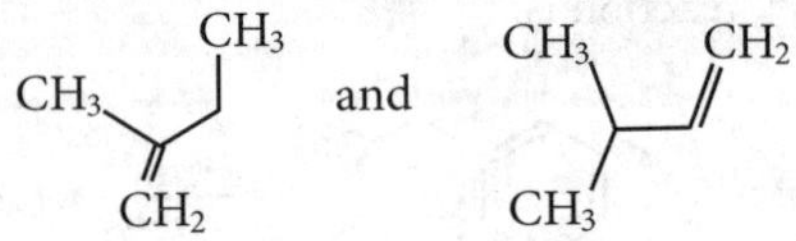

(c) 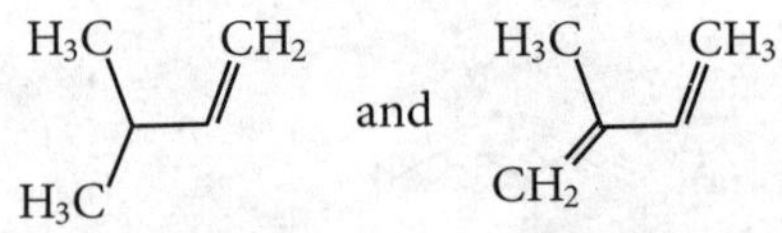

(d) 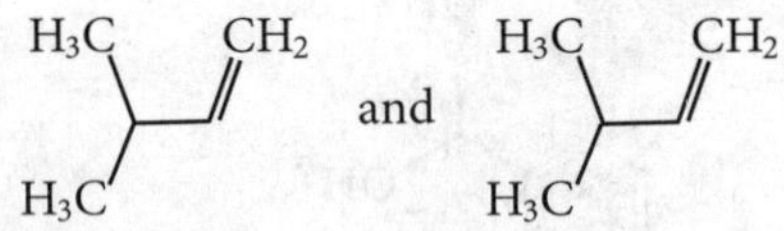

80. Which of the following reactions is correctly matched with the major product?

(a) 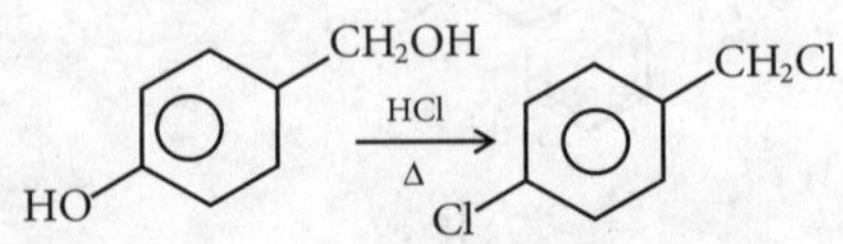

(b) $CH_3CH_2Cl \xrightarrow{AgNO_2} CH_3CH_2ONO$

(c) 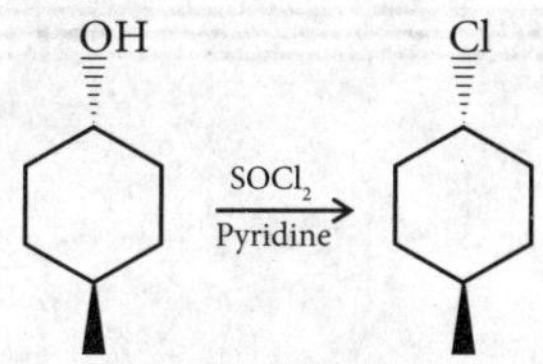

(d) $CH_3CH_2OH \xrightarrow[443\ K]{H_2SO_4} CH_2{=}CH_2$

81. Which of the following statements is correct?
(a) p-Nitrophenol is more acidic than phenol.
(b) The boiling points of alcohols and ethers are high and nearly the same.
(c) The dipole moment of phenol is larger than that of methanol.
(d) The IUPAC name of $(CH_3)_2CHOCH_2CH_2CH_3$ is 2-ethoxy-2-methylethane.

82. The best sequence reagents for the given transformation are:

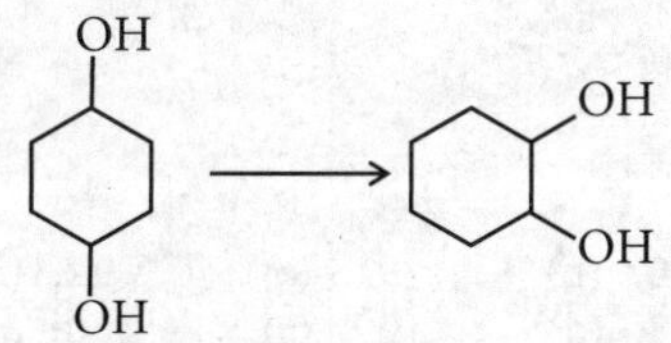

(1) Br_2/CCl_4
(2) H_2SO_4/Δ
(3) $KMnO_4/\overset{\ominus}{O}H/273\ K$
(4) $LiAlH_4/2$ mole
(5) CrO_3/H_2SO_4

(a) 2→1→4→3 (b) 2→1→3→4
(c) 1→2→3→4 (d) 4→3→2→1

83. Which of the following reagents cannot be used to convert the following into 1-chlorobutane?

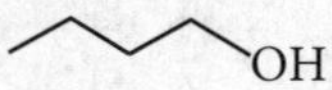

(a) HCl (b) $SOCl_2$
(c) HCl/ $ZnCl_2$ (d) Red P / Cl_2

84. Which of the following statements is correct?
(a) Addition reaction of water to but-1-ene in acidic medium yields butan-1-ol.
(b) Bond angle in ethers is slightly less than the tetrahedral angle.
(c) o-Nitrophenol is more soluble in water than the m- and p-isomers.
(d) The carbon–oxygen bond in phenol is slightly stronger than that in methanol.

85. The major product [B] in the following sequence of reactions is:

$CH_3{-}\underset{\displaystyle CH(CH_3)_2}{\underset{|}{C}}{=}CH{-}CH_2CH_3 \xrightarrow[(ii)\ H_2O_2,\ OH^{\ominus}]{(i)\ B_2H_6} [A] \xrightarrow[\Delta]{\text{Dilute } H_2SO_4} [B]$

(a) $CH_3{-}\underset{\displaystyle CH(CH_3)_2}{\underset{|}{C}}{=}CH{-}CH_2CH_3$

(b) $CH_2{=}\underset{\displaystyle CH(CH_3)_2}{\underset{|}{C}}{-}CH_2CH_2CH_3$

(c) $CH_3{-}\underset{\displaystyle \underset{H_3C\quad CH_3}{C}}{\underset{\|}{C}}{-}CH_2\ CH_2CH_3$

(d) $CH_3{-}\underset{\displaystyle CH(CH_3)_2}{\underset{|}{CH}}{-}CH{=}CH{-}CH_3$

86. The major product of the following reaction is:

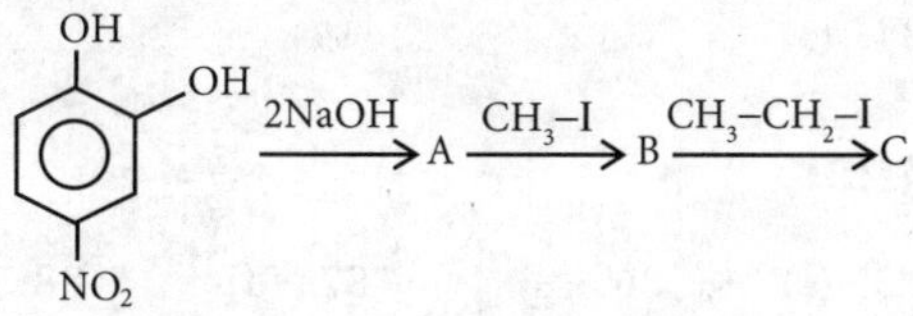

(a) 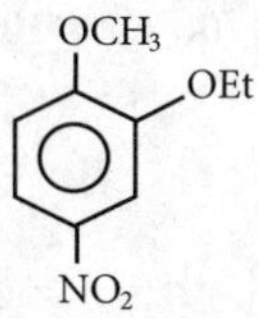

(b) 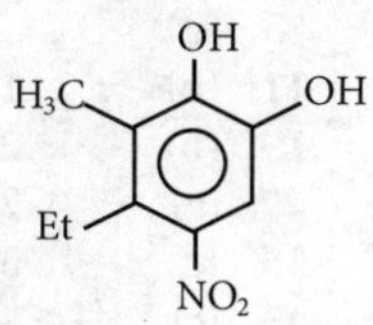

(c) 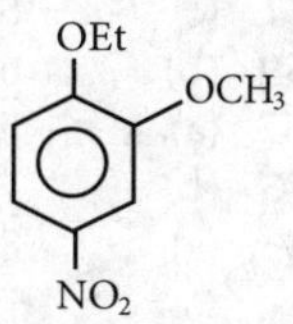

(d) 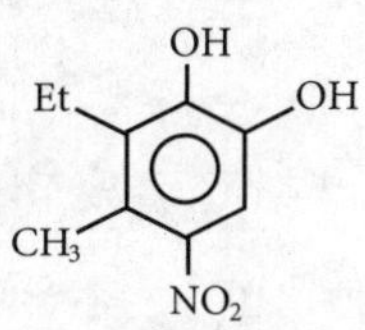

Answer Key

Level-1

Alcohol

1. (a)	**2.** (c)	**3.** (a)	**4.** (d)	**5.** (d)	**6.** (c)	**7.** (c)	**8.** (d)
9. (c)	**10.** (a)	**11.** (c)	**12.** (c)	**13.** (c)	**14.** (b)	**15.** (a)	**16.** (d)
17. (b)	**18.** (d)	**19.** (d)	**20.** (a)	**21.** (a)	**22.** (b)	**23.** (a)	**24.** (a)
25. (b)	**26.** (b)	**27.** (d)	**28.** (c)	**29.** (c)	**30.** (b)	**31.** (d)	**32.** (c)
33. (a)	**34.** (d)	**35.** (c)	**36.** (d)	**37.** (c)	**38.** (a)	**39.** (c)	**40.** (a)
41. (c)	**42.** (b)	**43.** (a)	**44.** (d)	**45.** (b)	**46.** (a)	**47.** (b)	**48.** (c)
49. (d)	**50.** (a)	**51.** (a)	**52.** (c)	**53.** (b)	**54.** (b)	**55.** (a)	**56.** (d)
57. (a)	**58.** (d)	**59.** (c)					

Phenol

60. (d)	**61.** (b)	**62.** (a)	**63.** (c)	**64.** (c)	**65.** (b)	**66.** (b)	**67.** (b)
68. (d)	**69.** (d)	**70.** (c)	**71.** (b)	**72.** (d)	**73.** (c)	**74.** (d)	**75.** (d)
76. (b)	**77.** (a)	**78.** (a)	**79.** (a)	**80.** (c)	**81.** (c)	**82.** (b)	**83.** (c)
84. (a)							

Ether

85. (c)	**86.** (d)	**87.** (d)	**88.** (a)	**89.** (c)	**90.** (b)	**91.** (a)	**92.** (b)
93. (a)	**94.** (c)	**95.** (d)	**96.** (a)	**97.** (c)	**98.** (d)	**99.** (a)	**100.** (c)
101. (c)	**102.** (a)	**103.** (a)	**104.** (c)	**105.** (c)	**106.** (b)	**107.** (a)	**108.** (b)
109. (c)							

Level-2

1. (d)	**2.** (c)	**3.** (d)	**4.** (d)	**5.** (b)	**6.** (d)	**7.** (d)	**8.** (c)
9. (c)	**10.** (d)	**11.** (b)	**12.** (b)	**13.** (d)	**14.** (a)	**15.** (d)	**16.** (d)
17. (d)	**18.** (d)	**19.** (b)	**20.** (d)	**21.** (c)	**22.** (c)	**23.** (d)	**24.** (b)
25. (c)	**26.** (d)	**27.** (a)	**28.** (a)	**29.** (b)	**30.** (d)	**31.** (c)	**32.** (d)
33. (a)	**34.** (c)	**35.** (d)	**36.** (a)	**37.** (a)	**38.** (a)	**39.** (c)	**40.** (a)
41. (b)	**42.** (b)	**43.** (c)	**44.** (b)	**45.** (d)	**46.** (a)	**47.** (c)	**48.** (b)
49. (a)	**50.** (d)	**51.** (c)	**52.** (c)	**53.** (c)	**54.** (b)	**55.** (b)	**56.** (d)
57. (d)	**58.** (d)	**59.** (b)	**60.** (c)	**61.** (c)	**62.** (b)	**63.** (c)	**64.** (a)
65. (b)	**66.** (b)	**67.** (a)	**68.** (a)	**69.** (a)	**70.** (b)	**71.** (b)	**72.** (c)
73. (c)	**74.** (d)	**75.** (b)	**76.** (c)	**77.** (a)	**78.** (c)	**79.** (a)	**80.** (d)
81. (a)	**82.** (b)	**83.** (a)	**84.** (d)	**85.** (c)	**86.** (c)		

Solutions

Level-1

1.

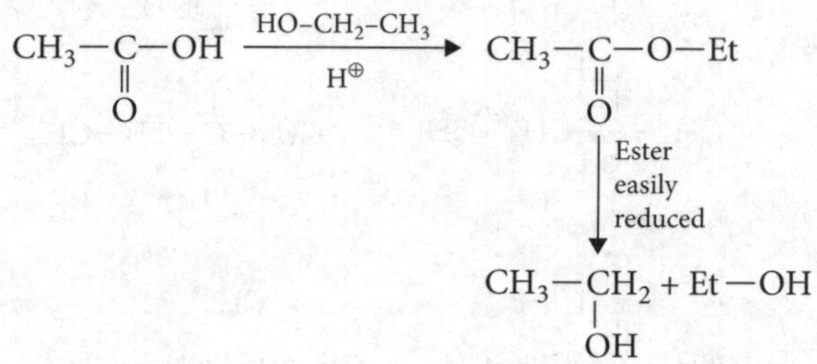

3.

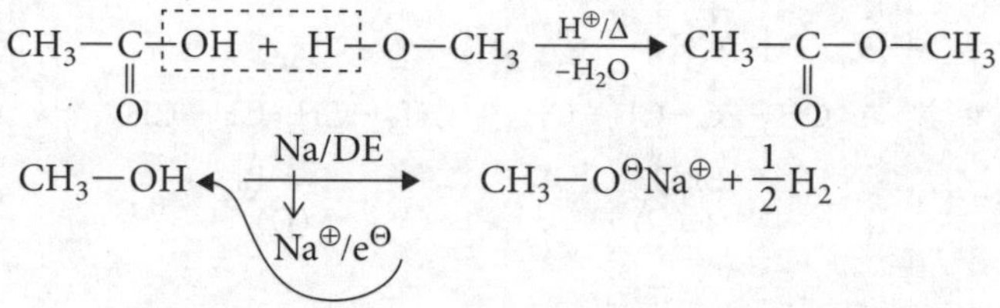

5. $3CH_3{-}CH_2{-}OH + PBr_3 \rightarrow 3CH_3{-}CH_2{-}Br + H_3PO_3$

6. Dehydration of alcohol $\propto$ Stability of carbocation

7.

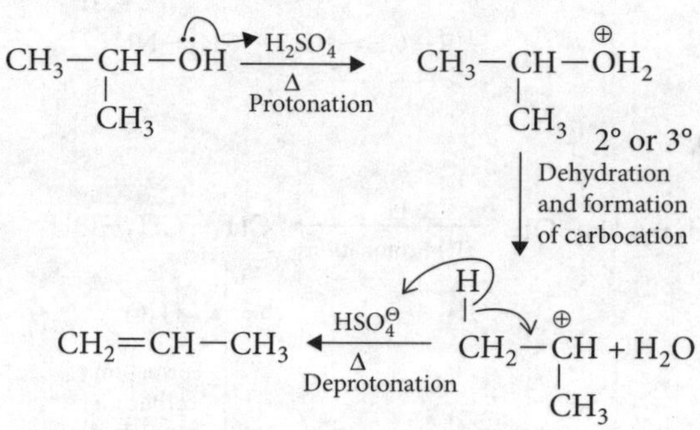

8.

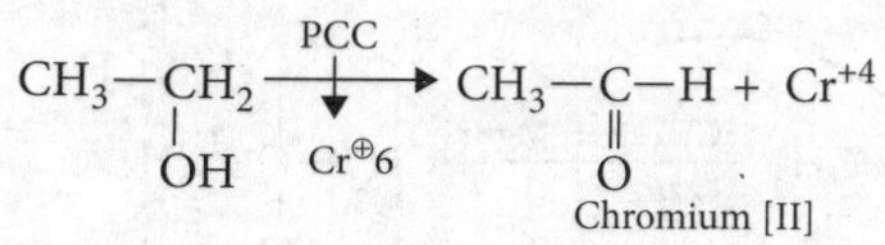

9.

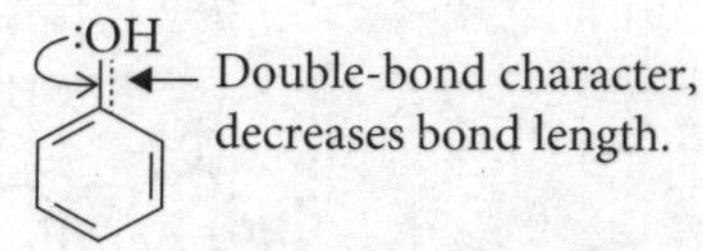

11. Methanol is poisonous.

12. $\text{Sugar} \xrightarrow[\text{Absence of } O_2 \text{ [by Yeast]}]{\text{Fermentation}} CH_3{-}CH_2{-}OH + CO_2$

14. Denatured spirit or denatured alcohol.

17. Fermentation occurs in the absence of oxygen by the enzymes invertase and zynase.

19. Alcoholic drinks contain ethanol as a major ingredient, not methanol.

21.

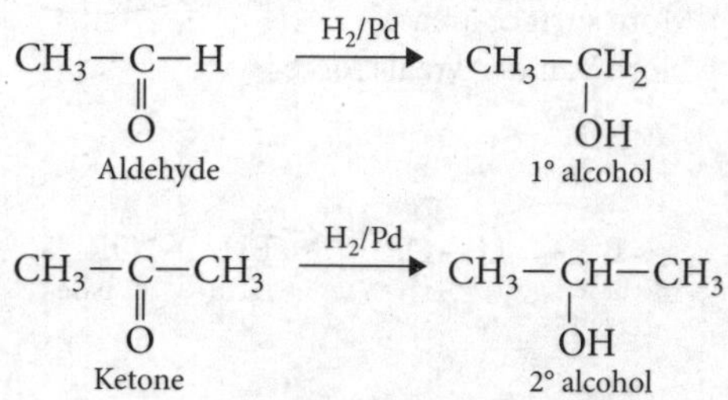

22.

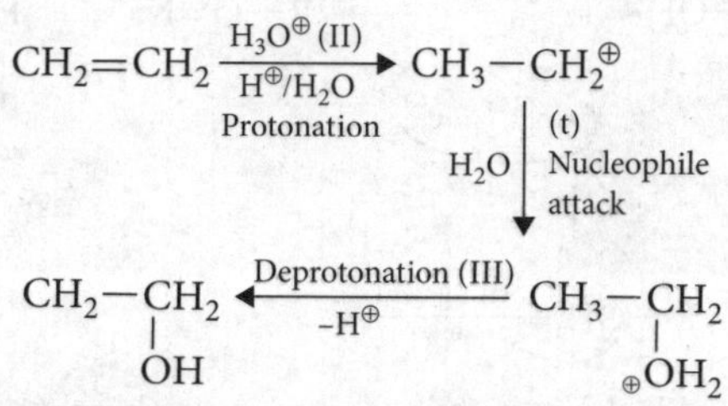

23. Direct reduction of carboxylic acid to alcohol by hydrogenation (H_2/Ni) is not possible.

25.

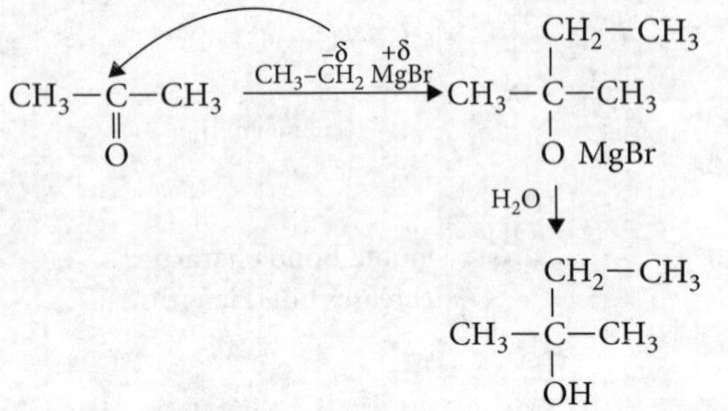

26. Ethanol forms hydrogen bonds; so the boiling point is much higher than in propane, but the molecular weight is almost the same.

29.

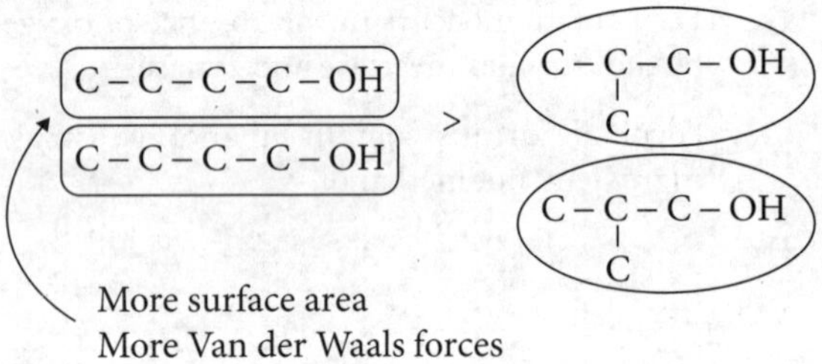

30.

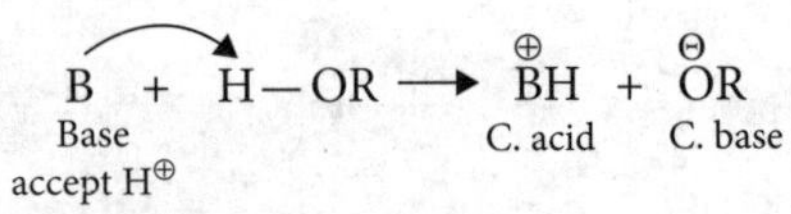

31.

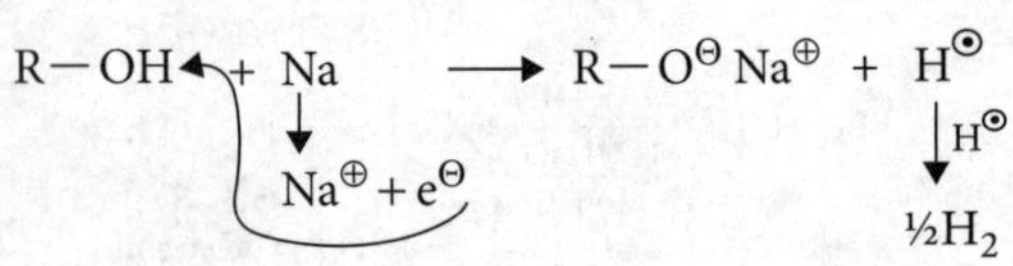

32.

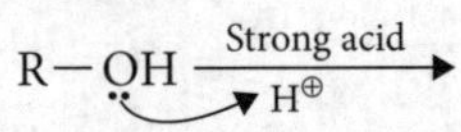

Alcohol acts as a base due to the presence of lone pair on oxygen.

34. By nucleophilic substitution by addition elimination (S_NAE), an ester is formed.

36. Tertiary alcohol forms the most stable carbocation and the fastest reaction by S_N1.

37.

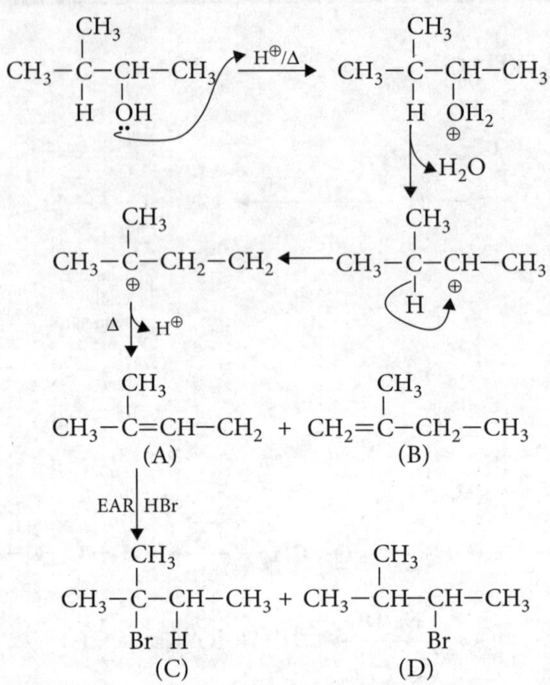

38.

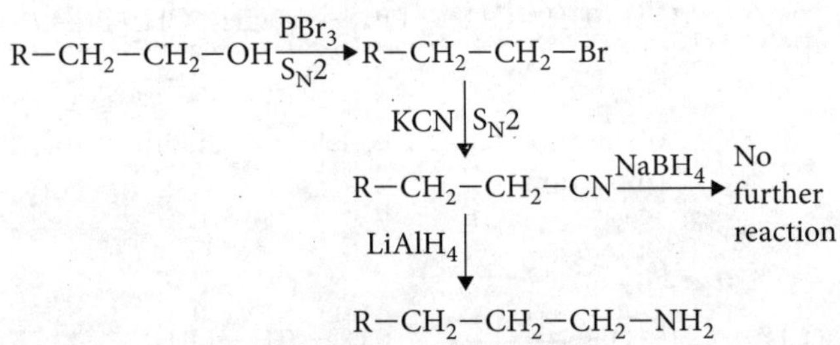

39.

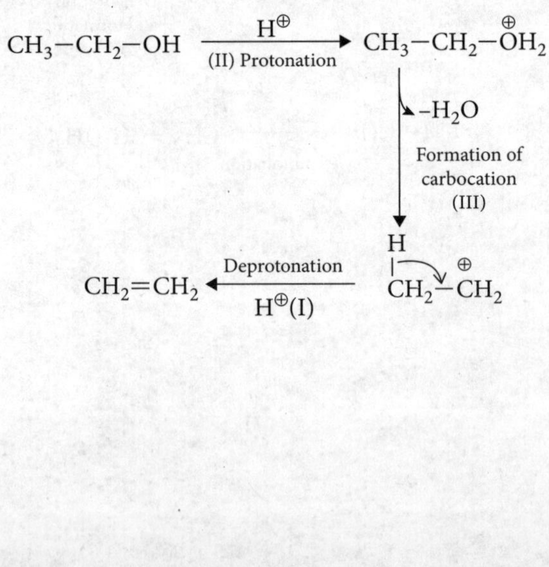

40.

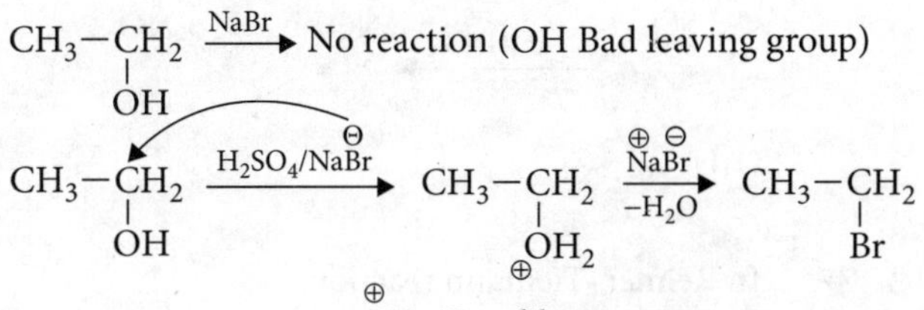

$\overset{\oplus}{-OH_2}$ Good leaving group

41. Reactivity depends on the stability of carbocation.

42. PCC (mild oxidizing agent) does not reduce π bond and 3° alcohol is not oxidized. It dehydrates into alkene.

44. Mild oxidizing agent (like PCC or Cu/300° or anhydrous CrO_3) oxidizes primary alcohol to aldehyde but strong oxidizing agents like $KMnO_4$ oxidize up to acid.

45.

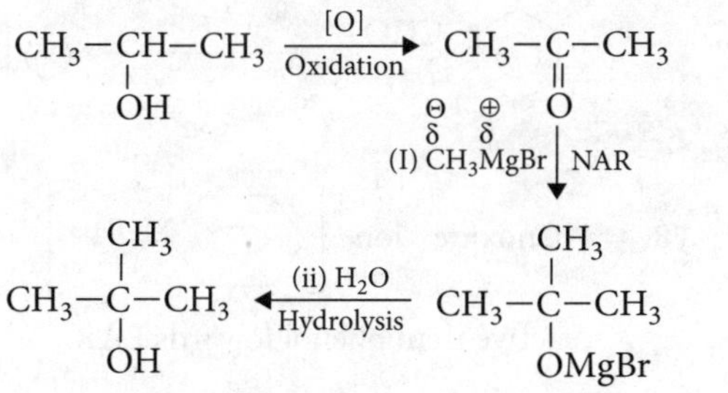

46.

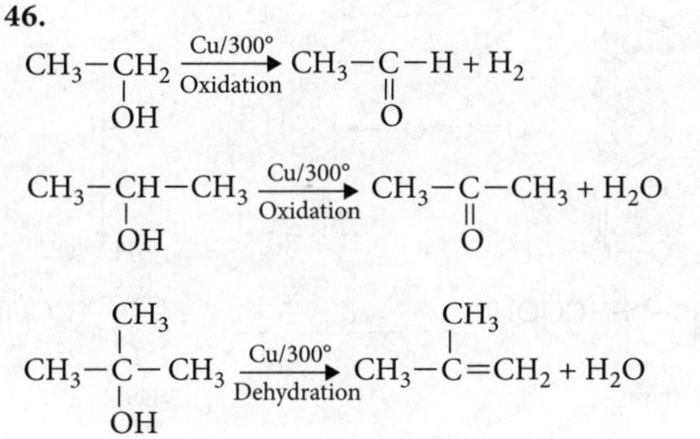

47.

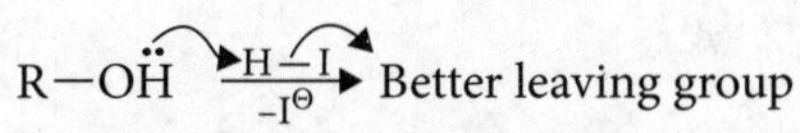

Stability $I^{\ominus} > Br^{\ominus} > Cl^{\ominus} > P^{\ominus}$
Due to size

48. Anhydrous $ZnCl_2$ acts as catalyst and increases the rate of reaction.

50.

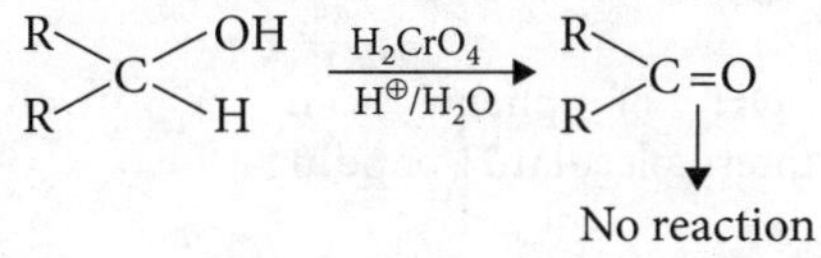

51.

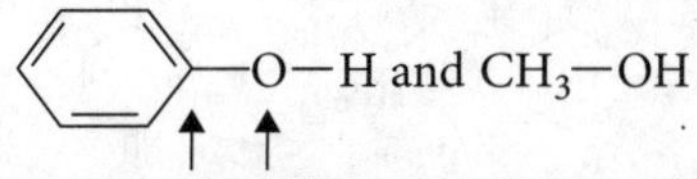

EN difference is less, so dipole moment is less.

52. Destructive distillation of wood = Wood spirit (methanol).

59. Methanol $\xrightarrow{\text{in liver cell}}$ HCOOH
Formic acid [methanoic acid] does not further convert to methanol.

61.

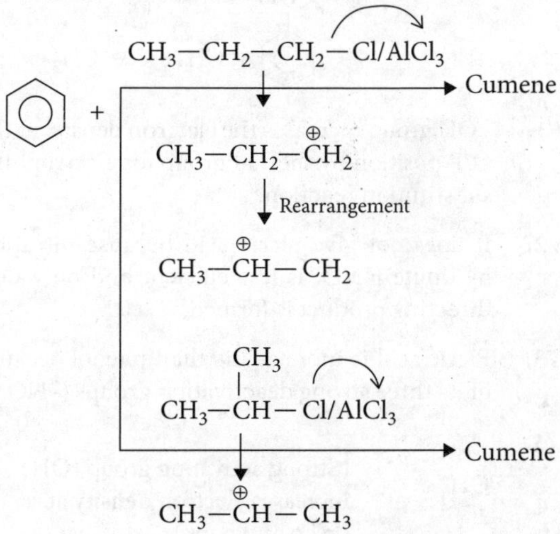

62. At room temperature and one atm pressure, S_NAr is not possible.

63. Due to intramolecular H-bonding

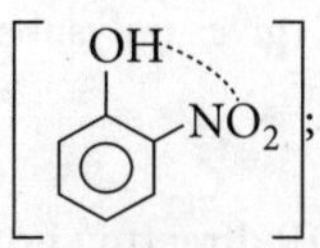

; o-nitrophenol has a lower boiling point than p-nitrophenol due to intramolecular H-bonding.

64. 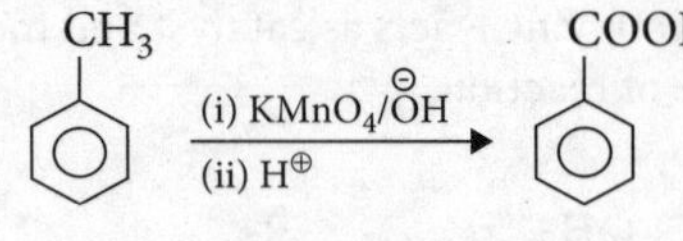

65. –OH of phenol can be involved in intermolecular H-bonding.

67.

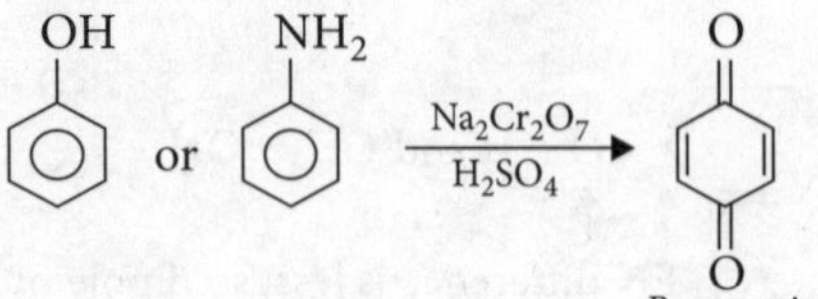

Benzoquinone

69.

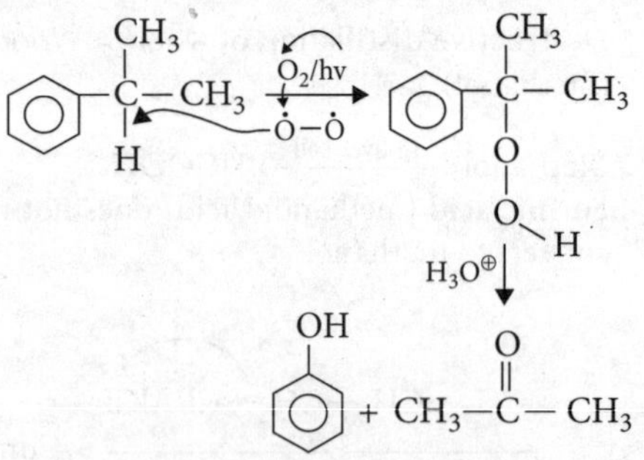

71. –OH group increases the electron density at the O/P position by the +M group for electrophilic substitution reaction.

72. It does not give picric acid because nitration by dilute HNO_3 is less efficient and only O/P directing product is formed.

73. Picric acid is more acidic than phenol because of its three strong deactivation groups ($-NO_2$).

74.

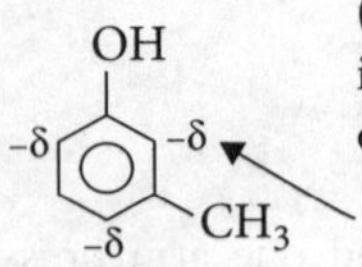

(Strong activating group (OH) increases electron density at ortho and para.)

Due to steric, not ESR.

75.

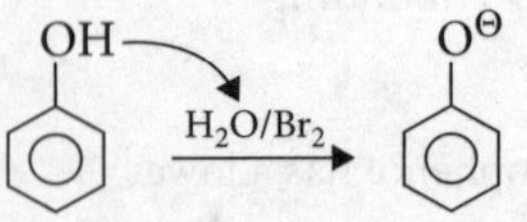

Strong activating group ($-O^{\ominus}$) gives polysubstitution

76. –OH of phenol is the O/P directing group and not meta-directing, and

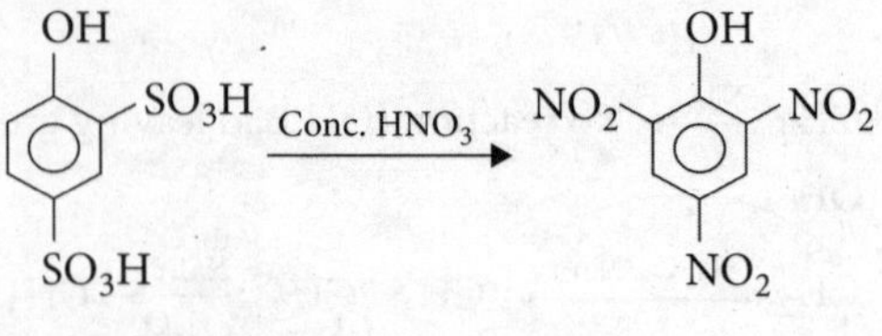

77. In Reimer–Tiemann reaction

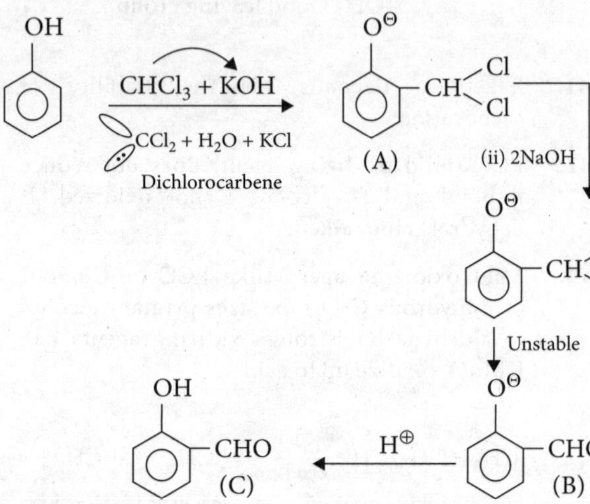

78. Phenoxide ion 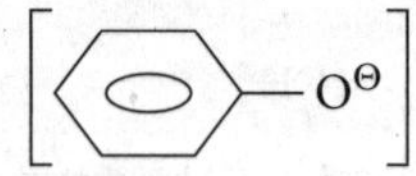 is more reactive than phenol towards EAR.

79.

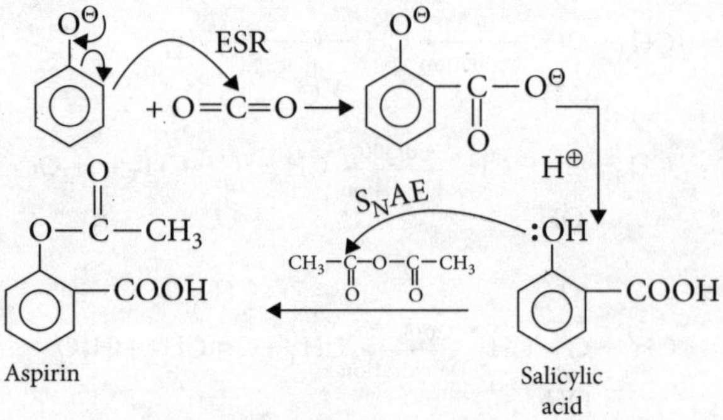

81.

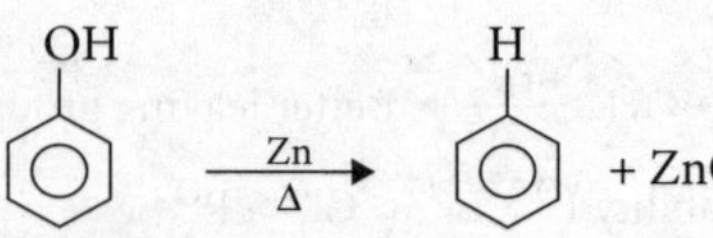

83. –OH group of phenol is highly activating due to +M; it brominates even in the absence of Lewis acid.

84. Phenol is oxidized into benzoquinone (quinone) in the presence of light and air.

85.

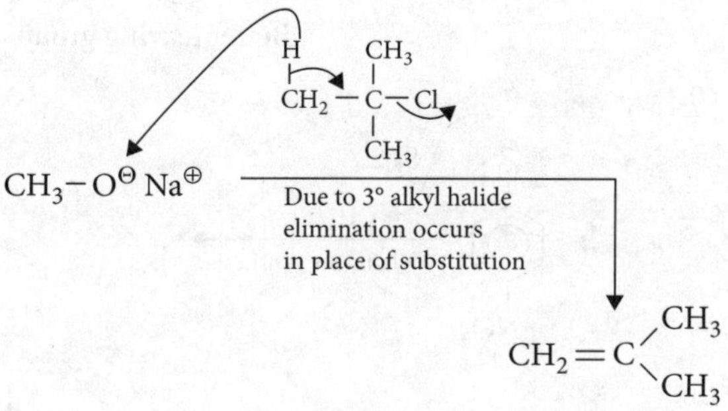

86. In alcohol, there is intermolecular H-bonding, but due to weak ionic interaction of ethers, it becomes volatile.

88.

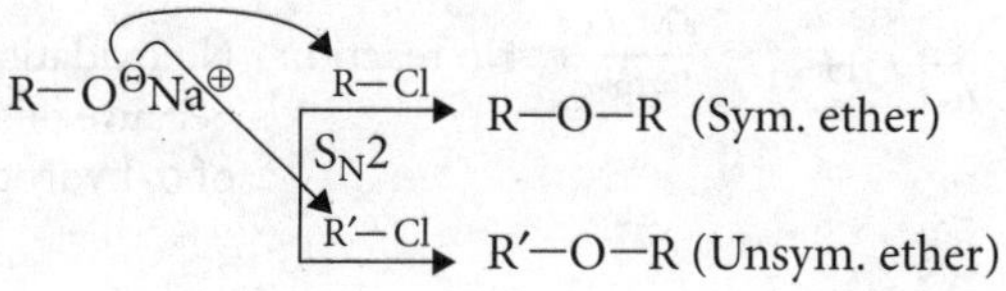

89. I is E_1 reaction and II is S_N2 (Williamson continuous ether synthesis)

90. $R-\overset{\ominus}{O}\overset{\oplus}{Na} \xrightarrow[S_N2]{R'-Cl} R'-O-R'$

93.

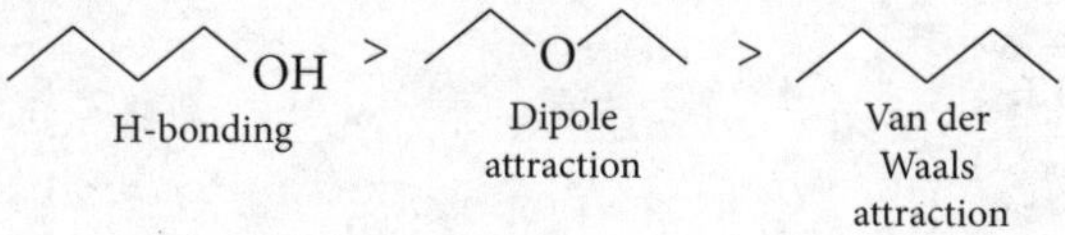

94. Hydrogen bonding is the most powerful interaction between molecules.

95. Due to intermolecular hydrogen bonding, alcohol is less volatile.

95. Alcohol and ether interact with water; so they are always miscible to the same extent. However, pentane is non-polar; so it is not miscible with polar solvent water.

97. In excess of HX, oxygen of ether forms an oxonium ion and will make a better leaving group.

99.

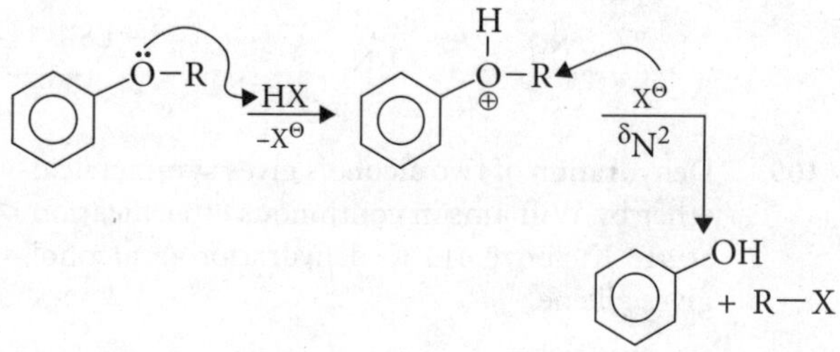

100. Better leaving group order ($I^{\ominus} > Br^{\ominus} > Cl^{\ominus}$).

103.

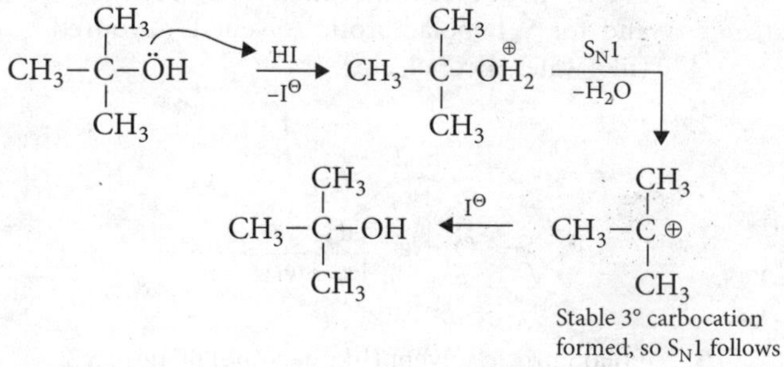

104. See Q.99.

105.

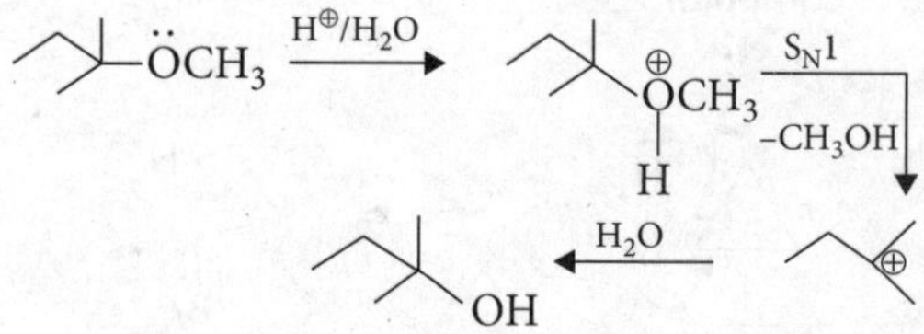

106. Due to the O/P directing group ($-OCH_3$), both output isomer products are formed and ortho is minor due to steric group $-OCH_3$.

107. This is because the steric group is at ortho, so para is major (90%).

108.

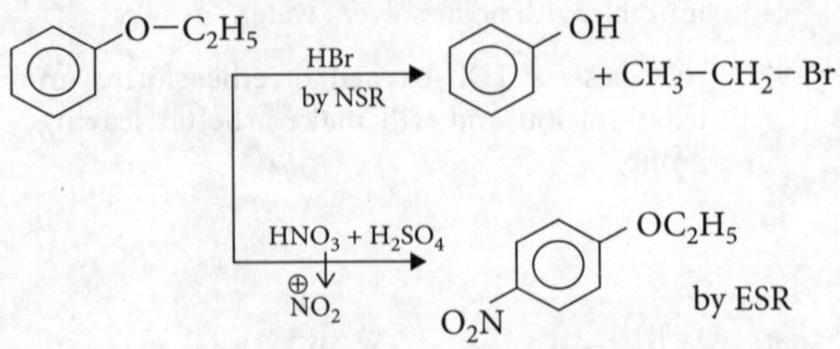

109. Dehydration of two alcohols gives symmetrical ether by Williamson continuous etherification at 413 K; above 413 K, dehydration of alcohol gives alkene.

Level-2

1. 3° alkyl halide; so the reaction follows only S_N1, and for S_N1, polar protic solvent is favoured (like water, alcohol, etc.).

2.

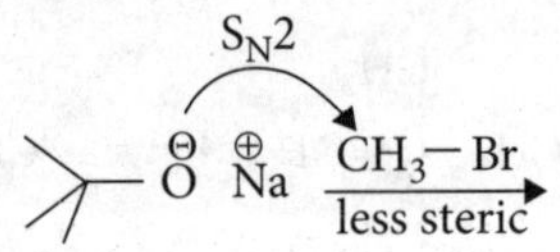

3. Polar aprotic solvent (like acetone) favours S_N2.

4. Grignard's reagent gives CH_4 (alkane) when it reacts with acidic hydrogen (like water) and with more acidic hydrogen containing compounds.

5.

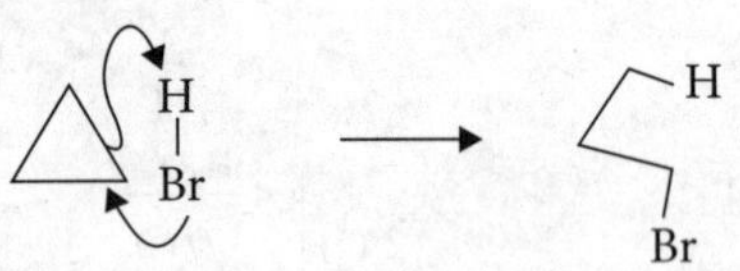

7.

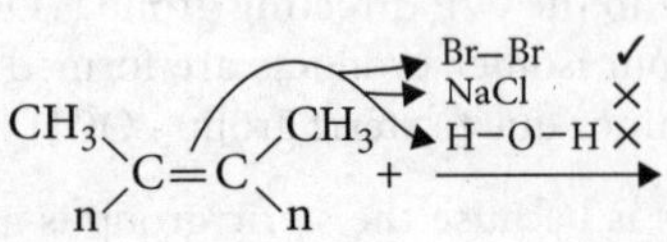

Electrophile will be bromine and threo product is formed.

8. Lone pair of chlorine by resonance gives orientation of product; this means the output product and reactivity is less than benzene because of dominant inductive effect over mesomeric.

9. $CH_3-\ddot{O}-CH=CH-CH_2-Br$

Better leaving group

10.

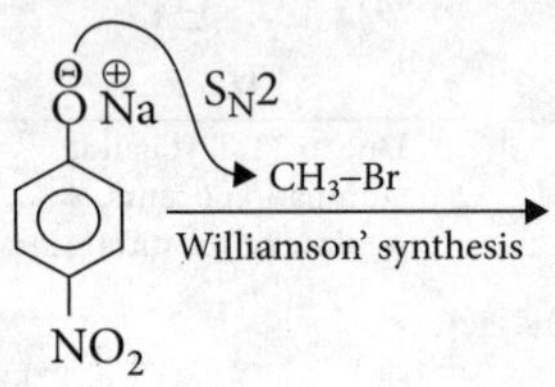

11.

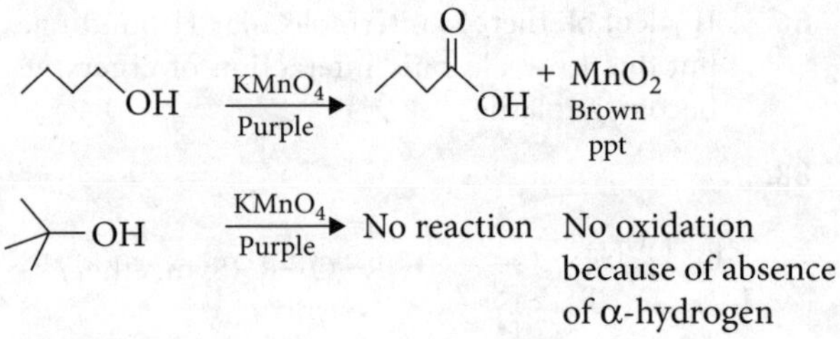

12.

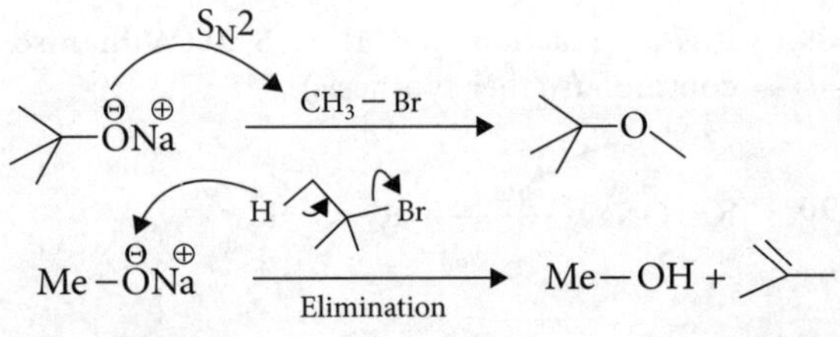

13.

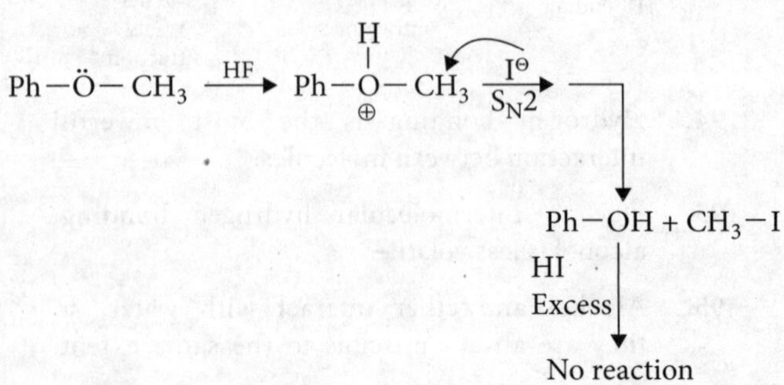

14.

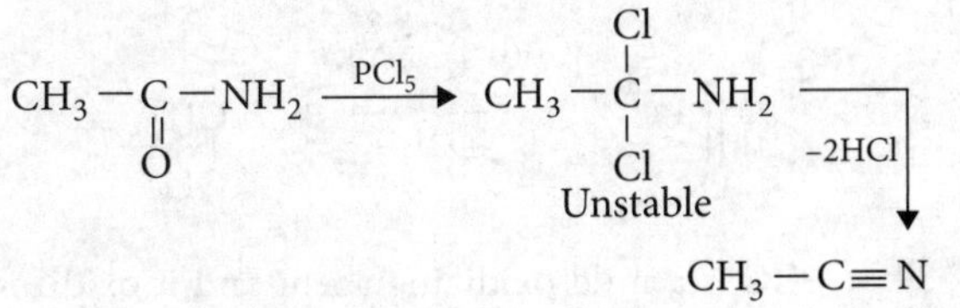

15.

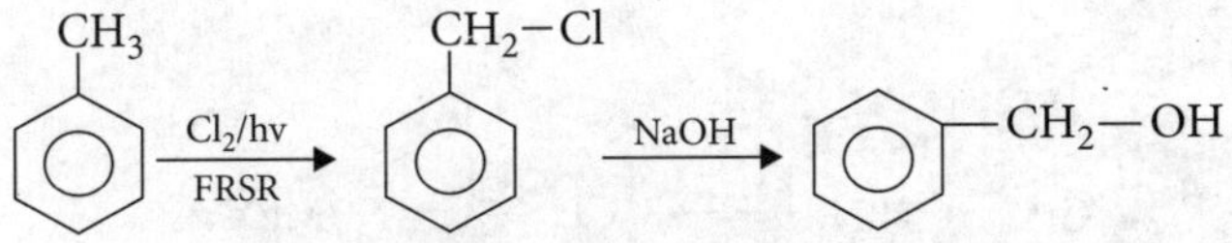

16. Those in which S_N2 is not possible; they are not formed by Williamson synthesis.

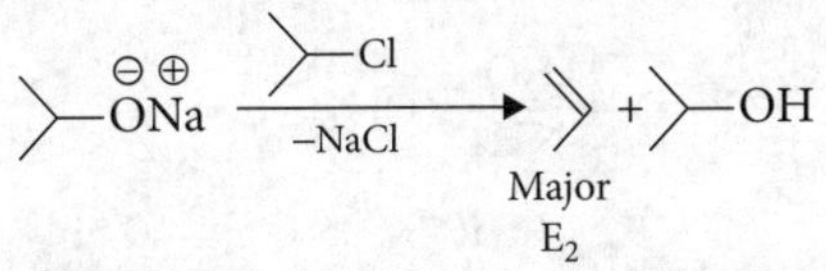

17. Stability of intermediate carbocation gives fastest dehydration of alcohol.

18.

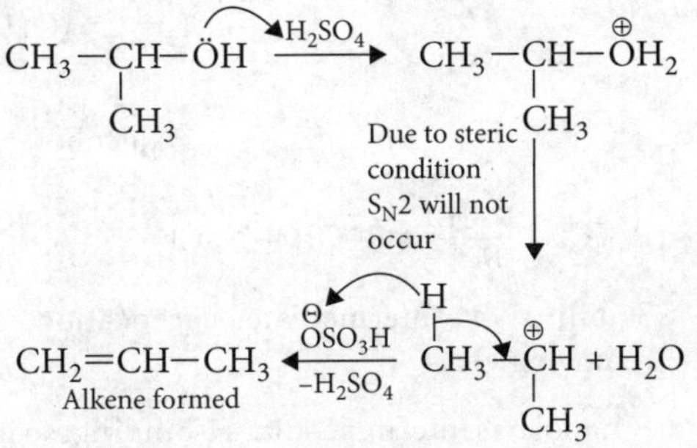

19. It follows S_N1, so concentrated HI is used for the formation of alkyl iodide and alcohol.

20. Zeisel method for ether cleavage is not applied.

21.

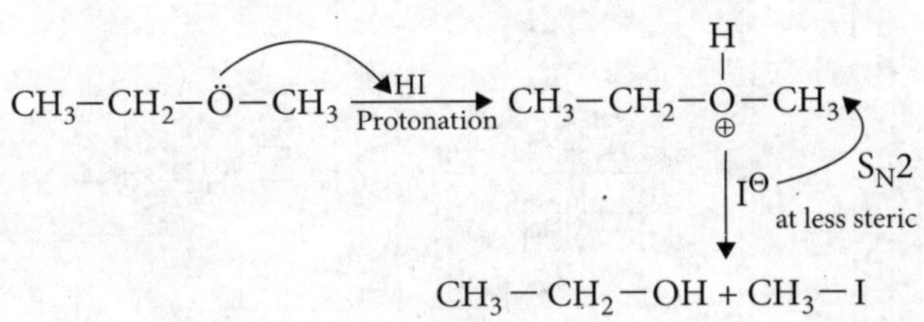

22.

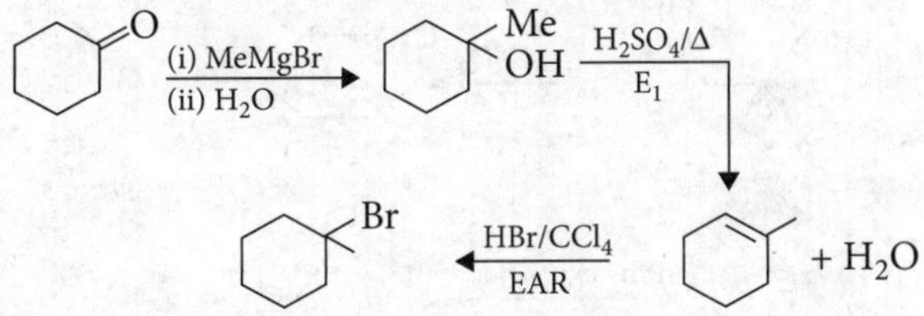

23. Homologous means member of the same family (functional group) but the number of carbon atoms is different (CH_2 or $CH_2 \times n$).

24. $CH_3-CH_2-OH \xrightarrow[H_3PO_4]{KI}$

H_3PO_4 is used for protonation of alcohol to create a good leaving group in place of H_2SO_4 because H_2SO_4 is an oxidizing agent and KI is a reducing agent. NaCl and NaBr are not reducing agents, so for formation of alkyl chloride or alkyl bromide, H_2SO_4 is possible.

25.

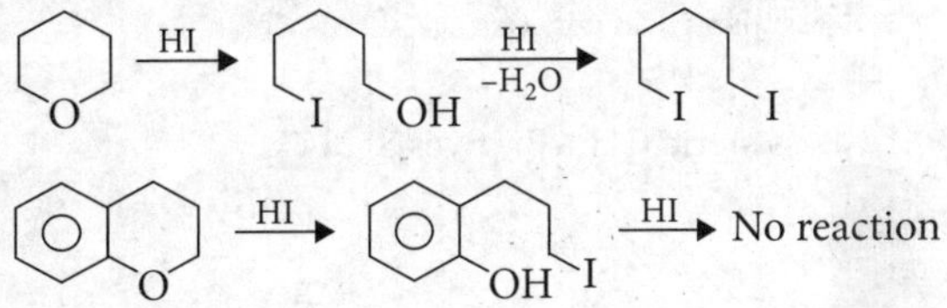

26.

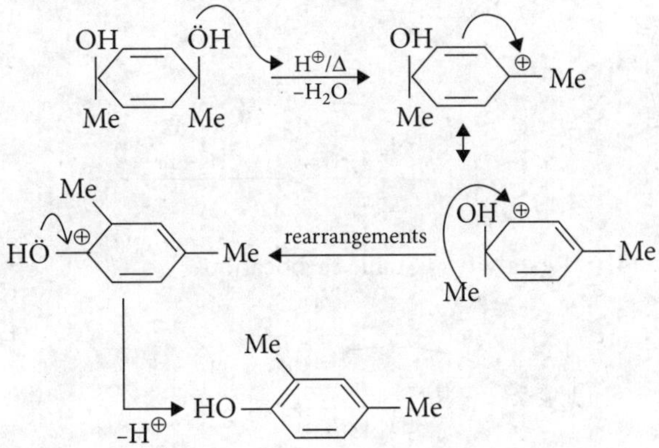

27. C_2 alcohol has two methyl groups, so it is more basic than C_5 alcohol.

28.

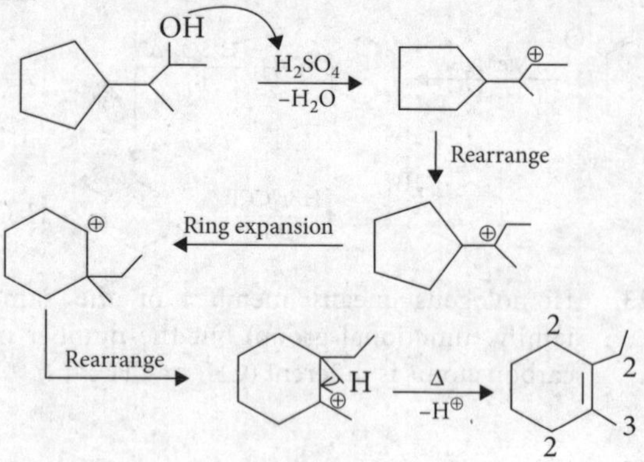

29.

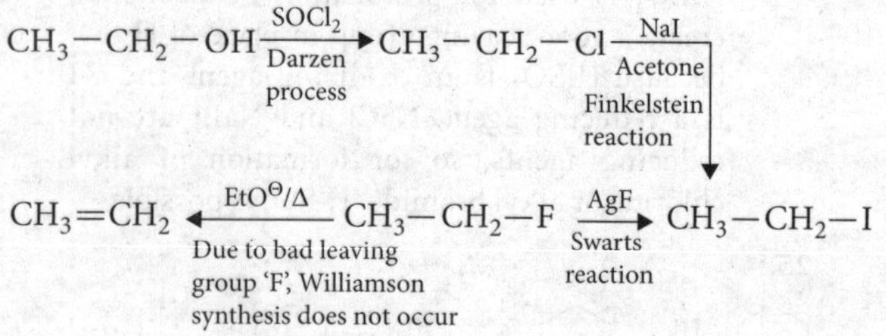

30. Less steric CH_3–Br gives S_N2.

32.

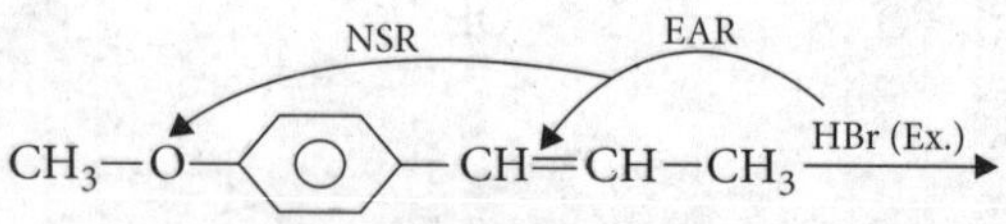

33.

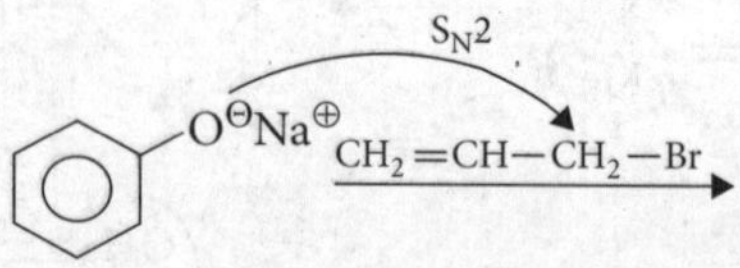

34. Reactivity ∝ Stable carbocation

35.

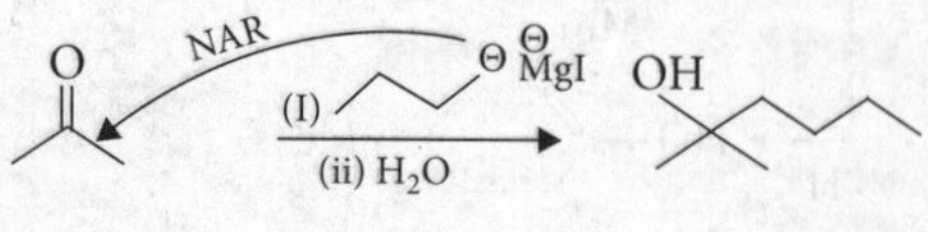

36.

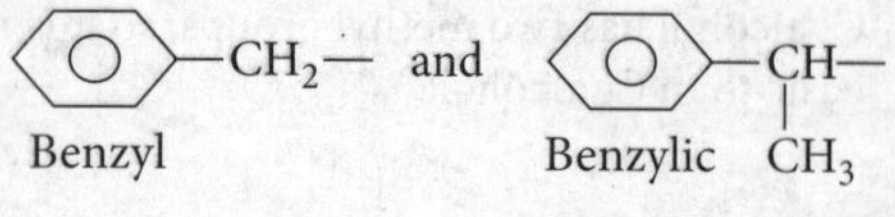

38.

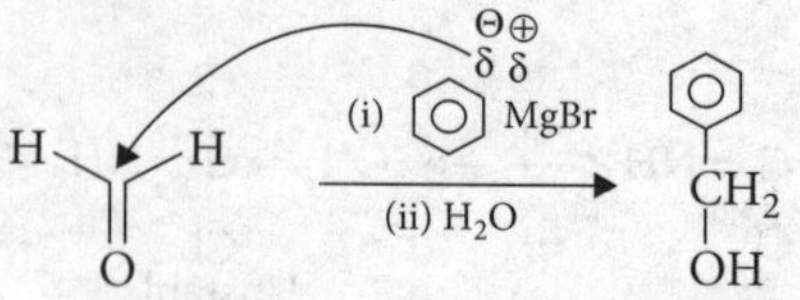

39. PCC is a mild oxidizing agent and it oxidizes alcohol to carbonyl compound only.

40. Intermediate carbocation

41.

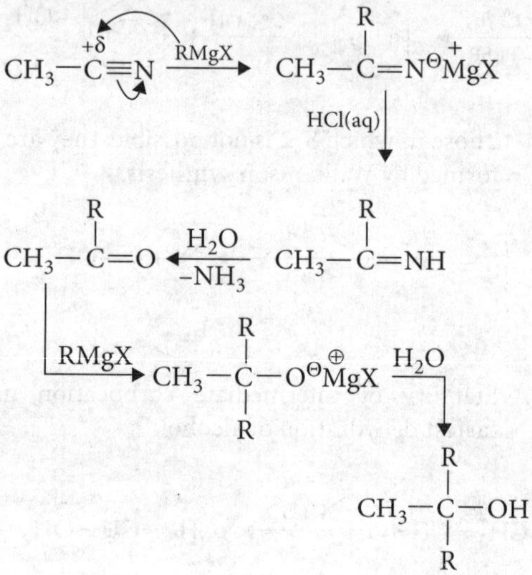

3° alcohol

42. $R-Cl \xrightarrow[NSR]{NaOH} R\text{-}OH + NaCl$

43. Stability of intermediate carbocation after removing OH.

45. Ethanol has intermolecular H-binding; so it has a higher boiling point than methoxymethane.

46.

$$\underbrace{C_2H_5-OH}_{\text{H-bonding}} > \underbrace{C_2H_5Cl}_{\text{Strong dipole}} > \underbrace{C_2H_5OCH_3}_{\text{Less dipole}} > \underbrace{CH_3-CH_2-CH_3}_{\text{No dipole moment}}$$

47.

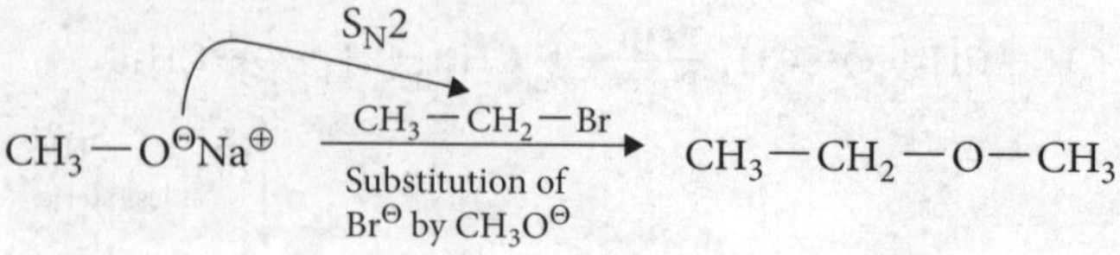

48.

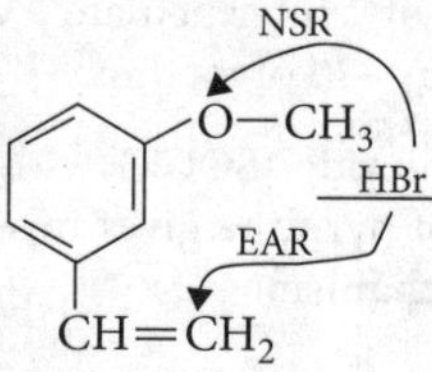

49.

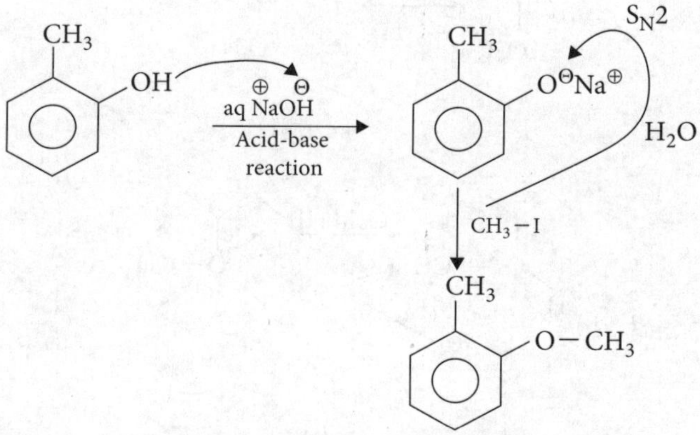

50. The boiling point also depends on molecular weight, which is directionally proportional.

52. 1° carbocation does not form quickly.

53.

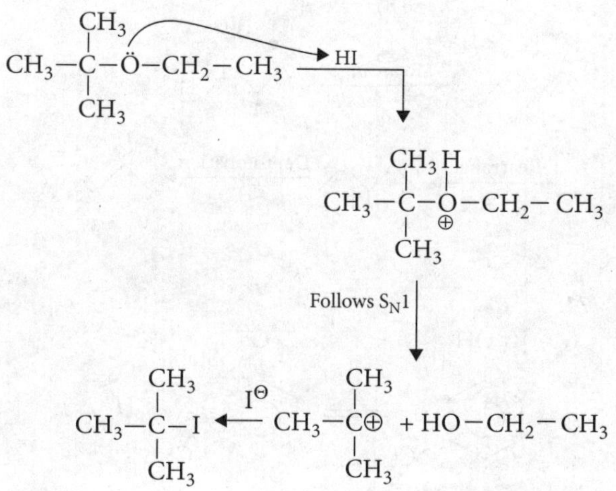

54.

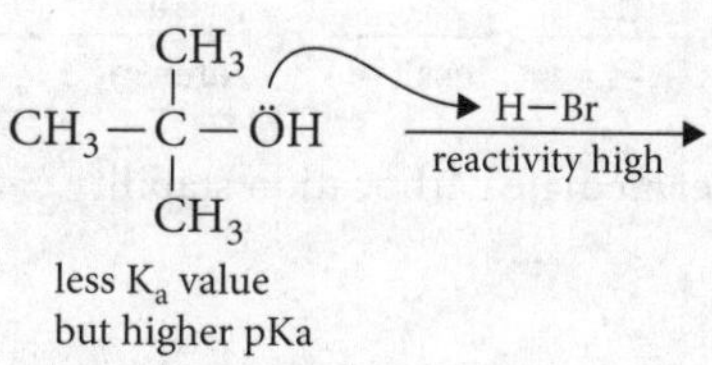

55. Stability of anion is favourable for leaving groups.

56.

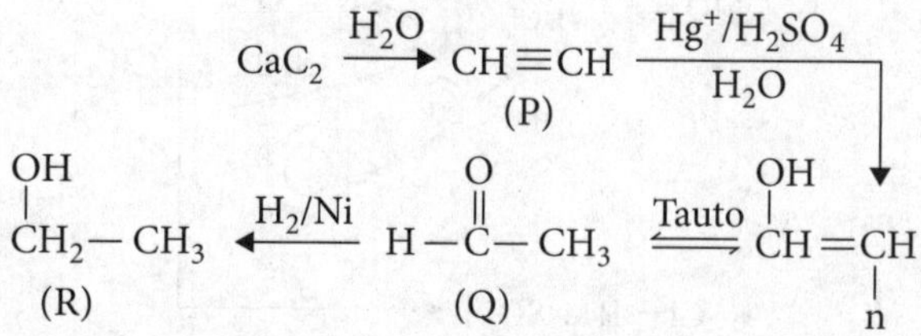

57.

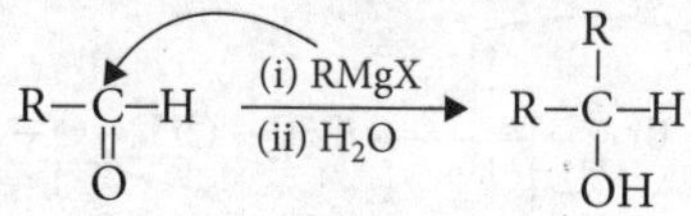

58.

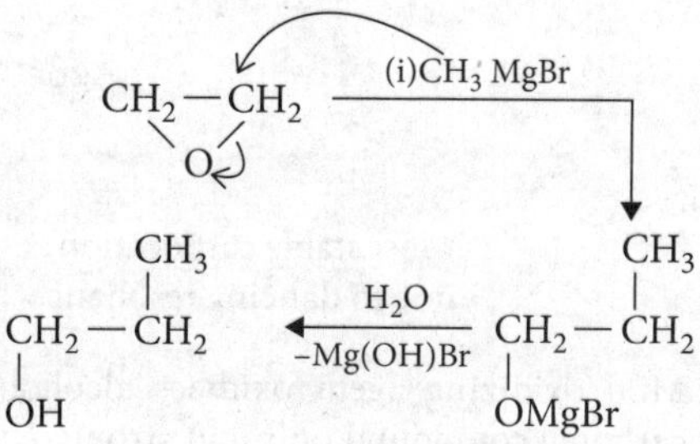

59.

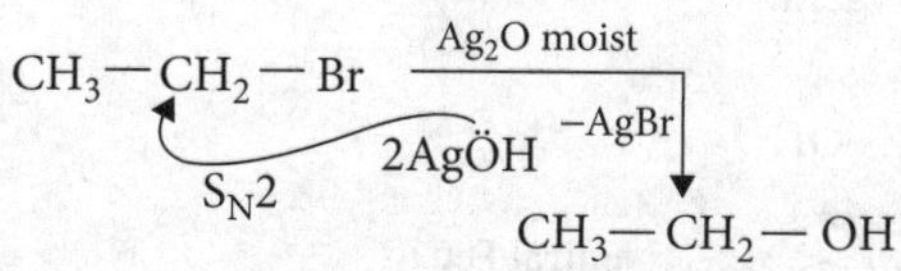

60.

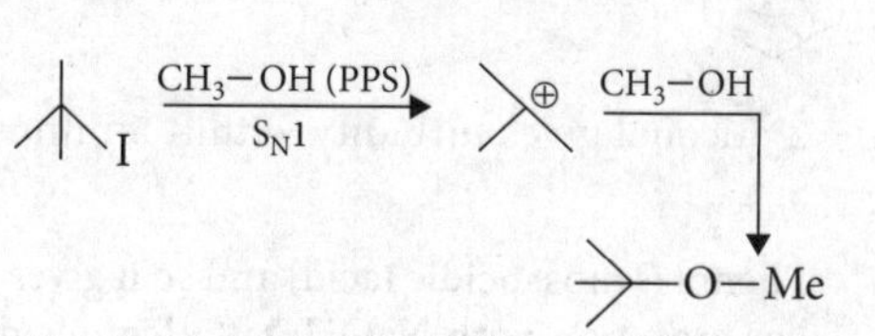

61.

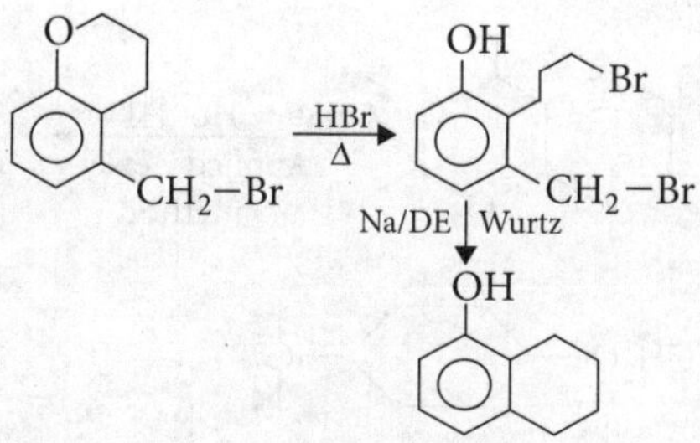

62.

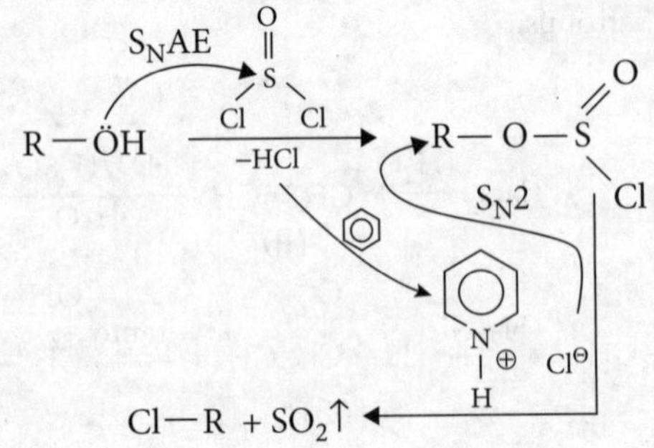

63.

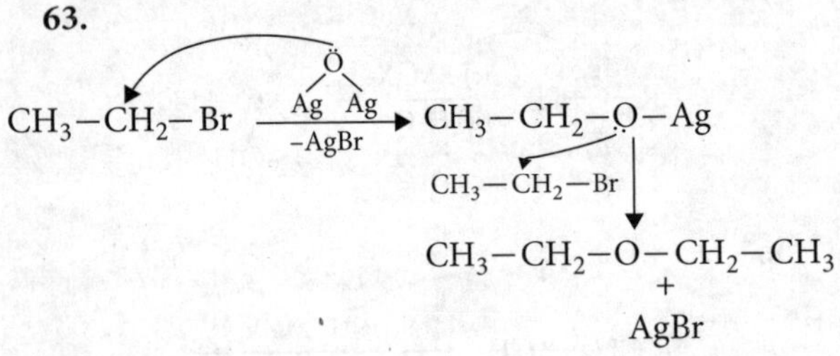

64.

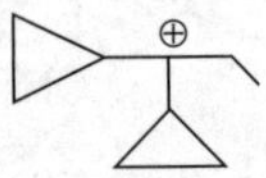

Most stable carbocation due to dancing resonance

65. Mild oxidizing agent oxidizes alcohol up to carbonyl compound only, but strong oxidizing agent (like $KMnO_4$, $K_2Cr_2O_7$) oxidizes up to acid.

66.

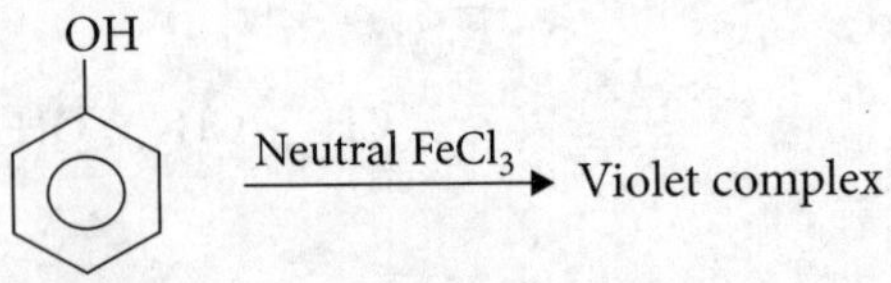

67. 2° alcohol gives turbidity within 5 minutes by S_N1.

68. Phenol is most acidic (acid) and so it gives acid–base reaction with NaOH; but alcohols do not give acid–base reaction with NaOH.

69.

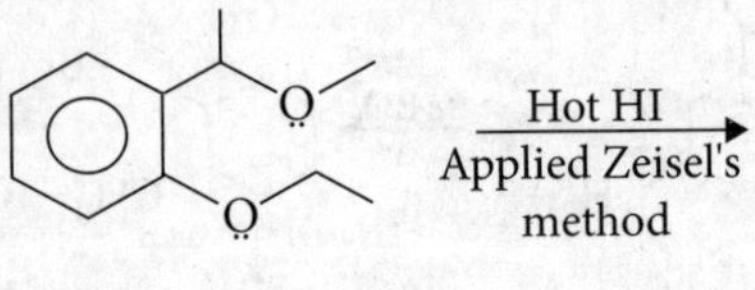

70.

Stability of intermediate carbocation is increased by +M of methoxy.

71. Thionyl chloride ($SOCl_2$) with alcohol in the presence of pyridine gives inversion produced by S_N2 mechanism.

72.

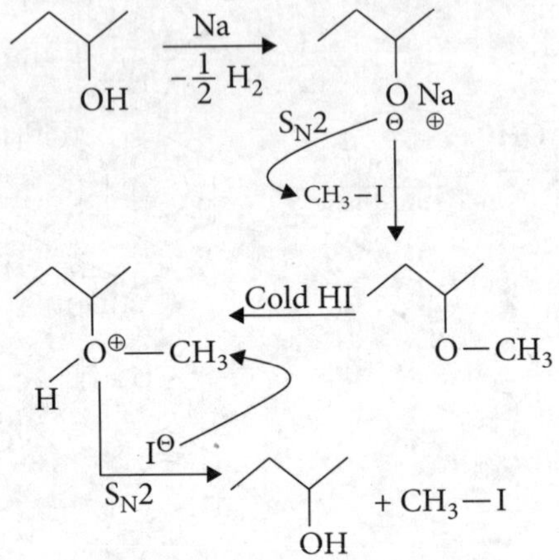

73.

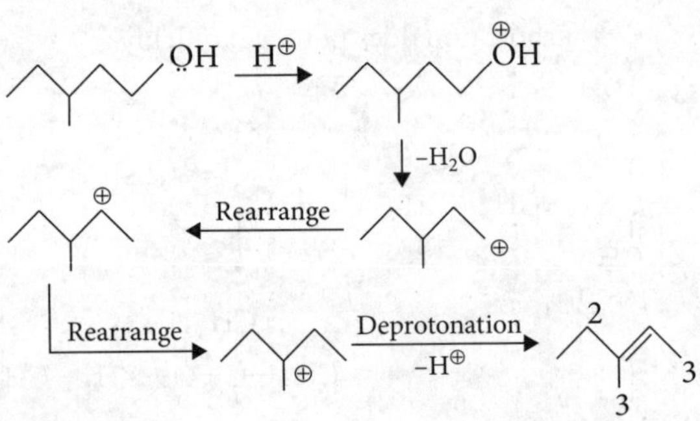

74.

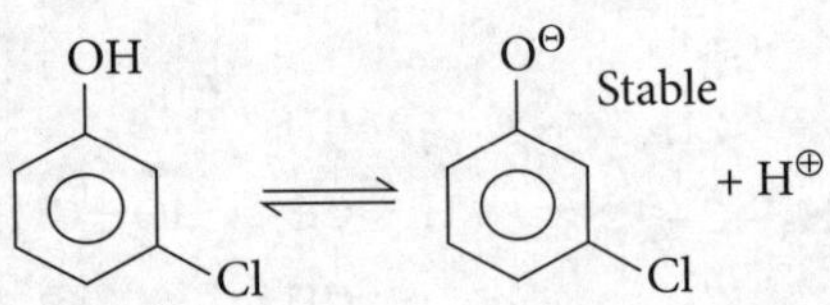

75.

b (–M) > d (–I) > c (less (–I)) > a (reference) > e (+M)

76. Intermediate carbocation stability

77. Boiling point $\propto \dfrac{\text{Molecular weight}}{\text{Branching}}$

78. Ortho-substituted aniline is a weaker base than aniline because of SIP (steric inhibition of protonation).

79. Stable alkene is major

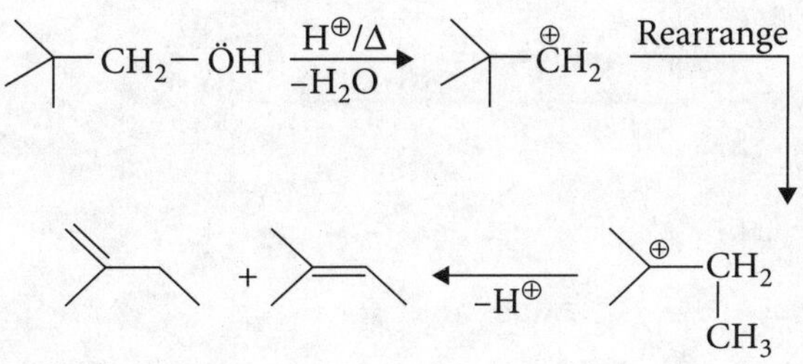

81.

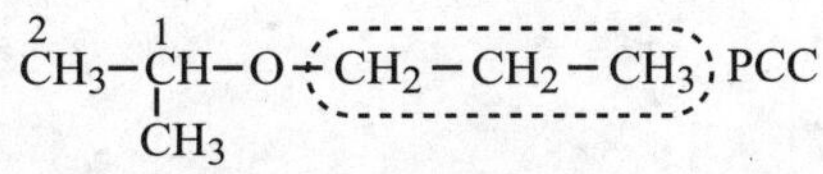

1-[1-methylethoxy] - propane

82.

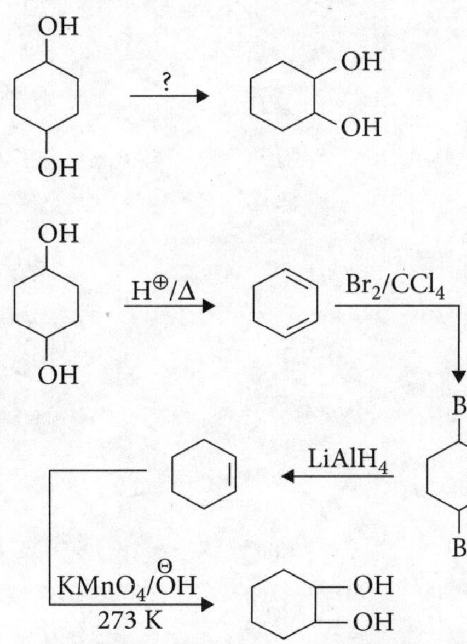

83.

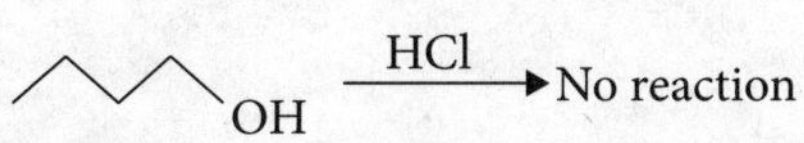

and others follow S_N2 mechanism.

84.

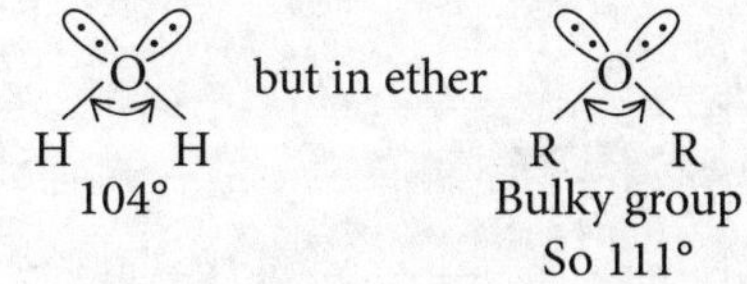

85.

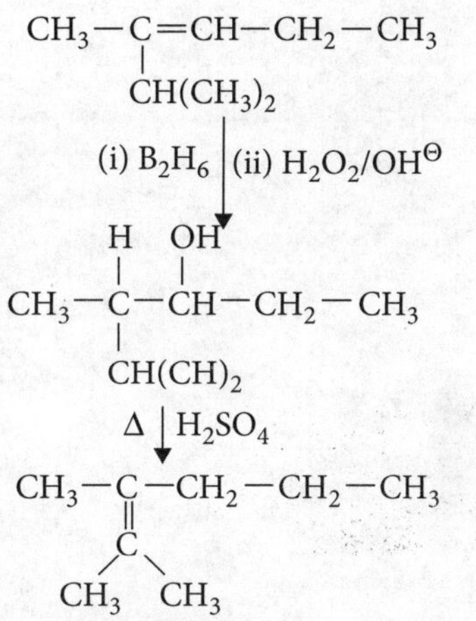

More stable alkene

86.

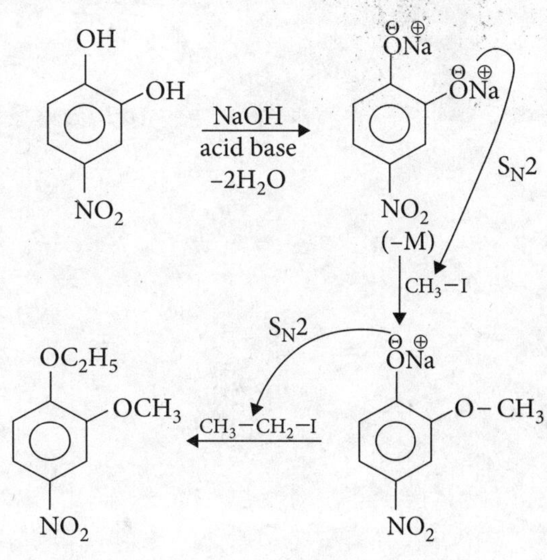

CHAPTER 8

Aldehyde, Ketone and Carboxylic Acid

Level-1

ALDEHYDE AND KETONE

1. Benzophenone can be obtained by_______________.
   (i) Benzoyl chloride + Benzene + $AlCl_3$
   (ii) Benzoyl chloride + Diphenylcadmium
   (iii) Benzoyl chloride + Benzyl magnesium chloride
   (iv) Benzene + Carbon monoxide + HCl/$AlCl_3$
   (a) (i) and (ii) (b) (ii) and (iii)
   (c) (iii) and (iv) (d) (i), (ii) and (iv)

2. Which of the following is the correct representation of carbonyl compounds?
   (a) 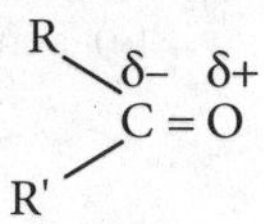
   (b) 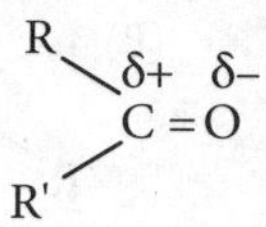
   (c) 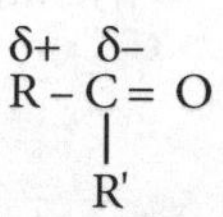
   (d) 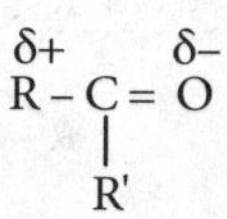

3. Read the following statements and choose the correct option:
   (i) The carbonyl carbon atom is sp^2 -hybridized
   (ii) The carbonyl carbon is an electrophilic (Lewis acid) centre
   (iii) The carbonyl oxygen is a nucleophilic (Lewis base) centre
   (iv) Carbonyl compounds are non-polar in nature
   (a) (i), (ii) and (iv) are correct
   (b) (i), (ii) and (iii) are correct
   (c) (ii), (iii) and (iv) are correct
   (d) (ii) and (iv) are correct

4. Read the following statements and choose the correct option:
   (i) The boiling points of aldehydes and ketones are lower than those of alcohols of similar molecular mass.
   (ii) Alcohols show intermolecular hydrogen bonding whereas aldehydes and ketones do not show intermolecular hydrogen bonding.
   (iii) The lower members of aldehydes and ketones are miscible with water in all proportions, because they form hydrogen bonds with water.
   (iv) The solubility of aldehydes and ketones increases rapidly on increasing the length of the alkyl chain.
   (a) TTFF (b) TFFT
   (c) FTTT (d) TTTF

5. **Assertion (A):** The boiling points of aldehydes and ketones are higher than hydrocarbons and ethers of comparable molecular mass.
   Reason (R): There is a comparatively stronger molecular association in aldehydes and ketones arising out of the dipole–dipole interactions.
   (a) Assertion is correct, reason is correct; reason is a correct explanation for assertion.
   (b) Assertion is correct, reason is correct; reason is not a correct explanation for assertion
   (c) Assertion is correct, reason is incorrect
   (d) Assertion is incorrect, reason is correct.

6. Aldehydes are generally more reactive than ketones in nucleophilic addition reactions. Which of the following statements accounts for this?
   (i) Sterically, the presence of two relatively large substituents in ketones hinders the approach of nucleophile to carbonyl carbon.
   (ii) Aldehydes show resonance whereas ketones do not.

(iii) Electronically, the presence of two alkyl groups in ketone reduces the electrophilicity of the carbonyl carbon more effectively.
(iv) Electronically, the carbonyl carbon atom in ketones is more electrophilic than in aldehydes.

(a) (i) and (iii) (b) (i) and (iv)
(c) (ii) and (iii) (d) (ii) and (iv)

7. Which of the following compounds is most reactive towards nucleophilic addition reactions?

(a) $CH_3-\overset{\overset{O}{\|}}{C}-H$

(b) $CH_3-\overset{\overset{O}{\|}}{C}-CH_3$

(c) 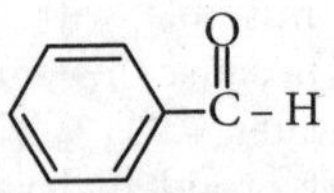

(d) 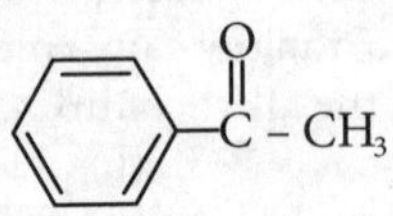

8. Benzaldehyde is less reactive than propanal because:
(i) The carbon atom of the carbonyl group of benzaldehyde is less electrophilic than that of propanal.
(ii) The carbon atom of the carbonyl group of benzaldehyde is more electrophilic than in propanal.
(iii) The carbonyl group in benzaldehyde is more polar due to resonance.
(iv) The carbonyl group in benzaldehyde is less polar due to resonance.

(a) (i) and (iii) (b) (i) and (iv)
(c) (i) only (d) (iv) only

9. Addition of hydrogen cyanide to aldehydes and ketones occurs in the presence of a base. The role of the base is to:
(i) Catalyse the reaction
(ii) Generate the CN^- ion
(iii) Slow down the reaction
(iv) Stabilize the cyanohydrins

(a) (i) and (iii) (b) (i) and (ii)
(c) (i) and (iv) (d) (ii) and (iv)

10. Which of the following products is formed when benzaldehyde is treated with CH_3MgBr and the addition product so obtained is subjected to acid hydrolysis?
(a) 1-Phenylethan-1-ol
(b) 2-Phenylethan-1-ol
(c) Phenol
(d) Benzyl alcohol

11. Read the following statements regarding the reaction of carbonyl compounds with $NaHSO_3$:
(a) The position of equilibrium lies largely to the right for most aldehydes and left for most ketones.
(b) The hydrogen sulphite products are water insoluble.
(c) This reaction is used for separation and purification of aldehydes.

The correct set of statements is:
(a) a, b (b) b, c
(c) a, b, c (d) a, c

12. Match the columns:

Column I	Column II
(A) $\begin{array}{l}R\\ \quad C=NH\\ R\end{array}$	(p) Oxime
(B) $\begin{array}{l}R\\ \quad C=NOH\\ R\end{array}$	(q) Semi-carbazone
(C) $\begin{array}{l}R\\ \quad C=N-NH_2\\ R\end{array}$	(r) Imine
(D) $\begin{array}{l}R\\ \quad C=NNH\overset{\overset{O}{\|}}{C}NH_2\\ R\end{array}$	(s) Hydrazone

(a) A – (q), B – (s), C – (p), D – (r)
(b) A – (r), B – (p), C– (s), D– (q)
(c) A – (r), B – (s), C – (p), D– (q)
(d) A – (s), B – (r), C – (q), D– (p)

13. Acetal formation is a reversible reaction:

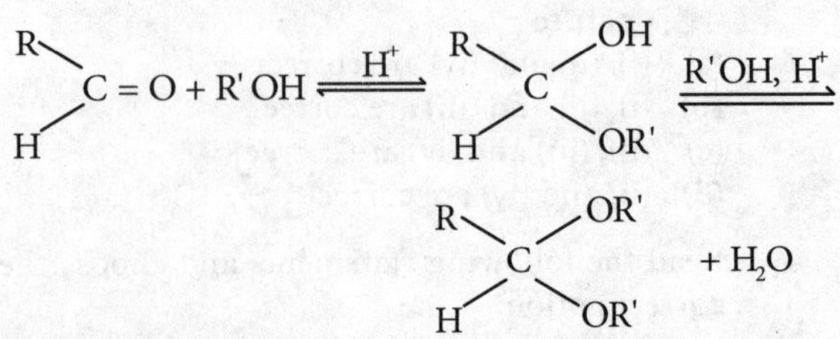

Under what conditions can the reaction be forced to proceed only in the right (forward) direction?
(a) Using excess of alcohol only
(b) Using low temperature
(c) Using dilute acid and alcohol
(d) Using dry acid and excess of alcohol

14. Which of the following conversions can be carried out by Clemmensen reduction?
(i) Benzaldehyde into benzyl alcohol
(ii) Cyclohexanone into cyclohexane
(iii) Benzoyl chloride into benzaldehyde
(iv) Benzophenone into diphenylmethane
(a) (ii) and (iv) (b) (i) and (iv)
(c) (i) and (iii) (d) (iii) and (iv)

15. Match the columns:

Column I (Reactions)	Column II (Reagents)
(A) Benzophenone → Diphenylmethane	(p) $LiAlH_4$
(B) Benzaldehyde → 1-Phenylethanol	(q) $SnCl_2$, HCl, H_3O^+
(C) Cyclohexanone → Cyclohexanol	(r) Zn(Hg)/Conc HCl
(D) Benzonitrile → Benzaldehyde	(s) CH_3MgBr, H_3O^+

(a) A – (p), B – (s), C – (r), D – (q)
(b) A – (q), B – (s), C – (p), D – (r)
(c) A – (s), B – (r), C – (q), D – (p)
(d) A – (r), B – (s), C – (p), D – (q)

16. Which of the following undergoes haloform reaction ?
(i) $CH_3CH_2COCH_2Cl$
(ii) $C_6H_5COCH_3$
(iii) Ph–CO–Ph
(iv) CH_3CH_2OH
(a) Only (ii) (b) (ii) and (iv)
(c) (i), (ii) and (iv) (d) All the four

17. The difference between aldol condensation and the Cannizzaro reaction is that:
(a) The former takes place in the presence of the α-H-atom.
(b) The latter takes place in the presence of the α-H-atom.
(c) The former takes place in the presence of the β-H-atom.
(d) The former is disproportionation while the latter is dehydration.

18. Which of the following pairs of compounds will undergo aldol and Cannizzaro reaction, respectively?
(i) Acetone, benzaldehyde
(ii) Acetaldehyde, butan-2-one
(iii) Propanone, formaldehyde
(iv) Cyclopentanone, benzaldehyde
(a) (i), (ii) and (iii) (b) (ii) and (iii)
(c) (i), (iii) and (iv) (d) (iii) and (iv)

19. Match the columns:

Column I	Column II
(A) $R-CO-CH_3 \xrightarrow{Zn-Hg/HCl} R-CH_2-CH_3$	(p) Friedel–Crafts reaction
(B) $2C_6H_5CHO \xrightarrow{NaOH} C_6H_5COONa + C_6H_5CH_2OH$	(q) Kolbe's reaction
(C) $C_6H_6 + CH_3COCl \xrightarrow[AlCl_3]{Anhydrous} C_6H_5COCH_3$	(r) Clemmensen reaction
(D) $C_6H_5OH \xrightarrow[(ii)H^+]{(i)CO_2,NaOH} HOC_6H_4COOH$	(s) Cannizzaro reaction

(a) A – (p), B – (q), C – (r), D – (s)
(b) A – (q), B – (p), C – (r), D – (s)
(c) A – (r), B – (s), C – (p), D – (q)
(d) A – (s), B – (r), C – (p), D – (q)

20. Alcohol vapours are passed over which of the following catalysts to give aldehydes and ketones?
(a) Zn or Ni (b) Ag or Cu
(c) Au or Pt (d) O_2 or N_2

21. Match the reactions given in Column I with the suitable reagents given in Column II and choose the correct option from the codes given below:

Column I (Reactions)	Column II (Reagents)
A Ethanenitrile to ethanal	1 O_3,Zn/H_2O
B Allyl alcohol to acrylaldehyde	2 (DIBAL-H)
C But-2-ene to ethanal	3 PCC

Codes

	A	B	C
(a)	1	2	3
(b)	3	2	1
(c)	2	3	1
(d)	2	1	3

22.

$$\text{Ethyne} + H_2O \xrightarrow[H_2SO_4]{HgSO_4}$$

The product formed in the given reaction is:
(a) Benzaldehyde
(b) Acetaldehyde
(c) Ethanoic acid
(d) Ethanoyl chloride

23.

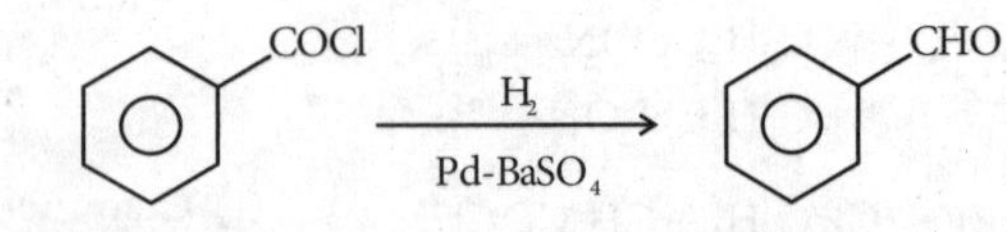

Benzoyl chloride Benzaldehyde

The above reaction is known as:
(a) Stephen reaction
(b) Rosenmund reduction
(c) Clemmensen reaction
(d) Reimer–Tiemann reaction

24. Select the reagent and the intermediate formed in the Stephen reaction:

Reagent	Intermediate
(a) DIBAL-H	Aldehyde
(b) Stannous chloride	Imine
(c) Stannous chloride	Aldehyde
(d) DIBAL-H	Imine

25. Which of the following substrates gives the same product on reduction with DIBAL-H?
(a) $CH_3(CH_2)_9CN$ and $CH_3(CH_2)_9COOH$
(b) $CH_3(CH_2)_9CN$ and $CH_3(CH_2)_9COOC_2H_5$
(c) $CH_3(CH_2)_9COOH$ and $CH_3(CH_2)_9CHO$
(d) $CH_3(CH_2)_9COOH$ and $CH_3(CH_2)_9COOC_2H_5$

26. Match the names of reagents given in Column II to bring about the conversions given in Column I and choose the correct option from the codes given below:

Column I (Conversion)	**Column II (Reagents)**
A. Hexan-1-ol to hexanal	1. $C_5H_5{}^+NHCrO_3Cl^-$ (PCC)
B. Cyclohexanol to cyclohexanone	2. CrO_3 in the presence of acetic anhydride
C. p-Fluorotoluene to p-fluorobenzaldehyde	3. $K_2Cr_2O_7$ in acidic medium

Codes

	A	B	C
(a)	1	2	3
(b)	2	3	1
(c)	1	3	2
(d)	2	1	3

27. Select the structure of the chromium complex formed when toluene reacts with chromyl chloride, which gives benzaldehyde on hydrolysis:

(a) 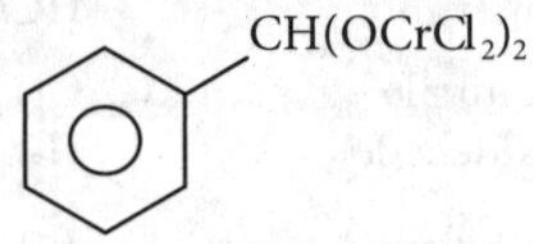

(b) 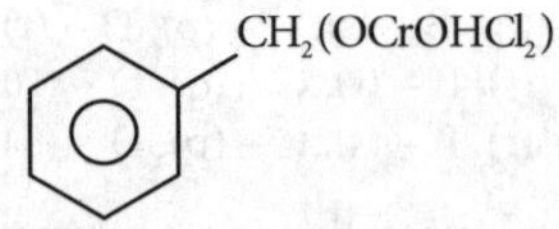

(c) 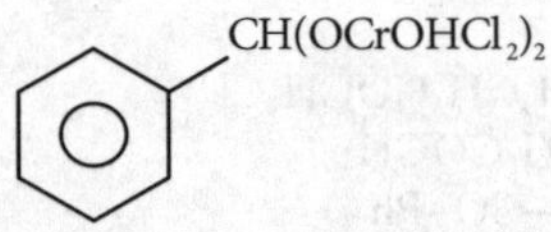

(d) 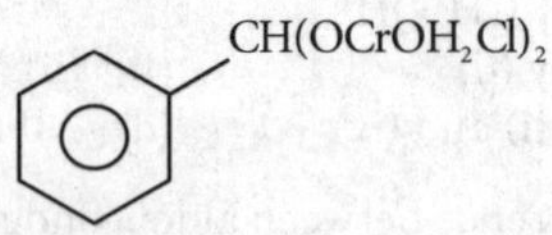

28. Toluene on treating with chromic oxide in acetic anhydride followed by aqueous acid gives:
(a) Benzyl diacetate
(b) Benzaldehyde
(c) Benzyl acetate
(d) Benzylidene diacetate

29. Choose the Gattermann–Koch reaction:

(a)

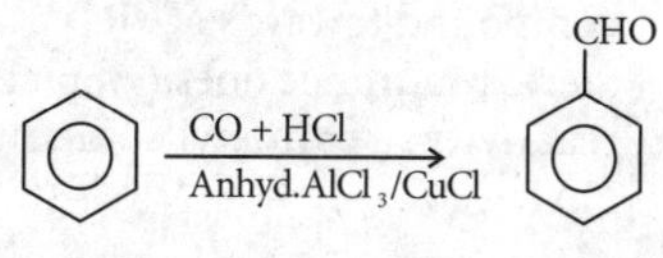

(b)

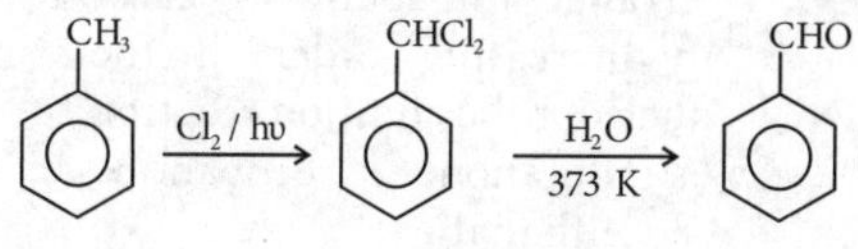

(c)

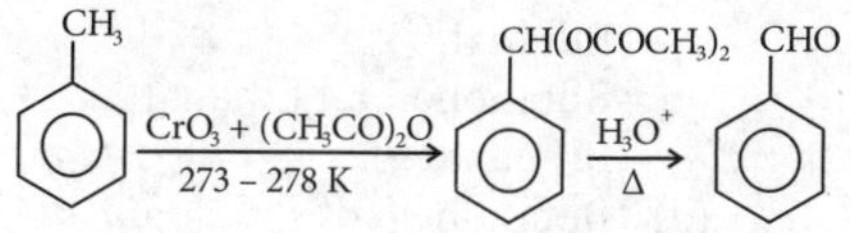

(d)

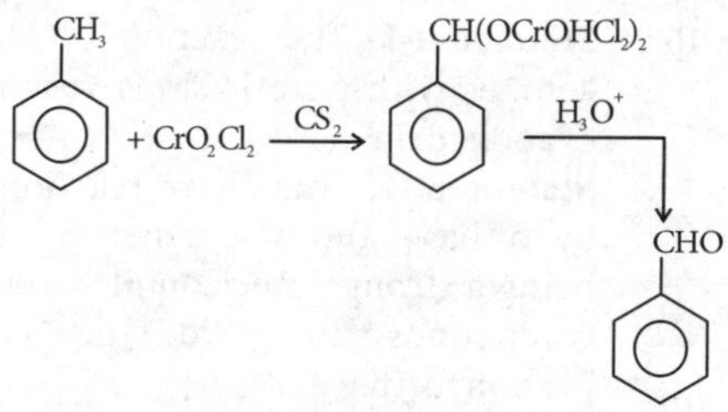

30. Which of the following reactions is/are correct regarding the preparation of ketone?

(a) Treatment of acyl chlorides with dialkyl cadmium, prepared by the reaction of cadmium chloride with the Grignard reagent, gives ketones.
(b) When benzene or substituted benzene is treated with acid chloride in the presence of anhydrous aluminium chloride, it gives the corresponding ketone.
(c) Treating a alkyl nitrile with the Grignard reagent followed by hydrolysis yields a ketone.
(d) All of the above

31. Methanal, ethanal and propanone are miscible with water because they interact with water by:

(a) Van der Waals forces
(b) Hydrogen bonding
(c) Dipole–dipole forces
(d) Dispersion forces

32. **Statement-I:** Aldehydes and ketones have larger dipole moments (2.3–2.8D).

Statement-II: The high polarity of the carbonyl group can be explained by resonance, involving neutral and dipolar structure.

(a) Both Statement-I and II are correct and Statement-II is the correct explanation of Statement-I.
(b) Both Statement-I and II are correct and II is not the correct explanation of Statement-I.
(c) Statement-I is correct, Statement-II is incorrect.
(d) Statement-I is incorrect, Statement-II is correct.

33. Choose the correct alternative from the following regarding the physical properties of carbonyl compounds:

(a) When the size of aldehyde increases, odour becomes less pungent and more fragrant.
(b) They are insoluble in organic solvents.
(c) Solubility increases rapidly on increasing the length of the alkyl chain.
(d) None of the above.

34. Arrange the following compounds in the increasing order of their boiling points:

$CH_3CH_2CH_2CHO$ (I) $\quad CH_3CH_2CH_2CH_2OH$ (II)

$H_5C_2OC_2H_5$ (III) $\quad CH_3CH_2CH_2CH_2CH_3$ (IV)

(a) IV < I < II < III
(b) IV < III < II < I
(c) IV < III < I < II
(d) IV < II < III < I

35. Select the correct dissimilarities between the C=O and C=C bonds:

(a) The carbon–oxygen double bond is polar but the carbon–carbon double bond is non-polar.
(b) The carbon–oxygen bond is shorter (123 pm) than that of the carbon–carbon bond (134 pm).
(c) Carbonyl compounds undergo nucleophilic addition reactions but compounds containing C=C double bonds undergo electrophilic addition reactions.
(d) All of the above

36. **Statement-I:** The carbonyl carbon is a nucleophilic centre and the carbonyl oxygen is an electrophilic centre.
Statement-II: The carbon–oxygen double bond is polarised due to higher electronegativity of oxygen relative to carbon.
(a) Both Statement-I and II are correct and Statement-II is the correct explanation of Statement-I.
(b) Both Statement-I and II are correct and II is not the correct explanation of Statement-I.
(c) Statement-I is correct, Statement-II is incorrect.
(d) Statement-I is incorrect, Statement-II is correct.

37. Study the mechanism given below carefully:

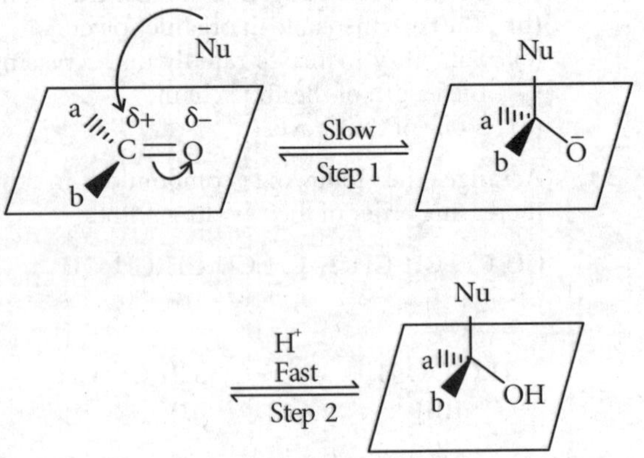

Select the correct statement(s) for the above diagram from the options given below:
(a) A nucleophile attacks the electrophilic carbon of the polar carbonyl group from a direction parallel to the plane of the sp^2-hybridized orbitals of the carbonyl carbon
(b) The hybridization of carbon changes from sp to sp^2 in this process
(c) The net result is the addition of nucleophile and H^+ across the carbon–oxygen double bond
(d) Step 2 is the rate determination step

38. Choose the correct alternative from the following:
(a) Ketones are more reactive than aldehydes towards NAR
(b) Aldehydes are more reactive than ketones towards NAR
(c) Formaldehyde is the least reactive carbonyl compound towards NAR
(d) Steric hindrance does not play a role in the reactivity of carbonyl compounds towards NAR

39. Arrange the following carbonyl compounds in increasing order of their reactivity in nucleophilic addition reaction:
(a) Butanone < Propanone < Propanal < Ethanal
(b) Butanone < Propanal < Propanone < Ethanal
(c) Butanone < Ethanal < Propanone < Propanal
(d) Butanone < Ethanal < Propanal < Propanone

40. **Statement-I**: The reaction of aldehydes and ketones with pure HCN is very slow to yield cyanohydrin.
Statement-II: The above reaction is catalyzed by a base and the generated cyanide ion, being a stronger nucleophile, adds to carbonyl compounds to yield the corresponding cyanohydrin.
(a) Both Statement-I and II are correct and Statement-II is the correct explanation of Statement-I.
(b) Both Statement-I and II are correct and II is not the correct explanation of Statement-I.
(c) Statement-I is correct, Statement-II is incorrect.
(d) Statement-I is incorrect, Statement-II is correct.

41. **Statement-I:** Sodium hydrogen sulphite adds to aldehyde, and ketones are a useful method for separation and purification of aldehydes.
Statement-II: The hydrogen sulphite addition compound is water soluble and can be converted back to the original carbonyl compound by treating it with dilute mineral acid or alkali.
(a) Both Statement-I and II are correct and Statement-II is the correct explanation of Statement-I.
(b) Both Statement-I and II are correct and II is not the correct explanation of Statement-I.
(c) Statement-I is correct, Statement-II is incorrect.
(d) Statement-I is incorrect, Statement-II is correct.

42.

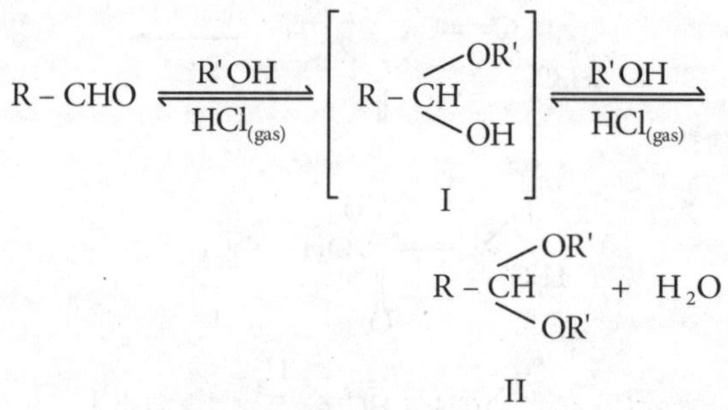

Identify the abbreviation used for I and II for the given reaction:

I	II
(a) Acetal or gem-dialkoxy	Hemiacetal or alkoxy alcohol
(b) Acetal or alkoxy alcohol	Hemiacetal or gem-dialkoxy
(c) Hemiacetal or alkoxy alcohol	Acetal or gem-dialkoxy
(d) Hemiacetal or gem-dialkoxy	Acetal or alkoxy alcohol

43. Which of the following options is incorrect for the treatment of ketones with ethylene glycol in the presence of dry HCl?
(a) The product obtained is ethylene glycol cyclic ketal
(b) The reaction is an example of electrophilic addition reaction
(c) HCl protonates the oxygen of the carbonyl group
(d) The reaction can be reversed by treating the product with aqueous mineral acid

44.

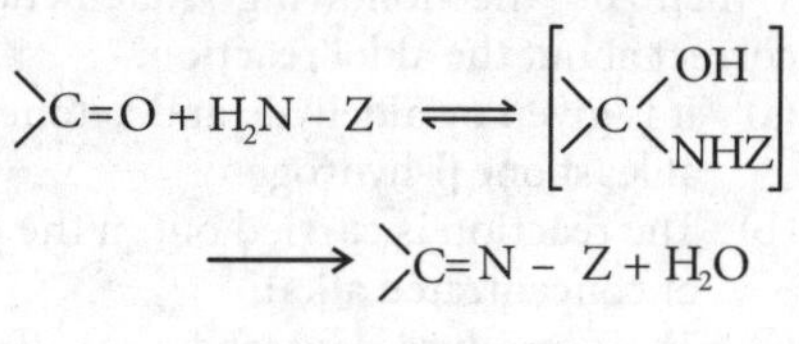

Which of the following statements is/are true about the above reaction?
(a) H_2N–Z tends to add to the carbon of the carbonyl group of aldehydes and ketones
(b) The reaction is reversible and catalysed by acid
(c) The equilibrium favours product formation due to rapid dehydration of the intermediate
(d) All of the above

45. Some N-substituted derivatives of aldehydes and ketones ($>C{=}N{-}Z$) are:

Z	Reagent name	Carbonyl derivative	Product name
–H	Ammonia	I	Imine
–R	Amine	$>C=NR$	II
III	Hydroxylamine	$>C{=}N-OH$	Oxime
$-NH_2$	IV	$>C{=}N-NH_2$	Hydrazone

Identify I, II, III and IV in the given table:

	I	II	III	IV
(a)	$-C\equiv N$	Schiff's base	–OH	Hydrazine
(b)	$>C=NH$	Substituted imine	–H	Hydrazine
(c)	$-C\equiv N$	Substituted imine	–OH	Hydrazine
(d)	$>C=NH$	Schiff's base	–OH	Hydrazine

46. Identify the example of the nucleophilic addition elimination reaction of carbonyl compounds:
(a) Addition of HCN
(b) Addition of $NaHSO_3$
(c) Addition of the Grignard reagent
(d) Addition of alcohols

47. Reagent(s) used for the reduction of aldehydes and ketones is/are:
(a) $LiAlH_4$
(b) $NaBH_4$
(c) Catalytic hydrogenation
(d) All of these

48. **Assertion (A):** A bright silver mirror is produced during the warming of an aldehyde with freshly prepared ammoniacal silver nitrate solution.
Reason (R): A bright silver mirror is produced due to the formation of silver metal during the reaction.
(a) Both A and R are correct; and R is the correct explanation of A.

(b) Both A and R are correct; but R is not the correct explanation of A.
(c) A is correct; but R is incorrect.
(d) R is correct; but A is incorrect.

49. Which of the following statements is/are correct?
(a) Aldehydes are generally oxidised under vigorous conditions
(b) Ketones are easily oxidised to carboxylic acids even under mild oxidising agents
(c) Oxidation of ketone involves carbon–carbon bond cleavage to give a mixture of carboxylic acids having fewer number of C-atoms than the parent ketones
(d) Ketones possess oxidisable hydrogen while aldehydes lack it.

50. An organic compound X having molecular formula $C_5H_{10}O$ yields phenyl hydrazone and gives a negative response to the iodoform test and Tollens' test. It produces n-pentane on Clemmensen reduction. X could be:
(a) Pentanal (b) Pentan-2-one
(c) Pentan-3-one (d) Pentan-2-ol

51. The composition of Fehling's solution A and Fehling's solution B is:
(a) Aqueous copper sulphate and alkaline sodium potassium tartrate (Rochelle salt), respectively
(b) Alkaline sodium potassium tartrate (Rochelle salt) and aqueous copper sulphate, respectively
(c) Aqueous copper sulphate and acidic sodium potassium tartrate (Rochelle salt), respectively
(d) Acidic sodium potassium tartrate (Rochelle salt) and aqueous copper sulphate, respectively

52. The composition of silver mirror in Tollens' test and red brown precipitate in the Fehling test are, respectively:
(a) Ag_2O, Cu_2O (b) Cu_2O, Ag
(c) Ag, Cu_2O (d) Cu_2O, Ag_2O

53. Which of the following carbonyl groups gives a positive Fehling test?
(a) Aliphatic aldehydes
(b) Aromatic aldehydes
(c) Ketones
(d) Both (a) and (b)

54. Identify the product formed by the reagent in this reaction:

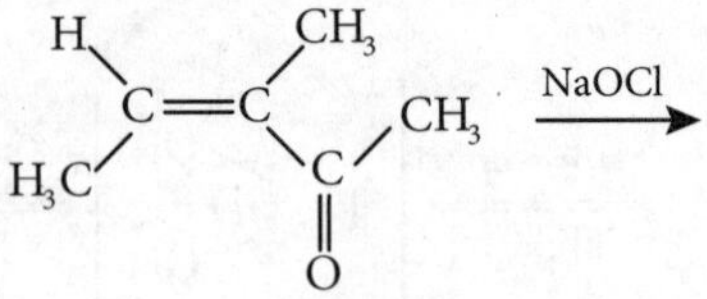

(a) 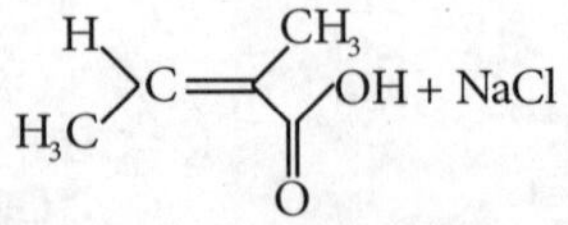

(b) 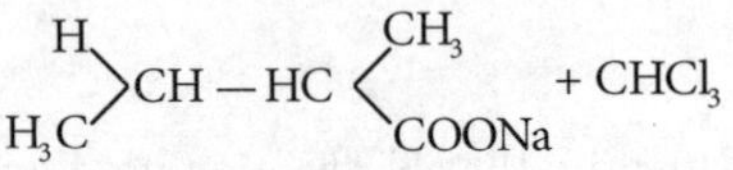

(c) 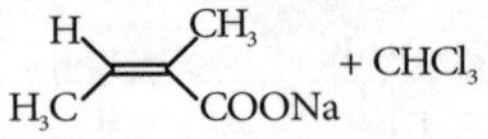

(d) 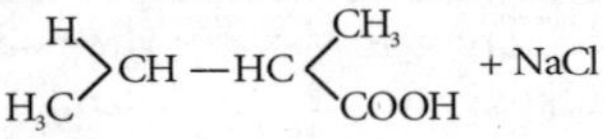

55. Which of the following ketones will give a positive iodoform test?
(a) 3-Hexanone
(b) Cyclohexanone
(c) 2-Methyl-3-pentanone
(d) 2-Hexanone

56. **Assertion (A):** α-hydrogen atoms of carbonyl compounds are acidic.
Reason (R): The acidity of α-hydrogen is due to the strong electron withdrawing effect of the carbonyl group and resonance stabilisation of the conjugate base.
(a) Both A and R are correct; and R is the correct explanation of A.
(b) Both A and R are correct; but R is not the correct explanation of A.
(c) A is correct; but R is incorrect.
(d) R is correct; but A is incorrect.

57. Which of the following statements is/are correct about the aldol reaction?
(a) It is given by aldehyde and ketones having at least one β-hydrogen
(b) The reaction is carried out in the presence of concentrated alkali
(c) The product formed is β-hydroxy aldehydes (aldol) or β-hydroxy ketone (ketol)
(d) It is an irreversible reaction

58.

$$2CH_3COCH_3 \xrightleftharpoons{Ba(OH)_2} X \xrightarrow[-H_2O]{\Delta} Y$$

Identify X and Y in the given reaction:

(a) 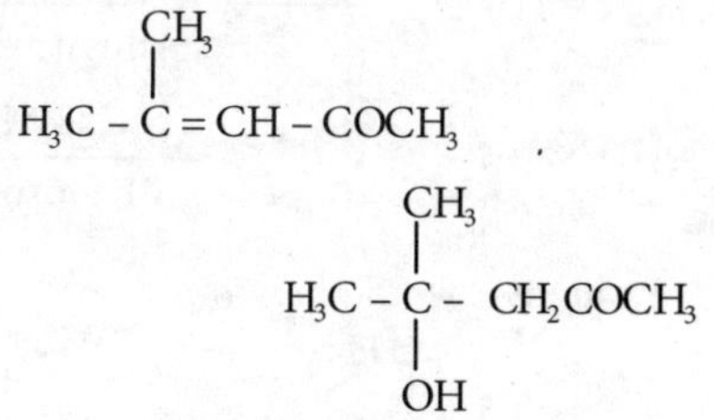

(b) 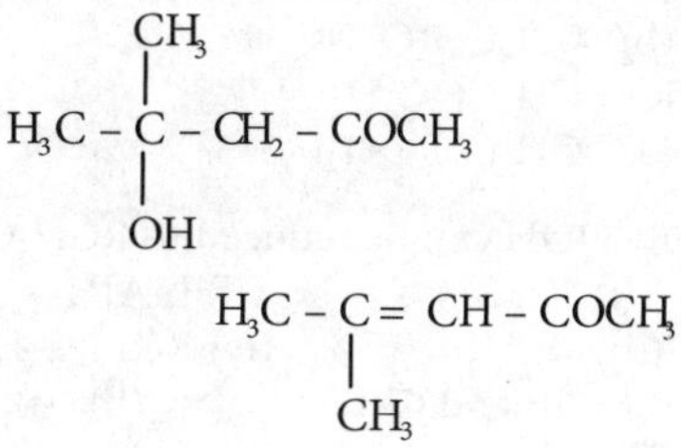

(c) 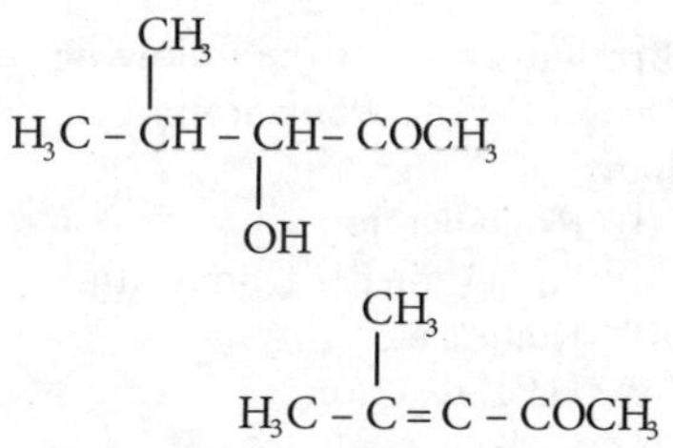

(d) 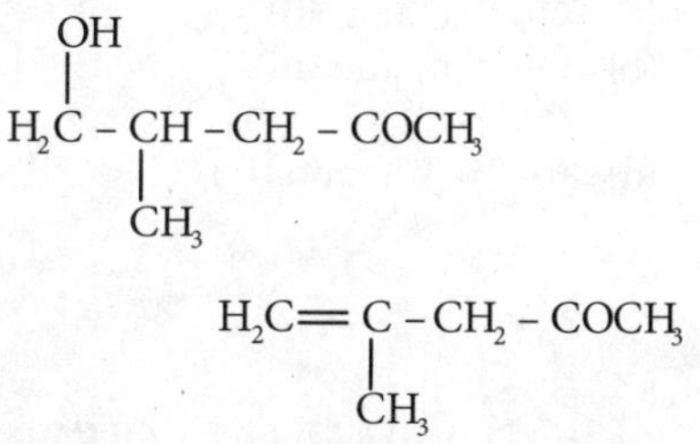

59. **Statement-I:** Benzaldehyde on heating with concentrated alkali gives α, β-unsaturated carbonyl compound.

Statement-II: Benzaldehyde does not have an α-H-atom.

(a) Both Statement-I and II are correct.
(b) Both Statement-I and II are incorrect.
(c) Statement-I is correct; but Statement-II is incorrect.
(d) Statement-I is incorrect; but Statement-II is correct.

60. **Assertion (A):** The nitration of benzaldehyde is slower than benzene, and m-nitrobenzaldehyde is the product.

Reason (R): The –CHO group acts as a deactivating and meta-directing group.

(a) Both A and R are correct; and R is the correct explanation of A.
(b) Both A and R are correct; but R is not the correct explanation of A.
(c) A is correct; but R is incorrect.
(d) R is correct; but A is incorrect.

61. Formaldehyde solution which is well known for preserving biological specimens is:

(a) Acetylene (40%) solution
(b) Acetylene (70%) solution
(c) Formalin (40%) solution
(d) Formalin (70%) solution

62. Choose the correct option from the following:

(a) Acetone is a common industrial solvent
(b) Formalin is used as a specimen preservative
(c) Butyraldehyde is used in perfumery
(d) All of the above

63. Which of the following is not a use of formaldehyde?

(a) Preservation of biological specimens
(b) Manufacturing of bakelite
(c) Silvering of mirrors
(d) Preparation of acetic acid

64. Many aldehydes and ketones are well known for their:

(a) Reactive nature towards the ortho and para positions during electrophilic substitution
(b) Non-polar nature
(c) Odour and flavour
(d) Inertness towards nucleophilic addition reaction

65. Match the following carbonyl compounds given in Column I with their uses given in Column II and choose the correct option from the given codes below:

Column I (Carbonyl compounds)	**Column II (Uses)**
A. Formaldehyde	1. Perfumery and dye industries
B. Acetaldehyde	2. Bakelite
C. Benzaldehyde	3. Odours and flavours
D. Vanillin, butyraldehyde	4. Manufacture of vinyl acetate and ethyl acetate

	A	B	C	D
(a)	1	2	3	4
(b)	2	3	4	1
(c)	1	3	4	1
(d)	2	4	1	3

Carboxylic Acid

66. Methyl cyanide can be converted into acetic acid by one of the following reactions:
(a) Reduction
(b) Hydrolysis
(c) Electrolysis
(d) Decarboxylation

67. Ethanoic acid cannot be obtained by which of the following reactions?

(i) $C_2H_5Cl \xrightarrow[(ii) H_3O^+]{(i) KCN}$

(ii) $CH_3Cl \xrightarrow[(ii) H_3O^+]{(i) AgCN}$

(iii) $CH_3CH=CH_2 \xrightarrow[Heat]{KMnO_4/OH^-}$

(iv) $CH_3Br \xrightarrow[(ii) CO_2,\ (iii) H_3O^+]{(i) Mg}$

(a) (iii) and (iv) (b) (i) and (ii)
(c) (ii) and (iii) (d) (i) and (iv)

68. **Assertion (A):** The molecular mass of acetic acid in benzene is 120 instead of 60.
Reason (R): The carboxylic acids exist as cyclic dimers in which the two molecules of the acid are held together by strong intermolecular hydrogen bonds.
(a) Assertion is correct, reason is correct; reason is a correct explanation for assertion.
(b) Assertion is correct, reason is correct; reason is not a correct explanation for assertion
(c) Assertion is correct, reason is incorrect
(d) Assertion is incorrect, reason is correct.

69. Acetic anhydride is obtained by the reaction of:
(a) Sodium and acetic acid
(b) Ammonia and acetic acid
(c) Ethanol and acetic acid
(d) P_2O_5 and acetic acid

70. In a set of the given reactions, the acetic acid yielded a product C:

$$CH_3COOH + PCl_5 \longrightarrow A \xrightarrow[\text{Anhydrous } AlCl_3]{C_6H_6} B \xrightarrow[(ii) \text{Hydrolysis}]{(i) C_2H_5MgBr} C$$

Product C would be:

(a) $CH_3-\underset{}{\overset{C_2H_5}{\overset{|}{C}}}(OH)C_6H_5$
(b) $CH_3CH(OH)C_2H_5$
(c) $CH_3COC_6H_5$
(d) $CH_3CH(OH)C_6H_5$

71. RCOOH can be reduced to RCH_2OH by:
(i) $NaBH_4$ (ii) $LiAlH_4$
(iii) B_2H_6 (iv) Red P + HI
(a) (ii) and (iii) (b) (i) and (iii)
(c) (i), (ii) and (iv) (d) (i), (iii) and (iv)

72. Through which of the following reactions can the number of carbon atoms be increased in the chain?
(i) Esterification
(ii) Soda lime decarboxylation
(iii) Kolbe's electrolysis
(iv) HVZ reaction
Choose the correct option:
(a) Only (i) and (iii)
(b) Only (ii) and (iii)
(c) Only (iii) and (iv)
(d) (i), (ii), (iii) and (iv)

73.

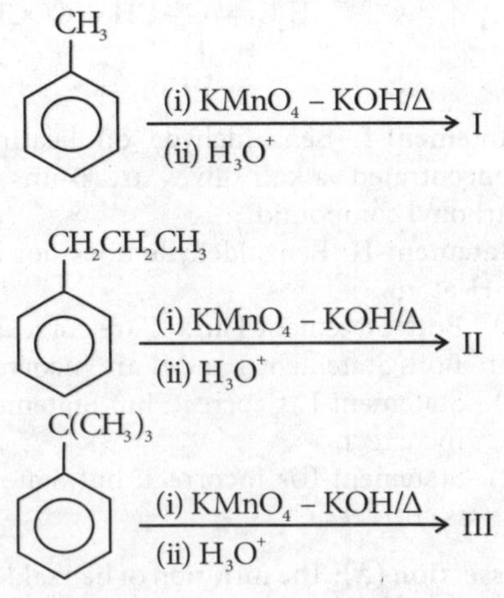

Identify the products formed in the given reaction:

I II III

(a) 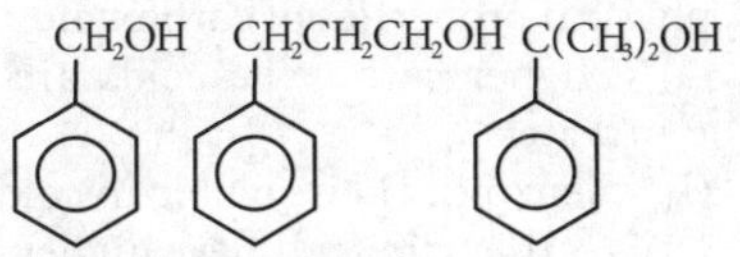

(b) 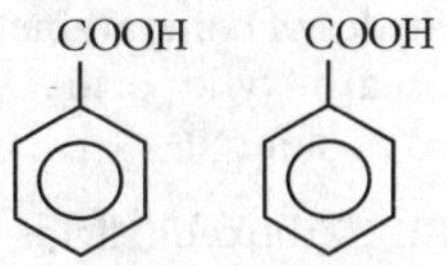

$(CH_3)_3C{-}COOH$

(c) 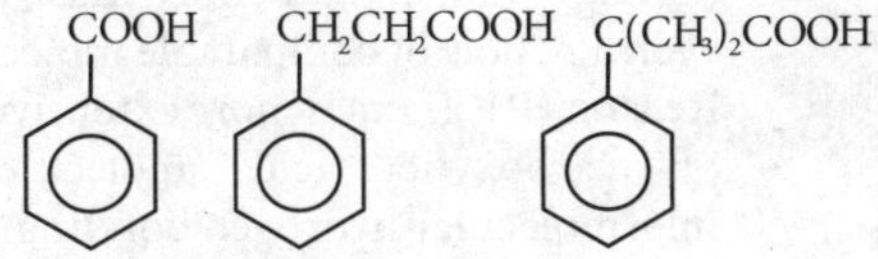

(d) 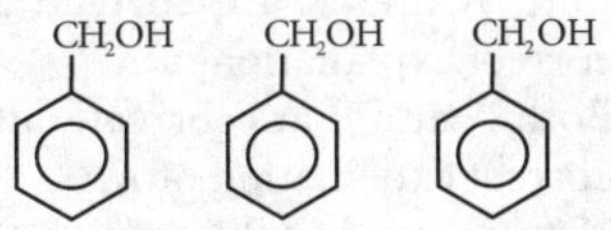

74. Select the correct statement(s) for the following:
(a) Nitriles are hydrolysed to amides and then to acids in the presence of H^+ or OH^- as catalyst
(b) Mild reaction conditions are used to stop the reaction at the amide stage during the hydrolysis of nitriles
(c) The Grignard reagent reacts with dry ice to form salts of carboxylic acids which in turn give the corresponding carboxylic acids after acidification with mineral acid
(d) All of the above

75. Select the acid(s) which cannot be prepared by the Grignard reagent?
(a) Acetic acid (b) Benzoic acid
(c) Formic acid (d) All of these

76. Match Column I with Column II and choose the correct option from the codes given below:

Column I (Starting material)	Column II (Reagents with product)
A. Cyclohexene	a. (i) Mg / ether (ii) Dry ice (iii) H_3O^+ → 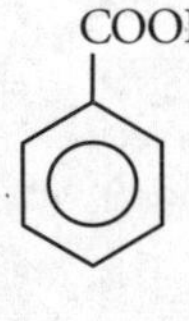
B. Bromobenzene	b. (i) $KMnO_4$ / KOH/Δ (ii) Dilute H_2SO_4 → 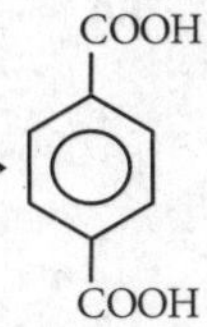
C. 4-Methylacetophenone	c. $KMnO_4/H_2SO_4/Δ$ → 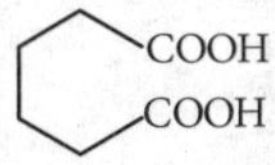

Codes

	A	B	C
(a)	a	b	c
(b)	c	b	a
(c)	c	a	b
(d)	b	a	c

77. The correct order of rate of hydrolysis of ester, acid chloride and acid anhydride is:
(a) Acid chloride > Acidic anhydride > Ester
(b) Ester > Acidic anhydride > Acid chloride
(c) Ester > Acid chloride > Acidic anhydride
(d) Ester < Acid chloride < Acidic anhydride

78. Which of the following types of hydrolysis of esters directly gives carboxylic acids and carboxylates, respectively?
(a) Acidic hydrolysis and basic hydrolysis
(b) Basic hydrolysis and acidic hydrolysis
(c) Acidic hydrolysis and acidic hydrolysis
(d) Basic hydrolysis and basic hydrolysis

79. In the following reaction,

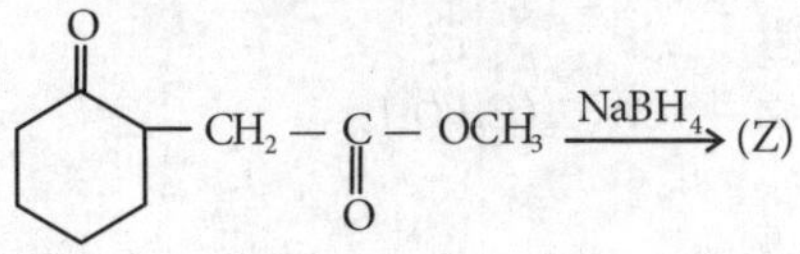

(Z) is:

(a) 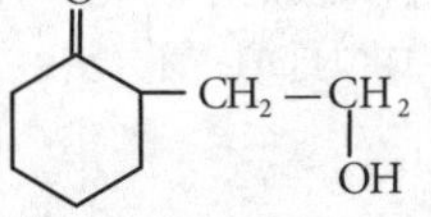

(b) 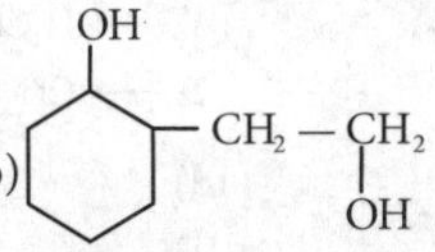

(c) 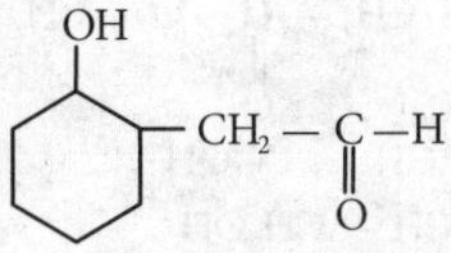

(d) 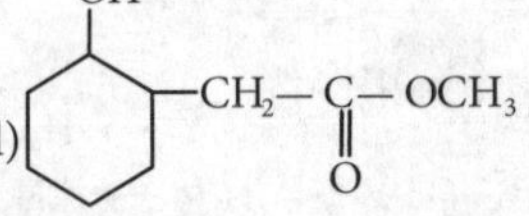

80. The following steps are given for the mechanism of esterification of carboxylic acids:

I. The protonated esters loses a proton to give the ester.

II. Protonation of the carbonyl oxygen activates the carbonyl group towards nucleophilic addition of the alcohol.

III. Proton transfer in the tetrahedral intermediate occurs.

IV. Nucleophilic attack of alcohol on the protonated carbonyl group.

Arrange the following steps in their correct sequence:

(a) I → II → IV → III
(b) I → IV→ III → II
(c) II → IV → III → I
(d) III → II → IV → I

81. An organic compound $X(C_8H_{16}O_2)$ was hydrolyzed with dilute H_2SO_4 to give carboxylic acid Y and alcohol Z. Oxidation of Z with chromic acid produced Y. Z on dehydration gives but-2-ene.

Identify X, Y and Z and choose the correct option:

(a)

$X \rightarrow H_3CCH_2-CH_2CH_2-\underset{\underset{O}{\|}}{C}-OCH_2CH_2CH_3$

$Y \rightarrow CH_3CH_2CH_2COOH$

$Z \rightarrow CH_3CH_2CH_2OH$

(b)

$X \rightarrow CH_3\underset{\underset{CH_3}{|}}{CH}\,CH_2-\underset{\underset{O}{\|}}{C}-OCH_2CH_2CH_3$

$Y \rightarrow H_3C-CH_2\underset{\underset{CH_3}{|}}{CH}-COOH$

$Z \rightarrow CH_3CH_2CH_2OH$

(c)

$X \rightarrow CH_3CH_2\,CH_2-\underset{\underset{O}{\|}}{C}-O-CH_2CH_2CH_2CH_3$

$Y \rightarrow H_3CCH_2CH_2-COOH$

$Z \rightarrow CH_3CH_2CH_2CH_2OH$

(d)

$X \rightarrow CH_3CH_2\,CH_2-\underset{\underset{O}{\|}}{C}-O-CH_2-\underset{\underset{CH_3}{|}}{CH}-CH_3$

$Y \rightarrow H_3CCH_2CH_2-COOH$

$Z \rightarrow CH_3-\underset{\underset{CH_3}{|}}{CH}-CH_2OH$

82. Choose the incorrect option regarding the physical properties of carboxylic acid:

(a) Higher carboxylic acids are insoluble in water
(b) Benzoic acid is soluble in cold water
(c) Carboxylic acids have higher boiling point than aldehydes of comparable mass
(d) Aliphatic carboxylic acids up to four C-atoms are coloured

83. **Assertion (A):** Carboxylic acids are higher boiling liquids than aldehydes, ketones and even alcohols of comparable molecular mass.

Reason (R): There is more extensive association of carboxylic acid molecules through intermolecular hydrogen bonding.

(a) Both A and R are correct; and R is the correct explanation of A.
(b) Both A and R are correct; but R is not the correct explanation of A.
(c) A is correct; but R is incorrect.
(d) R is correct; but A is incorrect.

84. **Assertion (A):** The melting points and boiling points of aliphatic acids are usually lower than those of aromatic acids of comparable molecular mass.

Reason (R): The planar benzene ring in the aromatic acids can fit more closely in the crystal lattice than the zig-zag structure of aliphatic acids.

(a) Both A and R are correct; and R is the correct explanation of A.
(b) Both A and R are correct; but R is not the correct explanation of A.
(c) A is correct; but R is incorrect.
(d) R is correct; but A is incorrect.

85. $2RCOOH + 2Na \longrightarrow 2RCOO^-Na^+ + X$

$RCOOH + NaHCO_3 \longrightarrow RCOO^-Na^+ + H_2O + Y$

Identify X and Y in the given reactions:

	X	Y
(a)	H_2	CO
(b)	H_2O	CO_2
(c)	H_2	CO_2
(d)	H_2O	CO

86. **Assertion (A):** Carboxylic acids are more acidic than phenols.

Reason (R): The carboxylate ion is less stabilised than the phenoxide ion.

(a) Both A and R are correct; and R is the correct explanation of A.

(b) Both A and R are correct; but R is not the correct explanation of A.
(c) A is correct; but R is incorrect.
(d) R is correct; but A is incorrect.

87. Several simple chemical tests are given to distinguish between a pair of compounds. Which of the following pairs is correct?
(a) Propanal and propanone → Silver mirror test
(b) Acetophenone and benzophenone → Iodoform test
(c) Ethanal and propanal → Fehling's test
(d) Benzoic acid and ethylbenzoate → Sodium bicarbonate test

(a) a, b, c (b) a, b, d
(c) b, d (d) a, b, c, d

88. Which of the following reagents is used for the conversion of ethanoic acid to ethanoic anhydride?
(a) $SOCl_2, \Delta$ (b) PCl_3, Δ
(c) P_2O_5, Δ (d) All of these

89.

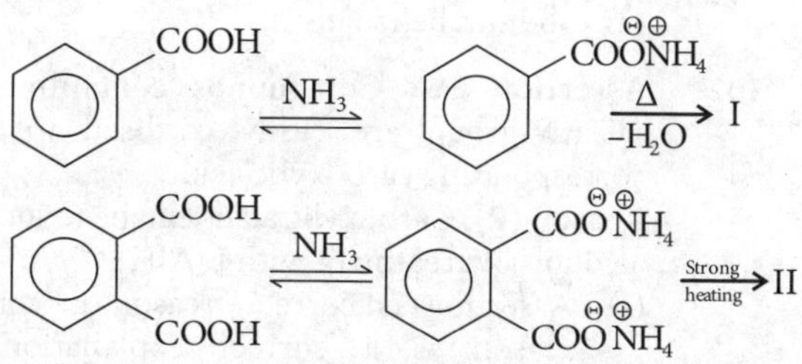

Identify I and II for the above reactions and choose the correct option:

I II

(a) 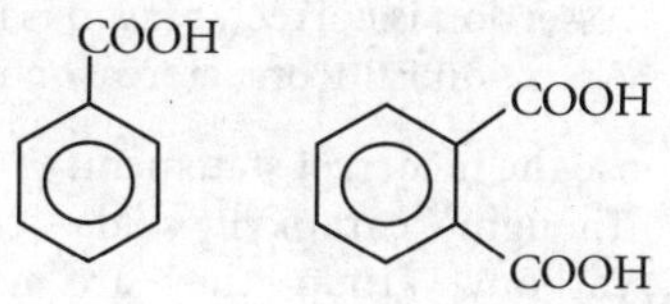

(b) 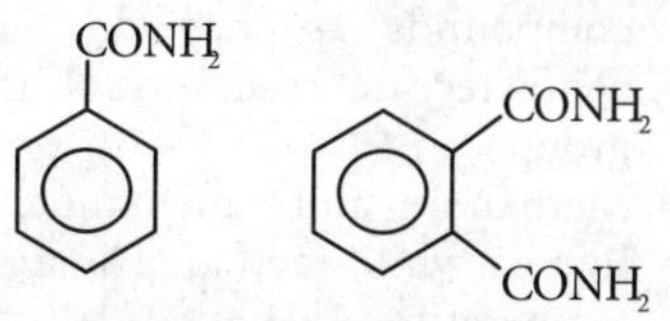

(c) 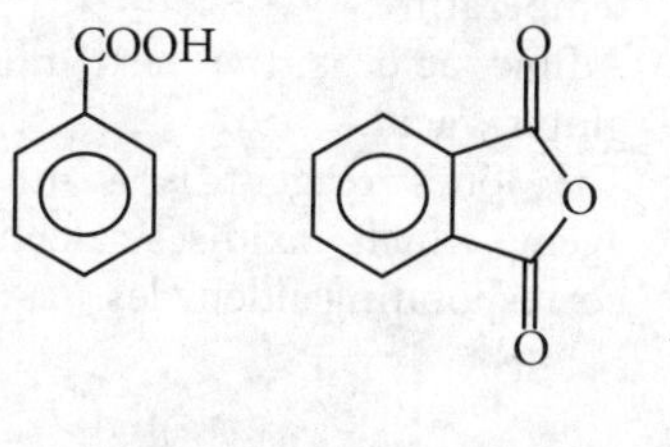

(d) 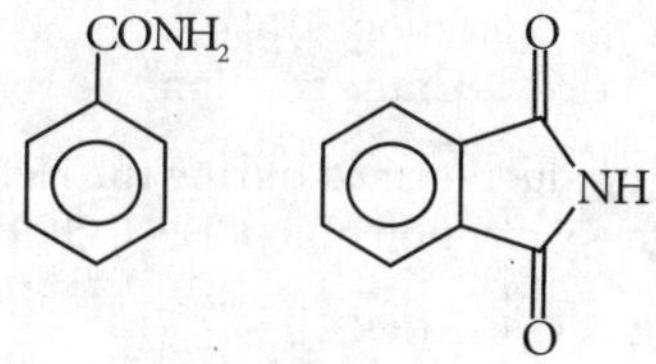

90. $CH_3-COO-CH_3 \xrightarrow{\text{DIBAL-H}} A + B$
Products A and B are:
(a) Aldehyde, ketone
(b) Aldehyde, acid
(c) Aldehyde, alcohol
(d) Ketone, alcohol

91. Diborane easily reduces functional groups such as:
(a) Acid (b) Ester
(c) Nitro (d) Halo

92. Rate of the decarboxylation by soda lime of the given compounds:

(a) 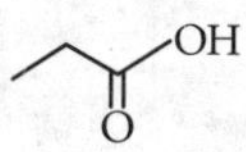 (b) 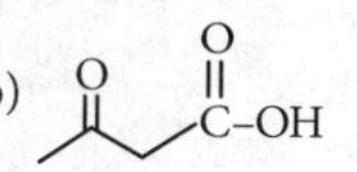

(c) 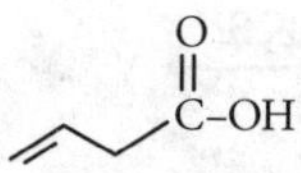 (d) 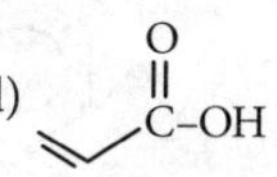

(a) a > b > c > d (b) b > c > d > a
(c) b > d > c > a (d) b > c > a > d

93. Soda lime is a mixture of:
(a) NaOH and CaO in the ratio 3:2
(b) NaOH and CaO in the ratio 1:3
(c) NaOH and CaO in the ratio 3:1
(d) NaOH and CaO in the ratio 2:3

94. What is the byproduct formed in this reaction?

$$R-COONa \xrightarrow[\Delta]{\text{NaOH, CaO}} R-H + ?$$

(a) $NaHCO_3$ (b) CO_2
(c) Na_2HCO_3 (d) Na_2CO_3

95. Name the product formed during decarboxylation of malonic acid by heating:
(a) Acetic acid (b) Ethanone
(c) Propanone (d) Formic acid

96. Alkali metal salts of carboxylic acids undergo decarboxylation on electrolysis of their aqueous solutions and form hydrocarbons having twice the number of C-atoms in the alkyl group of the acid. The reaction is known as:
(a) Kolbe's electrolysis
(b) Decarboxylation

(c) HVZ reaction
(d) Friedel–Crafts reaction

97. The product formed during the Hell–Volhard–Zelinsky reaction of R–CH_2–COOH is:

(a) R– CH(X) – COOH

(b) R– CH_2 – COX

(c) R –CH=CH –CHO

(d) R– CH(X) – CH_2 – COOH

98.

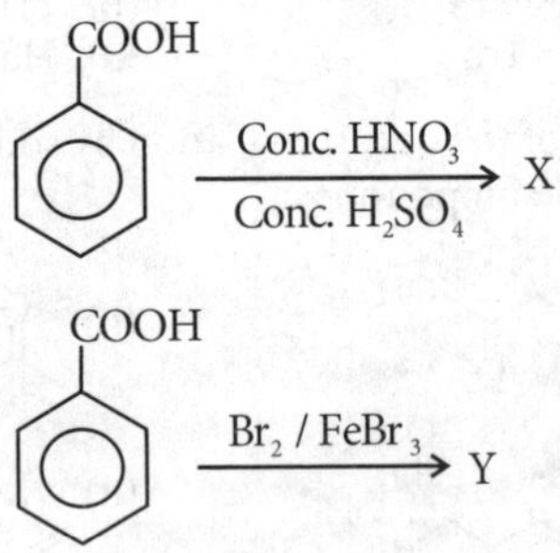

Identify X and Y for the above reaction:

X Y

(a) 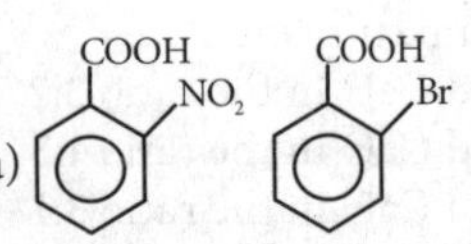 (b) 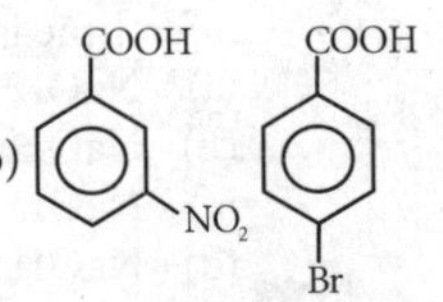

(c) 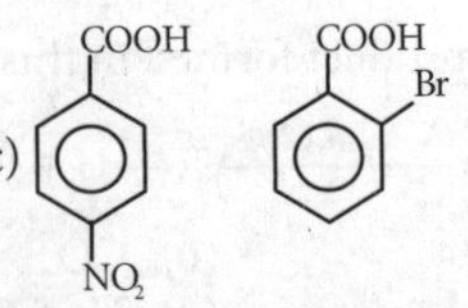 (d) 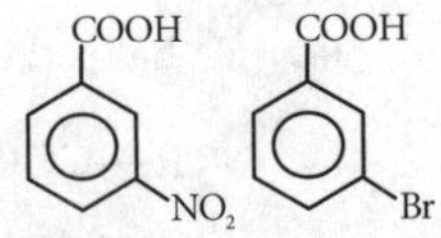

99. **Assertion (A):** The aromatic carboxylic acids do not undergo the Friedel–Crafts reaction.
Reason (R): The carboxyl group is a deactivating group.
(a) Both A and R are correct; and R is the correct explanation of A.
(b) Both A and R are correct; but R is not the correct explanation of A.
(c) A is correct; but R is incorrect.
(d) R is correct; but A is incorrect.

100. Match the compounds given in Column I with their uses given in Column II and choose the correct option from the codes given below:

Column I	Column II
A. Ethanoic acid	1. Soaps and detergents
B. Hexanedioic acid	2. Nylon-6,6
C. Sodium benzoate	3. Food preservative
D. Fatty acids	4. Vinegar

Codes

	A	B	C	D
(a)	4	2	3	1
(b)	1	2	3	4
(c)	1	3	2	4
(d)	4	3	2	1

101. Which of the following acids is used in the rubber, textile, dyeing, leather and electroplating industries?
(a) Hexanedioic acid
(b) Ethanoic acid
(c) Methanoic acid
(d) Sodium benzoate

102. **Assertion (A):** Compounds containing the –CHO group are easily oxidised to their corresponding carboxylic acid.
Reason (R): Carboxylic acids can be reduced to alcohols by treatment with $LiAlH_4$.
(a) Assertion is correct, reason is correct; reason is a correct explanation for assertion.
(b) Assertion is correct, reason is correct; reason is not a correct explanation for assertion
(c) Assertion is correct, reason is incorrect
(d) Assertion is incorrect, reason is correct.

103. Choose the incorrect statement:
(a) Thought carboxyl acids contain the carbonyl group, they are not carbonyl compounds as they do not give the characteristic reactions of the carbonyl group.
(b) Methanol and methanoic acid are liquids while methanal is a gas at room temperature.
(c) Adipic acid is the next homologue of glutaric acid.
(d) The Jones reagent is a mild oxidising agent which oxidises alcohol into its corresponding aldehydes.

Level-2

1. Which is the correct representation of the intermediate of the nucleophilic addition reaction?

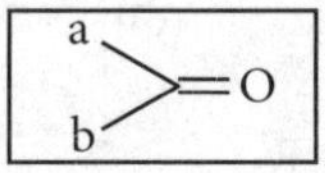

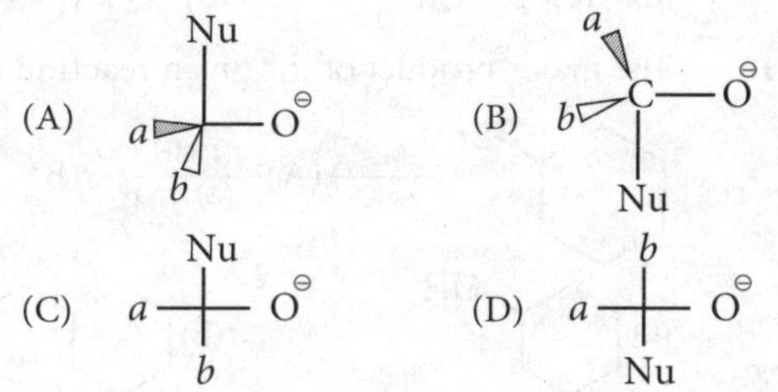

(a) Both C and D (b) Both A and B
(c) Only A (d) A, B, C, D

2. Which of the following compounds is most reactive towards nucleophilic addition reaction?

(a) $CH_3-\overset{O}{\overset{\|}{C}}-H$ (b) $CH_3-\overset{O}{\overset{\|}{C}}-CH_3$

(c) 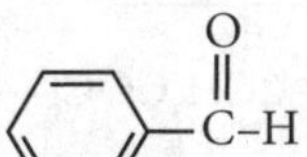 (d) 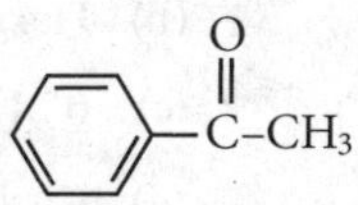

3. The correct order of increasing acidic strength is:
(a) Ethanol < Chloroacetic acid < Acetic acid
(b) Ethanol < Acetic acid < Chloroacetic acid
(c) Acetic acid < Ethanol < Chloroacetic acid
(d) Chloroacetic acid < Acetic acid < Ethanol

4. The compound phenyl benzoate can be prepared by the reaction of:
(a) Phenol and benzoic acid with NaOH
(b) Phenol and benzoyl chloride with pyridine
(c) Phenol and benzoyl chloride with $ZnCl_2$
(d) Phenol and benzaldehyde

5. The reagent which does not react with both acetone and benzaldehyde is:
(a) Sodium hydrogen sulphite
(b) Phenyl hydrazine
(c) Fehling's solution
(d) The Grignard reagent

6. Which product is formed when the compound benzaldehyde is treated with KOH solution?

(a) 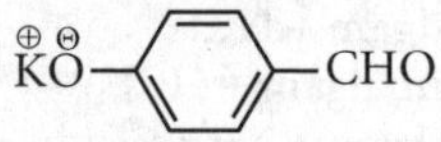

(b) 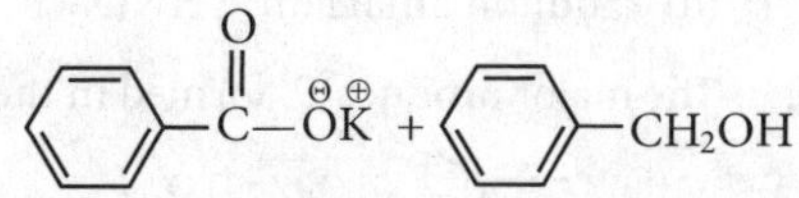

(c) 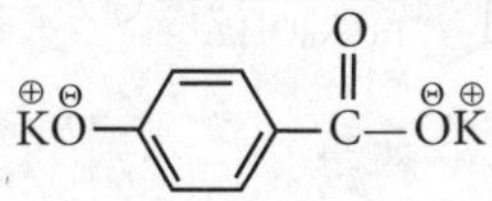

(d) 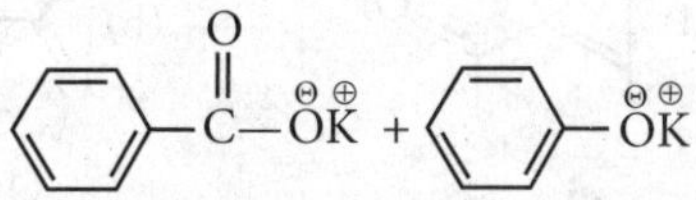

7. Structure of 'A' and type of isomerism in the given reaction, are, respectively:

$$CH_3-C\equiv CH \xrightarrow[1\%HgSO_4]{40\%H_2SO_4} A \xrightarrow{\text{Isomerisation}} \text{Acetone}$$

(a) Prop-1-en-2-ol, metamerism
(b) Prop-1-en-1-ol, tautomerism
(c) Prop-2-en-2-ol, geometrical isomerism
(d) Prop-1-en-2-ol, tautomerism

8. Compounds A and C in the following reaction are:

$$CH_3CHO \xrightarrow[\text{(ii)}H_2O]{\text{(i)}CH_3MgBr} (A) \xrightarrow{H_2SO_4,\Delta} (B) \xrightarrow{\text{Hydroboration oxidation}} (C)$$

(a) Identical isomers
(b) Positional isomers
(c) Functional isomers
(d) Optical isomers

9. Which is the most suitable reagent for the following conversion?

$$CH_3CH=CHCH_2\overset{O}{\overset{\|}{C}}CH_3 \longrightarrow CH_3CH=CHCH_2\overset{O}{\overset{\|}{C}}OH$$

(a) Tollens' reagent
(b) Benzoyl peroxide
(c) I_2 and NaOH solution
(d) Sn and NaOH solution

10. Which of the following compounds will give butanone with alkaline $KMnO_4$ solution?
(a) Butan-1-ol (b) Butan-2-ol
(c) Isobutanol (d) Butane

11. In Clemmensen reduction, the carbonyl compound is treated with:
(a) Zinc amalgam + HCl
(b) Sodium amalgam + HCl
(c) Zinc amalgam + Nitric acid
(d) Sodium amalgam + HNO_3

12. The major product 'P' formed in the reaction is:

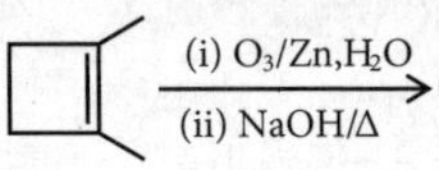

(a) 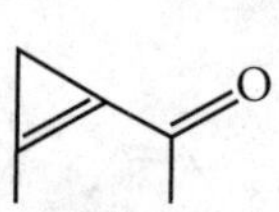 (b) 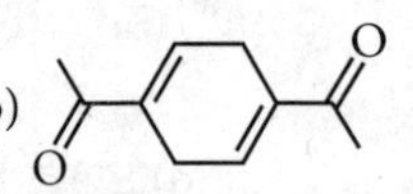

(c) 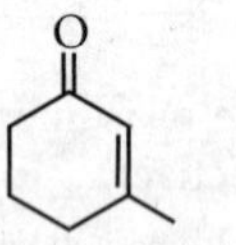 (d) 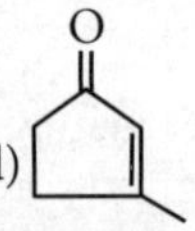

13. The following reaction is:

$$\text{Ph-}\overset{\text{O}}{\overset{\|}{\text{C}}}\text{-}\overset{\text{O}}{\overset{\|}{\text{C}}}\text{-H} \xrightarrow[\text{(ii) H}^+]{\text{(i) NaOH}}$$

(a) Intramolecular aldol
(b) Cross Cannizzaro
(c) Cross aldol
(d) Intramolecular Cannizzaro

14. Which of the following reactions will not form benzaldehyde as the major product?

(a) 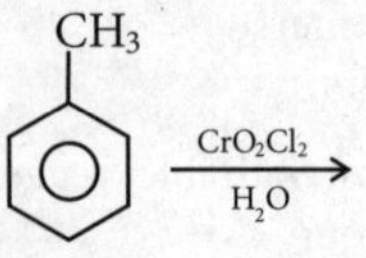 (b) 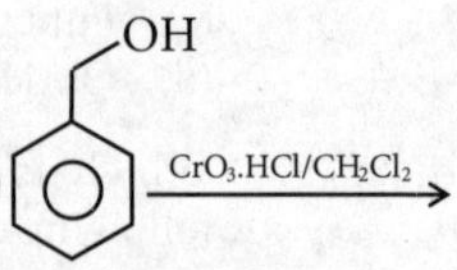

(c) 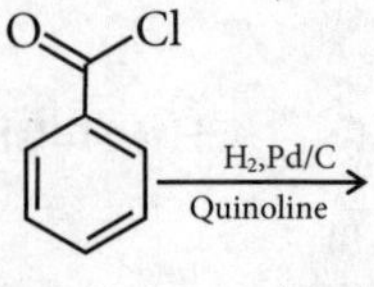 (d) 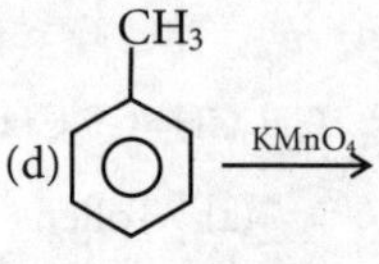

15. The correct order of nucleophilic addition is:

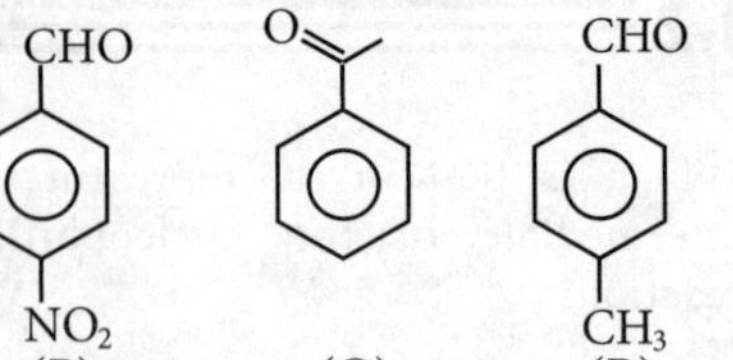

(P) (Q) (R)

(a) P > Q > R (b) P > R > Q
(c) R > P > Q (d) Q > P > R

16. The major product of the given reaction is:

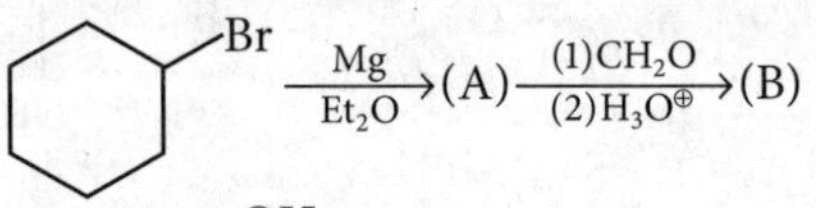

(a) 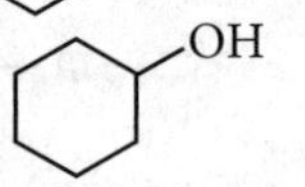 (b) 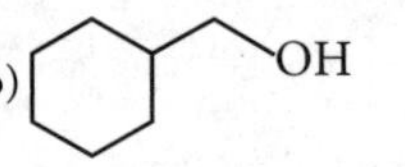

(c) 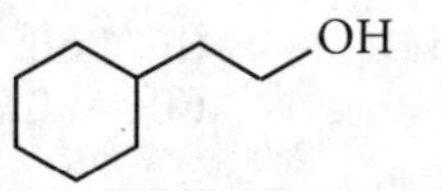 (d) 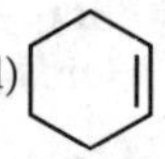

17. Which of following reactions will produce aldehyde as the major product?
(a) $CH_3-C\equiv CH \xrightarrow[H_2SO_4]{Hg^{2+}}$
(b) Hexan-1-ol $\xrightarrow[CrO_3]{\text{Anhydrous}}$
(c) $(C_6H_5CH_2)_2\,Cd + 2CH_3COCl \longrightarrow$
(d) Cyclohexanol + $C_5H_5\overset{\oplus}{N}H.CrO_3Cl^{\ominus} \longrightarrow$

18. Which of the following reactions will give 1° alcohol as the major product?
(a) $CH_3-\overset{O}{\overset{\|}{C}}-H \xrightarrow[HCl]{Zn-Hg}$
(b) $CH_3-CH_2-\overset{O}{\overset{\|}{C}}-H \xrightarrow[CaCO_3]{H_2-Pd}$
(c) $CH_3-\overset{O}{\overset{\|}{C}}-Cl \xrightarrow[\text{in } H_2O]{NaBH_4}$
(d) $CH_3-CH=CH_2 \xrightarrow[\text{(ii) } H_2O]{\text{(i) } B_2H_6}$

19. The major product of the given reaction is:

$$Ph-CH_2-\underset{OH}{\underset{|}{CH}}-CH_3 \xrightarrow{Na} \xrightarrow{C_2H_5Br} (A)$$

(a) Ph–CH$_2$–CH(OEt)–CH$_3$, (inversion)

(b) Ph–CH$_2$–CH(OEt)–CH$_3$, (retention)

(c) Ph–CH$_2$–CH(OEt)–CH$_3$, (racemic)

(d) Ph–CH=CH–CH$_3$

20. What is the major product expected from the following commercial reaction?

$$\text{Toluene} \xrightarrow[\text{(ii)}H_2O, 100°C]{\text{(i)}Cl_2/h\nu}$$

(a) PhOH (b) PhCHO
(c) PhCH$_2$Cl (d) Benzene

21. Which of following gives a positive Tollens' test?

(a) 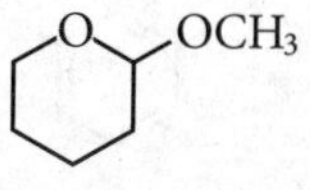
(b) 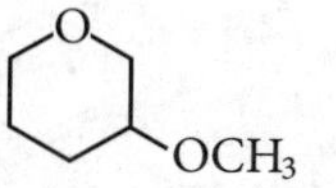
(c) 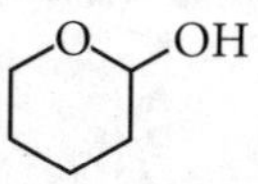
(d) 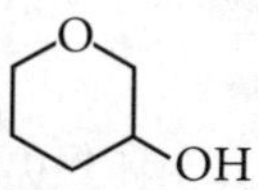

22. Which of the following compounds undergoes aldol condensation?

(a) 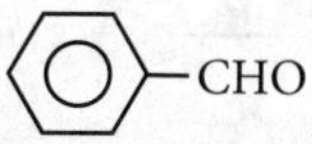
(b) $CH_3-C(CH_3)_2-CHO$
(c) 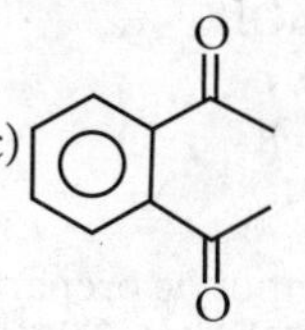
(d) OHC–CHO (CH(=O)–CH(=O))

23. Product (X) and (Y) can be differentiated by:

$$CH_3-C\equiv CH \xrightarrow[\text{dil.}H_2SO_4]{HgSO_4} (X)$$

$$CH_3-C\equiv CH \xrightarrow[\text{(ii)}H_2O_2/\overset{\ominus}{O}H]{\text{(i)}BH_3-THF} (Y)$$

(a) 2, 4-DNP (b) NaOI
(c) Na-Metal (d) NaHSO$_3$

24. Which of the following does not dominantly exist in gem-diol form?

(a) HCHO (b) Chloral
(c) 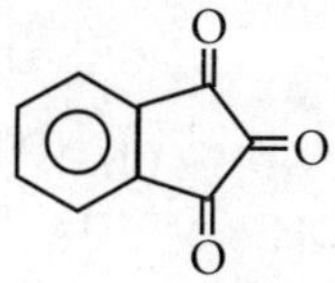 (d) Acetone

25. The correct order of boiling point for the following compounds is:

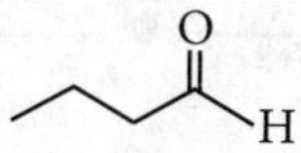
(P)
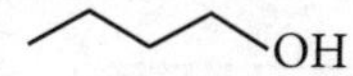
(Q)
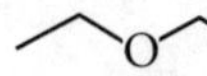
(R)

(S)

(a) P > Q > R > S (b) Q > R > P > S
(c) P > R > Q > S (d) Q > P > R > S

26. The major product (R) of the following sequence is:

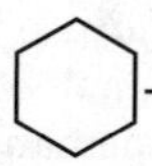 $\xrightarrow[h\nu]{Br_2} P \xrightarrow[\Delta]{EtONa} Q \xrightarrow[H_2SO_4,\ \Delta]{KMnO_4} R$

(a) Malonic acid (b) Fumaric acid
(c) Adipic acid (d) Glutaric acid

27. Which of the following statements is incorrect?

(a) The Grigand reagent should be prepared under anhydrous conditions.
(b) Alkyl halides, though polar, are immiscible with water.
(c) p-Dichlorobenzene has a lower melting point than o- and m-isomers.
(d) Ortho nitro phenol is more acidic than ortho methoxy phenol.

28. Which of the following compounds on reaction with NaCN/HCN produces racemic mixture?

(a) 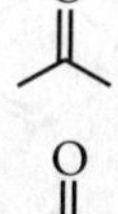 (b) CH$_3$CHO
(c) 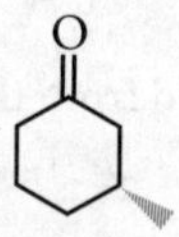 (d) 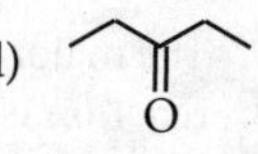

29. Acetaldehyde on reaction with sodium hydrogen sulphite produces:

(a) 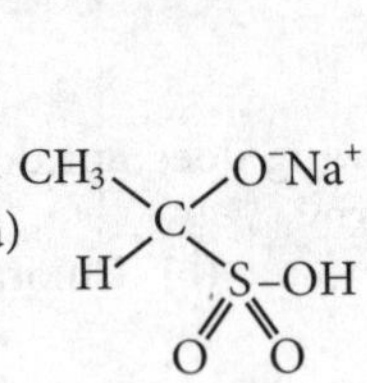
(b) 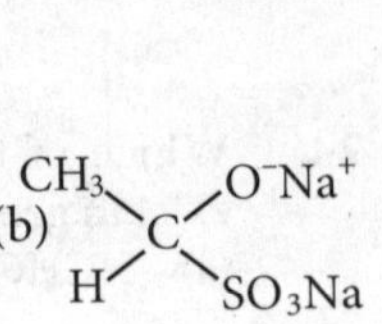

(c) 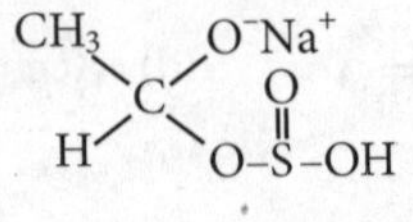
(d) 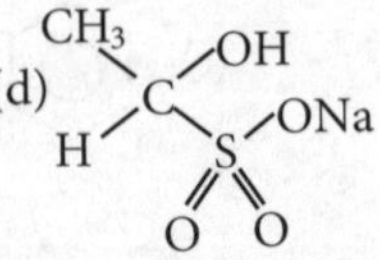

30. The major products Q and R are, respectively:

$$CH_3{-}C{\equiv}CH \xrightarrow[\text{liq. } NH_3]{NaNH_2} P \xrightarrow{CH_3{-}I} Q \xrightarrow[\text{Liquid } NH_3]{Na} R$$

(a) But-1-yne, but-1-ene
(b) But-2-yne, cis-but-2-ene
(c) But-1-yne, 2-methyl propene
(d) But-2-yne, trans-but-2-ene

31. Under Wolff–Kishner reduction conditions, the conversions which may be brought about are:
(a) Benzaldehyde into Benzyl alcohol
(b) Cyclohexanol into Cyclohexane
(c) Cyclohexanone into Cyclohexanol
(d) Benzophenone into Diphenylmethane

32. Among the following compounds, which will react with acetone to give imine?
(a) $(CH_3)_3N$ (b) $C_6H_5NHC_6H_5$
(c) $(CH_3)_2NH$ (d) $C_6H_5NH_2$

33. The reactant (P) will be:

$$(P) \xrightarrow{O_3/Zn/H_2O} (Q) \xrightarrow[\Delta]{NaOH}$$ 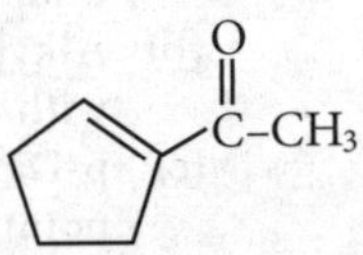

(a) 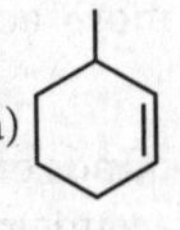 (b) 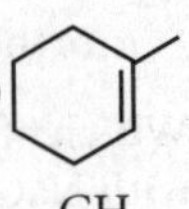

(c) 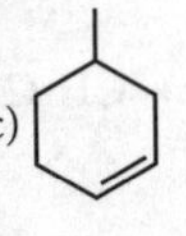 (d) 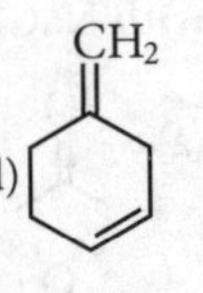

34. The major product expected from the following reaction is:

$$CH_3{-}C{\equiv}N \xrightarrow[\text{(ii) } H_2O]{\text{(i) PhMgBr}}$$

(a) CH_3CHO (b) PhCHO
(c) $PhCOCH_3$ (d) $PhCH_2CHO$

35. The increasing order of reactivity of the compounds in the nucleophilic addition reaction is:
(a) Benzaldehyde < Butanone < Propanone < Propanal
(b) Benzaldehyde < Propanal < Propanone < Butanone
(c) Propanal < Propanone < Butanone < Benzaldehyde
(d) Butanone < Propanone < Benzaldehyde < Propanal

36. The increasing order of the following compounds towards HCN addition is:

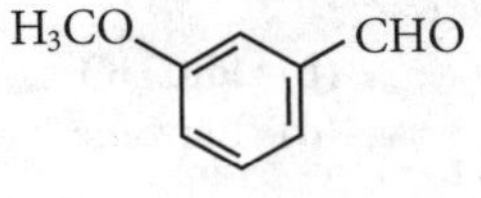
(i)

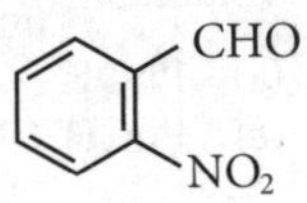
(ii)

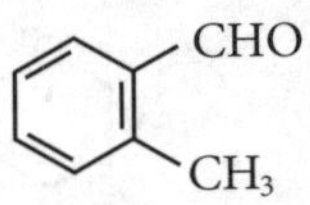
(iii)

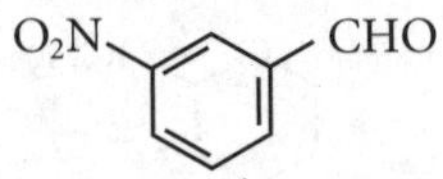
(iv)

(a) (iii) < (iv) < (i) < (ii)
(b) (iii) < (i) < (iv) < (ii)
(c) (i) < (iii) < (iv) < (ii)
(d) (iii) < iv) < (ii) < (i)

37. In the following reaction, the best combinations are:

$$\text{Aldehyde} + \text{Alcohol} \xrightarrow{HCl} \text{Acetal}$$

HCHO t-BuOH
or CH_3CHO or MeOH

(a) CH_3CHO and t-BuOH
(b) HCHO and t-BuOH
(c) CH_3CHO and MeOH
(d) HCHO and MeOH

38. 2-Phenyl-2-butanol cannot be prepared by:
(a) $PhCOCH_3 + CH_3CH_2MgX$
(b) $PhCOCH_2CH_3 + CH_3MgX$
(c) $HCHO + PhCH(CH_3)CH_2MgX$
(d) $CH_3CH_2COCH_3 + PhMgX$

39. In the following reaction, the rate of the reaction is the highest for:

$$\text{Carbonyl compound} + \text{MeOH} \xrightarrow{HCl} \text{Acetal}$$

(a) Acetone as substrate and methanol in excess
(b) Acetone as substrate and methanol in stoichiometric amount

(c) Propanal as substrate and methanol in excess
(d) Propanal as substrate and methanol in stoichiometric amount

40. Which is the most suitable reagent for the following transformation?

$$CH_3-CH=CH-CH_2-\underset{}{\overset{OH}{\overset{|}{C}H}}-CH_3 \longrightarrow$$

$CH_3-CH=CH-CH_2CO_2H$

(a) CrO_2Cl_2/CS_2
(b) Alkaline $KMnO_4$
(c) $I_2/NaOH$
(d) Tollens' reagent

41. Which one of the following undergoes reaction with 50% sodium hydroxide solution to give the corresponding alcohol and acid?
(a) Phenol (b) Benzaldehyde
(c) Butanal (d) Benzoic acid

42. Acetal or ketal is:
(a) Vic dialkoxy compound
(b) α, ω-dialkoxy compound
(c) α-alkoxy alcohol
(d) Gem-dialkoxy compound

43. Which of the following is reduced with Zn-Hg/HCl to give the corresponding hydrocarbon?
(a) Acetone (b) Acetic acid
(c) Acetamide (d) Ethyl acetate

44. Rate of reaction is fastest when X is:

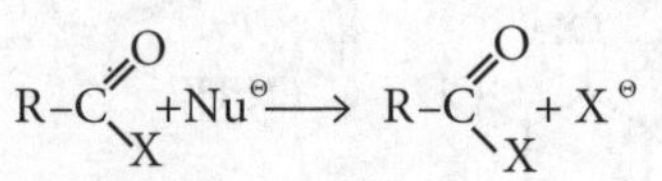

(a) NH_2 (b) Cl
(c) OCOR (d) OC_2H_5

45. In the following sequence of reactions, the correct statement is:
$CH_3CH{=}CHCH_3 \xrightarrow{O_3} A \xrightarrow[Zn]{H_2O} B$
(a) A is ethanol
(b) B is monozonide
(c) A is monozonide
(d) All of these

46. Arrange these compounds in decreasing order of reactivity for a nucleophilic attack:
(I) Acid chloride (II) Aldehyde
(III) Ketone (IV) Ester
(a) I > II > III > IV
(b) IV > III > II > I
(c) III > II > I > IV
(d) I > IV > II > III

47. Which of the following will produce 3-hydroxy-2-methyl butanal on reaction with dilute NaOH?
(a) CH_3–CH_2–CHO and CH_3–CH_2–CHO
(b) CH_3–CHO and CH_3–CH_2–CHO
(c) CH_3–CHO and CH_3–CHO
(d) CH_3–CHO and $CH_3-\overset{CH_3}{\overset{|}{\underset{CH_3}{\underset{|}{C}}}}-CHO$

48. An alkene on ozonolysis gives two moles of an aldehyde having a mass of 30 u. The alkene is:
(a) Ethene (b) 2-Hexene
(c) Ethyne (d) 2-Butene

49. The formation of cyanohydrin from a ketone is an example of:
(a) Electrophilic addition
(b) Nucleophilic addition
(c) Nucleophilic substitution
(d) Electrophilic substitution

50. Gem-dihalide on hydrolysis gives:
(a) Vic diol
(b) Gem-diol
(c) Carbonyl compound
(d) Carboxylic acid

51. The enolic form of acetaldehyde contains:
(a) 6 sigma bonds, 1 pi bond and 2 lone pairs
(b) 8 sigma bonds, 2 pi bonds and 2 lone pairs
(c) 5 sigma bonds, 1 pi bond and 2 lone pairs
(d) 6 sigma bonds, 2 pi bonds and 2 lone pairs

52. The order of reactivity of phenyl magnesium bromide with the following compounds is:

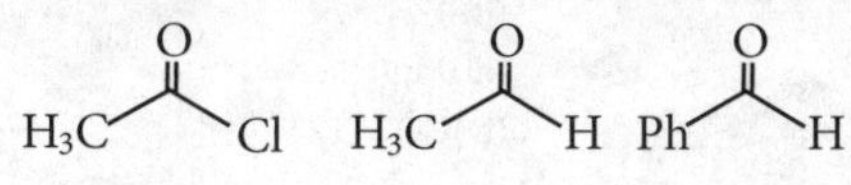

(I) (II) (III)

(a) II > III > I (b) I > III > II
(c) II > I > III (d) I > II > III

53. Which of the following orders is incorrect for boiling point?
(a) Pentan-1-ol > Butan-1-ol > Butan-2-ol
(b) Bromoform > Bromomethane > CH_3Cl

(c) Butan-1-ol > Ethoxyethane > n-Butane
(d) Propanal > Acetone > Methoxyethane

54. In the reaction sequence, (Z) will be:

Cyclohexane $\xrightarrow{hv/Cl_2}$ (X) $\xrightarrow{alc.KOH/\Delta}$ (Y) $\xrightarrow[(ii)H_2O/Zn]{(i)O_3}$ (Z)

(a) Hexanal (b) 2-Hexanone
(c) 3-Hexanone (d) Hexanedial

55. The cyanohydrin of which compound on hydrolysis will give lactic acid?
(a) C_6H_5CHO
(b) HCHO
(c) CH_3CHO
(d) $CH_3–CH_2–CHO$

56. Which of the following compounds will give aldol condensation?
(a) Acetaldehyde (b) Formaldehyde
(c) Pivaldehyde (d) Benzaldehyde

57. A mixture of Ph–CHO and HCHO is treated with NaOH. Then the Cannizzaro reaction involves:
(a) Oxidation of HCHO
(b) Reduction of HCHO
(c) Oxidation of Ph–CHO
(d) All of these

58. Consider the following reactions; the compound P is:

P $\xrightarrow[(ii)H_3O^+]{(i)CH_3MgBr}$ Q $\xrightarrow[573K]{Cu}$ 2-Methyl-2-butene

(a) Propanone
(b) Butanal
(c) Butanone
(d) 2-Methyl propanal

59. The major product of the following reaction is:

Hex–3–ynal $\xrightarrow[(ii)PBr_3 \ (iii)Mg/ether \ (iv)CO_2/H_3O^+]{(i)NaBH_4}$

(a) 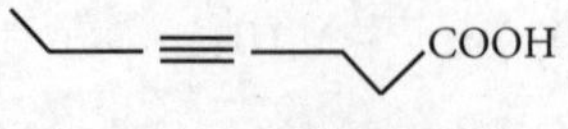
(b) 
(c) 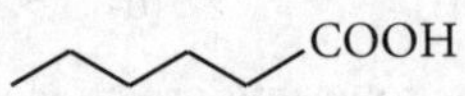
(d) 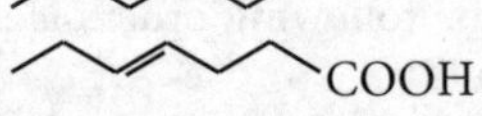

60. Trans-alkenes are formed by the reduction of alkynes with:
(a) Sn/HCl
(b) H_2-Pd/C, $BaSO_4$
(c) $NaBH_4$
(d) Na/liquid NH_3

61. The but-2-ene reaction with alkaline $KMnO_4$ at high temperature followed by acidification will give:
(a) One CH_3CHO and one CH_3COOH
(b) 2 molecules of CH_3CHO
(c) 2 molecules of CH_3COOH
(d) 2,3-Butandiol

62. The major product of the following reaction is:

$$R-C\equiv N \xrightarrow[(2)H_2O]{(1)AlH(i-Bu_2)}$$

(a) RCHO (b) RCOOH
(c) RCH_2NH_2 (d) $RCONH_2$

63. The major product 'X' formed in the following reaction is:

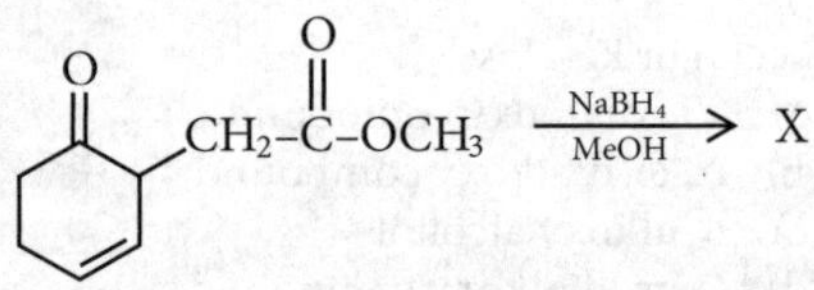

(a) 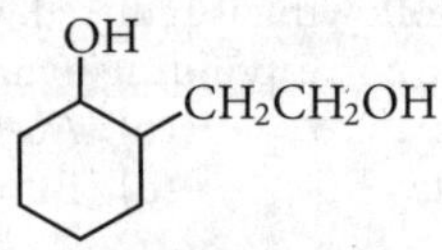

(b) 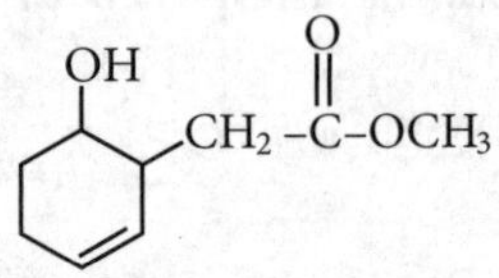

(c) 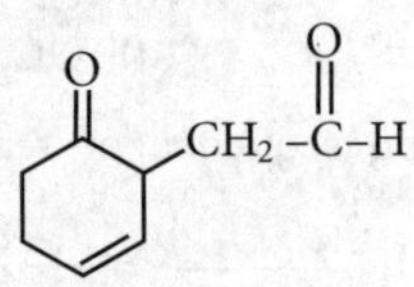

(d) 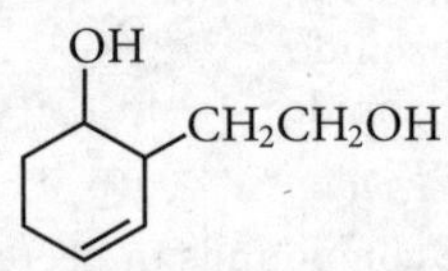

64. The acid derivative which reacts fastest towards hydrogenation but slowest with B_2H_6 is:
(a) Acid (b) Acid anhydride
(c) Acid halide (d) Ester

65. In the reaction sequence, the product (A) is:

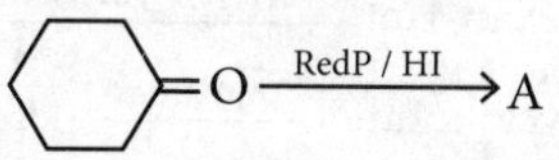

(a) 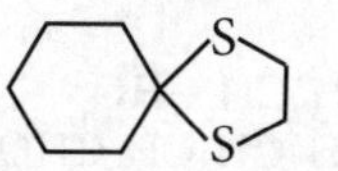

(b) 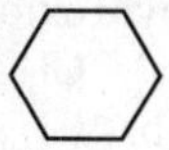

(c) 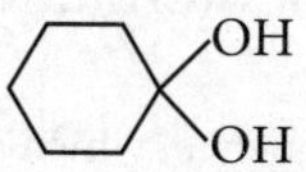

(d) 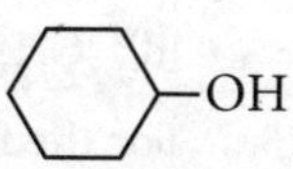

66. The major product of the following reaction is:

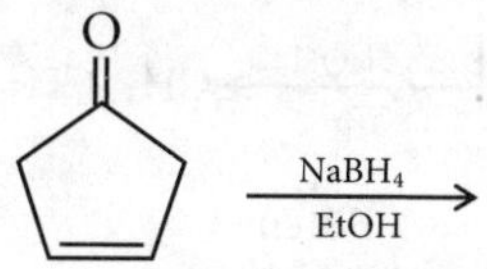

(a) 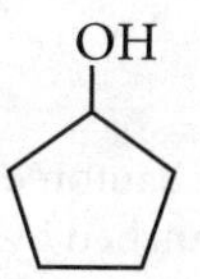

(b) 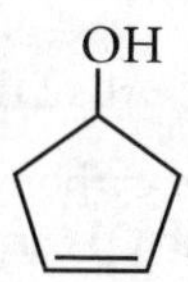

(c) 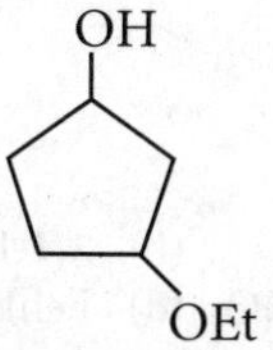

(d) 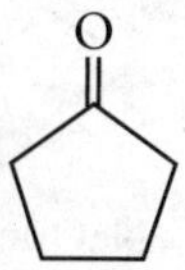

67. The major product of the following reaction is:

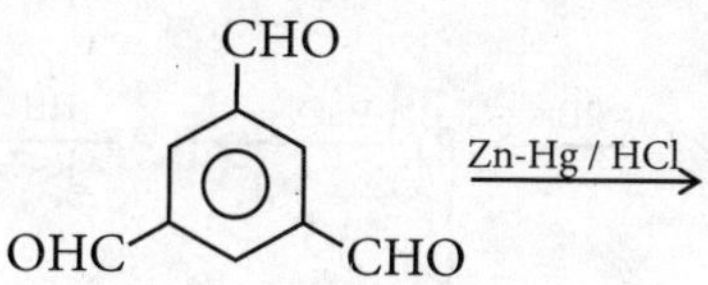

(a) 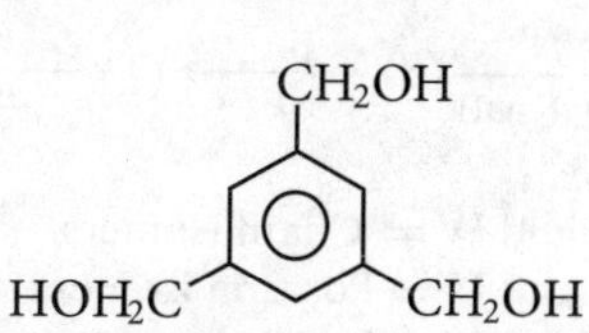

(b) 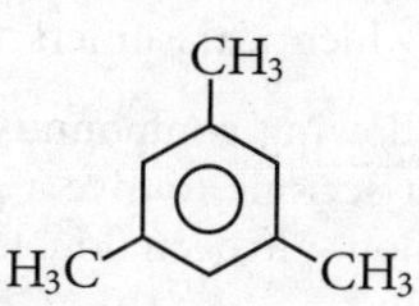

(c) 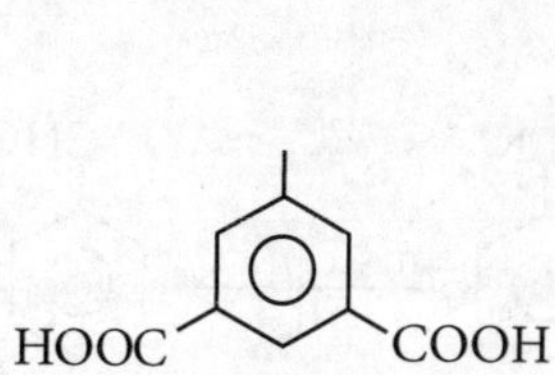

(d) 

68. The product of the following reaction is:

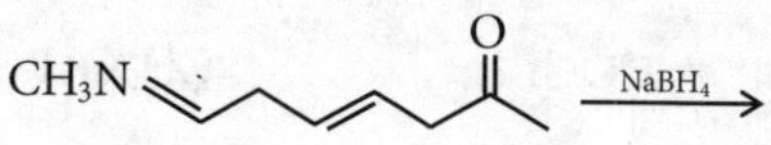

(a) 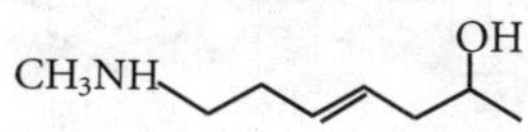

(b) 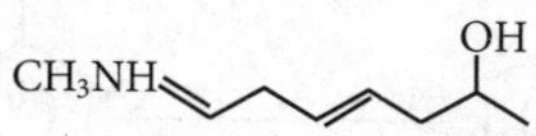

(c) 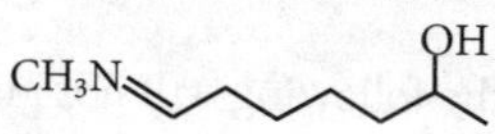

(d) 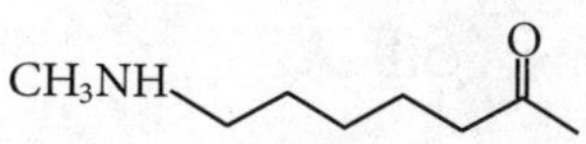

69. Which of the following on reaction with propanal gives a hydrazone derivative?

(a) $NH_2CONHNH_2$ (b) CH_3-NH_2

(c) NH_2-OH (d) $PhNHNH_2$

70. The major product obtained from the following reaction is:

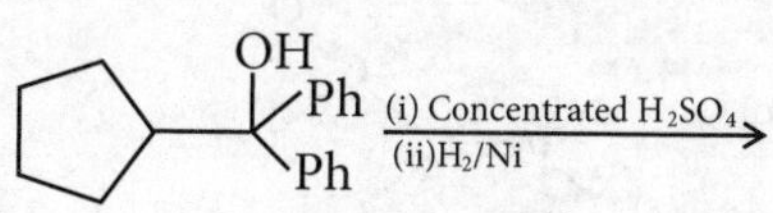

(a) 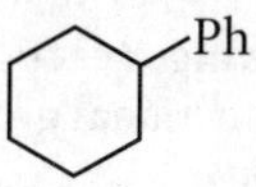

(b) 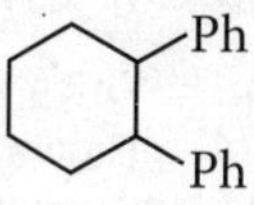

(c) 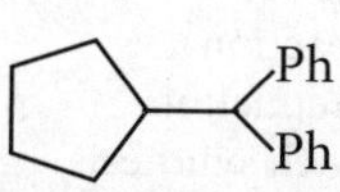

(d) 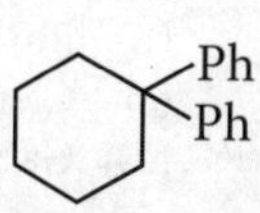

71. Which of the following is incorrectly matched with the major product?

(a) 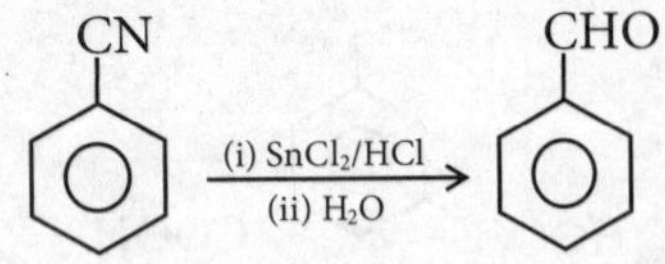

(b) 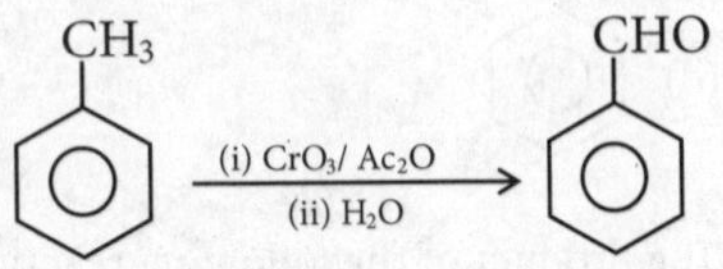

(c) 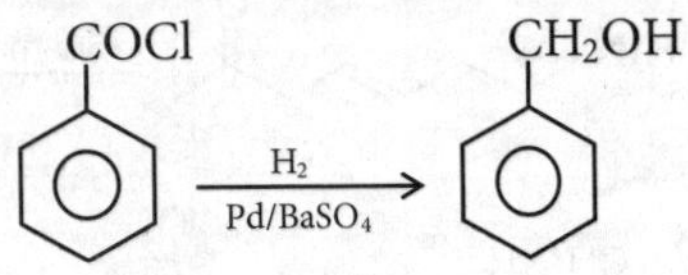

(d) 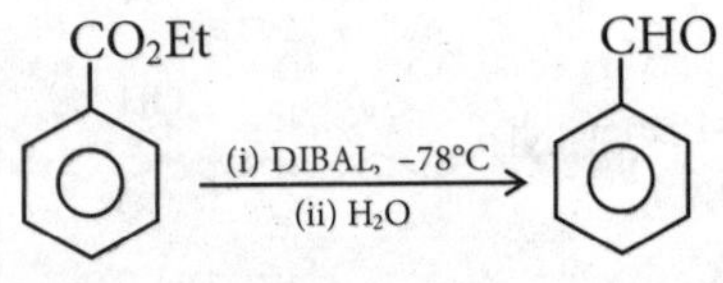

72. Which of the following will not give a positive Tollens' test?

(a) 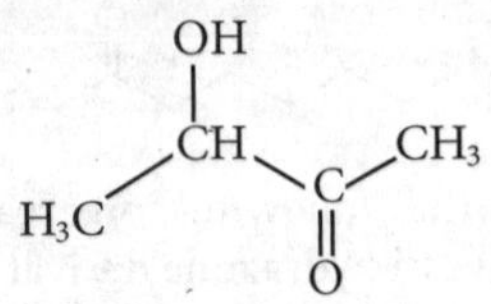

(b) 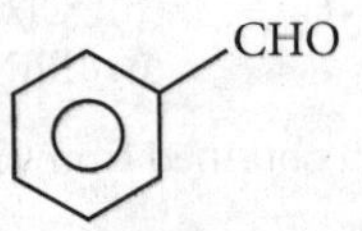

(c) 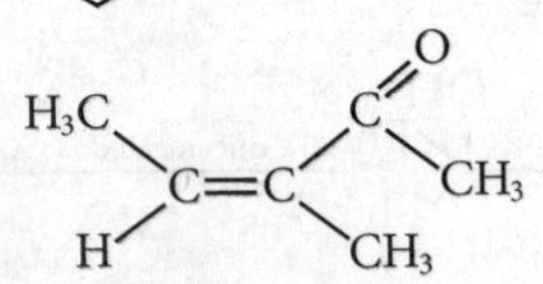

(d) CH_3–CHO

73. Which of the following reactions cannot produce an aldehyde functional group?
(a) Stephen's reduction
(b) Rosenmund reaction
(c) Clemmensen reduction
(d) Gatterman–Koch synthesis

74. Which of the following reactions is incorrectly matched with the major product?

(a) Ethane nitrile $\xrightarrow[\text{(ii) } H_2O]{\text{(i) DIBALH}}$ Propanal

(b) Allyl alcohol $\xrightarrow[CH_2Cl_2]{\text{PCC}}$ Propenal

(c) Hexan-1-ol $\xrightarrow{[C_5H_5NH]Cl.CrO_3}$ Hexanal

(d) Cyclohexanol $\xrightarrow[CrO_3]{\text{Anhydrous}}$ Cyclohexanone

75. Propanal on treatment with dilute sodium hydroxide gives:
(a) $CH_3CH_2CH_2CH_2CH_2CHO$
(b) $CH_3CH_2CH(OH)CH_2CH_2CHO$
(c) $CH_3CH_2CH(OH)CH(CH_3)CHO$
(d) CH_3CH_2COOH

76. For the following sequence, which is correctly matched?

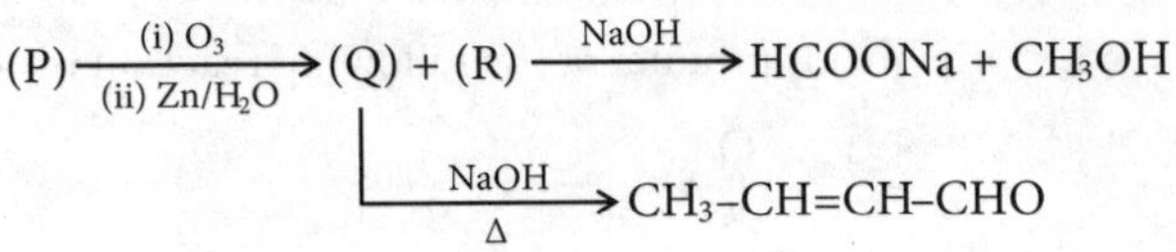

(a) (P) ⇒ 1-Butene
(b) (Q) ⇒ Propanal
(c) (R) ⇒ Formaldehyde
(d) All of these

77. The carbonyl obtained by tautomerism of (P) and (Q) cannot be distinguished by:

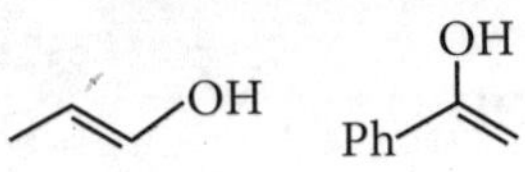

(P)

(a) NaOBr (b) 2,4-DNP
(c) Ammoniacal $AgNO_3$ (d) Fehling test

78. Which of the following reactions is correct for the following sequence?

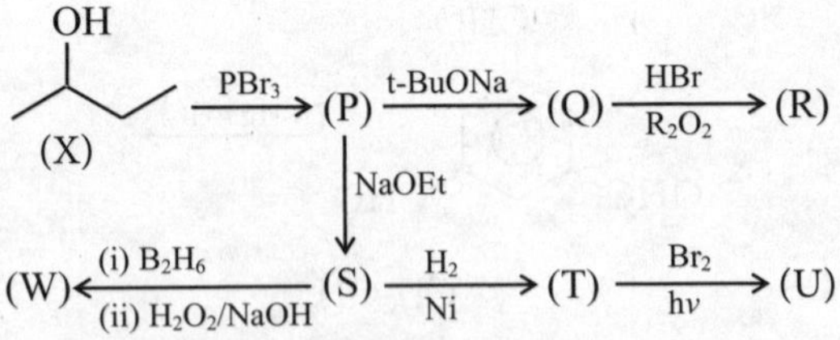

(a) X and W ⇒ Chain isomers
(b) R and U ⇒ Position isomers
(c) P and U ⇒ Position isomers
(d) R and P ⇒ Identical isomers

79. Among the following compounds, which one will react with acetone to give a product that contains a carbon–nitrogen double bond?
(a) Ph–NH–Ph (b) $(CH_3)_3N$
(c) $(CH_3)_2NH$ (d) Ph–NH–NH_2

80. Two unknown compounds X and Y having molecular formula C_4H_8O are, respectively:

	X	Y
1. Bromine water	Decolourizer	No reaction
2. Na metal	Bubbler	No reaction
3. Chromic acid	Orange to green	No reaction
4. Lucas reagent	No reaction	No reaction

(a) $CH_3-CH_2-C(=CH_2)-CH_3$ 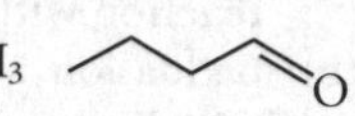

(b) 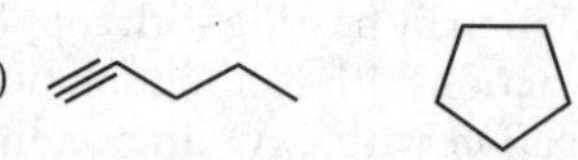

(c) 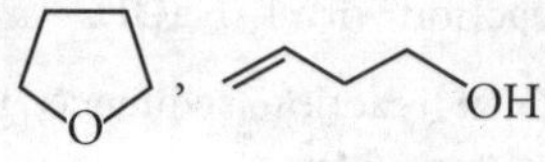

(d) $CH_3-CH_2-CH_2-C(=O)-H$, 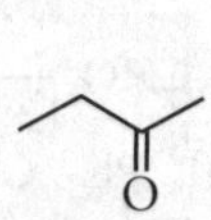

81. In the given reaction, Q undergoes Cannizzaro reaction but not haloform. Then P can be:

$$P \xrightarrow[\text{ii) } Zn/H_2O]{\text{i) } O_3/CH_2Cl_2} \underset{(C_8H_8O)}{Q}$$

(a) 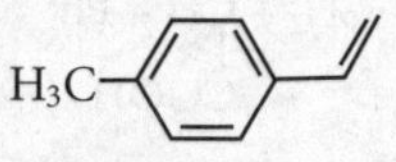

(b) 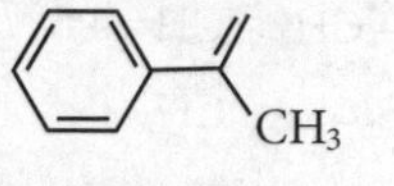

(c) 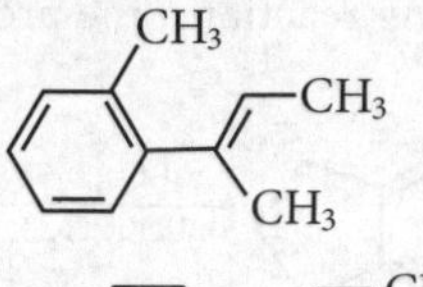

(d) 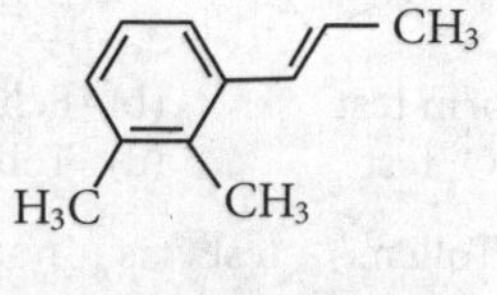

82. An unsaturated hydrocarbon X absorbs two hydrogen molecules on catalytic hydrogenation and also gives the following reaction. Then X will be:

$$X \xrightarrow[Zn/H_2O]{O_3} A \xrightarrow{[Ag(NH_3)_2]^+} B\text{(3-Oxo-hexandioic acid)}$$

(a) 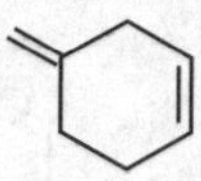 (b) 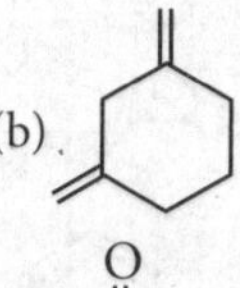

(c) 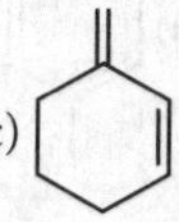 (d) 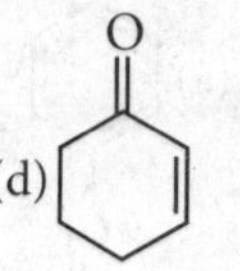

83. The major product formed in the following reaction is:

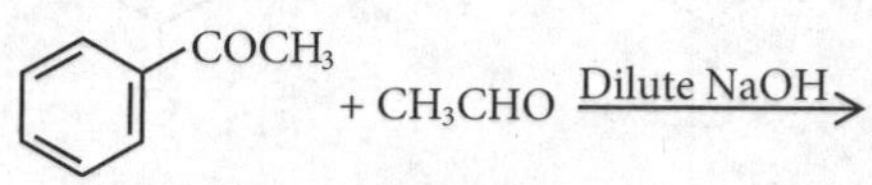

(a) 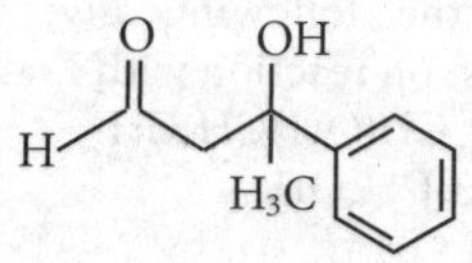

(b) 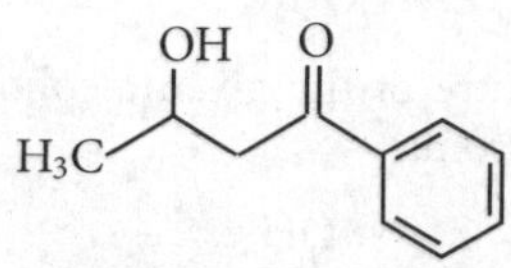

(c) 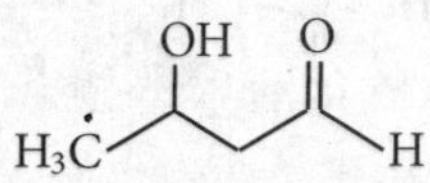

(d) 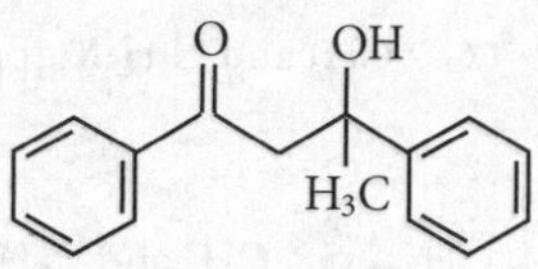

84. A compound has vapour density 29. On warming with a solution of iodine in alkali, it gives a yellow precipitate. The compound is:

(a) CH_3CH_2CHO

(b) CH_3COCH_3

(c) $CH_3CHOHCH_3$

(d) $CH_2=CHCH_2Br$

85. The major product of the following reaction is:

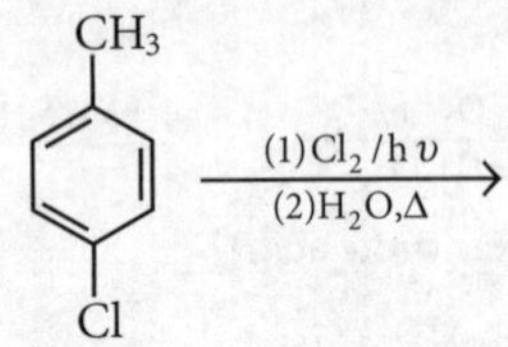

(a) 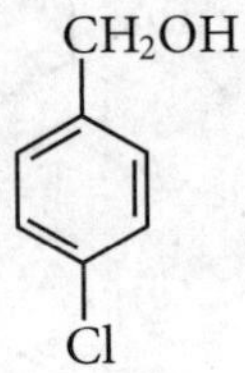

(b) 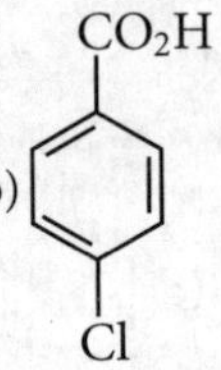

(c) 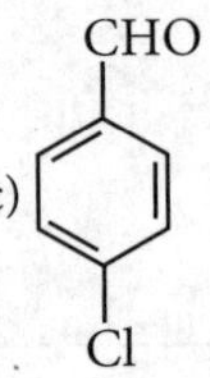

(d) 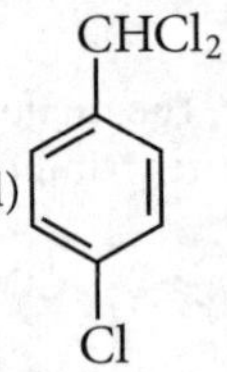

86. Which of the following gives a positive iodoform test on reaction with I_2 and NaOH?

(a) $CH_3CH_2CH(OH)CH_2CH_3$

(b) $C_6H_5CH_2CH_2OH$

(c) CH_3CH_2OH

(d) $CH_3CH_2CH_2OH$

87. The structure of the given alcohol cannot be prepared from:

$$C_6H_5-\underset{C_2H_5}{\overset{OH}{\underset{|}{\overset{|}{C}}}}-CH_3$$

(a) $C_6H_5-\overset{O}{\overset{\|}{C}}-CH_3$ and C_2H_5MgBr

(b) $CH_3-CH_2-\overset{O}{\overset{\|}{C}}-CH_3$ and C_6H_5MgBr

(b) $C_6H_5-\overset{O}{\overset{\|}{C}}-C_2H_5$ and CH_3MgBr

(d) $C_6H_5-\overset{O}{\overset{\|}{C}}-Cl$ and C_2H_5MgCl

88. In the Cannizzaro reaction given below, the slowest step is:

$$2PhCHO \xrightarrow{:\overset{\ominus}{O}H} PhCH_2OH + PhCO_2^{\ominus}$$

(a) Abstraction of proton from the COOH

(b) Deprotonation of $PhCH_2OH$

(c) Attack of NaOH at the carboxyl group

(d) Transfer of hydride to the carbonyl group

89. A compound with molecular formula $C_4H_{10}O_4$ on acylation with acetic anhydride gives a compound with molecular formula $C_8H_{14}O_6$. How many hydroxyl groups are present?

(a) One (b) Two

(c) Three (d) Four

90. 1-Propanol amd 2-propanol cannot be best distinguished by:

(a) Oxidation with Jones reagent followed by reaction with Fehling solution

(b) Oxidation with PCC followed by reaction with Tollens' reagent

(c) Oxidation by heating with copper followed by reaction with Fehling solution

(d) Oxidation with CrO_3 in acetone followed by reaction with I_2/NaOH

91. In the given reaction sequence, product (X) will be:

$$Ph-CH_2-CHO \xrightarrow{NaOH} \xrightarrow{\Delta} \xrightarrow{H_2/Ni} (X)$$

(a) $Ph-CH_2-\underset{OH}{\underset{|}{CH}}-\underset{CHO}{\underset{|}{CH}}-Ph$

(b) $Ph\ CH_2-CH_2-\underset{CH_2OH}{\underset{|}{CH}}-Ph$

(c) $Ph-CH_2-CH_2-\underset{COOH}{\underset{|}{CH}}-Ph$

(d) $Ph-CH_2-CH_2-\underset{CH_3}{\underset{|}{CH}}-Ph$

92. In the following reactions, the product R does not give:

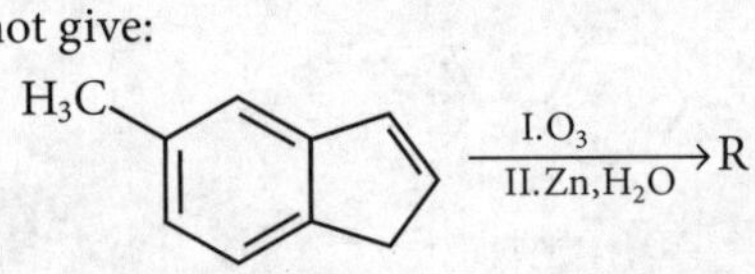

(a) Haloform test (b) Fehling test

(c) $NaHSO_3$ test (d) Tollens' test

93. Positive Tollens' test is not observed for:

(a) 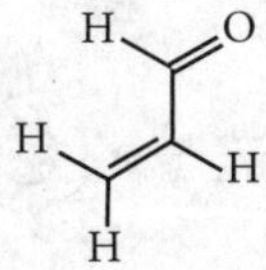 (b) 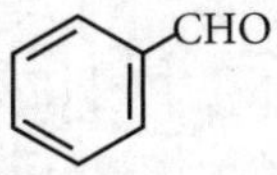

(c) 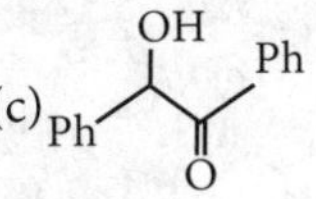 (d) 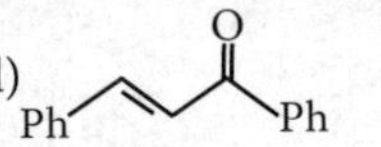

94. An organic compound (a), $C_5H_{10}O$, reacts with hydrazine to form a hydrazone derivative (b). The hydrazone (b) on being heated with KOH at about 180°C, gives n-pentane. The compound (a) does not respond positively to Tollens' reagent and to the iodoform test. The compound (a) is:

(a) 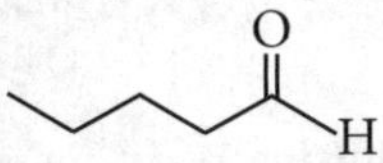 (b) 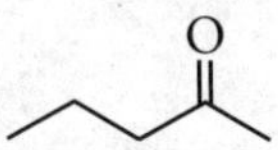

(c) 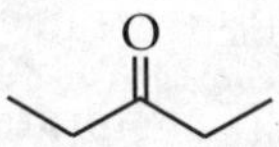 (d) 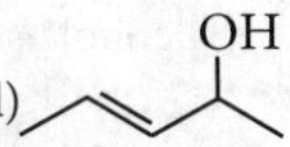

95. An organic compound reacts neither with the Lucas reagent nor with the Fehling solution. It, however, reacts with the Grignard reagent and gives a positive iodoform test. The compound is:

(a) 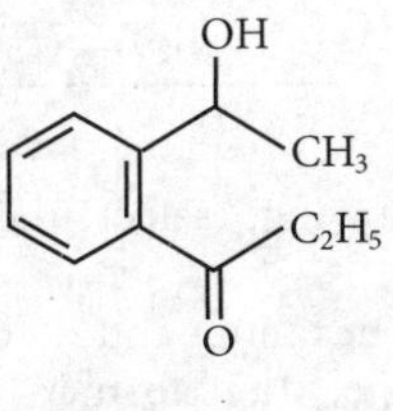 (b) 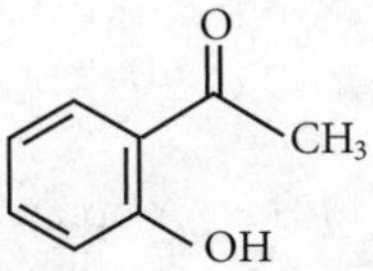

(c) 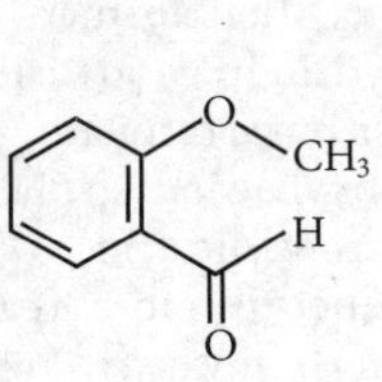 (d) 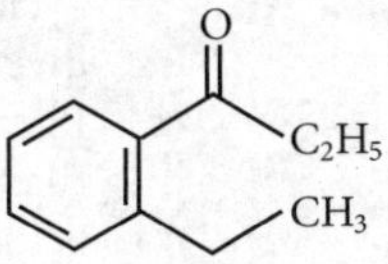

96. Among the following, the incorrect option is:
(a) Ammoniacal silver nitrate solution : Tollens' reagent
(b) Aqueous copper sulphate + Sodium citrate : Fehling's reagent
(c) Rosaniline hydrochloride + SO_2 : Schiff's reagent
(d) 2,4-Dinitro phenyl hydrazine : Brady's reagent

97. In the following sequence of reactions, the products (A) and (B) are, respectively:

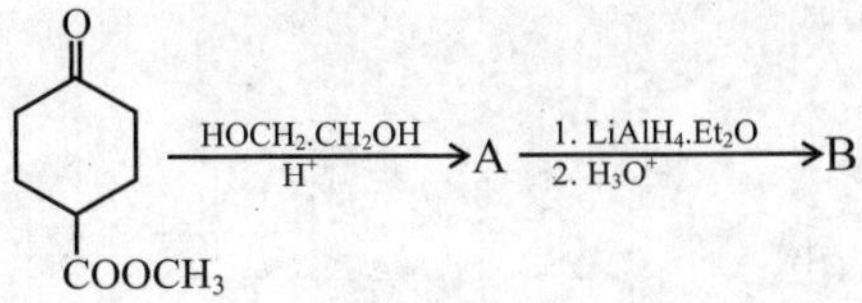

(a) 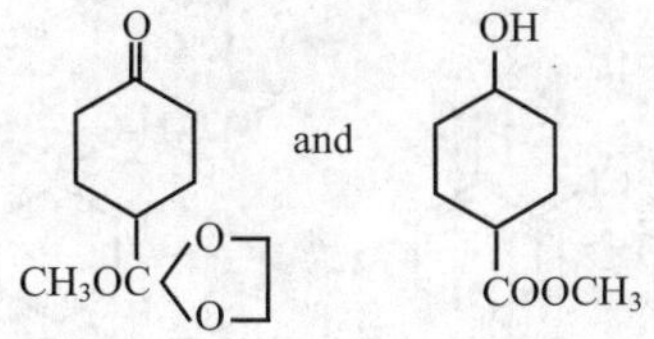

(b) 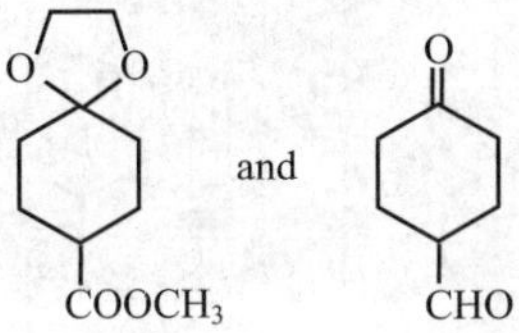

(c) 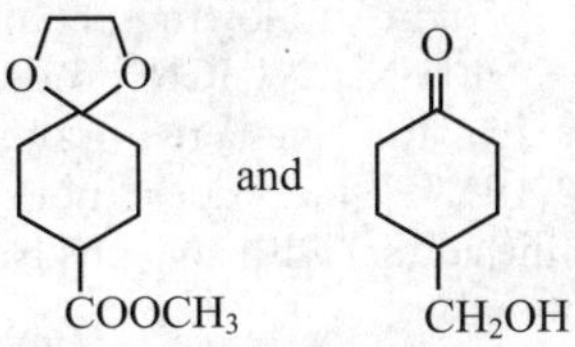

(d) 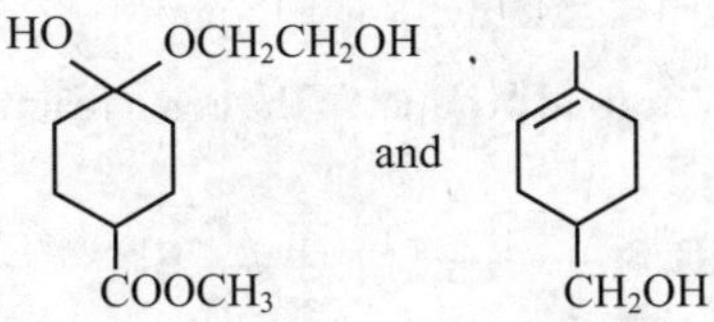

98. Choose the correct option for the following set of reactions:

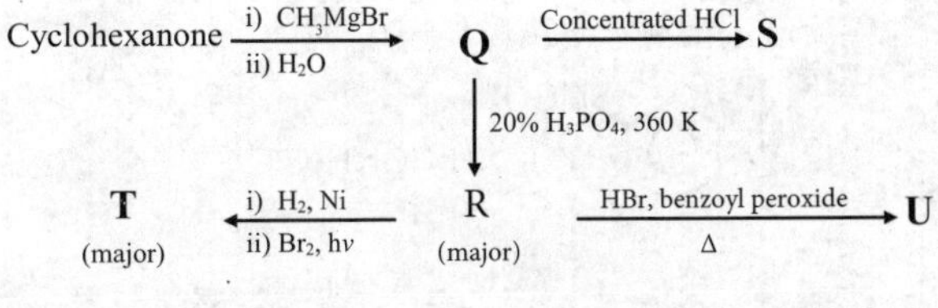

(a) 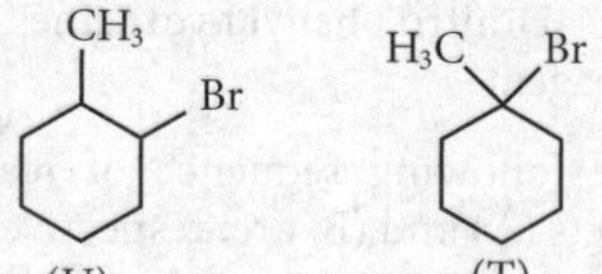
(U) (T)

(b) 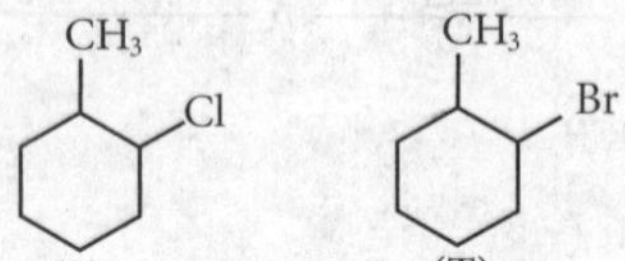
(S) (T)

(c) 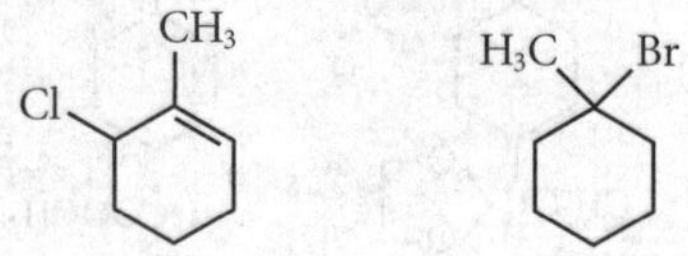
(S) (T)

(d) 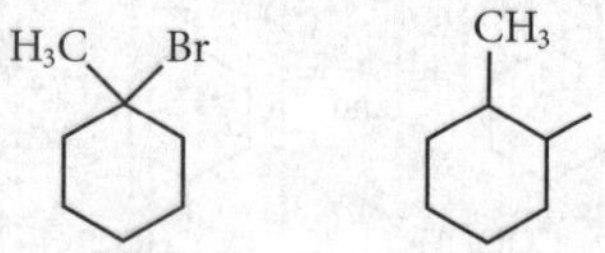
(U) (S)

99. Which of the following compounds on reaction with NaCN/HCN produces racemic cyanohydrin and gives a red-orange precipitate with 2,4-DNP but does not give white crystalline adduct with aqueous $NaHSO_3$?

(a) Butanal
(b) 3-Pentanone
(c) Cyclohexanone
(d) 2-Methyl-3-hexanone

100. The final product in the given reaction sequence is:

$$CH_3Br \xrightarrow{KCN} [A] \xrightarrow{H_3O^{\oplus}} [B] \xrightarrow{LiAlH_4} [C]$$

(a) Acetaldehyde (b) Ethyl alcohol
(c) Acetone (d) Methane

101. Which of the following reactions is incorrectly matched?

(a) 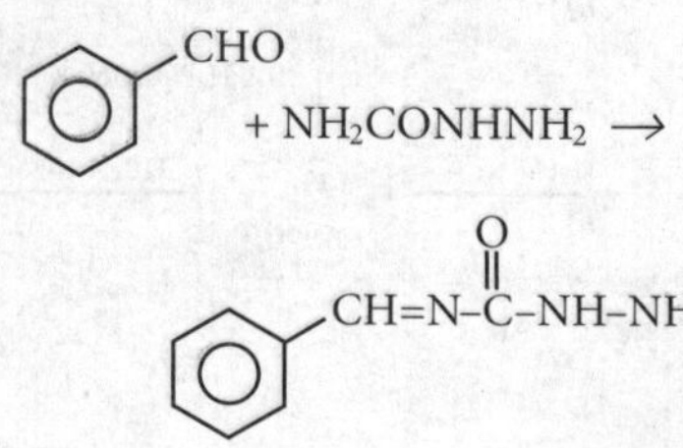

(b) 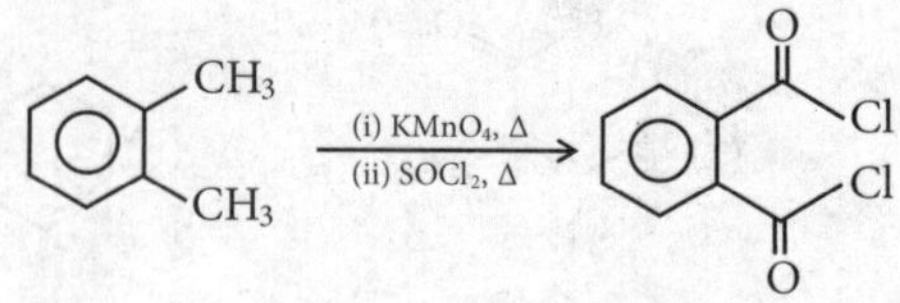

(c) 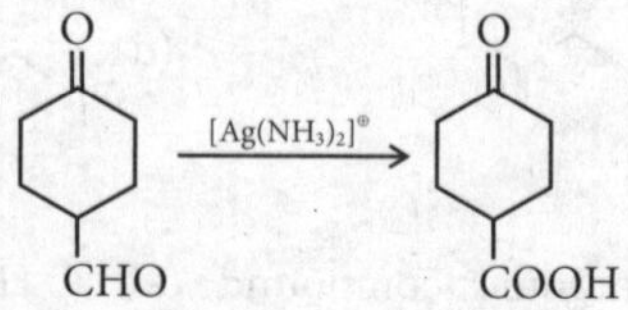

(d) 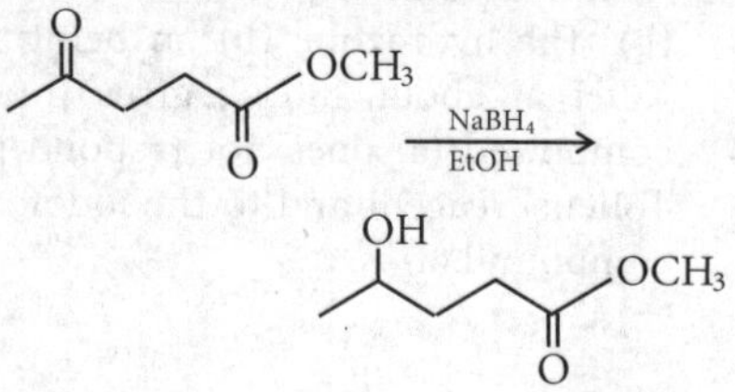

102. Which of the following reactions will give 3° alcohol as a major product?

(a) $CH_3-CH_2-\overset{O}{\overset{\|}{C}}-NH_2 \xrightarrow[\text{(ii) } NaNO_2/HCl]{\text{(i) LAH}}$

(b) $H-\overset{O}{\overset{\|}{C}}-OMe \xrightarrow[\text{(ii) } H^+]{\text{(i) } CH_3MgX(\text{excess})}$

(c) $H_3C-\underset{O}{HC-CH_2} \xrightarrow[\text{(ii) } H^+]{\text{(i) RMgX}}$

(d) $CH_3-\overset{O}{\overset{\|}{C}}-Cl \xrightarrow[H^+]{CH_3MgX(\text{excess})}$

103. Among the following, select the incorrect statement:

(a) Among cyclohexanone and 2,2,6-trimethyl cyclohexanone, the former compound gives cyanohydrin in good yield.
(b) Phenoxide has more resonating structures than the carboxylate ion; so phenol is more acidic than carboxylic acid.
(c) Aryl alkyl ether is more reactive than benzene ring towards electrophilic substitution.
(d) Ortho and para nitrophenol can be separated by steam distillation.

104. Which of the following is most appropriate for the given conversion?

(a) (i) O_3 (ii) $Zn-H_2O$

(b) (i) HBr/H_2O_2 (ii) NaOH (iii) CrO_3, H_2SO_4
(c) (i) BH_3–THF (ii) H_2O_2/NaOH (iii) PDC
(d) (i) HCl/H_2O_2 (ii) H_2O (iii) PCC

105. The major product of the following sequence cannot give:

$$CH_3CH_2Cl \xrightarrow[\text{(ii) } CdCl_2 \text{ (iii) } CH_3COCl]{\text{(i) Mg/ether}}$$

(a) Yellow crystal with NaOI
(b) Silver mirror with Tollens' reagent
(c) White crystal with aqueous $NaHSO_3$
(d) Precipitate with 2,4-DNP

106. Which of the following reactions is correctly matched?

(a)
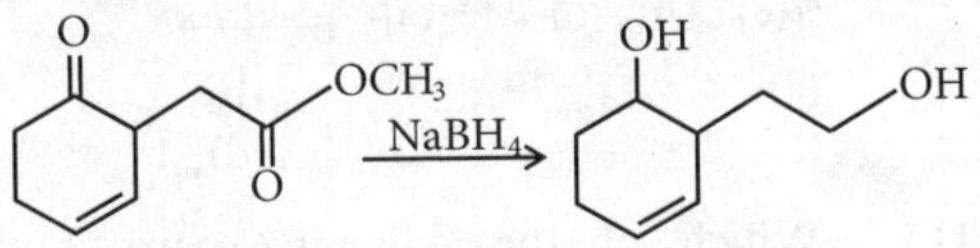

(b)
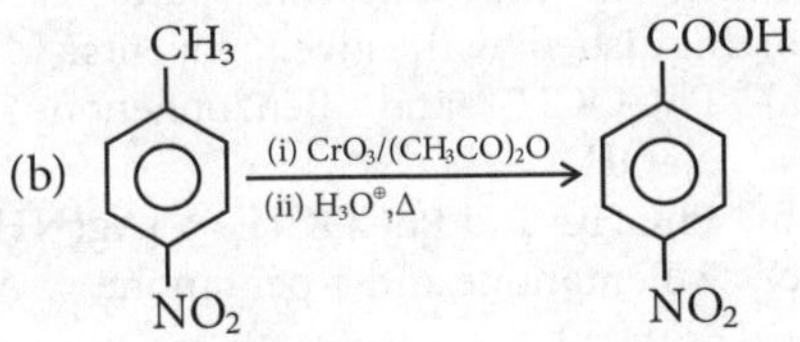

(c)
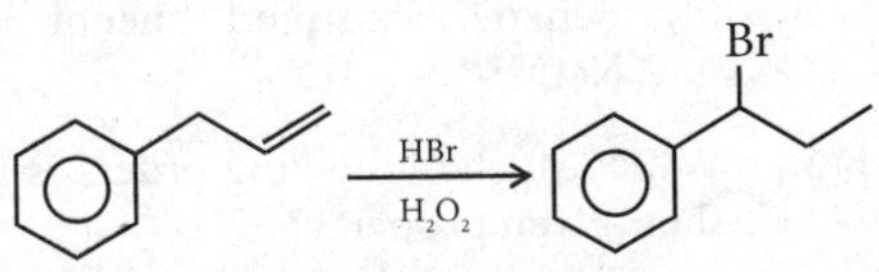

(d)
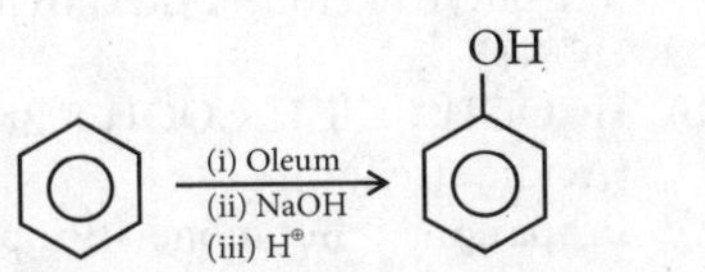

107. A in the given reaction cannot be prepared by:

$$A \xrightarrow[\Delta]{KOH} PhCOOK + PhCH_2OH$$

(a) Ph CH_2–OH $\xrightarrow{NBS}$

(b) Ph–CH_3 $\xrightarrow[\text{(ii) Aq.KOH}]{\text{(i) } Cl_2/hv}$

(c) Ph–CN $\xrightarrow[\text{(ii) } H_3O^{\oplus}]{\text{(i) DIBAL-H}}$

(d) PhMgBr $\xrightarrow[\text{(ii) } H_3O^{\oplus}]{\text{(i) CH≡CH}}$

108. The reaction which will give racemic mixture is:

(a)
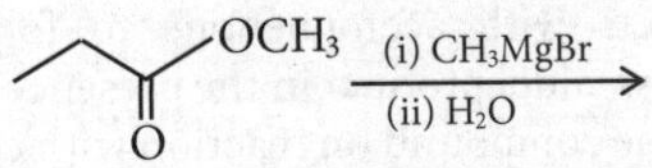

(b)
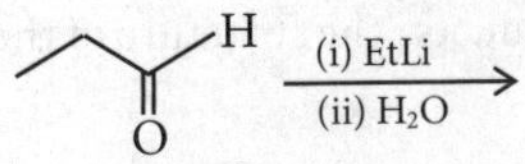

(c)
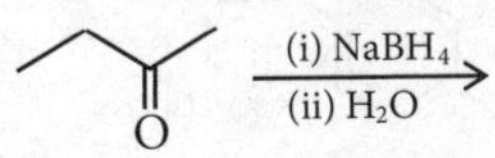

(d)
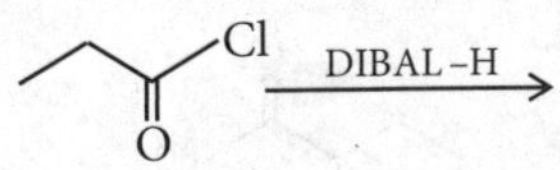

109. Which one of the following products is not obtained during the following reaction?

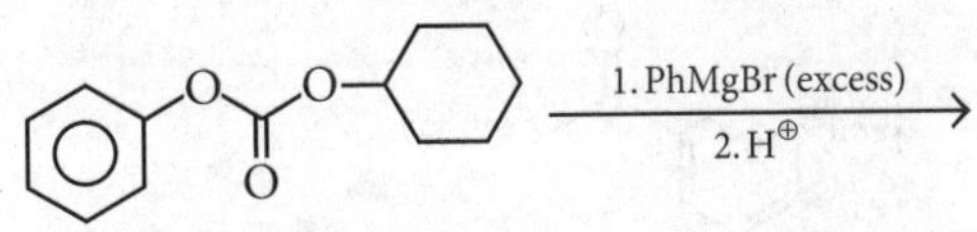

(a)
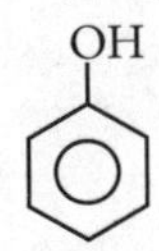

(b)
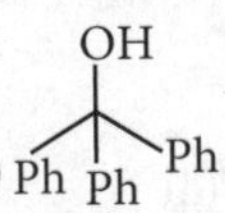

(c)
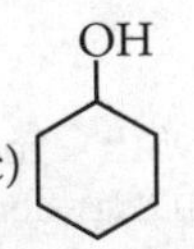

(d)
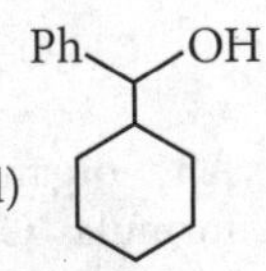

110. Which of the following reactions is correctly matched?

(a) CH_3–C≡C–CH_3 $\xrightarrow[Pd/BaSO_4]{H_2}$ Trans-2-butene

(b)
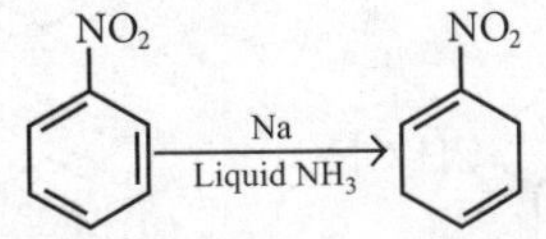

(c)
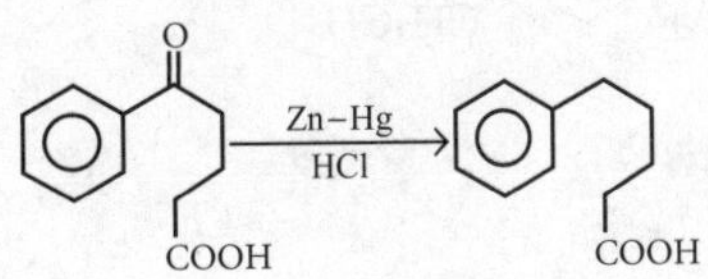

(d) 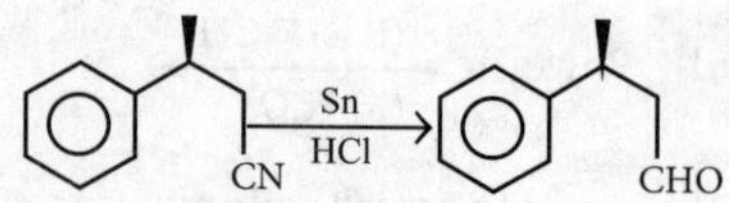

111. A compound with molecular formula $C_8H_8O_2$ reacts with acetophenone to form a single cross-aldol product in the presence of base. The same compound on reaction with concentrated NaOH forms benzyl alcohol derivative as one of the products. The structure of the compound is:

(a) 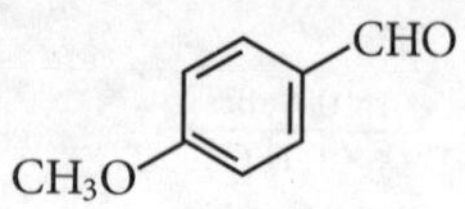

(b) 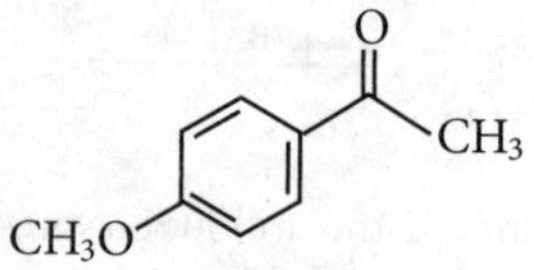

(c) 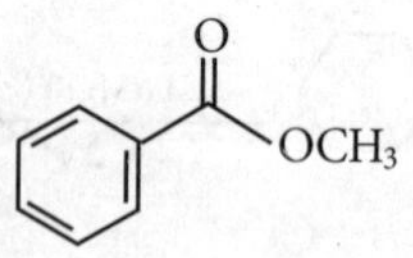

(d) 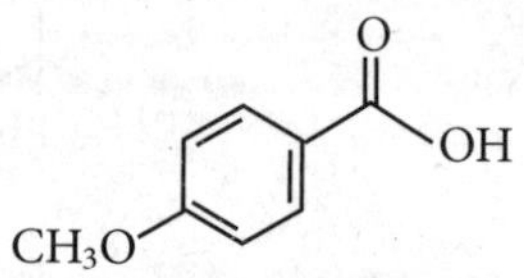

112. An organic compound with molecular formula "$C_9H_{10}O$" forms 2,4-DNP derivatives and reduces Tollens' reagent. It cannot show Cannizzaro reaction but shows aldol reaction. On oxidation with $KMnO_4$, Δ, it produces 1,2-benzene dicarboxylic acid. The compound is:

(a) 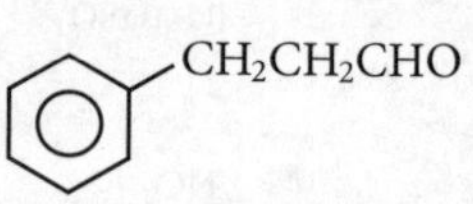
(b) 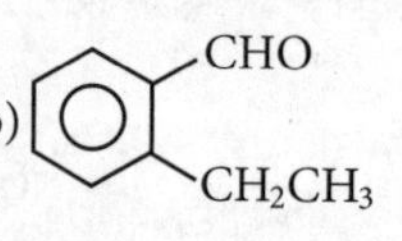

(c) 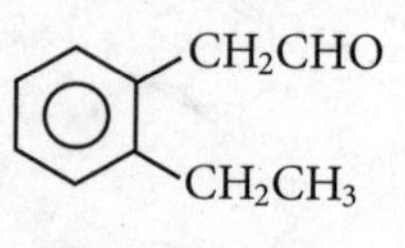
(d) 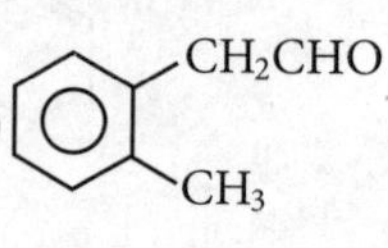

113. If both P and Q can give yellow crystal with I_2/NaOH, then R and R' can, respectively, be:

$$\text{RCOOR'} \xrightarrow[\text{(ii) } H_2O]{\text{(i) } LiAlH_4} P + Q$$

(a) $-CH_3$ and $-CH_3$
(b) $-CH_3$ and $-C_2H_5$
(c) $-C_2H_5$ and $-CH_3$
(d) $-C_2H_5$ and $-C_2H_5$

114. How many of the following reactions will produce carboxylic acid salt?

(i) $CH_3CH_2CN \xrightarrow[\text{(ii)} NH_4Cl]{\text{(i)} CH_3MgBr}$

(ii) $CH_3-CHO + 2[Ag(NH_3)_2]^+ + 3\overset{\ominus}{O}H \rightarrow$

(iii) Ph–CHO + Fehling solution →

(iv) $HCHO + NaOH \xrightarrow{\Delta}$

(a) 4 (b) 3
(c) 2 (d) 1

115. Which of the following pairs cannot be distinguished by the given reagents?
(a) $PhCOCH_3$ and Benzophenone ⇒ I_2/NaOH
(b) PhCHO and $PhCOCH_3$ ⇒ $[Ag(NH_3)_2]^{\oplus}$
(c) 2-Pentanone and 3-pentanone ⇒ Aqueous $NaHSO_3$
(d) Benzoic acid and phenol ⇒ Aqueous NaOH

116. Which of the following orders is correct with their given property?
(a) Acetone > Di-tert-butyl ketone > Methyl tert-butyl ketone (Reactivity towards HCN)
(b) HCOOH > $ClCH_2COOH$ > $BrCH_2COOH$ (Acidic strength)
(c) Propanone > Butanone > Propanal (Nucleophilic addition)
(d) p-Toluidine > Aniline > p-Nitro aniline (Carbyl amine reaction)

117. An organic compound containing one oxygen gives colour with the Victor Meyer test, decolourises alkaline $KMnO_4$, responds to iodoform test and shows geometrical isomerism. It should be:
(a) $Ph-CH=CH-CH_2-OH$
(b) $Ph-CH=CH-CH(OH)-CH_3$
(c) $Ph-CH=CH-CO-CH_3$

(d) $Ph-CH_2-CH(OH)-CH_3$

118. An alkene 'P' (2-methyl-2-butene) on ozonolysis gives a mixture of two compounds R and S. On the basis of the following observations, select the incorrect option:

Compound/Test	Fehling	Iodoform
R	✔	✔
S	×	✔

(a) Isopropanol + CrO_3/Acetone ⟶ (S)

(b) 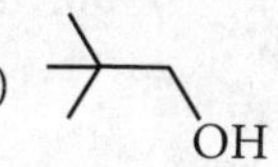 + H_2SO_4 $\xrightarrow{\Delta}$ (P)

(c) $CH_3-COCl + H_2/Pd \xrightarrow{\text{Quinoline}} (S)$

(d) $CH_3-CN \xrightarrow[\text{(ii)}H_2O]{\text{(i)}SnCl_2/HCl} (R)$

119. A compound (P) (propanal) produces cyanohydrin (Q) with HCN/NaCN. (Q) on reaction with dilute H_2SO_4 and heating produces (R). The major product R is:

(a) 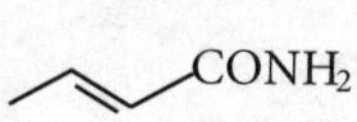
(b) 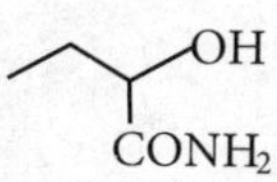
(c) 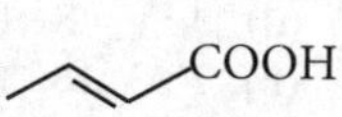
(d) 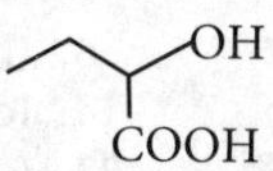

120. The major products of the following reaction are:

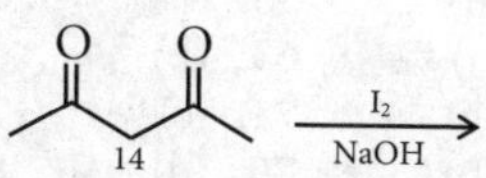

(a) CH_3COONa and $^{14}CHI_3$
(b) $^{14}CH_3COONa$ and CHI_3
(c) $NaOOC^{14}CH_2COONa$ and CHI_3
(d) $^{14}CH_3COONa$ and $^{14}CHI_3$

121. Hydrolysis of A gives positive Tollens' test. Then compound A is:

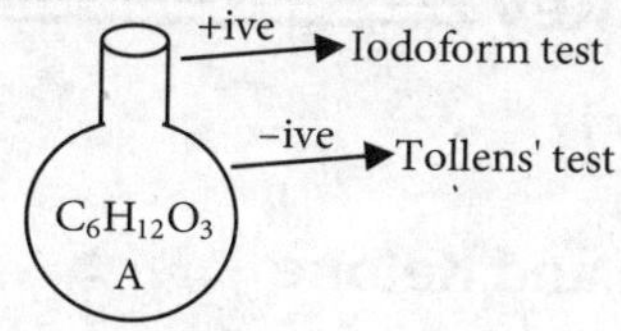

(a) $H-\overset{O}{\overset{\|}{C}}-C(OCH_3)_2-CH_2-CH_3$

(b) $CH_3-\overset{O}{\overset{\|}{C}}-C(OCH_3)_2-CH_3$

(c) $CH_3-\overset{O}{\overset{\|}{C}}-CH_2-CH(OCH_3)-OCH_3$

(d) $H-\overset{O}{\overset{\|}{C}}-CH_2-CH_2-CH(OCH_3)-OCH_3$

122. Two reactions which are examples of nucleophilic attack are given below:

I: $R_1R_2C=O + HCN \xrightarrow{pH=x}$

II: $R_1R_2C=O + NH_2-\overset{O}{\overset{\|}{C}}-NH-NH_2 \xrightarrow{pH=y}$

The values of x and y are, respectively:

(a) ≤ 4.5 and 4.5 (b) 6 and 1.5
(c) > 7 and 4.5 (d) 9 and 9

Answer Key

Level-1

Aldehyde and Ketone

1. (a)	2. (b)	3. (b)	4. (d)	5. (a)	6. (a)	7. (a)	8. (b)
9. (b)	10. (a)	11. (d)	12. (b)	13. (d)	14. (a)	15. (d)	16. (c)
17. (a)	18. (c)	19. (c)	20. (b)	21. (c)	22. (b)	23. (b)	24. (b)
25. (b)	26. (c)	27. (c)	28. (b)	29. (a)	30. (d)	31. (b)	32. (a)
33. (a)	34. (c)	35. (d)	36. (d)	37. (c)	38. (b)	39. (a)	40. (a)
41. (a)	42. (c)	43. (b)	44. (d)	45. (d)	46. (d)	47. (d)	48. (a)
49. (c)	50. (c)	51. (a)	52. (c)	53. (a)	54. (c)	55. (d)	56. (a)
57. (c)	58. (b)	59. (d)	60. (a)	61. (c)	62. (d)	63. (d)	64. (c)
65. (d)							

Carboxylic Acid

66. (b)	67. (b)	68. (a)	69. (d)	70. (a)	71. (a)	72. (a)	73. (b)
74. (d)	75. (c)	76. (c)	77. (a)	78. (a)	79. (d)	80. (c)	81. (c)
82. (d)	83. (a)	84. (a)	85. (c)	86. (c)	87. (b)	88. (c)	89. (d)
90. (c)	91. (a)	92. (b)	93. (c)	94. (d)	95. (a)	96. (a)	97. (a)
98. (d)	99. (a)	100. (a)	101. (c)	102. (b)	103. (d)		

Level-2

1. (d)	2. (a)	3. (b)	4. (b)	5. (c)	6. (b)	7. (d)	8. (b)
9. (c)	10. (b)	11. (a)	12. (d)	13. (d)	14. (d)	15. (b)	16. (b)
17. (b)	18. (c)	19. (b)	20. (b)	21. (c)	22. (c)	23. (b)	24. (d)
25. (d)	26. (c)	27. (c)	28. (b)	29. (d)	30. (d)	31. (d)	32. (d)
33. (b)	34. (c)	35. (d)	36. (b)	37. (d)	38. (c)	39. (c)	40. (c)
41. (b)	42. (d)	43. (a)	44. (b)	45. (c)	46. (a)	47. (b)	48. (a)
49. (b)	50. (c)	51. (a)	52. (d)	53. (d)	54. (d)	55. (c)	56. (a)
57. (a)	58. (c)	59. (a)	60. (d)	61. (c)	62. (a)	63. (b)	64. (c)
65. (b)	66. (b)	67. (b)	68. (a)	69. (d)	70. (b)	71. (c)	72. (c)
73. (c)	74. (a)	75. (c)	76. (c)	77. (b)	78. (b)	79. (d)	80. (b)
81. (a)	82. (a)	83. (b)	84. (b)	85. (c)	86. (c)	87. (d)	88. (d)
89. (b)	90. (a)	91. (b)	92. (a)	93. (d)	94. (c)	95. (b)	96. (b)
97. (c)	98. (a)	99. (d)	100. (b)	101. (a)	102. (d)	103. (b)	104. (c)
105. (b)	106. (d)	107. (d)	108. (c)	109. (b)	110. (c)	111. (a)	112. (d)
113. (b)	114. (c)	115. (d)	116. (d)	117. (b)	118. (c)	119. (c)	120. (a)
121. (c)	122. (c)						

Solutions

Level-1

1.

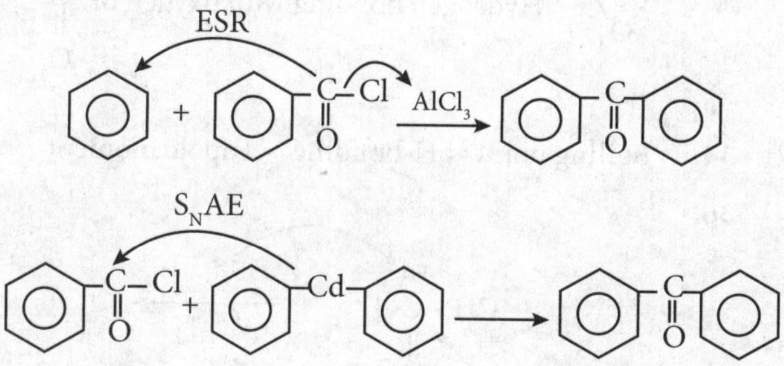

2. The π bond breaks towards more EN atoms. It induces $-\delta$ charge on the more EN atoms and $+\delta$ on the less EN atoms.

3.

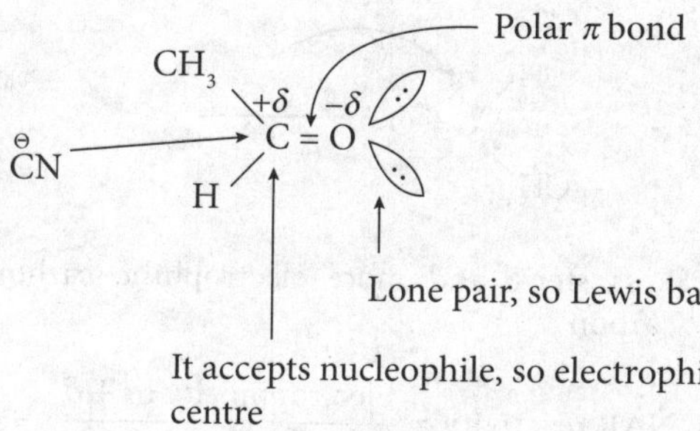

4. Due to stronger intermolecular hydrogen bonding by alcohol, it has a higher boiling point than carboxyl compounds of similar molecular mass.
Solubility of the molecule decreases with increase in the alkyl group.

5. Carbonyl compounds have higher dipole moment (μ). Hence, they are polar and have higher intermolecular attraction due to pole attraction. This results in a higher boiling point.

7.

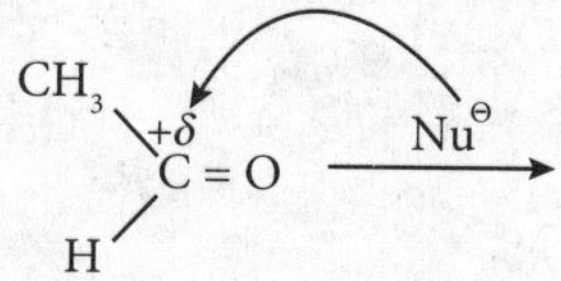

Less steric and higher electrophilicity

9.

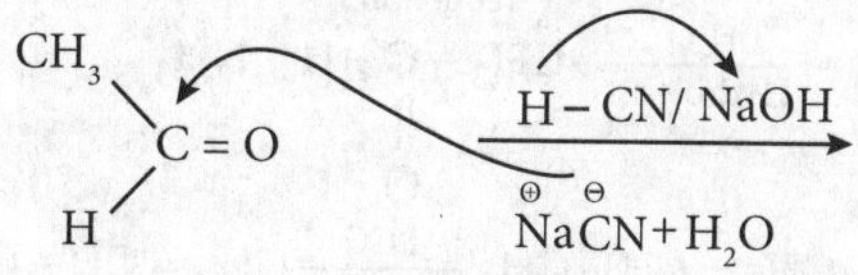

NaOH generates $\overset{\ominus}{C}N$ (good nucleophile) and at the end of the reaction, NaOH regenerates and returns to its original state. So it is a catalyst.

10.

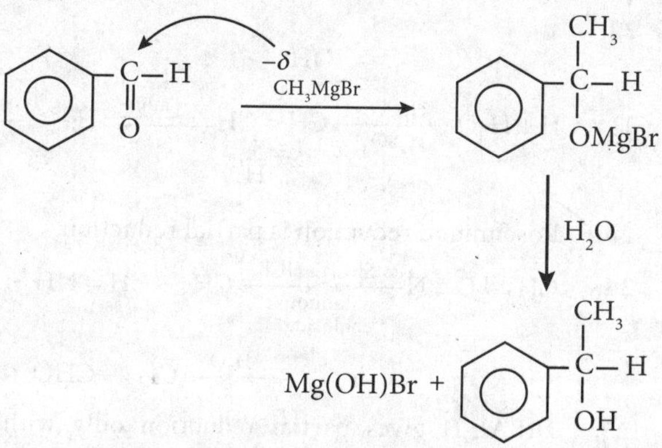

11. $NaHSO_3$ is a bulky nucleophile, so it is more reactive with aldehyde and less reactive with ketone. The product comprises white crystals, which are polar and so they are water soluble.

13. Dry acid removes water and substitutes another alcohol. So alcohol is in excess.

14. In Clemmensen reduction (Zn-Hg/HCl), the carbonyl compound is completely reduced to alkane.

16. For haloform reaction, the $CH_3-\underset{\underset{O}{\|}}{C}-H/R$ group is required and $CH_3-\underset{\underset{OH}{|}}{CH}-H/R$ can be oxidized to the same. Hydrogen that is replaced by halogen $(CH_2Cl-\underset{\underset{O}{\|}}{C}-H/R)$ also gives haloform reaction.

18. α-hydrogen containing aldehyde gives aldol reaction and absence of α-hydrogen containing aldehyde gives Cannizzaro reaction.

20. Alcohol is oxidized to carbonyl compound in the presence of heat and catalyst Ag or Cu.

21. $CH_3-C\equiv N \xrightarrow[\text{Partial reduction}]{\text{DIBAL-H}} CH_3-CH=NH$

$\xrightarrow[\text{Hydrolysis}]{H_2O} CH_3-\underset{\underset{O}{\|}}{C}-H + NH_3$

$CH_2=CH-\underset{\underset{OH}{|}}{CH_2} \xrightarrow{\text{PCC}} CH_2=CH-\underset{\underset{O}{\|}}{C}-H$

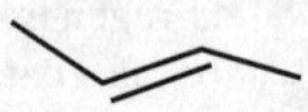 $\xrightarrow[\text{Ozonolysis}]{O_3/Zn/H_2O} 2CH_3-CHO$

22.

$CH\equiv CH + H_2O \xrightarrow[H_2SO_4]{HgSO_4} \underset{\underset{H}{|}}{\overset{\overset{OH}{|}}{CH=CH}} \xrightleftharpoons{\text{Tauto}} H-\overset{\overset{O}{\|}}{C}-CH_3$

23. Rosenmund reduction is partial reduction.

24. $CH_3-C\equiv N \xrightarrow[\text{Stannous chloride}]{SnCl_2+HCl} CH_3-CH=NH$

$\xrightarrow{H_2O} CH_3-CHO$

25. DIBAL-H gives partial reduction only with cyanide and ester, and it forms aldehyde.

27.

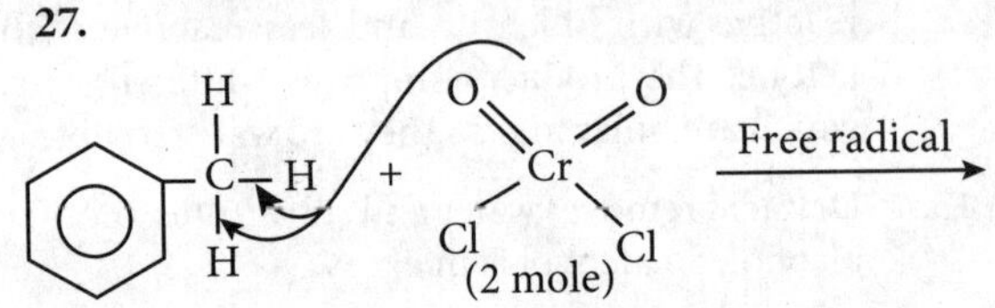

28.

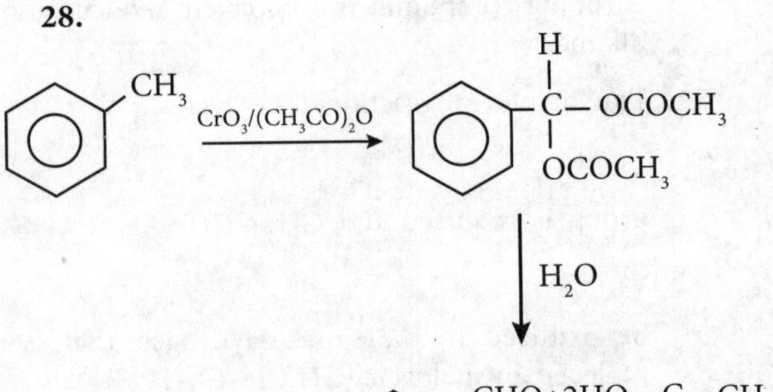

31.

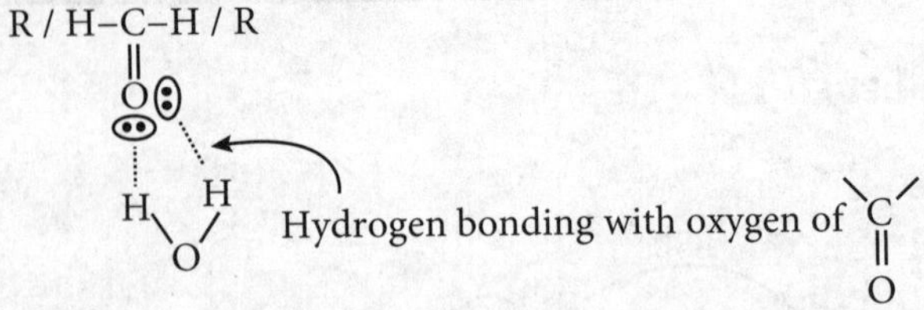

34. Boiling point ∝ H-bonding ∝ Dipole moment

36.

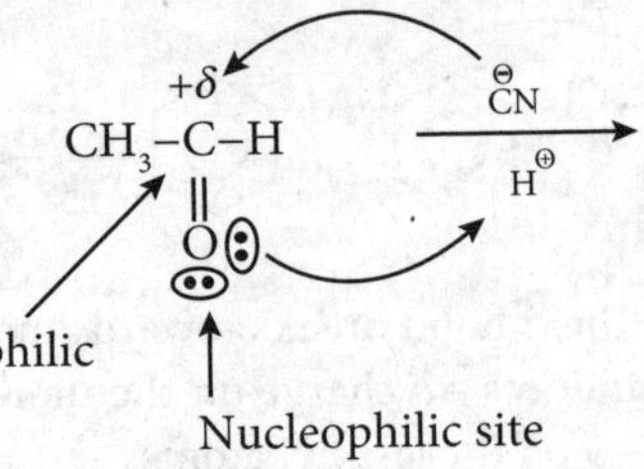

38.

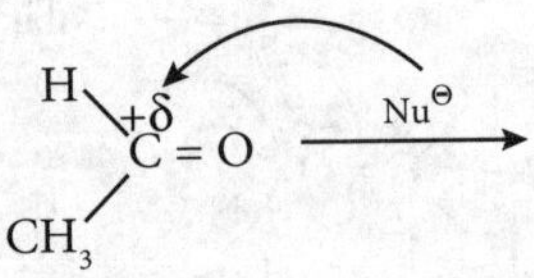

Less steric and more electrophilic carbonyl carbon

39. $\text{NAR reactivity} \propto \dfrac{\text{Electrophilicity or } +\delta}{\text{Steric}}$

40. Pure $\overset{+\delta}{H}-\overset{\delta}{C}N$ bond is bad nucleophile due to covalent bond between H and C and base (NaOH) pulls out H from H – CN and forms good nucleophile $\overset{\ominus}{C}N$.

41. $NaHSO_3$ reacts with aldehyde and forms white crystal, which is soluble in water.

43.

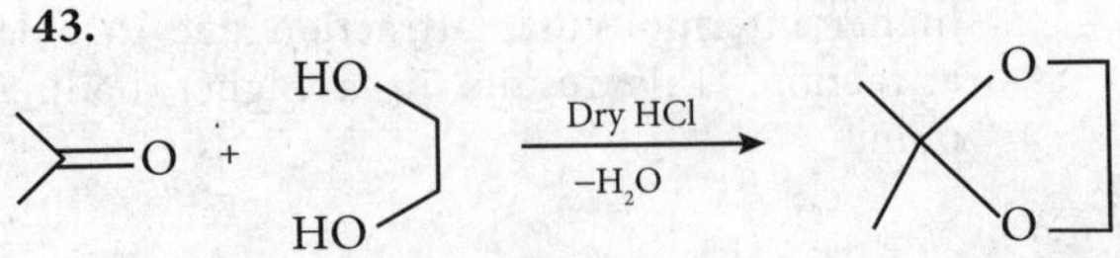

46.

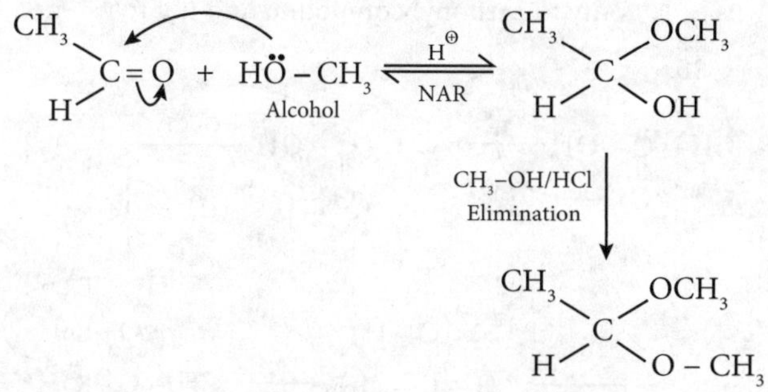

48. By Tollen's reagent with aldehyde, $Ag^{\oplus}$ is reduced to Ag.

49. Aldehyde is easily oxidized to acid because of the presence of oxidizable bond.

50. $C_5H_{10}O$ gives phenylhydrazone. This means it is a carbonyl compound and it does not give the test with Tollen's reagent. This means it is not an aldehyde and it does not give iodoform test. This means it does not contain methyl carbonyl. So it is $CH_3-CH_2-\underset{\underset{O}{\|}}{C}-CH_2-CH_3$

53. α-hydrogen containing aldehydes only gives Fehling test. This means aromatic aldehyde does not give the test.

54. NaOCl is a haloform reagent.

55. $\underbrace{CH_3-\underset{\underset{O}{\|}}{C}}-CH_2-CH_2-CH_2-CH_3$

This group is responsible for positive iodoform test.

58.

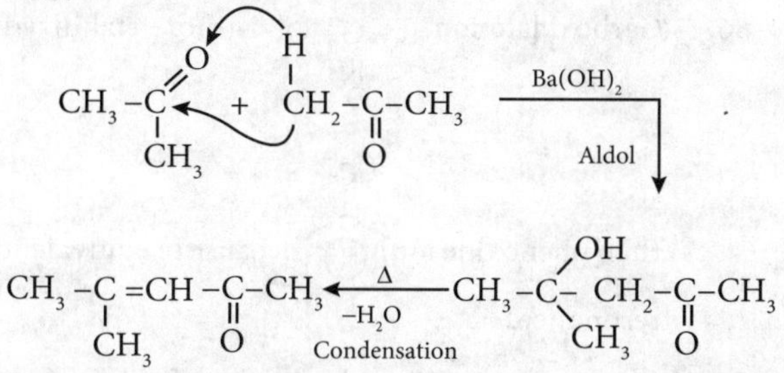

59. In benzaldehyde, α-hydrogen is absent. So it does not give unsaturated α-β carbonyl compounds.

61. Formalin is used as specimen preservative.

63. $CH_3-\underset{\underset{O}{\|}}{C}-OH$

(Acetic acid) is not formed by $H-\underset{\underset{O}{\|}}{C}-H$

66. $CH_3C\equiv N \xrightarrow[\text{Acidic hydrolysis}]{H_2O/H^{\oplus}} CH_3-\underset{\underset{O}{\|}}{C}-OH+NH_3$

67. $CH_3-CH_2-Cl \xrightarrow[SN^2]{KCN} CH_3-CH_2-CN$

$\xrightarrow[-NH_3]{H_3O^{\oplus}} CH_3-CH_2-COOH$

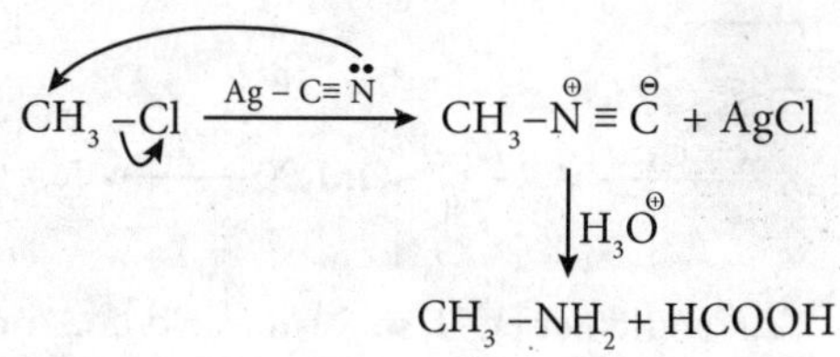

68.

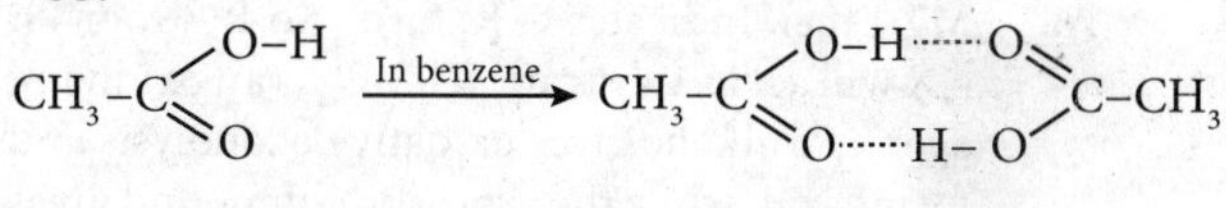

Due to dimer formation

69.

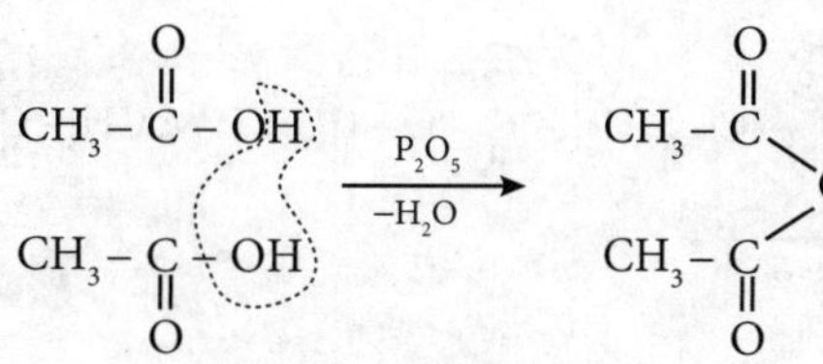

70.

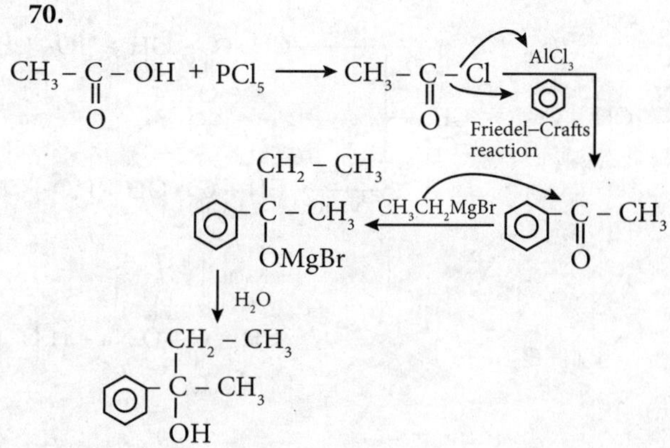

71. $NaBH_4$ is a weak reducing agent and cannot reduce to acid. Red P + HI is a strong reducing agent and it reduces to alkane.

72. By soda lime decarboxylation, one carbon atom will be less. In the HVZ reaction, the number of carbons is unchanged.

73. $KMnO_4$ is a strong oxidizing agent and it gives benzoic acid from at least one α-hydrogen containing benzene derivative, but

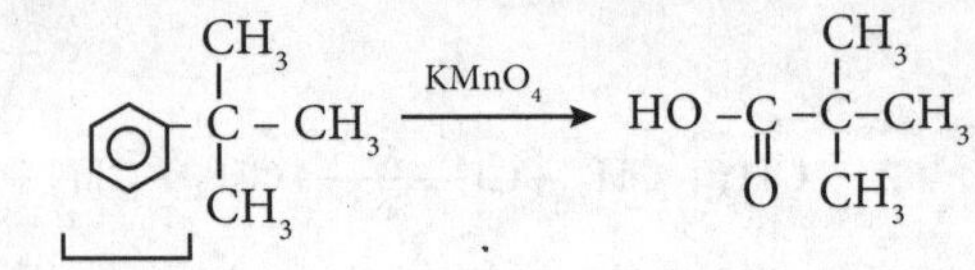

Oxidizing part

75.

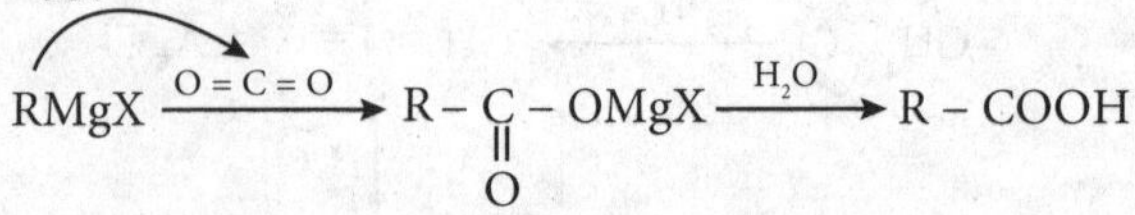

R could not be H; so formic acid does not form from Grignard reagent.

76. Mg/Ether, indicates G.R. form. So R – X or Ph – X will act as substrate. $KMnO_4$ is an oxidizing agent. So alkene gives oxidative ozonolysis and forms acid, while the aromatic compound gives aromatic acid.

77.

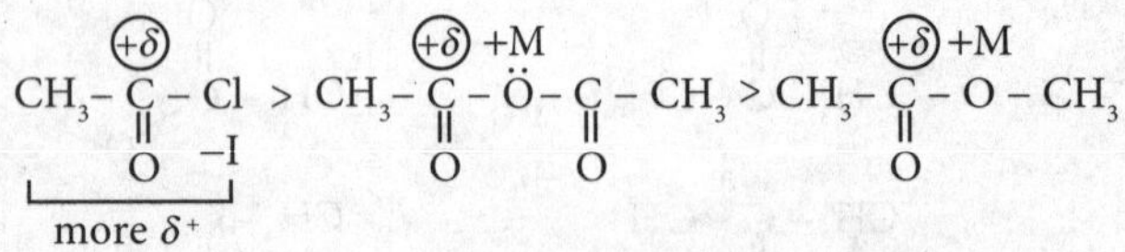

78.

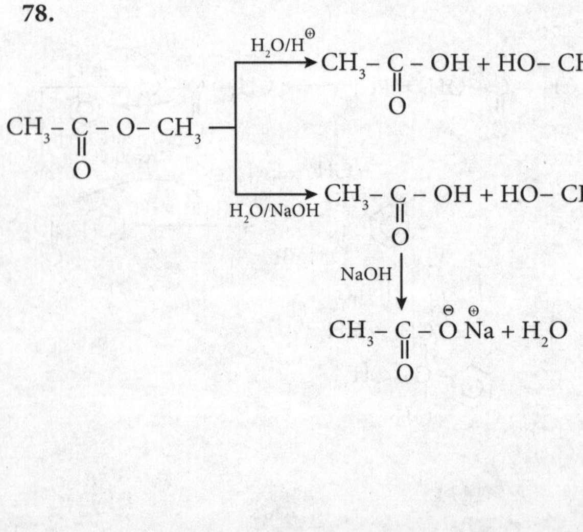

79. $NaBH_4$ is a weak reducing agent. So it reduces only to carbonyl compound and not to ester.

80.

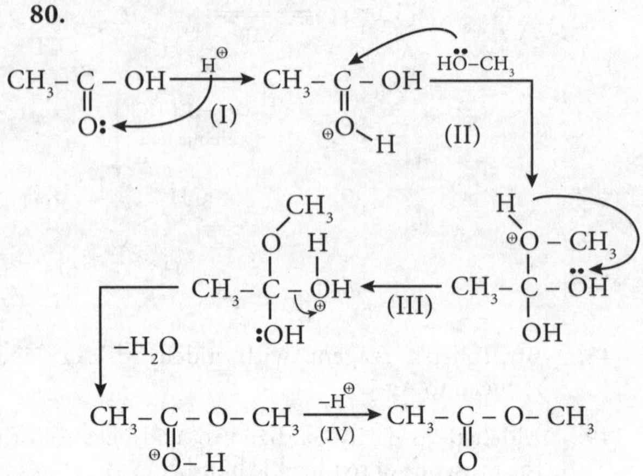

81. Hydrolysis gives acid and alcohol. This means $C_8H_{16}O_2$ is an ester and alcohol (Z) on oxidation gives carboxylic acid Y. The number of carbons is the same in esters on both sides of the valency.

82. Up to nine aliphatic monocarboxylic acids are colourless.

85.

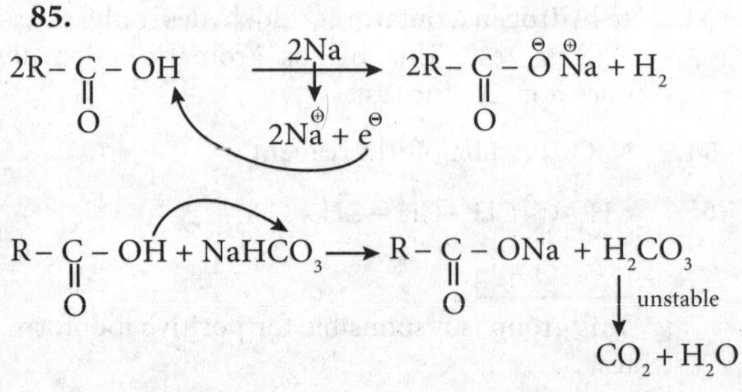

86. Carboxylate ion 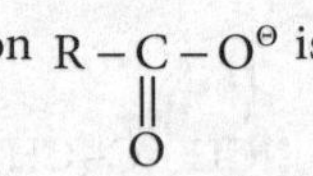 is more stabilized than phenoxide ion 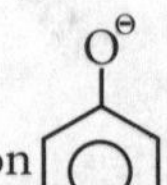 because of equivalent resonance.

87. Ethanal and propanal gives the Fehling test, because both are aliphatic aldehydes.

88. Only P_2O_5/Δ acts as a dehydrating agent.

89. On heating, ammonium salt of acid gives primary amide with release of water. On strong heating, two amides give imide after removal of ammonia.

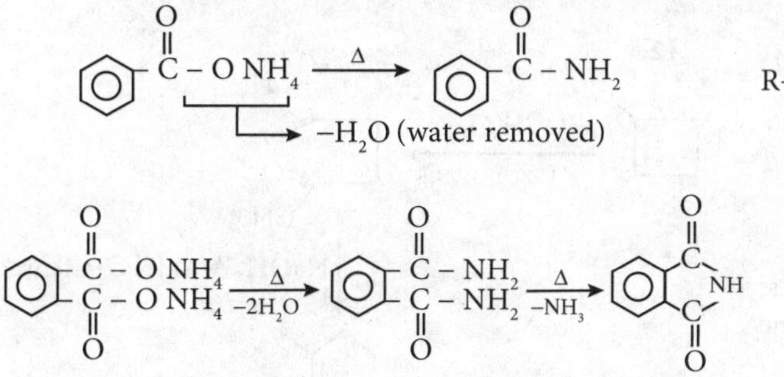

90.

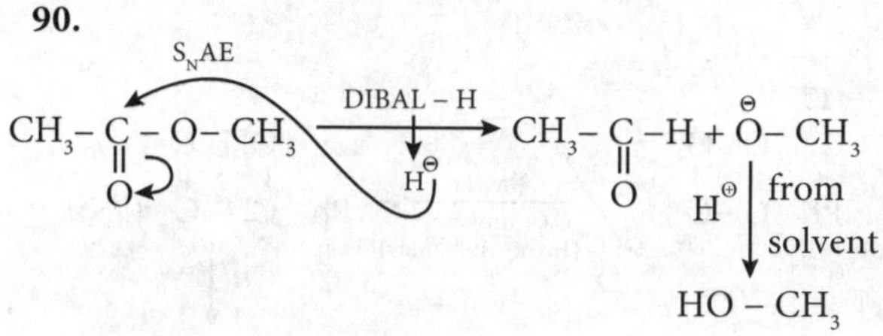

91. B_2H_6 reduces to acid, amide and nitrile to alcohol or amine but not to acid halide, anhydride and ester.

92. Rate of decarboxylation ∝ Stability of intermediate carbanion

94.

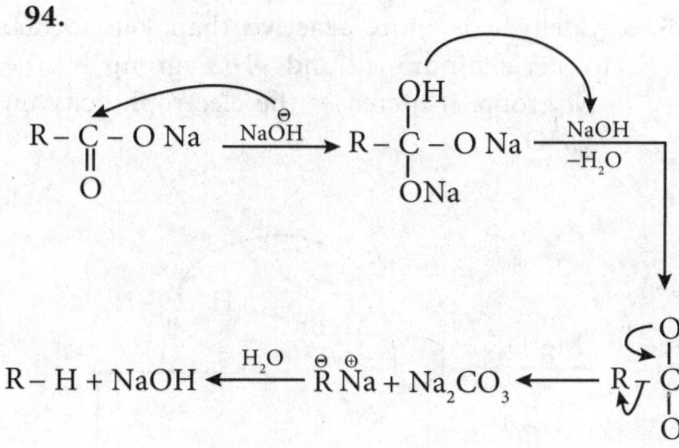

95. $$CH_2(COOH)_2 \xrightarrow[-CO_2]{\Delta} CH_3-COOH$$

96. $$R-COOH \xrightarrow{K.E.} R-R+Na_2CO_3$$

97.

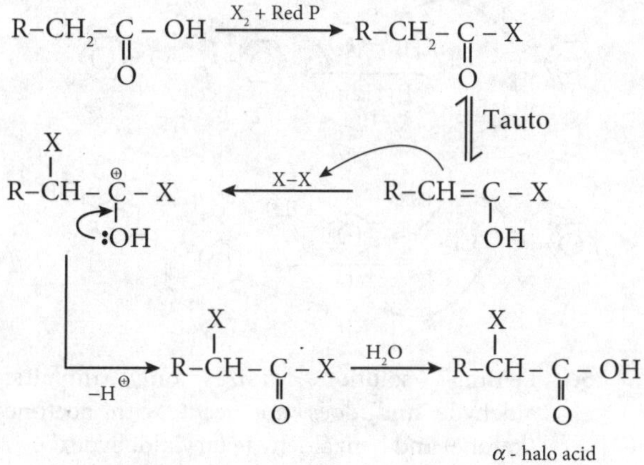

98. –COOH is a deactivating group for ESR and a meta directing group.

99. COOH group is strong deactivating group, and deactivating group never gives F.C. reaction.

100. Memory base

101. Memory base

102. –CHO has an oxidizable bond and so is oxidized to –COOH. $LiAlH_4$ is a strong reducing agent.

103. Jones' reagent (CrO_3 + H_2SO_4) is a strong oxidizing agent and it oxidizes primary alcohol to acid and not aldehyde.

LEVEL-2

1. Carbonyl compounds are planar structures and they are converted to tetrahedral structures by attack of nucleophile on both sides.

2.

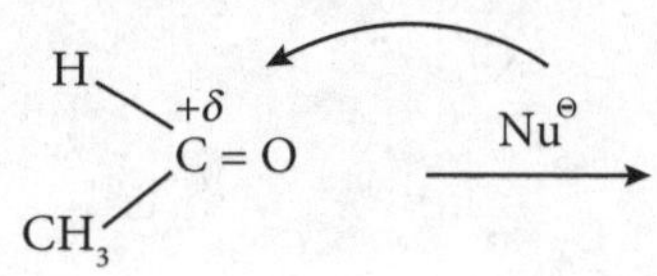

Less steric and high electrophilicity

3.

$$\underset{\displaystyle Cl}{CH_2}-COO^- > CH_3-COO^- > CH_3-CH_2-O^-$$

Stability of conjugate base

4.

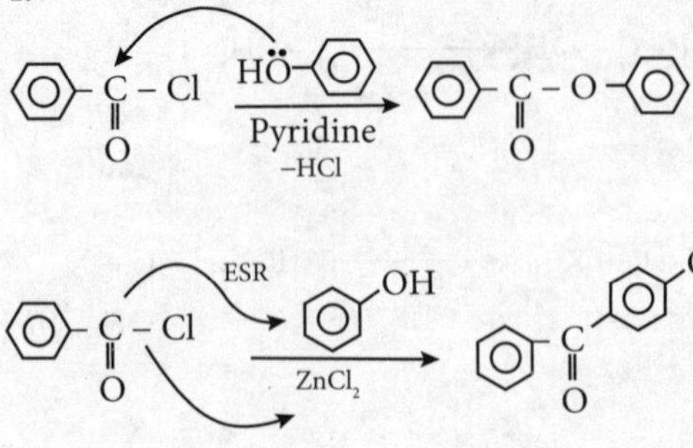

5. Fehling's solution oxidizes only aliphatic aldehyde and does not react with acetone (ketone) and benzaldehyde (arylaldehyde).

6. In the absence of α-hydrogen, benzaldehyde gives Cannizzaro reaction.

7.

$$CH_3-C\equiv CH \xrightarrow[Hg^{++}]{40\%\ H_2SO_4} CH_3-\underset{}{\overset{OH}{\overset{|}{C}}}=CH_2 \underset{\text{Tautomerisation}}{\overset{\text{Isomerisation}}{\rightleftharpoons}} CH_3-\overset{O}{\overset{\|}{C}}-CH_3$$

8.

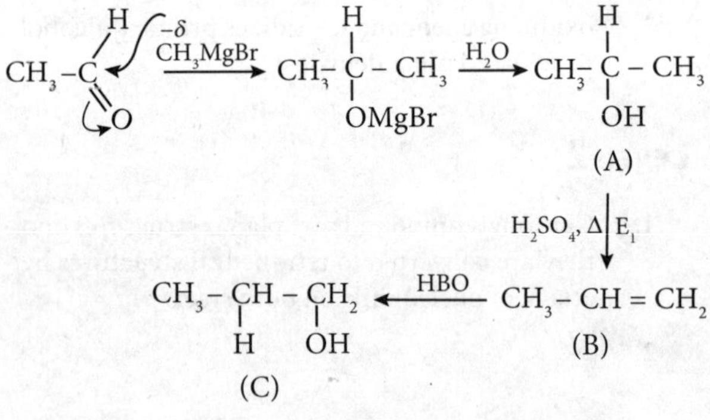

9.

$$CH_3-CH=CH-CH_2-\overset{O}{\overset{\|}{C}}-CH_3 \xrightarrow[\text{Haloform reaction}]{I_2 + NaOH}$$

$$CH_3-CH=CH-CH_2-\overset{O}{\overset{\|}{C}}-\overset{\ominus}{O}\overset{\oplus}{Na} + CHI_3$$

10.

$$CH_3-CH_2-\underset{OH}{\underset{|}{CH}}-CH_3 \xrightarrow[\text{Oxidation}]{KMnO_4/\overset{\ominus}{O}H} CH_3-CH_2-CO-CH_3$$

12.

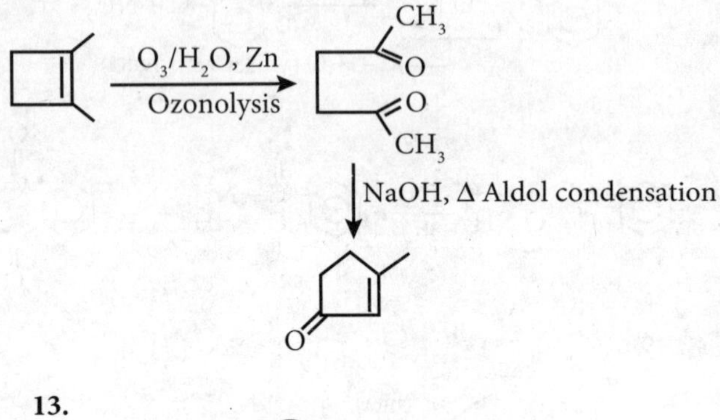

13.

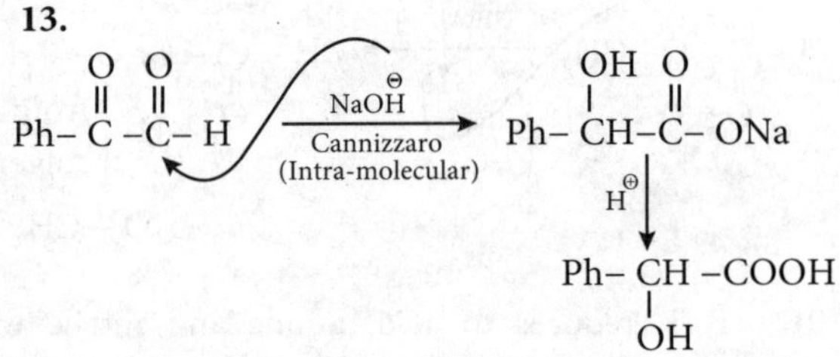

14.

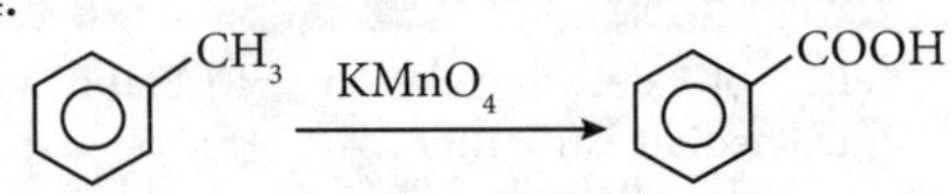

15. Aldehyde is more reactive than ketone due to steric hindrance and $-NO_2$ group by the –M group. It increases the electrophilicity on –CHO.

16.

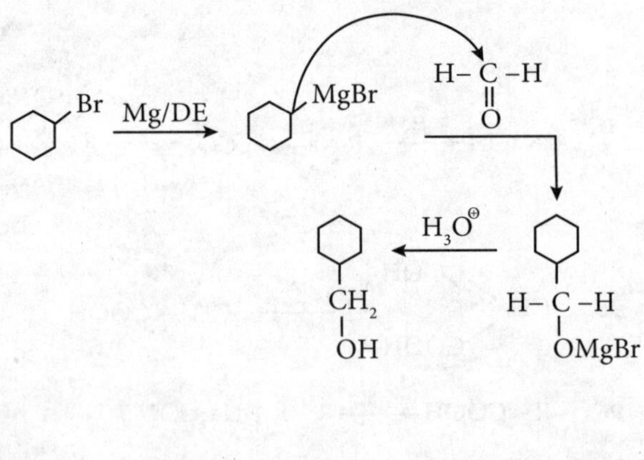

17.

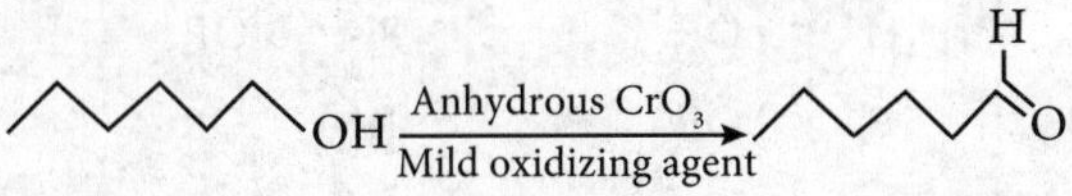

18. $CH_3-CHO \xrightarrow[HCl]{Zn-Hg} CH_3-CH_3$

$CH_3-CH_2-\overset{O}{\overset{\|}{C}}-H \xrightarrow[CaCO_3]{H_2-Pd} \times$

$CH_3-COCl \xrightarrow[\text{and } H_2O]{NaBH_4} CH_3-CH_2-OH$

$CH_3-CH=CH_2 \xrightarrow[(ii)\ H_2O]{(i)\ B_2H_6} CH_3-CH_2-CH_3$

19.

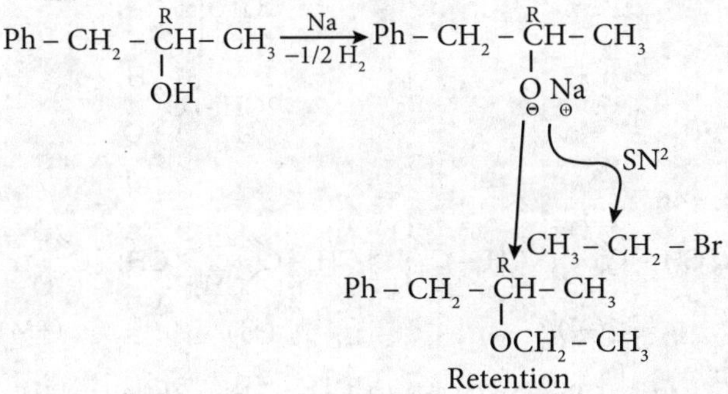

20.

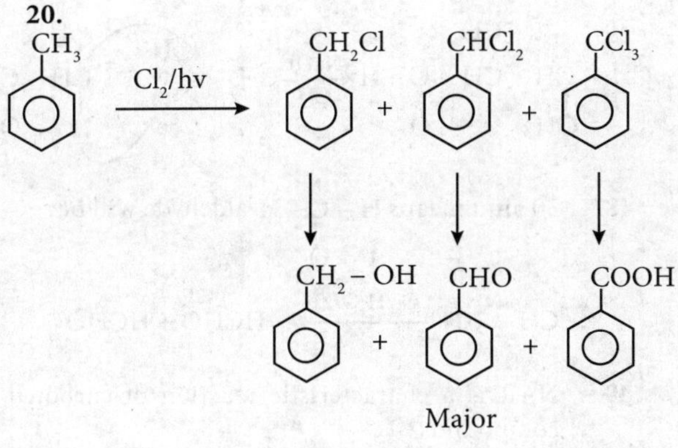

21. 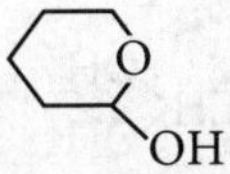 Hemiacetal

22. Presence of α-hydrogen (6α-H).

23.

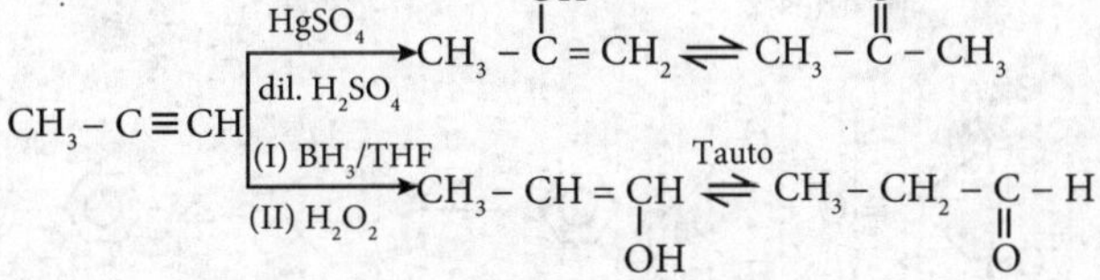

24. Acetone is less reactive. Stability of diol form is the least.

25. Boiling point $\propto$ Hydrogen bonding $\propto \dfrac{1}{\text{Branching}}$

26.

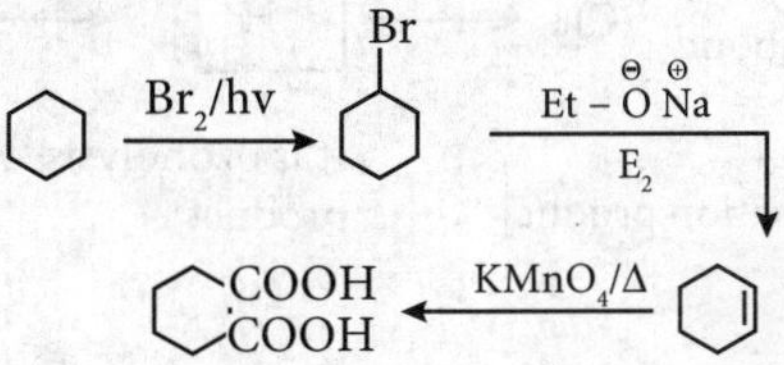

Adipic acid

27. Due to symmetry in para-di-chloro benzene and better fit, it is in crystal form.

28.  Symmetrical carbonyl compound does not give active stereoisomers.

29.

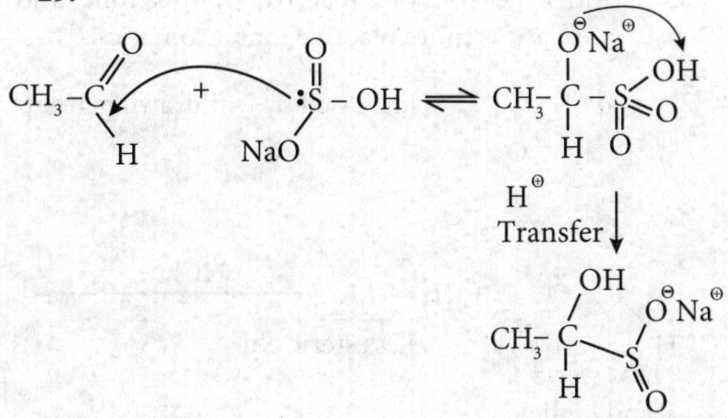

White crystal

30.

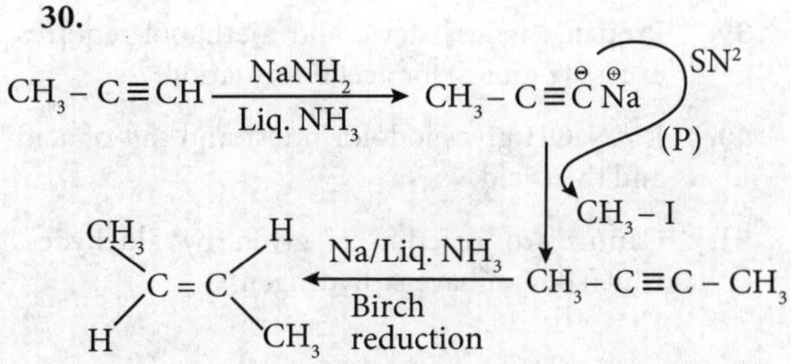

31. Complete reduction of carbonyl compounds to alkanes.

32.

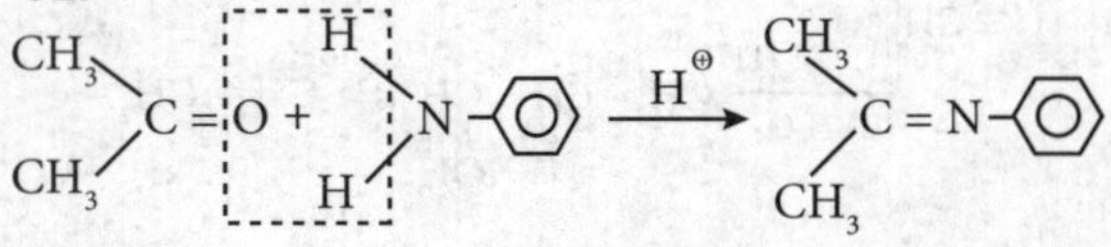

Imine

33.

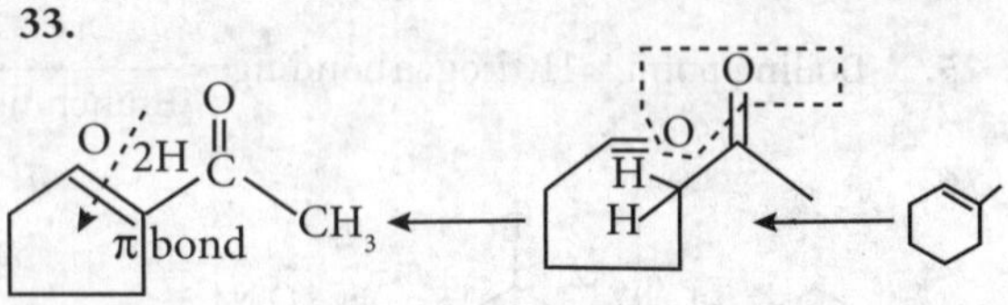

It is aldol condensation product

It is ozonolysis product

34.

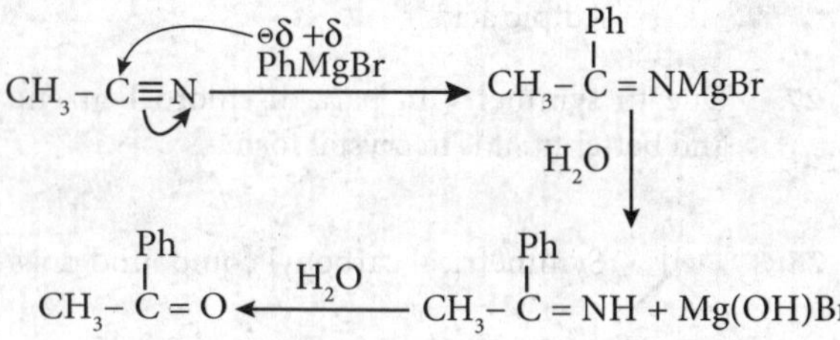

35. Aldehyde is more reactive than ketone and aliphatic is more reactive than aromatic.

36. $\overset{\oplus}{\delta}$ of $-\underset{\underset{O}{\|}}{C}-H$ is increased by withdrawing group.

37.

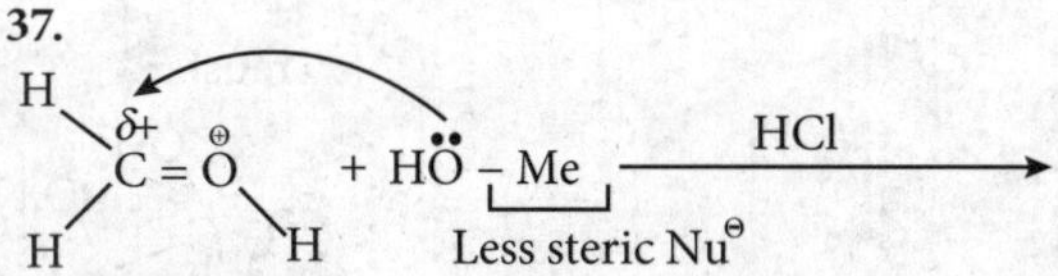

Less steric and high electrophilicity

39. Propanal is less steric and methanol requires excess (2 moles) for acetal formation.

40. I_2 / NaOH gives iodoform test and salt of acid and then acid.

41. Cannizzaro reaction is given by aldehydes, which do not have α-hydrogen.

42.

Acetal Ketal

43. Clemmensen reduction is used for carbonyl compounds.

44. $\overset{\ominus}{Cl}$ is the better leaving group.

45.

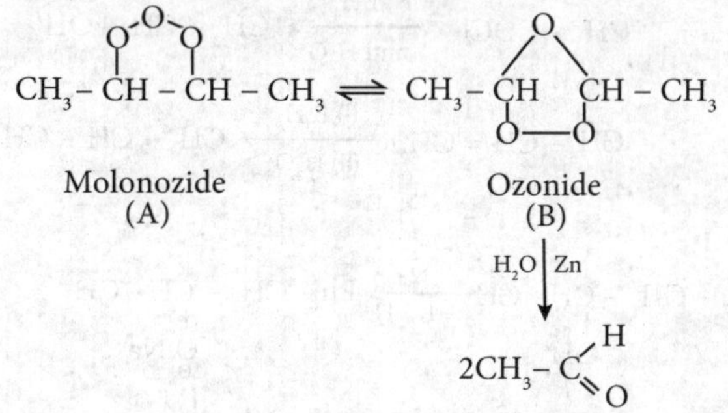

46.

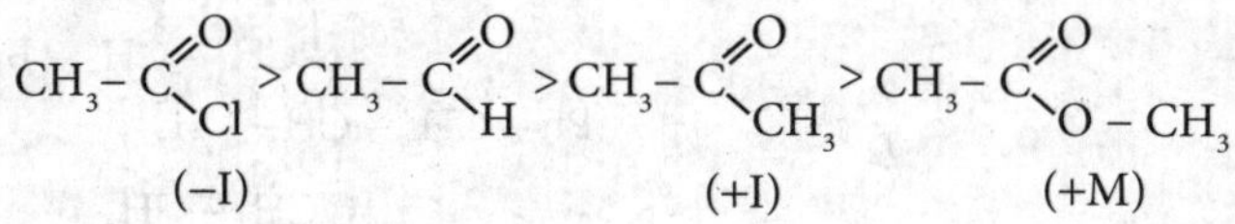

47. Dilute NaOH and 3-hydroxy give a hint of aldol reaction and not aldol condensation.

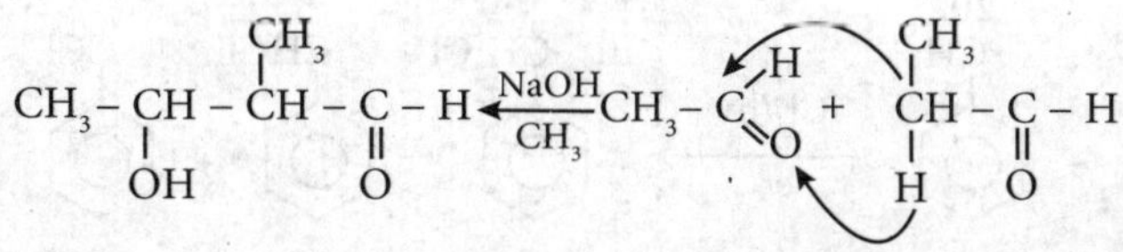

48. 30 amu means $H-\underset{\underset{O}{\|}}{C}-H$ aldehyde will be

$$CH_2=CH_2 \xrightarrow{O_3/H_2O/Zn} HCHO + HCHO$$

49. NAR is a characteristic reaction of carbonyl compounds.

50.

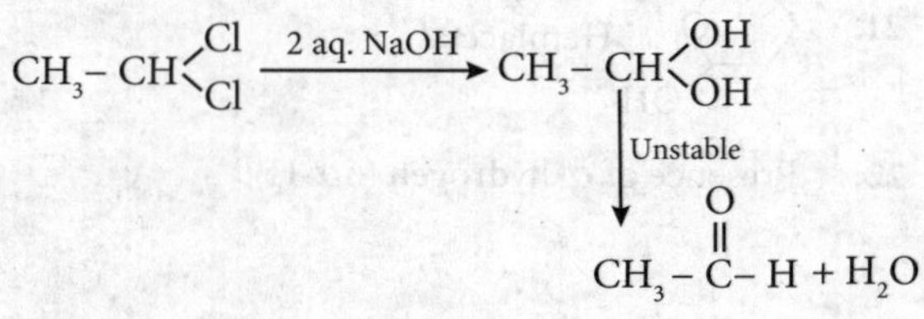

51.

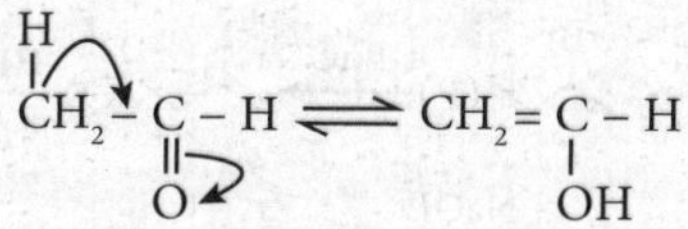

Number of π bonds, σ bonds and lone pairs remains the same in enol form.

52. Electrophilicity of $-\underset{\underset{O}{||}}{C}-$ $\propto$ Reactivity.

53. Boiling point $\propto$ Molecular weight $\propto$ $\xrightarrow[\text{Branching}]{\text{Hydrogen bonding}}$

54.

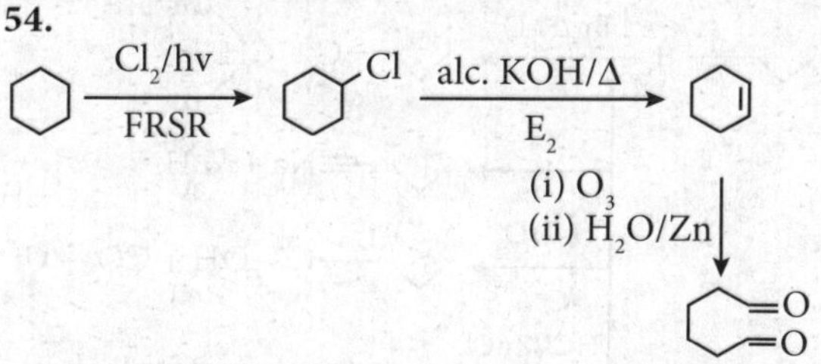

55.

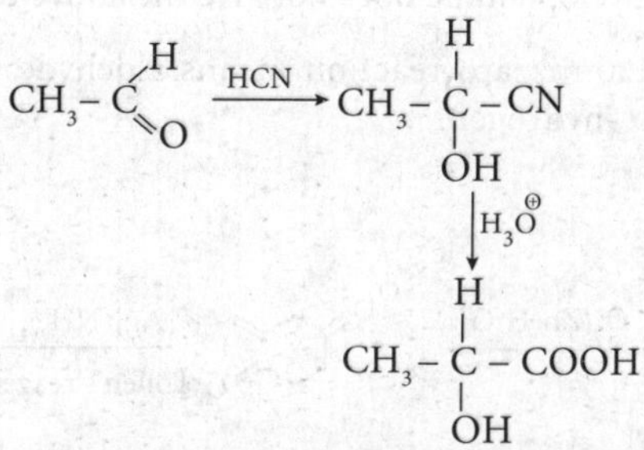

56. α-hydrogen containing carbonyl compound.

57.

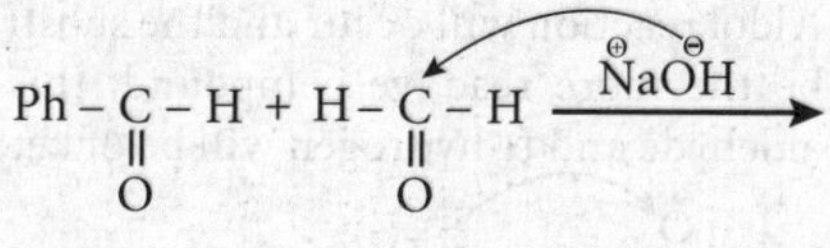

More reactive is oxidized and the other is reduced.

58.

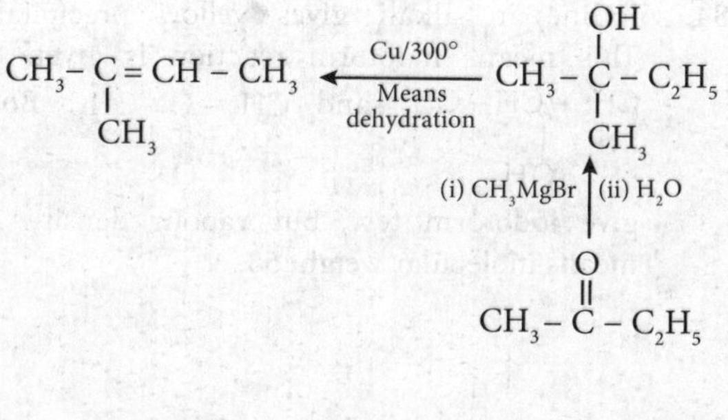

59.

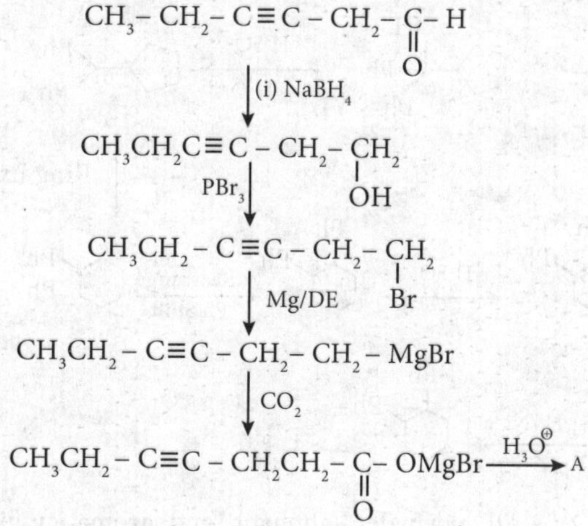

60. Birch reduction gives partial reduction and trans product.

61. Alkaline $KMnO_4$ with alkene followed by hydrolysis gives oxidative ozonolysis.

62.

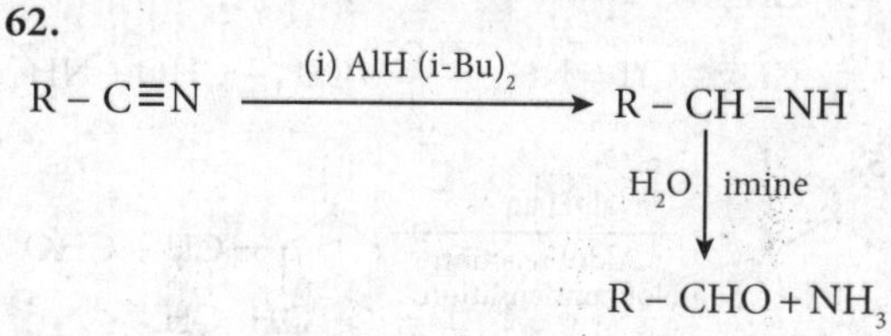

63. $NaBH_4$ is a weak reducing agent and reduces only the polar π-bonds of carbonyl compounds.

64. B_2H_6 shows electrophilic character and acid chloride also has highest electrophilicity character. So they are the least reactive.

65. Red P + HI is the strongest reducing agent and it reduces all compounds to alkanes.

66. $NaBH_4$ with ethanol reduces only to polar π-bonds of carbonyl compounds.

67. Zn-Hg/HCl (Clemmensen reduction) reduces carbonyl compounds to alkanes.

68. $NaBH_4$ reduces the polar π-bonds of carbonyl compounds and also imine and acid halide.

69. Phenylhydrazine gives phenylhydrazone.

70.

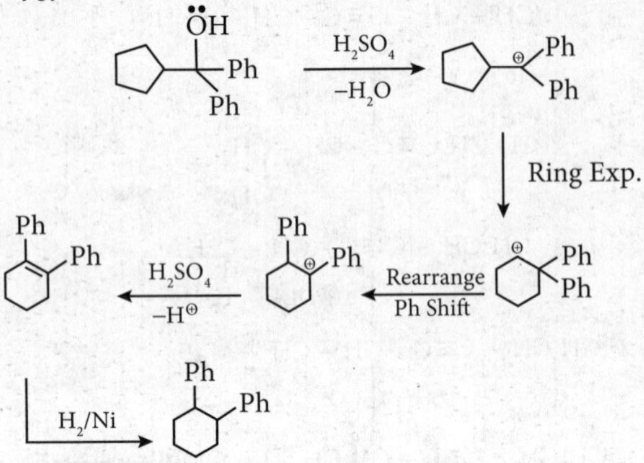

72. All aldehydes (aliphatic and aromatic) give Tollen's test.

73. Clemmensen is a reduction reaction and it reduces carbonyl compounds into alkanes.

74. $CH_3-C\equiv N \xrightarrow{\text{DiBAL-H}}$

$CH_3-CH=NH \xrightarrow{H_2O} CH_3-CHO+NH_3$

75.

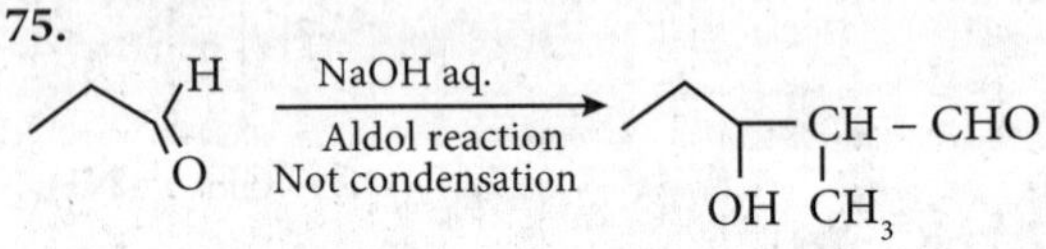

76. R gives salt of acid (HCOONa) and methanol by NaOH, so it confirms Cannizzaro reaction. This means R is HCHO and Q gives $\alpha-\beta$ unsaturated carbonyl compound. This confirms aldol condensation; means Q is CH_3–CH=O.

77.

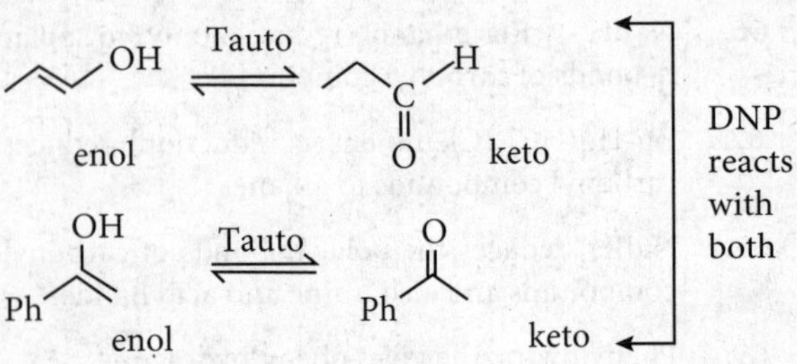

78.

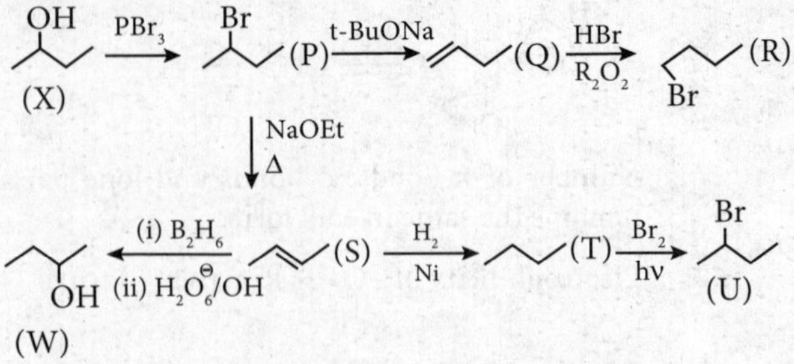

79. Nitrogen, which contain two 'H' atoms.

80.

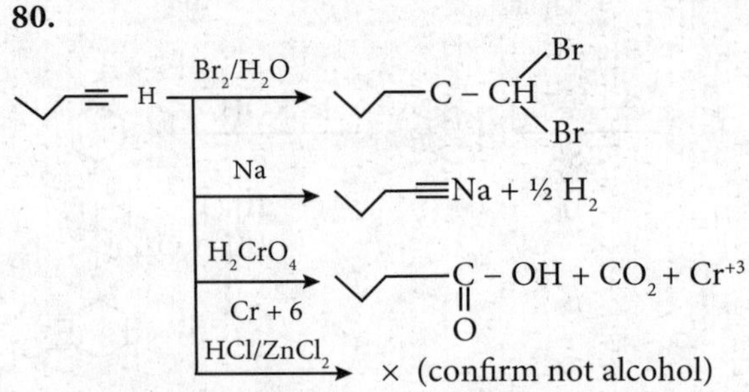

Cyclopentane does not give the above reaction.

81. Cannizzaro reaction means aldehyde without α–hydrogen.

82.

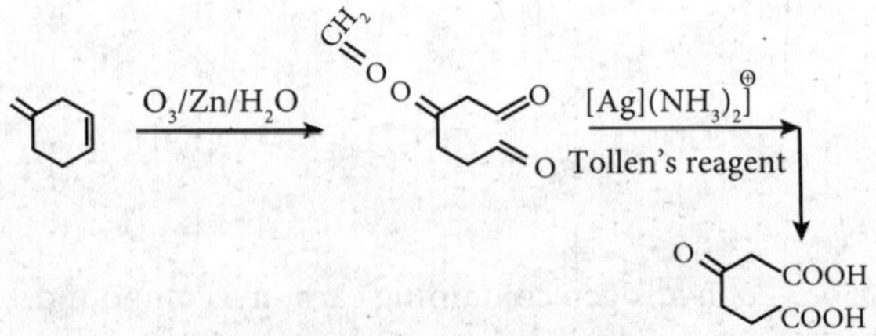

83. Aldol reaction will occur and the substrate will be the more reactive compound; this means aldehyde and α-hydrogen will be of ketone.

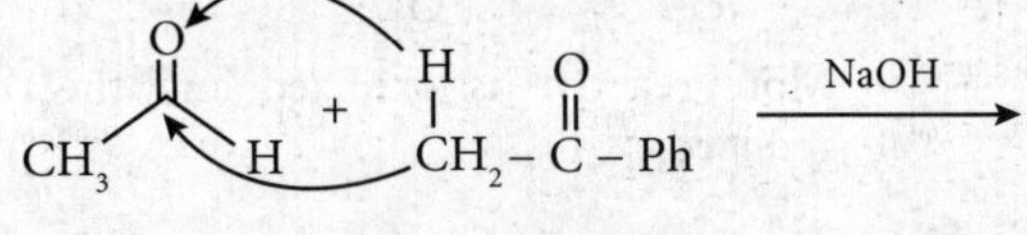

84. Iodine in alkali gives yellow precipitate. This means haloform reaction is given by $CH_3-\underset{\displaystyle OH}{\underset{|}{CH}}-CH_3$ and $CH_3-\underset{\displaystyle O}{\underset{\|}{C}}-CH_3$. Both give iodoform test, but vapour density 29 means molecular weight 58.

85.

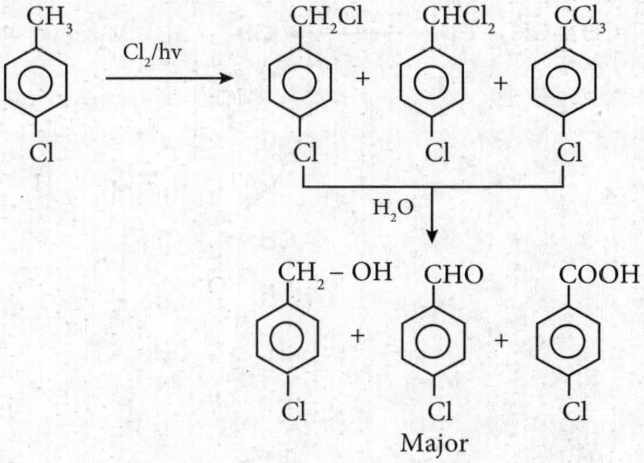

86. Haloform reagent is also a mild oxidising agent and it oxidises ethyl alcohol to acetaldehyde, which gives iodoform test.

87. Acid chloride reacts with Grignard reagent.

88. Transfer of H⁻ is slow and rate determination step.

89. On acetylation of one OH group, the molecular weight increases by 42. So

$$\text{No. of OH group} = \frac{\text{M. wt of } C_8H_{14}O_6 - \text{M. wt of } C_4H_{10}O_4}{42}$$

$$= \frac{206-122}{42} = \frac{84}{42} = 2$$

90. $CH_3-CH_2-OH \xrightarrow[\text{reagent}]{\text{Jones}} CH_3-COOH$

$CH_3-\underset{\displaystyle OH}{\underset{|}{CH}}-CH_3 \xrightarrow[\text{reagent}]{\text{Jones}} CH_3-\underset{\displaystyle O}{\underset{\|}{C}}-CH_3$

$\downarrow$

$CH_3-COOH + HCOOH$

91. NaOH and Δ means aldol condensation:

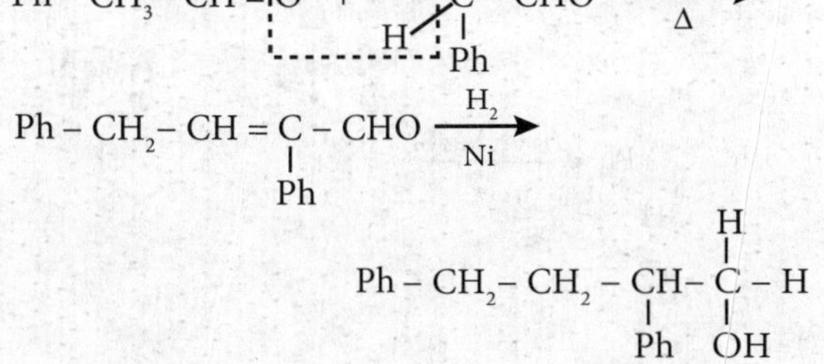

92.

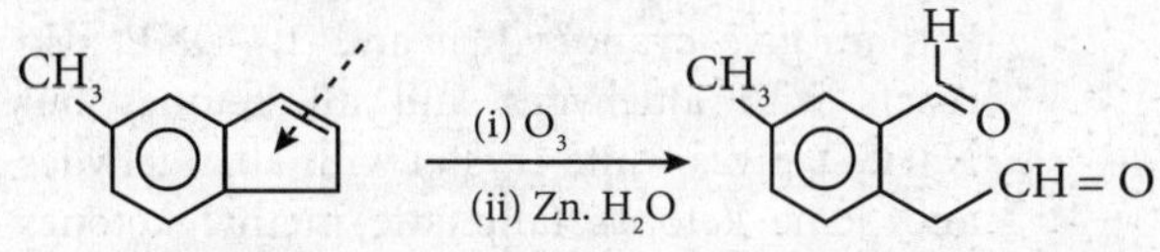

$CH_3-\underset{\displaystyle O}{\underset{\|}{C}}-H$ is absent, so does not give haloform reaction.

93. Ketone does not give Tollen's test but α-hydroxy ketone gives Tollen's test.

94. $C_5H_{10}O$(a) gives hydrazone with hydrazine and on heating with KOH, it gives n-pentane (alkane). It means Wolf–Kishner reduction. It does not give Tollen's test and iodoform test. This means the $-\underset{\displaystyle O}{\underset{\|}{C}}-$ group will be in hindered position. This means $CH_3-CH_2-\underset{\displaystyle O}{\underset{\|}{C}}-CH_2-CH_3$

95. Lucas's test is a test for alcohol. So, the compound does not have alcohol and Fehling's solution gives the test with aliphatic aldehyde and not with aromatic aldehyde. So it could not be aromatic aldehyde.

96. Aqueous $CuSO_4$ + Sodium citrate = Benedict's solution

97.

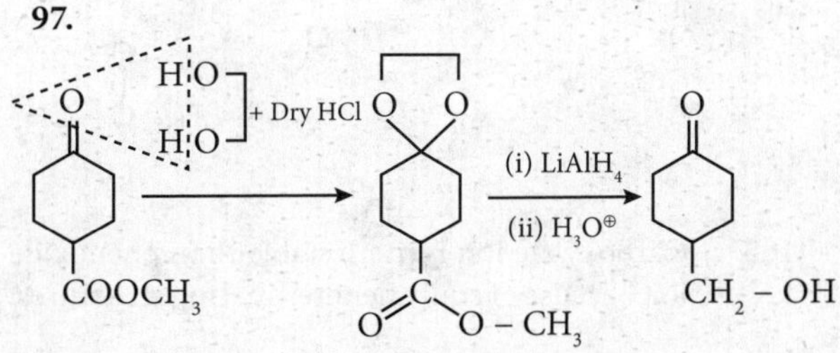

98.

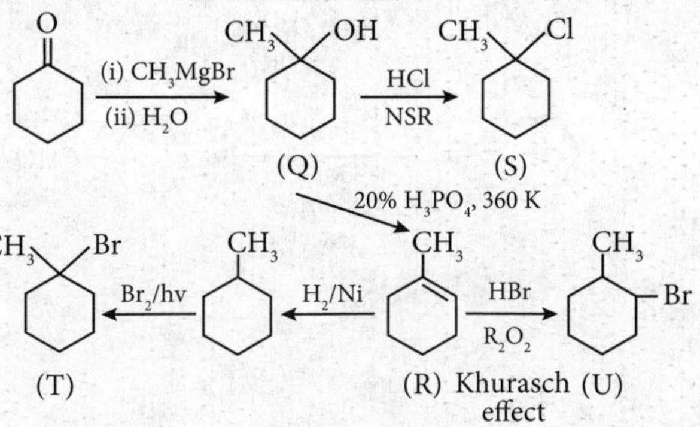

99. NaCN/HCN reacts with all aldehydes. All ketones give cyanohydrin and 2,4-DNP also reacts with aldehydes and all ketones but $NaHSO_3$ gives white crystal with all aldehydes and some ketones (aliphatic methyl ketones only).

100.

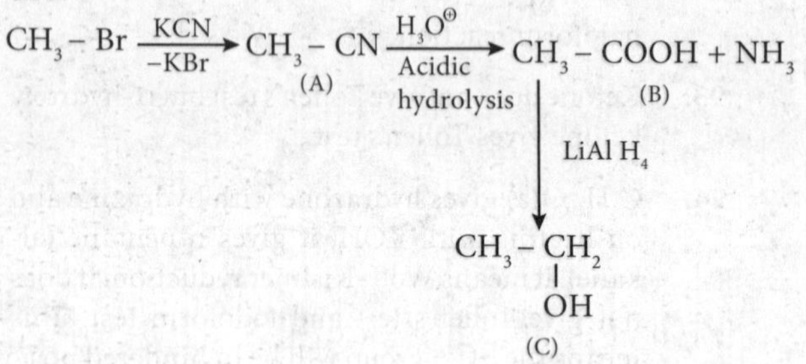

101.

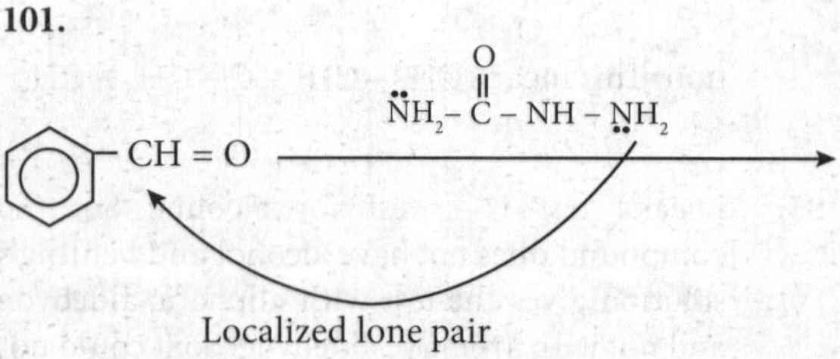

102.

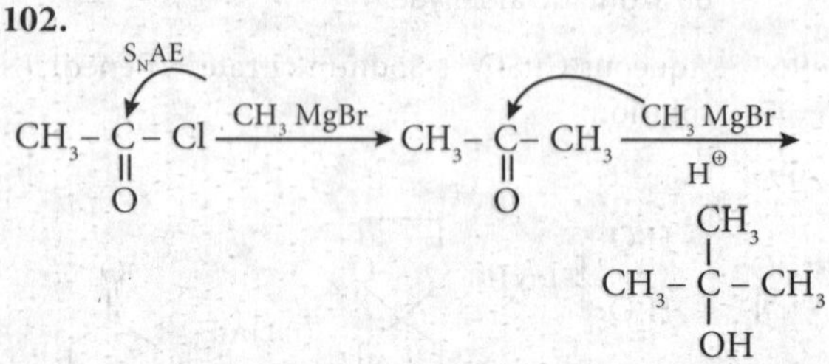

103. Carboxylate ion is more stable than phenoxide ion because of equivalent resonating structures.

104.

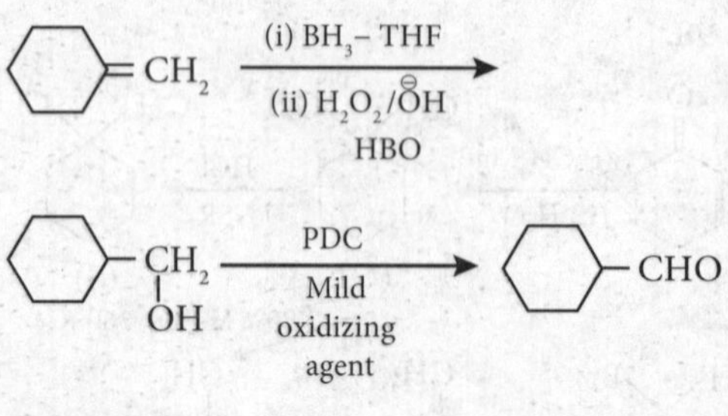

105.

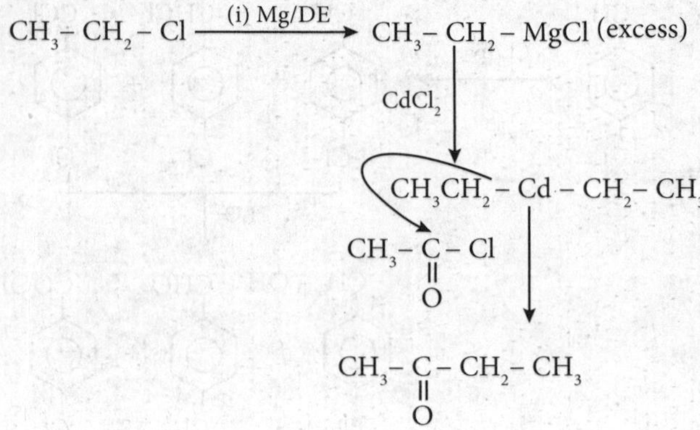

106.

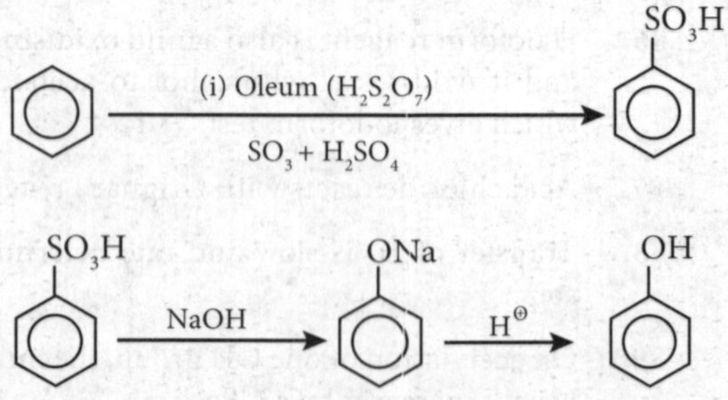

107. Salt of acid and alcohol is formed in the presence of NaOH/Δ. This means Cannizzaro reaction. So A is

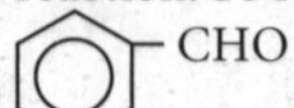

108.

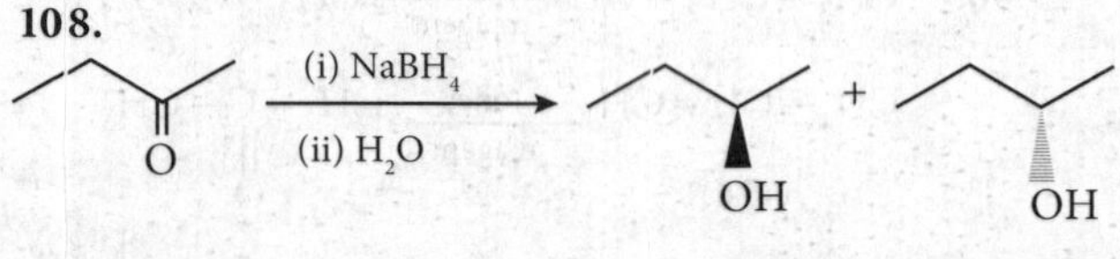

109.

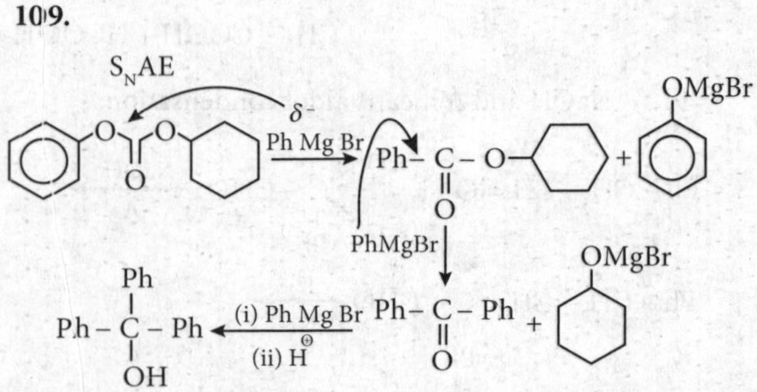

110. In Clemmensen reduction [Zn–Hg/HCl], the only carbonyl compound is reduced to alkane.

111. With NaOH/Δ gives benzyl alcohol. This means the Cannizzaro reation confirms aromatic aldehyde. So

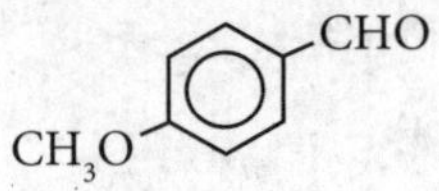

112. Does not give Cannizzaro reaction, but it gives aldol reaction. This means α-hydrogen is present and total number of carbons must be 9 because of the molecular formula.

113.

$$R-\underset{O}{\underset{||}{C}}-O\,R' \xrightarrow[\text{(ii) } H_2O]{\text{(i) LAlH}_4} R-\underset{OH}{\underset{|}{CH_2}} + HO-R'$$

On oxidation by $NaOH/I_2$, both alcohols are converted to aldehydes. So R = $-CH_3$ and R'– = CH_3–CH_2–.

114. Alkyl cyanide with Grignard regent gives imine and on hydrolysis gives ketone, while Fehling's solution reacts with only aliphatic aldehyde.

115. Phenol acid and benzoic acid react with NaOH.

116. Carbylamine reaction ∝ Nucleophilicity of arylamine

117.

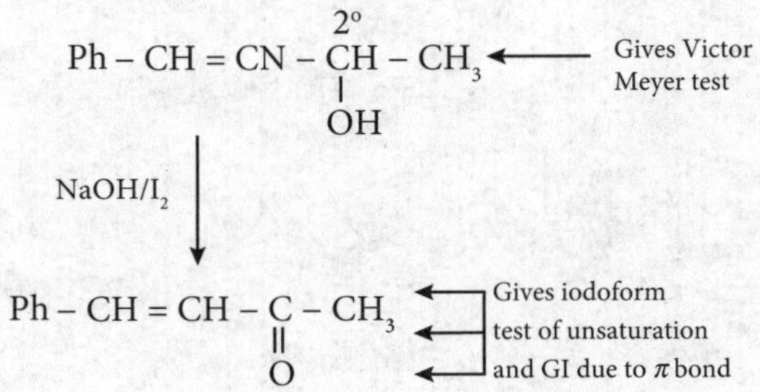

118.

$$CH_3-\underset{CH_3}{\underset{|}{C}}=CH-CH_3 \xrightarrow[\text{(ii) } H_2O/Zn]{\text{(i) } O_3} \underset{\text{(S)}}{CH_3-\underset{CH_3}{\underset{|}{C}}=O} + \underset{\text{(R)}}{O=CH-CH_3}$$

119.

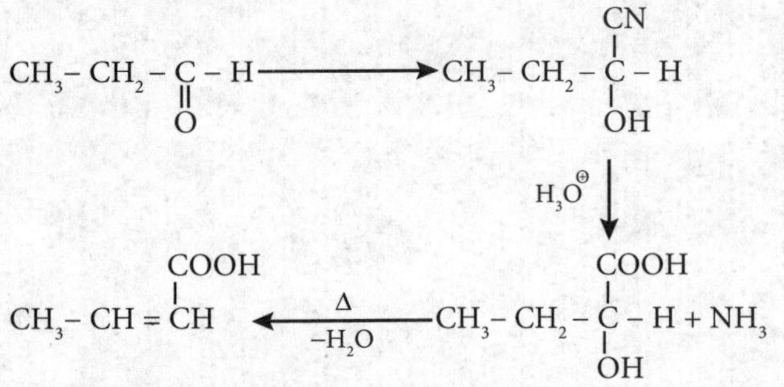

120.

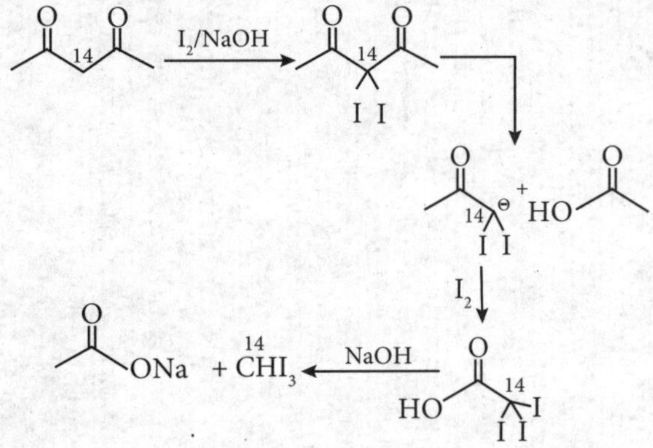

121.

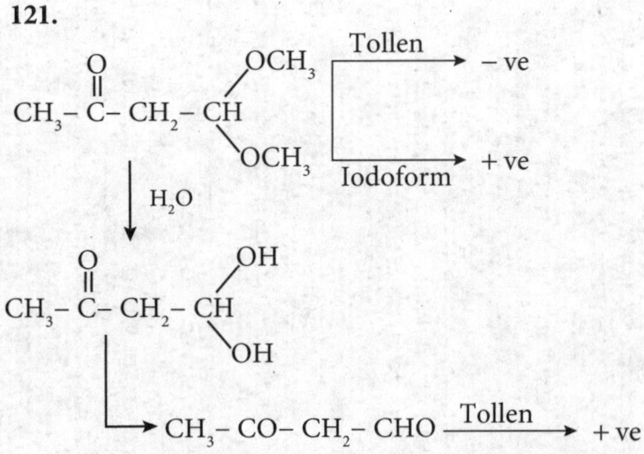

122. HCN is a poor nucleophile. So, in the presence of base, $\underset{(pH=7)}{(NaOH)} \xrightarrow[-H_2O]{H-CN} NaCN$ (Good $\bar{N}u$) and ammonia derivatives react in mild acidic medium (pH = 4.7)

CHAPTER **9**

Amines

Level-1

1. **Assertion:** Aromatic 1° amines cannot be prepared by Gabriel phthalimide synthesis.
Reason: Aryl halides cannot undergo nucleophilic substitution with the anion formed by phthalimide.
(a) Assertion is correct, reason is correct; reason is a correct explanation for assertion.
(b) Assertion is correct, reason is correct; reason is not a correct explanation for assertion
(c) Assertion is correct, reason is incorrect
(d) Assertion is incorrect, reason is correct.

2. Gabriel phthalimide synthesis is used for the preparation of:
(a) Primary aromatic amines
(b) Secondary amines
(c) Primary aliphatic amines
(d) Tertiary amines

3. Which of the following will give a primary amine in good yield?
(i) $R–X + NH_3$(excess)
(ii) $R–CN + Na–Hg/C_2H_5OH$
(iii) $R–CN + H_2O/H^+$
(a) (i) and (ii) (b) (i) and (iii)
(c) (ii) and (iii) (d) (i), (ii) and (iii)

4. Match the columns:

Column I	Column II
(A) Ammonolysis	(p) Amine with fewer number of carbon atoms
(B) Gabriel phthalimide synthesis	(q) Detection test for primary amines
(C) Hofmann bromamide reaction	(r) Reaction of phthalimide with KOH and R–X
(D) Carbylamine reaction	(s) Reaction of alkyl halides with NH_3

(a) A – (s), B – (r), C – (p), D – (q)
(b) A – (r), B – (p), C – (r), D – (s)
(c) A – (q), B – (r), C – (s), D – (p)
(d) A – (s), B – (p), C – (q), D – (r)

5. Which of the following methods of preparation of amines will produce amines with fewer number of carbon atoms than the substrate?
(a) Reaction of nitrile with $LiAlH_4$.
(b) Reaction of amide with $LiAlH_4$ followed by treatment with water.
(c) Heating alkyl halide with potassium salt of phthalimide followed by hydrolysis.
(d) Treatment of amide with bromine in aqueous solution of sodium hydroxide.

6. Read the following statements and choose the correct set of statements:
(i) The nitrogen atom in amines is sp^3-hybridized.
(ii) The geometry of amines is pyramidal.
(iii) The angle C–N–C or C–N–H is slightly more than 109.5°.
(a) (i), (ii) and (iii) (b) (i) and (ii)
(c) (i) and (iii) (d) (ii) and (iii)

7. Which of the following statements are correct?
(i) Lower aliphatic amines are soluble in water.
(ii) Solubility increases with increase in the molar mass of amines.
(iii) Higher amines are insoluble in water.
(iv) Amines are soluble in organic solvents.
(a) (i), (ii) and (iii) (b) (i), (iii) and (iv)
(c) (ii), (iii) and (iv) (d) (i) and (iv)

8. Which of the following statements are correct?
(i) Primary amines show more intermolecular association than secondary amines.
(ii) Tertiary amines do not show intermolecular association.
(iii) The boiling points of isomeric amines follow the order 3° > 2° > 1°

(a) (i) and (iii) (b) (i) and (ii)
(c) (i), (ii) and (iii) (d) (ii) and (iii)

9. Aniline is less soluble in water than ethyl amine due to:
(a) Planar structure
(b) +M effect of the $-NH_2$ group
(c) More hydrophobic nature of the C_6H_5 group than the C_2H_5 group
(d) More hydrophilic nature of the C_6H_5 group than the C_2H_5 group

10. Aliphatic amines are ________ basic than NH_3 but aromatic amines are ________ basic than NH_3:
(a) More, less (b) Less, more
(c) More, more (d) Less, less

11. The acylation reaction of aromatic amines is carried out in the presence of pyridine because:
(i) Pyridine is a weaker base than aromatic amine.
(ii) Pyridine is a stronger base than aromatic amine.
(iii) Pyridine removes the HCl formed and shifts the equilibrium to the right.
(iv) Pyridine removes the HCl formed and shifts the equilibrium to the left.
(a) (i) and (iii) (b) (ii) and (iv)
(c) (ii) and (iii) (d) (i) and (iv)

12. The hydrogen attached to nitrogen in sulphonamide is strongly ________ due to the presence of a strong electron-withdrawing sulphonyl group. Hence, it is ________ in alkali.
(a) Basic, insoluble (b) Acidic, soluble
(c) Acidic, insoluble (d) Basic, soluble

13. A compound with the molecular formulae C_3H_9N shows the following characteristics:
(i) Is dissolved in an acidic medium
(ii) Does not react with benzoyl chloride
(iii) Does not give the carbylamine test
(iv) Does not liberate nitrogen gas on reacting with HNO_2
The structure of the compound is:
(a) Trimethylamine
(b) Isopropylamine
(c) Propylamine
(d) None of the above

14. Read the following statements and choose the option containing the correct set of statements:
I. During ammonolysis, a primary amine is obtained as a major product by taking an excess of ammonia.
II. Secondary and tertiary amines can be distinguished by the carbylamine test.
III. The quantitative evolution of nitrogen during the reaction of amines with nitrous acid is used in the estimation of amino acids and proteins.
IV. N,N-diethylbenzenesulphonamide is not acidic, and hence, insoluble in alkali.
(a) I, II (b) I, II, III
(c) I, III, IV (d) I, II, IV

15. The reaction,
$C_6H_5NH_2 + ClCOC_6H_5 \longrightarrow C_6H_5NHCOC_6H_5$
is called:
(a) Friedel–Crafts' reaction
(b) Claisen condensation
(c) Benzoylation or Schotten–Baumann reaction
(d) None of the above

16. **Assertion:** Aniline does not undergo Friedel–Crafts' reaction.
Reason: The $-NH_2$ group of aniline reacts with $AlCl_3$ (Lewis acid) to give an acid–base reaction.
(a) Assertion is correct, reason is correct; reason is a correct explanation for assertion.
(b) Assertion is correct, reason is correct; reason is not a correct explanation for assertion
(c) Assertion is correct, reason is incorrect
(d) Assertion is incorrect, reason is correct.

17. Aniline and other aryl amines are usually colourless but become coloured on storage due to__________.
(a) Hydrolysis
(b) Dehydration
(c) Reduction
(d) Atmospheric oxidation

18. What is the reason for the stability of aromatic diazonium salts?
(a) Dispersal of negative charge over the benzene ring
(b) Dispersal of positive charge over the benzene ring
(c) Bond between diazonium group and anion
(d) High electronegativity of anion compared to the N atom

19. Which of the following statements are correct?

(i) In the Sandmeyer reaction, nucleophiles like Cl^-, Br^- and CN^- are introduced in the benzene ring in the presence of the Cu^+ ion.

(ii) In the Gattermann reaction, nucleophiles are introduced in the benzene ring in the presence of copper powder and HCl.

(iii) The yield in the Gattermann reaction is found to be better than that in the Sandmeyer reaction.

(a) (i) and (ii) (b) (i), (ii) and (iii)
(c) (ii) and (iii) (d) (i) and (iii)

20. Match the columns:

Column I	Column II
(A) Benzenesulphonyl chloride	(p) Zwitter ion
(B) Sulphanilic acid	(q) Hinsberg reagent
(C) Alkyl diazonium salts	(r) Used to prepare dyes
(D) Aryl diazonium salts	(s) Conversion to alcohols

(a) A – (s), B – (q), C – (r), D – (p)
(b) A – (q), B – (p), C – (s), D – (r)
(c) A – (r), B – (s), C – (p), D – (q)
(d) A – (s), B – (p), C – (r), D – (q)

21. **Assertion (A):** Fe + HCl is preferred as a reagent in the reduction of nitroalkanes to alkanamines.

Reason (R): Iron scrap and HCl are cheap.

(a) Both A and R are correct; R is the correct explanation of A
(b) Both A and R are correct; R is not the correct explanation of A
(c) A is correct; R is incorrect
(d) A is incorrect; R is correct

22. The alkyl or benzyl halide on reaction with an ethanolic solution of ammonia yields a product through:

(a) Nucleophilic substitution reaction
(b) Electrophilic substitution reaction
(c) Nucleophilic addition reaction
(d) Electrophilic addition reaction

23. Select the correct statement(s) about ammonolysis:

(a) It is the process of cleavage of the C–X bond by the ammonia molecule
(b) This reaction is carried out in an open tube at 373 K
(c) It is an electrophilic addition reaction
(d) None of the above

24. **Assertion (A):** Reduction of nitrobenzene to aniline can occur by H_2 / Pd, EtOH and Fe / HCl.

Reason (R): Reduction with Fe / HCl gives better yield of aniline than H_2 / Pd, EtOH.

(a) Both A and R are correct; R is the correct explanation of A
(b) Both A and R are correct; R is not the correct explanation of A
(c) A is correct; R is incorrect
(d) A is incorrect; R is correct

25. Which of the following statements is/are true about the Hofmann bromamide reaction?

(a) In this reaction, migration of an alkyl or aryl group takes place from a nitrogen atom of the amide to the carbonyl carbon
(b) The amine so formed contains one carbon more than that present in the amide
(c) It is a degradation reaction
(d) None of the above

26. Regarding the given figure,

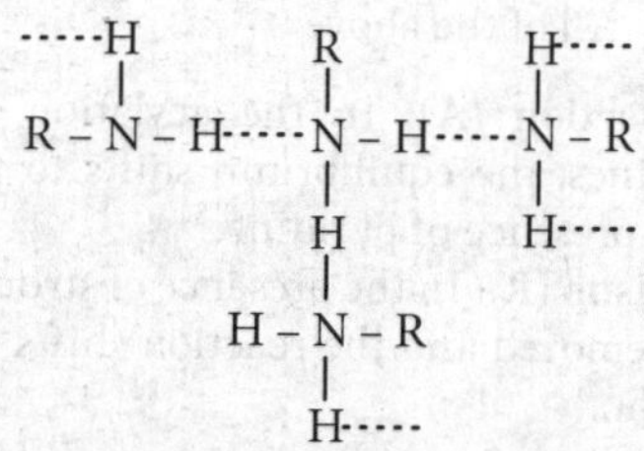

Which of the following statements is true?

(a) Intramolecular hydrogen bonding is present in primary amines
(b) Intermolecular hydrogen bonding is present in primary amines
(c) Intramolecular hydrogen bonding is present in secondary amines
(d) Intermolecular hydrogen bonding is present in tertiary amines

27. **Assertion (A):** Aliphatic amines are weaker bases than ammonia and aromatic amines are stronger bases than ammonia.

Reason (R): The +I-effect of alkyl groups on aliphatic amines increases electron density on the nitrogen atom. Aromatic amines are weaker due to the electron-withdrawing nature of the aryl group.
(a) Both A and R are correct; R is the correct explanation of A
(b) Both A and R are correct; R is not the correct explanation of A
(c) A is correct; R is incorrect
(d) A is incorrect; R is correct

28. Which of the following statements is/are true?
(a) Primary and secondary amines react with acid chlorides, anhydrides and esters by nucleophilic substitution reaction.
(b) In the acylation reaction of amines, there is replacement of the hydrogen atom of NH_2 or the NH group by the acyl group.
(c) The products obtained in the acylation reaction of amines are amides.
(d) All of the above

29. Regarding the dehydration of acetamide to acetonitrile, which of the following is correct?
(a) P_2O_5 can be used as the dehydrating agent
(b) Hybridization of carbon in the reactant to product changes from sp^2 to sp
(c) Product (acetonitrile) is more basic than reactant (acetamide)
(d) All of the above

30. **Assertion (A):** In the acylation reaction of amines, the equilibrium shifts to the right in the presence of pyridine.
Reason (R): In the presence of strong base, HCl is removed and the reaction shifts towards the right.
(a) Both A and R are correct; R is the correct explanation of A
(b) Both A and R are correct; R is not the correct explanation of A
(c) A is correct; R is incorrect
(d) A is incorrect; R is correct

31. The stability of an arene diazonium ion is explained on the basis of resonance. Which of the following resonating structures is incorrect?

(a) 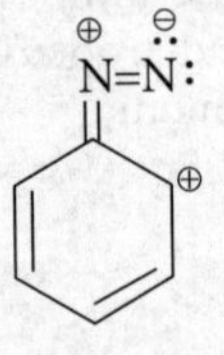

(b) 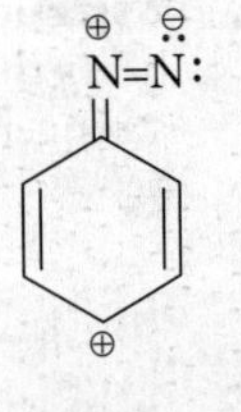

(c) 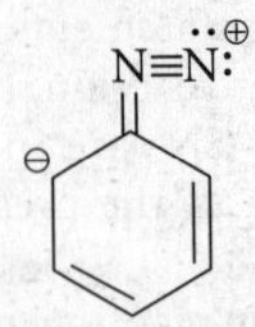

(d) 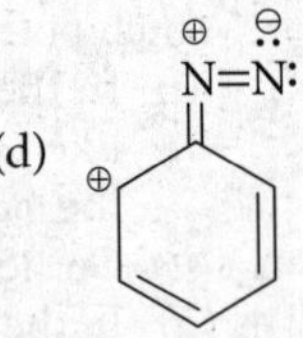

32. **Assertion (A):** Benzenediazonium salts are soluble in water.
Reason (R): They are covalent in nature, so they are soluble in water.
(a) Both A and R are correct; R is the correct explanation of A
(b) Both A and R are correct; R is not the correct explanation of A
(c) A is correct; R is incorrect
(d) A is incorrect; R is correct

33. Benzenediazonium chloride reacts with hypophosphorous acid to produce:
(a) Benzene
(b) Phenol
(c) Phenol isocyanide
(d) Phenyl phosphate

34. Consider the following sequence of reactions:

$$X(C_3H_9N)\xrightarrow{HNO_2}C_3H_8O\xrightarrow[H_2SO_4]{K_2Cr_2O_7}C_3H_6O$$

The compound (X) is:
(a) $CH_3CH_2NHCH_3$
(b) $(CH_3)_2CHNH_2$
(c) $(CH_3)_3N$
(d) None of the above

35. Which of the following statements is incorrect?
(a) Benzenediazonium chloride is not stored and is used immediately after its preparation
(b) Acetylation of the $-NH_2$ group of aniline increases its activating effect
(c) Pyridine in the acylation reaction of amines is used to remove the HCl
(d) Aniline is soluble in aqueous HCl due to the formation of salt

36. Which of the following reactions does not involve the degradation of the carbon chain?
(a) Soda lime decarboxylation
(b) Hell–Volhard–Zelinsky reaction
(c) Haloform reaction
(d) Borodine–Hunsdiecker reaction

37. Carboxylic acid is halogenated at the α-position on treatment with chlorine in the presence of red phosphorous. This is known as:
(a) Gabriel phthalimide synthesis

(b) Hell–Volhard–Zelinsky reaction
(c) Darzen process
(d) Ammonolysis reaction

38. In the given reaction, [X] will be:
[X] + Acetic anhydride → Aspirin
(a) Benzoic acid
(b) o-Methoxybenzoic acid
(c) o-Hydroxybenzoic acid
(d) p-Hydroxybenzoic acid

39. The decreasing order of ease of alkaline hydrolysis for the following esters is:

I. 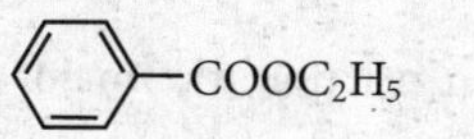

II. 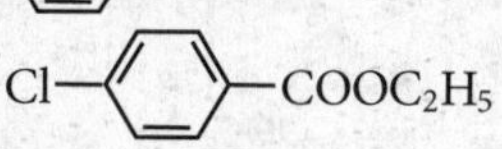

III. 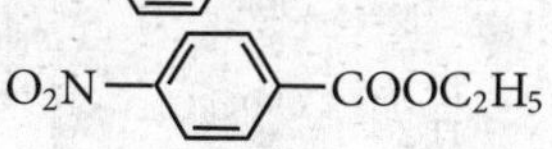

IV. 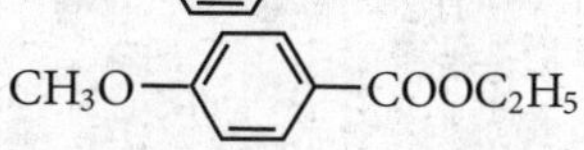

(a) IV > II > III > I
(b) II > III > I > IV
(c) III > II > I > IV
(d) III > II > IV > I

40. Which dicarboxylic acid in the presence of a dehydrating agent is the least reactive to give an anhydride?

(a) 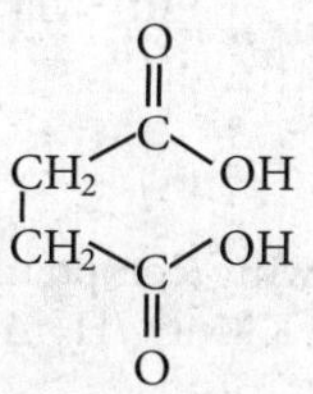

(b) 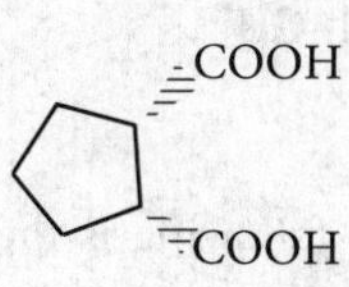

(c) 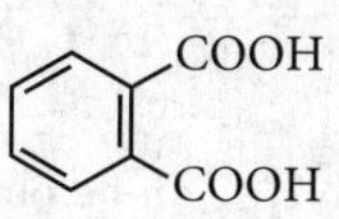

(d) 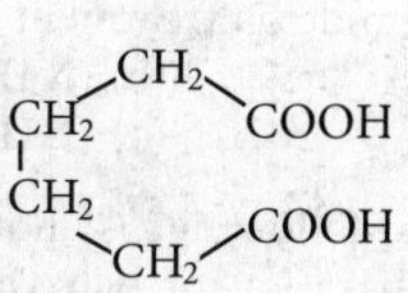

41. The major product of the following reaction is:

$CH_3CH(OH)CH_2CH_2NH_2 \xrightarrow[\text{Triethylamine}]{\text{Ethyl formate (1 equiv.)}}$

(a) $CH_3-CH(OH)-CH=CH_2$
(b) $CH_3CH=CH-CH_2NH_2$
(c) $CH_3CH(OH)CH_2CH_2NHCHO$
(d) $CH_3CH(OCHO)CH_2CH_2NH_2$

42. Arrange these esters in decreasing order of ease of esterification with $CH_3OH/H^{\oplus}$:
(I) $CH_3-CH(CH_3)-COOH$
(II) $CH_3-CH(CH_3)-CH_2-COOH$
(III) $CH_3-C(CH_3)_2-COOH$
(IV) $(CH_3-CH_2)_3C-COOH$
(a) II > I > III > IV
(b) I > II > III > IV
(c) III >IV > II > I
(d) IV > III > II > I

43. Sodium bicarbonate reacts with salicylic acid to form:
(a) C_6H_5ONa

(b) 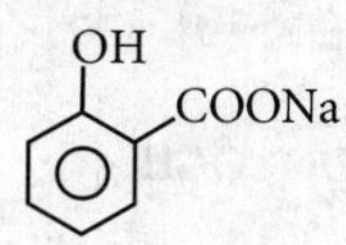

(c) 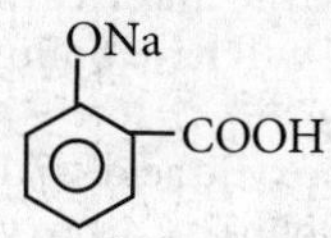

(d) 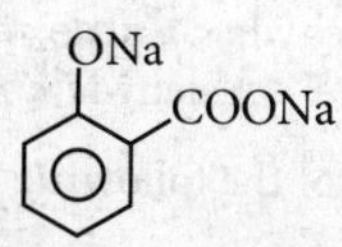

44. Which will form lactone on treatment with NaOH?
(a) α-Bromo acid
(b) β-Bromo acid
(c) β-Hydroxy acid
(d) δ-Bromo acid

45. Which acid can be oxidised by Fehling's solution?

(a) Malonic acid (b) Acetic acid
(c) Oxalic acid (d) Formic acid

46. The treatment of an open chain ester with $LiAlH_4$ followed by acid hydrolysis produces:

(a) Two aldehydes
(b) One carboxylic acid and one alcohol
(c) Two alcohols
(d) Two acids

47. The sodium salt of which monobasic acid on electrolysis does not give hydrocarbon?

(a) C_6H_5COOH
(b) HCOOH
(c) Me–COOH
(d) COOH–CH=CH–COOH

48. The major product of the following reaction is:

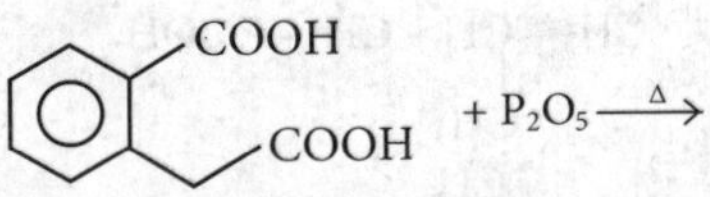

(a) 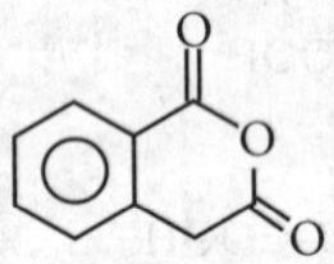

(b) 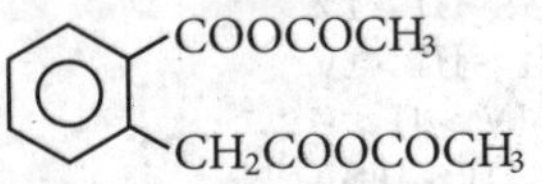

(c) 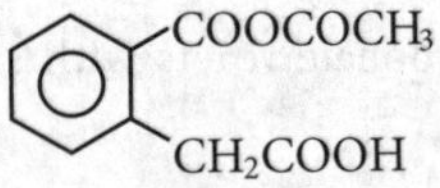

(d) 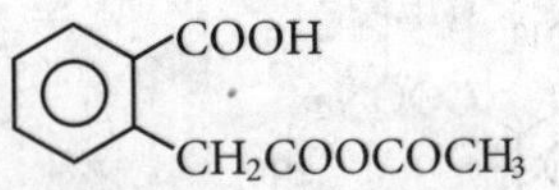

49. An alcohol, an aldehyde and a carboxylic acid of comparable mass will have boiling points in the order:

(a) Alcohol < Carboxylic acid < Aldehyde
(b) Aldehyde < Alcohol < Carboxylic acid
(c) Alcohol < Aldehyde < Carboxylic acid
(d) Carboxylic acid < Aldehyde < Alcohol

50. The major product of the following reaction is:

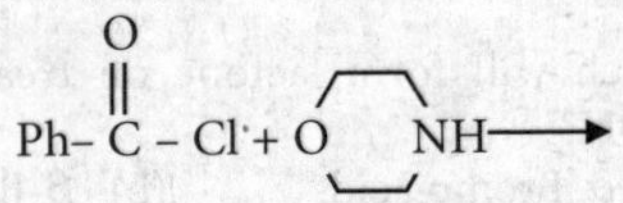

Morpholine

(a) 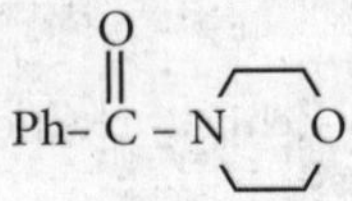

(b) 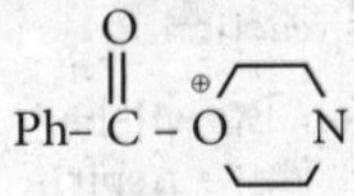

(c) 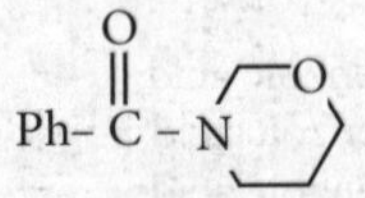

(d) 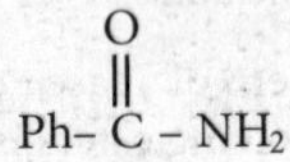

51. In the given reaction, the major product will be:

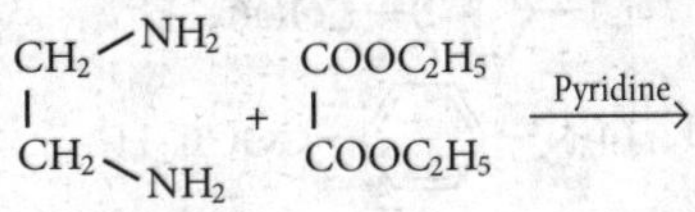

(a) Barbituric acid (b) 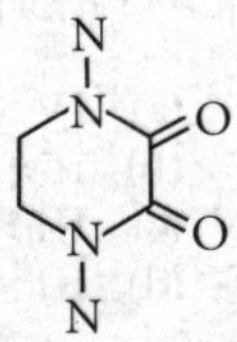

(c) 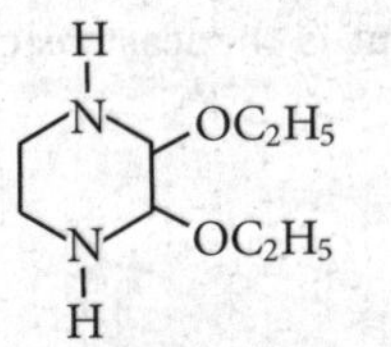 (d) Veronal

52. Which of the following compounds will not give acetic acid with $KMnO_4/H^{\oplus}/\Delta$?

(a) CH_3–CHO
(b) CH_3–CH=CH–CH_3
(c) CH_3–C≡C–CH_3
(d) CH_3OH

53. Which one of the following is the most basic compound in water?

(a) C_2H_5–NH_2 (b) C_2H_5–NHC_2H_5
(c) C_6H_5–$N(CH_3)_2$ (d) $C_2H_5N(C_2H_5)_2$

54. Ethylamine ($C_2H_5NH_2$) can be obtained from N-ethyl phthalimide on treatment with:

(a) NaOH (aq.) (b) $NaBH_4$
(c) CaH_2 (d) NH_3

55. Which of the following is not a correct method of preparation of benzylamine from cyanobenzene?

(a) H_2/Ni

(b) (i) HCl/H_2O (ii) $NaBH_4$
(c) (i) $LiAlH_4$ (ii) H_3O^+
(d) (i) $SnCl_2 + HCl(gas)$ (ii) $NaBH_4$

56. Which of the following amines can be prepared by Gabriel phthalimide reaction?
(a) Neo-pentyl amine (b) n-Butyl amine
(c) Triethyl amine (d) t-Butyl amine

57. The best reagent for converting 2-phenyl propanamide to 2-phenylpropanamine is:
(a) Excess H_2
(b) Br_2 in aqueous NaOH
(c) Iodine in the presence of red phosphorus
(d) $LiAlH_4$ in ether

58. The best reagent for converting 2-phenylpropanamide to 1-phenylethanamine is:
(a) Excess H_2/Pt (b) $NaOH/Br_2$
(c) $NaBH_4$/Methanol (d) $LiAlH_4$/Ether

59. The Hinsberg reagent is:
(a) $SOCl_2$ (b) $(COCl)_2$
(c) C_6H_5COCl (d) $C_6H_5SO_2Cl$

60. Instead of the Hinsberg reagent, nowadays which reagent is used?
(a) $SOCl_2$
(b) $p\text{-}CH_3C_6H_4SO_2Cl$
(c) C_6H_5COCl
(d) $C_6H_5SO_2Cl$

61. In the chemical reaction $CH_3CH_2NH_2 + CHCl_3 + 3KOH \rightarrow (1) + (2) + 3H_2O$, (1) and (2) are:
(a) C_2H_5CN and 3KCl
(b) $CH_3CH_2\,CONH_2$ and 3KCl
(c) C_2H_5NC and K_2CO_3
(d) C_2H_5NC and 3KCl

62. Which of the following compounds can be prepared in good yield by Gabriel phthalimide synthesis?

(a) 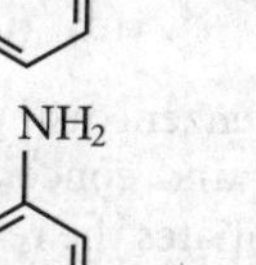

(b) 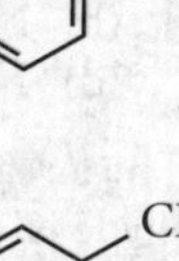

(c) 

(d) $CH_3CH_2NHCH_3$

63. A compound 'X' on treatment with Br_2/NaOH, provides C_3H_9N, which gives a positive carbylamine test. Compound 'X' is:
(a) $CH_3CH_2COCH_2NH_2$
(b) $CH_3COCH_2NHCH_3$
(c) $CH_3CON(CH_3)_2$
(d) $CH_3CH_2CH_2CONH_2$

64. The source of nitrogen in the Gabriel synthesis of amines is:
(a) Sodium azide, NaN_3
(b) Sodium nitrite, $NaNO_2$
(c) Potassium cyanide, KCN
(d) Potassium phthalimide, $C_6H_4(CO)_2N^-K^+$

65. In the Hofmann bromamide degradation reaction, the number of moles of NaOH and Br_2 used per mole of amine produced is:
(a) Four moles of NaOH and one mole of Br_2
(b) One mole of NaOH and one mole of Br_2
(c) Four moles of NaOH and two moles of Br_2
(d) Two moles of NaOH and two moles of Br_2

66. Amongst the given set of reactants, the most appropriate for preparing 2° amine is:
(a) 2° R—Br + NH_3
(b) 2° R—Br + NaCN followed by H_2/Pt
(c) 1° R—NH_2 + RCHO followed by H_2/Pt
(d) 1° RBr + Potassium phthalimide, then H_3O^+

67. The final product 'P' obtained from the following reaction is:

(a) 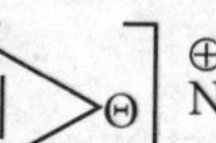

(b) 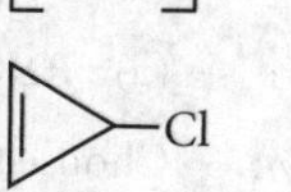

(c) 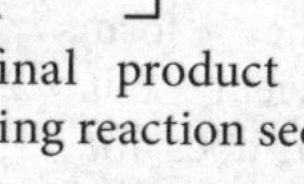

(d) 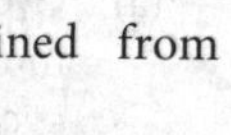

68. The final product 'Z' obtained from the following reaction sequence is:

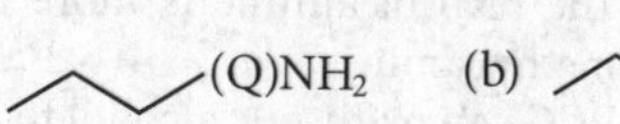

(a) 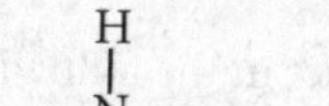

(b) 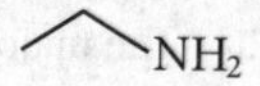

(c)

(d)

69. Which of the following pKb orders is correct?

Compound	pKb
(P) Benzenamine	(a) 9.30
(Q) N-methylaniline	(b) 8.92
(R) Phenylmethanamine	(c) 9.38
(S) N,N-dimethylaniline	(d) 4.70

(a) P-c, Q-a, R-b, S-d
(b) P-d, Q-a, R-c, S-b
(c) P-d, Q-b, R-d, S-c
(d) P-c, Q-b, R-d, S-a

70. Which of the following cannot be used for the separation of primary, secondary and tertiary amines?
(a) Hinsberg test
(b) Fractional distillation
(c) Carbylamine test
(d) None of the above

71. Nitriles can be converted into amines by reaction with:
(a) Na(Hg)/EtOH
(b) $LiAlH_4$
(c) H_2/Ni
(d) All of the above

72. Which of the following statements is incorrect?
(a) 1° Amine gives carbylamine reaction
(b) 1° Amine forms salt with excess HI
(c) 1° Amine gives hydrogen with sodium
(d) 1° Amine gives alcohol by hydrolysis

73. Which of the following reactions does not give a primary amine as a major product?
(a) Amide + KOBr $\rightarrow$
(b) Primary acid amide + $LiAlH_4 \rightarrow$
(c) Phthalimide + KOH $\xrightarrow[\text{(ii)}\,H_2O]{\text{(i)}\,Ph-X}$
(d) RNCO + NaOH $\rightarrow$

74. Choose the incorrect option:
(a) Cyclohexanone forms cyanohydrin in good yield but 2,2,6-trimethyl cyclohexanone does not.
(b) Tertiary amines have higher boiling point than primary amines.
(c) The pKb of aniline is more than that of methyl amine.
(d) PCC can oxidise 1° alcohol to aldehyde.

75. The major product in the following reaction is:

$$NH_2-\overset{\overset{\large O}{\|}}{C}-NH_2 \xrightarrow[Br_2]{NaOH}$$

(a) NH_2-COOH
(b) NH_2-OH
(c) H_2N-NH_2
(d) $NH_2-CONH-OH$

76. The incorrect statement for the given reaction is:

$$RNH_2 \xrightarrow[KOH]{CHCl_3}$$

(a) The reaction is known as the carbylamine reaction
(b) Four moles of KOH are required
(c) The major product is alkyl isocyanide
(d) The reaction involves dichlorocarbene

77. Which one of the following compounds gives carboxylic acid with HNO_2?
(a) $C_6H_5CH_2NH_2$ (b) $C_6H_5CONH_2$
(c) CH_3CH_2OH (d) $PhNH_2$

78. Ethylamine reacts with HNO_2 to form:
(a) $C_2H_5-O-N=O$ (b) CH_3-O-CH_3
(c) C_2H_5OH (d) CH_3CHO

79. The gas evolved when benzylamine reacts with nitrous acid is:
(a) NH_3 (b) N_2
(c) H_2 (d) C_2H_6

80. N-methyl pthalimide on hydrolysis gives:
(a) Methyl alcohol (b) Methylamine
(c) Dimethylamine (d) Diethylamine

81. Which of the following diazonium salts is relatively stable at 0–5°C?
(a) $\{CH_3-N\equiv N\}^{\oplus}Cl^-$
(b) $\{CH_3C(CH_3)-N\equiv N\}^{\oplus}Cl^-$
(c) $\{C_6H_5-N\equiv N\}^{\oplus}Cl^-$
(d) $\{(CH_3)_3C-N\equiv N\}^{\oplus}Cl^-$

82. Which of the following can be detected by the carbylamine reaction?
(a) Urea (b) CH_3CONH_2
(c) $C_2H_5NH_2$ (d) $(CH_3)_2NH$

83. In the nitration of benzene using a mixture of concentrated H_2SO_4 and concentrated HNO_3, the species which initiates the reaction is:
(a) NO_2 (b) NO^+
(c) NO_2^+ (d) NO_2^-

84. The compound obtained by a reaction between primary amine and aldehyde is:

(a) An amide (b) Imine
(c) Nitrite (d) Enamine

85. Which of the following amines reacts with the Hinsberg reagent to give a base-soluble product?
(a) Neopentyl amine
(b) Acetamide
(c) Diethyl amine
(d) Ethyl methyl amine

86. Hofmann degradation is not given by:
(a) Benzamide
(b) $RCONH_2$
(c) $CH_3CONHBr$
(d) N-methyl ethanamide

87. The correct IUPAC name for $CH_2{=}CHCH_2NHCH_3$ is:
(a) Allylmethylamine
(b) 2-Amino-4-pentene
(c) 4-Aminopent-1-ene
(d) N-methylprop-2-en-1-amine

88. Among the following, the strongest base in aqueous medium is:
(a) CH_3NH_2 (b) $NCCH_2NH_2$
(c) $(CH_3)_2NH$ (d) $C_6H_5NHCH_3$

89. Which of the following is the weakest Bronsted base?

(a) 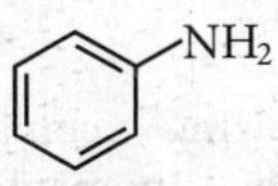

(b) 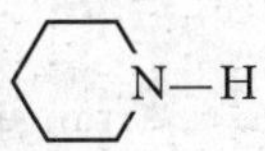

(c) 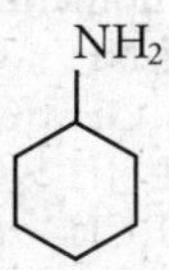

(d) CH_3NH_2

90. Which of the following is a 3° amine?
(a) 1-Methylcyclohexylamine
(b) Triethylamine
(c) tert-Butylamine
(d) N-Methylaniline

91. Which of the following alkylhalides is best suited for this reaction through the S_N1 mechanism?
$C_6H_5CH_2NH_2 + R—X \rightarrow C_6H_5CH_2NHR$
(a) CH_3Br (b) C_6H_5Br
(c) $C_6H_5CH_2Br$ (d) C_2H_5Br

92. Which of the following reagents would not be used for reducing an aryl nitro compound to an amine?
(a) H_2 / Pd, EtOH
(b) $NaBH_4$ in methanol
(c) Fe and HCl
(d) Sn and HCl

93. In order to prepare a 1° amine from an alkyl halide with simultaneous addition of one CH_2 group in the carbon chain, the reagent used as a source of nitrogen is:
(a) Sodium amide, $NaNH_2$
(b) Sodium azide, NaN_3
(c) Potassium cyanide, KCN
(d) Potassium phthalimide, $C_6H_4(CO)_2N^-K^+$

94. The Hofmann bromamide degradation reaction is shown by:
(a) $ArNH_2$ (b) $ArCONH_2$
(c) $ArNO_2$ (d) $ArCH_2NH_2$

95. Reduction of aromatic nitro compounds using Fe and HCl gives:
(a) Aromatic oxime
(b) Aromatic hydrocarbon
(c) Aromatic primary amine
(d) Aromatic amide

96. The correct increasing order of basic strength for the following compounds is:

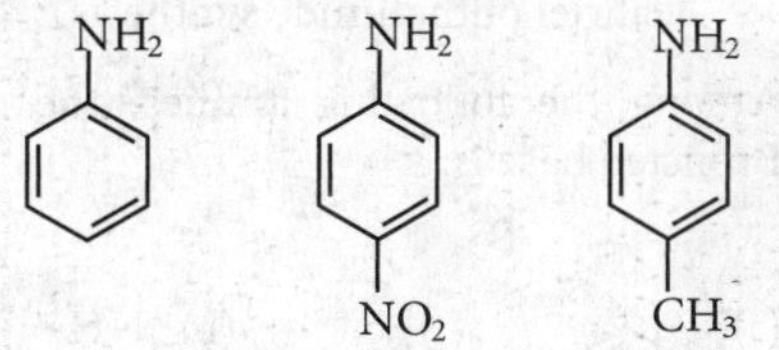

(I) (II) (III)

(a) II < III < I (b) III < I < II
(c) III < II < I (d) II < I < III

97. The most reactive amine towards dilute hydrochloric acid is:
(a) $CH_3–NH_2$ (b) 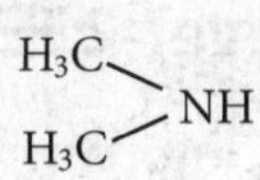

(c) 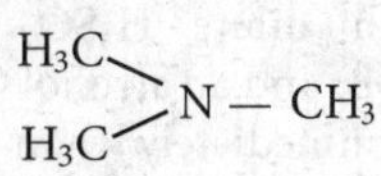

(d) $Ph–NH_2$

98. Acid anhydrides on reaction with primary amines give:
(a) Amide (b) Imide
(c) Secondary amine (d) Imine

99. The best method for preparing primary amines from alkyl halides without changing the carbon atoms in the chain is:

(a) Hofmann bromamide reaction
(b) Gabriel phthalimide synthesis
(c) Sandmeyer reaction
(d) Reaction with NH_3

100. Which of the following compounds is the weakest Bronsted base?

(a) 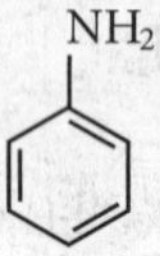
(b) 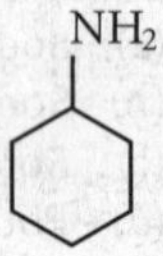
(c) 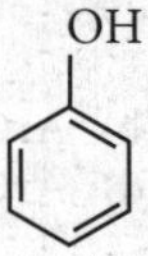
(d) 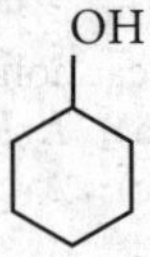

101. Which of the following statements is correct?
(a) Hofmann's bromamide reaction is given by primary amines.
(b) Primary amines are more basic than secondary amines in water.
(c) N-Ethylbenzene sulphonamide is soluble in alkali.
(d) Aromatic 1° amines can be prepared by Gabriel phthalimide synthesis.

102. Among the following amines, the strongest Bronsted base is:

(a) 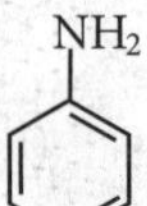
(b) NH_3
(c) 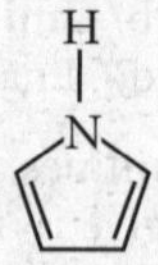
(d) 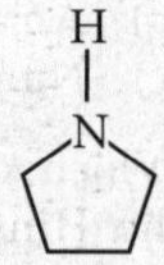

103. Which of the following statements is incorrect?
(a) Hydrogen attached to nitrogen in sulphonamide is strongly acidic.
(b) N,N-Diethylbenzenesulphonamide is insoluble in alkali.
(c) Only a small amount of HCl is required in the reduction of nitro compounds with iron scrap.
(d) Acetanilide is more basic than aniline.

104. The correct decreasing order of basic strength of the following species is:
H_2O, NH_3, OH^-, NH_2^-
(a) $NH_2^- > OH^- > NH_3 > H_2O$
(b) $OH^- > NH_2^- > H_2O > NH_3$
(c) $NH_3 > H_2O > NH_2^- > OH^-$
(d) $H_2O > NH_3 > OH^- > NH_2^-$

105. Which of the following should be the most basic in the gas phase?
(a) $CH_3CH_2CH_2NH_2$ (b) $(CH_3)_3N$
(c) CH_3CH_2–NH–CH_3 (d) $CH_3CH_2CH_3$

106. Arrange the following compounds in increasing order of dipole moment:
(a) $CH_3CH_2CH_3 < CH_3CH_2NH_2 < CH_3CH_2OH$
(b) $CH_3CH_2CH_3 < CH_3CH_2OH < CH_3CH_2NH_2$
(c) $CH_3CH_2CH_3 > CH_3CH_2NH_2 > CH_3CH_2OH$
(d) $CH_3CH_2NH_2 < CH_3CH_2CH_3 < CH_3CH_2OH$

Level-2

1. An organic compound ($C_6H_{12}O_2$) was hydrolyzed with dilute H_2SO_4 to give a carboxylic acid (B) and an alcohol (C). 'C' gives white turbidity immediately when treated with anhydrous $ZnCl_2$ and concentrated HCl. The organic compound is:

(a) 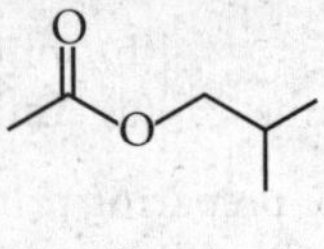
(b) 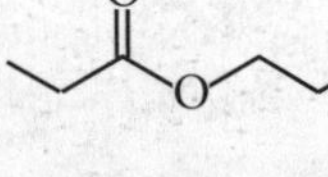
(c) 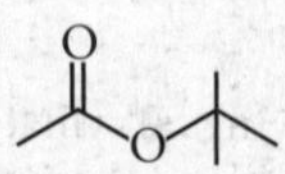
(d) 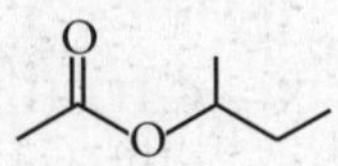

2. An organic compound [A] was hydrolyzed with dilute sulphuric acid to give a carboxylic acid [B] and an alcohol [C]. Oxidation of [C] with CrO_3–H_2SO_4 produces [B]. Which of the following structures is not possible for [A]?

(a) $(CH_3)_3CCOOCH_2C(CH_3)_3$

(b) $CH_3-CH_2-CH(CH_3)-COOCH(CH_3)-CH_2CH_3$

(c) $CH_3-CH_2-CH(CH_3)-COOCH_2-CH(CH_3)-CH_2CH_3$

(d) $CH_3CH_2CH_2COOCH_2CH_2CH_2CH_3$

3. For the following reaction, the most stable conformation for R is:

Acetone $\xrightarrow[NaOH]{I_2}$ Q $\xrightarrow{Electrolysis}$ R

(a) Eclipsed (b) Staggered
(c) Gauche (d) Anti

4. The major product obtained in the following reaction is:

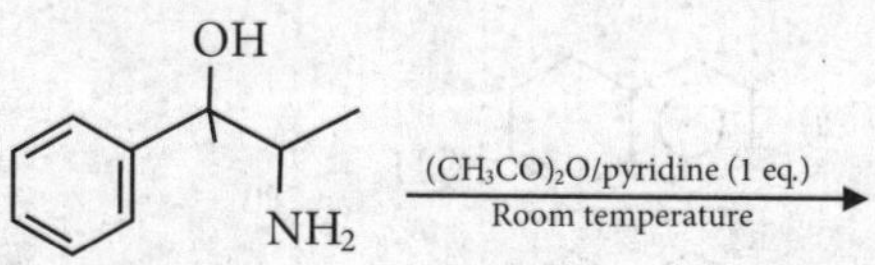

(a) 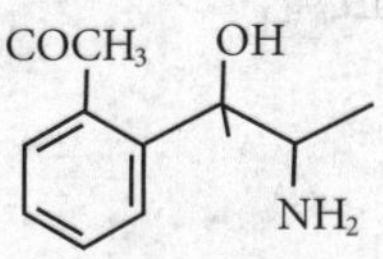

(b) 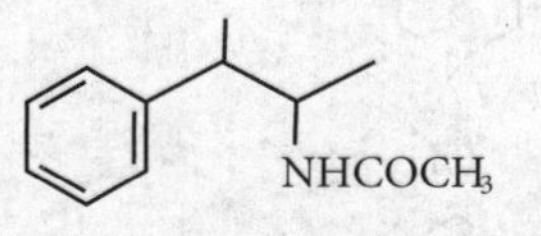

(c) 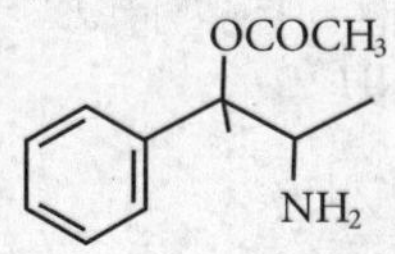

(d) 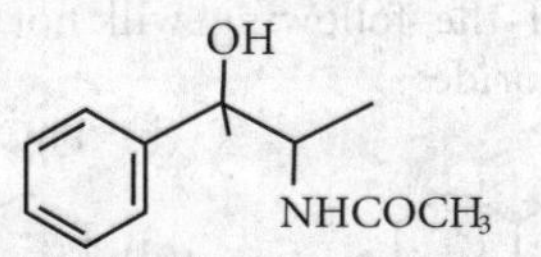

5. The molecule mass of the major product (P) obtained in the following reaction is:

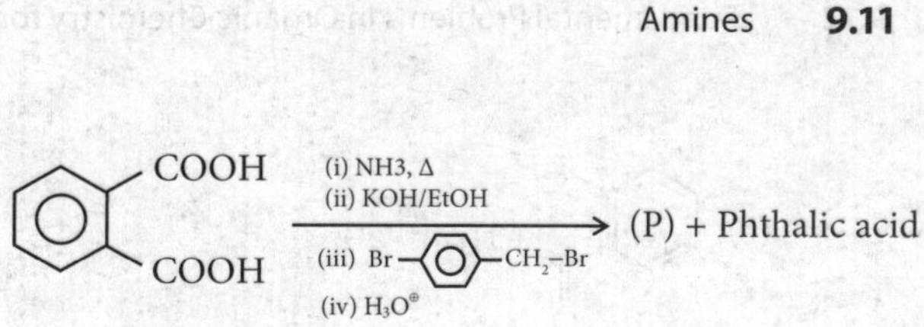

(a) 186 (b) 180
(c) 160 (d) 168

6. The major product obtained in the following reaction is:

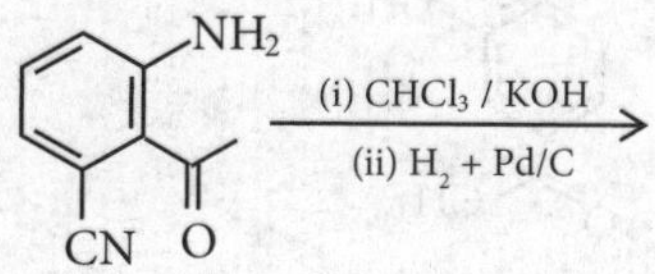

(a) 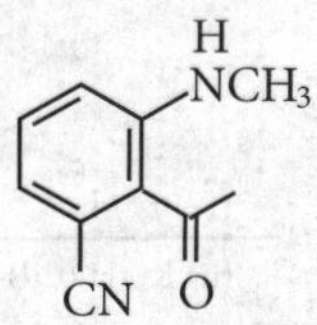

(b) 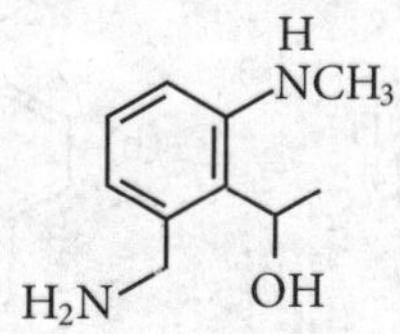

(c) 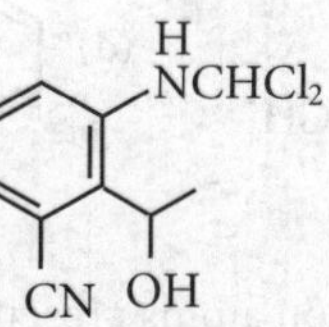

(d) 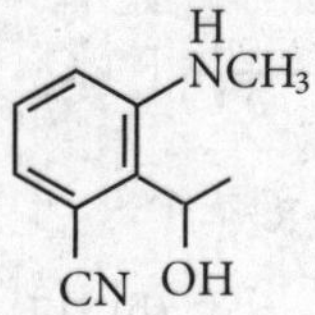

7. Compound A ($C_9H_{10}O$) shows positive iodoform test. Oxidation of A with $KMnO_4$/KOH gives acid B($C_8H_6O_4$). Anhydride of B is used for the preparation of phenolphthalein. Compound A is:

(a) 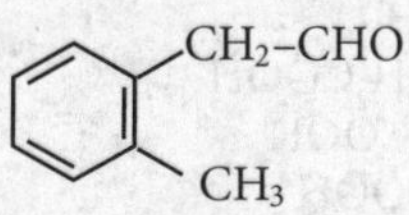

(b) 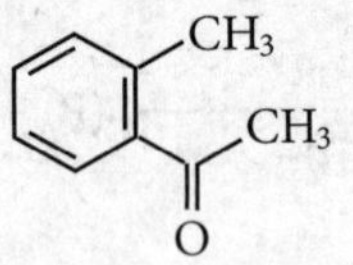

(c) 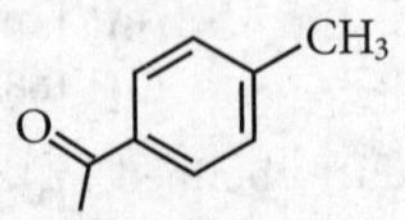

(d) 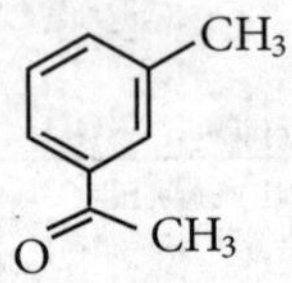

8. The major product of the following reaction is:

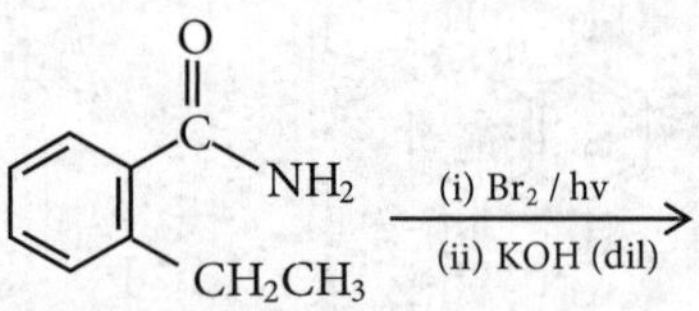

(a) 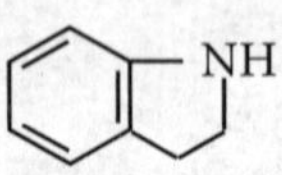
(b) 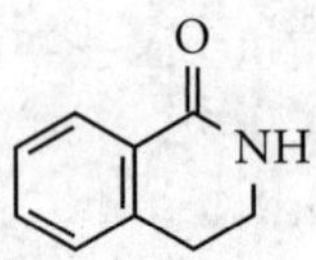

(c) 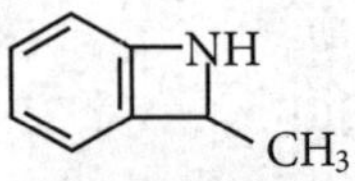
(d) 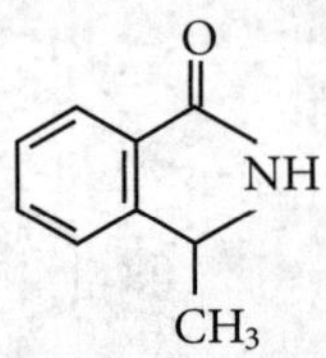

9. The total sp^2 carbon atoms present in R is:

(i) 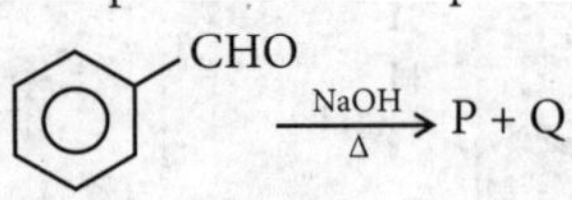

(ii) $P + Q \xrightarrow{H^+} R$

(a) 7 (b) 12
(c) 8 (d) 13

10. An organic compound A, upon reacting with NH_3, gives B. On heating, B gives C. C, in the presence of KOH, reacts with Br_2 to give isopropanamine. Then A is:
(a) CH_3COOH
(b) $CH_3CH_2CH_2COOH$
(c) $(CH_3)_2CHCOOH$
(d) CH_3CH_2COOH

11. Which of the following reactions does not yield an alkyl amine?
(a) $R-X + NH_3 \rightarrow$
(b) $R-CH = NH + NaBH_4 \rightarrow$
(c) $R-C \equiv N + H_2O \xrightarrow{H^{\oplus}}$
(d) $R-\overset{\overset{O}{||}}{C}-OH \xrightarrow[\text{(ii) } \Delta \text{ (ii)} LiAlH_4]{\text{(i) } NH_3}$

12. An organic compound P on reduction gives compound Q, which on reaction with chloroform and KOH forms R. The compound R on catalytic reduction gives N-methylaniline. The compound P is:
(a) Nitrobenzene (b) Nitromethane
(c) Methylamine (d) Aniline

13. The major product of the following reaction is:

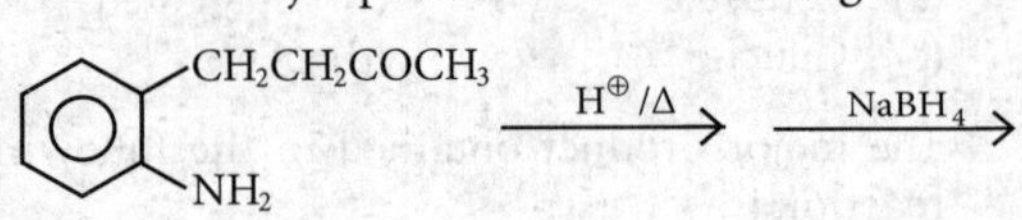

(a) 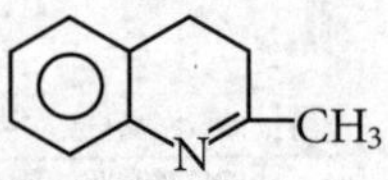

(b) 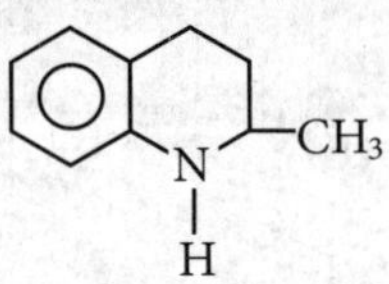

(c) 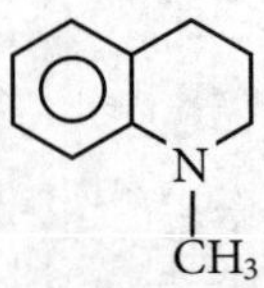

(d) 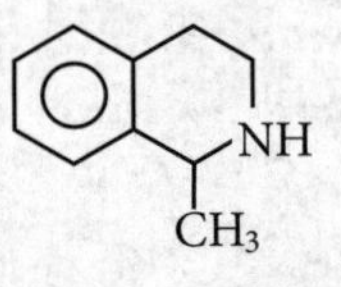

14. Which of the following will not react with acetyl chloride?
(a) H_2O (b) $PhCH_2OH$
(c) 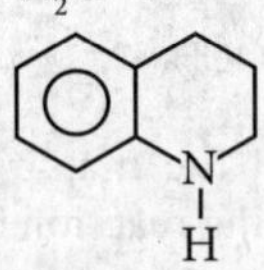 (d) 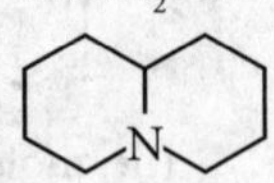

15. The compound (P) in the following sequence is:

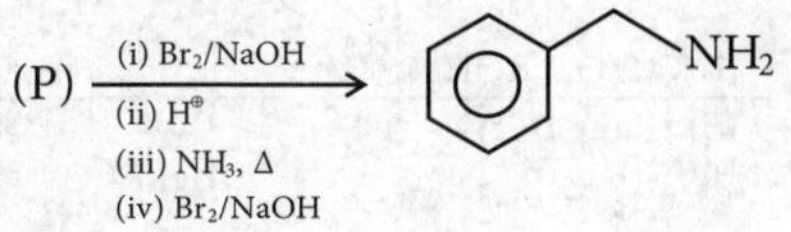

(a) 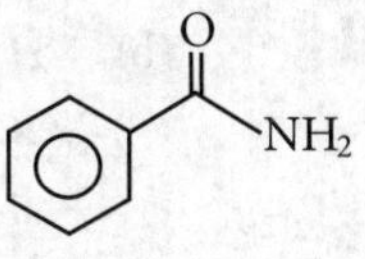 (b) 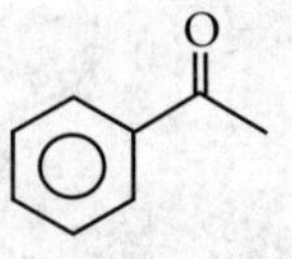

(c) 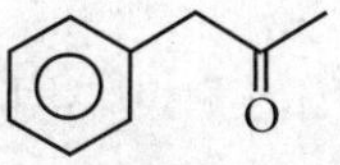 (d) 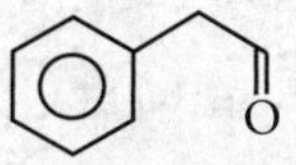

16. If the major product of the following sequence gives acid on further hydrolysis, then the major product is:

$$CH_3-\overset{\overset{\displaystyle O}{\|}}{C}-NH_2 \xrightarrow[\text{(ii) } H_3O^{\oplus}]{\text{(i) } P_2O_5,\ \Delta}$$

(a) CH_3-COOH (b) CH_3-NH_2
(c) CH_3CONH_2 (d) CH_3-CN

17. The major product of the following sequence is:

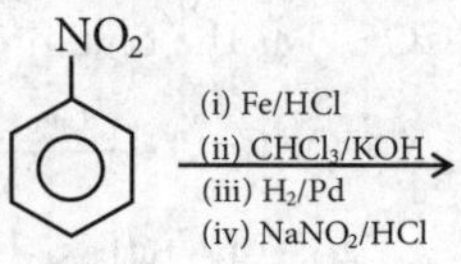

(a) 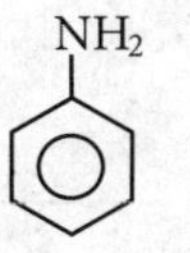 (b) 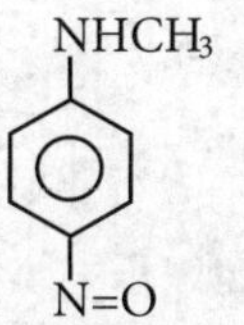

(c) 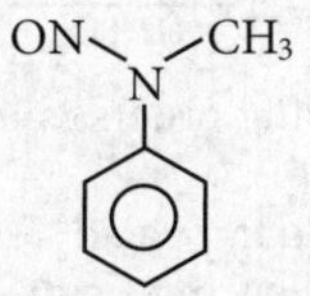 (d) 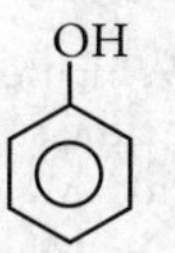

18. Which of the following reactions does not require aqueous KOH?
(a) Gabriel phthalimide amine synthesis
(b) Hofmann bromamide degradation
(c) Carbylamine reaction
(d) HVZ reaction

19. Which of the reactions/observations cannot be shown by aniline?
(a) Foul-smelling compound with $CHCl_3$/KOH
(b) Base-soluble product with the Hinsberg reagent
(c) White precipitate with bromine water
(d) Increase of 84 g mass with CH_3COCl/pyridine

20. For the following sequence, P and Q are related as:

$$\underset{(P)}{C_6H_5COOH} \xrightarrow[\text{(ii)HBr}]{\text{(i)LiAlH}_4} \xrightarrow[\text{(ii)}H_3O^{\oplus}]{\text{(i)KCN}} (Q)$$

(a) Chain isomers
(b) Identical isomers
(c) Position isomer
(d) Homologues

21. Which of the following statements is correct?
(a) Acidic medium hydrolysis of ester is known as saponification.
(b) Alkyl isocyanate on hydrolysis produces secondary amine.
(c) The Hinsberg reagent gives tertiary sulphonamide with tertiary amine.
(d) Acid amides are the least reactive towards hydrolysis.

22. 4-Oxobutanoic acid is reduced with sodium borohydride followed by aqueous acid. The major product is:

(a) 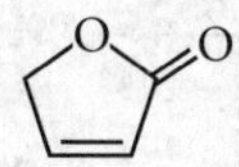

(b) 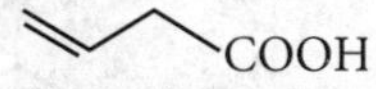

(c) 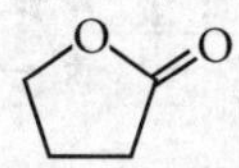

(d) 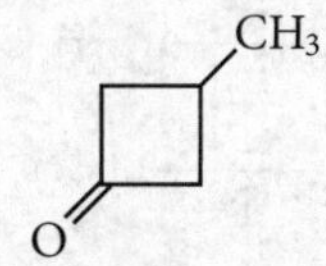

23. Which of the following statements is correct?
CH_3-NH_2 and $CH_3-NH-CH_3$
(a) Both are obtained by Gabriel phthalimide
(b) Both produce base-soluble product with $PhSO_2Cl$
(c) Both will produce N_2 with $NaNO_2$/HCl
(d) Both are more basic than NMe_3 in water

24. For the following sequence, compound (X) is:

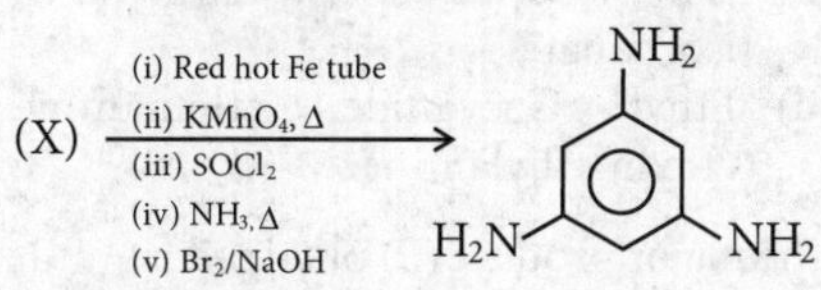

(a) $HC\equiv CH$ (b) $CH_3-C\equiv CH$

(c) $CH_3-C\equiv C-CH_3$ (d) 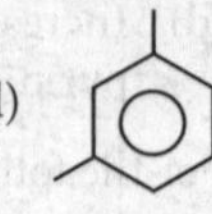

25. Select the correct statement for the following compounds:

(P)

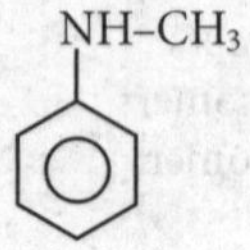
(Q)

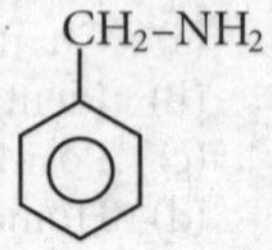
(R)

(a) Among P, Q and R, Q is the most basic compound
(b) Both P and R can be obtained in good yield by Gabriel phthalimide synthesis
(c) Both P and R will produce foul-smelling compound with $CHCl_3$/KOH
(d) Q on reaction with the Hinsberg reagent will produce a base-soluble sulphonamide

26. Which of the following reactions is correctly matched as major product?

(a) $CH_3CH_2COOH \xrightarrow[\text{(ii) NaOBr, (iii) NaNO}_2\text{/HCl}]{\text{(i) NH}_3,\Delta} CH_3CH_2Cl$

(b) $C_6H_5NO_2 \xrightarrow[\text{(ii) CHCl}_3\text{/KOH}]{\text{(i) Fe/HCl}}$ 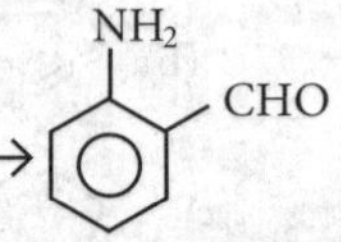

(c) $C_6H_5CH_2Cl \xrightarrow[\text{(ii) H}_2\text{/Ni}]{\text{(i) Ethanolic NaCN}} C_6H_5CH_2NH_2$

(d) $CH_3CN \xrightarrow[\text{(ii) Red P / Br}_2]{\text{(i) H}_3\text{O}^{\oplus},\Delta} BrCH_2COOH$

27. A, B and C, respectively, in the given reaction sequence are:

Bromo ethane $\xrightarrow{AgCN} A \xrightarrow{H_3O^+}$ Acid + B,

$B \xrightarrow[KOH]{CHCl_3} A \xrightarrow{\text{Reduction}} C$

(a) Ethane amine, methane nitrile and diethylamine
(b) Carbylamino ethane, ethaneamine and secondary amine
(c) Ethyl isocyanide, ethylamine and methyl isocyanate
(d) Ethyl isocyanide, ethanamine and ethylmethylamine

28. The major product (P) obtained is:

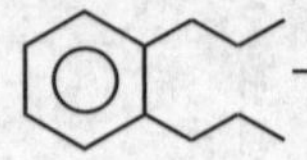 $\xrightarrow[\text{(ii) Dilute H}_2\text{SO}_4\text{, (iii) NH}_3,\Delta]{\text{(i) KMnO}_4\text{, KOH},\Delta} \xrightarrow[\text{(iii) CH}_3-\text{CH}_2-\text{Br, (iv) H}_3\text{O}^{\oplus}]{\text{(i) }\Delta\text{, (ii) NaOH}}$ (P)

(a) 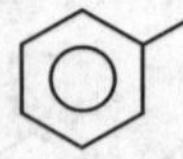 (b) $CH_3-CH_2-NH_2$

(c) 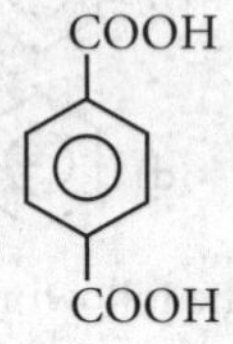 (d) $CH_3-NH-CH_3$

29. The major product (Z) of the following sequence of reactions is:

$CH_3CH_2CH_2CONH_2 \xrightarrow[\Delta]{KOH + Br_2}$

$X \xrightarrow{HNO_2} Z$

(a) $CH_3CH_2CH_2NH_2$ (b) $CH_3CH_2CH_2Cl$
(c) $CH_3CH(OH)CH_3$ (d) CH_3CH_2COOH

30. Which of the following sets of reactions cannot prepare RCOOH as the final product?

(a) $R-MgX + O=C=O \xrightarrow{\text{Dry ether}}$

(b) $R-CN \xrightarrow[\text{(ii) H}_2\text{O/H}^+]{\text{(i) SnCl}_2\text{ + HCl}}$

(c) 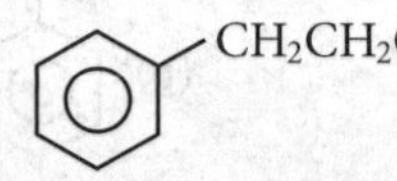 $\xrightarrow[\Delta]{KMnO_4/\overset{\ominus}{O}H}$

(d) $CH_3(CH_2)_8CH_2OH \xrightarrow[H_2SO_4]{CrO_3}$

31. Which of the following orders is incorrect for acidic strength?
(a) Maleic acid > Fumaric acid
(b) Malonic acid > Succinic acid
(c) Salicylic acid < Benzoic acid
(d) Formic acid > Benzoic acid

32. A compound of molecular formula $C_8H_8O_2$ reacts with acetophenone to form a single cross-aldol product in the presence of base. The same compound on reaction with ammoniacal $AgNO_3$ gives silver mirror. The structure of the compound is:

(a)

(b) 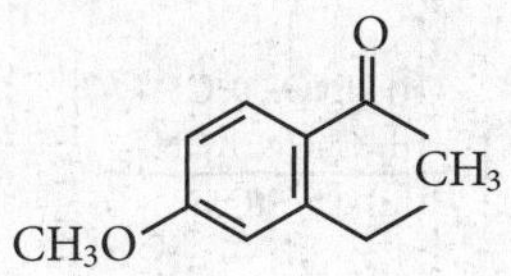

(c) 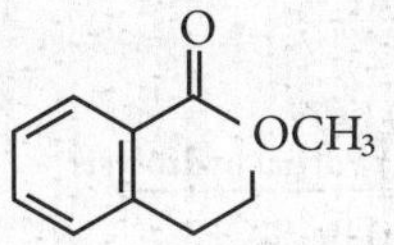

(d) 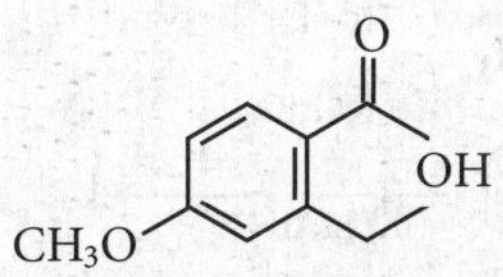

33. Which of the following statements does not involve hydrogen bonding in a primary role?

(a) Triethylamine is more Lewis base than primary amine in water.
(b) Carboxylic acids are higher boiling liquids than aldehydes and ketones.
(c) Ethanol and propane have comparable mass, but they differ in boiling point.
(d) The boiling point of alkyl halide is higher than a hydrocarbon of comparable mass.

34. Arrange the following in decreasing order of their acidic strength:

(a) $FCH_2COOH > ClCH_2COOH > C_6H_5CH_2COOH > CH_3COOH > CH_3CH_2OH$
(b) $ClCH_2COOH > FCH_2COOH > C_6H_5CH_2COOH > CH_3COOH > CH_3CH_2OH$
(c) $C_6H_5CH_2COOH > ClCH_2COOH > FCH_2COOH > CH_3COOH > CH_3CH_2OH$
(d) $FCH_2COOH > ClCH_2COOH > CH_3COOH > C_6H_5CH_2COOH > CH_3CH_2OH$

35. Among the following, which statement is incorrect?

(a) Acetic acid will not respond to haloform test
(b) Schiff's regent and Schiff's base are different compounds
(c) Fehling's solution is a good reagent to detect aromatic aldehydes
(d) Both aldehyde and ketone can react with Brady's reagent

36. Compound 'A' was prepared by oxidation of compound 'B' with alkaline $KMnO_4$. Compound 'A' on reduction with lithium aluminium hydride is converted back to compound 'B'. When compound 'A' is heated with compound B in the presence of H_2SO_4, it produces a fruity smell of compound C. Which option is incorrect?

(a) A = Aldehyde
(b) B = Alcohol
(c) C = Ester
(d) A = Carboxylic acid

37. For the following compounds, choose the incorrect option:

(P) $CH_3 - NH_2$ (Q) $Ph–NH_2$

(a) (P) is more basic than (Q)
(b) Both (P) and (Q) will give a foul-smelling compound with $CHCl_3$, KOH
(c) Both (P) and (Q) will form a base-soluble sulphonamide with the Hinsberg reagent
(d) Both (P) and (Q) can be obtained by Gabriel phthalimide synthesis

38. Compound C cannot show:

$$CH_3 - Br \xrightarrow{Mg/ether} (A) \xrightarrow[\text{(ii) Water}]{\text{(i)} CO_2} (B) \xrightarrow[\Delta]{CH_3OH/H^+} (C)$$

(a) Metamerism
(b) Tautomerism
(c) Functional isomerism
(d) Position isomerism

39. For the given reaction, X is a tertiary alcohol. Choose the incorrect option about the reactant amine:

$$C_4H_{11}N + HNO_2 \rightarrow X\ (C_4H_{10}O)$$

(a) It will give a foul smell in the carbylamine test
(b) The reaction involves the formation of nitrogen gas
(c) In total, two amines are possible for the reaction
(d) It gives a base-insoluble product with $PhSO_2Cl$

40. The best route by which the following conversion can be accomplished is:

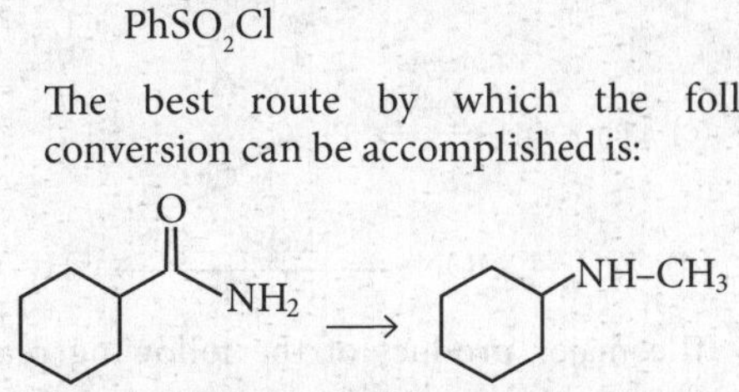

(a) (i) Br_2/KOH (ii) CH_3Br
(b) (i) $CHCl_3$/KOH (ii) Br_2/KOH
(c) (i) Br_2/KOH (ii) $CHCl_3$/KOH (iii) H_2/Ni
(d) (i) $LiAlH_4$ (ii) $CHCl_3$/KOH (iii) H_2/Ni

41. Which of the following statements is incorrect?

(a) Formaldehyde is a planar molecule.

(b) Carboxylic acids can be reduced to alcohols by treatment with $LiAlH_4$.
(c) Aromatic aldehydes are almost as reactive as formaldehyde.
(d) Compounds containing the CHO group are easily oxidised to their corresponding carboxylic acids.

42. An optically active compound 'X' has molecular formula $C_4H_8O_3$. It evolves CO_2 with aqueous $NaHCO_3$. 'X' reacts with $LiAlH_4$ to give an achiral compound. 'X' is:
(a) $CH_3CH_2\underset{OH}{\underset{|}{C}}HCOOH$
(b) $(CH_3)_2CH(OH)COOH$
(c) $CH_3\underset{CH_2OH}{\underset{|}{C}}HCOOH$
(d) $CH_3\underset{OH}{\underset{|}{C}}HCH_2COOH$

43. Which of the following reactions cannot be catalysed by HCl?
(a) $CH_3-CHO + (CH_2OH)_2 \rightarrow$ Acetal
(b) $CH_3COOH + CH_3CH_2OH \rightarrow$ Ester
(c) $CH_3COCH_3 + HCN \rightarrow$ Cyanohydrin
(d) $CH_3COOCH_3 + H_2O \rightarrow$ Acid

44. Which of the following reactions is incorrectly matched with their major product?
(a) $CH_3-COOH \xrightarrow[\Delta]{P_2O_5}$ 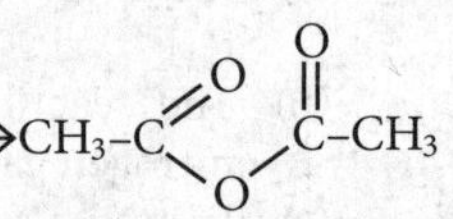
(b) $CH_3CH_2COOH \xrightarrow[\text{(ii)} H_2O]{\text{(i) Red P}/Cl_2} CH_3-\underset{Cl}{\underset{|}{C}}HCOOH$
(c) $PhCOOH \xrightarrow{SOCl_2}$ 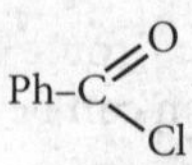
(d) $CH_3-COONa \xrightarrow[\Delta]{NaOH, CaO} CH_3-OH$

45. The major product of the following reaction can be obtained by:

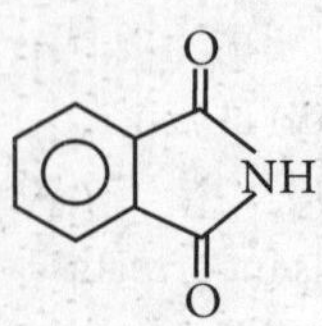 $\xrightarrow[\text{(ii) } PhCH_2Br \text{ (iii) } H_3O^{\oplus}]{\text{(i) KOH/EtOH}}$ (P) (Positive isocyanide test)

(i) 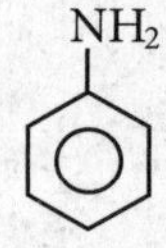 $\xrightarrow[\text{(iii) Na/EtOH}]{\text{(i) } HNO_2, 0°C \text{ (ii) CuCN/KCN}}$

(ii) 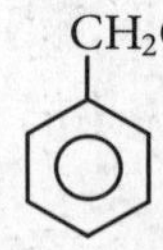 $\xrightarrow[\text{(iii) } Br_2/KOH]{\text{(i) KCN (ii) Partial hydrolysis}}$

(iii) 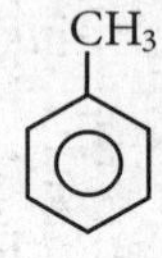 $\xrightarrow[\text{(iii) } LiAlH_4]{\text{(i) } KMnO_4, \Delta \text{ (ii) } NH_3/\Delta}$

(iv) 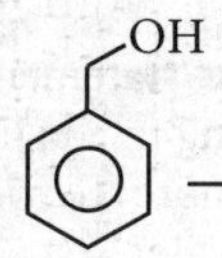 $\xrightarrow[\text{(iii) } H_2/Ni]{\text{(i) PCC (ii) } NH_3}$

(a) i, ii, iii (b) ii, iii, iv
(c) i, ii, iv (d) i, ii, iii, iv

46. The order of basic strength of NR_3 in aqueous state is given below.

NR_3 →
- $(CH_3)_2NH > CH_3NH_2 > (CH_3)_3N > NH_3$ when $R = -CH_3$
- $(C_2H_6)_2NH > (C_2H_5)_3N > C_2H_5NH_2 > NH_3$ when $R = -C_2H_5$

The observed pattern of basic strength cannot be explained by:
(a) The steric effect of the alkyl group
(b) The electronic effect of the alkyl group
(c) The extent of hydrogen bonding in water
(d) The solvation of the alkyl group

47. Which of the following reactions cannot give alcohol as a major product?
(a) $RCOR + R'Mgx \rightarrow$
(b) $CH_3-CH=CH_2 \xrightarrow[\text{(ii)} H_2O]{\text{(i)} BH_3-THF}$
(c) $R-COOH \xrightarrow[H^+]{ROH} \xrightarrow[\text{Catalyst}]{H_2}$
(d) $CH_3-CN \xrightarrow[\text{(ii)} H_2O \text{ (iii)} NaBH_4]{\text{(i)} SnCl_2/HCl}$

48. Chloroform on reaction with acetone in the presence of caustic soda gives:
(a) Acetylene (b) Chloretone
(c) Chloroform (d) Chloroacetone

49. The major products of the following reaction are:

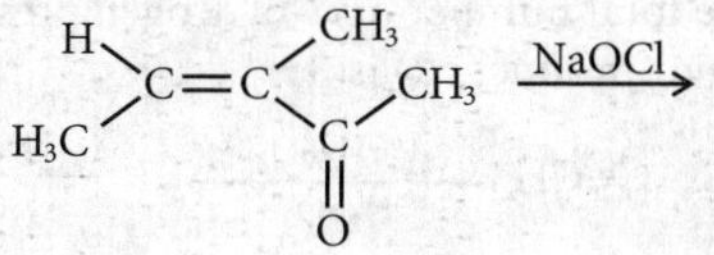

(a) 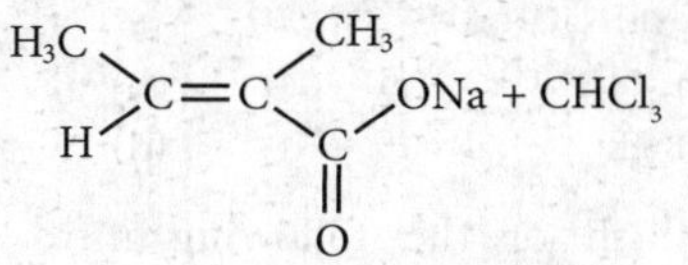

(b) 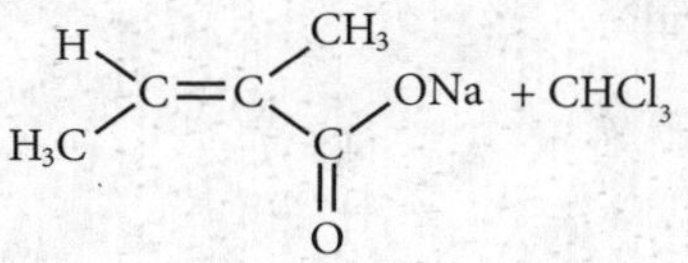

(c) 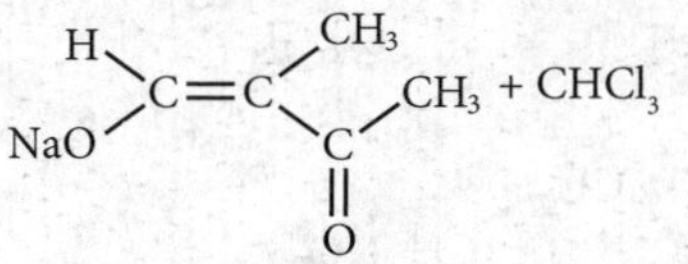

(d) 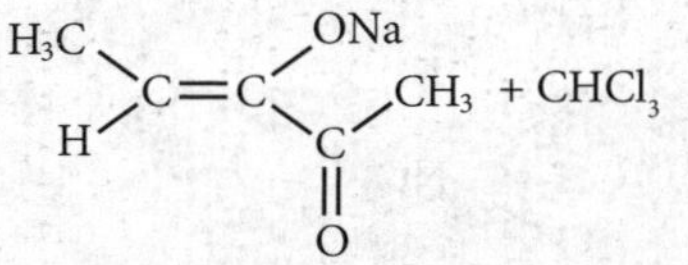

50. The total number of compounds which form foul-smelling compound with $CHCl_3$ and NaOH are:

(a) $PhNH_2$ (b) $Ph-NH-CH_3$

(c) 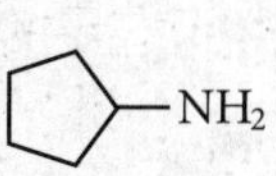 (d) 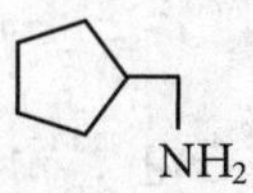

(e) 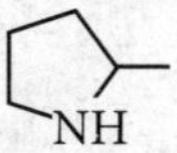 (f) 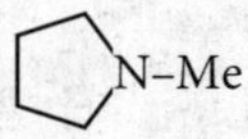

(g) Me_3N (h) Me_2NH

(i) Me_2CHNH_2

(a) 2 (b) 3
(c) 5 (d) 4

51. The total number of amines which can be prepared by Gabriel phthalimide synthesis are:

(a) 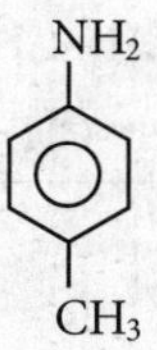 (b) Aniline

(c) 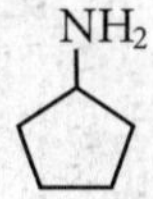 (d) 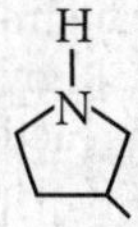

(e) 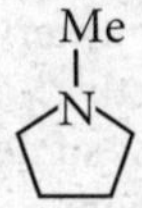 (f) 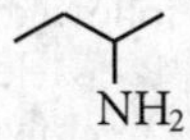

(g) 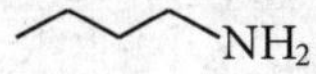 (h) 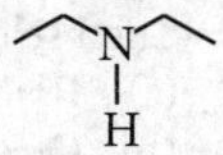

(i) 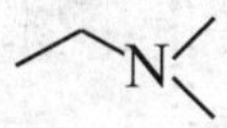 (j) 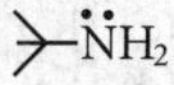

(a) 2 (b) 3
(c) 5 (d) 4

52. An aromatic compound 'A' having molecular formula $C_7H_6O_2$, on being treated with aqueous ammonia and heating, forms compound 'B'. The compound 'B' on reaction with molecular bromine and potassium hydroxide provides compound 'C' having molecular formula C_6H_7N. The structure of 'A' is:

(a) 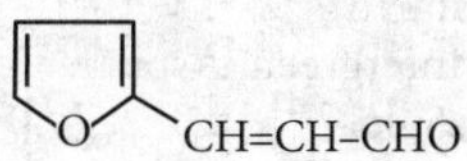

(b) 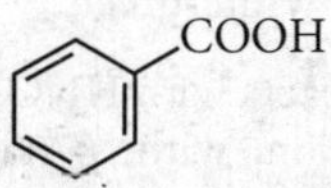

(c) 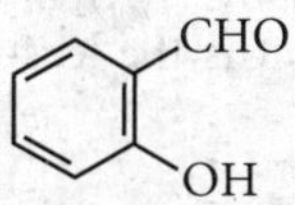

(d) 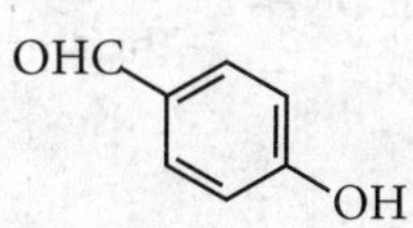

53. In the given reaction, the major product on reaction with the Hinsberg reagent gives:

$$C_6H_5-\overset{O}{\overset{\|}{C}}-NHCH_3 \xrightarrow{LiAlH_4}$$

(a) Base-soluble primary sulphonamide
(b) Base-insoluble tertiary sulphonamide
(c) Base-insoluble secondary sulphonamide
(d) Base-soluble secondary sulphonamide

54. A mixture of 1°, 2° and 3° amines can be separated by:

(a) Hinsberg's method
(b) Hofmann's isocyanide test
(c) Gabriel phthalimide synthesis
(d) Hofmann's mustard oil test

55. A hydrocarbon 'P', (C_4H_8) on reaction with HCl, gives a compound 'Q', (C_4H_9Cl), which on reaction with 1 mol of NH_3 gives compound 'R' ($C_4H_{11}N$). On reacting with $NaNO_2$ and HCl followed by treatment with water, compound 'R' yields an optically active alcohol, 'S'. Ozonolysis of 'P' gives 2 mols of acetaldehyde. Then select the incorrect option:

(a) P = 2-butene
(b) Q = 1-chlorobutane
(c) R = 2-butanamine
(d) S = 2-butanol

56. The major products (P) and (Q) of the following reaction are known as:

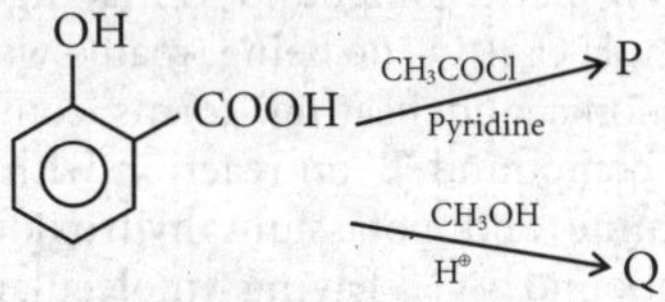

(a) Salol, Aspirin
(b) Oil of wintergreen, Aspirin
(c) Aspirin, Salol
(d) Aspirin, Oil of wintergreen

57. A compound (A) reacts with HNO_2 to produce (B). (B) on reaction with β-naphthol can produce a colourful dye. (A) has molecular formula C_7H_9N and it is the least basic in its isomers. Then (A) is:

(a) 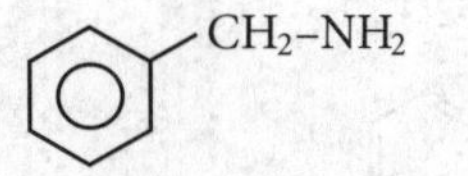

(b) Ph–$NHCH_3$

(c) 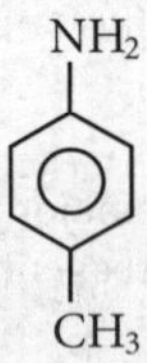

(d) 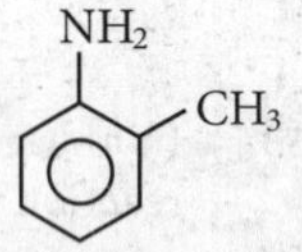

58. The total number of α-hydrogen present in the major product (R) is:

$$CH_3–C{\equiv}CH \xrightarrow[H_2SO_4]{1\%\ HgSO_4} P \xrightarrow[\Delta]{NaOH} Q \xrightarrow[(ii)\ NaOH,\Delta]{(i)\ N_2H_4} R$$

(a) 4 (b) 6
(c) 8 (d) 9

59. Which of the following nitro compounds produces (x)-type compound with nitrous acid?

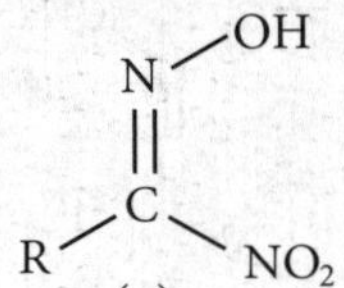

(x)

(a) 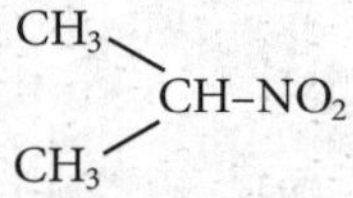

(b) 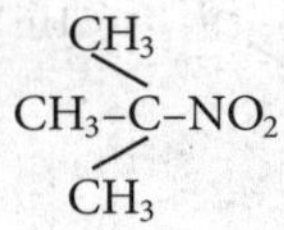

(c) 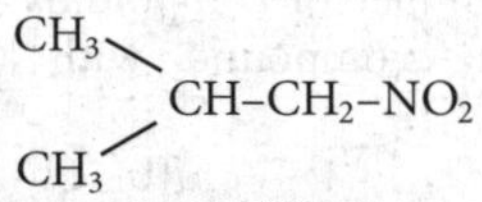

(d) 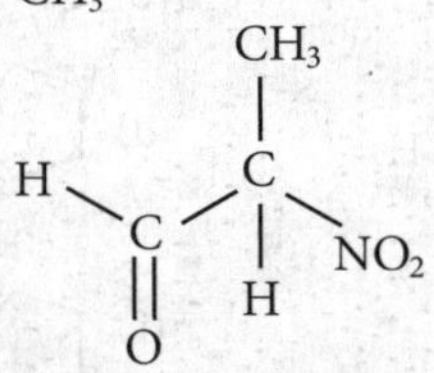

60. Which of the following reactions is incorrectly matched with the name of the reaction and the major product?

Reaction	Name	Product
(a) $PhNH_2 + CH_3COCl$	Schotten–Baumann reaction	Ph–$NHCOCH_3$
(b) $CH_3–CH_2–NH_2 + CHCl_3 + KOH$	Carbylamine reaction	$CH_3–CH_2–NC$
(c) $CH_3CN+SnCl_2+HCl$ followed H_2O	Stephen's reduction	$CH_3–CHO$
(d) $PhCHO+CH_3COONa+(CH_3CO)_2O$	Perkin reaction	Ph–CH=CH–CHO

61. Which of the following is correctly matched with the product and the name of the reaction?

(a)	$HCHO + NaOH \rightarrow$	$HCOONa + CH_3OH$	Aldol reaction
(b)	CH_3–Cl (excess) + $NH_3 \rightarrow$	Methyl amine	Hydrolysis
(c)	CH_3–NH_2 + PhCOCl/Pyridine $\rightarrow$	$CH_3NHCOPh$	Acetylation
(d)	$CH_3\text{–}COOH \xrightarrow[Br_2]{Red\ P}$	$BrCH_2COOH$	HVZ reaction

62. Which of the following reactions is correctly matched with the product and reactant?

(a)	Wurtz–Fittig reaction	$Ph\text{–}Br \xrightarrow[\Delta]{Na}$	Ph–Ph
(b)	Ammonolysis reaction	CH_3–Cl + NH_3 (excess) $\rightarrow$	Ammonium salt
(c)	Kolbe's electrolysis	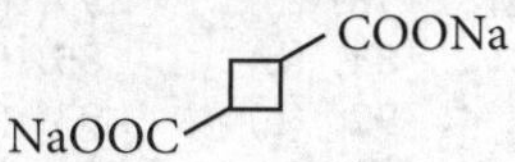	
(d)	Williamson's continuous ether	$EtOH \xrightarrow[140°C]{Conc.\ H_2SO_4}$	CH_3–CH_2–O–CH_2–CH_3

63. The major product (S) of the following sequence is:

$$CH_3CO_2Et \xrightarrow{LiAlH_4} (P) \xrightarrow[300°C]{Cu} (Q) \xrightarrow[H_2SO_4]{CrO_3} (R) \xrightarrow{Red P/Br_2} (S)$$

(a) CH_3COBr
(b) $BrCH_2COBr$
(c) $BrCH_2COOH$
(d) $CH_3CH(Br)COOH$

64. The major product of the following reaction is:

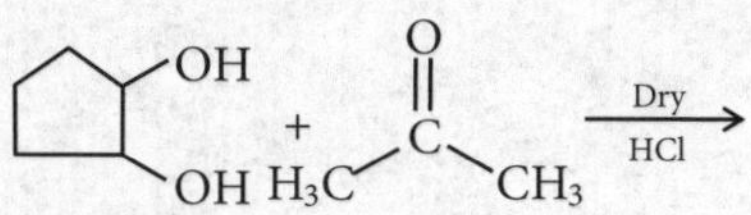

(a) 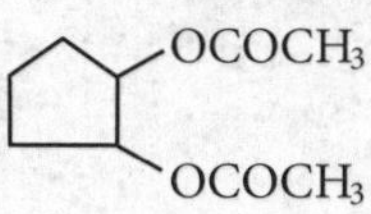 (b) 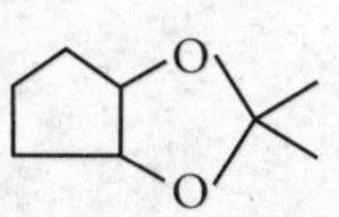

(c) 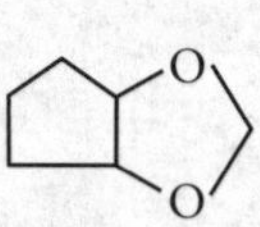 (d) 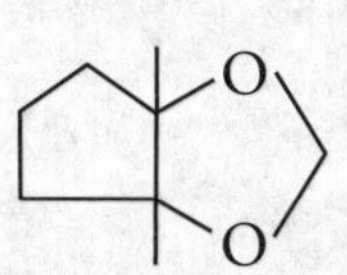

65. Choose the incorrect option:
(a) Acid amide does not react with CH_3COCl
(b) MnO_2 oxidises allylic and benzylic alcohol
(c) Hydrazine gives hydrazone with acetone
(d) Ammonolysis is a nucleophilic addition reaction

66. Choose the incorrect option regarding the following compounds:

CH_3–CHO (P) Ph–CHO (Q)

(a) (P) gives aldol condensation with NaOH, Δ
(b) (Q) gives PhCOONa with NaOH, Δ
(c) (P) and (Q) can be distinguished by Fehling's solution
(d) Only (P) forms cyanohydrin with HCN/NaCN

67. Which of the following reactions is incorrectly matched?
(a) CH_3–OH + $CH_3MgBr \rightarrow CH_4$
(b) HC≡CH + Na $\rightarrow$ $HC{\equiv}C^{\ominus}Na^{\oplus}$
(c) PhN_2Cl+ $H_2O \rightarrow$ Phenol
(d) Phenol + $PhN_2Cl \rightarrow$ Yellow dye

Answer Key

Level-1

1. (a)	**2.** (c)	**3.** (a)	**4.** (a)	**5.** (d)	**6.** (b)	**7.** (b)	**8.** (b)
9. (c)	**10.** (a)	**11.** (c)	**12.** (b)	**13.** (a)	**14.** (c)	**15.** (c)	**16.** (a)
17. (d)	**18.** (b)	**19.** (a)	**20.** (b)	**21.** (c)	**22.** (a)	**23.** (a)	**24.** (b)
25. (c)	**26.** (b)	**27.** (d)	**28.** (d)	**29.** (d)	**30.** (a)	**31.** (c)	**32.** (c)
33. (a)	**34.** (b)	**35.** (b)	**36.** (b)	**37.** (b)	**38.** (c)	**39.** (c)	**40.** (d)
41. (c)	**42.** (a)	**43.** (b)	**44.** (d)	**45.** (d)	**46.** (c)	**47.** (b)	**48.** (a)
49. (b)	**50.** (a)	**51.** (b)	**52.** (d)	**53.** (b)	**54.** (a)	**55.** (b)	**56.** (b)
57. (d)	**58.** (b)	**59.** (d)	**60.** (b)	**61.** (d)	**62.** (a)	**63.** (d)	**64.** (d)
65. (a)	**66.** (c)	**67.** (b)	**68.** (b)	**69.** (d)	**70.** (c)	**71.** (d)	**72.** (d)
73. (c)	**74.** (b)	**75.** (c)	**76.** (b)	**77.** (b)	**78.** (c)	**79.** (b)	**80.** (b)
81. (c)	**82.** (c)	**83.** (c)	**84.** (b)	**85.** (a)	**86.** (d)	**87.** (d)	**88.** (c)
89. (a)	**90.** (b)	**91.** (c)	**92.** (b)	**93.** (c)	**94.** (b)	**95.** (c)	**96.** (d)
97. (c)	**98.** (a)	**99.** (b)	**100.** (c)	**101.** (c)	**102.** (d)	**103.** (d)	**104.** (a)
105. (b)	**106.** (a)						

Level-2

1. (c)	**2.** (b)	**3.** (b)	**4.** (d)	**5.** (a)	**6.** (b)	**7.** (b)	**8.** (d)
9. (d)	**10.** (c)	**11.** (c)	**12.** (a)	**13.** (b)	**14.** (d)	**15.** (c)	**16.** (a)
17. (c)	**18.** (d)	**19.** (d)	**20.** (d)	**21.** (d)	**22.** (c)	**23.** (d)	**24.** (b)
25. (c)	**26.** (d)	**27.** (d)	**28.** (b)	**29.** (c)	**30.** (b)	**31.** (c)	**32.** (a)
33. (d)	**34.** (a)	**35.** (c)	**36.** (a)	**37.** (d)	**38.** (d)	**39.** (d)	**40.** (c)
41. (c)	**42.** (c)	**43.** (c)	**44.** (d)	**45.** (d)	**46.** (d)	**47.** (b)	**48.** (b)
49. (b)	**50.** (d)	**51.** (b)	**52.** (b)	**53.** (c)	**54.** (a)	**55.** (b)	**56.** (d)
57. (d)	**58.** (c)	**59.** (c)	**60.** (a)	**61.** (d)	**62.** (d)	**63.** (c)	**64.** (b)
65. (d)	**66.** (d)	**67.** (d)					

Solutions

Level-1

1.

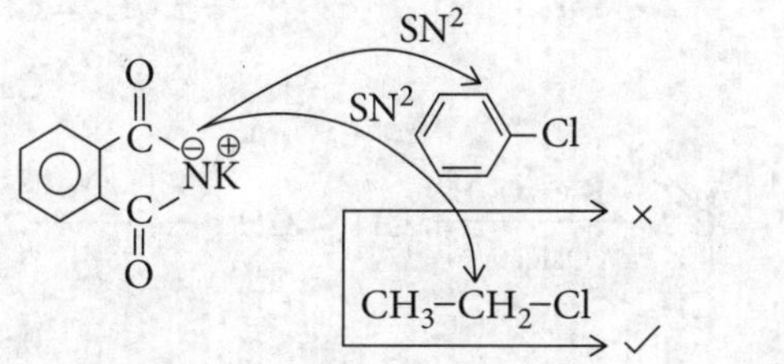

2. Steric factor and due to monovalency of halogen.

3. $R-C\equiv N \xrightarrow[\text{Acidic hydrolysis}]{H^+/H_2O} R-\underset{\underset{O}{\|}}{C}-OH+NH_3$

5. $CH_3-\underset{\underset{O}{\|}}{C}-NH_2 \xrightarrow[-NaBr,\ -H_2O]{Br_2+NaOH} CH_3NH_2+Na_2CO_3$

6.

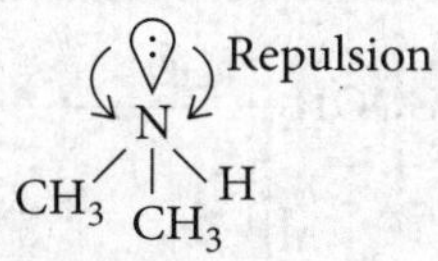

1 lone pair + 3 σ bond = 4, so sp^3 nitrogen; and due to lone pair–bond pair repulsion, the angle is less than 109.5°.

7. Solubility decreases with increase in molar mass.

8. More intermolecular association such as hydrogen bonding increases the boiling point.

$R-NH_2 > R-NH-R > R-\underset{\underset{R}{|}}{N}-R$

No hydrogen for hydrogen bonding

10. Lone pair of $R-\ddot{N}H_2$ (aliphatic amine) is localized; so more availability for donation.

11. Pyridine has a localized lone pair; so it is a good base for removing HCl.

12. $R-\underset{\underset{O}{\|}}{\overset{\overset{O}{\|}}{S}}-NH_2 \rightleftharpoons R-\underset{\underset{O}{\|}}{\overset{\overset{O}{\|}}{S}}-\overset{\ominus}{N}H+H^+$

Strong acid because of stable conjugate base (stable anion); so it is easily soluble in basic medium (NaOH).

13. Does not react with 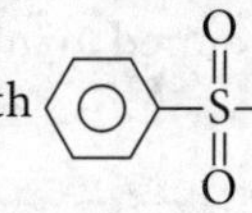 ; this means it is a 3° amine.

14. Carbylamine test is used for only 1° amines.

15. Benzoylation is also known as Schotten–Baumann reaction.

16.

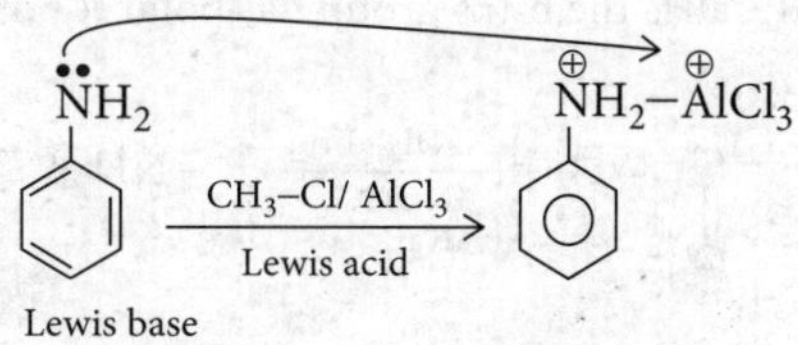

Deactivating group is formed, which does not give Friedel–Crafts reaction.

17.

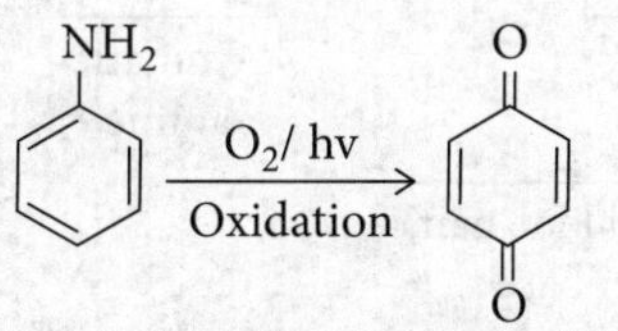

Benzoquinone (Pink)

18.

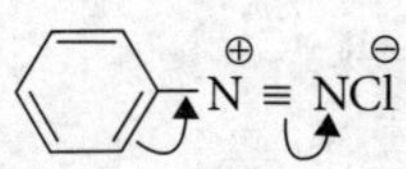

Due to resonance between π bond of ring and nitrogen, a +ve charge disperses on the ring and it acquires a double-bond character.

19. Sandmeyer reaction gives better yield than Gattermann reaction because Sandmeyer reaction produces only one salt but Gattermann reaction produces two salts. Hence, it is better.

20.

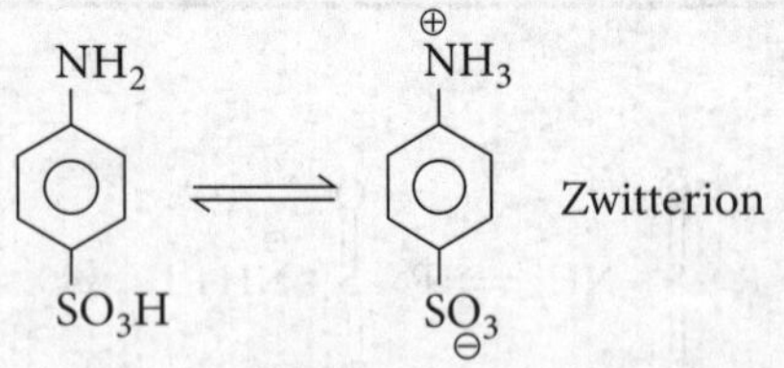

21. Fe + HCl is preferred for reduction of nitroalkane to alkanamine because in this reaction, $FeCl_2$ is formed and it hydrolyses with water and releases HCl. Thus, only a small amount of HCl is required to initiate the reaction.

22.

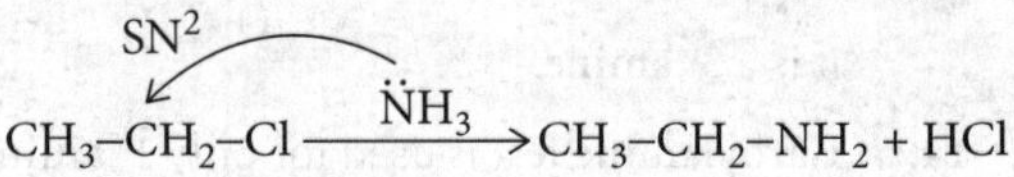

23. Ammonolysis occurs at 373 K in a sealed tube because NH_3 is gas.

24. Because the nitro group has polar π bonds.

25. $$R-\underset{\underset{O}{||}}{C}-NH_2 \xrightarrow[\substack{-Na_2CO_3 \\ -NaBr \\ -H_2O}]{NaOH+Br_2} R-NH_2$$

27.

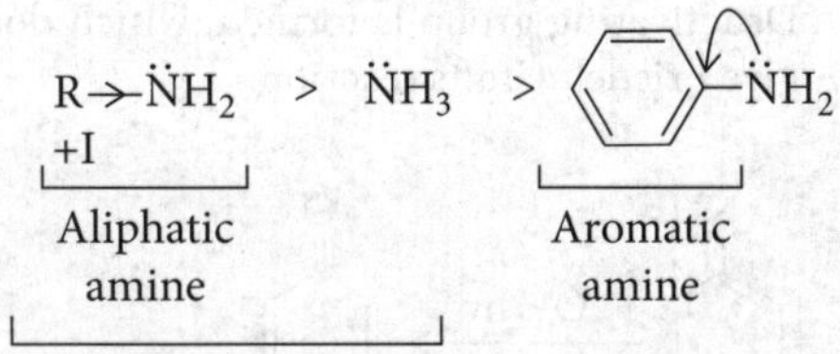

28. Primary and secondary amines have acidic hydrogen attached to nitrogen.

29. $$R-\underset{\underset{O}{||}}{C}-NH_2 \xrightarrow{P_2O_5} R-C\equiv N$$

31. Nitrogen cannot form 5 bonds.

32. Due to its polar nature, it is soluble in polar solvent water.

33.

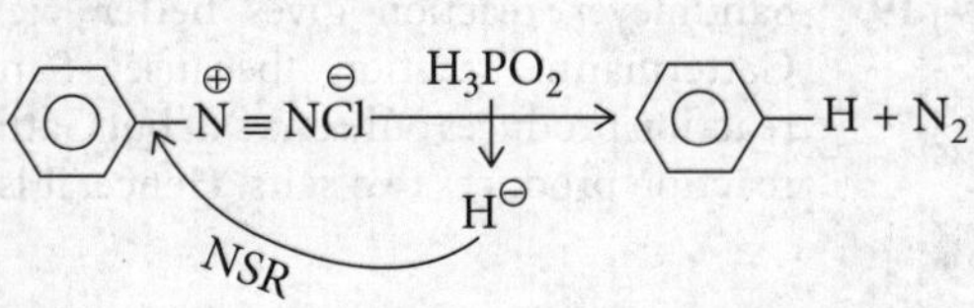

34.

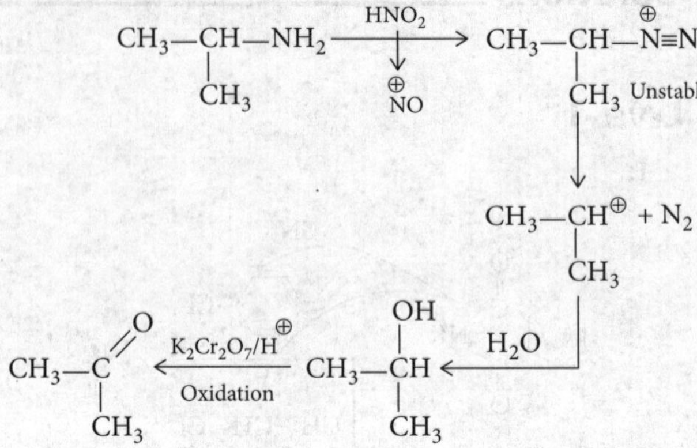

35.

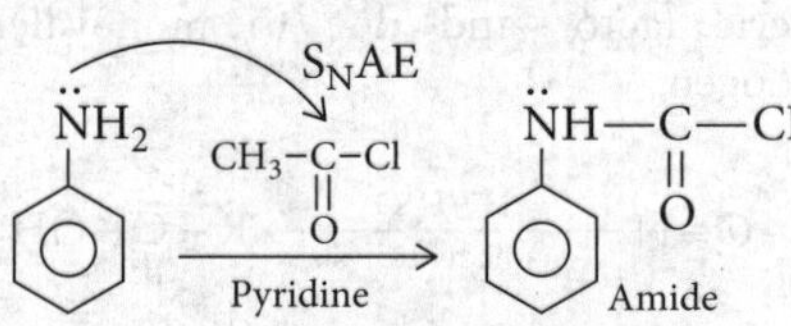

Due to delocalization of a lone pair with the $-\underset{\underset{O}{||}}{C}-$ group of amides, it is a bad base.

36. HVZ reaction is a substitution reaction.

$$CH_3CH_2COOH \xrightarrow{\text{Red P+Cl}_2} CH_3\underset{\underset{Cl}{|}}{C}HCOOH$$

α-halo acid

37. See Q36.

38. X = 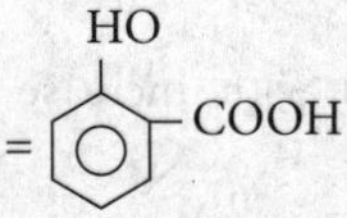 (salicylic acid)

39.

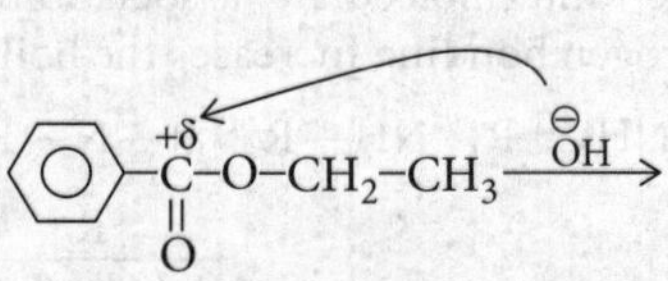

More electrophilicity ∝ Reactivity

40. Cyclic anhydride of seven-member ring is more unstable than five-member ring.

41.

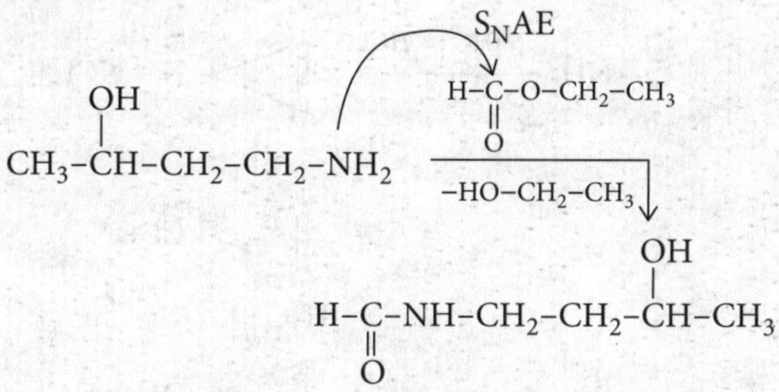

42. $\text{Esterification} \propto \dfrac{\text{Electrophilicity of carbonyl group}}{\text{Steric hindrence}}$

43.

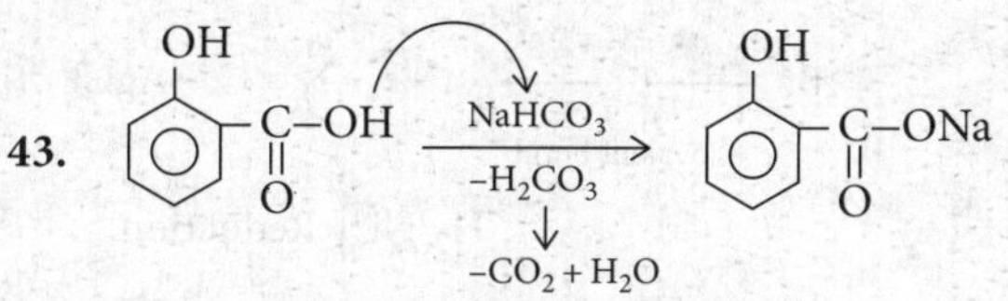

44.

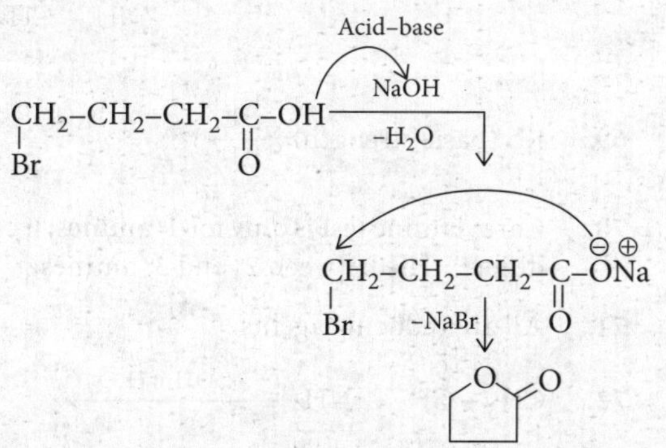

45.

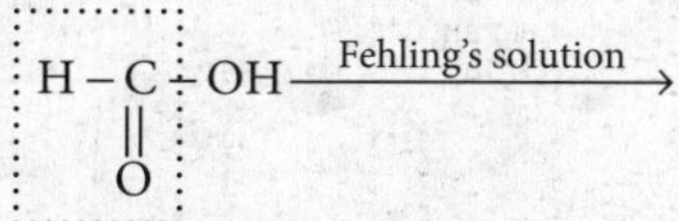

Oxidizable part is present.

46.

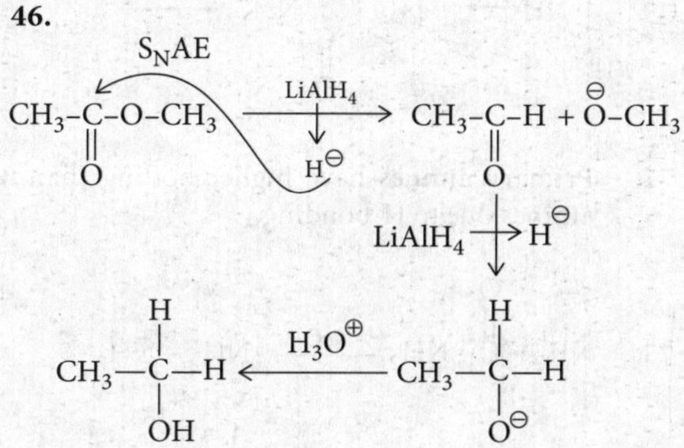

47.

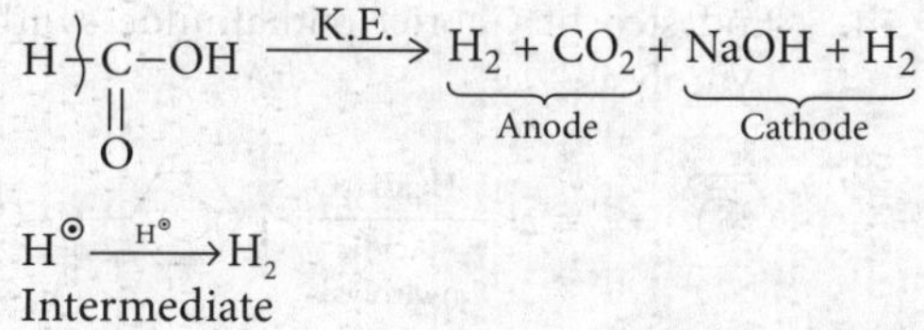

48.

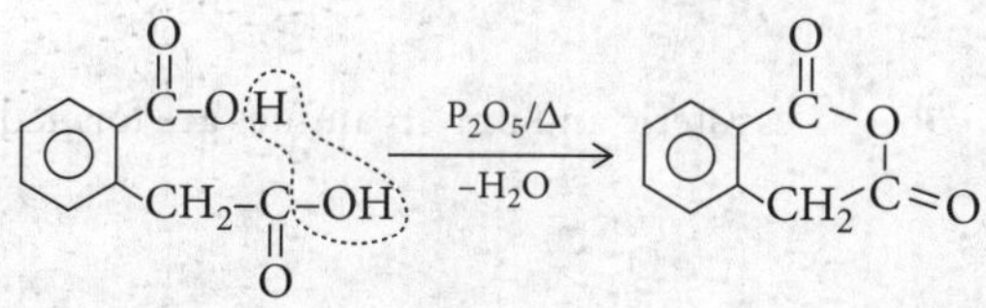

49.

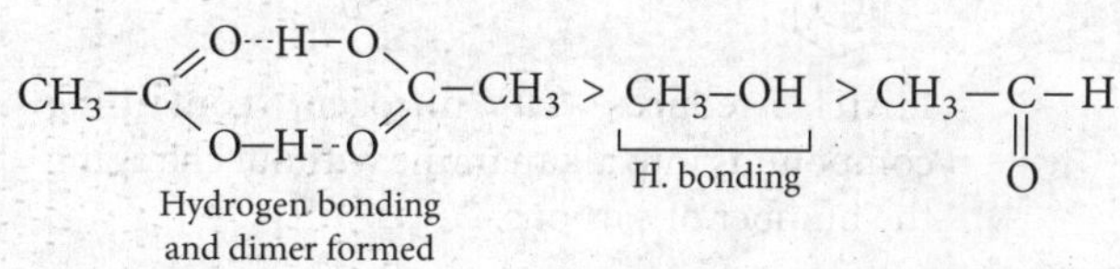

50.

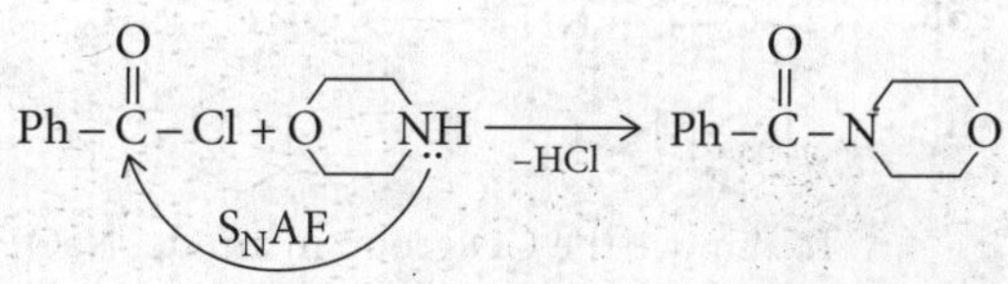

51.

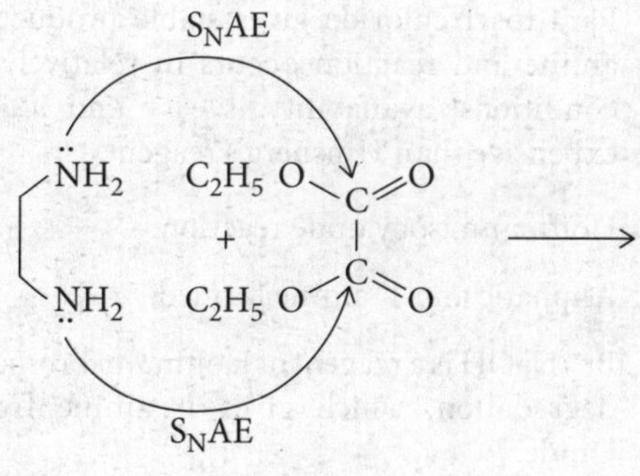

52. $CH_3-OH \xrightarrow{\text{Oxidation}} H-\underset{\underset{O}{\|}}{C}-OH \xrightarrow{\text{Oxidation}} CO_2 + H_2O$

53. Due to solvent factor, 2° amines are more basic than 3° amines.

54. End step of Gabriel phthalimide synthesis is hydrolysis.

55.

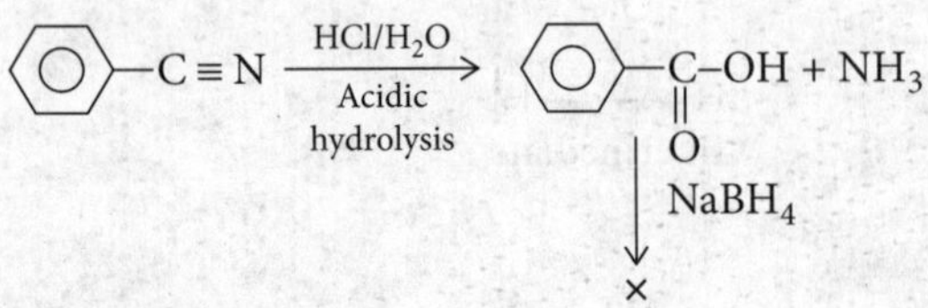

56. Less steric and only 1° amines are formed.

57.

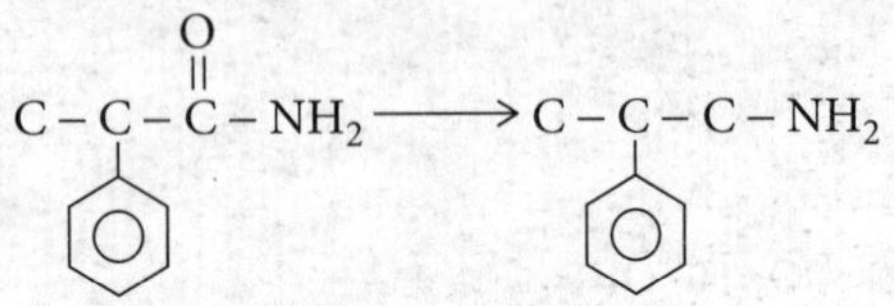

$LiAlH_4$ reduces all nitrogen containing compounds into alkanamine without changing the number of carbons.

58.

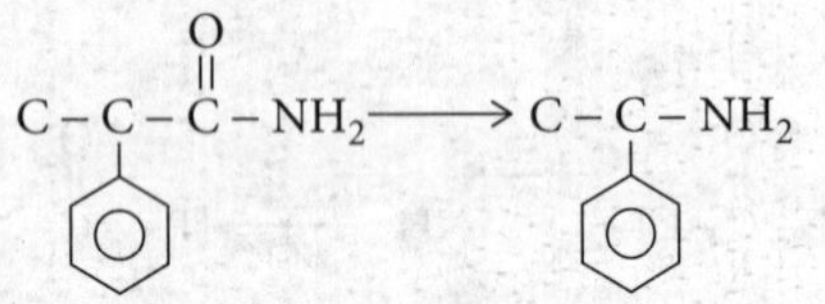

To remove the CO group in amide, NaOH/ Br_2 agent of Hoffmann bromamide degradation is required.

60. Para tosyl chloride gives stable product with amine and reaction occurs in relatively mild conditions; availability is easy and it is less expensive than Hinsberg's reagent.

61. Hoffmann isocyanide reaction

62. Aliphatic and 1° amine formed.

63. Br_2/NaOH is a reagent of Hoffmann bromamide degradation, which gives 1° amine from 1° amide.

66.

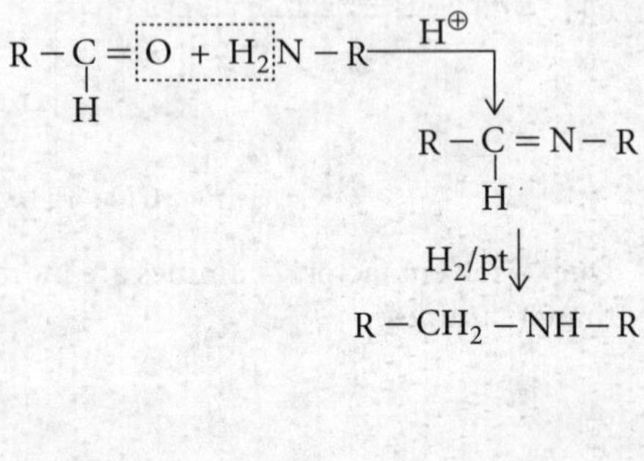

67.

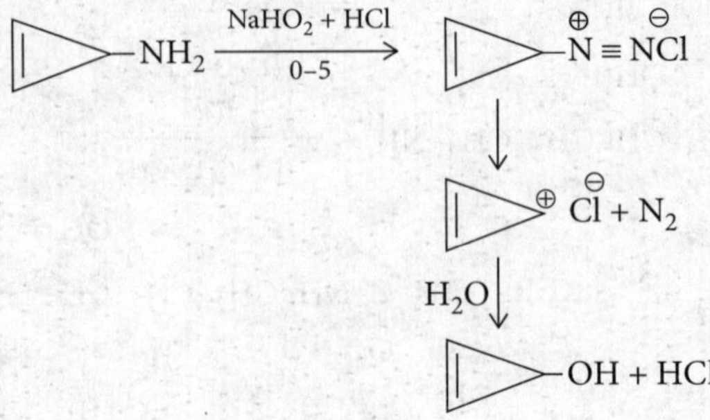

68.

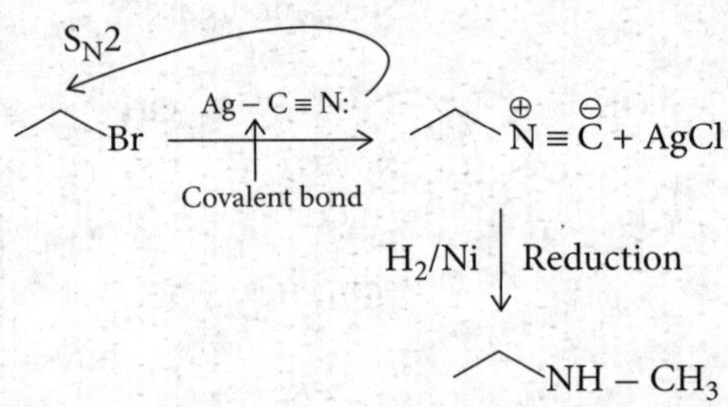

69. Kb (basic strength) $\propto \frac{1}{p^{Kb}}$

70. Carbylamine test is only for 1° amines; it cannot differentiate between 2° and 3° amines.

71. All are reducing agents.

72. $CH_3-CH_2-NH_2 \xrightarrow{\text{NaOH or } H_2O} \times$ (NH_2: Bad Leaving Group)

73.

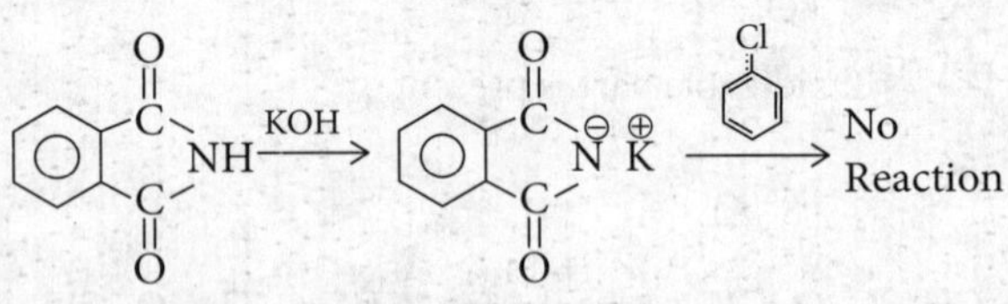

74. Primary amines have higher boiling than 3° amines due to H-bonding.

75. $NH_2-\overset{O}{\overset{||}{C}}-NH_2 \xrightarrow[Br_2]{NaOH} NH_2-NH_2$

76.

$$R-NH_2 \xrightarrow{CHCl_3+3KOH} R-NC$$

77.

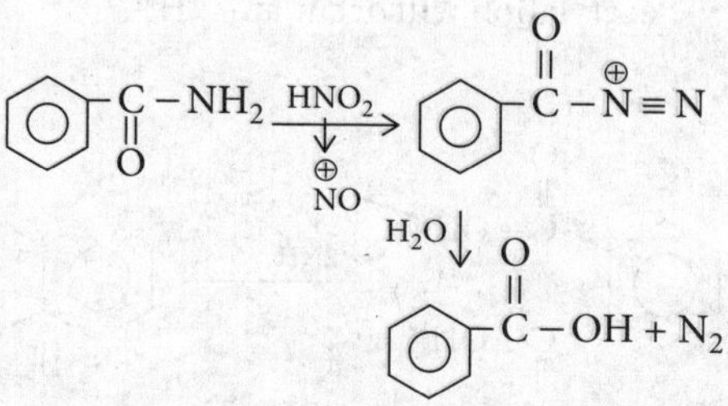

78.

$$CH_3-CH_2-NH_2 \xrightarrow{HNO_2} CH_3-CH_2-\overset{\oplus}{N}\equiv N \longrightarrow CH_3-\overset{\oplus}{C}H_2 + N_2 \xrightarrow{H_2O} CH_3-CH_2-OH$$

79.

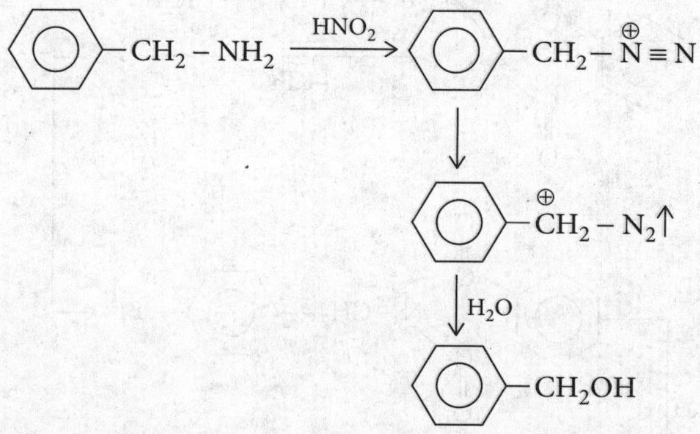

80.

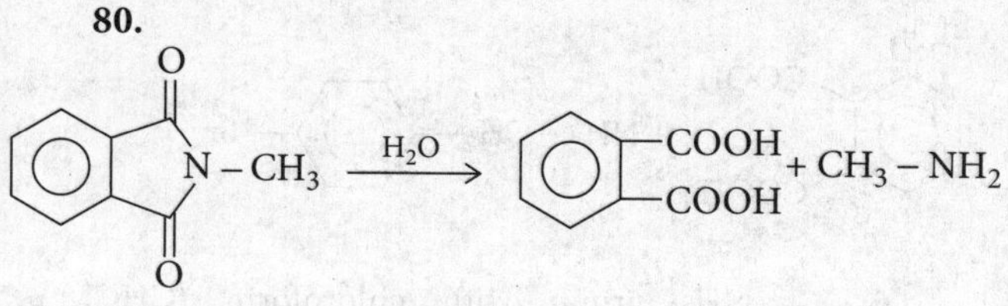

81.

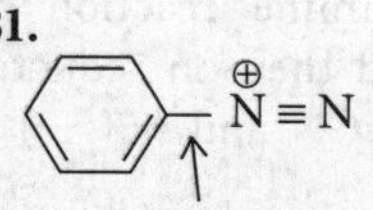

Double-bond character due to resonance

82. This reaction is for 1° amines only.

83.

$$H\ddot{O}-NO_2 + H_2SO_4 \xrightarrow[-OSO_3H]{} H_2\overset{\oplus}{O}-NO_2 \longrightarrow H_2O + \overset{\oplus}{N}O_2$$

84.

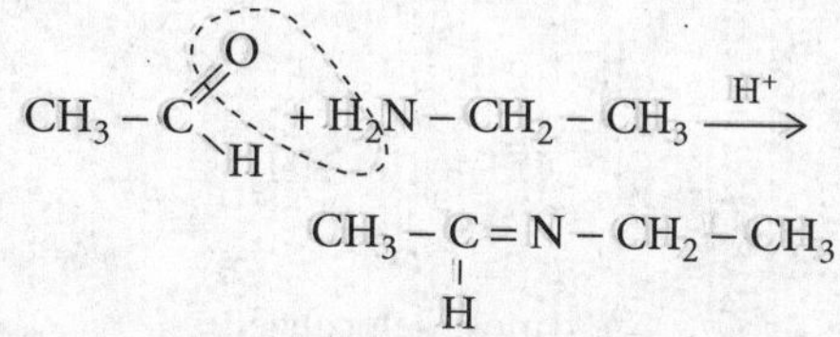

Imine

85. Primary amine

86. 2° amides do not give this reaction.

87. $\underbrace{CH_2=CH-CH_2}_{PCC}-NH-CH_3$

88. 2° amines are the most basic due to two factors: solvation and + I group.

89. Delocalized lone pair is a bad base.

91. Stable carbocation

92. $NaBH_4$ is a weak reducing agent for polar π bond.

93. $R-X \xrightarrow[-KX]{KCN} R-CN \xrightarrow{H_2/Pd} R-CH_2-NH_2$

94. 1° amide only

95.

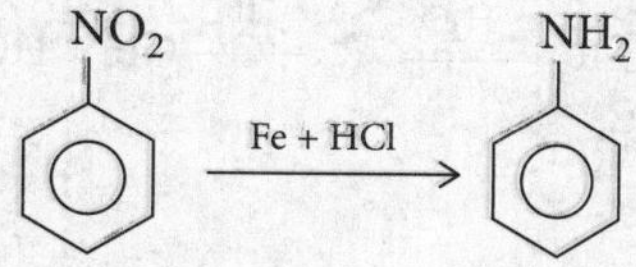

96. Electron releasing group favours basicity while withdrawing group is unfavourable.

97. Most basic

98.

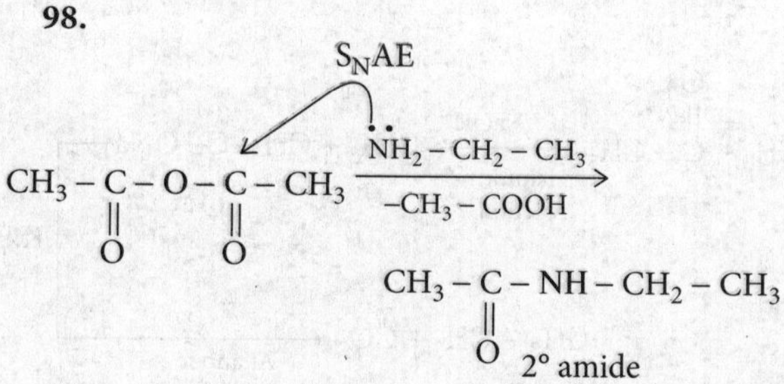

2° amide

99. Side product is precipitate, so pure liquid amine is obtained.

100. Localized lone pair and less EN-containing atom, so more likely to donate lone pair to proton.

102. Localized lone pair of 2° amine

103.

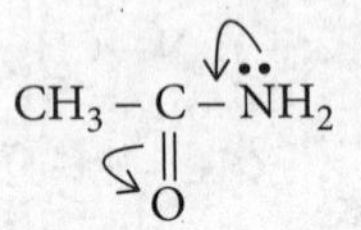

(most delocalized lone pair)

104. Anion is good base and less EN atom donates lone pair easily.

105. In gaseous stage, 3° amines have more electron density on nitrogen due to the +I alkyl group.

106. More polar, have more dipole moment.

Level-2

1. $C_6H_{12}O_2$, its DU = 1 and it may be an ester. On hydrolysis, alcohol and carboxylic acid are obtained; then it is confirmed as ester. If alcohol is produced immediately, it must be a 3° alcohol.

$$R_1-\overset{\overset{\displaystyle O}{\|}}{C}-O\,R_2 \xrightarrow{H_2O} R_1-\overset{\overset{\displaystyle O}{\|}}{C}-OH + HO-R_2$$

3° alcohol

2. B is carboxylic acid and alcohol C on oxidation gives B. C must be a primary alcohol because 2° alcohols on oxidation give ketone and tertiary alcohol does not oxidize.

3.

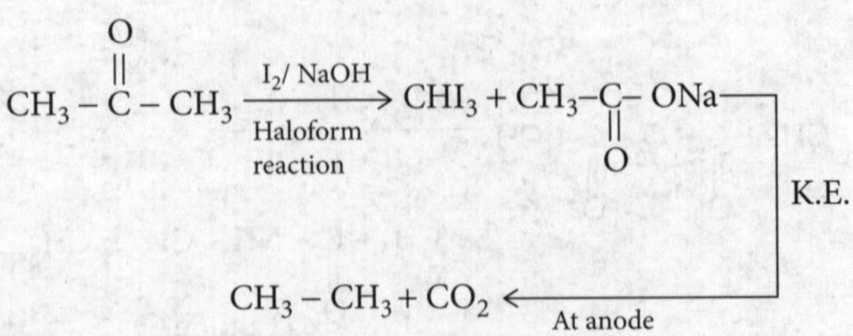

Staggered conformer is the most stable form of ethane.

4. – NH_2 is a better nucleophile than –OH; so acetylation will occur at $-NH_2$

5.

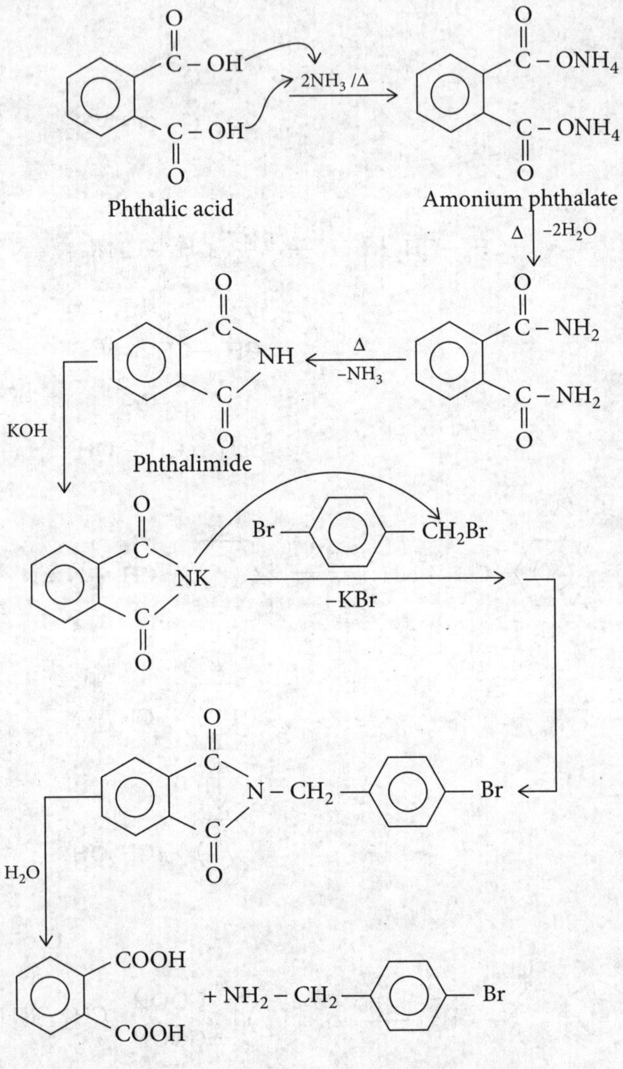

6. – NH_2 group with chloroform ($CHCl_3$) gives Hoffmann carbylamine reaction and isocyanide is formed and then on reduction, all three groups (–NC, –CN and —C(=O)—) are reduced.

7. For idoform test, $\underset{\underset{O}{\|}}{-C}-CH_3$ is required and for phthalic anhydride 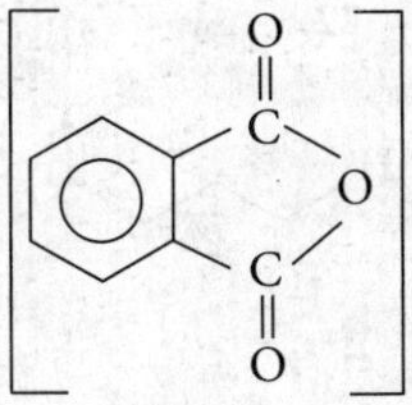 formation, the carbon must be at the ortho position.

8.

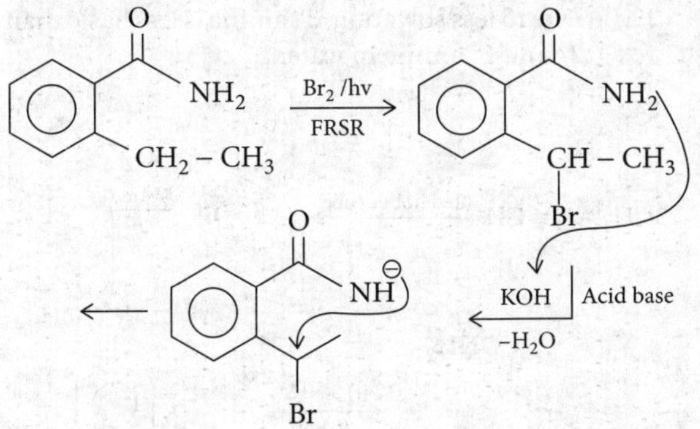

9.

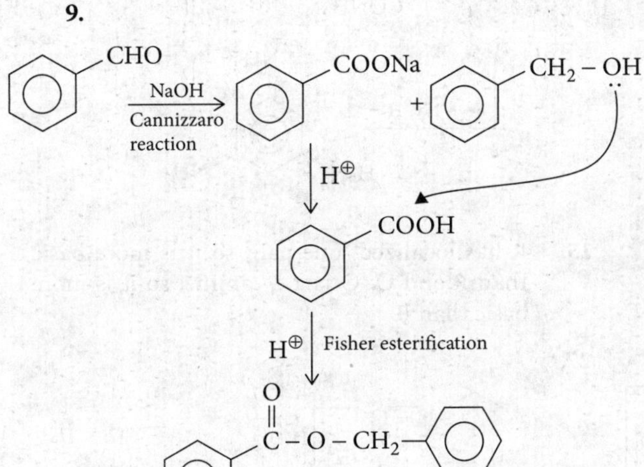

10. A must be acid because NH_3 with acid gives ammonium salt of acid, which on heating gives 1° amide; this gives 1° amine by Hoffmann bromamide degradation.

11. $R-C\equiv N \xrightarrow[\text{Hydrolysis}]{H_2O/H^{\oplus}} R-COOH+NH_3$

12. $P \xrightarrow{\text{Reduction}} Q \xrightarrow{CHCl_3+KOH} R \xrightarrow{\text{Reduction}}$

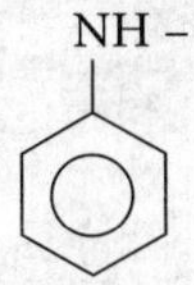

$CHCl_3$ + KOH is a reagent for Hoffmann isocyanide test; so Q is X $-NH_2$ compounds and R is 'X'$-N\equiv C$ and X $-N\equiv C$ gives 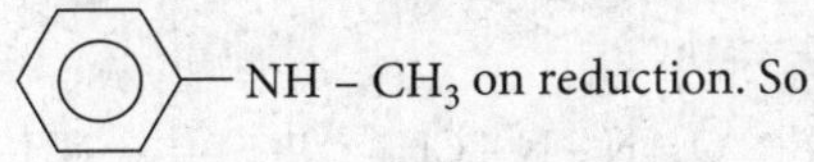 on reduction. So

X = 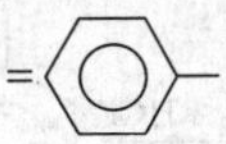 and P = 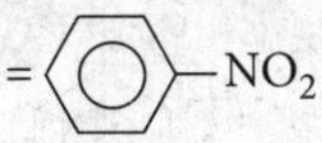

13.

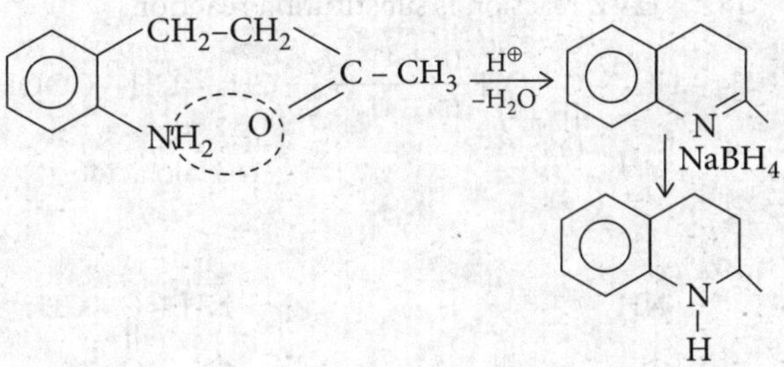

14. N- does not have hydrogen for deprotonation to be stabilized.

15.

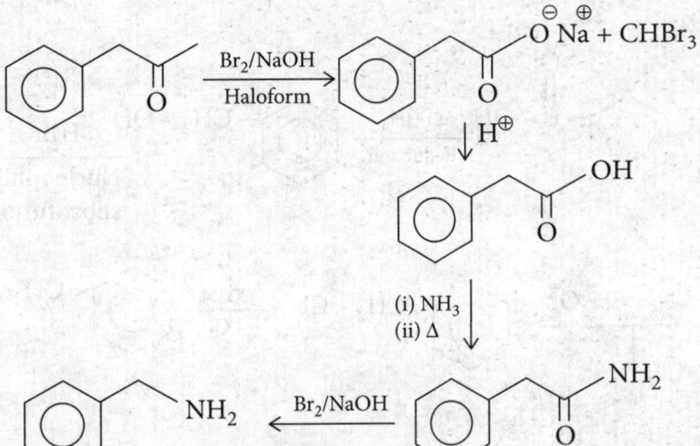

16.

$$CH_3-\overset{O}{\overset{\|}{C}}-NH_2 \xrightarrow[-H_2O]{(i)\ P_2O_5} CH_3-C\equiv N \xrightarrow{H_3O^{\oplus}} CH_3-COOH + NH_3$$

17.

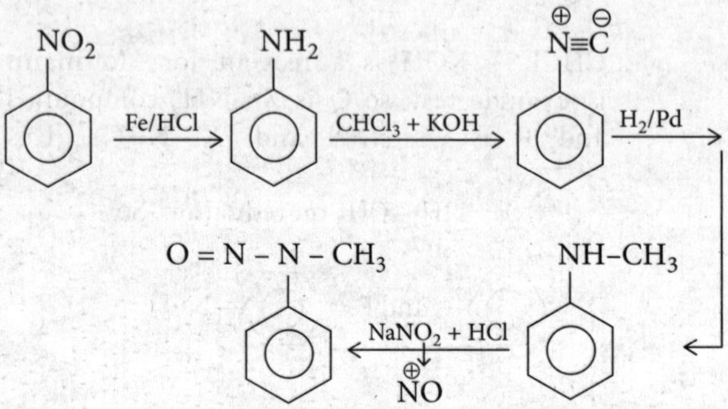

18. HVZ reaction is substitution reaction.

$$CH_3-CH_2-\underset{O}{\underset{\|}{C}}-OH \xrightarrow[(ii)\ H_2O]{(i)\ Red\ P + X_2} CH_3-\underset{X}{\underset{|}{C}H}-COOH$$

α-Halo acid

19.

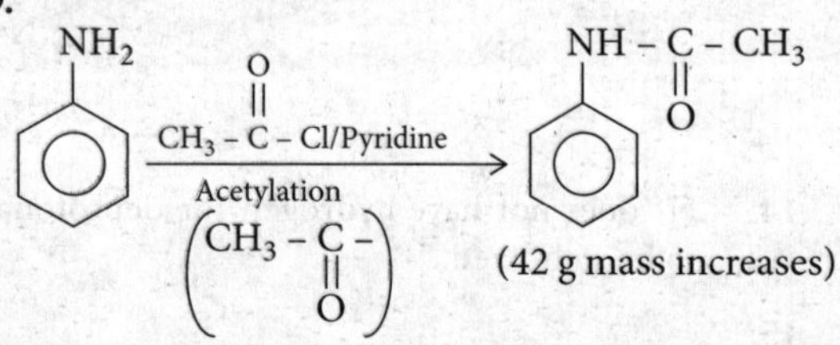

20.

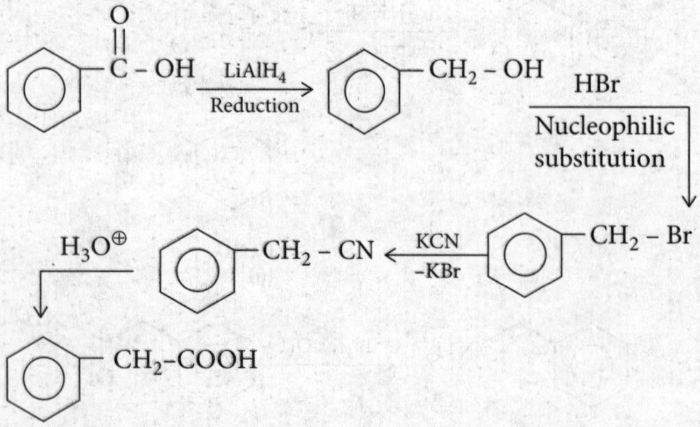

→ CH_2 is different between P and Q and the same functional group.

22.

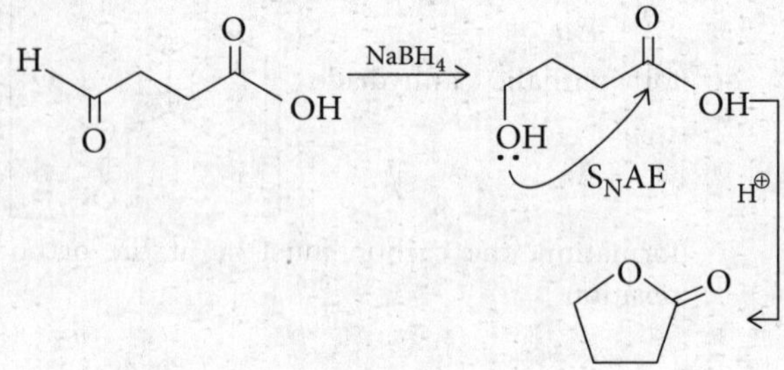

23. Due to less solvation, 3° amine is less basic than 2° and 1° amine in water.

24.

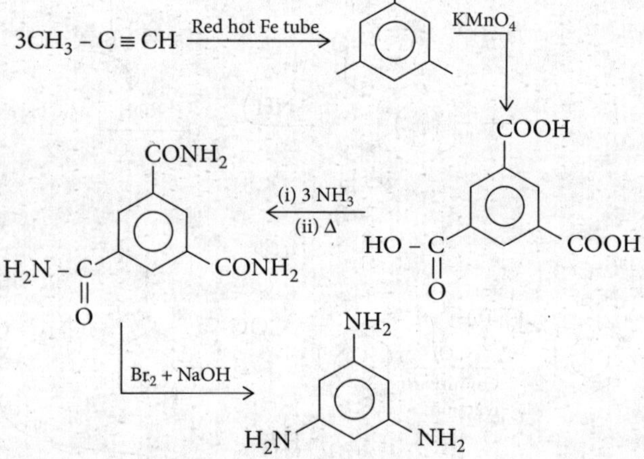

25. R has localized lone pair, so it is more basic than P and Q. Q is a 2° amine, so it is more basic than P.

27.

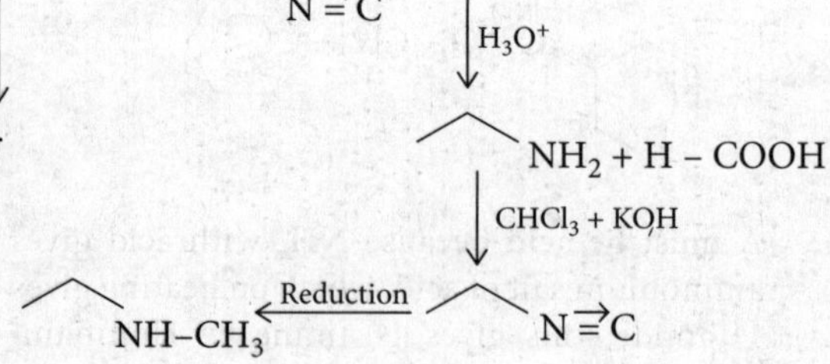

28.

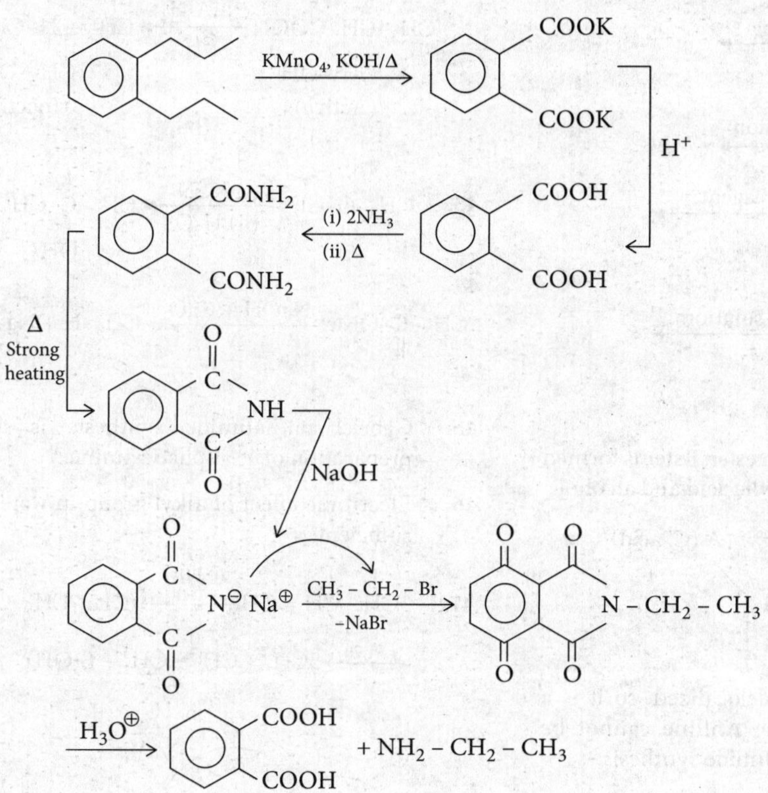

29.

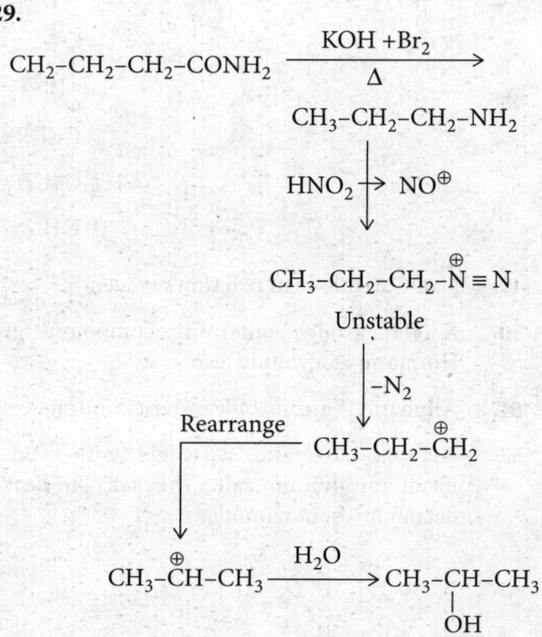

30. $R\text{–}C \equiv N \xrightarrow{SnCl_2 + HCl} R - CH = NH \xrightarrow{H_2O} R - CHO + NH_3$

31.

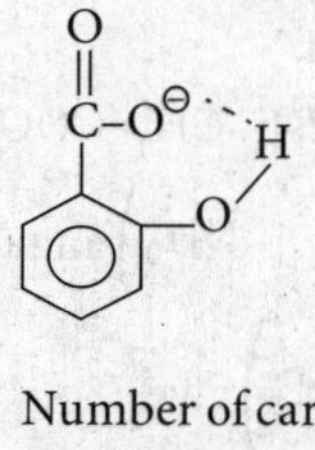

32. Number of carbons is 8 and only aldehyde gives positive test with Tollen's reagent.

33. Boiling point of alkyl halide is higher than in alkane because of dipole moment, not because of hydrogen bonding.

34. –I effect increases acidic strength.

35.

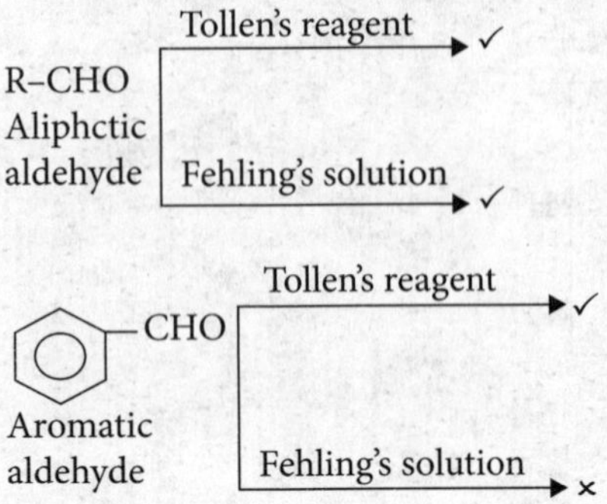

36. Fruity smell means it is an ester. Ester is formed by the reaction of carboxylic acid and alcohol.

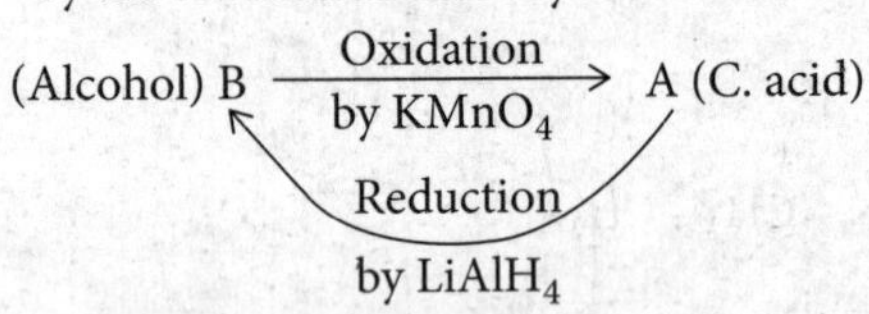

37. Lone pair in aniline is delocalized, so it is a poorer base than amine. Aniline cannot be formed by Gabriel phthalimide synthesis.

38. Product 'C' is ester $[CH_3-\underset{\underset{O}{\|}}{C}-O-CH_3]$

So its metamer is $H-\underset{\underset{O}{\|}}{C}-O-CH_2-CH_3$

Its tautomer is $CH_2=\underset{\underset{OH}{|}}{C}-O-CH_3$

Its functional isomer is CH_3-CH_2-COOH

39. → Isobutyl amine (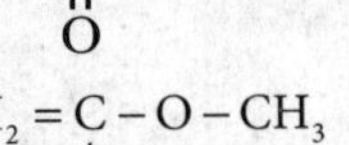) and tertiary butyl amine (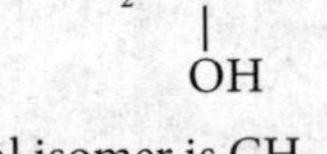) give the same product (3° alcohol)

→ With base, insoluble product is given by 2° amine.

41. Aromatic are less reactive than formaldehyde.

42.

$$\underset{(Active)}{CH_3-\overset{\star}{C}H(CH_2-OH)-COOH} \xrightarrow{LiAlH_4} \underset{(Inactive)}{CH_3-CH(CH_2-OH)-CH_2-OH}$$

43. $CH_3-\underset{\underset{O}{\|}}{C}-CH_3 \xrightarrow[(ii)\ H_2O]{(i)\ KCN} CH_3-\overset{\overset{CN}{|}}{\underset{\underset{OH}{|}}{C}}-CH_3$

44.

$$CH_3-\underset{\underset{O}{\|}}{C}-ONa \xrightarrow[\Delta]{NaOH + CaO} CH_3-H + Na_2CO_3$$

45. Gabriel phthalimide synthesis is for the preparation of 1° aliphatic amine.

46. Electronic effect of alkyl group in water is not sufficient.

47. $3CH_3-CH=CH_2 \xrightarrow{(i)\ BH_3/THF} (CH_3-CH_2-CH_2)_3B$

$$\xrightarrow{H_2O} 3CH_3+CH_2-\underset{\underset{H}{|}}{CH_2}+B(OH)_3$$

48.

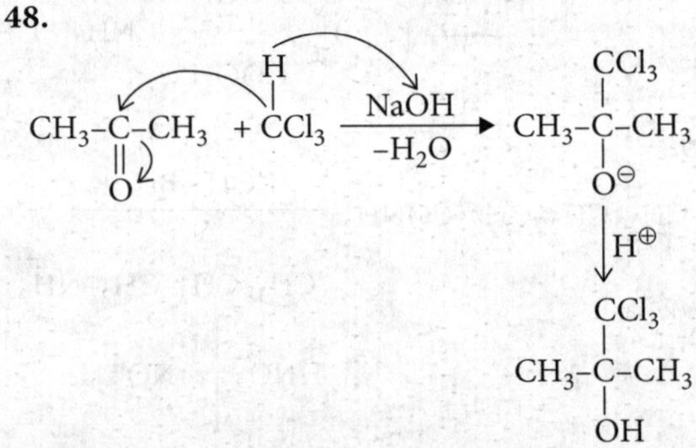

49. NaOCl (Haloform reaction's reagent)

50. X–NH_2 group containing compound gives Hofmann isocyanide test.

51. Aliphatic 1° amine of less steric hindrance.

52. NH_3 is base and it reacts with acid to form ammonium salt. The salt on heating decomposes into amide.

53.

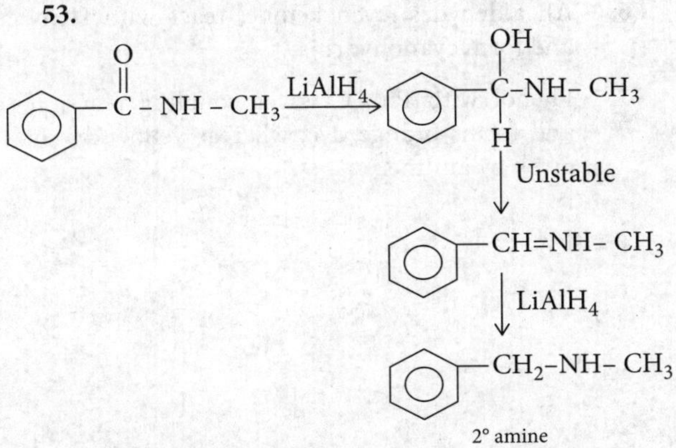

54. Hinsberg's method is based on the number of hydrogen atoms attached to nitrogen.

55.

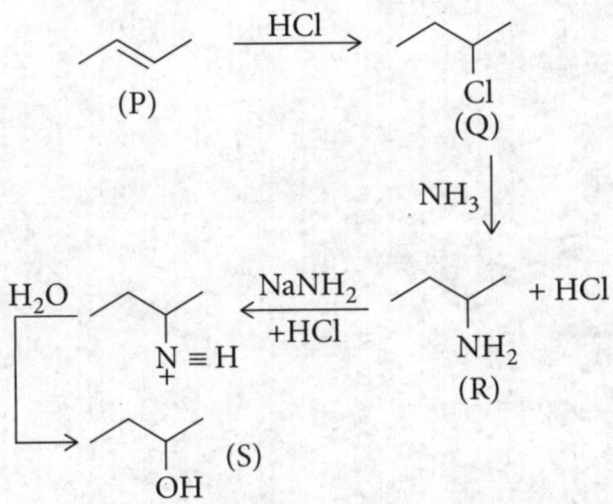

56. Acetylation of the –OH group of salicylic acid gives aspirin; esterification of salicylic acid with methanol gives oil of wintergreen (ester).

57. Derivative of aniline gives diazotization reaction and forms benzenediazonium salt; this means $-NH_2$ must be directly attached to benzene and to be least basic, aniline must have ortho substituent that gives SIP effect to it.

58.

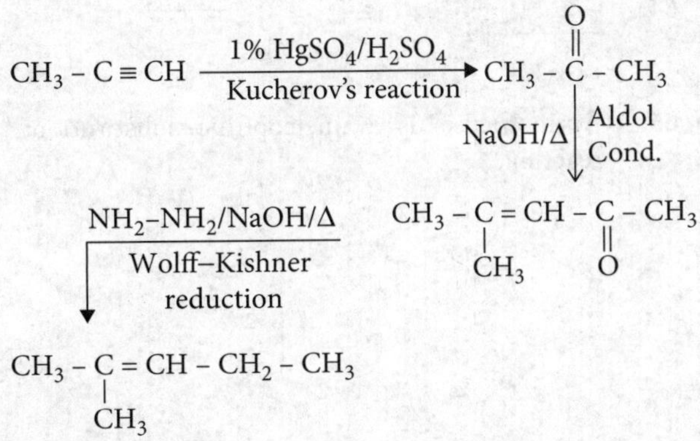

59.

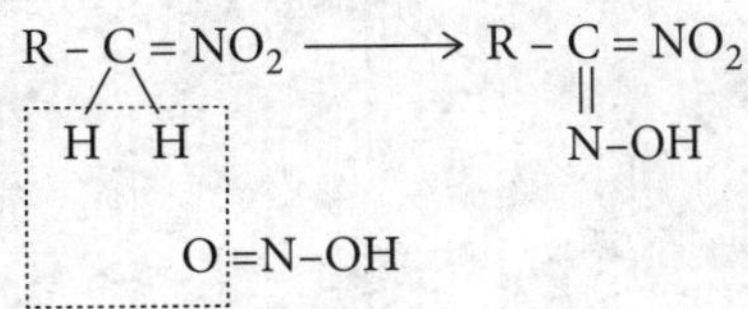

60. Schotten–Baumann reaction is benzoylation of aniline, not acetylation.

61. (a) Cannizzaro reaction
(b) Ammonolysis
(c) Benzoylation

63.

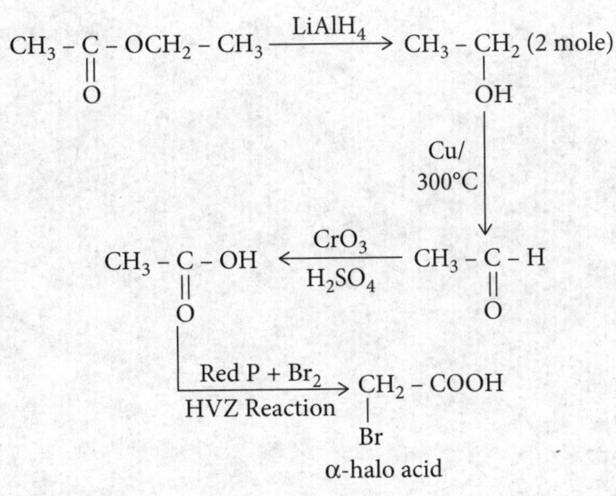

64. 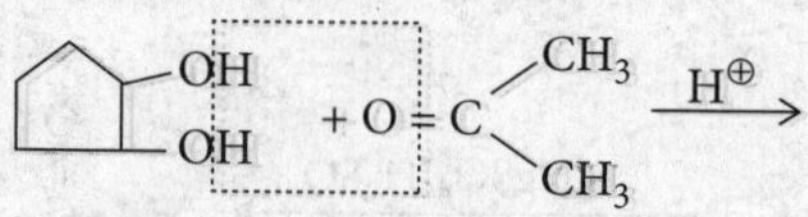

65. Ammonolysis is a nucleophilic substitution reaction.

66. All aldehydes, even ketone, react with HCN and form cyanohydrins.

67. Phenol with PhN_2Cl gives coupling reaction and forms orange dye; whereas yellow dye is given by aniline.

CHAPTER 10

Aromatic Compounds

Level-1

1. Which of the following groups is monovalent?
(a) Benzoyl (b) Benzyl
(c) Benzal (d) Benzylidene

2. How many p electrons are there in the following species:

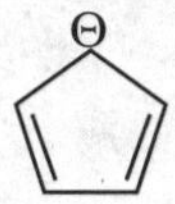

(a) 2 (b) 4
(c) 6 (d) 8

3. The number of benzylic hydrogen atoms in methylbenzene is:
(a) 3 (b) 5
(c) 2 (d) 7

4. The correct match between Item I (starting material) and Item II (reagent) for benzaldehyde is:

Item I	Item II
(I) Benzene	(P) HCl and $SnCl_2$, H_3O^+
(II) Benzonitrile	(Q) H_2, Pd-$BaSO_4$, S and quinoline
(III) Benzoyl chloride	(R) CO, HCl and $AlCl_3$

(a) (I)-(Q), (II)-(R) and (III)-(P)
(b) (I)-(R), (II)-(Q) and (III)-(P)
(c) (I)-(R), (II)-(P) and (III)-(Q)
(d) (I)-(P), (II)-(Q) and (III)-(R)

5. In the sulphonation and acetylation of benzene, the group of effective electrophiles would be:
(a) $SO_3^+, CH_3C\equiv\overset{+}{O}$
(b) $SO_3, CH_3-C\equiv\overset{+}{O}$
(c) SO_3, CH_3CHO
(d) HSO_3, CH_3CHO

6. Which can be used to generate NO_2^+ in the nitration of the benzene ring?
(a) $HNO_3 + H_2SO_4$
(b) $HNO_3 + HClO_4$
(c) N_2O_5
(d) All of the above

7. The product obtained when benzoyl acetic acid is heated with soda lime is:
(a) 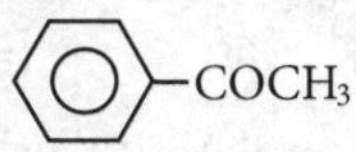
(b) 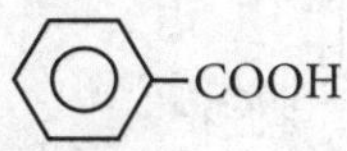
(c) PhCHO
(d) Toluene

8. For the electrophilic substitution reaction involving sulphonation, which of the following sequences regarding the rate of reaction is true?
(a) $k_{C_6H_6} > k_{C_6D_6} > k_{C_6T_6}$
(b) $k_{C_6H_6} < k_{C_6D_6} < k_{C_6T_6}$
(c) $k_{C_6H_6} = k_{C_6D_6} = k_{C_6T_6}$
(d) $k_{C_6H_6} > k_{C_6D_6} < k_{C_6T_6}$

9. p-Nitrotoluene on further nitration gives:
(a) 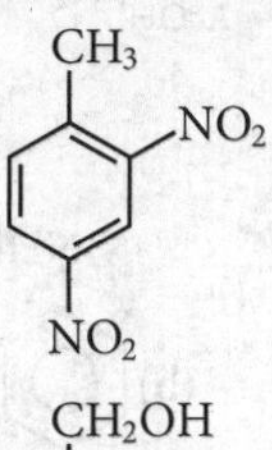
(b) 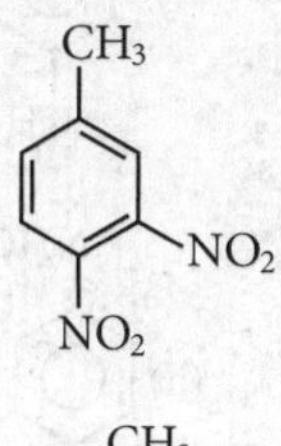
(c) 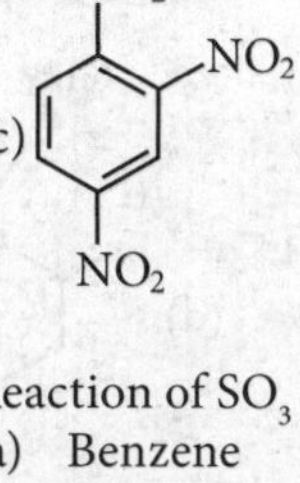
(d) 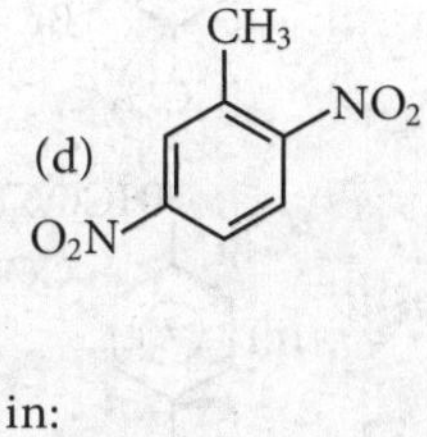

10. Reaction of SO_3 is easier in:
(a) Benzene (b) Anisole
(c) Nitrobenzene (d) Chlorobenzene

11. The major product of the following reaction is:

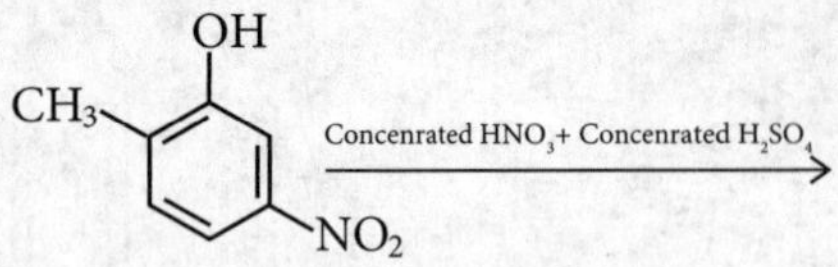

(a) 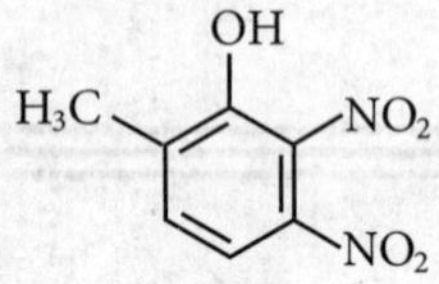

(b) 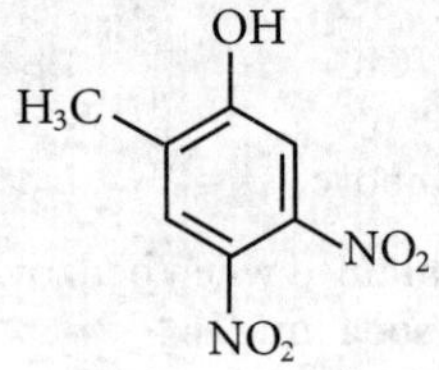

(c) 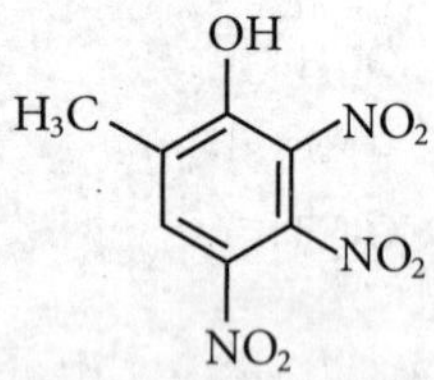

(d) 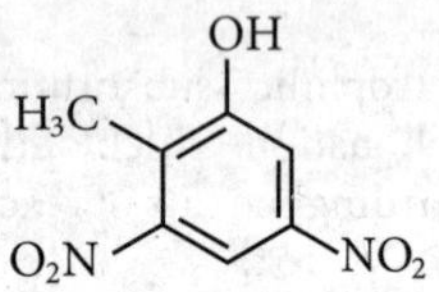

12. In the following reaction sequence, the major product Q is:

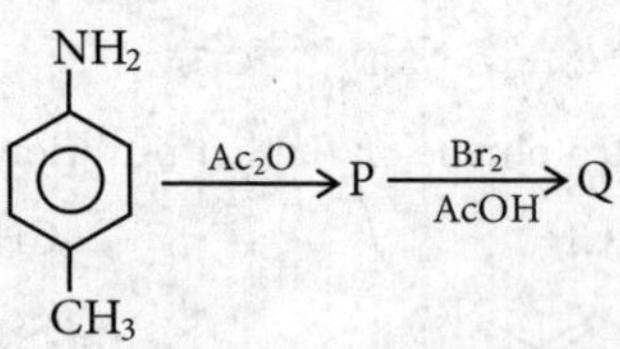

(a) 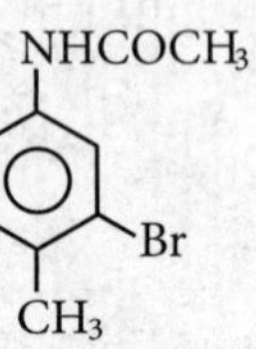

(b) 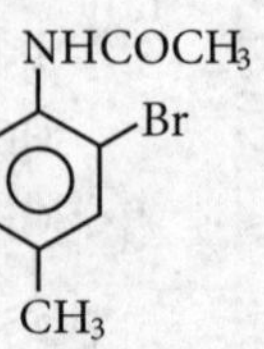

(c) 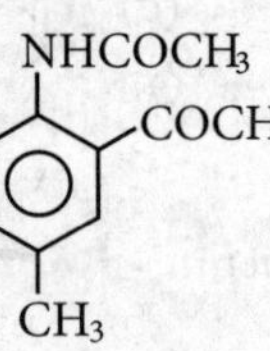

(d) 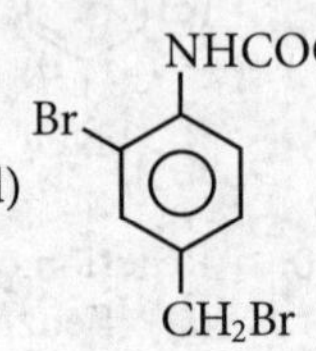

13. Which order is correct for the decreasing reactivity of monobromination of the following compounds:

(I) $C_6H_5OCH_3$ (II) $C_6H_5COOCH_3$
(III) C_6H_6 (IV) $C_6H_5NO_2$

(a) I > II > III > IV
(b) I > III > II > IV
(c) II > III > IV > I
(d) III > I > II > IV

14. Which of the following will undergo sulphonation at the fastest rate?

(a) 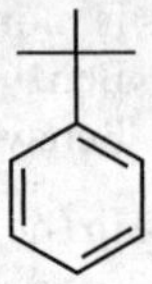

(b) 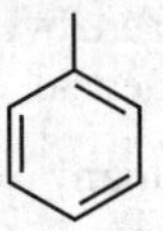

(c) 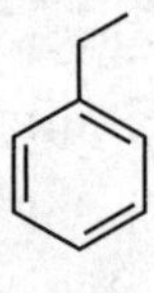

(d) 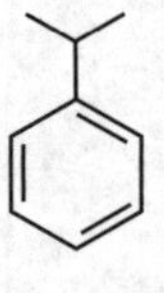

15. An aromatic compound of molecular formula $C_6H_4Br_2$ was nitrated. Then, only one isomer of the formula $C_6H_3Br_2NO_2$ was obtained. The original compound is:

(a) o-Dibromobenzene
(b) m-Dibromobenzene
(c) p-Dibromobenzene
(d) Both (a) and (b)

16. Which of these will produce the highest yield in the Friedel–Crafts reaction?

(a) 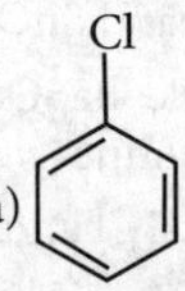

(b) 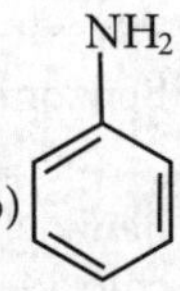

(c) 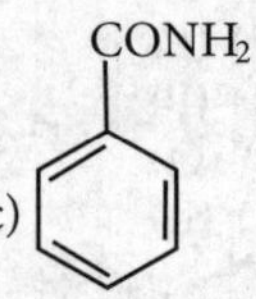

(d) 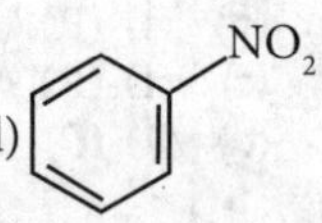

17. The products formed in the reaction of cumene with O_2 followed by treatment with dilute HCl are:

(a) 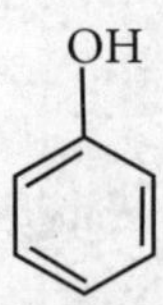 and 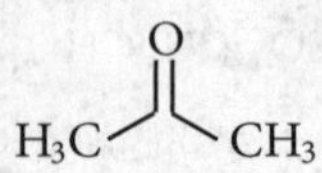

(b) 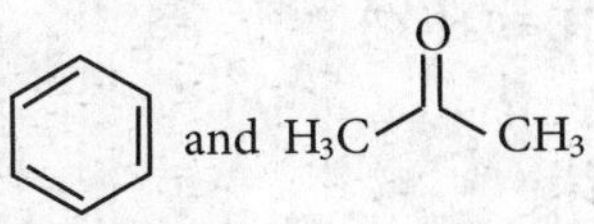

(c) 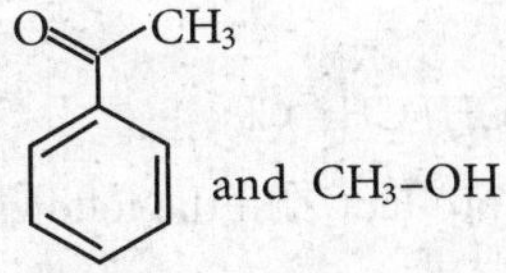

(d) 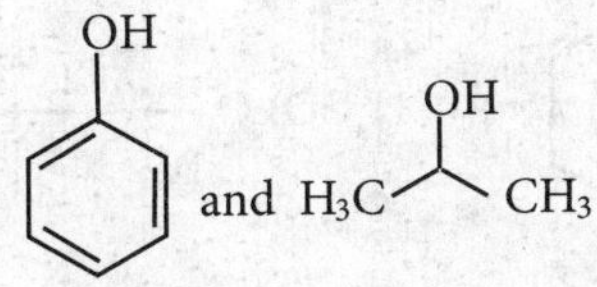

18. Benzene diazonium salt on reaction with KI produces:
(a) Benzene (b) Iodobenzene
(c) Fluorobenzene (d) No reaction

19. Which ring nitration of dimethyl benzene results in the formation of only two nitro dimethyl benzene?

(a) 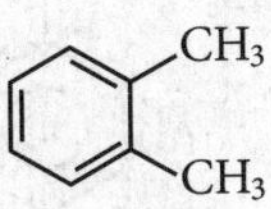

(b) 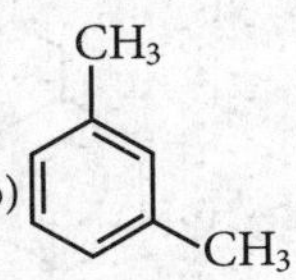

(c) 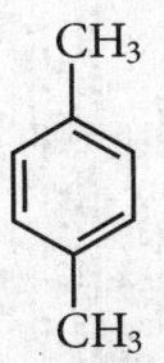

(d) None of these

20. If p-methoxytoluene is nitrated, the major product is:

(a) 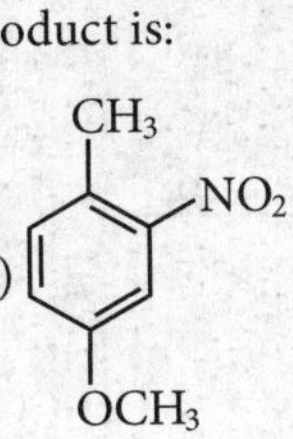

(b) 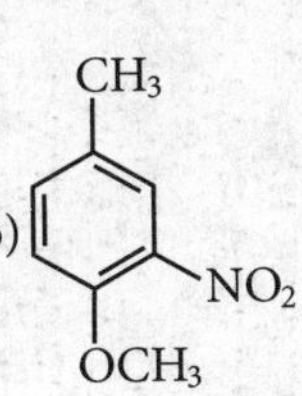

(c) 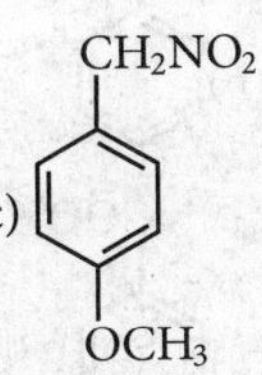

(d) No reaction

21. The major product of the following reaction is:

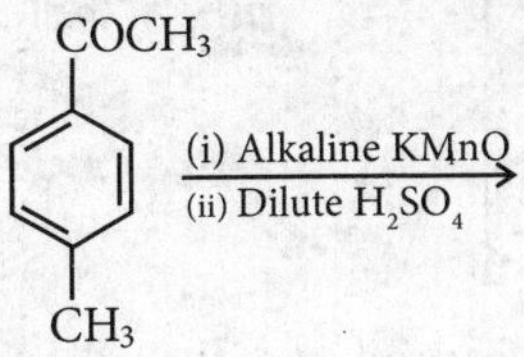

(a) 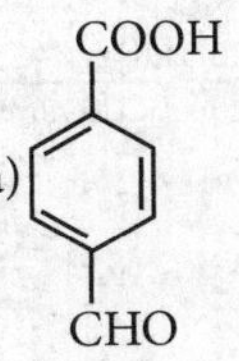

(b) 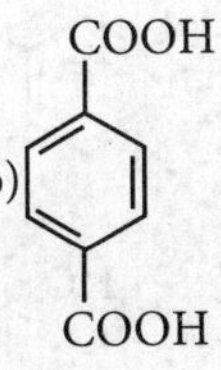

(c) 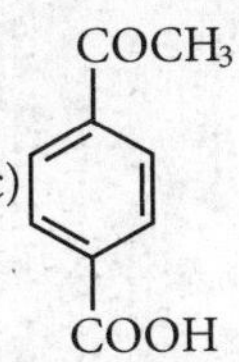

(d) 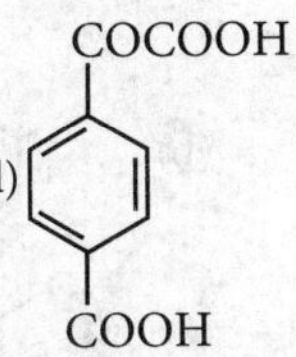

22. Compounds A and B are, respectively:

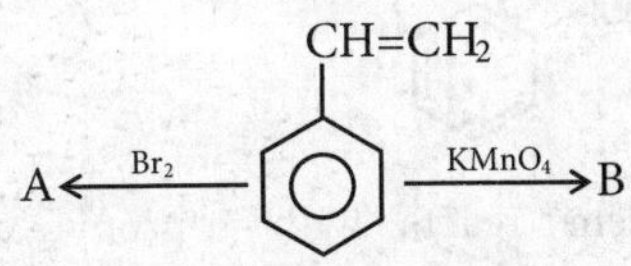

(a) o-Bromostyrene, benzoic acid
(b) p-Bromostyrene, benzaldehyde
(c) m-Bromostyrene, benzaldehyde
(d) Styrene dibromide, benzoic acid

23. A mixture of the following four aromatic compounds on oxidation by $KMnO_4$,Δ gives:

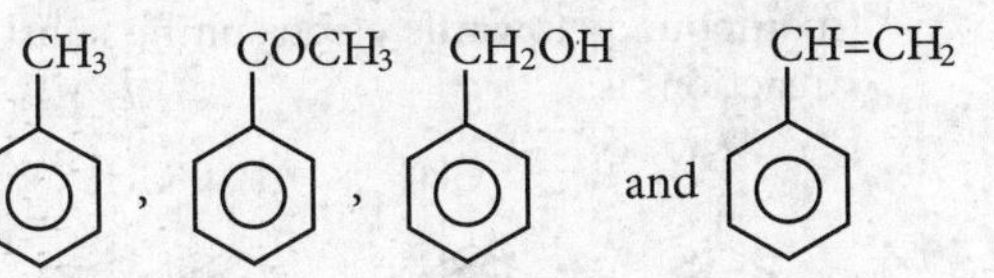

(a) Mixture of $C_6H_5CH_2OH + C_6H_5COOH$
(b) Mixture of $C_6H_5CHO + C_6H_5COOH$
(c) Only C_6H_5COOH
(d) None of the above

24. Which of the following can be isolated as the product of this reaction?

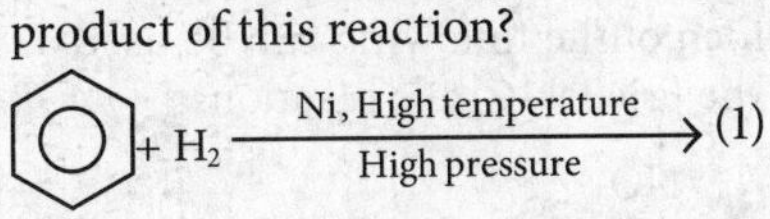

(a) 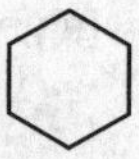 (b) 

(c)  (d) 

25. The major product of the following reaction is:

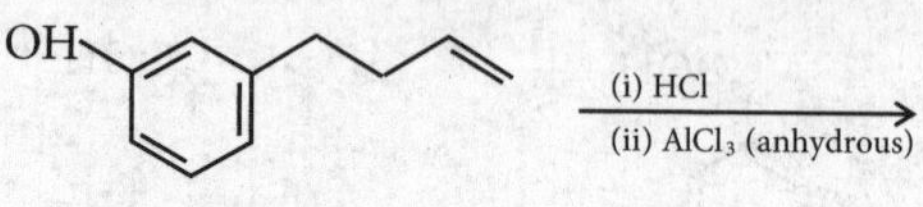

(a) 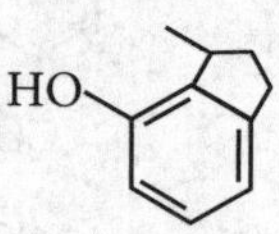

(b) 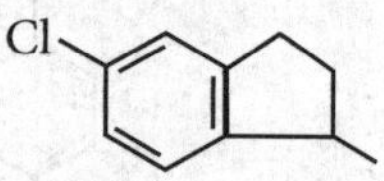

(c) 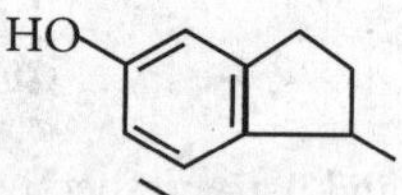

(d) 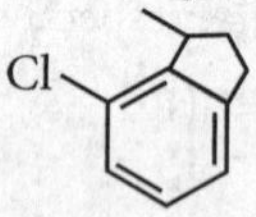

26. Benzene reacts with n-propyl chloride in the presence of anhydrous $AlCl_3$ to give predominantly:
(a) n-Propylbenzene
(b) Benzene
(c) 3-Propyl-1-chlorobenzene
(d) Cumene

27. The order of the reactivity of the following compounds towards electrophilic substitution reactions is:

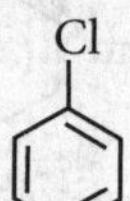 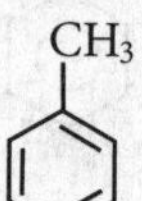 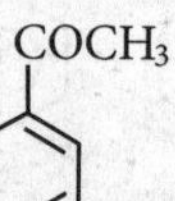

(I) (II) (III)

(a) III < II < I (b) I < III < II
(c) II < I < III (d) III < I < II

28. Which of the following can be used as reagent in the Friedel–Crafts reaction?

(a) 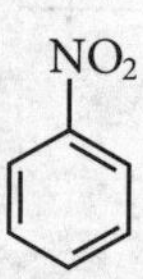

(b) CH_2=CH–Cl

(c) 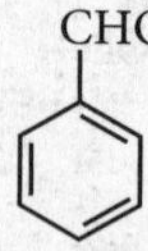

(d) CH_2=CH–CH_2–Cl

29. The major product Z in the following reaction is:

 + $(CH_3CO)_2O \xrightarrow{AlCl_3} X$

$\xrightarrow[HCl]{Zn-Hg} Y \xrightarrow{NBS} Z$

(a) 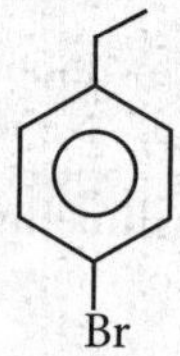 (b) 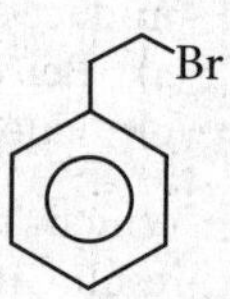

(c) 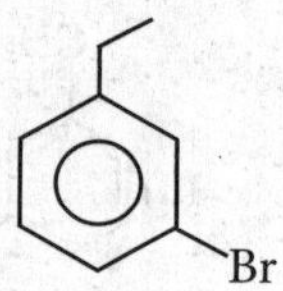 (d) 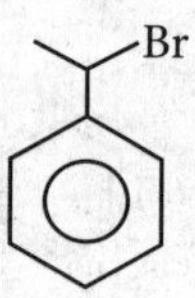

30. Poly substitution is a major drawback in:
(a) Friedel–Craft's alkylation
(b) Friedel–Craft's acylation
(c) Acetylation of aniline
(d) Reimer–Tiemann reaction

31. The major product of the following reaction is:

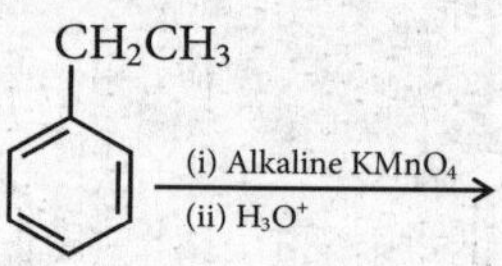

(a) 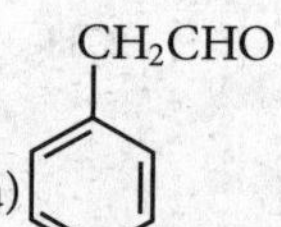 (b) 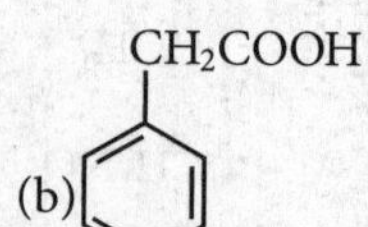

(c) 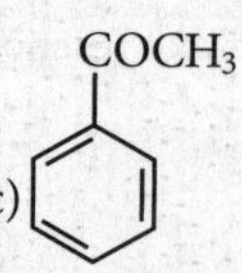 (d) 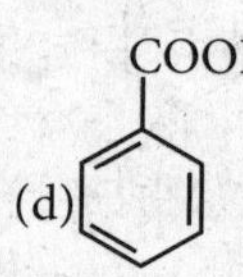

32. The increasing order of reactivity of the following compounds towards aromatic electrophilic substitution is:

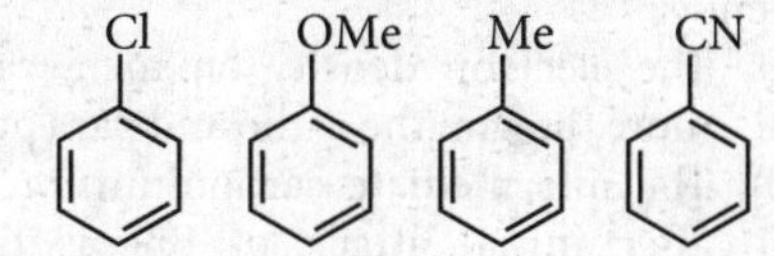

(A) (B) (C) (D)

(a) A < B < C < D (b) D < B < A < C
(c) D < A < C < B (d) B < C < A < D

33. The organic compound that gives the following qualitative analysis is:

Test	Inference
(a) Dilute HCl	Insoluble
(b) NaOH solution	Soluble
(c) Br_2/water	Decolourization

(a) 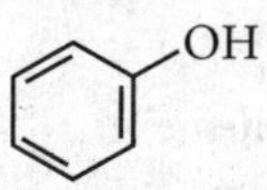 (b) 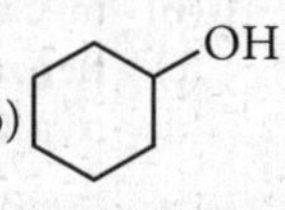

(c) 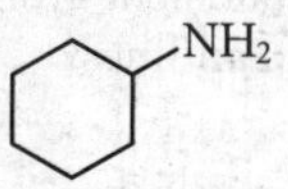 (d) 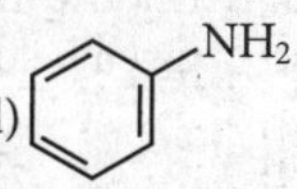

34. Which of the following gives a Friedel–Crafts reaction?

(a) 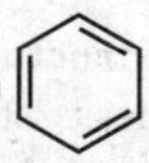 (b) 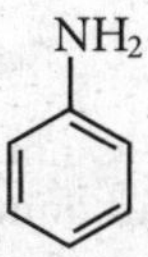

(c) 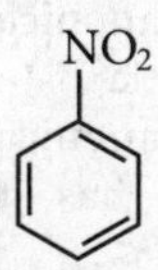 (d) 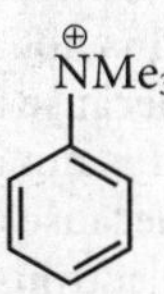

35. Which of the following is not classified as aromatic?
(a) 1, 2, 3-Triphenylcyclopropenium cation
(b) Cyclooctatetraenyl dianion
(c) Azulene
(d) Annulene [10]

36. Which of the following is the name of 1,2,3,4,5,6-hexachlorocyclohexane?
(a) Lindane
(b) Gammexane
(c) Benzene hexachloride
(d) All of the above

37. Which of the following σ-complexes is of the lowest energy?

(a) 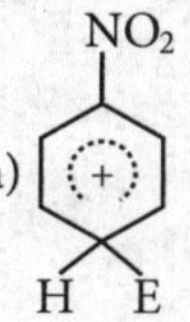 (b) 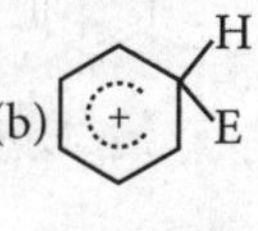

(c) 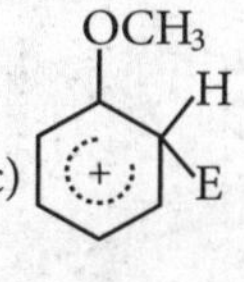 (d) 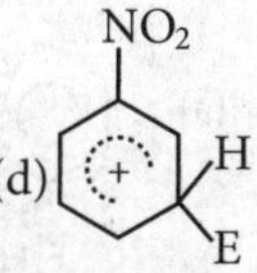

38. In the given chemical reaction, the compounds 'A' and 'B' are, respectively:

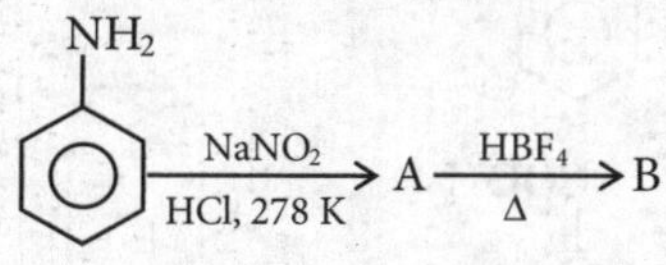

(a) Nitrobenzene and chlorobenzene
(b) Nitrobenzene and fluorobenzene
(c) Phenol and benzene
(d) Benzenediazonium chloride and fluorobenzene

39. The gas that leaked from a storage tank of the Union Carbide plant in the Bhopal gas tragedy was:
(a) Methylisocyanate (b) Methylamine
(c) Ammonia (d) Phosgene

40. The major product C would be:

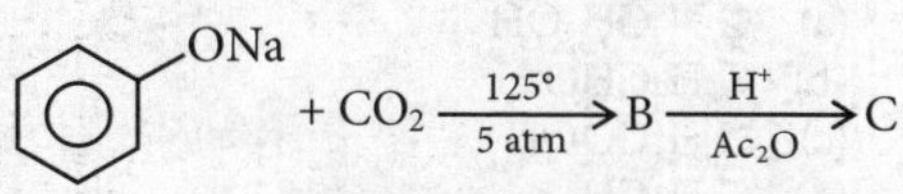

(a) 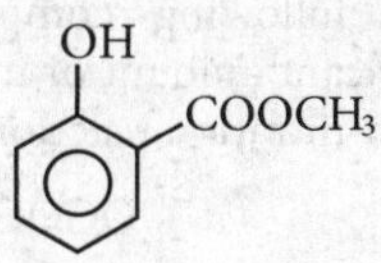 (b) 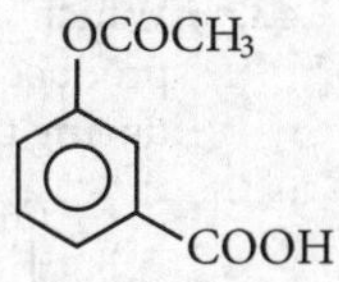

(c) 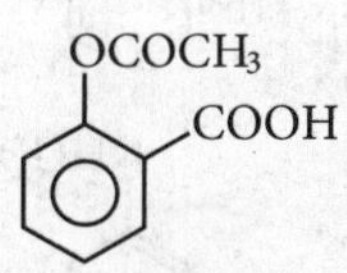 (d) 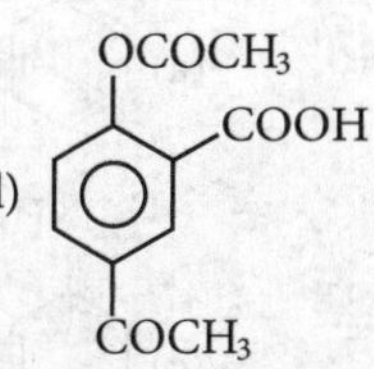

41. In the reaction, the product E is:

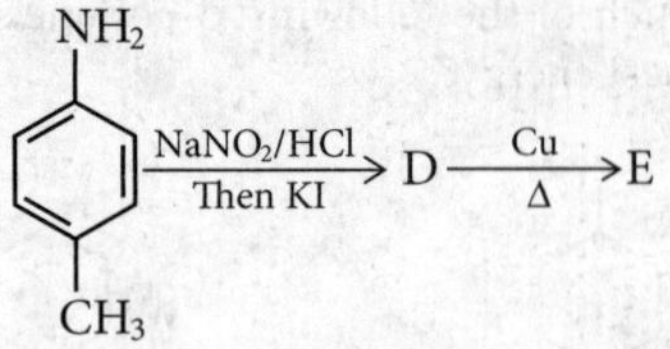

(a) 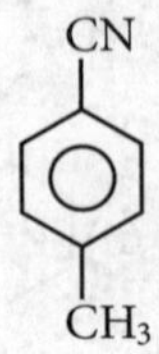

(b) 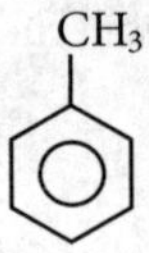

(c) 

(d) 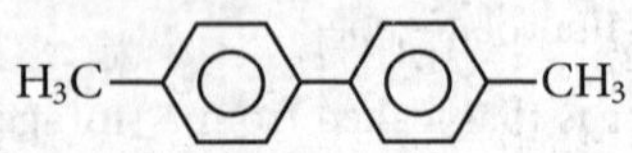

42. In the following sequence of reactions, the product C is:

$$\text{Toluene} \xrightarrow{KMnO_4} A \xrightarrow{SOCl_2} B \xrightarrow[BaSO_4]{H_2/Pd} C$$

(a) $C_6H_5CH_2OH$
(b) C_6H_5CHO
(c) C_6H_5COOH
(d) $C_6H_5CH_3$

43. Which of the following compounds will produce a significant amount of meta product during the mono-nitration reaction?

(a) 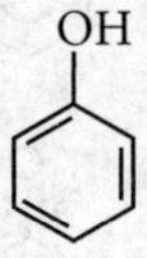
(b) 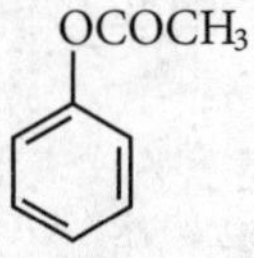

(c) 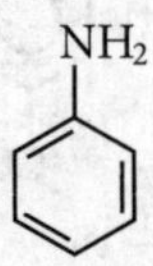
(d) 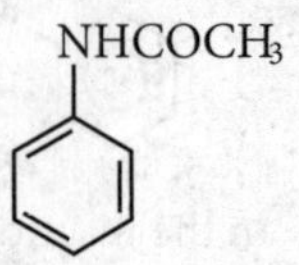

44. When nitrobenzene is treated with Br_2 in the presence of $FeBr_3$, the major product formed is m-bromonitrobenzene. The incorrect statement is:
(a) The electron density on meta carbon is more than on the ortho and para positions.
(b) The intermediate carbonium ion formed after initial attack of Br+ is the least destabilised at the meta position.
(c) Loss of aromaticity occurs when Br^+ attacks at the ortho and para positions and not at the meta position.
(d) Easier loss of H^+ to regain aromaticity occurs from the meta position than from the ortho and para positions.

45. The chlorination of toluene in the presence of ferric chloride gives predominantly:
(a) Benzyl chloride
(b) m-Chlorotoluene
(c) Benzal chloride
(d) o- and p-Chlorotoluene

46. Choose the correct statement from the ones given below for the two anilines:

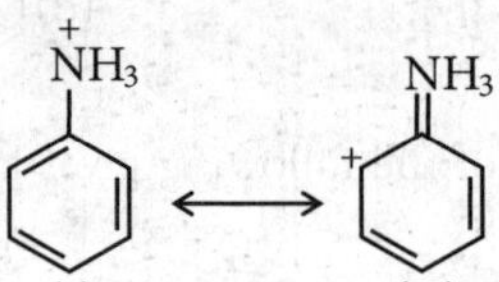

(I) (II)

(a) II is not an acceptable structure because carbonium ions are less stable than ammonium ions
(b) II is not an acceptable canonical structure because it is non-aromatic
(c) II is not an acceptable canonical structure because the nitrogen has 10 valence electrons
(d) II is an acceptable canonical structure

47. Arrange in order of decreasing trend towards S_E reactions:
(I) Chlorobenzene
(II) Benzene
(III) Anilinium chloride
(IV) Toluene
(a) II > I > III > IV (b) III > I > II > IV
(c) IV > II > I > III (d) I > II > III > IV

48. Among the following statements on the nitration of aromatic compounds, the false one is:

(a) The rate of nitration of benzene is almost the same as that of hexadeuterobenzene.
(b) The rate of nitration of toluene is greater than that of benzene.
(c) The rate of nitration of benzene is greater than that of hexadeuterobenzene
(d) Nitration is an electrophilic substitution reaction.

49. Nitrobenzene can be prepared from benzene by using a mixture of concentrated HNO_3 and concentrated H_2SO_4. In the nitrating mixture, HNO_3 acts as a:
(a) Base (b) Acid
(c) Reducing agent (d) Catalyst

50. Benzene diazonium chloride on reaction with phenol in a weakly basic medium gives a colour dye:
(a) o-Hydroxyazobenzene, yellow
(b) p-Hydroxyazobenzene, orange
(c) o-Hydroxyazobenzene, orange
(d) p-Hydroxyazobenzene, red

51. Toluene, when treated with Br_2/Fe, gives p-bromotoluene as the major product, because the CH_3 group:
(a) Is para directing
(b) Creates hindrance at the ortho position
(c) Activates the ring by hyper-conjugation
(d) All of the above

52. The major products P and Q are:

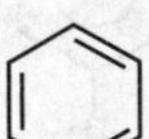 + Cl – CH_2CH_2–CH_3

$\xrightarrow{AlCl_3} P \xrightarrow[(ii)\,H_2O^+]{(i)\,O_2/\Delta} Q + \text{Phenol}$

(a) 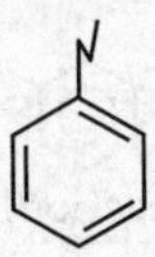 and CH_3CH_2CHO

(b) 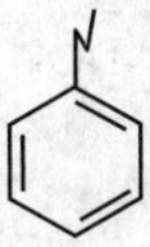 and CH_3COCH_3

(c) 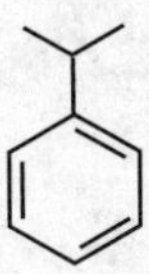 and CH_3COCH_3

(d) 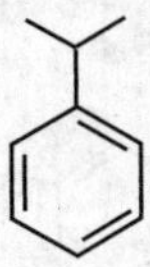 and CH_3CH_2CHO

53. The major product of following reaction is:

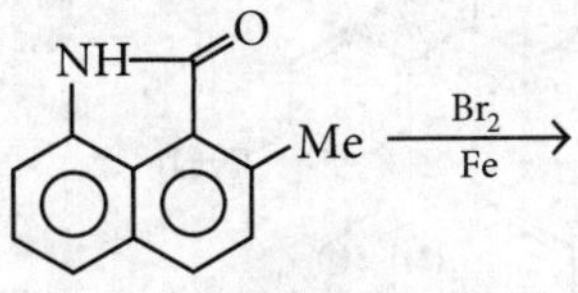

(a) 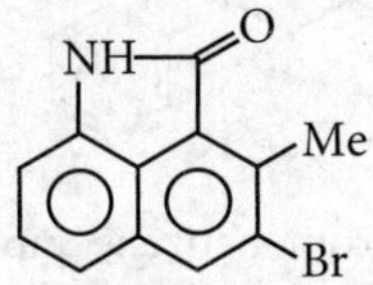

(b) 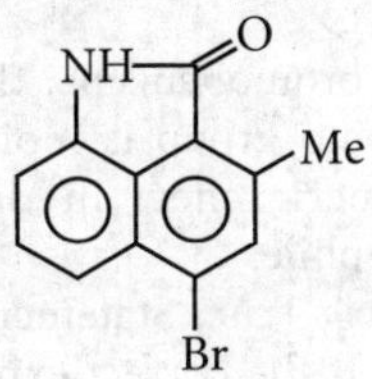

(c) 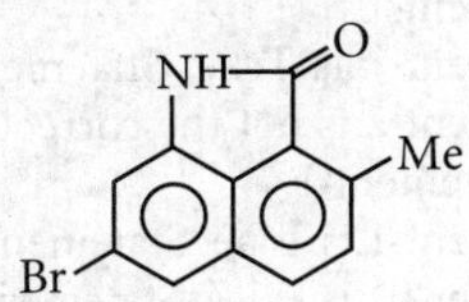

(d) 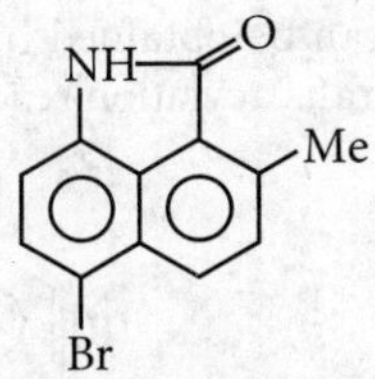

54. In the following reaction, the structure of the major product 'X' is:

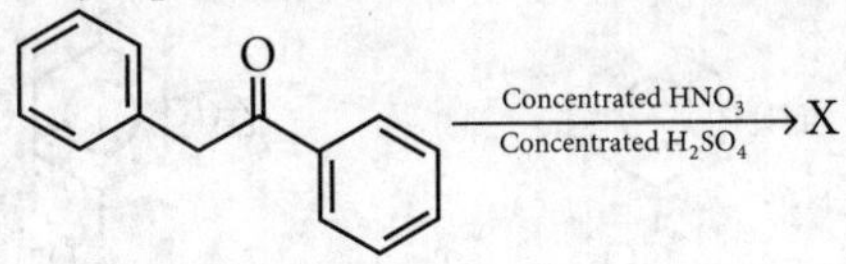

(a) 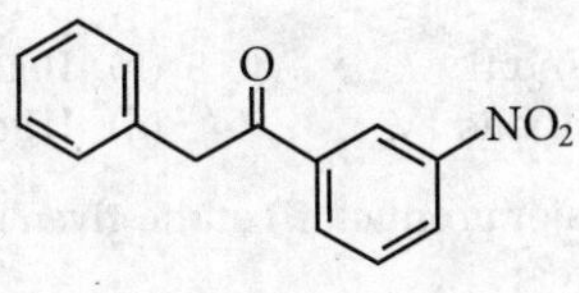

(b) 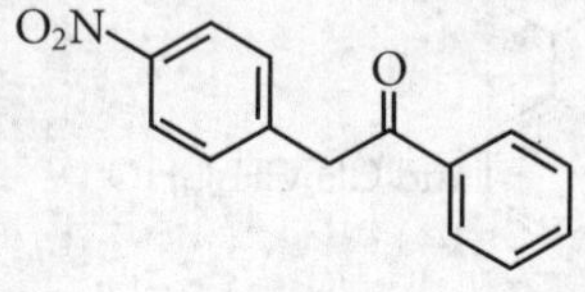

(c) 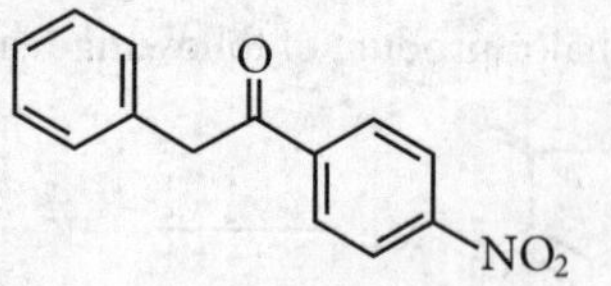

(d) 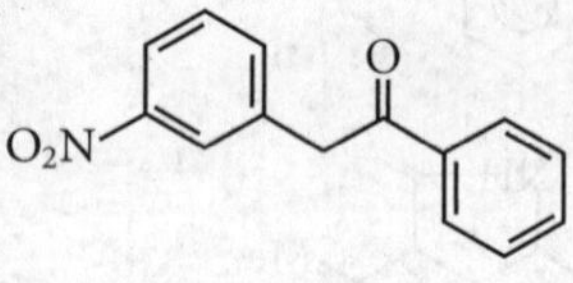

55. **Statement-1:** Bromobenzene upon reaction with Br_2 / Fe gives 1,4-dibromobenzene as the major product.
Statement-2: In bromobenzene, the inductive effect of the bromo group is more dominant than the mesomeric effect in directing the incoming electrophile.
(a) Statement-1 is True, Statement-2 is True; Statement-2 is the correct explanation for Statement-1
(b) Statement-1 is True, Statement-2 is True; Statement-2 is not the correct explanation for Statement-1
(c) Statement-1 is True, Statement-2 is False
(d) Statement-1 is False, Statement-2 is True

56. Which ketones can be obtained in good yield by the Friedel–Crafts acylation reaction?

(I) 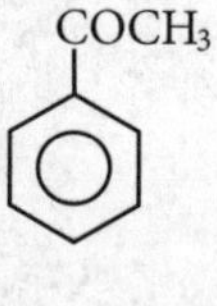
(II) 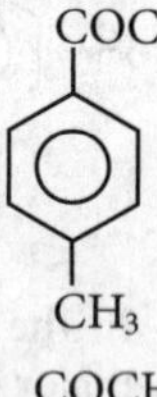

(III) 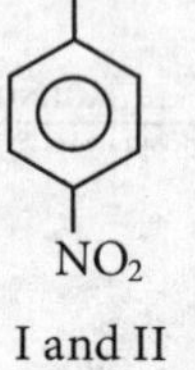
(IV) 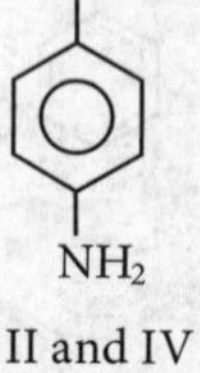

(a) I and II
(b) II and IV
(c) I, II and IV
(d) III only

57. The major product (P) of the given reaction will not give?

$$\text{Cumene} \xrightarrow[\text{(ii) } H^{\oplus}/H_2O]{\text{(i) } O_2/h\nu} \text{Acetone} + (P)$$

(a) 1% $FeCl_3$ test
(b) Na metal test
(c) Iodoform test
(d) White precipitate with Br_2/H_2O

58. Which of the following compounds is more reactive towards electrophilic attack?

(a) 
(b) 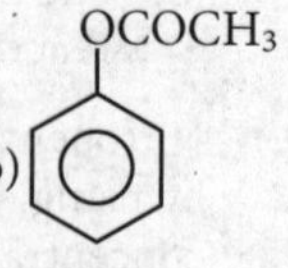

(c) 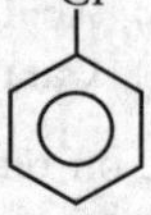
(d) 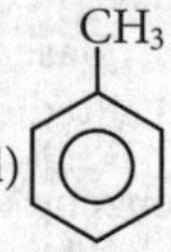

59. The major product of the following reaction with $CH_3Cl/AlCl_3$ produces:

$$\text{Hexane} \xrightarrow[\Delta,\ pr]{Al_2O_3,\ V_2O_5}$$

(a) 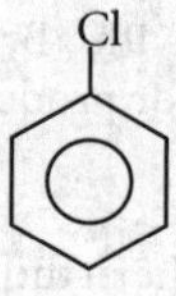
(b) 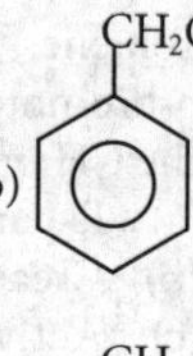

(c) 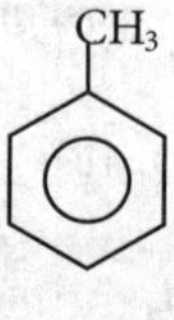
(d) 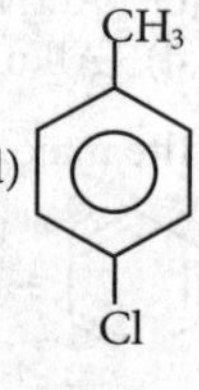

60. Which of the following reactions is incorrectly matched?

(a) 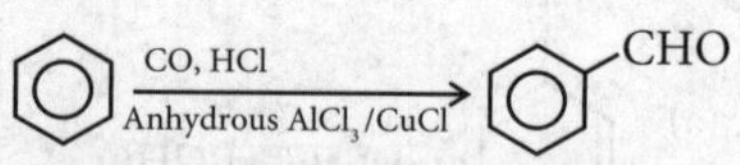
(Gattermann–Koch reaction)

(b) $CH_3–NH_2 \xrightarrow[3KOH]{CHCl_3} CH_3–NC + 3KCl + 3H_2O$
(Carbyl amine reaction)

(c) 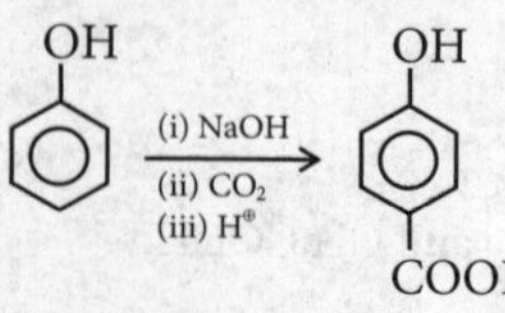
(Kolbe's reaction)

(d) 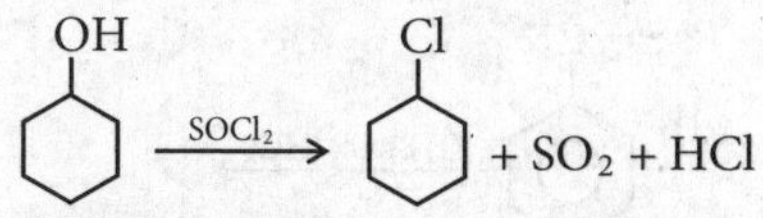

(Darzen process)

61. The major product 'Z' obtained during the following reaction sequence is:

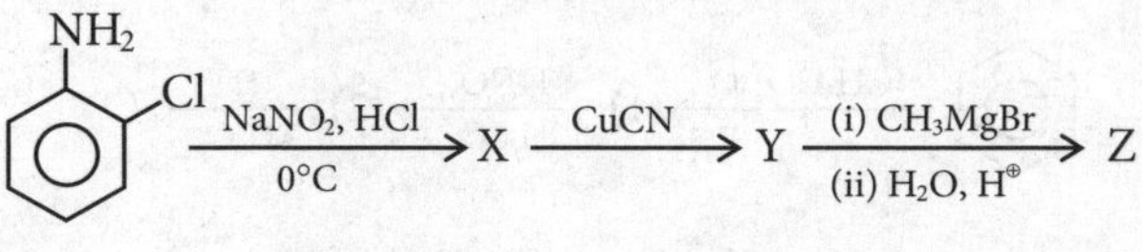

(a) 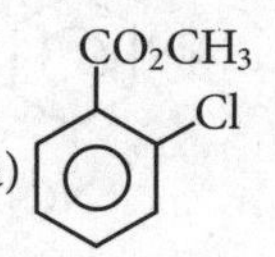

(b) 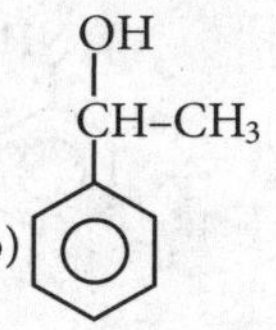

(c) 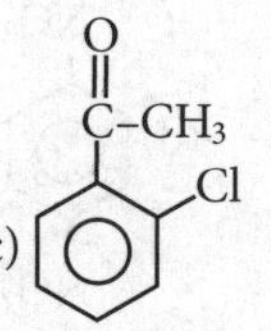

(d) 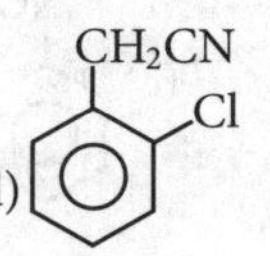

62. The major product of the following reaction is:

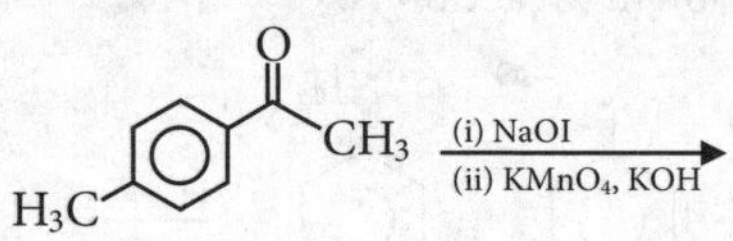

(a) 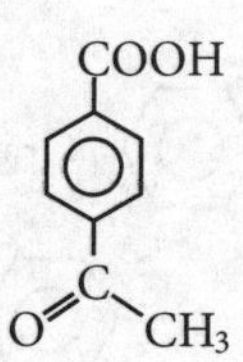

(b) 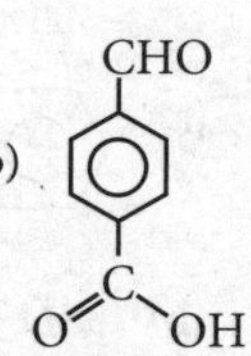

(c) 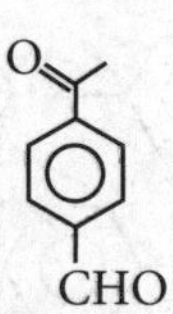

(d) 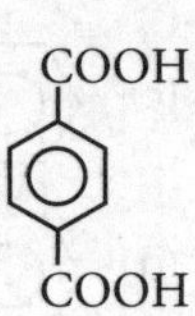

63. Which of the following reagents cannot be used for the protection of the amine ($-NH_2$) group of aniline during electrophilic aromatic substitution reaction, and that too, without changing the orientation effect?

(a) $(CH_3CO)_2O$/py.
(b) CH_3CO_2H/Al_2O_3
(c) $KMnO_4/OH^-$
(d) C_6H_5COCl/py.

64. Which one of the following compounds undergoes hydrolysis most readily by aqueous NaOH?

(a) 

(b) 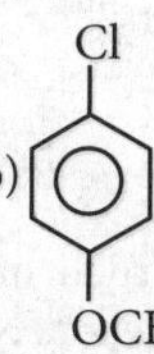

(c) 

(d) 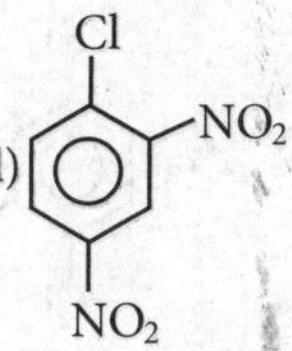

65. For the following sequence, (P) cannot give?

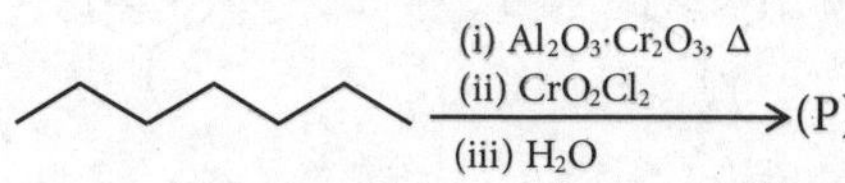

(a) Tollens' test
(b) Cannizzaro reaction
(c) Fehling's test
(d) 2,4-DNP test

66. (1) and (2) in the following reactions are:

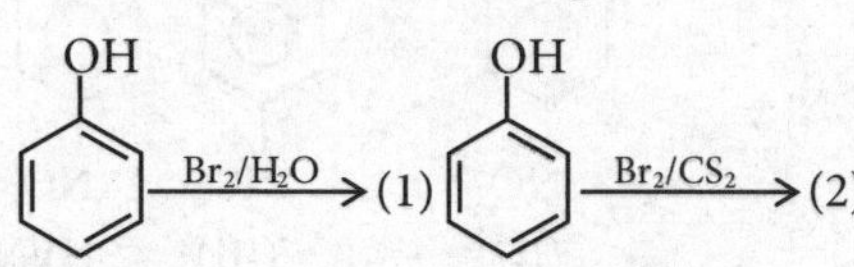

(a) 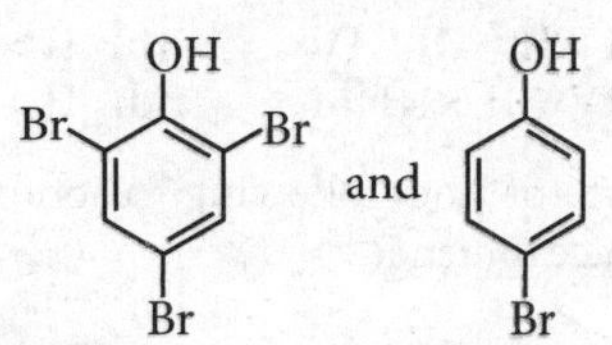

(b) 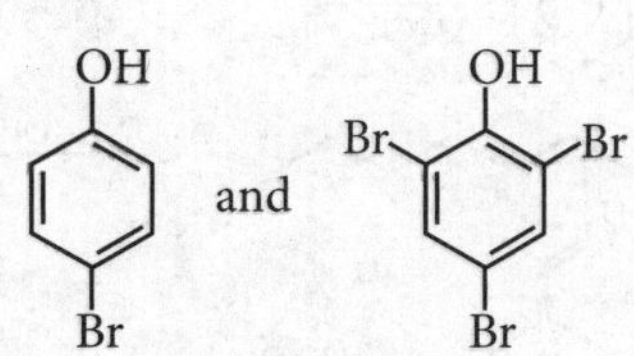

(c) 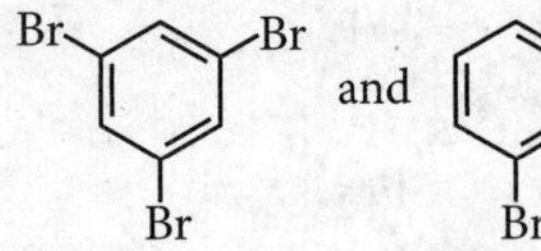

(d) 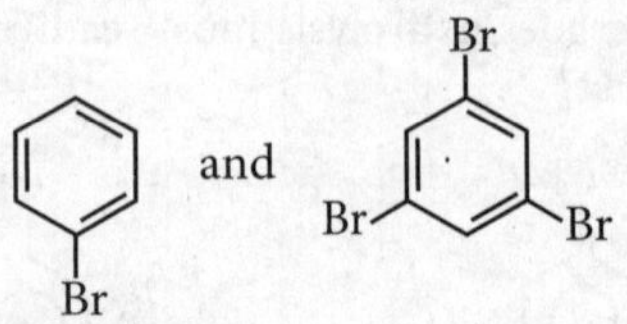

67. Which of the following is the most reactive towards NaOH?

(a) 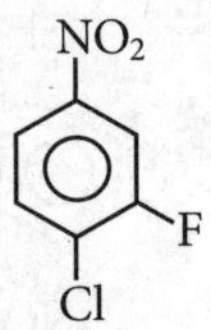
(b) 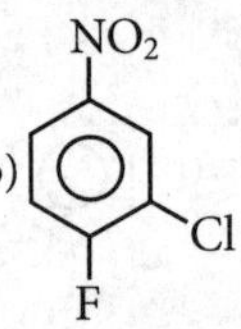
(c) 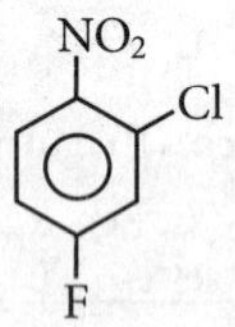
(d) 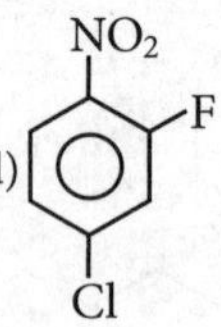

68. The order of reactivity of the given compounds towards nucleophilic substitution with aqueous NaOH is:

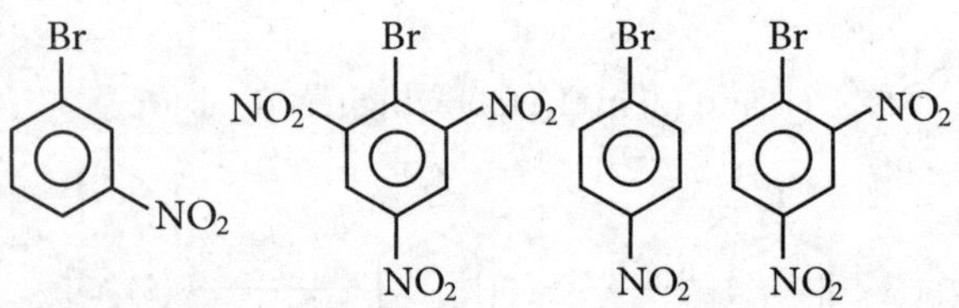

(I) (II) (III) (IV)

(a) I > II > III > IV
(b) II > IV > III > I
(c) IV > II > III > I
(d) II > IV > I > III

69. Which of the following reactions will not produce toluene?

(a) 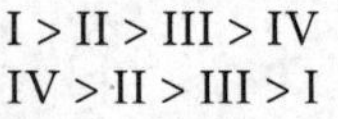

(b) 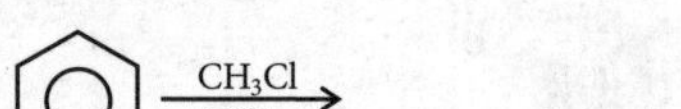

(c) 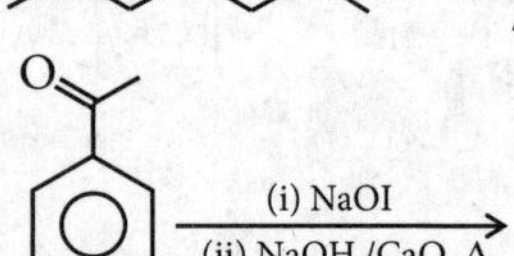

(d) 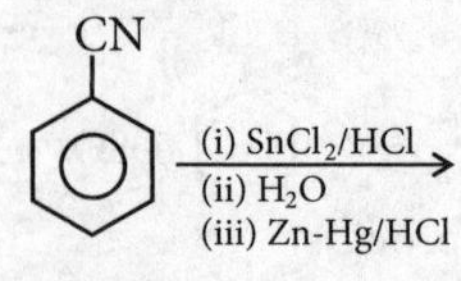

70. The major product of this reaction is:

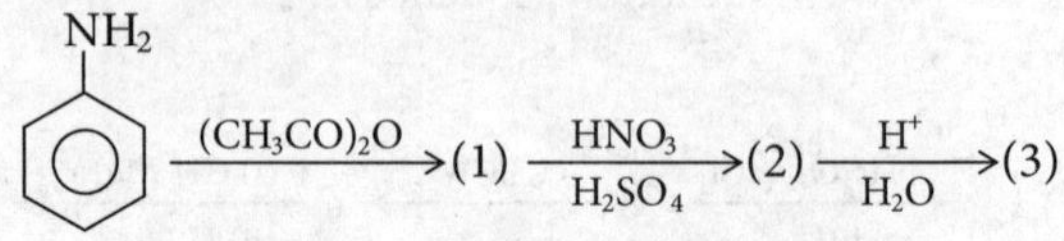

(a) 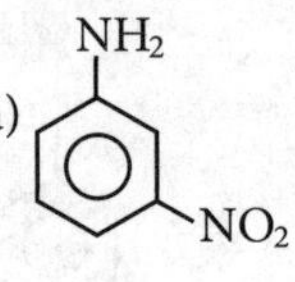
(b) 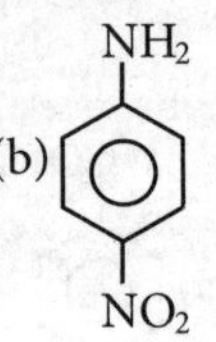
(c) 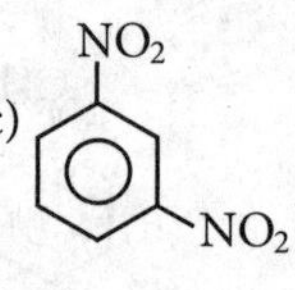
(d) 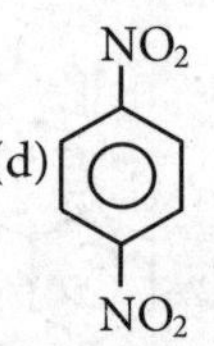

71. The major product and its colour in the following reaction is:

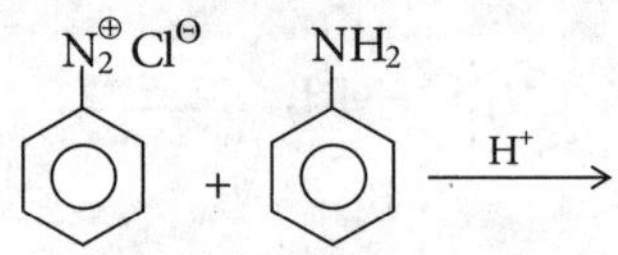

(a) 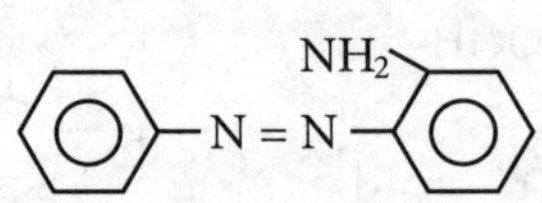 , Orange

(b) 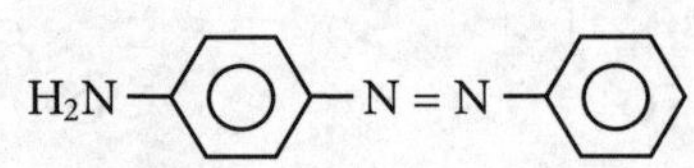 , Red

(c) 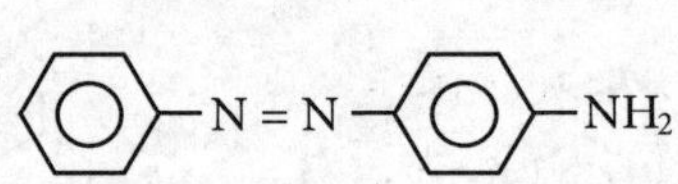 , Yellow

(d) 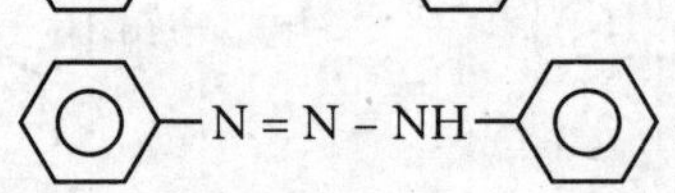 , Orange

72. Aniline (P) on reaction with HNO_3/H_2SO_4 produces three mononitro derivatives Q, R and S in 51%, 2% and 47%, respectively. Which of the following compounds is the least basic?

(a) P
(b) Q
(c) R
(d) S

73. The major product 'Q' of the following reaction is:

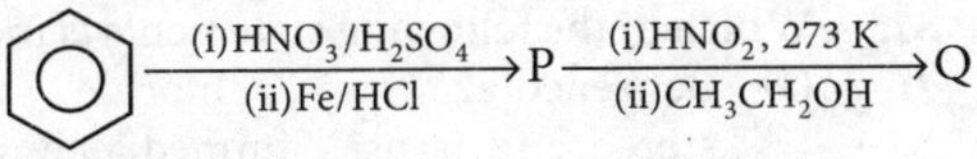

(a) 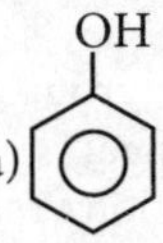
(b) 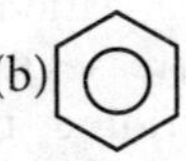
(c) 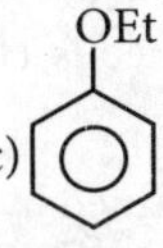
(d) 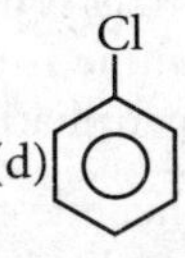

74. Which of the following compounds will show faster aromatic nucleophilic substitution reactions?

(a) 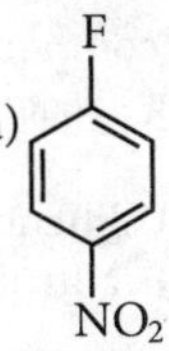
(b) 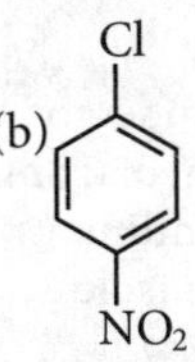
(c) 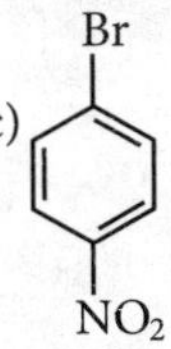
(d) 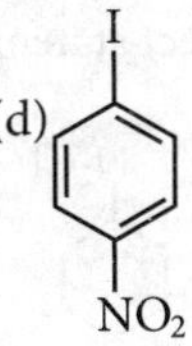

75. Which of the following is the best method to prepare picric acid from phenol?
(a) Concentrated HNO_3
(b) HNO_3/H_2SO_4, 100°C
(c) Dilute HNO_3
(d) (i) Concentrated H_2SO_4, (ii) Concentrated HNO_3

76. Identify the compound Y in the following reaction:

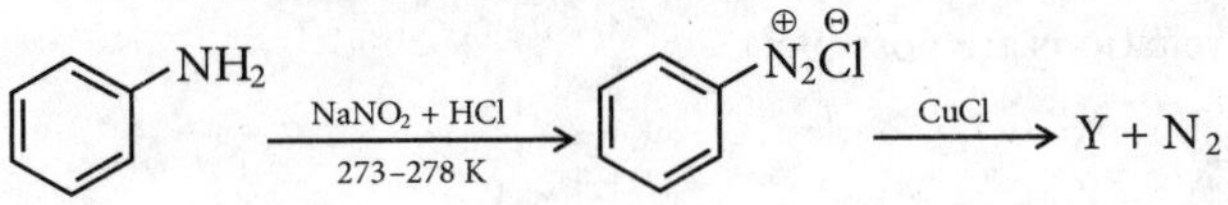

(a) 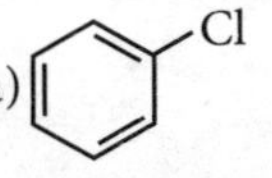
(b) 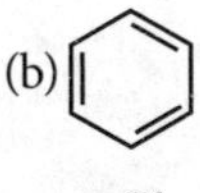
(c) 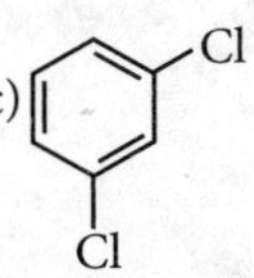
(d) 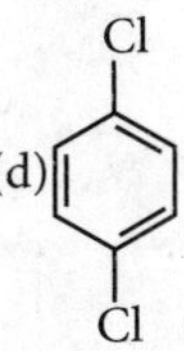

77. Toluene reacts with a halogen in the presence of iron(III) chloride, giving the ortho and para halo compounds. The reaction is:
(a) Electrophilic elimination reaction
(b) Electrophilic substitution reaction
(c) Free radical addition reaction
(d) Nucleophilic substitution reaction

78. Chlorobenzene is formed by the reaction of chlorine with benzene in the presence of $AlCl_3$. Which of the following species attacks the benzene ring in this reaction?
(a) Cl^- (b) Cl^+
(c) $AlCl_3$ (d) $[AlCl_4]^-$

79. Which of the following statements is incorrect?
(a) tert-Butyl bromide undergoes Wurtz reaction to give 2,2,3,3-tetramethylbutane.
(b) Presence of a nitro group at the ortho position increases the reactivity towards nucleophilic substitution.
(c) Aryl iodides can be prepared by the reaction of arenes with iodine in the presence of an oxidising agent.
(d) It is difficult to replace chlorine with –OH in chlorobenzene in comparison to that in chloroethane.

80. The reaction $Ar\overset{+}{N_2}Cl^- \xrightarrow{Cu/HCl} ArCl + N_2 +$ CuCl is called:
(a) Sandmeyer reaction
(b) Gattermann reaction
(c) Claisen reaction
(d) Carbylamine reaction

81. Which of the following cannot be prepared by the Sandmeyer reaction?
(a) Chlorobenzene
(b) Bromobenzene
(c) Iodobenzene
(d) All of the above can be prepared

82. Reduction of nitrobenzene by which of the following reagents does not give aniline?
(a) Sn/HCl (b) Fe/HCl
(c) H_2-Pd (d) Sn/NH_4OH

83. The reagents that can be used to convert benzenediazonium chloride to benzene are:
(a) $SnCl_2/HCl$ (b) CH_3OH
(c) H_3PO_2 (d) $LiAlH_4$

84. The arenium ion not involved in the bromination of aniline is:

(a) 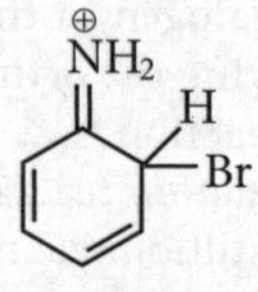

(b) 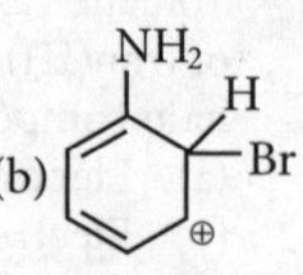

(c) 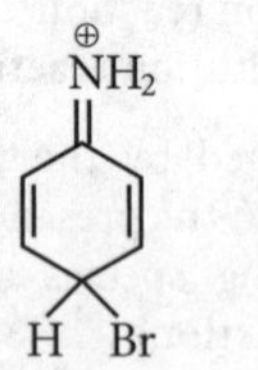

(d) 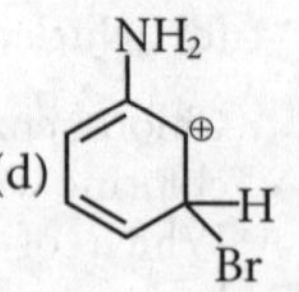

85. Which of the following reactions belongs to electrophilic aromatic substitution?
(a) Bromination of acetaldehyde
(b) Coupling reaction of aryl diazonium salts
(c) Diazotisation of aniline
(d) Acylation of aniline

86. How will you bring out the following conversion?

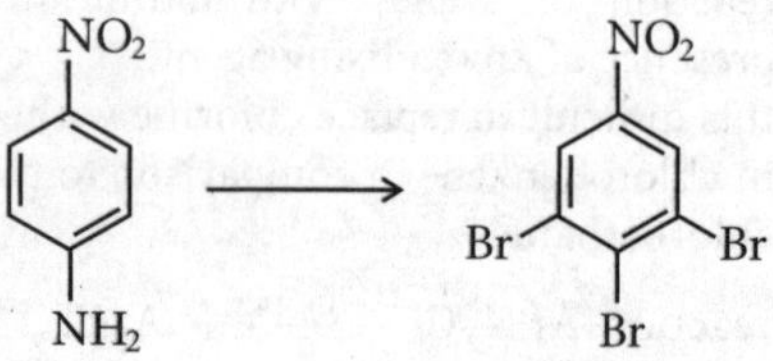

p-Nitroaniline 3,4,5-Tribromonitrobenzene

(a) (i) Br_2/CH_3COOH (ii) HNO_2 (iii) Cu_2Br_2/HBr
(b) (i) Sn/HCl (ii) Br_2/H_2O (iii) HNO_2 (iv) Cu_2Br_2/HBr
(c) (i) HNO_2 (ii) Cu_2Br_2/HBr (iii) Br_2/Fe
(d) (i) H_2/Ni (ii) HNO_2 (iii) Cu_2Br_2/HBr

87. Which of the following statements is incorrect?
(a) Benzenediazonium chloride is not stored and is used immediately after its preparation
(b) Acetylation of the $-NH_2$ group of aniline increases its activating effect
(c) Pyridine in the acylation reaction of amines is used to remove HCl
(d) Aniline is soluble in aqueous HCl due to the formation of salt

88. Acetophenone cannot be obtained by:
(a) Acetyl chloride + Benzene + $AlCl_3$
(b) Benzoyl chloride + Dimethyl cadmium
(c) Methyl benzoate + PhMgCl
(d) Phenyl acetylene + $HgSO_4$ + H_2SO_4

89. Which of the following compounds will not undergo azo coupling reaction with benzenediazonium chloride?
(a) Aniline (b) Phenol
(c) Anisole (d) Nitrobenzene

90. For the following compounds, choose the incorrect statement:

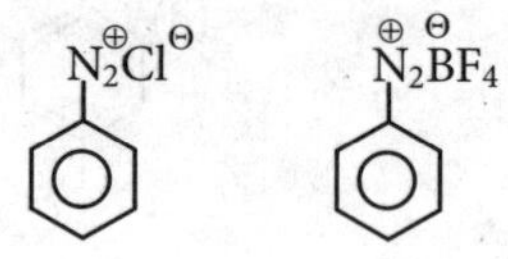

(P) (Q)

(a) P is stable and Q is unstable at room temperature
(b) P is a crystalline, colourless solid
(c) P is readily soluble in water while Q is not
(d) Q, on strong heating, produces N_2 gas

Level-2

1. Consider the following reactions. Which of these reactions are possible?

(a) 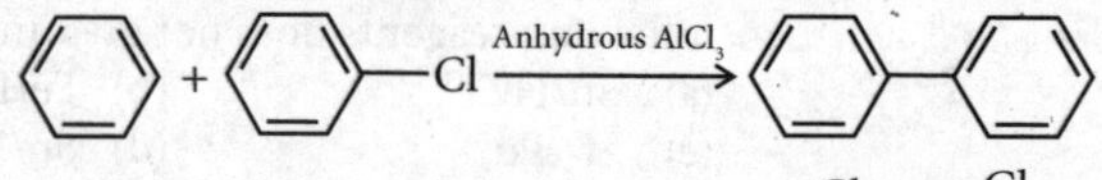

(b) 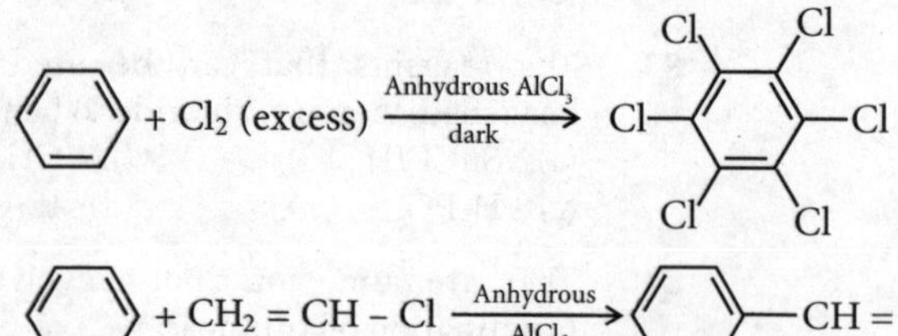

(c) 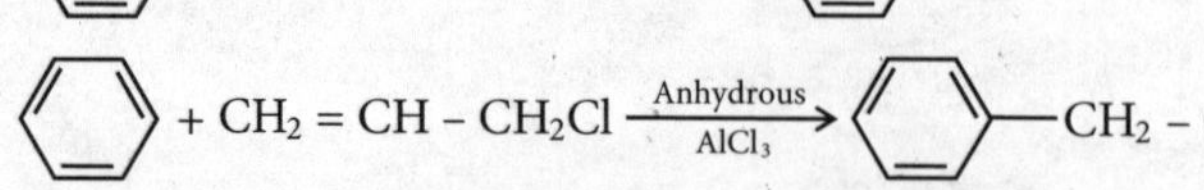

(d) 

(a) (b) and (d) (b) (b), (c) and (d)
(c) (a) and (d) (d) (b) and (b)

2. Consider the following reactions. The compound [P] is:

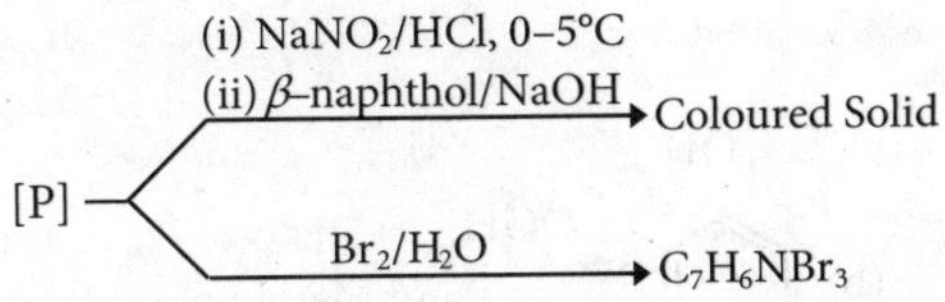

(a) 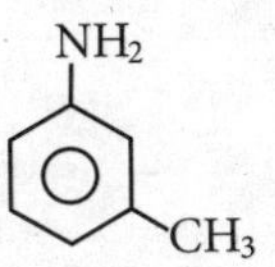
(b) 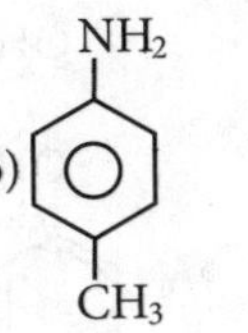
(c) 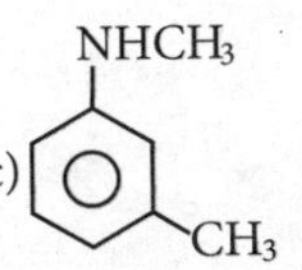
(d) 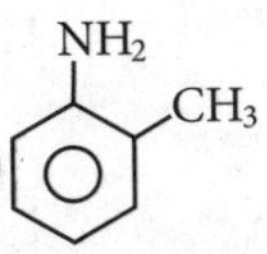

3. The product of which reaction is non-aromatic?
(a) Oxidation of toluene by chromyl chloride
(b) Oxidation of toluene by alkaline $KMnO_4$
(c) Passing propyne in a red hot iron tube
(d) Reaction of benzene with Cl_2 in UV light

4. The compounds A and B in the following reaction are, respectively:

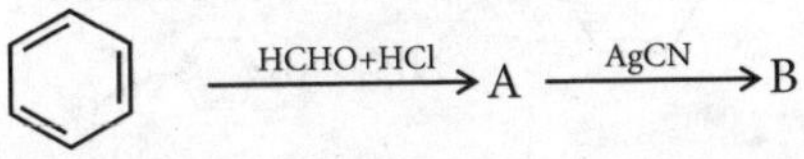

(a) A = Benzyl alcohol, B = Benzyl isocyanide
(b) A = Benzyl alcohol, B = Benzyl cyanide
(c) A = Benzyl chloride, B = Benzyl cyanide
(d) A = Benzyl chloride, B = Benzyl isocyanide

5. The reaction which gives the correct major product is:

(a) 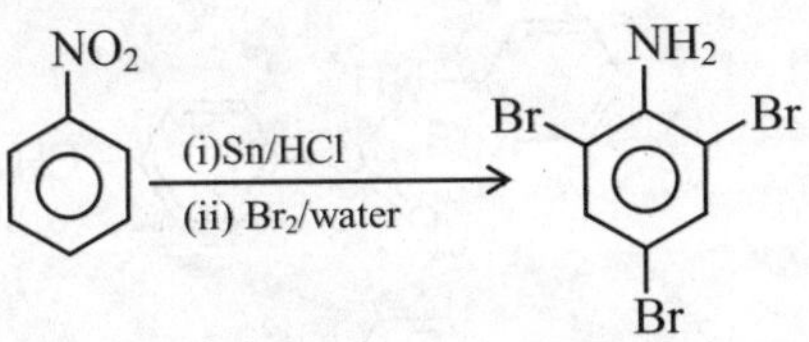

(b) 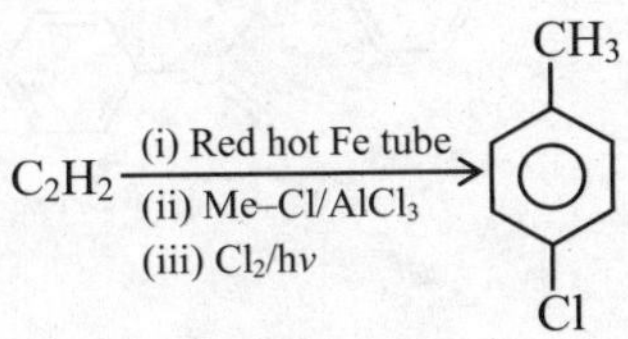

(c) 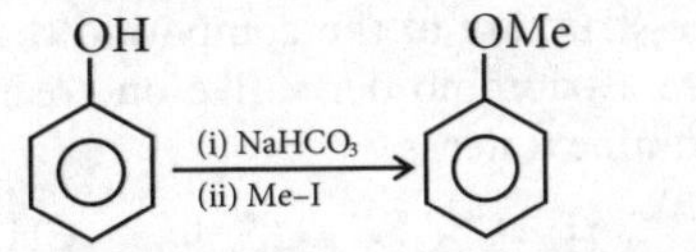

(d) 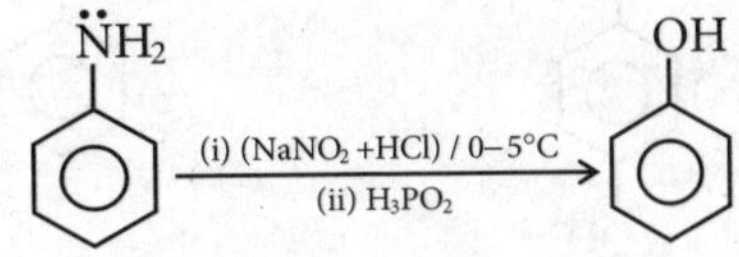

6. The major product of the following reaction is:

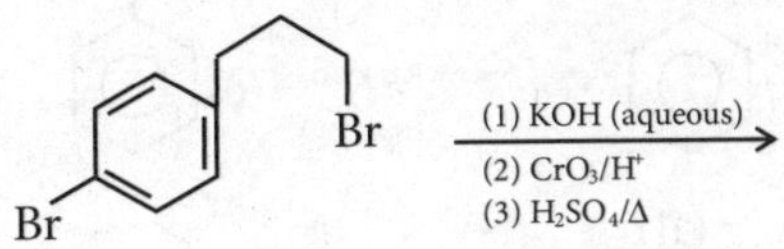

(a) 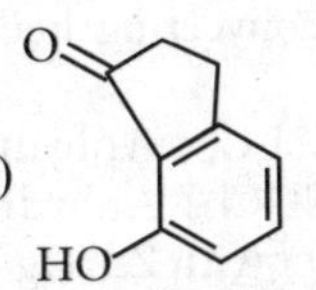
(b) 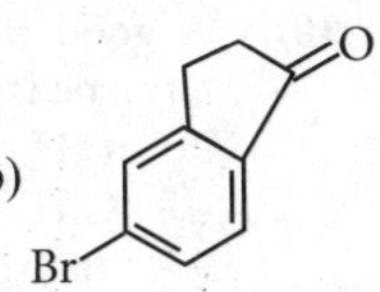
(c) 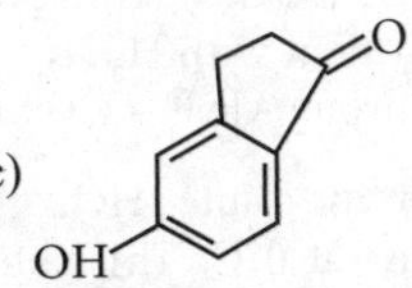
(d) 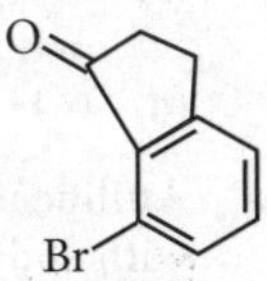

7. In which of the following reactions is t-butyl benzene not formed?
(a) Benzene + Isobutyl chloride, $AlCl_3 \longrightarrow$
(b) Benzene + $(CH_3)_2C = CH_2 \xrightarrow{BF_3.HF}$
(c) Benzene + t-Butyl alcohol $\xrightarrow{H_2SO_4}$
(d) Benzene + 2-Butene / $H_2SO_4 \longrightarrow$

8. The major product Z obtained in the following reaction of m-bromoaniline (P) is:

$$P \xrightarrow[273-278\ K]{NaNO_2/HCl} X \xrightarrow{Cu,\ Br_2} Y \xrightarrow[H_2SO_4]{HNO_3} Z$$

(a) 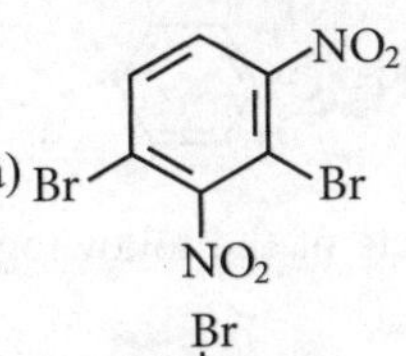
(b) 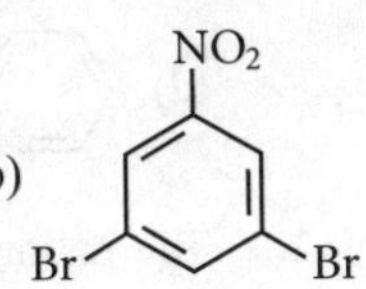
(c) 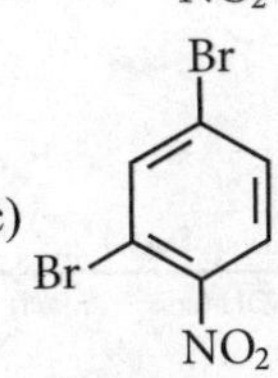
(d) 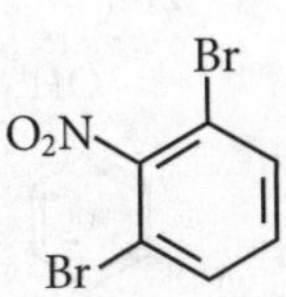

9. The structure of the compound that does not give a tribromo derivative on treatment with bromine water is:

(a) 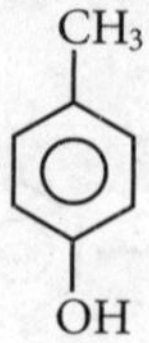
(b) 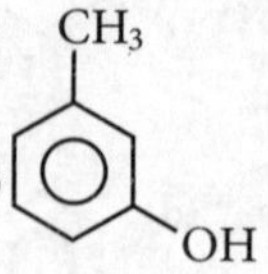
(c) 
(d) 

10. A good method for converting benzene into cumene is:

(a) $C_6H_6 + CH_3CH_2CH_2Cl$ + Anhydrous $AlCl_3$

(b) $C_6H_6 + CH_3CH_2COCl$ + Anhydrous $AlCl_3$ and then treatment with Zn/Hg/HCl

(c) $C_6H_6 + CH_3CH_2COCl$ + Anhydrous $AlCl_3$ and then treatment with H_2 Ni

(d) C_6H_6 + Anhydrous $AlCl_3$ + Cyclopropane

11. Aniline dissolved in dilute HC1 is reacted with sodium nitrite at 0°C. This solution was added drop-wise to a solution containing an equimolar mixture of aniline and phenol in dilute HC1. The major product is:

(a) 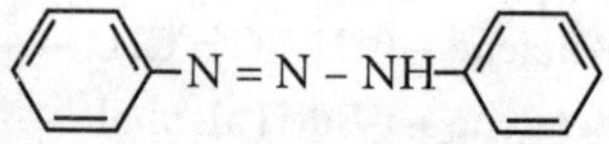
(b) 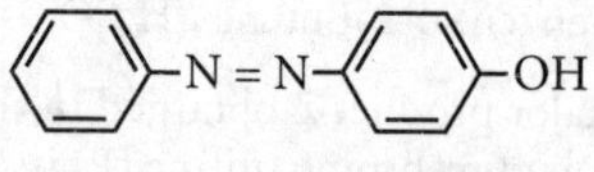
(c) 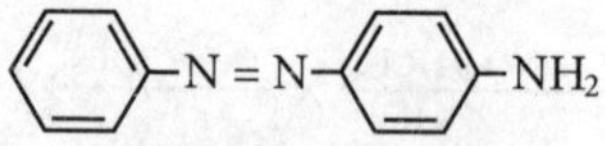
(d) 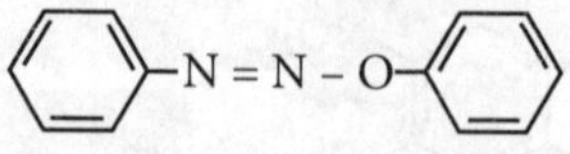

12. The major products of the following reaction are:

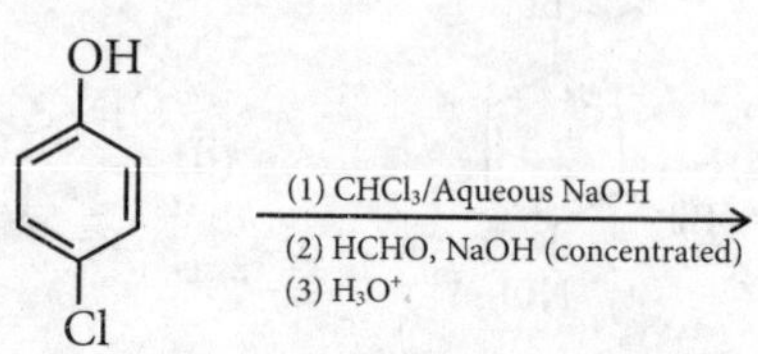

(a) 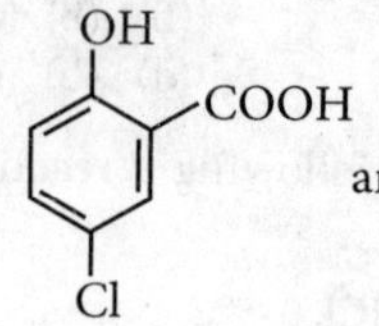 and Methanol

(b) 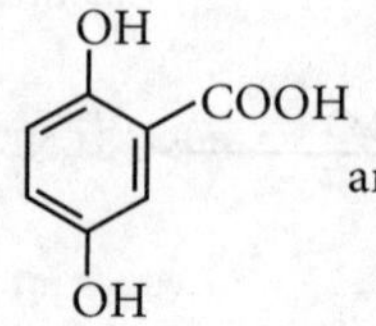 and Methanol

(c) 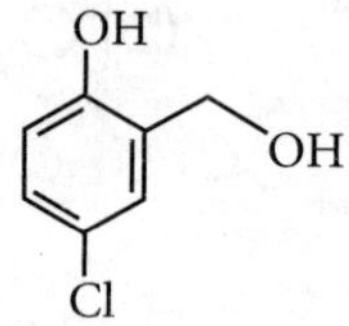 and Formic acid

(d) 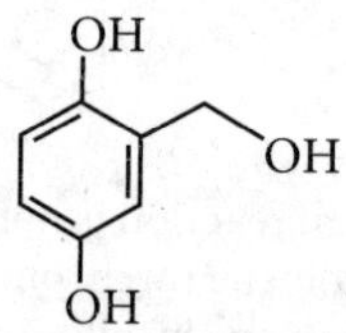 and Formic acid

13. In the Schotten–Baumann reaction, the structure of the product T is:

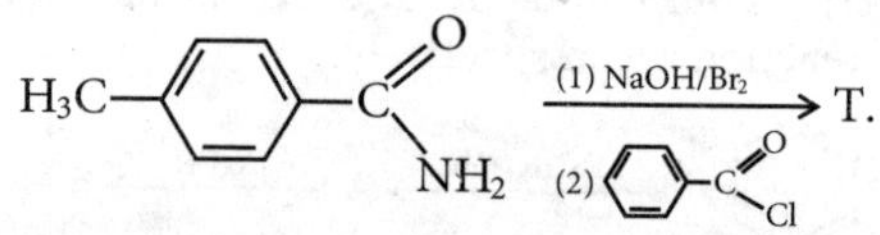

(a) 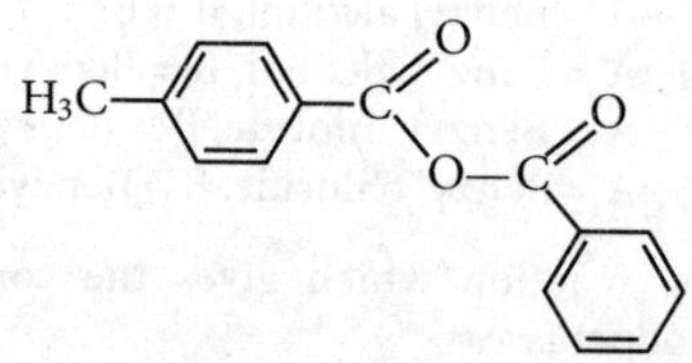
(b) 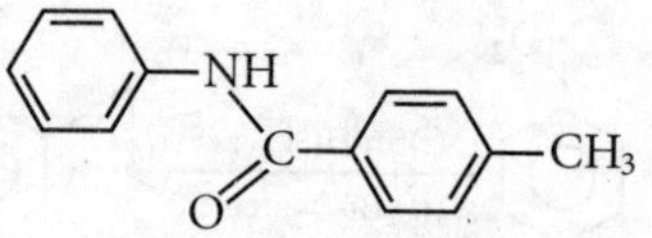
(c) 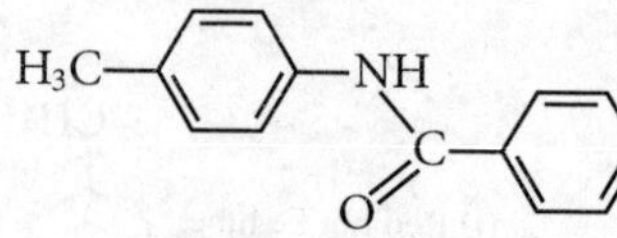

(d) 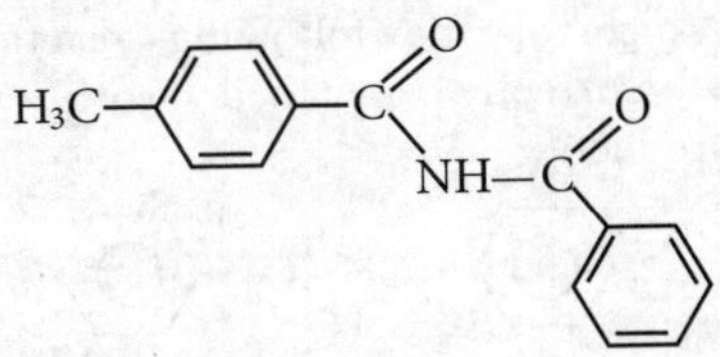

14. In which of the following compounds is F substituted when it reacts with hot NaOH?

(A) 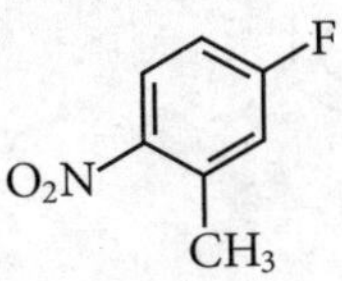 (B) 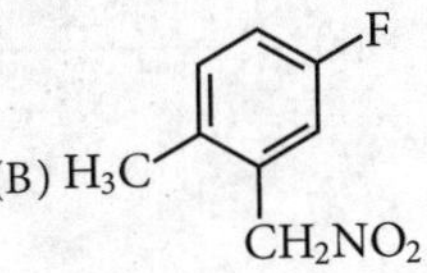

(a) Only A
(b) Only B
(c) Both A and B
(d) None of the above

15. Which of the following reagents cannot be used to convert styrene to benzoic acid?

(a) (i) $KMnO_4$, KOH (ii) Dilute H_2SO_4
(b) (i) $H_3O^{\oplus}$ (ii) I_2, NaOH
(c) (i) O_3 (ii) H_2O_2/H_2O
(d) Cold 1% $KMnO_4$

16. In the reaction shown below, the major product formed is:

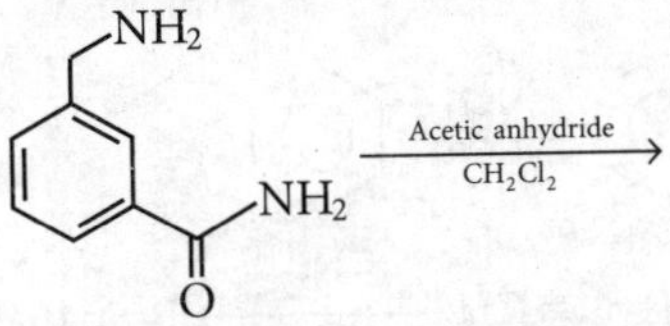

(a) 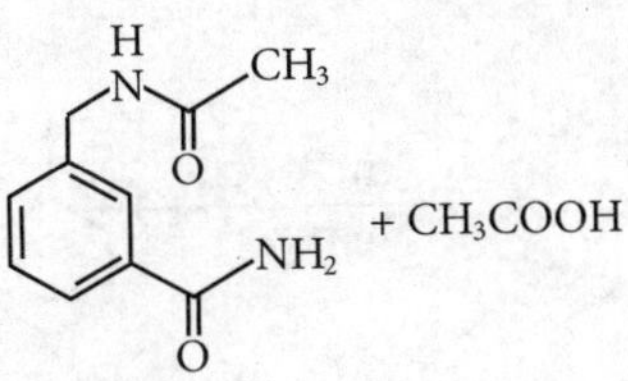

(b) 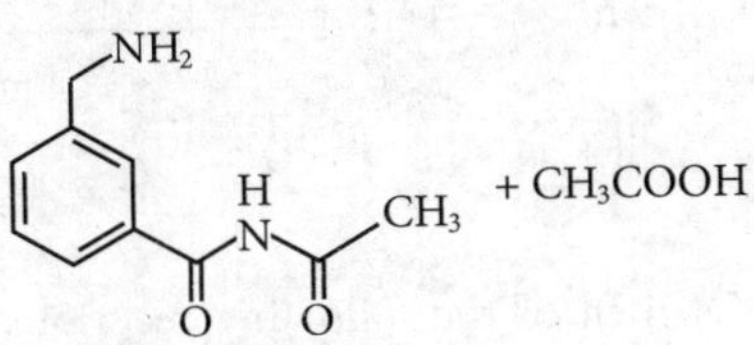

(c) 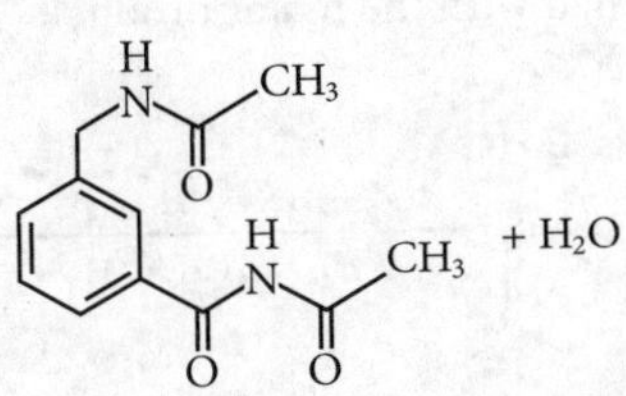

(d) 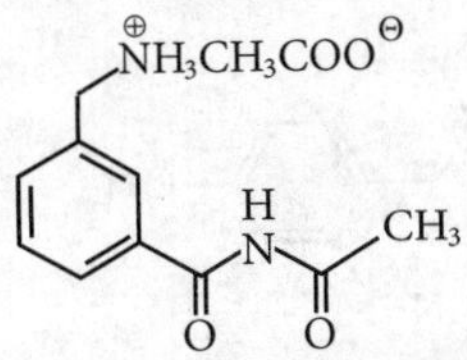

17. The major product U in the following reaction is:

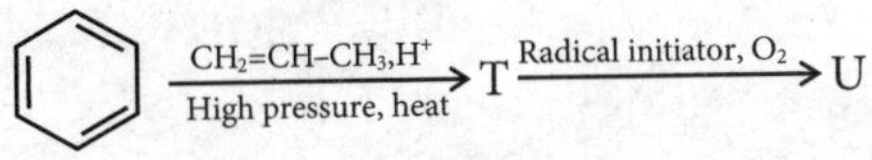

(a) 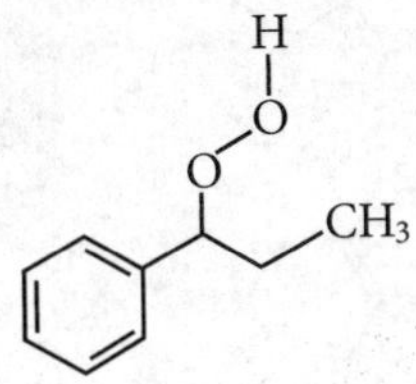

(b) 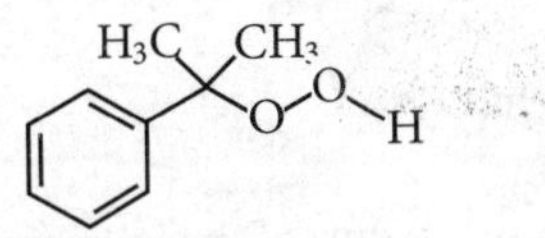

(c) 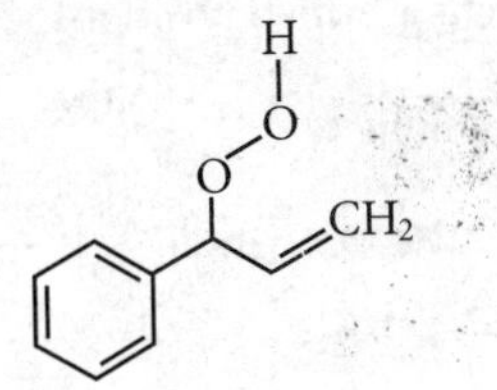

(d) 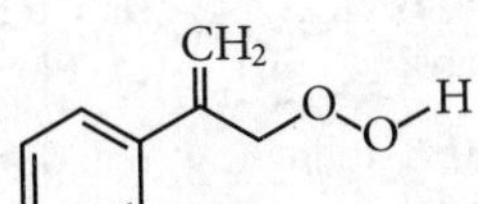

18. In the following reactions, the red-coloured major product **W** is:

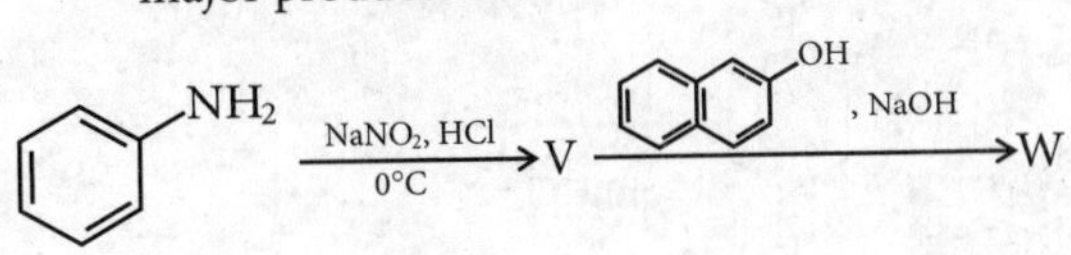

(a) 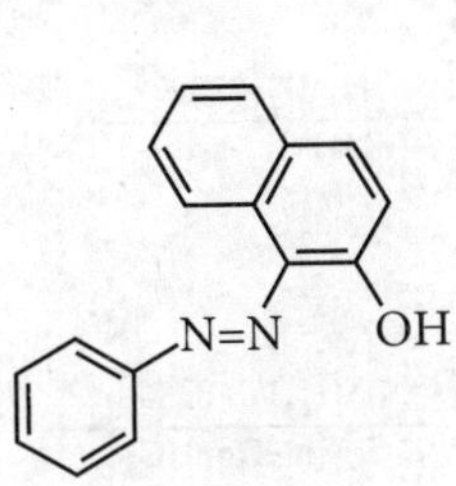

(b) 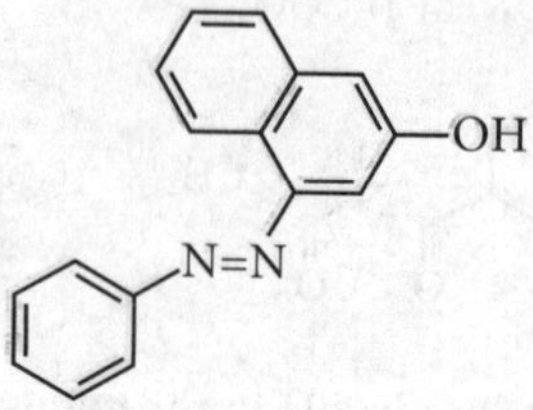

(c) 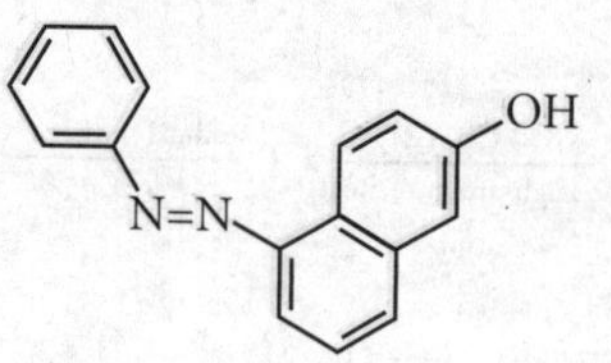

(d) 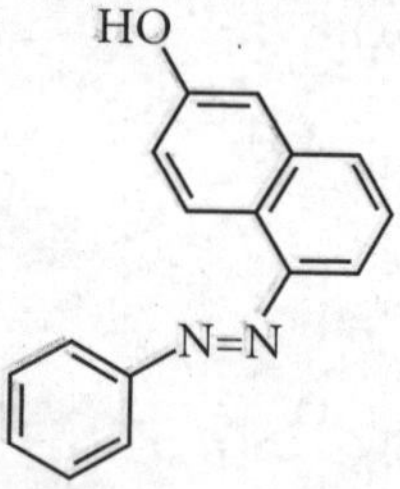

19. In the major product of the following reactions, NO_2 is present at which positions?

(i) 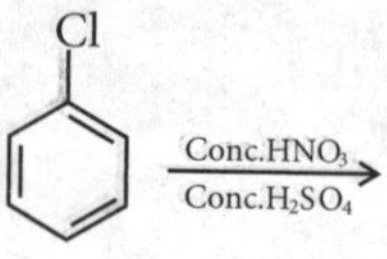 (ii) 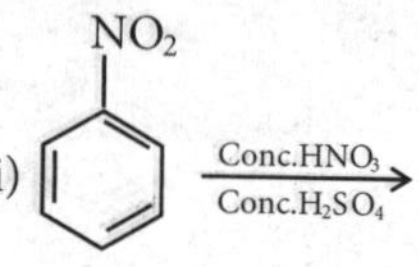

(a) Para, para (b) Meta, meta
(c) Meta, para (d) Para, meta

20. Which of the following reactions will not produce phenol?

(a) 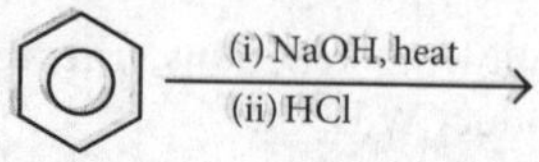

(b) 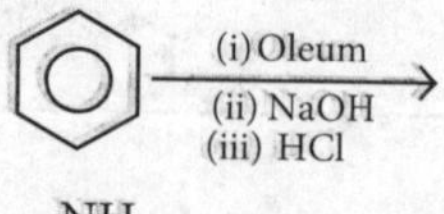

(c) 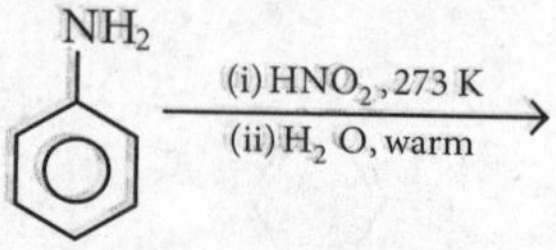

(d) 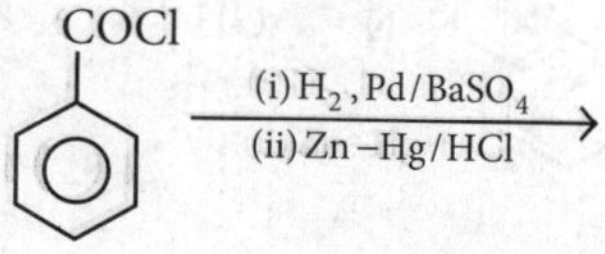

21. Which of the following reactions of (P) is correctly matched with the major product?

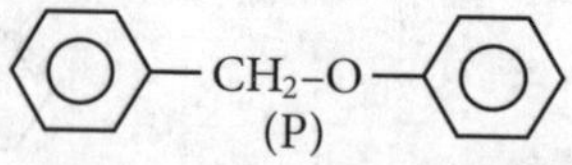

(a) 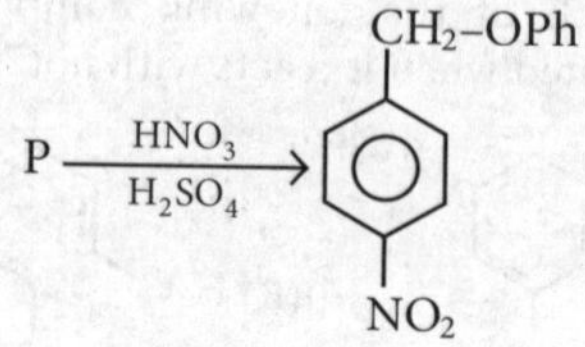

(b) 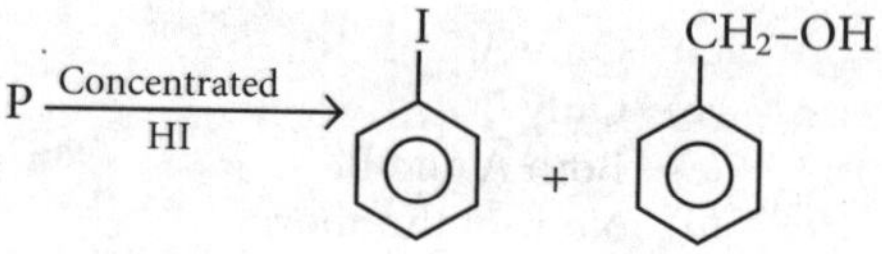

(c) 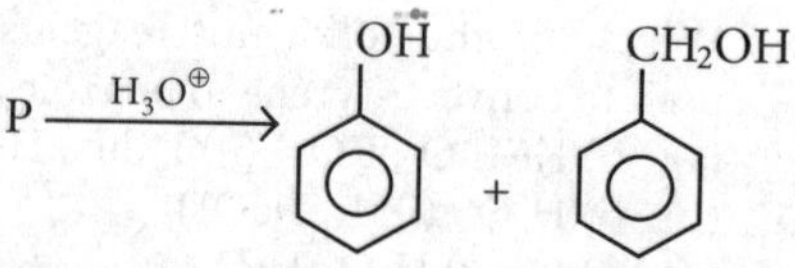

(d) All of these

22. Which of the following reactions is correctly matched with the major product?

(a) 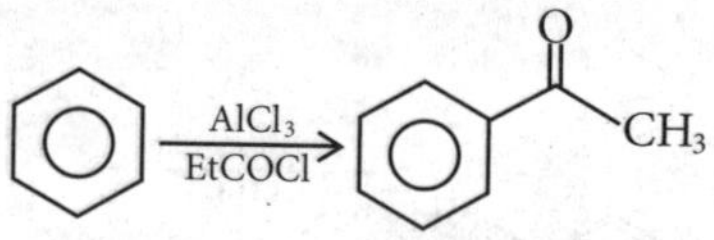

(b) $CH_3-C\equiv CH \xrightarrow[H_2SO_4]{Hg^{2+}}$ Propanal

(c) 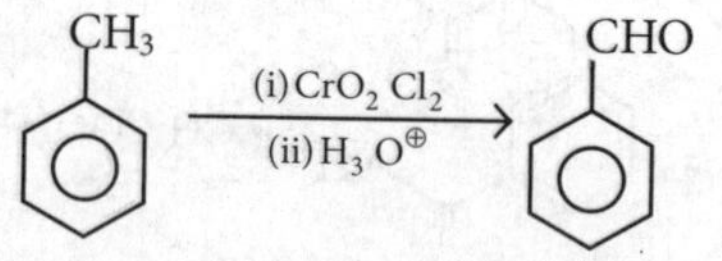

(d) $(C_6H_5CH_2)_2Cd \xrightarrow{CH_3COCl}$

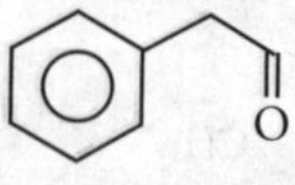

23. Which of the following reactions is correctly matched with the major products?

(a) 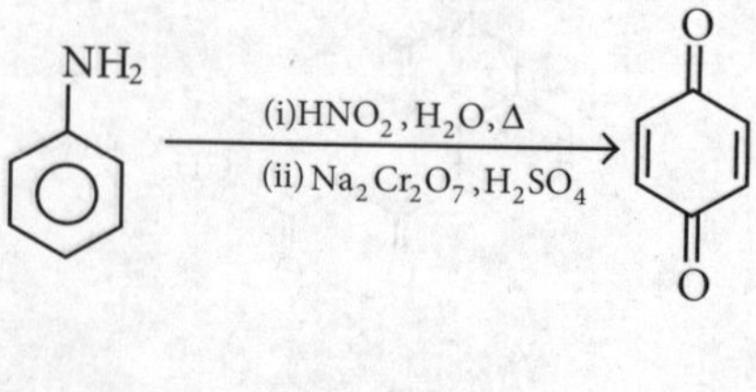

(b) 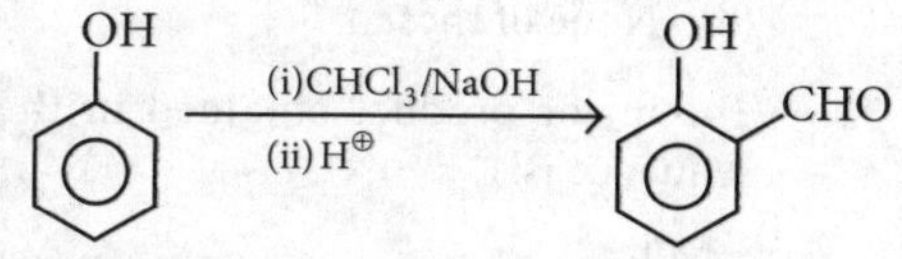

(c) 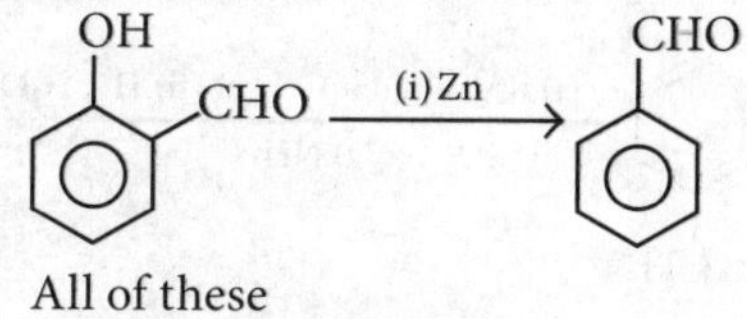

(d) All of these

24. The reaction among the following that is not correctly matched with the major product is:

(a) 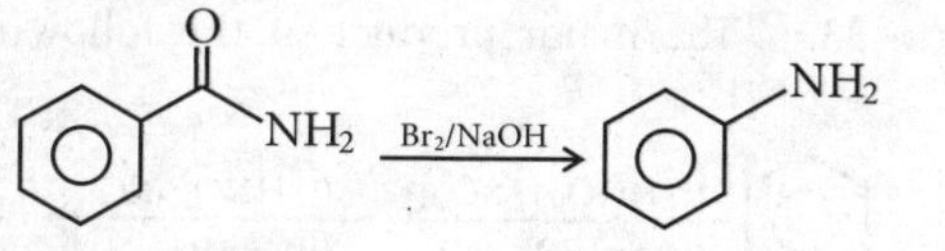

(b) 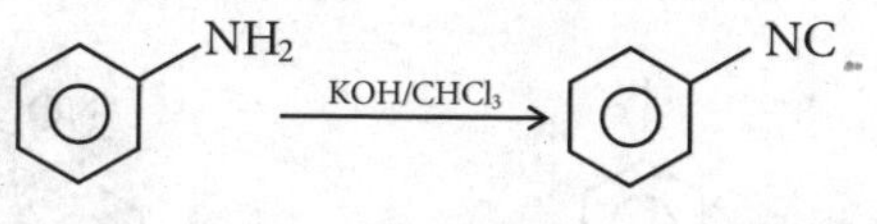

(c) 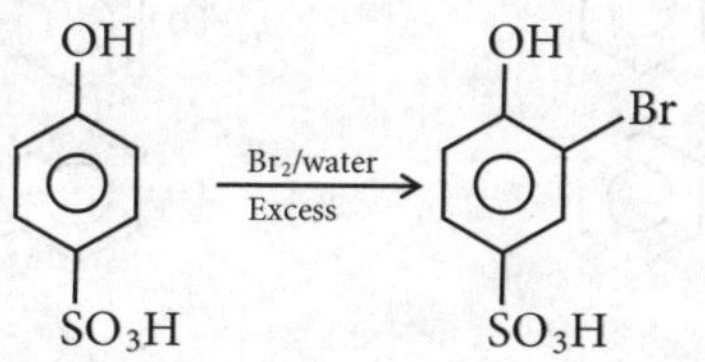

(d) 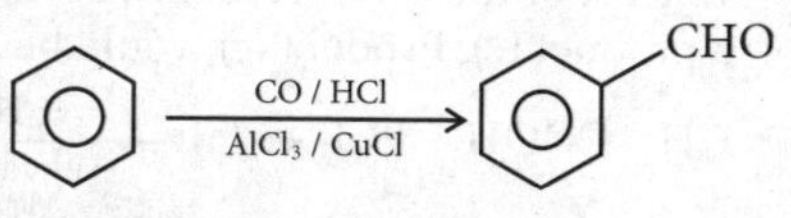

25. By considering the major product in each step, compounds A and D are:

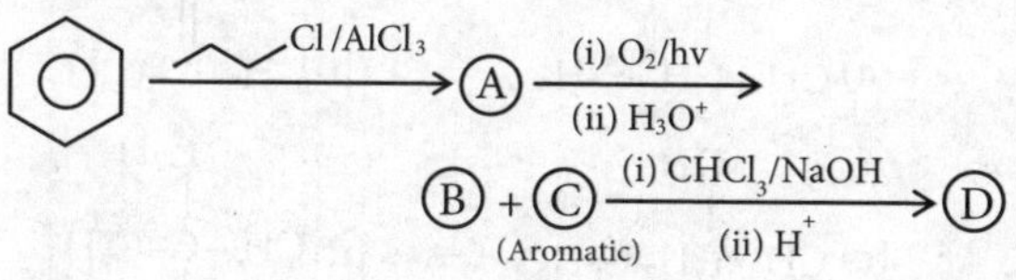

(a) 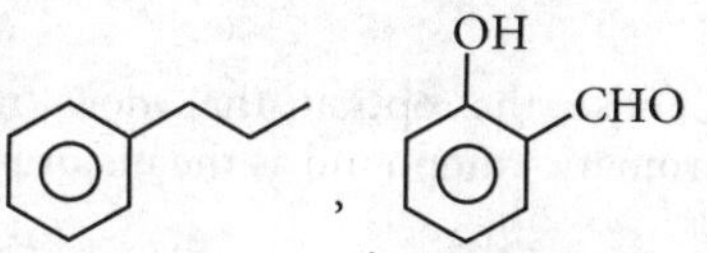

(b) 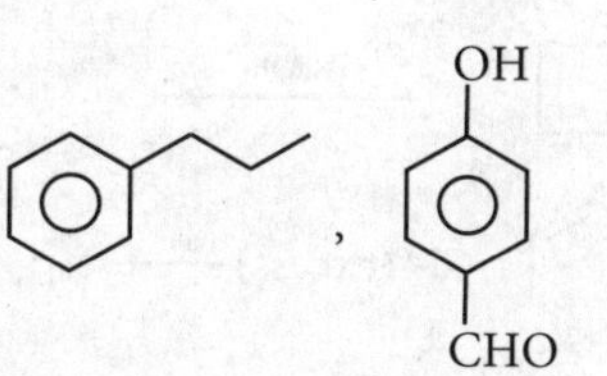

(c) 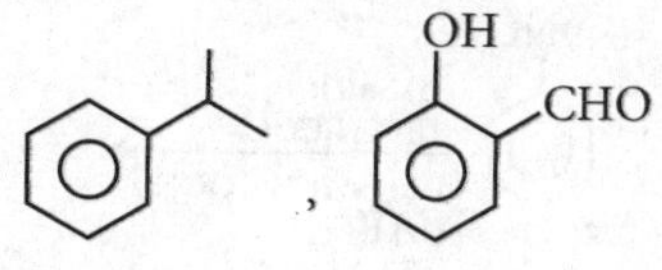

(d) 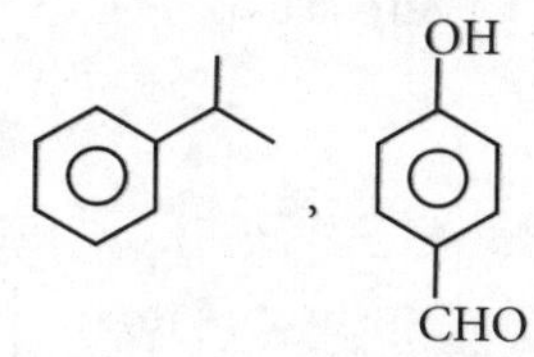

26. Which of the following reactions will produce chlorobenzene as a major product?

(a) $C_6H_5NH_2 \xrightarrow[HCl;0°C]{NaNO_2} \xrightarrow{Heat}$

(b) $C_6H_5NH_2 \xrightarrow[HCl;0°C]{NaNO_2} \xrightarrow{CuCl}$

(c) $C_6H_6 + C_6H_5COCl \xrightarrow{AlCl_3}$

(d) $C_6H_6 + Cl_2 \xrightarrow{h\nu}$

27. Which of the following reactions involves the S_N2 mechanism with a carbanion intermediate?

(a) 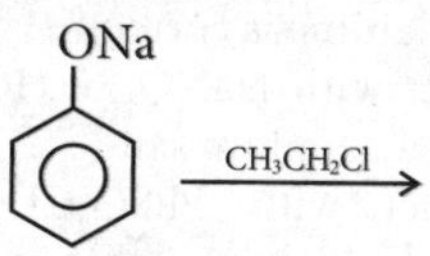

(b) 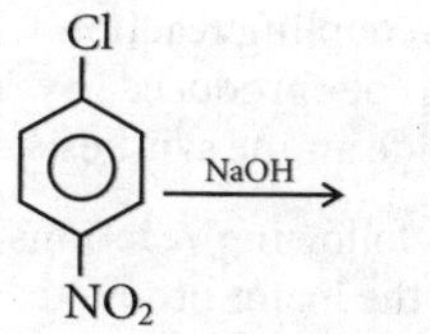

(c) $CH_3–CHO \xrightarrow[\Delta]{NaOH}$

(d) 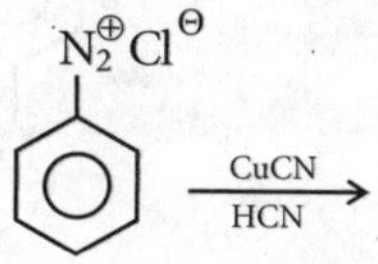

28. The major product of the given sequence is:

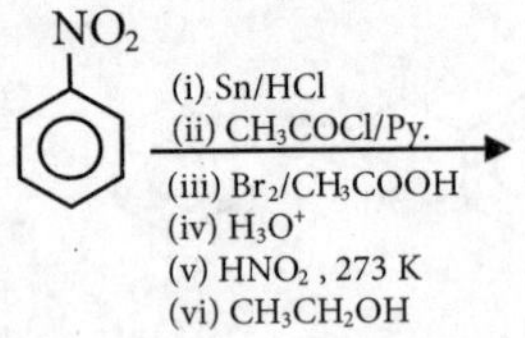

(a) 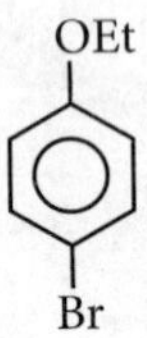

(b) 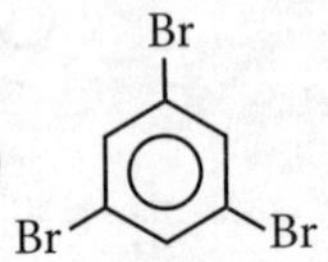

(c) 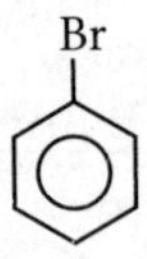

(d) 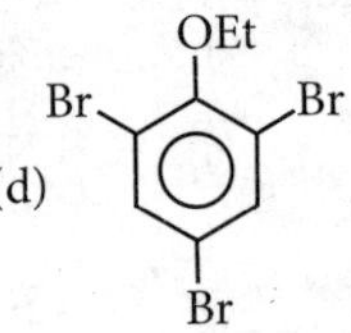

29. Benzenediazonium chloride will not produce:
(a) Phenol with steam
(b) Benzene from H_3PO_2
(c) Bromo benzene with Cu/HBr
(d) Red precipitate with phenol/NaOH

30. Which of the given characteristics of aniline and cyclohexylamine is correct?
(a) Both react with $NaNO_2$ + HCl at 0–5°C and form diazonium salt
(b) Both react with $PhSO_2Cl$ to give a compound which is soluble in KOH
(c) Both give coupling reaction with phenol
(d) Both can be produced by the Gabriel phthalimide amine synthesis

31. Which of the following reactions is correctly matched with the major product?

(a) 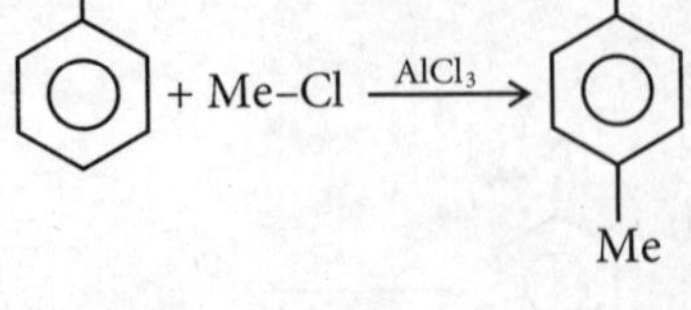

(b) 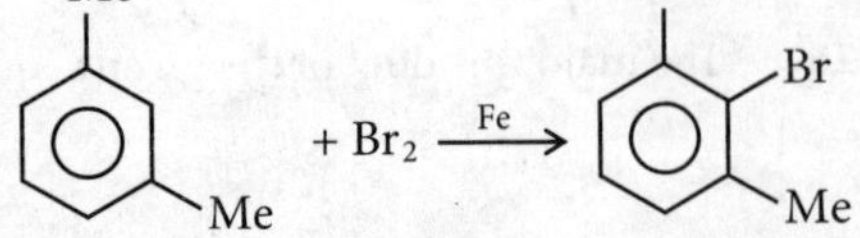

(c) Me–C≡CH + Na/Liq NH_3 ⟶ Propene

(d) None of these

32. The major product obtained in the following sequence is:

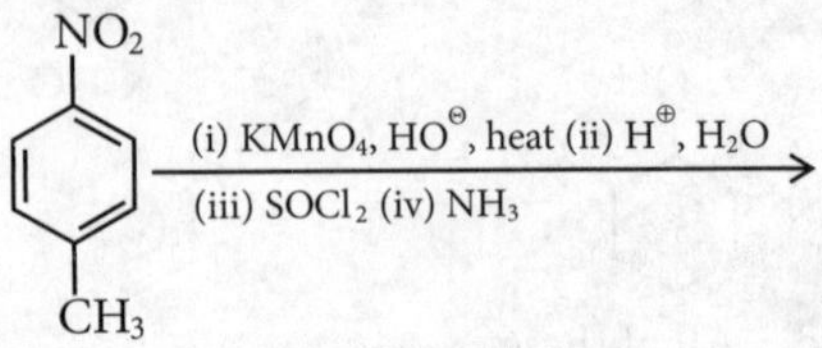

(a) $C_7H_6N_2O_3$ (b) $C_6H_5NO_4$
(c) $C_6H_6N_2O_2$ (d) $C_6H_5NO_3$

33. The major product of the following reaction is:

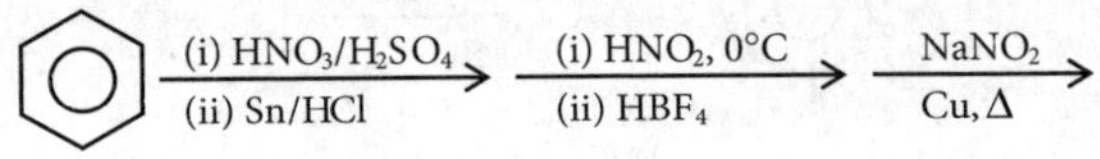

(a) 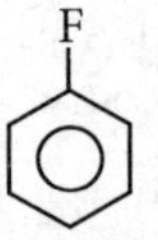 (b) 

(c)  (d) 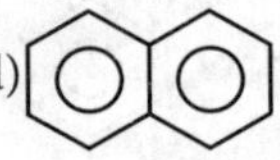

34. In a set of the given reaction, acetic acid yields a product (c). Product (c) would be:

$$CH_3\text{–}COOH + PCl_5 \rightarrow (a) \xrightarrow[\text{Anhydrous } AlCl_3]{C_6H_6}$$

$$(b) \xrightarrow[\text{(ii) } H^{\oplus}]{\text{(i) } C_2H_5MgBr/\text{ether}} (c)$$

(a) $CH_3\text{–}CH(OH)\text{–}C_2H_5$ (b) $CH_3\text{–}C(=O)\text{–}C_6H_5$

(c) $CH_3\text{–}CH(OH)\text{–}C_6H_5$ (d) $CH_3\text{–}C(C_2H_5)(OH)\text{–}C_6H_5$

35. Choose the option that does not give an aromatic compound as the major product:

(a) 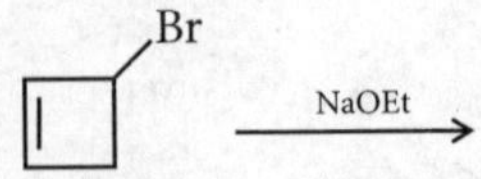

(b) 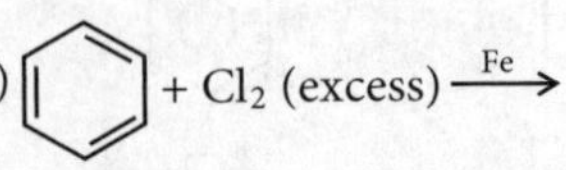

(c) 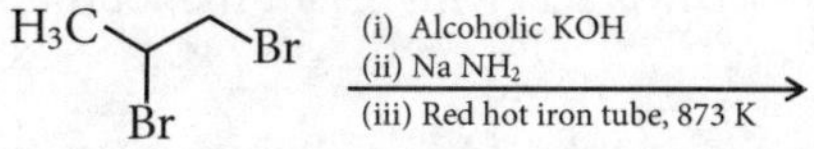

(d) 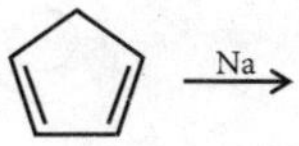

36. The major product (Q) of the following sequence is:

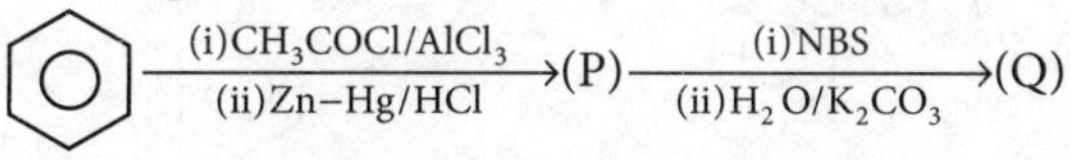

(a) 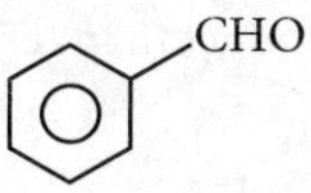

(b) 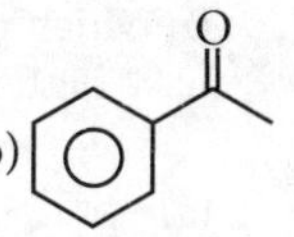

(c) 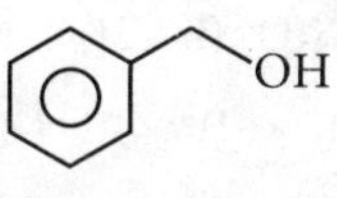

(d) 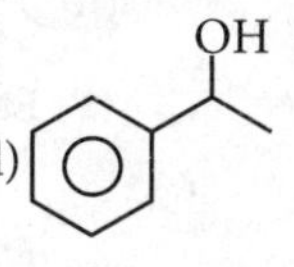

37. Which has a faster rate of electrophilic aromatic substitution than benzene?

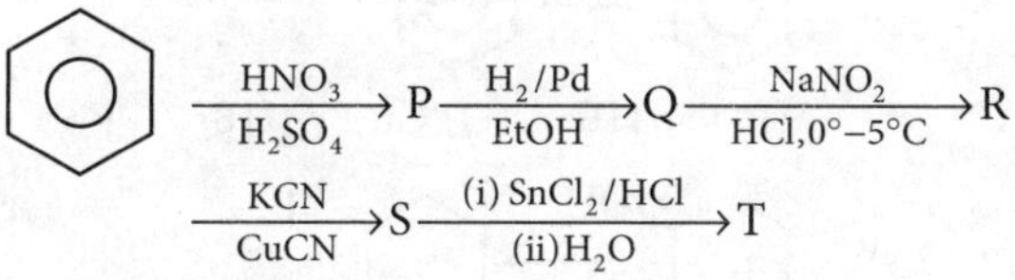

(a) P (b) Q
(c) S (d) T

38. The major product (Q) of the following sequence is:

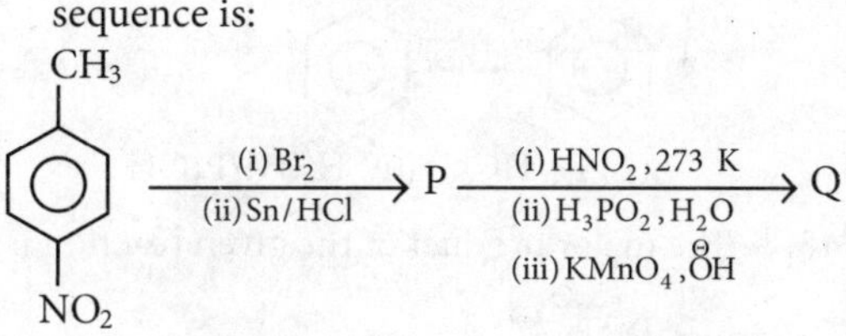

(a) 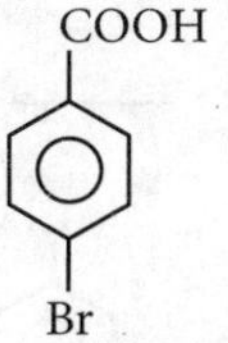

(b) 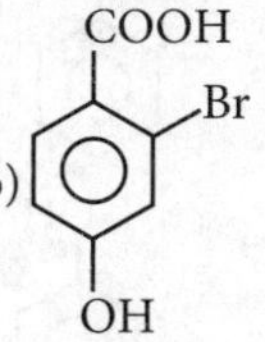

(c) 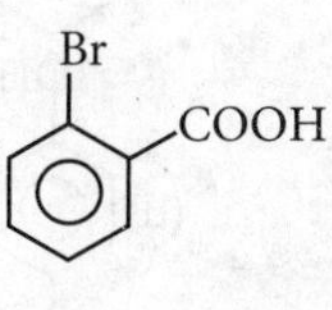

(d) 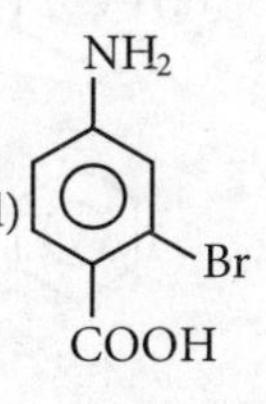

39. Among the following, the incorrect statement is:

(a) Phosphinic acid on reaction with benzenediazonium chloride produces benzene
(b) Above 283K, diazonium salt produces phenol as the major product
(c) Phenol with concentrated HNO_3 produces picric acid in very poor yield
(d) Benzenediazonium fluoroborate on heating produces biphenyl

40. Which of the following compounds will not undergo the Friedel–Craft reaction with benzene?

(a) 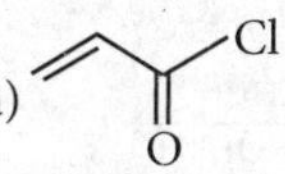

(b) 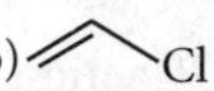

(c) 

(d) 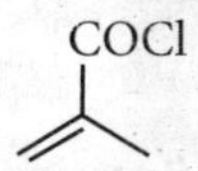

41. Choose the incorrect statement?

(a) During the formation of ester from acid and alcohol, water should be removed as soon it is formed.
(b) Ethyl amine is soluble in water whereas aniline is not.
(c) Aniline does not undergo Friedel–Craft's reaction.
(d) The pKb of methylamine is more than that of aniline.

42. Reactions in which phenol is obtained as a major product are:

(A) 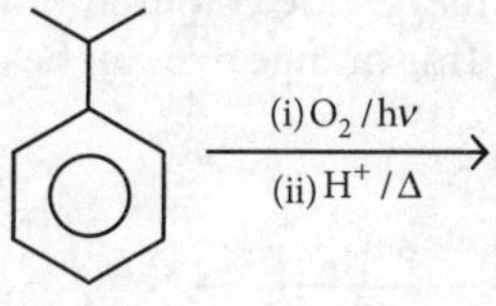

(B) 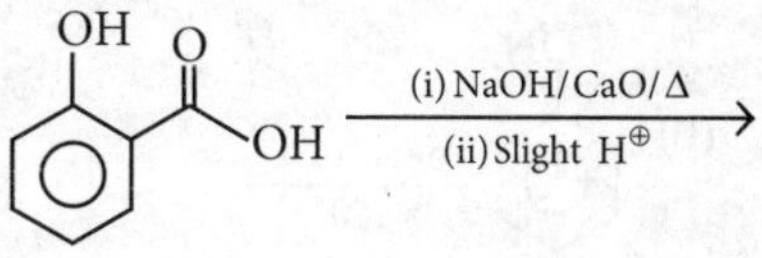

(C) 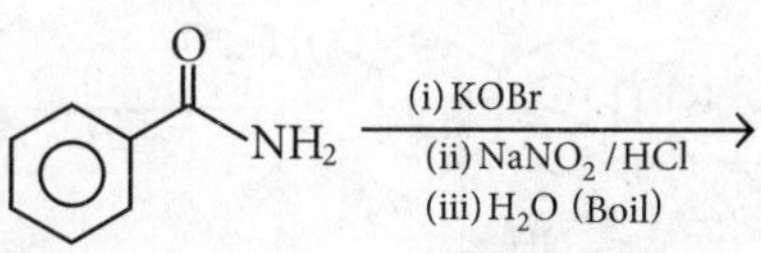

(a) A, C (b) A, B
(c) A, B, C (d) Only B

43. Suggest the best reaction condition for the synthesis shown below:

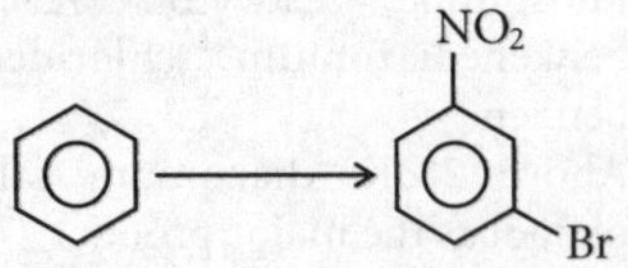

(a) (1) HNO_3, H_2SO_4 (2) Fe/HCl (3) Br_2/Fe
(b) (1) Br_2 (2) HNO_3, H_2SO_4
(c) (1) CH_3–Br, $AlBr_3$ (2) HNO_3, H_2SO_4
(d) (1) HNO_3, H_2SO_4 (2) Br_2, $FeBr_3$

44. Which of the following options is incorrect for the given reactions?

Reaction I : 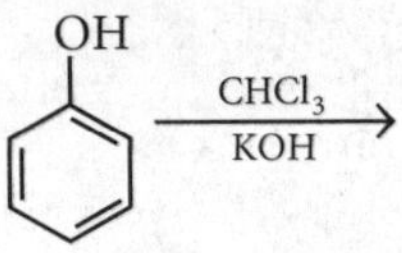

Reaction II : 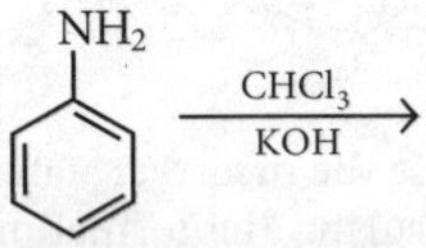

(a) Reaction II requires 4 moles of KOH for 1 mole of aniline.
(b) Major product of reaction I shows violet colour with neutral $FeCl_3$.
(c) Both the reactions proceed with dichlorocarbene as an intermediate.
(d) Reaction I is a substitution reaction and the major product is steam volatile.

45. Paul Ehrlich was working on an azo dye as antibiotic because it is similar to salvarsan. He noted that tissues are coloured orange by dyes selectively. This orange dye can be obtained by:

(a) 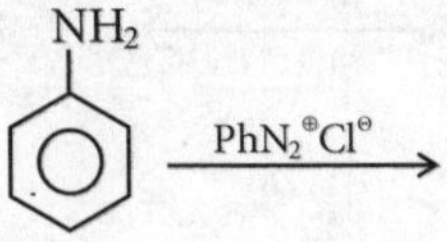

(b) 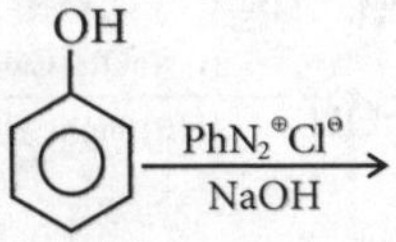

(c) 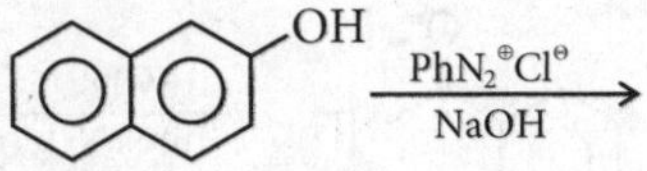

(d) 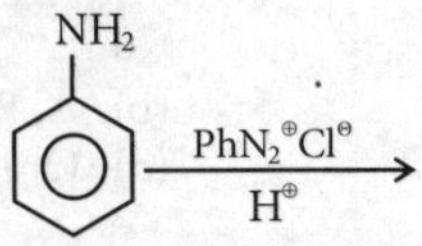

46. Which of the following compounds will require Lewis acid with Br_2 for monobromination?

(a) 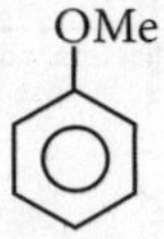

(b) 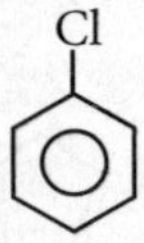

(c) 

(d) 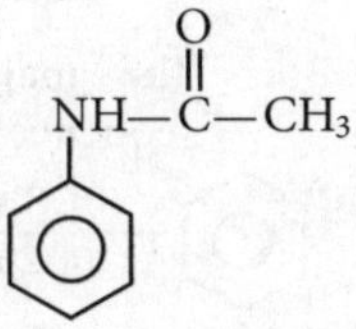

47. In which of the following conversions will (P) have better yield of product than (Q)?

(a) 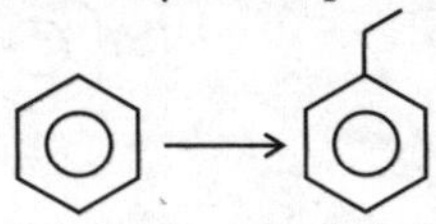

(P) EtCl/$AlCl_3$ (Q) (i) $CH_3COCl/AlCl_3$ (ii) Zn – Hg / HCl

(b) 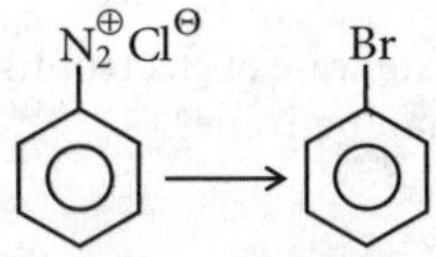

(P) Cu/HBr (Q) Cu_2Br_2/HBr

(c) 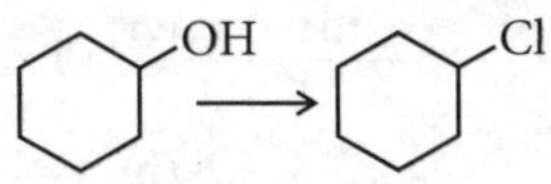

(P) HCl/$ZnCl_2$ (Q) $SOCl_2$

(d) 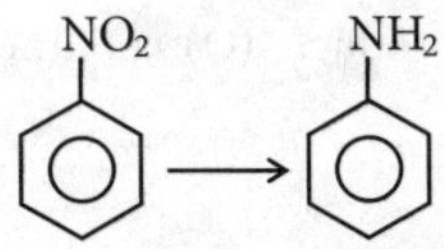

(P) Fe/HCl (Q) H_2,Pd/EtOH

48. The major product of the given reaction is:

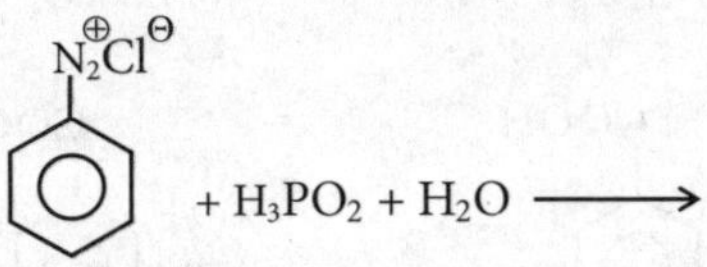

(a) 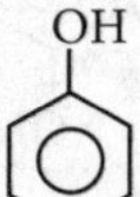

(b) 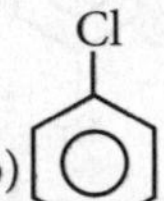

(c) 
(d) 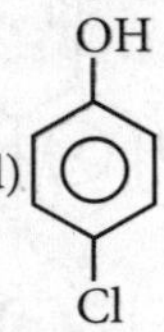

49. The major product (Q) of the following sequence is:

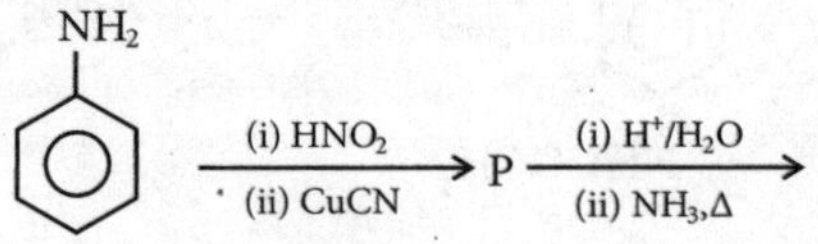

(a) 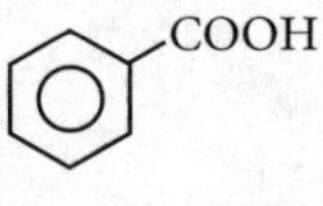

(b) 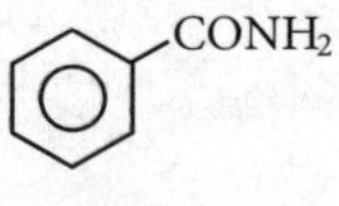

(c) 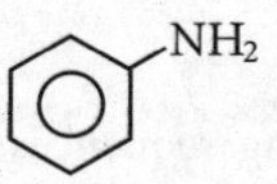

(d) 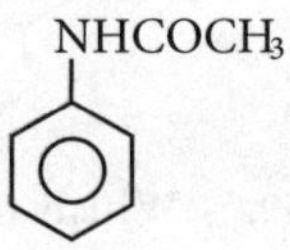

50. Which of the following compounds, on warm H_2O, gives a nucleophilic substitution reaction?

(a) 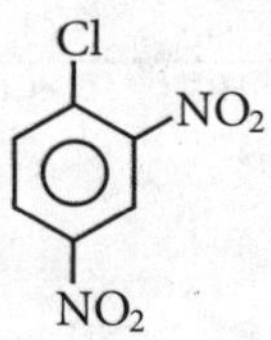

(b) 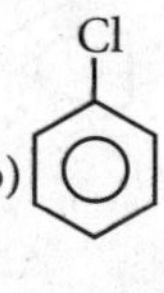

(c) 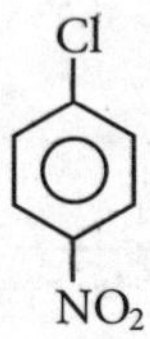

(d) 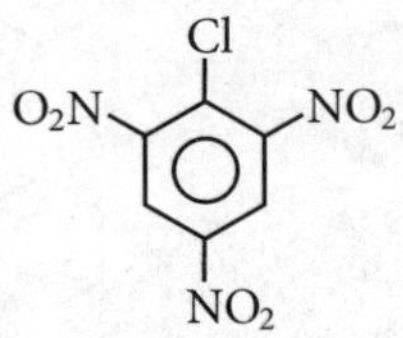

51. The pKa values for the given phenol and its derivatives are, respectively:

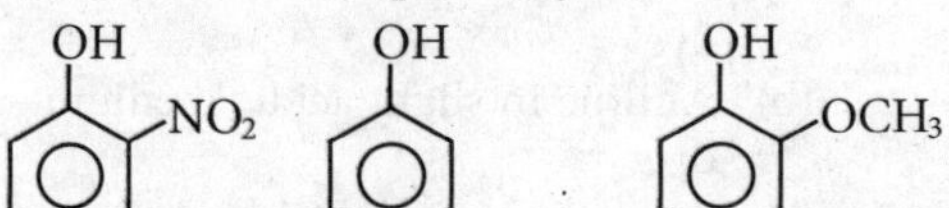

(a) 7.2, 10.0, 10.2 (b) 10.2, 7.0, 10.0
(c) 7.2, 10.2, 10.0 (d) 10.2, 10.0, 7.21

52. Which of the following reactions is incorrectly matched with the major product for the given compound (P)?

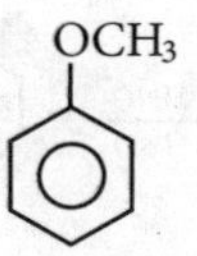

(a) (P) $\xrightarrow{CH_3Cl/AlCl_3}$ 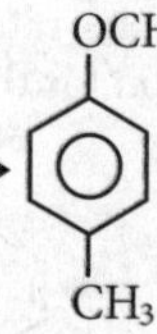

(b) (P) $\xrightarrow[H_2SO_4]{HNO_3}$ 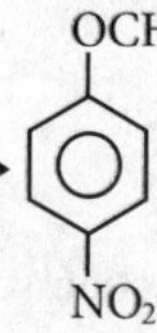

(c) (P) $\xrightarrow[HI]{\text{Concentrated}}$ 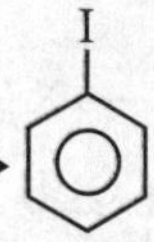

$+ CH_3I$

(d) (P) $\xrightarrow[\text{Ethanoic acid}]{Br_2}$ 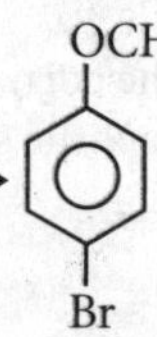

53. In which of these reactions is aldehyde not obtained as a major product?
(a) Stephen reaction
(b) Gattermann–Koch
(c) Etard reaction
(d) Sandmeyer reaction

54. The product of the following reaction sequence is:

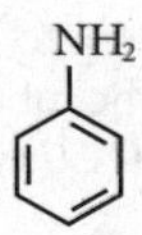

(i) Acetic anhydride/pyridine
(ii) Br_2 /Fe
(iii) H_3O^+, heat
(iv) $NaNO_2$ /HCl, 273–278 K
(v) Cu/HBr

(a) 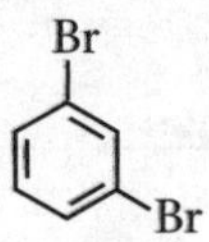

(b) 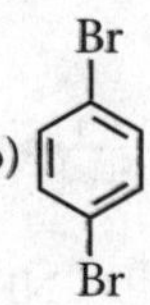

(c) 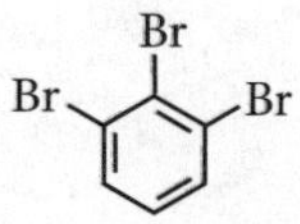

(d) 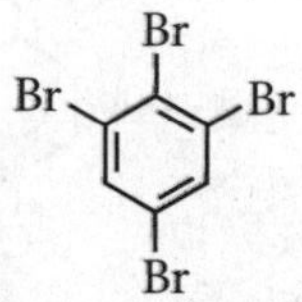

55. Compare the rate of reaction of electrophilic substitution for the given position:

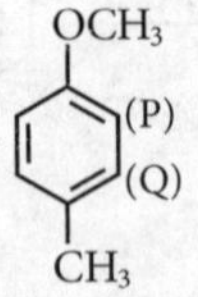

(a) P < Q (b) P > Q
(c) P = Q (d) Cannot predict

56. In the reaction sequence, the major product Y will be:

$$CHCl_3 \xrightarrow{Air/h\nu} X \xrightarrow{C_6H_6/\text{Anhydrous } AlCl_3} Y$$

(a) $C_6H_5COCH_3$ (b) $C_6H_5COC_6H_5$
(c) $COCl_2$ (d) C_6H_5CHO

57. What is the correct order of reactivity towards the electrophilic substitution reaction?

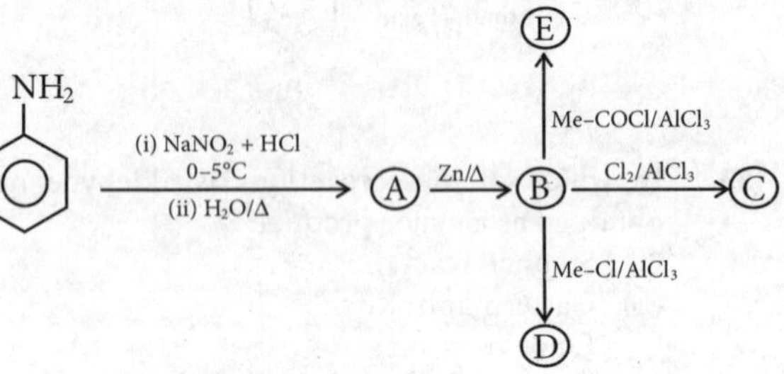

(a) A > D > B > C > E
(b) D > A > B > C > E
(c) D > A > C > B > E
(d) A > D > C > B > E

58. Phenacetin, an analgesic, can be obtain by the reaction of 'S' with CH_3COCl/py. Then phenacetin is:

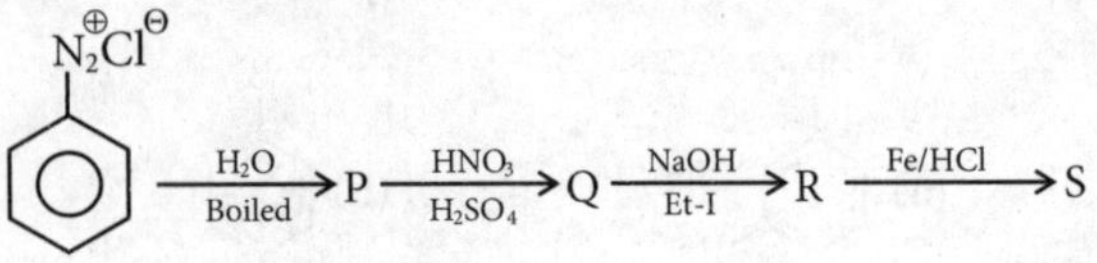

(a)
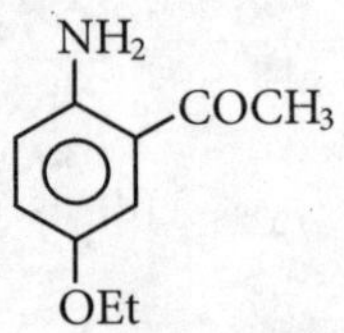

(b)
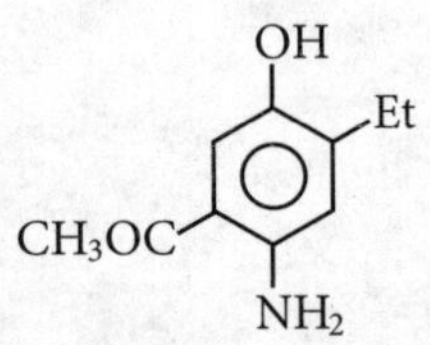

(c)
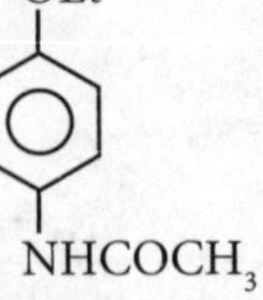

(d)
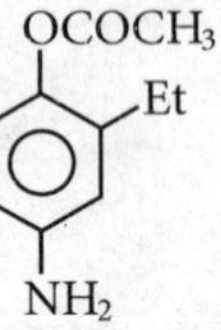

59. Which of the following sequences is used to prepare m-chloronitrobenzene in best yield?

(a)
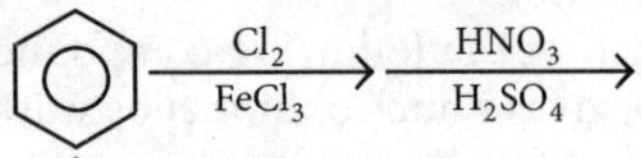

(b)
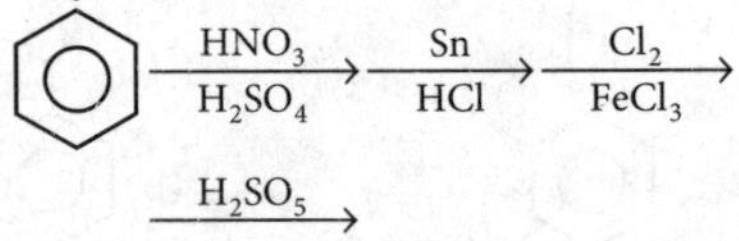

(c)
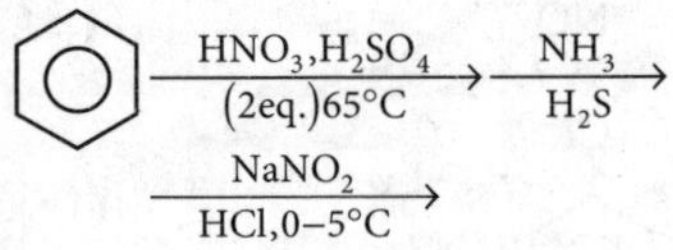

(d)
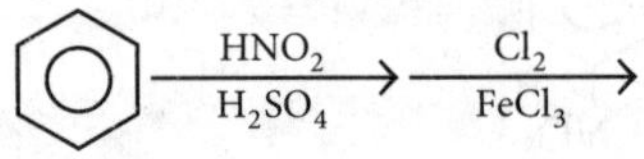

60. Which of the following products is incorrectly matched with benzenediazonium chloride?
(a) Phenol in slight basic medium → Orange dye
(b) Aniline in slight acidic medium→ Yellow dye
(c) β-napthol in slight basic medium→ Red dye
(d) Copper in the presence of hydrochloric acid → Biphenyl

61. Which of the following reactions is incorrect corresponding to the major products?

(a)
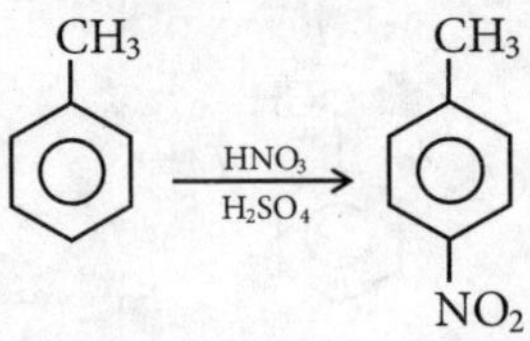

(b)
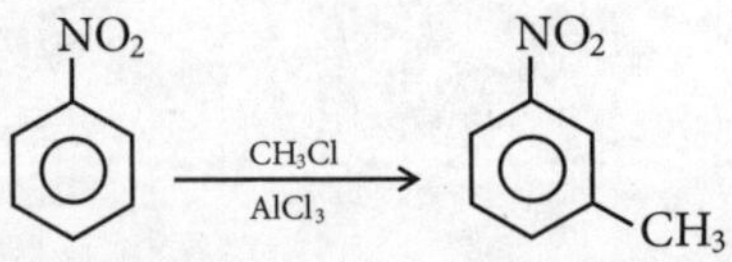

(c) 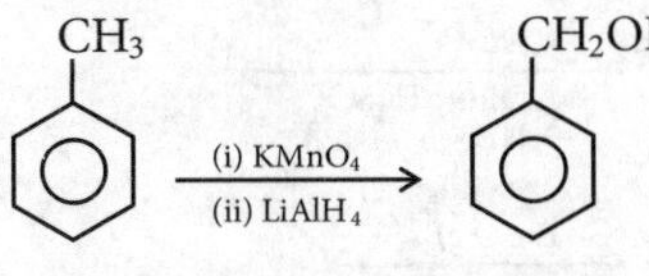

(d) 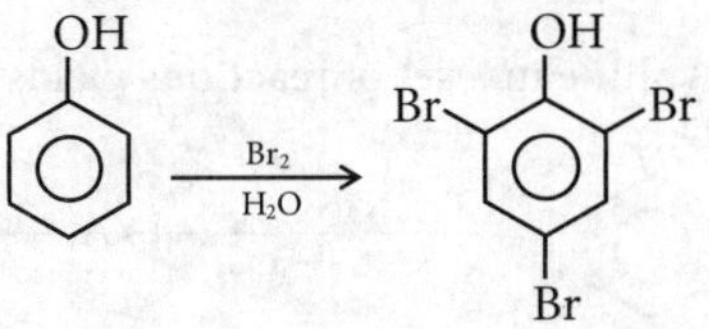

62. If (P) is phthalic acid, then the total number of bromine present in the final major product will be:

(P) $\xrightarrow[\substack{\text{(ii) } Br_2/NaOH \\ \text{(iii) } Br_2/H_2O \\ \text{(iv) } NaNO_2/HCl, 0^\circ C\text{(excess)} \\ \text{(v) Cu/HBr}}]{\text{(i) } NH_3\text{(excess)}, \Delta}$

(a) 4 (b) 5
(c) 6 (d) 3

63. Which of the following compounds on reaction with Zn produces benzene?

(a) 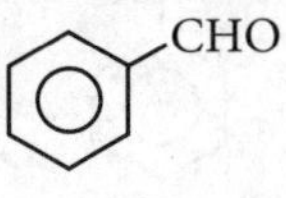 (b) 

(c) 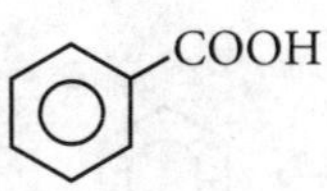 (d) 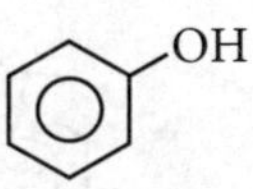

64. The maximum number of atoms present in 'C' in one plane is: (A is the lowest molecular weight alkyne)

$A \xrightarrow[\text{Fe tube}]{\text{Red hot}} B \xrightarrow[\text{Anhydrous } AlCl_3]{CH_3Cl\text{(1.eq.)}} C$

(a) 8 (b) 13
(c) 15 (d) 12

65. 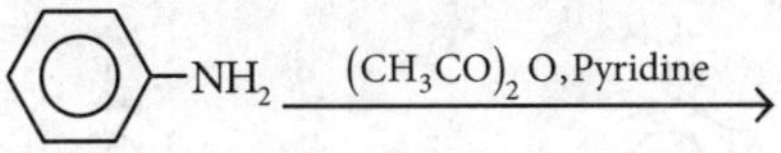

(I)

$\text{(II)} \xrightarrow[\text{(ii)} H_2O]{\text{(i)} LiAlH_4} \text{III}$

The basicity order of I, II and III is:
(a) III > I > II
(b) I > II > III
(c) III > II > I
(d) II > III > I

66. 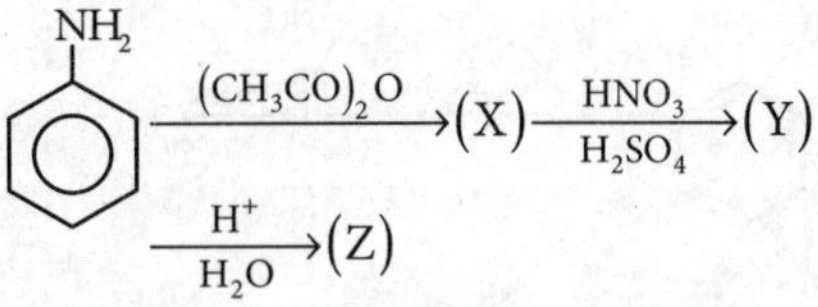

Product Z of the reaction is:

(a) 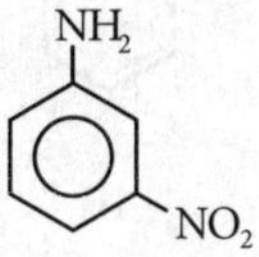 (b) 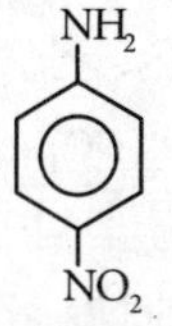

(c) 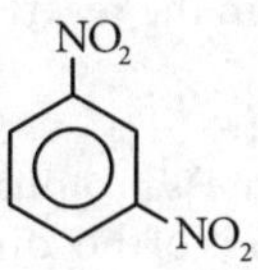 (d) 

67. In the given reaction,

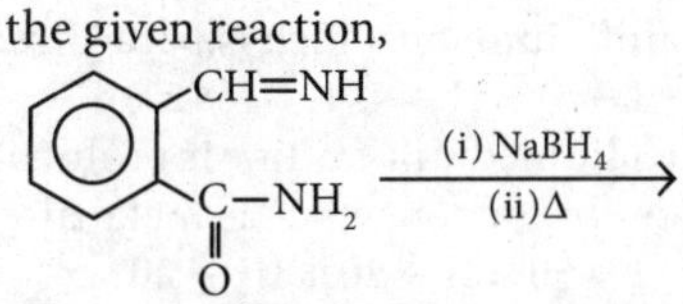

What would be the final product formed?

(a) (b) 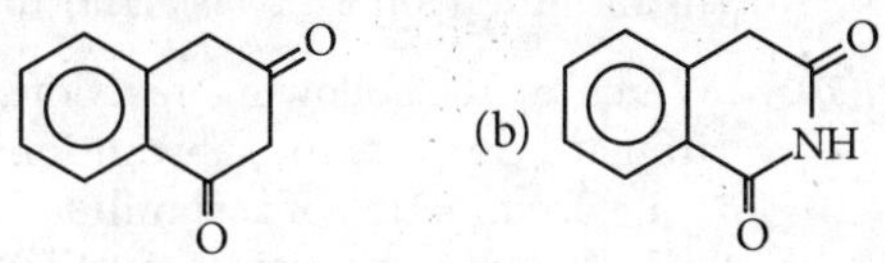

(c) (d) 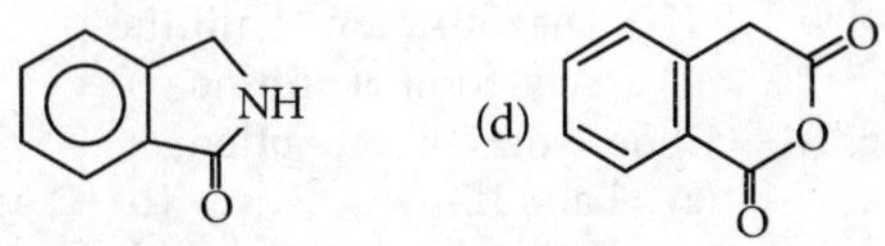

68. Under which of the following reaction conditions would aniline give p-nitro derivative as the major product?

I. Acetyl chloride/pyridine followed by reaction with concentrated H_2SO_4 + concentrated HNO_3.
II. Acetic anhydride/pyridine followed by concentrated H_2SO_4 + concentrated HNO_3.
III. Dilute HCl followed by reaction with concentrated H_2SO_4 + concentrated HNO_3.
IV. Reaction with concentrated HNO_3 + concentrated H_2SO_4.

(a) I and II (b) II and III
(c) III and IV (d) I and IV

69. 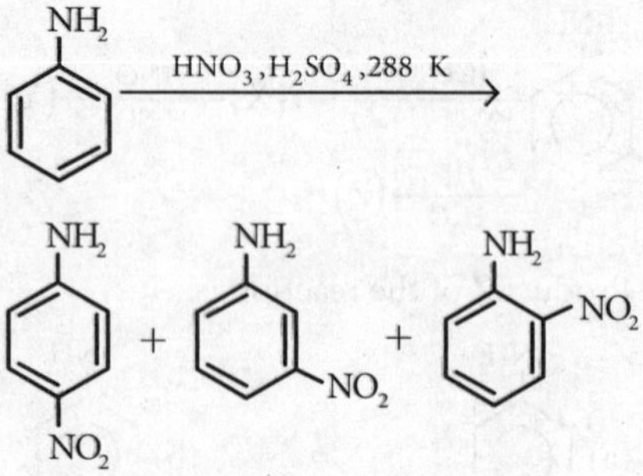

I. II. III.

Select the percentage in which these amine derivatives are formed in the reaction mixture, along with the reason:

(a) I → 2% II → 47% III → 51%
In acidic medium, aniline is protonated to form an anilinium ion which is ortho-directing

(b) I → 51% II → 2% III → 47%
In acidic medium, aniline is protonated to form an anilinium ion which is para-directing

(c) I → 51% II → 47% III → 2%
In acidic medium, aniline is protonated to form an anilinium ion which is meta-directing

(d) I → 50% II → 20% III → 20%
In acidic medium, aniline is protonated to form an anilinium ion which is ortho-directing

70. Which of the following reactions belongs to aromatic electrophilic substitution?

I. Bromination of acetanilide
II. Coupling reaction of aryl diazonium salts
III. Diazotisation of aniline
IV. Acylation of aniline

Choose the correct option:

(a) I and II (b) II and III
(c) III and IV (d) I and IV

71. 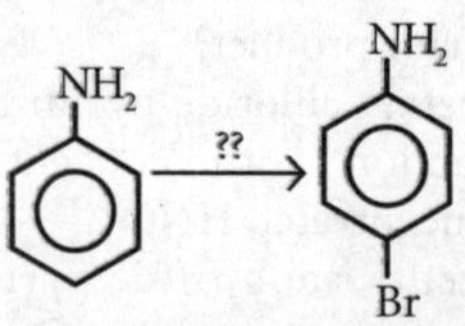

Which of the following reagent systems will be most suitable for this conversion?

(a) $\xrightarrow{}$ 1. H_2SO_4 2. Ac_2O 3. Dilute H_2SO_4/Δ 4. Br_2

(b) $\xrightarrow{}$ 1. Ac_2O 2. $Br_2/FeBr_3$ 3. Dilute H_2SO_4/Δ

(c) $\xrightarrow{}$ 1. Ac_2O 2. Dilute H_2SO_4 3. HBr

(d) $\xrightarrow{Br_2/FeBr_3}$

72. Aniline in a set of reactions yields end product D:

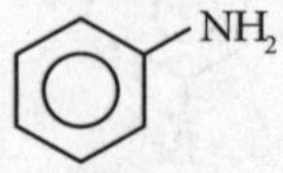

$\xrightarrow[0-5^\circ C]{NaNO_2+HCl}$ A $\xrightarrow{CuCN}$ B $\xrightarrow[Ni]{H_2}$ C $\xrightarrow{HNO_2}$ D

The structure of the product D would be:

(a) $C_6H_5CH_2OH$
(b) $C_6H_5CH_2NH_2$
(c) C_6H_5NHOH
(d) $C_6H_5NHCH_2CH_3$

73. Which reaction gives the incorrect product?

(a) 

(b) 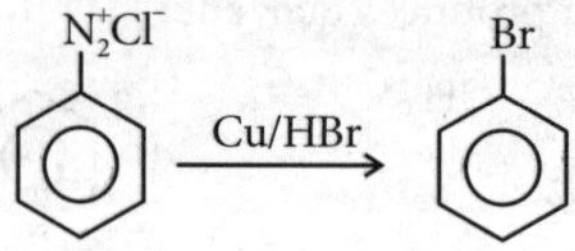

(c) 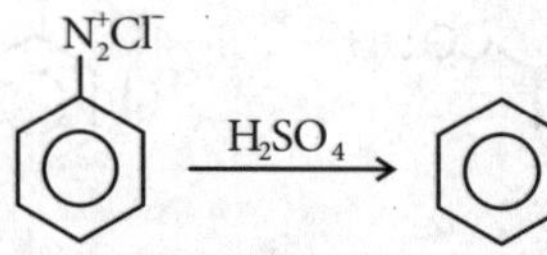

(d) 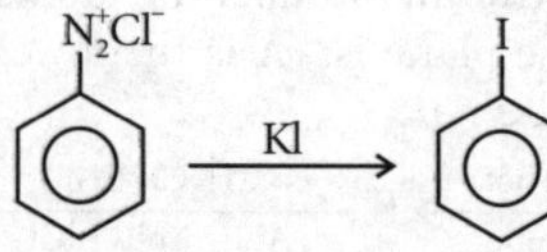

74. When p-toluidine reacts with chloroform and alcoholic KOH, the product is:

(a) 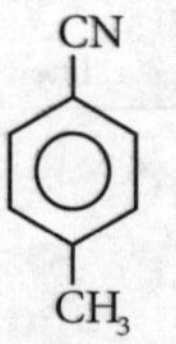

(b) 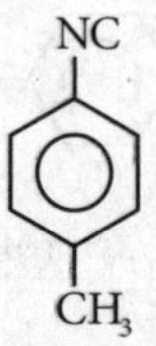

(c) 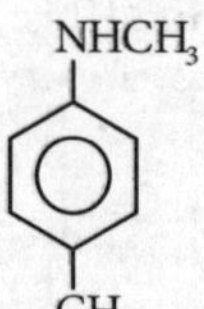

(d) 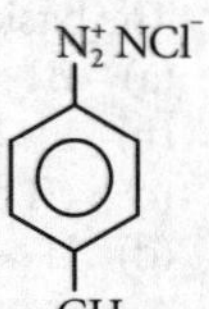

Answer Key

LEVEL-1

1. (b)	**2.** (c)	**3.** (a)	**4.** (c)	**5.** (b)	**6.** (d)	**7.** (a)	**8.** (d)
9. (a)	**10.** (b)	**11.** (b)	**12.** (b)	**13.** (b)	**14.** (b)	**15.** (c)	**16.** (a)
17. (a)	**18.** (b)	**19.** (a)	**20.** (b)	**21.** (b)	**22.** (d)	**23.** (c)	**24.** (a)
25. (c)	**26.** (d)	**27.** (d)	**28.** (d)	**29.** (d)	**30.** (a)	**31.** (d)	**32.** (c)
33. (a)	**34.** (a)	**35.** (d)	**36.** (d)	**37.** (c)	**38.** (d)	**39.** (a)	**40.** (c)
41. (d)	**42.** (b)	**43.** (c)	**44.** (c)	**45.** (d)	**46.** (c)	**47.** (c)	**48.** (c)
49. (a)	**50.** (b)	**51.** (d)	**52.** (c)	**53.** (d)	**54.** (b)	**55.** (c)	**56.** (a)
57. (c)	**58.** (b)	**59.** (c)	**60.** (c)	**61.** (c)	**62.** (d)	**63.** (c)	**64.** (d)
65. (c)	**66.** (a)	**67.** (b)	**68.** (b)	**69.** (c)	**70.** (b)	**71.** (c)	**72.** (c)
73. (b)	**74.** (a)	**75.** (d)	**76.** (a)	**77.** (b)	**78.** (b)	**79.** (a)	**80.** (b)
81. (c)	**82.** (d)	**83.** (c)	**84.** (d)	**85.** (b)	**86.** (a)	**87.** (b)	**88.** (c)
89. (d)	**90.** (a)						

LEVEL-2

1. (a)	**2.** (a)	**3.** (d)	**4.** (d)	**5.** (a)	**6.** (b)	**7.** (d)	**8.** (c)
9. (a)	**10.** (a)	**11.** (c)	**12.** (c)	**13.** (c)	**14.** (a)	**15.** (d)	**16.** (a)
17. (b)	**18.** (a)	**19.** (d)	**20.** (d)	**21.** (c)	**22.** (c)	**23.** (d)	**24.** (c)
25. (c)	**26.** (b)	**27.** (b)	**28.** (c)	**29.** (d)	**30.** (b)	**31.** (d)	**32.** (a)
33. (b)	**34.** (d)	**35.** (a)	**36.** (d)	**37.** (b)	**38.** (c)	**39.** (d)	**40.** (b)
41. (d)	**42.** (c)	**43.** (d)	**44.** (a)	**45.** (b)	**46.** (b)	**47.** (d)	**48.** (c)
49. (b)	**50.** (d)	**51.** (a)	**52.** (c)	**53.** (d)	**54.** (b)	**55.** (b)	**56.** (b)
57. (a)	**58.** (c)	**59.** (d)	**60.** (d)	**61.** (b)	**62.** (c)	**63.** (d)	**64.** (b)
65. (a)	**66.** (b)	**67.** (c)	**68.** (a)	**69.** (c)	**70.** (a)	**71.** (b)	**72.** (a)
73. (c)	**74.** (b)						

Solutions

Level-1

1. 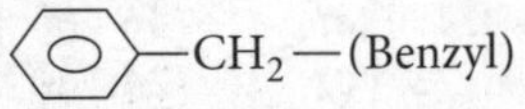

2. 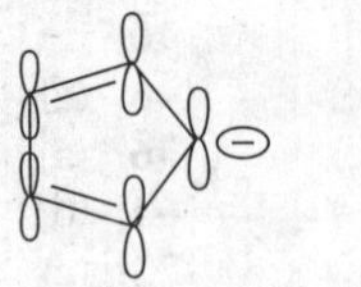

4 π electrons and 2 p-orbital electrons of lone pair = $6e^-$

3. 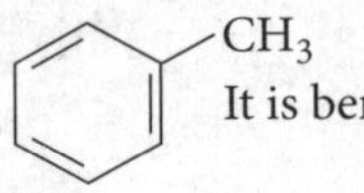

It is benzylic hydrogens.

5. 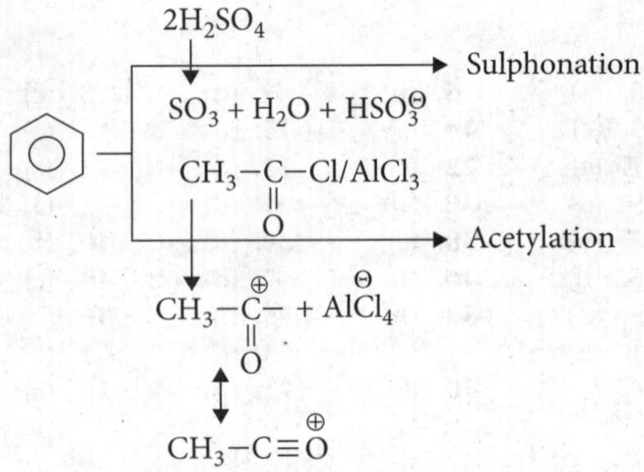

6. 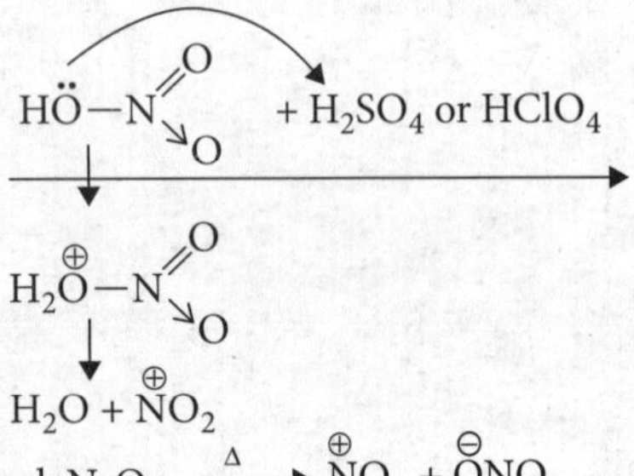

7. 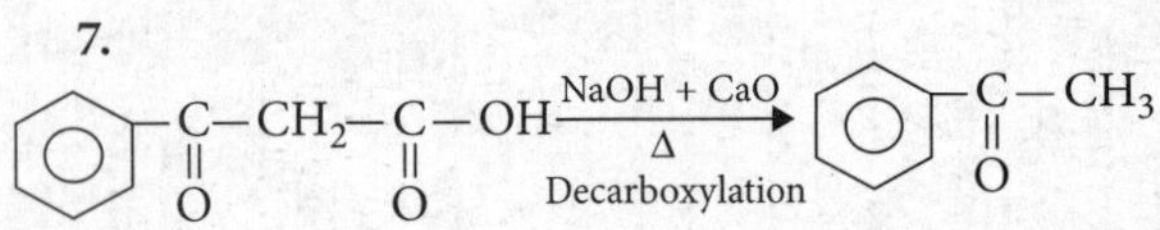

8. In sulphonation and iodination, isotopic effect is observed. This means the second step is rate determining step; so removal of $H^{\oplus} > D^{\oplus} > T^{\oplus}$ is in order.

9. 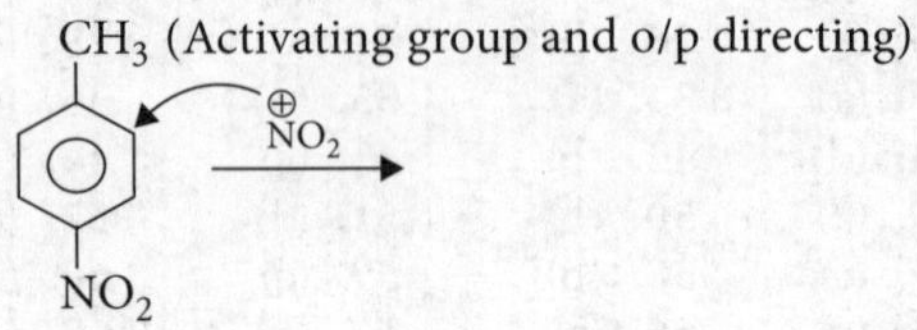

10. 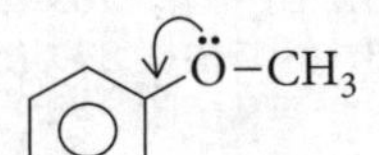

(By +M, it activates the ring for electrophiles)

11. 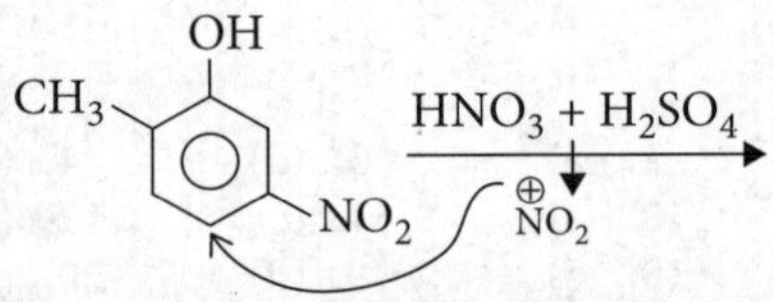

–OH is a stronger activating group than $-CH_3$. So it dominates for ESR in the O/P direction.

12. 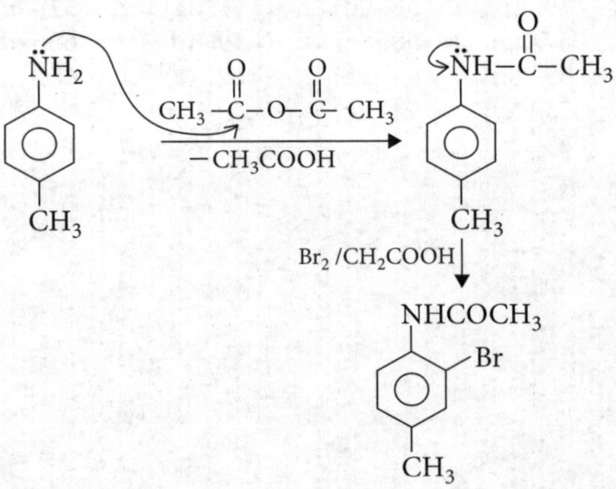

13. 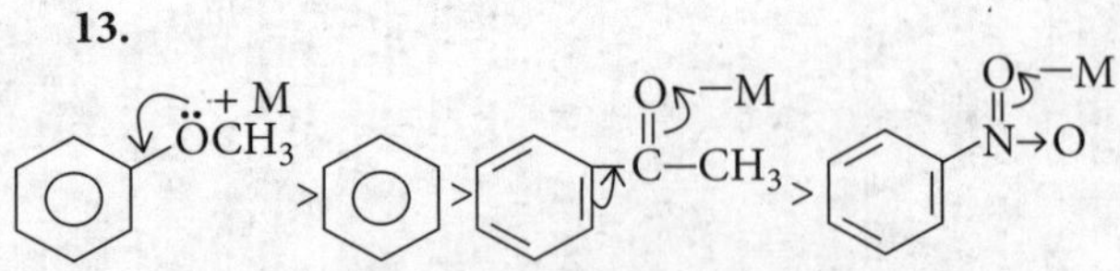

14. More α-hydrogen (more hyperconjugation). This results in greater activation of the ring.

15. 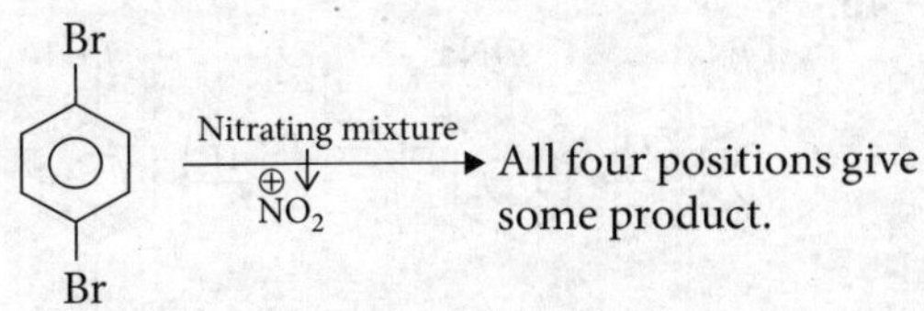

16. Strong deactivating group does not give Friedel–Crafts reaction. Aniline, in the presence of catalyst Lewis acid $AlCl_3$, deactivates the ring and the Friedel–Crafts reaction does not occur.

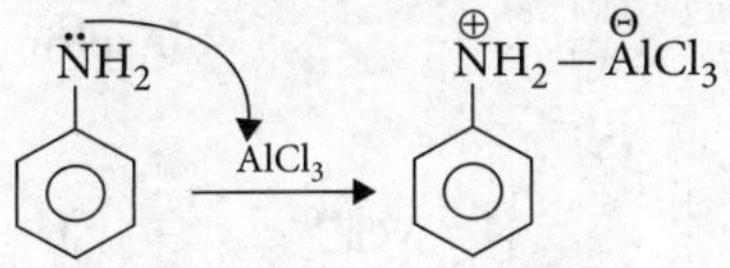

17. 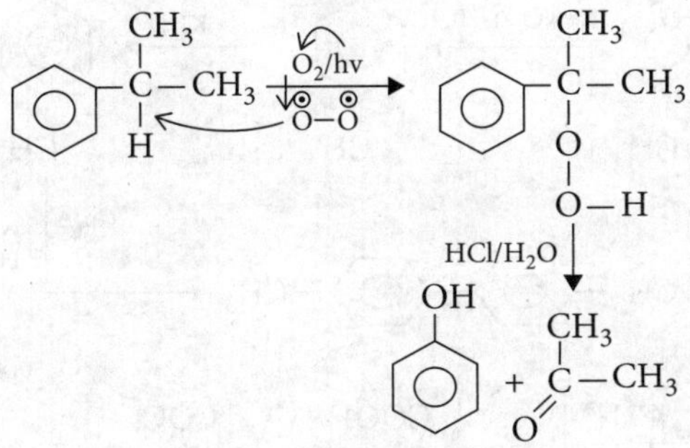

18. 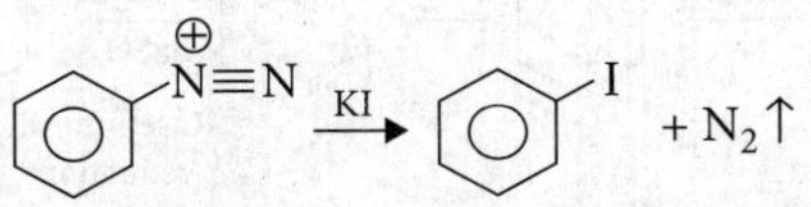

19. 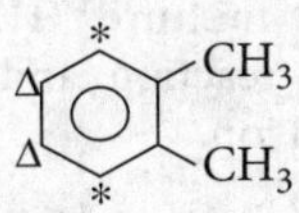

20. 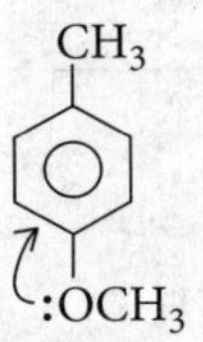

+M strong activating group decides the position of attack of the electrophile.

21. $KMnO_4$ oxidizes the carbon of the side branch of the ring to carboxylic acid as benzoic acid.

22. 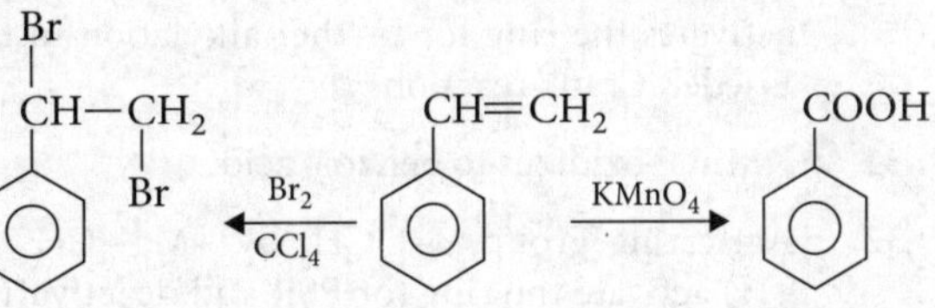

Styrene dibromide

Benzoic acid

23. All the carbons are present just outside the ring (benzene); they are oxidized to acid as benzoic acid.

24. On hydrogenation, all π bonds are hydrogenated if excess of hydrogen is taken in the presence of catalyst.

25. 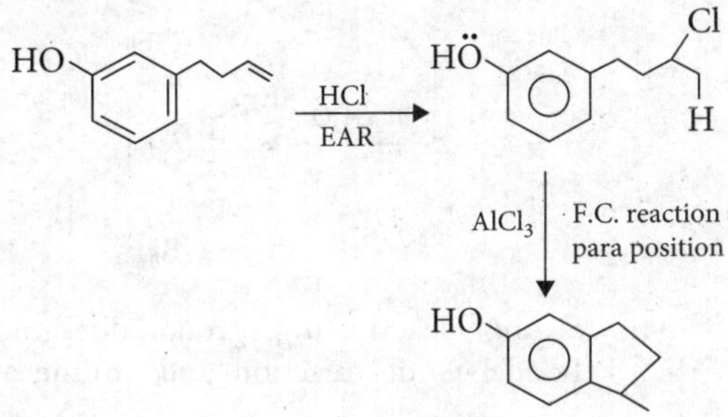

26. 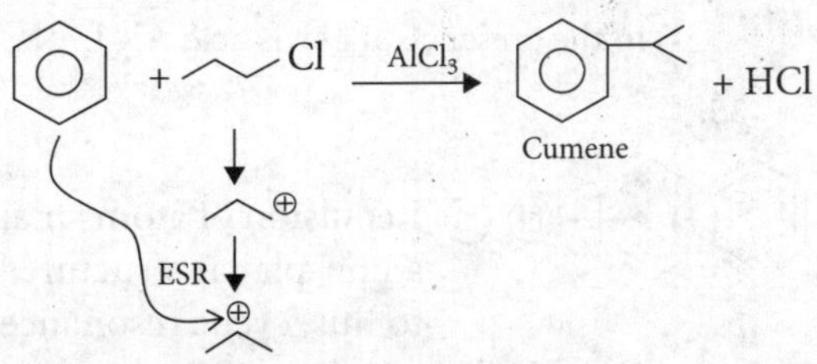

27. $-CH_3$ (by (+H)) activates the ring; –Cl (by (–I)) deactivates the ring; $-COCl_3$ (by (–M)) strongly deactivates the ring.

28. Nitrobenzene is a strong deactivating group, so it does not take part in Friedel–Crafts reaction. But it is a polar solvent, so it promotes ionization of the reagent for the reaction.

29. 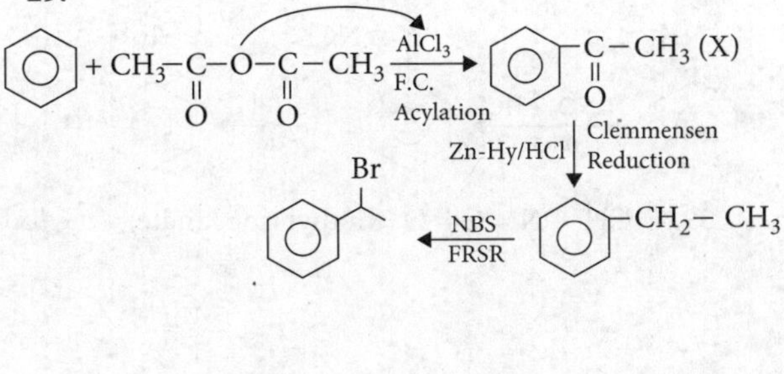

30. On alkylation of benzene, the alkyl group activates the ring for further alkylation in the Friedel–Crafts reaction.

31. $KMnO_4$ oxidizes to benzoic acid.

32. Activating groups ($-OCH_3$ by +M, $-CH_3$ by +H) activate the ring for ESR and deactivating groups (–Cl by (–I) and –CN by (–M)) deactivate the ring.

33.

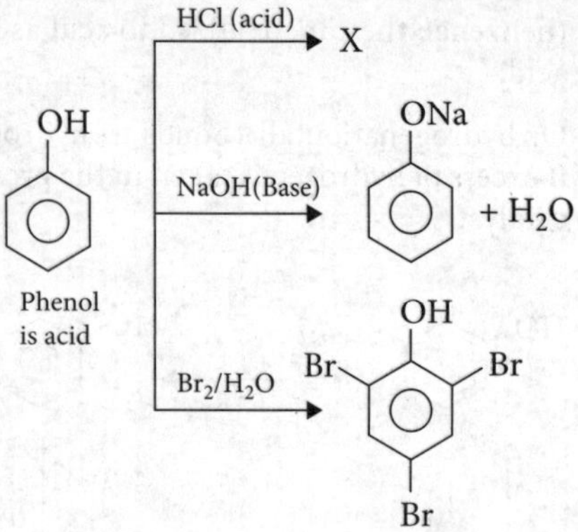

34. Strong deactivating group does not give Friedel–Crafts reaction and aniline also becomes deactivating anilinium ($C_6H_5-\overset{\oplus}{N}H_2-\overset{\ominus}{Al}Cl_3$) in the presence of Lewis acid $AlCl_3$.

35.

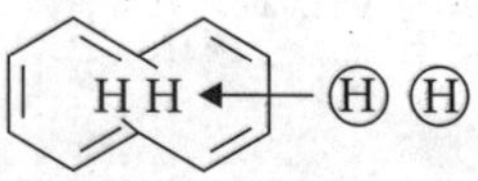

Repulsion of atoms makes a non-planar structure; due to this, cyclic resonance is restricted. So it is non-aromatic.

37. Lowest energy means the most stable.

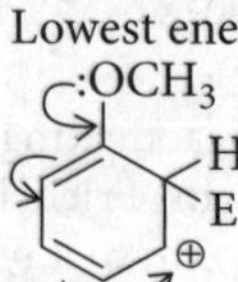

38.

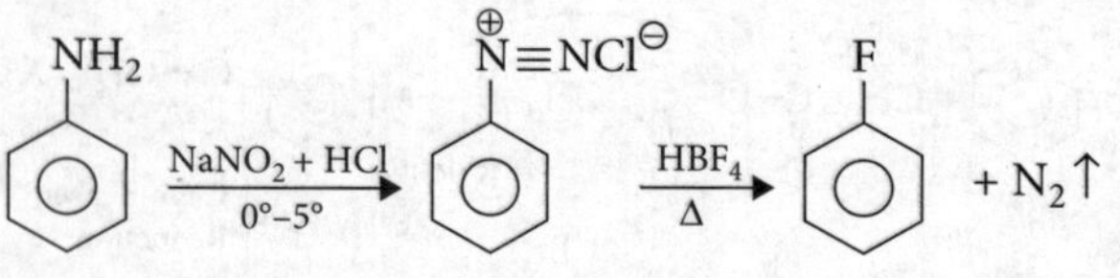

39. $CH_3-N=C=O$ (Methyl isocyanate)

40.

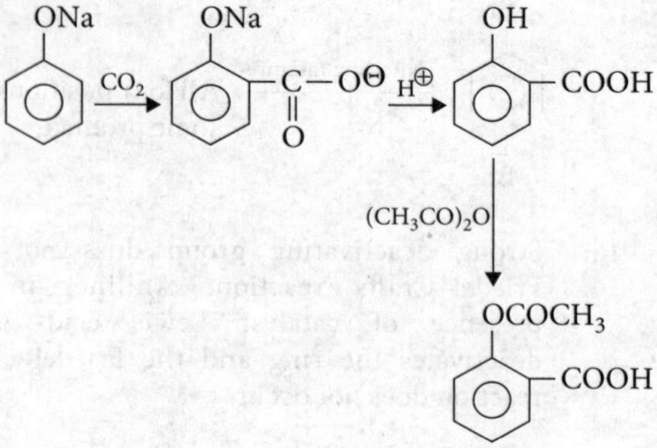

Aspirin

41.

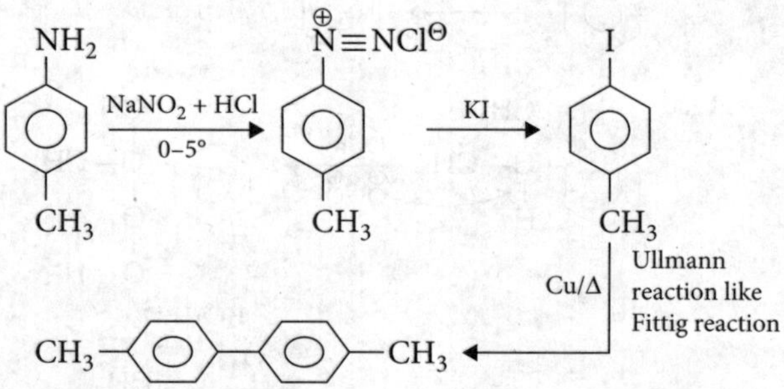

42.

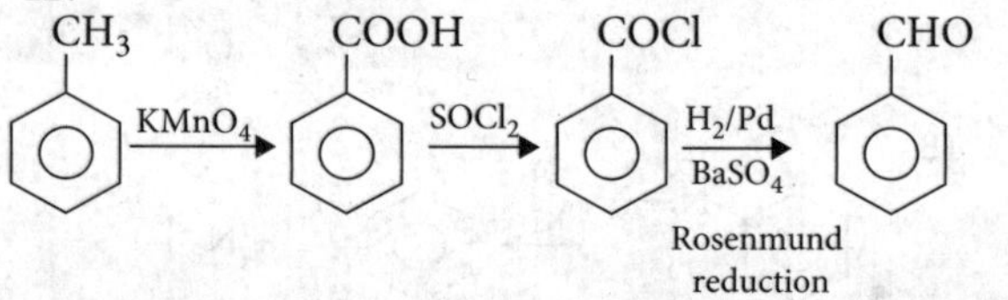

43. Aniline with nitrating mixture (HNO_3 + H_2SO_4) gives acid–base reaction and forms meta-directing anilinium ion.

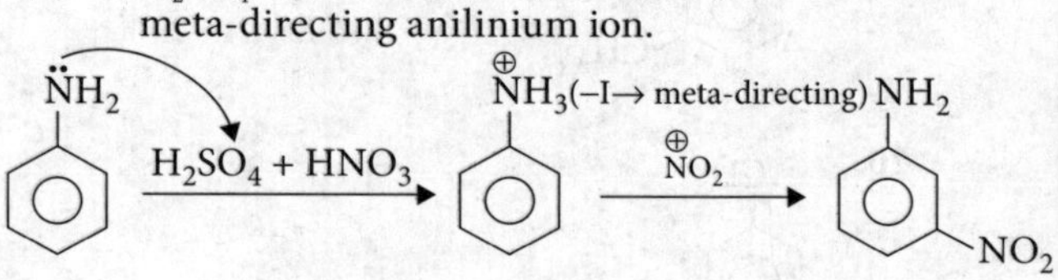

45.

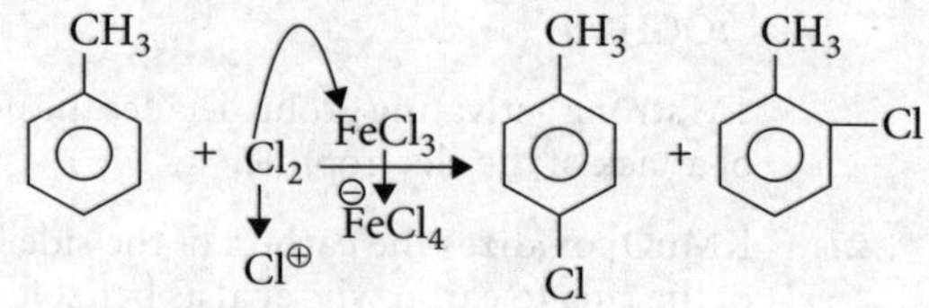

46. 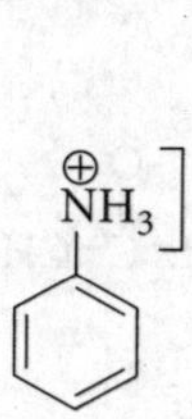

Octet complete and vacant orbital is not available; so it does not accept π electrons.

47.

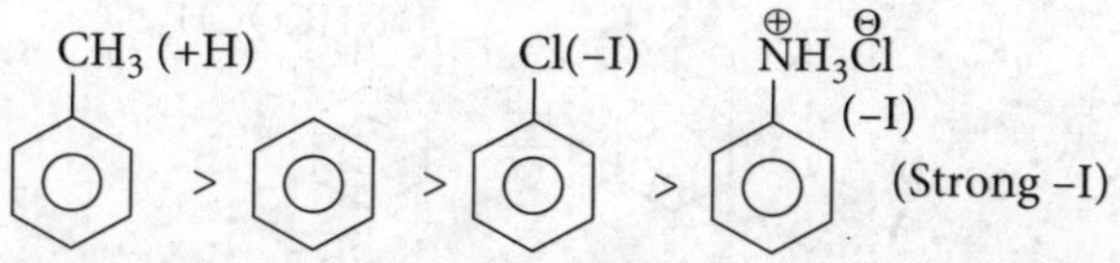

48. In nitration, the second step (deprotonation) is not a rate determining step. So the rate of reaction does not depend on atoms (H or D) of the benzene ring.

49.

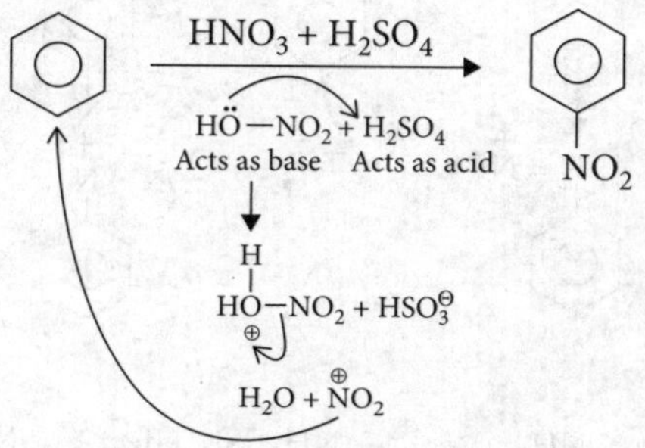

50.

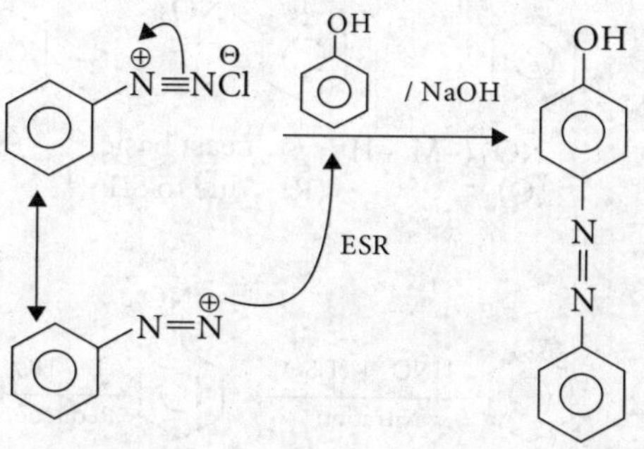

Orange dye

52. See Q17

53. Nitrogen has a lone pair, so it activates the ring by +M strongly at the o/p position. The ortho position shows some steric condition, so the para position gives the major product.

54. Nitration will be at the first ring because it is activated by +H (2α - H) and the para position has high density and less steric hindrance.

55. Direction of electrophile is decided by mesomeric effect of halogen.

56.

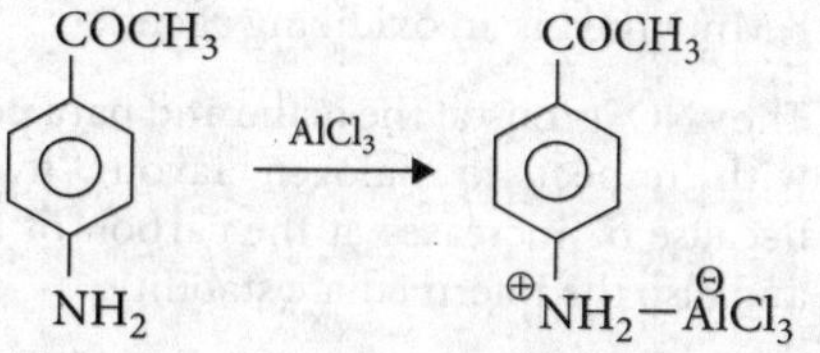

Both groups are deactivating in (IV) and (III). So (I) and (II) are the most preferred options.

57. See Q17. ‘P’ is phenol, so phenol does not give iodoform test.

58. 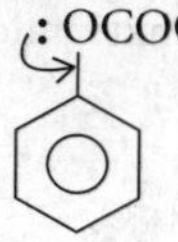 $:OCOCH_3$ (Activating group by +M)

59.

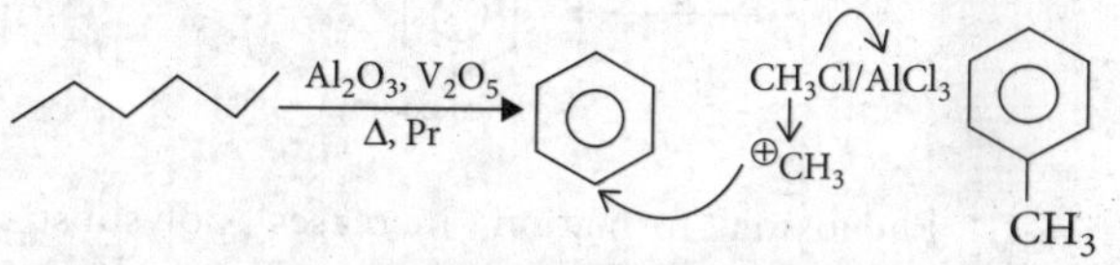

60. In Kolbe's reaction, the major product is formed at the ortho position. This is because of higher electron density at the ortho position by the $-O^{\ominus}$ group of phenoxide and a stable product.

61.

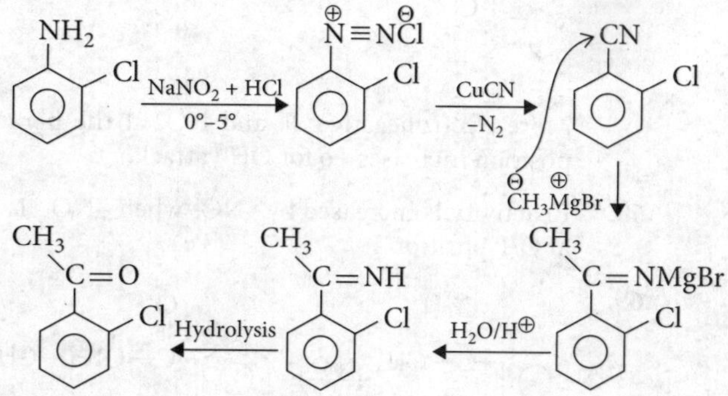

62.

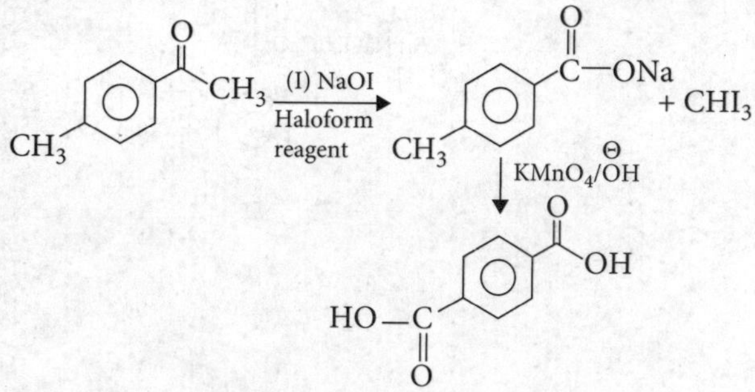

63. $KMnO_4/\overset{\ominus}{O}H$ is an oxidizing agent.

64. The $-NO_2$ group at the ortho and para positions with respect to halogen favour hydrolysis because $\delta^{\oplus}$ increases at the carbon of halogen and also the intermediate stability.

65.

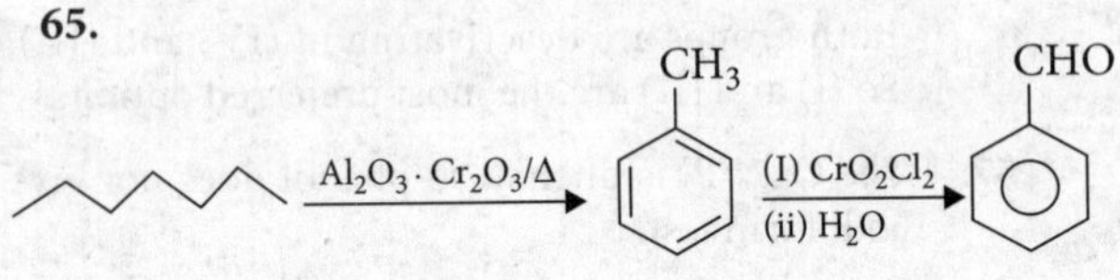

Fehling's test is given by aliphatic aldehyde, and not by aromatic aldehyde.

66.

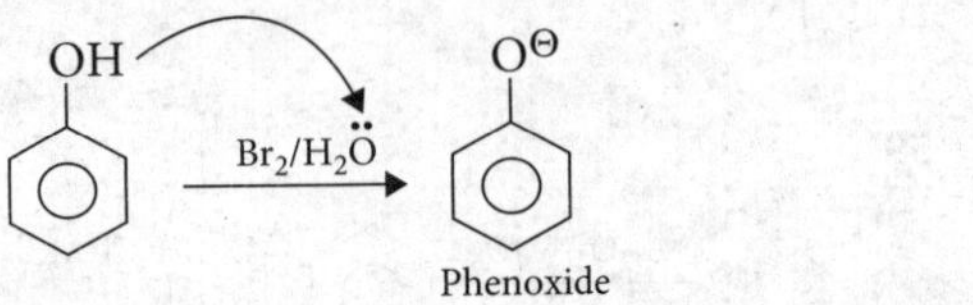

Phenoxide formation increases polysubstitution, but phenol gives only ortho and para products and the para product is major.

67.

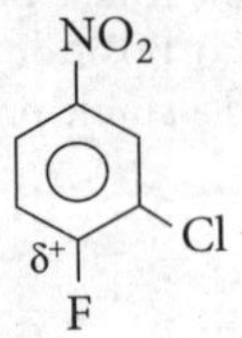

More electronegative 'F' and NO_2 at the para position increases $+\delta$ for $OH^{\ominus}$ attack.

68. Reactivity is increased by $-NO_2$ when $-NO_2$ is at O/P position.

69.

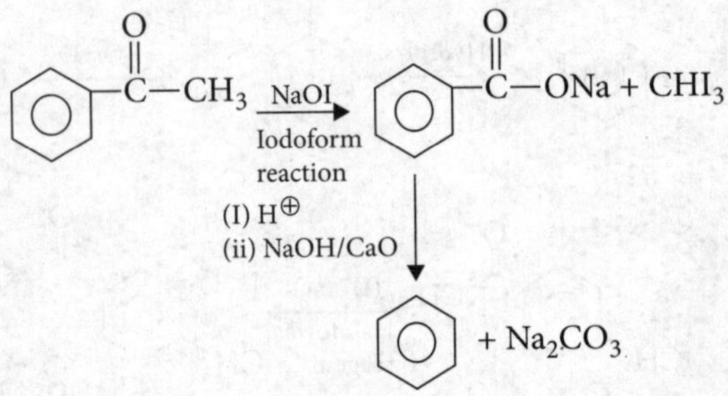

70.

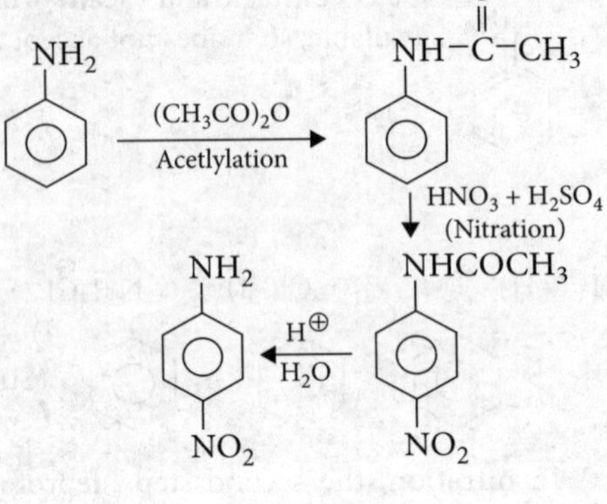

71.

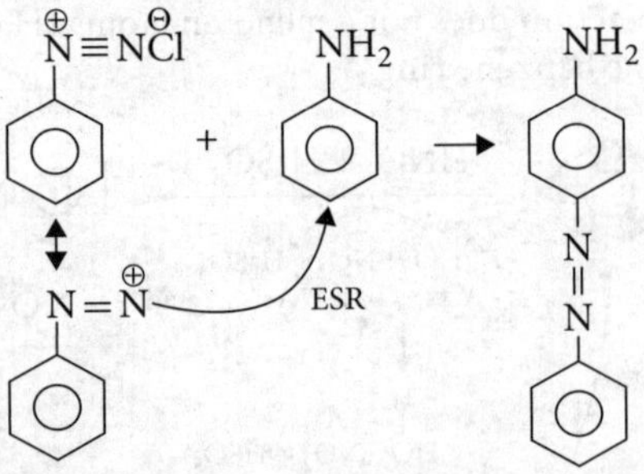

Yellow dye.

72.

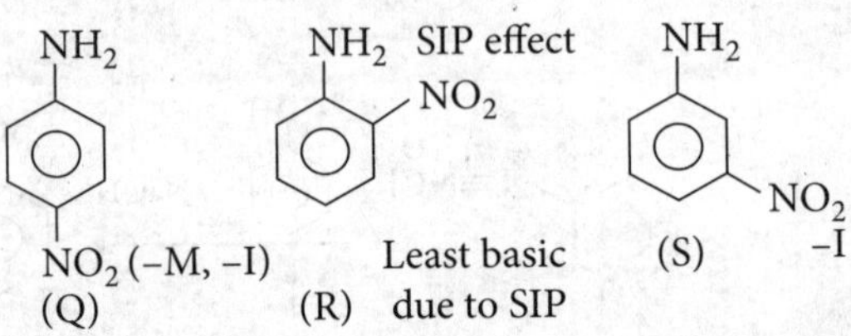

73.

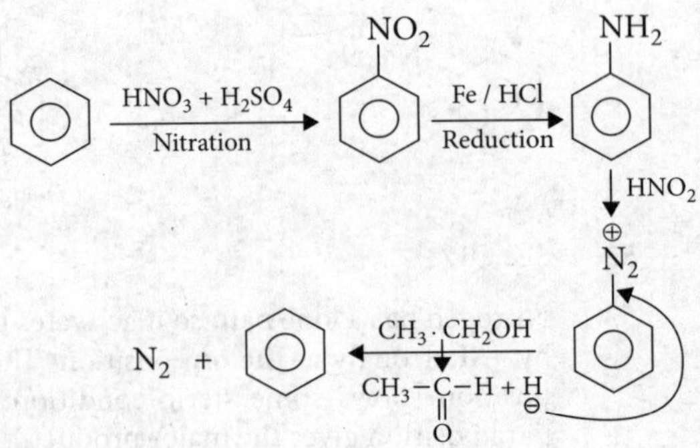

74. Fluorine develops more $\delta^{\oplus}$ on carbon for attack of nucleophile.

75. After nitration, 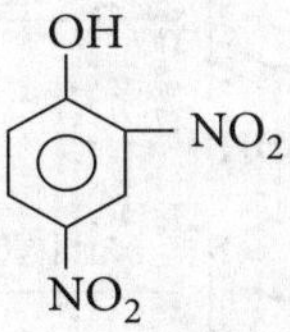 It is oxidized for the next nitration, but nitration after formation of

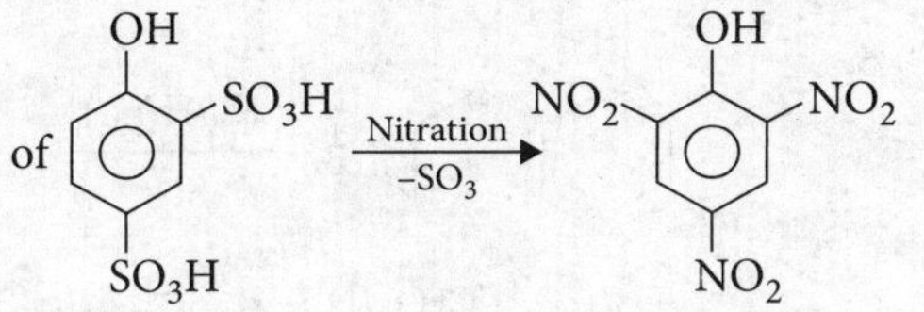

76.

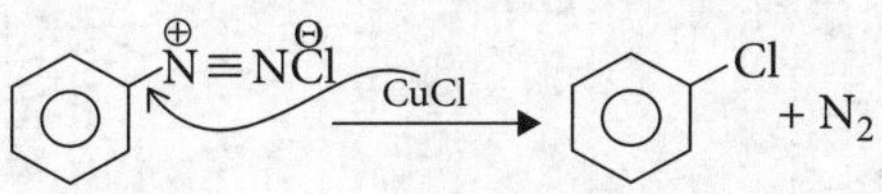

77. Electrophilic substitution reaction is a characteristic reaction of aromatic compounds.

78.

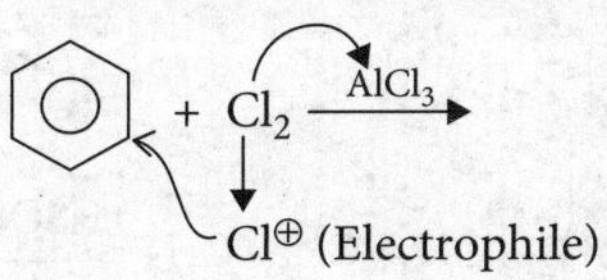

79. Due to steric hindrance, radical combination product does not give major product; disproportionation product is the major product.

82. Sn/NH_4OH is a weak reducing agent; it is partially reduced to nitrobenzene.

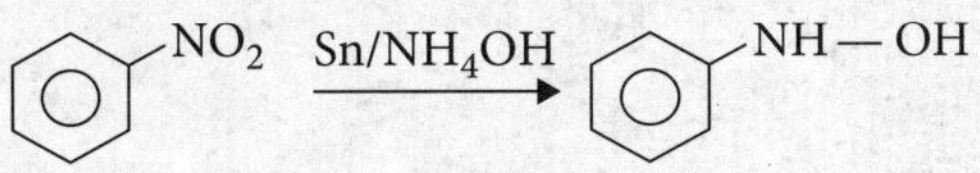

83.

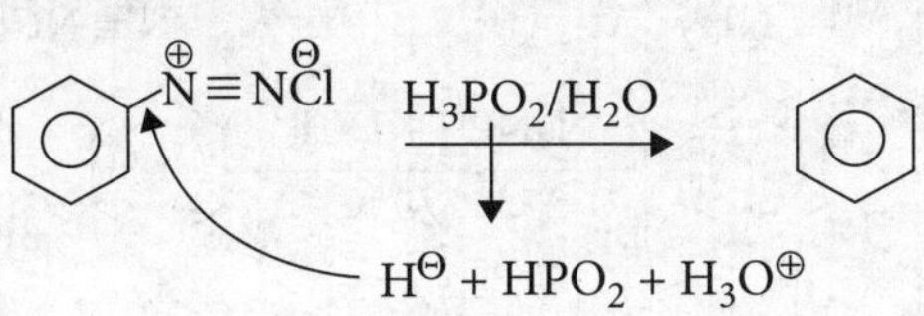

84.

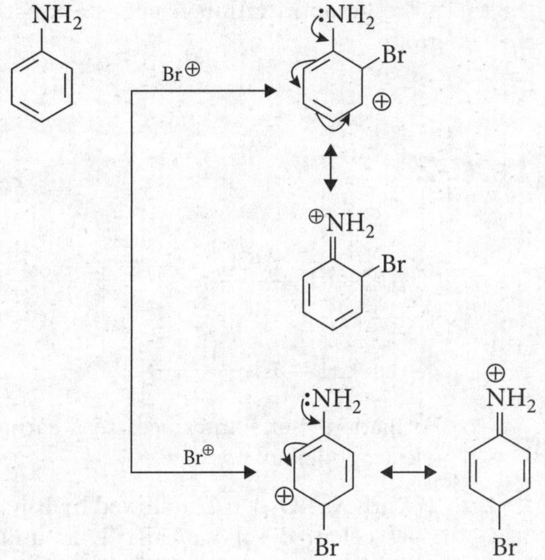

86.

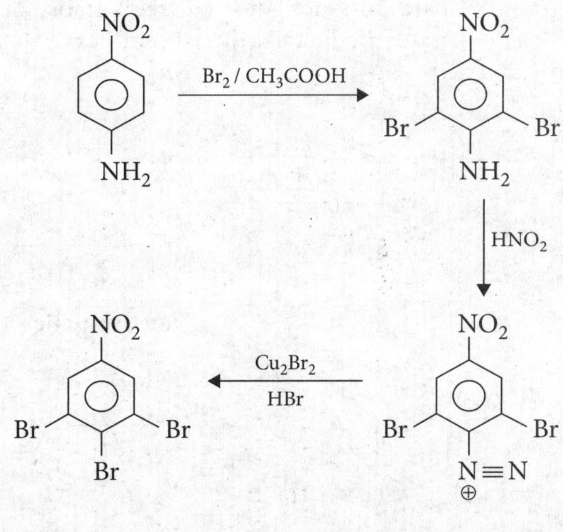

87.

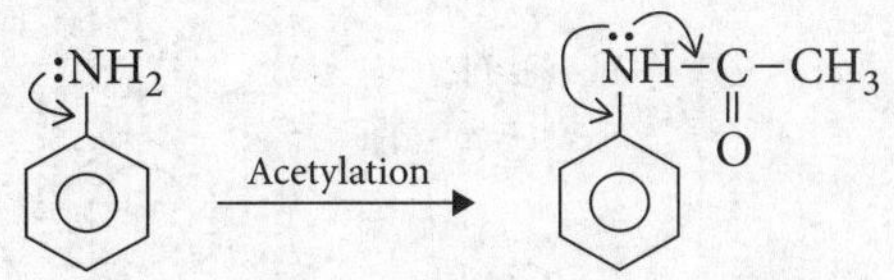

88.

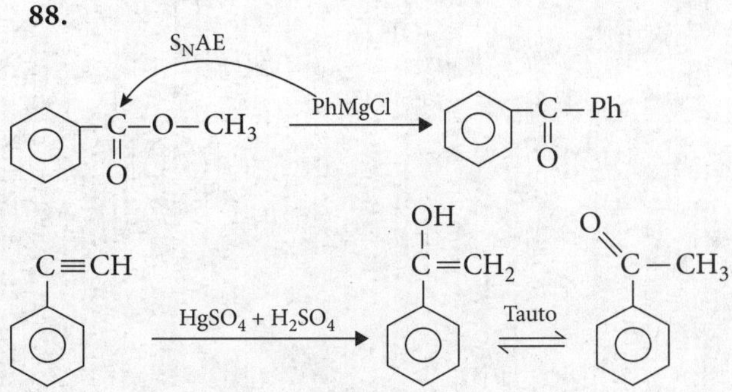

89. Nitro group in nitrobenzene is a deactivating group.

LEVEL-2

1.

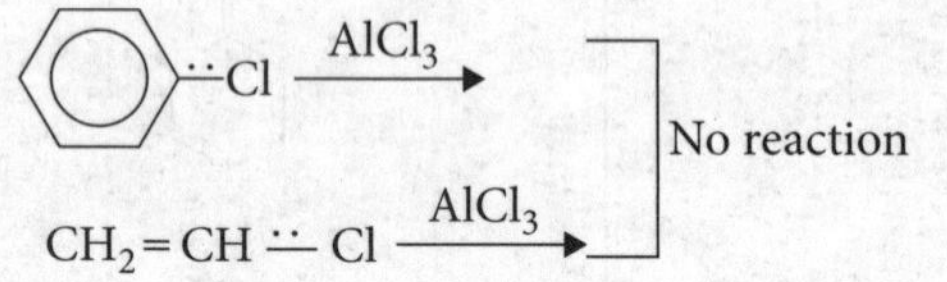

Formation of intermediate carbocation (electrophile) not possible.

2. 'P' with $NaNO_2$ + HCl followed by B-naphthol gives coloured solid means 'P' is aniline or aniline derivative in which both the ortho and para positions must be free because bromine water product has three bromines.

3.

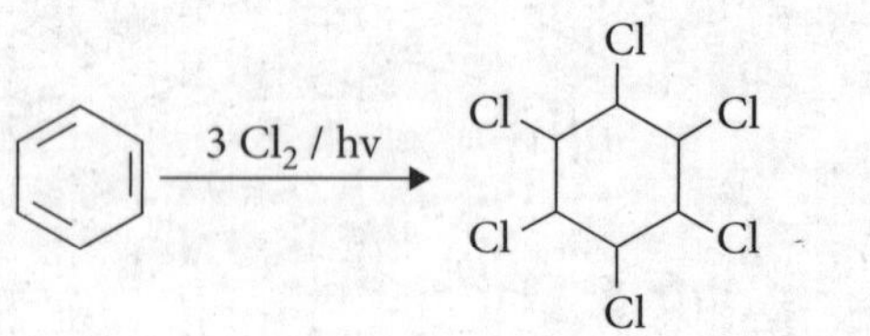

Non-aromatic

4.

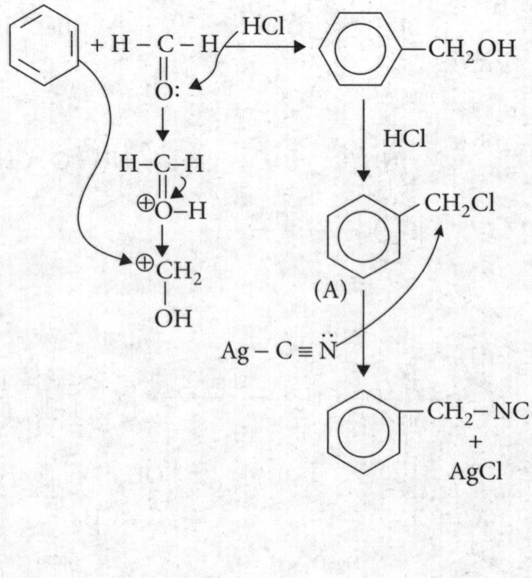

5.

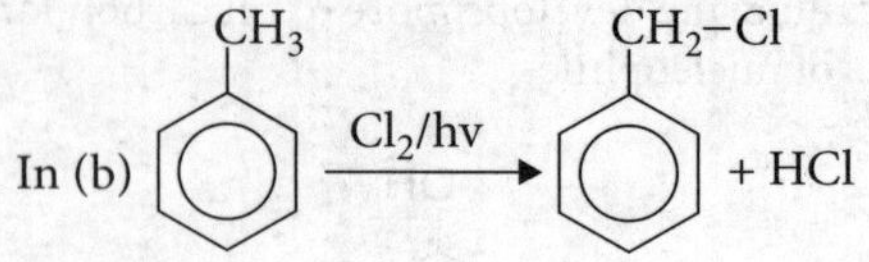

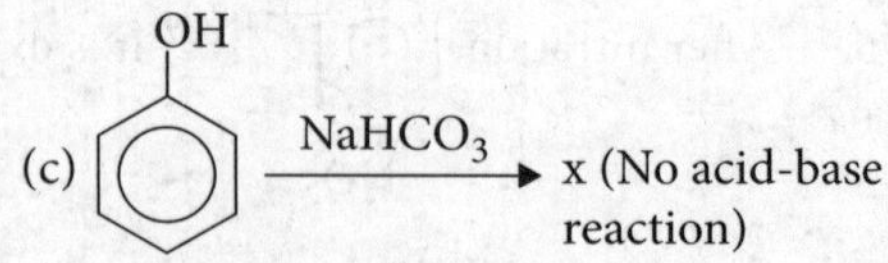

(d) gives benzene not phenol

6.

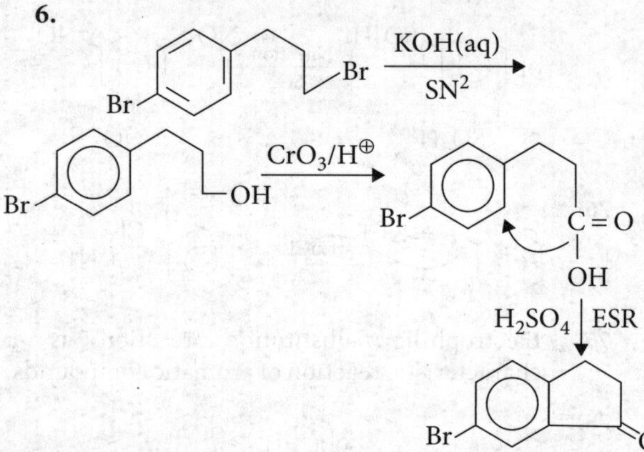

7.

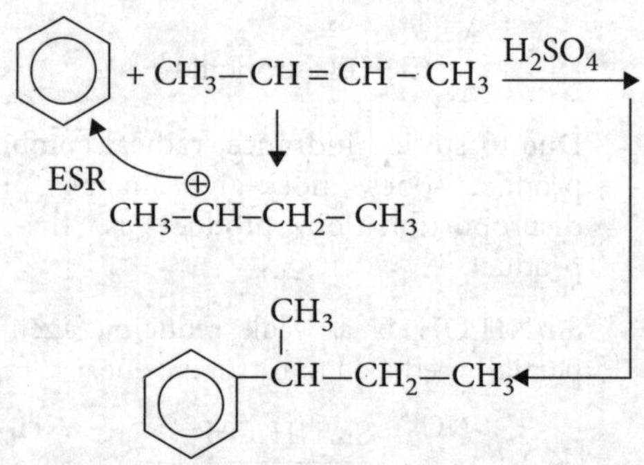

8.

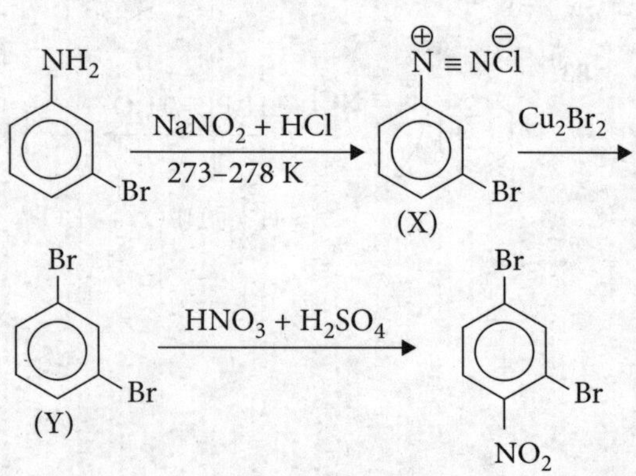

9.

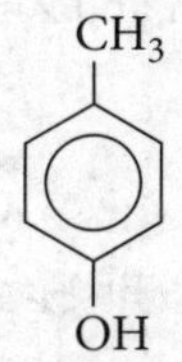

In this compound, $Br^{\oplus}$ (electrophile) does not substitute CH_3, but in 'C', $-SO_3H$ is easily substituted.

10.

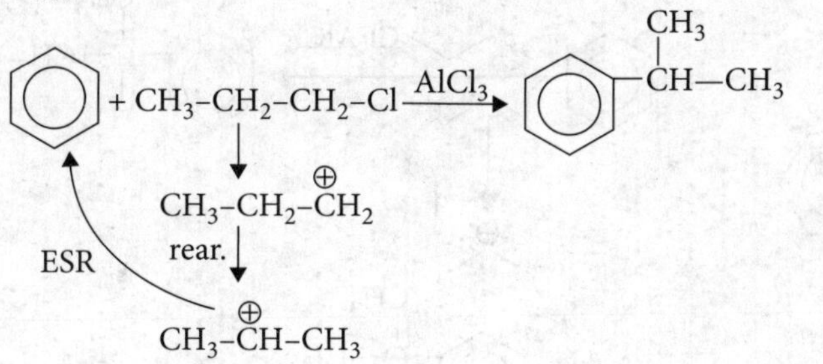

11.

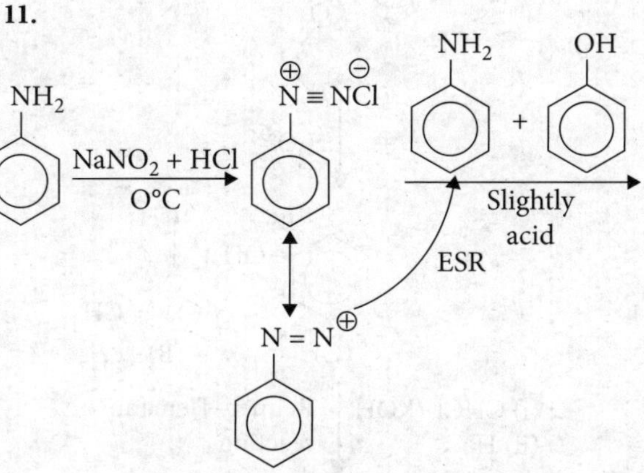

12.

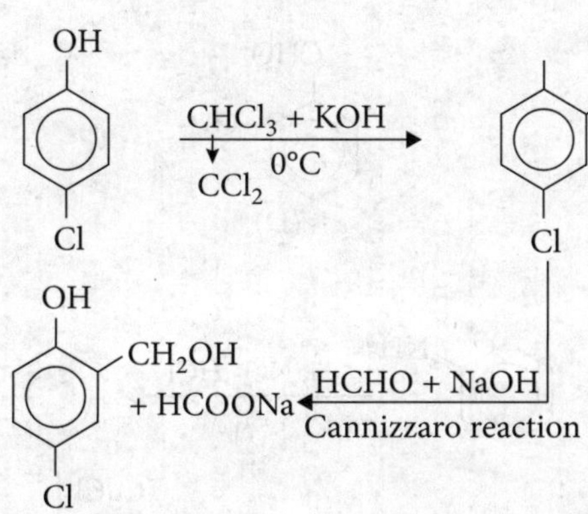

13.

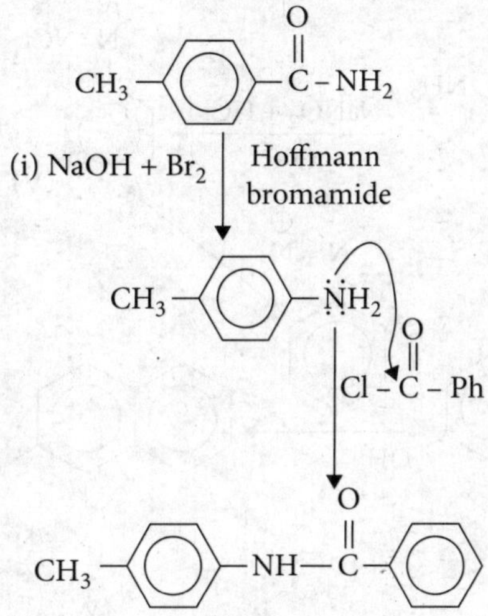

14. The $-NO_2$ group is at the para position with respect to F; so nucleophilic substitution will occur.

15.

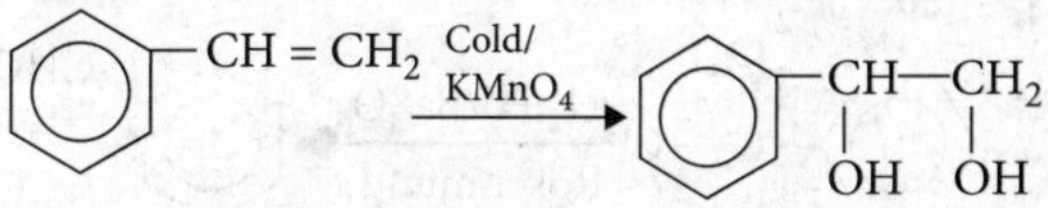

16.

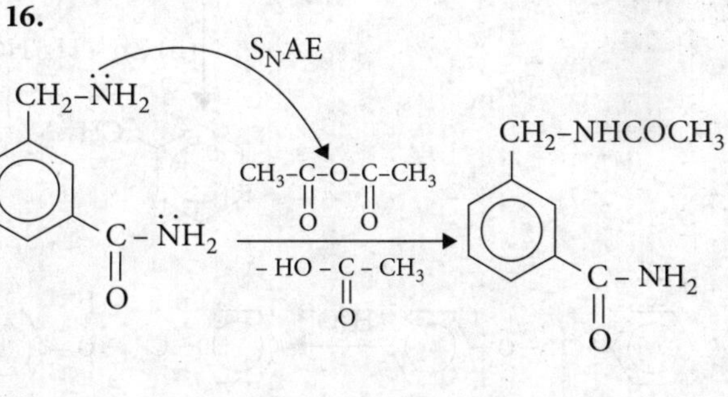

17.

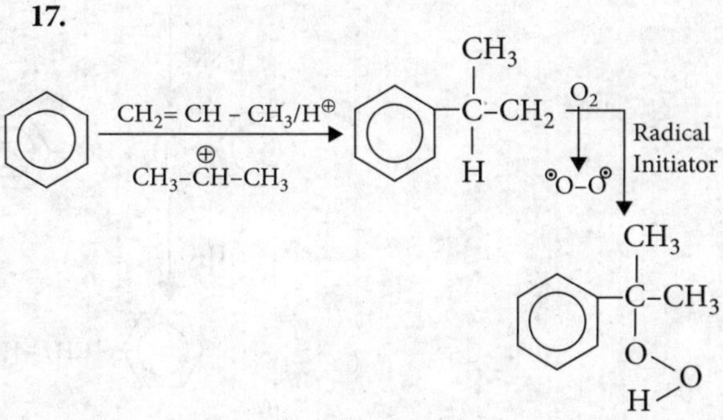

18.

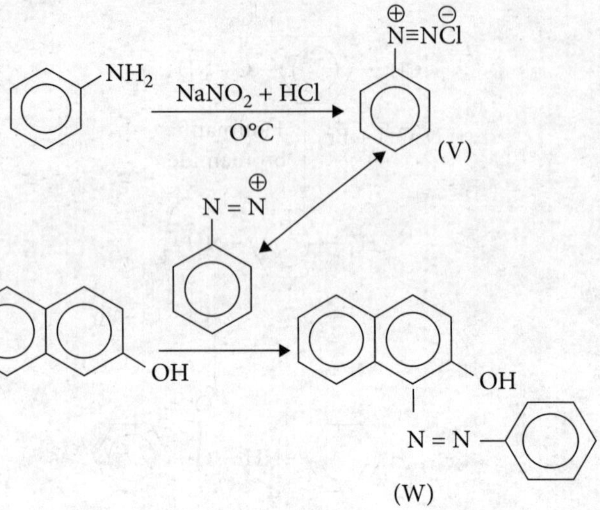

19. –Cl is the o/p directing group due to lone pair (+M) and – NO_2 is the meta directing group.

20.

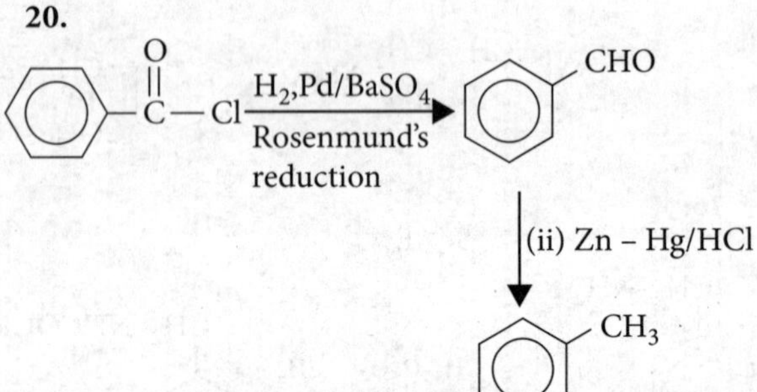

21.

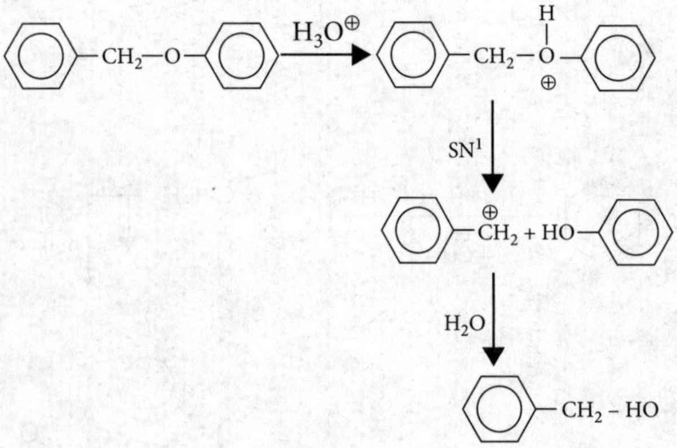

22. Etard reaction is correctly explained.

23. HNO_2 forms benzene diazonium salt and after hydrolysis is converted into phenol, which is oxidized into benzoquinone.

(b) is Reimer–Tiemann reaction and Zn is the reducing agent

24.

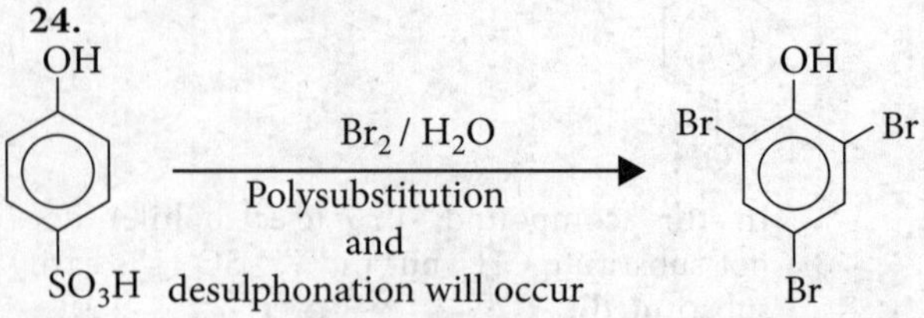

25.

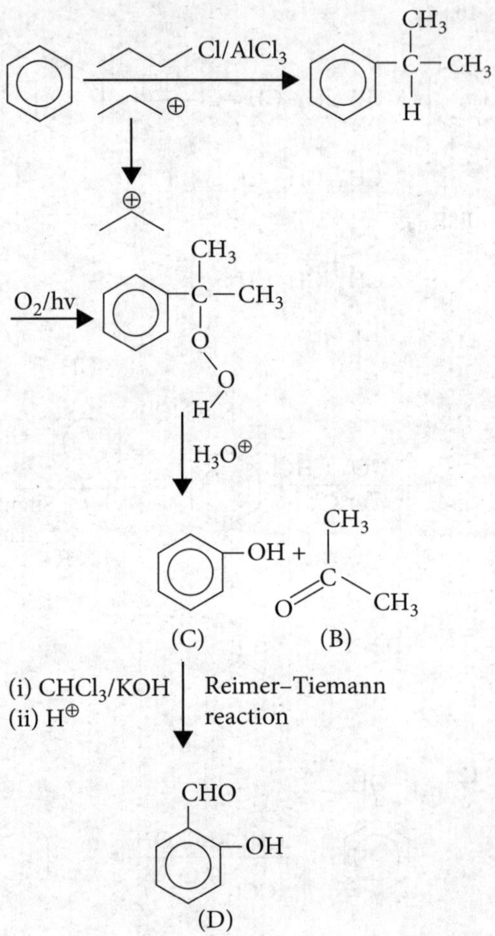

26.

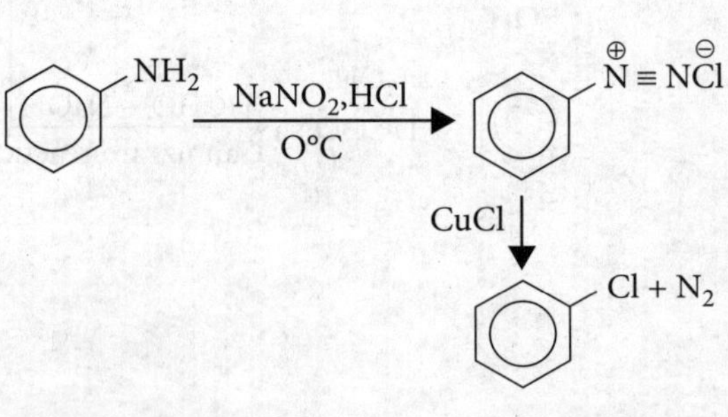

27.

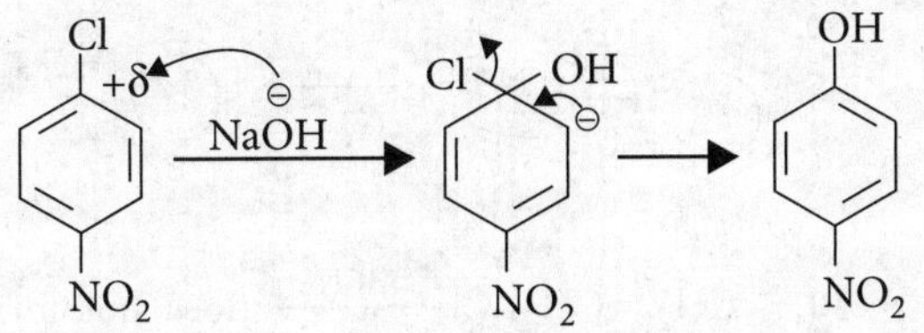

28.

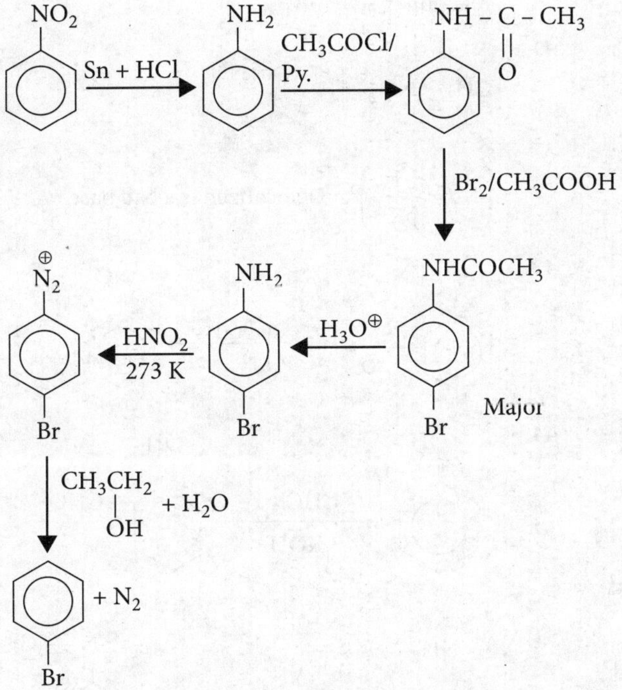

29. With phenol, benzene diazonium chloride gives coupling reaction and forms orange dye and not red dye.

31.

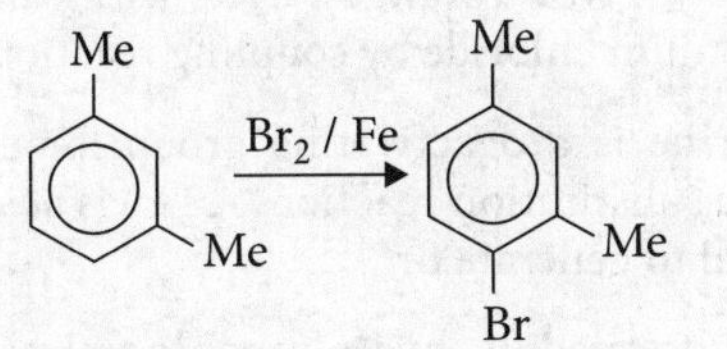

Aniline does not give Friedel–Crafts reaction and terminal alkyne does not gives Birch's reduction due to acid-base reaction, which occurs in the presence of acidic hydrogen.

32.

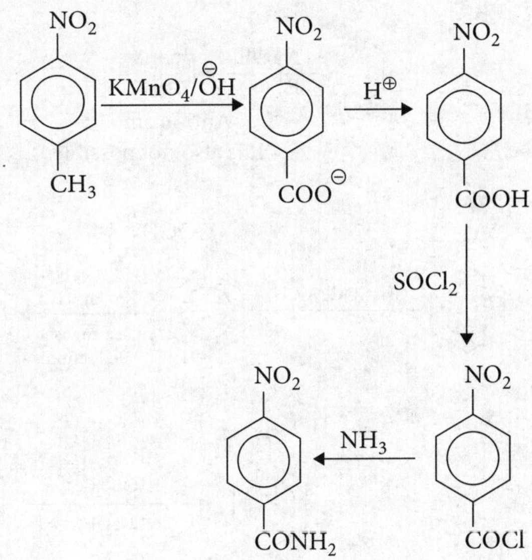

33.

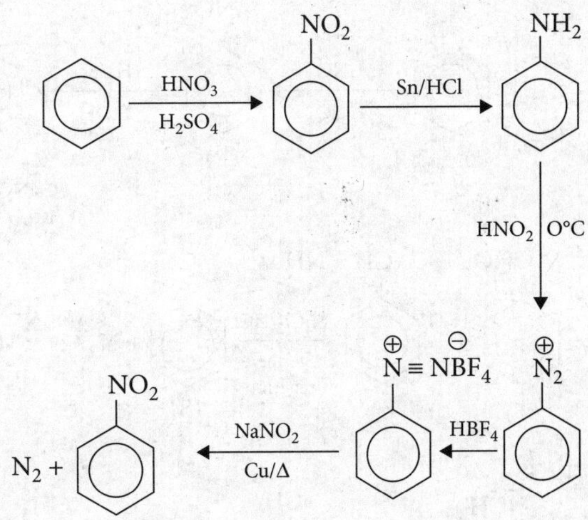

34.

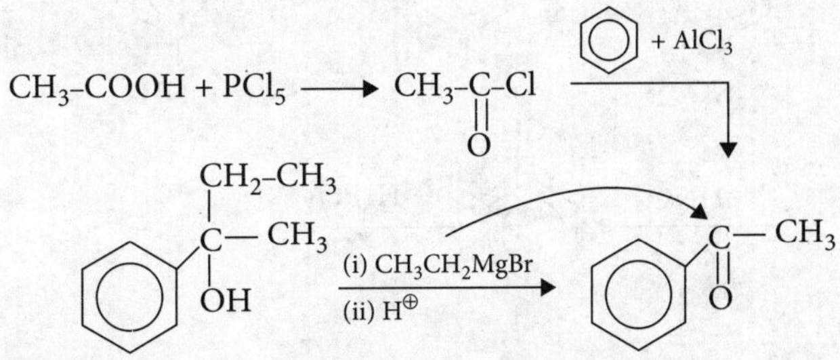

35.

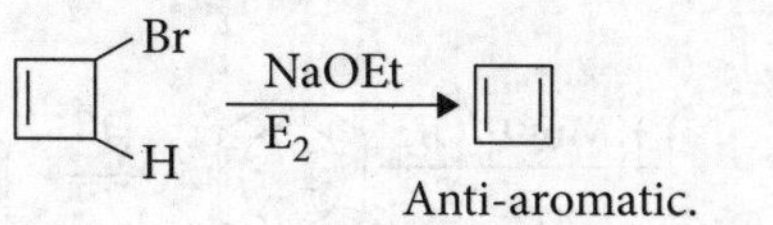

Anti-aromatic.
It is also not possible.

36.

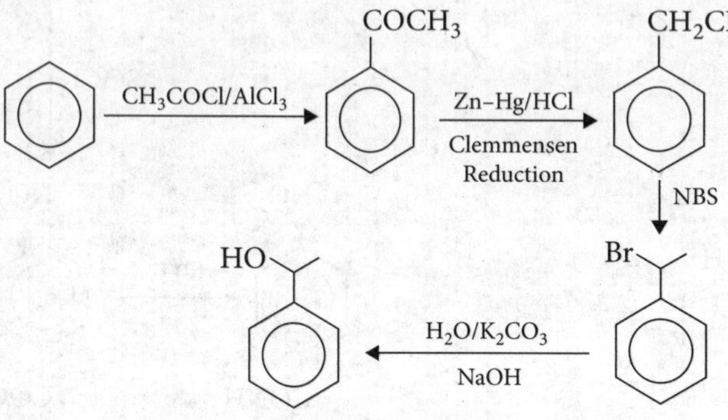

37.

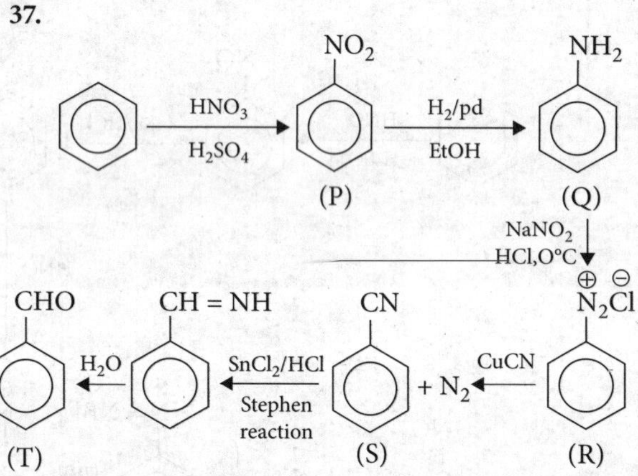

38.

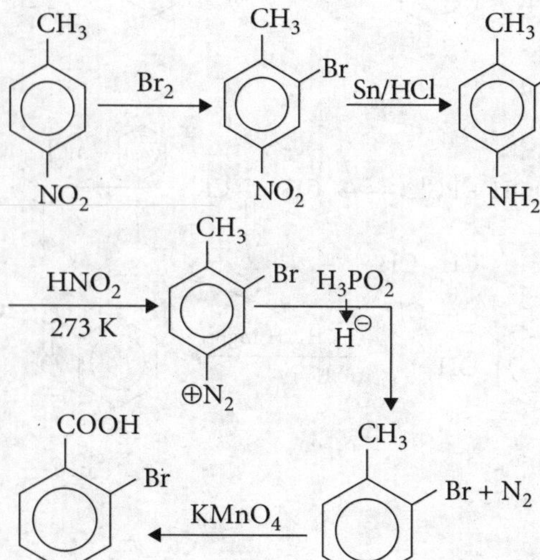

39.

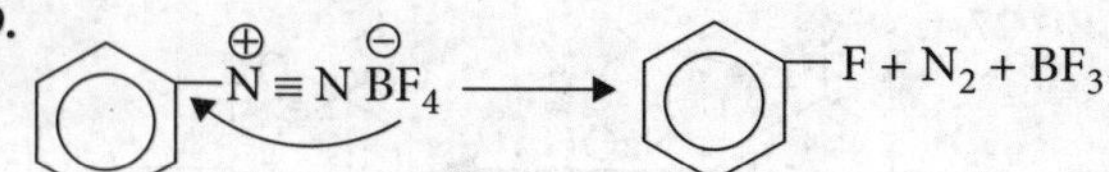

40. $CH_2 = CH \cdots Cl \xrightarrow{AlCl_3}$ does not form carbocation; so it does not give the Friedel–Crafts reaction.

41.

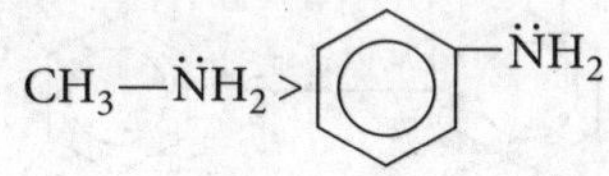

$\left(Kb \propto \frac{1}{pKb}\right)$ Delocalized is a bad base.

43.

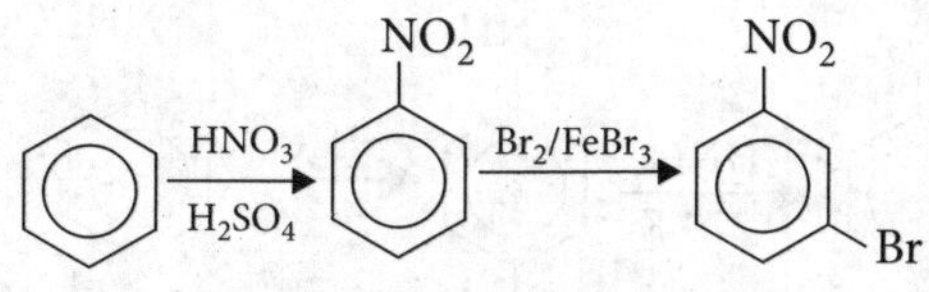

44.

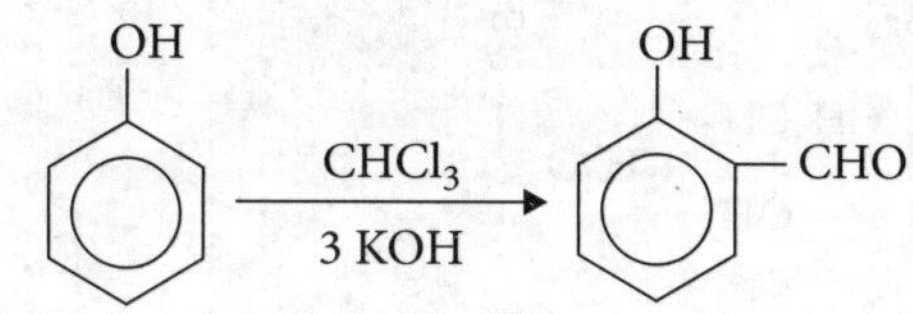

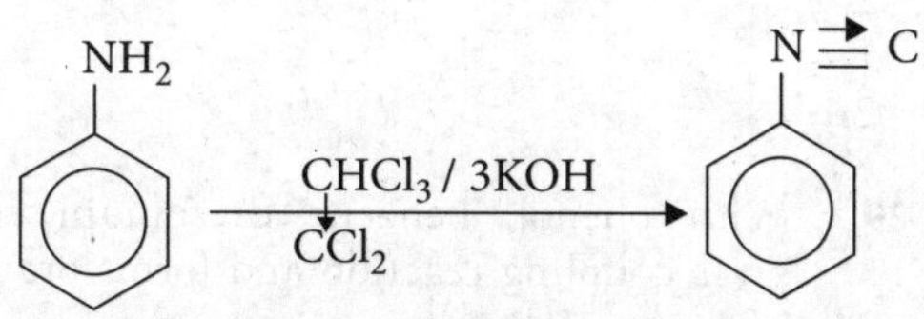

45. Phenol gives orange dye with benzene diazonium chloride by coupling reaction.

46. Chlorine is a deactivating group for electrophilic substitution reaction. A Lewis acid is required to generate Br^+.

47. $FeCl_2$ formed is hydrolyzed to release HCl during the reaction. Thus, only a small amount of HCl is required to initiate the reaction.

48.

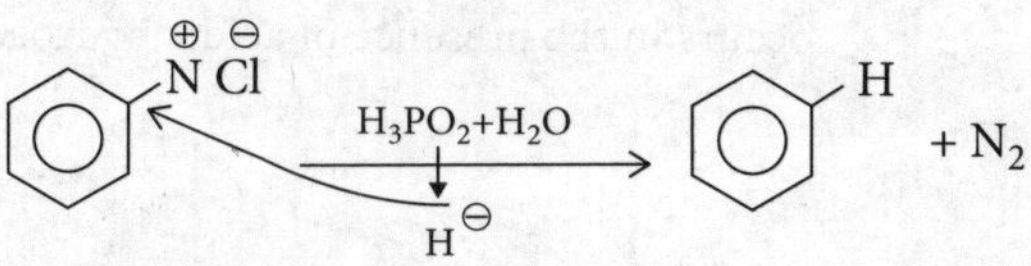

49.

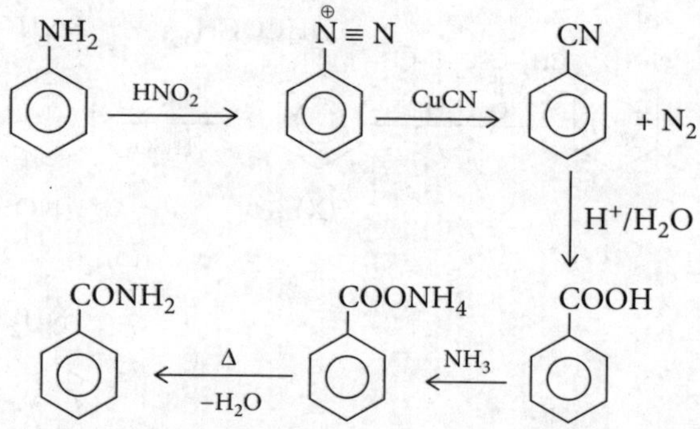

50. Three $-NO_2$ strongly increases aromatic nucleophilic substitution reaction.

51. $-NO_2$ (by -M) increases acidic strength (Ka) and OCH_3 (by +M) decreases acidic strength (Ka).

$$Ka \propto \frac{1}{pKa}$$

52.

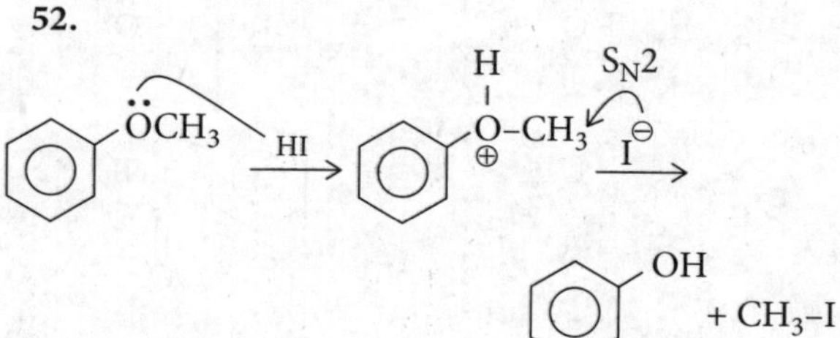

53. Sandmeyer reaction is aromatic nucleophilic substitution reaction for the formation of aryl chloride, aryl bromide and aryl cyanide.

54.

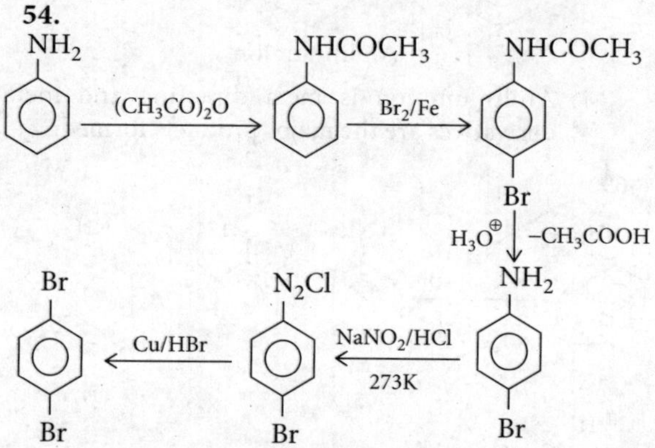

55. $-OCH_4$ is the o/p directing and activating group, so (p) will be the answer.

56.

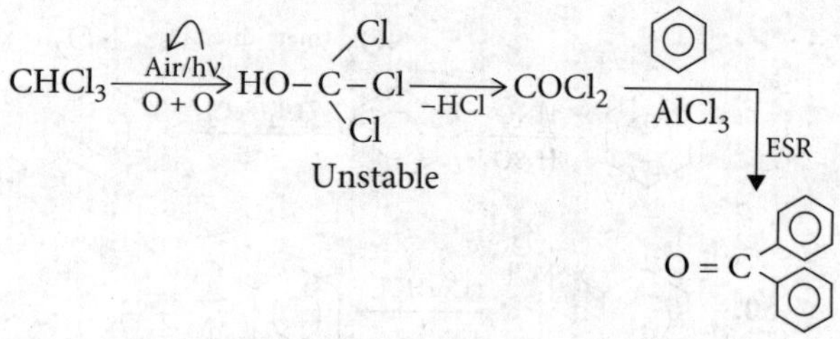

57.

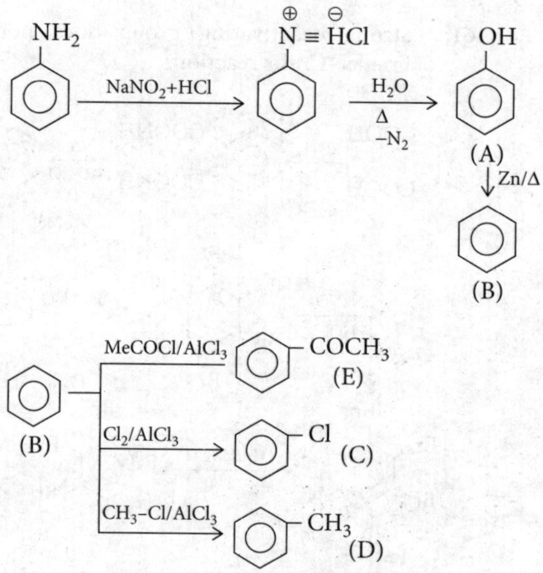

58.

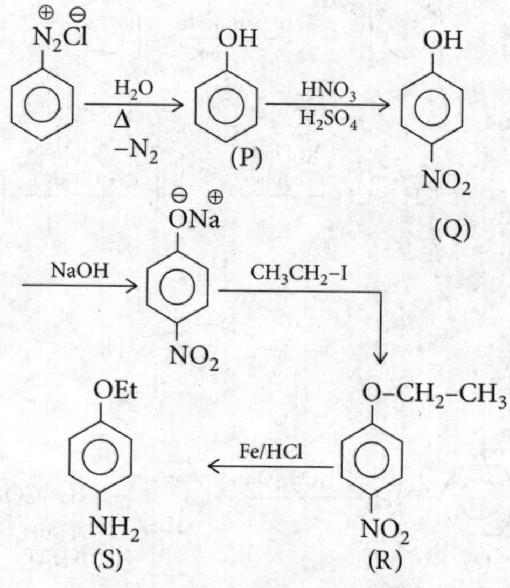

59.

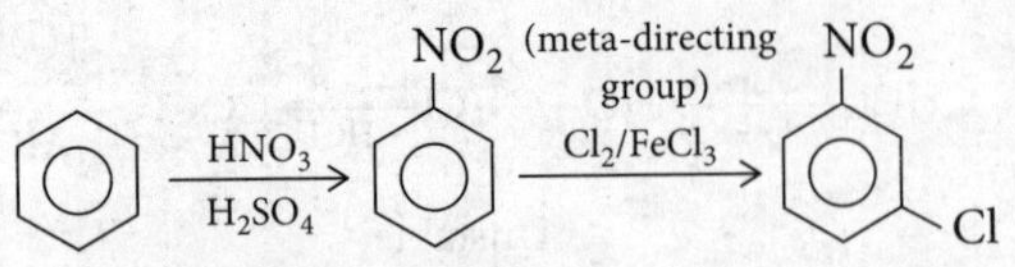

60.

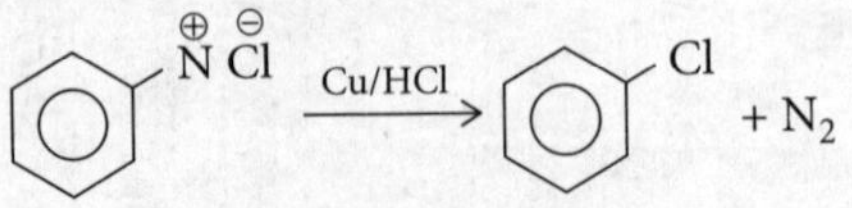

61. Strong deactivating group does not gives Friedel–Crafts reaction.

62.

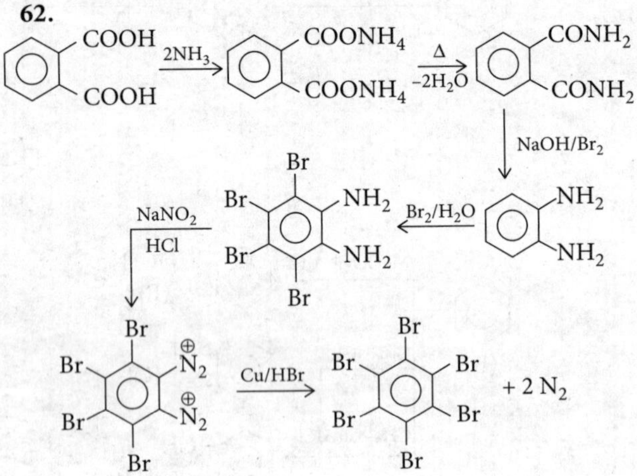

63.

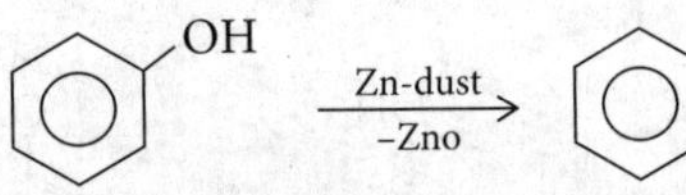

64.

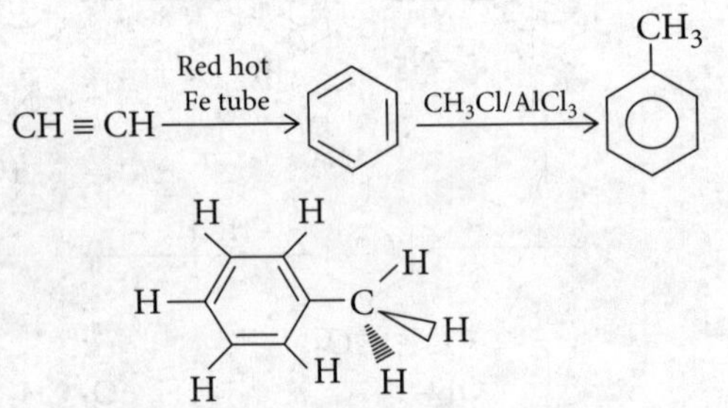

65.

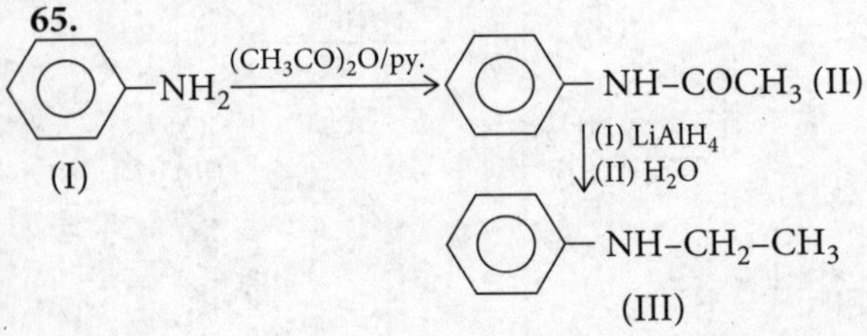

66.

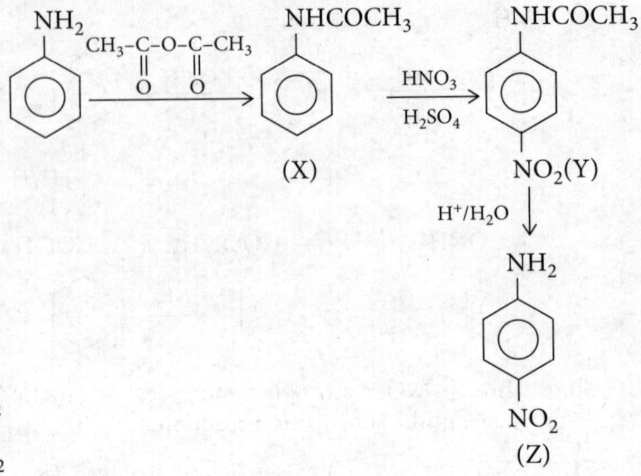

67.

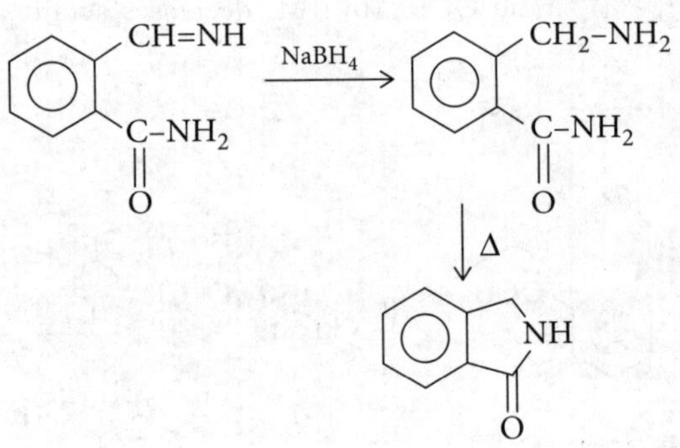

68.

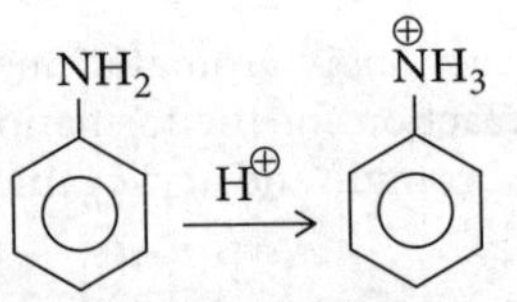

Anilinium ion

Anilinium ion is meta directing and meta derivatives are the major products formed.

69.

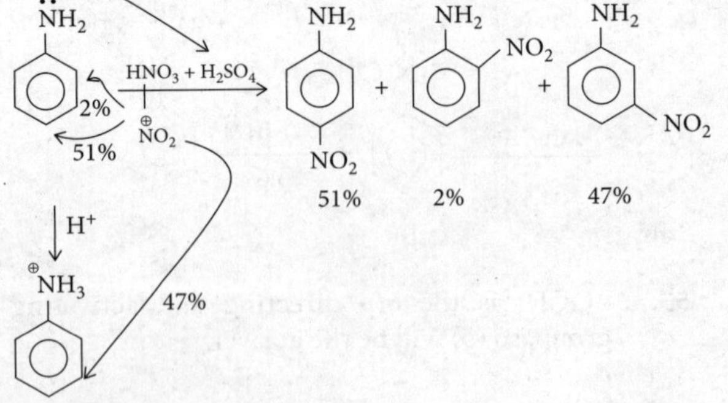

71.

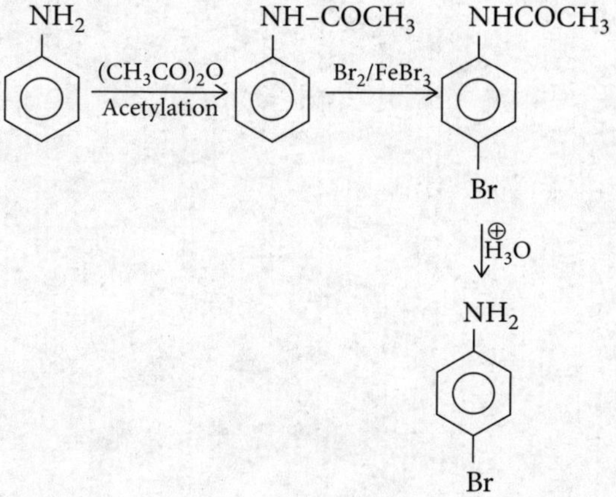

72.

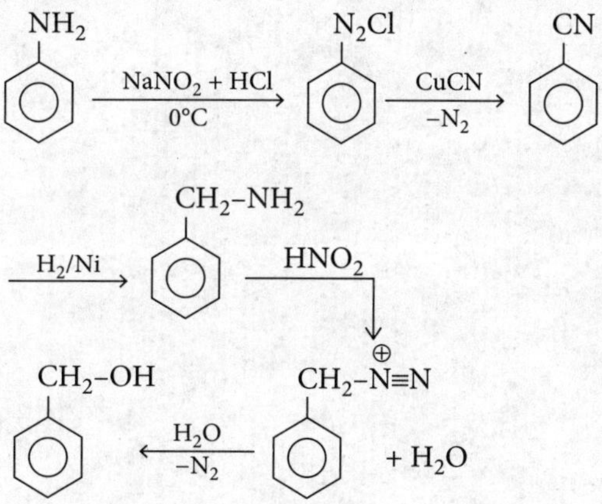

73.

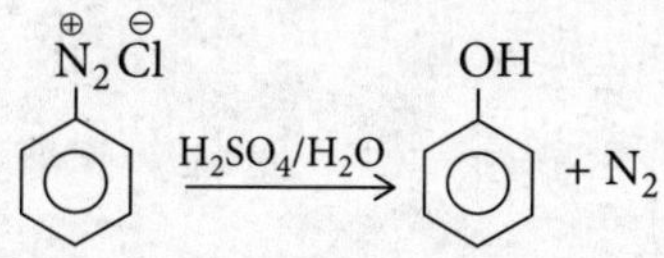

74.

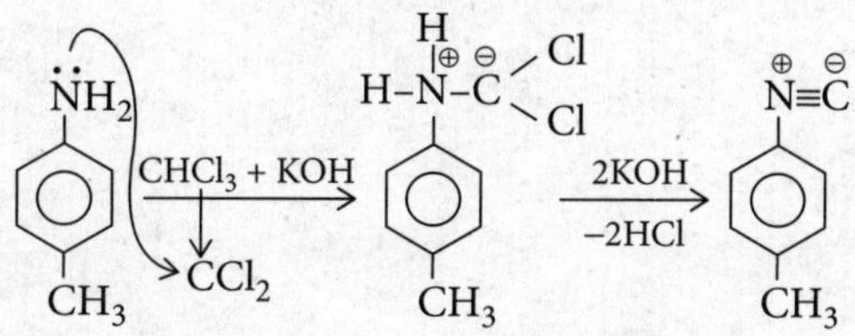

CHAPTER **11**

Biomolecules

Level-1

Carbohydrates-I (Monosaccharides)

1. Which of the following properties of glucose explains its open chain structure?
   (i) Glucose does not form hydrogen sulphite with $NaHSO_3$.
   (ii) On oxidation with HNO_3, glucose gives saccharic acid.
   (iii) Glucose is found to exist in two different crystalline forms, namely, α and β.
   (a) (ii) only (b) (i) and (iii)
   (c) (ii) and (iii) (d) (i) and (ii)

2. Which of the following statements is incorrect regarding glucose?
   (a) It is an aldohexose.
   (b) It is also known as dextrose.
   (c) It is a monomer of cellulose.
   (d) It is the least abundant organic compound on earth.

3. Glucose gives the silver mirror test with Tollens' reagent. It shows the presence of:
   (a) Acidic group
   (b) Alcoholic group
   (c) Ketonic group
   (d) Aldehyde group

4. Glucose is found to exist in two different α and β crystalline forms. These forms can be obtained by:
   (i) The α form of glucose is obtained by crystallization from a concentrated solution of glucose at 303 K.
   (ii) The β form of glucose is obtained by crystallization from a concentrated solution of glucose at 303 K.
   (iii) The β form is obtained by crystallization from a hot and saturated aqueous solution at 371 K.
   (iv) The α form is obtained by crystallization from a hot and saturated aqueous solution at 371 K.
   (a) (i) and (iii) (b) (ii) and (iv)
   (c) (ii) and (iii) (d) (i) only

5. Reduction of glucose by HI suggests:
   (a) Presence of OH groups
   (b) Presence of –CHO group
   (c) Cyclic structure of glucose
   (d) Six carbon atoms are arranged in a straight chain

6. Which of the following statements is correct about fructose?
   (a) It is a dextrorotatory compound.
   (b) It exists in two cyclic forms which are obtained by the addition of OH at C5 to the >C=O group.
   (c) It exists as a six-membered ring.
   (d) It is also called furanose as it contains one oxygen and six carbon atoms.

7. Which of the following monosaccharides are present as a five-membered cyclic structure (furanose structure)?
   (i) Ribose (ii) Glucose
   (iii) Fructose (iv) Galactose
   (a) (i) and (ii) (b) (i) and (iii)
   (c) (iii) and (iv) (d) (ii) and (iii)

8. Read the following statements:
   (i) Pyran is a cyclic organic compound with one oxygen atom and five carbon atoms.
   (ii) The cyclic structure of glucose is correctly represented by the Haworth structure.
   (iii) The five-membered cyclic structure of glucose is called the pyranose structure.
   Which of the following statement(s) is/are true?
   (a) (i) and (iii) (b) (i) and (ii)
   (c) Only (iii) (d) (i), (ii) and (iii)

9. Match the columns:

Column I **Reaction of glucose**	Column I **Characteristic of the glucose molecule**
A. 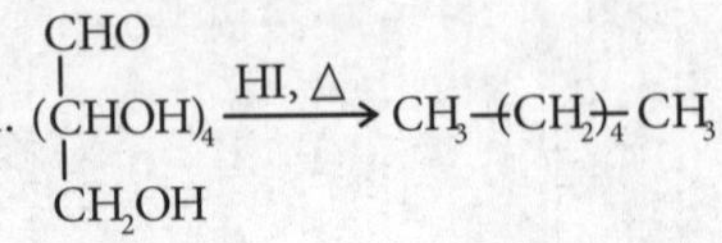	p. Presence of $>C=O$ group.
B. 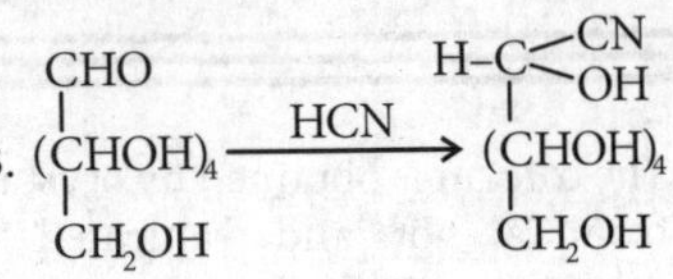	q. Presence of aldehydic group.
C. 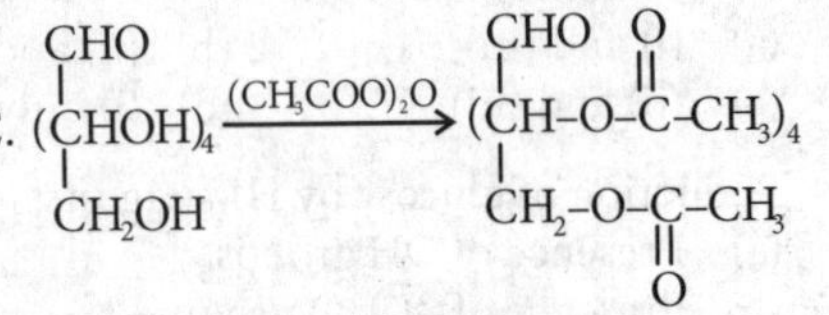	r. All six carbon atoms are linked in a straight chain.
D. 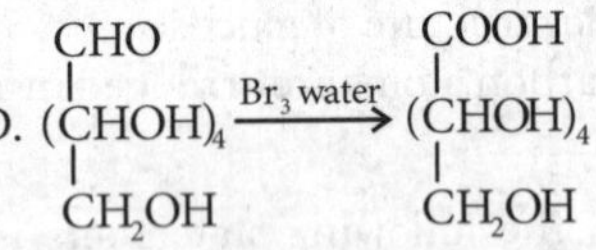	s. Presence of five –OH groups.

(a) A – p, B – r, C – s, D – q
(b) A – r, B – s, C – p, D – q
(c) A – r, B – p, C – s, D – q
(d) A – r, B – p, C – q, D – s

10. Read the following statements:
(i) The Haworth structure of α-D-glucose will be

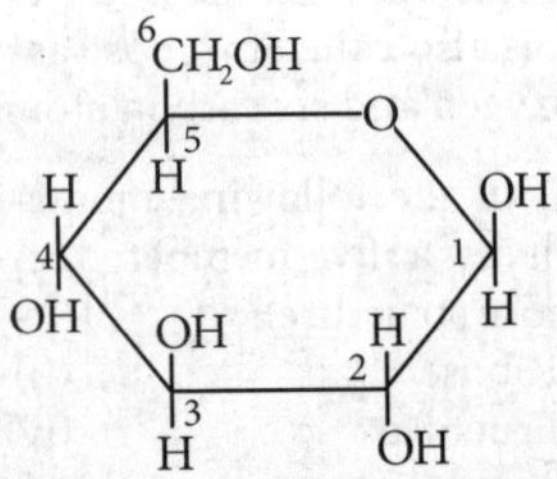

(ii) Fructose belongs to the D-series and is a laevorotatory compound.
(iii) The Haworth structure for β-D-fructose will be

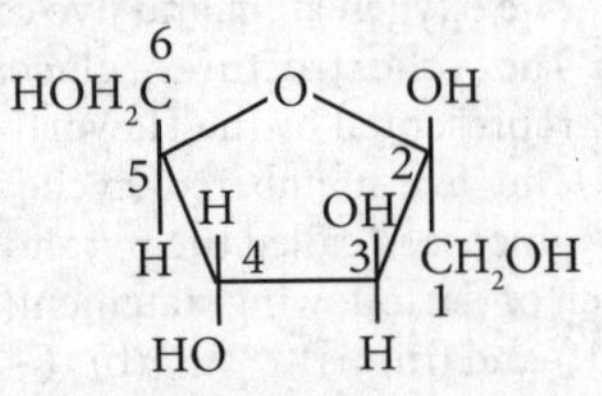

(iv) Fructose contains a ketonic functional group at the C-2 carbon atom.
Which of the following is the correct code for the statements above?

(a) FTTT (b) FFTT
(c) TFFT (d) FTFT

11. Which of the following monosaccharides is present as a furanose structure?
(a) Ribose (b) Glucose
(c) Mannose (d) Galactose

12. The number of stereo centres present in the linear and cyclic structures of glucose are, respectively:
(a) 4 and 4 (b) 4 and 5
(c) 5 and 5 (d) 5 and 4

13. Glucose and galactose have identical configuration in all positions, except:
(a) C5 (b) C3
(c) C2 (d) C4

14. Which of the following pairs represents anomers?

(a) 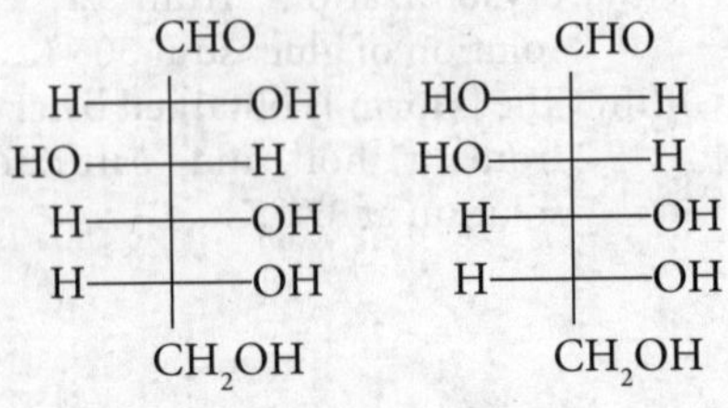

(b) 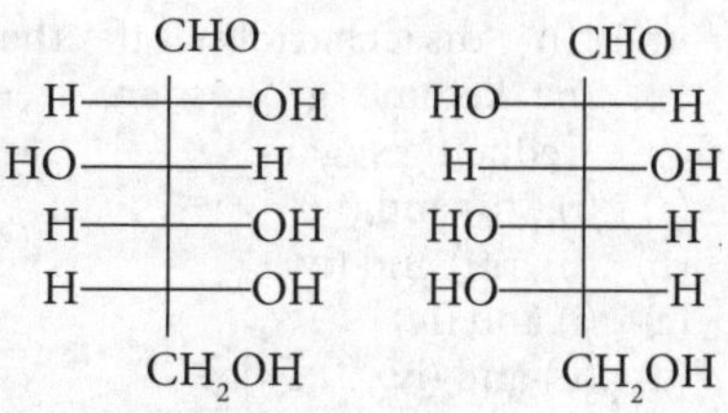

(c) 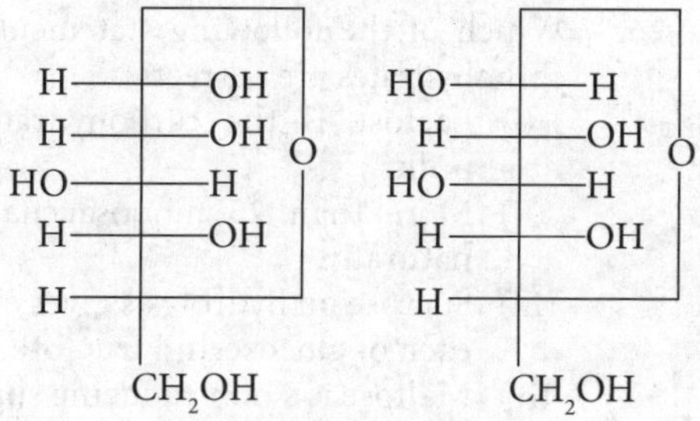

(d) 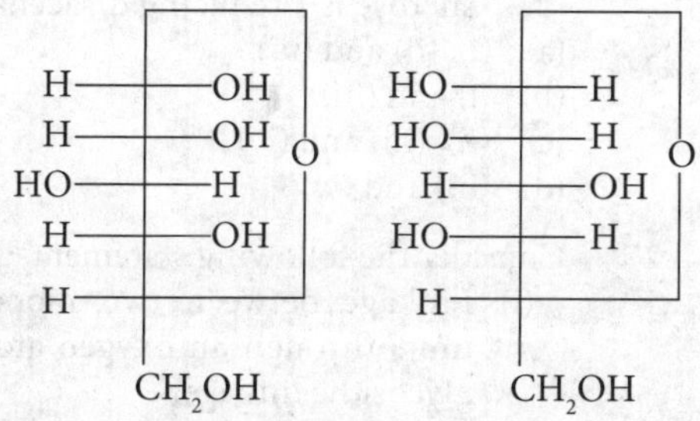

15. Which of the following represents the anomer of the compound shown?

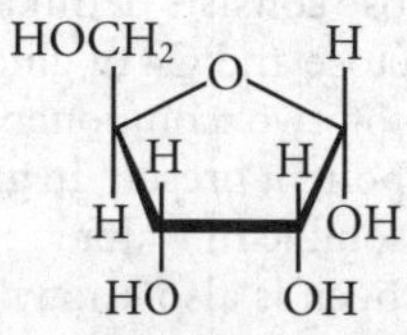

(a) 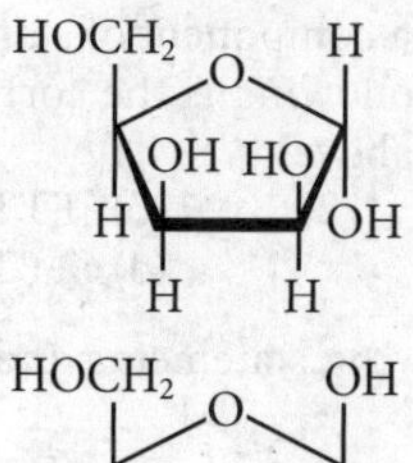

(b) 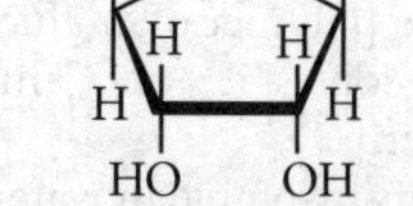

(c) 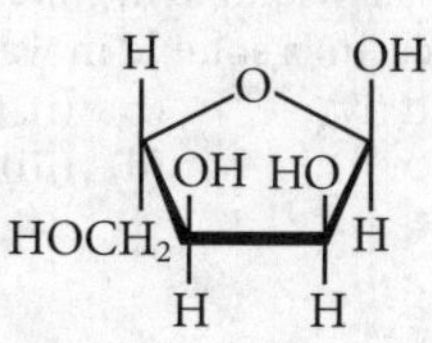

(d) 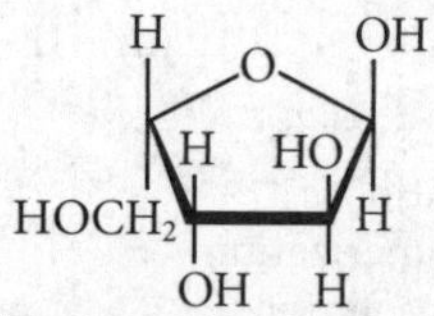

16. D-glucose and D-fructose can be differentiated by which of the following tests?

(a) 2,4-DNP test (b) Tollens' test

(c) Br_2/Water test (d) Lucas' test

17. What is the structure of L-glyceraldehyde?

(a) 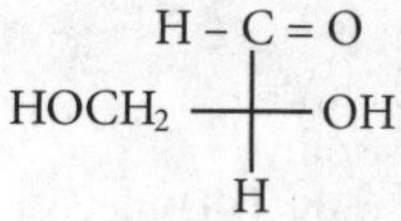

(b) 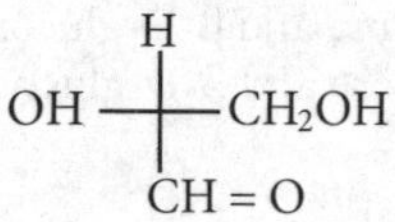

(c) 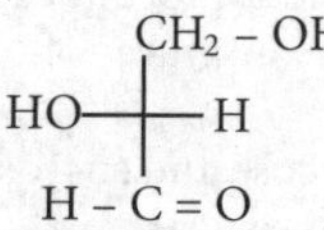

(d) Both (a) and (b)

18. What is the structure of L-glucose?

(a) 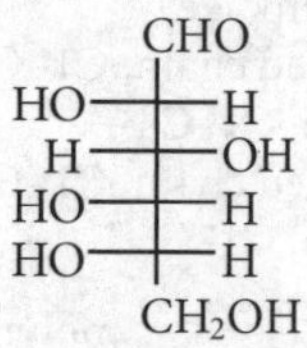

(b) 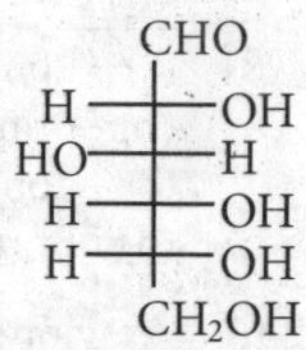

(c) 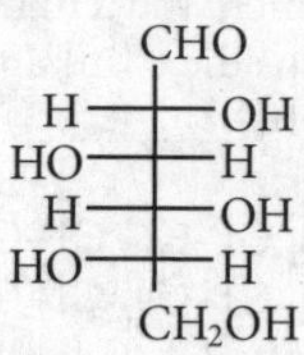

(d) None of these

19. Optical rotations of some compounds along with their structures are given below. Which of them have D configuration?

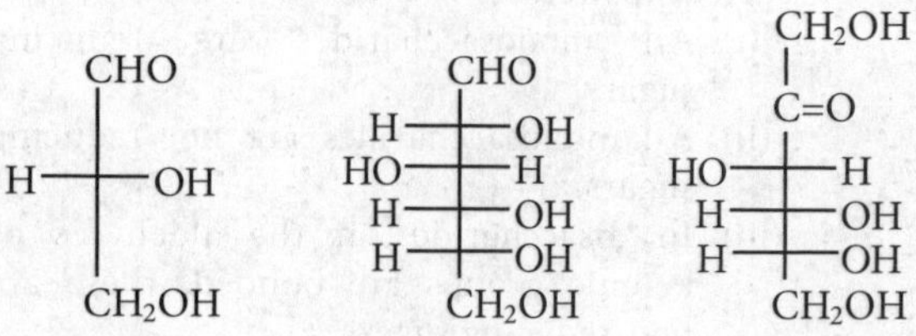

(+) rotation (I) (+) rotation (II) (–) rotation (III)

(a) I, II, III (b) II, III
(c) I, II (d) III

20. Mutarotation involves:
(a) Racemization
(b) Diastereomerization
(c) Optical resolution
(d) Conformational inversion

Carbohydrates-II (Disaccharides and Polysaccharides)

21. Lactose is made of:
(a) α-D-glucose only
(b) α-D-glucose and β-D-glucose
(c) α-D-galactose and β-D-glucose
(d) β-D-galactose and β-D-glucose

22. Invert sugar is:
(a) Chemically inactive form of sugar
(b) Equimolecular mixture of glucose and fructose
(c) Mixture of glucose and sucrose
(d) A variety of cane sugar

23. Chemically, amylose is a _________ with 200–1000 α-D-(+)-glucose units held by ______ glycosidic linkage:
(a) Long unbranched chain, C1–C6
(b) Branched chain, C1–C4
(c) Long unbranched chain, C1–C4
(d) Branched chain, C1–C6

24. Amylopectin is a ________ polymer of α-D-glucose units in which the chain is formed by ________ glycosidic linkage, whereas branching occurs by ________ glycosidic linkage:
(a) Branched chain, C1–C6, C1–C4
(b) Branched chain, C1–C4, C1–C6
(c) Unbranched chain, C1–C4, C1–C6
(d) Unbranched chain, C1–C6, C1–C4

25. Read the following statements and choose the correct answer:
(i) All monosaccharides are reducing sugars.
(ii) All monosaccharides are not reducing sugars.
(iii) In disaccharides, if the aldehydic or ketonic groups are bonded, these are non-reducing sugars.
(iv) In disaccharides, if the aldehydic or ketonic groups are free, these are reducing sugars.
(a) (i), (iii) and (iv)
(b) (ii), (iii) and (iv)
(c) (i) and (iv)
(d) (ii) and (iv)

26. Which of the following statements regarding carbohydrates are correct?
(i) Lactose is the carbohydrate found in milk.
(ii) More than 25 monosaccharides occur naturally.
(iii) Sucrose on hydrolysis gives one molecule each of glucose and fructose.
(iv) Maltose is a non-reducing sugar, whereas sucrose is a reducing disaccharide sugar.
(a) (i), (ii) and (iii)
(b) (i) and (iii)
(c) (ii), (iii) and (iv)
(d) (iii) and (iv)

27. Consider the following statements:
(i) Linkage between two monosaccharide units through an oxygen atom is called glycosidic linkage.
(ii) Sucrose on hydrolysis gives an equimolar mixture of fructose and glucose, which is dextrorotatory.
(iii) Lactose consists of linkage between C1 of galactose and C4 of glucose.
(iv) Out of two components of starch, the component present in greater proportion is insoluble in water.
(v) Glycogen is also known as animal starch because it is structurally similar to amylose, a component of starch.

Which of the following is the correct code for the statements above?
(a) FFFTT (b) FTTTF
(c) TFTFT (d) TFTTF

28. Read the following statements and choose the correct option:
(i) Starch is a polymer of α-glucose.
(ii) Starch consists of amylose and amylopectin.
(iii) Amylose is insoluble in water.
(iv) Amylopectin is soluble in water.
(a) (i) (iii) and (iv) (b) (i), (ii) and (iii)
(c) (i) and (ii) (d) (iii) and (iv)

29. In disaccharides, if the reducing groups of monosaccharides, that is, aldehydic or ketonic groups, are bonded, these are non-reducing sugars. Which of the following disaccharides is a non-reducing sugar?

(a) 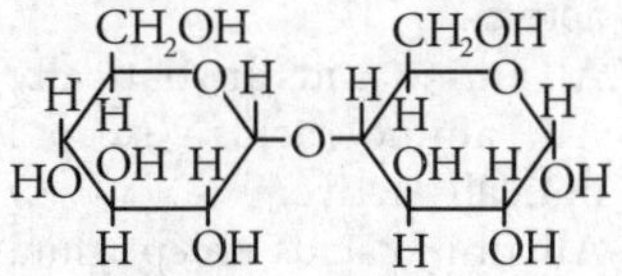

(b) 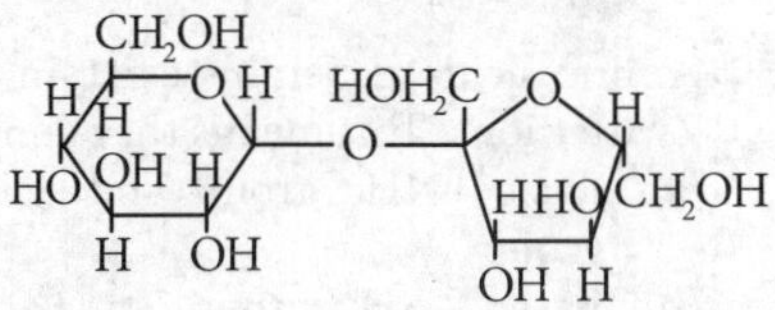

(c) 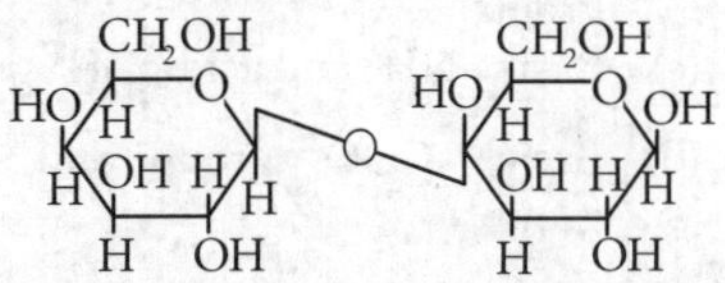

(d) 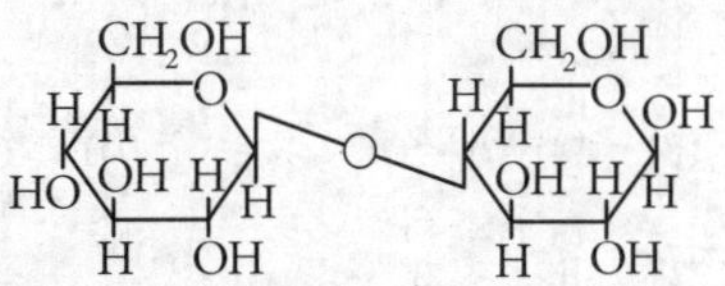

30. **Assertion (A):** β-glycosidic linkage is present in maltose.

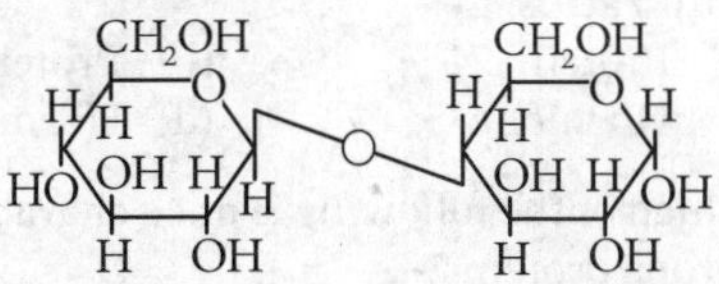

Reason (R): Maltose is composed of two glucose units in which C1 of one glucose unit is linked to C4 of another glucose unit.

(a) Assertion is correct, reason is correct; reason is a correct explanation for assertion.
(b) Assertion is correct, reason is correct; reason is not a correct explanation for assertion.
(c) Assertion is correct, reason is incorrect.
(d) Assertion is incorrect, reason is correct.

31. Starch molecules are polymers with repeating glucose units. Select the incorrect statement:

(a) Glucose units are joined through α-glycosidic linkage.
(b) The branches of amylopectin are linked to the chain with α-1,6'-glycosidic linkages.
(c) The linear linkages of amylopectin are formed by α-1,6'-glycosidic bonds.
(d) Amylose has an unbranched skeleton of glucose molecules with α-1,4'-glycosidic linkages.

32. Which of the following carbohydrates is a branched polymer of glucose?

(a) Amylose (b) Starch
(c) Cellulose (d) Glycogen

33. Three structures are given below in which two glucose units are linked. Which of these linkages between glucose units are between C1 and C4 and which linkages are between C1 and C6?

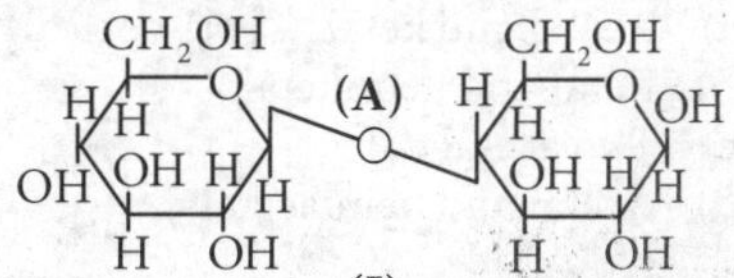

(I)

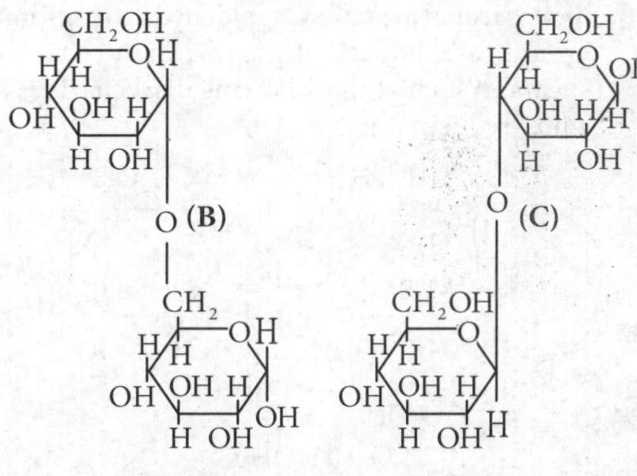

(II) (III)

(a) (I) is between C1 and C4, (II) and (III) are between C1 and C6
(b) (I) and (II) are between C1 and C4, (III) is between C1 and C6
(c) (I) and (III) are between C1 and C4, (II) is between C1 and C6
(d) (I) and (III) are between C1 and C6, (II) is between C1 and C4

34. The structure of a disaccharide formed by glucose and fructose is given below. Identify the anomeric carbon atoms in the monosaccharide units:

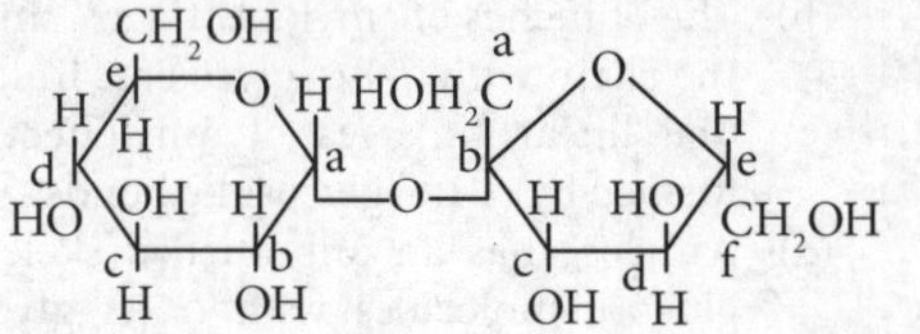

(a) 'a' carbon of glucose and 'a' carbon of fructose
(b) 'a' carbon of glucose and 'e' carbon of fructose.
(c) 'a' carbon of glucose and 'b' carbon of fructose
(d) 'f ' carbon of glucose and 'f ' carbon of fructose.

35. What are the functional groups present in the structure of maltose?
(a) Acetal and ketal
(b) Ketal and hemiketal
(c) Two acetal
(d) Acetal and hemiacetal

36. In disaccharides, if the reducing groups of monosaccharides, that is, aldehydic or ketonic groups, are bonded, these are non-reducing sugars. Which of the following disaccharides is a non-reducing sugar?

(a) 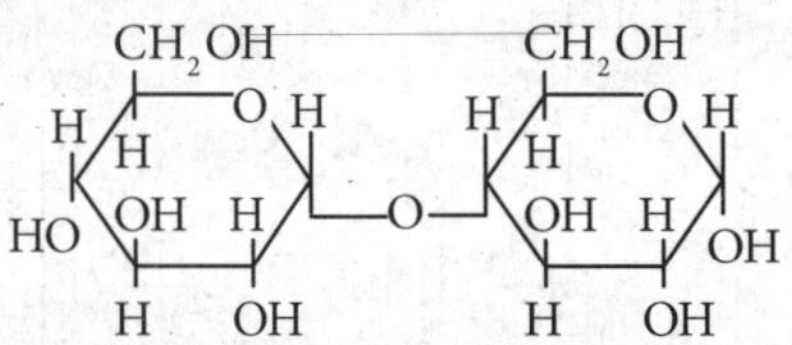

(b) 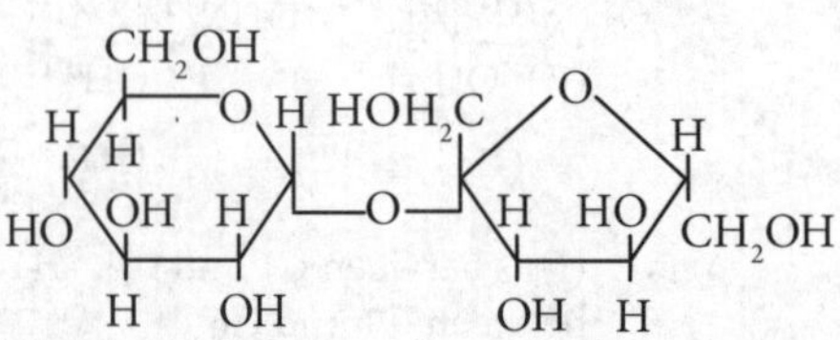

(c) 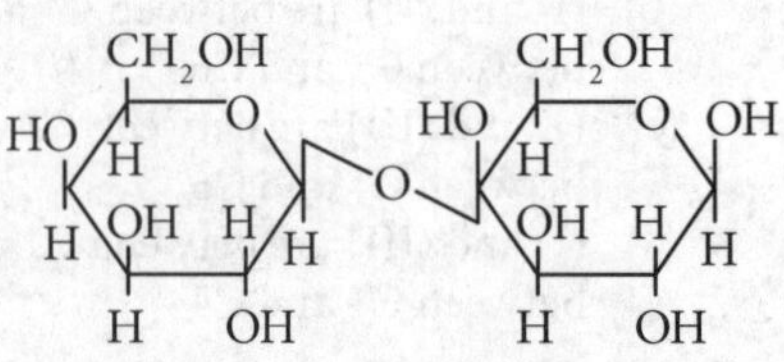

(d) 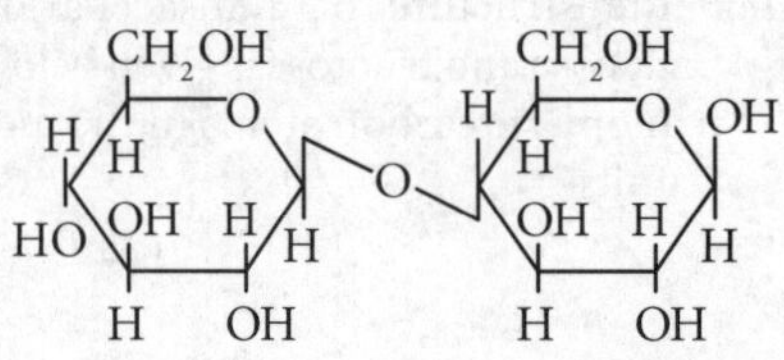

Amino Acids and Proteins

37. Which one of the following statements is correct?
(a) All amino acids except lysine are optically active.
(b) All amino acids are optically active.
(c) All amino acids except glycine are optically active.
(d) All amino acids except glutamic acids are optically active.

38. Amino acids generally exist in the form of Zwitter ions. This means they contain:
(a) Basic $-NH_2$ group and acidic $-COOH$ group
(b) Basic $-\overset{+}{N}H_3$ group and acidic $-COO^-$ group
(c) Basic $-NH_2$ and acidic $-H^+$ group
(d) Basic $-COO^-$ group and $-\overset{+}{N}H_3$ acidic group

39. The linkage present in proteins and peptides is:
(a) $-\overset{O}{\overset{\|}{C}}-NH-$ (b) $-\overset{O}{\overset{\|}{C}}-O$
(c) $-\overset{O}{\overset{\|}{C}}-O-\overset{O}{\overset{\|}{C}}-$ (d) $NH-$

40. An insulin is a ______ which contains _____ amino acids:
(a) Protein, 74 (b) Protein, 51
(c) Hormone, 51 (d) Hormone, 74

41. Which of the following is not a characteristic of fibrous proteins?
(a) In fibrous proteins, the polypeptide chains are held together by hydrogen and disulphide bonds.
(b) These have a fibre-like structure.
(c) These are generally soluble in water.
(d) These have an elongated shape.

42. The primary structure of a protein is:
(a) Sequence in which α-amino acids are linked to one another.
(b) Sequence in which amino acids of one polypeptide chain are joined to the other chain.
(c) The folding patterns of polypeptide chains.
(d) The pattern in which the polypeptide chains are arranged.

43. Which of the following statements is incorrect?
(a) In α-helix structure, a polypeptide chain forms all possible hydrogen bonds by twisting into a right-handed screw.
(b) In β-structure of proteins, all peptide chains are stretched out to nearly maximum extension.
(c) During denaturation, 1° and 2° structures are destroyed but 3° structures remain intact.
(d) All of the above statements are incorrect.

44. Which of the following statements is not true about the secondary structure of proteins?
(a) Alpha helix, beta-pleated sheet and beta turns are examples of the secondary structure of proteins.
(b) The ability of peptide bonds to form intramolecular hydrogen bonds is important to the secondary structure.
(c) The steric influence of amino acid residues is important to the secondary structure.
(d) The hydrophilic/hydrophobic character of amino acid residues is important to the secondary structure.

45. Which of the following statements are correct?
(i) Proteins on hydrolysis give only α-amino acids.
(ii) Gln stands for glutamic acid.
(iii) Amino acids with equal number of amino and carboxyl groups are neutral.
(iv) All naturally occurring α-amino acids are optically active.
(a) (i) and (iii)
(b) (i), (ii) and (iv)
(c) (iii) and (iv)
(d) (ii), (iii) and (iv)

46. Which of the statements about "denaturation" given below are correct?
(i) Denaturation of proteins causes loss of secondary and tertiary structures of the protein.
(ii) Denaturation leads to conversion of double strand of DNA into single strand.
(iii) Denaturation affects the primary structure, which gets distorted.
(a) (ii) and (iii)
(b) (i) and (iii)
(c) (i) and (ii)
(d) (i), (ii) and (iii)

47. The peptide linkage in Gly-Ala contains:
(a) Free $-NH_2$ on alanine
(b) Chiral centre on alanine
(c) Free –COOH on glycine
(d) All of these

48. Amino acids are classified as acidic, basic or neutral depending upon the relative number of amino and carboxyl groups in their molecule. Which of the following are acidic?
(a) $(CH_3)_2CH-CH(NH_2)-COOH$
(b) $HOOC-CH_2-CH_2-CH(NH_2)-COOH$
(c) $H_2NCH_2CH_2CH(NH_2)-COOH$
(d) All of these

49. Which of the following amino acids is aromatic?
(a) Serine (b) Tryptophan
(c) Valine (d) Alanine

50. Which of the following is not an essential amino acid?
(a) Leucine (b) Lysine
(c) Valine (d) Tyrosine

51. Which amino acid does not contain a chiral centre?
(a) Valine (b) Leucine
(c) Glycine (d) Iso-leucine

52. Peptide linkage is:
(a) $-C(=O)-O-$ (b) $-C(=O)-NH_2$
(c) $-C(=O)-NH-$ (d) $-C(=O)-NH-NH_2$

ENZYMES AND VITAMINES

53. Which of the following is incorrect regarding enzymes?
(a) Most of them are globular proteins.
(b) They are very specific for a particular reaction, but not for a particular substrate.
(c) They are generally named after the compound or class of compounds upon which they work.
(d) All of the above statements are incorrect.

54. Which one of the following statements is incorrect about enzyme catalyst?

(a) Enzymes are mostly proteinous in nature.
(b) Enzyme action is specific.
(c) Enzymes are denaturated by ultraviolet rays and at high temperature.
(d) Enzymes are least reactive at optimum temperature.

55. The function of enzymes in the living system is to:
(a) Transport oxygen
(b) Provide energy
(c) Provide immunity
(d) Catalyse biochemical reactions

56. Which of the following statements is incorrect?
(a) Enzymes are organic catalysts.
(b) Enzymes have a very large turnover number.
(c) Enzyme action is specific.
(d) Enzymes always require a coenzyme in their catalytic action.

57. Of the following statements about enzymes, which ones are true?
(i) Enzymes lack nucleophilic groups.
(ii) Enzymes are highly specific, both in binding chiral substrates and in catalysing their reactions.
(iii) Enzymes catalyse chemical reactions by lowering the energy of activation.
(iv) Pepsin is a proteolytic enzyme.
(a) (i) and (iv) (b) (i) and (iii)
(c) (ii), (iii) and (iv) (d) (i)

58. Match the columns:

Column I (Enzyme)	Column II (Reaction)
A. Invertase	p. Decomposition of urea into NH_3 and CO_2
B. Maltase	q. Conversion of glucose into ethyl alcohol
C. Pepsin	r. Hydrolysis of maltose into glucose
D. Urease	s. Hydrolysis of cane sugar
E. Zymase	t. Hydrolysis of proteins into peptides

(a) A – s, B – r, C – t, D – p, E – q
(b) A – r, B – q, C – s, D – p, E – t
(c) A – q, B – p, C – r, D – s, E – t
(d) A – s, B – p, C – t, D – q, E – r

59. Which of the following statements are correct?
(i) Vitamins A, D, E and K are insoluble in water.
(ii) Vitamins A, D, E and K are stored in the liver and adipose tissues.
(iii) Vitamin B and vitamin C are water soluble.
(iv) Water-soluble vitamins should not be supplied regularly in diet.
(a) (i), (ii) and (iv) (b) (i), (ii) and (iii)
(c) (i) and (iv) (d) (ii) and (iv)

60. Match the columns:

Column I	Column II
A. Vitamin A	p. Scurvy
B. Vitamin B_{12}	q. Hemorrhagic condition
C. Vitamin C	r. Sterility
D. Vitamin E	s. Xerophthalmia
E. Vitamin K	t. Pernicious anemia

(a) A – t, B – s, C – p, D – r, E – r
(b) A – s, B – t, C – p, D – q, E – r
(c) A – s, B – t, C – p, D – r, E – q
(d) A – t, B – s, C – p, D – r, E – q

61. **Assertion (A):** Vitamin D cannot be stored in our body.
Reason (R): Vitamin D is a fat-soluble vitamin and is stored in fatty tissue and the liver.
(a) Assertion is correct, reason is correct; reason is a correct explanation for assertion.
(b) Assertion is correct, reason is correct; reason is not a correct explanation for assertion.
(c) Assertion is correct, reason is incorrect.
(d) Assertion is incorrect, reason is correct.

62. Vitamin C must be supplied regularly in diet because:
(a) It is water soluble and hence excreted in urine and cannot be stored in the body.
(b) It is fat soluble and hence stored in the body and cannot be used on a regular basis.
(c) It is required in large amounts by the body and hence supplied regularly.
(d) It is water soluble and hence used by the body on a daily basis and is to be supplied regularly.

63. Which one of the following options is correct?
(a) Only aliphatic amines give isocyanide test
(b) Vitamin C is water insoluble
(c) Gly-Ala and Ala-Gly are different dipeptides
(d) Starch contain only 1,4 glycosidic linkage

64. The activation energy for the acid-catalysed hydrolysis of sucrose is x kJ mol^{-1}, while the activation energy is y kJ mol^{-1} when hydrolysis is catalysed by the enzyme sucrase. Then x and y are:
(a) 6.62, 6.22 (b) 2.15, 6.62
(c) 6.62, 2.15 (d) 2.15, 2.15

65. Which of the following acids is a vitamin?
(a) Aspartic acid (b) Ascorbic acid
(c) Adipic acid (d) Saccharic acid

66. Which of the following B-group vitamins can be stored in our body?
(a) Vitamin B_1 (b) Vitamin B_2
(c) Vitamin B_6 (d) Vitamin B_{12}

67. Which of the following terms are correct about enzymes?
(a) Proteins (b) Dinucleotides
(c) Nucleic acids (d) All of these

68. Which of the following vitamins contains cobalt?
(a) Vitamin A (b) Vitamin C
(c) Vitamin B_{12} (d) Vitamin K

Nucleic Acids

69. In DNA, the complementary bases are:
(a) Adenine and thymine; guanine and cytosine
(b) Adenine and thymine; guanine and uracil
(c) Adenine and guanine; thymine and cytosine
(d) Uracil and adenine; cytosine and guanine

70. Which of the following structures represents thymine ?

(a) 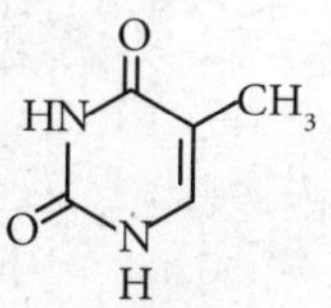

(b) 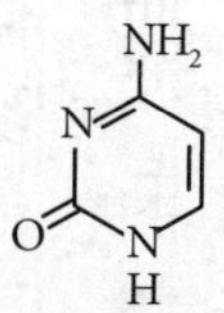

(c) 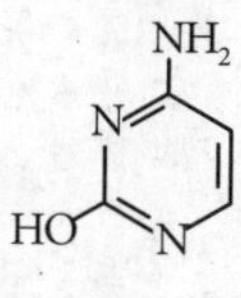

(d) 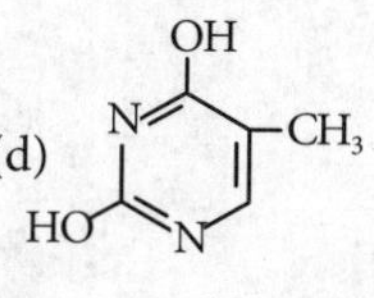

71. Which of the following statements regarding DNA fingerprinting is incorrect?
(a) It is used in forensic laboratories for identification of criminals.
(b) It cannot be altered by surgery.
(c) It is different for every cell and cannot be altered by any known treatment.
(d) It is used to determine the paternity of an individual.

72. The function of DNA in an organism is:
(a) To assist in the synthesis of the RNA molecule.
(b) To store information about heredity characteristics.
(c) To assist in the synthesis of proteins and polypeptides.
(d) All of these.

73. DNA has deoxyribose, a base and a third component, which is:
(a) Phosphoric acid (b) Ribose
(c) Adenine (d) Thymine

74. When adenine is attached to ribose sugar, it is called adenosine. To make a nucleotide from it, it would require:
(a) Oxygenation
(b) Addition of a base
(c) Addition of phosphate
(d) Hydrogenation

75. Which of the following statement(s) is/are correct?
(i) Information regarding the sequence of nucleotides in the chain of a nucleic acid is called its primary structure.
(ii) In the secondary structure of DNA, adenine forms hydrogen bonds with guanine whereas cytosine forms hydrogen bonds with thymine.
(iii) RNA molecules are of three types: m-RNA, r-RNA and t-RNA; and they all perform different functions.
(a) (ii) only (b) (i) and (iii)
(c) (ii) and (iii) (d) (iii) only

76. Consider the following statements:
(i) Nucleic acids are long-chain polymers of nucleotides.
(ii) Sugar moiety in DNA molecules is β-D-ribose, whereas in RNA molecules it is β-D-2-deoxyribose.
(iii) RNA contains four bases, namely, adenine (A), guanine (G), cytosine (C) and uracil (U).

(iv) Nucleotide is a nucleoside linked to phosphoric acid at the 4-position of the sugar moiety.

Which of the following is the correct code for the statements above?

(a) TFFT (b) TFTF
(c) FFTT (d) FTFF

77. In both DNA and RNA, heterocylic base and phosphate ester linkages are at:
(a) C_5' and C_1', respectively, of the sugar molecule.
(b) C_1' and C_5', respectively, of the sugar molecule.
(c) C_2' and C_5', respectively, of the sugar molecule.
(d) C_5' and C_2', respectively, of the sugar molecule.

78. In DNA, the linkages between different nitrogenous bases are:
(a) Peptide linkage
(b) Phosphate linkage
(c) H-bonding
(d) Glycosidic linkage

79. Dinucleotide is obtained by joining two nucleotides by phosphodiester linkage. Between which carbon atoms of pentose sugars of nucleotides are these linkages present?
(a) 5' and 3' (b) 1' and 5'
(c) 5' and 5' (d) 3' and 3'

80. Nucleic acids are the polymers of:
(a) Nucleosides (b) Nucleotides
(c) Bases (d) Sugars

81. The monomer of nucleic acids are held together by:
(a) Phosphodiester linkage
(b) Amide linkage
(c) Glycosidic linkage
(d) Ester linkage

82. Which of the following statements is not true about RNA?
(a) It always has a double-stranded α-helix structure
(b) It usually does not replicate
(c) It is present in the nucleus of the cell
(d) It controls the synthesis of proteins

83. Which of the following is present in DNA but not in RNA?

(a) 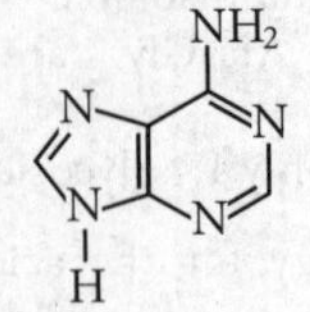
(b) 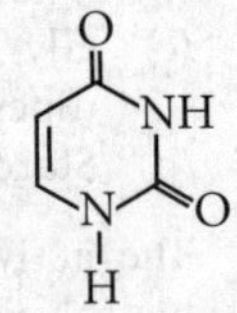
(c) 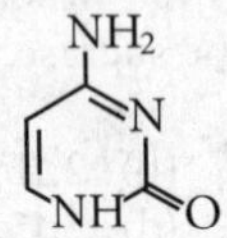
(d) 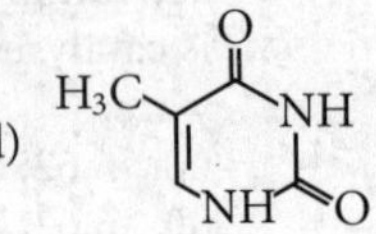

84. Which one of the following is a nucleotide?

(a) 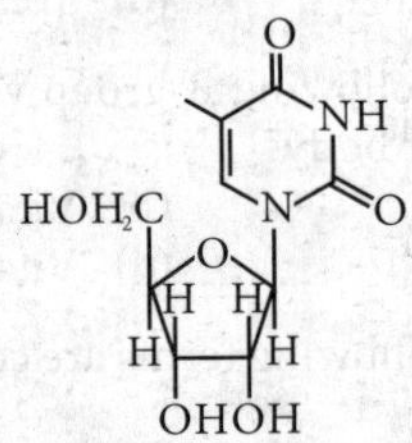
(b) 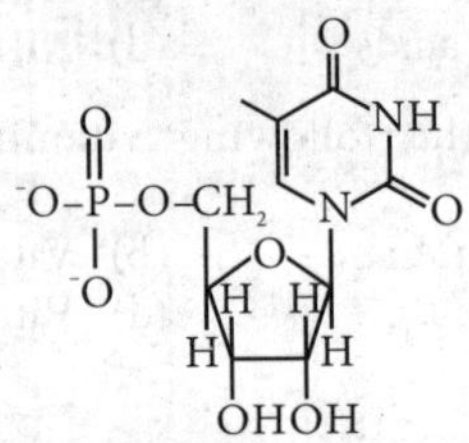
(c) 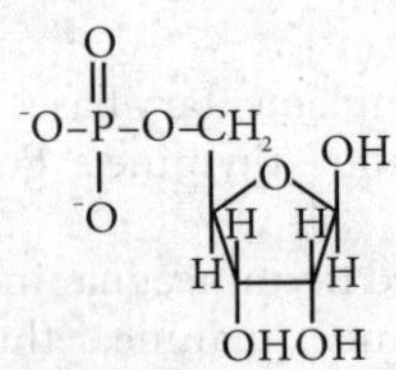
(d) 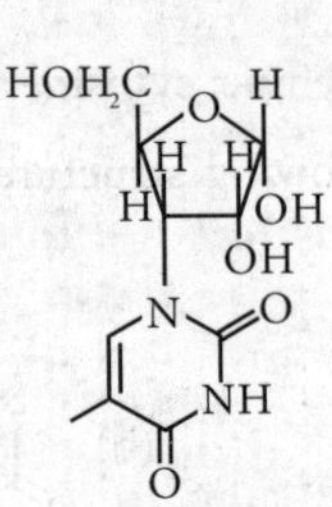

85. Which pair of purine bases is present in DNA?

(a) 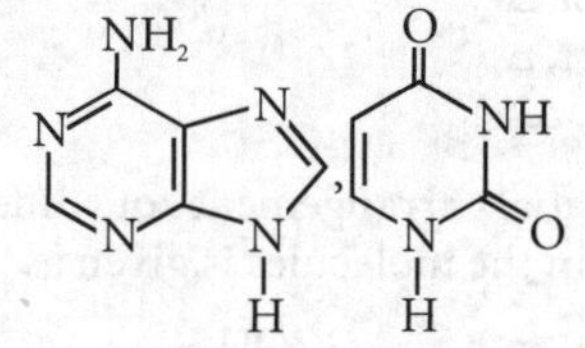

(c) 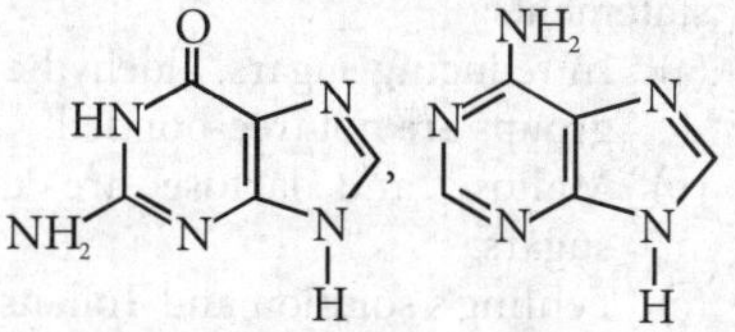

(b) 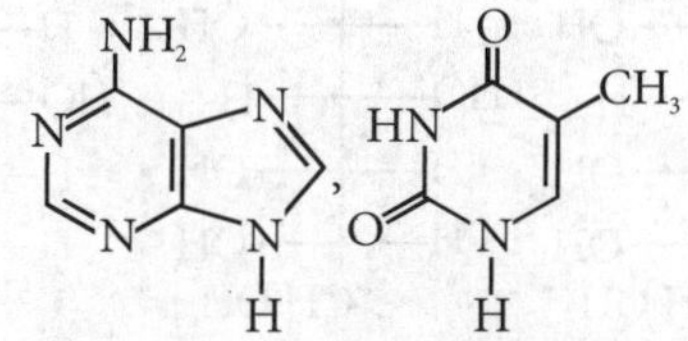

(d) 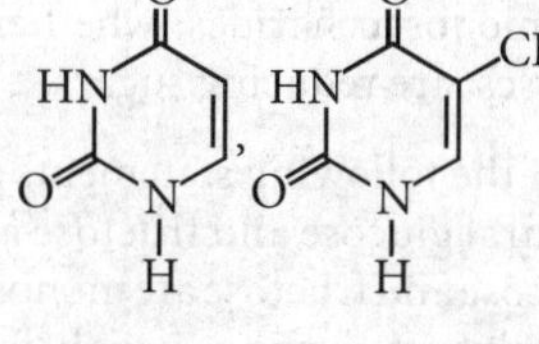

Level-2

1. Consider the following statements:

I. Carbohydrates, proteins, nucleic acids and lipids are all biomolecules.

II. Biomolecules are organic compounds.

III. Plants and animals are made up of biomolecules.

Select the correct statements and mark the correct option:

(a) Only I (b) Only II
(c) Only III (d) I, II and III

2. Which of the following statement(s) is/are false about carbohydrates?

I. They have the general formula, $C_x(H_2O)_y$.

II. They are hydrates of carbon.

III. The molecular formula of glucose is $C_6H_{12}O_6$ and the general formula is $C_6(H_2O)_6$.

Choose the correct option:

(a) Only I (b) Only II
(c) II and III (d) Only III

3. Carbohydrates are classified on the basis of their behaviour on hydrolysis. They have been broadly divided into:

(a) Two groups (b) Three groups
(c) Four groups (d) Five groups

4. **Assertion (A):** Acetic acid is a carbohydrate.
Reason (R): Acetic acid fits in the general formula of carbohydrates, $C_x(H_2O)_y$.

(a) Both A and R are correct; R is the correct explanation of A.
(b) Both A and R are correct; R is not the correct explanation of A.
(c) A is correct but R is incorrect.
(d) R is correct but A is incorrect.

5. How many natural monosaccharides are known to occur in nature?

(a) 5 (b) 10
(c) 15 (d) 20

6. **Assertion (A):** Oligosaccharides are classified as disaccharides, trisaccharides, and tetrasaccharides.
Reason (R): It depends upon the number of monosaccharides produced on hydrolysis.

(a) Both A and R are correct; R is the correct explanation of A.
(b) Both A and R are correct; R is not the correct explanation of A.
(c) A is correct but R is incorrect.
(d) R is correct but A is incorrect.

7. Why are polysaccharides called non-sugars?

(a) They yield a large number of monosaccharides on hydrolysis.
(b) They do not taste sweet.
(c) They are reducing sugars.
(d) They are non-reducing sugars.

8. Select the incorrect statement about sugar:

(a) It is sweet to taste.
(b) Sugar present in milk is called sucrose.
(c) The Greek word 'sakcharon' means sugar.
(d) Not all carbohydrates are called sugars.

9. Find out the correct option among the following statements:
   (a) In reducing sugars, aldehydic and ketonic groups are not free-bonded.
   (b) Maltose and lactose are non-reducing sugars.
   (c) Fehling's solution and Tollens' reagent are for non-reducing sugars.
   (d) All monosaccharides, whether aldoses or ketoses, are reducing sugars.

10. Which of the following statements are correct?
   (a) Natural glucose and fructose are D-forms.
   (b) Glucose and fructose are monosaccharides.
   (c) A solution having equal molecules of D-glucose and D-fructose is termed invert sugar.
   (d) Aldohexoses exists in 2^6 optical forms.
   (a) a and b (b) a, b, c
   (c) Only a (d) Only d

11. Select the correct statements from the following:
   (a) Glucose exists in two different crystalline forms, α-D-glucose and β-D-glucose.
   (b) α-D-glucose and β-D-glucose are enantiomers.
   (c) Cellulose is a straight-chain polysaccharide made up of only β-glucose unit.
   (d) The cyclic structure of α-D-glucose and β-D-glucose is called pyranose structure.
   (a) a and b (b) a, c, d
   (c) Only a (d) Only d

12. **Assertion (A):** D-(+)-glucose is dextrorotatory in nature.
   Reason (R): 'D' represents its dextrorotatory nature.
   (a) Both A and R are correct; R is the correct explanation of A.
   (b) Both A and R are correct; R is not the correct explanation of A.
   (c) A is correct but R is incorrect.
   (d) R is correct but A is incorrect.

13. Name the reagent and condition required for carrying out the following reaction:

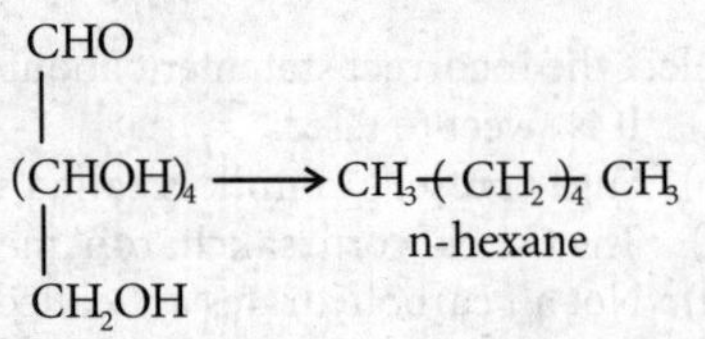

   (a) HF, Δ
   (b) HCl, Δ
   (c) HBr, Δ
   (d) HI, Δ

14. The spatial arrangement of different –OH groups in the molecules is given as

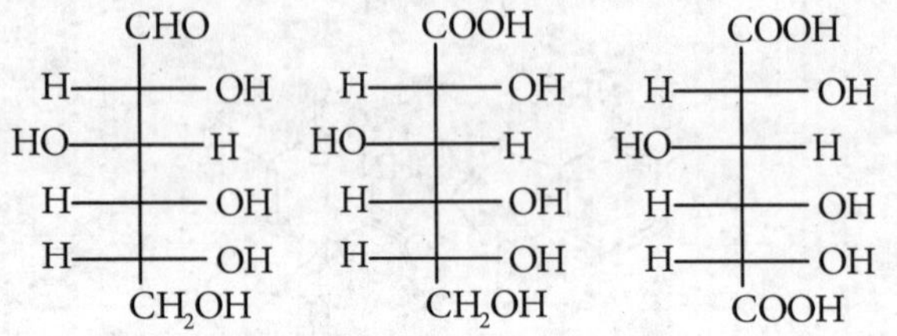

I II III

Choose the correct option with names for I, II and III:
   (a) I → Gluconic acid II → Glucose, III → Saccharic acid
   (b) I → Saccharic acid, II → Glucose, III → Gluconic acid
   (c) I → Glucose, II → Gluconic acid, III → Saccharic acid
   (d) I → Glucose, II → Saccharic acid, III → Gluconic acid

15. Select the incorrect statement about cyclic glucose:
   (a) If the –OH group is added to the –CHO group, it will form a cyclic hemiacetal structure.
   (b) Glucose forms a six-membered ring in which –OH is at the C5 position.
   (c) The melting point of α-glucose is 423 K and of β-glucose is 419 K.
   (d)

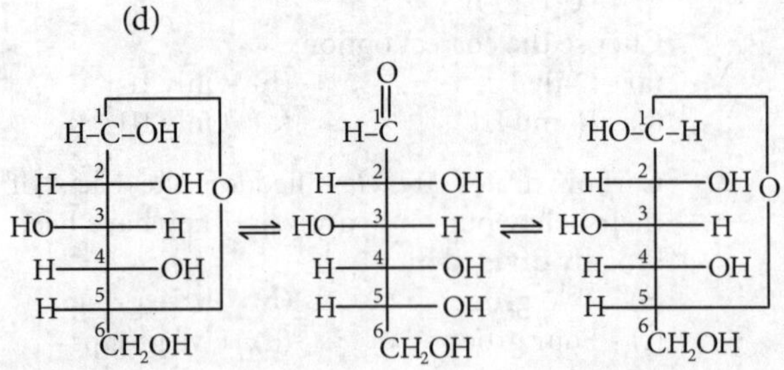

α-D-(+)-glucose β-D-(+)-glucose

16. Identify α-D-(–)-fructofuranose and β-D-(–)-fructofuranose from the following structures:

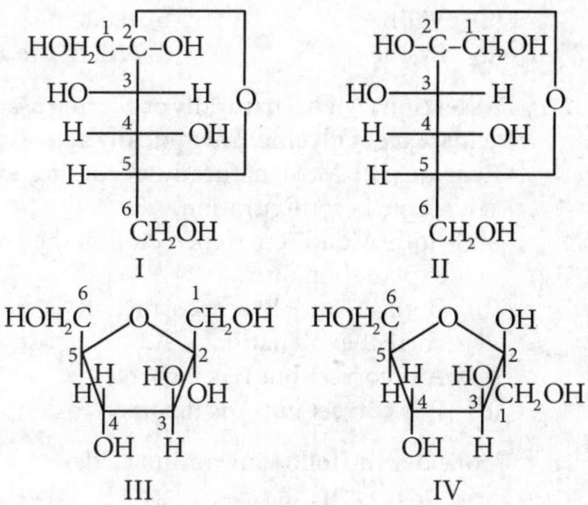

Choose the correct option:

	α-D-(-)-fructofuranose	**β-D-(-)-fructofuranose**
(a)	I and II	III and IV
(b)	I and III	II and IV
(c)	II and III	I and IV
(d)	II and IV	I and III

17. **Assertion (A):** Cellulose cannot be digested in the human body.
Reason (R): The human system contains the cellulase enzyme which hydrolyses cellulose into glucose.
(a) Both A and R are correct; R is the correct explanation of A.
(b) Both A and R are correct; R is not the correct explanation of A.
(c) A is correct but R is incorrect.
(d) R is correct but A is incorrect.

18. **Assertion (A):** β-glycosidic linkage is present in maltose.
Reason (R): Maltose is composed of two glucose units in which the C1 of one glucose unit is linked to the C4 of another glucose unit.
(a) Both A and R are correct; R is the correct explanation of A.
(b) Both A and R are correct; R is not the correct explanation of A.
(c) A is correct but R is incorrect.
(d) R is correct but A is incorrect.

19. Consider the following statements:
I. Disaccharides on hydrolysis with dilute acid give three molecules of the same or different monosaccharides.
II. Disaccharides are formed by the loss of water and have an oxide linkage.

Choose the incorrect statement about disaccharide and select the most appropriate option:
(a) Only I (b) Both I and II
(c) Only II (d) None of these

20. Consider the following structure:

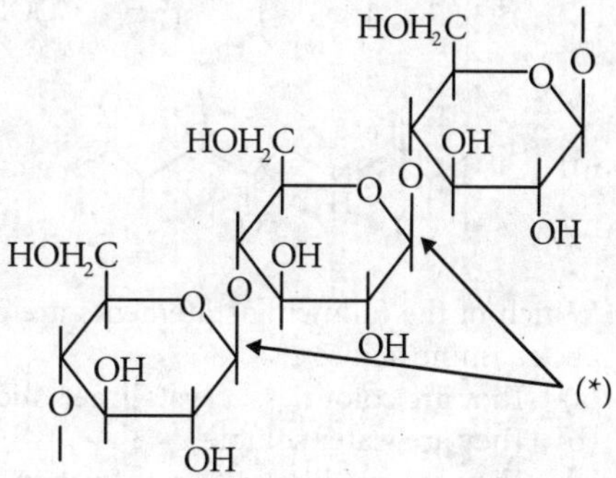

Name the kind of linkage which has been indicated with (*) in the above figure:
(a) α-linkage (b) β-linkage
(c) γ-linkage (d) δ-linkage

21. Which of the following are true about amino acids?
(a) Glycine is the only naturally occurring amino acid which is optically inactive.
(b) Most naturally occurring amino acids have D-configuration.
(c) Alanine has one amino and one carboxylic group.
(d) Amino acids are the constituents of all proteins.
(a) a, c, d (b) a, b, c
(c) Only a (d) a, b, c, d

22. Which of the following statements is/are correct about proteins?
(a) Proteins form the basis of the structure and functions of life.
(b) They are required for growth and maintenance of the body.
(c) They are polymers of α-amino acids.
(d) All of the above.

23. Which one of the following is the correct representation of tripeptide (alanine-glycine-alanine)?

(a) 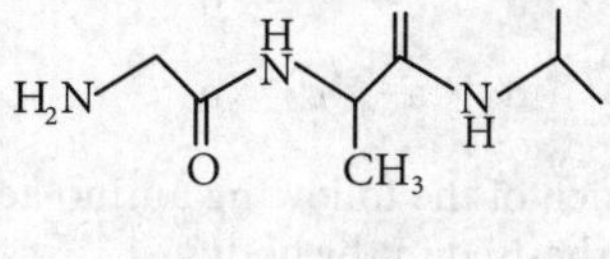

(b) 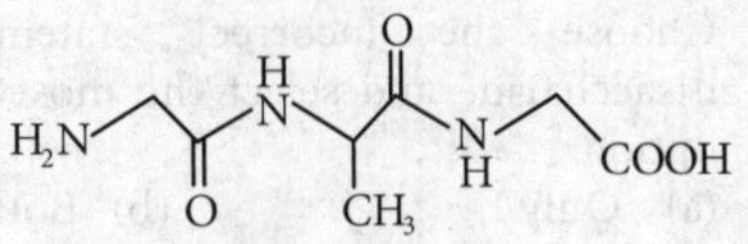

(c) 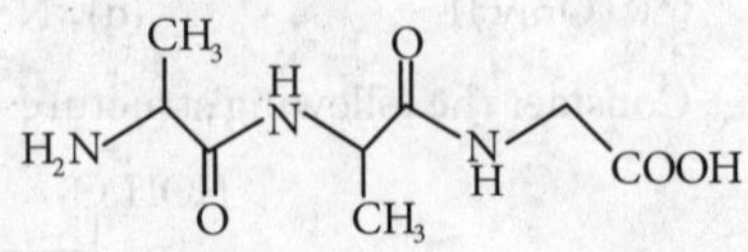

(d) 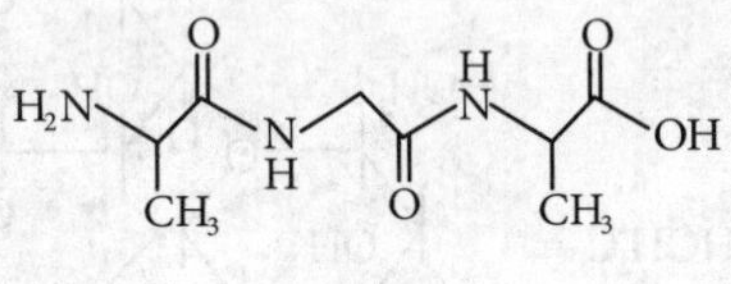

24. Which of the following statements are correct about amino acids?
(a) They are colourless, crystalline solids.
(b) They are water soluble.
(c) They behave like salts rather than simple amines or carboxylic acids.
(d) They are high-melting-point solids.
(a) a and b
(b) a and c
(c) Only a
(d) a, b, c and d

25. Match the amino acid in Column I with their characteristic feature of side chain in Column II and select the appropriate option from the codes given below:

Column I	Column II
A. Asparagine (Asn, N)	a. 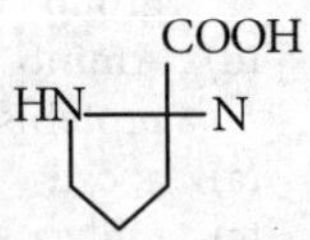
B. Proline (Pro, P)	b. $HOOC-CH_2-CH_2-$
C. Glutamic acid (Glu, E)	c. $HO-CH_2-$
D. Serine (Ser, S)	d. $H_2N-COCH_2-$

Codes

	A	B	C	D
(a)	d	a	b	c
(b)	d	b	a	c
(c)	d	c	a	b
(d)	d	a	c	b

26. Which of the following amino acids cannot be synthesised in the body?
(a) Valine (b) Leucine
(c) Lysine (d) All of the above

27. **Assertion (A):** All naturally occurring α-amino acids, except glycine, are optically active.
Reason (R): Most naturally occurring amino acids have L-configuration.
(a) Both A and R are correct; R is the correct explanation of A.
(b) Both A and R are correct; R is not the correct explanation of A.
(c) A is correct but R is incorrect.
(d) R is correct but A is incorrect.

28. Consider the following amino acids:
I. $(CH_3)_2CH-CH(NH_2)-COOH$
II. $HOOC-CH_2-CH_2-CH(NH_2)-COOH$
III. $H_2N-CH_2-CH_2-CH_2-COOH$
IV. $HOOC-CH_2-CH(NH_2)-COOH$

Which of these are acidic amino acids? Choose the correct option:
(a) I and II (b) II and III
(c) III and I (d) II and IV

29. Consider the following statements:
I. Proteins are the polymers of α-amino acids and they are connected to each other by glycosidic linkage.
II. In globular proteins, chains of polypeptides coil around each other to give a spherical shape.
III. The structure and shape of globular protein can be studied at three different levels.

Select the correct statement(s) and mark the correct option.
(a) Only I
(b) Only II
(c) Both II and III
(d) All the statements are correct

30. Select the correct statements:
(a) There are 20 essential amino acids.
(b) L-amino acids are represented by writing the $-NH_2$ group on the left.
(c) Only α-amino acids are obtained on hydrolysis of proteins.
(d) The amino acids which are synthesised in the body are known as non-essential amino acids.

(a) a and b (b) a, b, c
(c) b, d and c (d) a and d

31.

$$H_2NCH_2COOH + H_2N-\underset{\displaystyle CH_3}{\underset{|}{CH}}-COOH \xrightarrow[-H_2O]{} H_2NCH_2CONH-\underset{\displaystyle CH_3}{\underset{|}{CH}}-COOH$$

Name the dipeptide formed in the above reaction:
(a) Alanglycine
(b) Glycylalanine
(c) Alaninglycine
(d) Glycinalanine

32. Which of the following statements is/are correct?
(a) When four, five or six amino acids are linked, the respective products are known as tetrapeptide, pentapeptide or hexapeptide.
(b) Polypeptide with more than 100 amino acid residues, having molecular mass higher than 10000u, is called protein.
(c) Polypeptide with fewer amino acids are called proteins if they have well-defined conformation of amino acids such as insulin.
(d) All of the above.

33. Which of the following statements are correct about globular proteins?
(a) Globular proteins are usually soluble in water.
(b) In these proteins, chains of polypeptides coil around each other to give a spherical shape.
(c) Insulin is an example of a globular protein.
(d) Albumin is an example of a globular protein.
(a) a, b, c and d (b) a, b, c
(c) Only a (d) a and b

34. On what basis are fibrous and globular proteins classified?
(a) On the basis of the number of amino acids
(b) On the basis of their molecular shape
(c) On the basis of the type of the amino acids
(d) On the basis of molecular weight

35. "When the polypeptide chains that run parallel are held together by hydrogen and disulphide bonds, a fibre-like structure is formed. Such proteins are generally insoluble in water."
Name the type of protein which favours the above information:
(a) Fibrous protein
(b) Globular protein
(c) Primary protein
(d) Tertiary protein

36. Which of the following statements is incorrect about the secondary structure of protein?
(a) It refers to the shape in which the long polypeptide chain can exist.
(b) It exists in two different types of structures, α-helix and β-pleated sheet structure.
(c) The structure arises due to regular folding of the backbone of the polypeptide chain.
(d) There is covalent bonding between the >C=O and –NH groups of the peptide bond.

37. The main forces which stabilise the 2° and 3° structures of proteins is/are:
(a) Hydrogen bond
(b) Disulphide bond
(c) Van der Waals forces
(d) Electrostatic forces of attraction
(a) a and b (b) a, b, c
(c) a, b, c, d (d) Only d

38.

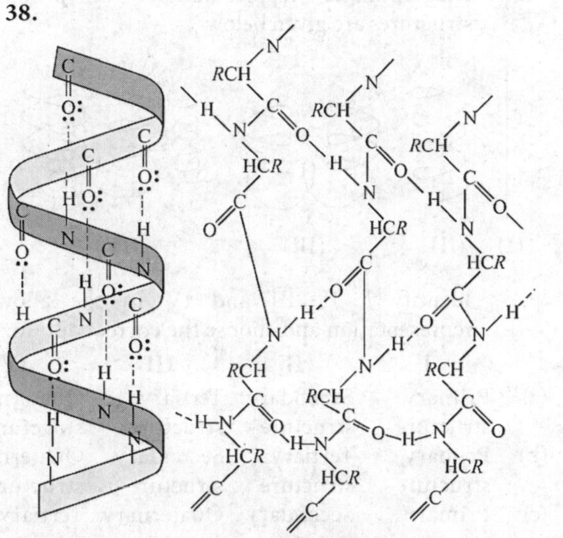

I II

Identify I and II in the given figure.

	I	II
(a)	α-helix structure of protein	β-pleated sheet structure of protein
(b)	α-helix structure of DNA	β-pleated sheet structure of protein
(c)	α-helix structure of protein	β-pleated structure of DNA
(d)	2-helix structure of DNA	β-pleated structure of DNA

39. The spatial arrangement of two or more polypeptide chains with respect to each other is known as:
(a) Primary structure
(b) Secondary structure
(c) Tertiary structure
(d) Quaternary structure

40. Lysine, $H_2N-(CH_2)_4-\underset{NH_2}{\underset{|}{CH}}-COOH$, is a/an:

I. α-amino acid
II. Basic amino acid
III. Amino acid synthesised in the body
IV. β-amino acid

Select the correct option:
(a) I and II (b) II and III
(c) III and IV (d) IV and I

41. Diagrammatic representations of protein structures are given below:

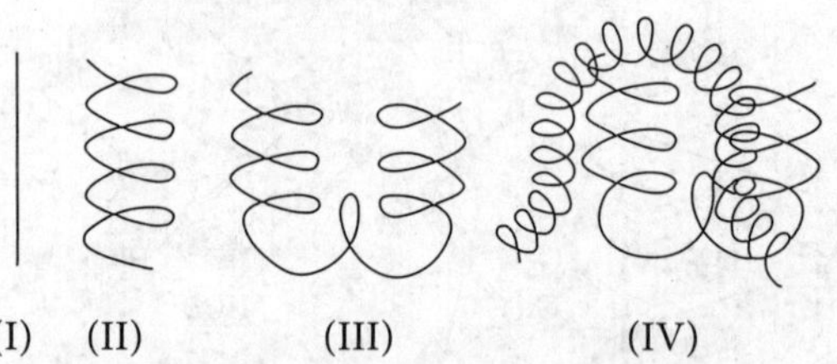

(I) (II) (III) (IV)

Identify I, II, III and IV in the above representation and choose the correct option:

	I	II	III	IV
(a)	Primary structure	Secondary structure	Tertiary structure	Quaternary structure
(b)	Primary structure	Tertiary structure	Secondary structure	Quaternary structure
(c)	Primary structure	Secondary structure	Quaternary structure	Tertiary structure
(d)	Quaternary structure	Tertiary structure	Secondary structure	Primary structure

42. Consider the following statements:

I. Tripeptide contains three amino acids linked by three peptide linkages.
II. In β-pleated sheet structure, all peptide chains after maximum extension are laid side by side and held together by intramolecular H-bonds.
III. The tertiary structure of proteins arises due to further folding of the secondary structure.

Select the correct statements and mark the correct option:
(a) Only I (b) Only III
(c) II and III (d) None of these

43. **Assertion (A):** α-helix structure of proteins is in the shape of a right-handed screw.
Reason (R): There is a hydrogen bond between the >NH group of each amino acid and the >=O of an adjacent turn of the helix.
(a) Both A and R are correct; R is the correct explanation of A.
(b) Both A and R are correct; R is not the correct explanation of A.
(c) A is correct but R is incorrect.
(d) R is correct but A is incorrect.

44. Select the correct statement about the denaturation of protein:
(a) During denaturation, the 1° and 2° structures of proteins are destroyed but the 3° structure remains intact.
(b) During denaturation, the 2° and 3° structures of proteins are destroyed but the 1° structure remains intact.
(c) During denaturation, the 1° and 3° structures of proteins are destroyed but the 2° structure remains intact.
(d) During denaturation, the 1° and 4° structures of proteins are destroyed but the 3° structure remains intact.

45. Which of the following is/are example(s) of denaturation of proteins?
(a) Coagulation of egg white
(b) Clotting of blood
(c) Curdling of milk
(d) Both (a) and (c)

46. Mark the correct statements about denaturation of proteins:
(a) After denaturation, the biological activity of the protein is destroyed.

(b) The primary structure of the protein does not change.
(c) Fibrous proteins are converted into globular proteins.
(d) Curdling of milk is an example of denaturation of protein.

(a) a and b (b) a, b, c
(c) Only a (d) a, b, d

47. **Assertion (A):** There is coagulation of egg white on boiling.
Reason (R): Denaturation of protein occurs when its native form is subjected to physical change or chemical change.
(a) Both A and R are correct; R is the correct explanation of A.
(b) Both A and R are correct; R is not the correct explanation of A.
(c) A is correct but R is incorrect.
(d) R is correct but A is incorrect.

48. **Assertion (A):** Activation energy for acid-catalysed hydrolysis of sucrose is 6.22 kJ mol^{-1}, while activation energy is only 2.15 kJ mol^{-1} when hydrolysis is catalysed by the enzyme sucrase.
Reason (R): Biocatalysts reduce the magnitude of activation energy by providing an alternative path. In the hydrolysis of sucrose, the enzyme reduces the activation energy from 6.22 kJ mol^{-1} to 2.15 kJ mol^{-1}.
(a) Both A and R are correct; R is the correct explanation of A.
(b) Both A and R are correct; R is not the correct explanation of A.
(c) A is correct but R is incorrect.
(d) R is correct but A is incorrect.

49. Name the enzyme that catalyses the reaction given below:

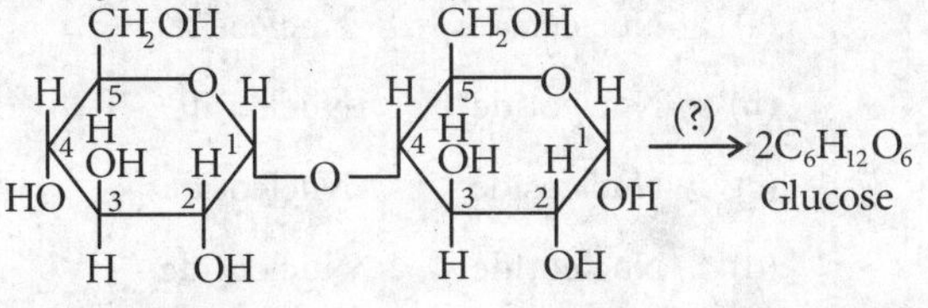

(a) Talose (b) Lactose
(c) Pepsin (d) Maltase

50. Consider the following statements regarding vitamins:

I. Vitamins are organic compounds required in small amounts in the diet but their deficiency causes specific diseases.
II. Vitamins cannot be synthesised by plants but our body can synthesise them.
III. Vitamins are necessary to perform specific biological functions for the normal maintenance of optimum growth and health of the organism.

Select the incorrect statement about vitamins and choose the correct option:
(a) Only I (b) Only II
(c) I and II (d) II and III

51. **Assertion (A):** Vitamins A, D, E and K are stored in the liver and adipose tissue.
Reason (R): Vitamins A, D, E and K are soluble in fats and oils.
(a) Both A and R are correct; R is the correct explanation of A.
(b) Both A and R are correct; R is not the correct explanation of A.
(c) A is correct but R is incorrect.
(d) R is correct but A is incorrect.

52. Match the vitamins given in Column I with their deficiency disease given in Column II and select the correct option from the codes given below:

Column I (Vitamin)	**Column II (Disease)**
A. Vitamin B_{12}	a. Increased blood clotting time
B. Vitamin C	b. Pernicious anemia
C. Vitamin D	c. Increased fragility of RBCs and muscular weakness
D. Vitamin E	d. Scurvy
E. Vitamin K	e. Rickets and osteomalacia

Codes

	A	B	C	D	E
(a)	a	b	d	c	e
(b)	b	d	e	c	a
(c)	b	e	c	d	a
(d)	a	b	c	d	e

53. **Assertion (A):** Fresh tomatoes are a better source of vitamin C than those which have been stored for some time.
Reason (R): On prolonged exposure to air, vitamin C is destroyed due to aerial oxidation.
(a) Both A and R are correct; R is the correct explanation of A.
(b) Both A and R are correct; R is not the correct explanation of A.
(c) A is correct but R is incorrect.
(d) R is correct but A is incorrect.

54. **Assertion (A):** DNA is responsible for maintaining the identity of different species of organisms over millions of years.
Reason (R): The DNA molecule is capable of self-duplication during cell division and identical DNA strands are transferred to the daughter cell.
(a) Both A and R are correct; R is the correct explanation of A.
(b) Both A and R are correct; R is not the correct explanation of A.
(c) A is correct but R is incorrect.
(d) R is correct but A is incorrect.

55. Which of the following matches is correct between nucleic acid and its respective sugar base?
(a) DNA $\rightarrow$ β-D-3-deoxyribose
(b) DNA $\rightarrow$ β-D-1-deoxyribose
(c) RNA $\rightarrow$ β-D-ribose
(d) RNA $\rightarrow$ β-D-3-deoxyribose

56. Consider the following structures:

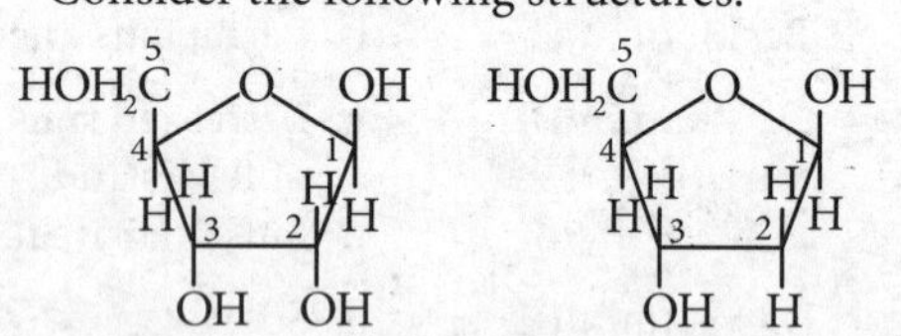

I II

Identify structure I and II and choose the correct option:

	I	II
(a)	β-D-ribose	β-D-2-deoxyribose
(b)	α-D-ribose	β-D-3-deoxyribose
(c)	β-D-deoxyribose	β-D-ribose
(d)	β-D-deoxyribose	α-D-ribose

57. **Assertion (A):** The two strands of DNA are complementary to each other.
Reason (R): Adenine forms hydrogen bonds with guanine and thymine forms hydrogen bonds with cytosine.
(a) Both A and R are correct; R is the correct explanation of A.
(b) Both A and R are correct; R is not the correct explanation of A.
(c) A is correct but R is incorrect.
(d) R is correct but A is incorrect.

58. Select the base which is not common between DNA and RNA:
(a) Adenine (A)
(b) Guanine (G)
(c) Cytosine (C)
(d) Uracil (U)

59. What will be the sequence of complementary strands of DNA, if one strand of DNA has the sequence of TATGACTG?
(a) ATACACTC
(b) ACGTTGAC
(c) ATACTGAC
(d) ATACTGCA

60. Consider the following structures:

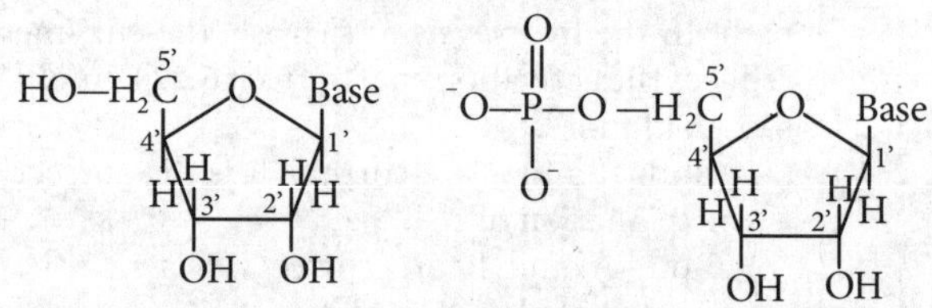

I II

Identify I and II in the above structures and mark the correct option:

	I	II
(a)	Nucleoside	Nucleosite
(b)	Nucleotide	Nucleosite
(c)	Nucleoside	Nucleotide
(d)	Nucleotide	Nucleoside

61. Match the structure of base given in Column I with their name given in Column II and select the correct option from the codes given below:

	Column I	Column II
A.	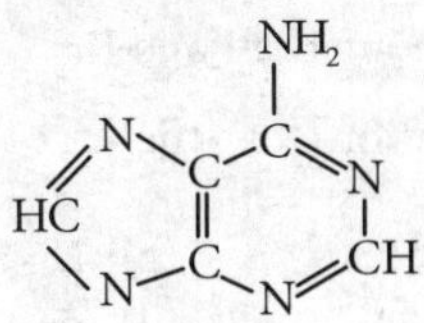	a. Thymine (T)
B.	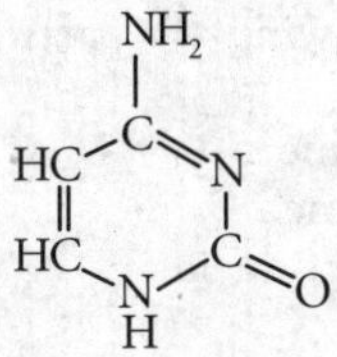	b. Guanine (G)
C.	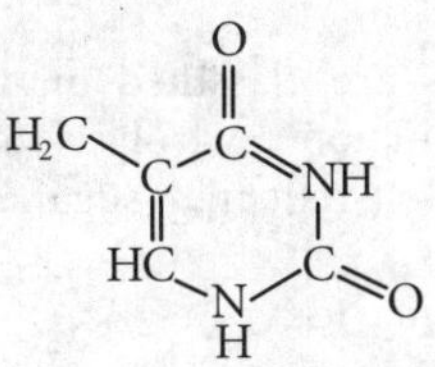	c. Cytosine (c)
D.	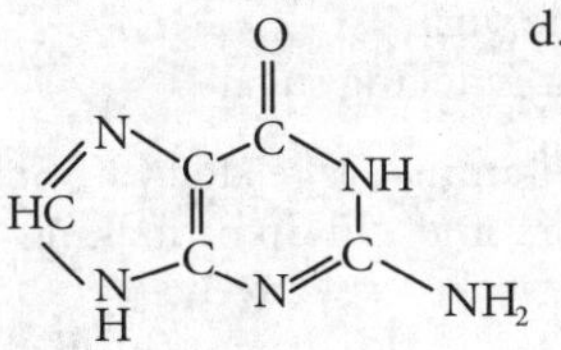	d. Uracil (U)
E.	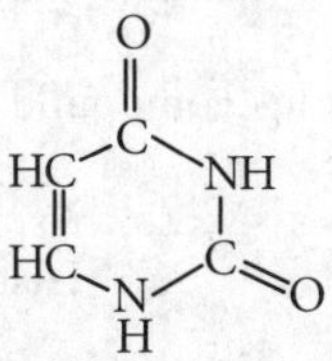	e. Adenine (a)

Codes

	A	B	C	D	E
(a)	e	c	b	d	a
(b)	e	a	b	d	c
(c)	b	c	a	e	d
(d)	e	c	a	b	d

62. Complete hydrolysis of DNA/RNA yields:
(a) A pentose sugar
(b) Phosphoric acid
(c) Base (nitrogen containing heterocyclic compounds)
(d) All of these

63. Which of the following statements is/are true?
(a) Every individual has unique fingerprints and they occur at the tips of the fingers.
(b) A sequence of bases on DNA is also unique for a person and information regarding this is called fingerprinting.
(c) Fingerprints can be altered by surgery.
(d) All of the above.

64. Which of the following is/are application(s) of DNA fingerprinting?
(a) In forensic laboratories for the identification of criminals.
(b) To identify radical groups to rewrite biological evolution.
(c) To determine the paternity of an individual.
(d) All of the above.

65. The optically active amino acid obtained by hydrolysis of the given compound is:

$$NH_2-\underset{}{\overset{CH_3}{\overset{|}{C}}}H-\overset{O}{\overset{||}{C}}-NH-CH_2-\overset{O}{\overset{||}{C}}-OH$$

(a) Alanine (b) Glycine
(c) Leucine (d) Valine

66. Which L-sugar on oxidation gives an optically active dibasic acid?

(a) 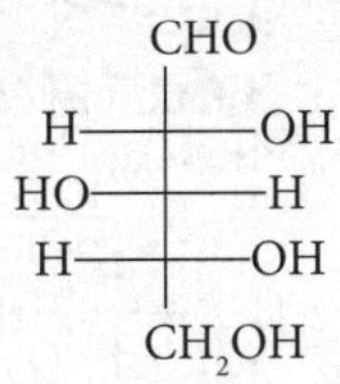 (b) 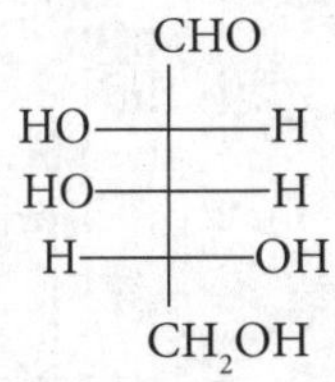

(c) 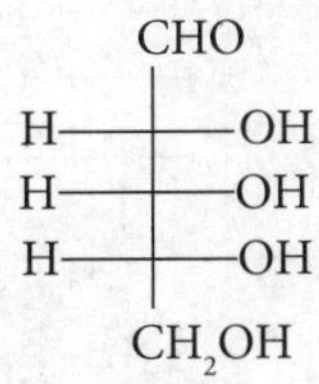 (d) 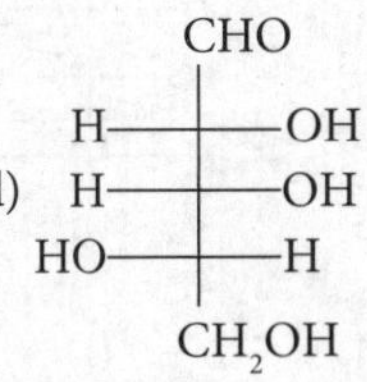

67. Each polypeptide in a protein has amino acids linked with each other in a specific sequence. This sequence of amino acids is said to be the:
(a) Primary structure of proteins
(b) Secondary structure of proteins
(c) Tertiary structure of proteins
(d) Quaternary structure of proteins

68. Which statement among the following is correct?
(a) Uracil is an N-base present in DNA but not in RNA.
(b) Vitamin A is fat soluble.

(c) Ortho-salicylic acid reacts with Me–OH/H^+ to form aspirin.
(d) Deficiency of vitamin D causes night blindness.

69. Open D-glucose and α-D-glucose can be differentiated by:
(a) Fehling's solution (b) Tollens' reagent
(c) Benedict's test (d) Schiff's test

70. Which of the following statements is not true for glucose?
(a) Glucose reacts with hydroxylamine to form oxime
(b) Glucose gives Schiff's test for aldehyde
(c) Glucose exists in two crystalline forms, α and β
(d) The pentaacetate of glucose does not react with hydroxylamine to give oxime

71. Which of the following statements is correct?
(a) Gluconic acid is a partial oxidation product of glucose
(b) Gluconic acid can form a cyclic (acetel/hemiacetal) structure
(c) Gluconic acid is a dicarboxylic acid
(d) Gluconic acid is obtained by oxidation of glucose with HNO_3

72. Three cyclic structures of monosaccharides are given below. Which of these are anomers?

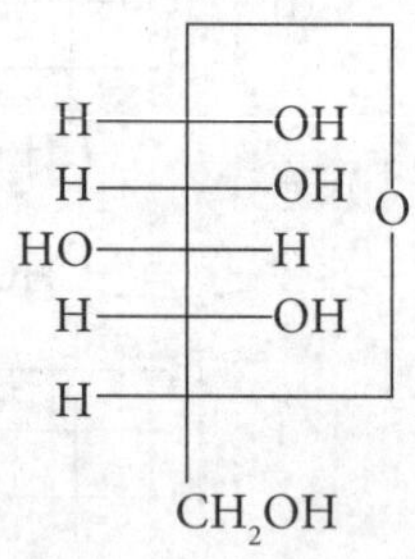

(I)

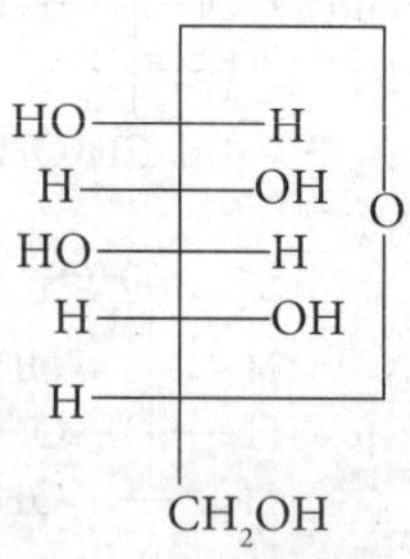

(II)

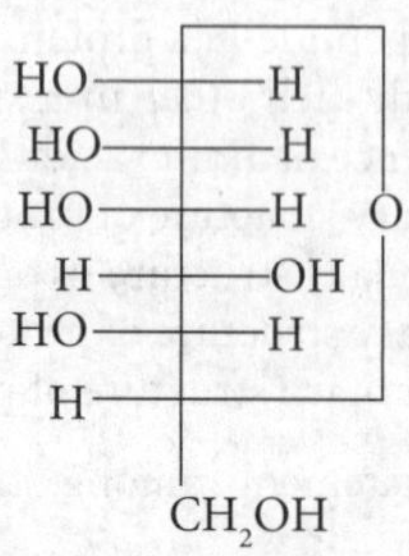

(III)

(a) I and II
(b) II and III
(c) I and III
(d) III is an anomer of I and II

73. The configuration of the C2 epimer of D-glucose is:
(a) 2R, 3S, 4R, 5S (b) 2S, 3S, 4R, 5R
(c) 2S, 3R, 4S, 5R (d) 2R, 3S, 4R, 5R

74. Which of the following are parts of essential amino acids?
A : Valine B : Leucine
C : Serine D : Proline
E : Lysine F : Aspartic acid
(a) A, B, C (b) B, C, F
(c) A, C, D (d) A, B, E

75. Carbohydrates are classified on the basis of their behaviour on hydrolysis and also as reducing or non-reducing sugars. Sucrose is not a:
(a) Monosaccharide
(b) Disaccharide
(c) Cane sugar
(d) Non-reducing sugar

76. Which vitamins are related with acute bleeding in minors and children, making their bones soft and weak, respectively?
(a) C, D (b) B_{12}, C
(c) A, D (d) A, K

77. Among the following compounds, the most basic amino acid is:
(a) Leucine (b) Asparagine
(c) Serine (d) Histidine

78. Which of the following amino acids contains a thioether functional group?
(a) Cystine (b) Serine
(c) Cysteine (d) Methionine

79. Which of the following carbohydrates develops blue colour on treatment with iodine solution?
(a) Glucose (b) Maltose
(c) Starch (d) Fructose

80. Carbohydrates are essential for life in both plants and animals. The carbohydrates that are used as storage molecules in plants and animals and which are present in wood or the fibre of cotton cloth are:
(a) Plants - Cellulose
(b) Animals - Glycogen
(c) Wood - Starch
(d) All of these

81. Which of the following is a purine base?
(a) Guanine (b) Cytosine
(c) Thymine (d) Uracil

82. Which of the following is incorrect?
(a) Lactose is the sugar present in milk and such oligosaccharides are called disaccharides.
(b) Phosphoric acid is linked at the 5'-position of the sugar moiety of the nucleoside to give a nucleotide.
(c) The linkage connecting monosaccharide units to polysaccharides is glycosidic.
(d) Sucrose is laevorotatory but the mixture obtained after hydrolysis is dextrorotatory.

Answer Key

Level-1

1. (b)	**2.** (d)	**3.** (d)	**4.** (a)	**5.** (d)	**6.** (b)	**7.** (b)	**8.** (b)
9. (c)	**10.** (a)	**11.** (a)	**12.** (b)	**13.** (d)	**14.** (c)	**15.** (b)	**16.** (c)
17. (d)	**18.** (a)	**19.** (a)	**20.** (b)	**21.** (d)	**22.** (b)	**23.** (c)	**24.** (b)
25. (a)	**26.** (b)	**27.** (d)	**28.** (c)	**29.** (b)	**30.** (d)	**31.** (c)	**32.** (d)
33. (c)	**34.** (c)	**35.** (d)	**36.** (b)	**37.** (c)	**38.** (d)	**39.** (a)	**40.** (b)
41. (c)	**42.** (a)	**43.** (c)	**44.** (d)	**45.** (a)	**46.** (c)	**47.** (b)	**48.** (b)
49. (b)	**50.** (d)	**51.** (c)	**52.** (c)	**53.** (b)	**54.** (d)	**55.** (d)	**56.** (d)
57. (c)	**58.** (a)	**59.** (b)	**60.** (c)	**61.** (d)	**62.** (a)	**63.** (c)	**64.** (c)
65. (b)	**66.** (d)	**67.** (a)	**68.** (c)	**69.** (a)	**70.** (a)	**71.** (c)	**72.** (d)
73. (a)	**74.** (c)	**75.** (b)	**76.** (b)	**77.** (b)	**78.** (c)	**79.** (a)	**80.** (b)
81. (a)	**82.** (a)	**83.** (d)	**84.** (b)	**85.** (c)			

Level-2

1. (d)	**2.** (d)	**3.** (b)	**4.** (d)	**5.** (d)	**6.** (a)	**7.** (b)	**8.** (b)
9. (d)	**10.** (b)	**11.** (b)	**12.** (c)	**13.** (d)	**14.** (c)	**15.** (c)	**16.** (b)
17. (c)	**18.** (d)	**19.** (a)	**20.** (b)	**21.** (a)	**22.** (d)	**23.** (d)	**24.** (d)
25. (a)	**26.** (d)	**27.** (b)	**28.** (d)	**29.** (b)	**30.** (c)	**31.** (b)	**32.** (d)
33. (a)	**34.** (b)	**35.** (a)	**36.** (d)	**37.** (c)	**38.** (a)	**39.** (d)	**40.** (a)
41. (a)	**42.** (b)	**43.** (a)	**44.** (b)	**45.** (d)	**46.** (d)	**47.** (a)	**48.** (a)
49. (d)	**50.** (b)	**51.** (a)	**52.** (b)	**53.** (a)	**54.** (a)	**55.** (c)	**56.** (a)
57. (c)	**58.** (d)	**59.** (c)	**60.** (c)	**61.** (d)	**62.** (d)	**63.** (d)	**64.** (d)
65. (a)	**66.** (d)	**67.** (a)	**68.** (b)	**69.** (d)	**70.** (b)	**71.** (a)	**72.** (a)
73. (b)	**74.** (d)	**75.** (a)	**76.** (a)	**77.** (d)	**78.** (d)	**79.** (c)	**80.** (b)
81. (a)	**82.** (d)						

Solutions

Level-1

1.

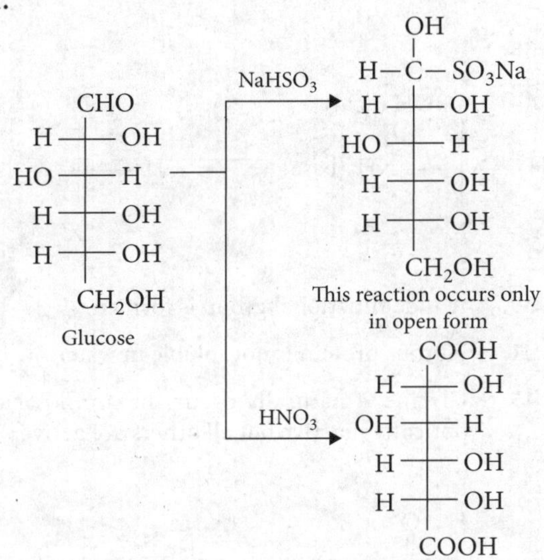

Glucose

Saccharic acid

This reaction occurs in both open and closed forms of glucose

Cyclic glucose exists in two α and β forms but open form is only in one form.

2. Glucose is the most abundant organic compound on earth.

3. Tollen's reagent is used for detection of –CHO group because it easily oxidizes to acid.

5. HI is the strongest reducing agent. It reduces glucose to n-hexane.

7.

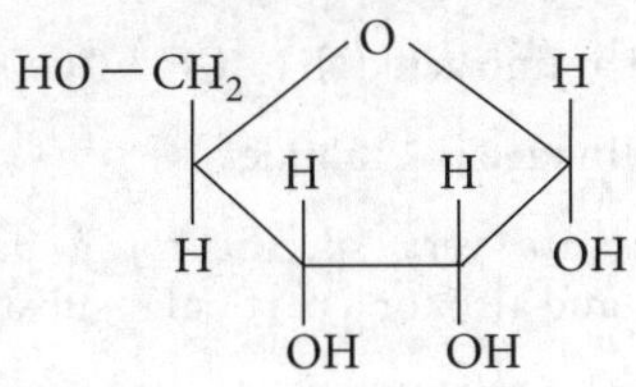

Ribose

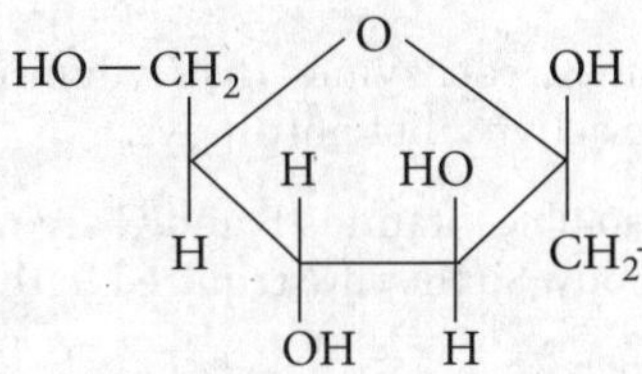

Fructose

11. Furanose structure is a 5-member ring in which there are 4 carbon atoms and one is an oxygen atom. Examples are ribose and fructose.

12.

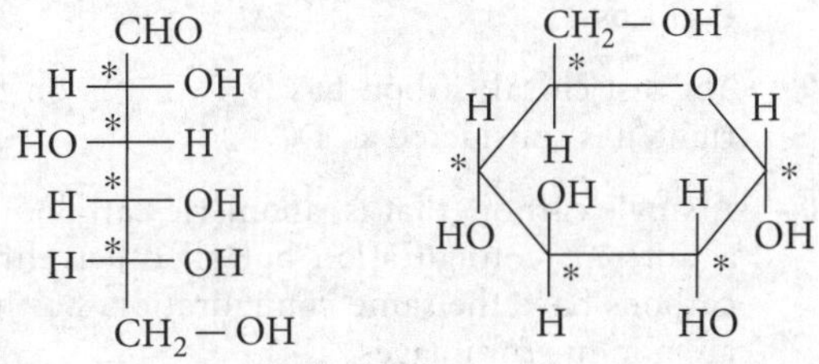

13.

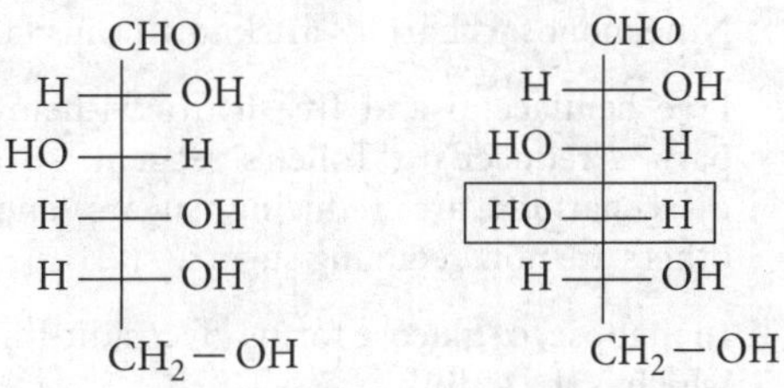

Glucose Galactose

14. First carbon of glucose (–CHO) has two different configurations and forms anomers.

15.

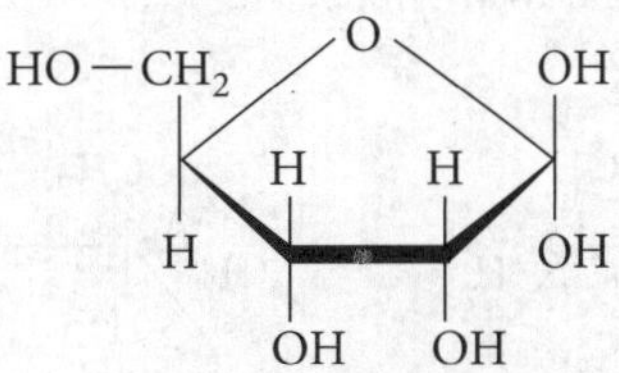

Ribose

First carbon has a different configuration but all the others are in the same configuration.

16. Br_2/H_2O oxidizes only free aldehyde to acid, not to α-hydroxy ketone.

17. After arrangement in a pattern.

(a)

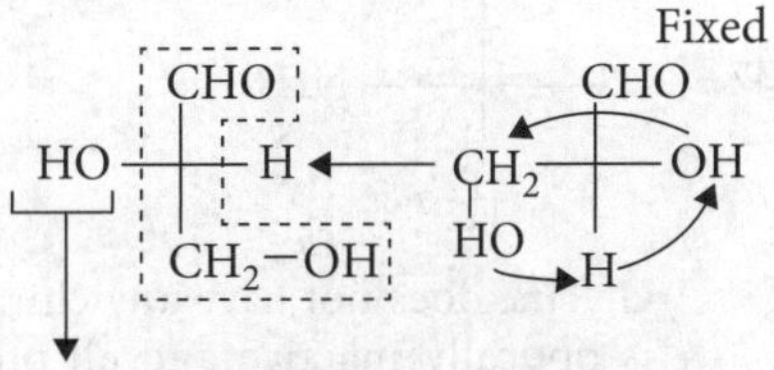

HO is on the left after rearrangement.

(b) 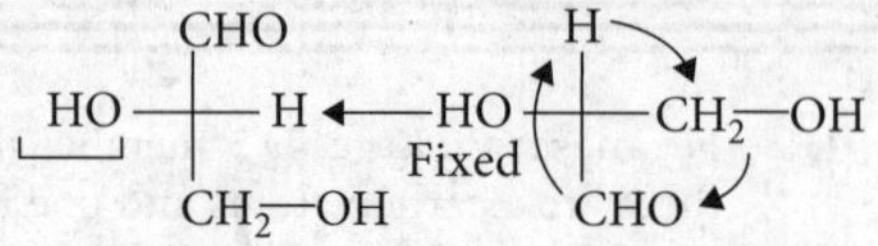

18. Complete mirror image of D-glucose is L-glucose.

19. The last chiral carbon has OH. If it is on the right, it is considered as 'D'.

20. A single carbon, that is, anomeric carbon, has a different configuration but all other chiral carbons have the same configuration. So they are non-mirror images.

22. Invert sugar is known as sucrose.

26. Nine monosaccharides are known thus far.

29. Free hemiacetal and free hydroxyl-hemiketal part is reduced to Tollen's reagent, so those disaccharides are reducing sugars and the others are non-reducing sugars.

30. In maltose, α-glucose forms glycosidic linkage, which is the α-link.

31. In linear linkage, 1-4' glycosidic bonds are formed.

32. Glycogen is animal starch and its structure is similar to amylopectin.

35.

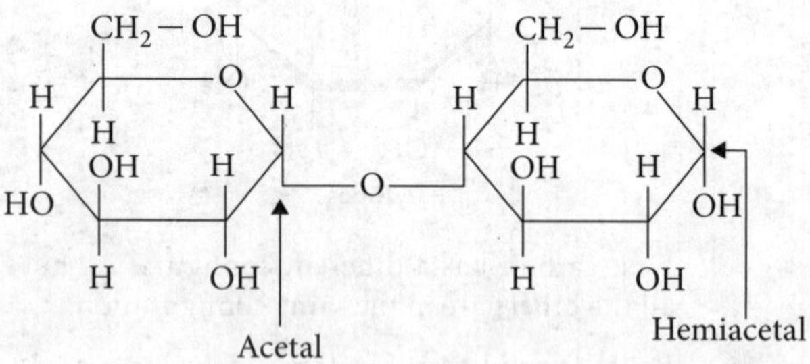

37. 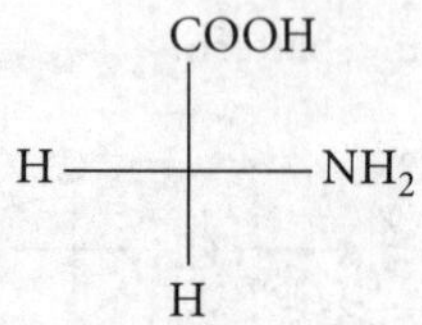

Glycine does not have any chiral carbon, so it is optically inactive and all others are active because of having at least one chiral carbon.

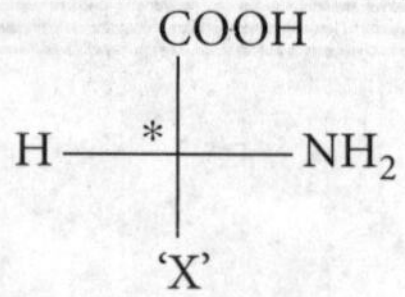

38.

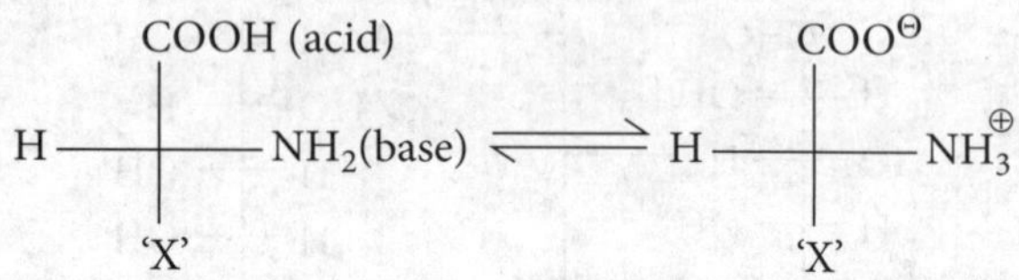

39. Amide functional group is formed.

41. Fibrous protein is not soluble in water.

45. Glycine, a naturally occurring amino acid, is optically inactive but all others are active.

47.

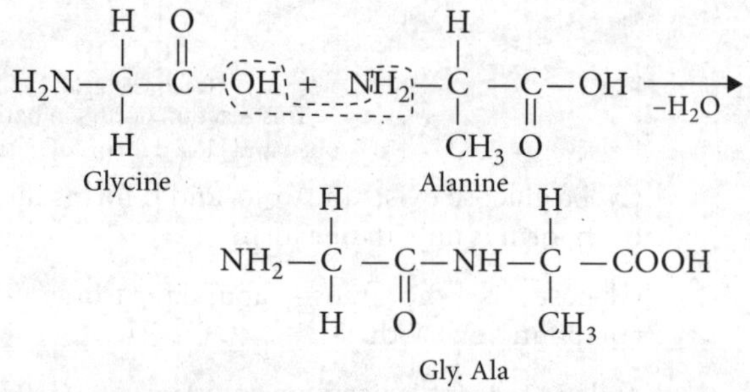

49. Memory bases

50. Essential amino acid is not formed in the human body. So they are essential in the diet.

51. Simplest amino acid (NH_2–CH_2–COOH)

52. Peptide linkage is 2° amide.

53. Enzymes are very specific for a particular reaction and also for a particular substrate.

54. Optimum temperature is the temperature that is favourable for enzyme activity.

56. Sometimes, coenzymes (like vitamin) enable enzyme activity, but not always.

59. Water-soluble vitamins B and C are not stored in the body. So they are required in the diet.

60. Memory base

61. Vitamin D is a fat-soluble vitamin and it is stored in our body.

62. Vitamin C is water soluble and it is excreted from the body in urine. So it is required in the diet.

64. The catalytic enzyme sucrase decreases activation energy. So, in the absence of catalytic enzymes, the activation energy is higher.

65. Ascorbic acid means vitamin C.

69. Adenine = Thymine
Guanine ≡ Cytosine

71. DNA fingerprinting is the same for every cell of any individual.

73.

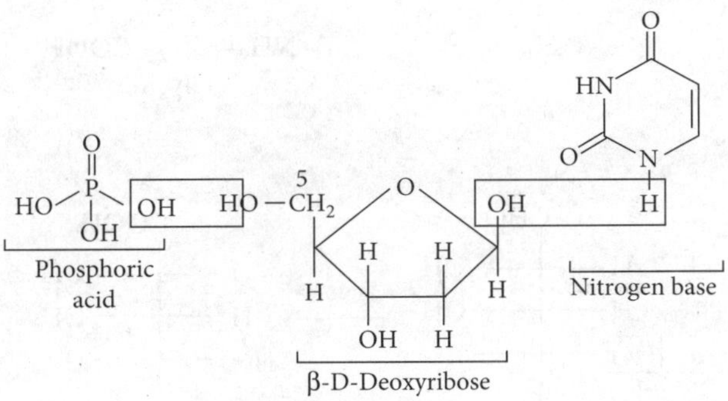

74. See Q73.

75. A = T
G ≡ C

77. See Q73.

78. N-base ::::: N-base
↑ H-bonding

79.

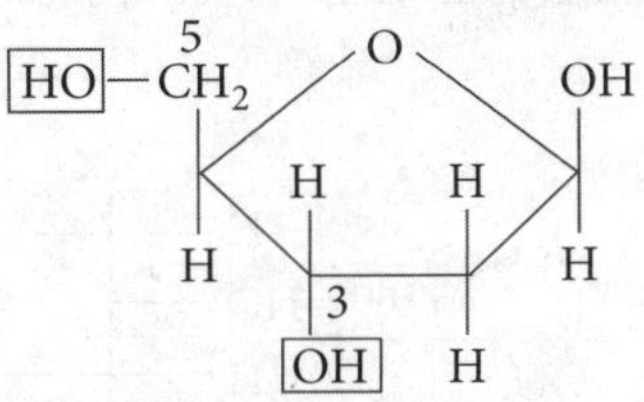

81.

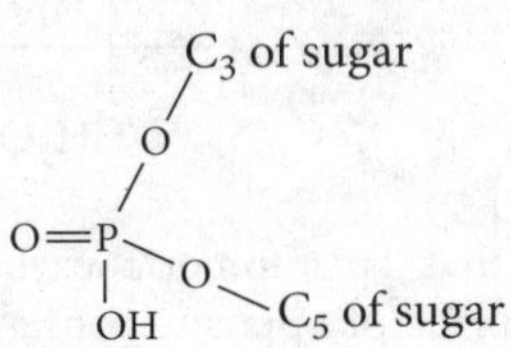

82. RNA is a single-stranded chain of nucleotide.

83. In RNA, uracil is present in place of thymine.

84. See Q73.

85. Adenine and guanine are purine bases.

Level-2

2. General formula of glucose is not $C_6(H_2O)_6$. It is the condensed molecular formula of glucose.

3. On hydrolysis, carbohydrates are classified as monosaccharides, oligosaccharides and polysaccharides.

5. Memory base

8. The sugar present in milk is lactose.

9. All monosaccharides have a non-bounded aldehyde and 2-hydroxy ketonic group.

10. Aldohexose, like glucose, has 4 chiral carbons. So 2^4 optical isomers.

11. α-D-glucose and β-D-glucose are diastereomers.

12. 'D' in glucose and other molecules represents the position of 'OH' of the last chiral carbon of the molecules. It is not related to specific rotation with respect to PPL.

13. HI is the strongest reducing agent.

15. β-glucose has a higher melting point (423 K) than α-glucose (419 K).

17. Cellulase, the enzyme, is absent in humans.

18.

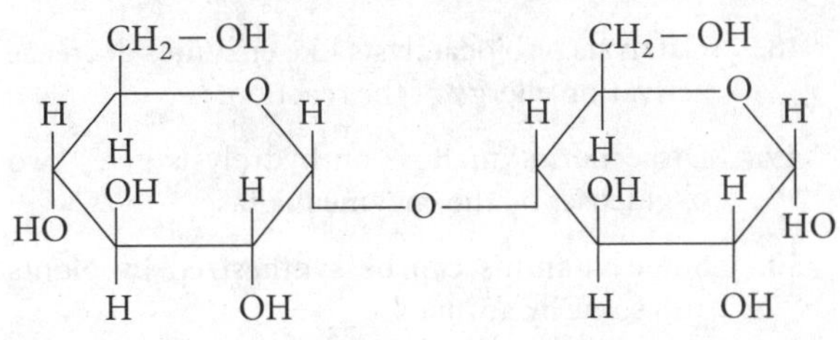

α-glucose + α-glucose = Maltose

19. Disaccharides on hydrolysis give two monosaccharides.

20. β-cellulose gives β-link.

23.

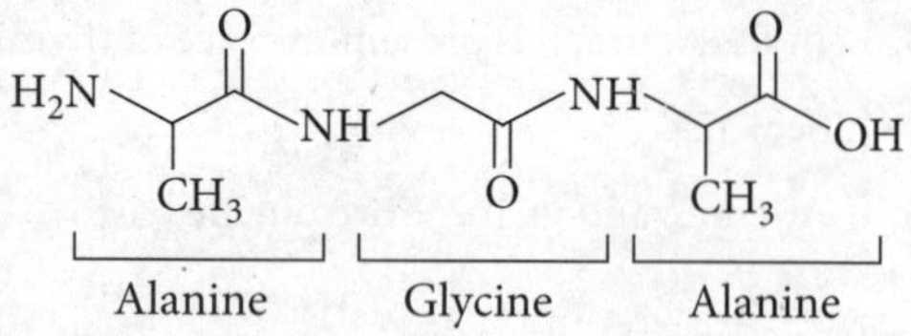

25. Memory base

26. They are also known as essential amino acids.

28. More than one COOH group.

29. In protein, peptide bonds are formed by amino acids and globular proteins have four levels of structures.

30. On hydrolysis of protein, only α-amino acids are obtained. Ten amino acids are essential and about 500 have been identified in nature.

36.

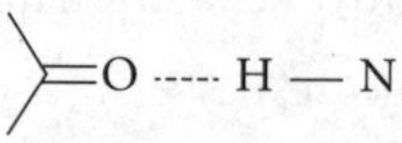

It is hydrogen bonding.

40. $\ddot{N}H_2-CH_2-CH_2-CH_2-CH_2-\overset{\alpha}{C}H(NH_2)-COOH$

Basic part extra

42. In α-helix structure, intramolecular H-bonding is seen. But in β-pleated sheet structure, intermolecular H-bonding is seen between two polypeptide chains.

44. In primary protein, strong polypeptide bond remains as such.

45. Denaturated proteins permanently lose their biological properties.

48. Catalysts or biocatalysts like enzymes decrease activation energy of the reaction.

49. Disaccharide maltose on hydrolysis gives two α-glucoses by the enzyme maltase.

50. Some vitamins can be synthesized by plants and some by animals.

55. DNA has β-D-2-deoxyribose, but RNA has β-D-ribose sugar.

56. Second carbon has lack of oxygen.

57. Adenine with thymine and guanine with cytosine.

58. In RNA, uracil is present in place of thymine.

59.

T A T G A C T G

↓ ↓ ↓ ↓ ↓ ↓ ↓ ↓

A T A C T G A C

60. Pentose sugar + Nitrogen base = Nucleoside
Nucleoside + Phosphoric acid = Nucleotide

65.

$$NH_2-\overset{\star}{C}H(CH_3)-\overset{O}{\overset{\|}{C}}-NH-CH_2-\overset{O}{\overset{\|}{C}}-OH \xrightarrow{H_2O} NH_2-\overset{\star}{C}H(CH_3)-COOH + NH_2-CH_2-COOH$$

Alanine (Active) + Glycine

66.

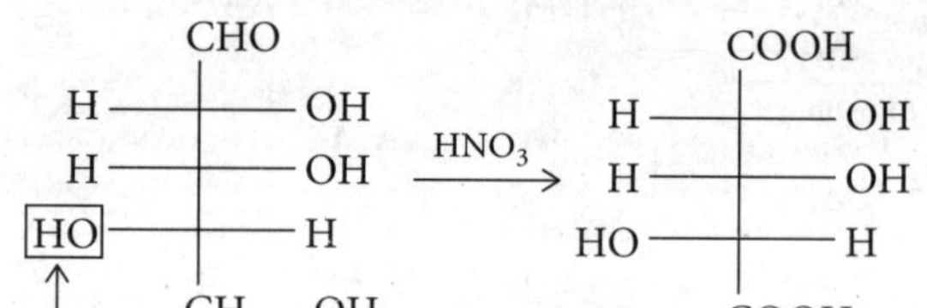

Presence of OH on the left means it is 'D' form

68. Memory base

69. Schiff's reagent gives test with open D-glucose because of free aldehyde group, but it does not give cyclic α- or β-D-glucose.

70. Only open-D-glucose gives Schiff's test.

71.

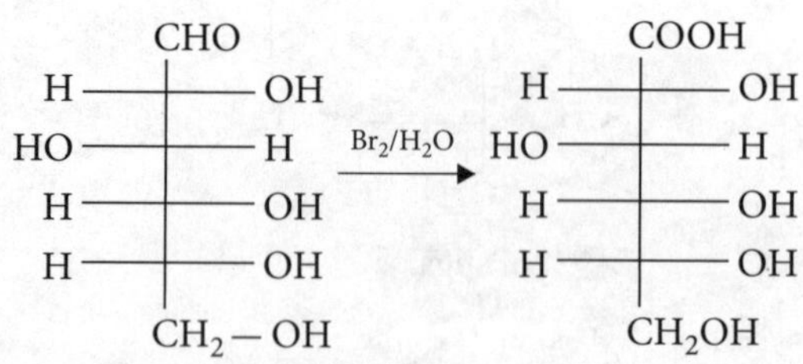

72. First carbon, that is, anomeric carbon, has two different forms of opposite configuration, known as anomers.

73.

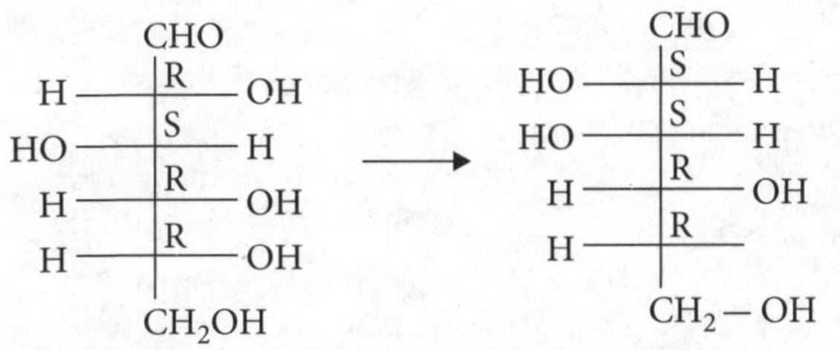

Glucose

C_2 epimer of glucose = Mannose

75. Sucrose in disaccharide of α-glucose and β-fructose.

76. Acute bleeding in minors is a symptom of scurvy. It is caused by deficiency of vitamin C. Bone weakness and softness in children are symptoms of rickets. It is caused by deficiency of vitamin D.

77.

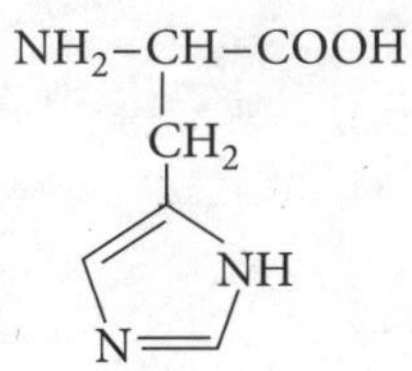

(Histidine is a basic amino acid)

78. $NH_2-CH(-CH_2-CH_2-S-CH_3)-COOH$ (Methionine)

79. Polysaccharide (starch) gives test with iodine solution.

80. The storage molecule in animals is glycogen. In plants, storage food is starch, and in wood and fibres, cellulose is present.

81. Adenine and guanine are purine nitrogen bases.

82. Sucrose is dextrorotatory (+66°), but after hydrolysis, there is a mixture of glucose (+52°) and fructose (–92°), which becomes laevorotatory. So sucrose is also known as invert sugar.